CHILD DEVELOPMENT

Early Stages Through Adolescence

10th Edition

Celia Anita Decker
Former Professor of Family and Consumer Sciences
Northwestern State University
Natchitoches, Louisiana

Julia McClannon
National Board-Certified Family and Consumer Sciences Teacher
Fuquay-Varina High School
Fuquay-Varina, North Carolina

Michelle McCoy
Texas Board-Certified Family and
Consumer Sciences/Early Childhood Education Teacher
Hendrickson High School
Pflugerville, Texas

Publisher
The Goodheart-Willcox Company, Inc.
Tinley Park, IL
www.g-w.com

About the Authors

Celia Decker is a former professor in the Department of Family and Consumer Sciences at Northwestern State University of Louisiana. She taught courses in early childhood education, child development, and family relations. Dr. Decker was coordinator of graduate studies in early childhood education. Before her position at Northwestern State University, she taught college courses at East Texas State University (now Texas A&M at Commerce) and at the University of Arkansas at Fayetteville. Dr. Decker also taught public school kindergarten in Kansas City, Kansas.

In addition to writing this text, Dr. Decker coauthors *Parents and Their Children* with Verdene Ryder. Dr. Decker has also published other books, numerous chapters in books, and articles. She presents papers at national and state annual meetings of professional associations, such as the National Association for the Education of Young Children, Southern Early Childhood Association, Association for Childhood Education International, National Association of Early Childhood Teacher Educators, and the Society for Research in Child Development. She does extensive consultant work for Head Start, Even Start, and local school systems.

During her years of teaching, Dr. Decker was named to Who's Who in Child Development Professionals, Who's Who in Personalities of the South, Who's Who in American Women, and the World's Who's Who in Education. In 1994, she was selected as the Outstanding Professor at Northwestern State University.

Julia McClannon is a National Board-Certified Family and Consumer Sciences teacher at Fuquay-Varina High School in Fuquay-Varina, North Carolina. She has over 10 years of experience in education. Julia has a Bachelor of Science degree in Family and Consumer Sciences from Meredith College and a master's degree in Curriculum and Instruction with a focus on Educational Psychology from North Carolina State University. Julia began her career teaching Teen Living and Foods and Nutrition courses. She was awarded the Diane Kent Parker First-Year Teacher Award for her district and Beginning Teacher of the Year for her school. After receiving her master's degree, Julia worked at Oxford University Press as a Product Trainer while co-authoring an e-book stemming from her master's thesis research on beginning teacher turnover.

In 2015, Julia returned to the classroom to teach early childhood and teacher training courses, serving as head of the Early Childhood Education program. She has served as department chair at her school, as well as a Professional Learning Team leader at the school and district levels. She is the lead advisor for Family, Career, and Community Leaders of America at her school and has led students to multiple state and national competitions. She is a teacher leader on the Human Services Career Advisory Team for her district, collaborating with business and industry partners to ensure alignment between school and business. Julia has presented at many professional conferences, including the North Carolina Career and Technical Education Summer Conference and various professional learning opportunities for her school and district. She won Teacher of the Year for Fuquay-Varina High School in 2019 along with the Fuquay-Varina Chamber of Commerce Excellence in Education award.

Michelle McCoy is a Family and Consumer Science teacher at Hendrickson High School in Pflugerville, Texas. Over the years she developed and supervised teen parenting, culinary arts, and hospitality programs and served on the boards for the San Patricio, Harris, and Bee County Fairs. She founded and served on numerous student organizations such as Family, Career and Community Leaders of America; the Texas Association of Future Educators; and Hawk Paintball.

Michelle has served as a board member, secretary, vice-president, and president of the Family and Consumer Sciences Teachers Association of Texas (FCSTAT) and as a board member, secretary, and chairperson for the Texas Career and Technology Council. Michelle has also served on the Texas A&M University Kingsville Department of Agriculture and Human Services

Advisory Council and the Human Services Alumni Association as historian and president. She writes curriculum for her district as well as for the Texas Education Agency Career and Technical Education state curriculum initiative. She wrote the pedagogy, teacher material, and workbook for Goodheart-Wilcox's *Principles of Human Services* textbook. She has presented at her district and at the FCSTAT summer and midwinter conferences.

Michelle is a member of the American Association of Family and Consumer Sciences, the National Association of Teacher of Family and Consumer Sciences, and Kappa Omicron Nu honor society. Twice she has received the FCSTAT Region V Teacher of the Year Award and was named the FCSTAT State Teacher of the Year in 2011. She earned a Master of Science in Human Services with a minor in Family Studies and Management and a Bachelor of Science in Human Services with a minor in Early Childhood Education from Texas A&M University–Kingsville. Michelle has over 30 years of experience teaching, writing, mentoring, and serving in the field of Family and Consumer Sciences.

Reviewers

The author and the publisher are grateful to the following reviewers who provided valuable input to this edition.

Calliope Capra
Teacher
Dearborn Public Schools
Dearborn, Michigan

Krista Carr
Teacher
Tempe Union High School District
Tempe, Arizona

Theresa Ettinger
Teacher
Tempe Union High School District
Tempe, Arizona

Pamela Flores
Teacher
Rio Rancho Public Schools
Rancho, New Mexico

Colleen Florkowski
Teacher
Toledo Public Schools
Toledo, Ohio

Michelle Griffin
Teacher
Tempe Union High School District
Tempe, Arizona

Mallory Seidlitz
Teacher
Unit Seven Schools
Tolono, Illinois

Deanna Smith
Teacher
Tempe Union High School District
Tempe, Arizona

Donna Yazzie
Teacher
Central Consolidated School District
Farmington, New Mexico

New to This Edition

The tenth edition of *Child Development: Early Stages Through Adolescence* has been revised and updated to reflect current practice. For instructor convenience, the chapters have been organized into lessons with corresponding review questions. STEM activities and technology engagement have been added in all curriculum-related chapters. New social studies strategies are included to promote inclusion and acceptance of diversity. In addition, content in individual chapters has been updated as follows:

Chapter 1: *Learning About Children* includes a new feature on genetics by way of twin studies.

Chapter 2: *New Directions in Learning* includes a case study that examines the use of technology on the developing brain and provides the latest advice from the American Academy of Pediatrics regarding children and digital devices. This chapter also includes a new feature on the impact of trauma on the developing brain and steps that can be taken via trauma-informed care to minimize negative effects and promote resilience in children.

Chapter 3: *Families Today* has an updated feature on the impact of media and technology on the family unit. It also includes an updated feature on the cost of raising a child.

Chapter 9: *Intellectual Development in the First Twelve Months* includes updated advice and activities designed to promote memory and intellectual development in infants.

Chapter 10: *Social-Emotional Development* includes a new Mental Health feature about post-partum depression and post-partum psychosis.

Chapter 13: *Social-Emotional Development of Toddlers* provides new information on how to help toddlers learn obedience.

Chapter 14: *Physical Development of Preschoolers* provides updated growth charts and physical milestones for preschoolers.

Chapter 16: *Social-Emotional Development of Preschoolers* includes information on gender identity in children.

Chapter 18: *Intellectual Development of School-Age Children and Adolescents* provides an updated feature on bilingualism. This chapter also explores the use of digital media in promoting literacy.

Chapter 23: *Meeting Children's Special Needs* provides current best practices on identifying and educating children with diverse needs.

Chapter 25: *Preparing for a Child-Related Career* gives students advice on how to research and pursue job opportunities in the field of child development.

Precision Exams by YouScience Certification

Goodheart-Willcox is pleased to partner with YouScience to correlate *Child Development: Early Stages Through Adolescence* with their Child Development certification standards. Students who pass the exams and performance portions of the exams can earn a Career Skills certification. Precision Exams by YouScience and Career Skills Exams were created in partnership with industry and subject matter experts to align real-world job skills with marketplace demands. Students can showcase their skills and knowledge with industry-recognized certifications—and build outstanding resumes to stand out from the crowd!

And for teachers, Precision Exams by YouScience provides:

- Access to a library of Career Skills Exams, including pre- and post-assessments for all 16 National Career Clusters
- Suite of on-demand reporting to measure program and student academic growth
- Easy-to-use, 100% online administration

To see how *Child Development: Early Stages Through Adolescence* correlates to Precision Exams by YouScience standards, visit the Correlations tab at www.g-w.com/child-development-2024. For more information about Precision Exams by YouScience, visit www.youscience.com/certifications/career-clusters/.

Guided Tour

The instructional design includes student-focused learning tools to help students succeed. This visual guide highlights the features designed for the textbook.

Essential Question provides a starting point for thinking about the material in the lesson.

Case Study describes a real-world scenario, with application questions to consider.

Focus on Careers feature identifies specific career paths in early learning environments.

Focus on Financial Literacy feature explores the costs of raising children in today's world.

Learning Outcomes clearly identify the knowledge and skills to be obtained when the lesson is completed.

Reading and Notetaking Activity provides reading comprehension advice at the beginning of each chapter.

Key Terms lists the vocabulary words to be defined in each lesson.

Investigate Special Topics feature provides insight into the latest research and topics in the child development field today.

Focus on Mental Health feature identifies policies and procedures that promote the mental health of children and caregivers.

Focus on Reading feature explores language and literacy topics relating to child development.

Focus on Social Studies feature identifies ethical guidelines to be followed in early learning environments.

Focus on Speech feature explores speech development and best practices for helping children with speech.

Focus on Health feature identifies policies and procedures that promote children's health.

Focus on Science feature explores STEM topics in the field of child development.

Chapter Summary feature provides an additional review tool and reinforces key learning outcomes.

Recall and Application reinforces the vocabulary words learned in each chapter.

Critical Thinking questions develop higher-order thinking and problem-solving, personal, and workplace skills.

Core Skills questions enhance students' understanding of the core material.

College and Career Portfolio helps students build and gather materials that will aid them in their job search in child-related fields.

Observations helps students interpret children's behaviors to gain a deeper understanding of child development.

TOOLS FOR STUDENT AND INSTRUCTOR SUCCESS

Student Tools

Student Text

Child Development: Early Stages Through Adolescence covers the knowledge and skills required to prepare students for a career in child care. The lesson-based structure includes extensive assessment opportunities as well as a selection of Focus on Careers features, which provide students with information about a variety of child care careers. The following supplemental materials are available for students with access to digital resources. The Workbook is also available in print.

Workbook

- Hands-on practice includes questions and activities.
- Organized to follow the textbook lessons to help students achieve key learning outcomes.

Companion Website

- E-flash cards and vocabulary exercises allow interaction with content to create opportunities to increase achievement.
- Interactive activities reinforce key concepts from the text with engaging and informational graphics.

Instructor Tools

G-W Ignite

G-W Ignite provides a seamless user experience for both you and your students. The easy-to-navigate interface and class rostering capabilities make setting up a course easy and intuitive. Instructors can quickly and easily share assignments with students. Auto-graded activities and assignments make grading easier than ever, and rubrics are provided for ease of grading when required. Extensive reporting capabilities allow instructors to view students' progress and evaluate performance against learning outcomes and key standards. Students have their own My Progress dashboard where they can view grades and comments from their instructor.

G-W Ignite provides a complete learning package for you and your students. The included digital resources help your students remain engaged and learn effectively.

- The **Online Textbook** is a reflowable digital textbook that works well on all devices. It also works well with screen readers and accessibility tools.
- The **Workbook** content in digital format provides opportunities for students to reinforce understanding of learning outcomes in the text. Instructors can easily assign activities and grade student work using the rubrics provided.
- **Drill and Practice Vocabulary Activities**, which are provided for all key terms in every lesson, provide an active, engaging, and effective way for students to learn the required terminology.

Use the **Pretests**, **Posttests**, and **Exams** to assess students' knowledge of learning outcomes and key standards. These prebuilt assessments help you measure student knowledge and track progress in achieving learning outcomes.

- The **Instructor Resources** provide instructors with time-saving preparation tools such as answer keys, editable lesson plans, and other teaching aids.
- **Instructor's Presentations for PowerPoint®** are fully customizable, richly illustrated slides that help you teach and visually reinforce the key concepts from each chapter.

See www.g-w.com/child-development-2024 for a list of all available resources.

Professional Development

- Expert Content Specialists
- Research-Based Pedagogy and Instructional Practices
- Options for virtual and in-person PD

Brief Contents

Contents

Feature Contents

Focus on Careers

Focus on Mental Health

Unit 1 Children and Families in Today's World

Career and Technical Student Organizations

Career and Technical Student Organizations (CTSOs) are valuable assets to any educational program. These organizations support student learning and the application of skills learned in real-world situations. There is a variety of organizations from which to choose, depending on the goals of educational programs.

One CTSO that fits well with child development is Family, Career and Community Leaders of America (FCCLA). Founded at a convention in Chicago, Illinois, in June 1945, FCCLA is the only CTSO with the family as its central focus. FCCLA helps youth develop leadership and workplace skills through Family and Consumer Sciences education, student leadership, and service learning. The mission of FCCLA is to prepare members for their roles as family members, wage earners, and community leaders.

Another CTSO related to child development is Educators Rising. Educators Rising, formerly known as Future Educators of America (FEA), is a CTSO for students interested in education-related careers. Educators Rising offers resources and opportunities that integrate directly into academic education programs at the high school level. This program also offers professional development tools to help prepare students for their future education careers.

Perhaps your school has a broader CTSO like SkillsUSA, which covers a variety of career clusters, ranging from A/V technology to transportation distribution. The Human Services career cluster would be most relevant to child development, offering a variety of career pathways that relate to families and human needs (e.g., counseling and mental health services, family and community services, etc.).

All of these CTSOs offer similar opportunities for their student members. National conferences offer students the chance to compete on a regional and national level, develop leadership skills, and network for future academic or workplace careers. Competitive events allow students to showcase their knowledge, skills, and leadership. CTSOs also provide scholarship opportunities for members.

1. Find out if your school has a local FCCLA, Educators Rising, or SkillsUSA chapter. Talk to your local advisor or instructor to find out more information.
2. Check out the organization websites to see what resources and events they offer.

Chapter 1

Learning About Children

Lesson 1.1 Understanding Child Development

Lesson 1.2 Principles and Theories of Growth and Development

Lesson 1.3 Studying and Observing Children

Essential Question

How do genes and environment work together to affect children's growth and development?

Case Study   Sanjay's Development

Read the case study and discuss/reflect on the questions that follow. After you finish studying the chapter, think about this case study again. Have your opinions changed based on what you learned?

Sanjay is a healthy and active 28-month-old child who attends a child care center during the day. Sanjay plays happily alongside peers, but doesn't engage much in cooperative play. Sanjay particularly loves to play with the center's wooden blocks, stacking them carefully one on top of the other.

Lately Sanjay's parent, Ashima, has been concerned about Sanjay's language development. Sanjay can say about 20 words clearly and a few more that only Ashima and Ashima's partner, Robert, can understand. Often Sanjay will point to something and grunt, throwing a tantrum if misunderstood.

Ashima wants to make an appointment with their pediatrician to discuss Sanjay's speech development. Ashima has noticed that the other children in the center have much larger vocabularies and speak more clearly than Sanjay. Ashima worries that if Sanjay's communication skills don't improve, the tantrums will get worse and lead to more serious behavioral problems.

Robert thinks Ashima is overreacting. Robert was a late talker as a child, and feels that Sanjay will speak when ready. Robert fears that receiving speech therapy too early may cause Sanjay to feel too pressured and not want to speak at all. Robert suggests that they wait another year before speaking to Sanjay's pediatrician.

Give It Some Thought

1. Do you agree with Ashima or Robert regarding when they should speak to the pediatrician? Explain your answer.
2. Do all children develop at the same rate? How do caregivers know when to become concerned?
3. If Sanjay is taken to the pediatrician right away, what do you think the doctor will say?

Understanding Child Development

Learning Outcomes

After studying this lesson, you will be able to

1.1-1 **define** the term *child development*.

1.1-2 **describe** and **organize** the three domains of child development.

1.1-3 **summarize** the six stages of the individual life cycle that involve children.

1.1-4 **differentiate** between heredity and environment and **synthesize** how they interact to influence growth and development.

Reading and Notetaking Activity

Based on your own experiences and observations, list what you think the six stages of child development are called. Then write two or three characteristics of each stage. As you read this lesson, list the six stages of child development and characteristics of each stage as noted by the author. Organize your notes around the information you already know, adding new information as needed. After you finish reading the lesson, compare the two lists. In what ways are they similar and different? Why do you think the six stages of child development are divided this way? Consider how your prior knowledge of the subject matter helped you understand this topic.

Introduction

Child development is one of the most fascinating subjects you can study. Children are constantly changing and exploring. They are also curious and creative. Who else would use a cardboard box for a house, a car, or a hiding place? If you spend any time with children, you know they can be lovable and challenging.

As you learn more about children, you will see that they go through many stages of growth and development. This book emphasizes the early years (before birth through adolescence). These years are the most important in shaping children's lives.

1.1-1 What Is Child Development?

For many years, scientists and researchers have been studying children. The goal of these professionals is to learn more about how children grow and develop. **Development** is the gradual process through which babies become adults. Development begins at conception and continues until death. The process of development has many stages, such as before birth, infancy, childhood, adolescence, and adulthood.

Child development is the scientific study of children from conception through adolescence. Child development is concerned with the whole child and the process or changes that occur in both growth and behavior. **Growth** is an increase in size, such as height, or in quantity, such as adding new vocabulary. Changes in behavior include any change in motor, thinking, and social skills.

By conducting research, experts in the fields of medicine, education, family and consumer sciences, psychology, and sociology help gather knowledge about children. People then use these facts to learn about and care for children. Anyone who interacts with children can benefit from this knowledge.

1.1-2 Domains of Child Development

Because the **domains** (areas) of child development are so highly related, child development experts must learn about all of the domains and how they interact. This text uses the following terms to describe the domains of child development:

- **physical development**—involves growth of the body and the development of both fine and gross motor skills.
- **intellectual development**—includes how people think and learn and how people express what they know through a variety of methods, especially language.
- **social-emotional development**—concerns interactions with people and social groups, disposition, and emotions.

The domains of development constantly interact and overlap (See **Figure 1.1**).

1.1-3 Individual Life Cycle

The **individual life cycle** is a description of the stages of change people experience throughout life (from birth through old age). To help them study development over time, experts divide life into age-related stages. Each stage of life has unique opportunities, achievements, and challenges. Thus, each stage requires different ways of supporting growth and development.

Each stage includes average ages to provide a basic idea of when stages may begin and end. The exact ages for a specific person varies because of the unique combination of biology and experiences for each individual. This book covers the first seven stages, which are those that involve children. See **Figure 1.2** to learn more about these seven stages.

PHYSICAL
Learning to walk leads the more mobile child to...

INTELLECTUAL
explore and learn about objects that can be used to...

SOCIAL-EMOTIONAL
aid in interactions with others and bring pleasure to the child.

Goodheart-Willcox Publisher

Figure 1.1 The domains of development constantly intercept and overlap. *Can you think of another physical milestone and how that overlaps into intellectual and social-emotional development?*

Figure 1.2 Child Development Stages

Stage	Definition	Appearance
Prenatal	Begins at conception and ends at birth (typically 9 months later). The rate of growth at this stage is the fastest it will be in life. In this stage, a fetus grows from a single cell to a complete organism. Even before birth, babies can move, recognize the pregnant person's voice patterns, and react to some strong stimuli.	PeopleImages/iStock via Getty Images Plus
Neonatal	Also known as newborn, this extends from birth to 1 month. During this period, the baby physically adapts to life outside the pregnant person's body.	Mehmet Hilmi Barcin/E+ via Getty Images
Infancy	Begins at 1 month and continues to 12 months. The infant develops the foundation for motor, thinking, language, and social skills.	MBI/Shutterstock.com
Toddler	Begins at 12 months and ends at 36 months (the child's third birthday). In the toddler stage, the child makes great strides in motor, thinking, and language skills and begins to be less dependent on adults.	digital skillet/iStock via Getty Images Plus
Preschool	Begins at 3 years and ends at 6 years. During this stage, the child becomes more self-sufficient, spends many hours in play exploring the physical and social world, and begins to develop knowledge of self.	LUNAMARINA/iStock via Getty Images Plus
School-age (middle childhood)	Begins at 6 years and ends at 12 years. This stage corresponds to the typical ages of children in the elementary school years. Achievement is the central goal of these years. School-age children become proficient in the basics of reading, writing, and arithmetic. They are exposed to many other learning opportunities, too. In school, children interact with peers more and learn by group instruction. Before the end of this stage, children have more stable feelings about self and know how others feel about them.	LUNAMARINA/iStock via Getty Images Plus
Adolescence	Begins at 12 years and ends around 18 years. This stage corresponds to the typical ages of children in middle school and high school and is marked by the onset of puberty. Adolescence is the stage during which a young person develops from a child to an adult.	Heather Preston

Figure 1.2 *How do you think these child development stages were determined? Why?*

1.1-4 Factors That Influence Growth and Development

Why is each child different? Two main factors influence growth and development: heredity and environment. **Heredity** includes all the traits that a child inherits from blood relatives. Sometimes heredity is called *nature*. **Environment** includes all the conditions and situations that surround and affect a child. Sometimes environment is called *nurture*. The way these two factors combine makes children unique, or different from one another. Experts continue to study how these two factors interact and affect children's growth and development.

Heredity

You have many traits in common with all the other members of your biological family. These traits pass to you in complex ways through your parents' genes at conception. Babies inherit about 23,000 genes from their biological parents. **Genes** are sections of the DNA molecule found in a person's cells that determine individual traits. You are born with genes carrying instructions that help make you who you are. For example, you might be born with genes for brown eyes or curly hair.

Genes affect almost every physical, intellectual, and social-emotional trait. Sometimes the effects of genes are so strong they are not easily changed by the environment. In other cases, the genetic impact is not as clear-cut and is more susceptible to outside influences. Following are examples of ways in which genes influence growth and development:

- Genes determine body features, such as blood type, facial structure, and color of hair, eyes, and skin (See **Figure 1.3**). Genes also determine whether a person has certain diseases, such as the inherited red blood cell disorder known as sickle-cell disease.
- Genes also determine, in part, our intellectual abilities and social-emotional traits. Shyness, or withdrawal from unfamiliar people, places, and things, seems to have a genetic component that appears early in life and remains stable over time. However, simple physical traits like blood type are more strongly influenced by genetics, while more complex personality traits, like shyness, are more affected by the environment.
- Some genes determine a trait's **potential**. (**Potential** is the greatest amount or level possible.) Whether a person will show or use that genetic (nature) trait to its potential depends on the person's environment (nurture). For instance, genes determine how tall you can grow, but good nutrition and healthy living conditions help determine whether you reach your height potential.

Environment

All people live in both a physical and social environment. The unborn baby lives primarily in a physical environment that is almost totally dependent on the pregnant person's physical condition. This environment may be beneficial due to proper prenatal care or harmful due to the lack of such care. After birth, physical conditions, such as food and rest, are part of the environment.

Beyond physical conditions, all other experiences are part of a person's social environment. To some degree, even unborn babies have a social environment. They can hear outside-the-womb sounds, especially the pregnant person's voice that may be soothing or startling due to fear or anger. These sounds are reinforced by physical signals—changes in blood pressure, breathing rate, and hormones, sent to the fetus by the pregnant person. After birth, the social environment affects the way a child grows and develops in every developmental domain.

Prostock-Studio/Shutterstock.com

Figure 1.3 Because they share genes, biological parents and children often look alike. *What physical traits do this father and son have in common?*

Heredity and Environment Combined

The concepts of nature and nurture have been around since ancient times, but the phrase nature versus nurture was popularized by Francis Galton in the 1800s to frame the discussion of the importance of heredity (nature) and environment (nurture) on human development.

Investigate Special Topics

Twin and Virtual Twin Studies

Raised in different Ohio cities, Jim Lewis and Jim Springer—known as the "Jim Twins"—are identical twins who didn't meet or even know of each other until they were nearly 40 years old. When they finally did meet, they discovered that they both bit their fingernails, both drove light blue Chevrolets, both liked to vacation on the same beach in Florida, and both named their sons James Alan. Also, not only did they both marry women named Linda, they both got divorced and then married women named Betty.

Sara and Julie Curry are what's known as virtual twins. *Virtual twins* are unrelated children of almost the exact same age raised in the same household. Because they were having difficulties conceiving, Sara and Julie's parents applied to adopt a baby. Shortly after they found out they could adopt Sara, they discovered Mrs. Curry was expecting Julie. The girls are only four months apart in age. Unlike the Jim Twins, Julie and Sara are very different from one another. Sara is talkative, but Julie is quiet. Sara likes to dress up, but Julie likes to dress casually. Sara hates extreme sports, but Julie likes to go skydiving.

Child development researchers have long been interested in the effects of heredity. They noted that identical twins, who have the same genetic code, were more alike in physical traits and intellectual abilities than are brothers and sisters or other family members. The same similarities were found in identical twins even when they were raised apart from each other in different environments.

Studies of virtual twins, however, revealed that although the environment would be very similar for both children, they were often very different in most traits. Thus, heredity has a major impact on growth and development.

Today, most studies of heredity are conducted in a laboratory. **Genetics** (juh-NET-iks) is the study of the factors involved in the passing of traits in living beings

Feature Viorika/E+ via Getty Images

from one generation to the next. In short, genetics is the study of heredity. *Geneticists* (biologists who study heredity) continue to make strides in learning which traits pass from biological parents to child.

Practice Your Skills

Compare and contrast what research into different types of twins tells us about the influence of heredity and the impact of the environment. Working in pairs or small groups, choose from the following types of twin studies: (1) Identical twins reared together; (2) Identical twins reared apart, (3) Fraternal twins, and (4) Virtual twins. Once you have your topic, search online to find what the latest research tells us about heredity and environment for the twins you are studying. You can also take advantage of any twins (identical, fraternal, virtual) that you personally know through interviews and anecdotes. Compile the key takeaways from the research/interviews into a presentation to share with the class, and then synthesize the findings from all the presentations to gain a broader understanding of the *nature/nurture* continuum.

In Galton's time, nature and nurture were seen as battling for supremacy, and people argued about which was more important. Today, the thinking is more about collaboration and how nature and nurture work together to shape us as human beings. Following are a few examples of the interaction of heredity and environment:

- Potential intelligence is inherited, but physical factors (nutrition and rest) and quality of experiences (high-quality child care; challenging and engaging teachers) determine whether the potential will be reached or not.
- Fear of new things is genetic trait that can clearly be seen in some children. These children tend to startle easily and avoid or withdraw from new situations. While fearful children may always be somewhat uncomfortable around new people, places, and things, that fear and discomfort can be greatly reduced by calm and patient parenting, positive early experiences, and repeated exposure to new things in a safe environment.

Heredity Affected by Environment

In recent years, geneticists have discovered genes are not fixed as once thought. The environment in which a person lives, both before and after birth, can alter genes through their epigenome. The **epigenome** (eh-pih-JEE-nohm), which means above the genes, consists of chemicals that can turn genes on and off. These chemicals tell the gene what to do, and where and when to do things. Thus, the epigenome is like the operating system of a computer or smartphone. The epigenome explains why even identical twins who have the same structural genome are somewhat different before birth, as discussed in the Investigate Special Topics section.

How does the epigenome affect who people are? The following in **Figure 1.4** is what is currently known:

Stressors are situations that cause worry and anxiety. Throughout the text you will learn about stress and **trauma** (experiences characterized by high levels of negative stress) and how these impact growth and development. Stress can be both beneficial and harmful depending on the level of stress and how often and how long the body's stress system is turned on. Having loving and responsive people in a person's life reduces the effects of stress. Without these people, problems may occur even in later life. See **Figure 1.5** to learn about the three types of stress.

Although the epigenome can change throughout life, positive and negative experiences from conception to 12 months have the most lasting effects. The brain is the most susceptible to changes in the epigenome. Adverse experiences are not erased but affect the person's overall well-being for the rest of their life. Changes in the epigenome—both positive and negative—can be passed down to the next generation if they occur prenatally. Generally the chemical tags are erased, but about one percent of these tags are not erased and are passed on to the offspring due to changes in the egg and sperm. In these cases, nurture becomes nature.

Positive environmental factors cause chemical compounds to turn on genetic potential. This helps the person become all they can be.

POSITIVE FACTORS
- Healthy diet and exercise
- Quality learning experiences
- Supportive and loving relationships

Negative environmental factors may lead to stress and trauma. This may cause harm in all domains of development.

NEGATIVE FACTORS
- Poor health practices
- Exposure to toxic substances and situations
- Lack of quality experiences with people and objects

EPIGENOME

Goodheart-Willcox Publisher

Figure 1.4 The epigenome consists of chemicals that turn genes on and off. *How does the epigenome affect who people are?*

Figure 1.5 Levels of Stress

Level	Definition	Examples	Results
Toxic	Strong and prolonged (over a long time) activation of the body's stress system	• Family and community violence • Multiple, repeated traumatic events	• Development of a smaller brain • Stress-related physical illness, such as heart disease, stroke, and possibly diabetes • Mental health problems, such as depression, anxiety disorders, and substance abuse
Tolerable	Not as long-lasting as toxic stress	• Death or serious illness of a loved one • Parental divorce	• Can be helped with loving and supporting relationships • Recovers with adult support • Becomes toxic without support
Positive	Moderate and short-lived stress	• Meeting new people • Attending a new child care and education program or a new school • Taking a test • Having a medical procedure	• Can become more serious if the setting is not warm or secure or if supportive adults are not available

Goodheart-Willcox Publisher

Figure 1.5. The three levels of stress have varying effects on children. *Think back on your own childhood. Did you experience all three levels of stress?*

 FOCUS ON MENTAL HEALTH

Toxic stress or prolonged and frequent tolerable stress can result in mental health issues throughout life. The government's Substance Abuse and Mental Health Services Administration (SAMHSA's) National Helpline is a confidential, free, 24-hour-a-day, 365-day-a-year, information service, in English and Spanish, for people facing mental and/or substance use disorders. This service provides referrals to local treatment facilities, support groups, and community-based organizations. Callers can also order free publications and other information.

Lesson 1.1 Review and Assessment

1. Child development is the scientific study of children from _____. (1.1-1)
   A. conception through adolescence
   B. infancy through adolescence
   C. birth through adolescence
   D. birth through toddlerhood

2. Which of the following is not a domain of child development? (1.1-2)
   A. Social-emotional   C. Trauma
   B. Intellectual   D. Physical

3. **True or False.** The individual life cycle is a description of the stages of change people experience during adolescence. (1.1-3)

4. Human development is affected by _____. (1.1-4)
   A. heredity and environment
   B. heredity only
   C. environment only
   D. neither heredity nor environment

Principles and Theories of Growth and Development

Learning Outcomes

After studying this lesson, you will be able to

1.2-1 **identify** key principles of growth and development.

1.2-2 **give examples** of the major principles of growth and development.

Reading and Notetaking Activity

Skim this chapter from top to bottom and from left to right and list all of the key headings. Then, identify key terms that you don't know and scan through the chapter to find their definitions. Write a "topic sentence" for each heading, using the key terms to explain what you think you will learn. After you read this chapter, write a new topic sentence for each section, outlining the main points you learned.

Introduction

Every science works on certain *principles*—basic truths or assumptions. For example, in physics, one principle is: Every effect has a cause. Principles are generated through countless research studies over time. When the same results come up over and over again, a principle is noted.

In child development, you know that each child is unique. Yet, through research observations, you know there are basic patterns of growth and development called *principles*. These principles are *universal* (apply to all children throughout all times), *predictable* (will occur in future observations), and *orderly* (patterns are sequenced and will occur at approximate times).

Why are principles of development important? When you make any decision about a child, taking into account these principles will aid development, but ignoring the principles will likely hinder development. Researchers and theorists use their existing knowledge about principles of growth and development as they develop new theories.

1.2-1 Principles of Growth and Development

Each person is unique, yet people are more alike than different. Experts study these likenesses to find patterns in the way people generally grow and develop. These patterns, or **principles of growth and development**, do not fit every person exactly. They are true enough to be used as a guide, however, when learning about children (**Figure 1.6**).

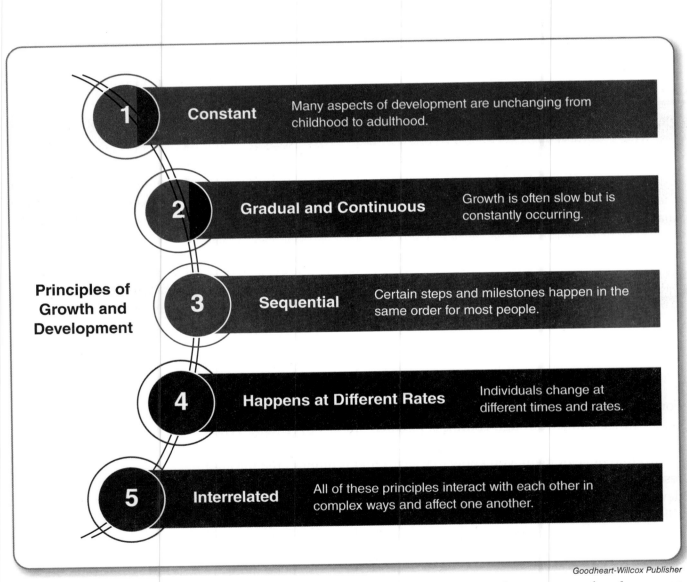

Principles of Growth and Development

1 **Constant** — Many aspects of development are unchanging from childhood to adulthood.

2 **Gradual and Continuous** — Growth is often slow but is constantly occurring.

3 **Sequential** — Certain steps and milestones happen in the same order for most people.

4 **Happens at Different Rates** — Individuals change at different times and rates.

5 **Interrelated** — All of these principles interact with each other in complex ways and affect one another.

Figure 1.6 The principles of growth and development do not fit every person exactly. *Do you know someone for whom one or more of the principles of growth and development does not fit?*

The following sections describe key principles of growth and development in more detail.

Principle 1: Growth and Development Are Constant

Many aspects of a person's growth and development are unchanging. This is called **constancy**. Traits that children possess today are a good hint—but not proof—of traits that will be present in the future. For example, tall two-year-olds tend to be tall adults. Children who are good students in elementary school are likely to be good students in high school. Happy, secure children tend to be cheerful, confident adults.

Why is this so? There are two reasons for constancy in growth and development. First, new growth, knowledge, and skills are always built on those already acquired. One stage always prepares the way for the next, such as making sounds before speaking words. Second, people often live in the same environment for years. For major changes to take place in growth and development, major changes must take place in the environment.

Principle 2: Growth and Development Are Gradual and Continuous

Growth and development are, for the most part, gradual and continuous. A child does not grow or develop overnight. Consider a baby taking their first steps on a certain date. Each day before walking, the baby grew, the body matured, and the baby practiced motor skills, such as crawling and pulling up to stand. All these small changes lead to the baby's first steps (**Figure 1.7**).

In a positive way, the principle suggests development does not reverse overnight. A few mistakes or stresses usually do not cause severe problems. As an example, a one-day junk food binge does not seriously harm a healthy person. The principle is also positive in that setbacks in development can be overcome with correct intervention and effort.

On the negative side, the principle can work to a person's disadvantage. It suggests that poor

Ivanko80/Shutterstock.com

Figure 1.7 Children must practice many motor skills before they take their first steps. *What are some of these motor skills?*

growth and development are not easily reversed. Consider a child with poor health due to a lifelong poor diet. It may take many months or years of eating a carefully planned diet to restore the child's health. In some cases, the body may never be able to overcome these obstacles. Consider, too, a child who lags in intellectual development due to the lack of quality experiences with adults and with toys and books. Once extremely behind in learning, it is difficult to overcome the learning gap between where the child is and where they should be.

Principle 3: Growth and Development Happen in Sequenced Steps

For growth and development to be continuous, change must build on what children have already learned. For instance, writing comes from making random marks. The steps in growth and development follow one another in a set order called **sequenced steps**. These sequenced steps are called *stages* or *milestones*. Researchers have **codified** (arranged in an orderly way) the milestones through many years of observations.

The sequence should always lead to greater complexity of behaviors, such as scooting to walking, thinking in prelogical to logical terms, and watching others play to interacting in team sports.

How do milestones aid those who are working with children? Milestones give adults ideas about teachable moments. A **teachable moment** is an optimal time when a person can learn a new task. Teachable moments occur when the body and mind are physically ready, when caregivers encourage and support the child, and when the child feels a strong desire to learn. If a child has not reached the teachable moment, they will feel stressed when trying to grasp a task or skill. Waiting too long after the teachable moment occurs may cause problems, too. For example, a child who is eager to learn to read but not given the opportunity may lose interest and not reach their full potential as a reader.

Principle 4: Growth and Development Happen at Different Rates

Growth and development happen at different rates for different people. All people change with time. Some people enter a stage earlier and some later than the typical age. Researchers know the typical time when a developmental milestone occurs. The timing is called an **age norm** and can be expressed as an average age or age range. The age norm simply predicts when development will likely occur.

Developmental acceleration occurs when a child performs like an older child. For example, a 30-month-old child who speaks in long, complex sentences is developmentally accelerated in language. A **developmental delay** occurs when a child performs like a younger child. For example, a three-year-old who speaks in two-word sentences may have a developmental delay in language.

Focus on Health

A Lesson on Safety

A *teachable moment* is any unplanned event that can be used as a learning opportunity. Teachable moments occur many times each day. By observing children, you can see these opportunities and teach to the moment. Children learn best when they show spontaneous interest and when learning is embedded in meaningful contexts.

Here is an example: A family is attending a barbecue at a friend's home. Their three-year-old child has never seen a grill and excitedly runs over and tries to touch it. Instead of scolding the child, the parent gently leads them away while explaining a grill is just like their kitchen stove, but it is outside. Thus, it is very hot and should not be touched.

The parent points out that the person cooking has special gloves and long-handled kitchen tools to protect them from the heat and fire. The parent positions their chair in view of the grill and sits with the child to watch the cooking. From time to time, the child mentions the heat and the leaping flames, occasionally saying, "Hot. Don't touch." The parent smiles and says, "Yes, that's right." The child smiles and nods her head in agreement, content with this new knowledge.

Look at the first paragraph again. How did this example fit the criteria of a teachable moment?

Photo: wavebreakmedia/Shutterstock.com

Why do the rates differ among people? The most common reasons include the following:

- The effects of genes and the epigenome differ in a given person. Even identical twins will vary in aspects of growth and development.
- Gender determines different growth rates. For example, the bones and organs of a biological female are more mature at all ages than those of a biological male.
- Environmental influences have a major impact on growth and development. Children need a supportive environment to grow at the best rate. A supportive environment includes much love and care and many ways to learn. If the environment is lacking, lags or delays in growth and development occur. On the other hand, an adult's attempts to hurry growth and development may cause a child harmful stress.
- **Motivation**, which is a child's desire to achieve, also makes growth and development rates vary (**Figure 1.8**). Some children are eager to achieve, and others are more poorly motivated.

Rates of growth and development also vary within the individual. Some of the rate changes are expected. Biological maturation, especially of the brain, determines typical periods of fast and slow growth and development in all people.

Beyond these expected differences in rates, other differences are mainly determined by a person's genetic makeup and environmental experiences. For example, a child may develop at a fast rate in motor skills and a slower rate in language usage. A child may be developmentally accelerated or delayed in one or more areas. It is even possible for a child to be delayed in one area and accelerated in another. A few children may be developmentally accelerated or delayed in most areas.

Principle 5: Growth and Development Are Interrelated

In this book, the physical, intellectual, and social-emotional aspects of growth and development are often discussed in separate chapters. This is so you can better understand each aspect. In reality, however, all aspects are **interrelated**, or they interact in complex ways.

People who work with children must understand how areas of growth and development affect one another. For instance, a teacher's job is to improve children's intellectual growth. If children come to school hungry or sleepy, however, they will not do well in learning activities. Studies have shown that unless children have positive feelings about themselves (social-emotional domain), they cannot devote the attention and energy needed for learning. Understanding these interrelationships improves the way people work with children.

1.2-2 Theories of Growth and Development

Several researchers who studied children extensively have developed theories. A **theory** is a set of statements offered as a possible explanation for a phenomenon, such as child growth and development. Child development theories

- describe changes (may also be called *stages*) over time within one or more domains (areas) of development
- show changes among domains of development
- explain why the changes occur

Amorn Suriyan/Shutterstock.com

Figure 1.8 Motivation is a person's desire to achieve or progress. *What are some qualities of a motivated person?*

Some theories deal with biology, others with the environment, and still others with both biology and the environment. See **Figure 1.9** for a detailed description of the theories. Because these theories cover many aspects of development, they are often referred to as the *grand theories*. Associated with these theories are the pioneering theorists whose works shape people's knowledge of child development.

Figure 1.9 Child Development Grand Theories

Theory	Description
Maturational	Arnold Gesell (1880–1961) believed that physical and intellectual development was determined by heredity and biological maturation. His theory established many of the age norms and ideas about "readiness."
Psychoanalytic	Sigmund Freud (1856–1939) believed personality (and mental health) was determined by how children coped with their physical drives. He examined how children regulate their desires and take on social norms. His theory was used primarily by psychiatrists.
Psychosocial	Erik Erikson (1902–1994) was concerned about conflicts that occur between a child's needs and social demands. He was a student of Anna Freud (1895–1982), the daughter of Sigmund Freud, and his work has close ties to Freud's psychoanalytic theory. Erikson believed that people who can cope with each conflict develop a healthy personality and vice versa. His theory is used in preventing and treating mental health problems.
Learning	Several theorists, including B.F. Skinner (1904–1990) and Albert Bandura (1925–present), focused on how the environments affect observable behaviors, not internal changes, such as personality and how you learn. They studied how behaviors can be reinforced (made stronger) or extinguished (stopped). Learning theories are mainly used in behavior modification or in intervention methods for children having learning or behavioral problems.
Cognitive-developmental	Jean Piaget (1896–1980) believed children think differently at different ages. He thought children constructed (built) their knowledge through experiences. As children learn new ideas, their minds adapt (change). His theory totally changed child development. Piaget's work has been carried on by his students such as Rheta DeVries (1936–2012) and Constant Kamii (1931–present) who have applied Piaget's theory to many aspects of education.
Sociocultural	Lev Vygotsky (1896–1934) disagreed with Piaget's theory that children totally construct their own knowledge. He believed that some knowledge was a personal construction, but much was a social construction (taught by people of one's culture). His idea of mentoring or tutoring learning is used in many schools today.
Ecological systems	Urie Bronfenbrenner (1917–2005) noted that children's development is influenced by both heredity and their environment (family, friends, schools, and health services) as well as their indirect environment (families' workplaces and general culture). He also believed that children affect their environment. For example, how children treat friends may affect their friendships. His theory has made people more aware of how the many contexts (systems) affect child development.

Goodheart-Willcox Publisher

Why are there so many theories? Why cannot just one theory be validated by research? Theorists experience the following problems:

- Development is too broad and complex for one theorist to study all aspects of development.
- Research is not completely objective. Theorists begin with their personal knowledge, interests, and hunches. Their hunches determine what questions they ask and how they set up their research.
- New research has to begin with what is known based on theory.
- New research relies on available research tools. Most of the child development theorists were doing their work before the time of computers or even calculators. Recording equipment was not available either, so all notes were handwritten. Technology, such as brain scans and computers, make a major difference in the ability to research child development. Even with the best of technology, however, research is a long and slow process.
- Theory development requires a knowledge network because answers come only when theories can be tested by others. Some child development theorists did work together, but most did not have easy access to the theories of others.

No one theory has been adequate to describe the complexity of child development. The grand theories have given direction for more research. The research done by others may **confirm** (prove accurate) or **disprove** (show to be wrong or false) a theory, expand the theory, or apply the knowledge based on the theory to practice, such as education or child guidance. Grand theories form the basis of *mini theories*, which are smaller theories that focus on particular aspects of a grand theory, rather than trying to explain all of growth and development. These smaller, more focused mini-theories are often easier to research. The grand theories and the works of some of the mini-theorists will be highlighted throughout the text.

Lesson 1.2 Review and Assessment

1. Each of the following is a key principle of growth and development except _____. (1.2.1)
   A. growth and development are constant
   B. growth and development happens in unpredictable stages
   C. growth and development are gradual and continuous
   D. growth and development are interrelated
2. Which theorist focused on conflicts that occur between a child's needs and social demands? (1.2.2)
   A. Erik Erikson
   B. Maria Montessori
   C. Jean Piaget
   D. Sigmund Freud
3. Which theorist believed that personality is determined by how children cope with their physical drives? (1.2.2)
   A. Erik Erikson
   B. Maria Montessori
   C. Jean Piaget
   D. Sigmund Freud
4. Which theorist believed that children construct their knowledge through experiences? (1.2.2)
   A. Sigmund Freud
   B. B.F. Skinner
   C. Jean Piaget
   D. Urie Bronfenbrenner

Lesson 1.3

Studying and Observing Children

Key Terms

advocates
child-centered society
direct observation
empathize
hierarchy
indirect observation
irreducible
self-actualization

Learning Outcomes

After studying this lesson, you will be able to

1.3-1 **recognize** the benefits of studying children.

1.3-2 **assess** Abraham Maslow's *hierarchy of human needs*.

1.3-3 **explain** Brazelton and Greenspan's seven basic needs of all children.

1.3-4 **develop** observation skills.

Reading and Notetaking Activity

In learning about children, you will also learn a great deal about yourself. As you read this lesson, consider what each concept you learn might teach you about yourself. Keep a list of these ideas, placing a star beside any concepts that especially interest you. After reading the lesson, pick two or three of these ideas and write a few paragraphs reflecting on how the content in this lesson helps you understand yourself.

Introduction

All sciences, including child development, are based on the idea that nature is orderly, and can be discovered through study and observation. People must have some understanding of children before they can understand their own "developmental roots" or be responsible for or take action on behalf of children. Much of a person's understanding can come from personal observations of children when these are combined with *informed knowledge* (knowledge from theory and research).

1.3-1 Benefits of Studying Children

How will studying children help you? Learning about children will help you to better understand yourself now and as you continue to develop. One of your future goals may be to become a responsible parent. You may even be interested in a career in a child-related field. All adults—regardless of parenthood or career—have responsibilities for protecting children.

Understand Yourself

Many times, adults are not fully aware that who they are today is a result of the children they once were. As you study children, you can gain insight into your own growth, development, and values. You can also understand how your values affect your feelings about, and reactions to, children. This knowledge can then help you to learn better ways to care for children.

Studying children can help you develop, too. It can help you appreciate all that goes into taking a first step or saying a first word. When you help a child overcome a fear or learn a skill, you feel good. Adults often enjoy just being with children. Children can share gifts that, sadly, adults often outgrow. Their awe of beauty, their frankness, and their magical thinking are charming to many adults.

Be a Responsible Parent

Parenting is a mind-boggling task. How much adults know about children, however, can determine the kind of parents they become. Parents who are responsible meet their children's needs. By studying children, parents know their children's needs at each stage of development. They also know the best ways to respond to those needs.

Work With Children

In the past, people thought all the knowledge and skills that adults need for child-related careers—including parenting—came naturally. Many felt just being raised in a family teaches adults all they need to know about children and child care skills.

Today, experts know that understanding children requires careful study. Changes continue to take place in society and in families. These changes require people to know more about children's growth and development than what they observe in their own families. Adults with child-related careers should study children. Some careers may seem to focus mainly on one aspect of children's development. The child is, however, a whole person. Anyone preparing for a child-related career should know some about all aspects of children's growth and development, since the domains of development are so interrelated. Learning more about children enables workers in child-related careers to provide better care for children. (Throughout the text you will note *Focus on Careers* features that highlight careers working with children.)

Protect Children's Rights

In the United States, people live in a **child-centered society**—a society that sees children as important, cares about their well-being, and works to meet their needs. However, some children experience a great deal of harm through abuse and neglect. Children need safe environments. They need homes, schools, and other places where they can develop to their full potential (**Figure 1.10**).

Halfpoint/Shutterstock.com

Figure 1.10 Children achieve their potential through different experiences and rates of growth; it is important that families recognize their children's strengths and weaknesses and nurture them accordingly. *Consider a child you know. What are their strengths and weaknesses? What experiences might encourage their growth and development?*

Children's Rights

Children are easily hurt because they are physically weaker than adults and cannot reason as adults. Society must protect them. By learning about children, lawmakers can pass laws that will keep children safe.

The Convention on the Rights of the Child (United Nations International Children's Education Fund) wrote 54 articles that set out the rights of every child in the world. These rights can be given under 11 major categories. The following categories explain children's rights to:

- **an identity** (government should protect children's names, family ties, and nationalities)
- **a family** (children should be able to live with their parents unless this is not in the children's best interest; parents have the responsibility for raising children with government support)
- **express themselves and have access to information** (children have the right to express their views; have freedom of thought, conscience, and religion; and obtain information)
- **a safe and healthy life** (children have the right to life; the government should do all it can to make sure children survive and develop; children should have access to medical services and a decent standard of living)
- **special protection in times of war** (children who are refugees are entitled to special protection; children who are under 15 should not take part in armed conflict)
- **an education** (primary education should be free and required of all children; secondary education should be accessible to all children)
- **special care for those with disabilities** (children with disabilities have the right to special care, education, and training)
- **protection from discrimination** (all rights apply to all children; children have the right to practice their own cultures, religions, and languages)
- **protection from abuse** (children shall be protected against abuse and neglect; government shall be involved with laws and programs concerned with abuse)
- **protection from harmful work** (children have the right to rest, leisure, play, and participation in cultural and artistic activities; children have the right to be protected from having to participate in work that threatens their health, education, and development)
- **special treatment if arrested** (children are entitled to assistance and treatment that respect their rights)

Discussion Activity

In small groups, list children's rights on the left side of a piece of paper. Then, brainstorm at least two practical situations in which each right can be applied. Use examples from everyday life and historical examples where needed. Choose one situation for each right and then share your group's examples with the rest of the class.

Photo: Tom Wang/Shutterstock.com

All children should have the chance to grow in an environment that promotes their health and well-being. By studying children, you will learn how to provide these safe places.

In the United States, parents have the rights of guardianship and determine their children's upbringing. For example, they control the children's level of financial support. They also control religious and moral teachings, as well as education and health care choices. The state can come between a parent and child only if the court feels the child needs more protection.

Each state makes laws and policies to protect children. The state can make laws to develop child welfare services. Each state has a department concerned with children's welfare and the obligations and responsibilities of families. These state departments are usually called *Department of Human Services* (with offices pertaining to children within the larger department) or *Child Protective Services (CPS)*. These offices are staffed with caseworkers who work to make sure laws and policies are being carried out by families with minor children.

For example, laws exist regarding the quality of child care programs, school attendance, child labor, and illegal drug sales to help protect children and society. State laws also protect children from the results of their own lack of judgment. For example, young children are not responsible legally for their contracts. Children are treated differently from adults in court. The state can make laws to develop child welfare services.

Children have gained rights, too. Examples are the rights of due process and fair treatment in schools and juvenile and family courts. In some states, children may receive medical help without parental consent.

Laws can be enacted on the local level, too. An example is a curfew law. In addition, local citizen groups often become **advocates** (people who actively support a cause) of children's rights. These groups attempt to get needed laws passed and notify the appropriate people when it seems a child's rights have been violated. People who are knowledgeable about child development make excellent advocates.

Focus on Careers

Child Care Worker

Child care workers work with young children who are not yet in school. They may also work with older children before or after school. Child care workers meet children's basic needs and provide activities to stimulate growth and development.

Career cluster: Education and training.

Education: Educational requirements vary greatly for each state. Requirements may include a Child Development Associate (CDA) credential or a bachelor's degree.

Job outlook: Future employment opportunities are expected to grow as fast as the average for all occupations.

To learn more about a career as a child care worker, visit the United States Department of Labor's *Occupational Outlook Handbook* website. You will also be able to compare the job responsibilities, educational requirements, job outlook, and average pay of child care workers with similar occupations.

Photo: michaeljung/Shutterstock.com

Child Protective Services

Because of deep concern for the welfare of children and their parents, each state has created an agency called *Child Protective Services (CPS)* or a child protection office under various titles within the state's Department of Human Services. The authority to provide certain services is vested in each agency through state laws and government policies.

The people who work in these agencies are caseworkers trained in social work. Besides their initial training, caseworkers can receive additional training specific to their jurisdictions through the National Resource Center for Child Protective Services (NRCCPS). This training is funded by the Children's Bureau, U.S. Department of Health and Human Services.

What are the basic responsibilities of caseworkers for CPS? Their roles include

- *providing services to families in their homes.* Caseworkers focus on family strengths and provide families with assistance when needed to protect children within their home.
- *investigating reports of child neglect and abuse.* If the reports are *substantiated* (found true), they can decide whether to remove children immediately or provide the families with assistance and continue follow-up visits.
- *placing children in the state's foster care program.* Caseworkers receive children who are abandoned, children they remove from homes, and children police remove from homes. They screen parents who have applied for the role of foster parents. Caseworkers also regularly visit foster homes after child placement.
- *placing children in adoptive homes.* In order to do this, parents either surrender their rights or caseworkers decide after a period of time that these children's parents will likely never

be able to provide safe homes. They screen parents who have applied to be adoptive parents. (The courts make all final adoption decrees.)
- *providing assistance to teens as they age out of the foster care system and make a transition to independent living as adults.* This assistance is primarily counseling in nature. In many states, the work of the CPS is coordinated with agencies or *offices of child care assistance.* These agencies provide financial help to pay for child care so teenage and low-income parents can get an education or work. CPS is also coordinated with *child support enforcement.* (Enforces monetary decisions made by the courts on behalf of children when parents have never married, separated, or divorced.) Caseworkers with social work training do the needed investigations. After the investigations, enforcement of child support decisions are done by the courts.

Research Activity

Conduct research to learn more about Child Protective Services in your community. Then, answer the following questions:

1. What services does Child Protective Services provide for your community?
2. What are the qualifications for becoming a CPS caseworker?
3. What should a person do if they are concerned for the welfare of a child?
4. How does CPS handle cases where a child's rights are being violated?

Photo: Tom Wang/Shutterstock.com

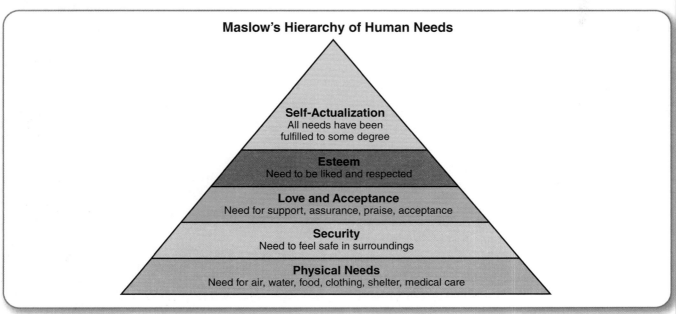

Focus on Careers

Child Advocate

Child advocates represent the best interests of children who have been abused or neglected. They promote and protect the rights of children.

Career cluster: Law, public safety, corrections, and security.

Education: Educational requirements vary for each state. Training in laws regarding children in the state in which advocates practice is often required.

Job outlook: Future employment opportunities for child advocates are expected to grow much faster than the average for all occupations.

To learn more about a career as a child advocate, visit the United States Department of Labor's *Occupational Outlook Handbook* website. You will also be able to compare the job responsibilities, educational requirements, job outlook, and average pay of child advocates with similar occupations.

Photo: Marina C/Shutterstock.com

1.3-2 Maslow's Hierarchy of Needs

Abraham Maslow, a noted psychologist, was one of the first researchers to study human needs.

Although his ideas were used to understand what motivates workers, his model was later extended to child development.

According to Maslow, people strive to fulfill their needs in a **hierarchy** (rank order). Maslow called this model *the hierarchy of human needs* (**Figure 1.11**).

Maslow's Hierarchy of Human Needs

Self-Actualization
All needs have been fulfilled to some degree

Esteem
Need to be liked and respected

Love and Acceptance
Need for support, assurance, praise, acceptance

Security
Need to feel safe in surroundings

Physical Needs
Need for air, water, food, clothing, shelter, medical care

Goodheart-Willcox Publisher

Figure 1.11 Maslow sees two kinds of needs in all humans—basic needs (physical and psychological needs) and higher-level needs (self-actualization needs). *Where would you place yourself on Maslow's hierarchy of needs? Which needs are met? Which needs are not met?*

The first four levels are *basic needs* (inborn needs). The first level includes all *physical needs*. The other three levels are the *psychological needs* (related to feelings) of security, love and acceptance, and esteem. In addition to basic needs, Maslow also created a fifth level for higher-level needs, which he called *self-actualization needs*. **Self-actualization** means to grow and feel fulfilled as a person. Self-actualization needs include the drive to pursue talents and hobbies, gain skills, and learn more about the world. Education helps to meet a person's self-actualization needs. Complete self-actualization is a lifelong process that many people never attain.

If people's basic needs are not satisfied in order of level, they will no longer be concerned about pursuing higher-level needs. Therefore, parents and other adults must first help children meet their basic needs. For instance, adults can offer children nutritious foods. Once the basic need for food is met, adults can help children turn their attention from eating to meeting their psychological needs. These needs might include building relationships with friends and being respected by others. Higher-level skills help children reach their full potential as adults.

1.3-3 Brazelton and Greenspan's Irreducible Needs

Two noted researchers and physicians, T. Berry Brazelton and Stanley I. Greenspan, researched the basic needs of all children. They identified seven needs children must meet to thrive and flourish for a lifetime, which they call the *irreducible needs of children*. (**Irreducible** means impossible to make smaller or simpler.) These needs include

- *ongoing nurturing relationships.* A nurturing relationship is critical for all development. Children from birth through the preschool years need nurturing interactions most of their waking hours. If this relationship is absent or interrupted, children are apt to develop disorders in their intellectual, social, and emotional development.
- *physical protection, safety, and regulation.* Children need an environment both before and after birth that protects them from physical and emotional harm. For example,

this includes appropriate food, clothing, and shelter and protection from toxins, harm, and any form of abuse.
- *experiences tailored to individual differences.* Each child has a unique temperament and way of relating to the world and the people in it. Families need to match the child's strengths and weaknesses with their experiences. In this way a child achieves their potential (**Figure 1.12**).
- *experiences that are developmentally appropriate.* Each child needs experiences tailored to their stage of development. Families and those working in child-related careers need to know and apply "best practices" for each stage of development as the child matures.
- *limit setting, structure, and expectations.* Children need both structure and discipline in their lives. Families and other adults need to **empathize** with children's feelings, or understand and relate to them, but set limits as well. In this way children can develop self-discipline and resolve conflicts in peaceful ways.
- *stable communities and cultural continuity.* Children need continuity of values in family, peer groups, and the broader community. Families and others who work with children must work together, not compete. For example, when two adults have different ideas about what they think is best for children and are unwilling to work together, this would be considered competing.

Tinna Pong/Shutterstock.com

Figure 1.12 Children need places where they can engage in fun and challenging activities that will encourage growth. *What activities do you think a child would consider fun and challenging?*

- *protecting the future.* People live in an interdependent nation and world. Adults must meet the needs of all children. To protect the future for one child, people must protect it for all.

1.3-4 Observing Children

Observation is the oldest, most common, and best way to learn about human behavior, including the behavior of children. You have all the equipment you need for observing—your senses. Because the senses are the main tools you use, you might think observation skills come naturally. To some extent, they do. You see and hear what goes on around you every day. It takes training, however, to interpret what you see and hear into information you can use. For this reason, many observation skills must be learned. These skills come with knowledge and practice. As an example, when you look at an X-ray or sonogram, you probably just see shadows and lines. Why would your doctor see more? With their training and experience, your doctor can see meaning in these images you may not notice.

Why Observe Children?

By observing children, you can learn about their growth and development. To observe children, you must focus on a task—what you want to learn. For example, "Are the children spending more time in the block center than in the dramatic play center, and if so, why?" As you observe, you learn more about children when using your mind to "see" more. Child development researchers often work on specific problems for years—even a lifetime.

During your course in child development, you will receive assignments requiring observation of children. These assignments are an important part of your class for the following reasons:

- Observing children will help you understand what you read in this book and what you hear about children. At the same time, what you learn from your reading and class activities will help you see more when you observe (**Figure 1.13**). What you observe will depend on the purpose of observation. Because this book looks at the sequence of children's growth and development, you will consider these principles when you observe.

- You, too, will notice behaviors that are not part of your assigned work. You will want to ask questions about what you see. This is how professional researchers learn.
- Like professional researchers, your assignment may cause you to want to learn more about a behavior. For example, you may hear three-year-olds reciting numbers from 1 to 10. Does this mean they can count objects to 10? To find out, you may need to observe behavior more closely.
- Observing children can help you better interact with the children in your care. You can learn this by observing how others work with children and how the children react to them. When you observe adults who work with children, you can learn to imitate their successful behaviors. For instance, if you observe a teacher sitting on the floor working with children, you might later try this, too. This can help you interact with children in a more positive way. Because many skills are learned through imitation, this type of observation is important.
- In some cases, you may be allowed to participate in the activities of children while observing. Extra "helping hands" are often needed and serve as a learning experience for you, too. In all cases, by watching carefully, you can respond quickly if dangers arise.

DGLImages/iStock via Getty Images Plus

Figure 1.13 Each time this student observes and takes notes, they see more. *What observations can you make about the children in this picture? Would you be able to "observe" more if you could hear what they were saying?*

Ways to Observe

There are many ways to observe children. The best way is to observe children directly. Many observations, however, are done indirectly.

Direct Observations

A **direct observation** means watching children in real time, typically in their natural environments. These environments include home, play groups, child care programs, schools, and public places, such as shopping centers, parks, and restaurants (**Figure 1.14**). Most direct observations occur in these types of places.

Sometimes it is not possible or practical to observe directly in the child's natural environment.

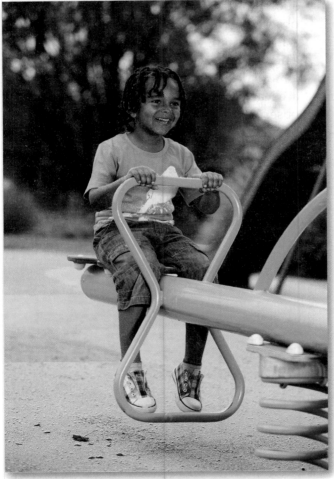

Samuel Borges Photography/Shutterstock.com

Figure 1.14 Playgrounds are one natural environment where direct observation may occur. *Why do you think it is better for direct observation to take place in a child's natural environment?*

In that case, researchers often set up special laboratory settings where they can do direct observations of behaviors that are more difficult to study in the natural environment. They may need to observe, for example, how a baby reacts when the mother leaves the room and a stranger enters. Researchers also use laboratory observations to speed up the observation process. Suppose researchers want to observe a child's balancing skills. If they go to a park with a balance beam, they may wait hours before they observe enough children to form a sample for their study. In a laboratory, however, children would arrive at the setting, walk the beam, and leave. Researchers also use laboratory settings when special equipment is needed.

Observations set in laboratories cannot answer all questions. For instance, it would be hard for researchers to know if children really like playing on a balance beam. Although some information in this book comes from research in the laboratory setting, this is not the way you will start observing. You will begin your observations in the natural setting, as do most researchers.

Indirect Observations

Although direct observation is the main way to learn about children, researchers also use other observation methods to study them. Sometimes they want to see something in more detail or check direct observations. One important method is **indirect observation**. This may include asking questions of families, teachers, or children. Indirect observation also includes observing products children make, such as artwork or the stories children dictate or write. It may involve watching videos or audio recordings of children. Studying test scores is an indirect observation. Generally speaking, a researcher can gather more data quickly through indirect observation than through direct observation.

Although you can learn a lot from indirect observations, such as children's artwork, you can learn even more when you observe children making these products. For example, by looking at a drawing, you can easily notice that a child has colored outside the lines. How can you tell if this is due to lack of motor control, a damaged crayon, or a rushed coloring job? Only direct observation will tell you.

Guidelines for Observing

Anyone observing children should follow certain guidelines. See **Figure 1.15** for a detailed description of these important standards. These guidelines are important for several reasons. First, they protect the rights of the subject and the observer. They also list proper behaviors you should follow when visiting a child care center. Finally, these guidelines will help you make meaningful and accurate observations.

Figure 1.15 Guidelines for Observations

Guidelines	Details About Guidelines
Know your objectives.	• Objectives tell you what age children to observe, what type of activity to observe, where to observe (in some cases), how much time to spend observing, what type of records to keep, etc.
Obtain permission to observe.	• In public places (a park or shopping center), you may observe children without permission. Families or other adults are more cooperative, however, when they know what you are doing. To observe in private places (homes or child care programs), you will need prior approval from your teacher and permission from the adult at the home or program. Observe only on dates and times approved by your teacher.
Know what to do at the site.	• Sites have different procedures. At some sites, you may observe in an observation room looking through a one way mirror. At other sites, you may help with the children. In still other sites, you might sit away from the children. Find out in advance what you will be expected to do. Also make sure to follow all health and safety procedures.
Ask questions at convenient times.	• Never interrupt a staff member who is engaged with children or an adult.
Be sure observations do not distract children from regular activities.	• Unless asked to help, do not get any closer to the children than necessary. If children come to you, answer them briefly, but encourage them to return to their activities. Also, avoid talking directly to children. Your objectives should never interfere with the program objectives.
Observe carefully and objectively.	• Only state facts; state what you see. If the child is speaking try to write exactly what they say. Observe closely so you can remember the situation vividly. Many situations can affect objectivity, such as distractions, fatigue, or discomfort. Biases also affect objectivity, so observers should be careful when they study their own children or children of close friends or relatives, and make note of any biases they might have. If possible, try and observe children who you don't know.
Record accurately.	• When recording information, try to be as detailed and organized as possible. Record information about where, when (exact times), who, what, etc. Checklists, charts, and tables can be developed that will help you organize your notes and record more accurately.
Protect the rights of all observed.	• People have privacy rights observers must protect in the following ways: • Never discuss a child in front of that child or an adult except the child's teacher. • Use no name or the child's first name only during class discussions. • Respect families' rights to refuse your request to observe. • Keep information confidential. • Destroy notes completely when they are no longer useful.

Goodheart-Willcox Publisher

1. Which of the following is not a benefit of studying children? (1.3.1)
   A. Being a responsible parent
   B. Protecting children's rights
   C. Learning which punishments work best
   D. Understanding children

2. Which of Maslow's hierarchy of human needs is described as a need to be liked and accepted? (1.3.2)
   A. Esteem
   B. Love and acceptance
   C. Security
   D. Physical needs

3. Which of these is not one of the seven irreducible needs of children as identified by Brazelton and Greenspan? (1.3.3)
   A. Ongoing nurturing relationships
   B. Physical protection, safety, and regulation
   C. Experiences tailored to individual differences
   D. Unlimited settings and expectations

4. A direct observation can take place in each of the following settings except _____. (1.3.4)
   A. home
   B. school
   C. office
   D. playground

Chapter

1

Review and Assessment

Chapter Summary

Lesson 1.1

1.1-1 Define the term *child development*. The scientific study of children is called child development.

1.1-2 Describe and organize the three domains of child development. Child development is generally classified into three categories or domains including physical, cognitive, and social-emotional.

1.1-3 Summarize the six stages of the individual life cycle that involve children. Children develop over six life cycle stages including one before birth (prenatal) and 5 after birth (neonatal or newborn, infancy, toddler, preschool, and school-age or middle childhood)

1.1-4 Differentiate between heredity and environment and synthesize how they interact to influence growth and development. Children's growth and development is influenced by heredity (genetics or nature) and environment (nurture) working together.

1.1-5 Define the term epigenome and analyze how it *influences* the heredity/ environment connection. Chemicals that can turn genes on and off are called the epigenome. They tell the gene what to do, and where and when to do things, and are an example of how the environment interacts with genetics.

Lesson 1.2

1.2-1 Identify key principles of growth and development. There are five key principles of growth and development. Growth and development are constant, gradual and continuous, sequential, happen at different rates, and are interrelated.

1.2-2 Give examples of the major principles of growth and development. The five key principles provide a framework for understanding growth and development and allow descriptions and examples.

Lesson 1.3

1.3-1 Recognize the benefits of studying children. Studying children helps you understand yourself and the children around you. It can help you as a parent and/or in a career working with children.

1.3-2 Assess Abraham Maslow's *hierarchy of human needs*. Maslow's hierarchy of human needs starts with 4 levels of basic needs: both physical and psychological. In addition to basic needs, Maslow also created a fifth level for higher-level needs, which he called self-actualization needs. Self-actualization means to grow and feel fulfilled as a person.

1.3-3 Explain Brazelton and Greenspan's seven basic needs of all children. Brazelton and Greenspan said all children have seven irreducible needs including: nurturing relationships, physical protection and safety, experiences tailored to individual differences and that are developmentally appropriate, limit setting and structure, stable communities and cultural continuity, and protecting the future.

1.3-4 Develop observation skills. Observation can be both direct and indirect. Following guidelines such as consent/permission, knowing objectives, and observing carefully and objectively can make your observations more effective.

College and Career Portfolio

Portfolio Foundations

When you apply for college admission, a job, or a community service position, you may need to tell others about your qualifications for the position. A portfolio is a selection of related materials you collect and organize. These materials show your qualifications, skills, talents, and interests. For instance, a certificate that shows you completed first aid and CPR training could help you get a summer job working with children through a park district program. An essay you wrote about protecting children from neglect may help you gain admission to the early childhood education college program you desire. A transcript of your school grades also shows your qualifications to a potential college.

There are a variety of methods for organizing and presenting your credentials in a portfolio format, including print versions, e-portfolios (using programs such as PowerPoint or Google Slides), and web sites to name a few. Your school may have specific programs available to you, or you might be encouraged to make your own choices regarding format.

Recall and Application

1. _____ is a change in size, such as height, or in quantity, such as vocabulary. (1.1.1)
   A. Gene
   B. Growth
   C. Heredity
   D. Development

2. Physical development involves _____. (1.1.2)
   A. growth of the body and the development of both large and small motor skills
   B. how people think and learn
   C. interactions with people in social groups, disposition, and emotions
   D. the rate at which a child learns to read

3. To help them study development over time, experts divide life into _____ stages. (1.1.3)
   A. age-related
   B. growth-related
   C. development-related
   D. gene-related

4. _____ are sections of the DNA molecule found in a person's cells that determine individual traits. (1.1.4)
   A. Epigenomes
   B. Domains
   C. Genes
   D. Stressors

5. Each of the following is a key principle of growth and development except _____. (1.2.1)
   A. growth and development are constant.
   B. growth and development happens in unpredictable stages.
   C. growth and development are gradual and continuous.
   D. growth and development are interrelated.

6. Which theorist disagreed with Piaget's theory that children totally construct their own knowledge? (1.2.2)
   A. Erik Erikson
   B. Maria Montessori
   C. Lev Vygotsky
   D. Sigmund Freud

7. _____ are people who actively support a cause. (1.3.1)
   A. Social workers
   B. Child care workers
   C. Theorists
   D. Advocates

8. _____ means to grow and feel fulfilled as a person. (1.3.2)
   A. Hierarchy
   B. Esteem
   C. Self-actualization
   D. Security

9. Families need to _____ with children's feelings, or understand and relate to them. (1.3.3)
   A. empathize
   B. argue
   C. work
   D. contend

10. If you ask a teacher or a parent for information about a child, you are conducting a(n) _____. (1.3.4)
    A. direct observation
    B. indirect observation
    C. formal assessment
    D. informal assessment

Critical Thinking

1. **Cause and effect.** Give an example of how learning a skill in one developmental domain affects other developmental domains.

2. **Draw conclusions.** What are the names of other stages in the life cycle that refer to teens and adults? What major developments or changes occur in these stages?

3. **Make inferences.** In what ways do you think you have developed from infancy until now?

4. **Determine.** Which of your traits were determined by genes that were passed to you by your biological parents?

5. **Identify.** Identify hereditary and environmental factors that make you unique.

6. **Cause and effect.** In small groups, discuss how developmental acceleration and developmental delay might affect a young child. Give examples of two developmental accelerations and two developmental delays and briefly summarize the impact they might have.

7. **Make inferences.** Trace the effects of a different problem, such as poor nutrition or lack of affection, on all areas of development. How are the areas of development interrelated?

8. **Compare and contrast.** Choose two theories of child development that are discussed in this chapter. Then, create a T-chart listing the components of each theory. Draw lines between components the theories have in common and highlight the differences between the theories. Discuss your charts in class.

9. **Assess.** Close your eyes and listen for sounds that could be used in an observation. What do you hear? How do you identify these sounds as ones being used in an observation?

10. **Draw conclusions.** What have you learned through observation?

Core Skills

1. **Writing.** Think of a child you know or have known at one of the childhood lifecycle phases. Write phrases describing that child. How is the child creative? How is the child challenging? How do you think studying child development can help you interact with this child?

2. **Reading.** Read an autobiography or biography about the life of a famous person in any career. Look for examples of constancy in the person's growth and development. How did this constancy lead to fame in their career? Summarize, in your own words, the information presented in the text in simple, but accurate terms. Share your findings with the class.

3. **Listening, speaking, and writing.** Conduct an oral history interview with an older family member or with an older adult you know. Acquire permission to audio- or video-record the interview and to take any photos. Then do the following:
   - Share with the person what you have learned about developmental tasks.

   - Ask the person to describe developmental tasks they became skilled at that people seldom learn today. Examples may include household tasks or chores, hobbies, games, and job duties of the past.
   - Listen carefully to encourage your interviewee. Use eye contact and nodding to give assurance you are listening.
   - Give a brief oral report to the class contrasting the accomplishment of developmental tasks in years past with those of today.
   - Use the interview as a foundation for creating a print or digital family history book. Add photos, written stories about family members, and memories to the history book. To take this project a step further, develop a self-directed FCCLA *Power of One* project on *Family Ties*. Use the *FCCLA Planning Process* to plan, carry out, and evaluate your project. Your FCCLA adviser can provide further information.

4. **Listening and speaking.** In small groups, discuss ways in which society is child-centered and ways in which society is adult-centered. Can a society resolve these dual interests? How can a new family find a balance for a happier family life? Build on one another's ideas and then express these ideas in a discussion with the rest of the class.

5. **Writing.** Write a one-page narrative on the history of the nature versus nurture debate. Within your narrative discuss how ideas about the importance of heredity and the environment have changed over time.

6. **Listening and speaking.** Interview a person working with children in a child-related career, such as a child care teacher or child care provider. What characteristics does this person need to work with children? What are the job responsibilities? What are the educational and training requirements for the career? Give a one-minute oral presentation of your findings in class.

7. **Research and writing.** According to researchers from the *Center on the Developing Child* at Harvard University, "the foundations of lifelong health are built in early childhood." Research the core roots of health that support physical and mental well-being from early childhood through the lifespan. Read at least three articles on this topic and summarize your findings in writing. Begin your research at the Harvard University website. As you read, ask yourself:
   - Who are the researchers, and why are they credible?
   - What foundations of health help nourish physical and mental well-being? Why are they important?
   - What do families and caregivers need to do to build a foundation of health?
   - How do the articles support the information in this chapter?
8. **CTE Career Readiness Practice.** Everyone has a stake in protecting the environment. Taking steps as an individual to be more environmentally conscious is a behavior of responsible citizens. From a business standpoint, it may also help a company be more profitable. In what ways can child care workers in a child care save energy or other resources (for example, creating electronic portfolios to document children's work)?

Observations

1. Observe a group of people in a public place such as a park or a shopping mall. List characteristics you see that are due to heredity and characteristics you see that are due to environment. Compare and discuss your lists in class.
2. In small groups, list some specific observation topics, such as sharing toys, participating during group time, and performing certain physical skills. Discuss what behaviors you might expect to observe in each of these observations. Then, compare and discuss your lists and ideas in class.
3. In indirect observations, children are not directly observed. Instead researchers observe children's work/products or interview caregivers for comments about children. In small groups, give examples of specific children's work/products that could be used in indirect observations to document children's growth and learning. Discuss the types of information you can gather from using this observation method.

Chapter 2

New Directions in Learning

Lesson 2.1 Brain Studies
Lesson 2.2 Acquiring Knowledge

Essential Question

How has recent brain research enlightened people's knowledge of child development?

Case Study — Technology and Brain Development

Read the case study and discuss/reflect on the questions that follow. After you finish studying the chapter, think about this case study again. Have your opinions changed based on what you learned?

Tom is a single parent with two children: Lamar, age four, and Lucinda, age two. Tom drops his children off at Penny Lane Child Care Center every day before work. By pick-up time at 5 PM, Tom is usually exhausted. After buckling the kids into their car seats, Tom hands a smartphone to Lamar to play with on the 20-minute drive home.

Tom remembers that they are out of groceries and stops on the drive back to pick up food for the week. Lamar continues to quietly play on the smartphone as Tom pushes the cart around the store. Lucinda starts to cry, and Tom produces a tablet that is loaded with toddler apps. Lucinda immediately stops crying and happily plays with the tablet while Tom finishes up the shopping.

When they get home, Tom sits both children down in front of the TV and unloads the groceries. Lamar already knows how to work the remote and quickly finds a show. Tom breathes a sigh of relief as the kids play in front of the TV for the next hour, allowing time to put the groceries away and get dinner on the table.

Give It Some Thought

1. Should Tom be worried about the amount of time the children spend using technology (smartphones, tablets, TV, etc.)? Why or why not?
2. What does current research tell us about the effects of technology on children's brain development?
3. What do organizations that focus on young children (e.g., National Association for the Education of Young Children, Zero to Three, American Academy of Pediatrics) recommend concerning technology use and young children? Do you agree with their recommendations?
4. Should two-year-old Lucinda be treated differently than four-year-old Lamar when it comes to access to technology? Why or why not?

Lesson 2.1

Brain Studies

Key Terms

axons
biochemistry
brain plasticity
critical periods
dendrites
firing process
glial cells
neurons
pruning
sensitive periods
sorting process
window of opportunity
wiring process

Learning Outcomes

After studying this lesson, you will be able to

2.1-1   **describe** how children learn.

2.1-2   **explain** the biological processes of brain function.

2.1-3   **compare** the critical and sensitive periods of brain development.

2.1-4   **explain** why having needed experiences is important to a child's brain development.

2.1-5   **identify** two offenders of normal brain functioning.

Reading and Notetaking Activity

Skim this chapter from top to bottom and from left to right and list all the headings. Then, identify key terms with which you are familiar and scan through the chapter to find their definitions. Write a "topic sentence" and brief summary for each heading, using the key terms to explain what you think you will learn. After you read this chapter, write a new topic sentence and summary for each section, outlining the main points you learned.

Introduction

The study of children has changed dramatically over the years. The scientific study of children emerged from the field of psychology. First it was called *child study* and then *child development.*

Researchers in child development aim to learn more about children. During the last half century, child development research has mainly focused on the intellectual (cognitive) theories of Piaget and Vygotsky. These theories remain important, but the "new" research frontier of the 21st century is brain studies.

Researchers have long been interested in the brain, but major technological advances allow for much more precise study. Because technology is changing so rapidly, research on brain development is constantly being updated.

2.1-1 How Do Children Learn?

In child development, people use the word *learning* in a broad sense. People might say *learning* is any permanent change in knowledge or behavior. The words *learning* and *development* are almost the same because both refer to changes in all domains. For example, a child

- learns motor skills like walking, throwing a ball, or cutting with scissors (physical development)
- acquires knowledge of people, places, objects, and events, and even learns how to think about thinking (what researchers call metacognition)
- learns to understand, speak, read, and write words (intellectual development)
- learns how to interact with others (social development)
- learns to express and understand emotions (emotional development)

Changes often result from experiences, such as personal experiences in the environment, imitation, guided discovery, or direct instruction. Although the whole body is involved in learning, the command center of the body is the brain. The brain is responsible for controlling most body functions. These include operation of the body systems, movements, thinking, memory, and feelings.

2.1-2 How the Brain Works

Scientists and other people who study and work with children have long been curious about the brain's growth, developmental change, activity, and potential damage. Until recently, the brain was mostly a mystery although brain development was inferred through observed behaviors in children, especially through Piaget's research on intellectual milestones (stages). In recent years, however, scientists have learned much more about brain development. Much of this knowledge is gained from the use of new technologies and advances in **biochemistry** (the chemistry of living organisms). **Figure 2.1** shows a *magnetic resonance image (MRI)*, which is a specific type of brain scan. Technology has opened so many new avenues of study, and although many questions have been answered, there is much to discover.

Knowing Brain Biology

Brain development begins shortly after conception. Before birth, about 250,000 brain cells are formed each minute. Full-term babies have about 100 billion brain cells. The brain, however, is the least developed organ at birth. A newborn's brain is only about 25 percent of the size of the adult brain.

Allison Herreid/Shutterstock.com

Figure 2.1 A magnetic resonance image (MRI) is a brain scan that can be used to diagnose diseases and disorders of the brain. These pictures of the brain have also helped scientists understand the brain at different stages of development. *Why do you think the ability to see a living brain at work and rest is so important to understanding it?*

After birth the newborn's brain develops rapidly in stages, which can be noted by

- increases in head circumference
- increases of 5 to 10 percent in brain weight during a stage (with only a 1-percent gain between each stage)
- changes in the cells

Brain growth occurs in a predictable, biological sequence that is the same for all people. Unlike body development that goes from head to foot (what scientists call cephalocaudal), brain development begins at the base (near the neck) and moves to the front of the brain.

A lot of brain development happens before you are even born, but did you know that your brain is still developing? It's amazing to think that your own brain will continue to grow and develop well into your 20s! While the fastest brain growth takes place before birth, the stages of fastest growth after birth are shown in **Figure 2.2**. The time between each stage is used for practicing and gaining expertise and efficiency in the skills developed in previous stages. For example, between four and six years of age, motor and sensory skills combine to develop eye-hand coordination needed for activities such as catching balls, drawing, writing, playing musical instruments, and eating with flatware.

Figure 2.2 **Stages of Fastest Brain Growth After Birth**

Age	Area Maturing
3–10 months	Activation (turning on) and control of motor actions.
2–4 years	Maturation of the senses. (The senses function near the adult level by the end of the stage.)
6–8 years	Emergence (beginning) of logical thinking about actual experiences. (Unlike the previous stages that are genetically programmed, logical thinking must be taught and practiced.)
10–12 years (biological females) and 12–14 years (biological males)	Beginning of generalized thinking beyond actual experiences—abstract reasoning. (This ability allows older children and teens to understand higher mathematics and science.)

The brain is made up of two types of cells—neurons and glial (GLEE-uhl) cells. **Neurons** (nerve cells) are brain cells that send and receive chemical and electrical impulses to direct the various tasks of the brain. There are three types of neurons (sensory, motor, interneurons), and each type has its own specific tasks and the following three parts (**Figure 2.3**):

Figure 2.3 **Neurons**

Types	Functions
Sensory neurons	Transfer information from the external environment to the central nervous system (CNS).
Motor neurons	Transfer information from the CNS to the external environment.
Interneurons (associative neurons)	Process information in the CNS and transfer information from one neuron to another within the CNS.

Parts of a Neuron

The cell body contains genetic information and proteins for cell maintenance.

Dendrites (DEHN-drights) branch out from the cell body much like the branches of a tree. Dendrites allow each neuron to receive signals sent by other neurons (the input function).

Axons are long, thick cables with terminal buttons (small knobs at the end of the axons) that transmit signals between neurons (the output function).

Glial cells are brain cells that support neurons. Glial is Greek for *glue* because originally glial were thought of as the "glue" that holds neurons together. Now we know that glial do much more than that. Not only do they hold neurons together, they also support neurons, provide nourishment, and aid in *neurotransmission*. About 90 percent of the cells in the brain are glial cells. Four types of glial cells support the neurons (**Figure 2.4**). Unlike neurons, glial cells divide—especially during times of fastest brain growth. Perhaps because neurons need differing amounts of support, glial cells vary in *density* throughout the brain. Glial cells are star-shaped, with legs extending out from the body.

Figure 2.4 Glial Cells That Support Neurons

Types	Functions
Astrocytes (AS-truh-sites)	Help neurons receive nourishment. Control chemical environment of the brain. Prevent certain substances from entering the brain.
Microglia (my-KRAWG-lee-uh)	Remove cellular waste.
Ependymal (eh-PEN-duh-muhl)	Form a protective covering around spinal cord and central brain cavities.
Oligodendrocytes (AW-lih-go-DEN-druh-sites)	Help insulate the axons with myelin.

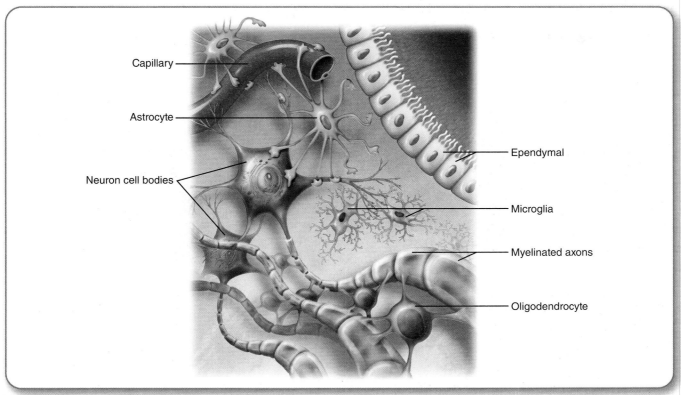

© Body Scientific International

Making and Sorting Connections

Each area of the brain is highly specialized (**Figure 2.5**). Before birth, all cells must migrate to their special location. This process is broken into four steps: the wiring process, the sorting process, the firing process, and the pruning process.

Reshaping Connections: Brain Plasticity

Until 10 years of age, children create many new connections in their brains. After age 10, pruning is rather aggressive. Does this mean the child who did not have quality experiences early in life cannot learn and possibly catch up with peers? Can a person who suffers a brain injury recover? Can adults who need to learn new skills for their careers do so? The answer to all these questions is *yes* because the human brain is adaptable and open to change.

The brain's ability to be shaped and reshaped is called **brain plasticity**. For many years, scientists thought the brain was only plastic during childhood. Now there is mounting evidence that our brains remain plastic and adaptable throughout our lives. Glial cells aid plasticity by dividing as a person needs more memory cells. Because the brain is plastic, a person can make up for a lost function, too.

Figure 2.5 Areas and Functions of the Brain

Types	Functions
Temporal lobe	hearing, smell, memory, speech
Frontal lobe	memory, intelligence, behavior, emotions, motor function, smell
Parietal (puh-RYE-uh-tuhl) lobe	pain, touch, sensations of hot and cold, speech
Occipital lobe	vision, speech
Cerebellum (ser-uh-BELL-uhm)	body movements and balance
Brain stem	breathing, heart rate, blood pressure, reflexes, sleep

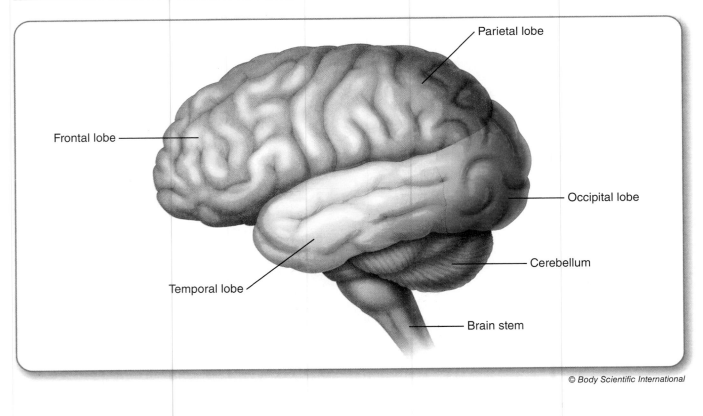

© Body Scientific International

For example, although damaged neurons cannot be replaced after an injury, nearby cells can change their functions to take on functions of the damaged cells. This is another example of plasticity. While adult brains have some plasticity, children's brains are much more plastic because:

- Children have more connections than they need to function. Adults have lost many of their connections. Rerouting communication among neurons is easier with more connections.
- Chemicals that aid in making connections are far more active in the earlier years. The brain of a three-year-old is two and a half times more active than an adult's brain.

- Connections are more flexible in the early years and become more stabilized as people age.

2.1-3 Timing of Experiences

Although the brain is plastic, timing is an important concept when it comes to brain development. The entire brain is not wired at one time. Years ago, brain wiring was noted by observing the developmental skills in children. They called these periods the *stages of development*. Today, brain researchers use brain scans to note optimal times for making connections.

Neuron Communication

- During the **wiring process**, a network of fibers is created. These fibers carry brain signals between neurons.
- During the **sorting process**, connections are formed when a chemical and electrical signal (called a *neurotransmitter*) jumps from one neuron to another.
- The **firing process** results in both strengthening the connections and forming more to enable more learning. Babies begin with about 1,000 trillion connections, which allows for very rapid learning during the early years.
- The brain weeds out connections that we rarely use in a process called **pruning**. Healthy pruning allows the remaining connections to become strong, which increases the speed and efficiency for often-used brain signals.

Designua/Shutterstock.om

Science

Technology and the Developing Brain

Early experiences have such a dramatic effect on brain wiring that they can increase or decrease the final number of synapses by as much as 25 percent. The effects this has on future learning potential are lifelong. Today, at home and at school, children grow up surrounded by a variety of technologies, including tablets, smartphones, gaming systems, and televisions. What role is screen exposure playing in healthy brain development?

In the past, the American Academy of Pediatrics (AAP) published strict guidelines regarding how much time children should spend looking at screens during different stages of development. Now, they've revised those rules with an approach that focuses more on the quality of the content to which children are exposed. The AAP still stresses that screen time has no shown benefits for children under the age of two, but they do make the following recommendations for families with children two and older:

Get involved. Don't just hand your child a device and walk away. Think of the device as just another playground or playroom, and play with your child. Be aware of which games they are playing, which media they are consuming, and to whom they are talking online.

Set limits. Research shows that young children develop language skills best via two-way conversation. Too much time watching passive video presentations may delay speech development. Also, too much time engaged in sedentary activities is not healthy for physical development. Children need opportunities to develop their **gross motor skills** (abilities that allow us to do tasks that involve large muscles in our torso, legs, and arms).

Content matters. The quality of the content is more important than the amount of time spent on the device. Know which apps your child is using and choose educational content whenever possible.

Create media-free times. This is especially recommended at mealtimes and bedtimes. This will encourage family time, healthier eating habits, and improved sleep.

Let your kids make mistakes. If your child is exposed to inappropriate content or engages in inappropriate behavior online, talk to them about it. Use the experience as a teachable moment and an opportunity to understand what is going on in their life.

Photo: SDI Productions/E+ via Getty Images

They note two types of periods in wiring—*critical periods* and *sensitive periods*.

Critical periods are times when some part of the body is very vulnerable to lack of stimulation or to negative experiences. For example, if babies are born with cataracts and do not have them removed in the first few months, they will forever be blind. Vision neurons die without light stimulation. The brain is not plastic when it comes to most wiring completed during the first six months of pregnancy and for vision after birth.

Sensitive periods are times when the brain is best able to wire specific skills for all children. Although the brain is plastic, matching the right skills to the sensitive times means easier learning, a better foundation for later skills, and performance at a higher level than if learned later.

Why is this information useful? Knowing these sensitive periods helps families and teachers offer the right kinds of experiences for a child at the best possible times. They will know which skills they should encourage most and which will likely come at a later time. This can help children's brains reach their full potential.

Offering the best experiences at the right times is called *using the windows of opportunity*. A **window of opportunity** is a prime period in a child's life for developing a particular skill. In this window, the child reaches a peak capacity to learn this skill if given the opportunity. At this time, a certain type of stimulation is more critical than others. The right stimulation at the right times is good for development. Just like there are windows of opportunity, there are also times when development is a greater risk of being impaired. We call these *windows of vulnerability*. During windows of vulnerability, a child might be more impacted by trauma or stress.

Each area has its own window of opportunity (**Figure 2.6**). Most windows are large, which means the favorable time for learning this skill is several years. Motor development is a good example.

Some windows are small, which means the most favorable time for learning is a few months, such as the window for vision.

Often, the windows of opportunity for various tasks overlap. This means a child will likely be learning those skills at the same time if given the opportunity. Many of the overlapping skills are related, such as social attachments and emotional control.

2.1-4 Providing Needed Experiences

Cutting-edge science on brain development confirms what many families and caregivers have known for years. The earliest years are the most important for all areas of growth and development (physical, intellectual, and social-emotional). All experiences affect the brain's performance.

Figure 2.6 Windows of Opportunity

Skill Area	Skills	Sensitive Time
Motor	• Posture and coordination • Large muscle • Small muscle	• Birth–2 years • Birth–5 years • 6 months–9 years
Vision	• Sight • Acuity • Binocular	• Birth–4 to 6 months • Birth–7 years • 1–3 years
Language	• Phonemes (FO-neems) in languages one will speak • Idea of connections between words and objects • Vocabulary • Syntax	• Birth–7 to 11 months • 4 months–1 year • Birth–3 years • Birth–6 years
Social	• Attachment • Independence • Cooperation	• Birth–2 years • 1½ years–3 years • 2–4 years
Emotional	• Trust • Intelligence (read other's emotions) • Control • Cope with stress	• Birth–14 months • Birth–4 years • Birth–3 years • Birth–2 years
Thinking skills (including math)	• Prelogical (perceptual) • Logical	• 6 months–5 years • 5 or 6 years–puberty
Music	• Absolute ("perfect") pitch • Appreciation • Learning	• Birth–5 years • Birth–9 years • 3–9 years

Goodheart-Willcox Publisher

The Impact of Trauma on a Developing Brain

As you are learning in this chapter, there are many processes involved in healthy brain development. How do you think these processes are impacted when a child experiences a trauma (a deeply distressing or disturbing experience)?

The U.S. Center for Disease Control defines Adverse Childhood Experiences (ACEs) as potentially traumatic events that occur in childhood. These events may include violence, abuse, neglect, death of a loved one, or growing up in a family with mental health or substance abuse problems. Exposure to trauma can create what is called toxic stress, which can disrupt healthy brain development and lead to chronic health problems, mental illness, and substance abuse in adulthood.

Trauma-informed care (TIC) is an approach to working with children who have suffered an ACE. Research suggests that TIC offers a variety of benefits for children, including a higher chance of returning to normal brain function. The National Child Traumatic Stress Network defines TIC as a seven-step approach and advises people who work with children to apply the following:

1. Routinely screen for trauma exposure and related symptoms;
2. Use evidence-based, culturally responsive assessment and treatment for traumatic stress and associated mental health symptoms;
3. Make resources available to children, families, and providers on trauma exposure, its impact, and treatment;
4. Engage in efforts to strengthen the resilience and protective factors of children and families impacted by and vulnerable to trauma;
5. Address parent and caregiver trauma and its impact on the family system;
6. Emphasize the continuity of care and collaboration across child-service systems; and

7. Maintain an environment of care for staff that addresses, minimizes, and treats secondary traumatic stress and that increases staff wellness.

If TIC is not administered after a trauma, the child has a higher chance of developing negative coping skills such as substance abuse, self-hate, and aggressive behaviors. The goal of TIC is to promote **resilience**. Resilience is the ability to move on from a traumatic event with positive coping strategies and habits. Trauma cannot be erased from the brain, but its negative effects can minimized with consistent, evidence-based TIC.

Writing Activity

Imagine you are a kindergarten teacher at an elementary school. You were recently informed that a child in your class suffered an ACE. The principal wants to make sure the child receives proper TIC. She asks you to screen for and document any trauma symptoms you observe in the child for the rest of the school year.

On your own or with a partner, research the signs and symptoms of ACEs. Make a list of the symptoms you will be looking for in your student. Then make a list of ways you could help foster resilience in your student. Using the items from your lists, write a one- or two-paragraph plan for creating the best possible environment for your student while collecting thorough and accurate data for your principal. Share your plan with your class.

Photo: Tom Wang/Shutterstock.com

The best experiences for young children include interaction with loving adults engaged in daily tasks and family-type activities. (Even child care programs for children under three years of age should have a home-like atmosphere.) Babies and very young children need not be taught in a formal way. Children learn by playing, especially with caring adults. Children need choices in what and how to learn. Closely observing children and following their lead in play activities is often "best practice." Children usually choose age-appropriate experiences that parallel the windows of opportunity. Children need time to practice and develop their skills. Repetition of experiences develops the brain and strengthens connections between neurons. Good books and a few quality toys that allow for open-ended, creative play (blocks, balls, art materials, sand, and water) are better than toys with limited possibilities. In future chapters, we will learn about how our knowledge of brain development helps shape and guide best practices to support and encourage optimal development.

2.1-5 Protecting the Brain

The brain is part of the human body. Nutrition, sleep, physical activity, and general health all affect a person's brain (**Figure 2.7**). For example, 60 percent of daily nutrients are used by the brain during the first year. The fat content in breast milk or formula for infants and whole milk for weaned toddlers is essential for myelin development. Do you know why tired people become fretful and say that their thinking is not clear?

Prostock-studio/Shutterstock.com

Figure 2.7 An infant or child's nutrition can dramatically affect their brain health and development. *Why do you think nutrition can have such an impact on the brain?*

Without rest, the neurotransmitters become depleted. Rest restores the working of the brain.

Without stimulation and quality early experiences, brain connections can be pruned too much and windows of opportunity missed. Overstimulation can be harmful, too. It can make children feel overwhelmed, tired, frustrated, and unable to focus. Overstimulation, such as loud music, can even cause hearing neurons to die.

Lesson 2.1 Review and Assessment

1. Which of the following is *not* something that children learn? (2.1.1)
   A. Motor skills like walking, throwing a ball, or cutting with scissors
   B. Public speaking skills
   C. Understanding, speaking, read, and writing words
   D. How to interact with others
2. Which of the following is *not* a characteristic of newborn brain development? (2.1.2)
   A. Increases in head circumference
   B. Increases of 5 to 10 percent in brain weight during a stage
   C. Changes in the cells
   D. Decreased activity in frontal lobe
3. **True or False.** Sensitive periods are times when some part of the body is very vulnerable to lack of stimulation or to negative experiences. (2.1.3)
4. The best experiences for young children include ____. (2.1.4)
   A. interaction with loving adults engaged in daily tasks and family-type activities
   B. regular introduction of new caregivers
   C. situations that make them uncomfortable so they learn to face their fears
   D. exposure to age-inappropriate toys
5. **True or False.** Nutrition, sleep, physical activity, and general health all affect a person's brain. (2.1.5)

Lesson 2.2

Acquiring Knowledge

Key Terms

cognitive flexibility
developmental tasks
essential life skills
executive functions (EFs)
inhibition
lifelong learning
reinforcement
working memory
explicit
implicit
manipulating
neuroscience

Learning Outcomes

After studying this lesson, you will be able to

2.2-1 **differentiate** between four types of knowledge.

2.2-2 **explain** how knowledge of child development is used in education.

2.2-3 **identify** and **describe** three executive functions.

2.2-4 **analyze** Galinsky's seven life skills.

Reading and Notetaking Activity

Before reading, skim the headings in this chapter. List the headings to create an outline for taking notes during reading and class discussion. Under each heading, list any key terms. Finally, write two questions you expect to have answered in class. After completing each chapter, ask your instructor any questions you still have about the concepts or terms you learned.

Robert Kneschke/Shutterstock.com

Figure 2.8 Child care and education centers are natural, ideal environments in which to watch children interact and learn. *What other locations or situations would make an ideal environment for observing children?*

Introduction

Child development involves the study of children and the adults in their lives. The first goal of child development research is to advance knowledge. The other goal is to apply knowledge. People who work with or for children, especially in education, not only use available research knowledge, but also create more knowledge. For example, child care and education programs are natural laboratories for the study of children (**Figure 2.8**). Schools for older children are also using child development research to guide curriculum decisions. Popular phrases in today's schools are words coming from brain studies, such as *windows of opportunity* and *brain-compatible learning*.

Professionals in health and protective services also contribute to the knowledge of child development. These experts try to prevent and treat mental health issues in children. They are returning to Erikson's theory and brain studies to provide more answers. It is becoming clear that the roots of mental health problems, for children and adults, are in the stressors of childhood. Although the scars of trauma and stress may be seen on the bodies of children and in their behaviors, the real scars may be within their brains.

2.2-1 Types of Knowledge

The last lesson posed the question "How do children learn?" You learned that biology coupled with broad experiences determined how children learn. Because the brain is so plastic, people can learn almost anything. Thus, the *how* question does not answer *what* children should learn.

In every culture throughout history, adults have asked, "What should children learn?" The answer has always been "Children need to know the values and practices of the culture and have the skills needed to thrive in their world." The answer to the question does not change, but the specifics do.

In this 21st century culture, the answer to the specifics of what children should learn rests in the educational system (the schools). Schools transmit the values of the culture and teach skills needed for the workforce. The responsibility of the schools, however, is no longer as simple as it was in the past.

Families are looking to the schools to help educate their children at younger ages than in the past. By law children must receive 12 or 13 years of education. Today, however, many children enter the educational system during infancy or the preschool years and continue their education through college.

Focus on Careers

Elementary School Teacher

An elementary school teacher is responsible for creating lessons and teaching students appropriate grade-level materials. One teacher may be responsible for multiple subjects, including math, reading, language, science, and social studies. Teachers monitor educational development, assess student learning, and prepare students for the next grade level.

Career cluster: Education and training.

Education: Educational requirements vary by state, but a bachelor's degree in elementary education is the minimum. Other requirements may include an additional degree in a specific subject area, a teaching certificate, and a master's degree.

Education requirements for private schools also vary. Continued education is also required.

Job outlook: Future employment opportunities for elementary school teachers are expected to grow as fast as the average for all occupations.

To learn more about a career as an elementary school teacher, visit the United States Department of Labor's *Occupational Outlook Handbook* website. You will also be able to compare the job responsibilities, educational requirements, job outlook, and average pay of elementary school teachers with similar occupations.

Photo: MBI/Shutterstock.com

In this century, schools can no longer determine the exact skills needed for the workforce of the future. Because knowledge is expanding and changing so rapidly, the needed skills of today will change before the current workforce retires. This means that learning must be ongoing, which is called **lifelong learning**. Workers must adapt to changing career demands or even to new careers. Furthermore, people in today's culture are part of a world community that requires broader knowledge, such as global economies and multicultural understandings. Schools today have a much broader responsibility for preparing students for today's world and giving them the skills to adapt to a changing world.

Today, schools are teaching four types of knowledge needed now and in the future. The specifics of what children should know are embedded in each type of knowledge and are sequenced in state curriculum standards and college-degree programs. Your textbooks, other learning materials, and achievement tests closely follow these standards.

Explicit Knowledge

Explicit knowledge refers to knowledge about "facts." It is sometimes called *codified knowledge* because it is written. When young children learn to name colors, shapes, animals, and objects, they are acquiring codified knowledge (**Figure 2.9**).

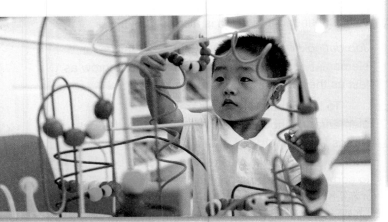

baona/E+ via Getty Images

Figure 2.9 Children gain explicit knowledge by learning the names of colors, shapes, animals, and objects. *What is one way you use explicit knowledge in your typical day?*

Schools require students to have a broad base of **explicit** (clearly described) knowledge. Because no one can learn more than a small amount of codified knowledge, education beyond high school focuses to a great extent on explicit knowledge in the specific area of study, such as computer technology, medicine, law, or child development.

Implicit Knowledge

Implicit knowledge (also called *experienced-based knowledge*) refers to skills-based knowledge. Think about the **implicit** (implied or understood without describing in detail) knowledge involved in specific tasks, such as teaching, managing a large corporation, or operating a complex machine. Often, this knowledge cannot be completely written. Young children begin acquiring implicit knowledge when they learn to ride a bike, swim, or balance blocks while building a structure (**Figure 2.10**). In school, implicit knowledge is needed to turn ideas into an essay or project or to become a leader in a student organization.

wavebreakmedia/iStock via Getty Images Plus

Figure 2.10 Implicit knowledge is skill-based and can be gained by learning to swim, ride a bike, interact with people, or balance blocks on a structure. *What are some ways you use implicit knowledge in your everyday life?*

Scientific Knowledge

Scientific knowledge refers to the ability to create knowledge. This type of knowledge underlies new technological development, scientific discoveries, and process advances. Although the knowledge is often acquired in laboratories, it is used in many other careers. For example, as doctors learn about new drugs or procedures, they use them in their practices. Acquiring scientific knowledge begins when young children, even babies, try different actions with their toys (**Figure 2.11**). For example, their scientific questions might be "How can I make the pans sound louder or the boat move faster?" Part of the curriculum in schools involves critical thinking and problem solving. Some teens take this form of knowledge to a high level as seen in science project competitions.

Knowledge About Experts

Knowledge about experts (also called the *knowledge network*) involves knowing who has the other forms of knowledge. The knowledge network is used in all careers to get access to needed explicit, implicit, and scientific knowledge. Knowledge about experts is becoming more and more important. Again, even young children begin to acquire this knowledge. They quickly learn which parent, sibling, or friend has the knowledge or skills they desire. They even know whether this person gives them correct information.

Schools teach this type of knowledge when they require students to use valid and reliable sources of information. During this course, your teacher may ask you to interview someone or to give a group presentation. To do these activities will require you to choose someone who can share the information you need.

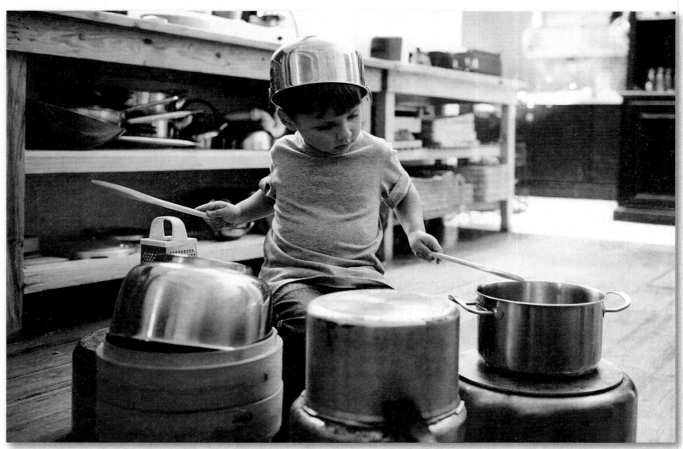

PeopleImages/E+ via Getty Images

Figure 2.11 Children gain scientific knowledge by experimenting with their toys and determining how their actions can affect objects in the physical world. *What do you think makes this type of knowledge scientific?*

Speech

Group Presentations

Break into small groups and create a presentation on one of the following types of knowledge: explicit knowledge, implicit knowledge, scientific knowledge, or knowledge about experts. In your presentation, analyze how this type of knowledge is learned and practiced over each of the six stages of child development. (Review Figure 1.2 for the six stages of child development.)

Complete the following steps to prepare your presentation:

1. In your group, discuss examples of your chosen type of knowledge for each of the six stages of child development. Consider the question: How does this type of knowledge develop in each stage?

2. After discussing, divide the stages of child development among all group members. Each group member should be responsible for presenting on one stage of child development.

3. Make notes on index cards about important points to present. Before presenting, evaluate each other's notes and offer suggestions.

4. Deliver your presentation to the class. The person presenting on the first stage of child development should go first, the person presenting on the second stage second, and so on. Be prepared to answer any questions your classmates have, and ask questions about the other presentations in your class.

Photo: naluwan/Shutterstock.com

Mastering this type of knowledge requires understanding what knowledge is needed, knowing who has this knowledge, and building a social relationship to get access to experts and their knowledge.

2.2-2 Linking Child Development Knowledge to Education

Until the 1950s, the schools were mainly concerned with preparing children to become productive workers for jobs in a slower-changing world. Schools could teach the needed skills for a lifetime career, such as typing and shorthand to students wanting to be secretaries. These skills were not expected to change. *Rote memorization*, or memorization without full comprehension, was the way children learned many facts. Learning theories seemed to be the "best fit" for this type of education.

Learning theories used **reinforcement** (rewards) for mastery of facts and skills. For example, children might be given a reward for learning multiplication tables. Rote learning did not work as well after the primary grades due to the complexity of many concepts and skills.

As the world changed, educators realized rote memorization was not best for learning needed skills. Robert Havighurst (1900–1991), a psychologist, began to develop educational theory based on child development concepts. His research led him to the concept of developmental tasks. **Developmental tasks** are skills that should be mastered at a certain stage in life. Havighurst coined the term *teachable moment* as the best time to teach a specific skill. He thought educators would be more effective if they used tasks for a particular level of development rather than using rote learning. Havighurst believed that the child's readiness for a developmental task came from the following three sources:

- *physical maturation.* A baby comes into the world as a helpless being. As their body matures, the child is able to learn many new skills, such as walking and reading.
- *social pressures.* Through rewards and penalties, society pressures the child to learn important tasks. Developmental tasks differ from culture to culture because each group may value different skills. Tasks differ from region to region, too. Over time, tasks also change to reflect changes in society.
- *inner pressures.* The actual push to achieve comes from within children. In the end, the child is responsible for mastering each task. Children work harder to learn tasks they like (**Figure 2.12**).

The United States is no longer an industrial economy but is a *knowledge-based economy* (knowledge and information along with technology drive the present production of goods and services and future economic growth). Children must be educated for today's world and also adaptable and creative for the future. Although the theories of Piaget and Vygotsky are not theories of education, these theories, rather than learning theories, are being used to inform "best practices."

Constance Kamii and Rheta DeVries, psychologists who studied under Piaget, have "translated" Piaget's theory into educational practice. Together and individually, they developed and researched specific math and physical knowledge curricular ideas for teachers using the *constructivist approach to education*. In this approach, the child does not ingest teacher-taught facts and procedures, which they see as a path to failure. Rather, the curriculum is designed to challenge groups of children to collaboratively work on inquiry-based learning activities, called *games*. Teachers encourage children to ask questions, explore, and assess their current knowledge through which children construct new knowledge at ever-higher levels.

2.2-3 Using Knowledge Effectively

For people to reach their full potential in school, in careers, and in their personal lives, they must not only acquire knowledge, but make good use of it. Everyone needs to know how to learn (study, recognize important information, remember, and make associations with other knowledge).

Figure 2.12 Developmental Tasks

Description	Tasks Arise from Three Sources:	Example of the Actual Push to Achieve
Area: Motor task **Task for middle childhood:** Learning skills needed for common games **Example of task:** Learning skills needed to play ball *kali9/E+ via Getty Images*	1. **Physical maturation.** Child needs bone and muscle growth. The child's eyes and hands must work smoothly together. 2. **Social pressures.** Other children reward skillful players (praise or accept them as friends) and punish failures (tease or reject them as friends). Families and coaches may also expect children to become proficient at the skills. 3. **Inner pressures.** Child desires to be admired by other children, families, and coaches.	**Child must see new possibilities for behavior.** • Child sees older children playing ball. **Child must form new concept of self.** • Child thinks, "I can be a player." **Child must cope with conflicting demands.** • Child thinks, "I can get hit with a ball or be teased for striking out, but if I do not play, the other kids will make fun of me, and my family and coaches will not consider me grown-up." **Child wants to achieve the next step in development enough to work for it.** • Child now spends hours in practice.

People also need to know how to make plans, organize and prioritize tasks, keep track of information, and communicate effectively. Knowing how to stay focused on the task at hand, but being able to return to the primary task after being interrupted are also important skills to learn. Some people, however, are weak in these skills. Often, they cannot achieve as much as they should and have problems in working effectively with and for others. The good news is that these skills can be improved.

Executive Functions

Executive functions (EFs) are cognitive functions people use to manage themselves and their resources (knowledge, time) to achieve goals. (EFs are also called *managing functions*.) EFs are used in achieving all tasks. Some researchers believe EFs may predict a person's success more than intelligence. Not all researchers list the same EFs, but the following three functions are always listed:

- **working memory**—storing, organizing, and **manipulating** (moving or changing) information while working on a task. Some people refer to *working memory* as *short-term memory*, but *short-term memory* refers only to storing information while working on a task.
- **cognitive flexibility**—being able to adjust to changing demands.
- **inhibition**—filtering thoughts and feelings so as not to act impulsively (**Figure 2.13**).

EFs have their developmental roots in early childhood, are easily seen around nine years of age, and mature at 25 years of age. The lack of EFs is most often seen in children with learning and behavioral problems. Many other children, however, have weak EFs. EFs are fragile, and the lack of EFs can be seen for a short time in anyone who is sleep deprived or stressed. During these times, people cannot focus and distractions seem to rule behavior.

The exact causes of weak EFs are not known. Adverse effects on EFs include a chaotic and stressful environment and child neglect and abuse. Treatments can only help, not cure, weak EFs.

Figure 2.13 **Symptoms and Aids for Weak Executive Functions**

Working Memory

Symptoms	Examples of Aids
• Has problems following multistep oral directions. • Cannot tell or write story details in order of occurrence. • Forgets a question or intended response while waiting. • Cannot remember a phone number while placing a call or a thought while writing it. • Forgets about assignments and projects. • In sounding out letters, has problems remembering the first sounds by the end of the word, so cannot combine sounds to form one word. • In reading a book section, has problems connecting concepts, so comprehension is weak. • Cannot remember oral messages. • In playing games, cannot keep track of moves (chess, checkers) or what has been played (dominoes, cards).	• Sort many objects by one attribute (color, shape, size). • Play memory games, such as *concentration*. • Engage in dramatic play. (Child must remember the specifics of the role and keep track of sequence.) • Play games with rules. • Play games that require memory of moves or what has been played. • Break oral instructions into small chunks. • Use lists or drawings or repeat information to aid comprehension. • Establish routines. • Use calendars and assignment planners. • Organize materials and prioritize tasks. • Remove distracters. • Make plans, follow plans, and discuss the activity at the end. • Use memory aids such as acronyms.

(Continued)

Figure 2.13 Symptoms and Aids for Weak Executive Functions (Continued)

Cognitive Flexibility

Symptoms	Examples of Aids
• Finds it difficult to change rules or directions, such as sort or classify by different attributes. • Has problems changing behaviors for different settings (inside/outside voices; behavior at ballgames versus behavior at a religious service; behaviors allowed at home versus school). • Cannot separate main ideas from supporting details. • Finds math word problems difficult due to the shift from words to equations. • Finds it difficult to see from another person's perspective.	• Sort or classify using the same materials, but changing attribute (use color then shape). • Do multiplicative classification, or recognize several possible categories for one object or person. • Engage in pretend play (changing roles and/or use the same prop, such as a block, to stand for different things). • Use words with multiple meanings, such as idioms, puns, and riddles. • Work jigsaw puzzles. • Take turns elaborating on a made-up story. • Learn more than one way to solve a problem. • Play "Turn It Around." (Say two things and have children reverse the order, such as "socks and shoes—shoes and socks.") • Ask about another person's perspective, such as "Why is Goldilocks afraid when the bears return?" (She's been in their house and knows they won't like it.)

Inhibition

Symptoms	Examples of Aids
• Cannot pause and think before acting. (If bumped in a line, never evaluates that the bump might have been accidental. Just becomes angry and hits.) • Finds it easier to "give up" than to cope with a small set-back. • Has problems resisting temptations, such as watching TV when homework needs to be done. • Becomes distracted when riding a bike or watching a program. • Has problems focusing on a conversation in a busy room. • Cannot hold a personal thought in order to not hurt someone else's feelings.	• Play "Simon Says" with new rules, such as do the action when Simon does not say it, or do the opposite of what Simon says, such as touch head when he says "toes." • Play a tapping game by doing the opposite of the adult. For example, if the adult taps twice, the child taps three times and vice versa. • Read color words written in the wrong color, such as RED written in green. • Delay gratification. (Get a bigger reward for waiting, such as saving money for a major purchase over several smaller purchases.) • Play games in which the child must wait for their turn.

2.2-4 Galinsky's Seven Essential Life Skills

Ellen Galinsky wanted to learn which skills had the greatest effects on children's development now and in the future. She spent eight years interviewing more than 75 of the leading researchers in child development and **neuroscience** (study of the brain) and filming aspects of their work.

Galinsky's study led her to identify seven basic skills, which she calls *essential life skills*. She defined **essential life skills** as the intellectual, social, and emotional skills that prepare children for the pressures of modern life. Following are Galinsky's *Seven Essential Life Skills*:

- *Focus and self-control.* Focus and self-control allow children to achieve goals in a rushed world filled with distractions and information overload. This skill involves being oriented toward achieving a goal by being alert and paying attention to get more out of information. It also requires having intellectual flexibility, and exercising self-control by not going on "automatic pilot" and by delaying gratification.
- *Perspective taking.* Perspective taking is the skill of figuring out what others are thinking and feeling. Understanding and respecting other's intentions are needed in a complex world.
- *Communicating.* Communicating is more than just listening, speaking, and writing correctly, although these skills are highly important. This skill involves reflecting on the message. While doing this, one person must listen and understand another person's perspective and realize how their communication will be understood by others.
- *Making connections.* Making connections is a skill most similar to *intelligence* itself. This skill involves seeing how things are the same or different and determining how bits of knowledge relate to each other. People who can see unusual connections between concepts and facts are creative and make advances in their fields.
- *Critical thinking.* Critical thinking involves obtaining and using valid and reliable knowledge to guide a person's beliefs, decisions, and actions. Critical thinking requires scientific reasoning to determine "what causes what."
- *Taking on challenges.* Taking on challenges is the willingness for a person to "stretch" themselves rather than simply doing what is comfortable. The skill is based on an understanding that a person's abilities can grow.
- *Self-directed and engaged learning.* Self-directed and engaged learning is the willingness to continue learning for a lifetime.

Everyone needs to find something they are passionate about and pursue the needed learning. This skill allows people to adapt to the changing world.

Essential life skills are closely related to EFs. For example, "perspective taking," one of Galinsky's seven skills, requires a person to remember all needed information about another person and to compare the current situation with similar situations (*working memory*). Perspective taking also requires the person to view the situation from both the other person's point of view and their point of view (*intellectual flexibility*). Finally, perspective taking requires the person to put their reactions aside while looking at another person's point of view (*inhibition*). For best results, these seven skills must be fostered beginning in early childhood.

Lesson 2.2 Review and Assessment

1. Which of the following is *not* one of the four types of knowledge? (2.2.1)
   A. Implicit
   B. Cognitive
   C. Explicit
   D. Scientific
2. **True or False.** Teachable moments are skills that should be mastered at a certain stage in life. (2.2.2)
3. Which of the following is the executive function that involves being able to adjust to changing demands? (2.2.3)
   A. Working memory
   B. Cognitive flexibility
   C. Inhibition
   D. Manipulating
4. **True or False.** According to Galinsky's study of essential life skills, focus and self-control allow children to achieve goals in a rushed world filled with distractions and information overload. (2.2.4)

Summary

Lesson 2.1

2.1-1 Because technology is changing so rapidly, research on brain development is constantly being updated.

2.1-2 Brain development begins shortly after conception.

2.1-2 The process by which your brain makes connections is broken into four steps: the wiring process, the sorting process, the firing process, and the pruning process.

2.1-3 The brain's ability to be shaped and reshaped is called brain plasticity.

2.1-4 Most jobs in early childhood require at least a certificate or a degree.

2.1-5 Nutrition, sleep, physical activity, and general health all affect a person's brain.

Lesson 2.2

2.2-1 In today's rapidly changing world, learning must be ongoing. This is called lifelong learning.

2.2-1 The four types of learning are explicit, implicit, scientific, and knowledge about experts.

2.2-2 Psychologist Robert Havighurst developed a list four of developmental tasks, or skills that should be mastered at a certain stage in life. The ability to perform these tasks derives from three sources: physical maturation, social pressures, inner pressures.

2.2-2 A teachable moment is the best time to learn a specific skill.

2.2-3 Executive functions are cognitive functions people use to manage themselves and their resources (knowledge, time) to achieve goals. These include working memory, cognitive flexibility, and inhibition.

2.2-3 Researcher Ellen Galinsky identified seven essential life skills: focus and self-control, perspective taking, communicating, making connections, critical thinking, taking on challenges, and self-directed and engaged learning.

College and Career Portfolio

Portfolio Objective

Begin by writing an objective for your portfolio. An objective is a complete sentence or two that states what you want to accomplish. The language should be clear and specific. The objective should contain enough details so that you can easily judge when it is accomplished. For instance, "I will create a portfolio for my future education" is too general. A better, more detailed objective might read: "I will work with my teacher and spend at least three hours per week creating, editing, and compiling items which will help me get into a college child care program." A clear objective is a good starting point for building a portfolio. As you think about building your portfolio, complete the following:

- Decide on the purpose of your portfolio—temporary or short-term employment, career, and/or college application.
- Research articles about writing objectives. Look for articles containing sample objectives.
- It can be helpful to examine the portfolios or resumes of others in the field in which you want to work or study. What objectives do they list, and can you adapt this for your own use?

Once you have completed the above steps, you are ready to write an objective for your portfolio.

Recall and Application

1. Although the whole body is involved in learning, the command center of the body is the _____. (2.1.1)
   A. heart
   B. eyes
   C. brain
   D. ears
2. Much of the knowledge scientists have gained about brain development comes from the use of high technology brain scans and advances in _____. (2.1.2)
   A. abundance
   B. biochemistry
   C. neurons
   D. dendrites
3. A _____ is a prime period in a child's life for developing a particular skill. (2.1.3)
   A. window of opportunity
   B. critical period
   C. sensitive period
   D. myelin
4. **True or False.** All experiences affect the brain's performance. (2.1.4)
5. Each of the following affects a person's brain *except* _____. (2.1.5)
   A. nutrition
   B. sleep
   C. physical activity
   D. clothing
6. Learning has to be ongoing. This is called _____. (2.2.1)
   A. explicit knowledge
   B. implicit knowledge
   C. lifelong learning
   D. cognitive flexibility

7. _____ are skills that should be mastered at a certain stage in life. (2.2.3)
   A. Executive functions
   B. Developmental tasks
   C. Inhibitions
   D. Scientific knowledge
8. Ellen Galinsky defined _____ as the intellectual, social, and emotional skills that prepare children for the pressures of modern life. (2.2.4)
   A. focus and control
   B. critical thinking
   C. communication
   D. essential life skills

Critical Thinking

1. **Cause and effect.** Review Figure 2.2 and the stages of brain growth after birth. Working with a partner, thinking about children you know in each of the stages, how do you think brain growth and development impact their behavior? Give one concrete example for each age range listed.
2. **Compare and contrast.** Use the internet to research the three types of neurons (sensory, motor, interneurons) and their functions. How are their structures and functions different? How are they similar? Use a Venn diagram like the one below to document the differences and areas of overlap.

3. **Make inferences.** Two-year-old Aiden fell off a slide and is now having vision problems. His mother took him to the eye doctor, but Aiden's eyes are fine. The eye doctor recommended they see a neurologist. Why? What problems might the eye doctor suspect?
4. **Cause and effect.** Think of a special skill at which you excel (e.g., art, sports, music, etc.). How did repetition and practice help you develop this skill? How do you think it impacted the wiring in your brain?
5. **Analyze.** Research shows that teens have less myelin in their frontal lobes compared to adults. More myelin allows for better flow of information between brain regions. How do you think less myelin in this particular brain region affects your own thinking?
6. **Determine.** When is the best time to guide a child in understanding or reading others' emotions? What might happen if a child is pressured to learn these concepts too early? too late?
7. **Draw conclusions.** Based on what you have learned in this chapter, how would being deprived of loving attention and learning experiences impact the developing brain of a young child?
8. **Compare and contrast.** In what ways do you use explicit knowledge, implicit knowledge, scientific knowledge, and knowledge about experts in your everyday life? Compare answers with a partner and discuss your differences.
9. **Identify.** Identify examples of social pressures that motivate children to learn. From where do these pressures originate? Are these social pressures always positive, or can they have negative effects if applied excessively?
10. **Evaluate.** List Galinsky's seven essential life skills and assess your strength in each of these skills. Where are you strongest? Where are you weakest?

1. **Research and writing.** Interview an older family member or friend. Find out what the roles and expectations were for children when they were a kid. Then, reflect on how these roles changed for your generation and how new brain discoveries may have been responsible for shifting views of childhood. Write a short essay comparing your experience to your interviewee's experience and how the differences in your childhoods may have affected the wiring of your brains.

2. **Reading.** With a partner, make flash cards of all the key terms in this chapter. On the front of the card, write the term. On the back, write the phonetic spelling of the word. (You may use a dictionary to find the phonetic spelling.) Practice reading and defining the terms aloud, clarifying pronunciations where needed.

3. **Using technology.** Using a graphics editing software, create a line drawing of a neuron and label its parts. Show your image to a partner and explain how an electrical signal is passed from neuron to neuron.

4. **Math.** Review the windows of opportunity in Figure 2.6. At what age, in months, does the latest window of opportunity begin?

5. **Listening, writing, and speaking.** Interview an early childhood (birth through age 8) educator about how they incorporate windows of opportunity into their teaching and/or caregiving. What age group do they work with? What specific skills and tasks are they working on with the children? What do they consider best practices for teaching and developing these skills? After the interview, create a presentation about the interview, highlighting how the educator does (or does not) take advantage of children's windows of opportunities. During your presentation, share with the class your own evaluation of the early childhood educator's practices and whether or not they are developmentally appropriate for that age group.

6. **Speaking.** Divide into teams and have each team select one of the following topics:
   - the four types of knowledge
   - the three executive functions
   - Galinsky's seven essential life skills

   In your team, identify the components of your topic and brainstorm as many everyday examples as possible. Present your findings to the class, using props or demonstrations to illustrate each component.

7. **Listening.** As your classmates present their findings from the previous activity, listen closely to your classmates' examples. Take notes on anything you find particularly interesting, or write any questions you think of during their presentations. Once they are finished presenting, share with the class one thought or question you had regarding their presentation. Do this for all the presentations in your class.

8. **CTE Career Readiness Practice.** Presume you are a teacher at a local preschool and kindergarten. The families of your children are concerned that you are not teaching some topics and skills early enough, and you have scheduled a collective "family-teacher conference" next week. To explain your teaching method, you decide to put together handouts about the following:
   - the windows of opportunity for children's learning
   - the four types of knowledge, the executive functions, and Galinsky's seven essential life skills—all of which you emphasize in your lessons

   Prepare these handouts and then write a short speech in which you acknowledge the families' concerns while educating them about child development and your teaching method. Distribute your handouts and give your presentation to the class.

Observations

1. In small groups, set up a time with a local child care facility to observe young children. If you do not have access to a child care facility, you can ask to observe a family friend's children. During your observation, assess the child's or children's readiness for developmental tasks, including

   • physical maturation
   • social pressures
   • inner pressures

   Afterward, discuss your observations with your group. Do your group members agree with your assessment? Why or why not? If there are differences of opinion, consider how two people can observe a child and see two different things.

   As a group, present a short summary of your observations and discussion to the class.

2. If abandoned or isolated from a young age, some children may never learn language skills or other developmental tasks. These children are known as *feral children*. Watch a documentary about a feral child. Documentaries can be found at a local library or online. Be sure to note the title and citation information of the documentary you chose. As you watch the documentary, note any observations you have. Then, write a one-page essay about the documentary you watched and about what you learned. Include citations for the documentary in the APA and MLA formats. Share your essay with the rest of the class.

Chapter 3

Families Today

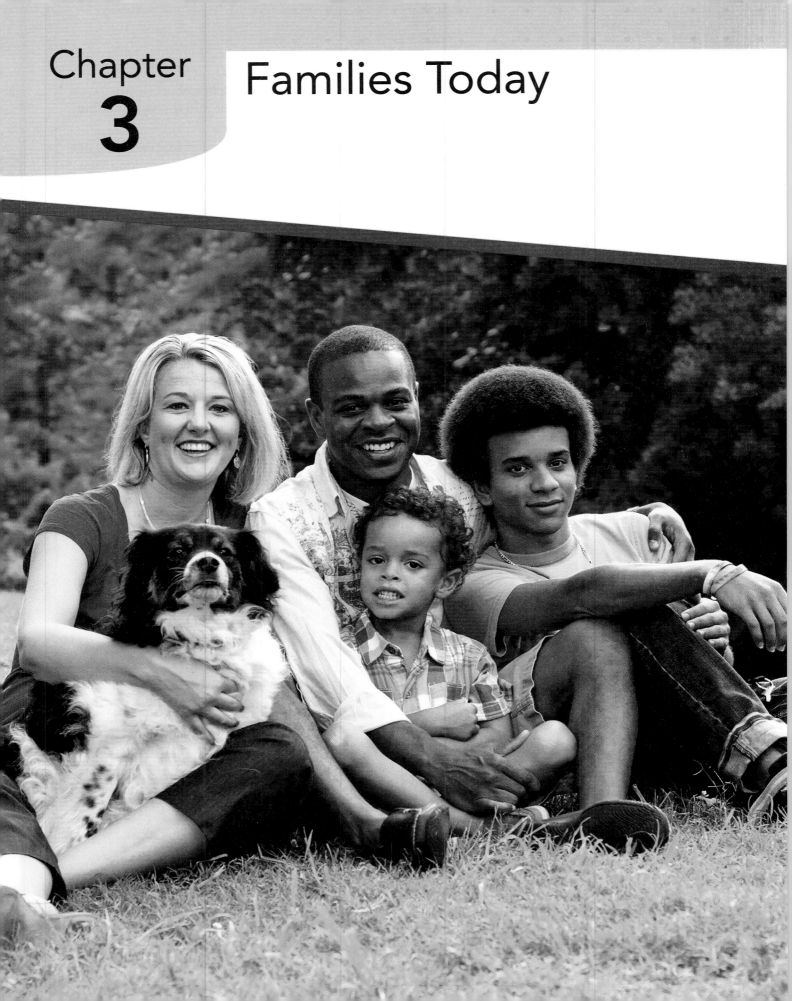

Essential Question

In what ways do family relationships affect children?

Case Study   How Can Cultural Differences in a Family Impact Childrearing?

As a class, read the case study and discuss the questions that follow. After you finish studying the chapter, discuss this case study again. Have your opinions changed based on what you learned?

Camila and Jim are looking for a place to live together after they get married next month. Camila sees a home for sale that is nearby many members of their family.

Jim finds Camila's family warm and welcoming but is not sure iving so close to them is such a great idea. The interactions among Camila's family members are constant—similar to an extended family, although each has their own home. Jim was raised in a nuclear family. They visited relatives mainly during holidays and vacation times, but otherwise lived as an independent family unit.

Jim understands that Camila's family means well, but feels smothered when they want details about everything and are free with their advice. Jim mentions this to Camila, who does not understand Jim's feelings. Jim does not know what to do and wonders whether this is just the beginning of problems due to differences in family culture.

Give It Some Thought

1. How can Jim explain his objections without hurting Camila's or Camila's family's feelings?
2. Is there a compromise that would make both Jim and Camila happy?
3. If Jim and Camila start a family of their own, how would their different ideas about family affect their parenting decisions?
4. Is Jim worrying needlessly, or can different family cultures make for long-term, serious marital and childrearing problems?

Rob Hainer/Shutterstock.com

Lesson 3.1

Healthy Family Development

Key Terms

active listening
beneficial
bias
body language
communication
comprise
cultural diversity
culture
detrimental
discontentment
essence
family life cycle
income
Industrial Revolution
inherent
marriage
multicultural family
norm

Learning Outcomes

After studying this lesson, you will be able to

3.1-1   **identify** criteria for a healthy family.

3.1-2   **assess** changes that take place during the family life cycle.

3.1-3   **describe** ways that culture influences the family.

3.1-4   **compare** past and present societal influences on families.

3.1-5   **determine** characteristics of healthy families.

Reading and Notetaking Activity

Imagine you are a family therapist. Your new clients are a family with two young children. The caregivers want to explore ways they could function better as a family and be happier. Write a two-paragraph speech recommending steps your clients can take to accomplish their goals. Incorporate information you have learned about child development and the kind of support children need. As you read the chapter, take detailed notes. After reading the chapter, read your speech again. With a partner, discuss what you would change about your speech based on any new information you have learned. Present your final speech to the class.

Introduction

How would you define *family*? The U.S. Census Bureau defines *family* as two or more people living in the same household who are related by blood (birth), marriage, or adoption. Perhaps your definition of family may be broader and include people who do not fit into the "traditional" definition. For example, many people consider other relatives or even close friends as family. If you were to ask others how they would define *family*, you would probably get many different responses.

The family is the oldest known social group. How well family members get along and work together help determine the stability of the family unit. Healthy families work on building healthy relationships. Families, just like individuals, change through the years, but continue to be the basic unit of society.

3.1-1 What Is a Family?

Why is it so difficult to define *family*? Every family is unique, and the relationships within the family are always special and complex. Adults bring to family relationships all of their childhood and adult experiences as well as their hopes and expectations. Children come into their families with certain inborn ways of reaching out to their parents to which parents respond.

Parent-child relationships are often embedded in relationships with other family members of different ages who will influence these relationships (**Figure 3.1**). The family also lives in a social and cultural setting that exerts its influence on the family. Thus, the family is not just simply two or more people related by blood, commitment, or **marriage** (a legal contract and, ideally an emotional and social union between two partners). The family is more than parents and their children, more than common ancestors, or more than people who share a household. It is this "more than" thinking—this **essence** (qualities that cannot be disregarded) that are **inherent** (basic) to all families, that makes the word *family* difficult to define.

skynesher/E+ via Getty Images

Figure 3.1 Establishing healthy relationships with family members is essential to the stability of the family unit and the health and development of any children. *How can you promote healthy relationships in your family?*

In this text, you will learn the following three things about families:

- Families can be classified by types (who belongs), and these types can change over time or with certain events.
- *Family dynamics*, the roles of family members and their patterns of relating within the family, can be **beneficial** (helpful) or **detrimental** (unhelpful or harmful) to a child's development.
- The family is the strongest and the most lasting influence in a child's life. The family is the foundation for all domains of the child's development.

Identifying Healthy Families

What makes for a healthy family? There are many criteria for a healthy family, and the more criteria the family meets, the greater the chance for its lasting health. The criteria include adults who are emotionally committed to each other and who feel accountable to each other and to their children even if conflicts and periods of **discontentment** (unhappiness) occur. The criteria also include adults who have established healthy family dynamics, such as

- encouraging all members of the family to work together for the well-being of the family
- keeping the avenues of **communication** (exchange of messages and information between at least two people) open through verbal messages, **active listening** (the receiver of a message provides feedback to the speaker, indicating the message is understood), and **body language**, which is the sending of nonverbal messages through body movements (**Figure 3.2**)
- establishing rules and boundaries that are clearly stated and evenly applied, but flexible enough to respond to each family member's needs
- creating expectations that are reasonable
- being models of family values and desired behaviors
- having fun and humor to ease the burden of family challenges

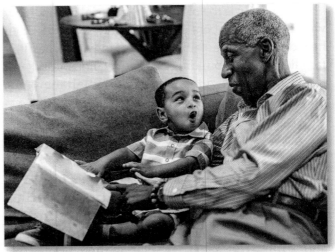

Lisa5201/E+ via Getty Images

Figure 3.2 Nonverbal communication includes facial expressions, eye contact, gestures, body movements, posture, and other elements of body language. All of these factors contribute to the message that is sent. *How are the two people in this photo communicating nonverbally? What messages are they sending?*

- allowing room for each family member to fulfill personal goals and to mature and change
- not keeping secrets from each other

Laying the Developmental Foundation for Children

Through family, children receive care during their dependent years. Adults are the decision-makers and providers of children's food, clothing, shelter, hygiene, and access to health care and education. Adults are the custodians of their children's schedules for all daily activities, such as eating, sleeping, and playing. They are also the role models for physical habits and a voice of influence when their children are cared for outside of the family.

The first and most continuous social relationships of children are familial. The family is where children acquire their first experiences of being loved and respected as individuals in their own right. The ability to meet life's demands and challenges is greatly influenced by the family dynamics of a child's home. The family instructs, gives guidance, and models social behaviors.

Even in the healthiest of families, harmony does not always prevail. So healthy families model and engage children in effective conflict resolution and problem-solving (**Figure 3.3**).

Healthy families sow the seeds for children to grow up with positive attitudes and life management skills. When families have unhealthy dynamics due to social strains, many children are unable to cope with stress and are at greater risk of becoming mentally unhealthy, having poor social skills, having weak impulse control (are "mad at the world"), and being poor problem-solvers. In short, all children depend on adults in their families to help them develop healthy human relationships.

3.1-2 The Family Life Cycle

Many parents and their children go through similar stages called the **family life cycle**. The traditional family life cycle consists of six stages (**Figure 3.4**). The *beginning stage* consists of an individual or a couple. During this time, they decide whether they want to become parents and, if so, how many children they want to have.

In the *childbearing stage*, parents give birth to or adopt one or more children and assume their roles and responsibilities in caring for and guiding children through their earliest years. If a couple or individual has more than one child, the childbearing and parenting stages often overlap.

Figure 3.3 Steps in Problem Solving

Step	Questions
Step 1. Identify the problem	• What is the problem that is getting in the way of achieving a goal? Be specific. • How is the problem affecting me? How is it affecting others? • What is happening? When is it happening? What causes the problem?
Step 2. Look at alternative solutions	• Brainstorm as many solutions as possible. • Do not discard any idea. Sometimes seemingly "bad ideas" can develop into "good solutions."
Step 3. Analyze the alternative solutions	• Write the good and bad points for each possible solution. • Group alternative solutions, when possible.
Step 4. Select a possible solution	• Decide which solutions might have the most impact on the problem. Decide if the solution is realistic and manageable. • As you consider possible solutions, think of the consequences of each. What is the extent of a risk involved in each possible solution? • Do not hurry this step. Talk to others, including those affected by the problem.
Step 5. Implement a solution	• After choosing a solution, plan how and when you will implement it. • Be specific on the steps to implement the plan. • Communicate the implementation steps to all involved.
Step 6. Evaluate the results	• Evaluate the effectiveness of the solution. Is the solution achieving the desired goal? Did the solution have any unforeseen risks? • If the problem has not been resolved, ask the following: Do I need to give it more time to work? Should I change the plan of action? Do I need to begin the entire process again? • If the problem seems to be resolved, continue to monitor. Problems do not always stay solved.

Goodheart-Willcox Publisher

Figure 3.4 **The Family Life Cycle**

Stage	Definition	Example
Beginning stage	Either a couple or an individual determines whether they want to embark on parenthood and, if so, how many children they would like to have. This stage lasts until the individual or couple has a child. Individuals and couples who remain childless stay in the beginning stage of the family life cycle until they reach the mid-years stage.	Rawpixel.com/Shutterstock.com
Childbearing stage	The individual or couple starts having children. The stages of the family life cycle for parents of multiple children are overlapping. The childbearing stage continues until individuals or couples have their last child.	Ground Picture/Shutterstock.com
Parenting stage	The individual or couple focuses on guiding their children through the school-age and teen years. Balancing children's school and extracurricular activities with family and work demands can pose many scheduling challenges during this stage.	Monkey Business Images/Stockbroker/ Monkey Business via Getty Images Plus;
Launching stage	The children begin leaving home to attend college, find a job and live on their own, or possibly start their own families. The individual or couple often begins to have more free time for themselves.	kali9/E+ via Getty Images
Mid-years stage	The individual or couple faces an *empty nest* when all of their children leave home, and they may feel a void in their lives without the busyness of taking care of their children. They refocus on planning for their future and possibly becoming grandparents. This stage lasts until the individual or couple retires.	adamkaz/E+ via Getty Images
Aging stage	The individual or couple retires and adjusts to this change in lifestyle. Their health may decline, which might result in grown children becoming caregivers of their parents. This stage lasts throughout the remainder of life.	Lordn/Shutterstock.com

Goodheart-Willcox Publisher

During the *parenting stage*, parents focus on guiding and nurturing their children through the school-age and teen years. They are preparing their children to become productive members of society. Children begin to learn more from teachers and peers. During adolescence, parents begin treating their children as adults. They also know when to provide guidance and help.

The *launching stage* brings new feelings for parents. During this stage, children start to leave home to make their own lives. As each child leaves home, parents may feel lonelier. They may also feel their children no longer need them. In this stage, parents must acknowledge their children are adults and their relationships may be more equal. Parents learn new ways to offer support to and interact with their grown children.

In the *mid-years stage*, parents may find more time for themselves than they did when their children lived at home. They may devote more time to new interests or hobbies. Keeping in touch with their children is still important, and they may become grandparents. The couple or individual also begins to focus on retirement.

In some cases, economic troubles, divorce, or other situations may cause grown children to return to the family home. Parents then have to learn new ways to relate to their children. They may have adjusted to their children becoming adults and do not know how to treat them as adults when they all live in the same home. Grandchildren may also come to live in the home. Open communication can help ensure that family members continue to get along.

The final stage of the family life cycle is the *aging stage*. This stage lasts from retirement to the death of a partner. In this stage, the couple or individual may pursue new hobbies and spend time with family and friends. They may have health conditions that cause them to need help from their children. The couple or individual may face different challenges and have new concerns. During this stage, family members may need to make many adjustments.

Keep in mind that while many families follow this traditional family life cycle in whole or in part, that does not mean all families do, and it does not mean that it is always the best way to do things.

Focus on Careers

Marriage and Family Therapist

Marriage and family therapists are professionals who work to improve the social and psychological functioning of children and their families and to maximize the family's well-being. They help families overcome stress, mental health issues, and behavioral problems.

Career cluster: Human services.

Education: Educational requirements often include a master's degree. All states have some licensure, certification, or registration requirement.

Job outlook: Future employment opportunities for marriage and family therapists are expected to grow much faster than the average for all occupations.

To learn more about a career as a marriage and family therapist, visit the United States Department of Labor's *Occupational Outlook Handbook* website. You will also be able to compare the job responsibilities, educational requirements, job outlook, and average pay of marriage and family therapists with similar occupations.

Photo: wavebreakmedia/ Shutterstock.com

There are many ways that healthy families form and evolve/change, and we need to remember that there is no one right way to make a family.

3.1-3 Cultural Influences on Families

Families may go through similar stages and are alike in many ways, but they may differ in the cultural groups to which they belong. **Culture**, a way of life within a group of people that includes language, beliefs, attitudes, values, rituals, and skills, greatly affects a family's life (**Figure 3.5**). Because not every family belongs to the same culture, the effects of culture differ widely from one family to the next.

People of many cultural groups live in the United States. Families who once came from many parts of the world call the United States home. The United States is an example of a nation with great **cultural diversity**, which means it has more than one culture represented among its people.

Figure 3.5 Aspects of a Person's Culture

- History, folklore, heroes
- Language (written, verbal, slang, body language, and gestures)
- Humor
- Names (surname and given name)
- Holiday celebrations, traditions, rites and rituals
- Methods of greeting (such as eye contact, handshakes, hugs, kisses, and bowing)
- Preferences about personal space and touching
- Cherished values and traits
- Foods, eating methods, eating manners
- Dress and body decorations
- Home furnishings and decorations
- Arts and crafts
- Music

Goodheart-Willcox Publisher

How Cultures Vary

Families often identify their culture in terms of their origin or ancestors. People often reference a region of origin, specific country, or language to identify their culture because of the customs, traditions, values, and religions that **comprise** (make up) each culture. These components help describe a family's cultural identification.

Each culture's practices support its beliefs and customs. For example, goals for achievement vary from culture to culture. Some cultures stress academic achievement as a way to honor the family and achieve economic success that will help the entire family. These families view academic learning as the top priority for children. Other cultures stress achievement in social interactions. In these cultures, showing dignity and respect in interactions with others brings honor to the individual or family. These families emphasize play as well as academic skills. Because they have such different views, these two types of families differ in their parenting practices, modeling, praise, and criticism regarding the role of education.

Cultures differ in the way they view the concept of family. In some cultures, *family* includes only the immediate family. In other cultures, this term has a broader meaning that includes other relatives, close family friends, and neighbors.

The importance of the family also varies from culture to culture (see **Figure 3.6**). In cultures with a group orientation, family is most important. Cultures with an individual orientation focus on each person as an individual more than on the family as a group.

Language and dialect can vary from one culture to the next, too. Families generally use their culture's native language and teach this language to their children. Using the language of their people can bring a sense of unity and belonging and contribute to their culture. Families may use language as a way to foster this involvement in the culture.

The use and meaning of body language can vary from group to group. This explains the well-known saying: *Not all people smile in the same language*. In some cultures, smiling expresses friendliness, pleasure, or understanding of humor.

In other cultures, a smile is used to acknowledge a fault. Some cultures might use smiling to mask emotion (hurt or disagreement) or avoid conflict.

In other cultures, people smile in response to a compliment if they feel verbal response would show a lack of modesty.

Figure 3.6 Cultures See Families Differently

Edwin Tan/E+ via Getty Images

kali9/E+ via Getty Images

Group-Oriented Culture	Individual-Oriented Culture
Family includes kin and perhaps others.	Family includes parents and their children.
Family members live in same house or near each other.	Family members live in different houses and may live far away from one another.
Status in the family (and possibly in the group) is achieved by age and/or gender.	Status in the family is determined by achievement.
Elders make decisions based on the welfare of the whole family (collective responsibility).	The individual considers their own welfare when making decisions for themselves (individual responsibility).
Members take pride in their family name, family history, and family honor.	Members take pride in their own talents, achievements, and status.
Family members conform to those in authority.	Family members may challenge or question those in authority.
Members value cooperation and togetherness.	Members value competition and achievement.
Family harmony is emphasized.	Individual happiness is emphasized.
Early dependence on group is encouraged.	Early independence is encouraged.
Group members help each other, even at their own expense.	Each person is expected to help themselves with little assistance from the family.
Parent-child bond is stressed. Children are seen as extensions of parents (children bring honor to and help the family throughout life).	Marital bond is stressed. Children are seen as individuals who as adults take care of themselves.
Family looks more to the past and traditions and has a more lax approach to time.	Family looks more to the future and values efficiency and timeliness.
Expression of emotion is more indirect (emotionally controlled; modest; formal toward elders to show respect).	Expression of emotion is more direct (emotionally expressive; more "I-centered"; informal).

Goodheart-Willcox Publisher

Social Studies

Cultural Diversity

Speaking different languages is not the only way communication differs across cultures. The role of language can differ, too. For instance, some cultures teach children to talk often, be open and direct, and be informal. These children might address people by their first names without asking and soon after meeting, use slang, and talk to strangers. Other cultures value silence—talking only when necessary. These cultures teach children to notice other body language clues (such as "reading the eyes") to help them understand without being told. These cultures prefer formal word choice and the use of courtesy titles when addressing elders or strangers. In these cultures, children are taught to address elders in a way that shows respect.

In what ways do you think your cultural background will influence the way you parent or care for children? How can children benefit from these influences?

Photo: wavebreakmedia/Shutterstock.com

Multicultural Families

As the United States increases in cultural diversity, the number of *multicultural families* continues to grow. A **multicultural family** is a family with members from two or more cultural groups. Multicultural families offer family members unique opportunities to learn about and experience different cultures' practices firsthand. In mixing and navigating different cultural expectations, multicultural families may experience many advantages as well as added challenges.

Adults in multicultural families know from the beginning that they must mix cultural backgrounds. They may often have to consider each cultural groups practices to decide

- where to live, such as near which relatives or in which community type;
- what religion to follow;
- what holidays to observe;
- if bilingual (speaking two languages), what language to speak;
- how to handle differences with relatives;
- what types of food to make; and
- how to handle childrearing.

There are several advantages of living in a multicultural family. Children are exposed to a broader cultural view. Many children in multicultural families also become bilingual at an early age, which is an advantage in today's global society. Most children raised in multicultural homes are happy and grow up to respect diversity and have a strong sense of self. Recent studies show that children in multicultural families may be more creative. Multicultural families that are strong seem to have much in common (**Figure 3.7**).

Figure 3.7 What Makes Multicultural Families Strong?

Studies have shown that strong multicultural families often share the following characteristics:
- Parents have strong cultural identities and feel good about their multicultural family.
- The family talks about cultural issues in the home.
- Parents and children develop creative ways to solve problems that show equal respect for both cultures.
- The family surrounds itself with supportive family and friends.
- Parents work with child care staff and teachers on behalf of their children.
- The family celebrates all cultures.
- Parents tolerate no biased remarks within their circle of family, friends, and peers.

Goodheart-Willcox Publisher

Unfortunately, multicultural families are more likely to experience **bias** (favoring; unequal treatment). Children of multicultural families may feel pressured to choose one culture over another. Despite these challenges, the diverse experiences of children in multicultural families gives them greater understanding of, and openness toward, other cultures.

3.1-4 Societal Influences on Families

Changes in society cause major changes in the family. In the past, before the **Industrial Revolution** (time in history in which society began to focus on industry and manufacturing), many families lived on farms and met most of their own needs. These families consisted of the immediate family (parents and their children) as well as grandparents and other family members. They often lived together or in nearby houses as part of an extended family group.

During the Industrial Revolution, many families left their farms and moved into the cities to work in factories, leaving behind relatives and friends. Away from other relatives, people began to turn to their immediate family members for companionship and emotional support. The immediate family became more important for love and security.

The societal views of children during this time were different from those of today. Children were considered an asset to the family because they helped the family earn money. When children reached four to seven years of age, they were expected to work long days in factories or on farms. Today, society values children and sees childhood as a special time. Labor laws changed the role children played in the economy while protecting them as individuals. Children now lead lives as *children*, not as a source of family **income** (money received for working). In the past, because children were a source of income, families tended to be larger, with many children. Today, children are a source of expense (costing money), and families tend to be much smaller.

Families continue to respond and adapt to societal changes, such as advancements in medicine and technology. Medical advances allow people to live longer. In the United States and elsewhere, the life expectancy rate has steadily increased in the past few decades. Technological advancements also change the **norm** (normal, socially acceptable pattern) of living. Electronic devices, such as home appliances, cell phones, tablets, televisions, and video consoles, affect how family members communicate with each other, use time for entertainment, and help complete tasks around the house. Technology also affects how people learn. Information is more readily available today than in the past.

3.1-5 Characteristics of Healthy Families

There is no magic recipe to create a healthy family. Families can be very different and yet strong. Some common characteristics are often seen in healthy families (**Figure 3.8**). The most common characteristic is that families share similar values.

Figure 3.8 Characteristics of a Healthy Family

- Relationships built on and directed by shared values
- Acceptance of family members' differences
- Expectation that family values and structure will change
- Willingness to adjust
- Mutual commitment to family life
- Others-centeredness, not self-centeredness
- Sharing of responsibilities
- Honesty and dependability
- Open, honest communication

Goodheart-Willcox Publisher

Viktorcvetkovic/E+ via Getty Images

Culturally Sensitive Trauma-Informed Care

In Chapter 2, you learned about the effects of Adverse Childhood Experiences (ACEs) on the developing brain. You also learned how important it is to implement trauma-informed care (TIC) to promote resilience in children who have suffered a trauma. But just as families from different cultures have different approaches to language, behavior, customs, and religion, they may also have different needs with regard to TIC.

Culturally sensitive TIC refers to the capacity for health care professionals to equally provide trauma-informed assessment and intervention that acknowledges, respects, and integrates families' cultural values, beliefs, and practices. Although research suggests that there is a universal biological response to trauma, cultural factors can affect the way a family reacts to highly stressful situations. When working with the family of a child who has experienced an ACE, it is important to listen carefully and be respectful of the family's culture.

Following is advice on applying culturally sensitive TIC:

Listen for variations in understanding. When viewed through their cultural lens, a family's perception of a traumatic event may differ from yours. It is helpful to ask families to explain what happened in their own words. Ask what is troubling them and the child the most and how the family feels about it.

Be open to involving others. One family may be **adamant** (refuse to change their minds) that extended families or other health care professionals be involved; others may want to involve as few people as possible. Some families may feel uncomfortable seeking resources outside their cultural community. It is important to listen with an open mind and understand that families need to feel safe before they can heal.

Be respectful of varying communication styles. All families are different. In some families, one family member makes most or all of the decisions. In others, decisions are more of a collaborative process. Some families take a more private approach to family business; others are more open and willing to share. Ask questions to find out how the family functions as a unit.

Look beyond your words. Some cultures are highly sensitive to nonverbal communication. Cues like eye contact, facial expressions, tone of voice, body language, and touch can mean different things to different people. For example, in some cultures it is considered highly disrespectful for a child to look an adult in the eye when being spoken to. If you ask them to look you in the eye, you could be asking them to do something that is very uncomfortable for them. Culturally appropriate communication practices have been shown to result in a higher level of trust between families and care professionals.

Application Activity

Research methods of nonverbal and verbal communication in three different cultures. On a piece of paper, draw three columns and label each with the name of one culture. Then list any communication conventions specific to each culture.

Find a partner and discuss your findings. Where there any communication styles that were the same across two or more cultures? What were the differences? How would you apply what you've learned if you were working with a family from each of these cultures?

Photo: Tom Wang/Shutterstock.com

They use these values to decide on goals together and guide them in raising their children.

Closely tied to shared values is the belief that family members are individuals. Strong families accept that even people who share many values will be somewhat different. They also realize life itself can change the family's goals. Healthy families are willing to adjust as needed.

Healthy families share a mutual commitment to family life. In these families, members want their own relationships to succeed. They want to be successful as a family unit. Part of the commitment involves growth—becoming more loving, caring, and understanding. These family members also want to do many activities as a family unit.

In healthy families, members want to help each other rather than being self-centered. Members share responsibilities. Although each family may divide tasks differently, healthy families seem to happily follow their own choices about duties. Each member can depend on the others to keep promises, fulfill commitments, and be honest.

Lesson 3.1   Review and Assessment

1. Which of the following is *not* a way to establish healthy family dynamics? (3.1.1)
   A. Encourage all members of the family to work together for the well-being of the family.
   B. Discourage the fulfillment of personal goals so that the focus remains on the family unit.
   C. Create reasonable expectations.
   D. Use fun and humor to ease the burden of family challenges.

2. There are _____ stages of the family life cycle. (3.1.2)
   A. 6
   B. 7
   C. 8
   D. 9

3. **True or False.** Culture is a way of life of a group of people that includes language, beliefs, attitudes, values, rituals, and skills. (3.1.3)

4. What is one way societal views of children today differ from societal views of children before and during the Industrial Revolution? (3.1.4)
   A. Children are considered lazy.
   B. Families want to send their children into the workforce at a younger age.
   C. Childhood is valued and seen as a special time.
   D. Companies no longer pay children for their labor.

5. Which of the following is *not* a characteristic of a healthy family? (3.1.5)
   A. Acceptance of family members' differences
   B. Expectation that family values and structure will change
   C. Avoiding difficult topics of conversation
   D. Willingness to adjust

Lesson 3.2

Family Types

Key Terms

adoption
adoption agency
child support order
closed adoption
consenting
custodial parent
extended family
foster family
guardian
illegal market adoption
independent adoption
joint custody
kin care
noncustodial parent
nuclear family
open adoption
recession
single-parent family
stepfamily

Learning Outcomes

After studying this lesson, you will be able to

3.2-1 **identify** various types of family structures and analyze the advantages and challenges of each.

3.2-2 **compare** and **contrast** different types of adoptions.

> ### Reading and Notetaking Activity
>
> How would you describe your ideal family? Before reading this lesson, write a one-page short story about your idea of a model family. Who would be a part of the family, and what kinds of relationships would you have with them? How would members of your family treat each other, and what values would they hold? Keep your short story, and after reading this lesson, title it with the family type that best describes your family. Write one paragraph justifying this title and then share your short story with a classmate whose short story had a different title.

3.2-1 Different Types of Families

There are many types of families that comprise the U.S. population. The family type describes which people live in the household and how these people are related. Children usually enter families through birth and live in these families throughout childhood. Some children, however, have families who form differently. In these cases, children can have more than one type of family. This lesson describes different family types and their effects on children.

Nuclear Families

Two parents and their biological child or children who live together form a **nuclear family**. This type of family exists in most societies. In nuclear families, children often leave home when they become adults, especially when they marry and have their own families.

Compared to other family types, nuclear families can have some disadvantages. Family members, such as grandparents or aunts and uncles, do not live in the home and children may lose out on the skills these other people can teach them. The family may live too far from relatives to rely on them for support in times of stress. Parents who do not get along may expose children to stress. This is especially true if the relationship is abusive.

On the other hand, nuclear families have some advantages. Both the adults and the children may have their needs met more easily because family members can share responsibilities. Children may be **apt** (likely) to learn more flexible home and child care roles in the nuclear family. Adults often share these tasks, and children who see role sharing may be better prepared for the future than those who do not. Children also have the chance to see how spouses relate to each other in positive ways.

Single-Parent Families

A **single-parent family** is made up of one parent and their child or children. Single-parent families can form in several different ways. Certain *circumstances* (situations or conditions) such as the death of a parent or a couple's marital separation or divorce can change a nuclear family to a single-parent family (**Figure 3.9**). Single-parent families may also form when parents never marry and live apart, or when a person decides to have a child on their own through adoption, surrogacy, artificial insemination or other means. In the majority of single-parent families, the mother is the **custodial parent** (the parent who heads the household and has legal responsibility for caregiving). A growing number of single fathers, however, are also becoming custodial parents.

One of the most common challenges single-parent families face is reduced resources, such as income, time, and energy. In a single-parent family, one custodial parent provides for the majority of the family's needs. This can put single-parent families at a disadvantage compared to families in which both parents work and take responsibility for providing for children. While the custodial parent is responsible for meeting children's needs, the **noncustodial parent** (parent who lives separately from their children), when present, may have a legal responsibility to contribute financially toward a child's care. If a noncustodial parent refuses to pay, a child support order can be issued by the court. A **child support order** is a judgment of the court that states how much the noncustodial parent must pay toward the child's expenses.

If children live with a single parent, this does not always mean the other parent cannot take an active role in the children's lives. When possible, parents can work together to raise children even if they do not live in the same house. Some co-parents go to court to seek **joint custody**, which is the shared legal right to provide care for, and make decisions about, their children's lives. Joint custody avoids the issue of determining which parent will be the primary caregiver.

MBI/Shutterstock.com

fizkes/iStock via Getty Images Plus

Figure 3.9 Any number of circumstances can change a nuclear family to a single-parent family. *What are some advantages of single-parent families? some challenges?*

Depending on the manner in which they form, single-parent families can face difficult emotional concerns. When death or divorce changes a nuclear family to a single-parent family, children feel the loss of a relationship and role model. In these families, children's daily routines change as one parent takes over the duties of two parents. Single parents must learn to **cope** (handle challenges in a healthy manner) with their own feelings about the change as well as help their children cope. When one parent is absent, children may wonder whether they caused the parent to abandon them. They may wonder why other children have two parents and they have only one. These children may feel a lasting sense of loss, especially if they have never known or no longer have contact with the second parent. They may feel anger toward either parent, which may cause strained family relationships.

If only one parent participates in the child's life, there are sources of support and help available. Other family members, friends, and neighbors may provide help in caring for the children. Adults from an organization such as Big Brothers Big Sisters of America can serve as role models for the children. Some single parents find support groups or social groups, such as Parents Without Partners®, helpful in providing social and emotional supports. Social service agencies may offer emotional, practical, and financial help, too.

Despite the challenges, children in single-parent families also have many advantages. Children in single-parent homes often have a less stressful and more secure environment than children in two-parent homes where the parents frequently argue. The relationship between children and their single parent is often very strong. Because single parents have such busy schedules, children are often encouraged to help out around the home and do things for themselves, which helps teach children to be independent and responsible.

Focus on

FINANCIAL LITERACY

Cost of Raising a Child

According to 2020 data from the US Department of Agriculture, the average cost of raising a child through age 17 is $233,610. The cost of raising a child includes monthly expenses such as:

- Housing
- Food
- Transportation
- Healthcare
- Child care
- Clothing
- Personal care items
- Entertainment

It also includes one-time expenses (such as car seats, cribs, strollers, etc.) and limited-time expenses (e.g., diapers, baby bottles). Using an online cost of raising a child calculator or data about expenses in your area (e.g., cost of housing, cost of child care), calculate how much money per month you would need to raise a child. How might decisions you make raise or lower these costs? Do you think these costs will increase or decrease as the child ages? What about the cost of college? How will that be funded?

Photo: Noam Armonn/Shutterstock.com

FOCUS ON MENTAL HEALTH

All families, regardless of the family type, face challenges, such as financial concerns or a family member's emotional problems. If these difficulties are not addressed, mental health problems may result. The government's Substance Abuse and Mental Health Services Administration (SAMHSA's) National Helpline is a confidential, free, 24-hour-a-day, 365-day-a-year, information service, in English and Spanish, for people facing mental and/or substance use disorders. This service provides referrals to local treatment facilities, support groups, and community-based organizations. Callers can also order free publications and other information.

Extended Families

An **extended family** is a household that includes the parent or parents and their children and other relatives. Other relatives who live in an extended family may include grandparents, aunts, uncles, and cousins. There are three extended family types:

- *One-generation extended family.* In a one-generation extended family, everyone in the household is of the same generation. Members of this family type might include a married couple and their siblings or cousins.
- *Two-generation extended family.* In a two-generation extended family, the family members span two generations. An example of this family type might include parents, their adult child, and their son-in-law or daughter-in-law.
- *Three-generation extended family.* A three-generation extended family is commonly called a *multigenerational family.* Parents, their children, and their aging parents living in the same household is an example of a multigenerational family.

Although there may be several generations of family members living together in an extended family, there is usually only one head of the household. For example, if a young couple moves into a parent's home, the young couple will likely consider the parent as the head of the household. If an older adult moves in with their adult child, the older adult will see the adult child as the head of the household.

Extended families are very common in many countries around the world. In the United States, extended families may form for many reasons. An extended family may form when a single parent and their children move in with other family members to combine resources and provide care for the children. Extended families may also form as aging family members move in with their adult children. When the economy is in **recession** (economic period with minimal or no growth), there are always more extended families due to financial circumstances. Other families choose this family structure due to cultural tradition.

Extended families experience certain challenges. Sometimes family members find they do not have enough privacy. There may be more disagreements among family members sharing spaces and resources. Also, decisions are more often made for the good of the entire family rather than the needs of each person.

Extended families also have many advantages. Children learn to interact with people of all ages because younger and older family members are in daily contact. Extended families are good at handing down family beliefs and *family history,* or stories of a family's past (**Figure 3.10**). Because there are so many members, extended families can perform more duties than small family groups.

wavebreakmedia/Shutterstock.com

Figure 3.10 Family history and beliefs can be passed down through conversations; through time spent together; through letters and heirlooms; or through scrapbooks, as shown in the picture above. *What family beliefs and history have been passed down to you?*

When stressful events happen in extended families, family members are there to help support one another.

Stepfamilies and Blended Families

A **stepfamily** forms when one or both adults in the relationship have children from a previous relationship living in the home. The terms *stepparent* and *stepchild* refer to the parents and children in the family who are brought together by the adults' relationship. In many cases, stepfamilies form when an individual remarries after divorce or death or when a single parent chooses to marry.

The stepfamily is a fairly common family form. Many of today's children have two stepfamilies—that of each parent and the parent's new partner. Often, children live with only one of these stepfamilies. Other times, children live with each stepfamily part of the year. Each situation is unique.

Many people use the terms *stepfamily* and *blended family* interchangeably. A *blended family* will start as a stepfamily, but members must then work together to merge, or blend, the families into a cohesive family unit that creates a healthy family bond. Adjustment challenges are common when blending families (**Figure 3.11**).

Figure 3.11 Adjustment Challenges of Blending Families

- Family members find themselves in instant relationships—stepparents must relate with stepchildren and stepchildren must relate with each other.
- Parents must adjust to their new roles as a married couple while dealing with children from the beginning of marriage.
- Both parents have to adjust from being heads of single households to sharing roles and discipline and guidance of children.
- Children usually maintain relationships with the family of their other parent, too. Many children must adjust to two sets of rules, which can be a major challenge for school-age children.
- Sibling rivalry is common in all families but can be worse among stepsiblings.
- Housing space may be a concern.

Goodheart-Willcox Publisher

Some ways stepparents can help create a family bond include
- letting stepchildren set the pace for their relationships with stepparents
- letting stepchildren know they are appreciated
- explaining to children that a stepparent is another person to love and support them
- encouraging stepchildren to have one-on-one time with both their biological parents
- planning activities with stepchildren, but avoiding attempts to "buy" their love
- insisting on respect, but letting biological parents remain primarily responsible for discipline until solid bonds are established
- avoiding showing favoritism among children by treating all children equally
- keeping family communication open and frequent

Blending two families requires many adjustments, but being part of a blended family offers many benefits, too. Parents can provide a strong emotional support system for each other and their children. Blended families are also able to combine resources and incomes to reduce stress related to lack of time, energy, or money. Children in blended families can benefit from the companionship, love, and support of new siblings and other relatives, such as grandparents, aunts, uncles, and cousins.

Families with Adopted Children

Adoption occurs when a child of one pair of parents legally becomes the child of other parents (or parent). Adoption legally ends the rights and responsibilities between a child and the birthparents (biological parents). The adoptive parents are then granted these rights. Many of the children available for adoption are older, have special needs, are born outside the United States, or are living in foster families and group homes. People often want to adopt for the following reasons:
- They cannot give birth or can give birth only with great difficulty.
- They may want to add to their current family.
- They know a child who needs a home.
- They want to be a parent and provide a home for children.

Children who are adopted generally have stable, happy home lives because their adopted families want and love them very much. Some challenges, however, may exist. In most cases, adoptive parents do not have the nine months of pregnancy to make the transition to parenthood. Instead, they take on their new roles very quickly. People wanting to adopt may be on a waiting list for many years. Then one day the adoption agency may call and announce a child will be ready for them the next day.

Other challenges may arise related to the adopted child's birthparents, especially if the adoption is closed. Birthparents may want to see the child or become part of the child's life. Adoptive parents may not agree that this is best for the child.

Children who are adopted often ask questions about the adoption. They may want to know about or meet their birthparents. Older children who lived with their birthparents and are then adopted by a new family need time to adjust. These children may miss their birthparents or want to be with them. To help these children adjust, adoptive parents can answer their children's questions about the adoption in direct and honest ways. Adoptive parents may also wish to seek counseling to help them guide the children and offer them the support they need to make the adjustment.

Adjustments to living in an adoptive family take time for all family members. Soon, however, families are likely to adapt. Many adoptive parents create a loving family life that helps adopted children overcome any stress they may feel.

Foster Families

A **foster family** is a family in which an adult provides a temporary home for a child who cannot live with their birthparents. Foster parents assume the parenting responsibilities for the children in their care. They fill these roles until children reunite with their birthparents, are adopted, or become adults. Some foster children live in institutions or group homes rather than in family settings.

Children often enter foster families because of problems in their birth families. These problems often include abuse, neglect, incarceration, or substance abuse by the birthparents or other family members. In these cases, the courts intervene to protect the children by placing them in a foster family and providing counseling, treatment, and other help for the birthparents. The goal is to reunite children with their birthparents if they are able to provide a safe, secure home for their children. In serious or prolonged cases of neglect or abuse, the court may **sever** (end or cut off) the rights of the birthparents. The children remain in foster care until they can be adopted and given a permanent home. Sometimes children can be adopted by their foster parents.

A foster family may have one or two parents, and may include other biological, adoptive, or foster children. A foster child may be placed with brothers and sisters or apart from them, depending on the situation. Foster families can offer a stable, secure home for children. Joining a foster family, however, is a major adjustment. In many cases, foster children need counseling for the problems they faced in their birth families. They may also miss their birthparents and other family members. To ease separation stress, contact or visitation is sometimes granted. Other children may grieve if they know they will never return to live with their birthparents. Each situation is unique. Foster parents need to be flexible, supportive, and understanding of the children in their care.

FOCUS ON MENTAL HEALTH

Children who live in an unstable home environment, especially one that involves abuse, neglect, or substance abuse, are at a greater risk of developing mental health problems, limiting children's success now and in the future. Children need a loving, stable home environment to promote healthy development.

If you or a child you know is experiencing abuse, you can call the National Child Abuse Hotline. Professional crisis counselors provide support and assistance 24 hours a day/7 days a week/365 days a year. Calls, texts, and chats are confidential.

Families with Guardians

A **guardian** is a person who is legally appointed by the court to take responsibility for a child in the event of the birthparents' death or extended absence. The guardian is often chosen by a child's biological parents and is usually someone who has close ties to the family, such as a relative or friend. The guardian assumes parental responsibilities. Some guardians manage the child's inherited money, while others take full financial responsibility for childrearing costs. The court supervises the guardian and may even make some decisions for the child. A child remains with their guardian until the child becomes a legal adult or the court terminates the relationship.

Kin Care

Growing numbers of children in the United States are living in households headed by grandparents and other relatives (**Figure 3.12**). This is called **kin care** (care of children by relatives other than the parents). These family heads often do not have legal guardianship, but assume the parenting responsibilities of a guardian. Not having legal rights as a guardian may present challenges for the children and the guardian.

Kin care may be provided by aunts, uncles, cousins, or even older siblings, but the most common type of kin care is grandparents raising grandchildren. While grandparents are often the safety net for their grandchildren, parenting grandchildren can be high-risk for grandparents. These risks include

- not being able to physically care for grandchildren until the children are grown. *Vigor* (strength and energy) and health decrease as grandparents age.
- having less income due to retirement or loss of a spouse. (About 20 percent of these grandparents live at the poverty level.)
- giving up plans for the retirement years, such as leisure, hobbies, or travel.
- grieving over their grandchildren's parents. Usually the need for grandparents to become the active parents is due to one of the *Four Ds*: drugs, divorce, desertion, or death. Because of the Four Ds, parenting the second time around is long-term.

Figure 3.12 Statistics on Raising Grandchildren

- Eighty percent of children who live with relatives are with grandparents.
- Over 33 percent of these households are without any parental help.
- Fifty-one percent of the children are younger than six years of age, which means many years of child-raising.
- Fifty percent of the children are raised by two grandparents, and fifty percent by grandmothers.
- Fifty percent of the households have two or more children.
- Almost 20 percent of the households are in poverty.
- Sixty-seven percent of grandparents are under 60 years of age.

Goodheart-Willcox Publisher

MBI/Shutterstock.com

- having anxiety about meeting the needs of grandchildren whose cultural and technological experiences are often so different from their own.
- dealing with their grandchildren's special needs, such as addictions, malnourishment, disabilities, and disorders, often due to earlier parental neglect and abuse.

On the positive side, grandparents often do an excellent job in raising their grandchildren. Grandparents usually have good parenting skills and they love their grandchildren unconditionally. Grandchildren typically respond in positive ways to their grandparents.

3.2-2 Different Types of Adoption

Most parents who adopt children spend much effort finding them. Buying or selling a child for adoption, which is called an **illegal market adoption**, is illegal in all states. Legal adoptions are expensive because parents pay providers for their time and expenses. For example, some expenses may include maternal expenses, such as health care not covered by insurance, salary and transportation costs for social workers, legal fees, and office expenses. Paying expenses, however, is different from buying and selling children. There are two ways to adopt children legally—through an adoption agency and through an independent source.

An **adoption agency** is an agency licensed by the state to handle adoptions. The agency works out the details between the birthparents and the adoptive parents. State courts handle the final legal aspects of the adoption. Adoption agencies are either state-funded or private (managed by a religious or a service organization).

In an **independent adoption**, a person, such as a lawyer or physician, works out the details between the birthparents and adoptive parents. Independent adoptions are handled in state courts and thus follow state laws. Foreign adoptions can be handled through an adoption agency or an independent source. **Figure 3.13** compares the pros and cons of each type of adoption.

Adoption Options and Rights

The laws of each state govern adoption options and rights. Adoption rights protect those involved in an adoption. In most states, the birthfather has legal rights. State laws may permit the birthfather to deny *paternity* (fathering of a child), give all rights to the birthmother, and give permission along with the birthmother for the child to be adopted. In some states, if the father cannot be found, steps can be taken to end his rights to make decisions about the child.

Focus on

Careers

Social Worker— Adoption Coordinator

Social worker is a category of careers in which professionals help families meet their basic needs. Some social workers, called *adoption coordinators*, work with adoption agencies to help families going through the adoption process. Adoption coordinators facilitate the placement of children for adoption. They conduct home studies and monitor children throughout the adoption process. Adoption coordinators must also possess a working knowledge of state laws as they relate to adoption.

Career cluster: Human services.

Education: Educational requirements include a bachelor's or master's degree in social work.

Job outlook: Future employment opportunities for social workers are expected to grow much faster than the average for all occupations.

To learn more about a career as an adoption coordinator, visit the United States Department of Labor's *Occupational Outlook Handbook* website. You will also be able to compare the job responsibilities, educational requirements, job outlook, and average pay of adoption coordinators with similar occupations.

Photo: Varina C/Shutterstock.com

Figure 3.13 **Pros and Cons of Agency and Independent Adoptions**

Type	Pros	Cons
Agency	• Agency handles the legal aspects to meet the needs of all involved. • Children are closely matched with adoptive families to ensure good placement. Emphasis is on meeting the child's needs. • Birthparents can request certain types of adoptive families. (They can choose or meet adoptive parents in an open adoption.) • Adoptive parent can choose a child of a certain gender, age, and family background. • Information is exchanged between birthparents and the adoptive family (non-identifying information only in a closed adoption). • Social workers counsel both sets of parents. • Adoptive families are supervised from the time children are placed until the time the adoption is final. • Cost may be lower for the adoptive parents. Agency may charge based on parents' ability to pay.	• Agency sets criteria for adoptive parents. Many suitable homes may be turned down in favor of "more qualified" homes. People who are newly married, remarried, single, gay/lesbian, or older may have a harder time using an agency. • Income, religious, and housing guidelines may also exclude some people wanting to adopt. • The study of people wanting to adopt is extremely detailed and goes into all aspects of personal and married life. • Fewer babies are available for adoption. Also, available children may not be of the same culture as the adoptive parents. • When fewer children are available for adoption, long waiting periods are common. • People wanting to adopt may wait a long time before a good match with a child is found.
Independent	• There are no stated qualifications for adoptive parents. Thus, many people who might not be chosen to adopt through an agency (people who are newly married, remarried, single, gay/lesbian, or older) can become adoptive parents. • If they wish, birthparents can arrange for someone they already know as adoptive parents. • It may be easier to adopt a baby or to adopt a child of the same culture as the adoptive parents.	• Less emphasis may be placed on the child's welfare. • Adoptive parents are screened less thoroughly. Placement occurs before a study is done, so the child may be in an unsuitable home. • Adoptive parents may receive less information about the child's background and health history. • Adoptive parents need to hire lawyers to help with legal details. • May be less privacy for both sets of parents than in an agency adoption. • Counseling is not provided as part of the adoption. • Cost may be higher than with an agency. (Some adoptive parents unknowingly enter illegal market adoptions.) • Birthparent(s) might change their mind and not follow through with the adoption or seek to regain custody of the child after placement

Both agency and independent adoptions may be either closed or open adoptions. A **closed adoption** (also called *confidential adoption*) is an adoption in which the identities of the birthparents and adopting family are not revealed. An **open adoption** is a type of adoption that involves some degree of communication between the birthparent(s) and adoptive family. Birthparents and adoptive parents can choose the type of adoption they prefer. The two options differ in how much information is exchanged and how much contact occurs between the birthparents and the adoptive family (**Figure 3.14**).

Figure 3.14 Differences in Closed and Open Adoptions

Adoption Options	Details
Closed	• Certain identifying information, as determined by state law, is kept private. This information most often includes names, addresses, and other identifying information about the birthparents and adopting families. • Sometimes even adopted children as adults cannot obtain information about birthparents. • Adoption is handled through an adoption agency, attorney, or doctor and is finalized in the courts. • Birthparents can get information on the type of home in which their child is placed. • Adoptive parents receive medical and social backgrounds of the child. • Sometimes birthparents write a letter for the child to read when they are old enough to understand. (This letter is often signed with a non-identifying signature, such as *Your Birthmom*.)
Open	• Birthparents often choose the adoptive parents from résumés and/or photographs sent to an agency or attorney. After the initial selection, identities of all parents are made known and birthparents may choose to meet the adoptive parents before making a final decision. • Information is exchanged between birthparents and adoptive families as an aid for parenting. • After the adoption, visitation and other forms of contact may continue between both families for as long as desired. • All adoption records are usually accessible to adopted children when they become adults. • Children benefit from knowing their adoptions are loving decisions that involve open communication between both sets of parents.

Goodheart-Willcox Publisher

For all adoptions, birthparents must sign papers **consenting** (giving permission) to the adoption. Adoption agencies will have a waiting period in which they determine "the fit" between the adoptive parents and the child. Then, the matter must be presented in court, and a judge must declare the adoption final. When the adoption is complete, the child's original birth certificate is placed under court seal. A new birth certificate is issued listing the adoptive parents as the child's parents.

Lesson 3.2 Review and Assessment

1. Which of the following is an advantage of the nuclear family? (3.2.1)
   A. Both the adults and the children may have their needs met more easily because family members can share responsibilities.
   B. Children can benefit from multi-generational influences in their home.
   C. Children can benefit from the companionship, love, and support of new step-siblings.
   D. Two parents don't have to agree on the rules.
2. Which of the following is *not* a way stepparents can help create a family bond? (3.2.1)
   A. Letting stepchildren set the pace for their relationships with stepparents
   B. Letting stepchildren know they are appreciated
   C. Explaining to children that a stepparent is another person to love and support them
   D. Discouraging stepchildren to have one-on-one time with both their biological parents
3. **True or False.** There is no difference between a *foster parent* and a *guardian*. (3.2.1)
4. **True or False.** In an independent adoption, a person, such as a lawyer or physician, works out the details between the birthparents and adoptive parents. (3.2.2)

Summary

Lesson 3.1

3.1-1 The family is the basic unit of society and is often the most lasting influence in a child's life.

3.1-1 How family members interact with one another can be helpful or unhelpful to a child's development.

3.1-1, 3.1-5
Healthy families work together for the well-being of the family. They communicate openly, respect one another, meet each other's needs, solve problems together, have fun together, and encourage one another to fulfill personal goals.

3.1-1, 3.1-5
Healthy families sow the seeds for children to grow up with positive attitudes and life management skills.

3.1-2 Changes take place during the six stages of the family life cycle. From the beginning stage through the childbearing, parenting, launching, mid-years, and aging stages, the family grows and develops.

3.1-3 Culture, which is identified in different ways, influences how each family lives.

3.1-3 Multicultural families offer family members unique opportunities to learn about and experience different cultures' practices firsthand.

3.1-4 Society influences the way families operate.

Lesson 3.2

3.2-1 Family types include nuclear, single-parent, stepfamilies, extended families, families with adopted children, foster families, families with guardians, and families with grandparents or other relatives as the head of household.

3.2-1 Each family type has unique challenges and strengths.

3.2-2 An adoption agency is an agency licensed by the state to handle adoptions.

3.2-2 In an independent adoption, a person, such as a lawyer or physician, works out the details between the birthparents and adoptive parents.

3.2-2 A closed adoption (also called *confidential adoption*) is an adoption in which the identities of the birthparents and adopting family are not revealed. An open adoption is a type of adoption that involves some degree of communication between the birthparent(s) and adoptive family.

College and Career Portfolio

Portfolio Organization

A portfolio is a collection of documents that represent the work you have done as a student. A portfolio may include examples of successful coursework, student assessments, proof of volunteer hours, a statement of your goals, letters of recommendation, awards, trainings, and degrees and certifications. The purpose of a portfolio is to provide insight into the kind of career you are interested in and the steps you are taking to achieve your goals.

As you collect items for your portfolio, you will need to keep your documents safe and well organized. Keep all your files in one place, and always keep back-up copies of everything. Before you begin collecting items for your portfolio, write a paragraph that describes your plan for storing and labeling the items. Refer to this plan each time you add items to the portfolio.

Recall and Application

1. _____ is when the receiver of a message provides feedback to the speaker, indicating the message is understood. (3.1.1)
   A. Body language
   B. Communication
   C. Active listening
   D. Discontentment

2. Many parents and their children go through similar stages called the _____. (3.1.2)
   A. family life cycle
   B. group-oriented culture
   C. steps in problem solving
   D. Industrial Revolution

3. The United States is an example of a nation with great _____, which means it has more than one culture represented among its people. (3.1.3)
   A. human services
   B. cultural diversity
   C. family life cycles
   D. group-oriented culture

4. A(n) _____ is made up of one parent and their child or children. (3.2.1)
   A. single-parent family
   B. nuclear family
   C. child support order
   D. extended family

5. A(n) _____ forms when one or both adults in the relationship have children from a previous relationship living in the home. (3.2.1)
   A. single-parent family
   B. nuclear family
   C. extended family
   D. stepfamily

6. A(n) _____ is a type of adoption that involves some degree of communication between the birth parent(s) and the adoptive family. (3.2.2)
   A. closed adoption
   B. open adoption
   C. foster family
   D. guardianship

Critical Thinking

1. **Analyze.** Analyze the different factors that affect how *family* is defined. How do a person's relationships affect this definition? How do cultural and social settings influence family dynamics? Write 3-4 sentences explaining how you would define your current family type(s) and family dynamics.

2. **Evaluate.** Before Adrian and Darryl can adopt a child into their family, a social worker must evaluate their family dynamics. The social worker's notes read as follows:
   - Established rules and boundaries clearly stated but applied unevenly
   - Adults model family values and desired behaviors
   - Unreasonable expectations for child achievement

   Evaluate the dynamics of Adrian and Darryl's family. Are these notes positive or negative? In which ways could this family improve their healthy dynamics?

3. **Make inferences.** Select one of the figures in this chapter and then write a short paragraph interpreting the body language in that image. Make inferences about what kind of situation is occurring.

4. **Cause and effect.** Identify two events that might cause a family to repeat stages of the family life cycle. For example, a grown child recently divorced and needs to move back into the parent's home. Then, describe how each event might affect the family.

5. **Draw conclusions.** Choose a current cultural or historical event. Then, describe how this event has impacted family life both positively and negatively.

6. **Analyze.** Because family is the basic unit of society, culture plays a large role in impacting family life. Conversely, family types and behaviors influence culture. Analyze how family life influences cultural trends and behaviors. For example, how does a shift in family living affect society at large? Share your thoughts with the class.

7. **Compare and contrast.** Choose two of the types of families discussed in this chapter. For each type, make a T-chart listing the pros and cons of living in that family. Finally, write a one-page paper comparing and contrasting the benefits and challenges of these family types.

8. **Identify.** On a piece of paper, list your friends and acquaintances, whether current or from the past. Then, identify what type of family that person has. Is one type of family predominant over the others?

9. **Determine.** Consider some possible benefits and challenges of open adoption for each of the following: birthparents, adoptive family, and the adopted child. Whose benefit do you think should take priority, and why? What factors should each party consider when deciding between an open and closed adoption?

Core Skills

1. **Listening.** Ask your family about the roles and responsibilities of being a caretaker. Demonstrate active listening by taking notes and being attentive. Ask if your family has any advice for you about forming healthy family dynamics. Share these pieces of advice with the class. Finally, as a class, discuss the best tips for forming healthy families and assess how effective these might be.

2. **Speaking.** In small groups, role-play the roles of family members in each stage of the family life cycle. In your role-plays, emphasize the changes that take place in each stage and how these changes impact relationships. After practicing, perform your role-plays for the class and ask the class to guess which stage of the family life cycle you are representing. Lead the class in a discussion about how roles changed during each stage.

3. **Research, social studies, and reading.** Choose a culture other than your own and then use a library or the internet to locate information about family living in that culture. Write a short essay summarizing your findings.

4. **History and research.** Use internet or print sources to research the Industrial Revolution time line. How did the Industrial Revolution affect families? How are families now different than during the Industrial Revolution? Share your findings with the class.

5. **Art and speaking.** Review the qualities of a healthy family listed in this chapter. Then, using this list, make a list of the qualities of an unhealthy family. Draw two pictures—one illustrating a healthy family and another illustrating an unhealthy family. Present and explain your drawings to the class.

6. **Math, technology, and speaking.** Visit the United States Census Bureau website and view the most current information about the marital statuses and living arrangements for adults of all races. Choose one marital status or living arrangement and note what percentage of the population it describes. Then, apply that percentage to the size of your class. Give a short presentation informing your class of how these statistics apply to them.

7. **Writing.** Write a fiction story entitled, "The Joys and Trials of Living in a _____ Family Type." Base the story on your own family type or describe what you think it would be like to live in a family type different from your own. Check your story for correct spelling, grammar, and punctuation.

8. **Listening.** Choose one family type you are not familiar with and interview a person living in that type of family. How did the person's family form? How long has the person been living in their type of family? In their opinion, what are the advantages and disadvantages of the family type? Take notes about the person's answers to these questions and then discuss with a partner.

9. **CTE Career Readiness Practice.** Presume you are a family counselor. Your interpersonal skills—your ability to listen, speak, and empathize—are a great asset in working with clients.

   You are currently counseling Dante and his teenage children, Vanita and Alex. Their mother pays child support to help Dante financially, but as a single father, Dante often resorts to ordering takeout for dinner or letting the laundry pile up because he does not have enough time to do everything. Sometimes, Dante gets discouraged about his success as a parent. How would you counsel Dante to improve his day-to-day schedule? What resources would you present to Dante for social, emotional, and practical support?

Observations

1. Watch one or two episodes of a television show that features an entire family. Try to identify where the family is on the family life cycle and assess how healthy the family is based on how the members interact. Write a short report summarizing your thoughts and then present your assessment to the class.

2. Choose a friend who has a different type of family from your own, and ask if you can come over for dinner one night. While at dinner, observe how the family interacts and consider how the family is similar to and different from yours. List these similarities and differences and write a short paragraph reflecting on how family types affect family living and behaviors.

Chapter 4

Preparing for Parenting

Lesson 4.1 — Deciding About Parenthood
Lesson 4.2 — Parenting Roles, Responsibilities, and Styles

Essential Question

How have the roles and responsibilities of caregivers and guardians changed in today's society?

Case Study — Are Some Forms of Discipline Better Than Others?

As a class, read the case study and discuss the questions that follow. After you finish studying the chapter, discuss this case study again. Have your opinions changed based on what you learned?

Andrea and Michael are polar opposites when it comes to disciplining their rather "headstrong" six-year-old, Jayden. Andrea, who has taken a child development course, believes the best way to discipline is to give Jayden reasons for expected behaviors and use nonphysical punishment when need be. Michael, who is a career military officer, believes in a more strict approach. Michael says the only reason Jayden needs for following instructions and behaving in certain ways is "because I said so." Michael backs this statement up with the point that children must respect their parents and not question their judgments. Michael believes that disobedience is grounds for a spanking and tells Andrea that perhaps giving reasons for certain behaviors helps some children, but not Jayden because Jayden is "headstrong."

Michael was spanked as a child and is well-adjusted and responsible adult, and so Michael believes this method of discipline will work for Jayden, too. Andrea agrees that Michael is well-adjusted and responsible, but also knows that Jayden's behavior has not improved under Michael's parenting method.

Give It Some Thought

1. Can children who are given reasons for certain behaviors develop respect for authority?
2. Do you think respect for authority is the same as "blind authority" (rules without reasons) and authority with reasons?
3. Do you think spankings are needed in the case of some children, such as those who are "headstrong"?
4. Do you think Jayden will respect the authority of teachers and other adults if Michael applies his parenting method? Why or why not?
5. As an adult, what type of employee or parent will Jayden likely be?

wavebreakmedia/Shutterstock.com

Lesson 4.1

Deciding About Parenthood

Key Terms

ample
birth control methods
depleted
direct costs
expenditures
family planning
foregone income
indirect costs
maturity
procreation
socioeconomic
stifle

Learning Outcomes

After studying this lesson, you will be able to

4.1-1 **analyze** motivations for choosing whether or not to become a parent.

4.1-2 **describe** aspects of parenting that people may want to consider before having a child.

4.1-3 **summarize** points people may want to keep in mind as they plan families.

Reading and Notetaking Activity

Before reading this chapter, skim the headings. List the headings to create an outline for taking notes during the reading and class discussion. Under each heading, list any key terms. Finally, write two questions you expect to have answered in class. After completing this chapter, ask your teacher any questions you still have about the concepts or terms you learned.

Introduction

People have different motivations for choosing whether or not to become parents. Some of these are described in this lesson. Before deciding about parenthood, however, people may want to consider all the aspects of parenting. Parenting comes with a lot of responsibilities, and once a person is a parent, their life will be forever changed.

4.1-1 Choosing Whether or Not to Parent

The decision to parent is unlike many life decisions in two ways. First, the decision to parent is a *permanent* choice. Once a child is born, they are part of the parent's life forever. A person can choose to change careers, but having a child is different. Once a person is a parent, they will always be a parent.

Second, a decision not to parent is not permanent. People have some time to decide whether to become parents. People have at least 15 safe childbearing years (**Figure 4.1**). The option of adopting a child may also be considered. Some people may want to be parents but choose to wait until a more appropriate time. Other people may not be sure about parenthood and will wait to decide. Even people who decide they never want children can later change their minds. In fact, many people are putting off having children until later in life when they are financially stable.

Reasons for Choosing Parenthood

People have various reasons for choosing parenthood. Although they may not always be able to explain why, they see children as part of their lives. The following are reasons people often give for wanting to become parents.

"We want to share our love and time with a child." This is perhaps the most important reason for wanting a child. A person's desire to share their love and time with a child is the best reason for parenthood. Parents should want a child with no strings attached. If parents hope a child will fulfill other needs or goals, the parent–child relationship may not be healthy.

PeopleImages/iStock via Getty Images Plus

Figure 4.1 The 15 safe childbearing years are between 20 and 35 years of age. *What complications might make childbearing less safe for people who are under 20 years of age?*

FOCUS ON MENTAL HEALTH

When a person is not ready to take on the responsibilities of becoming a parent, it can result in a relationship strain between the caregiver and child. The caregiver may have mental health issues related to stress and guilt for not wanting the child. This, in turn, may affect the child's mental health later in life. The caregiver can prevent these issues by seeking support systems to help ease the challenges of parenthood. They can also work these issues out with a mental health advisor.

"Wouldn't it be nice to have a cute little baby?" When some people see others with babies, they think it would be nice to have a baby, too. It is good for people to think positively about babies, but the problem is that babies are not always cute. All babies are sick, fussy, and cranky at times, and require round-the-clock care.

"Our parents want grandchildren." Some people want to fulfill their parents' wishes to be grandparents. Grandparents can give a child much love, but the question is, "Who is responsible for the care of the child?" It is more important for parents, not grandparents, to want and love a child.

"Our older child needs a sibling." When a person wants a playmate for an older child, they are fulfilling someone else's needs, not their own. Although a child might enjoy having a sibling, there are other ways to meet an only child's need for a playmate.

"A child can make us proud." Some people see children as sources of pride. They want children to carry on the family name and customs, inherit the family business or money, or achieve certain goals. It is good for families to be proud of their children and want them to achieve. They must be careful, however, not to let their hopes **stifle** (suppress) their children's goals. Parenthood is not a good choice if a child is wanted only to boost the parents' ego or meet their unfulfilled goals.

"A child will comfort us in our old age." Sometimes people think of children as sources of help in their old age. It is natural for people to think about being helpless or lonely when they grow old. An aging parent, however, cannot count on a child's help as you never know what will happen in life.

"A child will fix my problems." Some people hope that having a child will fix their problems by bringing joy and excitement into their lives. Children may indeed enrich family life for stable couples or individuals. Unstable individuals or couples, however, may find that the added responsibilities of having children makes their problems worse.

"My biological clock is ticking." Many people are putting off having children until later in life, then one day feel that they need to have a child before they get too old. While it is true that people only have about 15 safe childbearing years, it is important for people of any age to be sure they are ready for the challenges of parenthood before they make their decision.

Reasons for Not Choosing Parenthood

Some people plan to be childless permanently. Other people decide to postpone parenthood. Even people who consider having children may want to think about how children can change their lives. Below are some reasons people often give for not choosing parenthood.

"I'm not ready for a child." When people say they are not ready for children, they usually mean they need to mature. They may feel they need more time to grow as an individual. They may want to devote more time to their education or job. Many people want to establish themselves in a career before becoming parents.

"A baby costs a lot." Babies are expensive. At one time, a large family was an economic asset because children helped with the work. Today, due to child labor laws and a change in the way society views childhood, children cannot contribute to the family income. (Later in this lesson you will look more closely at the cost of having a child.)

"A child will tie me down." Unlike many other responsibilities, child care tasks cannot be put off until later. Parents are always called if children are hurt, ill, or need help. Even with the best babysitters in charge, parents cannot completely forget their roles.

"A child will interfere with my career." When tending to both their career and children, parents face two common problems. First, it is difficult for parents to have enough time and energy for both parenting and succeeding at work (**Figure 4.2**). Second, it is difficult to find good child care services.

Some careers make parenting easier than others. School teachers have hours and vacation times similar to those of their older children. Other careers make parenting more difficult by requiring parents to work long hours or travel frequently. Highly stressful jobs are also difficult for parents. People who combine these types of jobs with parenting must plan carefully. Some parents decide to stay at home while their children are younger, meaning the family survives on less income.

Jeff Randall/DigitalVision via Getty Images

Figure 4.2 The amount of time and energy a person wants to spend on their career is an important consideration when thinking about having children. *What are some other reasons a person might choose not to have children?*

"Our child could be sick or have a disability." There is no guarantee that children will be in perfect health when they are born. Babies can be born with disabilities or become seriously ill or injured. Good medical care before and after birth reduces—but does not eliminate—these risks. Children with disabilities or who are ill or injured have special needs beyond those of other children. Many parents, however, feel that raising children with disabilities is highly rewarding.

"My marriage could fail, and I don't want to be a single parent." If a person feels this way, they may want to seek help with their marital problems before having children. Whether a person willingly chooses single parenthood or not, being a single parent can be difficult. Single parents may lack money, help with household and child care tasks, and other supports a partner can provide. Without these resources, the single parent cannot always take part in adult activities, which can lead to feelings of isolation. Many single parents solve such problems by including their extended family in raising their children.

4.1-2 Aspects of Parenting

Parenting is both a rewarding and challenging task (**Figure 4.3**). Many people invest more money, time, and emotions in their children than they do in any other investment in their lives. Most parents hope their children will inherit all their strengths and avoid their weaknesses. They also hope their children will have opportunities they did not have. Before having a child, people must seriously consider all aspects of parenting.

Knowledge About Parenting

Upon the birth or adoption of a child, a person instantly becomes a parent. Few, if any, other jobs give a beginner such responsibility without training. Many people feel they need help in becoming good parents. Experienced family members or friends may help some new parents. Many places offer child care and parenting classes. Literature on parenting is plentiful, but sources may not always be reliable and accurate.

Figure 4.3 Challenges and Rewards of Parenting

Challenges

- Becoming parents means adjusting lifestyles. Lifestyles with children may be starkly different from lifestyles before children.
- Caregivers or guardians may feel they lack training and parenting skills. They can feel overwhelmed, especially as first-time parents. They may be unsure or unprepared for how to handle a situation.
- Roles change when people have children. Caregivers may disagree about parenting styles and how to handle certain situations. This may result in tension in relationships.
- The parent-child relationship is often one-sided. For many years, parents are "givers" and children are the "takers." Parents must put their children's needs before their own needs.
- Parenting can be physically draining. Caregivers are often fatigued from a lack of sleep, especially during the early years.
- Parenting is a full-time, nonstop job. Caregivers have less time to spend alone or with friends.
- Parenthood may impact career choices. Some parents may forego or give up career opportunities.
- Parenting is expensive. Meeting financial expenses is a major concern for most families. Families are financially responsible for a child until they are eighteen or graduate from high school.
- Parents may lack parenting support from their spouses. Similarly, relatives and close family friends may not have time or may live too far away to provide parenting support as modern families have moved away from where they grew up.
- Relatives, friends, and other parents may frequently offer parenting advice, even when not solicited.
- Parents may feel fear, frustration, and stress.

Goodheart-Willcox Publisher
(Continued)

Figure 4.3 Challenges and Rewards of Parenting (Continued)

Rewards
- Caregivers or guardians experience a new type of deep, unconditional love when they become parents.
- Building a family can positively add to the marriage dynamic when the marriage is healthy.
- Becoming parents can strengthen the couple's relationships with their own parents.
- Experiencing a child's first sounds, smiles, words, and steps can bring joy to parents' lives.
- Parenting can be an adventure. Caregivers or guardians gain new experiences through their children's points of view and can explore the world with their children. Children may introduce activities or knowledge to parents' lives.
- Children can be funny and make ordinary situations comical.
- Caregivers feel a sense of satisfaction when they can successfully provide for their children and see their children happy.
- Caregivers also feel a sense of satisfaction and happiness when their children grow up to be happy, independent, successful adults.

Maturity

Regardless of age, a person who may be biologically capable of conceiving a child may not have the *maturity* to become a parent. **Maturity** is having the intellectual and emotional capacity of a healthy, responsible adult. Maturity is different from age. People may be mature for their age, but there is a special type of maturity needed for parenting. Erikson's theory addresses this issue.

Erikson felt that teens and even young adults are not best suited for parenting. His theory states that teens need to explore their sense of independence and develop a sense of self. Young adults need time to find out what is important to them and what sort of person they want to be before entering into parenthood.

According to Erikson, at some point mature people want to contribute to the next generation by "making their mark in life" and making the world a better place. Some adults do this through careers or volunteer work, but many do it through parenting. Parenting at a mature level involves more than **procreation** (the producing of children). True parenting is not a self-centered activity. It is a way of looking outside of yourself and giving back to society by the way you parent.

Relationships

Children are born into a network of people and relationships. Some children are parented within a couple's relationship and the relationships that couple has with their family and friends. Other children are parented by a single parent and a support system of friends, family, and/or child care providers. Children affect these relationships and these relationships affect children. Relationships are a two-way street. People may want to think about what changes parenthood will bring to their relationships.

Children Affect Relationships

To prepare for parenthood, people need to know how children will change their lives. Unlike other relationships, parenting in the beginning is very one-sided. Babies are demanding of the parents' time and other resources. Babies have no idea that their parents are exhausted from round-the-clock care. Parents may even feel their needs go unnoticed by family friends when the focus is on the baby. Parenting during the first few months is quite challenging. Because parenting continues, parents must want more than to have a baby. They must want and be willing to change along with this baby over many years. In **Figure 4.4**, Ellen Galinsky, a psychologist, describes how parents develop.

Relationships Affect Children

People can begin looking at the relationships in their lives and asking questions about their feelings for others. These kinds of questions relate directly to parenting. For starters, people might ask themselves the questions in **Figure 4.5**.

Figure 4.4 Galinsky's Parenting Stages

Stage	Timing of Stage (based on child's age/stage)	Parenting Tasks
Image-making	Before birth	• Prepare for changes in their lives. • Form images of what their child will be like and their roles as parents.
Nurturing	Birth–2 years	• Try to balance their baby's needs with their own needs. • Provide loving and consistent care to their baby. (This stems from emotional bonds.)
Authority	2 years–4 to 5 years	• Change their role as the family's authority figures (called *parenting style*). • Teach their child the "rules of behavior" through reasoning, rewards, and punishments.
Interpretive	4 to 5 years–12 to 13 years	• Share their knowledge about the world with their child. • Interpret other authority figures, such as teachers or coaches, by explaining what they expect. • Teach values and morals as the need arises. • Help their child accept social reality, such as "life may not always be fair."
Interdependent	Teen years	• Cope with their teen's changing needs for closeness and distance. • Monitor teen's behavior and give guidance as needed. • Begin to give more freedom with boundaries to their teen.
Departure	Teen or early adult years	• Evaluate themselves as parents. • Redefine their relationship with their child, such as allowing their child to make their own decisions. • Provide guidance only when asked.

Goodheart-Willcox Publisher

Figure 4.5 Questions People May Ask to Learn About Their Feelings for Others

• Am I loving and sensitive to others' needs?
• Am I careful not to judge people and their ideas?
• Can I recognize and respect others' rights?
• Am I self-disciplined?

• Do I relate well to others?
• Am I flexible enough to accept changes?
• Am I brave about challenges?
• Am I honest about my feelings for others?

Goodheart-Willcox Publisher

People can also look at their present relationships with relatives and friends. Good relationships with others are a positive example for future children. People might want to ask themselves the questions in **Figure 4.6** about their relationships with others.

People also need to think about how their relationships with others can affect their children. There are at least three advantages to children's relationships with others. First, relatives and friends provide children with their first link to the outside world. Second, grandparents and older relatives can teach children about the past. Third, when many relatives and friends care for children, they feel more rooted to their family.

Figure 4.6 **Questions People May Ask to Learn About Their Relationships with Others**

- Do my relatives and friends share my basic values?
- Can I tolerate differences in beliefs?
- Can I ask for advice and also use my own judgment?
- Can I tell others about my needs and accept the help they offer?
- Can I recognize others' needs and offer my help?
- Can I avoid abusing others' generosity, including time and money?
- Can I share fun times with others?

Goodheart-Willcox Publisher

Investigate Special Topics

Developing Parenting Skills

Many people feel they need help learning how to become good parents. Finding the following resources can help people learn about child care and development:

- professionals and/or successful parents to give advice
- child development literature (books, journals, magazines) that is accurate, practical, and available
- child care and parenting classes (hospitals, community colleges, and local American Red Cross chapters may offer such classes)
- families with infants and young children (babysit and volunteer in schools and organizations to understand what it is like to care for children)

New parents should also realize there is not one right way to parent. Although some methods may be more respected than others, many factors influence parenting. The culture in which a child is raised affects how parents raise children. Also, what society considers important for children to learn may change with each generation. The personalities of parents and children also affect parenting. The ways people have seen their parents or friends care for children influences how they care for their own. Having a child who has colic versus a child who is easy going can impact a caregiver–child relationship. Parents can sometimes become frustrated when they can't figure out what's wrong with their child. Learning skills to cope with stress and frustration is a must for all caregivers and guardians. All these factors are important to think about when learning child care skills.

Research Activity

Choose one source of information people could access for parenting advice or education. This might be a parenting book, an interview with someone who is a parent, an online article, or a brochure about parenting. Skim this resource and write three to four interesting pieces of advice the resource provides. Share your findings with the class. Then, choose a partner and discuss which pieces of advice you thought were most helpful and why.

Photo: Tom Wang/Shutterstock.com

Because each relative and friend is unique, children learn to understand that people are different. They also learn to accept people's unique traits. This interaction will help children get along well with others as they grow.

Communication

In any relationship, communication is key. If more than one person is involved in the decision to become a parent, caregiver, or guardian of a child, both people need to communicate their expectations and concerns to each other. Without honest communication about how to raise, guide, and discipline the child, there can be friction between the adults. Planning ahead, checking in periodically, and updating or changing what they agree on helps maintain a healthy relationship.

Management of Resources

Parenting also involves management of time, energy, home care, careers, finances, and resources needed directly for children. Prospective parents may want to consider all these factors before having a child. Because these factors can change, parents may want to revisit their decisions before adding to their families, changing their jobs or careers, and other major life changes.

Time and Energy

Time and energy are both *limited resources* and are **depleted** (used up) very quickly during parenting. People considering parenting may want to identify current and future demands on their time. To make time for parenting, they may need to forego certain activities. They may also want to consider the availability of additional help if children take more parenting time than expected, such as with twins or triplets, or children with special needs.

Parenting is the most energy-depleting role a person will likely encounter. Without energy, parents cannot effectively take care of their children. A parent's energy is also depleted by other life activities, especially home care and career demands. People may want to consider their health, career demands, and current household tasks to determine if they have enough energy to effectively care for a child.

Home Care

Homes are resources for family life. Home is where people prepare meals, eat, sleep, groom, and store personal possessions. Home is the center of the family's relationships and where extended family members and friends may gather (**Figure 4.7**).

JohnnyGreig/E+ via Getty Images

Figure 4.7 Caring for the family's home is an important aspect of parenting because homes are centers of teaching, care, and family resources. *How do you help in caring for your family's home?*

Because of their many uses, homes require a great deal of care. Home care responsibilities use much time and energy.

For couples, they may want to consider how they currently share tasks and how they feel about this division of duties. Next, the couple may consider how children might affect how they share responsibilities. If they become parents, will there be major changes in the way they share responsibilities? Can they agree on how to divide home and child care tasks? How couples choose to divide tasks can depend on each person's needs. If couples plan carefully and try all ideas, they can divide tasks so both partners are satisfied.

In the case of a single parent, assessing the kind of support they will have with home care is important. Do they have family or friends who are willing to lend a hand? Can they afford to pay someone to help with house cleaning? It can be helpful to make a list of all home care chores and decide which need to be tended to immediately, and which can be handled less frequently.

Careers

Parenting is unlike other careers. Parents probably have studied and trained more for their careers than for their roles as parents. Their job skills may be better than their child care skills. A family's major financial resources come from their careers. Couples may want to decide whether they will both work or whether one will care for children at home. Single parents need to decide who will care for their child while they work. The parents' workplaces also help determine the **socioeconomic** (social and economic) level of the family, where they live, possible mobility, the work hours/workdays, and possibly the parents' stress levels.

Finances

The cost of raising a child is considerable. **Expenditures** (expenses) on a child from birth through 17 years of age are over $233,000. Lower-income families spend 27 percent of their before-tax income on a child, while middle-income families spend 16 percent. Higher-income families spend 11 percent.

The first year of childrearing is expensive, and expenses grow as the child grows. However, the largest expense of raising a child occurs between ages 15–17. During the teen years, children are involved in various activities as well as growth spurts that require caregivers to spend more money on food, clothing, and activities. Families are also preparing for the child to leave home to embark on post-secondary schooling or a career. The **direct costs**, or expenses related to raising a child, include clothing, food, housing, child care, education, and transportation. Other direct costs involve children's extra activities, such as toys, entertainment, and sports or music lessons. The first baby is often the most expensive. Additional children may use some of the firstborn's items. Each extra child increases the costs, and typically, a second child almost doubles the costs (**Figure 4.8**).

Figure 4.8 ## 2021 Cost of Having a Child

Cost of Having a Baby	Cost/Percentage of Income
Childbirth or adoption	$4,500 – $43,000 Based on insurance and adoption costs Infertility issues can add to this
Housing	$3750 per year = 29%
Food	$2794 per year = 18%
Child care and education	$37,400 total = 16%
Transportation	$1947 per year = 15%
Health care	$1168 per year= 9%
Clothing	$779 per year = 6%
Miscellaneous— personal items, entertainment. sports equipment	$909 per year = 7%
Total spent on one child	$2856 per year = 22% of income

Figure 4.8 The current cost of raising one child for one year is approximately 22% of an individual's or couple's income.

In addition to direct costs of having a child, there are indirect costs. **Indirect costs** are resources parents use to meet child-related costs that could have been used to meet other goals. Some indirect costs of having children include the following:

- *Foregone income.* **Foregone income** is the potential income given up by a parent who leaves the workforce and stays home to raise a child. Foregone income includes salary and wages, bonuses, and retirement or pension money. Foregone income increases with the salary or wage level. Foregone income can be estimated.
- *Foregone career opportunities.* A worker who is out of the workforce for several years may miss promotions and may even need to be retrained before working again. The cost of time out of the workforce is the most difficult indirect cost to calculate.
- *Time spent in child care.* Caring for children daily, driving them to activities, and using personal or sick days to care for a sick child are all indirect costs.

People should consider these when they estimate the direct and indirect costs of parenting.

Each family is different, and these differences show in the way families spend their money.

Carefully planning financial resources is important for everyone. In some ways, financial planning becomes more important when people think about children. This is because children rely on their parents for financial support for many years. Parents also model for their children either good or poor consumer practices. People may want to ask themselves the following questions about finances before becoming parents:

- How do I currently earn and spend my money?
- Am I satisfied with my budget? Does the budget fit my needs and allow for a few luxuries?
- Do I have regular savings I could use to meet child-related expenses? If not, can I adjust my budget to meet such expenses?
- Can I expect more income or lower expenses during the next few years to help offset child-related costs?
- What type of savings goals do I need for a child?
- What is an estimate of child-related expenses for the first and next several years?

FOCUS ON

FINANCIAL LITERACY

Parenting Costs

Families have many financial considerations, which vary according to factors such as number of people in the household, income earned, and individual needs. Some categories of expenditures, however, are predictable. For example, families in the United States spend a percentage of their incomes on average in the following categories:

- housing—25–35%
- transportation—15%
- food—10–15%
- child care and education—16%
- insurance (health, medical, auto, life—10–15%

- clothing—5%
- miscellaneous—7%

Using the percentages above, calculate the amount spent in each category of expenditures for a family with a $75,000 annual income. Do you think the percentages spent in each category would be the same for a family that makes $30,000 per year compared to a family that makes $250,000 per year? What factors might affect how much income is spent on each category of expenditures?

Photo: Noam Armonn/Shutterstock.com

Other Resources

People may also want to consider other resources children need, such as child care and education programs, schools, park and recreation services, health and medical services, youth organizations, community programs, and religious groups. Parents often like to live near these services, which might require a change in housing location or even a change in career.

4.1-3 Family Planning

Family planning involves decisions people make about whether or not they want to have children and when to have them. Family planning is a personal choice. There are some points people may want to keep in mind as they plan for their families. They can consult with a doctor while planning. Doctors may offer information and advice on the following:

- options in **birth control methods** (measures people use to help prevent pregnancy).
Figure 4.9 shows some questions people may want to ask their doctor to learn more about birth control methods.

- the impact their current health might have on a pregnancy.
- pre-pregnancy preparations, such as a nutritious diet, prenatal vitamins, and lifestyle changes (no smoking or alcohol; less caffeine).
- spacing of pregnancies. Doctors often advise a person to wait 18 to 23 months after delivery to become pregnant again to allow their bodies to recover to pre-pregnancy conditions.

Figure 4.9 Questions to Ask About Birth Control Methods

- How does the method work to prevent pregnancy? (For example, does the method block sperm's travel or provide hormones that prevent ovulation?)
- What is the time limit for the product's recommended use?
- How successful is the method at preventing pregnancy if properly used?
- What are the directions for using the method?
- What is the method's possible side effects and risks, including future fertility?
- What does the method cost?

Goodheart-Willcox Publisher

After consulting with a doctor, people may want to think about which birth control method they prefer. This might depend on their religious beliefs and their likes and dislikes of certain methods. Sometimes people change birth control methods due to side effects, needed changes after childbirth, or when their family is complete.

Although doctors can advise about the spacing of children or even whether to have another child, it is a personal decision. Not all people feel they can handle another child right away. These feelings depend on their finances, emotional and physical energy, career, age, and lifestyle.

People should not feel guilty if they want only one child or none at all. The best reason for a person to have another child is to share their love and time with this child, too.

For people who want to add to their families, a spacing of about three years is advised for developmental reasons. **Ample** (a generous amount of) spacing gives parents time to work with each child alone before they need to divide their attention. In addition, there is often less jealousy between children when there is a three-year age difference or more.

Lesson 4.1 Review and Assessment

1. Which of the following is *not* a poor reason to become a parent? (4.1.1)
   A. A child will take care of me in my old age.
   B. Our parents want grandchildren.
   C. I want to share my love with a child.
   D. I don't want my partner to leave.

2. Which of these is a reason people give for not choosing parenthood? (4.1.1)
   A. Having a child will mean I have more spare time.
   B. I can't afford to have a child.
   C. I want to feel more tied down.
   D. I would rather share my time and love with a child than focus on my career.

3. Which theorist stated that at some point mature people want to contribute to the next generation by making their mark in life? (4.1.2)
   A. Erikson
   B. Freud
   C. Skinner
   D. Piaget

4. Which of the following statements is a reward of parenting? (4.1.2)
   A. Parents are often fatigued from lack of sleep.
   B. Parenting can be an adventure.
   C. Family members may give unsolicited advice on how to raise a child.
   D. Parents must put their child's needs before their own.

5. _____ involves decisions people make about whether or not they want to have children and when to have them. (4.1.3)
   A. Forgone income
   B. Procreation
   C. Maturity
   D. Family planning

Lesson 4.2

Parenting Roles, Responsibilities, and Styles

Key Terms

authoritarian
authoritative
character
discipline
guidance
induction
love withdrawal
nurturance
overparenting
parental rights
parental responsibilities
permissive
power assertion
socialize

Learning Outcomes

After studying this lesson, you will be able to

4.2-1 **explain** caregivers' and guardians' roles and responsibilities involving nurturance, socialization, and guidance and discipline.

4.2-2 **differentiate** between the terms *guidance* and *discipline* and describe their effects on children.

4.2-3 **compare** and **contrast** the following parenting styles: authoritarian, permissive, authoritative, overparenting, and uninvolved.

Reading and Notetaking Activity

Read the key terms for this lesson and then write them on a separate piece of paper. Look up each of these terms in the glossary at the back of this textbook and then write the definition in your own words. Underneath each term and definition, write an example of the term's meaning in action. After reading this lesson, update your examples and share with a partner.

Introduction

People who choose to become parents have many roles and responsibilities. Family culture determines the specifics of how the childrearing function will be fulfilled, which is what people call parenting *roles*. Perhaps the most widely identified parenting responsibilities involve *nurturing* (caring for) and *socialization* (social training), including guidance and discipline. The parenting role of socialization begins after infancy. As parents guide and discipline their toddlers, one of four parenting styles emerges and becomes very consistent by the preschool years.

4.2-1 Parenting Roles and Responsibilities

Parents or guardians are responsible for the well-being of their children. Before making the decision to become a parent, people need to understand the rights and responsibilities that they are agreeing to by having or adopting a child. Historically, **parental rights** have gone hand in hand with **parental responsibilities**. If a parent does not uphold their responsibilities they may lose their parental rights and have the child(ren) taken away through the court system. In the United States parental rights include:

- physical custody. The child lives with the parent/guardian. In the case of a divorce this might be shared between two households.
- legal custody. This refers to the daily decisions that a parent makes for their child's upbringing. This includes choices about education, religion, and medical care.

Parental Responsibilities

Parents must meet their child's basic needs. This means that they give their child food, clothing, housing, education, and medical care. Parents are also responsible for meeting their child's emotional and physical needs, including protecting them from harm and abuse. A parent also has the responsibility of meeting their child's financial needs until the child is eighteen or graduates from high school. In some cases, if these needs are not met, the parent/guardian risks losing their parental rights. Parents can have their rights terminated for the following reasons:

- chronic or extreme abuse or neglect
- sexual abuse
- chronic drug or alcohol abuse that leads to the parent being incapacitated
- failure to maintain contact with the child
- abandonment
- some felonies
- an act of crime against the child or other family member
- long-term incarceration in conjunction with long-term foster care

So what are the roles and responsibilities that caregivers have? These roles and responsibilities mainly involve nurturance, socialization, and guidance and discipline. Children thrive in a nurturing environment. They learn to become responsible members of a community through socialization by their parents or guardians and other members of their family. Through their parents' guidance and discipline, children learn right from wrong.

Nurturance

Nurturance, in a narrow sense, includes the physical aspects of child care, such as feeding, dressing, and bathing children. In a broader sense, *nurturance* includes meeting intellectual needs, such as providing children with a stimulating environment. Allowing them to explore, learn, and interact mentally and physically creates a stimulating environment. *Nurturance* also includes meeting social-emotional needs, such as helping children feel secure and loved (**Figure 4.10**). Physical care, love, and concern are important for children's healthy growth. Both mothers and fathers play an important role in nurturing their children.

George Rudy/Shutterstock.com

Figure 4.10 Nurturance involves helping children meet their physical needs as well as their intellectual and social-emotional needs. *What are some examples of children's intellectual and social-emotional needs? How can parents help children meet these needs?*

Culture

Read all or some of the chapters from Laura Ingalls Wilder's books, *Little House in the Big Woods* and *Farmer Boy*. As you are reading, look for specific examples of how the parents socialized their children. What skills, customs, and values did the parents hand down to the children in the stories? How are these teachings different from what your parents have passed down to you about your culture? Record your findings and share them with the class.

Photo: Andy-pix/Shutterstock.com

Socialization

People are born into a community. From the beginning, people experience their world as one of relationships. Learning to form relationships is a key social need. Children need to form strong relationships with their family. These relationships can help children feel secure and teach them how to respond and relate to other people.

Children also need a sense of belonging. To build this sense, parents **socialize** their children, or train them to live as part of the larger social group. Parents teach children about the way of life within the family group as well as cultural and societal groups. Each social group may have its own language, beliefs, attitudes, values, rituals, and skills that children learn through a process called *socialization*. Socialization is a major role of parents, for it allows children to fit into their social group.

Another name for a social group is *culture*. From birth onward, children grow up in a culture, or sometimes cultures, that mold their belonging to the group. Parents, family members, schools, religious groups, and others influence children's cultural learning.

Parents model, reward, and praise what their culture values. They criticize and correct that which does not fit with their cultural beliefs. In this socialization process, children learn most of their culture's values at home. These concepts are also taught indirectly by living within the culture. Once a child begins socializing with others outside their immediate community they are exposed to other cultures and societal norms.

Some cultural concepts, such as history and heroes, are taught more directly. The reasons behind traditions of the culture are also often taught to children from an early age. Parents and other older family members may help **impart** (give or share) values to children through storytelling and answering children's questions about the culture or its practices.

Guardians also teach their children how to respond in a culturally diverse society. Caregivers who value diversity point out the benefit of learning from people who are not like themselves. These caregivers teach their children to appreciate people of all cultures. They believe each group is different from, but equal to, other groups. Other caregivers do not value diversity and believe that people of different groups should not interact with one another. Whatever their viewpoints, caregivers and guardians are passing these views to their children.

Before making the choice to become a parent or to abstain from having children, people must first understand the roles and responsibilities necessary for raising a child.

4.2-2 Guidance and Discipline

Child guidance and discipline are important responsibilities of parenthood. Parents guide their children in their daily interactions with them (**Figure 4.11**). **Guidance** includes the words and actions parents use to influence their children's behavior. For example, when parents face frustrations but react calmly, they guide their children to do the same. By showing children they are not upset when they do not get their way, caregivers are modeling good behavior. Guiding children in a positive way is an important parental role.

Discipline is part of guidance. **Discipline** is the use of methods and techniques to teach children self-control. Through discipline, children learn to act in ways that society finds acceptable. Punishment is not the same as discipline. *Punishment* is a consequence for a misdeed. For punishment to be effective, the negative consequences must fit the misdeed.

One major goal of guidance and discipline is to build character in children. **Character** is the principles and beliefs that guide a person's **conduct**

sirtravelalot/Shutterstock.com

Figure 4.11 The teaching of children does not just happen in the classroom or child care center. Parents guide and teach their children through their daily interactions with them. *What have your caregivers taught you through their interactions with you?*

(actions and manners) and define their personality and behavior. Through love and guidance, caregivers help their children grow into self-directed adults (**Figure 4.12**).

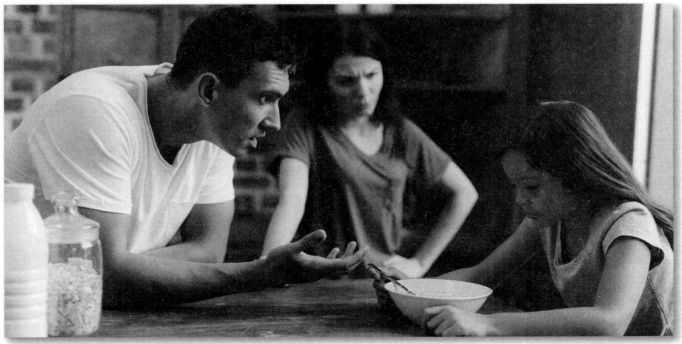

VGstockstudio/Shutterstock.com

Figure 4.12 Parents administer discipline and guidance in order to shape their children's characters and steer them toward becoming healthy adults. *What kinds of discipline might encourage children to have character? What kinds might not?*

Most caregivers would like to find the perfect method for handling their children's unpleasant or disruptive behaviors. Although there is no perfect method for use with every child, some forms of discipline are better than others. In choosing a method, parents need to remember that the goal is to teach children self-regulation, not just take care of the immediate misbehavior. This is important because parents will not always be able to guide children, especially as they become older. Studies report that caregivers use three types of discipline—power assertion, love withdrawal, and induction.

Power Assertion

Power assertion occurs when caregivers use or threaten to use some form of physical punishment (also called *corporal punishment*) or deny privileges. The American Academy of Pediatrics takes a strong stance against corporal punishment of any kind, including spanking. Research has shown that not only is it an ineffective form of discipline, but also can have negative long-term effects. Certainly, many people can name children who were occasionally spanked and are now healthy, happy adults. However, other forms of discipline are safer and more effective.

Below are the main reasons power-assertive techniques are not a healthy form of discipline:

- Power-assertive techniques are often used when caregivers are angry. If guardians are **prone** (likely) to lose their tempers, their intended light physical punishment could become abusive when done in anger. For this reason, corporal punishment is illegal in child care programs and some other settings.
- Power-assertion is based on making a child fearful of the larger (and louder) adult. As the child grows physically, however, fear lessens and the technique no longer works.
- Power-assertion involves the fear of being caught and punished. Many power-assertive adults will threaten, "Don't let me catch you doing that again!" Thus, the child weighs the chances of being caught and the likely punishment. The child is not being guided by what is right or wrong but what they think they can get away with.
- When a child is physically aggressive toward another child, such as hitting another child, corporal punishment seems like a double standard. The child may think, "You are hitting me; why can't I hit others?" This is a good example of the punishment not fitting the misdeed.
- Discipline techniques are imitated or modeled by children. Children disciplined through power assertiveness are more apt to use these methods in their own relationships. If they see their caregivers lose control, children may become violent during the teen years or abusive to their own spouses or children as adults.

Love Withdrawal

In a discipline technique called **love withdrawal**, caregivers threaten children with being unloved or suggest some form of parent/child separation. An example is caregiver or guardian telling children they do not want or love them. Some caregivers even tell their children they are going to give them away. Other forms of love withdrawal include ignoring the child or giving the child the "silent treatment." Experts consider love withdrawal to be emotional abuse. Love withdrawal creates stress and prevents the expression of feelings.

Induction

In the third technique, **induction**, caregivers discipline their children by reasoning and explaining to them why they should or should not use certain behaviors. The induction method involves several different techniques and is individualized to the child's age (**Figure 4.13**). Children disciplined by this technique tend to show better self-control, display more concern for others, and take responsibility for their own failures. Caregivers need to remember that what works for one child may not work for another child and tailor the discipline technique to the child.

Figure 4.13 Some Induction Techniques and Examples

Technique	Examples
Keep control as an adult.	• Stay calm. • Deal with issues quickly, but not impulsively. • Seek help if it becomes too difficult to remain calm.
Maintain realistic expectations in making decisions about what are and are not acceptable behaviors.	• Consider child's age/stage, temperament, and any special problems. • Try to prevent situations that lead to misbehaviors, such as child proofing and avoiding hunger, sleep deprivation, or overstimulation.
Be a positive model.	• Avoid doing or saying anything you would not want your child to model. • Avoid media that show aggressive acts. Choose books and media that have positive images.
Use positive words with children.	• Show respect when speaking to children. • Make the child's environment a "yes/yes/no" one rather than a ""no/no/yes" one. (Using "no" mainly for safety reasons makes for a more positive environment.) • With older children, stick to one issue at a time rather than bringing up all issues. • Know that it is fine to say "I'm sorry" to a child.
Provide structure and consistency in the environment.	• Make the environment physically suitable for the child. (For example, children will try unsafe ways to reach items beyond their floor reach. Within-reach storage also allows children to keep their areas neat.) • Have a routine that lessens stress for both children and adults. • Explain any changes in routines and even rehearse new expectations.
Distract and redirect infants and young toddlers.	• Remove from an unsafe situation. • Involve child in a new activity.
Set limits and reinforce them.	• State rules in positive words. • Make statements simple for young children. • Give options when possible.
Use problem-solving techniques with older children.	• Use the six steps in the problem-solving process. • Evaluate the effectiveness of the solution selected.
Use punishment with care.	• Help child see punishment as the result of their willful misbehavior. • Choose punishment that fits the misbehavior. • For toddlers and preschoolers, a *time-out* (removing a child from an activity or the presence of others for less than five minutes) often works for a temper outburst or aggression toward others. • Natural consequences (common results of misbehaviors, such as a broken toy caused by an action done in anger) teach children that actions have consequences. • Logical consequences (adult-planned consequences to show a direct link between misbehavior and consequences, such as having to park a tricycle if riding limits are disobeyed) also teach children results of a specific misbehavior.
Encourage and support children's efforts.	• Use verbal encouragement rather than tangible (material) rewards. • Tell children what behavior was acceptable, such as "Your room looks nice when you put away your belongings." • Encourage younger children by helping them with a task, such as putting away toys. Ask older children if they can use a helping hand.

Goodheart-Willcox Publisher

4.2-3 Parenting Styles

Most caregivers want to raise their children to become responsible, well-mannered adults. As children enter the toddler years, parents must begin using guidance and discipline. Within a year or two, parents develop a *parenting style* (an overall way of socializing children). The caregiver's own childhood experiences, beliefs, and temperament, as well as the temperament of the child influence parenting styles. Parenting styles are classified as *authoritarian, permissive, overparenting, uninvolved* and *authoritative*. **Figure 4.14** shows results these parenting styles may have on children.

Figure 4.14 **Possible Results of Parenting Styles on Children**

Parenting Style	Possible Results
Authoritarian	• Moody • Unhappy • Aggressive, including violence, or *passive aggressiveness* (indirect expression of hostility, such as resentment or sullenness) • Not friendly • Vulnerable to stress • Trouble getting along with those in authority • Unable to make a decision on their own • Act out when away from parental influence and on their own • Distrustful
Permissive/ laissez-faire	• Not self-controlled • Not self-reliant • Impulsive • Aggressive • Rebellious • Low achievement • Anxious about whether they are doing the right thing
Overparenting/ helicopter parenting	• High perfectionist strivings, but are not willing to take risks • Lack leadership traits • Have unrealistic achievement goals • Lack emotional self-regulation and psychological resilience to handle typical problems on the road to adulthood • Often do not achieve, but believe they are entitled to get what they want • May stay dependent on parents even as young adults
Authoritative	• Self-reliant • Self-controlled • Curious • Can handle stress • Engage in fewer risk-taking behaviors • Moral/good character • Cooperative • High achiever

Goodheart-Willcox Publisher
(Continued)

Figure 4.14 **Possible Results of Parenting Styles on Children** (Continued)

Parenting Style	Possible Results
Uninvolved	• Children raise themselves causing them to grow up too quickly • Struggle with self-esteem issues • Perform poorly in school • Frequent behavior problems • Rank low in happiness • Moody • Unhappy

Authoritarian

Some caregivers use an **authoritarian** parenting style, in which the main objective is to make children completely obedient. These caregivers think obedience is the most important behavior their children should learn. They expect children to respect their authority with little or no explanation as to why children should obey. Authoritarian parents most often use power assertion as their discipline technique. Although these children often obey their parents, they do not understand why they should act as their parents wish. Beyond not developing self-control, power assertion can result in unhealthy long-term behaviors.

Permissive

Caregivers who use the **permissive** parenting style give children almost no guidelines or rules. This style is often called laissez-faire. Caregivers feel children should make their own decisions about right and wrong. They may think setting limits for their children will make the children feel unhappy or unloved. Some permissive parents become **overindulgent** (provide everything the child wants).

The truth is, without guidelines, these children may feel lost. Permissive/laissez-faire parenting can also give children the impression that parents do not care enough to guide and teach them or that they are trying to buy their love. Permissiveness can result in unhealthy long-term behaviors.

 FOCUS ON MENTAL HEALTH

Of the three discipline methods, only induction aids children's self-control. When power-assertion or love withdrawal techniques become the primary forms of discipline, children often do not learn self-control, which can lead to mental health problems. Having positive role models in a child's life can help teach self-control if a parent is unable to.

 FOCUS ON MENTAL HEALTH

Four parenting styles—authoritarian, permissive, uninvolved and overparenting—produce children at risk for mental health problems later in life. Conversely, the authoritative parenting style is the only style that emphasizes self-control and handling stress. Parenting experts conclude that the authoritative parenting style is the healthiest for children and families.

Overparenting

Overparenting is a parenting style in which caregivers desire to provide for and protect their children beyond what is in the best interest of children. *Overparenting* can be defined as parenting by controlling every move of the child. This style is often called helicopter parenting, as the caregiver is over-involved in every aspect of the child's life.

Overparenting often begins in infancy and becomes apparent from the toddler years through the teen and even young adult years. Some common characteristics of overparenting include

- hiring tutors beginning in the toddler or preschool years
- doing their children's projects or homework
- resolving children's conflicts with adults and peers without allowing children to try resolving conflicts on their own
- discouraging their children from independent explorations by manufacturing almost every experience for their children
- contacting all adults who provide services for their children (teachers, coaches, youth directors) **incessantly** (constantly; without break) and supervising activities
- attending job interviews with their children and negotiating for them

Although many of these caregivers have good intentions, the results may not be positive for their children. These children may be more self-centered and have an exaggerated sense of **entitlement** (the right to particular privileges or benefits). They may also have more difficulty developing their own coping skills and can even be afraid to make decisions on their own.

Uninvolved

Uninvolved parenting is a parenting style in which the caregiver has little or no knowledge of what their children are doing. There tend to be few rules and children do not receive much in guidance, nurturing, or parental attention. Caregivers don't devote time or energy into meeting the child's basic needs. Sometimes, an uninvolved caregiver may have mental health issues or substance abuse problems that prevent them from being able to care for a child's physical or emotional needs consistently. Other times, an uninvolved caregiver may lack knowledge about child development and are overwhelmed with problems like work, paying bills, and/or managing a household.

Authoritative

Many caregivers find a compromise between the authoritarian and permissive styles of parenting. They use an **authoritative** (also called *assertive-democratic*) style, in which caregivers set some rules but allow children some freedom. Caregivers who typically use an authoritative parenting style also use the induction method of discipline. Their children learn self-discipline in a positive, encouraging setting. Parenting experts **endorse** (support) an authoritative parenting style as healthiest for children and families. The long-term results for children are most positive.

1. Which of the following are not part of a caregivers' roles and responsibilities? (4.2.1)
   A. Disciplining a misbehaving child
   B. Providing food, clothing, and shelter
   C. Ensuring a child gets an education
   D. Telling a child they are not loved

2. Nurturing includes all of the following *except* _____ (4.2.1)
   A. feeding the child
   B. bathing the child
   C. providing a stimulating environment
   D. acting as a role model

3. To build a sense of belonging and community, parents _____ their children, or train them to live as part of the larger social group. (4.2.1)
   A. socialize
   B. guide
   C. discipline
   D. nurture

4. Which of the following statements is true? (4.2.2)
   A. Guidance includes the words and actions parents use to influence their children's behavior.
   B. Discipline includes the words and actions parents use to influence their children's behavior.
   C. Guidance is the use of methods and techniques to teach children self-control.
   D. Nurturance helps children have a sense of belonging to a social group.

5. The goal of guidance and discipline includes _____. (4.2.2)
   A. building character
   B. modeling behavior
   C. teaching culture
   D. teaching social norms

6. Which of the following is *not* included in authoritative parenting? (4.2.3)
   A. Parents apply the induction method of discipline.
   B. Parents use the phrase "because I said so."
   C. Parents explain reasons behind rules.
   D. Children are allowed some freedom.

7. Which of the following is *not* part of permissive parenting? (4.2.3)
   A. Setting rules but not enforcing them
   B. Very rarely giving out consequences
   C. Not spending time with child
   D. Believing children learn best without interference

8. Parents who hover over their children and don't let them make any decisions are called _____. (4.2.3)
   A. permissive parents
   B. helicopter parents
   C. authoritative parents
   D. uninvolved parents

Review and Assessment

Summary

Lesson 4.1

4.1-1 People have different reasons for wanting or not wanting children.

4.1-1 There are a number of factors people must consider before making the decision to become a parent.

4.1-1 Before having children, people should determine whether their reasons for wanting to parent are good ones grounded in solid decision making and reality, or poor ones grounded in the expectations of others or a desire to solve their problems.

4.1-2 Parenting is challenging because it involves a great deal of maturity.

4.1-2 Parenting involves relationships, such as the parent-child relationship. This relationship changes over time due to the child's development and relationships with other family members, friends, and others.

4.1-2 Parenting involves management of critical family resources and good communication skills.

4.1-3 Many people today practice family planning. The use of birth control methods can make family planning more successful.

4.2-1 Parenting involves a number of roles and responsibilities including nurturance; the meeting of a child's needs; socialization; teaching children how to live in groups; and guidance and discipline.

Lesson 4.2

4.2-2 There are five different parenting styles: authoritarian, permissive, overparenting, uninvolved, and authoritative.

4.2-2 Parenting experts identify the authoritative parenting style as the healthiest for children and families.

College and Career Portfolio

Portfolio Organization

It's important to have a plan for storing and organizing your portfolio. Ask your instructor where to save your documents. Think about how to organize related files into categories. Also think about where to store this information when you leave the school. For example, school transcripts and diplomas might be one category, writing samples might be another category, and so on. Next, consider how you will name the files. The names for folders and files should be descriptive, but not too long. You will decide in a later activity how to present your electronic files for viewers. To begin organizing your portfolio, complete the following activities:

- Create a folder in which you will save your files.
- Write a few sentences to describe how you will name the subfolders and files for your portfolio.
- Create the subfolders to organize the files, using the naming system you created.

Recall and Application

1. Which of the following statements is true about a child raised in an authoritarian parenting style? (4.2.3)
   A. Child raises themself.
   B. Child is curious.
   C. Child is passive aggressive.
   D. Child is impulsive.

2. Which of the following statements is true about a child raised in an authoritative parenting style? (4.2.3)
   A. Child is curious.
   B. Child is anxious.
   C. Child performs poorly in school.
   D. Child is vulnerable to stress.

3. Which of the following statements are true about Galinsky's Interpretive Parenting Stage? (4.1.2)
   A. Teach rules of behavior to child.
   B. Begin to give more freedoms with boundaries.
   C. Share knowledge about the world with the child.
   D. Evaluate self as a parent.

4. Which of the following statements are true about Galinsky's Interdependent Parenting Stage? (4.1.2)
   A. Teach rules of behavior to child.
   B. Begin to give more freedoms with boundaries.
   C. Share knowledge about the world with the child.
   D. Evaluate selves as parents.

Critical Thinking

1. **Evaluate.** Keante and your friend, Aafia, have been married for six months and are considering having children. Aafia explains her reasons for wanting to be a parent and says the following:
   - Her parents and Keante's parents are getting old and want to have grandchildren before they die.
   - Aafia and Keante's marriage is strong and growing stronger, and they want to share their love with a potential child.

   Based on what she has said, evaluate your friend's reasons and how healthy they are. What, if any, follow-up questions would you ask Aafia?

2. **Make inferences.** If a married person chooses not to have children or wants to wait several years before having a child, what can they say to their parents who want grandchildren? Why do older people often want grandchildren? Besides having grandchildren, what are some ways older people can fulfill their need to be with young children?

3. **Cause and effect.** List the aspects of parenting discussed in this chapter and then find a partner. Together, discuss how having children affects each of these aspects and why it is important that potential parents consider these effects. Take turns presenting the highlights of your discussion to the class.

4. **Identify.** Identify the decisions that are involved in *family planning*. Why is it important that potential parents consider these decisions? How does family planning differ from the decisions about whether or not to parent?

5. **Compare and contrast.** Parents' roles and responsibilities fall into four main categories: nurturance, socialization, guidance, and discipline. Define these four words, according to the glossary and according to a dictionary. Then, write a two- to three-page essay comparing and contrasting examples of behaviors that fall into these categories. Share your essays with the rest of the class by giving a one-minute oral presentation. Hold a question-answer session after your essay and be prepared to answer any questions your classmates may have.

6. **Make inferences.** This chapter states, "One major goal of guidance and discipline is to build character in children." Does this mean that parents can determine the characters of their children? Why or why not? Use evidence from this chapter to support your argument.

7. **Determine.** Ling, a fourth-grader in your after-school program, seems sad and uninterested in playing one day. You ask him what is wrong, and he says that his mom will not talk to him since he failed his math test. You have a conference with Ling's parents tomorrow. What kind of discipline is Ling's mother using? What, if any, alternative types of discipline might you suggest during the conference?

8. **Draw conclusions.** Think of a time when you misbehaved as a young child and write a short paragraph describing the scenario. Then, use Figure 4.13 to imagine inductive techniques parents could use to respond to this scenario. Try to imagine how each inductive technique would play out in your scenario. Which technique do you think would work most effectively?

9. **Analyze.** Review the five parenting styles covered in this chapter. Then, in small groups consider the following questions:
   - What effects might each parenting style have on a child?
   - How likely do you think parents are to adopt the parenting style used by their parents?

After you have answered these questions, share your thoughts with the class. As other groups share, support or challenge their conclusions. As a class, analyze the variety of answers represented.

Core Skills

1. **Listening and speaking.** Interview an individual or couple who decided not to have children. What are their reasons? Present your findings to the class and discuss the most common reasons for choosing not to have children.

2. **Writing.** Compose a short paper giving your views on the kinds of maturity people should have before becoming parents. How should they exhibit this maturity? What are some signs of maturity? of immaturity? Check your paper for correct spelling, grammar, and punctuation.

3. **Art.** Children both affect and are affected by relationships. On a large piece of paper, draw the silhouette of a child. Then, as a class, draw arrows and illustrations pointing *in* to signify ways that children are affected by relationships. Draw arrows and illustrations pointing *out* to signify ways that children affect relationships. Then, review your class's final product and discuss the different factors you brought to each other's attention.

4. **Math.** Child care is an indirect cost of parenting when both parents work. Ask a local child care provider what rate is charged to provide child care for one infant full-time (nine hours a day, five days a week). Use this weekly rate to calculate the cost of child care during the first year of life (from age six weeks until the first birthday).

5. **Reading.** Search online or visit your local library to find and read a book about parenting. Create a bibliography that includes the title of the publication, name and address of the publisher, topics covered, ages of children discussed, and any information that you found particularly interesting. Share your findings with the rest of the class.

6. **Science and research.** In the case study for this chapter, Andrea was concerned about Michael using harsh punishments their child. Using online or print resources, find and read a scientific study about harsh punishments—including corporal punishment—and child development. After reading the study, write a short essay assessing its reliability and summarizing its results. Read and discuss your essays in class.

7. **Writing and technology.** Choose one parenting style and, in groups, write a short script about a day in the life of a child whose parents use that parenting style. Include specific situations and reactions. Present your script to the class and lead a discussion about which parenting style is being represented.

8. **CTE Career Readiness Practice.** As a journalist for a local newspaper, it has come to your attention that a high percentage of parents in your community yell at and physically punish their children.

Your assignment is to write a full-page public service announcement that captures attention and educates parents on effective styles and methods of parenting. In your research, identify certain types of discipline that do not teach children and a number of possible alternatives. Present and discuss your public service announcement in class.

Observations

1. In an informal setting, observe caregivers and guardians who are having a difficult time with a child. What kind of parenting styles and methods are they using? What parenting skills might they need to help them with their children?

2. Visit your local library or bookstore and choose a book about parenting methods and preparing for parenting. Skim the chapters of the book and read three separate anecdotes about parenting. An *anecdote* is a brief account of a situation or story. Summarize each anecdote and analyze how it could be applied to the lives of parents and their children.

Unit 2 Pregnancy and Childbirth

CTSOs and Competitive Events

Participating in competitive events is a key aspect of membership in any Career and Technical Student Organization (CTSO). Competing offers you an opportunity to expand your leadership potential and develop skills necessary in your family, community, and future workplace. These events allow you to demonstrate your knowledge, skills, and leadership while improving your creativity, commitment, and professionalism. Through competition, you can earn recognition, awards, travel opportunities, scholarships, and more!

To learn more about competitive events, complete the following activities.

1. Talk with the local adviser or contact the organization before the next competition. This gives you time to review and decide which competitive events are best for you and your team.
2. Make sure to follow national and local/state websites and social media accounts to stay up to date on important information.
3. Select one or two events of interest and print the event information. Competitive events may be written, oral, or a combination of both. Discuss the events with your instructor or adviser.
4. Read all event guidelines closely, including the rubrics against which you will be judged. To avoid disqualification from an event, strictly follow the rules and regulations.
5. Because communication plays an important role in competitive events, carefully research which communication skills are required in the event you select. Research and preparation are important factors in successful competition.

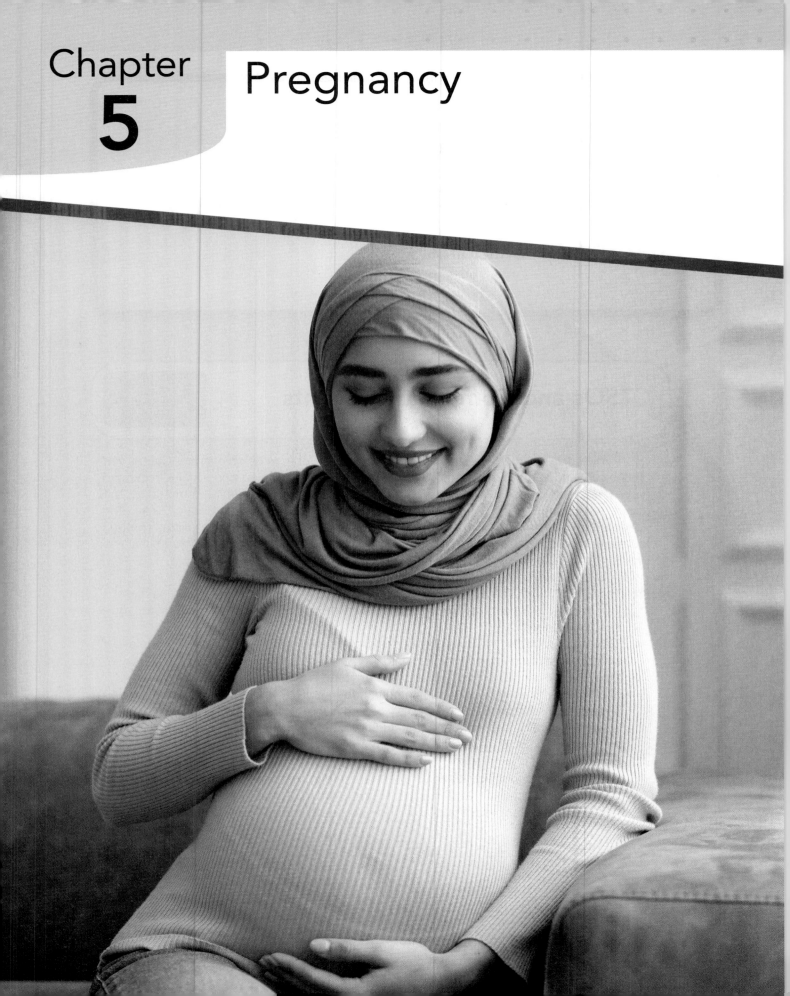

Chapter 5

Pregnancy

Lesson 5.1   Conception and Prenatal Development
Lesson 5.2   Factors That Affect the Unborn Baby
Lesson 5.3   Health Habits Prior to and During Pregnancy

Essential Question

How do biological processes create human life, and what factors affect a healthy pregnancy?

Case Study · Should Unborn Babies Have Health Protection Rights?

As a class, read the case study and discuss the questions that follow. After you finish studying the chapter, discuss this case study again to determine if your opinions have changed based on what you learned.

Emma and Cole are attending a party with their close friends, Kate and Satya. A few days ago, Kate excitedly told Emma and Cole she was five weeks pregnant.

During the party, Kate sips a glass of wine. Emma and Cole cannot believe Kate is drinking alcohol. Emma and Cole attended classes before the birth of their child and know the dangers of drinking alcohol while pregnant. Emma never touched alcohol while pregnant or breast-feeding.

As they watch Kate finish her drink, Cole whispers to Emma, "Shouldn't Kate be arrested for endangering the baby?" Emma thinks, then responds, "Don't pregnant people have their own rights, too?"

Give It Some Thought

1. Cole is not serious about having Kate arrested, but is concerned and upset by Kate's behavior. Do you share Cole's concerns? Explain your reasoning.
2. What do you think about Emma's response? Do you believe the law should require a pregnant person to give up some of their freedoms if they pose high risks for the unborn baby? Why or why not?
3. At what point in the pregnancy should concern for the well-being of the unborn baby overshadow the pregnant person's right to live as they choose?

Prostock-studio/Shutterstock.com

Lesson 5.1

Conception and Prenatal Development

Key Terms

age of viability
amnion
cell
cervix
chorion
conception
embryo
embryonic stage
fallopian tubes
fetal stage
fetus
germinal stage
ovaries
ovum
period of gestation
placenta
prenatal development
quickening
sperm
testes
umbilical cord
uterus
zygote

Learning Outcomes

After studying this lesson, you will be able to

5.1-1   **summarize** the biological processes that make conception occur.

5.1-2   **identify**, **compare**, and **contrast** the three stages of prenatal development.

5.1-3   **give examples** of developmental changes that occur month by month during pregnancy.

Reading and Notetaking Activity

Read the key terms for this lesson and look up any words you are unfamiliar with. Then, using all of the key terms, write two paragraphs summarizing what you already know about conception and prenatal development. If you do not know how a key term relates to either of these concepts, write that key term below your paragraphs. After reading, go back and explain how your unknown key terms relate.

Introduction

Pregnancy is the process through which a new human prepares to enter the world. This process begins with conception, when a baby is created inside a person's body. Even before a person knows they are pregnant, the baby affects their life. Their body changes to prepare for nine months of growth inside their uterus.

The prenatal period, from conception to birth, lasts about 280 days and is the shortest stage in the lifespan. This **formative** (shaping) stage is also the most critical time for a child's development. At no other time are two people closer than a pregnant person and baby during the prenatal period.

5.1-1 Conception

A **cell** is the smallest unit of life that is able to reproduce itself. Human bodies have two types of cells. One type is *body cells* that make up the tissues and organs of the body and reproduce themselves for growth and repair.

The other type is called *germ cells* or *sex cells*, the cells involved in reproduction or the creation of a baby.

A new life begins with the joining of two separate germ cells—one from the female reproductive system and one from the male reproductive system. The female germ cell is the **ovum** (often called *the egg*) and the male germ cell is the **sperm**. The joining of these two cells is called **conception** (**Figure 5.1**). This typically happens through sexual intercourse but can also occur through other methods (you'll learn more about these in the next chapter). At conception, the ovum and sperm combine to form a single cell called a **zygote** (ZIGH-goht), or *fertilized egg*.

The Female's Role

Before her own birth, the female produces and stores *ova* (eggs) in her **ovaries** (female reproductive glands). Inside the ovary, each ovum is stored in a small sac called a *follicle*. When the body becomes capable of reproduction through puberty, hormones cause some follicles to grow and fill with fluid each month. Around the middle of the menstrual cycle, one ovum is released from its follicle, and the other follicles that were growing typically become inactive. (Sometimes more than one ovum is released.) The release of the ovum is called *ovulation*.

Giovanni Cancemi/Shutterstock.com

Figure 5.1 Conception occurs when one sperm reaches the center (nucleus) of the ovum. *What type of cells are involved in reproduction?*

When the egg is released, it travels toward the fallopian tubes. The **fallopian tubes** are two hollow tubes that extend from the right and left sides of the uterus (**Figure 5.2**). The **uterus** is the reproductive organ in which the baby develops and is protected until birth. The **cervix** (SER-viks) is the lower, narrow portion of the uterus that connects the uterus to the vagina, or *birth canal*.

One end of each fallopian tube is connected to the uterus. The other end of each tube has fingerlike projections that lie near the ovary (they are not attached to the ovary). The fingerlike projections help gather the ovum as it emerges from the ovary. Once inside the fallopian tube, the ovum moves very slowly down the tube. Here, the ovum is ready and able to be joined by a sperm.

The Male's Role

Unlike a female who has all of her ova at birth, a male's **testes** (reproductive glands) do not produce sperm until the body is capable of reproduction at puberty. Sperm production continues throughout a male's lifetime. During typical conception, *semen*, a liquid which usually contains over 100 million sperm, enters the female's body during intercourse. The sperm leaves the male's penis and enters the female's vagina. These sperm travel from the vagina to the cervix and through the uterus to reach the fallopian tube. The sperm's journey to the ovum can take anywhere from 15 minutes to 12 hours, depending on the female's time of ovulation. Many sperm do not survive. Only 300 to 500 reach the correct fallopian tube to fertilize the egg.

Conception usually occurs when the ovum is less than one-third of the way down the fallopian tube. After that point, conception is unlikely because the ovum has a short lifespan—only living about 24 hours after ovulation. However, sperm can live inside a female's body for up to 5 days, so it is still possible for a person to get pregnant even if intercourse happens before ovulation.

Many sperm approach the ovum and try to break through its surface. Only one sperm successfully enters, or *fertilizes,* the egg. Once one sperm is accepted, no other sperm can enter the ovum. Conception has occurred, and the zygote forms.

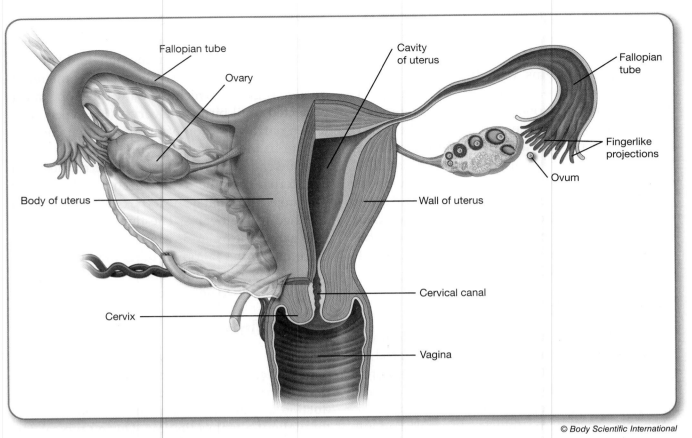

Figure 5.2 Eggs travel from the ovaries to the uterus via the fallopian tubes on either side of the uterus. *What route would sperm take to reach the fallopian tubes?*

Labels in figure:
- Fallopian tube
- Ovary
- Cavity of uterus
- Fallopian tube
- Fingerlike projections
- Ovum
- Body of uterus
- Wall of uterus
- Cervical canal
- Cervix
- Vagina

© Body Scientific International

5.1-2 Stages of Prenatal Development

Many changes happen in the time between conception and birth, called the **period of gestation** (pregnancy). This period lasts approximately nine months and is divided into three trimesters. A **trimester** is a period of three months. The baby's development that takes place during this time is called **prenatal development**. Prenatal development is divided into the germinal, embryonic, and fetal stages.

Germinal Stage

Conception marks the beginning of the first stage of prenatal development, the **germinal stage**. This stage covers the first two weeks of the pregnancy.

Once conception occurs, the fertilized egg (zygote) remains a single cell for about 30 hours before it starts to divide (**Figure 5.3**). On the third day, the zygote forms a solid ball of cells called a *morula*. By the fourth day, a fluid-filled cavity forms within the ball of cells, which is now called a *blastocyst* (BLAS-toh-sist). The blastocyst enters the uterus, where cells continue to divide rapidly for about three more days. During this time, the blastocyst floats freely in the uterus. Then, the blastocyst begins to **embed** (attach) itself in the wall of the uterus in a process called implantation. The cells continue to divide for several more days until implantation is complete. After implantation, the blastocyst will remain in the uterus until delivery; the inner cells will become the embryo in the next stage, and the outer cells will protect and nourish the embryo.

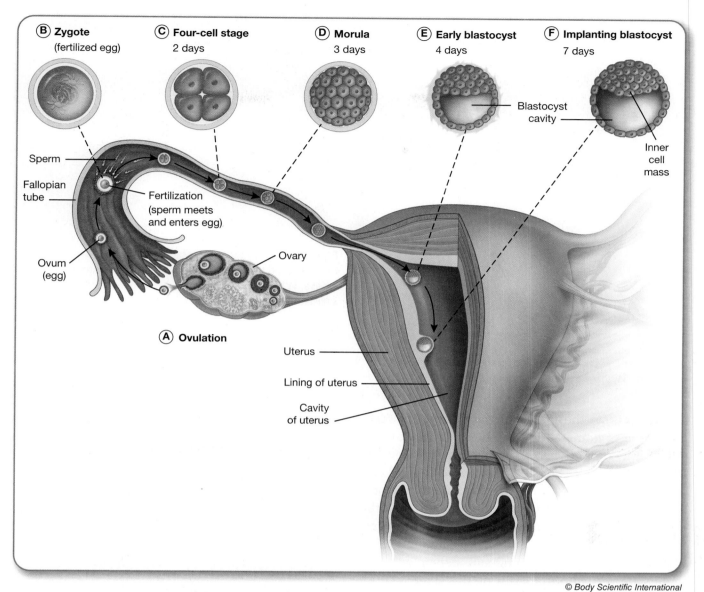

B Zygote
(fertilized egg)

C Four-cell stage
2 days

D Morula
3 days

E Early blastocyst
4 days

F Implanting blastocyst
7 days

Blastocyst cavity

Inner cell mass

Sperm

Fallopian tube

Fertilization (sperm meets and enters egg)

Ovum (egg)

Ovary

A Ovulation

Uterus

Lining of uterus

Cavity of uterus

© Body Scientific International

Figure 5.3 After 30 hours, the zygote divides rapidly, forming a *morula* and then a *blastocyst*. *What is the difference between a morula and a blastocyst?*

Embryonic Stage

The second stage of prenatal development is the **embryonic stage**, which lasts six weeks. During this stage, the baby is called an **embryo**. The following support systems for the pregnancy develop during the embryonic stage:

- The **chorion** (CORE-ee-ahn), the outermost membrane that surrounds the baby in the uterus, and the **amnion** (a fluid-filled sac) begin to form. They surround the embryo and protect the baby until birth (**Figure 5.4**).

- The **placenta** (pluh-SENT-uh), an organ filled with blood vessels, develops against the wall of the uterus. As the placenta develops, it will nourish the baby, remove the baby's wastes, exchange gases between pregnant person and baby, and provide the baby with needed hormones.

- The **umbilical cord** contains three blood vessels that connect the baby to the placenta. The umbilical cord grows out from the developing baby at the site of the future navel. It is connected to the placenta.

Figure 5.4 The chorion, amnion, placenta, and umbilical cord form. *What purpose does the placenta serve?*

Experts say the embryonic stage is the most critical stage of prenatal development because almost all of the unborn baby's body systems develop during this time. The baby receives both good and harmful substances from the pregnant person's placenta through the umbilical cord. Because the baby's body parts are developing so quickly, passing harmful substances to the child can affect them for life. Therefore, the pregnant person's health habits are very important during this stage.

Fetal Stage

The **fetal stage** of prenatal development begins nine weeks after conception. From this point until birth, a baby is medically known as a **fetus**. During the fetal stage, all parts of the unborn baby's body mature, and overall size increases quickly. By the fourth month, the fetus has usually grown enough to make the pregnant person's enlarged abdomen visible to others.

Several milestones that happen during the fetal stage are listed below:

- *Heartbeat.* The heartbeat of the unborn baby can be heard through the doctor's stethoscope (20 weeks) (**Figure 5.5**).

Figure 5.5 During the fetal stage, the baby's heartbeat can be heard through a doctor's stethoscope around 20 weeks. *When can the heartbeat first be detected with an ultrasound?*

- *Movements.* The baby's movements can be felt by the pregnant person, called **quickening** (18–20 weeks for first-time pregnancies; 15–17 weeks for following pregnancies).
- *Age of viability.* **Age of viability** is the time from when a baby can survive if born early. This time begins possibly as early as 23 weeks, but chances improve every week after until the full 40-week gestational period is over.

5.1-3 Month-by-Month Development

Although describing prenatal development by stages is accurate—the germinal stage, the embryonic stage, and the fetal stage—these basic descriptions do not explain much about *how* the baby is developing. All developmental changes begin during the germinal and embryonic stages, which last most of the first trimester of pregnancy. The fetal stage lasts about 32 weeks, beginning in the last one-fourth of the first trimester and continuing throughout the second and third trimesters of pregnancy. Due to the long time period of the fetal stage, it is difficult to easily describe how much a baby grows and changes.

It is most helpful to describe prenatal development in smaller segments. For instance, studying development month by month makes it easier to describe how a baby grows and develops before birth. **Figure 5.6** shows details on this development.

Figure 5.6 **Prenatal Development**
First Trimester

Month	Development
First month	• Baby begins as a *zygote*. It grows into a *blastocyst* and then into an *embryo*. • First signs of the baby's heart, lungs, face, arms, and legs show. • Heart begins beating and pumps blood through arteries. • Digestive system is forming. • Baby's brain and spinal cord develop from the neural tube. • Ears and eyes begin to form. • Tissue that will later form the baby's backbone, skull, ribs, and muscles can be seen on ultrasound. • By month's end, baby becomes an embryo and is ½ inch long. • By month's end, baby weighs much less than 1 ounce.
Second month	• Body organs and systems that began in the first month are continuing to develop. • Heartbeat can be detected by an ultrasound at around week 6 of pregnancy. • Liver and stomach start to work. • Head makes up nearly half of the embryo. • Brain grows quickly and directs the baby's movements. • Arms and legs become longer and take shape. • Fingers and toes develop. • Distinct wrists, elbows, and hands are present. • Distinct knees and feet are present. • Eyes take on color. • Eyelids form, but are sealed shut. • Ears, nose, and mouth take shape. • At month's end, embryo is 1 inch long. • At month's end, embryo weighs ⅓ ounce.
Third month	• Baby is now called a *fetus*. • Bones are growing. • Kidneys are working. • Fetus moves often, but cannot be felt by pregnant person. • Tooth sockets and buds for teeth forming in jawbone. • Fetus can open and close mouth and swallow. • Fingerprints appear. • All parts of the baby's body are formed by the end of the month. • At month's end, baby is 4 inches long. • At month's end, baby weighs 1 ounce.

Goodheart-Willcox Publisher; © Body Scientific International
(Continued)

Figure 5.6 **Prenatal Development** (Continued)
Second Trimester

Month	Development
Fourth month	• Baby's heartbeat is strong. • Baby's airways develop, but are not in use. • Skin is transparent and thin. • Fingernails appear. • Baby sleeps and wakes. • Baby moves and kicks. • Baby sucks their thumb. • Toward the end of the month, the pregnant person may feel the baby's movements. • Placenta is now formed. • Umbilical cord grows and thickens to carry enough blood and nourishment to baby. • Baby's nervous system and reproductive system develop. • By the end of the month, the baby is about 6 inches long. • By the end of the month, the baby weighs about 4 ounces.
Fifth month	• Baby's internal organs continue to grow. • Blood supply to the lungs increases. • Eyelashes and eyebrows appear. • Scalp hair appears. • Silky body hair called lanugo and a thick, white protective coating called *vernix* protect baby's skin from its watery surroundings. • Baby sleeps and wakes in a pattern. • Baby turns from side to side. • Baby kicks and moves a lot. • By month's end, the baby is about 10 inches long. • By month's end, the baby weighs about ½ to 1 pound.
Sixth month	• Baby's growth speeds up. • Baby opens and closes their eyes. • Baby can hear sounds. • Skin is red, wrinkled, and oily. • Baby stretches and kicks. • At month's end, the baby is about 12 inches long. • At month's end, the baby weighs almost 2 pounds.

(Continued)

Figure 5.6 **Prenatal Development** (Continued)
Third Trimester

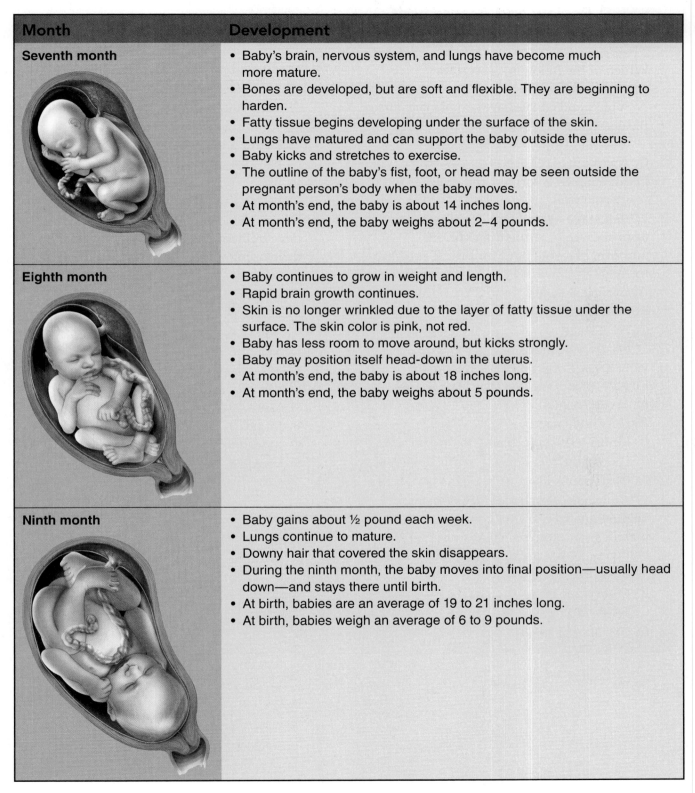

Month	Development
Seventh month	• Baby's brain, nervous system, and lungs have become much more mature. • Bones are developed, but are soft and flexible. They are beginning to harden. • Fatty tissue begins developing under the surface of the skin. • Lungs have matured and can support the baby outside the uterus. • Baby kicks and stretches to exercise. • The outline of the baby's fist, foot, or head may be seen outside the pregnant person's body when the baby moves. • At month's end, the baby is about 14 inches long. • At month's end, the baby weighs about 2–4 pounds.
Eighth month	• Baby continues to grow in weight and length. • Rapid brain growth continues. • Skin is no longer wrinkled due to the layer of fatty tissue under the surface. The skin color is pink, not red. • Baby has less room to move around, but kicks strongly. • Baby may position itself head-down in the uterus. • At month's end, the baby is about 18 inches long. • At month's end, the baby weighs about 5 pounds.
Ninth month	• Baby gains about ½ pound each week. • Lungs continue to mature. • Downy hair that covered the skin disappears. • During the ninth month, the baby moves into final position—usually head down—and stays there until birth. • At birth, babies are an average of 19 to 21 inches long. • At birth, babies weigh an average of 6 to 9 pounds.

1. Which of the following describes conception? (5.1.1)
   A. A male and female have sexual intercourse.
   B. One sperm fertilizes an ovum in the fallopian tube.
   C. An ovum is released from an ovary.
   D. An embryo is formed and attaches to the uterine wall.

2. Which stage of prenatal development lasts six weeks while the chorion, amnion, placenta, and umbilical cord are formed? (5.1.2)
   A. Germinal stage
   B. Embryonic stage
   C. Fetal stage
   D. Gestational stage

3. Which stage of prenatal development includes the blastocyst attaching to the wall of the uterus? (5.1.2)
   A. Germinal stage
   B. Embryonic stage
   C. Fetal stage
   D. Gestational stage

4. Which stage of prenatal development begins nine weeks after conception and includes milestones such as movements being felt by the pregnant person? (5.1.3)
   A. Germinal stage
   B. Embryonic stage
   C. Fetal stage
   D. Gestational stage

5. Month 6 of prenatal development includes which milestone? (5.1.3)
   A. Scalp hair appears
   B. Tooth sockets and buds for teeth forming in jawbone
   C. Baby's airways develop but are not in use
   D. Baby can hear sounds

6. During which month of prenatal development does fatty tissue begin developing under the surface of the skin? (5.1.3)
   A. Month 8
   B. Month 5
   C. Month 7
   D. Month 6

7. When will the fetus be 4 inches long? (5.1.3)
   A. Month 3
   B. Month 4
   C. Month 5
   D. Month 2

Factors That Affect the Unborn Baby

Learning Outcomes

After studying this lesson, you will be able to

5.2-1 **summarize** how genetic factors and heredity affect prenatal development.

5.2-2 **differentiate** between genetic and chromosomal disorders.

5.2-3 **explain** the role of the environment on prenatal development and give examples of environmental factors that can harm the fetus.

Reading and Notetaking Activity

Skim the lesson and consider what each section might teach you about factors that affect the unborn baby. Keep a list, placing a star beside any concepts that especially interest you. After reading this lesson, choose three concepts and write a few paragraphs about how these concepts can help you understand prenatal development. Use proper spelling and grammar in your paragraphs.

Key Terms

AIDS
chromosomal disorders
chromosomes
diabetes
dominant traits
Down syndrome
environmental factors
fetal alcohol spectrum disorders (FASDs)
genetic disorder
genetic factors
HIV
pregnancy-induced hypertension (PIH)
recessive traits
Rh factor
rubella
sexually transmitted infections (STIs)

Introduction

The moment a sperm enters an egg, the unborn baby forms traits from both the biological parents. These inherited traits, including any disorders, are merged into a unique new person and influence the child's growth and development throughout life. Development, however, is not determined solely by genetics. Immediately after conception, the environment also begins to **exert** (forcibly place) an influence on the unborn baby's traits.

5.2-1 Genetic Factors

Genetic factors are a person's inherited traits passed to them through the parents' genes at conception. This is also referred to as heredity. Each parent's genes combine to make a blueprint for the unborn child's growth and development. During pregnancy, this genetic blueprint, called a *genome*, guides growth and development. The *epigenome*, which can turn genes on and off, has a major impact on genes—altering how the genes may function throughout life.

Through the guidance of the genome and epigenome, the unborn baby changes from a zygote to a baby ready to be born. The child may look much like other members of the family. They will likely have abilities, interests, and personality traits similar to those of other family members, too.

During the prenatal period, the genetic blueprint also gives the fetus' cells instructions for family-like traits that will unfold throughout life.

For example, during the prenatal period, a biologically male baby's cells receive instructions on hair loss later in life. These instructions determine whether he will be bald, what the pattern of hair loss will be, and when hair loss will occur. Some people's genes lead them to lose hair, while others have genes that promote keeping a full head of hair. Heredity causes each person to be different.

Heredity and Genetics

All people begin life as a single-celled zygote. The *nucleus*, or center, of this cell contains a set of instructions to build a living being. These directions are written in what scientists call a *genetic code*. The genetic code is stored in DNA, or deoxyribonucleic (dee-OXY-rye-bo-new-KLEE-ic) acid. DNA is a chemical compound found in thread-like structures called **chromosomes** (KRO-muh-zomes). Chromosomes carry genes in living cells (**Figure 5.7**).

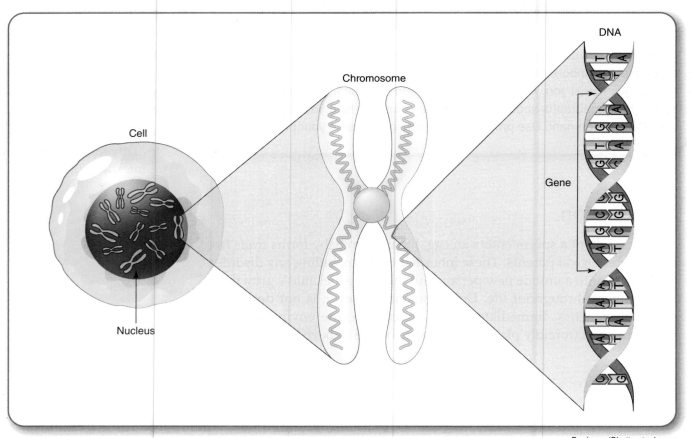

Figure 5.7 DNA contains the genetic instructions that guide the assembly of a living creature. *How are a cell, nucleus, chromosome, and DNA all related?*

Chromosomes and Genes

All living organisms have a certain number of chromosomes. Humans have 46 chromosomes—23 from each parent—that form 23 pairs in each of the body cells. The sperm and egg each have only 23 chromosomes, so when fertilization occurs, these pair up to create a zygote with 46 chromosomes. Each chromosome has about 20,000 genes. These genes and the epigenome determine a person's individual traits.

Dominant and Recessive Traits

The initial laws of heredity were discovered by Gregor Mendel (1822–1884), a **botanist** (person who studies plant life) from Austria. At first, Mendel thought traits were handed down equally from both parents and "averaged"; for example, a tall parent and a short parent would produce an average height "child." (Mendel was actually studying peas.)

Mendel's findings did not support the "averaging" idea. He soon discovered that the laws of heredity, which apply to all living beings, are based on dominant and recessive genes. For this reason, different traits come from each parent, and a child might express traits that both parents carry, but don't express.

Dominant traits are always expressed in a person even if only one gene of the gene-pair is inherited for that trait. **Recessive traits** are not typically expressed in a person unless both genes for the trait are inherited (one from each parent). A person who inherits only one recessive gene for a trait becomes a *carrier* of that trait. This makes it possible for the trait to be expressed in later generations.

Autosomes and Sex Chromosomes

Each human has 23 pairs of chromosomes in each cell. Chromosome pairs 1-22 are called *autosomes* (AW-tuh-zomes). Autosomes carry gene pairs (one from each parent) that follow dominant and recessive gene principles.

Focus on Science

Dominant and Recessive Genes

At the time of conception, your parents together gave you gene pairs that have determined your unique traits. Your traits were randomly selected from the traits of all generations of your blood relatives. Most traits, such as eye color, are the result of multiple gene pairs. Other traits, called *Mendelian inheritance*, are the result of one gene pair. Remember for a dominant trait, only one dominant gene in the pair is needed, which can come from one or both parents. For a recessive trait, both genes in the pair must be for the recessive trait, which means both parents either have the recessive trait or are carriers. Thus, dominant traits are more common in the general population.

Some typical dominant traits include: Dimples; cleft chin; ear lobe unattached from the head; right-handedness; freckles; blood types A, B, or AB (co-dominant); Rh+ blood factor; high blood pressure; nearsightedness; and baldness (in males). Recessive traits would be the opposites, such as no dimples, or another trait, such as blood type O.

From these options, make a list of your dominant and recessive traits. Who else in your family shares each trait with you? Research other Mendelian inheritance traits and share your findings with the class.

Photo: Otna Ydur/Shutterstock.com

Unlike the autosomes, the 23rd pair of chromosomes are called the *sex chromosomes* because they determine a person's biological gender (**Figure 5.8**). The sex chromosomes are labeled as X and Y, simply because that is what they look like under a microscope.

- If a person's 23rd pair of chromosomes was an X and X, that person would be biologically female. When a female's chromosome pair splits to form her eggs (ova), all ova will be X because they are coming from an XX chromosome pair.
- If a person's 23rd pair of chromosomes was an X and Y, that person would be biologically male. When a male's chromosome pair splits to form sperm, some will be X and some will be Y because they are coming from an XY pair.
- There are rare situations where sexual reproductive organs or specific genes of the unborn baby do not match with the typical definition of being biologically male or female. These are known as intersex conditions and can raise difficult gender-related questions and decisions for parents or caregivers.

All egg cells carry the X chromosome. If the egg is fertilized by a sperm carrying an X chromosome, the child will be biologically female (XX). If the sperm cell carries the Y chromosome, the child will be biologically male (XY). Because the father's sex chromosome is the one that varies (X or Y), the father's sperm always determines the gender of the child.

5.2-2 Genetic and Chromosomal Disorders

A **genetic disorder** is a defect caused by one or more **abnormalities** (flaws or irregularities) in the genome. Some disorders are inherited from parents as a dominant or recessive trait (**Figure 5.9**). Other defects are due to *mutations* (changes in the DNA). If the mutation is in the sex chromosome, it can be passed down to the next generation. Most genetic disorders are caused by a combination of small variations in genes and environmental factors (**Figure 5.10**).

Dee-sign/ Shutterstock.com

Figure 5.8 Karyotype means an individual's collection of chromosomes. Here, you can see the male and female karyotype. *If a male contributes an X chromosome to the genetic makeup of a baby, what gender will the baby be?*

Figure 5.9 Genetic Alterations: Single Gene
Dominant gene (50% chance a child will inherit)

Type of Alteration	Examples of Defects	Prevalence of Defects
Autosomal dominant polycystic kidney disease (ADPKD)	Clusters of cysts (fluid-filled sacs) develop in the kidneys and sometimes in the liver. High blood pressure and kidney failure often occur.	1 in 1,250 births
Marfan syndrome	Damages connective tissues that support the skeleton and body structures. These connective tissues lose their elasticity and strength. Body structure looks much like that of Abraham Lincoln (tall and thin). If heart and blood vessels are affected, the syndrome is life threatening.	1 in 4,000 births
Huntington's disease	Disease injures the brain, causing movement, intellectual, and psychiatric disorders. These disorders gradually worsen over time. Death occurs 10 to 30 years after disease onset. (If onset occurs in childhood, death often occurs within 10 years.)	1 in 10,000 births

Recessive gene (25% chance a child will have the disorder)

Type of Alteration	Examples of Defects	Prevalence of Defects
Sickle-cell anemia	Disease that causes an abnormality in the red blood cells. The cells are rigid, sticky, shaped like sickles (crescent moons), and break easily. These sickle cells often block blood flow, causing severe pain, damage to the retina, damage to the spleen (resulting in infections), and swelling in the hands and feet. Sickle cells live only 20 days compared to a normal cell's lifespan of 120 days, so people with Sickle-cell anemia do not have enough red blood cells to carry needed oxygen throughout the body. The disease is treated with blood transfusions, which can be risky.	1 in 625 births
Cystic fibrosis	Disease affects cells that produce mucous, sweat, and digestive juices. Secretions become thick and sticky, resulting in plugged passageways in the lungs and pancreas. Life expectancy for people with Cystic Fibrosis has increased due to medical advances; most babies born with the disease are expected to live into their mid-forties.	1 in 2,000 births
Tay-Sachs disease	A fatty substance in the child's brain builds up to toxic levels and affects neuron functioning. The disease leads to blindness, deafness, paralysis, and death. (In the infantile form, children die before the preschool years. In the juvenile form, death occurs in the mid-teen years.)	1 in 3,000 births
PKU or phenylketonuria (FEN-uhl-kee-tuh-NOOR-ia)	Disease causes an amino acid, phenylalanine, to build up in the body due to the lack of an enzyme to break down the amino acid. Without dietary treatment, stunted growth, small head size, severe intellectual disabilities, and behavioral problems occur.	1 in 12,000 births

Goodheart-Willcox Publisher
(Continued)

Figure 5.9 Genetic Alterations: Single Gene (Continued)

X-linked recessive (50% chance for biological males being affected)

Type of Alteration	Examples of Defects	Prevalence of Defects
Duchenne (doo-SHEN) muscular dystrophy	Muscle fibers are very susceptible to damage. Limbs contract, making victims wheelchair-bound. Disease affects heart, lungs, and ability to swallow. People with this disease often die of respiratory failure before they reach 40 years of age.	1 in 7,000 births
Hemophilia	Disease is a disorder of the blood-clotting system. Hemophilia causes severe bruising; internal bleeding; bleeding into the joints, urine, and stool; and extreme fatigue. Blood transfusions are used for treatment. Uncontrolled bleeding can lead to death.	1 in 10,000 births

Figure 5.10 Examples of Multiple Gene Alterations Combined with the Environment

- Asthma
- Autoimmune diseases, such as multiple sclerosis (MS), inflammatory bowel disease (IBD), and rheumatoid arthritis (RA)
- Cleft palate
- Diabetes
- Heart disease
- Mood disorders

Goodheart-Willcox Publisher

Chromosomal disorders are defects in the chromosomes. These defects are often more serious than single-gene defects because they involve so many genes. Chromosome disorders are caused by changes in the number of chromosomes or by an atypical chromosome structure, such as a deletion or duplication of part of the chromosome. Chromosomal defects usually occur due to an error in cell division. One example of a chromosomal condition is **Down syndrome**, which occurs when each body cell has three copies of chromosome 21 instead of two copies.

Most chromosome errors occur in the egg or in the sperm, so the defect is present in every body cell. In other cases, the defect occurs after conception, which means some cells carry the defect, but others do not. Parents' ages increase the risks of genetic and chromosomal disorders due to the aging of genetic materials in the germ (sperm and egg) cells.

5.2-3 Environmental Factors

Environmental factors are caused by a person's surroundings. The prenatal environment is the pregnant person's body, and the substances a pregnant person takes into their body also affect the developing baby. Environmental substances include foods, beverages, drugs, and environmental pollutants (lead, chemicals, pesticides, and herbicides). Each of these substances can negatively impact the developing fetus.

An unborn baby completely depends on its environment for a healthy start. People with good health habits and a healthy environment before pregnancy are more likely to have healthy babies. If unhealthy environmental factors are present, the pregnancy is called a *high-risk pregnancy*. Environmental factors that can affect the health of a pregnancy include the age of the baby's biological parents, the pregnant person's physical health, and even the pregnant person's emotional health.

Age of Biological Parents

Regarding health, the ideal time for a person to have a baby is between 21 and 28 years of age. Teens and people over 35 years old are considered high-risk populations. Because bodies are still developing during the teen years, a teen's body cannot always meet the needs of a developing baby. Pregnant people who are over 35 years of age have a higher rate of babies with health problems, disabilities, and disorders. They are also more likely to have their own health problems.

Careers

Genetic Counselor

Genetic counselors assess individual and family likelihood or risk for genetic disorders, syndromes, or certain birth defects. They analyze the genetics of patients through DNA testing.

Career cluster: Health care.

Education: Educational requirements include a minimum of a master's degree in genetic counseling or genetics. Some genetic counselors choose to further their education and earn a Ph.D. Most states also require certification and a license in genetic counseling.

Job outlook: Future employment opportunities for genetic counselors are expected to grow much faster than the average for all occupations.

To learn more about a career as a genetic counselor, visit the United States Department of Labor's *Occupational Outlook Handbook* website. You will also be able to compare the job responsibilities, educational requirements, job outlook, and average pay of genetic counselors with similar occupations.

Photo: Wild Squirrels/Shutterstock.com

Geneticists suspect that a biological male's age is also involved in some genetic disorders. Mutations in the sperm occur as men age, and the number of mutations rise **exponentially** (rapidly). For example, at 36 years old, men pass along twice as many new mutations as men who are 20 years old. By 70 years of age, men pass along eight times the number of new mutations seen in 20-year-olds. Most sperm mutations are harmless to children, but some may result in disorders.

Pregnant Person's Physical Health

Good health habits prior to and during pregnancy can promote a healthy pregnancy. Good health habits include eating nutritious meals, attending regular medical appointments, getting plenty of sleep and rest, and participating in enjoyable physical activity. When a pregnant person does not practice good health habits, the risk of complications rises. (You will learn more about health habits prior to and during pregnancy later in this chapter.) Other health issues that can cause harm to the unborn baby or pregnant person include certain illnesses and diseases, high-risk

behaviors like drug or alcohol use, and severe emotional stress.

Illnesses and Diseases in the Pregnant Person

Any health problems a person has before and during pregnancy may play a role in the pregnancy and affect the baby's health. People should ask their doctors (before pregnancy, if possible) how these problems might affect the pregnancy. In many cases, steps can be taken to lower these risks. The doctor will want to monitor health problems more closely during pregnancy. Special testing might be done, and medications or treatments might need to be adjusted for the safety of both the developing baby and the pregnant person.

Diabetes

Diabetes is a disorder caused by the body's inability to use sugar properly. In diabetes, the body inadequately produces or uses the hormone *insulin*. Some people might have diabetes before they become pregnant. If so, they should talk to their doctors about how to manage the disorder during pregnancy.

Another kind of diabetes, called *gestational diabetes*, can occur during pregnancy. Gestational diabetes appears in about 18 percent of people who did not have diabetes before pregnancy. Soon after pregnancy ends, gestational diabetes usually disappears; however, it leaves the person with a 35–60 percent chance of developing diabetes later in life. The chances of developing diabetes increase for their children, too.

A nutritious diet, physical activity, and medication (if needed) can keep both types of diabetes under control. Pregnant people with either of these conditions should work closely with their doctors and dietitians to plan for a healthy pregnancy.

Pregnancy-Induced Hypertension (PIH)

Pregnancy-induced hypertension (PIH) is the name for high blood pressure caused by pregnancy. This dangerous condition can also be referred to as *pre-eclampsia* or *toxemia* (**Figure 5.11**). It includes a sudden increase in blood pressure, protein in the urine, and swelling. PIH appears late in pregnancy, but its cause is unknown. If untreated, PIH can lead to damage or death of the pregnant person, baby, or both. Early treatment, which may include bed rest, medicine, and perhaps early delivery of the baby, can help both pregnant person and baby avoid serious health problems.

Rh Factor

The **Rh factor** is a protein substance found on the surface of red blood cells of about 85 percent of the population, mainly among Caucasians. People who have the substance are called *Rh positive (Rh+)*, and those who do not are called *Rh negative (Rh–)*.

The only time the Rh factor can cause a problem during pregnancy is when the male is Rh+ and the female is Rh–. If the baby inherits the Rh+ blood type from the male, the baby may develop Rh disease. *Rh disease* is a type of blood condition that destroys the baby's red blood cells.

Rh disease does not affect the Rh+ unborn baby during a person's first pregnancy. However, some of the baby's Rh+ cells may enter the pregnant person's bloodstream during birth. These cells are foreign to the pregnant person's Rh– system. Their body fights these Rh+ cells by making antibodies, which then makes the pregnant person immune to the blood cells of future Rh+ babies. In the next pregnancy, these antibodies cross the placenta. If this baby is also Rh+, the pregnant person's antibodies destroy the baby's red blood cells. A vaccine called *anti-Rh-immune globulin* greatly reduces the danger of Rh disease (the vaccine is 99 percent effective.)

Cytomegalovirus (CMV)

Cytomegalovirus (CMV) is a common virus that can cross the placenta during prenatal development and infect the unborn baby. CMV can be fatal for the embryo or young fetus. In older fetuses, CMV can cause brain, liver, and blood problems. Antiviral drugs may help reduce the severity of problems in newborns with CMV. According to the Centers for Disease Control and Prevention, approximately 50–80 percent of Americans have had CMV by the time they are 40 years old. CMV is contracted primarily through contact with bodily fluids of young children but can also be passed through sexual contact with an infected partner. Once a person contracts CMV, the virus remains in the body for life. People in close contact with young children are at greater risk for CMV exposure.

Sexually Transmitted Infections (STIs)

Sexually transmitted infections (STIs) are infectious illnesses contracted primarily through sexual intercourse. STIs are also known as *sexually transmitted diseases (STDs)*. The most dangerous STI is HIV/AIDS. **HIV** (human immunodeficiency virus) is the STI that causes the disease **AIDS** (acquired immunodeficiency syndrome). AIDS develops when HIV attacks the body's immune system until it is no longer able to fight illness.

Chompoo Suriyo/Shutterstock.com

Figure 5.11 Early detection and treatment are important for people who have pregnancy-induced hypertension (PIH). *What can people do to make sure pregnancy complications do not go undetected?*

HIV is spread through sexual relations or by contact with contaminated blood and bodily fluids. Among drug users, HIV can spread through the sharing of contaminated intravenous needles.

STIs can have serious effects on the unborn baby (**Figure 5.12**). For example, some STIs can enter the bloodstream of the pregnant person and cross the placenta to reach the fetus. Others infect the reproductive tract and can pass to the baby during delivery. Still other STIs can be passed to the baby during breast-feeding. STIs pose a high risk particularly because a pregnant person could be infected with an STI and not even realize it if they have no symptoms. If a person thinks there is a chance they were exposed to an STI, they should immediately communicate this to their doctor. Today, pregnant people under the care of a medical provider receive STI tests during pregnancy to protect both pregnant person and baby.

Rubella

Rubella (formerly called *German measles*) is a virus that can cross the placenta and affect the baby during the first three months of pregnancy. For the pregnant person, this disease is mild, but Rubella can cause blindness, deafness, intellectual disabilities, and/or heart problems for the baby if they are infected.

Figure 5.12 **STIs and Their Effects on the Unborn/Newborn**

STI	Transmission	Effects on Baby
Syphilis	Contracted by pregnant person through sexual activity. Crosses the placenta beginning in the eighteenth week of pregnancy.	Effects are prevented if treated before the sixteenth week of pregnancy. Untreated infection causes deafness, brain damage, skin lesions, bone and facial deformities, and fetal death.
Herpes simplex (herpes)	Contracted primarily by sexual relations. Transmitted to baby at or shortly before delivery by baby's contact with infected secretions.	Newborns develop skin lesions and brain damage. 50 percent death rate in newborns. May result in increased risk for mental health problems. No treatment available. C-sections may prevent contact with secretions.
Gonorrhea	Contracted by sexual relations. Transmitted to baby at or shortly before delivery by baby's contact with reproductive tract infection.	Blindness if untreated. Treatment includes placing silver nitrate or antibiotic ointment in the infant's eyes and treating baby with antibiotics.
Chlamydia	Transmitted through sexual relations. (Twice as common as gonorrhea.) Females rarely experience symptoms. May lead to sterility.	Miscarriage, low birthweight, and death of infants due to lung disorders.
Pelvic inflammatory disease (PID)	Complication of some STIs due to sexual relations with an infected partner.	Damages reproductive organs, making it difficult or impossible to conceive. Often the cause of PID is gonorrhea or chlamydia. (See these effects on baby.)
Human papillomavirus (HPV)	Transmitted by all forms of sexual relations. Incredibly common. Can cause genital warts and cancer. Vaccines are available to prevent HPV.	Warts may block the vaginal canal, requiring surgical delivery of the baby. Most babies overcome the virus without treatment. Babies may develop warts on the vocal cords (called *laryngeal papillomatosis*).
Acquired immunodeficiency syndrome (AIDS)	Acquired through sexual relations or contact with infected blood or body fluids. Infected pregnant people transmit the virus in 25 percent of births. (People who are pregnant usually have HIV only, with AIDS developing sometime after pregnancy.)	Illness and perhaps very early death of child. Treatment of symptoms. No cure.

Goodheart-Willcox Publisher

Pregnant people should have received an MMR (measles-mumps-rubella) vaccination for rubella during childhood. The MMR vaccine must be avoided during pregnancy, however, because the vaccine itself also presents a risk to a fetus.

Radiation Exposure

During pregnancy, X-rays should be avoided if possible. X-rays aimed toward the fetus increase the likelihood of childhood cancer. Some studies also link the use of X-rays in pregnancy to congenital disabilities in the fetus.

Pregnant people should inform their doctors or dentists of a possible or known pregnancy before X-rays are performed. They should also avoid working near X-ray or radiation treatment machines and should leave the room when an X-ray is being taken.

If an X-ray is necessary before delivery, it must be low in intensity, taken away from the fetus, and done only when the abdomen is shielded by a lead safety drape.

Drug and Alcohol Use

Harmful substances, such as nicotine, alcohol, medications, and drugs can enter the pregnant person's body, pass through the placenta, and reach an unborn baby. Some of these substances can harm the baby in the early months of pregnancy, and many can harm the baby throughout pregnancy. Other drugs, such as aspirin, are most hazardous near delivery.

Nicotine

When a pregnant person smokes, the baby feels the effects. Because nicotine is a *stimulant*, it raises the pregnant person's heart rate, blood pressure, and breathing rate. Nicotine also reduces the flow of blood. While a person is smoking, their baby's oxygen is greatly reduced. Babies need oxygen as they grow, especially during the prenatal period. A parent or parents who smoke during pregnancy usually continue to smoke after pregnancy, too. Thus, the child continues to be affected by secondhand smoke. **Figure 5.13** outlines the harmful effects of nicotine use during pregnancy.

Alcohol

Most doctors recommend completely avoiding alcohol during pregnancy. Any alcoholic drink can harm an unborn baby. Alcohol is a type of

FOCUS ON MENTAL HEALTH

Alcohol-Related Neurodevelopmental Disorder (ARND) can cause mental health problems in young children. To avoid any risk to your baby, commit to no drinking throughout your entire pregnancy. No alcohol means no chance of alcohol-related disorders!

depressant, which slows the central nervous system. A developing baby cannot process alcohol. Taking even one drink could possibly cause the baby to have birth defects.

Fetal alcohol spectrum disorders (FASDs) are a group of symptoms that occurs in babies who were exposed to alcohol during pregnancy. FASDs are comprised of the following conditions:

- *Fetal Alcohol Syndrome (FAS)*. FAS is at the severe end of the spectrum. These babies have abnormal facial features, growth problems, and brain disorders. They can have problems with learning, executive functions, vision, or hearing.
- *Alcohol-Related Neurodevelopmental Disorder (ARND)*. These babies may have learning and behavioral problems (poor judgment and impulse control), often first noted near school-age.
- *Alcohol-Related Birth Defects (ARBD)*. These babies often have problems with one or more of the following: heart, kidneys, bones, or hearing.

Figure 5.13 **Risks of Nicotine Use During Pregnancy**

- Low birthweight or premature birth
- Congenital disorders
- Abnormal brain development, which can lead to learning problems, hyperactivity, and poor attention spans
- Ear infections and breathing problems
- Cleft lip or palate
- Delivery complications
- Possible miscarriage
- Newborn or infant death

Goodheart-Willcox Publisher

Medications

The effects of most medications on unborn babies are unknown. Therefore, a pregnant person should not take any medication without consulting with their doctor. This includes prescriptions prior to the pregnancy, over-the-counter medications, dietary supplements, and even herbal or natural products. Taking more than the prescribed amount of a medication can be dangerous, too.

Drugs

Some babies are exposed to recreational drugs like cocaine, crack, heroin, marijuana, ecstasy, and other hallucinogens during their time in the womb. Some pregnant people also take powerful narcotics (pain-relieving or sleep-inducing drugs), with or without a prescription. Drugs can cross the placenta quickly and reach the baby. If a pregnant person is addicted to drugs, chances are their baby is, too.

Some of the effects of drugs can be seen immediately in babies, such as:

- early birth or death before birth
- *withdrawal symptoms* (high-pitched cry, shaking, twitching, vomiting, fever, trouble breathing, poor feeding, and rubbing the nose until the skin bleeds)
- damage to a baby's brain, eyes, heart, limbs, intestines, and urinary tract (with cocaine use)

By the school-age and teen years, children exposed to drugs during fetal development may show mood disorders and an inability to focus. In other words, the damage was done very early, but symptoms didn't appear until later in life.

Besides the direct effects of drugs, pregnant people who use drugs often neglect their own health. In many cases, these people eat poorly, smoke, or abuse alcohol in addition to drugs.

Some never see a doctor during pregnancy. For these reasons, babies who were exposed to drugs are much less likely to live a healthy life.

Emotional Health During Pregnancy

The pregnant person's emotional health can also impact prenatal development. Positive thoughts and feelings influence the health of a baby. When a pregnant person is happy and calm, their heartbeat and breathing slow down and their muscles relax. These factors lead to an easier pregnancy and delivery.

About one in eleven pregnant people experience depression and excessive stress during pregnancy, called *toxic stress*. These people are more likely to engage in unhealthy habits, refuse treatment for depression and stress, and skip prenatal visits.

Stress hormones cross the placenta to the baby. In the later stages of prenatal development, the baby can detect changes in the parent's heartbeat and breathing rates, too. The unborn baby can handle some stress, but if the stress is prolonged, severe, or frequent, it is dangerous. Toxic stress may result in the following outcomes:

- early birth and lower birthweight.
- lag in brain development.
- change in the epigenome, which "silences" the gene that controls overproduction of stress hormones. This causes the newborn to be more **vulnerable** (easily affected; sensitive) to the actions of others.
- fussy temperament and sleep problems.
- developmental delays and behavioral problems.

Focus on Mental Health

The best choice for anyone is to avoid exposure to illegal/recreational drugs, but for pregnant people, avoiding drugs can mean better mental health for their child during school age and teen years. Providing the best life for your unborn baby starts with your decisions during pregnancy. Make your choices count!

Focus on Mental Health

Your body has a gene that calms you after stress. A pregnant person's stress levels can affect this gene in an unborn child. Excessive or prolonged stress during pregnancy is detrimental to the baby's health; people who are pregnant should focus on mental health practices that boost resilience and contentment. Coping positively with stress while pregnant can give your unborn baby a head start at good mental health!

How Early Exposures to Substances Affect the Prenatal Brain and the Child After Birth

Children's first environment is one of chemicals—substances. Some chemicals, such as quality nutrients from a pregnant person's well-balanced diet, are essential to good health of the unborn and nursing baby. Some chemicals, however, are toxic and create devastating and lifelong impacts on children. Harmful substances are found in nicotine, alcohol, prescribed and over-the-counter medications, and in illegal recreational drugs. The effects of specific substances on the child are complex.

There are two ways that substances taken by a pregnant person can affect their baby. The first way is during pregnancy, when chemicals cross the placenta and enter the unborn baby's body. Many substances affect the neurotransmitters in the baby's brain, which are also chemicals. Neurotransmitters eventually help facilitate the process of learning in all developmental domains.

If harmful substances are present during the germinal stage, the baby usually does not survive. During the embryonic stage, harmful substances that reach the unborn baby's brain result in physical damage, such as a baby being born blind, deaf, without certain limbs, with heart problems, or with neural tube defects (defects related to the brain, spine, or spinal cord). If harmful substances affect the unborn during the fetal stage, neurotransmitters and brain processes are affected, causing intellectual and behavioral problems after birth.

The second way substance abuse alters a child's development is in the neonatal period—often beginning 72 hours after delivery and lasting throughout the neonatal (newborn) stage. The baby suffers from withdrawal symptoms called *neonatal withdrawal syndrome* or *neonatal discontinuation*. Substances taken by a pregnant person in the last trimester often lead to issues for the baby, such as preterm delivery, poor feeding and diarrhea, irritability, tremors, convulsions,

SciePro/Shutterstock.com

sleep disturbances, and respiratory problems. If the baby lives, the initial symptoms usually end within a month, but other effects, such as sensory-motor, intellectual, and behavioral problems, are seen throughout childhood and often beyond.

Thinking Activity

Many questions about the effects of toxicity remain unanswered. As a class, respond to the following questions.

1. Why do you think harmful practices, such as not getting adequate nutrition and substance abuse, often occur together?
2. What suggestions do you have for overcoming negative impacts on children due to exposure to harmful substances?
3. What is the best way to reach parents-to-be about the intake of substances under their control? How should substance abuse by pregnant people be handled in today's society?

Photo: Tom Wang/Shutterstock.com

Although some factors are uncontrollable during prenatal development, such as genetic factors, environmental factors are often controllable to a certain degree. A healthy pregnancy requires a strong support system, a hazard-free environment, adequate sleep, quality medical care, and proper nutrition.

Lesson 5.2 Review and Assessment

1. How does heredity affect the developing fetus? (5.2.1)
   A. Twenty-three chromosomes are given from each biological parent, and the genes that are paired up from each parent's chromosomes will determine all the child's traits.
   B. A child will inherit all the traits of his/her parents' chromosomes.
   C. Forty-six chromosome pairs determine all of the child's traits during conception.
   D. The sperm and egg both contain 23 pairs of chromosomes, which contain the DNA that will write the child's genetic code.

2. Which of the following is true about dominant and recessive traits? (5.2.1)
   A. Dominant traits must be inherited from both parents to present themselves in the child.
   B. Dominant traits will always present themselves in the child.
   C. Recessive traits always skip a generation because they do not always present themselves.
   D. Recessive traits are inherited from one parent who is a carrier of that trait.

3. A couple is trying to conceive their first child. What will determine whether the baby is a boy or a girl? (5.2.1)
   A. If the female contributes a Y sex chromosome, the baby will be a girl.
   B. If the male contributes an X sex chromosome, the baby will be a boy.
   C. If the female and male both contribute a Y sex chromosome, the baby will be a girl.
   D. If the male contributes a Y sex chromosome, the baby will be a boy.

4. Bryan and Arianna are adopting a child. They are worried their child might have a genetic disorder since they don't know the genetic history of the biological parents. What would cause their adopted baby to have sickle-cell anemia or cystic fibrosis? (5.2.2)
   A. Their adopted baby would only have to inherit a dominant trait from one parent.
   B. Their adopted baby would have to inherit a recessive trait from both parents.
   C. Their adopted baby would have to experience a chromosomal abnormality to have these diseases.
   D. Their adopted baby would have to inherit an X-linked recessive gene from both parents.

5. Which is an example of a chromosomal disorder? (5.2.2)
   A. Huntington's disease
   B. Duchenne muscular dystrophy
   C. Down syndrome
   D. Tay-Sachs disease

6. Sydney is pregnant. Her partner is verbally and emotionally abusive to her, causing Sydney to experience stress and depression. How does this affect her unborn baby? (5.2.3)
   A. This type of stress is unfortunate but does not pose a direct threat to the unborn baby.
   B. This type of stress can cause the unborn baby to inherit mood disorders like depression and anxiety, or to have stress-induced high blood pressure.
   C. Stress and depression can lead to heart problems for the pregnant person, causing strain on the developing baby.
   D. This type of stress can cause emotional and developmental delays, early birth, or behavioral problems.

Lesson 5.3

Health Habits Prior to and During Pregnancy

Key Terms

amniocentesis

chorionic villus sampling (CVS)

congenital condition

folic acid

MyPlate

nutrients

obstetricians

premature birth

prenatal supplement

ultrasound

Learning Outcomes

After studying this lesson, you will be able to

5.3-1 **analyze** the importance of good health habits prior to pregnancy.

5.3-2 **identify** signs of pregnancy.

5.3-3 **describe** medical and nutritional needs during pregnancy.

Reading and Notetaking Activity

How much do a person's daily habits affect their developing baby? Before reading this lesson, research this question using two to three sources. Then, write a one-page essay summarizing your findings. After reading this lesson, compare what you learned with your sources' information. How reliable were your sources?

Introduction

The March of Dimes, an organization specializing in healthy pregnancies, urges pregnant people to "be good to your baby before it is born." Pregnant people should take this message seriously. Because experts know more about pregnancy, childbirth, and infant care than ever before, there are many proven ways to keep both the pregnant person and developing baby healthy and safe.

Optimum (the best) health care begins before conception. Good health habits throughout the younger years help prepare a person for childbearing. It can take time for a person to prepare their body for a healthy pregnancy. Many doctors say that even for healthy person, prenatal care is at least a one-year event.

5.3-1 Health Habits Prior to Pregnancy

Health habits before pregnancy can impact a person's ability both to become pregnant and to carry that pregnancy to term. Annual medical exams are a form of preventive care that can help people achieve overall health and well-being. By visiting the doctor regularly, diseases or disorders may be prevented or diagnosed early and treated. Annual exams will also establish a baseline to compare to a person's health during pregnancy.

In addition to annual medical exams, people should also engage in other healthy habits to maintain good physical health prior to pregnancy. These healthy habits include:

- getting plenty of physical activity
- making nutritious food choices
- managing stress in healthy ways
- getting plenty of sleep
- avoiding high-risk behaviors, such as smoking, drinking, or abusing drugs

MyPlate is a food guidance system developed by the U.S. Department of Agriculture (USDA) to recommend nutritious food choices for people two years of age and older. The MyPlate website provides tools for people to develop their own daily food plans and to track the foods they eat each day. This system can help people create healthier eating habits. People should make nutritious meals a priority before becoming pregnant to ensure they are receiving the right amount of nutrients. **Nutrients** are substances found in food that the body needs to grow and function. There are six types of nutrients: carbohydrates, proteins, fats, vitamins, minerals, and water (**Figure 5.14**).

Anyone who is capable of becoming pregnant should also consume 400 micrograms of folic acid daily, either from a supplement or from fortified foods. **Folic acid** is the **synthetic** (not natural) form of the B vitamin folate. Folic acid is more readily absorbed by the body than folate. This B vitamin reduces a baby's risk for neural tube defects.

Figure 5.14 Types of Nutrients

Nutrient	What Does It Do?	Where Is It Found?
Carbohydrates	Supply energy to the body (short-term or long-term)	Fruits, vegetables, grains, dairy products
Proteins	Build and maintain the body's cells and tissues	Meats, poultry, fish, eggs, dairy products, legumes, beans, nuts and seeds, grains
Fats	Supply energy to the body and help the body absorb and transport certain vitamins	Meat and dairy products, vegetable oils, nuts and seeds, and other plant-based products
Vitamins	Regulate various body processes such as blood clotting, the immune system, and maintaining healthy skin	Various foods depending on type of vitamin; supplements
Minerals	Promote normal growth and development	Various foods depending on type of mineral; supplements
Water	Helps regulate body temperature, lubricates joints, protects sensitive tissues, helps get rid of waste, and moves oxygen and nutrients throughout body	It is recommended that people drink 8 to 10 cups of water per day

Goodheart-Willcox Publisher

5.3-2 **Signs of Pregnancy**

A person is unable to feel the sperm and egg unite. They cannot feel cells divide as the baby begins to develop. Typically, a person will not even realize that they might be pregnant until a couple of weeks after conception. Nevertheless, their body immediately nourishes and protects the new life. Hormones trigger changes in some of the person's organs. These changes show themselves as common signs of pregnancy.

The signs of pregnancy are divided into presumptive and positive signs (**Figure 5.15**). The *presumptive signs* could be signs of pregnancy or not. *Positive signs*, however, are determined by medical professionals as definitely being caused by pregnancy.

Figure 5.15 **Signs of Pregnancy**
Presumptive Signs

Amenorrhea (menstruation stops)—If the person is usually regular in their menstrual cycle, a delay of 10 or more days is a sign.

Nausea—Nausea is present in about ½ to ⅔ of all pregnancies. Because it often occurs in the morning hours, it is called *morning sickness*. Nausea may happen at any time of the day. Nausea occurring consistently or in a pattern from weeks 4–12 is a sign.

Tiredness—Many people feel tired during the first few months of pregnancy.

Frequency of urination—Hormones can cause more frequent urination. As the uterus expands, it puts pressure on the bladder.

Swelling and tenderness of the breasts—This is often the first sign.

Skin discoloration—Darkening of skin may occur on the face and nipples. Stretch marks may be seen as the breasts and abdomen enlarge.

Internal changes—Doctors often note softening of the cervix (Goodell's sign). There may also be a softening of the lower part of the uterus (Hegar's sign) and a bluish tinge to the vagina and cervix due to circulatory congestion (Chadwick's sign). The uterus is also enlarged with irregular areas of firmness and softness (Piskacek's sign).

Other signs—Other symptoms include backache, groin pains, dizziness, abdominal swelling, leg cramps, varicose veins, and indigestion.

Positive Signs

HCG (human chorionic gonadotrophin)—HCG is a hormone found in the blood and urine of pregnant people. Lab tests done at home or in the doctor's office can detect the hormone's presence toward the end of the first week of pregnancy. Over-the-counter home pregnancy tests provide privacy and fast results, but may be inaccurate due to testing too early (before a missed period) or not following directions exactly. When HCG tests are done by doctors, the hormone can be detected sooner, more accurately, and can result in other findings, such as the week of the pregnancy and if there are multiple embryos.

Fetal heartbeat—The baby's heartbeat can be detected through an ultrasound as early as six weeks in some cases. It can be heard through a special device called a doppler at 10–12 weeks and through a stethoscope at 18–20 weeks.

Fetal movement—Spontaneous movement of the baby begins at 11 weeks but is typically not felt until 16–18 weeks.

Fetal image—The baby's image may be seen with ultrasound scanning.

Fetal shape—The baby's shape may be felt through the abdominal wall.

Uterine contractions—A doctor can accurately detect these painless contractions.

Goodheart-Willcox Publisher

5.3-3 Health Habits During Pregnancy

Health habits for pregnant people are similar to good health habits for all people. When a person is pregnant, however, health habits have an even greater effect on their and their baby's overall health. Only a few health habits change during pregnancy. Because each pregnancy differs, people should ask their doctors for any specific health guidelines.

Medical Care

Medical care during pregnancy (prenatal care) is the best way to make childbearing safe and successful. If a person believes they are pregnant, they should make an appointment with a doctor as soon as possible whether the pregnancy is a first, second, or later pregnancy. Starting good prenatal care early in pregnancy greatly reduces the risk of complications. Many pregnant people choose to visit **obstetricians**, or doctors who specialize in pregnancy and birth.

The First Appointment

Scheduling a medical appointment as soon as a person discovers they are pregnant is critical. The first prenatal appointment sets a foundation for medical care throughout the pregnancy. If the person has a spouse/romantic partner or if they will have a birth partner, it is a good idea for that person to attend this appointment as well.

During the first appointment, the doctor will:
- gather general information and health history.
- gather details on reproductive health, menstrual cycles, and any past pregnancies.
- answer questions about pregnancy.
- perform a complete physical exam (**Figure 5.16**).
- give advice on health habits to follow.
- give an estimate of the baby's *due date* (given as the expected week). This might be adjusted later in the pregnancy. The length of a healthy pregnancy varies by as much as 37 days. Only about 5 percent of pregnant people deliver on their doctor's estimated due date, but 70 percent deliver within 10 days of this date.

Follow-Up Appointments

Usually the doctor sees a pregnant person once a month during the first six months of pregnancy. Visits increase to twice a month during the seventh and eighth months. During the ninth month, visits increase to once a week or more. If complications arise, or if the pregnant person is high-risk, there will be appointments more often.

Figure 5.16 **Physical Exam for Pregnant People**

- Blood pressure, pulse, respiration rates, and weight are recorded
- Breasts are examined
- Pelvic exam is performed, which may include a pelvic measurement
- A blood sample is collected to confirm pregnancy, check for blood type, rule out *anemia* (uh-NEE-me-uh) (condition caused by lack of iron), check blood sugar level, and test for diseases that can harm a baby
- Urine sample is collected

MBI/Shutterstock.com

Goodheart-Willcox Publisher

Going to each of the follow-up appointments is important. Doctors continue to carefully monitor the pregnancy. Through regular appointments, the chance of delivering a healthy baby increases, the discomforts of pregnancy may be lessened, and confidence is likely to build. Health care providers should be notified if any alarming symptoms arise between scheduled visits.

Prenatal Testing

As a pregnancy progresses, doctors may also perform several types of prenatal tests, which help to monitor the health of the baby and the pregnant person. These tests can help detect and, in some cases, correct abnormalities before they become too severe. They can also diagnose chromosomal disorders before birth and identify risk factors for the baby's development and delivery.

Blood Tests

There are three main blood tests that screen for major prenatal disorders (**Figure 5.17**). These tests are done by drawing blood from the pregnant person. Because a blood test is **noninvasive** (not requiring insertion or cutting) for the fetus, it poses no risk to the unborn baby.

Other blood tests are used to check for conditions other than possible abnormalities in the fetus. Blood tests can screen for sexually transmitted infections at a person's first medical visit. Another blood test, which is given at six or seven months, screens for gestational diabetes.

Ultrasound

An **ultrasound** is a test in which sound waves bounce off the fetus to produce an image of the fetus inside the womb. The picture of the fetus the ultrasound produces is called a *sonogram*. Sonograms are used to monitor the unborn baby.

To perform an ultrasound, a technician inserts a *transducer* into the pregnant person's vagina (for early pregnancy) or moves the transducer over the abdomen (later in pregnancy). The sound waves the transducer emits are **deflected** (changing direction) or absorbed at different rates, depending on whether they hit bone, organ tissue, blood, or water. These differences are changed into electrical impulses, which produce a visual image of the fetus on a monitor. From this image, the doctor can see whether the baby seems to be developing correctly.

A 3-D ultrasound can help specialists determine the **severity** (seriousness) of any structural defects. For example, these machines can detect the thickness of a fluid-filled area behind the unborn baby's neck (called *nuchal translucency*).

Figure 5.17 **Blood Tests That Screen for Major Prenatal Disorders**

Test	Description
First trimester screen	Offered to all pregnant people between weeks 11–14 of pregnancy. It measures AFP (alpha-fetoprotein), HCG (human chorionic gonadotropin), and estriol (a protein found during pregnancy). The screening assesses the risk for three chromosomal disorders (Down syndrome, Edward's Syndrome, and Patau Syndrome) with 88 percent accuracy.
Cell-free fetal DNA test (also called noninvasive prenatal diagnostic testing)	Offered to people at high risk for certain chromosomal disorders. People who are 35 years of age and older who did not take the *First Trimester Screen*, or who had abnormal results on the *First Trimester Screen* can take this test at 10 weeks' gestation or later. This test is 99 percent accurate and will also determine the unborn baby's gender.
Multiple marker screen	Given between 15–20 weeks gestation to people who did not take the *First Trimester Screen*, who are at high risk for chromosomal disorders, or who had ultrasound testing showing abnormalities. This test reveals the risk of a chromosomal disorder or a neural tube defect, such as *spina bifida*.

Goodheart-Willcox Publisher

Focus on Careers

Diagnostic Medical Sonographer

Diagnostic medical sonographers use equipment to collect reflected echoes to form an image that may be videotaped, transmitted, or photographed for interpretation and diagnosis by a physician. Obstetric and gynecologic diagnostic medical sonographers specialize in the imaging of the female reproductive system and the fetus of a pregnant person to track the baby's growth and health.

Career cluster: Health science.

Education: Educational requirements include an associate's degree and special certification.

Job outlook: Future employment opportunities for diagnostic medical sonographers are expected to grow much faster than the average for all occupations.

To learn more about a career as a diagnostic medical sonographer, visit the United States Department of Labor's *Occupational Outlook Handbook* website. You will also be able to compare the job responsibilities, educational requirements, job outlook, and average pay of diagnostic medical sonographers with similar occupations.

Photo: MBI/Shutterstock.com

This test can confirm Down syndrome early in the pregnancy and usually follows the *First Trimester Screen* if results of this test indicate abnormalities in the fetus.

Because ultrasounds are considered safe, they are used fairly routinely to check for abnormalities, size, gender, support systems (placenta, umbilical cord, amniotic fluid), multiple babies, and the baby's position prior to birth. A typical pregnancy will include two or three ultrasounds.

Chorionic Villus Sampling

Chorionic villus sampling (CVS) is a procedure for finding abnormalities in the fetus. CVS is only done on women whose unborn children are at high-risk for abnormalities or whose *First Trimester Screen* revealed potential problems. This procedure is performed by testing a small sample taken from the chorion, which will later develop into the fetal part of the placenta. CVS is used between weeks 10 and 12 of pregnancy. This test can detect serious problems with the fetus early in the pregnancy.

CVS is completed by inserting a hollow tube through the vagina and cervix, into the uterus, and then guiding it to the chorion. (Another method is guiding a needle through the abdomen to the uterus.) *Chorionic villi* are fingerlike projections that branch out from the surface of the chorion and transport nutrients to, and wastes from, the unborn. A small section of the chorionic villi is painlessly suctioned off and analyzed for congenital problems. CVS has a slight risk (one percent) of infection, which can result in the loss of the baby.

Amniocentesis

Amniocentesis (AM-nee-oh-sen-TEE-sis) is a prenatal test used to check for the presence of over 100 congenital conditions. A **congenital condition** is a physical or biochemical problem in a baby that is present at birth and may be caused by genetic or environmental factors. An amniocentesis is given using the same criteria that is used for CVS. Usually it checks for conditions such as Down syndrome, Tay-Sachs disease, sickle-cell anemia, and cystic fibrosis.

To perform the test, a medical specialist inserts a needle through the abdominal wall into the uterus. An ultrasound is performed at the same time to position the needle. The specialist draws a small amount of fluid from the amniotic sac.

Amniotic fluid provides much information because cells cast off by the fetus float in the fluid. These cells are cultivated in a lab for three to five weeks and are then checked for congenital problems.

Amniocentesis cannot be done until the fetus is 15–18 weeks old. At this time, there is enough amniotic fluid for the test. Due to the lab time required, a person will be 20–21 weeks pregnant when they learn the results. Amniocentesis is a safe procedure in 99.5 percent of cases, but it is not a routine procedure. This is because of the risks that may result, which include **premature birth** (born too soon) or even loss of the baby. Amniocentesis is used only when problems are suspected or if the age of the pregnant person is determined to be a risk factor.

Nutrition

During the first week after conception, the embryo gets all of its nutrients from the yolk sac, which is a temporary structure that nourishes the unborn baby in early pregnancy. By the twelfth week of pregnancy, the baby completely depends on the pregnant person for food. There is a direct link between what a pregnant person eats and the following factors:

- their weight
- the unborn baby's weight
- the baby's growth
- the baby's intellectual capacity
- the baby's physical performance

Good nutrition during pregnancy is vital because pregnant people have an increased need for iron, folate, protein, and choline. Pregnant people need 600 micrograms of folate daily. Green leafy vegetables, citrus, and whole-wheat bread are good sources of folate; however, doctors often recommend pregnant people take a **prenatal supplement** that contains folic acid.

Focus on Social Studies

The History of Ultrasound Technology

The science behind the ultrasound—in which sound waves are bounced off an area to create an image—was not discovered for the purpose of imaging fetuses and tracking their development. One of the earliest versions of ultrasound technology was what is now called SONAR (Sound Navigation and Ranging). Used by war ships during World War II, SONAR helped ships navigate unfamiliar and potentially dangerous seas by bouncing sound waves off the floor of the ocean and interpreting those sound waves to navigate and detect submarines. Because submarines were a common weapon during World War II, SONAR was an important and effective tactical tool.

It was not until the late 1940s that scientists began using ultrasound technology on the human body. Early ultrasound scans were conducted on patients who sat in water-filled gun turrets, and these scans looked similar to modern seismographs, which depict earthquake activity with a series of lines and spikes. Since then, science has come a long way to create the ultrasound technology doctors use to image babies in the womb. Based on what ultrasound technology is used for now and on what it has been used for in the past, what other applications of this technology do you think science could explore? What else could be achieved through ultrasound technology? Share your ideas with a classmate.

Photo: Roman Zaiets/Shutterstock.com

Prenatal supplements also supply iron and other important vitamins and minerals, but most do not contain choline. Pregnant people must be sure to include good food sources of choline, such as eggs or salmon, in their diets.

Pregnant people should also have at least eight 8-ounce glasses of water daily. Caffeine intake should be limited during pregnancy. Daily intake of caffeine from all sources (including coffee, tea, soft drinks, and chocolate) should not exceed 200 milligrams.

Seafood is the best source of omega-3 fats. These fats provide benefits to both the pregnant person and the baby. Some types of seafood, however, are also sources of contaminants, such as mercury. Too much mercury can damage the fetus's developing brain and nervous system. For these reasons, pregnant people are encouraged to eat 8–12 ounces of seafood each week, focusing on seafood that is lower in mercury.

MyPlate provides guidelines to help people meet their nutritional needs during pregnancy (**Figure 5.18**). To meet the nutrient needs for themselves and their babies, pregnant people often need about 340–450 more calories per day in the second and third trimesters.

Figure 5.18 MyPlate Guidelines for Pregnant Person

Trimester	1st Trimester	2nd Trimester	3rd Trimester
Calorie Guidelines	No added calories	May increase calories slightly (consult with a professional)	May increase calories slightly (consult with a professional)

Food	Guidelines		
Grains Make half your grains whole grains	Find whole-grain foods by reading the Nutrition Facts label and ingredients list.		
Vegetables Vary your veggies	Aim to eat dark green, red, and orange veggies; beans and peas; starchy veggies, and other forms of veggies		
Fruits Focus on whole fruits	Focus on eating the whole fruit. Choose fruits that are fresh, frozen, canned, or dried.		
Dairy Move to low-fat or fat-free milk or yogurt	Consider fat-free milk, yogurt, and soy beverages (soy milk) to cut back on your saturated fat.		
Protein Foods Vary your protein routine	Mix up your protein foods to include seafood, beans and peas, unsalted nuts and seeds, soy products, eggs, and lean meats and poultry.		
Sodium, Fat, and Added Sugars	Drink and eat less sodium, saturated fat, and added sugars.		

*These are general guidelines. Check with your health care provider to make sure you are getting adequate nutrition.

Goodheart-Willcox Publisher

Figure 5.18 Nutritional needs vary among individuals, so people should consult their doctors or dietitians about what to eat during pregnancy. *Based on these guidelines, what meals could a pregnant person have for breakfast, lunch, and dinner?*

Copyright Goodheart-Willcox Co., Inc.

Chapter 5 Pregnancy **151**

More calories might be added for multiple babies. A pregnant person should consult directly with reliable medical professionals and dietitians to determine their individual needs during pregnancy.

Weight Gain

Typical and recommended weight gain during pregnancy is approximately 25–35 pounds. The exact amount depends on the individual person and their health factors. Doctors make considerations for weight recommendations based on these factors. Some people may be advised to gain more or less than the typical 25–35 pounds. Additional weight gain might be needed to support the health of multiple births (twins, triplets, etc.). Much of the person's weight gain goes to the growing baby and the supporting tissues (**Figure 5.19**).

Doctors monitor weight during pregnancy. Added weight can cause strain on the pregnant person's heart and make them uncomfortable. Doctors also watch for sudden weight gain and unusual swelling. These conditions can be serious and require **prompt** (immediate) medical attention. Low weight gain can also be concerning. This can signal the baby is not growing properly or receiving enough nutrients.

Typically, a pregnant person will gain about 2–4 pounds during the first trimester. During the second and third trimesters, a gain of about 1 pound per week is common. Sudden weight loss or gain during pregnancy may indicate a medical problem.

Physical Activity and Exercise

Unless advised by their doctor to limit physical activity, a pregnant person can and should be active. Activity helps maintain body functions, strengthens muscles used in delivery, increases energy, and relieves tension (**Figure 5.20**).

ZephyrMedia/Shutterstock.com

Figure 5.20 Physical activity has many benefits for pregnant people. *What types of physical activities should pregnant people avoid?*

Figure 5.19 Weight Distribution During Pregnancy

Portion of Added Weight	Typical Weight in Pounds
Baby	7–8
Amniotic fluid	2
Placenta	1–2
Uterus growth	2
Extra blood volume	3–5
Breast tissue growth	1–2
Other body fluids	3–5
Fat stores and other body tissues	6–9
Total	**25–35 pounds**

Goodheart-Willcox Publisher

Many doctors advise pregnant people to avoid contact sports, activities that jolt the pelvic region, and activities that could result in falls. Walking, swimming, and yoga are all commonly recommended exercises during pregnancy. There are even special exercise classes for pregnant people.

In childbirth classes, people may learn conditioning exercises to relieve back and leg strain that often occur later in the pregnancy. They can also learn exercises that prepare the pelvic muscles for delivery.

Hygiene Practices

People should continue their normal grooming and body care habits during pregnancy. Regular hygiene prevents bacteria and possible infection.

Many doctors suggest pregnant people do the following:

- Have a dental checkup (**Figure 5.21**. Recent studies show a link between gum disease in pregnancy and early birth of the baby.
- Avoid very cold or very hot baths and hot tubs.
- Wear comfortable clothes with low-heeled or flat shoes.
- Replace baths with showers during the last four to six weeks of pregnancy. This practice helps to prevent internal infection.

Rest and Sleep

A pregnant person needs much rest and sleep (**Figure 5.22**). Many doctors advise eight to nine hours of sleep each night. In addition, pregnant people need at least one 15- to 30-minute rest (with or without sleep) during the day. Many people feel the most tired during the first few months and last weeks of pregnancy. Exhaustion is never good, especially in pregnancy. A sleepless night, however, is not dangerous. If a person has frequent sleep problems, they should talk with their doctor. They should never take sleep aids (even over-the-counter medications) unless prescribed or recommended by their doctor.

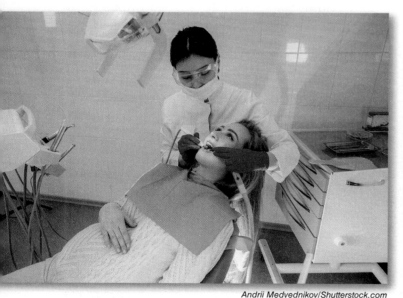

Andrii Medvednikov/Shutterstock.com

Figure 5.21 This pregnant person is having a dental checkup. *Why do you think it is important for pregnant people to keep up with their dental checkups?*

Ground Picture/Shutterstock.com

Figure 5.22 Getting enough rest is especially important during pregnancy. *Why do you think a pregnant person might be more tired than they were before they became pregnant?*

1. Why are a person's health habits prior to pregnancy important? (5.3.1)
   A. If a person becomes pregnant, all their previous health issues can transfer to the unborn baby through the placenta.
   B. A person's health habits can impact their ability to get pregnant or carry a pregnancy to term.
   C. If a person has good health habits before pregnancy, they will have good health habits during pregnancy.
   D. Health concerns before pregnancy are too risky to address during pregnancy because they may harm the unborn baby.

2. Which of the following are early signs of pregnancy? (5.3.2)
   A. Swollen, tender breasts and amenorrhea
   B. Fetal movement
   C. Increased urination due to pressure on the bladder from the uterus
   D. Skin discoloration

3. There are several prenatal tests that may be conducted. Which prenatal test can detect Down syndrome, Edward's Syndrome, and Patau Syndrome? (5.3.3)
   A. Multiple Marker Screen
   B. Amniocentesis
   C. Chorionic villus sampling (CVS)
   D. First Trimester Screen

4. Certain nutritional needs must be met during pregnancy. What substance is typically not included in prenatal supplements? (5.3.3)
   A. Folate
   B. Iron
   C. Choline
   D. Calcium

5. What is a recommended nutritional guideline for pregnancy? (5.3.3)
   A. Increasing caloric intake in the second and third trimesters
   B. Making sure to avoid red meat during pregnancy
   C. Following a strict diet to make sure specific nutritional amounts are reached
   D. Eliminating fat and sugar from the diet during the second and third trimesters

6. Four friends are pregnant at the same time. Who is practicing good health habits during their pregnancy? (5.3.3)
   A. Kisha gets plenty of physical activity and has kept up her participation in her recreational lacrosse league during pregnancy.
   B. Emily makes sure to eat a nutritious diet, walk daily, and take hot baths to unwind at the end of the day.
   C. Isabel started a prenatal yoga class to strengthen her pelvic floor muscles for childbirth. She makes sure to rest once a day to recharge.
   D. Brenna is waiting to go to her regular dental check up until after the baby is born to avoid any harmful practices.

Chapter 5

Review and Assessment

Summary

Lesson 5.1

5.1-1   Human life begins with conception. Conception occurs when the sex cells (germ cells) of a biological male and female meet, and one sperm penetrates the egg (ovum).

5.1-2   From conception until the birth of a baby, a person experiences pregnancy (also referred to as gestation). Pregnancy lasts nine months and is split into three three-month trimesters. The development of the baby (prenatal development) is divided into three stages, known as the germinal stage, embryonic stage, and fetal stage.

5.1-2   Distinct changes occur during each stage of prenatal development: The fertilized egg (zygote) becomes a blastocyst that attaches itself to the uterine wall, the baby's support systems are created, and all body parts and systems of the unborn baby develop and mature.

5.1-3   Important development occurs with each new month of pregnancy to both the pregnant person and the unborn baby.

Lesson 5.2

5.2-1   During pregnancy, genetic factors and environmental factors play a role in the baby's development and can cause certain conditions, defects, or disorders.

5.2-1   Humans have 23 pairs of chromosomes (23 from each biological parent, 46 chromosomes total). These chromosomes carry DNA and gene pairs that determine all of the baby's traits. Whether a gene is dominant or recessive determines its likelihood of inheritance.

5.2-1   If a baby receives a Y sex cell from the father, the baby will be biologically male. If a baby receives an X sex cell from the father, the baby will be biologically female.

5.2-1   Some disorders or conditions are inherited through dominant or recessive traits in single genes. Chromosomal disorders are issues that affect the number of chromosomes or the structure of the chromosome. These are typically more serious since they involve multiple affected genes. Down syndrome is an example of a chromosomal disorder.

5.2-2   Environmental factors can also impact the developing fetus. These are largely within a pregnant person's control and include things like nicotine, alcohol, drug or medication use during pregnancy, exposure to chemicals or x-rays, and even the pregnant person's emotional health. A person's medical health and the age of both biological parents can also play a role in healthy fetal development.

5.2-2   Good health habits before pregnancy will benefit both the pregnant person and the unborn baby. Poor health habits can lead to the inability to get pregnant or to carry a baby to term.

Lesson 5.3

5.3-1   Prenatal care from a health care provider is the best way to ensure a successful and healthy pregnancy. Many prenatal tests can be done to detect birth defects or anything that is atypical. Proper nutrition is also a huge factor in a healthy pregnancy.

5.3-2 Signs of pregnancy include amenorrhea (lack of menstruation), tender or swollen breasts, nausea or fatigue, or increased urination. At home pregnancy tests can detect the HCG (pregnancy) hormone but can give inaccurate results. A blood test performed by a medical professional will have the most accurate results.

5.3-3 Along with proper nutrition, other positive health habits during pregnancy include good hygiene, getting plenty of rest, sleep, and safe exercise, and avoiding high risk activities that could harm the pregnant person or unborn baby.

College and Career Portfolio

Portfolio Checklist

Now that you know the purpose of your portfolio and how you will organize your portfolio, consider what items you want to include. If your portfolio is for a college program, you might include transcripts, a statement of purpose, or samples of your work. As you progress through this book, you will be advised about additional items to include in your portfolio.

It is helpful to have a checklist of components that should be included in your portfolio. Your instructor may provide you with or guide you in creating a checklist. Make sure to create a checklist that works best for you and for the purpose of your portfolio. Complete the following steps to create your portfolio checklist:

Compile a checklist of the items you want to include. If you need guidance, talk to your teacher or to a college/career counselor at your school.

Save your checklist to an easy-to-access location in your portfolio. Also print a copy and place it somewhere you can easily reference it and cross things off as they are completed.

Recall and Application

1. What is considered to be the age of viability? (5.1.2)
   A. 20 weeks
   B. 32 weeks
   C. 23 weeks
   D. 28 weeks

2. Which prenatal test inserts a needle through the abdominal wall into the uterus to collect a small amount of fluid? (5.3.3)
   A. Chorionic villus sampling (CVS)
   B. Alpha-fetoprotein (AFP)
   C. Cell-Free Fetal DNA Test
   D. Amniocentesis

3. Which of the following gives the correct order of development from conception to the fetal stage? (5.1.2)
   A. Zygote, morula, blastocyst, embryo, fetus
   B. Embryo, zygote, blastocyst, morula, fetus
   C. Morula, blastocyst, zygote, embryo, fetus
   D. Blastocyst, zygote, embryo, morula, fetus
4. In which month of pregnancy does an unborn baby's heart begin beating? (5.1.2)
   A. Month 3
   B. Month 1
   C. Month 5
   D. Month 2
5. A pregnant person feels their baby kick for the first time. What is this called? (5.1.2)
   A. Quickening
   B. Lightening
   C. Lanugo
   D. Braxton Hicks contractions
6. Which is true about chromosomes? (5.2.1)
   A. All humans have 46 pairs of chromosomes.
   B. Sex chromosomes for males and females both involve X and Y.
   C. Chromosomes contain DNA and genes.
   D. Female and male sex cells are the only cells that do not carry chromosomes.
7. What threat does the Rh factor pose to an unborn baby? (5.2.2)
   A. It can cause high blood pressure and swelling.
   B. In certain cases, the pregnant person's antibodies may fight the baby's blood cells.
   C. It can cause brain, liver, and blood problems.
   D. It can cause the baby to be born blind, deaf, or with an intellectual disability.
8. What are the potential effects of Alcohol-Related Birth Defects (ARBD)? (5.2.3)
   A. Problems with the heart, kidneys, bones, or hearing
   B. Problems with learning, executive functions, vision, or hearing
   C. Ear infections and breathing problems
   D. Increased risk of congenital disabilities or childhood cancer

9. When does a fetus develop silky body hair and a protective coating on its skin during gestation? (5.1.3)
   A. Month 8
   B. Month 6
   C. Month 9
   D. Month 5
10. How does a pregnant person's emotional health affect the unborn baby? (5.2.3)
    A. If a pregnant person is happy and calm, the baby is more likely to be happy as a newborn.
    B. A person who has depression will also be affected by postpartum depression once the baby is born.
    C. Toxic stress of the pregnant person can cause developmental delays and behavioral problems in the baby.
    D. Anxiety can cross the placenta and cause the likelihood of an anxiety disorder in the unborn baby.
11. Which is true about nutritional needs of a pregnant person? (5.3.3)
    A. Pregnant people need to double their water intake during pregnancy.
    B. Pregnant people should eat 8-12 ounces of seafood per week.
    C. Caffeine is harmful and should be avoided during pregnancy.
    D. Pregnant people need 1200 micrograms of folate daily.
12. Which prenatal test can be done at 10 weeks of pregnancy? (5.3.3)
    A. First Trimester Screen
    B. Multiple Marker Screen
    C. Ultrasound
    D. Cell-Free Fetal DNA Test
13. Which recessive genetic disorder causes thick, sticky mucous secretions and clogs passageways in the lungs and pancreas? (5.3.3)
    A. Sickle-cell anemia
    B. Cystic fibrosis
    C. Tay-Sachs disease
    D. PKU or phenylketonuria

14. Which is an example of both a genetic and environmental defect? (5.3.3)
    A. Down syndrome
    B. Hemophilia
    C. Cleft palate
    D. Marfan syndrome
15. Which is true about female and male biological processes related to conception? (5.1.1)
    A. A female produces eggs each month, beginning at puberty.
    B. A male produces sperm until around the age of 75.
    C. A female is born with all her eggs.
    D. A male sperm dies within one hour if it doesn't reach the egg.

Critical Thinking

1. **Make inferences.** The basic principles of growth and development state that growth and development are constant, happen in sequenced steps, happen at different rates, and have interrelated parts. How do the stages in prenatal development follow the principles of growth and development? Give specific examples as part of your explanation.
2. **Identify.** Create a checklist that contains all the prenatal changes described in this lesson. Color code your checklist so that each color represents a different stage of prenatal development. Have a partner look over your checklist for accuracy.
3. **Compare and contrast.** On separate index cards, write three to five factors that might affect an unborn baby. Then, in small groups, combine everyone's index cards and determine whether they are genetic factors or environmental factors. Sort into two piles.
4. **Draw conclusions.** Two parents with blood types A and B want to have a child with blood type O. Is this possible? Are there any circumstances that would allow this couple to have a child with blood type O? Explain.

5. **Cause and effect.** Divide a piece of paper into two columns—one labeled *negative effect* and the other labeled *positive effect*. Then, list at least twelve potential behaviors or habits of pregnant people, writing them under the correct columns.
6. **Analyze.** A young couple you know is trying to get pregnant, and recently they have splurged on junk food and stopped exercising, with the reasoning that they want to "have fun" before they become pregnant. Is this a good idea or a bad one? Analyze how, if at all, these actions might affect their planned pregnancy.
7. **Evaluate.** Imagine that you are a doctor, and a person has just come to your office telling you they are pregnant. Their breasts feel tender, they have been having morning sickness, and they always feel tired. Evaluate these signs as either positive or presumptive. What other signs might you check for?
8. **Determine.** Your friend has just become pregnant and feels overwhelmed by all of the medical appointments and lifestyle changes suggested. To help your friend cope, create an organized list of all the medical appointments your friend should schedule as well as any lifestyle changes worth considering. Break these goals down into small tasks to help your friend feel less overwhelmed.

Core Skills

1. **Writing and speaking.** Imagine you are a school teacher, and your next unit in class is about conception. You must teach this concept to a class of sixth graders and a class of tenth graders. For each class, write a one-page explanation appropriate for that age group. Choose one explanation and give this speech to your class.

2. **Art, technology, and speaking.** Using material or electronic supplies, create a month-by-month illustration of a developing baby during gestation. (See Figure 5.6 for example.) Once you have finished these illustrations, compile them into a slideshow presentation describing the developmental changes that occur during the months of gestation. Deliver your presentation to the class.

3. **Writing.** Write a story about prenatal development from the unborn baby's point of view. Use your creativity to explore what life might be like for the baby as new developments occur before birth. Check your story for correct spelling, grammar, and punctuation.

4. **Health and technology.** Create an electronic presentation entitled "Eating for Two Requires Careful Planning." Include sample menus for a pregnant person for one week. You might also include pictures or a list of some nonessential foods they should avoid. Share your presentations with the class.

5. **Reading, speaking, and listening.** Read at least three reliable articles concerning prenatal care. Write a brief essay describing the main points of each article. Include the title of each article and the author. Present your main points to the class. As you listen to other presentations, write three questions you have. Ask one of your questions and write the presenter's response.

6. **Research and advocacy.** Research organizations in your community that provide services for expectant parents. Do any of the organizations provide prenatal or childbirth classes? Are classes offered for parenting, providing daily care for infants, and first aid? Do any of the organizations use volunteers? Choose one organization to visit and learn more about its history and goals. Take it a step further and become a volunteer to help the organization.

7. **CTE Career Readiness Practice.** Complete an oral history by interviewing a relatively new parent about their pregnancy. If you are unable to interview someone, read one or more case studies about pregnancy from reliable internet or library resources. How does the information you learned from the interview or reading compare to information presented by the author of your text? Write a detailed summary of your interview or reading, describing the experience of pregnancy.

Observations

1. Observe a nuclear family with a biological mother, father, and children. Which features seem to come from the mother's family and which from the father's family? Which features are similar across siblings, if any?

2. Either online or at a local art gallery, observe works of art that illustrate pregnancy. What aspects of pregnancy do they emphasize? Are there any aspects of pregnancy they avoid? How reflective do you think this art is of a pregnant person's experience of pregnancy?

Chapter 6

Special Circumstances of Pregnancy

Lesson 6.1 Special Medical Concerns of Pregnancy
Lesson 6.2 Teen Pregnancy

Essential Question

What are some medical and social circumstances that may affect a pregnancy?

Case Study — What Are the Consequences of Teen Parenthood?

As a class, read the case study and discuss the questions that follow. After you finish studying the chapter, discuss this case study again. Have your opinions changed based on what you learned?

Kelly, a high school junior, and Brantley, a high school senior, have been dating for a while. Kelly and Brantley went to prom and ended the night by having sex for the first time. Kelly thought that after having sex with Brantley they would be even closer as a couple. Instead, they saw each other less and less. Then Kelly took a home pregnancy test, and it came back positive.

Brantley was furious and said, "Why weren't you using contraceptives? How do I even know the baby's mine? Maybe you should just get an abortion." Kelly tried to respond, but Brantley said, "I don't want anything to do with you or your baby."

Kelly was stunned and hurt by Brantley's reaction and didn't know what to do. Kelly's parents would likely be upset and disappointed. Kelly wanted to go to college, but that didn't seem likely now.

Kelly didn't believe in abortion, but raising a child alone seemed impossible. What if Kelly's parents wouldn't help financially? How would Kelly pay medical bills and pay for baby supplies?

Give It Some Thought

1. Is Brantley being fair to Kelly? Is Kelly being fair to expect Brantley to be involved? What legal responsibilities or problems might Brantley face? Explain your answers.
2. What problems will Kelly likely face now and for many years to come? What other options might Kelly have?
3. What plans does Kelly need to make?

Altrendo Images/Shutterstock.com

Lesson 6.1

Special Medical Concerns of Pregnancy

Learning Outcomes

After studying this lesson, you will be able to

6.1-1 **describe** three of the most common ART procedures, including the drawbacks of each.

6.1-2 **compare** and **contrast** the different types of multiple pregnancies.

6.1-3 **explain** complications of pregnancy and congenital conditions.

Reading and Notetaking Activity

Before reading, skim the headings and write each heading in a different color or font on a separate piece of paper or electronically. As you read the chapter, take notes in the color or font you used for each heading. Then draw or copy and paste a small illustration or visual next to the section that will help you remember what you learned.

Introduction

Birth rates in the United States are declining, leading to fewer babies being born than in previous years. One reason for this decline is that many people are delaying having children to focus on their careers. Many people also choose to wait until they are financially ready to have a child. For people trying to become pregnant, the usual course of events is to conceive a baby within a year. About 10 percent of people in the United States, however, are unable to get pregnant or stay pregnant. People who are unable to conceive may undergo fertility treatments to have a baby.

Closely connected to fertility treatments is the rising occurrence of multiple pregnancies. When fertility treatments include hormones, the ovaries are stimulated, and the risk of multiple pregnancies is somewhat increased. Similarly, just before the end of a female's reproductive years, the ovaries may produce more hormones for a few months, resulting in multiple pregnancies.

6.1-1 Infertility and Sterility

Most people who try to conceive are able to do so within a year. Individuals who try to conceive and are unable to do so within a year are known as **infertile**. If a person miscarries over and over, they may also be infertile. About 40 percent of infertile people do not want children. About two-thirds of infertile people who do want children will conceive if treated for infertility. The remaining people will not successfully conceive because one or both partners are sterile. Being **sterile** means the couple is permanently unable to conceive or the uterus is unable to carry their biological child.

People often think that biological females account for almost all fertility problems. In one-third of the cases, infertility is due to the biological female. In another one-third of the cases, it is due to the biological male. The remaining cases are caused by a combination of both partners or by unknown reasons. When both adults are infertile, they have a much lower chance to conceive than individuals with only one infertile partner.

Reproductive diseases and problems with the reproductive organs are the main causes of infertility and sterility (**Figure 6.1**). Certain diseases, such as diabetes, and some prescription drugs, such as those for high blood pressure, may lessen fertility. Being exposed to certain drugs, chemicals, and radiation can **hamper** (interfere with) fertility. The same is true of sexually transmitted infections and smoking. Excessive physical activity, being overweight or underweight, and aging can also lead to fertility problems.

Treating Infertility

Infertile individuals who want to pursue having biological children can seek fertility counseling. **Fertility counseling** is a medical evaluation that seeks to determine the reasons for fertility problems and explores available treatment options. Tests are given to determine the problem. If a problem is found, the doctor may suggest steps to restore fertility.

Assisted reproductive technologies (ARTs) are methods infertile individuals may use to help them conceive. The most common treatments include using hormones or drugs to stimulate ovulation or balance hormone levels. Sometimes surgery is used to repair problems with the reproductive organs. If these treatments cannot correct the problem, then other methods may help infertile individuals conceive. Following are three of the most common ART procedures:

- **Artificial insemination** (also called *intrauterine insemination*) occurs when the sperm is introduced into the vagina or uterus by a medical procedure rather than by intercourse.
- **In vitro fertilization (IVF)** occurs when some of the eggs are surgically removed and fertilized with sperm in a laboratory dish (**Figure 6.2**). After a few days, fertilized eggs are implanted in the uterus.
- **Gamete intrafallopian transfer (GIFT)** occurs when a mixture of sperm and eggs is placed in the fallopian tubes, where fertilization can occur. Because more than one egg is present, conception is more likely, but a *multiple pregnancy* can occur, too.

Figure 6.1 Major Causes of Infertility and Sterility

Females	Males
• Lack of ovulation	• Low sperm count
• Hormone deficiencies	• Hormone deficiencies
• Irregular ovulation	• Inability of sperm to move (called *motility problems*)
• Damage to reproductive organs	• Damage to reproductive organs

Goodheart-Willcox Publisher

tilialucida/Shutterstock.com

Figure 6.2 The in vitro fertilization process involves combining the egg and sperm in a petri dish and then implanting them into the person's uterus. *What fertility problems does this ART method seek to avoid?*

In some cases, problems exist with the sperm, eggs, or both the sperm and eggs of the individuals. For example, one or both partners may be sterile. When these problems exist, individuals may opt to use an ART with the germ cells (sperm, eggs, or sperm and eggs) donated by other people. These donor cells would be used to attempt conception usually through IVF or GIFT.

If the person cannot carry a baby, they might consider using a **surrogate**, or a person who bears (sometimes both conceives and bears) a child for other people. The surrogate would carry the baby in their uterus, give birth to the baby, and sign their parenting rights over to the individuals hoping for a baby. Surrogates can conceive using an ART with their own eggs or with the eggs of the individual hoping for a baby. **Figure 6.3** shows different ART methods and potential challenges for each method.

Figure 6.3 ART Methods

Method	Used to...	Problems
Artificial insemination (also called *intrauterine insemination*)	Provide increased number of sperm for conception in the uterus.	• Slight risk of infection • If sperm is not from the partner, moral issues and legal issues may arise surrounding the rights of the donor
Hormone therapy (fertility drugs)	Stimulate ovaries to function properly.	• Multiple pregnancies
Microsurgery	Attempt to open the fallopian tubes.	• Risks of surgery, such as anesthetic and infection risks
In vitro fertilization (IVF)	Allow a person with permanently blocked fallopian tubes to have their eggs surgically removed and fertilized with sperm in a laboratory dish. After a few days, the fertilized eggs are implanted into the uterus. Impregnate a surrogate.	• Risks of surgery • Multiple births • Moral and legal issues
Gamete intrafallopian transfer (GIFT)	Increase chances of conception if the sperm count is low or if there are issues with ovulation. (A mixture of sperm and several eggs are surgically placed in the fallopian tubes.)	• Risks of surgery • Multiple births
Surrogate	Replace the infertile couple's role in bearing a child. Surrogate may (a) bear a child who is the infertile couple's biological child conceived by in vitro fertilization, (b) bear a child with the surrogate's egg and the biological father's sperm that were introduced to the surrogate through artificial insemination, or (c) bear a child not biologically related to the infertile couple by using their own eggs and donor sperm introduced through artificial insemination.	• Moral issues • Legal issues

Goodheart-Willcox Publisher

Challenges of Fertility Treatments

Individuals and couples can face challenges when undergoing fertility treatments, such as:

- Fertility problems can be emotionally painful for individuals.
- Some may feel their privacy is violated during fertility testing and treatment.
- Less than half of the individuals having treatments succeed after just one treatment.

Older individuals often have the least chance of succeeding.

- Some treatments can be expensive. Additional expense may be incurred traveling to major hospitals for treatment.
- For some individuals, ethical issues are involved with the use of any ART. For many other people, ethical, legal, and biological issues are involved when donor egg and sperm are used or if a surrogate bears the baby (**Figure 6.4**).

Figure 6.4 Issues Involving ARTs

Issues	Description
Ethical issues	Ethical issues center on the artificial nature of conception. • Some couples do not approve of any ARTs, even when the procedure involves the couple's eggs and sperm. • More people believe ART is a moral issue when someone other than the couple is involved in the pregnancy by being an egg or sperm donor or serving as a surrogate. • For better outcomes for implanted embryos and the safety of the person trying to carry the child, most doctors today reduce the number of embryos to two or three before implantation in the IVF procedure. The age of the person trying to carry the child often determines how many are implanted (often three for an older person). The "quality" of the embryos may determine which ones are selected for implantation. The moral issue centers on the destruction of the embryos that are not implanted.
Legal issues	Legal problems center on contracts and fees. Contracts • What if the donor of the egg or sperm wants parenting rights or changes their mind? • What happens if the surrogate decides to keep the baby, who may also be the surrogate's biological child? • What happens if the couple decides they do not want this child because they have conceived or adopted in the meantime or the child has a disability? Fees • Who pays if the surrogate's and/or the newborn's medical fees are much higher than the contract fee? • Who pays if the contract is broken by either party? How much? Who pays more for legal fees, time spent, or possible psychological issues?
Biological issues	Biological problems center on heredity issues involved in close relatives parenting. • Should egg and sperm donors be allowed to parent many offspring? (Some biological females have donated eggs several times, and some biological males have parented hundreds of children through donations to sperm banks. For banks, donors receive money for their donated egg and sperm cells.) • How can couples know for sure they are not marrying close relatives, even half siblings? How can they be protected from the higher risk of having children born with genetic defects?

Goodheart-Willcox Publisher

Because of these challenges, some people choose not to pursue their options regarding ARTs. Others try but find they cannot restore their fertility. Both types of individuals may face or experience a crisis as they adjust to this reality. For some people who deeply desire children, there may be a lasting sense of being unfulfilled. Counseling may help them resolve these feelings. Other people become fulfilled parents through adoption or foster parenthood. Some childless individuals find fulfillment in other **endeavors** (attempts to achieve plans and goals) involving families and children.

6.1-2 Multiple Pregnancies

Sometimes two or more babies develop in the same pregnancy (called a **multiple pregnancy**). Multiple pregnancies are far less common than single pregnancies (**Figure 6.5**). Notice twins are more common than triplets, and triplets are more common than quadruplets. As many as seven or eight babies can be conceived in the same pregnancy in very rare cases.

Doctors are often concerned about the health of multiple births with three or more babies. Most babies in these births are born early and have low birthweights. A **low birthweight** is a weight under 5.5 pounds at birth for a single birth and under 3.3 pounds per baby in a multiple birth. This puts them at risk for severe vision, hearing, intellectual, and developmental disabilities. Twins are also almost five times (triplets almost 10 times) more likely to die in their first year than single-birth children.

Types of Multiple Pregnancies

Twin type or *multiple type* refers to the classifications of twins and larger sets of multiples. The most common way to describe multiples is by *zygosity* (zy-GAWS-uh-tee)—whether the multiples developed from one zygote or more. Types of multiple pregnancies include fraternal births, identical births, and higher-multiple births.

Fraternal Births

The most common multiple pregnancy is caused when multiple babies develop from two or more ova. Each ova is fertilized with a different sperm, which means each child has a different genetic makeup. These babies are as much alike or different as any other siblings. Children born in these multiple births are called **fraternal births** or *dizygotic* (DYE-zye-GAW-tik) *births*. (*Fraternal* comes from a Latin word meaning *brother*.)

Multiple ovulation, when more than one egg is released, makes fraternal multiples possible. Multiple ovulation is due to hormones that

Figure 6.5 Chances of Having Spontaneous Multiples*

Multiples	Chances
Twins	1 in 80 births
Triplets	1 in over 6 thousand births
Quadruplets	1 in over 500 thousand births
Quintuplets	1 in about 40 million births
Sextuplets	1 in about 3 billion births

*These numbers exclude pregnancies of people using ART.

Goodheart-Willcox Publisher

stimulate ovulation. The *Investigate Special Topics: Factors Affecting Fraternal Multiple Births* feature in this lesson explains this common factor. If you have a history of multiple births in your family, do you have a better chance of having multiple births? On a pregnant person's mother's side of the family, they have a better chance of having fraternal (not identical) births because the production of extra hormones is hereditary.

The most common type of fraternal births is fraternal twins. Fraternal twins represent about three-fourths of all twins. Fraternal children may or may not be the same gender. Of these fraternal twins, 25 percent are female pairs, 25 percent are male pairs, and 50 percent are female-male pairs.

Identical Births

In **identical births**, called *monozygotic* (MAWN-oh-zye-GAWT-ik) *births*, children develop from a single ovum fertilized by a single sperm. Before the zygote embeds in the uterine wall, the ovum splits to produce two or more children. These children are always the same biological sex. Scientists do not know why the ovum splits. Heredity does not seem to contribute to monozygotic births. Identical twins occur in about one-third of multiple pregnancies. Thus, the chances of identical births are much less than the odds for fraternal births (**Figure 6.6**).

Babies from an identical birth have the same genome. Because identical children are very similar in appearance, people sometimes confuse which child is which. Even family members may confuse them. Except for their genes, identical children are not exactly alike because their epigenome creates some differences. Their fingerprints, palm prints, and footprints are similar, but not exactly the same. Also, environment makes identical children different. For example, one child may be larger because of better nourishment, even before birth.

Some identical twins are *mirror twins*—they look the way you and your mirror image would appear. For instance, one may have a birthmark on the right shoulder and the other may have one on the left shoulder. One may be right-handed while the other is left-handed.

If the ovum does not completely split, the babies will be *conjoined twins*. The bodies of these twins are joined in one or more places. They may share external body parts, such as legs, or internal organs, such as the liver. Conjoined twins occur in about one in 200,000 live births.

Higher-Multiple Births

Higher-multiple births, three or more babies born from a single pregnancy, are sometimes called *super twins*. In these higher-multiple births, the children can be all identical, all fraternal, or mixed type. Of higher-multiple births, most are **mixed-type births** (two or more babies are identical and one or more are fraternal). If all the children are identical or fraternal, it is not a mixed-type birth.

Figure 6.6 ## Chances of Having Spontaneous Identical Multiples*

Multiples	Chances
Twins	1 in 250 pregnancies
Triplets	1 in almost 60 thousand pregnancies
Quadruplets	1 in 11 to 15 million pregnancies
Quintuplets	1 in almost 4 billion pregnancies

*These numbers exclude pregnancies of people using ART.

Goodheart-Willcox Publisher

Factors Affecting Fraternal Multiple Births

Although fraternal multiple pregnancies are not as common as single pregnancies, they have become more common. This is due to several factors.

Maternal age (Although it becomes more difficult for people to conceive as they age, those who do are more likely to have fraternal multiple births than younger people.)

- Rate doubles between 35 and 40 years of age.
- Rate decreases between 40 and 45 years of age.
- After 45 years of age, one in nine pregnancies are multiples.

Better nutrition

- Good nutrition aids hormones.
- Taller and heavier (not obese) people have more fraternal multiple births.

History of earlier pregnancies

- Compared to the first pregnancy, the rate increases four times for the fourth or fifth pregnancy.
- Rate is four times greater for pregnant people who have had multiples over those who have had singletons.

Fraternal multiple pregnancies on the maternal side of the family

- Production of extra hormones needed for multiple ovulation runs in families.
- Better nutrition from prenatal stage through childhood appears to run in families.

Use of ARTs

The hormones in fertility drugs stimulate ovulation. Thus, successful ARTs almost always produce fraternal multiple pregnancies. In the 1990s when ARTs were new, it was not uncommon for some of these people to have more than three babies. Higher-number multiples, however, are now on the decline due to improvements in ARTs.

Common factor in fraternal multiple births

Is there something common about these factors? Yes, they all increase the chances of multiple ovulation due to hormones.

Reading Activity

In small groups, write responses to the following questions. Then, pass your responses to the next group. Read the responses you receive and add any follow-up questions or comments.

1. What might be some benefits of having a multiple pregnancy?
2. What might be some challenges of having a multiple pregnancy?
3. How would having a multiple pregnancy change the way a person prepares for childbirth and parenting?

Photo: Tom Wang/Shutterstock.com

In mixed types of pregnancies, separate sperm fertilize two or more eggs (fraternal). Then, one or more of the fertilized ova may split (identical). Triplets are often from a mixed-type pregnancy, with two children identical and one fraternal (**Figure 6.7**). Quadruplets are often from a mixed-type birth. With quadruplets, there could be several combinations of fraternal and identical children.

Testing for Multiple Pregnancy Type

Mixed-gender children are always fraternal. Same-gender children may be identical or fraternal. In higher multiples, both fraternal and identical are common. Sometimes it is impossible to tell zygosity by looking at children. The way children look is not the same as the genome.

At one time, doctors determined whether children were identical or fraternal by examining the amniotic sacs after delivery. Identical births share the same sac, but fraternal children each have their own sac. Today, ultrasound can be used to see the sac or sacs before birth. More accurate testing is done through blood specimens taken from newborns or their placentas. Cells can also be collected by swabbing the inside of babies' cheeks and sent to labs for valid DNA testing.

Why is testing important? Mainly, knowledge of DNA is helpful for medical reasons. Caregivers can also use this information to help them understand differences and similarities in their children's growth and development.

6.1-3 Pregnancy Complications

Anyone can have pregnancy complications. Some pregnancies, however, are considered "high risk" because of a great chance of complications. High-risk people include teens, which is discussed in Lesson 6.2. Older pregnant people are also at greater risks for complications, and their babies are at an increased risk for abnormalities compared with those of younger people. Multiple births are high risk, especially higher-multiple births. Finally, anyone not in optimal health before pregnancy has increased risks of pregnancy complications.

Figure 6.7 A combination of fraternal and identical multiples is called a *mixed-type pregnancy. How do mixed-type pregnancies occur?*

digitalskillet/Shutterstock.com

Pregnant people can greatly reduce the chance of complications in their pregnancies by receiving prenatal care, following their doctors' advice, and practicing good health habits. Complications can occur, however, in any pregnancy. **Figure 6.8** describes the major complications of pregnancy. Complications can damage the pregnant person's health, and some can result in congenital conditions or the loss of the baby before birth. Prenatal care helps doctors note problems early, which allows for needed early treatment.

Congenital Conditions

Congenital conditions may be inherited, caused by environmental factors, or combined genetic and environmental factors. These disabilities and diseases occur with varying degrees of severity. **Figure 6.9** describes the most common congenital conditions.

Figure 6.8 Pregnancy Complications

Problem	Causes	Symptoms
Ectopic pregnancy (development of fetus outside of uterus)	Blocked fallopian tube	Spotting and cramping; uterus does not enlarge as it should; rupture of fallopian tube
Too much amniotic fluid	Uncontrolled diabetes; multiple pregnancy; incompatible blood types; congenital problems	Excessive pressure on pregnant person's body; breathing problems; congenital problems in the newborn
Too little amniotic fluid	Congenital problems; growth problems; death of fetus	Fetal movement slows or stops
Bleeding in late pregnancy	Placenta abruptio; placenta previa; vaginal or cervical infection	Bleeding—often heavy
Placenta abruptio (placenta becomes detached from the uterine wall before it should)	Unknown Occurs more in people who smoke, have high blood pressure, have had previous children or a history of detached placentas, suffered injury to the abdomen, or are carrying multiples	Bleeding; cramping; abdominal tenderness
Placenta previa (placenta attaches itself to the uterus near or covering the cervix rather than in the upper half of the uterus)	Scarring of the uterine wall from a prior pregnancy; tumors of the uterus; surgery of the uterus; more common among people who smoke or use drugs, are older than 35, and are carrying multiples	Bright red bleeding without pain or tenderness of the abdomen
Pregnancy-induced hypertension (also called preeclampsia or toxemia)	Multiple fetuses; teen pregnancy or pregnancy of people over 40 years of age; high blood pressure; kidney disease	Sudden swelling of hands and face; high blood pressure; headache; dizziness; fever; irritability; protein in urine; abdominal pain; blurred vision; seizures

Goodheart-Willcox Publisher

Figure 6.9 Congenital Conditions

Condition	Symptoms	Causes	Treatment
Chiari malformation	Headache, especially after sudden coughing, sneezing, or straining, neck pain, hearing or balance problems, muscle weakness or numbness, dizziness, difficulty swallowing or speaking, ringing or buzzing in the ears (tinnitus), curvature of the spine (scoliosis), problems with hand coordination and fine motor skills	Structural defects in the base of the skull and cerebellum, the part of the brain that controls balance, when part of the cerebellum extends below the spinal opening and into the upper spinal canal	Decompression surgery, surgery to reposition the spinal cord and close opening in back, inserting a shunt to relieve pressure and fluid from the head
Cleft lip/palate	Noticeable at birth. A cleft lip occurs when the two sides of the upper lip fail to grow together properly. A cleft palate occurs when an opening remains in the roof of the mouth. This creates problems in breathing, talking, hearing, and eating.	Variable; often caused by several factors working together. Smoking and severe dieting may be factors.	Corrective surgery and speech therapy
Cystic fibrosis	A chemical failure affects lungs and pancreas. Thick sticky mucus forms in the lungs, causing breathing problems. Reduced amounts of digestive juices cause poor digestion of food. An excess amount of salt is excreted in perspiration.	Recessive gene	No cure. Physical therapy, synthetic digestive enzymes, salt tablets, and antibodies can lessen the effect of the symptoms. May have shorter-than-normal lifespan because of higher susceptibility to respiratory diseases
Diabetes	Metabolic disorders cause high blood sugar. The person feels thirsty, hungry, and weak and usually loses weight.	A number of factors working together	No cure. Can be controlled by insulin injections, careful diet, and physical activity.
Down syndrome	Distinct physical features are evident, such as slanting eyes; large, misshapen forehead; oversized tongue; single crease across palm of each hand; and varying degrees of intellectual disabilities are typical.	Chromosome abnormality. More likely to occur when the pregnant person is over age 35.	Special educational needs. Lifespan may be nearly normal.

Goodheart-Willcox Publisher
(Continued)

Figure 6.9 **Congenital Conditions** (Continued)

Condition	Symptoms	Causes	Treatment
Huntington's chorea	The brain and central nervous system gradually deteriorate when the person is between 30 and 40 years old. This causes involuntary jerking, loss of mental abilities, insanity, depression, and finally death.	Dominant gene	None
Hydrocephalus	Extra fluid is trapped in the brain. The person's head is larger than normal.	A number of factors working together	Surgical removal of excess fluid. Without treatment, children rarely survive.
Muscular dystrophy	A group of disorders which damage muscles. They cause progressive weakness and finally death.	Often sex-linked	No cure. Therapy and braces offer some relief.
Phenylketonuria (PKU)	An enzyme deficiency makes the person unable to digest a certain amino acid. The baby appears normal at birth, but slowly develops intellectual disabilities because the amino acid builds up in the body and causes brain damage.	Recessive gene	A carefully prescribed diet that balances the enzyme deficiency. The effects of the disease can usually be avoided if treatment begins within the first six weeks of birth.
Sickle-cell anemia	Red blood cells are sickle shaped rather than round. They cannot carry oxygen efficiently throughout the body. People become pale, tired, and short of breath. They have occasional pains and low resistance to infection. Their lifespan is often shorter than normal.	Recessive gene often seen in people of African-American descent	No cure. Various treatments relieve some symptoms. Blood transfusions are needed occasionally.
Spina bifida (also called neural tube defect)	A condition that causes partial paralysis and urinary and bowel incontinence due to an incompletely formed spinal cord. Learning disabilities are also common. Condition varies due to severity.	Heredity and environmental factors	Corrective surgery, physical therapy, and lifelong antibiotics. Special educational needs.
Tay-Sachs disease	A lack of a specific chemical in the blood resulting in an inability to process and use fats. Leads to severe brain damage and death, often by age two or three years.	Recessive gene often seen in people of Eastern European Jewish descent	None

Preterm Birth

Preterm birth is a delivery that occurs before 37 weeks of pregnancy. Preterm births are higher for teen, older, and multiple-birth pregnancies. Some common factors also linked to preterm births include having

- a family history of preterm babies.
- a preterm baby in the past.
- the spacing between deliveries of less than 18 months.
- problems with the uterus or cervix.
- poor health habits during pregnancy.
- late or no prenatal care.

Preterm delivery results in a high rate of death during the first month after birth. Preterm delivery can also result in a high incidence of brain disorders, cerebral palsy, chronic lung disease, and developmental delays. Preterm births take an emotional and financial toll on families, too.

When a person goes into preterm labor, the doctor can try several treatments to prolong the pregnancy. Some treatments work to prevent early labor while others speed up the baby's lung development.

Loss of Baby Before Birth

A **miscarriage** is the **expulsion** (forcing out) of the baby from the uterus before week 20 of pregnancy. The medical term for miscarriage is *spontaneous abortion*. About 50 percent of all miscarriages occur around the time of the expected menstrual period, and the person is unaware that they were pregnant. About 10 to 25 percent of all *known* pregnancies end in the loss of the baby. Most of these miscarriages occur in the first 13 weeks of pregnancy. Although losses frequently occur for unknown reasons, some causes are known (**Figure 6.10**).

Often, the treatment for miscarriage occurring 10 to 12 weeks in the pregnancy is dilation and curettage (CURE-uh-tazh), which is usually called *D&C*. The purpose of a D&C is to remove small pieces of placenta not expelled during the miscarriage and to control heavy bleeding. The 10-to-15-minute outpatient or inpatient procedure involves anesthesia followed by dilating the cervix. The lining of the uterus and its contents are then scraped with a spoon-shaped instrument, called a *curette*, which prevents infections and excessive bleeding. Afterward, drugs to control bleeding and antibiotics are typically given.

Stillbirth is the loss of the fetus after 20 weeks of pregnancy. In a stillbirth, the baby is born dead. Stillbirth affects about 1 percent of pregnancies. The main causes of stillbirth include abnormalities present at birth, problems with the placenta, bacterial infections occurring between 24 and 27 weeks' gestation, and the failure of the baby to grow.

Figure 6.10 Common Causes of Miscarriage

- Chromosomal abnormality (due to damaged egg or sperm or to incorrect cell division of the zygote)
- Pregnant person's age (35 years old—15% chance; 36–45 years old—20% to 35% chance; over 45 years old—50% chance)
- Previous miscarriage
- Physical problems (hormones, infections, or other health problems)
- Lifestyle (exposure to health hazards)
- Trauma to the pregnant person (accident, extreme stress)

Goodheart-Willcox Publisher

Several factors increase the pregnant person's risk (**Figure 6.11**). A presumptive sign of stillbirth is when the person no longer feels the baby's movements. Stillbirth is often confirmed by ultrasound. Babies who are stillborn are delivered by either *induction* (drugs that start labor) or when labor begins spontaneously. Doctors need to make this call.

Caregivers and individuals grieve after the loss of their unborn. Most individuals cope with the support of family, close friends, religious groups, and/or professional groups.

Individuals often seek answers about the cause of a miscarriage or stillbirth to help prevent this in a future pregnancy. Having a miscarriage or stillbirth does increase the risk of another. With good medical care, however, many partners can conceive again and deliver healthy babies after the loss of a baby.

Figure 6.11 **Factors That Increase Risk of Stillbirth**

- Pregnant person is 35 years and older
- Malnutrition
- Use of drugs
- Stress
- Genetic and chromosomal disorders of the baby
- Separation of placenta from uterus (called *placental abruption*)
- Illness of the pregnant person (diabetes, liver condition, or blood clotting problems)

Goodheart-Willcox Publisher

Lesson 6.1 Review and Assessment

1. _____ refers to an individual who is unable to conceive after a year of trying. (6.1.1)
   A. Infertile
   B. Sterile
   C. Fertility
   D. ART procedure

2. _____ refers to individuals who are permanently unable to conceive or carry a biological child. (6.1.1)
   A. Infertile
   B. Sterile
   C. Fertility
   D. ART procedure

3. **True or False.** In fraternal births, children develop from a single ovum. (6.1.2)

4. **True or False.** Identical twins occur in one-third of multiple births. (6.1.2)

5. Which of the following is NOT a complication of pregnancy? (6.1.3)
   A. Preterm birth
   B. Miscarriage
   C. Mood swings
   D. Stillbirth

Teen Pregnancy

Learning Outcomes

After studying this lesson, you will be able to

6.2-1 **determine** risks of a sexual relationship.

6.2-2 **describe** the negative impacts of teen pregnancy.

6.2-3 **assess** support systems available for teen parents.

6.2-4 **evaluate** teen pregnancy prevention programs available to teens.

Key Terms

abstinence

adversely

friction

General Educational Development (GED) test

inconsolable

initiate

mortality rate

nonessential

practical

Reading and Notetaking Activity

Skim the headings in this lesson and consider what each concept might teach you about teen pregnancy. Keep a list, placing a star next to any concepts that particularly interest you. After reading the lesson, pick three concepts and write a few paragraphs about how these concepts can help you understand yourself. Use proper grammar and spelling in your paragraphs.

Introduction

The developmental changes that occur in the teen years often cause confusion. Teens' developmental quests result in conflicting feelings. Teens have a quest for closeness in shared relationships. As teens become more physically mature, they experience their flourishing sexuality. Many teens experience romantic love for the first time and, due to their feelings, may seek sexual relationships. These feelings often interact with other quests, such as desiring more independence, learning skills that will allow for their eventual independence, and searching for and finding their own identity (**Figure 6.12**).

Figure 6.12 Teens should consider their futures and plans when they make decisions about sexual activity. Some ways that teens can process these feelings and thoughts include talking with a trusted adult or journaling. *How do you think a person's future plans impact their sexual decisions?*

Because of these quests, teens are not ready to be caregivers, even though they are physically capable of reproducing. Parenthood requires they turn their time, energy, and attention away from their own quests and focus on the helpless baby they have brought into the world. This lesson looks at the medical and social consequences of teen parenthood for the teens themselves and for their babies.

6.2-1 Risks of Sexual Relationships

Many teens (and even adults) ask the question: Why should I wait for marriage to have sex if I am in love? First, what many mistake for love is a passing feeling that does not last. Entering a sexual relationship can make a person feel emotionally tied to the other person. Imagine how painful this would make a breakup.

The results of a sexual relationship can be life-altering and permanent. Two of the most troubling risks are unplanned pregnancy and STIs, such as HIV/AIDS. Many birth control methods are available to help reduce the risk of unplanned pregnancy

and STIs, but the idea of "completely safe sex" is a myth. The best way to avoid unwanted pregnancies and STIs is **abstinence** (refusal to engage in a sexual relationship).

Other risks of sexual relationships teens may experience include

- emotional scars that may follow a broken relationship.
- conflicts with caregivers and other adults who care for them.
- conflicts with their own consciences, goals, and values.

6.2-2 Negative Impacts of Teen Pregnancy

Many teens become pregnant in the United States each year. Over 75 percent of these pregnancies are unplanned. The rates for teen pregnancies in the United States are higher than in many other developed countries.

Teen parenting is not a random sample of the teenage population. For example, teens who are not active in school or engaged in learning are more likely than other teens to have a baby or be a partner to a person who has a baby. Teens who live in communities in which income and employment opportunities are limited are also more likely to become teen parents. Already being a caregiver is the greatest risk factor for a teen pregnancy.

Teen parenting is a major risk. Becoming a caregiver in the teen years has no advantages over becoming a caregiver between 20 and 35 years of age. The risks of teen pregnancy and parenting affect many aspects of the teens' lives, and it is impossible to reverse most of the consequences (**Figure 6.13**). Many of these problems relate to health risks, educational impact, financial concerns, lifestyle changes, and stress and violence. Many teens who choose to raise their babies become single parents. Being a single, never-married caregiver results in the highest risk for the child's overall well-being.

Health Risks

Teens' bodies are still growing and developing—only babies in the womb and infants develop more quickly. Because of all these physical changes, proper nutrition is crucial for a teen. When a teen is pregnant, their baby is dependent on them for nutrition, which depletes the teen's body of nutrients. Poor nutrition before or during pregnancy puts both the teen and the baby at risk.

The lack of medical care is another health risk for pregnant teens. All pregnant people need early and continuous prenatal care. They also need medical care for about two months after delivery. Unfortunately, some teens do not receive the level of care they need early in pregnancy. Some teens receive no prenatal care.

Focus on Health

Food Assistance Programs

Many teen parents have an incredibly difficult road ahead for themselves and their children for many reasons. One major consequence of teen parenting is the reality of poverty. Any family living near, at, or below the poverty level will find meeting their basic necessities, such as having an adequate amount of nutritious foods, difficult to impossible unless they receive assistance.

The U.S. government has two food assistance programs that can aid qualifying pregnant teens, teen caregivers, and their children. One program is the *Supplemental Nutrition Assistance Program (SNAP)*. SNAP is an entitlement program provided to all eligible households who apply. The applicant must meet certain requirements pertaining to household size, income, certain expenses, and resources. The program allows recipients to buy almost all food items, but excludes other items sold in grocery stores, such as pet foods, toiletries, cleaning products, and drugs. SNAP also provides information on food purchasing and preparation.

Another program is the *Special Supplemental Nutrition Program for Women, Infants and Children (WIC)*. Like SNAP, WIC provides supplemental nutritious foods, nutrition education, and counseling. Unlike SNAP, WIC is a "discretionary" grant program, which means WIC programs, such as county WIC offices, must stay within their budgets in making eligibility and benefit decisions. WIC serves pregnant, postpartum, and nursing people, and infants and children up to their fifth birthdays. WIC applicants must qualify based on income and be considered a "nutrition risk" by a health care provider.

Photo: wavebreakmedia/Shutterstock.com

Figure 6.13 Consequences of Teen Parenting

Affected	Consequences

For pregnant teens	• Health risks are greater for younger teens and for all teens who do not receive quality prenatal and postnatal care.
	• Many teens never complete high school.
	• Teens lack entry-level skills for the job market. Their income is usually much below that of people who have their first child after the teen years.
	• Teens who marry are at high risk for divorce. The divorce rate increases between the first and sixth year after marriage.
	• Married teens report major marital problems. These problems include the following:
	  • more sexual activity than they desire
	  • loneliness (Many times a teen partner maintains their social life while the primary caregiver assumes more child care responsibility. Also, most teen caregivers tend to lose touch with friends.)
	  • lack of support (Many times, older partners are not interested in marriage or parenting. The teen may not receive companionship, parenting support, or child support.)

For their partners	• Teens have poor school performance and many times drop out of high school. • Teens often lack education and training. For these reasons, they usually cannot earn adequate incomes to support their family. • Unmarried teens report not being able to see their babies when they wish. Married teens report problems with the child's grandparents. • Teen parents show less self-esteem than other teens because of less education and more financial problems.

For children of teen parents	• The mortality rate is high for babies born to someone age 15 years or younger. This death rate is twice as high as that for babies born to someone between ages 20 and 34 years.
	• Babies of teen parents are a greater risk for congenital problems.
	• Children of teens have lower achievement in school because of:
	  • having abnormalities present at birth
	  • being born too soon or too small
	  • having less family income
	• Children of teens are at a higher risk of being abused because of:
	  • having abnormalities present at birth
	  • being born too soon or too small
	  • having parents who do not know when a child is ready to do or learn a task
	  • crying when parents want to sleep, study, or socialize or when parents are depressed

For society	• Often extra child care tasks and the need for more income burden the grandparents of the teen's child. • Teen parents lose productive income because of their lower-income jobs or unemployment. • Society pays the costs of assistance programs to teen parents. • Society pays for assistance to children and loss of productive income in the next generation if children do not overcome their problems. • Societies may be more violent if children are abused. • The numbers of problems faced by single-parent, divorced, and remarried families may increase.

Goodheart-Willcox Publisher

Possible reasons for this lack of medical care may be that pregnant teens

- may think they are not pregnant.
- feel their caregivers will be upset by the pregnancy.
- are afraid their relationship with their partner will end once they learn about the pregnancy (**Figure 6.14**).
- lack money for medical care or do not know where to go for help.
- cannot find transportation to a medical facility.
- do not know that medical care is necessary.
- are afraid of medical procedures.

Both the pregnant person and baby are affected by these risks. Even with good health care, pregnant teens experience other health risks. These include longer labors and thus a great many surgical deliveries. Teen parents are at the highest risk of depression after pregnancy, too. Therefore, care after pregnancy is needed to protect both physical and mental health of the teen and the baby.

The **mortality rate** (rate of death) for the babies of teens is high. Many of the babies who survive have low birthweights. These small babies have higher rates of slow growth throughout childhood. They may have more learning problems in school and more social problems with peers. Health risks increase even more for both teen and baby if the teen smokes, drinks alcohol, or has an untreated STI. Health risks also increase for both teen and baby if the teen is younger than 15 years of age or has had more than one pregnancy in the teen years. Many teens have a repeat pregnancy before 20 years of age. On a positive side, with good nutrition and prenatal care, teens are capable of having a healthy pregnancy and a healthy baby.

Educational Impact

Teen pregnancy significantly impacts the educational outcomes of teen parents. Only about half of teens who give birth to babies graduate from high school. Their partners have a 25 to 30 percent lower probability of graduating from high school than their peers who are not parents.

Why is education often sacrificed? Teen parents find completing their education difficult or impossible for the following reasons:

- Adequate child care is unaffordable.
- The need for a job, even a low-paying one, may keep teen parents out of school.
- Teen parents' time to study is limited because of their parenting responsibilities.

Many teen-parent families live in poverty. Living in poverty causes problems that **adversely** (unfavorably) affect the lives of teen parents and their children.

Because schools are becoming more involved in educating teen parents, more teens are graduating.

Figure 6.14 Many pregnant teens do not receive prenatal care out of fear that the pregnancy will harm their relationships, either with their parents or with their partners. *Why should a pregnant teen seek prenatal care even if they are afraid of the pregnancy's impact on their relationships?*

fizkes/Shutterstock.com

Teens who do not graduate can receive a state-issued certificate of high school equivalency if they pass a **General Educational Development (GED) test**. A few teen parents who graduate from high school or pass a GED test go to college. In fact, some teen parents are very motivated to get an education to better provide for their children. Teens with a high school diploma or a certificate of high school equivalency earn 44 percent more per year than teens not finishing high school or its equivalent (**Figure 6.15**).

Financial Concerns

Prenatal care and delivery are expensive. If teens are covered by their parents' insurance policies, the costs of pregnancy and childbirth may not be covered. Even if the pregnant teen is covered, the baby may not be covered.

Health problems add to the costs for pregnant person and baby. The added expense of a baby is a real burden for teens, most of whom are financially strapped. Parents must pay for a baby's food, clothing, equipment, and perhaps child care. These costs increase as babies grow.

Sadly, these financial concerns can continue into adulthood. Studies show teens who become parents usually have financial problems all their lives. As discussed in Chapter 4, raising a child is expensive. Most families spend approximately 22 percent of their monthly income toward the care of their child. Refer back to Figure 4.8 for the expenses families incur each month.

Lifestyle Changes

When teens become parents, their lives change in dramatic ways. Those who marry because of a pregnancy may find themselves in unhappy marriages. They may encounter problems living with their baby in their parents' home. Besides financial pressures, many also socialize less often with friends because they have more responsibility, as well as no additional money to spend on going out as the baby's needs come first. Teen parents usually lead stressful lives.

Life at Home

Teen parents who continue to live with their own parents report additional **friction** (conflict; tension) at home. A teen's parents may have a difficult time adjusting to their teen's early parenthood. They may be disappointed and concerned. They may insist the baby's other biological parent stay out of the baby's life. Grandparents of the baby often feel the most stress because they are juggling child care, work, and other family obligations. There are often conflicts about childrearing between the teen and their parents. Conflicts may concern the general parenting style or possibly specific issues, such as taking responsibility for the child.

NotarYES/Shutterstock.com

Figure 6.15 Between the responsibilities of caring for a child and the financial need for a job, it can be difficult for teen parents to study and continue their education. Graduating from high school or earning a GED is important for teen parents because this education can help them obtain higher-paying jobs in the future. *How can the people around a teen parent encourage them to pursue an education?*

Social Life Changes

Before pregnancy, a teen's life focuses on school, social activities, and family. Once a teen becomes a parent, life changes (**Figure 6.16**). Now the teen focuses on the medical aspects of pregnancy, the costs of a baby, and ways to meet the baby's needs. Teen parents have little time to study or spend with friends because baby care takes too much time. Baby expenses leave little or no money to spend on **nonessential** (not vital) items.

Many teen parents say they feel isolated. Although friends usually stand by teen parents, they may not maintain the same social contact. This often happens during the pregnancy and after the baby is born, which can lead to depression and frustration for the teen parent.

Anastassiya Bezhekeneva/Shutterstock.com

Figure 6.16 Having a baby changes a person's life, and teen parents often find that their lives are consumed with the responsibilities of caring and providing for a child. This leaves little time for teens to spend with friends. *What are some other life changes that might come with having a baby?*

Focus on Careers

Social and Human Service Assistant

Social and human service assistants work with people in need to determine what type of benefits and community services are available to help them. They determine eligibility for services, such as food assistance or child care programs, and then help the clients complete the necessary paperwork to receive benefits. Social and human service assistants also check in with clients to make sure the services are meeting their needs. They may work under the direct supervision of social workers or other professionals who have more experience.

Career cluster: Human services.

Education: Educational requirements may include an associate's degree or certificate and on-the-job training.

Job outlook: Future employment opportunities for social and human service assistants are expected to grow much faster than the average for all occupations.

To learn more about a career as a social and human service assistant, visit the United States Department of Labor's *Occupational Outlook Handbook* website. You will also be able to compare the job responsibilities, educational requirements, job outlook, and average pay of social and human service assistants with similar occupations.

Photo: MBI/Shutterstock.com

Stress and Violence

Teen stress and frustrations may **initiate** (start) family violence. Spouse abuse may occur in unhappy marriages. Children of teens are at high risk for child neglect and abuse. Why does this happen? The major reasons include:

- Teens' needs, such as resolving their own identity, work, study, and socialization do not mesh well with their children's needs.
- Teen parents rarely have enough support in parenting tasks.
- Teens seldom know about child development and may expect their children to reach unreasonable goals. The parents' frustration with a child's "lack of progress" or the **inconsolable** (unable to be soothed) crying baby often leads to child neglect and abuse.

6.2-3 Support Systems for Teen Parents

Although teen parents face challenges, some overcome them and have positive experiences as young parents. Teen parents are individuals, so they differ some in their need for support. Teen parents who are successful, however, often have a strong support system. Teen parents with the most support believe their opportunities are not limited. They realize their success only comes from taking responsibility for the pregnancy and having the drive, dedication, and commitment to succeed.

What resources do teen parents need? They need to decide where they are going to live, and they need to explore other resources quickly because some take time to negotiate (**Figure 6.17**).

Figure 6.17 Possible Resources for Teen Parents

Resources	Health Care
Health care	• Health departments or university clinics offer free or low-cost prenatal care and have patient confidentiality policies. • Schools may have health care services or can advise the teen parent.

Education	• If you are pregnant or parenting, Title IX states that you may go to your school (do *not* have to go to an alternative school), participate in extracurricular activities, access the same quality of classes as other students, and will receive an excused absence from school during childbirth, recovery, and when your child is ill. (*Note:* All schools have a Title IX coordinator.)
	• Some schools are dedicated to serving teen parents and:
	  • have health care and child care services
	  • provide academic support
	  • provide group and individual counseling
	  • teach parenting skills
	  • collaborate with other community organizations
	• (*Note:* Often a school social worker coordinates the services.)

Financial support	• *Temporary Assistance for Needy Families (TANF).* Assistance can be provided to low-income teen parents who are in school and meet other qualifications. • *Supplemental Nutrition Assistance Program (SNAP).* Teens qualify if their parents qualify or if married and living with a partner who is financially needy. • *Women, Infants, and Children (WIC).* Provides food and health assistance, such as nutrition education for teens. • Child care assistance. Often local human resource departments issue a child care voucher for a discounted rate. Some states offer child care if the teen stays in school. Check with the local Child Care Resource and Referral Agency (CCRR).

Goodheart-Willcox Publisher

Teen parents also need people they can turn to for help. Joining support groups may be very helpful for both **practical** (useable; applicable) and emotional support. Teens can get information about parenting rights from their state Attorney General's office. In Texas, the biological partner's name only goes on the birth certificate if the parents are married or they have signed an acknowledgement of paternity form. Pregnant teens should check to see what their state has in place for teen parents.

6.2-4 Teen Pregnancy Prevention

Teens who have not yet become pregnant need support for pregnancy prevention. Basically, these teens need knowledge about the consequences of teen parenting and pregnancy prevention before they make decisions about sexual activity. Thus, support needs to include the following:

- knowing how to cope with peer sexual pressures, such as an understanding that most teens do not engage in sexual relationships during high school and ways to say "no."
- knowing how to prevent pregnancy (abstinence or correct and consistent use of effective contraceptive methods) and recognizing myths about pregnancy prevention, such as douching after intercourse.
- understanding that most contraceptives do not prevent STIs.
- being aware of the medical and social consequences of pregnancy (and STIs).

Many pregnancy prevention programs are available to teens through their schools, youth organizations, and religious organizations. Two national programs are the *National Campaign to Prevent Teen Pregnancy* and the *President's Teen Pregnancy Prevention Initiative (TPPI)*. Also, parents must guide their teens during their turbulent years by promoting responsible values and behaviors.

1. Which of the following is not a risk of sexual relationships? (6.2.1)
   A. Pregnancy or STI
   B. Emotional scars from a broken relationship
   C. Strengthening of relationship between partners
   D. Conflict with caregivers
2. Which of the following is NOT a reason that pregnant teens do not receive necessary parental care? (6.2.2)
   A. Do not realize they are pregnant
   B. Afraid to tell adults in their life for fear of their response
   C. Afraid their partner will not stay in their life
   D. They see no reason to spend money at a doctor's office when they can get prenatal vitamins over the counter
3. **True or False.** Only half of pregnant teens finish high school. (6.2.2)
4. **True or False.** There are no resources available to help pregnant teens. (6.2.3)
5. Which of the following is a pregnancy prevention program available to teens? (6.2.4)
   A. WIC
   B. National Campaign to Prevent Teen Pregnancy
   C. SNAP
   D. TANF

Summary

Lesson 6.1

6.1-1 People who try to conceive and are unable to do so within a year are known as infertile.

6.1-1 Assisted reproductive technologies (ARTs) are methods infertile people may use to help them conceive.

6.1-2 A multiple pregnancy is when two or more babies develop in the same pregnancy.

6.1-3 Congenital conditions, preterm birth, and loss of a baby before birth are all examples of pregnancy complications.

6.2-1 Sexual relationships have many risk factors, such as STIs, emotional scars, and unwanted pregnancies.

Lesson 6.2

6.2-2 There are many health risks for pregnant teens and their babies.

6.2-2 Only about half of teen parents graduate from high school.

6.2-2 Teen parents face major concerns with finances, lifestyle, education, and stress and violence.

6.2-3 There are resources available to help teen parents in the areas of health care, education, and financial support.

6.2-4 Many teen pregnancy prevention programs are available to teens through their schools, youth organizations, and religious organizations.

College and Career Portfolio

Portfolio Resources

Some components of your portfolio may require the help of an outside professional. Before you compile items for your portfolio, identify *where* you will acquire these items, *how* you will acquire them, and *what resources* you will need.

Locate your portfolio checklist and review the items you plan to include. Then, identify any items which you will need outside help to acquire. Identifying these items early will enable you to compile these items in a timely and organized manner.

As you review the items you plan to include in your portfolio, complete the following activities:
- Research how you will acquire each item and then make note of where you need to go or whom you need to talk with to include this item in your portfolio.
- Note the contact information of any people or resources that have been of help to you so far in constructing your portfolio.

Recall and Application

1. Which of the following is NOT a major cause of infertility and sterility in females? (6.1.1)
   A. Damage to reproductive organs
   B. Irregular ovulation
   C. Inability of sperm to move
   D. Lack of ovulation

2. Which of the following is NOT a major cause of infertility and sterility in males? (6.1.1)
   A. Damage to reproductive organs
   B. Hormone deficiencies
   C. Low sperm count
   D. Lack of ovulation

3. **True or False.** Fertility problems can be emotionally painful for individuals and partners. (6.1.1)

4. **True or False.** Older individuals have an easier time of succeeding with fertility treatments. (6.1.1)

5. Which of the following is a legal issue involving ARTs? (6.1.1)
   A. Some people do not approve of ART procedures.
   B. The surrogate wants to keep the baby.
   C. The number of embryo's implanted in the uterus.
   D. Researching to ensure children are not born with genetic defects.

6. Which of the following pregnancy complications has the symptoms of bleeding, cramping and abdominal tenderness? (6.1.3)
   A. Ectopic pregnancy
   B. Placenta abruptio
   C. Placenta previa
   D. Pregnancy-induced hypertension

7. Which of the following pregnancy complications has the symptoms of bright red bleeding without pain or tenderness of the abdomen? (6.1.3)
   A. Ectopic pregnancy
   B. Placenta abruptio
   C. Placenta previa
   D. Pregnancy-induced hypertension

8. Chiari malformation is caused by a(n) _____. (6.1.3)
   A. dominant gene
   B. recessive gene
   C. environmental factor
   D. inherited factor

9. Cystic fibrosis is caused by a(n) _____. (6.1.3)
   A. dominant gene
   B. recessive gene
   C. environmental factor
   D. inherited factor

10. Phenylketonuria (PKU) is caused by a(n) _____. (6.1.3)
    A. dominant gene
    B. recessive gene
    C. environmental factor
    D. inherited factor

11. Which of the following is NOT a consequence of teen parenting? (6.2.3)
    A. Lack entry level skills for the job market
    B. Do not finish high school
    C. Show more self-esteem than other teens
    D. Lack of support

12. **True or False.** Once a teen becomes pregnant, their focus should shift to the medical aspects of pregnancy, the costs of a baby, and ways to meet the baby's needs. (6.2.2)

13. **True or False.** Resources that help teen parents include health care, education, and financial support. (6.2.3)

Critical Thinking

1. **Cause and effect.** In small groups, use reliable resources to research reproductive diseases that can cause infertility or sterility. Choose three reproductive diseases and summarize their symptoms, causes, and treatments. How do these diseases cause infertility or sterility?

2. **Identify.** ART methods are expertly designed to treat specific fertility problems; therefore, the method of ART chosen depends on the symptoms of the individual or couple. Working with a partner, use Figure 6.3 to match each ART method to one or more major causes of infertility.

3. **Analyze.** Fraternal multiple births are known as *dizygotic*, and identical multiple births are known as *monozygotic*. With a partner, analyze these words and what they mean. How can they help you distinguish between fraternal and identical births?

4. **Make inferences.** Why do statistics for multiple births vary in different parts of the world? Discuss in terms of technology, medical practices, and methods of assisting infertile individuals and couples. Is there a connection between infertility treatments and multiple births? Explain.

5. **Compare and contrast.** Choose three congenital conditions discussed in this chapter and identify the causes of the conditions and the types and severities of the disabilities they may cause. Compare and contrast your findings for all three conditions.

6. **Evaluate.** Imagine that your friend has been dating someone at school for six months, and that one day they approach you for advice. Their dating partner wants to have sex, but your friend is not sure if that is a good idea. How would you advise your friend? Make a list of things you would tell them.

7. **Draw conclusions.** Write a short essay drawing conclusions about why mortality rates for pregnant teens are higher than they are for pregnant people of other ages. In your essay, cite examples from this textbook and from reliable scientific sources. Read and discuss your essays in class.

8. **Cause and effect.** Sit in a circle with your classmates and have a round-table discussion about the effects of teen pregnancy on teen lives. Go around the circle clockwise three times. During the first round, name effects on the pregnant teen. During the second round, name effects on the pregnant teen's partner. During the third round, name effects on families and society.

9. **Determine.** In some cases, teen parents' stress and frustration can lead to family violence. This can be devastating to both teens and their children. What are some ways your community can support teen parents and prevent family violence? Write a letter to your teacher with some recommendations.

Core Skills

1. **Research, speaking, listening, and writing.** As a class, choose an ART method and debate the medical effectiveness (drawbacks versus advantages) and ethics for that method. Divide into two teams. Each team should gather information in support of the method or in opposition to the method. Use your textbook as well as outside sources for support. Compose a presentation arguing for your stance and then deliver it to the other team. As the other team delivers its presentation, listen carefully to their arguments. Take notes on important points and write any questions that occur to you. Ask questions to obtain clarification or additional information, and, if possible, counter their information with information of your own.

2. **Reading.** Read about some court cases involving surrogates. What were the outcomes when the surrogate changed their mind about giving the child to the individual or couple as agreed? How might these problems impact the child involved? Write a short account of the court case as well as a summary of your thoughts.

3. **Writing and speaking.** Pick 5–10 key terms from this chapter and write a brief scene in which those 5–10 terms are used as you imagine them being used by medical professionals in a real-life context. Then, rewrite the dialogue using simpler sentences and transitions, as though an adult were describing the same scene to elementary or middle-school students. Read both scenes to the class and ask for feedback.

4. **Research and writing.** In small groups, choose one of the pregnancy complications discussed in this chapter. Identify reliable resources and research how the complication is treated, as well as the chances of survival for both the pregnant person and the baby. Compose a presentation on the complication and its treatments and deliver your presentation to the class. Include MLA citations for your sources in the presentation.

5. **Math.** Browse the job listings in your community until you find a job that does not require a high-school education. Note the salary for that job and calculate that employee's total revenue working maximum hours for a year. Compare that number with the current average cost of caring for a child for one year.

6. **Research, technology, and speaking.** Research teen pregnancy prevention programs available in your community. Then, create a brochure cataloging these resources and giving a brief explanation. Finally, give a short presentation introducing your brochure. If possible, make your brochure available somewhere in your community.

7. **CTE Career Readiness Practice.** The ability to read and interpret information is an important workplace skill. Presume you work for a company that administers ART methods to infertile people. The company is considering adding gamete intrafallopian transfer (GIFT) to its procedures but wants you to evaluate and interpret some research on the method. You will need to locate three reliable sources of the latest information and research on GIFT. Read and interpret the information. Then write a report summarizing your findings.

Observations

1. Observe fraternal or identical twins—either in person or in a video about twins online—and take notes about how similar or different they are. If possible, observe how these siblings' upbringings might differ from the upbringings of single children. Based on these observations, form a hypothesis on why multiple pregnancies are considered a special circumstance.

2. Talk to another teen (or watch a video about a teen) who has said *no* to sexual activity within their dating relationship. How did this teen handle pressures to be sexually active? What were their reasons for choosing abstinence? How do they feel about that choice?

Chapter 7

Childbirth

Essential Question

What biological, medical, and social/emotional factors contribute to the healthy delivery of a newborn and postpartum care for its caregivers?

Case Study How Can Parents Best Cope with a Preterm Birth Crisis?

As a class, read the case study and discuss the questions that follow. After you finish studying the chapter, discuss this case study again. Have your opinions changed based on what you learned?

Some babies are born prematurely, and no one knows the cause. So it was with Ariana and Andrew's baby who was born at 25 weeks. The baby, Jackson, was rushed from the delivery room to the neonatal intensive care unit (NICU). The neonatologist told Ariana and Andrew the baby had a very small chance of surviving, but everything possible would be done.

Andrew tearfully said to Ariana, "I'm not visiting Jackson in the NICU. Did you see how pathetic our baby looked? If I go and become attached and the baby dies, I think I would die, too. If I don't visit and we lose the baby, it will be easier. If Jackson survives and comes home, I'll give my love and attention then."

Ariana is unable to understand why Andrew will not see their baby and try to contribute to Jackson's survival chances. Ariana would never think of staying home, especially when this could be their only chance to be with the baby. Ariana tries to convince Andrew to visit the baby. Ariana insists they are both the baby's parents, and the baby needs them both.

Give It Some Thought

1. Andrew mentioned how "pathetic" their baby looked. How does a 25-week baby look?
2. If the baby dies, do you think staying away would help Andrew avoid possible pain or increase the pain in the future? Explain your answer.
3. If the baby survives, do you think Andrew will feel guilty for not helping during the long hospital stay?
4. How might Ariana deal with Andrew's reluctance to help?
5. If you were the neonatologist (a doctor who specializes in the care and treatment of newborn babies), would you intervene? Explain your answer.

Gorodenkoff/Shutterstock.com

Lesson 7.1

Decisions About Childbirth

Key Terms

certified nurse-midwife (CNM)

Family and Medical Leave Act (FMLA)

labor

maternity leave

natural childbirth

paternity leave

Pregnancy Discrimination Act (PDA)

pregnancy leave

Learning Outcomes

After studying this lesson, you will be able to

7.1-1   **identify** decisions families must make during pregnancy.

7.1-2   **describe** options for taking leave from work surrounding a pregnancy, including the *Pregnancy Discrimination Act* and the *Family and Medical Leave Act*.

7.1-3   **differentiate** among options for a birthplace and methods of delivery.

Reading and Notetaking Activity

Before reading this lesson, skim the headings and write each heading in a different color or font on a separate piece of paper or electronically. As you silently read the lesson and then listen to your teacher, take notes in the color or font you chose for each heading. After you finish taking notes for each section, draw or copy and paste a small illustration or visual next to the section that will help you remember what you learned.

Introduction

During pregnancy, family members can be involved in the excitement as they offer support to the pregnant person and help prepare for the baby's arrival. The middle part of pregnancy is often the most pleasant for the entire family; pregnant people usually feel their best. Family members are more aware of the baby because they can see the pregnant person's abdomen grow and feel the baby move. People who live in the home may decorate a nursery and gather items needed for the baby. Parents also take time to plan for the many aspects surrounding childbirth, such as scheduling time away from work, choosing a birthplace, and selecting a method of delivery.

7.1-1 Family Considerations

There are many decisions to make before a baby is born. Because these are important decisions, pregnant people need to research each topic thoroughly before making a decision. **Figure 7.1** shows decisions families may make during the prenatal period. At times, unexpected events may cause decisions to change.

One major decision families make is when to inform other children in the family about the pregnancy. Families often decide to tell young children about the new baby during the middle of the pregnancy. To some degree, the timing depends on the age of the other child or children in the home. Older children need to know by the time changes in the pregnant person's body are noticeable. In many cases, explanations occur over time, such as when the child asks questions and when preparations are being made.

Explanations about the new baby may be along the following lines:

- Explain about changes in the body of the pregnant person or how a baby is born, if asked.
- Familiarize an older child with a newborn of a friend or family member, or show them videos of newborns online. Explain how newborns look and act (**Figure 7.2**).

Figure 7.1 Decisions Facing Parents-to-Be

- Health care provider for prenatal care and delivery
- Birthplace (often tied to the choice of the health care provider)
- Health care provider for the baby
- Support person for delivery
- Name(s) for the baby (babies)
- Breast-feeding or formula-feeding
- Housing arrangements for the baby
- Clothing and equipment for the baby
- Support people to help after the baby is born, possibly including child care and education program
- Work and leave options

Goodheart-Willcox Publisher

wavebreakmedia/Shutterstock.com

Figure 7.2 Ways Parents Can Help Young Children Learn About Newborns

- Explain characteristics of "new" babies. For example, parents might say, "Crying is a baby's way of talking."
- Visit with (or babysit for) a friend with a newborn or young infant. Encourage the older child to observe and talk about the baby.
- Show the older child their baby book and photos.
- Read children's books about families with newborns.

Goodheart-Willcox Publisher

Rido/Shutterstock.com

- Assure an older child about what factors will remain the same, such as lots of love, certain activities, and specific housing arrangements.
- Explain and make any changes in housing arrangements or routines before the baby arrives. For example, if an older child is moving to a toddler bed or a new room, explain the reason is because they are growing up. Then wait a while before putting the crib in the area for the new baby.
- Engage the older child as a "special helper" to prepare the house for the new arrival.
- When receiving gifts before or after the baby's arrival, plan a small gift or something special for any older children, too.
- When the baby arrives, ask the other child or children to "introduce" the new baby to family members and friends. Give them a photo of the new baby to take to their child care program or school for "show-and-tell" if the option is available.

Children have both sad and happy emotions about a new baby. Families need to reassure older children they are loved and appreciated. Older children need to feel they are still a vital part of their family.

7.1-2 **Employment Considerations**

Before the arrival of the baby, parents decide how much time off from work they want to take when the baby is born. The amount of time parents schedule often depends on their employer's leave policies, the pregnant person's and baby's health during pregnancy, and the family's financial considerations.

Many pregnant people work until just before their babies are born. Pregnant people may require a **pregnancy leave** if they cannot work for part or all of the pregnancy due to health reasons. Many working people in the United States are covered by the **Pregnancy Discrimination Act (PDA)**, a law that protects the rights of pregnant people who work (**Figure 7.3**).

Employers may grant maternity and paternity leaves to new parents. **Maternity leave**, the time a pregnant person takes off from work for the birth or adoption of a child, is more common than pregnancy leave. Maternity leave allows a biological parent time to recover from childbirth and regain strength; it offers new caregivers from all avenues (biological, adoption, fostering, special circumstances) a chance to adjust to life changes and get to know their newborn. Life with a newborn is usually **hectic** (very busy) and exhausting for the first few weeks. The new parent needs time to rest, adjust to their new role, and bond with the baby.

Figure 7.3 **Pregnancy Discrimination Act (PDA)**

Who qualifies?
- Pregnant people working for companies employing 15 or more people.
- Both married and single people who are pregnant.
- Pregnant people who work in companies that provide job security and benefits for other medical conditions.

What is guaranteed under the law?
- Employer cannot fire a pregnant person due to pregnancy or force a maternity leave.
- A pregnant person is guaranteed the same health, disability, and sickness-leave benefits as other employees with medical conditions.
- A pregnant person may work as long as they can perform their job duties.
- Depending on company policy, pregnant people may be given modified tasks, alternate assignments, disability leave, or leave without pay upon request.
- Job security is guaranteed during a leave.
- A pregnant person continues to accrue seniority and remains eligible for pay increases or benefits during a leave.

Goodheart-Willcox Publisher

Some employers grant **paternity leave** to the other expectant parent in a relationship, which is time off (usually unpaid) for a set period after a child's birth or adoption. Paternity leave gives the other new parent time to care for their family and bond with the child. Partners who were not the birthing person may face challenges in taking paternity leave, such as economic hardship, if the leave is unpaid.

The **Family and Medical Leave Act (FMLA)** is a law that protects the rights of qualified employees to take unpaid leave for various family-related reasons, such as maternity or paternity leave (**Figure 7.4**). Not all employers are required to provide FMLA. These employers, however, may have their own maternity (and possibly paternity) leave policies.

The length of maternity leave varies from company to company. Six weeks is often the minimum length offered (up to 12 weeks if the employee is covered by FMLA). Maternity leave may be paid, partially paid, or unpaid. Companies may grant benefits and a percentage of salary during maternity leave. Other companies might grant a longer unpaid leave, such as several months or a year.

Figure 7.4 Family and Medical Leave Act (FMLA)

Who qualifies?
- Employees who have worked at least 12 months for a covered employer.
- Employees who provide employers 30 days' notice of the need to take leave when the need is foreseeable. Employees must provide evidence of the need for the leave.
- Workers in the following circumstances:
  - Worker or worker's spouse has just given birth to or adopted a child.
  - Worker must provide care for a seriously ill family member.
  - Worker has a serious health condition of their own.

What is guaranteed under the law?
- Qualified employees have up to 12 weeks of leave; time does not have to be taken in one block.
- Leave is unpaid. Employer can pay salary or wages during some or all of the leave time. Employer may require workers to use any accrued paid leave while taking FMLA leave.
- Employer guarantees an employee can have their job (or an equal job) upon return to work.
- Employee maintains all health care benefits during the leave time.

Goodheart-Willcox Publisher

Focus on Careers

Certified Nurse-Midwife

Nurse-midwives provide primary care to pregnant people, including gynecological exams, family planning advice, prenatal care, assistance in labor and delivery, and neonatal care.

Career cluster: Health science.

Education: Educational requirements include a master's degree with classroom and clinical experience. Programs also require candidates to become a registered nurse (RN) before pursuing higher education.

Job outlook: Future employment opportunities for nurse-midwives are expected to grow much faster than the average for all occupations.

To learn more about a career as a nurse-midwife, visit the United States Department of Labor's *Occupational Outlook Handbook* website. You will also be able to compare the job responsibilities, educational requirements, job outlook, and average pay of nurse-midwives with similar occupations.

Photo: MBI/Shutterstock.com

7.1-3 Delivery Considerations

Perhaps the most pressing decisions expecting parents make during pregnancy involve choosing a birthplace and method of labor and delivery. **Labor** is the process that moves the baby out of the pregnant person's body. When making these decisions, factors parents may want to consider include:

- the type of care the birthing person might require during childbirth
- whether the delivery will involve the use of drugs for pain relief

Choosing a Birthplace

Pregnant people have several options to consider before deciding where they want their baby to be born. Options may be limited by where the pregnant person lives, who will deliver the baby, health conditions of the pregnant person and baby, and extent of insurance coverage. A family's choice of birthplace may include the following:

- *Hospitals.* Hospital deliveries are the most common. In a hospital, the birthing person labors in a maternity room and is taken to a delivery room shortly before the baby's birth. Pregnant people who require surgical delivery of their babies use a surgical room. The delivery or surgical room in a hospital is the best place for high-risk deliveries. After the birth, the birthing person spends time in a recovery room before returning to their maternity room. Newborns stay in the hospital nursery.
- *Birthing room in a hospital.* Many hospitals offer the option of a homelike room in the hospital for low-risk deliveries. The birthing room is furnished like a bedroom but has all the needed hospital equipment. A nurse stays in the room during labor. The doctor and delivery nurses are present for delivery or if problems arise. The baby remains with the birthing person and any birth partners in the birthing room until the birthing person is discharged.
- *Birth center.* People who have low-risk pregnancies may opt for a birth center that provides health care before labor as well as delivery services. Birth centers are often located near hospitals and employ certified nurse-midwives. A **certified nurse-midwife (CNM)** is a nurse who has special training in delivering babies during low-risk pregnancies. Many CNMs work with hospitals where they can call for help if an emergency arises. One drawback of birth centers is that the birthing person is often released within hours after giving birth.
- *Home.* Pregnant people may choose to give birth in their own homes. Home births can be risky, especially when emergency services are not nearby. The risks of home births may be lessened by having a CNM present for the delivery. The newborn death rate for home births, however, is higher than for hospital births.

Choosing a Method of Delivery

Before choosing a method of delivery, the pregnant person can discuss their options with the health care provider. All methods of delivery try to make labor and delivery safer and more comfortable for both the birthing person and baby. When choosing a method of delivery, pregnant people may want to keep the following points in mind:

- The length of labor is unknown but tends to be longer for a person's first delivery.
- The amount of pain is unknown. Labor is difficult and requires the use of many muscles. Pain is a part of labor, but if muscles are tense, the birthing person has even more pain. Any complications will also increase the pain.
- Unforeseen complications may cause the method of delivery to change during labor.

Parental Leave Around the World

In the United States, the length or guarantee of parental leave after giving birth or adding a new baby to the family varies greatly. The United States is one of a handful of countries in the entire world that does not have a national paid parental leave policy. In other countries, however, parental leave is a priority, and many countries offer fully paid leave for one or both parents. Length of full paid time off varies from 2 months (Kenya) to 7 months (Czech Republic). Many other countries offer more time off for less pay (some have options for up to a year or more).

Research shows that having one or both parents home has great benefits for both the baby and the caregivers for up to at least 6 months. A longer parental leave can increase bonding, mental health of the birthing person or partner, and immune system of the baby, with less hospitalizations. If breastfeeding is chosen as the main method of nutrition, having a parent home longer to breastfeed can also be a nutritional benefit. Many researchers also suggest that having paid parental leave helps level the playing field between families who are economically disadvantaged and those who can afford to take unpaid time off from work. Long-term benefits of paid parental leave have not been measured precisely, but evidence shows that building caring and trusting bonds in the first year of life can affect social and emotional outcomes well into adulthood. You'll learn more about that in Chapter 10.

Photo: wavebreakmedia/Shutterstock.com

Natural Childbirth

Natural childbirth is a delivery method in which the pregnant person does not use any pain-relieving or other drugs during labor or delivery. There are many ways to ease the pain of natural childbirth, and pregnant people can take preparatory classes or educate themselves on these techniques. Techniques to relieve pain might include changing positions, using a birthing ball, meditation, massage, breathing techniques, heat or ice, and dim lighting, among other things. The *Lamaze (luh-MAHZ) method* is one type of preparatory class pregnant people might take with their birth partners. This method focuses on mental state and breathing practices from the birthing person and birth partner.

In natural childbirth, the birthing person might select a coach to play an active role in prenatal education and support during delivery. Some people use a *doula* (DOO-luh), a knowledgeable helper, who reassures and guides the birthing person through labor. Doulas, however, are not certified to deliver babies. CNMs or nurses can also aid the birthing person.

Doctors may use the natural childbirth method of delivery in hospitals. At birth centers, CNMs use this delivery method **exclusively** (not shared; the only one). Unless attended by a doctor, natural childbirth is the only method used for home deliveries.

Delivery with the Use of Drugs

Although it is important to some birthing persons to have a completely natural childbirth experience, many people opt for a more pain-free labor and delivery. Drugs are also used when complications of delivery arise. Birthing persons must be in the hospital (including a birthing room) to receive most drugs.

Drugs for labor and delivery can be grouped in three ways. *Sedatives* reduce anxiety and are used in the early stages of labor. *Analgesics* (ANN-uhl-GEE-siks) reduce pain, but they do not take it away. *Anesthesia* (ANN-uh-STEE-shuh), also called *anesthetics*, blocks pain. Drugs may be used separately or in combination. All drugs can have side effects, but general anesthesia has the most side effects.

Figure 7.5 describes options for using drugs for pain relief during labor and delivery. To make sure the drug is safe for both the birthing person and baby, the doctor must know the birthing person's health history as well as current health status and any food or drink intake during the last several hours. No matter what method of delivery a birthing person chooses, they should educate themselves on all methods to make the best choice for them and their body. Even once a person has chosen their birth method, complications can arise that shift their plan during the course of labor and delivery. Cesarean section surgery is another method of delivery that you will learn about in the next lesson.

Figure 7.5 Commonly Used Drugs for Labor and Delivery

Drug	Comment
Sedative	Drug given by injection or intravenously (IV) to help reduce pain and ease anxiety.
Local anesthesia	Drug injected to numb the vaginal area when birth is near, an incision will be made, or sutures (stitches) are needed.
Regional anesthesia	Drug injected to numb one area (region) of the body.
Epidural (eh-pih-DURE-uhl)	Drug given through a tiny tube (catheter) placed in the small of the back, just outside the spinal canal. Birthing person feels touch and pressure, but not pain.
Spinal	Drug administered into spinal canal. Side effects are similar to those of epidural, but may be more dangerous. Epidural has almost replaced the spinal, but spinals are used frequently for scheduled C-sections.
Combined spinal epidural (CSE anesthesia); also called walking epidural	A low dose is injected below the spinal cord into the spinal fluid. A combined diluted analgesic and anesthesia are given as an epidural. The low dose allows the birthing person to move and walk as desired.
General anesthesia	Drug given intravenously (by IV) or by breathing a gas that puts the birthing person to sleep. General anesthesia is reserved for when complications arise, such as when an emergency C-section must be done. General anesthesia has more side effects for both the birthing person and baby than other types of anesthesia.

Goodheart-Willcox-Publisher

Coaches as Helpers

Regardless of which method of delivery is chosen, the birthing person needs emotional support, especially during delivery. Family members can act as coaches and provide support and assistance during labor. Coaches tend to calm the birthing person and reduce their feelings of anxiety. Anxiety can be a problem in labor because it causes changes in the blood chemistry. These changes decrease the flow of blood to the baby, which can harm the baby, and slow contractions, resulting in a longer labor.

Another benefit of having labor and delivery coaches is family closeness. Family members who participate in labor and delivery are there to help welcome the child into the world.

Investigate Special Topics

Cord-Blood Banking

In addition to choosing a birthplace and delivery option, expectant parents also make decisions about cord-blood banking. *Cord blood* is blood drawn from the umbilical cord after the baby is born. When parents choose cord-blood banking, the blood is taken to a blood bank where stem cells are removed and stored for possible future use. Research is finding ways to transplant these stem cells into children with certain life-threatening illnesses. For example, some cancers (especially leukemia), blood disorders (various types of anemia), and immune deficiencies are being treated with cord blood. New studies are being conducted on the use of cord blood for treating sickle-cell anemia, cerebral palsy, type 1 diabetes, heart defects, and brain injuries.

Cord blood may be stored in a private bank or in a public bank. Cord blood stored in a private bank enables a child to use their own stem cells if necessary, which eliminates the need for doctors to find a match. The cord blood may also be used to help a parent or sibling. The American Academy of Pediatrics (AAP) suggests that parents use a private bank only if certain illnesses are common in their family because of the high cost associated with banking cells.

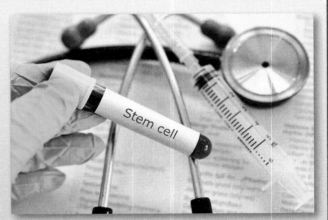
Jarun Ontakrai/Shutterstock.com

Donating the cord blood to a free, public bank is also an option parents may consider. Stem cells donated to a public bank are used to help other children or to aid research. Parents decide about cord-blood banking well before the baby's due date.

Speaking Activity

Take three to five minutes to consider the pros and cons of donating to a cord-blood bank. What legal, ethical, and personal issues might influence a parent's decision? With a partner, discuss your thoughts.

Photo: Tom Wang/Shutterstock.com

1. When do older siblings need to know about a new baby being added to the family? (7.1.1)

    A. It is best to tell them right away so they have time to get used to the idea.

    B. A good time is when changes in the pregnant person's body are noticeable.

    C. Telling older siblings close to the birth of the new baby is best.

    D. It is best to tell them when the family moves the older sibling to a new room.

2. . A child is upset about a new baby joining the family. What can the parents do to make their child feel better? (7.1.1)

    A. Explain they will have to share their parents now and it is going to take some getting used to.

    B. Promise they can be a big help when the baby arrives by doing chores to take pressure off their parents.

    C. Reassure the child and remind them they are loved and still an important part of the family.

    D. Give them a baby doll to play with to practice being a big sibling.

3. How long can an employee be out of work under the Family and Medical Leave Act (FMLA)? (7.1.2)

    A. 6 weeks

    B. 8 weeks

    C. 12 weeks

    D. 16 weeks

4. What is true about the Pregnancy Discrimination Act (PDA)? (7.1.2)

    A. The employee has guaranteed job security while they are out.

    B. A pregnant person may lose their medical benefits if they take maternity leave.

    C. Full pay is guaranteed during a maternity leave.

    D. It applies to any company of any size.

5. Which pain relief option helps reduce pain and ease anxiety? (7.1.3)

    A. Local anesthesia

    B. Spinal block

    C. Epidural

    D. Sedatives

6. What is natural childbirth? (7.1.3)

    A. Using a method of breathing and mental images to get through delivery

    B. Delivering a baby without the use of any medications or pain relief

    C. Giving birth in a tub, also called a water birth

    D. Giving birth at home without any medical intervention

Labor and Delivery

Learning Outcomes

After studying this lesson, you will be able to

7.2-1 **identify** and **describe** the signs of labor.

7.2-2 **explain** important events that occur during each of the three stages of labor.

7.2-3 **differentiate** among the most common procedures used for complications of childbirth.

7.2-4 **describe** the hospital stay following childbirth for both baby and birthing person.

Key Terms

bonding
breech birth position
cesarean section
contraction
dilation
episiotomy
forceps
lightening
vacuum extraction

Reading and Notetaking Activity

Skim this lesson from top to bottom and from left to right and list all the headings. Then, identify key terms with which you are unfamiliar and scan through to find their definitions. Write a "topic sentence" and brief summary for each heading, using the key terms to explain what you think you will learn. After you read this lesson, write a new topic sentence and summary for each section, outlining the main points you learned.

Introduction

The months of waiting and excitement during pregnancy come to an end sooner than expected as labor takes most parents by surprise. Labor may begin any time and any place—even in the middle of sleep. The first signs of labor let parents know the time for delivery is near. Once begun, labor and delivery can take anywhere from a few hours to more than 24 hours. Many deliveries happen without complications, but even in low-risk pregnancies, problems may still occur during or after childbirth.

7.2-1 Signs of Labor

Birth occurs about 266 days after conception (or about 280 days from the pregnant person's last menstrual cycle). During the last few weeks of pregnancy, especially for a first pregnancy, the pregnant person experiences **lightening**, or a change in the baby's position. When lightening occurs, the uterus settles downward and forward, and the baby descends lower into the pelvis. In most cases, the baby's body rotates so the head is toward the birth canal. In about five percent of the cases, however, the baby moves into a **breech birth position** in which the baby's feet, legs, or buttocks emerge first (**Figure 7.6**). When lightening happens, the pregnant person can usually breathe easier. Leg cramps may result, however, and frequent urination is often common due to the increased pressure of the baby on the bladder.

Because the pregnant person's body is preparing for labor during lightening, they may have a few **irregular** (occurring at different times; unusual) contractions. A **contraction** is the tightening or shortening of a muscle. Irregular contractions are known as *false labor*. These contractions are real, but true labor has not begun. Parents-to-be may go to the hospital only to find the contractions are false labor. Carefully timing the **intervals** or periods of time in between contractions can help parents know whether the pregnant person is really in labor.

Labor begins when a series of contractions in the uterine (YOO-teh-rhine) muscles move the baby out of the birthing person's body. These contractions are **involuntary** (not by choice); the birthing person cannot make these contractions happen. Natural signals from the body control the onset, duration, and strength of the contractions. Contractions occur at rather regular intervals that allow the birthing person's muscles to relax. As labor progresses, contractions increase in both duration and strength. The intervals of relaxation between contractions decrease. Parents who are in doubt about the type of contractions should call the health provider and go to the planned birthplace.

Besides regular contractions, there are several other signs of labor. One sign the birthing person may feel is a burst of energy due to increased adrenaline. Another sign of labor is the loosening of the mucous plug in the cervix. The small amount of blood in the mucous is called *the show*, which means labor may start within 24 hours. Another sign of labor may occur when part of the amniotic sac breaks before labor begins. (Often the sac breaks after labor begins.) If the mucous plug becomes **dislodged** (forcefully removed) or the amniotic sac breaks, the birthing person should notify their health care provider.

Complete Breech   Frank Breech   Incomplete Breech

Alila Medical Media/Shutterstock.com

Figure 7.6 In a breech birth, the baby is not in a head-first position. *How does breech birth position affect labor and delivery?*

7.2-2 Stages of Labor

In medical terms, labor is divided into three stages: (1) **dilation**, or opening, of the cervix; (2) delivery of the baby; and (3) delivery of the placenta (**Figure 7.7**).

Dilation of the Cervix

In the early part of labor, contractions come every 15–20 minutes and last about 30 seconds. In the middle part of the first stage of labor, contractions may last 45–60 seconds and are 2–4 minutes apart.

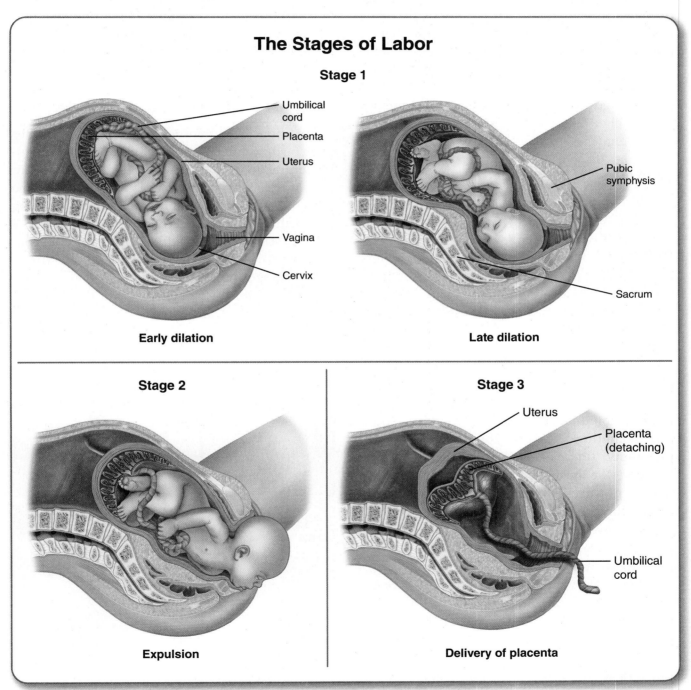

The Stages of Labor

Stage 1

Umbilical cord
Placenta
Uterus
Vagina
Cervix
Pubic symphysis
Sacrum

Early dilation

Late dilation

Stage 2

Expulsion

Stage 3

Uterus
Placenta (detaching)
Umbilical cord

Delivery of placenta

Figure 7.7 *Which stage of labor lasts the longest?*

The most difficult labor occurs in the later part of the stage, or the *transition*. Contractions last for 90 seconds and are so close apart they often feel continuous. Contractions cause the uterus to narrow, which straightens the baby's body and presses the baby's head (or buttocks) against the cervix. As the baby pushes against the cervix, the cervix flattens and opens (dilates).

If the amniotic sac has not broken, the doctor will break it when the cervix is fully dilated. Full dilation of the cervix measures about 4 inches (10 centimeters) in width, which is the size of a small grapefruit. The first stage of labor ends when the cervix is completely open. The length of time for this stage varies a great deal, but the average length is eight hours for a first pregnancy (less for later pregnancies).

Delivery of the Baby

After the transition phase of the first stage of labor, the second stage of labor begins with the lessening of contractions for about an hour. This allows the birthing person to rest before the very active delivery phase begins. During the delivery stage, the baby's head enters the birth canal and the birthing person's muscles push to move the baby down. The walls of the upper part of the birth canal are **elastic** (stretchable). The arrangement of muscles in the lower part of the canal, however, causes resistance and pain.

The doctor may have the birthing person use natural techniques, such as breathing, to reduce pain. Sometimes an **incision** (cut), called an **episiotomy** (ih-pea-zee-AW-tuh-mee), is made to widen the birth canal and prevent tearing. Another practice is to lubricate the birth canal to ease the baby out. After delivery, the doctor *sutures* (stitches) any incision.

The baby changes position during birth and faces downward as the widest part of the baby's head becomes visible (called *crowning*). Soon, the face appears from forehead to chin. The doctor usually suctions fluid from the mouth and nose and checks that the umbilical cord is not wrapped around the baby's neck. The baby's head turns to the side as the shoulders rotate inside the pelvis. This position allows one shoulder and then the other shoulder to emerge.

Finally, the baby's entire body comes out, often with the help of the doctor. The remaining fluid from the amniotic sac is expelled. Instruments are used to suction fluid from the baby's air passages, which helps the baby take their first breath.

The second stage ends when the baby is free of the birthing person's body. The time of birth is noted. The second stage usually lasts between two and three hours with the longer time required for first-time births. The doctor (or sometimes the birthing coach) clips the umbilical cord before the third stage begins (**Figure 7.8**).

Delivery of the Placenta

In about 5–10 minutes and up to 30 minutes after birth, the birthing person has a few irregular contractions. These cause the placenta to completely detach from the uterus and descend. The placenta and fetal membrane expelled following the birth of a baby are called the *afterbirth*. The drug *pitocin* is often used to help the uterus contract, which stops the main flow of blood. Nurses also massage the lower abdomen to aid contraction. As the third stage ends, the birthing person feels a little cold and tired. They also may feel relief and joy.

Paul Hakimata Photography/Shutterstock.com

Figure 7.8 Before the third stage of labor, the umbilical cord is clipped. *What was the function of the umbilical cord before birth?*

7.2-3 Complications of Childbirth

Complications may occur in childbirth that can put both the birthing person and baby at risk (**Figure 7.9**). When complications arise, special medical care involving the use of delivery-aid techniques protects the health of the birthing person and baby. Which technique is used depends on the nature of the problem. Each technique poses risks but has important advantages. Before delivery, a doctor explains any technique, risks, and advantages. The birthing person can then decide whether to have the procedure. The most common procedures used for complications of childbirth are drug-assisted deliveries, vaginal-assisted deliveries, and surgical removal of the baby.

Drug-Assisted Deliveries

Complications of childbirth increase pain. If complications occur, doctors administer or increase the amount of drugs, such as anesthesia and sedation.

Figure 7.9 Complications of Childbirth

Complication	Explanation
Premature delivery	Baby may not be mature enough to survive. Baby is often not in the correct position for delivery.
Premature rupture of membranes (PROM)	Amniotic sac breaks, but labor does not begin. Infection is a danger. Baby who is mature will be delivered. With a premature baby, drugs are given to prevent infection until delivery.
Prolonged and too quick of delivery	Both birthing person and baby are at risk for other complications.
Abnormal position for delivery	Baby may be injured and uterus may rupture. Sometimes the position may be corrected; if not, the baby must be surgically removed.
Cephalopelvic (SEF-a-low-PEL-vik) disproportion	Baby's head is too large to pass through birthing person's pelvic bones. Baby is often surgically removed.
Umbilical cord problems	*Compression*—hollow cord is wrapped around the baby's body. *Prolapsed*—cord slips into the birth canal and is trapped between the baby and canal. The umbilical cord supplies oxygen. A baby who is deprived of oxygen may be born with cerebral palsy, visual problems, and brain damage, or may even die. If the cord cannot be returned to the proper position, the baby is surgically removed.
Asphyxia (as-FIX-eeuh)	Oxygen supply is cut off due to problems with the placenta or umbilical cord, which can cause brain damage or death. After birth, breathing problems may result if lungs contain fluid or waste materials. Chest massage, drugs, and respirators can be used to stimulate breathing.
Meconium (mih-KO-nee-uhm) aspiration	If the baby passes a stool before birth, the meconium in the amniotic fluid may be swallowed or aspirated (breathing it in), and the baby may be covered in meconium. Swallowing sterile meconium is not a problem. Aspirating it will cause the baby to have mild to severe breathing problems, which can last for years. Doctors attempt to suction meconium from the baby's nose and mouth before the first breath.
Postpartum bleeding	The uterus should contract and squeeze the blood vessels shut that supplied blood to the uterus during pregnancy. Massage and hormones are given to help the uterus return to its original size. In rare cases, surgery may be needed to close the blood vessels and stop bleeding.

Goodheart-Willcox Publisher

Other drugs are used if an episiotomy is needed, and still other drugs are used for excessive bleeding during the third stage of labor. (Refer to Figure 7.5 to review different options for using drugs for pain relief during labor and delivery.)

Vaginal-Assisted Deliveries

About five percent of all deliveries in the United States are vaginal-assisted deliveries. Doctors may offer the following two types of assistance:

- *Manual assistance.* Doctors often use *version*, or manually rotating the unborn baby into the correct position for delivery. If the baby's shoulder is caught after the head is free of the birth canal, manual assistance is one of several options to free the shoulder.
- *Operative vaginal delivery.* The doctor may choose to use **forceps**, a curved instrument that fits around the sides of a baby's head. Forceps aid in easing the baby down the birth canal during a contraction. Forceps can also be used safely with premature babies and can be used to aid version. Forceps may cause more trauma for the birthing person than the baby. The other option is **vacuum extraction**, in which suction is used to attach a cuplike device around the top of the baby's head. Vacuum extraction allows the doctor to gently pull the baby down the birth canal. Vacuum extraction may cause more trauma for the baby than the birthing person. The option usually depends on the nature of the complication.

Cesarean Section Deliveries

Many delivery complications are handled through the cesarean (sih-ZARE-ee-uhn) section (or C-section) method. In the **cesarean section**, the birthing person's abdomen and uterus are surgically opened and the baby is removed. The incisions are then closed as with any other surgery. **Figure 7.10** lists medical reasons doctors might use C-section deliveries.

C-sections have the same risks as other major surgeries. Recovery after childbirth is longer than for vaginal deliveries. Also, **sequential** (following in an order) C-sections might raise risks for future complications. Having one C-section does not mean that a person would have to have all following babies be delivered via C-section. Many people are successful with a vaginal birth after cesarean (VBAC).

7.2-4 The Hospital Stay

For parents who choose hospital births, both the birthing person and baby can expect to remain in the hospital for 24–60 hours after delivery. The stay will be longer for a complicated or C-section delivery. Babies who are born at-risk are placed in special nurseries, which you will learn more about in the next lesson. These babies are often kept beyond the normal hospital stay for the birthing person. Parents visit their babies in these special nurseries.

During the hospital stay, medical care is given to ensure the health and safety of both birthing person and baby. The birthing person is closely watched to ensure their body is recovering from the exhausting delivery. The baby must be monitored for health conditions and adjustments to life outside the birthing person's body.

Most hospitals have nurseries for a healthy baby's care. Nurses are on duty in the nursery at all times. Visitors may see the baby through the nursery window during certain times. Younger siblings may or may not be allowed to visit the hospital.

Figure 7.10 Medical Reasons for Cesarean Section Deliveries

- The birthing person's pelvis is small or not shaped for an easy birth.
- The baby or birthing person is at medical risk.
- The baby's head is large.
- Contractions are weak or absent.
- The baby is in an incorrect position for birth.
- The pregnancy is a multiple birth, although some multiple births are vaginal or vaginal-assisted deliveries.
- The doctor feels that previous uterine scar(s) could rupture during a vaginal delivery, although one cesarean birth does not mean all later births must be C-sections, too.

Goodheart-Willcox Publisher

Many hospitals today encourage a *rooming-in arrangement*. If the baby is healthy, they are in a bassinet in the room with the birthing person. The medical care of the baby can be given in the room, and nurses are still available to help the new parent or parents. The support person for the birthing person is provided with a bed in the room.

A rooming-in arrangement enables the parents to begin **bonding**, developing a feeling of affection, with their baby immediately. Bonding helps parents and their baby (**Figure 7.11**). The first hour after birth is perhaps the most sensitive time for parents to bond with their babies. The baby will watch, hear, and respond to the body movements, voice, and touch of the parents. Bonding continues during the next few weeks as parents become more and more attached to their babies.

Figure 7.11 **Benefits of Bonding**

To Babies
- Increased chance of survival
- Better weight gain
- Less crying, more smiles and laughter
- Fewer infections
- Possibly higher IQ
- Better language development

To Parents
- Less incidence of child abuse
- Faster recovery from delivery
- Longer breast-feeding
- More self-confidence as a parent
- Less incidence of depression after delivery

Goodheart-Willcox Publisher

monkeybusinessimages/iStock via Getty Images Plus

Review and Assessment

1. Which of the following is *not* a sign of labor? (7.2.1)
   A. Amniotic sac ruptures.
   B. Pregnant person gets a burst of energy.
   C. Mucous plug becomes dislodged.
   D. Pregnant person feels sharp pains in lower pelvis.
2. What signifies the end of the first stage of labor? (7.2.2)
   A. Contractions are five minutes apart.
   B. The cervix is fully dilated.
   C. The crown of the baby's head is seen.
   D. The birthing person pushes to free the baby of their body.
3. What is the third stage of labor? (7.2.2)
   A. The baby is born and umbilical cord is cut.
   B. Doctor makes a surgical cut called an episiotomy.
   C. The placenta is delivered.
   D. The birthing person pushes to free the baby of their body.
4. Why might a doctor use a C-section delivery? (7.2.3)
   A. A birthing person requests one for a faster delivery.
   B. The baby is not in the correct position for birth.
   C. The birthing person goes into premature labor.
   D. The doctor thinks that vaginal delivery will take too long.
5. What is a rooming-in arrangement? (7.2.4)
   A. The baby stays in the room with the birthing person if the baby is healthy.
   B. The birth partner may stay in the room with the birthing person.
   C. The birthing person can choose to hire a nurse to stay in the hospital room with them at all times.
   D. The birthing person and baby share a room with another new parent and baby for socializing and support.

Lesson 7.3

Newborn Medical Care

Key Terms

anemia

Apgar test

Brazelton scale

jaundice

metabolize

neonatal intensive care unit (NICU)

neonate

neonatology

pediatrician

well-baby checkup

Learning Outcomes

After studying this lesson, you will be able to

7.3-1 **describe** the first medical care newborns receive after birth, including screenings, tests, and procedures.

7.3-2 **compare** the types of care and treatment needed at birth for premature and other high-risk babies.

Reading and Notetaking Activity

Before reading, skim the headings in this lesson. List the headings to create an outline for taking notes during reading and class discussion. Under each heading, list any key terms. Finally, write two questions you expect to have answered in class. After completing the lesson, ask your teacher any questions you still have about the concepts or terms you learned.

Introduction

At birth, babies enter a more exciting world. They are exposed to light and noise. The newborn's life support system—the placenta and umbilical cord—stops functioning minutes after birth. The newborn's air passage is drained of water. The lungs expand as the baby takes their first breath.

Newborns can show physical signs that might worry parents and caregivers. They cough and sneeze to clear mucus from their air passages and lungs. They breathe unevenly, about 46 times per minute, from the diaphragm in the abdominal area. (Adults breathe about 18 times per minute, usually from the chest.) Newborns' heart rates are often between 120 and 150 beats per minute. (Adults' heart rates are between 60 and 100 beats per minute.) To ensure newborns are healthy, doctors perform a series of medical tests on the day of birth and in the following weeks. Babies who are born premature or born with other medical conditions receive special care.

7.3-1 First Medical Care of the Baby

From birth to one month of age, a baby is medically known as a **neonate**. (Neonate is from the Latin words *neo*, meaning new, and *natus*, meaning born.) Generally, in hospital births, a pediatrician comes to the delivery or birthing room just as the baby is born. A **pediatrician** is a doctor who cares for infants, children, and teens until adulthood when growth is complete. If the birthing person is using an obstetrician, this type of doctor continues to complete the delivery process (it may not be the same doctor due to the unpredictability of labor and whether the doctor is working at the time). Family doctors can also deliver babies, but they are not always as capable in high risk or emergency situations, especially if surgery is involved.

After delivery, the baby is often held head downward and the doctor suctions fluid from the nostrils and mouth. The birthing person may hold the baby on their abdomen until the cord is clipped. The nurse then takes the baby to a special table with a heater and dries the newborn with warm towels. A doctor oversees the medical testing and care of the new baby.

The Apgar Test

Medical professionals measure the newborn's chance of survival using the **Apgar test**. The Apgar test checks the baby's pulse, breathing, muscle tone, responsiveness, and skin color. The baby's heart rate and breathing are most important. Skin color, which is a sign of circulation, is least important. The test is given one minute and five minutes after delivery. The baby scores a 0, 1, or 2 in each of the five areas (**Figure 7.12**). The best total score possible is a 10. For the first scoring, the umbilical cord is often still working, but usually has been clipped for the second check. The score at five minutes should be higher.

Healthy babies often score 6 or 7 at one minute and 8 to 10 at five minutes. If a baby scores 7 or less at five minutes, they are tested again at ten minutes after birth. A low score means the baby needs special medical care. If the vital signs are not good, the doctor will attempt to **resuscitate** (bring to an active state; revitalize) and stabilize the newborn. If there are still problems or if the baby is a preterm birth, the doctor orders care by other means (as you will read later in this lesson).

Immediate Care

For healthy newborns, the nurses begin health care after the Apgar tests. Antibiotic drops are put into the newborn's eyes to protect from bacterial infections. Because a newborn's temperature is not very stable, a thermometer is attached to the chest, and the baby wears a snug cap. Newborns typically receive a vitamin K injection to help their blood clot. An injection of penicillin may be necessary for newborns fighting a possible strep infection they may have contracted during delivery.

Figure 7.12 Apgar Test Scores

Sign	0	1	2
Heart rate	Absent	Slow; fewer than 100 beats per minute	More than 100 beats per minute
Respiratory effort	Absent	Weak cry; hyperventilation	Good; strong cry
Muscle tone	Limp	Some flexing and bending of extremities	Well flexed
Reflex irritability	No response	Some motion	Cry
Color	Blue; pale	Body pink; extremities blue	Completely pink

Goodheart-Willcox Publisher

Nurses take a sample of cord blood to determine the newborn's blood type and antibody status. Before the newborn is taken from the delivery room, footprints are made and name bands are placed around the newborn's wrists and/or ankles for identification purposes. The doctor looks over the records and checks the newborn again.

Newborn Screening Tests

Before the birthing person and the newborn leave the hospital, the doctor will order other tests to determine the newborn's health status. Screening tests are performed within 24 to 48 hours of birth and are repeated in two weeks. Any tests with out-of-range results require further testing. These tests can make the difference between wellness and permanent disorders or death.

Blood Tests

Doctors conduct blood tests on newborns by collecting a few drops of blood from a heel prick. Screening can check for anemia, jaundice, and developmental disorders. **Anemia** is a condition that occurs when the level of healthy red blood cells, which carry oxygen to all parts of the body, becomes too low. Mild anemia often does not require any treatment, but a blood transfusion may be necessary to treat more severe anemia.

Jaundice is a liver condition that can make the skin, tissues, and body fluids look yellow. A buildup in the blood of *bilirubin* (bih-lih-ROO-buhn), a yellow pigment, causes jaundice. Newborns, especially premature babies, have problems handling bilirubin due to their immature livers. Doctors treat jaundice by using *light treatment* or *phototherapy* to help reduce the skin's yellow color (**Figure 7.13**). Hospitals may also treat newborn jaundice with *fiberoptic phototherapy* in which a flexible light pad is wrapped around the baby. More research needs to be done on this newer method. Current studies show it to be less effective than conventional methods for full-term babies, but equally effective in treating preterm babies.

Doctors also screen newborns for developmental disorders. The number of disorders a doctor will check varies depending on each state's screening program. Most states require tests to check for the following conditions:

- *Phenylketonuria (PKU)*—condition in which the body is unable to **metabolize** (break down in the digestive system) an amino acid, *phenylalanine* (FEN-uhl-AL-eh-neen). PKU is treated by diet. Untreated PKU can lead to seizures and impaired intellectual abilities. (All states check for this condition.)

Figure 7.13 In light treatment or phototherapy, the newborn is placed in a bassinet under special lights. A mask protects the baby's eyes from the lights. *Why might newborns develop jaundice?*

Doro Guzenda/Shutterstock.com

- *Hypothyroidism*—thyroid hormone deficiency that can lead to slow growth and abnormal brain development if left untreated.
- *Galactosemia*—condition in which the body is unable to digest the sugar in milk. Blindness, impaired intellectual abilities, and death may result if left untreated.
- *Sickle-cell anemia*—disease in which the body makes sickle-shaped red blood cells (**Figure 7.14**). The cells become blocked in the blood vessels, causing pain and body damage and increasing the risk of infection and possibly death. Blood specialists provide regular medical care for this disorder.

Hearing Test

Doctors often conduct hearing tests on newborns. To get accurate results, doctors first drain any fluids in the middle ear. The fluid is usually squeezed out during a vaginal delivery, but babies born via C-section should wait about 48 hours after delivery before being given a hearing test. A loss of hearing can delay language and concept development.

Heart Test

Life-threatening heart defects may affect the way babies' hearts function or the way their hearts are shaped. Heart defects may not be apparent at birth, but become evident or critical soon after birth. A group of severe heart defects is medically referred to as *critical congenital heart disease (CCHD)*. Doctors conduct newborn screening for CCHD by using *pulse oximetry* (AWK-sim-uh-tree), a noninvasive test that determines how much oxygen is in the newborn's blood.

Neonatal Behavioral Assessment Scale

The Neonatal Behavioral Assessment Scale, or the **Brazelton scale**, is a test doctors use to test newborns and babies up to two months of age. The Brazelton scale determines whether a baby has problems with the following:

- *interacting with the environment.* Checks alertness; attention to sound, light, and other factors; and tendency to cuddle.
- *handling motor processes.* Assesses general activity level and reflex behaviors.
- *controlling their physical state.* Looks at self-quieting behaviors and levels of excitement and irritability.
- *responding to stress.* Checks startle reactions and trembling.

Circumcision

In the United States, parents have a choice of whether they do or do not want their newborn boy to be circumcised. *Circumcision* is a surgical procedure that involves removing the skin from the end of the penis (called *foreskin*). Parents choose circumcision primarily for religious, cultural, and/or health reasons. The procedure is often performed one or two days after birth. Circumcision carries benefits and risks, and parents may wish to seek advice from their doctor or religious leader before making their decision.

Sickle Cell Anemia

Normal red blood cell with normal hemoglobin

Mutated hemoglobin forms strands that cause sickle shape

Alila Medical Media/Shutterstock.com

Figure 7.14 A newborn blood test checks for sickle-cell anemia, a condition in which the red blood cells are irregularly shaped. *Explain how sickle-cell anemia might damage the body.*

Well-Baby Checkup

Before the newborn leaves the hospital, the doctor will ask the parents to make an appointment for a well-baby checkup within three to five days. A **well-baby checkup** is a routine medical visit in which the pediatrician examines a baby for signs of good health and proper growth.

During this checkup, the nurse weighs the newborn and measures the length, head, and chest. The pediatrician reviews the family's health history, examines the newborn, answers parents' questions, and makes recommendations. Parents then schedule their baby's next checkup.

7.3-2 Care for High-Risk Newborns

High-risk newborns are babies who are born premature, have a low birthweight, or have another high-risk condition, such as a congenital condition. In the United States, about 10 percent of newborns are born premature every year and about 8 percent have low-birthweights. Congenital conditions can affect the baby's heart, digestive tract, spine, or brain.

High-risk newborns are admitted into a **neonatal intensive care unit (NICU)**, also called an *intensive care nursery (ICN)*, where they receive immediate, specialized, round-the-clock care and treatment. NICUs are rated by level—1 to 4. Higher numbers are used for the treatment of high-risk newborns who are the smallest and most ill. The doctors and nurses who work in NICUs have special training in neonatology. **Neonatology** (NEE-oh-nay-TAW-lo-gee) is a branch of medicine concerned with the care, development, and diseases of newborns.

More lives are saved in NICUs now than in the past—due in part to medical and technological advances. A change in policy, however, also contributes to more newborns surviving. Today, NICUs throughout the United States implement *family-centered care policies*, which encourage parental presence in the NICU as well as parental involvement in the newborn's care and treatment. Parents are encouraged to visit the NICU and feed, touch, talk, and sing to their newborns. Hospitals even employ surrogate nonfamily members in the NICU to hold and rock babies. Family-centered

Focus on Careers

Physician—Neonatologist

Physician is a category of health careers in which health professionals provide physical care to patients. *Neonatologists* are physicians who specialize in the care of premature and ill newborns in a neonatal intensive care unit. Neonatologists diagnose and treat a variety of ailments specific to newborns.

Career cluster: Health science.

Education: Educational requirements include an advanced degree, four years of medical school, and three to seven additional years of internship and residency. Licensure is also required.

Job outlook: Future employment opportunities for neonatologists are expected to grow faster than the average for all occupations.

To learn more about a career as a neonatologist, visit the United States Department of Labor's *Occupational Outlook Handbook* website. You will also be able to compare the job responsibilities, educational requirements, job outlook, and average pay of neonatologists with similar occupations.

Photo: Photodisc/Photodisc via Getty Images

care policies promote a developmentally supportive environment, which provides newborns with the love, attention, and support they need for healthy growth and development (**Figure 7.15**).

Figure 7.15 NICU Developmentally Supportive Environment

- Each baby (and family) is assigned one medical team.
- Except for emergencies, medical and nursing care coincides with the baby's sleep-wake cycles.
- Parents are encouraged to participate in their baby's care by feeding, rocking, and doing skin-to-skin holding.
- The NICU is decorated and parents have their own space around their baby's NICU bed.
- Soft lighting and low noise levels provide a soothing environment.

Goodheart-Willcox Publisher

FOCUS ON MENTAL HEALTH

Preterm babies need a developmentally supportive environment in the NICU, including parents who regularly help with their babies' care. This boosts their mental health, which can have great health benefits as well. For a baby's mental health, a supportive environment must be continued after babies are discharged, too.

1. When is the Apgar test conducted on a newborn? (7.3.1)
   A. Within 24 hours of birth
   B. Within 30 minutes of birth
   C. At one minute and five minutes after birth
   D. At five minutes and eight minutes after birth

2. Which of the following is *not* a medical screening conducted on a newborn right after birth? (7.3.1)
   A. Injection of vitamin K
   B. Hearing test
   C. Apgar test
   D. Antibiotic eyedrops

3. What is true about the neonatal intensive care unit (NICU) for high-risk newborns? (7.3.2)
   A. They are rated from level 1-4, with level 4 representing the highest need.
   B. Parents/guardians are not allowed inside the NICU due to low immune systems of newborns.
   C. Newborns in the NICU are not expected to live long.
   D. The NICU is run exclusively by OB doctors.

Postpartum Care

Key Terms

baby blues

paternal postpartum
  depression (PPPD)

perinatal depression

postpartum depression
  (PPD)

postpartum psychosis
  (PPP)

postpartum care

postpartum mood
  disorder (PPMD)

Learning Outcomes

After studying this lesson, you will be able to

7.4-1 **describe** physical care needed for the birthing person during the postpartum period.

7.4-2 **identify** postpartum mood disorders and treatment options for both partners.

7.4-3 **exemplify** ways caregivers can meet their own needs while caring for a newborn.

Reading and Notetaking Activity

Create a table like the one shown. Include as many rows as you need. Before reading the lesson, list facts you already know about what is included in postpartum care for the birthing person and baby in the *Give One* column. In the *Get One* column, list facts you learn as you read the lesson. If you have any questions about what you are reading, raise your hand and ask your teacher. After you finish reading the lesson, team up with a classmate and discuss each other's lists. Are there items you would add to your list?

Give One	Get One
List facts you already know	List facts you learned

Introduction

A birthing person's body undergoes changes from conception to delivery; new changes occur again once the baby is born. Most of these changes help the birthing person's body recover from pregnancy and childbirth. Physical and psychological changes during the postnatal period are normal. Abnormal side effects of pregnancy and labor may occur, however, and are warning signs needing immediate medical attention.

Postnatal care for the birthing person is important not only for their health, but also for the well-being of the baby. Poor health of the birthing person impedes and delays their ability to meet the baby's care needs. Studies show that poor physical health of the birthing person negatively affects a baby's development in all domains through the infant and toddler years. Depressive symptoms have an even greater impact on children than poor physical health. Parent/guardian mood disorders adversely affect children's intellectual and emotional development throughout childhood.

7.4-1 Postpartum Physical Care

Postpartum care, or *postnatal care*, is the care the birthing person receives during the 6 to 8 weeks following the birth of a baby. People who had cesarean births may need 12 weeks of recovery time. Birthing persons may experience typical side effects of delivery during this postpartum period (**Figure 7.16**).

The first hour after birth is a critical time for restoring the birthing person's body stability. Vital signs (pulse, respiration, and other body functions) are measured every few minutes just as they would be following surgery. Doctors want to make sure the uterus contracts properly.

To regain their strength and avoid health concerns, the birthing person does not remain in bed for long after childbirth. After a few days, the doctor might allow the birthing person to perform certain

Figure 7.16 Typical Side Effects of Delivery

- Mild cramping
- *Lochia* (LO-kia), or vaginal bleeding caused by the shedding of the uterine lining
- Some loss or thinning of hair
- Facial blemishes or acne
- Night sweats
- Frequent urination to eliminate excess body fluid
- Urinating "accidents" due to the weakening of bladder muscles (called *stress incontinence*)
- Sore nipples and engorgement of breasts if breast-feeding
- Extra soreness due to any delivery complication

Goodheart-Willcox Publisher

exercises that will help tone the abdominal muscles. These exercises are done slowly and gradually for safety.

If the birthing person does not nurse their baby, they can return to their pre-pregnancy healthful eating patterns during the postpartum period. Nursing, however, requires more nutrients to create the breast milk that sustains babies. A doctor or dietitian can help determine nutritional and activity needs after pregnancy.

Doctors often want the birthing person to schedule a postpartum checkup about six weeks after delivery. At this appointment, doctors check to see how well the birthing person is recovering; if they must return to work before the end of the postpartum period, nurses and doctors can provide special guidance. The key to complete recovery, whether at home or on the job, is to get plenty of rest and to go slow with activity. Too much activity may hinder the recovery process.

7.4-2 Postpartum Mood Disorders

Parents often think the time after the birth of their baby will be happy and exciting. Sometimes, however, one or both partners may experience a **postpartum mood disorder (PPMD)**, a mental health condition characterized by feelings of sadness, guilt, or depression after the birth of their baby. PPMDs are made worse by other stressors, such as financial challenges, social isolation without parenting support, family conflicts, health concerns, increased work schedules, mood disorder in the partner, and a fussy baby.

Mood Disorders in Birthing Person

Approximately 15 percent of people who give birth experience depression during or after pregnancy. People who are depressed during pregnancy are also often depressed during the postpartum period and even afterward. For these people, the most vulnerable time is between 12 and 24 months post-delivery. Because of the timing before and long after delivery, **perinatal** (per-ih-NAY-tuhl) **depression** is the newer term used.

Mood disorders experienced in the postpartum period range from mild to severe (**Figure 7.17**). Each PPMD has its own symptoms. **Baby blues**, the most common mood disorder, is a mild postpartum mood disorder that goes away on its own. Baby blues usually begin one to three days after childbirth and disappear within a few days. **Figure 7.18** lists suggestions for coping with baby blues. **Postpartum depression (PPD)** is a serious form of depression that occurs less frequently than baby blues. **Postpartum psychosis (PPP)** is a rare and extremely severe mental illness. (*Psychosis* means *mental illness*.) Additionally, some people who give birth are also affected by postpartum anxiety, which can be caused from hormonal changes, sleep deprivation, feelings of being overwhelmed, or a combination of factors. The birthing person may feel restless, unable to relax, or feel a constant sense of worry. Anxiety can be treated by getting more sleep, receiving support and help with the baby, exercising or meditating, and talking to a professional. Sometimes, medication is also appropriate.

Generally, PPD and PPP occur a little later than baby blues and do not **subside** (lessen in severity) without treatment. In these cases, negative thoughts and feelings go beyond common negative thoughts, such as "I look awful," or "My baby is so fussy." People with serious mood disorders may think about harming themselves, their babies, and even older children. Some actually do cause harm.

Although the exact causes of postpartum mood disorders are unknown, scientists believe causes may be due to a variety of factors, including genetics, chemical changes, and stress. All birthing persons in the postpartum period are at risk of developing a PPMD. Some people, however, have more risk factors. These additional risk factors for developing a PPMD may include the following:

- age in the teen years or over 40 years of age
- family history of mood disorders
- family history of thyroid problems
- mood swings during the menstrual cycle—often called *PMS*
- migraine headaches when taking hormones (including birth control pills)
- fertility problems
- severe family stress
- lack of support from family and friends
- previous postpartum mood disorder

Figure 7.17 Postpartum Mood Disorders of the Birthing Person

Name	Rate of Incidence	Symptoms	Appearance and Duration
Baby blues	60–80% of all deliveries	Irritability; anxious spells; sleep and appetite problems; weeping; feeling tired	Peaks between 3 and 5 days postpartum. Often resolves itself within a few days.
Postpartum depression (PPD)	10–15% of all deliveries (Rates are higher for teen deliveries)	Restlessness; exhaustion; inability to concentrate; memory loss; uncontrollable crying; trouble making decisions; lack of interest in pleasurable activities; appetite and sleep problems; overconcern or lack of interest in baby; fear of harming self or baby; guilt	Occurs within first 6 weeks postpartum. Treatment recommended. If untreated, may last a year or longer. Often happens again in future deliveries.
Postpartum psychosis (PPP)	0.1–0.2% of all deliveries (1 to 2 in 1,000)	Severe mental illness; includes delusions that often focus on the infant dying; sees the infant as either perfect or defective; desires to kill self or infant	Occurs between 1 and 3 months postpartum with a second peak at 18 to 24 months postpartum. Continues until treated.

Goodheart-Willcox Publisher

Figure 7.18 Coping with Baby Blues

- Remember the feelings are temporary. The "blues" are due to a drop in the hormones estrogen (ES-truh-jehn) and progesterone (pro-JES-teh-rohn); recovery from pregnancy, labor, and delivery; and stress caused by the new parental role.
- Maintain good hygiene habits.
- Use physical activity as a way to increase *endorphins* (feel-good hormones). A 30-minute walk alone, with a family member or friend, or with the baby in a stroller is most helpful to the new parent's physical and psychological well-being.
- Make sure to get some sunshine.
- Sleep, nap, or relax whenever possible.
- Snack on nutritious foods.
- Take a few minutes daily to do something beyond baby care, such as chat with friends or family, or run an errand.
- Ask for child care help.
- Lower expectations concerning household responsibilities.
- Keep visitors to a minimum.
- Cry if needed, but practice positive coping skills. Doctors can help if crying is too frequent or uncontrollable.
- Do not expect to be completely comfortable in the new "parental shoes." Forget ideas of perfect parent and perfect baby. Within an instant, a person becomes a parent, but the parenting role evolves over many years.

Goodheart-Willcox Publisher

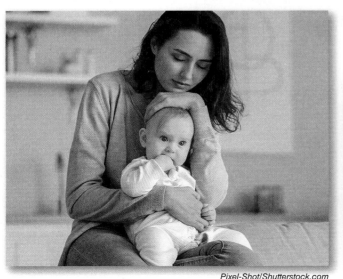

Pixel-Shot/Shutterstock.com

Mood Disorders in Partners

About 10 percent of partners show signs of depression during the birthing person's pregnancy through six months after delivery. The percentage spikes to approximately 26 percent from three to six months after delivery. This timing **coincides** (happens together) with the timing of when many birthing persons return to work. Depression is more likely if the birthing partner is experiencing it, too.

Mood disorders that appear in men and partners are often called **paternal postpartum depression (PPPD)**. Fathers and partners experience similar problems as the birthing person, such as a change in hormones and additional stressors. Certain PPPD symptoms are common (**Figure 7.19**). Most research has been conducted on traditional nuclear families, but either partner or new parent can experience postpartum depression, even in cases of adoption, same-sex relationships, or other family structures.

Figure 7.19 Symptoms of Paternal Postpartum Depression (PPD)

- Appear sad and quiet or irritable and agitated.
- May experience heart palpitations and shortness of breath.
- May experience panic attacks.
- Lose interest in hobbies and socializing.
- Feel worthless.
- Lose appetite and become sleep deprived.
- Work excessively (60+ hours per week).
- May engage in risky behaviors (substance abuse, gambling).

Goodheart-Willcox Publisher

Lopolo/Shutterstock.com

Treatment for Mood Disorders

Mood disorders are just as common and real as physical disorders. If untreated, like other problems, they can have devastating effects on the entire family. Treatment is critical because mood disorders not only cause problems for parents but can be devastating for the newborn.

Treatments for mood disorders vary due to the severity of the condition. Examples may include medication or behavior therapy. Training in parent-child interactions, participating in support groups, and receiving help with childrearing are other examples of treatment options.

7.4-3 Meeting the Needs of Caregivers

Once the newborn is home, roles and responsibilities of caregivers change. The first few weeks with the newborn are especially difficult. Parents find every waking moment dedicated to their newborn and family and may soon feel overwhelmed. As parents care for their newborn during the postpartum period, they also need to care for themselves. Parents can meet their own needs while being wonderful parents to their newborn by:

- *getting enough rest.* Being tired can lead to illness, irritability, and depression. Therefore, resting whenever possible is especially important for parents. Sleeping or resting while babies sleep can help immensely. If there are two partners in the family, taking turns getting up with the baby at night can also help parents get the rest they need.
- *maintaining a healthful diet.* Eating nutritious meals and snacks helps parents have the energy needed for parenting (**Figure 7.20**). Keeping it simple and planning or preparing meals ahead of time can save time and money.
- *being physically active.* Being physically active for 30 minutes each day has many benefits. Putting the baby in a stroller and going for a walk outside can be excellent for a parent's physical health and mood. Likewise, if there is someone who can stay with the baby, the parent can get some exercise while having a short break of alone time.

pixelfit/E+ via Getty Images

Figure 7.20 Preparing meals ahead of time and freezing them for a later date can be an easy and efficient way of planning ahead for postpartum nutritional needs. *What healthy freezer meals could a parent prepare?*

- *staying organized.* Parents can save time and frustration by keeping baby items organized and easily accessible. A bulletin or dry erase board in a convenient location may be useful for posting doctors' recommendations, appointments, bills, shopping lists, and other reminders.
- *taking care of legal matters.* While in the hospital, parents can apply for their baby's birth certificate and Social Security number. (Social Security numbers are needed for tax forms, bank accounts, savings bonds, and medical coverage.) Parents may also enroll their baby in a family health care policy and add the baby as a beneficiary to life insurance policies, investment accounts, and their will.
- *socializing.* Spending time with other new parents provides socialization opportunities for the parents and their newborns. Hiring a **competent** (knowledgeable) and trustworthy babysitter can also help parents have outings without babies (**Figure 7.21**).

The healthy development of newborns depends on the parent-child relationship. With their own needs met, parents are better able to meet their newborn's needs. Babies whose needs are met by loving parents are off to a good start.

MBI/Shutterstock.com

Figure 7.21 Parents need to spend time together away from the home and with other adults to restore their physical and mental energy. *What types of socialization opportunities might be available for parents and their newborns?*

1. How long does the postpartum period last for someone who has just given birth? (7.4.1)
   A. 2 weeks
   B. 6 weeks
   C. Up to 12 weeks
   D. Up to 6 months
2. What should someone keep in mind if they have just had a baby? (7.4.1)
   A. Get plenty of rest and slowly introduce activity.
   B. Start pre-pregnancy exercise back up as soon as possible.
   C. Breastfeeding a baby is natural and requires no extra nutrients.
   D. Bedrest is necessary to regain strength.
3. Which postpartum mood disorder is characterized by delusions that often focus on the infant dying, and seeing the infant as either perfect or defective? (7.4.2)
   A. Postpartum depression (PPD)
   B. Baby blues
   C. Postpartum psychosis (PPP)
4. What is one way a new parent can meet their own needs while caring for a newborn? (7.4.3)
   A. Ask a family member to move in temporarily to help with the baby.
   B. Try to get house chores completed while the baby sleeps to keep up with responsibilities.
   C. Stop going out or doing things with friends until they have a grip on their new responsibilities at home.
   D. Get 30 minutes of exercise each day and prepare meals ahead of time.

Chapter 7

Review and Assessment

Summary

Lesson 7.1

7.1-1 All family members can be involved in the period of pregnancy. Family decisions to be made before birth include where the baby will be born and which method of delivery will be used.

7.1-1 Other decisions before the birth of a baby include choosing a care provider, childcare options, equipment and housing arrangements for the baby, choosing a baby name, telling any other siblings, and whether to breastfeed or use formula.

7.1-2 There are many options for taking leave from work to have a baby. Two legal acts that protect pregnancy leave are called the Pregnancy Discrimination Act and the Family and Medical Leave Act.

7.1-3 Options for birthplace include hospital deliveries, birthing room in a hospital, a birthing center, or at home.

7.1-3 Delivery methods include natural or drug-assisted childbirth. C-section births may be medically necessary in cases of breech birth, multiple births, or when other pregnancy complications arise.

Lesson 7.2

7.2-1 Signs of labor include lightening when the baby lowers into the pelvis, a burst of energy in the pregnant person, the dislodging of the mucous plug, the amniotic sac rupturing or "water breaking," and contractions.

7.2-2 There are three stages of labor. In the first stage of labor, the cervix becomes fully dilated to 10cm in width. The second stage of labor includes the baby coming out of the birthing person's body and the umbilical cord being cut. The third stage of labor involves delivery of the placenta.

7.2-3 Common procedures used when delivery complications arise include the use of drugs such as anesthesia or sedatives, manual rotation of the unborn baby to change its position (called version), the use of forceps or a vacuum extraction, and C-section surgery.

7.2-4 The hospital stay can be anywhere from 24 hours to a few days, depending on several factors for both the baby and the birthing person. Medical care is given to both the birthing person and newborn, and both are monitored closely. Many hospitals use a rooming-in approach where the baby stays in the birthing person's hospital room for more close bonding.

Lesson 7.3

7.3-1 New babies receive immediate medical care and numerous tests at birth, including the Apgar test, antibiotic eye drops, a vitamin K injection, blood tests for detecting several conditions, hearing tests, and heart tests. Vitals and measurements are also taken immediately. The Neonatal Behavioral Assessment Scale, or Brazelton scale, is taken before the baby is two months old.

7.3-2 Premature and other high-risk babies are admitted to a neonatal intensive care unit (NICU), where they receive special individualized care around the clock with the latest technology and medical advancements. Most NICUs around the United States use family-centered care policies, inviting parents to visit, feed, touch, talk to, and sing to their newborns.

Lesson 7.4

7.4-1 The postpartum period lasts up to 12 weeks and requires special care for the person. The birthing person will experience typical side effects of delivery during this period, such as vaginal bleeding, cramping, hair loss or thinning, acne, night sweats, frequent urination and urinating accidents, and soreness. Other side effects will be present if the birthing person is breastfeeding, such as sore nipples and engorged breasts.

7.4-1 Getting plenty of rest and taking it slow are the best ways for the birthing person to recover from delivery. C-section deliveries typically take longer to recover from than vaginal deliveries.

7.4-2 Postpartum mood disorders can affect one or both partners due to stress, lack of sleep, and hormonal changes. Some form of baby blues is normal and affects most people who have given birth. Other disorders include postpartum depression, paternal postpartum depression, and postpartum psychosis.

7.4-2 Treatment for mood disorders varies and includes behavior therapy, support groups, education, medication, and receiving help caring for the baby.

7.4-3 New parents can make sure their needs and their newborn's needs are met by getting plenty of rest, staying organized, handling legal matters like securing insurance and a social security number for the baby, eating well, exercising regularly, socializing with other new parents, and having outings together without the baby.

College and Career Portfolio

Portfolio Prioritization

Identifying priorities is an essential part of any project and is especially important for a self-guided project like compiling a portfolio. Before you begin compiling your portfolio, identify which items are most important. Your priorities will depend on the purpose of your portfolio and on where your strengths lie.

When prioritizing, consider which items best showcase your work and talents. Also consider where you can compensate for any weaknesses. To identify your priorities as you compile a portfolio, complete the following activities:

- Consider which items will best highlight your strengths and which items are most important to your objective.
- Highlight the most important items in your portfolio. These will be your top priorities.

Recall and Application

1. What is a good way to prepare an older sibling for a new baby? (7.1.1)
   A. Teach them about newborns and let them spend time around a newborn if possible.
   B. Let them know that things in the family are going to change and they need to be a tough big brother or sister.
   C. Help them make a welcome gift for their new baby sister or brother.
   D. Explain to the older sibling that a new baby is not going to cause any changes in the family dynamic.

2. Which of the following is a law that protects the rights of qualified employees to take unpaid leave for various family-related reasons, such as maternity or paternity leave? (7.1.2)
   A. Pregnancy Discrimination Act
   B. Family and Medical Leave Act
   C. Civil Rights Act
   D. Pregnant Workers Fairness Act

3. Who qualifies for the Pregnancy Discrimination Act? (7.1.2)
   A. Married or single people who are pregnant that work for companies with 15 or more employees that provide job security and benefits for other medical conditions
   B. Employees who have worked at least 12 months for a covered employer
   C. Employees who provide employers 30 days' notice of the need to take leave when the leave is foreseeable
   D. Married or single people who are pregnant and may not be covered by health insurance for the delivery of their child

4. Which birthplace option is ideal for low-risk pregnancies and employs certified nurse-midwives (CNMs)? (7.1.3)
   A. Hospital
   B. Birthing room
   C. Birthing center
   D. Home birth

5. What is the difference between a natural childbirth and a vaginal delivery? (7.1.3)
   A. Natural childbirth involves the use of drugs, and vaginal deliveries don't.
   B. Vaginal deliveries can be natural or can involve the use of drugs.
   C. Natural childbirth is the best option, while vaginal delivery just means the baby is delivered through the vaginal canal.
   D. A vaginal delivery can also include C-section surgery when medically necessary.

6. What is a sign that labor may be coming soon? (7.2.1)
   A. The pregnant person feels extremely fatigued and uncomfortable.
   B. The baby lowers down into the pelvis and the pregnant person experiences lightening.
   C. The pregnant person has a feeling that the baby is ready to be born.
   D. Contractions begin, but they do not come in regular intervals yet.

7. What should a pregnant person do if their amniotic sac breaks? (7.2.1)
   A. Call their healthcare provider.
   B. Stay calm until contractions are 5 minutes apart.
   C. Wait for other signs of labor to confirm that it's time to prepare for delivery.
   D. Head immediately to the birthplace.

8. In the first stage of labor, how wide does the cervix have to be to be considered fully dilated? (7.2.2)
   A. 5 centimeters
   B. 8 centimeters
   C. 10 centimeters
   D. 13 centimeters
9. On average, about how long does the first stage of labor last for a first pregnancy? (7.2.2)
   A. 8 hours
   B. 24 hours
   C. 2 hours
   D. 15 hours
10. During the second stage of labor, the widest part of the baby's head becomes visible. What is this called? (7.2.2)
    A. Crowning
    B. Episiotomy
    C. Transition
    D. The show
11. What occurs during the delivery of the placenta? (7.2.2)
    A. The birthing person may feel a sense of dread and extreme sadness due to hormones.
    B. The doctor will make a small incision to allow for the extraction of the placenta.
    C. The nurse massages the birthing person's abdomen to aid contraction of the uterus.
    D. The birthing person gets in a special position to allow gravity to pull the placenta away from the uterus.
12. Which of the following is used to help guide the baby's head through the birth canal during a contraction? (7.2.3)
    A. Vacuum extraction
    B. Forceps
    C. Version
    D. Pitocin

13. What is one positive result of rooming-in at the hospital after delivery? (7.2.4)
    A. The new parents don't have to worry about the security of their baby.
    B. The nurses in the nursery can focus more on the other babies who need it.
    C. Breastfeeding is much easier because the baby is close by.
    D. Bonding occurs more easily.
14. Which of the following is a yellow pigment that causes jaundice in newborns? (7.3.1)
    A. Phenylketonuria (PKU)
    B. Galactosemia
    C. Bilirubin
    D. Anemia
15. Doctors test the newborn's blood for hypothyroidism. What is this condition? (7.3.1)
    A. A deficiency that can lead to slow growth and abnormal brain development if left untreated.
    B. A condition in which the body is unable to digest the sugar in milk.
    C. A condition in which the body is unable to metabolize a specific amino acid.
    D. A liver condition that can make the skin, tissues, and body fluids look yellow.
16. What is the primary reason parents might choose for their newborn to have a circumcision? (7.3.1)
    A. For cosmetic purposes
    B. Due to the recommendation from the doctor
    C. For religious, cultural, and/or health reasons
    D. To make sure the baby would have no reproductive medical problems later in life
17. How many newborns in the United States are born premature each year? (7.3.2)
    A. 25 percent
    B. 10 percent
    C. 8 percent
    D. 5 percent

18. Which of the following is not a typical delivery side effect that might be experienced during the postpartum period? (7.4.1)
    A. Hair loss or thinning
    B. Vaginal bleeding
    C. Urinary accidents or stress incontinence
    D. Bruises/markings around the vaginal area
19. Which of the following creates a higher risk for experiencing a postpartum mood disorder? (7.4.2)
    A. Age between 25 and 35 years old
    B. Family history of mood disorders
    C. No prior experience with newborns
    D. Excessive visitors after delivery
20. What benefit does physical activity have for new parents? (7.4.3)
    A. It helps the birthing parent lose their extra baby weight.
    B. It keeps a regular routine for the newborn.
    C. It can improve physical health and overall mood.
    D. It is a way to get a break from the baby.

Critical Thinking

1. **Identify.** At one time, pregnancy and childbirth were considered a "woman's affair." Now this event is thought of as a family affair. What changes in society have led to pregnancy and childbirth being a family affair? Are there ways in which society still considers pregnancy and childbirth a "woman's affair"? Identify ways family members can be involved.
2. **Determine.** Imagine you are a doctor and your patient is nearing their due date. The patient expresses concern that their four-year-old son might be upset about the new baby. Even though the patient has explained to their son that the baby is coming, he seems anxious and has been misbehaving at the child care program. With a partner, role-play this scenario, and determine what advice you would give to your patient.
3. **Compare and contrast.** Compare and contrast the birthplaces and methods of delivery available to pregnant people.

Create a resource for pregnant people, listing these options and identifying three pros and three cons for each.
4. **Evaluate.** Evaluate the benefits of bonding within the first weeks after birth. What are the benefits to babies, and what are the benefits to parents? What additional benefits are there for bonding in the first hour after birth?
5. **Draw conclusions.** Why is it best for the baby to be in a specific position for childbirth? Review the information in this chapter about lightening, childbirth, and breech birth position. Draw conclusions about why the ideal position for childbirth is ideal. What are the disadvantages if a baby is in the wrong position?
6. **Analyze.** Review the Apgar test and Brazelton scale and consider: how exactly do these measurements determine the health of a newborn? Why would a low score indicate that a newborn needs special medical attention? Why would a high score indicate a healthy baby?
7. **Make inferences.** Imagine a parent with a premature baby who will likely remain hospitalized for several weeks. What challenges might the parent face in terms of bonding? What can family and friends do to help?
8. **Cause and effect.** Imagine you are a counselor, and you are talking with a parent experiencing PPD and PPPD. How would you explain the causes of these conditions? How would you respond to the parent's feelings that something is "wrong" with them?

Core Skills

1. **Research and writing.** Maternity, paternity, and family leave policies vary by company and by country. Research the legal requirements for leave policies in the United States and in at least two other countries. How are the legal requirements similar? How are they different? Based on your research, how, if at all, would you change leave policies in the United States? Write a two- to four-page essay summarizing your research and proposing any changes.

2. **Art and writing.** Imagine you are teaching the stages of labor to a group of students who learn best when they create models and replicate processes with their hands. In small groups, devise a hands-on activity that simulates and teaches the process of childbirth, using classroom materials or materials from home. The activity should be school appropriate. Write a two-page proposal describing your activity and its educational merit.

3. **Speaking and listening.** Once your activity idea for #2 has been approved, acquire all the materials you will need for your class to participate in this hands-on activity. Create and pass out a sheet of instructions. Then, as a group, lead your class through the hands-on activity you devised. Be prepared to clarify any steps and to answer questions from your classmates. Participate fully and ask questions during all the activities devised for your class.

4. **Reading and writing.** Locate a book written for pregnant people and read the chapters on childbirth. Consider the language and tone. How does the book's coverage of childbirth differ from this textbook's coverage? Write a short essay identifying the audience of the book you read and analyzing why the author might have chosen the tone and language they did.

5. **Technology and speaking.** Review the Apgar test, Brazelton scale, and newborn screening tests covered in this chapter. Then, using digital resources, create a newborn "report card." Your report card should be an easy-to-use, easy-to-read log where parents can record their newborn's test results and easily reference them. Present your "report card" to the class and explain your rationale for the design.

6. **Listening and speaking.** In small groups, discuss with your classmates your knowledge about childbirth and postpartum care. Conduct this discussion as though you had never read the chapter. Take notes on the observations expressed. Then review the points discussed, factoring in your new knowledge about childbirth. Develop a summary of what you have learned and present it to the class, using the terms you have learned in this chapter.

7. **Math.** Review the rates of incidence for postpartum mood disorders in Figure 7.17. Research the total number of births in the United States in the current year, and using that number, calculate how many new parents should statistically have experienced each type of postpartum mood disorder.

8. **CTE Career Readiness Practice.** Historically, childbirth has claimed the lives of many birthing persons and children. Medical advances have reduced the number of fatalities due to childbirth, but in some areas of the world, childbirth can still be a hazardous affair. Using online or print resources, identify areas where childbirth fatalities are still high. What are the reasons for these fatalities? What are the social and economic impacts? What steps can these areas and the world take toward reducing the number of fatalities due to childbirth? Write a report of your findings to share with the class.

Observations

1. As a class, organize a trip to a local hospital or birthing center, and tour the facility. Observe how the facility is organized, what amenities are available, and what kind of environment is created by the decorations and staff. Discuss why the facility may have chosen to arrange and decorate as it did and how other facilities might differ depending on their purposes and locations.

2. Interview two people in your family or in a friend's family who gave birth two or three generations apart. Ask each to describe the childbirth experience. Where did they give birth, and who was allowed to be with them? What rules did they have to follow in pregnancy and childbirth? How much technology was involved in the birth? Summarize your interviews in a written report.

Unit 3 Infancy

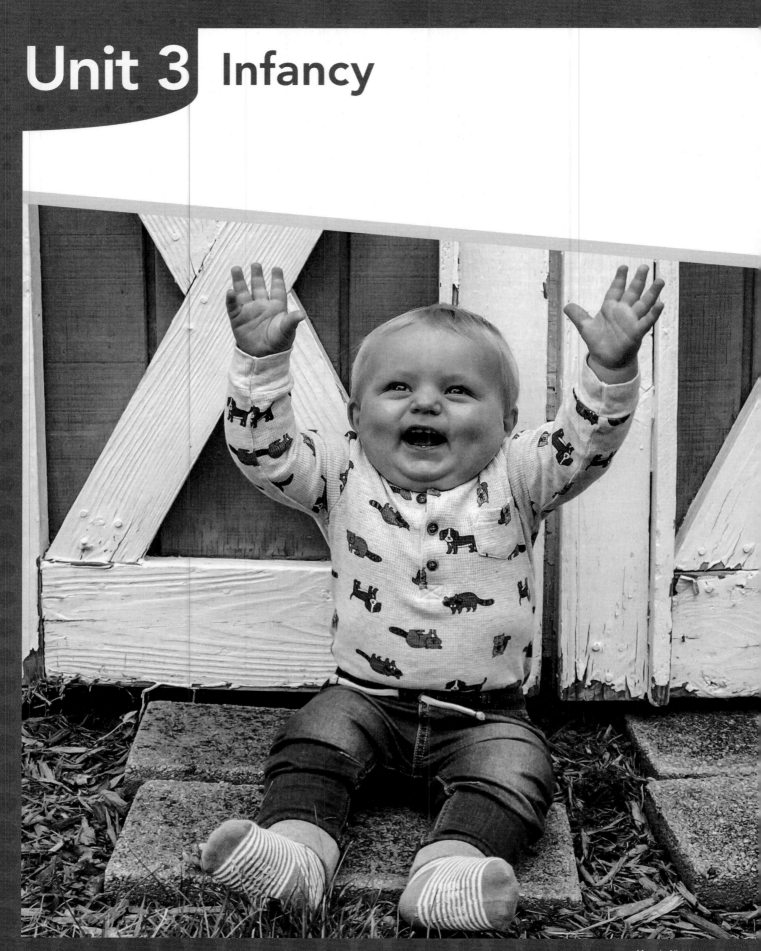

Maggie Albert

Community Service Project

An entire CTSO chapter typically carries out a community service project, which often takes several months to a year to complete. There may be several parts to this type of event—written and oral. The event may also involve preparation of a display or portfolio. The CTSO chapter designates several members to represent the team at the competitive event.

To prepare for a community service project, complete the following activities:

1. Read and analyze the event rules and guidelines.
2. Select a theme for your chapter's community service project as a team.
3. Identify the target audience of the community service project. Your project may include businesses, schools, and community groups.
4. Decide on which roles the team needs to carry out the plan, such as a team captain, secretary, or treasurer.
5. Use a decision-making planning process to create a project rationale that identifies the project goals and needs. What is the desired end result of this project? What are the benefits of supporting and completing the project? Identify goals, tasks, and ways to execute the plan.
6. Have group members report on progress during regular chapter meetings. Create a draft report based on guidelines from your CTSO organization. Update and refine your group's written report, creating necessary visuals or a portfolio until the project is complete. Include an analysis of the success of your report as part of the presentation.
7. Practice the presentation for the competitive event. Chapter members and the advisor can serve as judges during practice. Incorporate suggestions for refinement.

Chapter 8

Physical Development in the First Twelve Months

Essential Question

How do babies grow and develop physically in the first twelve months of life, and how do parents and caregivers provide for babies' physical needs?

Case Study — Why Do Some Newborns Fail to Thrive?

As a class, read the case study and discuss the questions that follow. After you finish studying the chapter, discuss this case study again. Have your opinions changed based on what you learned?

Before leaving the birthing center with their baby, Connor and Bella were reminded by the certified nurse-midwife to feed the baby every three hours. At the end of the first week, Bella took the baby for its first well-baby checkup. Although the doctor mentioned the baby's weight loss, all seemed to be well. At the baby's second checkup a week later, the doctor frowned and said, "I thought we would at least see the baby back at birthweight by now." Because the baby had gained only a very small amount, the doctor wanted to weigh the baby again in three days. After examining the baby for the third time, the doctor wrote on the baby's chart, "failure to thrive." He lectured Bella about feeding him more often—every two hours—so he would gain weight.

Those words, "failure to thrive," shook Bella's confidence. Bella believed they were doing everything right. Bella said to Connor, "How could the doctor use such horrible words? What kind of parents don't feed their baby and take care of it?

We have kept our baby clean, warm, dry, and content. We have such a dreamy baby who sleeps for long periods of time. What's wrong with our baby?"

Give It Some Thought

1. Why do you think the doctor waited until the third appointment before mentioning more frequent feeding? Explain your answer.
2. Why might the doctor suspect inadequate nutrition as the cause of the "failure to thrive"? Besides loss of weight, what other signs might the newborn have shown?
3. Should a caring parent be embarrassed by the words, "failure to thrive"? Why or why not?
4. If the baby had inadequate nutrition, hypothesize why it did not cry and become more distressed. Why did the baby sleep for extended hours?

Marlon Lopez MMG1 Design/Shutterstock.com

Growth and Development in the First Twelve Months

Key Terms

body proportions

cephalocaudal development

crawl

creep

cruising

deciduous teeth

developmental milestones

failure to thrive

fine-motor skills

gross-motor skills

infancy

motor development

ossification

proximodistal development

reflexes

skeletal system

voluntary grasping

Learning Outcomes

After studying this lesson, you will be able to

8.1-1 **describe** a child's physical growth in the first year.

8.1-2 **compare** and **contrast** different types of reflexes.

8.1-3 **differentiate** between gross-motor skills and fine-motor skills and the patterns in which they develop in the first year.

8.1-4 **give examples** of physical developmental milestones children might achieve in the first year.

Reading and Notetaking Activity

Before reading this lesson, skim the headings and write each heading in a different color or font on a separate piece of paper or electronically. As you silently read the chapter and then listen to your teacher, take notes in the color or font you chose for each heading. After you finish taking notes for each section, draw or copy and paste a small illustration or visual next to the section that will help you remember what you learned.

Introduction

Physical growth and development during the first year of life are exciting because children grow and develop new skills each day. Of all the changes that occur during infancy, physical growth is the most noticeable. People often remark, "Look how the baby has grown!" Growth occurs both outward, such as height and weight, and inward, such as tissue and organ growth. A person's physical growth may continue until the early years of adulthood. This growth period is longer than that of any other living creature.

From birth, children make great physiological adaptations (change from being helpless newborns to being "up and about" infants) in their new world outside the womb. These adaptations occur due to their impressive advances in motor skills. Development proceeds in two directions—from the head downward and from the center of the body to the *extremities* (fingers and toes).

Through biological maturation and experiences in the first year of life, the infant's world becomes more accessible.

8.1-1 Physical Growth in the First Twelve Months

As you may recall, from birth to one month of age a baby is medically known as a *neonate* or *newborn*. Between one month and one year after birth, a baby is commonly called an *infant*. The stage of development during this first year of life is known as **infancy**.

Much physical growth and development occur during infancy. At birth, a newborn looks much different from the plump infants you see in the media who are usually several months old (**Figure 8.1**). Besides changes in physical traits during the first year, changes also occur in organ maturation and skeletal growth.

Maturation of Organs

The brain grows faster than any other tissue or organ in the child's body during the first year. Most neurons develop during the prenatal period, but "fine tuning" occurs during infancy. The neurons increase in size, more glial cells form, more dendrites develop, and myelination continues to speed up connections. The brain weighs one pound at birth and two pounds at one year of age. You will learn about specific areas of brain growth as you read about intellectual development in the first year.

Newborns are born with a complete set of immature muscles. During infancy, muscles increase in size through physical activity and hormones. The infant's strength and **stamina** (ability to continually do something) increase with muscle development.

After birth, the child's digestion is aided by "friendly" intestinal bacteria, increased stomach size, and salivation. During the first year, the digestive system remains immature. Caregivers see evidence of this through frequent spitting up and partially digested foods in the child's stools.

As a child's lung capacity increases and the lungs mature, the child's breathing rate decreases. This decreased breathing rate does not negatively affect oxygen transfer to the bloodstream. Like newborns, infants still breathe from the diaphragm in the abdominal area rather than from the chest like adults. Infants' lung tissue is highly vulnerable to viruses, bacteria, and pollution (including secondhand smoke).

Newborns' hearts are immature but improve in strength throughout infancy. The pumping of the blood becomes better regulated, which lowers blood pressure. During this first year, the heart becomes stronger, giving the infant more stamina.

Figure 8.1 Changes in Appearance Between Birth and Six Months of Age

Age	Changes
Newborn *Konorieva Alina/Shutterstock.com*	• Eyes are dull gray-blue • Stomach protrudes; pelvis and hips are narrow • Legs are drawn up • Skin is blotchy; some blood vessels are visible
Three months *MBI/Shutterstock.com*	• Round and chubby • Body and limbs begin to stretch out • Head is large compared to body
Six months *Irina Wilhauk/Shutershock.com*	• Eye color develops • Rapid increase in length of body • Chest becomes larger in circumference than the head

Goodheart-Willcox Publisher

Skeletal Growth

The **skeletal system** is the framework of the body that consists of cartilage, bones, and teeth. Skeletal growth refers to the changes in a child's length and weight, body proportions, and bones and teeth.

Length and Weight

A child's length and weight change quickly during the first year. (The term *length* is used for the first year because the child does not stand. Once the child can stand, the term *height* is used.) Changes happen so quickly that even people who see the child daily are amazed at how fast they grow.

All children grow at individual rates, but the average length of a newborn is 20 to 21 inches. Many children increase their birth lengths by about 30 percent in the first five months. They often grow about 9 to 10 inches and almost triple their weight during the first year (**Figure 8.2**).

Around nine months of age, an infant is rather chubby because of an increase in fat tissues under the skin. After this time, fat tissues begin to decrease.

A child's *rate of growth* is more important than their actual length and weight. The pediatrician uses a growth chart to record the child's growth at each checkup. This growth chart shows several measurements for the child compared to average growth rates. The pediatrician will compare the child's actual measurements to the growth rates. As long as growth continues at a constant rate, the pediatrician will not likely be concerned.

Sometimes, however, children may experience a **failure to thrive**, which means they fail to grow at a healthy rate. A child's failure to thrive may indicate a health condition exists. In this case, the growth chart would show a steady growth rate and then a decline. Possible causes of failure to thrive include the following:

- diseases that prevent all or some nutrients from being absorbed or that cause nutrients to be quickly expelled from the body
- insufficient nutrients in the baby's food—diluted formula or poor quality or insufficient amount of breast milk caused by the nursing parent's malnutrition (called *marasmus*)
- infrequent or short feeding times
- abuse or neglect—the baby is not held, touched, or talked to enough

With the proper care and attention, the child's health can often be restored. How long this will take depends on the **onset** (beginning) and severity of the problem.

Body Proportions

A child's **body proportions** (relative size of body parts) differ from those of an adult during the first year. For example, an infant's head is about one-fourth their total length, while an adult's head is one-eighth of their total height (**Figure 8.3**). An infant also has a tiny jaw and chin, a long trunk, a "pot-bellied" abdomen, and short legs.

Figure 8.2 Average Length and Weight During the First Year

Age in Months	Length in Inches	Weight in Pounds
Birth	19.55	7.28
3	23.85	13.56
6	26.85	17.53
9	28	18.84
12	29.45	20.63

Figure 8.3 An infant's head is about one-fourth of their length, whereas an adult's head is about one-eighth of their height. *Do these proportions match what you typically see in everyday life?*

More than half of the total growth of a child's head occurs during the first year of life. The head **circumference** (linear distance around the edge of a closed curved or circular object) grows from an average of 13.5 to 18.5 inches in the first year. From birth until six months of age, the child's head is larger than the chest, but in many six-month-old children, the chest becomes larger. The difference in the distance around the chest as compared to the distance around the head continues to increase with age.

A child's gain in length during the first year is because the trunk grows. The legs do not grow much longer at this time. The abdomen **protrudes** (sticks out) because the internal organs are large for the child's small body. Because the center of gravity is high on the child's body, the result is poor balance.

Bones and Teeth

At birth, newborns have *fontanels* (FAHN-ta-NEHLS), or *soft spots*, where the skull is not closed.

Fontanels enable the baby's skull to compress while passing through the birth canal. Fontanels also allow the skull and brain to grow. The fontanels fill with bone as the skull grows. The skull completely closes in about two years.

A baby's skeleton is mainly made of **cartilage** (firm, but flexible connective tissue found in parts of the body). Some of a baby's bones are made entirely of cartilage while others are partly made of cartilage. There are large spaces between the baby's "bones" to help the joints bend easily without breaking. Young babies can suck their toes with no trouble, but sitting and standing are impossible because their skeletons are not sturdy.

Due to their softness, a newborn's or infant's bones can easily become misshapen. For example, the soft bones of a newborn's skull may be molded into an egg shape to make birth easier. The molded shape of the head will disappear in a couple weeks. A misshapen skull can also result from lying in one position all the time, causing an infant's head to flatten in one place.

This has become more common in recent years with the need for babies to sleep on their backs for safety reasons, which you will learn more about later in this chapter. Severe head flattening can be prevented by methods shown in **Figure 8.4**. When these methods do not work, or in more severe cases, helmet molding therapy may be recommended by a doctor.

During the first year, three changes occur in a child's bones. First, the length of the bones increases. Second, **ossification** (AWS-sih-fih-CAY-shun), the hardening of bones caused by the depositing of the minerals *calcium* and *phosphorus*, begins. Ossification helps the skeletal frame become sturdy, which in turn helps the infant to sit and eventually walk. Third, the number of bones changes. For example, a baby's body has about 300 bones at birth. These eventually fuse (grow together) to form the 206 bones that adults have. Throughout infancy, these bones are made partly or entirely of cartilage. During childhood, the cartilage grows and is slowly replaced by bone, with help from calcium.

Teeth, a part of the skeletal system, begin forming in the sixth week of prenatal life. By birth, all 20 **deciduous** (deh-SID-joo-uhs) **teeth** (also called *nonpermanent teeth* or *baby teeth*) and a few permanent teeth are developing deep in the jaw.

Deciduous teeth are the first set of teeth, which will later be replaced by permanent teeth. The deciduous teeth may begin appearing during the second half of the first year. The sequence (order) of teething is easier to predict than when teeth will appear (timing). In fact, some newborns are born with one or more teeth, although it is rare. Other children are more than a year old when their first teeth appear.

8.1-2 Reflexes

Newborns enter the world with some **innate** (inborn; natural) **reflexes** (automatic, unlearned movements in response to stimuli) needed for survival. For example, the *rooting reflex* helps newborns search for food by turning their heads and moving their mouths in response to a touch on the cheeks or mouth. After finding objects with their mouths, newborns begin to suck, which is called the *sucking reflex*. Newborns also come into the world with the *palmar (grasping) reflex*, which enables them to automatically grasp objects placed in their hands. **Figure 8.5** illustrates some major reflexes that help newborns and infants survive and learn.

Figure 8.4 **Prevent Head Flattening**

- Change the position of the sleeping baby's head from day to day, but do not take the baby off their back.
- Take an alert baby out of the crib.
- Use baby seats, bouncers, and swings for only a little while at a time.
- Remove a sleeping child from a car seat when not traveling.
- Use "tummy time," or time spent on the stomach, several times a day when babies are awake.
- Move objects of interest to encourage the baby to look from side to side when on their back.
- Encourage the infant to sit with support around three or four months. (Hold your hand a short distance behind their head to provide head support if needed.)

Goodheart-Willcox Publisher

Handcraft Films/Shutterstock.com

Figure 8.5 **Major Reflexes in Newborns and Infants**

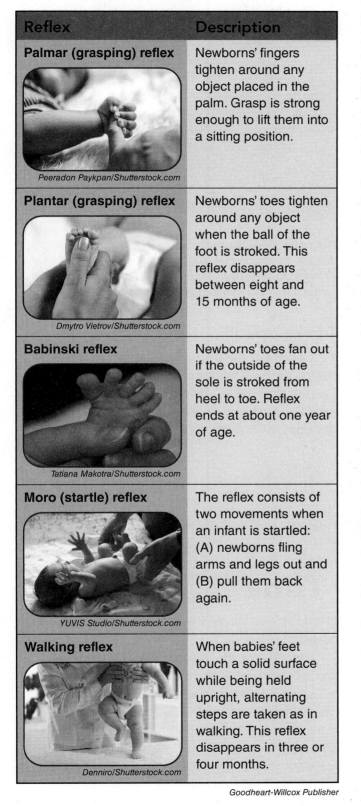

Reflex	Description
Palmar (grasping) reflex *Peeradon Paykpan/Shutterstock.com*	Newborns' fingers tighten around any object placed in the palm. Grasp is strong enough to lift them into a sitting position.
Plantar (grasping) reflex *Dmytro Vietrov/Shutterstock.com*	Newborns' toes tighten around any object when the ball of the foot is stroked. This reflex disappears between eight and 15 months of age.
Babinski reflex *Tatiana Makotra/Shutterstock.com*	Newborns' toes fan out if the outside of the sole is stroked from heel to toe. Reflex ends at about one year of age.
Moro (startle) reflex *YUVIS Studio/Shutterstock.com*	The reflex consists of two movements when an infant is startled: (A) newborns fling arms and legs out and (B) pull them back again.
Walking reflex *Denniro/Shutterstock.com*	When babies' feet touch a solid surface while being held upright, alternating steps are taken as in walking. This reflex disappears in three or four months.

Goodheart-Willcox Publisher

Some reflexes, like the rooting reflex, disappear within a few months, while other reflexes remain the same throughout life, such as your knee jerking when tapped with a mallet. Still other reflexes lead to learned, voluntary behaviors essential for development. For example, when infants are about four months old, the grasping reflex is replaced by **voluntary grasping** (the intentional grasping of objects). Babies' first grasps are awkward, but with practice, infants refine their skills as they learn to grab and hold many objects.

Reflexes are a clue to the health and maturity of the nervous system. The absence or weakness of a reflex may result from premature birth or a congenital condition. For example, pricking the soles of newborns' feet causes them to jerk or withdraw their legs (called the *withdrawal reflex*). The withdrawal reflex continues throughout life, and its absence may be a sign of brain damage. Reflexes that should disappear in time, but do not disappear, may also signal a problem.

8.1-3 Motor Development

Motor development is the use and control of muscles that direct body movements. Children develop **gross-motor skills** as they learn to use and control large muscles—the trunk, arms, and legs—to roll over, sit, crawl, stand, and walk. Being able to control the small muscles, such as those in the fingers and hands, leads children to develop **fine-motor skills**. Having control over the body is a sign of children's growth and development.

A child's motor skills develop in three main patterns that build on the order of brain development. The following list shows the patterns of motor development:

1. Until brain firings are hardwired, babies move slowly because they must think as they move.
2. Babies' reactions develop from general to specific. For example, if young infants see something they want, they wiggle all over. Older infants smile and reach for the object.
3. Motor development occurs in two directions—from head to foot and from the center of the body to the extremities (from the spine area of the trunk out to the hands and feet).

Head-to-Foot Development

Head-to-foot development, **cephalocaudal** (sef-uh-lo-KAW-dahl) **development**, describes the progression of development beginning with the head and moving down to the feet. Cephalocaudal development begins before birth. The fetus's head develops, then arm buds, and then leg buds. At birth, newborns have well-developed facial muscles, but less well-developed leg muscles. During infancy, children develop head and neck control more quickly than trunk and leg control.

Head and Neck Control

Newborns need to have their heads continually supported because their muscles are not strong enough to hold their heads steady themselves (**Figure 8.6**). Some newborns can raise their unsteady heads briefly, however, when lying on their stomachs during supervised tummy times. By two months of age, many infants spend a great deal of time with their heads raised. By three months of age, most infants can hold their heads and chests up with arm support. Head control is almost complete when infants are about five months old. By this time, infants can raise their heads briefly while lying on their backs. They can also hold their heads steady while sitting in a high chair.

Rudi Silva/via Getty Images E+

Figure 8.6 Because newborns are not strong enough to hold their heads steady, their large heads must be supported at all times. *By what age are infants usually able to spend a great deal of time with their heads raised?*

Trunk Control

Control of the trunk develops more slowly than control of the head. Infants placed on their stomachs can lift their heads before they can lift both their heads and chests. Trunk control enables infants to develop motor skills, such as rolling over and sitting.

Focus on Health

Tummy Time

Child development experts recommend that newborns and infants sleep on their backs, mostly for safety reasons. Lying on their backs, however, does not strengthen babies' neck muscles and upper bodies. Professionals recommend "tummy time" as an activity parents can do with their babies to promote motor skills, such as rolling over, reaching, and crawling. During tummy time, infants and newborns are lying on their bellies to play. Tummy time may begin with a few minutes several times a day. Additional minutes can be added to tummy time as infants develop more head and neck control.

Tummy time should occur only when both parent and baby are alert. Parents should always supervise the baby's movements and awareness and end tummy time before a baby gets drowsy. Parents might read to their babies during tummy time or provide toys that encourage babies to lift their heads and reach. These exercises and challenges promote motor development, aid in bone growth, and stimulate babies' brains.

Photo: People Image Studio/Shutterstock.com

Infants often learn to roll over between two and five months of age. Usually, they first learn to roll over from stomach to back. Then, about a month later, they learn to roll over from back to stomach. Infants have an easier time lifting their heads and trunks while lying on their abdomens than while lying on their backs.

Learning to sit takes several months. Infants must first gain strength in their necks and backs and be able to control their heads. Infants can sit briefly with support (being held or with pillows placed at their backs) at three or four months of age. By seven months of age, infants can often sit for a short time without support. For longer periods of sitting, infants lean forward and support themselves with their arms and legs but may topple over if distracted. Progress becomes rapid during the next few months, and by nine months of age, many infants can sit unaided.

Leg Control

Leg control is the last phase of head-to-foot development. As infants gain leg control, many go through the stages of crawling, creeping, standing, and walking.

- *Crawling.* Around five or six months of age, some infants learn to **crawl** by pulling with their arms, but not lifting their abdomens from the floor. The common term for this is *belly-crawling*.
- *Creeping.* Between 6 and 8 months of age, some infants learn to **creep** by lifting their abdomens off the floor and using their hands and knees or hands and feet to move. The common term for creeping is *knee-crawling*. Many people use the term "crawling" interchangeably for both creeping and crawling. These are not critical developmental milestones; many infants skip both of these steps and are perfectly healthy. In 2022, the Centers for Disease Control and Prevention updated their developmental milestone lists, removing crawling altogether.
- *Standing.* Around 6 months of age, infants enjoy standing as they push with their feet and bounce while parents provide support under their arms. A few months later, infants can usually pull themselves into a standing

position and then hold onto something for support. Many children first learn to stand alone between 12 and 14 months of age.
- *Walking.* After infants learn to stand alone, they usually begin **cruising** (walking by holding onto something for support). As leg control develops, infants can stand further away from objects and hold on with only one of their hands to maintain balance. Infants also take a few cautious steps between objects and people. Around 18 months of age, many children are able to walk alone. (**Figure 8.7** illustrates the stages of standing and walking.)

dekazigzag/Shutterstock.com

pikselstock/Shutterstock.com

Figure 8.7 At around 9 months, infants pull themselves into a standing position and hold onto something for support. Around 18 months of age, many children are able to walk alone. *How would you explain the stages of development between pulling to stand and walking to a new parent?*

Center-to-Extremities Development

The direction of development from the center of the body to the extremities is called **proximodistal** (prahk-sum-oh-DIS-tahl) **development**, or center-to-extremities development. In center-to-extremities development, control of the top half of the body begins with the trunk, then arms, hands, and fingers. Likewise, control on the bottom half of the body begins with the hips and extends to the legs, feet, and toes.

Center-to-extremities development aids infants' abilities to move about. For example, infants use their arms and hands to crawl and creep and as a balancing aid for standing and walking. For the most part, however, center-to-extremities development aids in the performance of fine-motor skills. These skills begin with the palmar reflex and are soon followed by voluntary swiping at objects. With time and experience, babies soon begin to grasp objects and even their own feet with their palms and fingers, but not with their thumbs. Near the second half of the first year, babies begin using the thumb and fingers with greater and greater skill until they can hold small objects between the tips of the thumb and the index finger. Typical fine motor skill milestones are shown in **Figure 8.8**.

8.1-4 Physical Developmental Milestones

Developmental milestones are physical, intellectual, and social-emotional tasks many children learn to accomplish by a certain age. Developmental milestones identify predicted ages for when children, on the average, can demonstrate certain growth and development tasks. Each child, however, develops at their own rate. The rate is affected by heredity, nutrition, illnesses, and activity. Whether a child is praised and encouraged (environment) can also make a difference.

Some infants develop more quickly than the predicted age while others lag behind. A particular infant may also develop quickly in one area, but more slowly in another. For example, rolling from stomach to back is a developmental milestone for a five-month-old infant. Some infants, however, will roll later.

Figure 8.8 Fine Motor Skill Milestones

Age	Fine Motor Skill
Birth to three months	• Brings hands to mouth • Moves arms and may swing them at toys • Hands open more as time progresses
Three to six months	• Holds small objects • Can hold hands together • Reaches for toys • Briefly holds a toy • Follows objects with eyes (called tracking)
Six to nine months	• Shakes and bangs toys • Brings toys to mouth • Uses raking grasp • Can pass objects from one hand to the other • Hands are open most of the time • Can start to pick up small items and food (like Cheerios)
Nine to twelve months	• Can release objects in hands • Gives toys to other people if prompted • Bangs two items together • Can turn pages of a book (may grab a few at once) • Starts to be able to put objects into a container • Points at objects • Can stack a couple of blocks

Goodheart-Willcox Publisher

Physical developmental milestones concern the development of gross-motor skills and fine-motor skills. Many researchers classify these skills as *postural*, *locomotor*, and *grasping* skills. *Postural skills* have to do with aligning the body in an erect position and maintaining the position through balance. Postural skills include holding the head erect, sitting erect, and standing erect without leaning or support. *Locomotor skills* involve the ability to move from place to place using the arms, legs, and feet. Locomotion includes rolling over, crawling, creeping, and walking. *Grasping skills* have to do with small movements of the hands, wrists, and fingers and often require the use of the eyes to coordinate movements. Examples of grasping skills are picking up, carrying, and manipulating small objects. **Figure 8.9** lists physical developmental milestones for the first year of life.

Figure 8.9 Newborn and Infant Physical Milestones

Age	Milestones
One month *220 Selfmade Studio/Shutterstock.com*	• Has reflexive movements. • Roots for food source. • Keeps hands in closed fists. • Attempts to lift head when on tummy.
Two months *Richard Semik/Shutterstock.com*	• Has more voluntary actions. • Smoother movements using both arms and legs. • Holds head up when on stomach. • Uses a reflexive grasp and opens hands briefly.
Three months *Mallory Dufek*	• Raises head and chest when on stomach. • Moves arms and legs easily and often. • Opens and closes hands. • May swipe at dangling objects. • Grasps and shakes objects.
Four months *AMR Studio/Shutterstock.com*	• Rocks from side to side. • Holds head steady without support. • Pushes up on elbows/arms when on stomach. • Holds toys and objects in hand. • Pulls objects placed in hand toward mouth.
Five months *Heather Preston*	• Rolls from stomach to back; some may roll from back to stomach. • May sit upright with support. • Grasp is stronger.
Six months *mpyrozhenka/Shutterstock.com*	• Rolls from back to stomach. • Supports body on both legs when held in standing position; may bounce. • May make crawling motions with arms and legs. • Opens hands wider for larger objects than for smaller objects. • Supports self with hand to sit.
Seven months *Mallory Dufek*	• Sits without support for a few minutes. • Reaches for items with one hand. • Uses raking grasp for items.
Eight months *Heather Preston*	• Can get in hand and knees position. • Can get into sitting position without help. • Enjoys bouncing on both feet when in a supported standing position.

Goodheart-Willcox Publisher
(Continued)

Copyright Goodheart-Willcox Co., Inc. Chapter 8 Physical Development in the First Twelve Months **237**

Figure 8.9 **Newborn and Infant Physical Milestones** (Continued)

Age	Milestones
Nine months sandsun/Shutterstock.com	• Can sit fully without support. • Pulls up to stand using people or furniture for support. • Stands holding with one hand while leaning on something. • Passes things from one hand to the other.
Ten months MBI/Shutterstock.com	• May walk when led by an adult. • Grasp and use of hands improves. • Can use thumb and forefinger to pick things up. • Can clap and wave.
Eleven months sandsun/Shutterstock.com	• Spends more time upright. • Skills and independent movements increase. • May stand a few seconds without support or take a few steps. • May crawl up stairs with supervision.

Lesson 8.1

Review and Assessment

1. Which part of the infant's body grows the fastest in the first year of life? (8.1.1)

   A. Lungs
   C. Brain
   B. Kidneys
   D. Heart

2. What are deciduous teeth? (8.1.1)

   A. Permanent teeth
   C. Molars
   B. Baby teeth
   D. Canine teeth

3. Which of the following is true about reflexes? (8.1.2)

   A. We keep all of the reflexes we are born with.
   B. Babies are born with specific reflexes that all fade within the first year.
   C. Reflexes can show a person's age.
   D. Some reflexes fade, while others remain the same throughout life.

4. Motor development occurs in two main patterns, which are _____. (8.1.3)

   A. head-to-foot and center-to-extremities
   B. foot-to-head and extremities-to-trunk
   C. head/neck and trunk/limbs
   D. large muscle groups and small muscle groups

5. Which of the following are locomotor skills? (8.1.4)

   A. Hand-eye coordination, grasping objects, and picking things up
   B. Rolling over, crawling, creeping, and walking
   C. Holding the head erect, sitting up erect, and standing erect
   D. Being able to control the small muscles in the hands and fingers

Meeting Nutritional Needs in the First Twelve Months

Learning Outcomes

After studying this lesson, you will be able to

8.2-1 **describe** how to meet nutritional needs from birth to six months of age.

8.2-2 **describe** how to meet nutritional needs from six months to one year of age.

8.2-3 **Explain** the concepts of self-feeding and baby-led weaning.

Key Terms

colic
intolerance
lactation consultant
solids
weaning

Reading and Notetaking Activity

Imagine you are a registered dietitian and your client wants to learn more about feeding their infant. Write a two-paragraph speech recommending steps your client can take to make sure their baby gets the best nutrition and self-feeding skills. Incorporate information you already know about infant nutrition and feeding, and anything from your personal experiences. As you read this lesson, take detailed notes. After reading the lesson, go back over your speech. With a partner, discuss what you would change about your speech based on any new information you have learned. Present your final speech to the class.

Introduction

A well-balanced diet provides the essential nutrients a child needs to grow, explore, and develop in the first year. Meeting a baby's food and nutrition needs quickly alleviates (relieves) hunger. Responding promptly to the baby's need for food teaches the baby their needs will be met. Erikson calls this learning a sense of *basic trust*. A healthy relationship with food begins in infancy, and it is a caregiver's job to foster that relationship by providing opportunities for positive mealtimes.

Babies go through different stages of the feeding process. For the first six months of life, newborns and infants are completely dependent on breast milk or formula. Around six months, infants may begin eating solid foods.

By the end of the first year or earlier, infants are beginning to self-feed using their hands and fingers. As infants are developing new feeding skills, mealtimes can be frustrating and messy. Remaining calm can help make mealtimes pleasant for infants and their parents.

In all situations, parents and other caregivers need to make a priority of meeting their infants' nutritional needs. Nutrition during the first year of life can affect development in all areas later in life. The American Academy of Pediatrics (AAP) has made recommendations for meeting infants' nutritional needs.

8.2-1 Nutrition in the First Six Months

Because babies grow quickly throughout the first year, their nutritional needs are especially important. Parents can meet these needs by either breast-feeding or formula-feeding. Both methods provide opportunities for parents to bond with their babies as they hold and cuddle them during feeding times. See **Figure 8.10** for the pros and cons of breast and bottle feeding.

Figure 8.10 **Considerations for Breast Milk and Formula Feeding***

Breast Milk	Formula
• Breast milk contains the right proportions of proteins, carbohydrates, fats, vitamins, minerals, and water. This makes it easier to digest than formula. • Breast milk changes to fit the changing needs of the baby. • Breast-feeding has health benefits for the birthing person, such as causing the uterus to contract to original size and helping bones regain minerals. • Using breast milk exclusively can save the family money because there is no cost of formula. • The nursing parent's immunities to certain diseases are passed to the baby for the duration of using breast milk. • Breast milk is sterile (unless put in a bottle) and is ready immediately, unless the nursing person is struggling with milk production. • The nursing parent has to be cautious about their diet and any medicines taken. Everything in the nursing parent's diet can be passed to the baby through breast milk. Exclusive breast-feeding (no use of a bottle): • Vigorous sucking required for breast-feeding satisfies the need for sucking and may promote straighter teeth. • Babies rarely choke because they can control the flow of milk. • If the nursing parent returns to work, it may be difficult to find a private place or time to pump milk for bottle feeding when they are away from their child.	• Infant formula is a healthy and safe alternative to breast-feeding. It provides the needed nutrients for infants to grow and thrive. Formula may be more difficult to digest for some babies. • Formula is not as complex as breast milk and does not change with the baby's needs. • Health benefits for the birthing person may include increased mental wellness and reduced stress due to the obstacles that some parents face with breast-feeding. • Formula contains certain vitamins and nutrients that breastfed babies might need supplements for. • Using formula is convenient and flexible. Anyone can feed the baby. This is also true for parents who provide breast milk in a bottle. • Infant formula does not provide the immunities to certain diseases that breast milk does. • Specialty formulas needed for certain babies may be difficult to find. • The parent does not need to worry about their diet affecting their baby.

*Breast-feeding, bottle feeding breast milk, and formula feeding in a bottle are all healthy ways to feed a baby in the first year of life. Close bonding can occur with all methods of feeding. Though breast milk has the most optimal nutrition for babies, formula is a healthy and nutritious alternative. Many parents choose to use a combination of breast milk and formula at some point throughout the infant's first year.

Goodheart-Willcox Publisher

Breast-Feeding

In the first six months, breast milk best meets the baby's nutritional needs. The AAP recommends breast-feeding continue for at least the first 12 months of life if that is the chosen method of feeding.

People who breast-feed their babies have higher nutritional needs for some vitamins and minerals. Nursing parents can help meet their nutritional needs by choosing foods high in vitamins and minerals from each of the food groups—fruits, vegetables, dairy, grains, and proteins. In addition to a healthful diet, doctors may recommend some nursing parents take a vitamin and mineral supplement to help meet their nutritional needs.

Fluid needs also increase while breast-feeding. People who are breast-feeding need to drink plenty of water to meet these needs and satisfy their thirst. One way to help meet their fluid needs is to drink a glass of water each time they are breast-feeding or pumping their breast milk for use in a bottle. Drinks that contain alcohol, caffeine, or added sugars should be limited or avoided. These substances can affect the breast milk and the baby.

Any over-the-counter drugs taken can also pass from the parent's breast milk to the baby. Therefore, nursing parents should check with a doctor before taking any drugs. For breast-feeding advice, people may wish to consult with a doctor, nurse, or **lactation consultant** (breast-feeding expert).

Focus on Health

Bottle-Feeding

Whether parents are feeding their baby breast milk, formula, or both, it is important to follow certain safety and sanitation procedures when bottle-feeding an infant. The following guidelines are precautions caregivers should follow while bottle-feeding their baby:

- Keep mixed and ready-to-use formula refrigerated to prevent the growth of bacteria.
- Breast milk can stay in room temperature safely for four hours before being moved to the refrigerator, and formula can stay in room temperature for two hours. Once mixed, formula can stay in the refrigerator for 24 hours before being thrown out. Breast milk can stay in the refrigerator for up to four days but can last for months in the freezer if stored properly.
- Boil any water added (including bottled water) to powdered or liquid concentrate formulas for one to two minutes and then cool.
- Keep utensils, bottles, and nipples completely clean.

- Check the quality of bottle nipples. Large or clogged holes cause feeding problems. Torn or worn nipples could cause the baby to choke. Buy special nipples for premature and sick infants so they can nurse successfully.
- Do not prop the bottle. Babies can choke while feeding. (If a baby chokes, parents should turn the baby on their side or abdomen, then pat them on the back.)
- Report any digestive upsets or rash to the baby's doctor. These problems might indicate the baby is reacting to the ingredients in the formula or to something in the nursing parent's system that is passing through the breast milk.
- Once feeding begins, throw away all formula the baby does not finish within one hour (two hours for breast milk). The baby's saliva causes bacteria to grow.

Why are these safety precautions necessary when preparing a bottle?

Photo: Rido/Shutterstock.com

Formula-Feeding

Many families choose breast-feeding, but some cannot breast-feed or choose not to for a multitude of reasons. Many families also choose to use both breast milk and formula to meet their babies' needs. Parents who choose formula-feeding may want to consult with a doctor about the type and amount of formula to use. Most formulas are based on cow's milk, but soy formulas are often used for babies who have problems digesting milk-based formulas.

When formula-feeding, parents should only use commercially prepared (store bought) formulas that are regulated by the Food and Drug Administration (FDA), not homemade formulas or whole cow's milk. Commercially prepared formulas contain specially processed milk products that provide the needed nutrients for the baby. These formulas are processed in a way to make it easier for the baby to digest. Commercially prepared formulas are available in powdered, liquid concentrate, or ready-to-feed forms.

Burping the Baby

No matter the method of feeding, babies must be burped. Burping rids the body of the air swallowed while sucking or crying. To burp a baby, complete the following steps:

- Place the baby in a sitting position on your lap with a hand on the collarbone and under the chin. You may also lay the baby down on their stomach across your lap with baby's face toward your knees. (You may burp a newborn on your shoulder, but this position is easier when the baby is larger.)
- Lightly pat or rub the baby's back once they are in position. Continue for two or three minutes unless the baby burps sooner. If the baby does not burp, change positions and try again.
- Burp a baby midway and/or after feeding. Some babies are extra gassy and need more frequent burping.

The Feeding Schedule

Daily feeding schedules depend on babies' unique needs. Doctors suggest newborns feed on demand and mothers watch for clues of hunger (newborns are alert, mouthing, and rooting).

Newborns typically eat about every 2 hours, or 8 to 12 times in 24 hours. If they are nursing, they will breast-feed until **satiety** (being full), which takes at least 15 minutes per breast. Doctors suggest arousing a sleeping newborn every 3 or 4 hours for feedings. **Figure 8.11** shows a typical daily feeding schedule for the first six months.

Many babies will establish eating patterns as they get older. Some infants prefer smaller, more frequent meals while others prefer to eat more food less often. Even with established eating patterns, infants will be hungrier some days more than others. Feeding on demand will help parents address infants' hunger needs. How much food infants need depends on their size and how fast they are growing. Infants' health, heredity, and level of activity also affect their needs. As infants' growth rates slow toward the end of the first year, their appetites typically decrease, too.

Weaning

Weaning is the gradual process of taking infants off the breast or bottle. Weaning from the breast cannot be **abrupt** (sudden; unanticipated) for infants or the nursing parent. Abrupt weaning for infants is stressful because they need time to learn a new way to drink. For the person who is breast-feeding, abrupt weaning can cause blockage of the milk ducts and possible depression.

Figure 8.11 Daily Feeding Schedule

Months	Hours Between Feedings (breast milk)	Hours Between Feedings (formula-fed)
Less than one	1–3	2–3
One to five	2–4	3–4
Six	On demand with introduction of solids*	On demand with introduction of solids*

*Nutritious snacks of regular baby food (cereals, vegetables, fruits, etc.) or breast milk or formula and water should be offered about halfway between feedings (2½ to 3 hours after each feeding) if the infant is awake. Until a sufficient quantity of solids is given, breast milk or formula must be part of the snack.

Goodheart-Willcox Publisher

When weaning occurs gradually, both parties have time to adapt to this change.

When to begin weaning depends on the infant's age and whether the infant is fed breast milk or formula. If weaning from breast milk before one year of age, the AAP recommends giving babies iron-fortified formula for the remainder of the first year. At one year of age, doctors suggest switching from iron-fortified formula to whole cow's milk. Weaning from a bottle to a cup may begin as early as the child can use the cup and shows interest in doing so (**Figure 8.12**). Although this may be as early as 9 months of age, the recommended age to start weaning from the bottle to a cup is 12 months. At this time, whole cow's milk can be given instead of formula or breast milk.

Shanta Giddens/Shutterstock.com

Figure 8.12 A child's cup has two handles and is weighted to prevent tipping. Some cups also offer features that make liquid less likely to spill. *How could a parent determine when their child is ready to use a cup?*

To begin weaning, parents may gradually offer the new liquid (formula or whole milk, depending on age) as part of one feeding. Increase the amount of the new liquid at this feeding until the baby takes an entire feeding by bottle or cup for several days. Wait at least three days before replacing another feeding with the bottle or cup. Then, apply the same steps to other feeding times.

8.2-2 Nutrition from Six Months to Twelve Months

Around six months of age, while continuing on breast milk or formula, infants may be ready to start eating solid foods from a spoon. **Solids** for infant feedings are semiliquid, mushy foods, such as cereals, vegetables, and fruits. Solid foods include commercially prepared baby foods and homemade mashed, pureed, or strained table foods. Doctors often recommend a commercially prepared single grain, iron-fortified cereal as the first solid food. Pureed vegetables should be the next food offered around six months of age. To encourage eating vegetables, they should be the first food offered to infants at mealtime. Fruit juice should not be offered to children during the first 12 months of life. Avoid feeding infants hard, round foods and sticky, hard-to-swallow foods because they may cause choking (**Figure 8.13**).

Figure 8.13 Food Choking Hazards

- Rounded, small foods, such as carrots, berries, grapes, and raisins
- Thick-skinned fruits, such as raw apples (unless peeled)
- Stringy foods, such as celery or spaghetti
- Hard candy
- Nuts and peanut butter
- Cherries with pits
- Hot dogs sliced in rounds
- Meat with bones
- Pretzels
- Whole kernel cooked corn and popcorn
- Soft, sticky foods, such as large marshmallows, jelly, gummy candies, and nut butters

Goodheart-Willcox Publisher

The AAP advises parents to wait until infants are around six months old before starting solids for the following reasons:

- Babies are not born with the ability to swallow solids. Their jaw and throat muscles must develop before swallowing is easy and safe.
- Infants do not have the needed *enzymes* (special proteins that aid digestion) or saliva for digesting solid foods before six months of age.
- Until infants are 16 to 18 weeks old, they have an *extrusion reflex* (the tongue thrusts forward when touched by an object) that causes them to push foods out of their mouths.
- Infants do not need more nutrition than breast milk or formula until they reach 13 to 15 pounds, which is near five to six months of age.
- Infants may have an increased risk of developing chronic conditions, such as high blood pressure or obesity, later in life from starting solids too soon.

Spoon-Feeding

Like many other skills, eating from a spoon is a developmental milestone that many parents are excited to see their infants achieve. For the first spoon-feedings, parents often mix single grain, iron-fortified baby cereal with two tablespoons of breast milk or formula. Using breast milk or formula rather than water provides more nutrients and offers a familiar taste.

To feed an infant with a spoon, parents may place a small amount of the cereal on the tip of the spoon. A few bites of cereal about halfway through breast-feeding or formula-feeding times are often enough for the first spoon-feedings. Very gradually, parents can make the cereal thicker at each spoon-feeding as infants learn to use their tongues and tolerate the texture.

Using a small spoon with a long handle may make spoon-feeding easier. Also, a plastic-coated baby spoon is better for the infant's sensitive gums than a metal spoon (**Figure 8.14**).

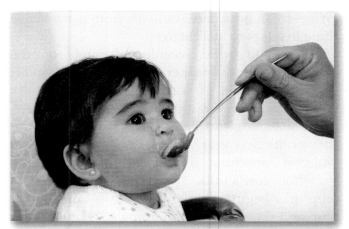

Marcos Messa Sam Wordley/Shutterstock.com

Figure 8.14 By six months, most infants are ready to start solid foods. *What reasons does the AAP give for waiting until this time?*

During spoon-feedings, parents hold the infant in their lap in an almost upright position. Later, infants can sit in an infant seat or high chair for spoon-feedings.

Once infants turn their heads or close their mouths during spoon-feeding times, parents may stop feeding the solids and give babies a sip or two of water. Then, breast-feeding or bottle-feeding can resume so babies' meals begin and end with the familiar taste of breast milk or formula.

Introducing New Solids

Many doctors recommend offering infants new solids early in the day and no later than early afternoon. They advise this because infants are more apt to have *colic* in the evening hours. **Colic** is a condition in which a baby has intense abdominal pain and cries inconsolably. Also, an allergic reaction following a night feeding would occur in the wee hours of the morning rather than during the early evening. As cereal and other solids are introduced, infants will need water for proper kidney action. A pediatrician can advise parents how much water to offer each day.

When feeding new solids to infants, parents may want to introduce one food at a time in small amounts, such as a bite or two. To see whether foods have any **adverse** (harmful) effects on infants, wait at least three days before introducing another new food.

If infants exhibit negative effects after eating a new food, they may have an intolerance to that food. **Intolerance** is a negative physical reaction that eating a certain food can cause. For example, intolerance to foods may result in infants becoming fussy, developing rashes, or having upset stomachs. If infant's stools are loose, watery, or contain mucous, parents should inform the infant's pediatrician.

Food intolerance among infants often shows one to four days after trying a new food. Many pediatricians suggest waiting until after the infant's first birthday before retrying an offending food. If too many foods cause a negative reaction, doctors can test the infant and prescribe a special diet if needed.

gennady/ Shutterstock.com

Figure 8.15 Fine-motor skill development is evident when infants self-feed and can grasp finger foods, such as bite-sized pieces of bagel or bread. *What are some other examples of safe finger foods for infants?*

8.2-3 Self-Feeding

Near the end of the first year, infants often develop the skill of self-feeding finger foods around the same time they develop the pincer grasp. Finger foods aid the infant's growing independence as well as grasping and chewing skills (**Figure 8.15**). Examples of foods infants can eat using their fingers include:

- bite-sized pieces of toasted bread or bagels
- O-shaped toasted oat cereal
- cooked diced vegetables, such as carrots or sweet potatoes
- small chunks of fruit, such as bananas, peaches, or pears

As infants begin self-feeding, parents may want to choose from the foods they know their infants already tolerate. Eating finger foods is fun, but can also be hazardous because infants may choke or gag at the new textures. For this reason, infants need supervision when they are eating.

Around eight or nine months of age, infants often let their parents know they are ready to self-feed. For example, infants may want to help their parents by grabbing the spoon during a feeding. They may also try to grab food off their parents' plates. Giving infants a spoon to hold or letting infants use the spoon on the last few bites is good practice for self-feeding skills needed during the toddler years.

Baby-Led Weaning

Some parents choose to encourage self-feeding earlier with their babies, around six months of age, in an evidence-based feeding method called baby-led weaning. This method encourages letting the baby take the lead in self-feeding; it also discourages the use of spoon-feeding from the caregiver to help the infant learn important skills for self-feeding and build independence. With baby-led weaning, the family makes one meal and everyone, including the infant, eats from that meal. The infant receives food with safe texture, size, and shape for their development (typically this is anything that the infant can grasp and bring to its mouth, avoiding anything that could cause choking). Examples of foods babies might eat using the baby-led weaning approach could include soft fruits, steamed vegetables, shredded meat, cheese, bread, eggs, and pasta. Foods used for baby-led weaning are typically stick-shaped or in a ball (not small enough to choke on).

Readiness signs for baby-led weaning are similar to traditional guidelines for starting solids. The infant needs to be able to sit up independently, have a strong palmar grasp, and have a diminished extrusion reflex. Hand-eye coordination is key so they can bring food to their mouth. Showing an interest in food is also important.

Baby-led weaning has many benefits. Parents like this approach because they do not have to buy or make special food for the baby, which saves them time and money. Developmentally, baby-led weaning allows the infant to practice and develop their coordination and fine motor skills. Baby-led weaning also promotes a healthy and positive relationship with food because infants get to try new things, explore, and decide on their own terms when they are full or hungry, since they are in charge of their food intake. Studies have shown that the risk for choking is not higher with baby-led weaning if it is done correctly. Parents should always consult with a doctor and research all options to make the best decision for their families. Many parents choose to do a mixture of traditional baby food and baby-led weaning. Formula and breast milk will still provide the bulk of the child's nutrition until the age of one.

Lesson 8.2 Review and Assessment

1. Which of the following is true about burping a baby? (8.2.1)
   A. Parents only need to burp their baby after they finish breast-feeding or bottle-feeding them.
   B. All babies have to be burped, regardless of whether they are formula- or breast-fed.
   C. Burping a baby must be done over the caregiver's shoulder for the best positioning.
   D. Burping a baby with colic could cause more gas to build up.

2. How long can breast milk be left out at room temperature? (8.2.1)
   A. 24 hours
   B. 8 hours
   C. 4 hours
   D. 2 hours

3. What do doctors typically recommend as the first solid food for infants? (8.2.2)
   A. Anything the parent eats, as long as it is soft enough to swallow
   B. Commercially bought baby food such as pureed fruits or vegetables
   C. Something soft and mushy like mashed potatoes or yogurt
   D. Single-grain, iron fortified cereal

4. What is a benefit of baby-led weaning? (8.2.3)
   A. It promotes developmental skills and independence for the infant.
   B. It allows the parents to control how much the infant eats.
   C. It is the best way to get a variety of nutrients into the infant's system.
   D. It allows infants to try new foods without the fear of gagging or choking.

Physical Care During the First Twelve Months

Learning Outcomes

After studying this lesson, you will be able to

8.3-1 **describe** clothing considerations for babies during infancy.

8.3-2 **demonstrate** how to bathe newborns and infants.

8.3-3 **demonstrate** how to diaper a baby.

8.3-4 **give examples** of sleep recommendations, including steps parents can take to protect their babies from SUID.

8.3-5 **identify** ways parents can encourage physical activity during infancy.

Key Terms

bassinet
immerse
play yard
sponge bath
sudden infant death syndrome (SIDS)

Reading and Notetaking Activity

Before reading this lesson, scan the lesson headings. Write a paragraph describing what you already know about these topics. Explain where you got the information you have—from conversations, the media, or research, for example. As you are reading, compare and contrast the information in the chapter with your prior knowledge. Organize your notes around the information you already know. After reading, consider how your prior knowledge of the subject matter helped you understand this topic.

Introduction

Babies depend on others to meet all their physical needs. When physical needs are not met, it affects other areas of development. Babies who are hungry, tired, or sick suffer in physical, intellectual, social, and emotional ways. For example, a baby who is fed late may not want to play and explore. The baby may also be fussy.

As you may recall, Maslow noted that physical needs are the most basic needs of humans. These needs must be met before other needs can be met. In Lesson 8.2, you learned about meeting nutritional needs in the first year. In this lesson, you will learn about meeting other physical needs during infancy, such as clothing and dressing, bathing, and diapering babies. You will also learn about meeting babies' needs for rest and sleep and physical activity.

8.3-1 Clothing and Dressing Babies

One basic human need is clothing. During the first year, babies need clothing items that are comfortable, easy to put on and take off, suitable for weather and temperature, and safe. Soft, loose-fitting clothes are easy for infants to move around in and are comfortable. Uncomfortable clothes include those with too much fabric, skin irritants (flat seams and fasteners), and fuzzy trims that tickle or itch. Because the AAP recommends no blankets in the first year, clothing that can keep infants warm is a good choice. Layering clothing is a good way to keep babies warm. Parents need to be careful, however, not to overdress babies. They can overheat easily. A good rule of thumb is to dress an infant in one more layer than you would dress yourself in.

Clothes for infants must also be safe. Clothes that have ties, buttons, bows, or hooks can be choking hazards for infants. Clothing items that are loosely knitted may also pose a safety hazard because they can trap babies' fingers or toes. Clothes with drawstrings are a strangulation hazard. To protect infants from burns, sleepwear must be made of **flame-resistant** (resist burning) fabric or must fit snugly.

Shopping for Clothing

Babies grow quickly and outgrow their clothing several times in the first year. Because of their rapid growth, babies, especially newborns, do not need too many clothes. During the first year, length and weight are better indicators of clothing size than age. Baby clothes in stores, however, are usually based on age. Companies use different sizes, so reading sizing charts and hangtags carefully before buying is necessary to select the right size for the baby.

When purchasing baby clothes, parents may want to look for clothes with built-in growth features that can help clothes last longer, such as a double row of snaps or buttons at the waistline. Knit garments and clothes with stretch waists and stretch leg and arm openings are also good choices. Clothes that must be hand-washed, dry-cleaned, or ironed are not practical.

Parents may consider buying baby shoes, but shoes are not needed until infants walk outdoors. Shoes protect and cushion the feet from outside dangers. Indoors, infants should walk without shoes to prevent flat-footed walking. Most shoes that infants wear in the first year are for decoration. These shoes have soft, cloth soles. Babies need to wear socks or footed clothing in cool weather to keep their feet warm.

Because baby clothes are so cute, parents can easily make unwise financial choices. Parents can stay within their clothing budget by watching for sales and borrowing baby clothes. Choosing gender-neutral clothes (and storing for the next child) is also cost-effective. Another cost-effective idea is for parents to buy or make clothes the baby can grow into.

Dressing Babies

Newborns are easier to dress than older infants because they do not squirm as much. To make dressing babies easy and safe, parents can have the baby's clothes ready and undo any buttons or snaps before getting the baby. Remembering to support the baby's head while lifting them is also important to avoid unnecessary jostling. Because newborns cannot push, parents need to pull babies' arms and legs through garment openings (**Figure 8.16**). If babies become upset, parents can cuddle them before continuing to dress them.

Anna Nahabed/Shutterstock.com

Figure 8.16 When dressing a newborn, a parent must pull the newborn's arms and legs through the garments. *What types of garments would be easy for dressing a newborn? What types of garments would be more difficult?*

Finally, parents can use dressing times to talk with their babies and even tell them what they are doing. ("I'm snapping your shirt. Snap…snap…snap.")

Caring for Baby Clothes

Many parents store baby clothes for future children or as keepsakes. Before storing, clothes need to be clean. Soiled spots change over time, and then stains cannot be removed. When clothes are clean and dry, they are ready to be stored. Parents can care for baby clothes properly by following these practices:

- Read labels and tags before cleaning clothes. Follow the directions.
- Pretreat stains before washing clothes to prevent the stains from setting. Also, mend tears before washing to prevent them from getting larger.
- Choose a gentle detergent or rinse babies' and children's clothing more often than other clothes. Extra rinses help remove detergent from clothes. Babies' skin is more sensitive than adults' skin.

- Avoid using fabric softener when washing sleepwear. The chemicals in fabric softeners can reduce the flame-resistant qualities of the clothing.

8.3-2 Bathing

Newborns do not need baths every day because they do not get too dirty except for their faces, necks, and diaper areas. Parents keep these areas clean as they burp and diaper their babies. Newborn skin can also dry out easily if it is washed too often. Parents can bathe their newborns several times a week by giving sponge baths. In a **sponge bath**, parents do not **immerse** (cover in liquid) the baby in water, but instead use a washcloth or sponge to wash the baby's body. Doctors recommend sponge baths for newborns until the navel heals completely—up to three weeks after birth. (Keep the cord stump dry and never pull on it even when it starts coming loose. The doctor will tell parents any other procedure in cord care.)

Focus on Careers

Physical Therapist

Physical therapists help people improve movement and manage pain. Pediatric physical therapists help patients under 18 years old improve their range of motion, strength, and flexibility. This could be due to injury, specific conditions, or developmental delays. If children are not meeting their gross motor skill milestones, your pediatrician may refer you to a pediatric physical therapist.

Career cluster: Healthcare.

Education: Educational requirements include a doctor of physical therapy degree (DPT). All states require a license to practice physical therapy.

Job outlook: Future employment opportunities for physical therapists are projected to grow much faster than the average for all occupations.

To learn more about a career as a physical therapist, visit the United States Department of Labor's *Occupational Outlook Handbook* website. You will also be able to compare the job responsibilities, educational requirements, job outlook, and average pay of physical therapists with similar occupations.

Photo: SylwiaMoz/Shutterstock

Tub bathing can begin as soon as the newborn's navel has healed. If the baby was circumcised, the circumcision also needs to be healed. The preparation steps for tub bathing are the same as those for sponge bathing. The only difference is that a small tub is filled with about three inches of comfortably warm water. Tub baths should be given carefully and quickly for the baby's comfort and safety. Whether giving babies sponge baths or tub baths, parents should *never* leave their babies unattended—even for a second.

As babies are bathed, they enjoy parents who talk, sing, cuddle, and smile. Babies often respond well because warm water is relaxing. As infants grow, they enjoy kicking and splashing in the water as their parents hold them. Water play is good for babies' developing motor skills as well as being lots of fun.

8.3-3 Diapering

Babies require frequent diaper changes throughout the first year. Parents can use either disposable or cloth diapers for babies. Both disposable and cloth diapers have advantages and disadvantages. When deciding which type of diapers to use, parents often consider cost and convenience.

Disposable diapers are more costly but can be easy and convenient for parents. There are many different brands and sizes of disposable diapers available from which parents can choose. Newborn disposable diapers have a cutout in front so the baby's cord stump does not get wet. Disposable diapers have waterproof outer layers. For child care, disposable diapers are often required.

Cloth diapers are less expensive than disposable diapers but can also be less convenient because parents have to spend time washing them. Babies who wear cloth diapers also need to wear waterproof cloth diaper covers to protect from leaks. Some parents prefer to use cloth diapers because they are **eco-friendly** (not harmful to the environment). In some places, parents have the option of using a diaper service that picks up soiled diapers and delivers sterilized cloth ones.

Once the type of diaper is selected, parents are ready to change the baby's diaper (**Figure 8.17**).

Figure 8.17 **How to Diaper a Baby**

1. Gather diapering materials before you get the baby. You will need the following:
   - changing pad for baby to lie on (if not using a changing table)
   - clean diaper (if using cloth diapers, have diaper folded and ready for use)
   - clean cloth, such as a burp cloth
   - fasteners for pre-folded cloth diapers
   - baby wipes
   - lotion or diaper rash ointment may be recommended by doctor
2. Wash and dry your hands and then remove the baby's clothing.
3. Place the baby on the changing pad on a safe, firm surface. Using a changing table with a safety strap enables you to fasten the baby to the changing table to prevent falls.
4. Unfasten, remove, and dispose of the soiled diaper. If diapering a baby with a penis, place a clean cloth over the penis to prevent spraying.
5. Use baby wipes to clean the baby's genitals and buttocks from front to back. Be sure to also clean between skin folds.
6. With one hand, grasp the baby's ankles and slide a fresh diaper under the baby's bottom. Apply any necessary lotion or diaper rash ointment. Then, pull the front of the diaper up between the baby's legs.
7. Fasten the diaper. When using disposable diapers, the tape fastens from the back to the front. Some cloth diapers use Velcro or snaps as fasteners while other cloth diapers use diaper safety pins as fasteners. Place two fingers in the top front of the fastened diaper to make sure it is not too loose or too tight.
8. Redress the baby and return them to a safe place.
9. Wash your hands thoroughly.
10. Do not forget to clean and disinfect the changing table or wash the changing pad.

Goodheart-Willcox Publisher

Josep Suria/Shutterstock.com

Older infants wiggle more and may protest when diapered, which makes the task harder for adults. To keep the infant's interest, parents may talk, sing, and play with the infant during diaper changes. Parents and other caregivers should wash their hands (and the baby's hands and any toys the baby is holding) after each diaper change.

Diaper rashes may develop from wet or soiled diapers if they are not changed frequently enough, or from sensitive skin issues. In a diaper rash, bacteria grow rapidly on the warm, moist, and air-free skin. Most babies develop diaper rash at one time or another. The most common treatment is to change the baby's diaper more often to keep it dry and use petroleum jelly or a rash ointment on the affected area when diapering. If the rash persists following several days of treatment, parents should consult a pediatrician.

To prevent the spread of germs, diaper-changing areas need to be clean. When cleaning a diaper-changing table, clean any visible soil with a detergent and water mixture and rinse with water. Then, spray the entire changing surface with a sanitizing solution, such as one teaspoon of household bleach per one cup of water. Finally, leave the solution in contact with the surface for two minutes and allow to air-dry or wipe-dry with a clean cloth.

8.3-4 Resting and Sleeping

Babies vary in the amount of rest and sleep they need. Because newborns grow so rapidly, their tiny bodies need lots of rest. On average, newborns need 14 to 17 hours of sleep per day for the first three months. (Some sleep less than this, while others, especially preterm babies, sleep as many as 23 hours per day.) Newborns have a 24-hour feeding and sleep cycle and will only stay awake for 1 to 3 hours at a time.

Between 4 and 12 months of age, infants need 12 to 16 hours of sleep per day, including naps. As infants grow, they can sleep for longer periods. By the time infants are 9 months old, they may be able to sleep for at least 8 to 10 hours through the night without a feeding. To get the remaining hours of sleep, infants typically take 1 to 4 naps per day, between 30 minutes and 2 hours at a time.

Sudden Unexpected Infant Death

Sudden infant death syndrome (SIDS) is a condition in which a sleeping baby dies without warning. Up until 2022, the cause of SIDS remained unexplained; no medical reason could be given for infants who died from SIDS. In 2022, however, groundbreaking research from The Children's Hospital Westmead in Sydney, Australia found a potential link between SIDS and a defect in the area of the brain dealing with arousal from sleep. This study supported the theory that infants with this brain defect would be unable to awaken themselves if they stopped breathing during sleep. While SIDS is a tragic condition, ongoing research following this study might help prove the cause of SIDS. Knowing the cause can pave the way for screenings and hopefully a cure.

SIDS is part of a broader category of *sudden unexpected infant death (SUID)*, which includes infant deaths from SIDS, accidental suffocation or strangulation in bed, and other unknown causes. SUID is the leading cause of death in babies between one month and one year of age. In many cases, seemingly healthy babies simply stop breathing in their sleep. Though the cause of all SUID is unknown, some risk factors are known (**Figure 8.18**).

Figure 8.18 Risk Factors for Sudden Unexpected Infant Death (SUID)

- Teen pregnancy
- Insufficient prenatal care
- Exposure to tobacco, alcohol, or illegal drugs (especially cocaine) before birth
- Premature birth (especially for infants born more than two weeks before due date)
- Low-birthweight (less than 5½ pounds)
- Multiple births (especially if weighing less than 3.3 pounds)
- Exposure to cigarette smoke after birth
- Occurrence of an older sibling who died of SIDS
- Babies who are biologically male and have other risk factors listed above
- Infants between two and four months of age
- Sleep-deprived infants

Goodheart-Willcox Publisher

Circadian Rhythms and Routines

Babies, especially newborns, are well-known for not sleeping through the night. This is because babies are still developing circadian rhythms. The *circadian* (sir-CAY-dee-uhn) *rhythm*, also known as the *sleep-wake cycle*, is an internal system that regulates feelings of sleepiness and alertness. Circadian rhythms are regulated by hormone (serotonin) production in the brain. Lightness and darkness in the environment also guide circadian rhythms. Light triggers feelings of alertness, and darkness triggers feelings of sleepiness. Since babies' sleep-wake cycles are immature, however, they do not follow these signals in the environment for sleep and wake time.

Establishing routines is important to help babies develop and maintain regular sleep habits. Routines also help babies develop a basic sense of trust. Babies feel secure because they know what to expect. To make sure routines fit babies' and adults' needs, parents can develop a nighttime ritual (routine) for putting a baby to bed. This needs to be a quiet time. Some parents bathe their infants before bedtime. Reading a story or listening to some quiet music may also be part of nighttime rituals. Babies need to be soothed until they are drowsy. Crying babies need parents to help them calm down and feel comfortable. Parents may darken a room to induce feelings of sleepiness.

Routines need to be flexible and change as infants mature. For example, the many short daytime and nighttime naps are gradually replaced by fewer, but longer, daytime naps and longer periods of sleep at night. If the infant does not sleep well at night, parents may try to rearrange

Photo: kanyanat wongsa/Shutterstock.com

the schedule. Waking infants after four hours of daytime sleep may help infants sleep longer at night. Eventually, circadian rhythms stabilize between three and six months of age and most infants sleep through the night.

Reading Activity

Managing infants' sleep-wake cycles is a major topic for new parents, many of whom grow tired from waking up to soothe their infants. In small groups, research books or articles that give advice to new parents about managing their infants' sleeping schedules. As a group, discuss the following questions:

1. How authoritative are the sources your group chose? How do you know?
2. How do the stated pieces of advice help new parents manage their infants' sleeping schedules?

Photo: Tom Wang/Shutterstock.com

Until the cause and prevention of all conditions under SUID are found, parents can take the following positive steps to protect their babies:

- Avoid as many of the risk factors as possible both before and after the baby is born.

- Place the baby on their back to sleep during naps and at night. Remember the saying, "Back to sleep." Placing the baby on their stomach increases the chance of SUID. Stomach-sleeping may put pressure on the baby's jaw and narrow the airway.

It also increases the risk of the baby rebreathing exhaled air (which contains carbon dioxide rather than oxygen). Caregivers should never place babies on their sides to sleep because babies can roll from their sides to their stomachs.

- Place the baby on a firm surface to sleep. Cribs should meet current safety standards with no broken or missing parts or drop-side rails. Babies should not sleep on chairs, sofas, cushions, sheepskins, beanbag chairs, or waterbeds.
- Do not use fluffy blankets, comforters, throws, stuffed toys, or pillows in the crib or **play yard** (an enclosed play space for babies; formerly called a *playpen*). Soft items and loose bedding in these areas can increase the risk of suffocation or strangulation.
- Use a car seat for transport only. A baby's position in a car seat reduces their breathing capacity. Babies sleeping in car seats, swings, and baby seats are more prone to SUID.
- Make sure the baby does not get too warm while sleeping. The temperature of a baby's room should be comfortable. Babies who become very warm may go into a deeper sleep and find it more difficult to wake up. Because of this, it is best not to overdress the baby for sleep.
- Offer a pacifier for sleep from birth and continue its use for sleep even after the baby no longer uses a pacifier while awake.
- Avoid sharing a parent bed with a baby (called *co-sleeping* or *co-bedding*). Young babies are safest in their own crib in their parent's room. Babies should not sleep with older children either.
- Encourage adequate sleep (**Figure 8.19**).

- Attend regular well-baby checkups.
- Breast-feed the baby for at least seven months and preferably for one year.
- Keep the baby away from people who smoke and places where people smoke.
- Do not use breathing monitors and alarms or specialized products that claim to reduce the risk of SUID unless recommended by a doctor.

Bedding Safety

A bed is one of the most essential pieces of furniture a baby needs. During the first few weeks after birth, parents may prefer their newborns sleep in a cradle or small **bassinet** (basketlike bed). As babies grow, they will need a crib. Some parents are purchasing *convertible furniture*, or furniture that easily becomes useful for other purposes. Convertible furniture can grow with the child. For example, some cribs can be converted to youth or even adult beds.

Safety in the baby's bedding and supplies is essential. A baby bed should be high and stable enough to prevent young children or pets from tipping it over. If the cradle or bed has slats, distance between the slats must be 2⅜ inches or less. This prevents infants from wiggling feet first through the slats until their heads are caught, which could cause serious injury or death. The mattress on the bed should be snug-fitting and any sheets should be firm-fitting, not loose-fitting. Loose fabric can tangle around the baby and smother or strangle them. Also, drop-side cribs and bumper pads should not be used.

8.3-5 Encouraging Physical Activity

Movement is a large part of life—before and after birth. Watch the constant movement of newborns lying awake on their backs. Physical activity is important for muscle development, coordination, and even relaxation. Helping babies move their muscles may help the general development of the muscles.

Asia Images Group/Shutterstock.com

Figure 8.19 Sleep deficits of even two hours on a given day are associated with SUID. *What can parents do to make sure they are giving their infants enough sleep time?*

To help babies with physical activity, parents often engage their babies in tummy time several times each day (**Figure 8.20**). Play yards also provide a safe place for infants to play. Parents should limit total time spent in a play yard, however, to no more than two hours per day. Infants need to be able to move and explore freely in order to develop gross motor skills.

Physical activity, if started early in life, may become a daily, lifelong habit. Daily physical activity is also a way to have fun with babies and develop a warm relationship. Many families find that doing physical activities together is great family fun.

Paul Hakimatta Photograpahy/Shutterstock.com

Figure 8.20 Tummy time both provides physical activity for infants and aids in their motor development. *Why do you think tummy time is considered physical activity for infants?*

Lesson 8.3 Review and Assessment

1. What is one thing to keep in mind when choosing infant clothing? (8.3.1)
   A. Built-in growth features can help make clothes last longer.
   B. New clothing is better than used clothing because you know it hasn't been damaged.
   C. Babies get cold easily, so they need several extra layers.
   D. Most infant clothing is manufactured to be water resistant to repel urine.

2. When bathing a newborn, what is most important? (8.3.2)
   A. Use a small tub filled with comfortably warm water.
   B. Toys and bubbles can make bath time enjoyable for infants.
   C. Only give sponge baths until the navel has healed completely.
   D. Bathe newborns daily to keep their sensitive skin clean.

3. After a caregiver removes the soiled diaper during a diaper change, what comes next? (8.3.3)
   A. Slide a new diaper underneath the baby while holding its legs up by the ankles.
   B. Wipe the genitals and buttocks from front to back.

C. Caregiver should wash their hands again to prevent spreading bacteria.
   D. Disinfect the diaper changing area to make sure it is clean before the next step.

4. Which of the following is *not* a safe sleep recommendation for infants? (8.3.4)
   A. Do not use soft items like fluffy blankets or stuffed animals inside the crib.
   B. Offer a pacifier to infants before bedtime or naptime.
   C. Make sure the baby does not get too warm during sleep.
   D. Lay infants on their sides in case they vomit in their sleep.

5. How should parents and caregivers encourage physical activity of infants? (8.3.5)
   A. By having the infant participate in tummy time once daily
   B. By allowing the infant to move and explore freely
   C. By letting the infant play in a safe place like a play yard for several hours a day
   D. By bringing the infant along whenever they exercise to be a good role model

Chapter 8

Review and Assessment

Summary

Lesson 8.1

8.1-1 The infant's brain grows the fastest out of all the organs in the first year.

8.1-1 Infants grow about 9 to 10 inches and almost triple their weight during the first year.

8.1-1 Children who do not grow at a healthy rate may be diagnosed with failure to thrive.

8.1-1 Deciduous teeth, or baby teeth, begin to appear in the first year, typically during the second half of the first year.

8.1-2 Newborns have a rooting reflex, sucking reflex, palmar and plantar (grasping) reflex, withdrawal reflex, Babinski reflex, Moro (startle) reflex, and walking reflex.

8.1-3 Motor development involves the use and control of muscles that direct body movements.

8.1-4 Physical developmental milestones are classified as postural, locomotor, or grasping. Infants reach these milestones at individual rates, but there are predictable ages for each milestone.

Lesson 8.2

8.2-1 From birth to six months old, infants get all their needed nutrients from breast milk or formula.

8.2-1 Babies need to be burped during and after every feeding.

8.2-2 Babies need to wean off breast milk or formula gradually. Cow's milk can be given at age one instead of formula or breast milk; a gradual weaning helps everyone adapt to the change.

8.2-2 Around six months of age, infants may be ready to start eating solid foods. Many parents choose to start with spoon-feeding infant cereal mixed with formula or breast milk.

8.2-2 It is important to space out the introduction of new foods at least three days and one at a time. This helps the parents and caregivers notice any adverse reactions like allergies or intolerances.

8.2-3 Self-feeding usually begins near the end of the first year, when infants develop the pincer grasp. Infants always need supervision when self-feeding.

Lesson 8.3

8.3-1 Infants need comfortable, safe, soft clothing that is easy to put on and off. Sleepwear should be flame-resistant or fit snugly.

8.3-2 Newborns do not need a bath every day and should only have sponge baths until the navel is completely healed.

8.3-2 For tub bathing, a small tub should be filled with about three inches of comfortably warm water. Bath time should be enjoyable; water play is good for developing motor skills.

8.3-3 Babies require frequent diaper changes in the first year. Diaper choices include cloth or disposable diapers.

8.3-4 Newborns need lots of rest, averaging 14 to 17 hours of sleep per day in the first three months. This gradually changes to 12 to 16 hours of sleep per day as the infant gets older. Sleeping through the night takes time.

8.3-4 Sudden Unexpected Infant Death (SUID) is a category of infant death that includes Sudden Infant Death Syndrome (SIDS), accidental suffocation or strangulation in bed, and other unknown causes. To prevent these conditions, parents should follow several positive sleep safety recommendations.

8.3-5 Physical activity is key to development. Parents and caregivers should engage their babies in tummy time, let them explore freely, and limit time spent in play yards to no more than two hours per day.

College and Career Portfolio

Portfolio Transcripts

One of the most important elements of a portfolio—whether for college or for a first job—is a transcript. Transcripts take time to request and receive.

Procedures for requesting a transcript vary depending on your school and the purpose of the transcript. If you need to request a transcript, it is best to do so well in advance, since they take time to generate. To include a transcript in your portfolio, complete the following steps:

- Research how to request a transcript from your school. If you need help, ask your teacher or consult a career counselor. In a college or university, students' transcripts are available in the Office of the Registrar.
- Follow the procedure to request your transcript in advance. Seek help if necessary.

Recall and Application

1. How long is a baby considered a neonate, or newborn? (8.1.1)
   A. From birth to two weeks
   B. From birth to one month
   C. From birth to two months
   D. From birth to three months
2. What does frequent spitting up and partially digested foods in the child's stools show evidence of? (8.1.1)
   A. A food intolerance or allergy
   B. The infant's difficulty digesting breast milk
   C. Starting solids too early
   D. An immature digestive system
3. Which of the following is NOT a cause of failure to thrive? (8.1.1)
   A. Insufficient nutrients in the infant's food
   B. Using formula to feed the infant
   C. Infrequent or short feeding times
   D. Abuse or neglect
4. Which infant reflex is characterized by the infant turning their head and moving their mouth in response to a touch on the cheek or mouth? (8.1.2)
   A. Sucking
   B. Moro (startle)
   C. Rooting
   D. Walking

5. Which infant reflex is characterized by the infant's toes fanning out if the outside of the foot is stroked from heel to toe? (8.1.2)
   A. Babinski
   B. Walking
   C. Plantar grasp
   D. Rooting

6. Which is an example of gross-motor skills? (8.1.3)
   A. Sitting
   B. Standing
   C. Walking without support
   D. Eating with utensils

7. How are physical development milestones classified? (8.1.4)
   A. Fine-motor skills, gross-motor skills, and reflexes
   B. Cephalocaudal and proximodistal development
   C. Postural, locomotor, and grasping
   D. Skeletal, muscular, and reflexes

8. When is the best time for introducing new solids to infants? (8.2.2)
   A. In the evening
   B. Before bedtime
   C. At lunchtime
   D. Early in the day

9. Which of the following is NOT a safe food for an infant to eat using their fingers? (8.2.3)
   A. Rounded, small foods, such as carrots, berries, grapes, and raisins
   B. O-shaped toasted oat cereal
   C. Cooked diced vegetables, such as carrots or sweet potatoes
   D. Small chunks of fruit, such as bananas, peaches, or pears

10. How can parents and caregivers care for infant clothing? (8.3.1)
    A. Use a gentle detergent or rinse babies' clothing more often than other clothes.
    B. Use fabric softener so clothes will be extra soft.
    C. Pretreat stains and mend tears before washing clothes.
    D. Read labels and tags before cleaning clothes.

11. How often should newborns be bathed? (8.3.2)
    A. Every day
    B. Once a week
    C. Several times a week
    D. Newborns do not need any type of bath until their navels are healed

12. What is the first step to changing an infant's diaper? (8.3.3)
    A. Wash and dry your hands.
    B. Gather diapering materials.
    C. Remove the baby's clothing.
    D. Clean and disinfect the changing table.

13. How much sleep does a newborn need per day? (8.3.4)
    A. 10 to 12 hours
    B. 12 to 15 hours
    C. 18 to 21 hours
    D. 14 to 17 hours

14. Which of the following is true about physical activity for infants? (8.3.5)
    A. Parents and caregivers should engage their babies in tummy time several times a day.
    B. Parents and caregivers should make sure infants are always enclosed in a play yard if they are going to explore.
    C. The more parents and caregivers exercise, the more likely their baby will be to enjoy physical activity.
    D. Parents and caregivers should encourage older siblings to help the infant get physical activity.

Critical Thinking

1. **Compare and contrast.** Using a life-size doll, demonstrate each reflex and identify what stimulus causes each response. Then, as a class, compare and contrast reflexes during infancy.

2. **Cause and effect.** Identify the two directions of a baby's physical development in the first year. Then, imagine you are trying to explain these directions to a student you are tutoring. Use visual methods to explain the two directions of development and to assess how they affect a child's development.

3. **Draw conclusions.** Using Figure 8.10, describe a baby of an age you choose using the developmental milestones listed. Then, close your book and find a partner. Give your partner a brief description of the milestones the baby you chose has achieved. Then, ask your partner what age they think the baby is. Switch roles and listen to your partner's description. Then, discuss your answers with your partner.

4. **Analyze.** After discussing your answers to the #3 activity, find a different partner. As a pair, consider the following questions:
   - How easy was it to identify a baby's age based on milestones?
   - How difficult do you think it is to do this in real life?

5. **Determine.** Many parents track their baby's physical and motor development, and may worry if their child does not mature or achieve milestones as they think they should. In small groups, consider under what circumstances a parent might worry about their baby's lack of development. What should a parent then do to resolve these concerns?

6. **Evaluate.** Child development experts often advise parents to follow the baby's lead. Brainstorm with classmates how you can follow a baby's lead in meeting their needs. Are there times when newborns should follow their parents' leads? Why or why not?

7. **Identify.** Imagine that one of your friends is a new parent and is nervous about the processes of breast-feeding, weaning, and introducing solid foods. Your friend is insecure in their ability to wean their child and is embarrassed about asking. With a partner, role-play this conversation, and identify methods of weaning and introducing solid foods for your friend. Encourage them to seek advice from their doctor as well.

Core Skills

1. **Math.** Interview at least six parents whose children were full-term or almost full-term. Ask each parent what the child's weight and height were at birth, six months, and one year. Record these figures in a master list. Showing your work, figure the average weight and height for this group of babies at each age.

2. **Speaking.** Find a quality infant toy that would encourage an infant to develop gross- and fine-motor skills. Determine the children's ages for which the toy would be safe. Make an oral presentation to the class showing how your selected toy promotes both types of skills and explaining what age range should use the toy and why.

3. **Writing.** Write a paragraph from the perspective of a baby during the first year of life, describing what the baby can and cannot do, how they feel, and what they are learning to do.

4. **Technology, writing, and speaking.** As a group or class project, create a one- or two-page brochure that explains both the skeletal and organ maturation that occurs during infancy and the milestones parents can expect babies to meet. Your goal is to create a brochure that will help parents keep track of what changes they should see in their babies during the first year of life. List all the milestones and significant physical changes described in this chapter, and then choose the ones you think parents will most easily recognize and most worry about. Then, organize the information and discuss how you will lay out your brochure. Finally, arrange the information in a logical and easy-to-understand way. Use pictures to accent the information described in your brochure. Finally, present your brochure to the class and explain why you chose certain changes and milestones.

5. **Listening and speaking.** Organize a debate about breast-feeding versus formula-feeding. Divide into two teams—one to argue in favor of breast-feeding and the other to argue in favor of formula-feeding. For each method, emphasize the physical, social, emotional, and intellectual aspects; parental bonding issues; adaptations for working parents; and costs. During the debate, deliver persuasive opening statements, arguments, and closing statements. Afterward, discuss the issues raised as a class.

6. **Reading.** Locate a book or collection of recipes for infants up to one year of age and then read at least five recipes. Take notes on the types of foods described and consider how safe and healthy the recipes are based on what you learned in this chapter. Then, choose two recipes and evaluate them in terms of nutrition, safety, and age-appropriateness. Present your findings to the class.

7. **Health safety.** Use a life-size infant doll to demonstrate the following skills needed for infant care: feeding, sponge and tub bathing, diapering, putting a baby to bed, and dressing. Treat the doll as you would a newborn, being gentle with the baby and supporting its head. Which skills were easiest for you, and which will take much more practice? In what ways might these tasks be different with a real infant than with a doll?

8. **CTE Career Readiness Practice.** The director of the child care center where you work overheard you explaining to parents the precautions they can take against SUID. Your center has recently hired a new employee, and your director asks you to train this new employee on methods of preventing SUID and on educating parents about these methods. In preparation for training, develop materials for the new employee, including

A. authoritative information about SUID and what resources provide accurate information about it

B. the precautions your child care center takes against SUID

C. a script in which you train the employee to talk with parents about SUID

Observations

1. Observe two infants who are the same age. How do they differ in their physical maturity? How do they differ in their motor skills? Does one infant have an acceleration or delay in maturity or skills?

2. Many parents keep a "baby book," a small book that contains pictures of the baby at each month for the first year, as well as some descriptions of when the baby achieved certain milestones. Read your own baby book or a classmate's baby book, and write observations about changes in size, shape, and motor skills.

Chapter 9

Intellectual Development in the First Twelve Months

Lesson 9.1   How Infants Learn in the First Twelve Months
Lesson 9.2   What Infants Learn in the First Twelve Months
Lesson 9.3   Meeting Intellectual Needs in the First Twelve Months

Essential Question

How do infants make sense of their world, and how can parents and other caregivers support their baby's learning?

Case Study — Can Baby Signing Delay Learning to Talk?

As a class, read the case study and discuss the questions that follow. After you finish studying the chapter, discuss this case study again. Have your opinions changed based on what you learned?

Olivia and Noah began to teach their child, Harper, *Baby Signs* at 6 months of age. By 8 months, Harper was signing back and learned new "words" quickly. Olivia's friends, Mia and Elijah, began teaching their child, Liam, *Baby Signs* at 6 months of age, too. Liam also learned and used many signs in just a few months, and by 12 months, Liam was beginning to say a few of the signed words out loud.

At Harper's 12-month-old well-baby checkup, Olivia and Noah told the pediatrician that Harper was not talking yet. The pediatrician replied, "Oh, I'm sure that will happen soon." As the months passed, Harper continued to smile, gesture, and use *Baby Signs*, but didn't talk. Harper's grandparents said that *Baby Signs* had probably kept Harper from talking because "babies don't talk unless they need to talk."

Olivia was becoming concerned that something might be wrong with Harper and began thinking that maybe they should take Harper to see a child development expert.

Give It Some Thought

1. Harper's grandparents said that *Baby Signs* probably kept Harper from talking because "babies don't talk unless they need to talk." Do you think they made a good point? Why or why not?
2. Do you think the lack of spoken vocabulary words at 12 months of age should concern the pediatrician? Why or why not?
3. Do you think Harper needs to see a child development expert? Why or why not?
4. What might be some disadvantages of baby signing in settings in which people do not know signing, during the stage in which infants naturally focus on the speaker's mouth, and in the joint adult-child interactions required in gazing and pointing?

Stefan Tomic/E+ via Getty Images

Lesson 9.1

How Infants Learn in the First Twelve Months

Key Terms

binocular vision
cognition
explicit memory
implicit memory
perception
perceptual learning
scaffolding
sensorimotor stage
sociocultural
stimuli
theory of development
zone of proximal
   development (ZPD)

Learning Outcomes

After studying this lesson, you will be able to

9.1-1   **describe** how brain development supports learning.

9.1-2   **explain** the concept of perceptual learning.

9.1-3   **compare and contrast** two major cognitive/intellectual development theories.

Reading and Notetaking Activity

Before reading this lesson, skim the headings and write each heading in a different color or font on a separate piece of paper or electronically. As you silently read the chapter and then listen to your teacher, take notes in the color or font you chose for each heading. After you finish taking notes for each section, draw or copy and paste a small illustration or visual next to the section that will help you remember what you learned.

Introduction

As you may recall, intellectual development is how and what people learn and how they express what they know through language. Intellectual development is also called cognitive development. During the baby's first year, intellectual development happens as quickly as physical development. The learning process begins right after birth. In fact, the brain and some of the senses are active before birth. Learning, however, involves more than physical growth and development. Many researchers in child development believe babies *want* to learn. Each month babies exert more and more effort to explore their world. Because learning begins so early, parents are a child's first teachers.

9.1-1 Brain Development Supports Learning

Newborns come into the world using all their sense organs (eyes, ears, nose, tongue, and skin), which are rapidly maturing. Environmental **stimuli** (light, sound, heat, texture) are agents that affect the sensory organs causing a person to react. Early reactions are mainly reflexive. For example, when babies see a bright light (stimulus), they close their eyes (reaction). As their senses develop, babies use stimuli to learn. For example, when handed an object (stimulus), infants will look at it (reaction) and mouth it (reaction).

Brain research has noted much activity in the vision and motor centers of the baby's brain during the first year. As motor skills develop, infants are able to move toward many sights, sounds, and other stimuli. While taking in sensory and motor experiences, the brain is wiring the thinking and memory centers. **Figure 9.1** shows the functions of the brain.

Vision Center

The vision center of the brain allows babies to process the sights of their world into information. The brain makes some connections from the sensory receptors before birth but wiring increases dramatically after birth. Vision dominates how babies interpret their world early in life. For this reason, the vision center is very active in early infancy. The window of opportunity for sight is from birth to four to six months of age. During this time, a baby's vision matures rapidly in the following areas:

- *Acuity*—the ability to see clearly in each eye. To see clearly, muscles must contract and relax the lens of each eye, so an image is projected clearly on the retina. (**Figure 9.2** shows the internal structures of the eye.) Because babies do not have good control of the lens muscles, their focus is often not correct for distance. They may focus in front of or behind the object. Acuity is also dependent on the maturity of the retina and the brain. Early blurry vision does not last long. The newborn's acuity is about 20/120 (top letter on an eye chart). By four months of age, acuity is about 20/60. By eight months of age, acuity is about 20/30 (normal adult acuity is 20/20). Going from 20/30 acuity to 20/20 acuity takes years. The window of opportunity for acuity is from birth to seven years of age.

- voluntary eye movement
- motor and speech production
- Higher intellect
- Self control
- Inhibition
- Emotions
- voluntary movement
- motor skills development
- Sensation
- Language comprehension
- Vision
- Memory
- Equilibrium and muscle coordination
- Auditory

Functions of **the Brain**

Figure 9.1 Different sections of the brain are responsible for different functions. *How do you think the divided responsibilities within the brain affect how surgeons diagnose localized brain injuries?*

Monkik/Shutterstock.com

Figure 9.2 The Internal Structures of the Eye

Structure	Description
Cornea	Transparent covering that protects the eye.
Aqueous (AY-kwee-us) humor	Liquid that fills the cavity between the cornea and pupil of the eye; maintains the eye's shape.
Pupil	Opening through which light passes into the interior of the eye.
Iris	Structure that widens or narrows the size of the pupil, controlling how much light enters the eye; gives the eye its color.
Lens	Transparent, curved structure that changes shape to clearly focus on objects at various distances.
Vitreous (VIT-ree-us) humor	Liquid that fills the cavern of the eye behind the lens; maintains the eye's shape.
Retina	Innermost layer of the eye, which contains light-sensitive nerve endings.
Choroid (KOR-oyd) layer	Middle layer of the eye, which contains blood vessels that nourish the eye.
Optic nerve	Nerve that transmits electrical impulses from the eye to the brain.

Goodheart-Willcox Publisher

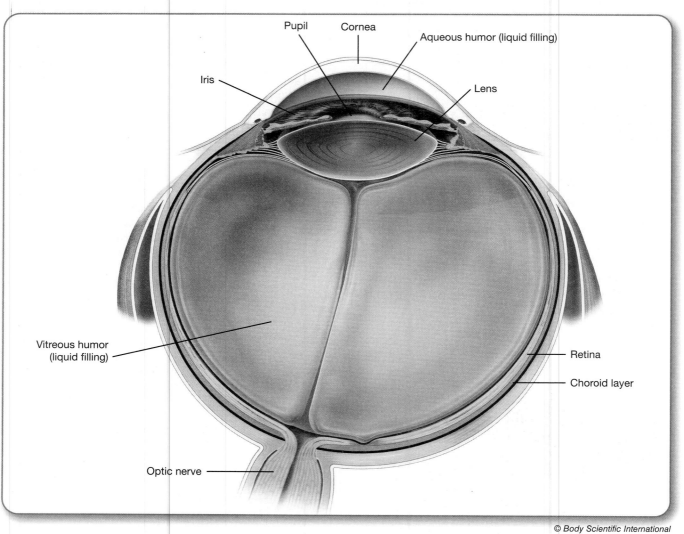

© *Body Scientific International*

- *Contrast sensitivity*—the ability to see objects with varying degrees of contrast from their background. Objects and their backgrounds have differing degrees of contrast. The contrast between an object and its background is given as a percentage. Higher percentages mean more contrast while lower percentages mean less contrast. For example, a light gray object on a white background has low contrast, making the object more difficult to detect. An example of high contrast would be a white object on a black background. Newborns can only see objects that have high contrast, such as black and white, which is a 100 percent contrast. By nine weeks of age, an infant's contrast sensitivity is near the adult level. They can see objects on backgrounds with as low as a 0.2 percent contrast (almost the same color intensity).

- *Color sensitivity*—the ability to see color. When matched for contrast, two-week-old newborns can distinguish red from green objects. Color receptors are not yet mature, so newborns may not be able to distinguish between **subtle** (not obvious) color differences (blue versus aqua) or among very light pastel colors.

- *Eye movements and coordination*—the ability to move both eyes perfectly together so a person sees the world as a fused picture. Between one and three months of age, infants begin to look at objects with both eyes. Watching a young infant, the adult may notice their eyes do not seem to work together. Often, one of the baby's eyes will drift off focus. At first, the baby's brain "sees" two slightly separated images of the same object. Around three months of age, the infant's brain can fuse the images together. To fuse an image requires the eyes to stay focused together on the object. Fusing images typically happens naturally unless the baby has weak eye muscles. Once the infant can use both eyes in unison, equally and accurately, to fuse in the brain the two images into one image, they have **binocular vision**. The window of opportunity for binocular vision is from one year to three years of age.

Focus on Careers

Physician— Pediatric Ophthalmologist

Many physicians work in medical specialties and even subspecialties. For example, an *ophthalmologist* is a highly trained medical doctor who is an eye specialist. A *pediatric ophthalmologist* further specializes in working with children. Pediatric ophthalmologists examine children's eyes and treat eye conditions, diseases, and illnesses. They can perform eye surgery, if necessary. Babies should have a six-month appointment with a pediatric ophthalmologist or at least an ophthalmologist.

Career cluster: Health science

Education: Educational requirements include an advanced degree, four years of medical school, and three to seven additional years of internship and residency. Licensure is also required.

Job outlook: Future employment opportunities for pediatric ophthalmologists are expected to grow faster than the average for all occupations.

To learn more about a career as a pediatric ophthalmologist, visit the United States Department of Labor's *Occupational Outlook Handbook* website. You will also be able to compare the job responsibilities, educational requirements, job outlook, and average pay of pediatric ophthalmologists with similar occupations.

Photo: MBI/Shutterstock.com

- *3-D vision*—the ability to see the world in three dimensions. The focus on the eye's retina is always two-dimensional (flat). Seeing in three dimensions requires the brain to interpret the image from each eye. Each eye sees an image somewhat differently because of the space between a person's eyes. The image must also be fused through binocular vision. Infants develop 3-D vision between three and six months of age.

Motor Center

As reflexes **wane** (diminish) during infancy, much activity occurs in the motor center of the baby's brain. Fast brain wiring in the motor center often starts around two months of age. At this time, infants begin the multiyear process of learning voluntary gross-motor movements. Wiring for fine-motor movements begins around two or three months of age when infants make their first attempts to grasp objects.

During infancy, babies depend on their motor skills as they react to environmental stimuli. These motor experiences within their environment enable infants to learn about important ideas, such as space, weight, and depth. For example, when an infant sees something interesting, they move toward the object. As the infant reaches for the object, using 3-D vision, they must assess the space between their hand and the object to know how far to reach for the object. Young infants look back and forth between hand and object, which slows the movement. After many experiences, infants have an understanding of space and can grasp objects with just a quick glance.

Thinking Center

Thinking requires more than the physical ability of the sensory organs to receive input from stimuli. Thinking also requires the ability to interpret sensory information the brain receives. A sensory association area of the brain inputs the basic sensory information received, such as shape, color, pitch, and location, and processes it into recognizable objects, such as dogs, trees, and faces. Recognizing a parent takes thousands of neurons firing in the brain. Repeat experiences help infants make these sensory associations.

Just as babies need good nutrition for physical growth, they also need quality experiences for intellectual development. Interesting things to see, hear, and touch are "food for thought." Because the world is new to babies, common objects and experiences in their environment provide quality learning opportunities. The adult's face, a cardboard box, some pans and spoons, or a trip to the yard can provide good learning experiences. **Figure 9.3** shows how babies change their seeing, hearing, and touching preferences for experiences as they try to learn about their new world.

Figure 9.3 Babies' Preferences for Sensory Experiences

Approximate Age	Sensory Experience (S) = Seeing, (H) = Hearing, (T) = Touching
Birth to 3 months	• Prefers patterns to solids. (S)
3 to 6 months	• Prefers some colors to others as vision develops. (S) • Enjoys mirrors but does not know their own image until after 1 year of age. (S) • Likes small objects. (S)
6 to 9 months	• Takes pleasure in hearing singing and tries to sing along. (H) • Prefers toys with moving parts such as dials and wheels. (T)
9 to 12 months	• Shows less interest in faces except to quickly identify familiar faces and strange faces. (S) • Watches dropped objects with interest to see whether they roll, break, or bounce. (S) • Likes hiding games, such as peek-a-boo. (S) • Takes pleasure in hearing own name. (H) • Enjoys self-feeding. (T) • Likes dropping objects into pails and boxes. (T) • Enjoys stacking blocks and knocking them down. (T) • Shows interest in nesting (putting smaller into larger) objects. (S and T)

Goodheart-Willcox Publisher

Memory Centers

Thinking and learning require memory, and memory abilities begin very early in life. There are two main categories of memory. **Explicit memory** is the conscious, intentional recalling of experiences and facts, or the "knowing what" memory. For example, explicit memory involves remembering a person's name, a pet's name, or even landmarks on the way to a park. **Implicit memory** is the unconscious awareness of past experiences to perform tasks, or the "knowing how" memory. Examples of implicit memory include rolling over, walking, or playing a familiar game.

Although infants' memories are much more fragile than adults' memories, infants (and people of all ages) remember better when:

- they are directly engaged in an experience rather than just watching
- experiences are meaningful
- experiences happen over and over (reinforced)
- cues (or reminders) are used, such as showing an object or picture or seeing a landmark

Memories are important even to babies because the brain draws on past learning experiences to build new learning experiences. Think about how difficult it would be to start learning from "scratch" every day.

9.1-2 Perceptual Learning

Perceptual learning, which is the process of making sense out of sensory stimuli, is highly important in infancy. Perceptual learning happens because the sense organs mature, the brain develops, and preferences for certain stimuli change. To learn, infants must choose from among stimuli. Researchers believe babies have inborn abilities to choose the stimuli that will most help them learn. **Figure 9.4** shows how babies' preferences, or choices, for certain objects change during infancy.

Figure 9.4 **How Babies' Preferences for Certain Objects Change**

Preferences change from parts of objects to complete objects.
At first, babies react to, or study, parts of objects. Later, they pay more attention to the entire object. For instance, two-month-old babies smile at eyes drawn on a blank background. At three months of age, they study a picture that has eyes and a nose. By five months of age, they smile only at the picture of the full face. At this point, infants prefer the complete objects rather than parts of objects.

Preferences change from simple to complex objects.
Until babies are almost two months old, they do not prefer one object to another. After that, infants prefer more complex objects. For example, infants prefer 3-D objects over 2-D pictures. They prefer patterned or textured cards over plain white or solid-colored cards. Infants also prefer a drawn human face over any other drawn pattern or solid-colored card. Other preferences include slow-moving objects over nonmoving objects and curved lines over straight lines. They may show little or no reaction to complex stimuli because they cannot understand them.

Preferences change from familiar to new objects.
After two months of age, infants begin to explore objects that are new to them. They ignore objects that are too different because they may not understand them.

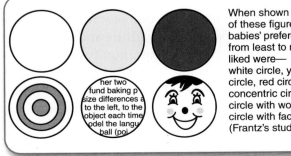

When shown each of these figures, babies' preferences from least to most liked were— white circle, yellow circle, red circle, concentric circles, circle with words, circle with face (Frantz's study).

When shown each of these pairs of lines, infants liked the curved lines more than the straight lines (Frantz's study).

Goodheart-Willcox Publisher

The outcome of perceptual learning is called **perception**. Perception involves

- *organizing information that comes through the senses.* This is a major step in learning. People perceive by noting how objects are alike and different in size, color, shape, and texture. Perceptions about form, space, weight, and numbers come through the senses, too.
- *how fast the brain organizes information.* For example, a mature reader can tell the difference between the letters *b* and *d* faster than a beginning reader.
- *the way a person reacts to different sensory experiences.* For example, a child in a room crowded with strangers may run to their caregiver and play with a toy while sitting on the caregiver's lap. If the child is alone with the mother, however, they may play with a toy on the floor rather than on the mother's lap.

9.1-3 Cognitive (Intellectual) Development Theories

Cognition is the act or process of knowing or understanding. Cognition gives meaning to perceptions. The baby's brain begins to piece together perceptions to form a picture in the mind.

Two highly recognized cognitive (intellectual) psychologists who described how children learn are Jean Piaget and Lev Vygotsky. Both men agreed that children construct their knowledge from their experiences. They believed learning attempts must be respected by allowing the child to take the lead. Their ideas influence education even today.

Piaget's Cognitive-Developmental Theory

Piaget thought children learn through their environment by making their own discoveries. He felt that the role of the adult was to provide a stimulating environment. Piaget's research led

him to believe that children go through four stages of cognitive development (sometimes called intellectual development). His theory is known as the *cognitive-developmental theory* (**Figure 9.5**).

Because babies explore with their senses and motor actions, Piaget called the first stage of cognitive development the **sensorimotor stage**. This stage begins at birth, and most children complete it in two years. During this stage, children use their senses and motor skills to learn and communicate. Piaget described learning experiences of the sensorimotor stage through six substages. As you can see by looking at Figure 9.5, babies work through four of the six substages during their first year. (You will learn about the last two substages later in this text.) Learning during the sensorimotor stage is particularly important because this stage is the basis for all future intellectual development.

In the beginning of the sensorimotor stage, connections babies make between themselves and the environment are accidental. Later, infants note the repeated connections between what they do (action) and what happens (response). This is the beginning of seeing cause and effect. Infants repeat their actions many times (called *circular*) to verify the results and bring pleasure.

During the third and fourth substages, infants learn by **imitating**, or copying another person's actions. Imitation is an important way that infants learn. Between 8 and 12 months, infants have goals, such as wanting a toy, which direct their actions. They can now combine several actions to achieve their goals or *problem solve*.

Vygotsky's Sociocultural Theory

Like Piaget, Vygotsky believed children's thinking changes as they develop. Although he knew children learned some skills through their own discoveries, he felt children learned mainly through interactions with others within their culture. Vygotsky believed the culture and social environment (family, school, community) in which a child is raised determine how a child will think and the skills they will develop. His theory is known as the **sociocultural theory of development**.

Figure 9.5 Piaget's Cognitive-Developmental Theory

Stages and Substages	Characteristics
Stage 1: Sensorimotor stage (birth to 2 years)	• Children learn through the senses and physical actions in six substages.

Substages 1 and 2 involve the baby's own body.

Stages and Substages	Characteristics
Substage 1: Practicing reflexes (birth to 1 month)	• Find stimulation through inborn reflexes, such as sucking and looking. • Practice these reflexes to make them strong and more efficient.
Substage 2: Primary circular reactions (1 to 4 months)	• Use voluntary actions that came from the reflexes, such as sucking at will. • Adapt these basic actions, such as sucking with more force for nourishment and with less force for pleasure (pacifier or hand).

Substages 3 and 4 involve people and objects.

Stages and Substages	Characteristics
Substage 3: Secondary circular reactions (4 to 8 months)	• Notice some responses to their actions, such as crying bringing a nearby parent and kicking making the mobile bounce (cause and effect). Practice their action-response sequences. • Can imitate some actions of others.
Substage 4: Coordination of secondary circular reactions (8 to 12 months)	• Begin to have goals, such as wanting a toy. • Problem-solve by combining two or more actions, such as *crawling* toward a toy and then *grasping* it. • Use a few tools to attain goals, such as using an object's string to pull it within reach.

Substages 5 and 6 involve creative actions and thinking before acting. (12 to 24 months)

Stages and Substages	Characteristics
Stage 2: Preoperational stage (2 to 7 years)	• Children learn through symbols, but with logical limitations.
Stage 3: Concrete operational stage (7 to 11 years)	• Children begin to think logically, but base their logic on past experiences.
Stage 4: Formal operational stage (11 years of age and older)	• Older children, teens, and adults reason abstractly.

Goodheart-Willcox Publisher

Vygotsky's **sociocultural** (relating to social and cultural factors) theory emphasizes how more knowledgeable adults and even older children guide younger children's discoveries (called *assisted discoveries*). Vygotsky saw teaching children as the basic sociocultural activity of humans. He believed teaching occurs through modeling, instructing, and working together on tasks or projects. The varying levels of instructional support given to help children learn a new concept or skill is called **scaffolding**.

To be effective as a teacher (or anyone who helps a child learn) Vygotsky thought it was most important to provide instructional supports at the right moments. For each concept or skill, teachers must first find the level in which a child can learn with help. This level is called the **zone of proximal development (ZPD)**. The match is correct when the child can be challenged to learn new concepts or skills but will not be overwhelmed. Working within a child's ZPD shows respect for what the child is learning and their interests, which is called *following the child's lead*. It also ensures that a child will not be pushed beyond their intellectual limits, which can have negative effects.

Once in the child's ZPD, teachers provide much scaffolding at first. After many experiences, some scaffolding or help is reduced. Once all the scaffolding is removed for a given learning experience, a new ZPD appears, and the child becomes ready for a higher level of learning. The gradual withdrawal of help makes the child more self-confident, too.

During infancy, parents can best scaffold through emotional communication. In the very early months, parents try to interpret their baby's cries or sucking behaviors. Around four months of age, infants' signals become clearer as they use body language. For example, infants may kick when they want out of a high chair or turn their head away when bored. Babies become calm when parents scaffold correctly. If parents read the cues and respond, the foundation for learning begins.

1. Infants are most likely to create a memory of an experience when which occurs? (9.1.1)
   A. They watch something happen.
   B. They experience something once.
   C. They engage in an experience.
   D. They are included in adults' normal routine.
2. Which is true about babies two months and older? (9.1.2)
   A. They prefer 2-D pictures to 3-D objects.
   B. They prefer non-moving objects over slow-moving objects.
   C. They prefer solid-colored cards over textured cards.
   D. They prefer a drawn human face over any other drawn pattern.
3. **True or False**. Piaget thought children learn by making their own discoveries through their environment. (9.1.3)

What Infants Learn in the First Twelve Months

Learning Outcomes

After studying this lesson, you will be able to

9.2-1   **explain** the concepts infants develop and differentiate among them.

9.2-2   **identify** examples of brain wiring and social interactions for language learning.

9.2-3   **summarize** communication development during infancy.

9.2-4   **identify** intellectual developmental milestones infants might achieve in the first year.

Key Terms

active vocabulary
auditory
babbling
categorization
concept
coo
depth perception
inflections
object concept
object constancy
object identity
object permanence
parentese
passive vocabulary

Reading and Notetaking Activity

Skim this lesson from top to bottom and from left to right and list all of the headings. Then, identify key terms with which you are unfamiliar and scan through the chapter to find their definitions. Write a "topic sentence" and brief summary for each heading, using the key terms to explain what you think you will learn. After you read this lesson, write a new topic sentence and summary for each section, outlining the main points you learned.

Introduction

How babies learn is related to what babies learn. As motor skills and the brain continue to develop, babies are better able to make sense of their surroundings. Babies develop many ideas about their environment during infancy. They learn about objects and people in their environments, and relationships between objects and themselves.

Babies also learn about language and communication. At birth, the main sound newborns make is crying. By the end of the first year, infants recognize many words, and some can even say a few words. Babies also know the tones of a language and may recognize the meaning of body language, such as shaking the head or smiling. Some babies, if taught, also learn sign language.

As you read in the previous lesson, newborns learn through their senses and reflexes and show they are learning by their behavior. When newborns are learning, their eyes are more alert, they become quiet, and their heart and breathing rates increase. During infancy, newborns can learn to:

- remember an object for a short time (beginning of memory)
- use a different sucking technique on a breast, bottle nipple, and pacifier
- become aware of the space around them
- imitate the actions of another person, such as facial expressions and hand gestures
- differentiate between speech and other sounds and recognize parents' voices
- exercise their reflexes (firings in the brain will lead to voluntary motor skills)

9.2-1 Concept Learning

As babies explore their world, they learn many concepts. A **concept** is an idea formed by combining what is known about a person, object, place, quality, or event. Thinking is organized through concepts. For example, if you see an animal you believe is a cat, you immediately think of all you know about cats. Then you note how this animal is like or unlike the cats you recall.

Concepts change throughout a person's life as they learn more. For example, you likely know more about children now than you did when you began studying child development. Your concepts have developed (changed). Concepts change by shifting from:

- concrete to abstract
- subclass to class (Sometimes children use a *class name*, such as "money," before they use the *subclass names*, such as penny or nickel. This is only due to the names used by parents or caregivers.)
- simple to complex
- incorrect to correct

Concepts are different for each person, because no two people have exactly the same experiences. Also, many concepts involve emotions. For example, the concept of school may be pleasant for one person, but unpleasant for another. During the first year, babies form many concepts. These concepts help children make sense of their world and further their intellectual development.

Perceptual Concepts

Babies form perceptual concepts by making sense out of what they see, hear, smell, taste, and touch and mentally organizing this information. Infants are able to develop perceptual concepts through many experiences in their world. The following sections describe major perceptual concepts children learn in the first year.

Object Constancy or Sameness

Object constancy refers to knowing that objects remain the same even if they appear different. For example, a child may see a large airplane with bright colors take off and then look small and gray in the distance. Children learn that, although the airplane may look different in size, shape, or color, it is still the same plane. Object constancy begins during the first year but is not fully developed until the second or third year.

Object Concept

Object concept is the understanding that objects, people, and events are separate from a person's interactions with them. Object concept has two parts—object identity and object permanence. **Object identity** is knowledge that an object stays the same from one time to the next (**Figure 9.6**).

denniro/Shutterstock.com

Figure 9.6 Object identity, the knowledge that an object stays the same from one time to the next, can be learned through something as simple as repeatedly touching a toy bunny or other object. *What would your perception be like if you had no grasp of object identity?*

For example, each time a child sees a toy bunny, the bunny is the same. **Object permanence** is knowledge that people, objects, and places still exist even when they are no longer seen, felt, or heard. For example, an infant may know their parent is still present in the house, even though they are not in the same room.

Like other concepts, object permanence develops with many experiences over time. The concept begins to develop as early as one to two months of age and often involves the baby's own hands that come in and out of view. At this time, infants will stare for a second at the place where an object or person was just seen but has disappeared. A few months later, infants will gleefully recover an object partially hidden. Toward the end of infancy, infants will search for objects that adults have completely hidden from view.

Spatial Concepts

Infants learn about **spatial** (pertaining to space) concepts in many ways. Some examples include visually *tracking* (following with one's eyes) the movements of people and objects or fitting objects into openings, such as placing shapes into shape sorters. Squeezing their bodies into tight spaces, hiding behind furniture, and looking at objects from different perspectives are other examples of ways infants learn about space.

One important spatial concept infants form, after they develop binocular vision, is **depth perception** (the ability to tell how far away something is). Accurate depth perception enables infants to judge how far to reach for an object. Using binocular vision, the eyes guide the hand in knowing how far the arm must extend before the hand can grasp the object (**Figure 9.7**). As children learn to walk, depth perception is necessary to keep them from stepping off an object far from the ground and falling. The eyes guide the feet in knowing how far up, down, or away the next step will be. Infants often develop depth perception by seven to nine months of age. Even with some depth perception concepts, babies are not safe from falls.

Number Sense

Infants' brains appear to be wired for understanding numbers. Brain scans show that both infant and adult brains light up in the same area when processing numerical information.

Research suggests babies can detect changes in quantities (numbers) of items. When babies were repeatedly shown the same number of objects on a screen, although the arrangement of the objects changed, they became familiarized and bored. When the numbers changed, they became interested again. The amount of change in quantity needed for babies to detect difference depended on the babies' ages. (Under six months required a 1:3 ratio change—4 to 12 dots; six-month-olds needed a 1:2 ratio change—6 to 12 dots; and nine-month-olds only needed a 1:1.5 ratio change—8 to 12 dots). Babies can also detect these same changes in quantities when they are presented as distinct sounds (taps on a drum).

Infants can also keep track of an added object. Researchers noted that five-month-old infants would watch while a single toy was placed on a table. Then a screen was placed in front of the toy. Next a hand placed, or seemed to place, a second toy behind the screen. The screen was removed to reveal one or two toys. If only one toy was behind the screen, the baby would stare longer than if two toys were shown. The longer stare is the baby's way of saying, "This was unexpected. I should see more toys."

Infants can also recognize exact amounts. Researchers showed six-month-olds three pictures —one with one dot, one with two dots, and one with three dots. After the researcher tapped on a drum one to three times, the baby's eyes would focus on the corresponding picture.

wavebreakmedia/Shutterstock.com

Figure 9.7 Depth perception involves learning how far one has to reach to touch an object. *How do you use your depth perception in your daily life?*

Physical Concepts

Infants understand two physical concepts, object solidity and gravity, very early. *Object solidity* means one solid object cannot move through another solid object and *gravity* involves objects falling to the floor or ground (**Figure 9.8**).

When experiments are done that have unexpected results, infants stare longer. For example, in experiments on object solidity, infants were shown a glass with dyed blue water and another glass with blue solid matter. The experimenter moved a straw in and out of the water. The infants stared longer when the straw would not **penetrate** (enter) the blue solid matter, which looked like the glass with water. Conversely, when the experimenter first showed how a straw could not penetrate the blue solid matter, the infant stared longer when the straw was easily moved in and out of the glass with the dyed water. In experiments on gravity, when helium-filled balloons were released, the infants saw the floating balloons as unexpected and stared longer because they are familiar with objects falling. These experiments show that infants are learning about their physical world in a perceptual way or based on expectations.

Relationship Concepts

Relationship concepts differ from perceptual concepts. Whereas perceptual concepts occur in the physical world, relationship concepts occur in the mind. Infants are aware of relationships between objects in their physical world.

One relationship concept is called **categorization**, or grouping similar objects or events into a group. For example, red objects, letters, or foods may be grouped together because they are the same color. Categorization reduces the amount of new information people have to learn. By three months of age, infants can recognize same shapes, colors, and sizes. With quality experiences, six-month-old infants can form other categories, such as foods, toys, animals, and vehicles. By one year of age, infants note subtle differences in the features of objects, such as differences between butterflies and birds.

Because infants do not sort objects into groups, how do researchers test these abilities? Researchers show infants several objects, one at a time, within a category, such as animals, until the infants are habituated. Then, researchers bring out two more objects at the same time—one in the original category (another animal) and one in a new category (a car, for example). Infants ignore the object from the old category (animals) and focus on the object from the new category (vehicles).

Figure 9.8 Gravity can be understood by observing an object falling after it is thrown into the air. An experience as simple as playing in leaves can teach this concept. *What would your perception be like if you had no understanding of gravity?*

evgenyatamanenko/iStock via Getty Images Plus

dszc/E+ via Getty Images

Figure 9.9 Infants can learn cause and effect by making things happen, such as pressing a piano key in order to hear a sound. *What other activities can help infants learn cause and effect?*

Infants are also interested in cause and effect (**Figure 9.9**). Infants see cause and effect as they smile at or cry for a nearby parent and get a response. They also learn cause and effect by making things happen while playing with their toys. For example, kicking their feet (cause) makes their mobile shake (effect) or knocking over a block tower (cause) makes a loud noise (effect).

9.2-2 Language Learning

Language is a complex system of sounds, words, grammar, letters or symbols, and social knowledge. To a great extent, language is a unique human endeavor. Although animals communicate, they cannot master the complex language systems of people. Language learning begins early. Two processes—brain wiring and social interactions involving language—interact in helping infants learn language.

Brain Wiring for Language

Brain development research shows language wiring begins at birth, if not before. The first wiring has to do with the sounds of language, which are needed to understand speech and to speak.

Brain wiring follows a sequence. During the first 6 months, infants distinguish small differences in sounds. They are prepared to learn any language. At 6 months of age, brain pruning begins because there are so many connections. Infants come to notice only major differences in sounds in the languages they hear from caring adults. By 12 months of age, infants complete the **auditory** (relating to hearing) maps needed for their primary language(s). Learning to speak another language without an accent becomes much more difficult as the wiring for the sounds of other languages begins to be pruned away. Around 9 to 12 months of age, wiring in the brain's speech center also begins.

The windows of opportunity for language are early in life. For example, studies of babies who are born deaf show waiting until two years of age to restore hearing through surgery results in language lags. If surgery occurs after four years of age, language delays are profound and lifelong. Other studies of immigrants show that as the age of immigration increases, **proficiency** (mastery of a skill) in the second language decreases. This is because a language different from their primary language is being learned outside the windows of opportunity for language development.

Social Interactions Involving Language

Many language development experts believe language development occurs due to the interaction between brain wiring and social interactions involving language. The following types of social language interactions seem to be the most important for encouraging language development:

- *Turn-taking.* Parents and other caregivers need to respond to babies' sounds from birth. As babies listen to spoken language, they make more sounds. Infants' pre-talk includes many language sounds. By 8 to 10 months of age, infants' "talk" reflects the sounds and pitch patterns of the language or languages heard. Infants also learn turn-taking in conversations if adults respond after a baby finishes a sound sequence.

Speech

The Greatest Language Achievements Occur in Infancy

Language development is somewhat of a mystery. During the first six months, babies cry, coo, and babble with or without social interactions. Language development changes around the second half of the first year. At this point, social interactions are necessary for continued language development. Otherwise, development is arrested. Language development is now something infants and their parents or caregivers do together. The following two critical achievements occur:

Babies develop a desire to communicate so they can achieve their personal goals. Because they are still in the pre-speech stage, they use gestures, especially gazing, and vocalizations to send their messages. Parents and caregivers know what infants mean and know hollering will soon start if they do not respond.

Babies discover people and things have "sound names." Their brains are wired to catch and remember these arbitrary symbols necessary for communication, and their vocal apparatus is quickly becoming ready to make these sounds.

Without these two achievements, oral language would not exist. Language development of infants is perhaps the best example of how all developmental domains work together—the physical, intellectual, and social-emotional. Exactly how it works remains a mystery debated by linguists. Yet, the same language milestones occur across cultures at nearly the same ages. How do you think language development occurs?

Photo: naluwan/Shutterstock.com

- *Parentese.* Parents and other caregivers often use **parentese**, an infant-directed, singsong, and high-pitched speech, when speaking to babies (**Figure 9.10**). Parentese helps babies clearly hear the sounds of language, learn facial expressions, and note *boundaries of words* (where words start and stop).
- *Connecting objects with words.* Because sounds have *referential meaning* (refer to something), parents and caregivers must help infants make associations. When babies see connections, they are *mapping words*. To do this, the adult simply looks at or points to the object or the person they are talking about. Even 3- to 4-month-old infants gaze in the same general direction adults are looking. By 10 to 12 months

of age, infants realize the purpose of the adult's gaze—to talk about an object or person. Infants begin to point around eight months of age. Joint attention by gazing and pointing contributes greatly to word mapping.

Figure 9.10 Characteristics of Parentese

- Vocal range—two-octave, rather than the typical one-octave, speaking range
- Sing-song sound
- Slow with clear pronunciation of sounds
- Short phrases and sentences
- Exaggerated facial expressions—joy, surprise, concern and comfort
- Face often close to the child's face

Goodheart-Willcox Publisher

- *"Face time."* Parents and caregivers need to provide quality "face time" to help babies **articulate** (clearly vocalize) sounds (**Figure 9.11**). When talking to infants, 4-month-olds gaze mostly at the eyes of the adult. By 6 months of age, infants spend equal amounts of time looking at the eyes and the mouth. The 8- to 10-month-old mainly looks at the mouth. By 12 months of age, infants once again look at the eyes more in "face time" talk. If a second language is introduced to 1-year-old infants, they will once again "lip read."
- *Language-rich environment.* Parents and caregivers need to be talkative. Children do not learn language by watching television or online videos. Children from talkative families with good vocabularies learn many more words than children from less talkative families.
- *Imitation.* Spoken language is mainly learned through imitation. By participating in a language-filled world, babies learn the sounds, vocabulary, facial expressions, and turn-taking aspects of language.

9.2-3 Communicating

From the time babies are born, they are communicating. Through the sounds they make, others learn to understand their language.

Stages in Communication

Before the baby's first birthday, they have made impressive gains in speaking and understanding language. From birth, babies listen to language and make speech-like sounds. Within a few months, they recognize facial expressions that accompany language, know what some words mean, and understand the idea of turn-taking in conversations. During the latter part of the first year, they may say their first words.

Crying and Cooing

Newborns do not have control over the sounds they make. They make many noises while eating and sleeping. They swallow, smack, burp, yawn, and sigh. During the first two months, babies mainly cry. Parents can quickly learn what their baby's cries mean.

Between the sixth and eighth week, infants often begin to **coo**—a vowel-like sound (*ah-ah-ah*; *oh-oh*; *ooh-ooh*) made in the back of the throat. Coos are light, happy sounds. The coo sounds are often made at different pitches. Along with cooing, infants will smile, blow bubbles, gurgle, and squeal. Infants coo more when others talk to, smile at, and touch them. Because turn-taking in conversations is so new to infants, they seldom coo on cue. Infants are more likely to respond to parentese by smiling and wiggling all over.

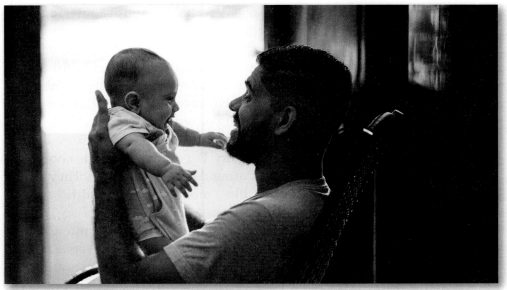

Figure 9.11 Long before they learn to speak, infants make speech-like sounds. *How does making speech-like sounds prepare babies to eventually speak?*

skaman306/E+ via Getty Images

Babbling

Cooing is slowly replaced by **babbling** (using the tongue and the front of the mouth to make a consonant-vowel sound, such as *ba*). Babbling is an important pre-talking skill. When babbling begins, infants practice all the sounds of most of the world's languages. Babies are ready to learn any language or languages they hear. Around one year of age, infants make only the sounds needed to speak the languages they hear. This is because the brain has pruned away the connections needed to make sounds from other languages. Infants who are deaf, however, babble very little after six months of age and do not learn the sounds of their culture's language.

Babbling is not **monotone** (single pitch without variation). Infants babble with **inflections** (changes of pitch) to express happiness, requests, commands, and questions. An infant often babbles with so much feeling you can almost guess what they are saying. Language experts refer to three types of babbling (**Figure 9.12**).

Figure 9.12 Types of Babbling

Type	Description
Marginal babbling	Between 4 and 6 months of age, the infant combines consonant-vowel single sounds (*baaa*) or vowel-consonant single sounds (*uuum*). Marginal babbling is mixed with squeals and coos.
Reduplication babbling	Between 6 and 10 months of age, infants repeat the same syllable over and over, such as *da-da-da-da*. During this stage, infants do a great deal of *reciprocal* (turn-taking) babbling.
Nonreduplicated babbling	Between 9 and 12 months of age, varied babbling sounds begin to sound more like words, such as *gima*. Infants have excellent inflectional changes in this stage. For example, their babbling sounds as if they are asking questions, exclaiming, or making statements.

Goodheart-Willcox Publisher

First Words

Infants may begin talking as early as nine months of age, but many start talking later. Before talking, infants must do the following:

- understand object permanence
- understand that people, objects, places, and events have names
- remember words that go with people, objects, places, and events
- have the ability to make the sounds
- realize talking is important

Many experts believe a sound counts as a word only when the same sound is used each time to refer to a specific person, object, place, or event. Most first words are *protowords* (*proto* means *first*), which are not words listed in a dictionary. Protowords are also different from babbling and are usually only one or two syllables. Each protoword consistently refers to something concrete. These made-up words for family members, food, a special toy, or a pacifier are important ways for infants to communicate. Parents and caregivers learn what the child means. Sometimes protowords are sounds similar to a word, such as *baba* for *bottle*. Most frequently, the protoword is completely unique to the baby, such as *gaga* for *ice*. Infants will soon begin to say their first "real words," but protowords may long remain part of the child's store of words.

Passive Versus Active Vocabulary

A person's vocabulary consists of the words they understand and use. Although infants can say only a few words, they understand many more. The words people understand, but do not speak or write are called their **passive vocabulary**. In contrast, **active vocabulary** includes the words used in speaking or writing.

Infants' passive vocabulary far exceeds their active vocabulary. For example, infants know their own names around 16 weeks of age. They recognize words like "mommy" and "daddy" around six months of age. At eight months of age, infants know about 36 words, and at ten months they know about 67 words. **Conversely** (versus; on the other hand), infants' active vocabularies are about 3 words by their first birthday.

Once infants get the idea that objects in their world have names, they learn these names quickly. They even understand phrases and sentences that refer to part of their daily routines such as, "Time for breakfast." Soon their favorite spoken word may be *whaddat* (What is that?) as they begin to learn language.

Baby Signing

With their limited active vocabularies, babies cannot tell others what they want or need, but they may make up signs for certain objects. Based on this information, Linda Acredolo and Susan Goodwin, professors in California universities, developed *Baby Signs*, a formal sign language for hearing infants. The gestures come from American Sign Language (or ASL, the sign language for people who are deaf) and from infant-friendly modifications of ASL gestures.

Infants can use their hands before using the more **intricate** (complex) throat, tongue, and mouth muscles needed for many words. Research shows that when parents begin signing to six- or seven-month-old infants, the infants will often begin signing about two months later. Although some research studies point to positive outcomes for infants, there have been very few studies on baby signing. Thus, more studies are needed before advantages and disadvantages of baby signing can be determined.

9.2-4 Intellectual Developmental Milestones

As you can see, babies learn many new concepts and abilities during infancy. **Figure 9.13** outlines intellectual developmental milestones from birth through 11 months of age. These milestones are simply a guide because infants will develop at their own rate. Also, many factors will influence infants' rates of intellectual development. Understanding intellectual milestones, however, can help parents and caregivers plan appropriate activities to help meet infants' intellectual needs.

Figure 9.13 **Newborn and Infant Intellectual Milestones**

Age	Milestones
One month *Heather Preston*	• Remembers objects if they reappear in a couple of seconds. • Recognizes primary caregiver's voice and smell. • Cries for assistance. • Is alert for more time than at birth.
Two months *Chin Kit Sen/ Shutterstock.com*	• "Sees" connections within their own body (uses mouth and thumb to suck). • Looks for a few seconds where object or person was last seen (beginning of object permanence). • Follows slow movement of objects with eyes (called *tracking*). • Discriminates among voices, people, tastes, and objects. • Attends and responds to voices. • Cries and coos some.
Three months *kupa_rock / iStock /Getty Images*	• Studies own hands. • Seeks sources of sound by turning head and neck. • Cries less. • Gurgles and coos. • Recognizes familiar objects or people from a distance.

Goodheart-Willcox Publisher
(Continued)

Figure 9.13 **Newborn and Infant Intellectual Milestones** (Continued)

Age	Milestones
Four months *MBI/Shutterstock.com*	• Notices response of an object to their own action; repeats action to get same response. • Remembers object for 5 to 7 seconds. • Likes detail in objects. • Recognizes specific characteristics of some things in the environment (bottle, family pet, a toy). • Makes new sounds. • Vocalizes to social stimulation; begins making sounds back to adults.
Five months *Arina P Habich/Shutterstock.com*	• Learns new actions to repeat. • Looks around when in new places. • Wants to explore objects. • Utters a few consonants. • Babbles one syllable repeatedly, such as *baa* (called *marginal babbling*). • Imitates sounds and gestures with model present.
Six months *pixelheadphoto digitalskillet/ Shutterstock.com*	• Inspects objects for a long time. • Reaches for toys they want. • Looks at objects upside down to create a new perspective. • Compares two objects. • Connects own actions to environmental response (shaking rattle causes the sound). • Utters more and more consonants. • Takes turns making sounds with caregivers.
Seven months *Juergen Faelchle/Shutterstock.com*	• Discriminates between familiar and unfamiliar adults. • Full-color vision is achieved and distance vision has matured. • Searches for an object partially hidden (object permanence is well underway). • Picks out their name in a conversation. • Makes more consonant-vowel combinations. • Babbles two syllables by repeating the first syllable (*ma ma*).
Eight months *Nadya Chetah/Shutterstock.com*	• Begins to have goals and combines actions to achieve goals (pushes a pillow away to reach a block). • Imitates somewhat new actions and makes some effort to improve imitation. • Babbles by repeating one syllable many times close together, such as *da-da-da-da* (called *reduplication babbling*); may use inflections while babbling. • Understands about 36 words. • Follows a one-step command if adult also gestures.
Nine months *Daxiao Productions/Shutterstock.com*	• Actively tries to recover a totally hidden toy where last seen (object permanence is mature). • Remembers games played on previous day. • Bangs objects together to explore. • Understands and uses gestures (shaking head and waving). • Responds to the word *no*. • Babbles nonreduplicated syllables. • Follows a one-step command without adult gestures.

(Continued)

Figure 9.13 **Newborn and Infant Intellectual Milestones** (Continued)

Age	Milestones
Ten months *durganand/iStock/Thinkstock*	• Tries to fit things together. • Responds to commands. • Understands idea of verbal labeling (people and things have names). • Understands about 67 words.
Eleven months *behindlens/Shutterstock.com*	• Imitates inflections and speech rhythms. • Begins to understand more and more labels (words) for people and things. • Says first words, which may be protowords. May use exclamations, such as, "oh oh!" • May call a parent by their special name ("mama," "dada," or something else). • May make sounds of some animals. • Uses a variety of methods to explore objects, like banging, throwing, dropping, shaking, etc. • Finds hidden objects with ease. • Puts objects into containers, like dropping toys into a cup or bowl.

Lesson 9.2 Review and Assessment

1. An infant's ability to group blue blocks together in a separate pile is an example of which relationship concept? (9.2.1)
   A. Categorization
   B. Cause and effect
   C. Solidity
   D. Depth perception

2. In the sequence of brain wiring for language, when do infants complete the auditory maps they need for their primary language(s)? (9.2.2)
   A. Before birth
   B. By age 6 months
   C. By age 9 months
   D. By age 12 months

3. **True or False**. As infants develop their ability to speak and understand language, babbling is an important step that occurs before cooing. (9.2.3)

4. Which intellectual developmental milestone typically occurs by age 2 months? (9.2.4)
   A. Recognizing their mother's voice and smell
   B. Remembering an object for 5 to 7 seconds
   C. Attending and responding to voices
   D. Looking around when in a new location

Lesson 9.3

Meeting Intellectual Needs in the First Twelve Months

Key Terms

baby agenda
coordination
enriched environment
holistic
sensory stimulation

Learning Outcomes

After studying this lesson, you will be able to

9.3-1 **differentiate** between learning during infancy and learning during later childhood.

9.3-2 **describe** guidelines for helping babies learn and reinforce concepts, including specific activities to aid babies' intellectual development in different areas.

Reading and Notetaking Activity

Imagine you are a child development expert, and your client wants to learn more about helping their infant learn new concepts. Write a two-paragraph speech recommending steps your client can take to make sure their baby gets the best learning experience in their first year of life. Incorporate information you already know about infant intellectual development, and anything from your personal experiences. As you read this lesson, take detailed notes. After reading the lesson, go back over your speech and make changes based on any new information you have learned.

Nicky Lloyd/E+ via Getty Images

Figure 9.14 Playing with toys and spending time with caregivers can provide babies with opportunities to learn problem-solving, motor, sensory, memory, and language skills. *What skills is this baby learning by playing with her toy?*

Introduction

Just as parents need to meet babies' physical needs, they also need to meet intellectual needs. Babies need an environment that offers them chances to learn (called an **enriched environment**). Adults can provide learning experiences for babies soon after birth. In fact, the sooner adults provide activities, the more babies want to learn. There are many activities that can help babies improve their sensory, motor, memory, language, and problem-solving skills (**Figure 9.14**). These activities help form the baby's enriched environment.

Remember, however, that babies learn at different rates. The rate of learning cannot increase with lots of activities and toys. Babies can only take in so much. Too many activities and toys can overstimulate the baby causing the baby to become overwhelmed or to tune out stimuli for self-protection.

9.3-1 Learning During Infancy vs. Childhood

How babies learn is very different from how older children learn. Babies have a **baby agenda** that is not culture specific but is universal to all babies due to genetic brain wiring. This means that learning certain concepts and skills happens around the same time for most babies, regardless of culture. The baby agenda has been the same for all periods of time and in all cultures. According to Ronald Lally, a noted psychologist, the main aspects of a baby's agenda include the following:

- developing motor skills
- learning language
- understanding how objects work
- seeking significant relationships for nurture, protection, and love
- learning ways to interact with others

The type of learning during infancy differs from learning during later childhood. Learning during infancy is more **holistic** (whole; complete) as opposed to the "bits and pieces" learning of older children. For example, when playing with balls, infants may learn about the colors of balls, how they roll, words associated with balls, and play approval from the adult all in one experience. Older children, however, may learn about naming the colors of the balls or sorting the balls by color.

Because a baby also has their own learning agenda, adults who try to "teach" something may slow the learning process and frustrate the baby. For example, an adult might hope a baby would use a color sorter to put all the red discs on one peg, but the baby's agenda might be to mouth them or mix discs of all colors over the pegs. Parents and caregivers need to trust a baby's own agenda for learning as best for babies.

9.3-2 Helping Infants Learn

A skillful parent or teacher uses activities to meet intellectual needs during infancy. The following are some guidelines for helping babies learn and reinforce concepts:

- Let babies try activities on their own to help them learn to solve problems. Piaget thought this was crucial for learning.
- Let the baby begin most activities and then expand them. For example, an infant may be patting a high chair tray. Expand the activity by patting a different sounding object or by patting the tray harder, softer, faster, or slower than the infant.
- Watch for signs of the baby's interest in certain experiences. To check for interest, show the baby how to use a toy, and then give them a turn. Repeat several times. If there is little or no interest, the toy or game is probably too advanced for the baby. Try again in a few days or weeks. Parents who match a toy or game with their child's abilities and interests are working in the child's zone of proximal development (ZPD).
- Repeat games many times. Using games over many months helps the baby retain the skills learned by playing each game.
- Weave words, songs, and games into daily routines, such as feeding, bathing, and diapering. Adults do not need to have a set schedule of daily games. The number and types of games are not as important as the warmth and care adults show for babies.

Activities for Newborns

Most of the stimulation for newborns comes from being near parents and other caregivers. Newborns are fascinated at seeing faces, hearing sounds, and feeling warm and loved when cuddled. Warm and expressive talk stimulates newborns. Newborns love to hear singing and other soothing sounds, such as a wind chime, music box, or soft music.

Newborns enjoy looking at objects with certain features (**Figure 9.15**). Because their distance vision is limited, newborns often cannot see mobiles hung above their beds. Newborns can see, however, objects attached near to or in the corners of their beds as they tilt their heads back or turn their heads left and right. Changing objects frequently or rotating them prevents newborns from getting bored. (Well into infancy, babies see rotated objects as "new.") Since grasping objects during the newborn stage is a reflex action, objects should be securely fastened, nontoxic, and too large to swallow.

Figure 9.15 Visual Preferences of Newborns

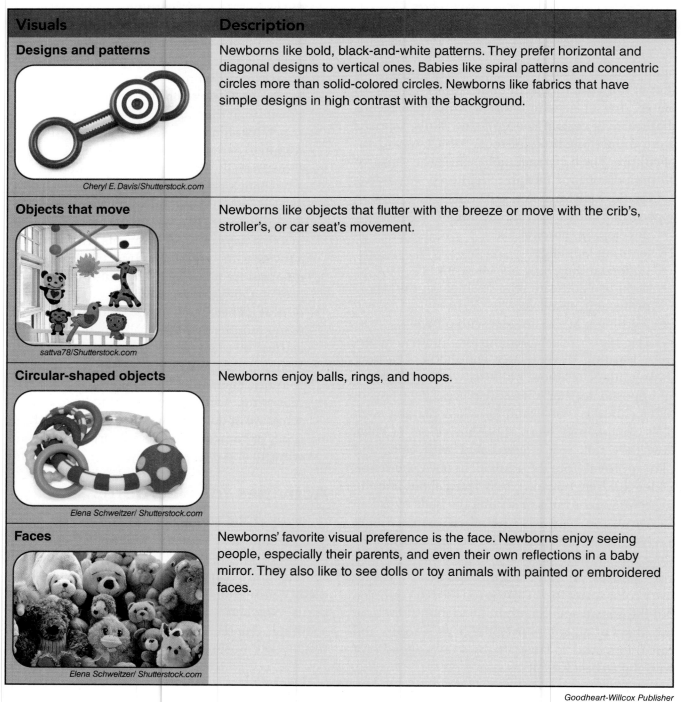

Visuals	Description
Designs and patterns Cheryl E. Davis/Shutterstock.com	Newborns like bold, black-and-white patterns. They prefer horizontal and diagonal designs to vertical ones. Babies like spiral patterns and concentric circles more than solid-colored circles. Newborns like fabrics that have simple designs in high contrast with the background.
Objects that move sattva78/Shutterstock.com	Newborns like objects that flutter with the breeze or move with the crib's, stroller's, or car seat's movement.
Circular-shaped objects Elena Schweitzer/ Shutterstock.com	Newborns enjoy balls, rings, and hoops.
Faces Elena Schweitzer/ Shutterstock.com	Newborns' favorite visual preference is the face. Newborns enjoy seeing people, especially their parents, and even their own reflections in a baby mirror. They also like to see dolls or toy animals with painted or embroidered faces.

Goodheart-Willcox Publisher

Tune into Infants' Cues for Stimulation

The message is out that infant experiences set the foundation for all later learning. The commercial world has responded to this knowledge through an explosion of media and "must-have" products aimed at enhancing infant development.

Babies need an enriched environment, but there are no "must-have" products. Babies need many sensory experiences naturally available in most homes and yards. A few toys that react to a baby's actions are desirable, such as an activity gym, squeeze toys, colorful ball, rattle, two or three soft blocks, an unbreakable mirror, and a few baby books. A warm social environment is most important. Babies are stimulated by the vocalizations and talk of people, their movements, smiles, and the baby games (gentle touching and peekaboo) they initiate.

Beyond the basic environment, parents need to tune in to infant cues for stimulation. Following are some hints:

- Stimulation is most effective during alert times. Alertness differs in babies. Newborns tend to sleep more than older infants, but even babies of the same age differ in their hours of being alert.
- Babies differ in their desire for stimulation. Some seem to be always eager to explore and master while others show less interest and energy.
- Babies differ in their abilities to prevent overstimulation. Some babies cannot sleep after much play and seem frustrated about missing out on anything. Other babies give very exact cues about the need to tune out and may even fall asleep on a pile of toys.

How do parents or caregivers handle these differences? Babies who are alert and interested, but also tune out on their own, get the right amount of stimulation without much adult help. Babies who are on-the-go and cannot tune out on their own are in danger of possible overstimulation. Parents can help by reducing the number of stimuli at one time (rotating toys) and having only quiet interactions before naps and bedtime. For the least alert babies, the danger is understimulation. Parents need to try to increase periods of alert time and keep the baby engaged while alert.

The bad news about stimulation is that adult actions can also lead to both overstimulation and understimulation. Parents may decide that if a little is good, more is better, and they may provide too many toys. Because these babies are often so overstimulated, they may tune out normal stimuli and attend only to intense stimuli. On the other hand, through neglect or abuse adults may deprive babies of almost all stimuli. The tragic results of severe understimulation are long-term developmental delays and depression. The good news is that most babies have a normal number of stimuli in their environments, and they can and do match the amount of stimulation to fit their own needs.

Research Activity

In small groups, choose two baby products that are advertised as "must-haves." Using reliable resources, answer the following questions.

1. On what basis do the manufacturers claim that these products are "must-haves"? What intellectual value do these products have?
2. What experiences or activities could replicate what these products provide?
3. How might these products contribute to overstimulation or understimulation?

Photo: Tom Wang/Shutterstock.com

Sensory Activities

Sensory stimulation involves using the senses to learn about the environment. According to Piaget, babies use their senses as a major way of learning. Babies use their senses to explore objects and to discover how objects operate.

For the baby to develop fully, all five senses (sight, hearing, touch, taste, and smell) must be stimulated. One example of a sensory stimulation activity is to let the baby touch a number of safe objects around the room or outdoors. For example, letting the baby touch the bark of a tree helps improve sensory development. Placing a mobile on the baby's crib or play yard also provides sensory stimulation.

Motor Activities

Movement is important for babies. As babies explore, motor activity helps their coordination and intellectual development. **Coordination** is the working together of muscles to form movements, such as walking. Although motor nerves are not fully developed for four or five years, coordination improves quickly after birth.

If babies are free to move, they engage in many motor activities on their own. Babies do, however, need some encouragement from caregivers. Infants use their large muscles as they perform gross-motor skills, such as rolling over, sitting, crawling, standing, and walking. An example of an activity that encourages gross-motor skills is crawling in and out of boxes or cartons. Coordination in the small muscles, especially those in the fingers and hands, is evident in the use of fine-motor skills. Playing with blocks is a fine-motor skill that requires coordination of the small muscles (**Figure 9.16**).

Memory Activities

As you read earlier, babies' explicit and implicit memories are rapidly developing. Even a newborn recognizes a caregiver's voice. The following are suggestions for how parents can aid their baby's memory:

- Have consistent routines so babies remember and anticipate activities.
- Keep toys in the same place because babies watch as parents get them. Once their motor skills are advanced, infants will seek the toys and pull them from shelves or out of containers.

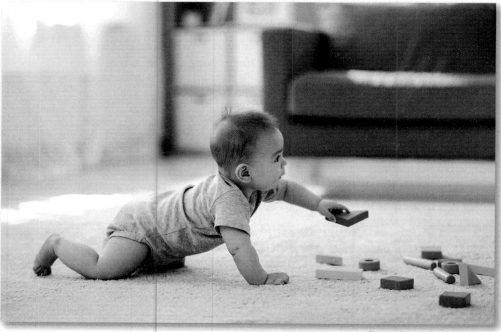

Figure 9.16 A baby can learn fine-motor skills by using blocks in different ways, such as stacking them, hitting them together, or placing them in a line. *Why do you think blocks are such a popular toy for babies? What other skills can blocks help babies learn?*

Ground Picture/Shutterstock.com

- Sing songs, say rhymes, and read books many times the same way with the same actions.
- Use the baby's name when speaking and referring to their toys and other items. Also, use family names consistently without switching to nicknames or other versions of names.
- Engage in turn-taking conversations to help the baby remember the back-and-forth patterns of conversations.
- Make associations between words and objects and between short phrases and sentences with actions. Use gazing and pointing gestures to connect words with people and objects and some safe and appropriate actions to give meaning to action words.
- Create a photo album of the baby's activities and show it often. (Children will not recognize themselves until the toddler years, but they will recognize their toys.)
- Give the baby a toy, such as a rattle or pull-apart toy. Once they learn the skill, take the toy away for a couple days and then reintroduce the toy. Note whether the skill is learned more quickly the second time. Repeat the sequence.
- Make sure the baby gets enough sleep to **consolidate** (combine) and retain memories.

Problem-Solving Activities

As babies use their senses to observe their world, they try to make sense of what they see, hear, smell, touch, and taste. In an enriched environment, babies learn how their world works as they explore.

Because babies learn in a holistic way, they make connections with objects in their environment and larger concepts. Babies will often problem-solve during play, but this problem-solving usually goes unnoticed by adults (**Figure 9.17**). The following are some examples of "hidden" problem-solving by infants:
- putting an object on a shelf or trying to crawl behind a couch (spatial relationships)
- placing a toy in front, behind, to the side, and on top of another object or container (spatial relationships)

Jose Luis Pelaez Inc/ Getty Images

Figure 9.17 Babies can learn problem-solving skills that relate to spatial relationships by placing objects inside other objects. *What is this baby learning about spatial relationships?*

- knocking over a block tower and throwing toys while sitting in a high chair, crib, or play yard (physical knowledge of gravity)
- putting like-items together, such as farm animals, cars, or certain blocks, in a container (categorization)
- dropping an object (physical knowledge of gravity; cause and effect—what happened to the object on impact, including the sound)
- looking at an object on the floor from different perspectives (object constancy)
- playing peekaboo (object permanence)

Language Activities

Babies learn language by hearing people talk. Adults can talk about the foods, toys, people, and routines that are part of the baby's world. Exact words are not as important to the baby as hearing language. How should adults talk to babies?

Some ideas are given in **Figure 9.18**. Although it does not matter exactly which words parents use, words should be pronounced correctly. Changing pitch or singing also varies the sound and adds interest. Adults can encourage infants to talk, too, such as by asking a question and then pausing before continuing to talk to the baby. Often, the infant will babble in response.

Figure 9.18 **Talking to Babies**

- Use complete short sentences. Remember that the last word is the one the infant will most note, such as "See the ball."
- Use nouns more than pronouns. For example, refer to yourself by name rather than *I*.
- Use lots of adjectives to describe nouns (*red* ball).
- Model language by using gestures to give meaning to words, such as pointing to the object being named or described.
- Expand single words an infant uses. For example, if the infant says, "Daddy," respond by saying, "Yes, Daddy is home."
- Ask questions even though the baby cannot respond at first.
- Describe the baby's feelings although the baby will not yet understand, such as "Kelly fell. Kelly is crying because falling hurts."
- Talk during routine care. For example, while dressing a baby, the caregiver could say, "Grammy is putting on Jack's green shirt. Does Jack like green?"

Goodheart-Willcox Publisher

Reading to infants daily exposes babies to new words and ideas. Even babies who cannot comprehend the words benefit from having books, magazines, and newspapers read to them. Time spent reading and hearing words is important at all ages.

Language games can be worked into daily routines and can provide a special time of sharing for babies and adults. Perhaps one of the earliest language action games infants enjoy is pat-a-cake.

Lesson 9.3 **Review and Assessment**

1. Which is true about a baby agenda? (9.3.1)
   A. It is influenced by an infant's culture.
   B. It would include learning the names of flowers in a garden.
   C. It is a list of learning goals the parents set for their baby.
   D. It would include learning how to interact with a sibling.
2. An example of an activity to aid a baby's problem-solving ability is _____. (9.3.2)
   A. playing with blocks
   B. peekaboo
   C. asking the baby questions
   D. reading the same books to the baby

Chapter 9

Review and Assessment

Summary

Lesson 9.1

9.1-1 An infant's brain development and wiring support learning and affects the sensory, motor, thinking, and memory centers of the brain. Quality experiences aid this fast-paced wiring.

9.1-1 As their senses develop, babies use stimuli to learn. The vision and motor centers of the baby's brain are highly active during a baby's first year.

9.1-1 The window of opportunity for sight is from birth to 4-to-6 months of age.

9.1-1 Fast brain wiring in the motor center starts around age 2 months as infants learn voluntary gross-motor movements; wiring for fine-motor movements begins around ages 2 or 3 months.

9.1-1 Repeat experiences help infants make the sensory associations related to thinking ability. Two main categories of memory are explicit memory and implicit memory.

9.1-2 Through perceptual learning, infants make sense out of sensory stimuli—choosing from among various stimuli to organize information.

9.1-2 Perception is the outcome of perceptual learning; it involves the organizing of information from the senses, the speed at which the brain organizes this information, and the way the person reacts to different sensory experiences.

9.1-3 Piaget's cognitive-developmental theory found that children learn about their environment by going through substages before they discover new ways to solve problems.

9.1-3 Vygotsky's sociocultural theory of development saw children's development determined by culture and the social environment. To be effective, teachers must find the child's zone of proximal development (ZPD) level, then provide scaffolding to help a child learn a new concept or skill.

Lesson 9.2

9.2-1 Perceptual concepts include object constancy or sameness, object concepts, spatial concepts, number sense, and physical concepts.

9.2-1 Relationship concepts occur in the mind as infants become aware of relationships between objects in their physical world. They include categorization and cause and effect.

9.2-2 Brain wiring for language development follows a sequence, beginning at birth and completing at 12 months of age when the auditory maps needed for their primary language(s) are complete. Wiring in the brain's speech center begins around 9 to 12 months.

9.2-2 Social language interactions that are most important for encouraging language development are turn-taking, "parentese," connecting objects with words, "face time," a language-rich environment, and imitation.

| 9.2-3 | Babies go through the following communication stages as they make and understand communication: crying, cooing, babbling (marginal, reduplication, nonreduplication), protowords, and real words. |

| 9.2-3 | Infants have passive and active vocabularies. |

| 9.2-3 | Baby Signs is a formal sign language for hearing infants to help them communicate. More studies are needed to determine the advantages and disadvantages of baby signing. |

| 9.2-4 | Intellectual developmental milestones for infants serve as a guide, but infants will develop at their own rate. |

Lesson 9.3

| 9.3-1 | To develop intellectually, children need an enriched environment; but the best learning agenda for infants is the baby's agenda, not an adult's agenda. |

| 9.3-1 | Learning during infancy is more holistic as opposed to the "bits and pieces" learning of older children. |

| 9.3-2 | Babies need activities that stimulate all the senses. As babies use their senses to observe their world, they try to make sense of what they see, hear, smell, touch, and taste. |

| 9.3-2 | Motor activities help infants' coordination and intellectual development. |

| 9.3-2 | Memory and problem-solving activities facilitate learning. |

| 9.3-2 | For language development to take place, it is important to talk to children and encourage them to make sounds and words. |

College and Career Portfolio

Portfolio Letters of Recommendation

Whether for a college or job application, most schools and employers require applicants to provide letters of recommendation or references. Letters of recommendation and references can take time to acquire.

Consider which teachers, employers, or other adults can best speak about your skills and work.

Then, decide on two to three individuals you want to ask to be your references, and complete the following activities:

Ask the individuals if they would be willing to be your reference. Make sure to be polite and grateful and give them time to respond.

If the purpose of your portfolio requires a letter of recommendation, ask the individuals you chose to write it for you. Be courteous, and make sure to communicate the deadline for your application.

Recall and Application

1. An infant's ability to see clearly in each eye is called _____. (9.1.1)
   A. contrast sensitivity
   B. acuity
   C. binocular vision
   D. 3-D vision

2. **True or False**. An example of explicit memory is singing a familiar song. (9.1.1)

3. At which age do babies enjoy hearing their own names? (9.1.2)
   A. Birth to 3 months
   B. Ages 3 to 6 months
   C. Ages 6 to 9 months
   D. Ages 9 to 12 months

4. According to Piaget, infants in Substage 4 do which of the following? (9.1.3)
   A. Practice inborn reflexes
   B. Imitate some actions of others
   C. Begin to have their own goals
   D. Learn through symbols

5. **True or False.** Vygotsky believed that for each concept or skill, teachers must first find the zone of proximal development (ZPD), or the level in which a child can learn with help. (9.1.3)

6. Knowing that objects remain the same even if they look different is _____. (9.2.1)
   A. depth perception
   B. object solidity
   C. spatial awareness
   D. object constancy

7. **True or False**. Infants learn language by watching television or online videos. (9.2.2)

8. Which best describes an infant's cooing? (9.2.3)
   A. A high-pitched sing-song
   B. A vowel-like sound
   C. A series of syllables
   D. A consonant-vowel sound

9. Which intellectual developmental milestone typically occurs by age 5 months? (9.2.4)
   A. Recognizing their mother's voice and smell
   B. Vocalizing to social stimulation
   C. Looking for a sound's source by turning their head
   D. Learning new actions to repeat

10. **True or False**. Because their concept of object permanence is mature, by age 7 months most babies will actively try to find a totally hidden toy where they last saw it. (9.2.4)

11. **True or False**. Understanding how objects work is a main aspect of a baby's agenda. (9.3.1)

12. An example of an activity to aid a baby's memory is _____. (9.3.2)
    A. placing a mobile on the baby's crib
    B. crawling on a grassy surface
    C. following a consistent routine
    D. pronouncing words correctly

Critical Thinking

1. **Analyze.** New, quality experiences are vital to development of the infant's thinking center. In small groups, visit a new location, and note everything about the location that is "new" to you. Then, compare lists and analyze how this new experience fosters learning.

2. **Identify.** Identify three examples of perceptual learning that you experience daily. In what situations do you have to sort through sensory stimuli? Choose one example and explain how it results in the three outcomes of perceptual learning.

3. **Make inferences.** Why is it important to "follow the child's lead" when teaching new concepts and activities in a child's zone of proximal development? Why does this approach differ from learning approaches used with older children?

4. **Evaluate.** For each of the four directions of concept development (concrete to abstract, subclass to class, simple to complex, and incorrect to correct), write a short paragraph illustrating the direction. Then, trade papers with a partner. Evaluate your partner's illustrations and identify which directions each paragraph describes. Discuss your answers with your partner.

5. **Compare and contrast.** In small groups, compare and contrast active vocabulary and passive vocabulary. List at least ten examples of each and deliver a presentation summarizing your discussion to the class.

6. **Determine.** Few studies have been conducted on the advantages and disadvantages of baby signing. As a class, debate the possible advantages and disadvantages of baby signing. Research the topic beforehand and come to class with a stance on the technique.

7. **Analyze.** In small groups, analyze the idea that babies have a baby agenda for learning that is not culture specific. What does this mean for babies around the world? How does the baby agenda differ from learning (such as school learning) later in life?

8. **Draw conclusions.** Bring an infant toy to class with you and trade toys with another student. Then, handle the toy and describe what an infant might perceive about the object, including its size, shape, color, texture, weight, and number. Write two to three paragraphs summarizing your observations.

Core Skills

1. **Science and technology.** Use reputable online sources to research brain development in the first year. Choose a specific research topic that interests you, such as "How is brain development affected by nutrition?" or "Which influences brain development more: genes or the environment?" Then, type a digital report of your findings. Check your paper for correct spelling, grammar, and punctuation. Adhere to all copyright laws and cite any sources you may use for the report.

2. **Technology and speaking.** Imagine you are a parenting educator who is teaching Piaget's and Vygotsky's theories to a class of expectant parents. Create a lesson plan and electronic presentation that will help you teach and reinforce the information. Present a three-minute sample of your lesson to the class. For each presentation, provide feedback for the presenter, and take notes on the feedback you receive.

3. **Math.** Within the first year, children develop "number sense," or the ability to detect changes in numbers and recognize amounts. Imagine you are a child care worker who needs to develop an activity to reinforce babies' number senses. Outline an age-appropriate activity to help babies recognize number changes and number amounts. Conduct your activity within your class and then explain how the activity reinforces number sense.

4. **Art and speaking.** In small groups, review the intellectual milestones children achieve within the first year of life. Then, using art supplies or electronic resources, collaborate to create an easy-to-follow visual representation of the milestones an infant achieves during each of the first twelve months. Your illustration should include drawings or pictures of infants achieving milestones during each month and should be an effective study tool and synthesis of the information you learned in this chapter. After completing your illustration, present it to the class and make it available for other students to reference while studying.

5. **Reading and writing.** Using online or print resources, find a nonfiction book that describes stimulating activities for babies. Read at least two chapters of the book, noting where the book overlaps with your textbook and where it might differ. Finally, write a report comparing the activities covered in the book you chose with the activities covered in your textbook. Incorporate quotations from both books and cite these quotations using MLA style.

6. **Writing.** Review the ways that caregivers can talk to babies, even when babies cannot yet talk back. Then, write short scenarios for at least three of the ways suggested in your textbook. For each scenario, explain how talking to the baby is helping the baby learn language.

7. **Research and listening.** Interview a *child development professional* (person with a college degree in child development, child and family studies, or early childhood education) regarding ways parents and caregivers can stimulate brain development in infants. What types of stimulation appear to be best for babies? What is the professional's opinion regarding the use of "brain development aids," such as flash cards, videos, and kits marketed to "boost a baby's brain power"? If the professional does not recommend these techniques, what techniques do they recommend?

8. **CTE Career Readiness Practice.** Use Internet or print resources, or the help of a science teacher, to examine how brain wiring changes in the first year of life. Prepare a storyboard with diagrams that illustrate what happens as babies learn new concepts and develop language skills. Explain how quality experiences and the baby agenda influence the wiring process.

Observations

1. For one week, observe an infant exploring their world for 30 minutes per day. Record what the baby does during this time. What senses were used? What concepts and skills might the baby have been learning?

2. As a class, assign groups to record or find recordings of sounds made by two- to twelve-month-old babies. In your group, listen to the recording you created or found. Distinguish between the sounds babies make and identify sounds such as cooing and babbling. Play your recording for the class and deliver a presentation identifying these sounds.

Chapter 10

Social-Emotional Development in the First Twelve Months

The Social-Emotional World of Babies

Meeting Social-Emotional Needs in the First Year

Essential Question

What is taking place in the first social-emotional interactions among babies and adults, and how can caregivers lay the "best" foundations for this relationship?

Case Study — Can an Infant's Caregivers Be *Too* Cautious?

As a class, read the case study and discuss the questions that follow. After you finish studying the chapter, discuss this case study again. Have your opinions changed based on what you learned?

The Millers have been very protective of their child since birth. Once the child started crawling, everything in the house seemed dangerous, even though a professional had childproofed their home. The Millers purchased pillows, cushions, and mats to protect their child from germs on the floor and from bumping into furniture. They even bought a helmet and special pants with kneepads.

During the last few well-baby checkups, the pediatrician noted how the Millers constantly said no to their child if they reached for items in the examination room because these "had germs." When the pediatrician notices the helmet, they remark to the Millers that the baby needs a balance between natural risk taking and safety precautions.

Stunned by this comment, the Millers sat in silence. What does the pediatrician mean? Wasn't it their job to keep their child healthy, safe, and happy? Shouldn't they always be protective?

Give It Some Thought

1. What does the pediatrician mean by finding a balance between the baby's natural risk taking and the parents' safety practices? Do you think there is just one balance point or could there be more than one? Explain your answer.
2. How might allowing some risk-taking keep children safer in the long run?
3. What beliefs and negative emotions might the Millers be possibly instilling in their child?
4. In some medical circles, there is a belief called the "hygiene hypothesis." This hypothesis suggests infant exposure to some bacteria and viruses builds a strong immune system and protects children from allergies, asthma, and autoimmune diseases during adulthood. Exposure during the first year of life may also promote less body inflammation associated with other diseases, such as heart disease. What do you think about the "hygiene hypothesis"?

RichLegg/E+ via Getty Images

Lesson 10.1

The Social-Emotional World of Babies

Key Terms

age-appropriate
  behaviors
anxiety
attachment
attachment behaviors
disposition
emotions
high-reactive infants
low-reactive infants
separation anxiety
temperament

Learning Outcomes

After studying this lesson, you will be able to

10.1-1 **identify** the three main aspects of social-emotional development.

10.1-2 **describe** the social-emotional developmental milestones children might achieve in the first twelve months.

Reading and Notetaking Activity

Before reading, skim the headings in this chapter. List the headings to create an outline for taking notes during reading and class discussion. Under each heading list any key term. Finally, write two questions you expect to have answered in class. After completing the chapter, ask your teacher any questions you still have about the concepts or terms you learned.

Introduction

Social-emotional development is an important type of development that happens as quickly during the first year as physical and intellectual development. A baby enters the world with unique traits, which are the roots of the child's later personality. By the end of the first year, personality traits are even more evident. As a baby's social-emotional world expands, they form ideas about themselves and whether the world is a friendly place. The baby begins to express feelings with different emotions.

10.1-1 Aspects of Social-Emotional Development

Social-emotional development involves a person's concepts about themselves as well as concepts about others. There are three main aspects or parts of social-emotional development.

1. **Disposition** or general mood of a person. Some people have a more cheerful disposition, and others are moodier.
2. Social relations, such as interactions with people and social groups. These interactions may include family members, friends, schools, and clubs (**Figure 10.1**).
3. Ways people express feelings through **emotions** (thoughts that lead to feelings, such as joy, fear, and anger, and cause changes in the body). For example, if you are upset at someone or something (a thought), you may become angry (a feeling), which may increase your heart rate (a change in the body). Even babies have emotions, which they display through their interactions with others.

Temperamental Differences in Babies

Temperament is the inherited tendency to react in a certain way, such as being cheerful or grumpy. Sometimes the word *disposition* also defines the ways people react consistently in different settings and over a long period of time.

Jerome Kagan, a well-known psychologist and researcher, has extensively studied personality, including temperament, in children. He theorizes that temperament is inherited and very noticeable by three months of age. Some children inherit genes that cause them to become overexcited and have problems calming down whereas other babies are rather easy-going.

Kagan believes temperament does not determine behavior but does push a child to react in a certain way. In his research, Kagan compared infants who are *high reactive* and *low reactive*, and then studied the same children as teens. **High-reactive infants** react to anything new with caution and can easily become physically agitated and distressed. **Low-reactive infants** tend to be sociable and bold (trying new challenges).

High-reactive infants are irregular in their habits. They may withdraw or protest—even scream—when facing new situations. High-reactive infants often have a rough start, which may cause caregivers increased feelings of anxiety. Low-reactive infants are cheerful, have regular habits, such as eating and sleeping, and respond quickly to a new situation. Low-reactive infants usually get off to a good start with their caregivers.

Figure 10.1 Social relations, one of the three aspects of social-emotional development, involve interactions with family members, friends, and other people. *What are the most important social relations in your life? With whom do you interact the most?*

kate_sept2004/E+ via Getty Images

Through his studies, Kagan found the following parenting behaviors (environmental factors) negatively influence high-reactive children's temperaments:

- *Inadequate soothing.* High-reactive children need caregivers who help them calm down and regulate their emotions. Without help, these children become more reactive.
- *Alarmist behavior.* Caregivers who are alarmist see dangers everywhere. Infants can sense caregivers' feelings of anxiety and become anxious themselves.
- *Intrusive behavior.* Caregivers who are **intrusive** (controlling) become overprotective. These children may have difficulty developing their own coping skills.

Kagan's research showed that no high-reactive child later became a low-reactive child. Caregivers can affect a compromise, however, by working on their high-reactive child's temperament. Good, consistent care of high-reactive babies may make them happier (**Figure 10.2**). Easing these children into new situations and alerting them to upcoming changes are also helpful strategies. As children get older, caregivers can even rehearse certain expectations with them.

Social Relations

Social refers to a relationship between two or more people. Social development in the first year is shaped by how other people affect the baby and how the baby affects other people. By the end of the first year, social development is well underway.

Interacting with Others

Human relationships are the building blocks of healthy development. Babies are born with tools for social development. At birth, newborns can turn their heads in the direction of the human voice. They move their arms in rhythm of human speech. They like to look at people's faces.

Positive interactions between babies and their caregivers are sometimes called "serve and return," like the game of tennis. Babies understand social messages by the way others talk to, look at, or hold them. Babies send signals to others through their cries, coos, and smiles. These "serve

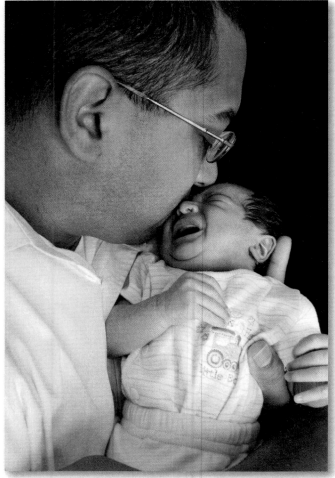

Tony Wear/Shutterstock.com

Figure 10.2 Supportive care of high-reactive babies includes extra holding, cuddling, and soothing. *Were you a low-reactive or high-reactive baby? Explain.*

and return" signals change in the following ways throughout the first year:

- Signals begin as early as two weeks after birth. Smiles with expressive eyes often occur around the fifth or sixth week.
- From three to six months, infants become even better at understanding and sending social signals. They also begin to distinguish between those who care for them and strangers.
- Once infants have better arm and hand control and can easily creep, they initiate social contact. For example, infants may follow other family members around the house. Infants will also reach with their arms to signal they want to be held.

Interacting with Adults

Babies thrive most when they are held, talked to, cuddled, and comforted. They are often happier babies, crying less than those who receive little attention. Caregivers help their baby's intellectual development, as well as social development, by providing lots of loving care. At this stage, caregivers are in Galinsky's nurturing stage of parenting (**Figure 10.3**). (You can review Galinsky's parenting stages in Figure 4.4 of the text.)

Grandparents, friends, babysitters, and others are helpful to a baby's total development. When these people care for and show an interest in them, babies learn to understand and trust others, which helps expand their social environment.

If the baby's first relationships are negative due to caregiver depression, conflicts in the home, or other crises, social connections in the baby's brain do not form properly. This is because "serve and return" relationships are faulty. In these faulty relationships, the adult does not "serve," or when the child "serves," the adult either does not return or returns without sensitivity.

Interacting with Other Children

Infants enjoy being around **siblings** (brothers and sisters) and other children, and tend to watch and follow them. Infants learn from older children and like to play with older children's toys. Older children can learn lessons in loving and caring for others from infants, too. All children benefit in these relationships.

Showing Attachment

Attachment is closeness between people that remains over time. As you may recall, *bonding* (developing a feeling of affection) is a special type of attachment between caregivers and their children. Bonding begins at birth and continues throughout infancy. Bonding happens through closeness, feeding times, bathing, and playtime. This connection lays the foundation for forming an attachment (**Figure 10.4**).

Figure 10.4 Attachment and Bonding

Relationship	Term Used
Caregivers come to love their babies soon after birth. Adult→ Baby	Bonding
Babies whose needs are met come to love their caregivers. Infants realize this tie after six months of age. Baby → Adult	Attachment

Goodheart-Willcox Publisher

Figure 10.3 Galinsky's *nurturance* parenting tasks include balancing a baby's needs with personal needs and providing loving and consistent care to a baby. *How do you think parenting tasks change as a child ages?*

MBI/Shutterstock.com

Babies are motivated to form attachments. They need a caregiver's love and care to survive and feel secure. Thus, babies develop an attachment to those who care for them. They show this attachment through **attachment behaviors**, or actions one person demonstrates to another person to show closeness to that person. Attachment behaviors change from birth through the school-age years. Attachment is developmental, which means attachment behaviors often occur in a set order. The attachment behavior in infancy is called *focused attachment* (**Figure 10.5**).

Attachment is closely related to positive interactions with caregivers and with future health and well-being. Attachment is positive in the following ways:

- Everyone needs to love and to be loved. For healthy social-emotional development, attachment is critical. Establishing healthy attachments helps babies feel loved.
- Attachment helps intellectual development. Attached infants tend to explore their world through play more than infants who are not attached to others.
- Healthy brain development depends on attachment. Overcoming stress throughout life is easier for people who formed strong attachments early in infancy. For example, through attachment, the toddler and young preschooler learn to deal with the fear of strangers and the fear of being left alone in the care of other adults.

Some infants have attachment problems. The main causes of attachment problems are: loss of the primary caregiver, inconsistent or angry care by the primary caregiver, abuse, and changes in other caregivers (turnover of staff in child care). Poor attachment can cause social and emotional problems throughout life.

Expressing Emotions

After disposition and social relations, the third aspect of social-emotional development involves expressing feelings. Long before babies express feelings, the emotion center of the brain becomes active. Because feelings are complex and tied to thinking, memory, and even language, wiring for emotions takes four years to complete.

Brain development research shows that by two months of age, infants begin constructing emotions. Infants first get visual cues of emotions in others at this age. During the first three or four months, infants have two basic responses to their world. The first is distress, shown by crying and muscle tension. The second is excitement, shown by smiling, cooing, and wiggling the body. By the end of the first year, infants can express love, fear, anxiety, anger, jealousy, joy, and sadness. Infants who express a range of emotions, from happy to unhappy, show healthy development.

Figure 10.5 Focused Attachment Behaviors by Age

Approximate Age	Focused Attachment Behaviors
1 month	• Baby recognizes familiar and unfamiliar voices. • Baby turns toward familiar voices.
2 weeks to 2 months	• Baby smiles.
3 months	• Infant responds by giving joyful sounds (coos and gurgles) and movements (kicks). • Infant may laugh.
4 to 6 months	• Infant engages in more turn-taking games, such as peekaboo. • Infant begins to show a preference for familiar people. • Infant becomes still and breathing becomes shallow when unknown people are close.
7 to 12 months	• Infant shows a strong preference for primary caregivers. • Infant cries when a stranger is nearby—fear of strangers. • Infant cries when left alone in an effort to bring a caregiver back into their presence. (Object permanence allows infant to know caregiver exists even when not present.)

Goodheart-Willcox Publisher

Attachment Theorists

Most, but not all, of the original child development theorists primarily focused their research on the child's development with little emphasis on family life. For about the last 75 years, other researchers have directly focused on the effects of early significant social interactions of infants and children under three years of age. *Attachment studies*, as they are known, began with a focus on the primary caregiver–child relationship, but now encompass bonding, infant care, stranger fear, separation anxiety, and the effects of the relationship between the baby and all caregivers. Four major theorists have shaped current knowledge of attachment.

John Bowlby, the father of attachment theory, found WWII in Great Britain had ruptured many family bonds. Specifically, Bowlby found the lack of maternal care, distortions of maternal care (neglect and abuse), and discontinuity in maternal care (maternal separations and multiple mothering figures) all resulted in lifelong mental health problems. Bowlby advocated early intervention for the country's youngest citizens and worked to change government policies for families.

Mary Ainsworth, born in the United States, served as Bowlby's research assistant for three years. Her lifelong, cross-cultural studies led her to develop listings of baby indicators of attachment, such as an infant crying when the caregiver leaves the room, showing excitement when the caregiver returns, and staying close to the caregiver if a stranger is nearby. As a fastidious researcher, she came up with the well-known method of testing infant attachment called the *Strange Situation*. From these experiments, she developed lists of variables for secure and insecure attachments, which will be explained later in the text.

John Kennell and **Marshall Klaus** had a 40-year research collaboration. Their studies led to understandings about parent-newborn bonding. From their studies, they called for changes in the inflexible hospital practices that isolated babies from their caregivers. Their works led to the hospital birthing room, use of the doula during childbirth, parental holding in the NICU, and hospital classes on baby care. They also researched family problems (grief, depression, marital problems) that prevented optimal bonding.

T. Berry Brazelton focused on assuring caregivers about attachment. He promoted the idea of attachment as a gradual process. His *Touch Points* helped prepare guardians and caregivers for the infant's developmental changes. He believed in a close partnership between caregivers and child care providers and researched the infant's ability to form multiple attachments. Through his writings and mass media appearances, he provided know-how and encouragement to all families—single parents, working families, adoptive parents, and parents with ill newborns—to bond with their babies as a foundation for children's mental health.

Research Activity

In small groups, choose one of the theorists described above. Then find a reliable article describing the theorist's life and work. Read the article individually and then discuss as a group what facts were especially interesting to you. Present the highlights of your discussion to the class.

Photo: Tom Wang/Shutterstock.com

Love

As caregivers and guardians care for their babies and meet their needs, babies become attached to them and begin to feel and show love and affection. Babies show love not only to important adults, but also to children who keep them company.

Besides people, babies also become attached to objects, such as pacifiers or stuffed toys (**Figure 10.6**). Babies seem to need these objects even more when they are upset or afraid, or when routines change. Sometimes adults worry about children's love for these objects. Such attachments, however, tend to give babies security and are important to them. Children give up these objects in time.

Fear

The true emotion of fear is not present at birth. Instead, newborns react with the startle reflex when they hear loud sounds or do not have support for their bodies. The stimulus of a loud sound or bodily displacement causes the reflex. For example, by four or five months of age, infants may show some wariness of adult strangers, called *stranger fear*. They may even see adults they know

who have new hairstyles, hats, sunglasses, or other such changes as unfamiliar. Infants do not seem to have the same reaction to adults viewed from the back or to young children they do not know.

Fear, as an emotion, occurs around six months of age. To experience true fear, infants must know they can be hurt. Three kinds of fear include the following:

- *Fear of the unknown.* Infants fear adult strangers, a new bed, or a sudden movement. They also fear different sounds, such as thunder or a siren.
- *Fear learned from direct experiences.* Infants may fear getting soap in their eyes, being in a doctor's office, or seeing a snapping dog because of a negative past experience.
- *Fear learned from adult influence.* What adults say and how they act affect babies' fears. Adults who act or look fearful in a storm, for example, will cause children to be fearful. Adults who tell babies that many situations can hurt them teach children to fear.

Of course, some fear is good. Too much fear, however, is not healthy. Fear affects motor and intellectual development because fearful babies often will not welcome new experiences.

Figure 10.6 Babies may express love by becoming attached to objects, such as pacifiers. *How do you think babies' attachments to objects encourage the development of love?*

2p2play/Shutterstock.com

Anxiety

Anxiety is fear of a possible future event. Sometimes the words *worry* and *concern* are used to describe anxiety. The first anxiety of an infant is called **separation anxiety**, which is the fear that loved ones who leave them with other caregivers will not return. Separation anxiety is seen around 8 months of age and peaks between 10 and 18 months (**Figure 10.7**). The reason very young infants show little separation anxiety is because of their limited intellectual development. Young babies have not yet become attached to certain people. They do not know parents or main caregivers are somewhere else when out of sight or how long they will be gone. These young babies are accepting of all who care for them. There are some indications of anxiety, however, between 4 and 6 months of age. (Review Figure 10.5.)

Around 8 months of age, infants develop the idea about their loved ones being somewhere else when out of sight. They also begin to anticipate future events. During this time, infants become anxious when the adults they love must leave them for a time. This is common when a caregiver goes to work or leaves the house to run an errand.

The anxiety begins when the infant sees clues of the upcoming separation, such as a caregiver picking up car keys or telling the infant good-bye. Separation anxiety is more intense when strangers, such as new babysitters, are near. Infants cannot anticipate a reunion with their loved ones. Thus, during separations, they cry as though their hearts will break. When this occurs, infants are most difficult to console.

Reactions to anxiety normally fade when infants are around two years of age, which may be due to the following:

- Children younger than two years of age cannot understand why caregivers must leave whereas two-year-olds have some understanding about why their caregivers must leave them with others.
- Unlike two-year-olds who remember their caregivers have returned after each separation, infants do not have memories of past events.
- Infants are dependent on others to fulfill their needs whereas two-year-olds are more independent.
- Two-year-olds can express their needs better than infants who cannot express their needs to others well, especially to adults they do not know. Infants' inability to express themselves can lead to anxiety.

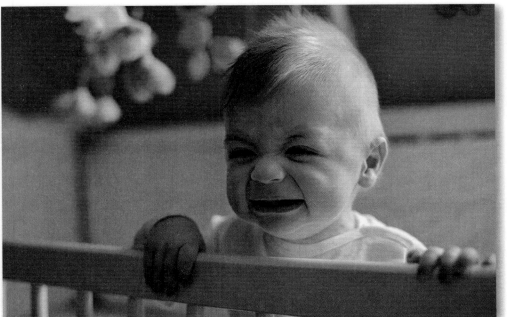

Figure 10.7 *Separation anxiety* is a baby's fear that a loved one who leaves them with other caregivers will not return. *What are some ways caregivers can soothe babies with separation anxiety?*

aywan88/iStock via Getty Images Plus

Anger

Just as the startle reflex **precedes** (comes before something) true fear, *infant rage* precedes true anger. Infant rage occurs when babies are distressed. When infants feel distressed, they may swing their arms and legs excitedly, turn red, and cry loudly (**Figure 10.8**). Infant rage is not true anger, because infant rage is an instinctive response with no thought. *True anger* is a feeling caused by frustration that is directed or focused toward a certain person or object.

By 8 to 10 months of age, infants develop true anger, which is often expressed in physical ways, such as kicking or hitting a person or object. Infants often show anger if

- they are being held, diapered, or dressed when they do not want to be. Being in a confined space (crib, high chair) when they do not want to be may make them angry, too.
- they cannot reach a toy they want or if toys are taken from them.
- their needs are not being met and caregivers are trying to distract them. For example, showing a crying, hungry infant a toy may cause the infant to cry louder and push the toy away.

Infants express their anger in physical ways because they lack language skills. Infants with calm dispositions may seem to show little anger during the first year. Infants whose dispositions tend to be negative may show much more anger. Meeting the infant's needs quickly often prevents anger. Staying calm by talking in a quiet voice and not looking upset are ways to show children how to control their anger. Caregivers might reduce an infant's anger by holding them close for a short time.

10.1-2 Social-Emotional Developmental Milestones

Sometimes adults say, "Children should act their age." This means that as people mature, the way they respond to their feelings changes. When people act their age, they use **age-appropriate behaviors** (proper or expected ways to express emotions at certain ages). For example, two-month-old infants will soothe themselves by sucking, which is an appropriate behavioral response for infants. This same response, however, may not be appropriate for school-age children.

Infants display many age-appropriate behaviors, which are also developmental milestones. **Figure 10.9** lists social-emotional developmental milestones during infancy. Understanding social-emotional milestones can help caregivers plan appropriate activities to meet babies' social-emotional needs.

Figure 10.8 Infant rage precedes true anger, which typically does not develop until around 8 to 10 months of age. *Do you think this baby is crying or showing infant rage? How would you describe infant rage to a new parent who is frustrated with their baby?*

Jaochainoi/Shutterstock.com

Figure 10.9 Newborn and Infant Social-Emotional Milestones

Age	Milestones
One month *Christoffer Askman/Image Source via Getty Images*	• Is quiet and still when looking at a face within 12 inches. • "Molds" to adult's body when held. • Responds to human voices by moving.
Two months *John and Stacy Richardson*	• Can be soothed by being held or rocked. • Soothes self by sucking.
Three months *Heather Preston*	• Shows excitement when people are nearby. • Smiles when stimulated by a face. • Tries to attract people's attention. • Shows delight and distress.
Four months *Heather Preston*	• Smiles broadly and laughs. • Vocalizes to initiate socializing. • Cries if play is disrupted. • Becomes easily excited or upset.
Five months *PeopleImages/iStock via Getty Images Plus*	• Imitates facial expressions. • Distinguishes strangers from family members. • Recognizes voices of family members. • Responds to their name.

Goodheart-Willcox Publisher
(Continued)

Figure 10.9 **Newborn and Infant Social-Emotional Milestones** (Continued)

Age	Milestones
Six months *Prostock-Studio/iStock via Getty Images Plus*	• Turns when name is said. • Becomes disturbed by the presence of strangers. • Reacts to differences in tones of voices. • Vocalizes pleasure and displeasure. • Protests if toys are taken.
Seven months *Andy Lim/Shutterstock.com*	• Pats mirror image. • Wants to be included in group. • Understands *no* by tone of adult voice. • Shows humor.
Eight months *MBI/Shutterstock.com*	• Pats, smiles, and kisses mirror image. • Shouts for attention. • Pushes away unwanted objects. • Becomes "angry" during confinement. • Shows some separation anxiety.
Nine months *Fuller Photography/Shutterstock.com*	• Performs for others. • Shows "focused attachment" to parents. • Initiates play. • Shows intense stranger anxiety.
Ten months *MIA Studio/Shutterstock.com*	• Seeks social approval. • Enjoys games, such as peekaboo. • Displays affection and anger.

(Continued)

Figure 10.9 **Newborn and Infant Social-Emotional Milestones** (Continued)

Age	Milestones
Eleven months 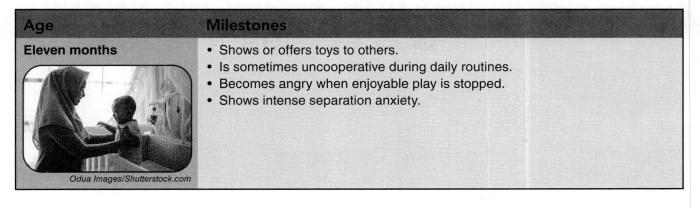 *Odua Images/Shutterstock.com*	• Shows or offers toys to others. • Is sometimes uncooperative during daily routines. • Becomes angry when enjoyable play is stopped. • Shows intense separation anxiety.

Lesson 10.1 Review and Assessment

1. Which of the following is *not* an aspect of social-emotional development during the first twelve months of life? (10.1.1)
   A. Expressing feelings
   B. General mood of the child
   C. Change in the body
   D. Interactions with others

2. _____ is the inherited tendency to react in a certain way, such as being cheerful or grumpy. (10.1.2)
   A. Anxiety
   B. Temperament
   C. Disposition
   D. Attachment

3. Which of the following is *not* a sign of a high-reactive infant? (10.1.2)
   A. Caution
   B. Physical agitation
   C. Distress
   D. Boldness

4. Which of the following is a sign of a low-reactive infant? (10.1.2)
   A. Boldness
   B. Caution
   C. Physical agitation
   D. Distress

Lesson 10.2

Meeting Social-Emotional Needs in the First Year

Key Terms

co-regulation
psychosocial theory
self-awareness
trust versus mistrust
unconditional love

Learning Outcomes

After studying this lesson, you will be able to

10.2-1 **describe** the conflict infants must resolve in the first stage of Erikson's psychosocial theory.

10.2-2 **describe** how parents can aid infant-adult interactions through "serving and responding."

10.2-3 **give examples** of ways infants develop self-awareness.

10.2-4 **identify** helpful tips for reducing a baby's stress.

> ### Reading and Notetaking Activity
>
> Before reading, skim the headings in this chapter. List the headings to create an outline for taking notes during reading and class discussion. Under each heading list any key terms. Finally, write two questions you expect to have answered in class. After completing this chapter, ask your teacher any questions you still have about the concepts or terms you learned.

Introduction

Babies have needs that must be met for healthy social-emotional development. Each baby is an individual. Some babies are more active, some like to be cuddled, some cry a lot, and others seem happy. This individuality influences the caregivers' responses to the baby, just like a person's personality affects the way others respond to them.

During the first year, social-emotional development seems to center on baby-adult interactions, the baby's developing self-awareness, and adults' ways of handling special problems. Social-emotional development affects the baby's mental health both now and in the future.

10.2-1 Erikson's Psychosocial Theory

Psychologist Erik Erikson was concerned about conflicts that occur between a child's needs and social demands. He theorized that people go through eight stages of personality development in their lifespan. His theory is known as **psychosocial theory**. Each stage of Erikson's **psychosocial** (relating to psychological and social aspects) theory of development presents a specific developmental task for each age group (**Figure 10.10**).

Figure 10.10 The Stages of Erikson's Psychosocial Theory

Approximate Age	Stage
Infancy (Birth to 1 year)	**Trust versus mistrust.** Newborns and infants need consistency in having their needs met and sameness in environment to develop a feeling the world is reliable—a sense of basic trust. If the world is not seen as a reliable place, the baby develops a sense of basic mistrust.
Toddler years (1 to 3 years)	**Autonomy versus shame and doubt.** Toddlers seek some autonomy so they can use their new skills and knowledge. They seek control over whether to rely on others as they see fit. Autonomy learned in this stage leads to pride. Failure to achieve autonomy leads to feelings of shame in front of others and self-doubt.
Preschool years (3 through 5 years)	**Initiative versus guilt.** Preschool children have growing abilities, much energy, and desire to engage in activities. They begin trying things on their own initiative. The sense of initiative learned at this stage leads to ambition and purpose. Too many failures and too many negative responses from adults lead to guilt and fear of trying new activities.
School-age years (6 through 12 years)	**Industry versus inferiority.** Middle childhood is the time for developing the tools of society in preparation for adult work. If children are encouraged to use these tools, they develop a sense of industry. If too little is expected or if children are criticized for their efforts, a sense of inferiority develops. Inferiority results in poor work habits, avoidance of competition, and the inability to cope with later tasks.
Adolescence (13 through 18 years or older)	**Identity versus role confusion.** Teens confront the question, "Who am I?" Role identity occurs when teens become certain about who they are in terms of career focus, important attitudes, and values. Role confusion results when others cannot confirm that teens are who they think they are and where they are headed.
Young adulthood (19 through 39 years)	**Intimacy versus isolation.** Intimacy results when a young adult can "lose and find themselves in another." Intimacy occurs when the young adult trusts they can surrender self (identity) to another person or relationship. Isolation occurs if the adult feels others cannot be trusted in an intimate way.
Middle adulthood (40 through 65 years)	**Generativity versus stagnation.** Generativity or productivity may be in the forming of a family, in achieving in one's career, and/or in providing significant services to others. This is the adult's way(s) of contributing to the next generation. Stagnation or self-absorption occurs when a person becomes concerned only with self.
Older adulthood (66 years and older)	**Integrity versus despair.** If older adults see their lives as unique and meaningful, they see a picture of a life well-spent. In this way integrity or the state of feeling complete has been achieved. Despair comes with feelings of regret about the way one's life was lived and causes anxiety about the end of life.

Goodheart-Willcox Publisher

Erikson believed that each task can have either a positive or negative outcome. Depending on the outcome of each stage, a person's personality could develop in healthy or unhealthy ways. If the person successfully resolves the conflict, they will feel a sense of achievement, resulting in healthy personality development. If the person is unsuccessful in resolving the conflict, they are more likely to feel inadequate, causing their personality to be more vulnerable during other stages. Erikson believed a person can overcome failures in resolving past conflicts, but positive changes later in life are more difficult. He saw the family and other factors as major influences on personality.

Infants are in the first stage of Erikson's psychosocial theory, called **trust versus mistrust**. In this stage, infants are tasked with learning whether to trust or mistrust others. Trust is a key part of social development. How much a person trusts or does not trust other people affects how they interact with them.

Erikson stated that two key factors are essential in whether infants learn to trust. First, infants need a consistent environment, which includes sameness in routines, caregivers, and surroundings. Second, infants learn to trust by having their basic needs met promptly each time. According to Erikson, if a baby's basic needs are consistently met, then babies feel the world is a good and happy place. This helps them learn to trust others and adapt to their world. If basic needs go unmet or partly met and the surroundings are unstable, then babies feel helpless and confused and develop mistrust.

10.2-2 Aiding Baby-Adult Interactions

Interacting with the baby is the baby's means to social contact. In an earlier chapter, you read about a baby's learning agenda. Part of a baby's agenda is seeking significant relationships and learning to interact with people. Just as caregivers aid their child's motor, sensory, concept, and language development, they must also aid social-emotional development through interactions with their baby. Caregivers can develop positive interactions with their baby by respecting the baby's temperament, interacting with newborns when alert, soothing infants when discomforted, serving and responding, and encouraging attachment.

Respecting the Baby's Temperament

One of the most important aspects of baby-adult interaction involves respecting the baby's temperament. Each baby comes into the world with a unique temperament. Adults respond positively or negatively toward the newborn's temperament and convey their feelings mainly through the way they hold, touch, and look at the baby. The newborn reacts to adults' feelings and actions (**Figure 10.11**). For example, if adults are tense or the newborn's needs are unmet, then they become fussy and difficult. On the other hand, when adults are relaxed and the newborn's needs are promptly met, they are more often quiet and cooperative.

Sometimes there is a *goodness of fit* between a caregivers' personality and a child's temperament. This means that the child's temperament matches the caregiver's ideal. Sometimes the fit is not so good. Adults who have good relationships with babies seem to respect their temperaments regardless of fit.

Anneka/ Shutterstock.com

Figure 10.11 Newborns are attuned to their caregivers' feelings and behaviors and may react to expressions of love and expressions of frustration or stress. *How can a caregiver avoid upsetting their baby when frustrated?*

Health

Optimal Infant Care Practices

Knowledge of optimal infant care practices has grown out of attachment studies. Two major researchers and teachers of infant care practices were Magda Gerber and Alice S. Honig.

Gerber advised caregivers and guardians to slow down, avoid exhaustion, and get to know the baby. She encouraged caregivers to provide a safe, challenging, and nurturing environment. Within this environment babies become independent by being active participants in routine care, exploring their environments, and having time to play alone. Gerber believed caregivers should give babies their full attention part of the time rather than half-attention all of the time. Her major point was for caregivers to live with babies in the moment—"to try less and enjoy it more."

Honig called for close observation of infants in order to provide needed nurturing. Her ideas included

- sending emotional signals (admiring eyes, crooning baby's name, loving tone of voice) so babies know they are cherished

- watching for signs of stress and providing nurturance through holding, staying nearby, and talking quietly
- creating loving, leisurely rituals for care
- knowing milestones and windows of opportunity and then "dancing up and down the developmental ladder" to provide the ability-activity match for babies
- helping babies rejoice in their mastery of skills

Honig emphasized these loving actions would become part of "body-memory" and nurture a baby's life journey toward positive relationships. Based on these guidelines, how do you think caregivers and guardians can balance maintaining their own health with optimizing the health of their infant? What strategies would you suggest to a caregiver who is struggling with their own health and is thus unable to promote an infant's health?

Photo: wavebreakmedia/Shutterstock.com

Two nationally-known infant educators, Alice Sterling Honig and Magda Gerber, have taught the need to respect each baby's individual temperament and interests. For example, active babies often get into places they do not belong. They require more watching than less active children. These caregivers need to adjust their own behaviors to provide this extra level of care.

Interacting with Newborns

Newborns need social interaction for development, too. Not only do babies seem to learn best when they are alert and inactive (not fussy), they

also develop warm relationships with others in this state. Newborns differ in alertness because of their individuality. For example, premature babies are often not as alert as full-term babies. Also, babies differ in the length of time they are alert. There seems to be a general pattern in the development of alertness.

Unless affected by drugs used in delivery, newborns are usually alert for a while after birth. Then, newborns tend to sleep a lot during the next few days. With each passing week, newborns spend more time in the alert-inactive stage. Newborns can also stay alert for longer periods of time in later weeks as they grow.

Caregivers work to establish a good relationship early in the newborn's life, even if the baby is sleepy or fussy most of the time. Caregivers communicate their feelings through facial expressions and vocalizations when engaging babies. Emotional wiring begins in newborns and young infants during times of adult-child interactions (feeding, other physical care tasks, comforting, and holding). Babies learn through the filter of feelings. If adults are harsh or nonresponsive because they are depressed, babies are likely to develop learning delays and social-emotional issues.

Adults need to cuddle and play with their babies in the alert state. They can try to soothe fussy newborns and enjoy them during their alert times. If caregivers are experiencing depression or having other issues, they should seek treatment and support.

Soothing a Fussy Newborn

All newborns cry, and some babies cry up to ¼ of each day, even when nothing is wrong. Caregivers who meet their newborns' needs should understand this crying is not related to their parenting abilities. Some babies just cry more and are harder to soothe than others.

Newborns cry for almost any reason, because crying is the way they "talk." They may cry because they are tired, hungry, lonely, or uncomfortable. Newborns also cry to relax from tension. *Colic* (a condition in which the baby has intense abdominal pain) is one major reason babies cry, especially during the first three months. There are many causes of colic, such as allergies, tension, swallowing air when sucking or crying, and hunger. Soothing a baby who has colic often works, but in severe cases of colic, a pediatrician may prescribe medication to treat the condition.

Caregivers will not spoil newborns by answering their cries and soothing them. Major stress relievers for newborns are hearing familiar voices talking quietly, feeding, and regulating temperature through contact with the parent's warm body. Swaddling a baby can also help.

FOCUS ON MENTAL HEALTH

Emotional wiring is based on early adult-child relationships. Adults who are depressed, harsh, or nonresponsive to their babies run a major risk of damaging the mental health of their babies. Most people experience "baby blues" after they give birth. This can include mood swings, crying spells, anxiety, and difficulty sleeping. Baby blues typically begin within the first two or three days after delivery and may last up to two weeks. Some people, however, experience a more severe, longer-lasting form of depression known as postpartum depression. The symptoms of postpartum depression are similar to the symptoms of baby blues, but are more intense, last longer, and may eventually interfere with the person's ability to care for the baby and handle daily tasks. Rarely, an extreme mood disorder called postpartum psychosis may develop after childbirth. Symptoms include confusion, disorientation, obsessive thoughts about the baby, sleep disturbances, and paranoia. Postpartum depression is not a character flaw or weakness, but rather a complication of giving birth. Partners of people who have given birth can also experience postpartum depression. Prompt treatment of postpartum depression can help caregivers manage their symptoms and bond with their baby. Speaking openly and honestly with their doctor is the best way for a caregiver to ensure they get the help they need.

Adults can *self-regulate* (calm down without help), but because this is a learned skill, newborns need help through co-regulation. **Co-regulation** is soothing the baby to aid them to calm down. A caregiver who soothes the newborn is called a *co-regulator*. Newborns who do not receive help in calming down feel vulnerable and often have difficulties with self-regulation later in life.

Soothing not only helps babies feel less alone in a big world, but also teaches self-regulation. Newborns may show the beginnings of self-regulation. For example, when startled or overstimulated, they may turn their heads, close their eyes, or suck their hands or fingers.

To soothe a newborn, a caregiver tries to interpret the baby's cry and then responds. **Figure 10.12** describes three distinct cries and how a person might respond to them. Following are some ways a caregiver might soothe a baby:

- Rock the baby in a vertical (over the shoulder) position. Place one hand behind the baby's head and rock quickly.
- Carry the baby around the house or yard.
- Sing and play music. Babies like the quiet tones of lullabies or even a steady tone, such as the hum of a ceiling fan or the bubbling sound from an aquarium.
- Take the baby for a car ride or a ride in a stroller.
- Stroke the baby to relieve tension.

A newborn's constant cries cause tension in caregivers. Relief from tension is good for family relationships. Using a babysitter for an hour or even an entire afternoon may help adults reduce their tension.

Serving and Responding

Babies need caregivers who serve and respond. Physical and vocal signals and responses shape the feelings between adults and their newborns. Babies feel love through physical contact with the adult. The quality of the relationship is influenced less by the total number of messages than by the quality of these messages. Even the most loving caregiver may miss a few opportunities to serve or respond because they are hurried or tense. In a healthy relationship, the balance must be on the positive side.

Child-adult relationships are mostly one-sided for many years. Infants may give some smiles and hugs, but adults do most of the giving. This giving is important, because the feelings adults show for babies help to shape the picture children form of themselves. Fostering good feelings in babies seems to increase the joy and love between children and their caregivers.

Figure 10.12 Soothing an Infant

Cause	Sounds of Cry	Ways to Respond
Pain	Cycle begins with shrill scream, followed by silence, and ends with short gasps. Cycle is repeated.	Respond immediately. Ease pain if possible. Cuddle baby to calm.
Hunger or boredom	Slow cries that become louder and rhythmic.	Feed if near feeding time. OR Entertain by giving baby a tour of the house or yard.
Upset	Fussy, rather quiet cry. Cry sounds a bit forced.	Cuddle or entertain.

Goodheart-Willcox Publisher

Selimaksan/E+ via Getty Images

Encouraging Attachment

The most important asset a child can have is the knowledge that someone has **unconditional love** (deep affection without limitations) for them and will always be supportive. A child becomes attached to this person. The quality of this attachment is a powerful **predictor** (something that is useful in making a prediction) of social-emotional outcome (**Figure 10.13**).

Many years will pass before children can verbally identify those who unconditionally love and support them. How do infants sense this love and support and develop attachments? Babies have needs and can signal these needs. Infants attach to caregivers who bring warmth, care, and security and make them feel loved, worthy of care, and safe. Through the nurturing relationship, positive connections are made in the brain. Depriving a child of the nurturing relationship leads to negative brain effects.

To encourage attachment, guardians and other caregivers need to understand and practice the following:

- Realize the most important adult behavior in forming attachment is correctly, consistently, and promptly responding to the baby's signals of needs in a loving way.
- Observe and learn to read the baby's signals and consider the baby's preferences for meeting needs. Babies prefer to be soothed in different ways.
- Allow the mobile infant to seek **proximity** (nearness) and maintain contact. For example, most infants prefer to play within a few feet of their caregivers—not in a far-off playroom or nursery. Ignoring or rejecting an infant's **overtures** (cues for positive relationship building) leads to insecurity for the infant.
- Minimize separation anxiety by leaving the infant for a short period of time, if possible, and with a familiar adult who will soothe them once the primary caregiver leaves. Infants can develop multiple attachments, which also depend on how other caregivers respond to the infant's needs.
- Realize attachment develops over time. No caregiver can be 100 percent correct and responsive in meeting each and every need of a baby. Because babies develop so rapidly, even the best adult observers can miss a cue. Like all other interactions, the balance of correct readings and consistent responses needs to be on the positive side.

Figure 10.13 A baby's attachment is a powerful influence on their social-emotional development. Without strong, positive attachment, babies may experience social-emotional developmental delays. *If a caregiver is worried that their baby is not forming attachment, what should they do?*

10.2-3 Helping Infants Develop Self-Awareness

Through infant-adult interactions, caregivers can help infants learn more about themselves. In the first year, an infant begins to develop **self-awareness** or an understanding of themselves as a unique person. As infants develop self-awareness, they form a mental picture of themselves and an idea of who they are and what they can do. Infants develop self-awareness in the following ways:

- *Hand regard.* Infants gaze at their hands for hours, making slight movements (called *hand regard*). As their brains process the sight and sensation of the moving hands, infants learn their hands are a part of their bodies.
- *Cause and effect.* Infants learn how their movements can affect other objects (**Figure 10.14**). For example, an infant might move a hand, bat a toy on an activity gym, and make the toy turn. This discovery teaches the infant which objects are part of them (the hand) and which are not (the toy and the activity gym). When an infant crawls to get a toy, the infant learns their actions can make things happen.
- *Name recognition.* By four months of age, infants recognize their names if used often. Calling the infant by name during happy times gives the infant positive feelings about their

name. Happy times include reunions between the adult and infant, such as after a nap or when the adult returns from work. Caregivers can also call the infant by name when talking to them during child care tasks or games.
- *Recognition of body parts.* During the second half of the first year, infants can learn to touch body parts (nose, ears, mouth, and hair) upon request and find these same body parts in other people and stuffed animals.
- *Mirror play.* Looking in mirrors also increases self-awareness. Infants enjoy seeing themselves in mirrors even before they know the images they see are their own. Calling the infant's image by name is helpful. Infants like trying to identify body parts in their mirror image. Adults may place infants in front of mirrors so they can watch themselves eat, dress, and move. Infants also enjoy having non-breakable play mirrors as toys.
- *Object possession.* Toward the end of the first year, infants become possessive about some objects. This should be encouraged, because infants' understanding that some objects belong to them is part of self-awareness. Also, infants must possess things before they can learn to share in a few years. Adults can help teach possession by making statements or asking questions, such as "Here's Adora's dress" or "Where are Will's blocks?"

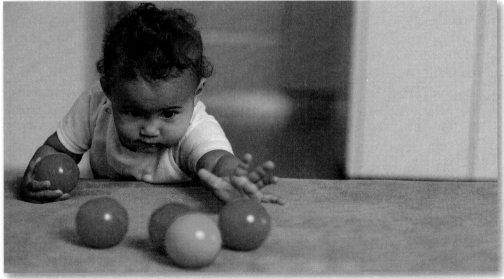

Figure 10.14 Infants develop self-awareness by learning cause and effect and by witnessing how their movement and actions affect the environment around them. *How can parents encourage their babies to learn about cause and effect?*

RuslanDashinsky/E+ via Getty Images

10.2-4 Handling Stress and Special Problems in Infancy

When guardians and other caregivers meet babies' needs, babies have surges of positive hormones. These babies signal, play, learn, and show affection. All babies, however, have some problems or causes of stress. These may include feeding and sleeping problems, fear of strangers, or excessive crying.

Sometimes, caregivers may **inadvertently** (unintentionally) cause stress in a baby's environment. Main stressors include not meeting a baby's physical needs, limiting a baby's body contact with a caregiver, and not being a co-regulator when the baby is stressed. Not providing the baby with "serve and return" signals or providing harsh signals can also cause stress for the infant.

When the baby's environment is neglectful or chaotic, the baby has to adapt either by showing little response to the environment or by over-responding (being hypersensitive) to it. In both cases, these babies have surges of negative hormones, especially *cortisol*. Chronic elevation of cortisol increases blood pressure, pulse, and blood sugar level and interrupts digestive and *excretory*

(kidney and bowel) functions. It also destroys brain cells, weakens attachment to caregivers, and is related to later depression.

Infants need constant emotional support. Caregivers can provide this support by responding to the baby's needs, holding the baby to their body, talking in a soothing voice, and being a co-regulator when the baby is distressed. Caregivers may also breast-feed to soothe the baby. (Compared with formula-feeding, breast-feeding reduces stress hormones.) Monitoring the baby's environment, such as keeping noise levels down, can also be helpful for reducing stress.

When problems arise, the following additional tips may help:

- *Decide if the problem is temporary.* If the baby seems ill, seek prompt medical attention. If the baby does not seem ill, wait a few days. Babies do have mood changes. Also, the problem may be because of a hurried or tense caregiver. In these cases, the problem will likely end as soon as the adult slows down or relaxes.
- *Get help when needed.* For example, caregivers who have a fussy baby may need to ask loving babysitters to give them time to rest or leave home for a few hours. Caregivers who need help coping with stressful situations may seek treatment from a mental health counselor.
- *Give in to an infant's demands sometimes, if the results are not serious.* Even infants have wills of their own, and letting them have their way sometimes is not going to spoil or harm them. For example, if an infant refuses to eat peas, try other vegetables with similar nutrients.
- *If the problem continues, talk to an expert.* A pediatrician or family doctor can determine if there are any underlying health issues.
- *Remain calm.* This helps the baby and the adult.

Experienced caregivers tend to almost ignore many common, not-too-serious problems. Experience teaches that all babies are different and many minor problems solve themselves in time.

Careers

Mental Health Counselor

Mental health counselors encourage clients to discuss their social-emotional problems. They work with their clients to develop skills that will help them cope with difficult situations. Mental health counselors help people understand and deal with their feelings. They also diagnose and treat mental health disorders, such as depression.

Career cluster: Human services.

Education: Educational requirements include a master's degree in a mental health field, such as social work, psychology, or counseling. Supervised clinical work and licensure are also required.

Job outlook: Future employment opportunities for mental health counselors are expected to grow much faster than the average for all occupations.

To learn more about a career as a mental health counselor, visit the United States Department of Labor's *Occupational Outlook Handbook* website. You will also be able to compare the job responsibilities, educational requirements, job outlook, and average pay of mental health counselors with similar occupations.

Photo: wavebreakmedia/ Shutterstock.com

Lesson 10.2 Review and Assessment

1. What conflict must infants resolve in the first stage of Erikson's psychosocial theory? (10.2.1)
   A. Autonomy versus shame and doubt
   B. Trust versus mistrust
   C. Industry versus inferiority
   D. Imitative versus guilt

2. Which of the following statements show a caregiver's respect for their baby's temperament? (10.2.2)
   A. Baby proof the house
   B. Ignore the child
   C. Tense and relax around the child as they cry
   D. Adjust caregiver behavior to provide care

3. **True or False.** Co-regulation is soothing a baby to aid them in calming down. (10.2.2)

4. Which of the following is *not* a way that infants develop self-awareness? (10.2.3)
   A. Gazing at their hands for hours making slight movements
   B. Learning how their movements can affect other objects
   C. Recognizing their name immediately
   D. Seeing themselves in the mirror

5. **True or False.** The main stressors for babies include not meeting their physical needs, limited body contact with caregiver, and not getting serve-and-return signals from caregivers. (10.2.4)

Summary

Lesson 10.1

10.1-1 Social-emotional development involves a person's basic disposition, social relations, and emotions.

10.1-1 Babies vary in their temperaments. High-reactive infants are the most vulnerable to stress and its effects, especially when parenting expectations are unrealistic.

10.1-1 Babies interact with others through a "serve and return" relationship. Without positive serve and return, social connections in the baby's brain do not form correctly.

10.1-2 Emotional wiring of the brain begins at birth and is completed in the preschool years. Emotions of love, fear, anxiety, and anger arise in all children. These emotions consist of thoughts that lead to feelings and, in turn, cause changes in the body. It is healthy for babies to express a wide range of emotions.

Lesson 10.2

10.2-1 According to Erikson's psychosocial theory, babies must resolve the conflict of trust versus mistrust. Babies learn trust by having their basic needs met.

10.2-2 Positive baby-adult interactions must be encouraged for healthy development.

10.2-2 Interactions should focus on respecting the baby's temperament and on correctly, consistently, and promptly responding to baby's signals of needs in a loving way.

10.2-3 The beginnings of self-awareness become obvious during the first year and should be encouraged.

10.2-4 Infants need constant emotional support. Caregivers can provide this support by responding to the baby's needs, holding the baby to their body, talking in a soothing voice, and being a co-regulator when the baby is distressed.

College and Career Portfolio

Portfolio Standardized Test Scores

For college portfolios and for some career portfolios, you may be asked to provide your standardized test scores. Standardized tests are national tests that assess your education level in general subjects, such as math, science, reading, and writing. Standardized tests vary by state and region, but include the ACT, PSAT, and SAT. To obtain your test scores, complete the following activities.

- Determine which, if any, standardized test scores you need to include in your portfolio. If you are unsure, ask your teacher or a guidance counselor.
- Research the steps for requesting your standardized test scores and submit the request or set a date to submit it based on the deadline for your portfolio. Request your scores well in advance of when they are needed.

Recall and Application

1. **True or False.** Disposition is the general mood of a person. (10.1.1)
2. Serve-and-return signals begin as early as _____ after birth. (10.1.1)
   A. two weeks
   B. four weeks
   C. six weeks
   D. eight weeks
3. Lacey is six months old and reacts to anything new with caution and becomes agitated easily in unfamiliar situations. Lacey is exhibiting characteristics of a(n) _____. (10.1.1)
   A. low-reactive baby
   B. high-reactive baby
   C. colicky baby
   D. alarmist
4. **True or False.** By the end of the first 12 months of life, babies are able to express love, fear, anxiety, anger, jealousy, joy, and sadness. (10.1.1)

5. Which of the following social-emotional milestones can be seen by the end of the first month after birth? (10.1.2)
   A. Initiates play
   B. Is quiet and still when looking at a face within 12 inches
   C. Can be soothed by being held or rocked
   D. Imitates facial expressions
6. **True or False.** In Erickson's trust versus mistrust stage of psychosocial theory, infants are tasked with seeking control over their skills and knowledge. (10.2.1)
7. **True or False.** Alice Sterling Honig and Magda Gerber taught the need to respect each baby's individual temperament and interests. (10.2.2)
8. Which of the following is *not* a way to sooth a newborn? (10.2.2)
   A. Carry the baby around the house or yard.
   B. Put the baby in their crib and walk away.
   C. Sing and play music.
   D. Take the baby on a ride in the car or stroller.

9. **True or False.** Caregivers should discourage infants from becoming possessive with objects. This will help infants develop self-awareness. (10.2.3)
10. **True or False.** When the baby's environment is neglectful or chaotic, the baby has to adapt either by showing little response to the environment or by over-responding to it. (10.2.4)

Critical Thinking

1. **Compare and contrast.** Review the three aspects of social-emotional development described in this text. Then, working with a partner, compare and contrast these three aspects. How are they alike? How are they different? Give concrete examples of each aspect.
2. **Evaluate.** Babies' temperaments often shape their personalities. How would you describe your temperament? Have you had these characteristics for a long time? Do others in your family have the same temperament?
3. **Draw conclusions.** Write four infant-adult scenarios that illustrate each of the four emotions infants develop in the first year. Then, trade papers with a partner. Draw conclusions about what emotions are being depicted in your partner's scenarios. After you have finished, discuss your answers.
4. **Cause and effect.** Feelings of mistrust and vulnerability in infancy can affect a child over the course of their life. How do you think feelings of mistrust surface in adults?
5. **Analyze.** Working with a partner, take turns explaining why interactions with caregivers are so important for infants' social-emotional development. Cite evidence from your textbook and create a compelling argument.
6. **Determine.** Some caregivers believe babies can be spoiled if people hold or soothe them when they do not have physical needs. Based on what you have read in this chapter, do you agree with this assessment? Explain why or why not.
7. **Make inferences.** Why do you think infant-adult interactions are described in terms of "serving and responding"? If you

were to create your own catchphrase to describe the dynamic of positive infant-adult relationships, what would it be?

8. **Compare and contrast.** Create a list of ten caregiver behaviors that inhibit attachment and ten caregiver behaviors that encourage attachment. Then, compare and contrast these behaviors. Write a short essay explaining what makes these caregiver behaviors positive or negative.
9. **Identify.** List ten attachment behaviors, both positive and negative. Then, trade papers with a partner and identify the behaviors your partner listed as indicative of weak or strong attachment.

Core Skills

1. **Technology.** In small groups, create a video tutorial on handling and interacting with high-reactive babies. Write a three-minute screenplay about two new caregivers interacting with a high-reactive baby. In your video tutorial, demonstrate proper techniques for holding infants and for soothing fussy or crying infants. Also, include a section about what caregivers should *not* do, and demonstrate those behaviors. After you have composed your screenplay, practice and then film your video tutorial. Present your tutorial to the class.
2. **Technology and science.** Use the internet to search for information about how brain development affects social-emotional development in the first year. Create an electronic presentation of your findings to share with the class. Adhere to all copyright laws and cite any sources you may use for the presentation.
3. **Research and writing.** Using reliable online or print resources, research how social-emotional development during infancy affects a person as a child, as an adolescent, and as an adult. As you conduct your research, assess the reliability of your sources, and compile a bibliography with citations in APA style. Take notes about facts or concepts that interest you and then compare notes with a partner.

After discussing your findings, write a collaborative four- to five-page essay detailing your findings and comparing them to the information in your textbook. Include a cumulative bibliography with your essay.

4. **Art and speaking.** In small groups, review the social-emotional milestones children achieve within the first year of life. Then, using art supplies or electronic resources, collaborate to create an easy-to-follow visual representation of the milestones a baby achieves during each month in infancy. Your illustration should include drawings or pictures of children achieving milestones during each month, and should be an effective study tool and synthesis of the information you learned in this chapter. After completing your illustration, present it to the class and make it available for other students to reference while studying.

5. **Writing.** Write a one- or two-page brochure about the importance of trust in the infant's life. Incorporate Erikson's psychosocial theory and explain how adults can promote trust in the infant. Check your brochure for correct spelling, grammar, and punctuation.

6. **Reading and writing.** Using online or print resources, find personal accounts of new parents caring for an infant who is twelve months old or younger. Read three of these accounts and take notes about the infants' social-emotional development and the interactions between the caregivers and infants described. Then, using what you have learned in this chapter, write a short essay relating these stories to infants' social-emotional development and evaluating whether the infant-adult interactions are positive or negative.

7. **Listening and speaking.** Interview two caregivers about the expanding social worlds of their babies. Prepare your list of interview questions in advance. Some questions might include: Besides parents or guardians, who are other important people in your baby's life? How does your baby react to siblings and other children? Did your baby become attached to an object? After the interview, consider what the caregivers' responses tell you about the differences in the social-emotional development of their babies. Report your findings to the class in an oral report.

8. **CTE Career Readiness Practice.** Suppose you work in an infant day care center where ensuring the health and safety of the children in your charge is of utmost importance. One day, you notice one of your coworkers becoming frustrated with a fussy infant and responding harshly to the infant's crying. In response, the infant cries more loudly, and, fearing that your coworker may shake the infant, you offer to hold the infant for a while. You finish the day without saying anything about the incident to anyone, but that night, you start to wonder if you should mention the incident to your supervisor. You begin to ask yourself, "Did I act responsibly by not talking to my boss about my coworker's behavior? Could I be legally liable, if abuse occurred, and I didn't report it?" In small groups, discuss this scenario. What is the responsible thing to do in this situation? Role-play a conversation in which you respond to the dilemma in an appropriate way.

Observations

1. In small groups, listen to recordings or videos of infants crying. If possible, listen to videos where caregivers respond to infants' cries. Then, individually, try to determine what each infant cry is communicating. Is the infant crying angrily? Is the infant afraid? Observe how the caregiver responds to the cry and assess how accurate your interpretations were. Afterward, reflect as a group on how caregivers learn to understand and respond to infants' cries.

2. Observe an infant with caregiver. How does the baby demonstrate attachment? How does the adult encourage attachment? Write a short report answering these questions, and then present your report to the class.

Unit 4 The Toddler Years

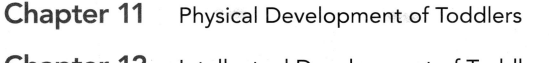

Chapter 11	Physical Development of Toddlers
Chapter 12	Intellectual Development of Toddlers
Chapter 13	Social-Emotional Development of Toddlers

Teamwork

Some CTSO competitive events have a performance section of the event. For a team event, the team making the presentation needs to prepare together to operate as a cohesive unit.

To prepare for team events, complete the following activities:

1. Read and follow the guidelines and regulations for team performances your organization provides.
2. Practice performing as a team by completing the team activities throughout this text.
3. Locate the rubric or scoring sheet for the event on your organization's website. Analyzing the scoring process offers insight into the criteria that judges use to assess your team.
4. Review the rules and regulations to confirm whether the judges will ask questions of the team or whether the team will need to defend a case or situation.
5. Make notes about important points and have team members evaluate one another's notes. You may also be able to use these notes during the event.
6. Assign each team member a role for the presentation and practice performing as a team. Have each team member introduce themself, review the case or point of the presentation, make suggestions, and conclude with a summary.
7. Ask your instructor to serve in the role of competition judge as your team practices its presentation. When your team finishes the presentation, ask your instructor for feedback on the performance. In addition, you may also consider having a student audience listen and give feedback.
8. Keep practicing. Use the feedback and evaluation requirements as a guide to polishing the presentation.

Chapter 11

Physical Development of Toddlers

Essential Question

How do toddlers physically grow and develop, and how can parents meet their toddler's physical needs while coping with the toddler's indomitable will?

Case Study   Should Parents Push Motor Skills?

As a class, read the case study and discuss the questions that follow. After you finish studying the chapter, discuss this case study again. Have your opinions changed based on what you learned?

Jamal is a sweet and playful 30-month-old toddler. Jamal didn't walk until 17 months of age and is still behind in motor skills. In fact, Jamal seems to have little interest in most gross-motor activities. Jamal's guardians are concerned, especially because they are both athletic and sports are an important value to them. Jamal's caregivers have even been planning to enroll Jamal in a T-ball program that Jamal's paternal figure has coached for several years.

Six months before the time to enroll Jamal in T-ball, Jamal's movements are still awkward. Jamal's caregivers want to enroll Jamal in a gymnastics program to help develop gross-motor skills. They also want Jamal to practice throwing and catching balls. Before enrolling Jamal in the gymnastics program, they took Jamal to a well-known doctor who treats children who have muscular-skeletal conditions. The doctor could not find anything wrong with Jamal. After Jamal's caregivers explain their plans, the doctor says, says, "I don't think it's best to overdo it."

Give It Some Thought

1. Do you think having athletic caregivers gives Jamal a better chance of being athletic compared with other children whose caregivers do not have these abilities? Why or why not?
2. How might the caregivers' plan help or hinder Jamal's development?
3. According to Galinsky, all caregivers go through an imaging stage of parenting. How long should caregivers pursue their dreams for their children? Should caregivers encourage a child to follow caregiver interests or should guardians follow the child's lead? Explain your answer.
4. What did the doctor mean by not "overdoing it"? What do you think are the doctor's concerns? Do you think Jamal's caregivers are apt to "overdo it"? Explain your answers.

Heather Preston

Lesson 11.1

Growth and Development of Toddlers

Key Terms

dexterity

eye-hand coordination

fine-motor skills

gross-motor skills

large-muscle
  development

muscle development

small-muscle
  development

Learning Outcomes

After studying this lesson, you will be able to

11.1-1 **describe** a child's organ maturation in the toddler years, specifically focusing on changes in the brain.

11.1-2 **explain** body growth and development in the toddler years in terms of changes in height and weight, body proportions, bones and teeth, and fat and muscles.

11.1-3 **distinguish** between *large-muscle development* and *small-muscle development* and give examples of major gross- and fine-motor skills children develop during the toddler years.

11.1-4 **give examples** of physical developmental milestones children might achieve in the toddler years.

Reading and Notetaking Activity

Before reading this chapter, skim the headings and write each heading in a different color or font on a separate sheet of paper or electronically. As you silently read the chapter and listen to your teacher, take notes in the color or font you chose for each heading. After you finish taking notes for each section, draw or copy and paste a small illustration or visual next to the section that will help you remember what you learned.

Introduction

Children between one and three years of age are called toddlers. This name fits them because toddlers toddle during almost all their waking minutes as they explore the world around them. As toddlers develop physically, their bodies mature, which helps them handle more complex tasks. Although toddlers do not grow as quickly as infants, they go through many important physical changes.

Toddlers' organs are maturing. By the end of the third year, the brain is four-fifths of its adult weight and closer to maturity than any other organ. The other body organs continue to mature, but they do so at a slower rate than the brain. (This is an example of the *head-to-foot* or *cephalocaudal principle*—developmental sequence from the brain down the spine.)

Newborns do not have much control over their muscles when they are born. By the end of their first year, infants are just learning to control voluntary muscle movements. These movements continue to improve during toddlerhood. In fact, both the gross- and fine-motor skills of toddlers improve so much that, by the end of their second year, toddlers can run, jump, throw, and feed themselves (**Figure 11.1**).

11.1-1 Maturation of Organs

From birth to one year of age, a child's brain doubles in size. Brain growth is particularly rapid in the areas that allow for the development of vision and other sensory organs, motor skills, memory, perception, and the sounds of language.

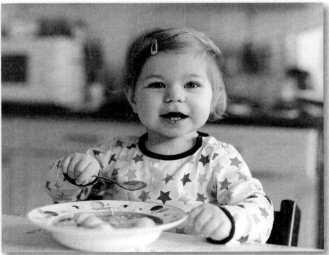

romrodinka/iStock via Getty Images Plus

Figure 11.1 By the end of the second year, toddlers are able to feed themselves. *How do you think a toddler's ability to self-feed impacts the toddler-caregiver relationship?*

The brain continues to mature in the toddler years. By three years of age, the brain reaches 80 percent of adult volume. Synaptic density also increases during toddlerhood. This means there are more dendrites, and they are closer together. Synaptic density permits additional connections and enables much faster learning. By two years of age, toddlers have as many synapses as the adult brain. By three years, the synapses are two times the density of the adult brain. These waves of brain growth—branching dendrites and connections—will not occur again at this rate until the teen years. The density in the toddler's brain aids coordination of sight with body movement, memory, comprehension, cognitive flexibility, the explosion of language, and self-awareness.

Myelination, the process by which myelin wraps around longer axons and cushions the cell bodies of neurons, aids the speed of neuron transmissions. Now toddlers can perform complex tasks and store memories through language, which supports learning. Myelination also aids the toddler's ability to be more aware of themselves and their emotions.

Brain growth is directly impacted by genes and the environment. During the toddler years, environmental experiences significantly affect the brain. Although connections allow for firings, experiences determine actual firings. Once the toddler period ends, serious pruning of connections begins. As the connections are pruned, the windows of opportunity begin to close. Researchers also believe that brain development during the toddler years plays a major role in mental health.

In addition to brain maturation, toddlers' other organs are maturing, too. The heart and lungs become more efficient. Between 12 and 24 months of age, the digestive system improves, making toddlers better able to digest fibrous foods. Between 18 and 24 months, toddlers can regulate their body temperature. Blood vessels in the skin's surface **constrict** (become smaller; more closed) to conserve heat when the body is cold. These blood vessels can also **dilate** (become larger; more open) to release heat when the body is hot.

Toward the end of the toddler years, the *excretory system*, which is responsible for removing waste products from the body, matures enough for toilet learning to begin (**Figure 11.2**).

11.1-2 Skeletal Growth

Toddlers grow at different rates due to heredity and environment. Because of these factors, toddlers sometimes grow at different rates than norms predict for their ages. In this section, you will learn about changes that occur in the toddler's height and weight, body proportions, bones and teeth, and fat and muscle.

Height and Weight

Heredity affects a toddler's height and how fast the toddler grows in height. Because genes determine height, they also influence weight.

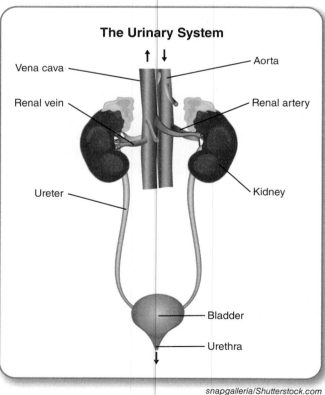

The Urinary System

- Vena cava
- Aorta
- Renal vein
- Renal artery
- Ureter
- Kidney
- Bladder
- Urethra

snapgalleria/Shutterstock.com

Figure 11.2 The urinary system is an important part of the excretory system. Other excretory system organs include the urinary system, lungs, skin, large intestine (colon), and liver. *What are the primary organs that make up the urinary system?*

(A person who is tall in **stature**—a person's height—usually weighs more than a person who is short in stature.) Other factors can also significantly affect their weight and even height, depending on nutrition. Some of the factors include a person's physical activity level, health, and even emotions. Because of heredity and other factors, the height and weight of toddlers can vary.

After a child's first birthday, body growth slows. For example, toddlers grow about half as much in height during the second year as compared with the first year. Children often triple their birthweight during the first year, then gain only one-fourth of that amount during the second year. Some toddlers grow a little faster than these norms in their second year. (They may be "catching up" to norms after a premature birth or first-year illness.) Females often reach half their adult height by 20 months of age while males achieve half their adult height by 27 months. Many factors can affect growth rates.

After 24 months of age, children grow at a slower, but steadier, rate. They tend to gain 2 to 3 inches and about 6 pounds per year throughout childhood. (This rate of growth continues until about 11 years for females and 13 years for males.) **Figure 11.3** shows the height and weight norms for children from 12 to 36 months of age.

Body Proportions

The body proportions of a two-year-old are not the same as those of an adult. At 24 months of age, the toddler's head is a little more than one-fifth of their total height. An adult's head is one-eighth of their height.

Figure 11.3 Average Height and Weight from 12 to 36 Months

Age in Months	Height in Inches	Weight in Pounds
12	30	21
18	32	24.5
24	34	27
30	36	30
36	38	32

Goodheart-Willcox Publisher

A 24-month-old toddler's chest and abdomen measurements are about the same circumference, but by 30 months, the chest is larger than the abdomen. As the child matures, the difference between chest and abdomen size becomes even greater. The child's body-build type becomes apparent during the toddler years, too.

Bones and Teeth

As toddlers grow, their bones continue to become harder, though the degree of ossification is not the same throughout the body. Due to the cartilage, the toddler's bones are more flexible and less likely to break than an adult's bones. The softer bones, however, are more prone to disease or **deformation** (abnormal or unusual formation). The toddlers' *fontanels* (gaps between the skull bones, also called *soft spots*) are closed or almost closed. The toddler's spine changes from the infants' C-shaped spine to the S-shaped spine of adults. The S-shape, called the *lumbar curve*, allows the posture to become straighter and more upright, making standing and walking easier.

Between two and three years of age, a child has the full set of deciduous teeth, or *baby teeth*. As you can see in **Figure 11.4** the emergence of deciduous teeth during infancy and toddlerhood occurs on a regular schedule. The teeth normally begin with the emergence of the bottom or lower central incisors then the upper central incisors. The early care of teeth is critical for lifelong dental health. A pediatric dentist needs to regularly examine a toddler's teeth. Caregivers must follow the dentist's suggestions for dental hygiene.

Fat and Muscle

Fat deposits under the skin decrease rapidly between 9 and 30 months, and the chubby baby becomes a slender child. The "baby fat" that is noticeable during infancy is decreasing and muscle is increasing as children grow and develop. Children who are still chubby at the end of the toddler years might not be at a healthy weight, and caregivers may wish to consult with a pediatrician or registered dietitian.

Figure 11.4 Order of Appearance of Teeth

Upper Teeth	Approximate Time of Teeth Emergence
Central incisor	8 to 12 months
Lateral incisor	9 to 13 months
Canine	16 to 22 months
First molar	13 to 19 months
Second molar	25 to 33 months

Lower Teeth	Approximate Time of Teeth Emergence
Central incisor	6 to 10 months
Lateral incisor	10 to 16 months
Canine	17 to 23 months
First molar	14 to 18 months
Second molar	22 to 31 months

Goodheart-Willcox Publisher

Belmane/Shutterstock.com

Forming healthy habits during the toddler years, such as eating nutritious meals and snacks and getting plenty of physical activity, can help shape children's eating habits throughout life. Following a nutritious diet, being physically active, and getting adequate rest and sleep can also help build muscles. **Muscle development** (the lengthening and thickening of muscles) is slow during the toddler stage.

11.1-3 Motor Development

As children grow and develop, their motor skills also develop. Toddlers improve the motor skills they developed as infants, and they learn many new skills. As toddlers practice these new skills, motor development improves even more.

Large-Muscle Development

Large-muscle development refers to the development of the trunk and arm and leg muscles. Movements, such as walking, jumping, and running, mainly depend on the large muscles. (These movements are examples of **gross-motor skills**.) During the first year, babies may develop these muscles at least to the point of standing and walking with support. After one year, children master walking and begin learning other motor skills. Toddlers love to run, jump, and use other large muscles. When children this age are held in one place too long, they often begin squirming, as if to say, "I want down!"

Walking and Running

Children learn to walk at different ages. Typically, children begin to walk without support within two to three months before or after their first birthday. Some children may take even longer to make walking attempts. Children learn to walk in their own time and in their own way—each child is unique. As children try to take their first steps, they need warm adult support, a positive reaction to walking attempts, and a safe area.

Regardless of age, beginning walkers often share some common traits, which include the following:

- Feet are wide apart, giving children a wider base of support.

- Feet are turned outward and knees are slightly flexed.
- First steps often seem like staggers. Children may also step backward or to the side, take irregular steps, lurch forward, and weave.
- Tiptoe walking may be common because children have not learned to lower their heels. (After three years of age, tiptoe walking is a developmental lag.)
- Arms are often held up or out for balance and do not swing alternately with foot movement (**Figure 11.5**).
- Posture may be slightly tilted forward when walking because the spine is not fully developed. (The development of the lumbar curve enables children to walk more upright and steadily.)
- Falls are likely due to poor balance caused by body proportions, such as large head size. Also, beginning walkers rarely go around small obstacles on the floor, such as a toy or book. They simply walk over these objects, which increases their chances of falling. (Toddlers must watch their foot placement while walking until almost three years of age.)

MBI/Shutterstock.com

Figure 11.5 When toddlers walk, they often hold their arms out for balance. *Are there situations in which adults hold their arms out for balance? Explain.*

As children's walking abilities improve, their walk may look more like a run, but it is not a run. In fact, toddlers take about 170 steps per minute and their stride is half the length of an adult's stride. Can you imagine doubling your steps, taking 170 steps per minute, and having someone hold onto your hand above your head? Yet, this is how many toddlers walk with adults.

True running (not just a hurried walk) often begins around two years of age. Two-year-olds are not skillful runners because their movements are still rather awkward. For example, toddlers tend to hold their arms up or out as they run and cannot start or stop quickly. With much practice, these skills improve.

Investigate Special Topics

The Muscular System

Muscles are soft tissues, which have blood vessels, *tendons* (fibrous tissue attaching muscle to bone), and nerves. The cells of the muscles do not increase in number after the prenatal and very early postnatal period. Muscle growth is seen in the increase of diameter and length of muscle fiber, but not in new muscles. Muscles make up half a person's weight, which is three times the weight of bones. Muscles give the body shape, hold the skeleton together, and are responsible for both internal and external movement and strength.

Muscles can be classified into the following three groups:

Visceral (also called smooth muscles). Seen only through a microscope, visceral muscles are in sheets or layers with one layer behind another. These muscles line the walls of blood vessels and most organs, such as the digestive tract, liver, kidneys, and uterus. Controlled in the unconscious part of the brain, they relax and contract allowing food to be digested, waste products to be excreted and retained, the baby to be pushed out at birth, and the eyes to focus.

Myocardium (also called the cardiac muscle). This muscle allows the heart to contract and relax (beat), which moves the blood. The myocardium is a *striated muscle* (striped with light and dark muscle fibers as seen through a microscope). Like the visceral muscles, the myocardium is unconsciously stimulated by hormones and signals from the brain, making the heart a natural pacemaker.

Striated muscles (also called skeletal muscles). About 700 skeletal muscles cover the entire skeleton of the body. These striated muscles are usually attached to two bones through tendons. Controlled consciously, one bone is pulled closer to another bone across a joint to another bone that remains stationary. This allows for movement. Skeletal muscles keep a person's body upright, allow for voluntary movements, control the tongue in eating and talking, permit facial movements, and give overall power and strength to the body. Most of these highly specialized muscles are named based on their location, size and direction, or function.

Throughout life, muscles need to grow in size, strengthen, and repair their microscopic cellular tears due to activity. Muscle growth, strength, and repair in children come from eating a variety of nutritious foods, doing lots of physical activities, and getting enough sleep. It does not come from eating a special diet and "working out."

Research Activity

In small groups, choose one muscle in the body—a muscle that you think is especially important. Use reliable online or print resources to research whether that muscle is *visceral* or *striated* as well as how the muscle achieves movement in the body. Give a short presentation about the muscle to your class.

Photo: Tom Wang/Shutterstock.com

Climbing and Jumping

Children may begin to climb as soon as they can crawl or creep. Between 15 and 18 months, toddlers will climb onto furniture. They will walk up and down stairs by holding onto the stair railing or balusters and the adult's hand. They may also turn to the side and hold the railing or balusters with both hands (**Figure 11.6**). For toddlers, going up stairs is easier than coming down stairs. Toddlers do not alternate feet while climbing until after their second birthday.

There is not a set time for when climbing begins. Climbing ability relates to the kinds of stairs and other objects near the toddler. Toddlers can more easily climb if stairs are enclosed and not too steep. Climbing also relates to courage. A courageous toddler is likely to try climbing sooner than a physically **timid** (shy) one.

Stepping off low objects at about 18 months is the way children learn to jump. Before two years of age, children may step off a low object and remain suspended in air for a brief moment. Around two years of age, children can jump off low objects with both feet. They move their arms backward, however, instead of helping the jump by swinging their arms forward.

Throwing and Catching

Around one year of age, children may begin throwing or dropping items on purpose, usually from a sitting position, such as from the high chair (**Figure 11.7**). After toddlers feel secure standing or walking, they throw from standing positions.

Eran Yardeni/Shutterstock.com

Figure 11.7 Toddlers throw or drop objects from a sitting position. *Should parents discourage their toddlers from throwing objects? Explain.*

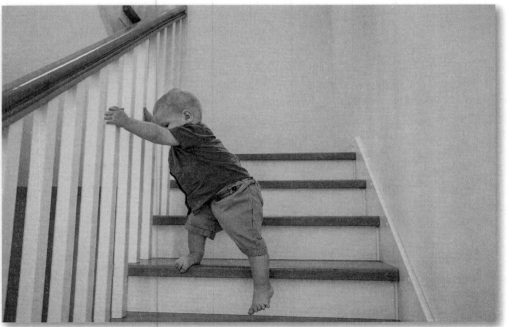

Sunflower Light Pro/Shutterstock.com

Figure 11.6 When toddlers walk up or down stairs, they often hold the railings or balusters with both hands. *How does holding onto railings or balusters help stabilize toddlers as they learn to climb up and down stairs?*

Children less than three years of age are not very skillful throwers. These children typically use a **rigid** (stiff; restricted) throw and do not shift their weight. In fact, when throwing with one hand, they often step with the same-side foot. They also cannot release the ball at the right time, which sends the ball in almost any direction.

Children first learn to "catch" by squatting and picking up an object. Around two years of age, children will bend at the waist to pick up the thrown object. Two- and three-year-olds may try to catch by standing in one position with arms extended and elbows stiff. For the child to catch a ball, it must be exactly on target, because the child does not move toward the ball. In fact, many children close their eyes as the ball comes toward them.

Small-Muscle Development

Small-muscle development refers to the development of small muscles, especially those in the hands and fingers. The movements that depend on these muscles are **fine-motor skills**. Fine-motor skills depend on a child's level of **eye-hand coordination**, which is the ability to coordinate sight with movement of the hands. Eye-hand coordination matures because of brain development. As small muscles and eye-hand coordination develop, toddlers can better handle complex fine-motor skills. With time and experience, clumsy and difficult movements become smoother and require less effort, which is called **dexterity**.

By 12 months of age, children begin to develop the pincer grasp, which helps them learn many new fine-motor skills. One of the major changes in fine-motor skills in the toddler years is the ability to grasp writing tools (**Figure 11.8**). Toddlers use both hands to some extent and often switch hands. A definite hand preference for right or left hand, however, usually does not occur until the preschool years.

Between 12 and 18 months, toddlers can hold spoons in their fists, feed themselves, and drink from cups. They can also fill and empty containers, insert rather large objects into holes, and build a tower of two or three soft blocks.

Figure 11.8 Toddlers' Ability to Grasp Writing Tools

Age	Grasp
About 18 to 24 months	Toddlers hold a crayon or pencil with the thumb on one side and fingers on the other side.
	Digital Vision/Photodisc via Getty Images
About 24 to 26 months	Toddlers hold a crayon or pencil with the thumb and fingers in an adult-like grasp.
	ziggy_mars/iStock via Getty Images Plus

Goodheart-Willcox Publisher

Throughout the toddler years, children's fine-motor skills continue to improve. With practice and better eye-hand coordination, toddlers become better at feeding themselves. Between 18 and 24 months of age, children are able to turn door knobs, hit pegs with a hammer, and string large beads on cords. After 24 months, toddlers can draw or copy vertical lines and build a straighter tower with blocks.

11.1-4 Physical Developmental Milestones

The refinement of brain wiring, greater muscle control, and a positive environment enable toddlers to develop their physical capabilities rapidly. **Figure 11.9** lists physical developmental milestones throughout the toddler years. Parents and caregivers study these charts to better meet toddlers' physical needs.

Lesson 11.1   Review and Assessment

1. What substance aids the speed of neuron transmissions, enabling toddlers to perform more complex tasks? (11.1.1)
   A. Synaptic density
   B. Dendrites
   C. Myelin
   D. Cephalocaudal

2. Which of the following factors do *not* impact a person's weight and height? (11.1.2)
   A. Heredity
   B. Physical activity level
   C. Emotions
   D. Self feeding

3. Which of the following teeth comes in first? (11.1.2)
   A. Lower central incisor
   B. Upper central incisor
   C. Lower lateral incisor
   D. Upper lateral incisor

4. **True or False.** Gross motor development refers to the small and fine muscles. (11.1.3)

5. Which movements do *not* depend mainly on the large muscles? (11.1.3)
   A. Push, pull and dump objects
   B. Step off low objects
   C. Turns pages in a book one at a time
   D. Climb on play equipment

6. Which of the following physical developmental milestones do toddlers achieve between 12 to 18 months? (11.1.4)
   A. Uses cup and holds spoon in palm
   B. Helps wash hands
   C. Climbs on furniture
   D. Unscrews lids from jars

Figure 11.9 Toddler Physical Milestones

12 to 18 months

- Takes a step or two without support (12 months).
- Walks without assistance (13 to 14 months).
- Walks sideways (16 months) and backward (17 months).
- Creeps up and down stairs (14 months) and walks up and down stairs with help (16 months).
- Squats or stoops without losing balance.
- Throws ball while sitting.
- Pushes, pulls, and dumps objects while sitting.
- Uses cup and holds spoon in palm and attempts to feed self (messy).
- Fills and empties containers.
- Picks up small objects with thumb and index finger.
- Makes a few marks on paper.
- Places pegs in a pegboard.
- Turns two or three book pages at one time.
- Builds a crooked tower of two or three blocks.

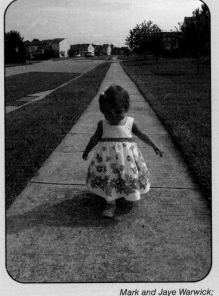

18 to 24 months

- Pushes and pulls objects while walking.
- Does a hurried walk that resembles a run (both feet do not leave surface as they do in running).
- Steps off low objects (first stage in jumping).
- Stands on one foot unsteadily.
- Climbs on furniture.
- Walks stairs without adult help, but needs hand railing or baluster; does not alternate feet.
- Throws ball while standing.
- Squats or bends to "catch" a ball.
- Turns pages in a book one at a time.
- Builds a crooked tower of three or four one-inch cube blocks.
- Strings one to three large beads on a cord.
- Imitates horizontal and vertical lines drawn on paper.
- Tries to fold a piece of paper in half (edges will not meet).
- Holds crayons or pencils with the thumb on one side and fingers on the other side.
- Helps wash hands.
- Scribbles.

24 to 36 months

- Carries a large toy or several smaller ones while walking.
- Stands on tiptoes.
- Runs awkwardly, but cannot stop or change directions easily.
- Jumps down with both feet (24 months); jumps up with both feet (28 months).
- Bends over easily without falling.
- Kicks ball with legs straight and little body involvement.
- Climbs on play equipment.
- Rides push and pedal toys and starts to pedal a tricycle, but finds it difficult.
- "Catches" a ball by bending at the waist to pick it up or by responding to an aerial ball with delayed arm action.
- Strings four beads on a cord.
- Holds pencil or crayon with the thumb and fingers in an adult-like grasp.
- Drinks from a straw; feeds self with a spoon (less messy).
- Uses a fork (awkwardly) to pierce food.
- Builds a somewhat straighter tower of several blocks.
- Unscrews lids from jars.
- Cuts snips in paper.
- Rotates handle (like on a jack-in-the-box toy).
- Is ready to start toilet learning due to the ability to manage pull-down clothing.

Mark and Jaye Warwick;   *John and Stacy Richardson*   *maroke/iStock via Getty Images Plus*

Goodheart-Willcox Publisher

Lesson 11.2

Meeting Nutritional Needs of Toddlers

Key Terms

complementary foods
food allergy
oils
table foods

Learning Outcomes

After studying this lesson, you will be able to

11.2-1 **explain** how a child's eating experience changes during the toddler years.

11.2-2 **describe** the nutritional needs of one- to two-year-old toddlers.

11.2-3 **identify** common feeding problems that might occur during the toddler years and give examples of possible ways to solve these problems.

Reading and Notetaking Activity

Create a table like the one shown. As your teacher presents this chapter, list the main topics and what foods to offer a toddler to reach their nutritional needs. Identify healthful food choices, foods to avoid, and how to prevent feeding problems. Then, team up with a classmate to discuss each other's lists. What items do you need to add? If there is anything you do not understand, seek clarification from your teacher.

The Toddlers' Eating Experience	Healthful Food Choices	Preventing Feeding Problems	MyPlate
Nutritional Needs of One- to Two-Year-Olds			Food Groups
Nutritional Needs of Two- to Three-Year-Olds			What makes a serving?
Special Nutrition Needs			

Introduction

Eating experiences change in the toddler years. Toddlers make a transition from breast- or formula-feeding to eating a variety of table foods with their new tastes and textures. Caregivers often overestimate their toddler's appetite. Toddlers' growth slows after infancy, but toddlers are much more active than infants. Pound for pound, toddlers have lower caloric needs than infants. The importance of good nutrition through a balanced diet is not diminished, however. In fact, a diminished appetite means every bite needs to count.

Getting any toddler to eat a balanced diet every day is quite a challenge. Many toddlers do not achieve this goal. If consistently offered a balanced diet through tasty foods, however, most toddlers eat well. Caregivers should talk with a registered dietitian or a doctor if concerned.

Caregivers often make two mistakes due to their concerns. First, turning mealtimes into sparring matches seldom works and often makes toddlers less likely to comply. Caregivers need to offer the right foods, serve as a good-eating model, and not provide "junk foods" to meet the balance of toddlers' caloric needs. Second, when self-feeding begins, some adults start emphasizing table manners. Due to their lack of eye-hand coordination, toddlers' eating styles define the term "mess hall." Eventually, eating behaviors become more civilized and then table manners can be introduced.

11.2-1 The Toddler's Eating Experience

During the toddler years, the eating experience changes. Children graduate from drinking breast milk or formula and eating baby foods to eating **table foods** (foods prepared for the entire family). In preparing table foods for toddlers, caregivers can use the helpful hints shown in **Figure 11.10**.

Toddlers' appetites decrease as their physical rate of growth slows. Instead of caregivers feeding them every few hours, toddlers are feeding themselves and joining the family for meals. Toddlers' self-feeding skills improve as they learn to use a cup and spoon instead of their fingers.

Figure 11.10 Preparing Table Foods

- Avoid adding salt or sugar to the food served to toddlers. (Caregivers can separate the toddler's serving from the dish before adding these for other family members.)
- Cook and refrigerate all foods properly.
- Continue to introduce new foods at five-day intervals to check for allergies and intolerances.
- Mash foods or cut them into bite-sized pieces for toddlers.
- Offer toddlers six offerings of food (meals and snacks) per day. Use a toddler-sized plate to avoid overwhelming the toddler with too much food.

Goodheart-Willcox Publisher

Because their fine-motor skills are not mature, toddlers can still be messy eaters.

Toddlers are often picky eaters, developing definite food likes and dislikes. In fact, toddlers frequently get on "food kicks" in which the same foods are preferred for days or even weeks and perhaps rejected later. Being assertive about foods and eating is part of what it means to be a toddler.

Because toddlers have so much energy, they often prefer nibbling foods while on-the-go rather than sitting to eat a full meal. Skipping a meal or two and then eating as though they are starved a few hours later is also common. Caregivers often worry that these **erratic** (unusual; inconsistent) eating habits may cause the child harm. Feeding toddlers a variety of healthy, nutritious meals and snacks, however, can help meet their nutritional needs during these active years.

11.2-2 Healthful Food Choices

Meeting nutritional needs in the toddler years is a top priority because children need a variety of nutritious foods for bodily growth and repair. During toddlerhood, the nutritional needs of one- to two-year-olds are different from the nutritional needs of two- to three-year-olds. Some children have special nutritional needs.

Nutritional Needs of One- to Two-Year-Olds

Solid foods that provide the nutrients infants and toddlers need in addition to their breast milk, formula, or whole cow's milk are called **complementary foods**. Having nutritional needs met in this way for infants and toddlers, 6 to 24 months of age, is called *complementary feeding*. Complementary feeding is a transitional diet that bridges exclusive breast- or formula-feeding to family foods.

Two changes occur in the complementary feeding of toddlers from 12 to 24 months. First, with each passing month, toddlers' nutritional needs are met more and more through complementary foods. Second, children who are breast-fed or formula-fed at 12 months of age are then changed to whole cow's milk. (Toddler formulas should not be used unless medically advised, and reduced-fat cow's milk is not usually recommended before two years of age.) Pediatricians may advise a later change to whole cow's milk for toddlers who were premature infants or who have certain illnesses.

Toddlers eat smaller amounts of food than infants or adults, and their daily caloric intakes vary depending on age, size, and activity level. To meet their nutritional needs, toddlers should eat a variety of nutritious foods each day, such as vegetables, fruits, whole-grain breads or cereals, lean meats, and beans. Toddlers also need about two cups of whole milk each day (**Figure 11.11**). Juices should not be served in place of milk because these drinks do not provide the calcium and other minerals toddlers need for proper bone growth and ossification. Furthermore, intake of 100 percent juice should not exceed four ounces daily for this age group.

Caregivers may have difficulty determining their child's varying food needs during the first year of toddlerhood. Following the toddler's cues for fullness and hunger is especially important. Typically, toddlers eat three small meals and two or three snacks each day. Caregivers should let toddlers eat a variety of nutritious foods until they are full. The exception to this recommendation would be if a toddler has a health concern that **merits** (deserves; warrants) a special nutritional plan.

Nutritional Needs of Two- to Three-Year-Olds

Caregivers of two- and three-year-old toddlers can refer to the MyPlate food guidance system to help them determine their child's nutritional needs.

Figure 11.11 In addition to milk, calcium-rich foods, such as yogurt, cheese, and cottage cheese can be offered as part of toddlers' meals and snacks. *Besides milk, what calcium-rich foods do you consume on a daily basis?*

The United States Department of Agriculture (USDA) designed this system to help people two years of age and older make more healthful food and physical activity choices. MyPlate has five major food groups, excluding oils. The following groups are included in the MyPlate plan:

- *Vegetables.* The vegetable group includes a variety of colorful foods, such as spinach, tomatoes, pinto beans, corn, and squash. Vegetables provide vitamins, minerals, and fiber, and most are low in fat and calories. Prepare and serve vegetables without added salt or solid fat.
- *Fruits.* Examples of foods in the fruit group include apples, pears, oranges, bananas, and berries. Fruits supply potassium, fiber, vitamin C, and folate that are often lacking in diets. Choose fresh, frozen, canned, and dried fruits more often and limit intake of 100 percent fruit juice. Unlike whole fruit, 100 percent juice does not contain fiber.
- *Dairy.* The dairy group includes milk and milk products that retain their calcium content, such as cheese and yogurt. Calcium-fortified soy milk is also in this group. These foods provide calcium, protein, potassium, and some are fortified with vitamin D. One- to two-year-olds should have two cups of whole milk daily to support bone growth. Two- to three-year-olds should have two cups of reduced-fat dairy daily to support bone growth.

- *Grains.* Examples from this group include tortillas, breads, and pasta. Grains are an important source of fiber, several B vitamins, and some minerals. Some grains are refined while others contain the entire grain kernel and are thus called *whole grain.* Half the grains a person consumes should be whole grains, such as oatmeal, bulgur, brown rice, or whole-wheat crackers (**Figure 11.12**).
- *Protein foods.* This group includes meat, poultry, fish, beans and peas, eggs, processed soy products, seeds, and nuts. (Nuts are a choking hazard and not recommended for this age group.) Foods in this group provide protein, B vitamins, minerals, iron, and zinc. Meats that are high in saturated fats should be limited. Some types of seafood supply the beneficial omega-3 fatty acids; however, young children should be offered seafood that is lower in mercury such as salmon, trout, and cod.

Although oils are not a food group, oils are essential to a healthy diet. **Oils** are fats that are liquid at room temperature, such as vegetable oils used in cooking. Oil is the main ingredient in mayonnaise, some salad dressings, and margarine spreads. Nuts, olives, seeds, and some fish are naturally high sources of oil. Because oils contain essential fatty acids, there is a limited allowance for oils in the food guide.

Figure 11.12 Whole-grain foods (bottom row) contain the entire grain kernel, whereas refined grains (top row) have been processed for a finer texture and increased shelf life. Whole grains are a more nutritious source of carbohydrates. *How could you identify whole-grain foods in a grocery store?*

Ami Parikh/Shutterstock.com

The USDA recommends offering smaller portion sizes to two- and three-year-olds. By preparing small, healthy meals or snacks five or six times a day at regular intervals, toddlers can often learn to recognize when they are full or hungry. The MyPlate website offers food plans for people according to age, weight, height, gender, and level of physical activity. These food plans show a person's daily recommended amount from each food group. **Figure 11.13** shows a daily food plan for a two-year-old toddler.

Figure 11.13 MyPlate Plan

Food Group Amounts for 1,000 Calories a Day*

Fruits	Vegetables	Grains	Protein	Dairy	Limit
1 cup	1 cup	3 ounces	2 ounces	2 cups	Limit
Focus on whole fruits.	Vary your veggies.	Make half your grains whole grains.	Vary your protein routine.	Move to low-fat or fat-free milk or yogurt.	Drink and eat less sodium, saturated fat, and added sugars.
Focus on whole fruits that are fresh, frozen, canned, or dried.	Aim for this much **each week:** Dark green veggies—½ cup Red and orange veggies—2½ cups Beans and peas—½ cup Starchy veggies—2 cups Other veggies—1½ cups	Find whole-grain foods by reading the Nutrition Facts label and ingredients list.	Mix up your protein foods to include seafood, beans and peas, unsalted nuts and seeds, soy products, eggs, and lean meats and poultry.	Choose fat-free milk, yogurt, and soy beverages (soy milk) to cut back on your saturated fat.	Limit: Sodium to **1,500 milligrams** a day. Saturated fat to **11 grams** a day. Added sugars to **25 grams** a day.
Fruits ChooseMyPlate.gov	Vegetables ChooseMyPlate.gov	Grains ChooseMyPlate.gov	Protein ChooseMyPlate.gov	Dairy ChooseMyPlate.gov	Limit ChooseMyPlate.gov

Be active your way: Children 2 to 5 years old should play actively every day.

Courtesy of the United States Department of Agriculture

Figure 11.13 For good health, a two-year-old needs physical activity as well as these recommended amounts from each food group of MyPlate every day. *Why is it so important to find the balance between food and physical activity?*

Figure 11.14 gives an examples of a menu for one day for a toddler. Food should be cut into bite sized or palm sized pieces making it easier for the toddler to pick up and feed themselves.

Special Nutritional Needs

Food intolerances and allergies require a special diet. A **food allergy** is an abnormal response to a food triggered by the body's immune system. Allergic reactions can be very severe, sometimes causing serious illness or even death. Foods that are responsible for a large percentage of food allergies include milk, eggs, peanuts, fish, shellfish, wheat, soy, and tree nuts. All food labels are required to list the presence of these eight ingredients.

Figure 11.14 Toddler One-Day Menu

Meal	Menu
Breakfast	• Mini oatmeal pancakes with sliced bananas and nut butter • Breastmilk or milk in a cup
Morning snack	• Ripe melon pieces • Plain, vanilla, or fruit yogurt • Water
Lunch	• Meatballs (cut into small pieces) • Plain macaroni or penne pasta • Cooked sweet potato • Breastmilk or milk in a cup
Afternoon snack	• 100% whole wheat unsalted crackers • Cheese cubes • Water
Dinner	• Baked risotto with salmon • Carrots and parsnips • Breastmilk or water
Bedtime snack	• Muffin with applesauce • Breastmilk or milk in a cup

Goodheart-Willcox Publisher

Figure 11.14 Here is an example of a balanced meal for a toddler. Remember that toddler foods should be cut into bite size or sliced into palm size for ease of eating. *What foods do you eat regularly that you think would be good for a toddler to eat?*

A physician or registered dietitian nutritionist can develop a meal plan for children who have food intolerances and allergies. These professionals may also make special food recommendations for the following reasons:

- height and weight are significantly out of the norms
- family history of weight gain
- physical activity level
- anemia and other illnesses
- disorders present at birth, such as PKU and galactosemia

11.2-3 Preventing Feeding Problems

Just like infants, toddlers need to be carefully watched while eating because they can easily choke on foods. Toddlers who are crawling, creeping, walking, or running while eating are more likely to choke than those who are sitting or standing still while eating. Foods that are choking hazards during infancy remain choking hazards during toddlerhood. Examples of foods to avoid include popcorn, hard candies, grapes, raisins, hot dogs sliced in rounds, and peanut butter. Softer raw foods may be safer in larger pieces than in finely chopped pieces because they are easier for the older toddler to hold.

Sometimes toddlers develop feeding problems, such as refusing to eat a meal or new foods, taking only a few bites, or showing a lack of self-feeding skills. Many of these problems stem from the toddler's stage of development—the slowing growth, improving motor and learning skills, and changing social needs. Toddlers work out most feeding problems in time with the help of patient adults.

Careers

Registered Dietitian

A registered dietitian (RD), also called a *registered dietitian nutritionist (RDN)*, has special training in food and nutrition. Registered dietitians assess group or individual nutrition needs, plan food and nutrition programs, and evaluate the effectiveness of a dietary plan. They prevent and treat illnesses by promoting healthy eating habits and recommending dietary modifications.

Career cluster: Health science.

Education: Educational requirements typically include a bachelor's degree in dietetics, foods and nutrition, or a related area and an internship. Many dietitians have advanced degrees.

Licensure and certification requirements vary by state.

Job outlook: Future employment opportunities for RDs or RDNs are projected to grow much faster than the average for all occupations.

To learn more about a career as a registered dietitian nutritionist, visit the United States Department of Labor's *Occupational Outlook Handbook* website. You will also be able to compare the job responsibilities, educational requirements, job outlook, and average pay of registered dietitians with similar occupations.

Photo: Keith Weller/ARS–USDA

Lesson 11.2 Review and Assessment

1. Toddlers slowly graduate from consuming breast milk or formula to consuming _____. (11.2.1)
   A. milk
   B. table food
   C. finger food
   D. juice

2. **True or False.** A one- to two-year-old's diet is in transition. (11.2.2)

3. **True or False.** Two- to three-year-olds should begin eating according to the MyPlate guidelines based on their age, height, weight, gender, and physical activity level. (11.2.2)

4. Which of the following foods may be choking hazards for toddlers? (11.2.3)
   A. Applesauce
   B. Hot dogs
   C. O-shaped cereal
   D. Banana

Meeting Other Physical Needs of Toddlers

Learning Outcomes

After studying this lesson, you will be able to

11.3-1 **list** features to consider when choosing garments for toddlers.

11.3-2 **describe** water play learning experiences during the toddler years.

11.3-3 **explain** the process of toilet learning and identify factors involved.

11.3-4 **identify** children's needs for physical activity during the toddler years.

11.3-5 **identify** children's needs for rest and sleep during the toddler years.

Key Terms

regression
toilet learning
training pants

Reading and Notetaking Activity

In learning about children, you learn a great deal about yourself. As you read this lesson, create a list of the main topics and identify concepts that might teach you about yourself. Place a star beside any concept that especially interests you. After reading the lesson, pick two or three of these ideas and research resources you could use in teaching these concepts to a toddler. Share the resources you found with your classmates.

Introduction

During the toddler years, children still depend on adults to provide for their needs and to keep them healthy and safe. To meet toddlers' physical needs, adults make sure toddlers are fed, clothed, cleaned, and rested. Adults also guide toddlers' self-care skills, such as dressing themselves, bathing, and toileting. As toddlers learn self-care skills, they can begin to meet their physical needs.

As you read in the opening of Lesson 11.2, meeting a toddler's nutritional needs can be challenging due to the toddler's growing will. In like manner, the **indomitable** (incapable of being subdued; stubborn-like) will of the toddler also affects meeting other physical needs. For example, toddlers often take issue with wearing clothing appropriate for the weather or activity. They may also refuse to cooperate with or learn skills needed for grooming or toileting. Success occurs only with adult patience and some creative methods of getting the toddler to comply.

11.3-1 Clothing

Choosing the right clothes and shoes for toddlers is important. Proper clothing helps toddlers stay active, comfortable, and safe. Clothing also stands the strain of constant movement and messy play.

Choosing Garments

Although toddlers grow more slowly than infants, they still outgrow their clothes quickly. The way clothing fits is important for the toddler. Clothes that are too tight can bind and restrict movement while clothes that are too loose can be uncomfortable and unsafe.

To ensure proper fit, caregivers often have toddlers try on garments rather than rely on garment sizing, which can be confusing. For example, some companies use descriptive terms, such as *small*, *medium*, and *large*, as their sizes. Other companies set sizes by age, such as *18 mo. (1T)*, *24 mo. (2T)*, *3T*, and *4T*. The most accurate sizing method for toddlers' garments is the weight range or weight and height ranges. A few companies provide more than one type of sizing on their labels for easy comparison. Sizes vary from one company to the next, but an example is provided in **Figure 11.15**.

During the toddler years, children are learning how to undress and dress themselves. Undressing is always easier than dressing. For example, it is easier to pop open snaps than match both sides of snaps and press them together. Toddlers can often push down their clothes for toileting, but may find it difficult to get both under- and outer-garments

up and straight when dressing. Because of this, caregivers often consider self-dressing features when choosing clothing for toddlers.

Figure 11.15 **Toddler Clothing Sizes**

Size	Height in Inches	Weight in Pounds
18 mo./1T	30¾ to 32	22 to 24
24 mo./2T	32½ to 35½	24½ to 28
3T	36 to 38½	28½ to 32
4T	39 to 41	32½ to 36
5T	41½ to 43	36½ to 41

Goodheart-Willcox Publisher

Kamira/Shutterstock.com

Self-dressing features in toddlers' clothes make dressing and undressing without help easier. Some self-dressing features are critical when toddlers begin toilet learning because they must be able to remove clothing very quickly to avoid toileting accidents. For example, teachers of toddlers in group settings often request toddlers wear elastic-waist pants or shorts instead of jumpsuits or overalls. Belts and difficult clothing fasteners, such as small buttons, are also a problem.

In addition to self-dressing features, caregivers consider other features when choosing garments for toddlers. These features may include safety, comfort, growth features, quality construction, and easy care. **Figure 11.16** shows some examples of each of these features.

Fitting Shoes

Toddlers need shoes to protect their feet from cold, dampness, and harmful objects. Shoes that fit properly have ½ inch of space between the large toe and shoe when the toddler stands. They also have a flexible sole and snug-fitting heel. New shoes are recommended over hand-me-downs, except for rain or snow boots worn over shoes.

Figure 11.16 Important Features in Toddler Clothes

Feature	Examples
Safety	• Flame-resistant (will burn, but smolders slowly rather than flaming when on fire) • No drawstrings or loose buttons, fasteners, or trim • Belts, ties, and sashes fastened to the garment securely to prevent tripping, choking, or strangling • Bright-colored clothing (increases ability to see toddlers)
Comfort	• Made of lightweight and absorbent fabrics • Made of stretch fabrics • Elastic encased or nonbinding • Fullness in pant legs to permit knee bending and stooping with ease • Collars and sleeves that do not rub or bind • Coats, sweaters, and jackets that can fit over clothes without binding • Underwear that is not binding • Neck openings large enough for ease of dressing
Growth features	• Made of stretch fabrics • Dresses without definite waistlines • Pants and skirts with elastic or adjustable waistbands • Adjustable shoulder straps • Clothes with deep hems, large seams, and pleats or tucks that can be easily let out • Two-piece outfits
Quality construction	• Reinforcement at points of strain such as seams, knees, pockets, and pocket edges • Stitches that are even and not too long • Seams that are flat, smooth, and finished • Securely attached fasteners and trims • Built-in growth features, such as deep hems • Patterns are matched at seams
Easy care	• Washable (especially machine washable with other colors) • Little or no ironing needed • Easy to mend

Goodheart-Willcox Publisher

Each foot is shaped differently. With even a little wear, shoes conform to a person's foot.

Because the bones and muscles of the foot are developing, shoe fit is very important for toddlers' proper growth and comfort. Shoes that fit improperly can cause permanent damage to the child's feet. Toddlers often outgrow their shoes before they wear them out. The average rate of foot growth for toddlers is one shoe size every one to two months.

During the toddler years, children have flat feet because their arches are relaxed. For many children, this flat-footed look disappears around three years of age. Going barefooted or wearing socks without shoes is good for the development of the arch. Shoes, even high-top shoes, do not provide support.

11.3-2 Bathing

Although toddlers may want to try to bathe themselves, they are not yet able to do so. Toddlers still need close supervision and are not safe to be left alone. Caregivers should never leave toddlers unattended or unsupervised while they are in or near water—not even for a minute. Toddlers can drown in just 1 inch of water.

Regular bathtubs are quite spacious for toddlers. Young toddlers may feel more secure bathing in a child's tub placed inside the regular bathtub. Other caregivers find their toddlers enjoy special bathtub seats designed specifically for toddlers.

Toddlers have fun during bath time splashing water and trying to hold slippery soap. Bath time for toddlers is a good opportunity to engage in water play. Children can learn many concepts from playing in the tub (**Figure 11.17**). Special bath toys are available for toddler water play, but toys can also be made easily from household objects. Unsafe items for toddler floor play are also unsafe for tub play.

11.3-3 Toilet Learning

Toilet learning is one of the most discussed aspects of the toddler years. **Toilet learning** is the process by which adults help children control their excretory systems, namely bowel movements and urination. Experts have found two things are certain in toilet learning. First, the timing of learning varies from toddler to toddler. Some children may be ready to begin toilet learning around 18 to 24 months of age while others are not ready until much later. Second, many toddlers do not complete the learning process quickly. Learning may take most of the toddler years and perhaps even longer to complete.

Figure 11.17 Water Play Learning Experiences

- Some toys float and some sink.
- Water power, such as moving water with your hands or feet, can push floating toys.
- Water can be held for a brief time in the cupped hand or in a toy with "holes."
- Water makes all things wet.
- Water can splash, squirt, and drip.
- The bottom of the tub can be seen through clear water. Bubbles make it harder to see the bottom.
- Soap makes bubbles that pop and disappear.
- Solid objects can be pushed down through the water.
- Play can be described by naming objects (boat, cup, bubbles) and actions (push, pop or burst, splash, squirt, drip, float, or sink).

Goodheart-Willcox Publisher

OlgaKorica/iStock via Getty Images Plus

Health

Physical and Emotional Factors of Toilet Learning

Toilet learning involves factors like physical development, motor skills, and emotional readiness. The physical and motor skills include the ability to

- feel a full bowel and bladder. Until about 15 months of age, children have bowel movements and pass urine without knowing in advance or realizing they have done so. Many disposable diapers and disposable pull-up pants do not help with the feeling of wetness because they are designed to keep the skin drier.
- know what the sensation of needing to eliminate means in time to get to the potty.
- control muscles used for holding in or letting go. These muscles, which are low in the body, are among the last to develop. (This is a good example of the cephalocaudal development principle.) Nerves can control these muscles around 18 months of age. Children tend to learn to control bowel movements before they learn to control their bladders.
- walk (or often run) to the potty.
- remove or push down clothes.
- redress and wash hands with help.

For toilet learning to work, emotional readiness must occur at the same time the child is physically developed. Toddlers must see the need to use the potty. Busy toddlers often do not want to sit on the potty for the needed amount of time. Saying *no* to using the toilet is part of the self-will toddlers want to express. Toddlers may also need to master fears of falling in, the flushing water, and even fear of bowel movements.

Photo: wavebreakmedia/Shutterstock.com

Readiness for Toilet Learning

Before toddlers can begin toilet learning, they must be developmentally ready. Toddlers vary in age of complete control, or ability to wait until they are at the toilet to release bodily waste. The average age for complete day control is 28 months of age, but the normal range varies greatly. Usually, a child must be able to stay dry for two or more hours before he or she can begin to learn.

Three years of age is often a difficult time to begin toilet learning. This is because three-year-old toddlers experience a brief, but intense stage of *regression* in their desire to be independent. **Regression** means going back to an earlier stage of development. A toddler should not begin toilet learning during regression or periods of family or child stress.

Even before toddlers are ready for toilet learning, adults can help them see what is expected. If an adult notes the child is eliminating, they can say something to make the child aware of it. Adults can also show the child the potty they will use. Special equipment available for toilet learning may include a child-sized toilet, a potty chair, or a potty seat that fits on many standard-sized toilet seats. When standard toilets are used (with or without toddler seats), toddlers often need a sturdy stool near the toilet to climb onto and turn around before sitting. Some toddlers want to sit on the potty first with their clothes on to check it out.

Starting Toilet Learning

Once toilet learning begins, adults need to provide a supportive learning environment for the toddler and accept success and failure in a matter-of-fact way. Toddlers need some encouragement, but too much adds pressure.

No matter how much care is taken, accidents will happen. Being prepared, however, helps prevent accidents from causing too much stress for toddlers or adults. **Training pants** (pants made of disposable diaper material, pants with a multi-layered cotton fabric crotch, or specially designed pants for wading or swimming use) help lessen the mess of accidents. Using diapers during sleep times, when traveling, or when away from home for long periods makes learning less stressful, too. Caregivers should stop the learning routine during an illness or if a child shows signs of stress.

If the toddler is in a group program, toilet learning must be a team effort—child, family, and caregivers. Toilet learning is something adults do *with* a child. A constant exchange of information between the home and the program is needed. Child care programs are often good places for toilet learning. This is due to the experience of the staff, child-sized bathrooms, and the program focus on helping children develop competence in self-care. Toddlers in child care programs often learn rapidly because they see their friends learning toileting skills.

11.3-4 Physical Activity

Physical activity is important for toddlers because it increases the strength and endurance of the cardiac and skeletal muscles and improves motor skills. Physical activity encourages attention during quiet learning times because it prevents restlessness.

Because most toddlers are so active, they usually get all the exercise they need. A few toddlers, however, are too **sedentary** (characterized by little physical activity). Sedentary toddlers spend up to 75 percent of their waking day in non-active ways. Most research suggests toddlers spend at least 50 percent of each day in active play. How can caregivers encourage sedentary toddlers to be

more active? The following ideas can encourage an active lifestyle:

- Eliminate or reduce time spent on all digital media to one hour or less daily.
- Select play equipment designed for active movement, such as balls and pedal riding toys.
- Plan a few movement activities, such as moving to music or navigating an obstacle course.
- Take the toddler to a playground daily, if possible (**Figure 11.18**).
- Plan activities keeping in mind motor milestones.
- Set an example of an active lifestyle and include toddlers in it.

11.3-5 Rest and Sleep

Toddlers often sleep fewer hours and take fewer naps than infants. Between one and three years of age, children typically need 11 to 14 hours of sleep. Around 18 months, toddlers often reduce naps to once daily for about one to three hours. Between 31 and 36 months, naps begin to disappear.

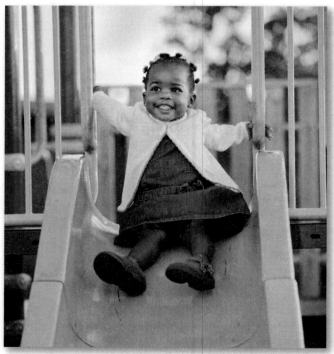

Flashon Studio/Shutterstock.com

Figure 11.18 Taking toddlers to the playground is an effective way of encouraging physical activity in their lives. *What kinds of physical activities can toddlers participate in at playgrounds?*

Toddlers, even when tired, are more likely than babies to resist rest and sleep. Bedtime problems stem partly from the toddlers' struggle for independence. Often, caregivers become physically tired from coping with toddlers who resist sleep. They may even feel stress if bedtime becomes a battle of wills. The following tips may help caregivers handle naptime and bedtime problems:

- Avoid scheduling naptime too close to bedtime.
- Maintain a consistent sleep schedule. Have the toddler go to bed at the same time every night. If the schedule must be adjusted, shift the toddler's bedtime gradually.
- Notify the toddler about 20 minutes before naptime or bedtime. Use a neutral sign, such as a clock (not a person), to signal the hour.
- Set a bedtime ritual or routine that includes only restful activities, such as a warm bath, drink of water, story, song, and hug. Naptime rituals can be developed, too.
- Tell a toddler who resists sleep that they do not have to sleep, but do need to stay in bed. (Caregivers can purchase an alarm device that has a night-light that comes on after a set period of time. Children are taught to stay in bed until they see the light.) Refer to daytime naps as "rest" and provide the toddler with books.
- Comfort a fearful toddler or a toddler who wakes during the night with nightmares. Provide a night-light in the toddler's room to ease fears or encourage the use of a security object, such as a stuffed animal or blanket.
- Return the toddler to bed if they get up during naptime or bedtime. Meet any real needs, but calmly refuse nonessential requests.

Caregivers' actions determine toddlers' behavior. From adults' responses and actions, toddlers may learn to stay in bed during rest time. If caregivers are usually **lenient** (easy-going; not strict), however, toddlers may instead learn tricks to get what they want. Learning to stay in bed helps toddlers get their needed rest. Caregivers also need this time to meet their own needs.

Lesson 11.3 Review and Assessment

1. _____ features in toddlers' clothes make dressing and undressing without help easier. (11.3.1)
   A. Sizing
   B. Comfort
   C. Self-dressing
   D. Construction

2. **True or False.** Teachers of toddlers in group settings often request toddlers wear elastic-waist pants or shorts. (11.3.1)

3. Which of the following can toddlers *not* learn with water play learning experiences? (11.3.2)
   A. Some toys float and some sink
   B. Soap makes bubbles that pop and disappear
   C. Object permanence
   D. Solid objects can be pushed down through the water

4. At what age are children typically ready for toilet learning? (11.3.3)
   A. 6 to 8 months
   B. 8 to 12 months
   C. 12 to 18 months
   D. 18 to 24 months

5. Most research suggests toddlers spend at least _____ percent of each day in active play. (11.3.4)
   A. 50
   B. 75
   C. 25
   D. 10

6. Between one and three years of age, children typically need _____ hours of sleep. (11.3.5)
   A. 10 to 13
   B. 11 to 14
   C. 12 to 15
   D. 13 to 16

Chapter 11

Review and Assessment

Summary

Lesson 11.1

11.1-1 During the toddler years, a child's brain continues to mature. Brain volume, synaptic density, and myelination increase rapidly.

11.1-2 Toddlers grow more slowly than infants and grow at different rates due to heredity and environment.

11.1-2 Toddlers refine gross-motor skills, such as walking, climbing, and throwing. They also learn to run, jump, and catch objects.

11.1-3 Fine-motor skills, including the toddler's ability to grasp writing tools, depend on the child's eye-hand coordination.

11.1-4 The refinement of brain wiring, greater muscle control, and a positive environment enable toddlers to develop their physical capabilities rapidly.

Lesson 11.2

11.2-1 Toddlers eat table foods and can feed themselves.

11.2-2 One- to two-year-olds engage in a diet called complementary feeding, which is a transition diet that includes breast milk, formula, or whole cow's milk and solids.

11.2-2 Two- to three-year-olds should eat according to the MyPlate food guidance system's recommendations.

11.2-3 A number of feeding problems can arise because of toddlers' slowing growth rates and growing independence. In some cases, toddlers will have special nutritional needs due to food allergies or other factors.

Lesson 11.3

11.3-1 Important clothing features for toddlers include safety, fit, comfort, growth features, quality construction, and easy care.

11.3-1 Toddlers still need close supervision during bath time.

11.3-2 Before children can begin toilet learning, their bodies must be physically ready.

11.3-3 Children should not be shamed or punished when they have accidents. When successful, they need encouragement.

11.3-3 Toddlers should be encouraged to engage in physical activity so they can form healthy habits early in life.

11.3-4 Sleep and rest requirements for toddlers have changed since infancy. Bedtime problems can develop, but adults can establish quiet nighttime rituals and try other tips to lessen sleep problems.

College and Career Portfolio

Portfolio Samples

Portfolios for college or job applications often include *samples of work*. A sample of work might be an especially well-written paper, a persuasive presentation, or a hypothetical lesson plan. To identify your portfolio samples, complete the following activities.

- Review samples of your work of which you are most proud. These samples might be from your schoolwork, from your participation in an extracurricular activity, or from personal projects you have completed.
- Consult with your teacher or with a college and career counselor about which samples of work would be most appropriate for your portfolio. Create a list of samples you want to use.

Recall and Application

1. **True or False.** By three years of age, the brain reaches 80 percent of adult volume. (11.1.1)
2. **True or False.** A toddler's growth slows after their first birthday. (11.1.2)
3. **True or False.** Between two and three years of age, a child has a full set of deciduous teeth (baby teeth). (11.1.2)
4. **True or False**. Small muscle development refers to the development of the trunk and arm and leg muscles. (11.1.3)
5. At what age can a toddler catch a ball by bending at the waist to pick it up? (11.1.4)
   A. 12 to 18 months
   B. 18 to 24 months
   C. 24 to 36 months
   D. Any time during toddlerhood
6. **True or False.** Toddlers make a transition from breast or formula-feeding to table foods. (11.2.1)
7. **True or False.** Toddlers eat smaller amounts of food than infants and adults, and their daily caloric intakes vary depending on age, size, and activity level. (11.2.2)
8. **True or False.** Foods that are choking hazards during infancy are not choking hazards during toddlerhood. (11.2.3)
9. Toddler clothing sizes are listed by _____. (11.3.1)
   A. age   C. pattern size
   B. height or weight   D. style
10. **True or False.** Toddlers still need supervision during bath time. (11.3.2)
11. **True or False.** Until about 15 months of age, children have bowel movements and pass urine without knowing in advance or realizing they have done so. (11.3.3)
12. **True or False.** Physical activity is important for toddlers because it increases the strength and endurance of the cardiac and skeletal muscles and improves motor skills. (11.3.4)
13. Which of the following statements is *not* true regarding rest and sleep for toddlers? (11.3.5)
    A. Avoid scheduling naptime too close to bedtime.
    B. Maintain a consistent sleep schedule.
    C. Insist that a toddler sleeps during rest/nap time.
    D. Return the toddler to bed if they get up during naptime or bedtime.

Critical Thinking

1. **Identify.** Identify ways in which the brain develops and other organs mature during the toddler years that enable toddlers to engage in more activities and learn through new experiences. How important is biological maturation to toddler growth? Explain your answer.

2. **Make inferences.** Based on your own experiences and learning, which factor do you think affects height and weight more: heredity or environment? In teams, debate this topic and explain the reasoning behind your answer.

3. **Draw conclusions.** The text indicates that toddlers walk at a rate of about 170 steps per minute. Walk quickly, counting your own steps for one minute as a partner times you. How do your results compare with the average rate for toddlers? What conclusions can you draw from this experiment?

4. **Analyze.** One- to two-year-olds have a different eating experience than two- to three-year-olds. Analyze how these eating experiences differ, and imagine what it would be like to transition from eating during infancy to eating during late toddlerhood. Write two to three paragraphs reflecting on how a child's experience of eating might change.

5. **Compare and contrast.** Compare the MyPlate recommendations for toddlers with those for you—especially in terms of daily amounts for the food groups. What does this comparison indicate in terms of planning family meals?

6. **Determine.** Review the water play learning experiences described in Figure 11.17. Why are these learning experiences important? Determine how each learning experience prepares toddlers to learn more about themselves and their environments outside of the tub.

7. **Evaluate.** Evaluate ways in which toddlers' habits of physical activity and rest might affect them later in life. How might being sedentary during toddlerhood affect a child's physical activity in the future? How might not getting enough sleep as a toddler impact a young child's sleeping pattern?

8. **Cause and effect.** Review the tips for handling toddler bedtime problems, and then determine how each tip achieves its intended effect. Why does each tip succeed in encouraging rest and sleep? Based on the reasons for the tips covered in this chapter, write your own list of tips for toddlers' caregivers.

Core Skills

1. **Writing.** As a group or class project, write a one- or two-page brochure explaining the progression of toddlers' motor skills. Include information on the order (and approximate age) when toddlers learn motor skills. Also, explain the motor actions used when walking, running, climbing, jumping, throwing, and catching. Include illustrations for these actions. Have your teacher check your brochure, then make copies. Give copies to caregivers and adults at a program that serves toddlers, such as a child care program or preschool.

2. **Art and speaking.** As a class, divide into three groups, and assign each group one of the age ranges covered in this chapter's table of physical developmental milestones (Figure 11.8). Then, create an art project that involves drawing based on a model, coloring within lines, or assembling art supplies. Assign your art project to one of the other groups in the class, and then review the project you have been assigned. In your group, attempt to complete the art project with only the motor skills your age range of toddlers can perform. For example, using your assigned toddler age range and keeping in mind the milestones these toddlers have achieved and have yet to achieve, you must hold any art supplies or utensils and draw and color as these toddlers would likely perform. After completing your art projects, grade them as a class and discuss what you learned about toddlers' motor skills.

3. **Technology and speaking.** In child care centers, meeting the special nutritional needs of toddlers with food allergies can be challenging. Imagine you are a teacher at a child care center and several of your toddlers have food allergies. The caregivers have inquired as to how you will protect their children against food allergens. Create a slide show presentation outlining how you will keep the toddlers who have food allergies safe while still providing for their nutritional needs. Deliver your presentation to the class.

4. **Research, technology, and listening.** Using reliable online or print resources, research toddlers' feeding problems. Working with a partner, use a doll to role-play one feeding problem and employ some recommended methods for solving the problem. Film your role-play and play it for the class. Ask your classmates for any feedback they would give to the caregivers in the role-play. Listen closely to your classmates' role-plays so you can offer helpful feedback.

5. **Reading and writing.** Many products for toddlers are constructed with dressing ease in mind. Using online or print resources, find an advertisement for one of these products and then print it or make a copy. Read the advertisement and identify how the product makes dressing and undressing toddlers easier. Then consider: Would this product be effective? Is there anything that could be added to or changed about the product to make it even more effective? Write a two-page report detailing your findings and assessing the product.

6. **Research and writing.** In small groups, research toilet learning strategies currently popular among caregivers. You may find these strategies in parenting magazines, online, or in published parenting books. Choose three toilet learning strategies that especially interest you and then write a short article marketing these strategies. In your article, explain the benefits of your chosen strategies and argue for their effectiveness

based on the information covered in this chapter.

7. **CTE Career Readiness Practice.** As a new employee at a child care center, you are taking on the challenge of making your center a healthy environment for young children. Part of your job includes taking initiative to serve healthy meals and snacks. Use the menu planner on the MyPlate website to plan healthful meals, compare food choices to recommendations for meeting nutrient needs, and identify ways to improve physical activities. Plan a one-week menu (meals and snacks) for the two- to three-year-old toddlers at your center. Your menu should satisfy all of the daily values these toddlers should consume. Print your menu and bring it to class. Working with a partner, exchange menus and discuss the various options chosen.

Observations

1. Compare a picture of yourself as a baby to a picture of yourself as a toddler. If you do not have these pictures of yourself, then find two pictures of the same child—one from infancy and one from toddlerhood. Observe how height and weight, body proportions, bones and teeth, and fat and muscles change over time. Write a two- to three-page essay analyzing the changes that took place and relating them to what you learned in this chapter.

2. In small groups, visit a home with a toddler or a child care center and observe how the toddler walks. If you are unable to arrange a visit, watch a video of a toddler online. Which of the common walking traits described in this chapter does the toddler exhibit? Is the toddler in a safe and supportive environment for walking? Discuss each group member's observations. Finally, compile your findings into a digital presentation and share with the class.

Intellectual Development of Toddlers

Essential Question

How do toddlers make a transition to learning through mental rather than physical actions, and how can caregivers encourage toddlers' curiosity and active exploration?

Case Study   Which Language Should Be the Language of Instruction?

As a class, read the case study and discuss the questions that follow. After you finish studying the chapter, discuss this case study again. Have your opinions changed based on what you learned?

A new toddler-preschool program will serve children of Spanish-speaking families in a mostly English-speaking town. The teachers and director are deciding which language (Spanish or English) to use as the language of instruction in the center by considering the following factors:

- *The optimal time for learning a second language is before 10 years of age.*
- *When a second language is introduced to young children, the best technique is immersion in the language. Immersion, however, often results in children becoming less fluent in their first language.*
- *Many people who are bilingual are not equally fluent in both languages. They have a dominant or preferred language.*

Because English is the dominant language in the schools and community, the children may see English as the more valued language by the school-age years.

Give It Some Thought

1. Which language would you vote for to be the language of instruction in this center? Why?
2. How do you think these children's feelings of competence could be affected if English were chosen as the language of instruction? If Spanish were chosen?
3. When schools have more than two primary languages represented, which language should become the language of instruction?
4. Who should make decisions about the language of instruction? The parents? The local schools? The state government? The federal government? Why?

How Toddlers Learn

Key Terms

collective symbolism
deferred imitation
mental imagery
pretense
solitary symbolic play

Learning Outcomes

After studying this lesson, you will be able to

12.1-1 **summarize** brain development during the toddler years.

12.1-2 **describe** how Piaget believed toddlers complete the last two substages of his sensorimotor stage.

12.1-3 **explain** how scaffolding strategies can be used to assist with toddlers' learning according to Vygotsky's Sociocultural Theory.

Reading and Notetaking Activity

Before reading, skim the headings in this chapter. List the headings to create an outline for taking notes during reading and class discussions. As you read the lesson, record any questions that come to mind. Indicate where the answer to each question can be found within the text, by asking your teacher, in another book, on the internet, or by reflecting on your knowledge and experiences. After completing the chapter, ask your teacher any questions you still have unanswered.

Introduction

Toddlers are eager to learn and curious about everyone and everything. When learning about and working at a task they choose, toddlers stay with the task until they are satisfied with the results. Because toddlers have their own agenda, however, they may not always be interested in learning what adults want them to learn.

During the toddler years, children truly begin to understand their environment. They remain holistic learners. Toddlers younger than two years old learn about objects and what happens when they manipulate these objects. They must meet their goals through physical trial-and-error. Because older toddlers learn to think before acting, they plan new ways to achieve goals. Toddlers also become able communicators as they learn new words and speak in short sentences.

12.1-1 Toddlerhood: A Biologically Primed Time for Learning

As you read in the chapter on toddlers' physical development, the brain undergoes a growth spurt during toddlerhood. The toddler's brain becomes super dense in synapses and has a high concentration of neurotransmitters. Glial cells responsible for myelination are also very active. All of these happenings are genetically preprogrammed and should occur except in cases of brain abnormalities or trauma.

The dense wiring allows for new learning, and myelination increases speed of connections. Used wirings remain and become stronger, but unused wirings will be pruned soon after toddlerhood. The more a pathway is used the stronger the wiring becomes. The brain will prune wiring that is used less frequently. Often, the wiring is experience-dependent (**Figure 12.1**).

The toddler's brain continues to develop in the sensory and motor areas. Toddlers can make fine sensory discriminations, such as seeing various shades of a given color or hearing small differences in sounds. These sensory discriminations lead to rather accurate perceptual concepts, but not to logical understandings. Furthermore, gross- and fine-motor skills are becoming very coordinated, and motor activities, such as assembling take-apart objects, will enhance learning.

Brain development in toddlerhood allows for the great intellectual advance called **mental imagery** (seeing in the "mind's eye" or hearing in the "mind's ear" in the absence of a stimulus). Mental imagery will eventually lead to abstract thinking and creativity. Unlike infants who simply adjust their actions to the properties of objects (moving after a rolling ball; hitting metal objects to make loud sounds), toddlers begin to impose their mental ideas on objects as seen in pretend play. Soon a block is not just for stacking but can be a chair or a shaker for a spice.

Development in the language and memory areas of the brain aids toddlers' thinking. The language of their world aids toddlers by

- refining and extending current knowledge. Verbalization of adults helps toddlers see important criteria in their problem-solving activities. For example, the caregiver might say, "Because you kept your blocks *straight*, your tower will not fall so easily." Now the toddler sees one important criterion, alignment, for physical stability in block building.
- simplifying learning of difficult new concepts. Language clues help people think by focusing their attention on specific things. For example, in an experiment, toddlers were asked to match patterned blocks. Toddlers simply told to match the blocks had a more difficult time with the task than toddlers given some verbal clues about the different patterns—those with *stripes* and those with *dots*. Even mature listeners and readers get constant clues from language through words, such as *similar to, for example, in contrast, on the other hand, essential question, in three* ways, and *to summarize*.
- storing in memory what has been learned. Verbalization greatly aids remembering. For example, toddlers who tell about their trip to the zoo or who retell a story about the zoo by looking at the pictures in the book will retain more information than toddlers who do not verbalize their experiences. Frequent retelling makes the memory even stronger.

ArtMarie/E+ via Getty Images

Figure 12.1 Experiences dictate which brain connections are strengthened, and the lack of certain experiences determines which are pruned. These experiences are vital to learning within windows of opportunity. For instance, picking out clothes is giving this toddler experience in *independence*, a skill for which the window of opportunity ends in the toddler years. *What other windows of opportunity end in the toddler years? (Review Figure 2.8 for the windows of opportunity.)*

Brain development leads to many windows of opportunity for toddlers. On the other hand, toddlerhood is a period of vulnerability if environmental conditions are not optimal. Optimal conditions include nutrition adequate to support the fast-growing brain, general physical health, a rich play environment surrounded by quality language exposure, and an emotionally supportive, stress-free world.

12.1-2 Piaget's Cognitive-Developmental Theory

Piaget uses stages to describe children's intellectual development. In the first stage, called the *sensorimotor stage*, children from birth to two years of age learn through their senses and motor actions.

The sensorimotor stage includes six substages. During infancy, babies work through the first four substages. During the toddler years, Piaget believed children complete the last two substages (**Figure 12.2**).

In substage 5 (called *tertiary circular reactions*), younger toddlers, around 12 to 18 months of age, learn by discovering new ways to solve problems through physical trial and error. In substage 6 (called *mental imagery or representation*), older toddlers, around 18 to 24 months of age, begin to think about how to solve a problem without using physical actions. By the end of the toddler years, a few children may enter Piaget's second stage of intellectual development, called the *preoperational stage*. (You will learn about the preoperational stage later in this text.)

Figure 12.2 Piaget's Cognitive-Development Theory

Stages and Substages	Characteristics
Stage 1: Sensorimotor stage (birth to 2 years)	• Children learn through the senses and physical actions in six substages.
Substages 1 and 2	• Involve the baby's own body.
Substages 3 and 4	• Involve people and objects.
Substages 5 and 6 (12 to 24 months)	• Involve creative actions and thinking before acting.
Substage 5: Tertiary circular reactions (12 to 18 months)	• Sometimes called the substage of "little scientists." • Experiment with objects to receive various results. • Notice some attributes of objects (sometimes color, sometimes size). • Use physical trial and error to solve problems. • Imitate behaviors they have never done before; imitate only in the presence of the model. • Look for hidden objects in the last place seen.
Substage 6: Mental imagery or representation (18 to 24 months)	• Can think about different ways to solve problems without using physical actions in a trial and error way. • Can think through the sequence of a few steps to solve a problem. • Begin to do some deferred imitation. • Know all objects and people are someplace. Hunt for objects in every possible place (completion of object permanence).
Stage 2: Preoperational stage (2 to 7 years)	• Children learn through symbols, but with logical limitations.
Stage 3: Concrete operational stage (7 to 11 years)	• Children begin to think logically, but base their logic on past experiences.
Stage 4: Formal operational stage (11 years of age and older)	• Older children, teens, and adults reason abstractly.

Goodheart-Willcox Publisher

Substage 5

Piaget called children in substage 5 "little scientists" because they are so busy exploring and discovering the possibilities in their world. In substage 5 toddlers take another intellectual step as they further their curiosity and show lots of interest in new actions. After discovering one way to use an object, toddlers are interested in discovering what else they can do with the same object. Children in this substage vary their actions to see why different actions get different results.

As you read, Piaget called substage 5 *tertiary circular reactions*. He used the term **tertiary** (third in a sequence) because it is the third major change in intellectual development. (The first two changes happened during infancy.) He used the term *circular* because toddlers enjoy repeating their actions. Repeating actions helps toddlers verify their observations, which is similar to how scientific findings are verified through additional research and experiments. In substage 5, children's learning is characterized by working toward a goal, using imitation and pretense, and having a greater understanding of object permanence.

Working Toward a Goal

In this substage, toddlers' actions involve reaching a goal. Toddlers experiment by using physical trial and error methods to solve problems. They first try what worked in the past. If this is not successful, they change their behaviors. As toddlers are exploring, experimenting, and discovering ways to reach their goals, they get into everything and can cause **havoc** (chaos) in their environment.

To an adult, the toddler's goal may be obvious. For example, a toddler might try to take a lid off a container to see what's inside. Sometimes, the toddler's goal may not be so obvious to the adult. The child may seem to be only playing with or throwing objects. In **actuality** (reality; fact), the child is trying to figure out how these objects work. Young toddlers want to know what happens to objects when they roll, shake, throw, or move them in other ways. Repeating actions with minor changes helps toddlers learn the best way to reach their goals. These experiments are signs of developing intellectual skills.

Using Imitation and Pretense

A toddler's imitation with the model present is quick and accurate. For example, toddlers can watch others make facial expressions and gestures (nod, wave) and listen to others' sounds and words and quickly imitate these (**Figure 12.3**). Imitation is a major way of learning.

Figure 12.3 Toddlers are likely to imitate their caregivers, other adults, and other children. *What lessons have you learned through imitation? Why is imitation a valuable learning tool?*

Dragon Images/Shutterstock.com

Pretense, symbolic actions seen in play that mimic real situations, also begins. There are different levels of pretense. Piaget referred to the first level of pretense as **solitary symbolic play**. Young toddlers pretend using either real objects or realistic toys; they cannot use objects to represent something entirely different. At this level, the toddler pretends to do something that has to do with themselves. For example, the toddler might pretend to eat. The pretense does not involve dolls, stuffed animals, or other people, although the young toddler might try to get others to watch the play. The second level of pretense, called **collective symbolism**, occurs in substage 6.

Having Greater Understanding of Object Permanence

Toddlers develop a greater understanding of object permanence in substage 5. Before this stage, infants would look for a missing object where it was *first seen or found*. Infants cannot conceive that an object might be where they last saw it. Unlike infants, young toddlers will look for a completely hidden object where it was *last seen or found*. They cannot, however, imagine the object might be hidden in some other place. Therefore, understanding of object permanence is *almost* complete in substage 5.

Substage 6

Younger toddlers do not have very developed thought processes. They learn through trial-and-error methods. Around 18 to 24 months, toddlers' intellectual abilities change again as they enter substage 6. Toddlers this age and older now think about what they do before they do it. The three main characteristics that describe substage 6 are identified by thinking. Toddlers think to achieve goals, imitate and engage in pretense, and locate hidden objects.

When you see toddlers pause in mid-action, they are probably thinking. They will "figure things out" intellectually instead of testing them physically. For example, the two-year-old realizes a large object will not fit through a small opening in a container. They mentally visualize trying to put the object through the opening before concluding the object is too big to fit. A one-year-old, however, would try to push the large object through the small opening and then realize the object does not fit.

Older toddlers will mainly think in terms of actions. They even identify objects in terms of actions. For example, a 30-month-old toddler may answer the question, "What is a ball?" with the reply, "To play with," or "To roll."

Thinking to Achieve Goals

Thinking shows in the older toddler's way of reaching goals. For example, the toddler's goal may be to reach a toy on a high playroom shelf. The toddler thinks about the stepstool they use in the bathroom to reach the sink. The toddler then gets the stool to reach the object on the playroom shelf. If the toddler cannot bring the stool into the playroom, they may use another object as a stool to reach the toy on the shelf. The toddler has thought through how to reach the goal.

Thinking Involved in Imitation and Pretense

Young toddlers can only imitate a person's actions when the model is present. Older toddlers, however, can imitate a person's actions without the model present. The ability to recall and later imitate someone's behavior is called **deferred imitation**. (**Deferred** means delayed or postponed). Children use deferred imitation in both pretend play and language.

Symbolic play moves to another level, too. The older toddler extends pretend play beyond themselves in two ways. First, pretend play now includes others. Second, the toddler begins to use actions that are not part of their own personal **repertoire** (reh-pur-TWAHR), or skill set. For example, a toddler might use deferred imitation of an adult preparing a meal by pretending to chop vegetables (**Figure 12.4**).

Older toddlers also enter Piaget's second level of pretense called **collective symbolism**. By two years of age, toddlers can use one set of objects to represent another set of objects. For example, blocks can be cars and trucks, or leaves can be dishes. Pretense now extends beyond the toddlers

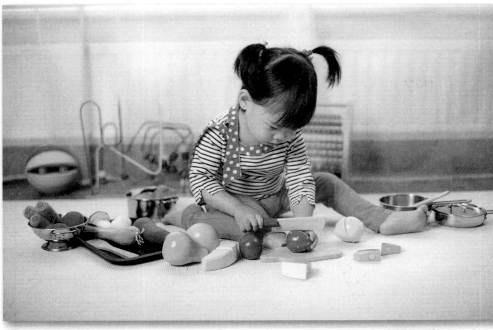

Mcimage/Shutterstock.com

Figure 12.4 Pretend play in the toddler years includes other people and objects. *What types of pretend play did you engage in as a young child?*

themselves and involves other people (caregivers) and objects (stuffed animals) as part of the play. At this age, a few toddlers can also combine actions, such as feeding a doll, "reading" the doll a story, and putting the doll to bed, but most toddlers just do one action at a time.

Thinking Involved in Locating Hidden Objects

During substage 6, children's understanding of object permanence is complete. Older toddlers may demonstrate this understanding by searching for hidden objects. For example, an adult might pretend to hide a toy in one place, but really hides it in another. The toddler knows the toy still exists (object permanence) and thinks about where the toy might be hidden. To find a hidden object, the toddler must also think in terms of spatial concepts. For example, the toddler considers which objects would be large enough to conceal the hidden toy.

12.1-3 Vygotsky's Sociocultural Theory

Vygotsky felt teaching children is a basic sociocultural activity. He believed "teachers" (anyone guiding a child in the learning process) should scaffold (help the child learn) within their zone of proximal development (ZPD). In most cultures, if not all, scaffolding begins during the toddler years. In a group-oriented culture, scaffolding is often done by caregivers, extended family members, and siblings. In an individual-oriented culture, caregivers are the primary teachers.

Scaffolding strategies used in teaching children are also affected by the culture and social environment in which a child is reared. Some families prefer to use direct methods of instruction to support children's learning. For example, some families direct the child's attention, model and instruct, help the child perform, and provide feedback. Others prefer less hands-on methods. These families might model but may not directly engage the child by getting their attention first and explaining exactly how to do a task.

What is taught to children involves cultural values of families, too. For example, some cultures like to show affection more than other cultures. In "teaching" pretend play, families in group-oriented cultures will show more affection (hugs and kisses) to dolls than families in individual-oriented cultures. (Review Figure 3.6 to see other ways in which group-oriented and individual-oriented cultures see families differently.)

Successfully Scaffold Toddlers' Learning

To successfully scaffold the toddler's learning, "teachers" need to first recognize the child's ZPD. Ways to recognize a toddler's ZPD include

- noting the toddler's explorations and interests
- observing the toddler's goals
- watching the toddler's body language and vocal cues for signs of pleasure or frustration during play
- recognizing the toddler's learning style, such as a preference for visual things

Once the ZPD is determined, the adult is ready to scaffold the toddler's learning. Some possible ways to support learning within the child's ZPD include

- watching and showing interest in a toddler's play through eye contact, smiles, and a few words
- changing the level of toy difficulty as needed
- showing pride in a toddler's new skill
- introducing novelty into an activity if the toddler appears uninvolved

- demonstrating the use of a toy, but not interrupting a toddler's use of a toy in a different way than usual, as long as it is safe
- offering help when the toddler is struggling to solve a problem, such as sorting toys
- showing pride in a toddler's new skill
- reacting with patience to a toddler's frustration

Application Activity

In groups, imagine you are teachers at a local child care center. The toddlers in your center vary widely in skill level and ZPD. Brainstorm ways your group can scaffold learning for the multiple skill levels and ZPDs in your center. Share your ideas with the class.

Photo: Tom Wang/Shutterstock.com

Lesson 12.1 Review and Assessment

1. Why is toddlerhood a biologically primed time for learning? (12.1.1)
   A. Toddlers are hands-on learners.
   B. Toddlers are holistic learners.
   C. The brain undergoes a growth spurt during toddlerhood.
   D. Sensory discrimination leads to perpetual concepts.

2. According to Piaget's developmental stages, substage 5 is called _____. (12.1.2)
   A. practicing reflexes
   B. primary circular reactions
   C. tertiary circular reactions
   D. mental imagery or representation

3. Which of the following is *not* a scaffolding technique that is used to help toddlers learn about their culture? (12.1.3)
   A. Direct the child's attention.
   B. Provide feedback.
   C. Model and instruct.
   D. Ignore cues from the child.

What Toddlers Learn

Learning Outcomes

After studying this lesson, you will be able to

12.2-1 **identify** the major areas of concept learning for toddlers and describe one skill a toddler might learn in each area.

12.2-2 **describe** the factors that contribute to the development of toddlers' communication skills.

12.2-3 **identify** intellectual developmental milestones toddlers might achieve.

Key Terms

articulation
bilingual
grammar
monolingual

Reading and Notetaking Activity

Before reading this chapter, skim the headings and write each heading in a different color or font on a separate piece of paper or electronically. As you silently read the chapter and listen to your teacher, take notes in the color or font you chose for each heading. After you finish taking notes for each section, draw, copy, or paste a small illustration or visual next to the section that will help you remember what you learned.

Introduction

During the toddler years, concepts become more complex and abstract, as seen through pretense and language. These concepts pave the way for what toddlers learn. Younger toddlers (12 to 18 months of age) work toward a goal, imitate others, and develop their understanding of object permanence. As ways of thinking about objects and people in the environment mature, older toddlers (18 to 36 months of age) further their comprehension of physics and the world around them. They learn to identify details of objects and solve problems. They begin to understand symbols and the language system and successfully communicate with others.

12.2-1 Concept Learning

Concepts infants start learning during infancy, such as object permanence, spatial relationships, and cause and effect, mature and become more **refined** (sophisticated; fine-tuned) during toddlerhood. It will be many more years, however, before these concepts are fully mature. The major areas of concept learning for toddlers include the following:

- distinguishing **attributes** (properties) of objects
- noting cause and effect
- using spatial relationships
- solving problems
- understanding quantity
- using symbols

Distinguishing Attributes of Objects

For young toddlers, noticing attributes of objects, such as their shape, size, color, and texture, is just beginning. Usually the first properties toddlers notice are major color and size differences in objects (**Figure 12.5**). Attributes become more important for creating mental images, especially as thought processes begin to form in older toddlers. For example, a toddler might often refer to attributes when talking about objects, such as a *red* ball or a *big* dog.

Toddlers often know the attributes of new objects based on prior experiences. They then use this knowledge in play. For example, suppose a child has already been exposed to the loud noise made by hitting metal objects and the lack of noise made by dropping soft objects. They will use this knowledge when given new objects for play. The child might immediately bang metal pans together but would not bang two balls of yarn together. This is a very valuable thinking skill.

Toddlers also begin to perceive differences in attributes. Noting these differences is a thinking skill because it requires comparison. This skill is needed to identify objects. For example, toddlers can distinguish between similar animals, such as ducks and geese, and between closely related

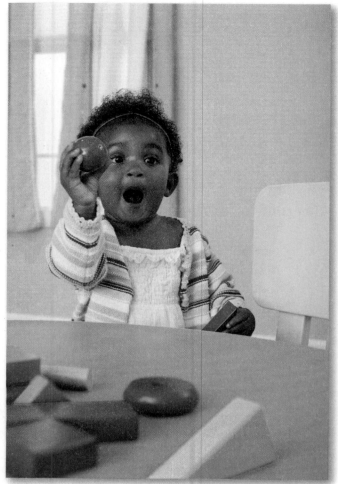

Jupiterimages/Stockbyte/Thinkstock

Figure 12.5 Young toddlers begin to distinguish between size and color differences in objects. *What size and color differences is this toddler observing?*

colors, such as red and pink. Toddlers mentally compare differences before they know the terms for objects. Although toddlers sometimes use the wrong word for an attribute, they do note the differences among objects. Seeing differences enables toddlers to sort information by attributes and to later classify objects.

Noting Cause and Effect

Young toddlers learn by throwing, rolling, shaking, or moving objects. Toddlers learn that round objects roll, and flat objects slide. They also learn that hard objects will make a loud noise when hit together, but soft objects will not. For the most part, young toddlers are learning physical knowledge concepts rather than the more advanced logical thinking skill—cause and effect.

Older toddlers, however, test their actions by repeating and varying them. For example, they may throw objects in different ways and note their **trajectories** (paths objects take). They hear the noise when the object lands and see what happens to the object upon landing (rolls, breaks). They can use different objects to hit pots and pans. While doing this, they may note different sounds caused by where the pan is hit, the type of object used to hit the pan, or the strength of the hit. Once older toddlers see the relationship between an action and the observable results, they are noting cause and effect (**Figure 12.6**).

Using Spatial Relationships

Toddlers learn about spatial relationships as they play. For example, toddlers learn how objects fit together as they nest containers and fit pieces into a puzzle board or shapes into a shape sorter. Toddlers also learn about spatial relationships as they move through spaces. For example, toddlers may crawl under or jump over objects in a simple obstacle course.

To test toddlers' abilities to mentally map space, an experimenter set up a small room with one piece of furniture on each wall. A toddler was

pavla/Shutterstock.com

Figure 12.6 Toddlers who can associate their actions with results begin to comprehend cause and effect. *What are some activities caregivers can do with toddlers to demonstrate cause and effect?*

brought into the room and given commands to walk to different pieces of furniture. Once the toddler was familiar with the setup, the toddler was taken out of the room. The furniture was rotated 90 degrees but kept in the same angular relationships. The toddler was then blindfolded and brought back into the room. Commands were once again given. Toddlers who were tested remembered the relationship of each piece of furniture to another. They had created a mental spatial map, which enabled them to walk through the room with ease.

Solving Problems

Toddlers solve their problems the best way they know how, which is by trial and error or by thinking through what solution will work. To problem-solve, toddlers combine actions and even use objects as tools to reach a goal. Because their understanding of cause and effect is somewhat limited, they do not think about the consequences of their actions. For example, to reach a piece of fruit on the kitchen table, a toddler may pull on the tablecloth until the fruit falls (along with other items on the table).

Understanding Quantity

By the toddler years, number words are a major part of language. Toddlers pick up on these words and use them, but often incorrectly. For example, "two" may mean any quantity greater than "one." Older toddlers often count by rote (memory), but many toddlers do not understand the quantity associated with each number.

Quantity concepts are much more difficult to grasp than noting the attributes of objects. Color, for example, is often **intrinsic** (naturally occurring trait) in a specific object. Numbers, however, are not inherent in an object. The number two, for example, only exists when combining a second object with a previous one. The combining of numbers is an intellectual act. What happens when a toddler counts two objects in reverse order? (The object called "two" is now "one" and vice versa.)

Using Symbols

Through pretend play, toddlers begin to use symbols (**Figure 12.7**). For infants and very young toddlers, a doll is an object. The doll is shaken, sucked on, thrown, dropped, and carried by its arm or leg or even by its hair. With the beginning of pretend play, however, toddlers think of the doll as a baby needing to be fed, rocked, and put to bed—and never treated as an object. Pretend play that begins in the toddler years is usually done alone.

Besides using objects in pretense and seeing pictures in books and drawings as symbols (not the real things), toddlers also begin to understand the complex system of letters, words, and numbers as symbols. These symbols are used as labels for people, objects, and ideas. Unlike other symbol systems, words do not sound or look like the people or objects they represent. Thus, *language* is the most abstract symbol system used by toddlers.

To learn language, children use two thinking skills. First, they must associate the word with the person or object to which it refers. Second, children must recall the word and its meaning when they hear the word or want to say it. Language requires high-level thinking skills.

12.2-2 Communicating

Spoken language develops at a faster rate between one and three years of age than at any other time in a person's life. Learning to talk takes time and effort, however, because speaking involves learning the sounds and meanings of words.

Learning to Articulate

Articulation refers to a person's ability to pronounce words that can be understood by others. If a child is to be **bilingual** (fluent in two languages), infancy is the best time to learn the **phonics** (sounds of letters and syllables) of both languages. Learning to control the tongue, lip muscles, and vocal cords to articulate the words of any language, however, takes practice. Toddlers do not pronounce sounds accurately each time. In fact, most toddlers have some problems making all the sounds in their spoken language.

Toddlers who cannot make one sound often substitute another. For example, they may use a *d* sound for a *th* sound, such as *dat* for *that*. Sometimes children can articulate the correct sound in one place in a word, but not in another. For example, a toddler may pronounce the *m* sound correctly at the beginning of a word, such as *milk*. The same toddler may have trouble, however, making the *m* sound in the middle of a word, such as *hammer*, or at the end of a word, such as *broom*.

Toddlers may also change the sound order of a word, such as saying *perslip* to mean *slipper*. They may even change an entire word, such as saying *book* to mean *bird*. Sometimes toddlers will drop a sound they cannot pronounce. For example, they may say *seepy* instead of *sleepy*.

Few children articulate sounds correctly from the beginning, but they tend to correct themselves over time. Pronouncing words correctly, even if the toddler's way of saying words sounds cute, sets a good example for children to follow. In time, children will learn from listening. Having children repeat a word again and again is not a recommended way to correct pronunciation because it may cause the child stress.

marcos77/E+ via Getty Images

Figure 12.7 Pretend play involves the use of *symbols*, usually objects that can be associated with actions or features. *How do you think toddlers begin to learn what actions and features are associated with certain objects?*

Learning Word Meanings

Learning the meanings of words is difficult. To do so, children must link certain features with a name. Older toddlers learn meanings better if parents show or point to what is being talked about or taught. Still, learning meanings is difficult because many objects with different names share some common features. For example, both dogs and ponies have four legs and run outside. Sometimes children confuse the meanings of words they hear. They may use a wrong name for an object, such as calling a cow *moo*, or a stove *hot*. Without meanings attached to spoken sounds, there would be no language. These meanings give children two new tools—communication and a new way to think.

Communication is the skill needed to understand others and be understood by them. Already, toddlers can understand many words and sentences. When they begin to talk, they want to be understood. Toddlers often use their communication for three reasons (**Figure 12.8**). All children communicate to achieve goals. Some toddlers primarily communicate to learn names that refer to people, places, and objects (nouns), explain actions (verbs), and describe nouns and verbs (adjectives and adverbs) to talk about their world. These toddlers' speech is referred to as *referential*. On the other hand, other toddlers primarily communicate with affective words (hug, kiss) to create social bonds with others.

Figure 12.8 Toddlers Three Reasons to Communicate

Reasons to Communicate	Examples of Communication
To achieve a goal	"Want cookie." (I want a cookie.) "Go bye-bye." (I want to ride in the car.) "No!" (I don't want _____.)
To identify an object	"See doggie." (I see a dog.) "Big!" (That is big.) "What dat?" (What is that?)
To create a bond with another person	"Mommy?" (Where are you mommy? I want you.) "Kiss." (I love you.) "Hurt." (Please help me.)

Goodheart-Willcox Publisher

These toddlers' speech is referred to as *expressive*. Although all toddlers use both types of vocabulary, most toddlers tend to use either more referential or expressive words in their spoken vocabulary.

Language is part of the thinking process. In other words, people learn to think in words. As children learn to talk, words go with actions. For example, toddlers will learn to say *goodbye* while waving. Later, children talk aloud to themselves as they play or lie in bed. They then often whisper words. Finally, they can just think with words, but without saying them aloud.

As children learn language, they develop both vocabulary and grammar. They attach meanings to words and to the order of words. This process, however, is gradual.

Vocabulary

Most children's vocabularies grow slowly until they are 18 to 24 months of age. The fastest growth occurs around 30 months of age. Toddlers vary in the number of words their vocabularies include at different ages. Variances in vocabulary occur for the following reasons:

- *Differences in environmental influences.* How many words a child understands or speaks is related to the quality of interactions the toddler has with caregivers. Caregivers who are talkative and use higher levels of vocabulary and sentence structure are providing quality learning experiences for their toddlers. Studies show that by 20 months of age, toddlers of talkative caregivers know more words than toddlers of less talkative caregivers. By 24 months of age, the gap doubles in favor of toddlers with talkative caregivers.
- *Bilingualism.* Bilingual toddlers divide their vocabulary evenly across two languages. For each language, their vocabulary is about half as large as the **monolingual** (speakers of one language) child's vocabulary. This difference disappears by the preschool years and is not considered a developmental delay.
- *Word usage.* Vocabulary count can also depend on whether all spoken words are counted or only those used correctly are counted as part of the vocabulary.
- *Frequency of word usage.* Toddlers may use words for a while, drop them, and pick them up again months later.

The size of the vocabulary is easier to measure in children three years of age and older than in younger children. Vocabulary by three years has a major impact on school achievement.

Toddlers use words that represent the actions they see and the people and objects they know (**Figure 12.9**). Thus, toddlers learn different types of words in a certain order. First words are usually nouns and simple action verbs. Nouns may include words such as *mama*, *daddy*, and *kitty*. Action verbs may include *run* and *fly*. Next, toddlers learn descriptive words (adjectives and adverbs), such as *big*, *hot*, *pretty*, *loud*, *quickly*, and *slowly*. Young children quickly learn words for human interactions, such as *hi* and *bye*, and words for love and affection, too, such as *hug*.

Cultural differences also affect the words children learn. Toddlers learn the words from their caregivers' career area, interests, and hobbies. Toddlers from individual-oriented cultures tend to have vocabularies with more referential than expressive words. On the other hand, toddlers raised in group-oriented cultures have vocabularies with more expressive than referential words.

antoniodiaz/Shutterstock.com

Figure 12.9 Toddlers learn words that represent the objects and actions they witness each day. A toddler who plays with their dog might learn the word *dog* sooner than they learn the word *cat*. *What were your first words? How, if at all, do you think they are representative of the objects and actions you witnessed as a young child?*

Grammar

Grammar is the study of word usage and order in a given language. Each language has grammar rules. Children begin to learn these rules during toddlerhood. This learning process begins with single-word "sentences" and often progresses to simple sentences of a few words during the toddler years.

Focus on Careers

Speech-Language Pathologist

Speech-language pathologists assess, diagnose, and treat disorders related to speech, language, cognitive-communication, voice, swallowing, and fluency. Many work with children who cannot produce speech sounds or cannot produce them clearly; those with speech rhythm and fluency problems, such as stuttering; and those with voice disorders.

Career cluster: Health science.

Education: Educational requirements include a master's degree and supervised clinical experience. Licensure is also required.

Job outlook: Future employment opportunities for speech-language pathologists are expected to grow much faster than the average for all occupations.

To learn more about a career as a speech-language pathologist, visit the United States Department of Labor's *Occupational Outlook Handbook* website. You will also be able to compare the job responsibilities, educational requirements, job outlook, and average pay of speech-language pathologists with similar occupations.

Photo: MBI/Shutterstock.com

Within six months of saying their first words, toddlers usually begin to put words together. Combining words is an advanced skill because word order affects the meanings of sentences.

By listening to adults and having good books read to them that reflect, celebrate, and honor all cultural backgrounds, toddlers learn the basic rules for the language they hear (**Figure 12.10**). They then apply these rules to their own phrases and sentences. If children are going to be bilingual, toddlerhood is the best time for learning the grammar of both languages.

Grammar knowledge develops in stages. First, toddlers learn single-word sentences. From 12 to 18 months of age, toddlers use sentences of only one word. This single word is often used by the toddler to mean different ideas at different times. For example, a child may say *bye-bye* both to identify a moving object (a car) and to make a request ("Let's go!"). To understand these meanings, the caregiver must note how the child says the word, what gestures they use, and what is happening at the time.

After 19 months, many children begin combining two or more words to form multi-word sentences. At the early stage of combining words, toddlers use only the most necessary words. By 24 to 30 months, many toddlers begin using three or more words in their sentences. When the child begins to use these multi-word sentences, the added words fill in the gaps of former simple sentences. For example, "Gone milk" becomes "Milk is gone." By the time the child uses three-word sentences, word order is often used correctly. The child may say, "Bird is flying," instead of saying, "Fly bird."

Different Rates of Learning to Talk

The rate at which toddlers learn to talk can vary by several months. Many adults worry about a slow talker, only to see the toddler become a nonstop talker a few months later. These toddlers are hearing sounds and learning meanings all along. When they begin to talk, they progress quickly.

A number of factors can affect language development. Learning to talk depends on the following factors:

- *Hearing.* A child must hear human speech clearly to learn to talk without special training. Even ear infections can delay speech in toddlers.
- *Interest.* Some active toddlers are more interested in motor skills than in talking. Within a few months, they often catch up to earlier talkers.
- *Intellectual abilities.* Because language is so closely related to thinking, a child with an intellectual disability is often slower to talk. On the other hand, the ability to talk early does not mean that a child has above average intellectual abilities. Children of average and even below average intellectual abilities may talk at a young age simply by repeating what they hear.
- *Gender.* From the first year of life, biological females tend to excel in verbal skills more than biological males. Researchers do not know whether this is due to heredity or the environment. (For example, adults may talk more often to girls than to boys.)

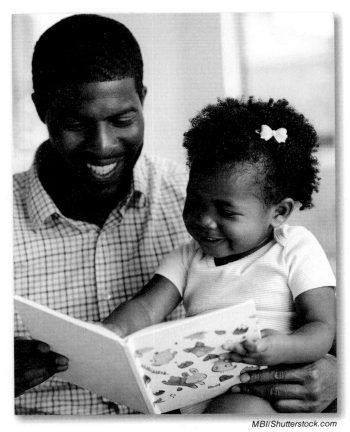

MBI/Shutterstock.com

Figure 12.10 Toddlers learn grammar by listening to others' speech and by being read to from books. Hearing correct grammar will encourage a toddler to use correct grammar. *To what extent do you think adults' communication is affected by what they read and hear?*

- *Need for speech.* Some children get what they need without saying anything. For example, if a toddler receives milk by pointing, holding a cup, or crying, there is no need for the child to learn to say, "I want milk."
- *Stimulating environment.* Just as adults have more to say when they have new experiences, so do toddlers (**Figure 12.11**).
- *Bilingualism.* Bilingual toddlers spread their learning of language across two languages. Unless other factors are involved, bilingual toddlers appear delayed, but are not.
- *Autism. Autism* (a developmental disorder) affects language. Language delays or losses are often early signs of autism. (Autism is discussed in more detail later in this text.)

In some cases, the rate of language development may lag far behind the norms. In these situations, children need professional help. Each child needs the best opportunity to develop language because language is essential to healthy intellectual and social-emotional development.

12.2-3 Intellectual Developmental Milestones

As toddlers explore and learn, they continue to achieve intellectual milestones. Pinpointing when toddlers learn a certain concept, however, becomes more difficult as the age of reaching milestones

Alina Demidenko/iStock via Getty Images Plus

Figure 12.11 Stimulating, new experiences encourage toddlers to learn and use new words. *What do you think are some stimulating experiences that might improve a toddler's vocabulary?*

begins to vary among children. Because the exact timing of achievements varies, intellectual developmental milestones in toddlerhood are grouped by months (**Figure 12.12**). Being aware of these developmental tasks and age groups can help caregivers create a stimulating environment for toddlers to help meet their intellectual needs.

Lesson 12.2 Review and Assessment

1. What are the three major areas of concept learning for toddlers? (12.2.1)
   A. Work toward a goal, imitate others, understand object permanence
   B. Distinguish attributes of objects, note cause and effect, solve problems
   C. Use spatial relationships, understand quantity, use symbols
   D. Articulate, learn word meanings, communicate
2. What does *articulation* mean? (12.2.2)
   A. Fluent in two languages
   B. Study of word usage and order in a language
   C. Ability to pronounce words that can be understood by others
   D. Fluent in one language
3. Which of the following factors do *not* influence vocabulary development in toddlers? (12.2.3)
   A. Differences in environmental influences
   B. Word usage
   C. Frequency of word usage
   D. Correcting their word usage
4. At what age would a toddler be able to sing a few songs? (12.2.3)
   A. 12 to 18 months
   B. 18 to 24 months
   C. 24 to 36 months
   D. 20 to 25 months

Figure 12.12 **Toddler Intellectual Milestones**

12 to 18 months	18 to 24 months	24 to 36 months
• Varies actions on objects to receive many results. • Notices attributes of objects. • Uses physical trial and error to solve problems. • Imitates others—coughing, sneezing, and making animal sounds. • Looks for hidden objects in last place seen (almost mature object permanence). • Points and vocalizes wants. • Points to named objects and animals in books. • Says 3 words (12 months) to 15 or more words (17 months). • Gestures when talking. • Uses one-word "sentences."	• Thinks how to solve some problems without using physical actions. • Solves simple problems requiring two or three steps. • Begins deferred imitation. • Hunts objects in all possible places (mature object permanence). • Pictures objects mentally. • Realizes words have referential meaning. • Says about 200 words. • Uses two- and three-word sentences. • Enjoys "singing" a few songs. • Understands questions, such as "Can you show me your eyes?" • Names pictures in a book. • Repeats actions of others (20 to 21 months).	• Involves others in play activities. • Begins to use a few symbols in pretend play, such as a doll for a baby. • Has many jumbled ideas (preconcepts). • Says up to 500 words. • Uses three- or more-word sentences. • Laughs at silly labels ("Cow goes quack, quack"). • Enjoys some books over and over. • Repeats a few rhymes. • Asks for information ("Why?" "What's dat?").

DragonImages/ iStock/Thinkstock

Jupiterimages/Stockbyte/Thinkstock

GrashAlex/iStock via Getty Images Plus

Goodheart-Willcox Publisher

Meeting Toddlers' Intellectual Needs

Learning Outcomes

After studying this lesson, you will be able to

12.3-1 **plan** developmentally appropriate activities and toys for stimulating motor, sensory, basic concept comprehension, symbolic learning, and emerging language skills for toddlers.

12.3-2 **evaluate** electronic media activities currently available for older toddlers to determine their educational value.

Reading and Notetaking Activity

While reading this lesson, place sticky notes next to sections that interest you or next to sections where you have questions. Write your questions or comments on the sticky notes. After reading, find a partner and share your questions and comments. If there are any questions that the two of you cannot answer together, then ask your teacher.

Introduction

Adults can use everyday activities to help meet toddlers' intellectual needs. For example, bathing and dressing provide the means for encouraging perceptual learning, good hygiene practices, and language and motor development. Helping with household tasks allows toddlers to develop spatial concepts as they put items in drawers or laundry in a basket. Vocabulary increases as toddlers learn the names of common objects found in the home and yard. Science becomes a part of everyday life as toddlers see how the vacuum cleaner picks up dirt, how air dries clothes, and how heat makes dough change into cookies.

Toddlers learn as they play in a safe environment with many objects to explore. Play enables toddlers to check and recheck concepts. Adults may play with toddlers sometimes. For the most part, however, adults should allow toddlers to play by themselves, and step in only when toddlers need help (Vygotsky's principle) or show a desire for adult participation. For example, a caregiver may show the toddler how to put a piece in a puzzle or introduce new play ideas to enrich toddlers' learning experiences.

12.3-1 Planning Developmentally Appropriate Activities

One of the main responsibilities of all caregivers of children is the responsibility to plan and implement intentional, developmentally appropriate learning experiences that promote the social and emotional development, physical development and health, cognitive development and general learning competencies of the children in their care. According to The National Association for the Education of Young Children developmentally appropriate practices are methods that promote each child's optimal development and learning. This learning is through a strength-based and play-based approach. To be considered developmentally appropriate, activities need to be culturally, linguistically, and ability-appropriate for the child. Also, it is important for caregivers to be aware of the child's strengths and abilities. Referring to the developmental milestones for each age grouping will help caregivers achieve that goal.

Focus on

Science

Using the Senses to Make Observations

Through the use of their senses, toddlers can learn about the world around them. They learn to distinguish sounds, identify smells, recognize sights, and remember the texture of an object. These lessons occur at a critical time of brain development. During the toddler years, a child's brain grows rapidly, and once the toddler years end, pruning of seldom used or unused brain connections increases. While toddlers learn many lessons through their own encounters with their environment, sensory stimulation activities can enrich what toddlers learn.

By providing opportunities for toddlers to use their senses, adults can encourage sensory learning. As toddlers play games, adults can teach them about their senses by talking through activities. For example, when a caregiver notices a toddler

hears a sound, the caregiver might stop briefly and listen. Then, the caregiver can point in the direction of the sound and say, "I hear a _____. Do you hear it, too?" This helps stimulate the toddler's sense of hearing. As another activity, caregivers can sniff loudly and tell toddlers what they smell. Later, they can ask the toddler, "What's cooking? What smells so good?" Caregivers can talk about a variety of odors. Flowers, an outdoor barbecue, and the rain all have distinct smells.

In small groups, brainstorm sensory stimulation activities for each of the major senses. Review the information you have already learned about toddlers' brain development and then discuss why sensory stimulation is vital to children during the toddler years.

Photo: otnaydur/Shutterstock.com

Motor Activities

During the toddler years, children develop both gross- and fine-motor skills quickly. Because toddlers are often on-the-go, they need few planned motor activities. As children run, climb, jump, and crawl, they are developing their gross-motor skills. Any activities that require the use of the small muscles help children develop their fine-motor skills.

Many fine-motor activities children perform aid other areas of learning. For example, drawing a picture, which requires the ability to grasp a writing tool, also aids symbol making and creativity. Building block towers, playing with shape sorters and puzzles, and stacking and nesting objects teach toddlers spatial concepts and physical knowledge. **Figure 12.13** lists common gross- and fine-motor activities that can help toddlers improve their skills.

Sensory Stimulation Activities

Through the senses, toddlers can learn about the qualities (also called *properties* or *attributes*) of objects. Through sight, for example, toddlers

Figure 12.13 Gross- and Fine-Motor Activities

Motor Activities	Skills
Gross-motor activities *leezsnow/E+ via Getty Images*	• Walk in different directions (sideways, backward) • Spin around and whirl • Roll and toss objects (beanbags and soft balls) • Use push and pull toys • Climb using low steps and couch cushions • Jump on mats or pillows with adult guidance • Build with large, hollow blocks • Crawl through tunnels • Play with sand and water • Slide down a child-size slide • Use push and pedal riding toys • Run outdoors
Fine-motor activities *Dan Howell/Shutterstock.com*	• Assemble and take apart items, such as MEGA Bloks® • Poke holes in soft objects • Use a hammer and peg set or beat a drum • Use Play-Doh® and finger paints • Build a tower with blocks • Use a shape sorter • Complete a simple jigsaw puzzle • Stack and nest objects • Turn pages in books • Cut paper with child safety scissors • Draw with thick crayons • Play with felt and stickers

Goodheart-Willcox Publisher

can learn about an object's color and size. Touch teaches toddlers whether objects are rough, smooth, hard, or soft. Through listening, toddlers learn the sounds of language. Taste teaches about different flavors, such as sweet, sour, salty, and bitter. Scent lets toddlers recognize familiar aromas in foods. Using the senses helps toddlers form concepts about objects.

When with toddlers, adults can name attributes of nearby objects, such as color and shape names, to help toddlers learn. Toddlers can do some sorting by attributes, such as putting all the farm animals in a picture-labeled basket or on a picture-labeled shelf. Toddlers enjoy matching socks by color or matching flatware in a drawer. Commercial materials are also available for sorting by color, shape, and size. Self-guided, hands-on play activities are excellent for sensory learning.

Basic Concept Activities

Basic concept activities encourage toddlers to try out their ideas (**Figure 12.14**). During the toddler years, many concept activities involve gross- and fine-motor skills. This is because toddlers, especially young toddlers, are still learning through physical trial and error. Therefore, toys

for toddlers need to be simple to use. For example, simple puzzles for young toddlers often include only a few pieces, and each piece shows an entire picture of an object. A knob on each puzzle piece aids fine-motor control. As older toddlers begin to think through problems, puzzles with a few more pieces may be more appropriate.

Symbolic Learning Activities

Toddlers 12 to 18 months of age use toys in the ways they are intended, such as using blocks for stacking and balls for throwing. Around 18 months, however, toddlers may engage in some symbolic play. By two years of age, more extended pretend play begins, which leads to the rich imaginary play seen in the preschool years.

Following are some suggestions for ways adults can encourage toddlers' symbolic play:
- Provide the toddler with toys that have a realistic purpose, such as a doll to represent a baby, when the toddler first begins symbolic play. Toy cars, trucks, planes, trains, animal figures, and stuffed animals are also good choices.
- Initiate pretend play, when the toddler is ready to include others, by asking to taste the "soup" or the "taco" or to "kiss" the stuffed toy or doll.

Figure 12.14 **Basic Concept Activities**

Opening lids. Place a small object in a container with a snap-on lid and then show the toddler how to open and close the lid. Then, let the toddler try to open and close the lid. When the toddler masters one type of lid, try another type, such as a screw-on lid. Do *not* use containers with safety caps.

Nesting and stacking. Give the toddler two or three objects for nesting and stacking or rings for sequencing. Add other objects or rings as the toddler masters the game. If there is very little difference in the size of the objects, the task becomes much more difficult and may be more appropriate for children who are a little older.

Where Am I? Hide from a toddler who is involved in another activity. Call the toddler's name and have them look for you. Praise the toddler for finding you. Of course, do not hide behind locked doors or other places where the toddler cannot look for you.

Rolling cars. Place toy cars on a flat board on the floor. (You may use chair cushions, sturdy cardboard lids, or trays as a board.) Point out to the toddler that the cars are not moving. Then, raise one end of the board and say, "Look at the cars go." After the toddler plays with the cars in this way many times, ask, "Can you make the cars go down the board fast (slow)?" See if the toddler increases (decreases) the slope of the board.

Through the tunnel. Show the toddler how to roll objects through a cardboard tube so the toddler learns how objects can go in one open end and come out the other end. After much play, some toddlers may learn to vary the slope of the tube to control the speed of the object's roll.

Goodheart-Willcox Publisher

- Play along when the toddler initiates ideas to include others in the pretend play. Allow the child to take the lead but extend the play if it seems appropriate. For example, if the toddler stirs a pot for a long time, suggest pouring the "soup" into the bowls.
- Do not interrupt a toddler who is talking aloud while playing. At this point, the toddler is in their own world of play and language.
- Include play animals and objects during story time. Finger puppets are also good in creating an imaginary world.
- Encourage the toddler to make sounds to represent animals and machines in their world. Read books with **onomatopoeic** (ahn-uh-mat-uh-PEE-ik) words, or words that imitate sounds, such as *pop*, *fizz*, and *buzz*, and ask the toddler to make these sounds.
- Encourage the toddler to "read" a book they enjoy to a favorite doll or teddy bear.
- Initiate a couple of pretend ideas when the toddler enters the second level of pretense and is ready to use one object to represent another object (*collective symbolism*). For example, ideas may include using a block for a car, a series of blocks for a train, a large box for a house, or a small container for a hat. Once the possibility is seen, toddlers come up with their own ideas (**Figure 12.15**).

kate_sept2004/E+ via Getty Images

Figure 12.15 Using boxes to represent cars, houses, or other objects can encourage pretend play in toddlers. *What are some stimulating pretend play activities that can be done with boxes?*

Language Activities

The toddler's active world needs a background of language. Talking with the toddler during games and daily routines and describing the actions being performed can enhance the toddler's use of language and conceptual development. Reading books and singing songs can promote language learning, too.

Talking with Toddlers

Adults can begin talking with the toddler in a conversational manner even before the child can respond verbally. For example, while preparing lunch, the adult might say, "Aren't you hungry?" and then pause briefly as though the child will answer. Then, the adult might respond to the child's imagined *yes* answer by saying, "Surely you are. Lunch smells good, doesn't it?"

Some general suggestions for talking experiences with toddlers include the following:

- Talk *with* not *at* the toddler and respond to the toddler's vocalizations.
- Name and describe objects, experiences, and the child's feelings.
- Discuss past experiences in rich and interesting detail with an older toddler, which help to create better memories in the toddler.
- Ask **open-ended questions** (questions that require a descriptive response for an answer) to aid conversation. Questions that only require a one- or two-word response, **closed-ended questions**, can limit conversation. For example, saying, "Did you like the zoo?" is a closed-ended question. Asking "What did you see at the zoo?" is more open-ended.
- Add descriptive words and sentences to the toddler's "talk." For example, if the toddler says, "ball," the adult might say, "Yes, the ball rolls and bounces."
- Use clear and simple speech and all types of sentences when talking with the toddler. Using statements, questions, and exclamations helps the toddler hear **intonation**, or the rise and fall of a person's voice while speaking.

- Make different sounds that go with toys, such as *rrr* for a siren, to help the toddler learn to make sounds.
- Match sentences to the child's level and pronounce words correctly. Explain new words using words the child already knows. Slightly challenging children helps their development. (This is Vygotsky's principle of using the child's ZPD.)

Adults are language models for toddlers. Children learn and repeat words they hear others say, including words or phrases that adults do not want children to use. If a toddler repeats unsuitable words, adults might correct the child by saying, "These are not words we use here (at home, at school)." By modeling correct language, adults can teach toddlers new words and correct toddlers' language errors. In each of the modeling examples in **Figure 12.16**, the adult does not point out the child's language error, but rather guides by expanding the toddler's sentence. Toddlers (and even older children) often feel defeated when adults only correct errors.

Reading with Toddlers

Reading books and saying poems and rhymes are activities adults can do with toddlers to help them develop language and literacy skills.

Typically, toddlers will not sit still and look at books for a long time. Young toddlers may enjoy glancing at a page and turning it. Using the motor skill of turning the page is often more fun for the toddler than looking at the pictures. Later, toddlers spend more time looking at the pictures, but they still may not want to hear the story. When choosing books for toddlers, look for books that

- are made of cloth, vinyl, and heavy cardboard with a plastic coating. These books are durable, sturdy, and washable.
- have pages that are easy for the toddler to turn and keep open.
- include colorful and simple pictures.
- contain story lines that focus on the toddler's favorite subjects, which may include animals, toys, fun places to visit, cars and trucks, or home and family. Whenever possible, link the book to events that occur in the toddler's real world. For example, if the toddler goes to the zoo, read a book about a zoo shortly thereafter. Talk with the toddler about the similarities between the book and the toddler's trip to the zoo.

Figure 12.16 Examples of Ways to Model Language to Toddlers

Purpose for Modeling Language	Example
To correct pronunciation	Toddler—"My wed (red) sooes (shoes)." Adult—"Yes, these are your pretty red shoes."
To correct grammar	Toddler—"I singed a song." Adult—"You sang a song about a rainy day."
To introduce a new word	Toddler—"See the plane go." Adult—"The plane flies fast."
To correct the meaning of a word	Toddler—"See the smoke." Adult—"It does look like smoke." Sniff loudly. "It doesn't smell like smoke though. We see fog. Fog is a cloud near the ground. Can you say *fog*?"

Goodheart-Willcox Publisher

To engage young toddlers in reading books, the adult can name and point to one object on the page. Then, the adult can ask the toddler to point to the object. As language develops, toddlers can name objects in the pictures and even make some sounds of animals or other objects. By two years of age, toddlers often enjoy hearing a whole story that contains only a short sentence or two for each picture page (**Figure 12.17**).

Many older toddlers (and even preschool children) insist on hearing the same story over and over. They often request the same story at bedtime. Routines, including favorite, repeated stories, help the toddler feel secure. The child knows what will happen in the story's beginning, middle, and end. Sometimes children will insist that not even a word be changed. The loving adult who reads daily to a child is likely to make the child feel more secure than the story itself.

Singing with Toddlers

Singing songs in which toddlers act out the meanings of words is a good way to help toddlers learn language. An example of an action song is "Here We Go 'Round the Mulberry Bush." While singing this song, toddlers get to act out lines such as "This is the way we eat our soup" and "This is the way we wash our hands." Toddlers can sing and act out many other verses, too. Adults and children can even make up new lyrics to fit almost any activity by using this so-called *mileage tune.*

Becky Lane

Figure 12.17 Young children's books are called *picture books* because pictures, rather than words, carry the story. Some picture books do not even have words. *What children's books did you enjoy as a child? Why?*

Other common mileage tunes children enjoy are "Do You Know the Muffin Man?"; "Twinkle, Twinkle Little Star"; and "London Bridge Is Falling Down." (**Figure 12.18** shows other language games that are fun and encourage children to use language.)

Figure 12.18 Language Games for Toddlers

Game	Directions
Show Me	Young toddlers enjoy running around and pointing to objects. When an adult names objects for the toddler to touch, the toddler's language skills improve. Make statements such as "Show me the door." As the toddler touches the door, praise them with a statement such as "You're right. That's the door."
Follow Directions	Give the toddler simple directions using familiar objects. For example, say, "Bring me the ball." Praise the toddler for following directions promptly. You may also play the game, "Follow the Leader." Give simple directions such as "clap your hands" or "pat your head."
Telephones	Listening to voices on a phone and talking into a phone can help language develop. Toddlers enjoy play phones. Talking on a real phone with adult supervision is also a good language practice.

Goodheart-Willcox Publisher

Electronic Media Activities

In today's world, children live in a media-rich environment. Companies specifically design television programs, videos, and interactive games for young children. Many child development experts and caregivers, however, question whether the impact of electronic media is helpful or harmful to their children's development.

The American Academy of Pediatrics (AAP) recommends caregivers of children younger than 18 months avoid use of screen media other than video-chatting. Why are digital mediums not good learning tools for children two years of age and younger? Consider the following:

- Media content is **vicarious** (experienced through another person or object). This means the toddler watches images instead of experiencing objects in real life. Because toddlers are still learning about objects, they may not be able to make the connection from images on the screen to objects in real life.
- Toddlers are still holistic learners, but the majority of children's media content is "bits and pieces learning," such as drills on shapes, colors, and letters. Young toddlers are not yet at this stage of learning.
- Around 30 months, toddlers' brains are laying the foundation for many skills requiring effort. Media tends to be a very passive way to learn. Children who watch television as toddlers have more learning problems in school.

For children between 18 months and three years of age, AAP recommends limiting screen time to one hour of high-quality media per day. When choosing electronic media activities, consider the educational value of the materials and set restrictions for when and where screen time takes place. Carefully selected television programs, videos, and interactive games may have a positive impact on children's learning. Through content-rich media interactions, older toddlers can begin to learn socially acceptable behaviors and math, language, and science concepts. Electronic media usage is best with adult supervision and when an adult describes a program's activities to the toddler.

Lesson 12.3 Review and Assessment

1. Which of the following is a developmentally appropriate fine motor activity for a toddler? (12.3.1)
   A. Build a tower with blocks.
   B. Use a push and pull toy.
   C. Build with large hollow blocks.
   D. Run outdoors.

2. Which of the following is *not* a way that caregivers can help toddlers develop language skills? (12.3.1)
   A. Talk with the toddler.
   B. Read with the toddler.
   C. Sing with the toddler.
   D. Correct the toddler's language and words.

3. What are two ways caregivers can enhance talking experiences with toddlers? (12.3.1)
   A. Ask open-ended questions and add descriptive words and sentences to toddlers' talk.
   B. Correct the toddler's language and use non-familiar words.
   C. Sing silly songs with the toddler while acting them out.
   D. Use finger puppets to act out stories.

4. For children between two and five years of age, child development experts recommend limiting screen time to no more than _____ per day. (12.3.2)
   A. 30 minutes
   B. 1 hour
   C. 1 1/2 hours
   D. 2 hours

Chapter 12

Review and Assessment

Summary

Lesson 12.1

12.1-1 During the toddler years, brain wiring is dense, making the toddler's brain ripe for learning.

12.1-1 After the toddler years, the brain will begin pruning seldom used or unused connections.

12.1-1 Toddlers develop mental imagery, which encourages pretend play.

12.1-2 Piaget categorizes toddler learning into two stages: substage 5 and substage 6. During substage 5, young toddlers learn using trial and error. Once they reach substage 6, older toddlers can think through actions.

12.1-3 Teaching by scaffolding also begins in the toddler years. Vygotsky's theory shows how cultural differences affect scaffolding.

Lesson 12.2

12.2-1 Concepts that children start learning during infancy mature during toddlerhood.

12.2-1 The major areas of concept learning for toddlers are distinguishing attributes, noting cause and effect, using spatial relationships, solving problems, understanding quantities, and using symbols.

12.2-2 Toddlers learn language by learning to articulate and learning word meanings.

12.2-2 Toddlers need experiences in hearing language. Toddlers first use single words before joining words to form sentences.

12.2-3 Several conditions—including hearing problems, interest in talking, intellectual abilities, gender, need for speech, environment, bilingualism, and autism—can affect and cause delays in language development.

Lesson 12.3

12.3-1 Toddlers learn through various play activities, such as motor activities, sensory stimulation activities, basic concept activities, symbolic learning activities, language activities, and electronic media activities.

12.3-1 Adults can enrich toddlers' learning environment by providing helpful materials and planning appropriate activities.

College and Career Portfolio

Portfolio Sample Editing

Portfolio samples are examples of your best work, so it is important to read and edit them. Correct spelling and grammar are important in school and in the workplace, and your best work should display your grasp of language. To make sure you are providing the best samples in your portfolio, complete the following activities:

- Proofread the samples for your portfolio. Check for spelling using a print or online dictionary. Check for grammar by reading aloud and researching grammar rules.
- Trade samples with a trusted classmate and proofread your classmate's samples for them. Afterward, review and incorporate corrections your classmate made to your samples.

Recall and Application

1. _____ increases the speed of connections in the brain. (12.1.1)
   A. Myelination
   B. Neurotransmitters
   C. Dendrites
   D. Synapses
2. **True or False.** Mental imagery is being able to see in the mind's eye or hear in the mind's ear in the absence of a stimulus. (12.1.1)
3. According to Piaget's developmental stages, substage 6 is called _____. (12.1.2)
   A. practicing reflexes
   B. primary circular reactions
   C. tertiary circular reactions
   D. mental imagery and representation
4. **True or False.** In teaching pretend play, families in group-oriented cultures will show less affection (hugs and kisses) than in individual-oriented cultures. (12.1.3)
5. **True or False.** The first properties toddlers notice are major color and size differences in objects. (12.2.1)
6. **True or False.** Young toddlers learn about cause and effect by throwing temper tantrums. (12.2.1)
7. If a child is bilingual it means they are fluent in _____ language(s). (12.2.2)
   A. one   C. three
   B. two   D. four
8. The fastest growth of vocabulary occurs around _____ months of age. (12.2.2)
   A. 18   C. 28
   B. 24   D. 30
9. **True or False.** Grammar is the study of word usage and order in a language. (12.2.4)
10. Which of the following is a gross motor activity? (12.3.1)
    A. Using finger paints
    B. Building with large hollow blocks
    C. Beating a drum
    D. Completing a jigsaw puzzle
11. Which of the following is *not* a basic concept activity for toddlers? (12.3.1)
    A. Opening lids
    B. Nesting and stacking
    C. Rolling cars
    D. Banging pots
12. **True or False.** Reading books and singing songs can promote language skills in toddlers. (12.3.1)

Critical Thinking

1. **Draw conclusions.** After the toddler years, the brain begins pruning connections; this makes toddlerhood the ideal period for learning skills and concepts. What do you think would happen if learning did not occur during the toddler years? Can a child learn a skill after this period closes?

2. **Cause and effect.** How does the development of language aid toddlers' thinking skills? Predict how a toddler's thinking would be affected if language development were delayed.

3. **Compare and contrast.** Review the discussion of *Piaget's Cognitive-Developmental Theory* in Lesson 12.1. Then, compare and contrast substages 5 and 6. Write a three- to four-paragraph essay explaining how the substages are similar and how they are different.

4. **Analyze.** Why is deferred imitation a more advanced intellectual ability than imitating while seeing an action performed?

5. **Evaluate.** Mikhail is 24 months old. In the past, when the caregivers have bought a stuffed animal or favorite superhero, Mikhail has chewed on the stuffed animal and thrown it around the room. This year, however, Mikhail has started reading to the stuffed animal and taking it on walks. Evaluate the situation. How would Piaget describe what Mikhail has learned?

6. **Determine.** Concept learning that begins in infancy advances during toddlerhood. Review the major concept areas of toddler learning, and if needed, review Chapter 9, *Intellectual Development in the First Twelve Months*. For each concept area, write a paragraph describing how the foundations of this concept are laid during infancy and determining how the concept lesson is refined during toddlerhood.

Core Skills

1. **Research and speaking.** Advances in neuroscience have helped experts understand childhood windows of opportunity and ideal periods for learning. Using reliable online or print resources, research how brain development affects when and how toddlers learn. Try to understand the anatomy that allows for learning and take notes on any facts or concepts that you find interesting. Finally, present your research to the class. Include a bibliography and be prepared to defend the reliability of the sources you used.

2. **Listening and speaking.** Imagine you are a third-grade teacher at a local elementary school and your curriculum requires you teach Piaget's *Cognitive-Developmental Theory* and Vygotsky's *Sociocultural Theory*, as they relate to toddlers. Review this chapter's information about the two theories and then draft an age-appropriate lesson plan to teach and then assess this knowledge in your students. Prepare two to three activities to reinforce these concepts and deliver your lesson in a small group.

3. **Math.** Conduct a survey asking caregivers how many words they would estimate their toddler knows. Try to survey at least 10 caregivers and make note of the toddlers' ages. Enter data into a spreadsheet. After compiling your results, calculate the average number of words a toddler knows. Show your work and turn in your spreadsheet and calculation to your teacher.

4. **Writing and speaking.** Review the table of intellectual milestones for toddlers (Figure 12.13), and in small groups, choose one of the three age ranges covered. Discuss in your group how a toddler changes when they cross into your chosen age range, and then create a brochure for parents and caregivers titled "What to Expect When Your Toddler Is _____ Months Old." In your brochure, detail the major changes a toddler undergoes and a parent or caregiver might observe. Make your brochure visually appealing and informative. Finally, distribute the brochure to the class and deliver a presentation about its contents.

5. **Reading.** With a partner, search online or visit a local library to find parenting books that advise caregivers how to improve their toddlers' language development and grammar. Read one of these books and take notes about strategies the book suggests. Assess these strategies against what you learned in this chapter and research additional sources to verify each strategy's effectiveness. Finally, write a two- to three-page book review evaluating the book's accuracy and helpfulness.

6. **Writing and art.** Reading with toddlers encourages visual imagery, language development, and fine-motor skills (involved in turning a book page). Review the considerations for choosing children's books and then identify a topic you think would be interesting to a toddler. Write a short children's book based on that topic and be sure to illustrate it with large, colorful pictures. Finally, bring your children's book to school and read it to the class. After reading, ask your class for feedback and take notes about what they would change.

7. **Research and technology.** Many electronic products claim to be effective teaching tools for toddlers. It is up to individual caregivers, however, to evaluate whether these tools are as helpful as they say. In small groups, choose an electronic product (such as a television program, video, or interactive game) that is marketed as being educational for toddlers. Conduct an investigation about how helpful the product actually is. This investigation might involve reading reviews or articles about the product or applying information about toddlers that you learned in this chapter. Once you have reached a consensus, create a poster that markets the product accurately and realistically.

8. **CTE Career Readiness Practice.** Imagine you are a new teacher at a local child care center. Your employer values your creativity and fresh take on planning activities for children, so she asks you to renovate the activities program for toddlers. She asks you to plan two weeks of activities for the toddlers' growth and development and to include a motor activity, sensory stimulation activity, basic concept activity, symbolic learning activity, language activity, and electronic media activity for each day. She also asks you to incorporate math, science, physical movement, outdoor play, art, and music into these activities. Create a two-week program of activities for toddlers at the child care center, including activity details, instructions, and time estimates. Once you have created your program, present it to the class and ask for feedback on how well you completed your employer's assignment.

Observations

1. In small groups, search online or at a local library for recordings or videos of toddlers and then analyze any articulation errors present in the toddlers' speech. Take notes about these errors and then play the recording or video for your class. Ask the students in your class to list the articulation errors they note and then lead a group discussion about your analysis and your classmates' responses.

2. As a class, visit a local child care center and observe several toddlers. For each toddler, note goals you witness the toddler striving to achieve. Record the actions the toddler uses and the outcomes of these actions. Note especially how thinking is evident. What concepts are the toddlers learning? What intellectual activities might be appropriate for them? Discuss your findings as a class.

Chapter 13

Social-Emotional Development of Toddlers

Essential Questions

What interrelated toddler developments serve as preparation for the emergence of a social child, and how can adults gradually and effectively begin to socialize their toddlers?

Case Study | How Can Toddlers' Separation Anxiety Be Handled?

As a class, read the case study and discuss the questions that follow. After you finish studying the chapter, discuss this case study again. Have your opinions changed based on what you learned?

Mariam, an attorney at a prestigious law firm, is going back to work after 13 months of family leave. Mariam does not want to leave their child, Avra, but must work to help support the family. While Mariam and Mariam's partner, Seth, are working, Avra will attend a toddler program.

To prepare Avra for the program, Mariam and Seth played "bye-bye" with Avra in the house by waving and going into another room. The family enjoyed the game. On Avra's first day at the center, however, Avra began crying after the realization that "bye-bye" meant that Mariam was gone. The next day, Avra began crying inconsolably as soon as the doors of the toddler center closed.

Mariam was upset about Avra's distress. Avra had stayed with unfamiliar caregivers before without crying. As the childcare worker approached, Mariam asked, "Did something go wrong yesterday? Avra has never cried like this before. Maybe you don't know how to handle my child."

The caregiver was offended and replied, "If you don't want Avra to cry, then don't leave your child with us."

The director, who overheard the exchange and noticed that Mariam was becoming even more upset, stepped in to defuse the situation.

Give It Some Thought

1. Why was Avra crying? What does this behavior show about Avra's relationship with the primary caregiver? Why do you think Avra had not cried during earlier child care situations?
2. Why was Mariam so upset on the second day? What other ways do primary caregivers react to their children's cries? Why?
3. Do you think the child care worker should have handled the situation differently? Explain your answer.

The Social-Emotional World of Toddlers

Key Terms

autonomy versus shame
   and doubt
gender identity
self-esteem
temper tantrum

Learning Outcomes

After studying this lesson, you will be able to

13.1-1 **describe** how self-awareness develops in toddlers.

13.1-2 **identify** the conflict toddlers must resolve in the second stage of Erikson's psychosocial theory.

13.1-3 **explain** how the adult-child relationship changes in the toddler years and how it is different than infancy.

13.1-4 **describe** secure attachments in toddlers and explain why insecure attachments lead to negative social-emotional outcomes.

13.1-5 **summarize** how children express their emotions in the toddler years.

13.1-6 **give examples** of social-emotional developmental milestones toddlers might achieve.

Reading and Notetaking Activity

Before reading, skim the headings in this chapter and list the headings to create an outline for taking notes during reading and class discussion. Under each heading list any key term. Finally, write two questions you expect to have answered in class. After completing the chapter, ask your teacher any questions you still have about the concepts or terms you learned.

Introduction

Most babies begin life surrounded by people who meet all their needs. Babies' needs are usually simple, so caregivers can meet most of them promptly. When their needs are met and their environments are consistent, babies develop focused attachment to their caregivers and, in turn, learn to trust their world.

As babies become toddlers, three changes happen. First, toddlers find out more about themselves as individuals and about their world. Second, toddlers realize the world is not solely devoted to meeting their needs.

Third, toddlers' emotions become more elaborate, specific to events, and intense (strong). Toddlers also directly sense the expressions of other people's emotions. Thus, during the toddler years, children develop self-awareness, achieve *autonomy*, and reach out to form social relations with others. They also begin to show attachments and express emotions. These three interrelated developments serve as a preparation for the emergence of a truly social being.

13.1-1 Developing Self-Awareness

Self-awareness (the understanding a person has of themselves) begins to develop at birth and continues to build throughout life. A good sense of self-awareness is essential to a person's well-being. Without a sense of self, children cannot develop close relationships and adults cannot share intimacy.

Self-awareness in the toddler years involves seeing oneself as a unique person, recognizing oneself (as in a mirror), and developing early feelings of self-esteem. Adults can readily note a toddler's emerging self-awareness when toddlers express possession (concerned about *me* and *mine*), identify their images as themselves, and are increasingly independent (**Figure 13.1**).

ikercelik/E+ via Getty Images

Figure 13.1 As toddlers become more self-aware, they also become more independent and more conscious of what they possess. *Why do you think self-awareness is a key component for independence? Could someone be independent without being self-aware?*

Seeing Oneself as a Unique Person

Around two years of age, toddlers begin to see themselves as separate from other people and objects. Toddlers demonstrate their understanding of being a unique person in the following ways:

- *Body awareness.* Toddlers become more aware of their bodies and what their bodies can do. By 24 months of age, children know and can name at least seven of their body parts. They can also distinguish their body parts from those of others, such as "my nose," "mommy's nose," and the "kitty's nose."
- *Sense awareness.* Toddlers know they can see, hear, touch, taste, and smell. They may not know; however, which body part controls each sense.
- *Gender identity.* Toddlers develop **gender identity**, the ability to label self and others as male or female (also called *gender labeling*). These labels are often based on physical differences, such as length of hair. Toddlers become upset if someone mislabels them.
- *Object possession.* Toddlers define themselves by what belongs to them, and will tell you so by saying, "Mine."
- *Family names.* Toddlers can state their own names and the names of family members.
- *Assimilate their culture.* Toddlers notice the physical traits of their ethnic group and the behaviors and values of their cultural group. They do not fully **assimilate** (fully understand and use knowledge of) their ethnicity and culture, however, for many years. For example, some verbal comparisons with other groups (expressions of self-awareness) are most often heard beginning in the preschool years.

Although toddlers are becoming **cognizant** (aware) of themselves, their understanding of self is still incomplete. For example, toddlers feel pain, but do not always know where the pain is located. Unless they can see a cut, scrape, or burn, they cannot tell someone where it hurts. More advanced body concepts develop later.

Recognizing Oneself

Toddlers can recognize themselves in mirrors between 15 and 18 months of age. Between 18 and 24 months, they can point to their reflection in the mirror, say their own names, and point to themselves in recent photos.

To study toddlers' ability to recognize themselves, researchers have conducted *mark and mirror* experiments. In one mark and mirror experiment, toddlers first looked at themselves in a mirror. While pretending to wipe the children's faces, the experimenter put dots of red lipstick on their noses. Once again the toddlers looked at themselves in a mirror. Toddlers who recognized themselves in the mirror wiped at their noses. Those who did not recognize themselves would wipe at the nose on the face in the mirror.

Once toddlers recognize themselves in mirrors, they enjoy looking at themselves, and begin to distinguish their physical features (**Figure 13.2**). Some child care and education programs use large, unbreakable mirrors near the floor to help

toddlers develop self-awareness. Toddlers and older children enjoy seeing how they look while playing.

TierneyMJ/Shutterstock.com

Figure 13.2 Mirrors help toddlers recognize themselves and develop self-awareness. In mirrors, toddlers can learn to distinguish their physical features and recognize those features as their own. *How does self-recognition contribute to self-awareness?*

Developing Early Feelings of Self-Esteem

A portion of **self-esteem** involves feelings of **worth** (usefulness; importance). Infants sense how others feel about them from the way they are spoken to and held. Toddlers can also sense how others feel about them. Toddlers must feel loved, even when they are difficult or make mistakes. If adults scold toddlers each time they do something wrong, toddlers will feel they are beyond being loved. With the help of caring adults, children develop good feelings of self-worth.

The confidence a person has in their own abilities (**competence**) is part of self-esteem. As toddlers achieve goals, their competence increases. Toddlers gain another aspect of self-esteem, **control** (influence over one's environment of people, things, and events), by figuring out what works and what does not. Adults who do not rescue toddlers from small frustrations too quickly are aiding a growing sense of control over outcomes and events. As toddlers make mistakes, try again, and practice what works, they will achieve autonomy.

As toddlers develop good feelings of self-worth, confidence in their own abilities, and gain control in their environment, they are developing self-esteem. When toddlers feel good about themselves, they seem to admire themselves and their growing control over their bodies. They are confident and like to show off their physical **feats** (accomplishments) for others. They will often clap for themselves and laugh with delight at their new skills.

Focus on

Health

Promoting Self-Esteem

Self-esteem tremendously impacts a person's well-being. Healthy self-esteem leads to joy. Low self-esteem causes anxiety and feelings of inadequacy. Because self-esteem can fluctuate, handling life's challenges is part of self-esteem.

Toddlers' feelings of self-esteem differ from those of adults. Adults' self-esteem is compartmentalized, but toddlers tend to see themselves as a whole. Self-esteem fluctuates only slightly in adults, but toddlers can go from a high (comparing themselves to superheroes) one minute to a low (inconsolable because something does not work) the next.

Caregivers can foster self-esteem in toddlers in the following ways:

Worth. The roots of worth are unconditional love. More than cuddling, this love requires giving undivided attention at times throughout each day. Toddlers need their words and feelings understood and validated ("I know you are sad about _____"). Feelings of worth also come from having behavioral limits that are reasonable, clearly stated, and consistently enforced.

Competence. Offering toddlers, a couple of toddler-friendly options says to the toddler, "I have faith in your decisions." Adults also build competence by acknowledging progress and supporting struggles in toddlers. Specific acknowledgement works, but general praise can erode toddlers' competence by making toddlers feel they are perfect or should be perfect, which is impossible.

Control. Toddlers need to pursue their own interests/goals. Adults should allow the child to take safe risks, make mistakes without saying, "I told you so," and recover from mistakes. Adults also aid toddlers' success by providing the appropriate books/toys, tools for self-help, and activities.

All three aspects of self-esteem work together. Over time, feelings of self-esteem should become stronger.

Photo: wavebreakmedia/Shutterstock.com

13.1-2 Achieving Autonomy

According to Erikson, social-emotional development begins in infancy when babies learn to trust or mistrust. Babies whose needs are met and who have a consistent environment develop a sense of trust. This sense of trust helps them as they enter Erikson's second stage of personality development, called **autonomy versus shame and doubt**. In this stage, toddlers are tasked with achieving **autonomy** (a form of self-governance in which a toddler seeks to do their own will). For most children, this stage begins sometime between 12 and 18 months of age and is completed at about 36 months. (You can review Erikson's theory in Figure 10.10 of the text.)

Autonomy builds on the toddler's expanding motor and intellectual skills. Toddlers are proud of their new skills and want to use them. They have the energy to carry out their goals. Because toddlers have much more "know how" than infants, they feel very independent. The independent feeling comes from toddlers' increasing self-awareness of their abilities. Erikson explained *autonomy* as the toddler's feeling of being able to do some tasks without help from others. He felt that caregivers should recognize toddlers' desire to be more independent and allow them to do what they can at their own pace.

Erikson believed damage occurs, however, when impatient caregivers' complete tasks that toddlers can do themselves. Consistently criticizing or overprotecting toddlers leads them to feel they cannot control themselves and their world. Erikson called this feeling *a sense of shame and doubt*.

13.1-3 Extending Social Relations

As children get older, their growing motor and intellectual abilities help them interact more with adults and other children. These early social interactions teach children new skills and attitudes, which help them get along with other people. This process of interacting with others socializes children.

Interacting with Adults

The caregiver-child relationship begun in infancy serves as the foundation for future social connections. Social relations with guardians, caregivers, and other adults, such as grandparents and family friends, become well established in the toddler years. Although toddlers know more people now, they need a great deal of guidance from primary caregivers and others to establish relationships with adults and other children.

Toddlers who have formed healthy attachments to caregivers have a safe base from which to meet people. Although toddlers continue to look to their main caregivers for social interaction, they now spend more time with adults other than their caregivers. These adults include babysitters, relatives, and neighbors. Having more than one caregiver often helps toddlers adjust to others and expect differences among people. When children have positive experiences with several adults, they develop trusting relationships with them. Having many caregivers, however, is not in the best interest of toddlers who need to develop secure attachments (as described later in the next section).

Interacting with Other Children

During the second year, toddlers tend to interact more with other children, although their first interactions are usually brief. For example, they often imitate each other's actions with a toy without talking to each other (**Figure 13.3**).

rSnapshotPhotos/Shutterstock.com

Figure 13.3 While children do not interact much during the toddler years, they do imitate one another before talking. *How does imitation lay a foundation for social interactions with other children?*

Later, they talk as they play. Toward the end of the toddler years, a couple of toddlers may play together. For example, they may help each other fill a dump truck with sand.

Toddlers are possessive of their toys and belongings when they play. Toddlers have not yet learned about ownership and, therefore, are not quite ready to share with other children. When toys are involved, they often grab, hit, or even bite. As they play, toddlers also explore other children in much the same way as they explore objects. They often feel that "overcoming" another child is positive. Harvey Karp, a popular writer of parenting books, jokingly says that toddlers have some "caveman-like qualities" when they play with other children.

With appropriate adult guidance, toddlers can learn to interact with other children in positive ways. For example, they can sometimes share, return a snatched toy, and show concern for someone who is hurt. When children are better able to communicate, getting along with playmates becomes much easier.

Investigate Special Topics

Establishing a Parenting Style in the *Authority Stage* of Parenting

The caregiver-child relationship changes in toddlerhood. In the first year of toddlerhood, caregivers are still in Galinsky's *nurturing stage* of parenting in which they try to read children's signals of need and then respond correctly, promptly, and consistently. As toddlers become more mobile, curious, and assertive, caregivers enter the *authority stage* of parenting.

In the *authority stage* of parenting, the parenting role includes shaping a child's social behaviors. Caregivers teach children to be *compliant* (agreeable) to caregivers' and other adult's wishes and to get along with other children.

The *authority stage* of parenting can be difficult to enter. The newly developed assertiveness of toddlers puts a strain on caregiver-child relationships. Toddlers seem to misbehave much of the time, partially because they explore everything. They frequently ignore caregivers' commands because they want to see whether the adults really mean what they say. Toddlers may laugh and continue to repeat their misbehavior.

As they respond to toddlers' assertiveness and start to shape and teach their children, caregivers begin to establish a parenting style.

As you have already learned, there are five types of parenting styles, which are uninvolved, permissive, authoritarian, overparenting, and authoritative. Use of the uninvolved, permissive, authoritarian, and overparenting styles often results in toddlers who are noncompliant and aggressive. Caregivers who try to see issues from the toddlers' perspectives and use the authoritative style, however, usually have more compliant and nonaggressive toddlers.

Critical Thinking Activity

Review the information about parenting styles in Lesson 4.2 and take notes about the behaviors associated with each parenting style. Then, in small groups, discuss what actions and responses shape caregivers' parenting styles. Consider how the way caregivers respond to children's assertiveness during toddlerhood affects which parenting style they use from that point onward.

Photo: Tom Wang/Shutterstock.com

13.1-4 Showing Attachments

A child's attachment to a caregiver begins in infancy and is completed between 12 and 18 months of age. Attachment has its biological roots in survival, but is learned by the child through correct, prompt, and consistent caregiving. A child shows attachment to their caregiver through attachment behaviors, which are seen when the toddler feels stress or anxiety. For example, the crying that occurs with separation anxiety is an attachment behavior. In these cases, the child seeks proximity with the caregiver to whom they are attached. The child views this adult as the person best able to cope with the world. Children are often attached to several people. Each attachment a child has is a positive force in their life.

When a toddler seeks out and tries to maintain proximity with a special caregiver, the toddler has a *secure attachment*. The child uses this caregiver as a secure base from which to explore an unfamiliar setting or approach an unfamiliar person. The child also seeks this caregiver's protection and comfort if a situation is perceived as dangerous or distressing. Secure family attachments often encourage out-of-family attachments.

After 18 months of age, if attachments are secure, toddlers are more apt to cooperate even when adult-child goals differ. When children who have secure attachments become adults, they will be able to

- calm themselves
- be confident in their abilities
- form lasting and positive relationships with others
- be overall well-adjusted

Toddlers who get inconsistent care, regardless of the reason, develop *insecure attachments*. Because of a lack of consistent care, toddlers are confused or feel they are not worthy of care or protection. A lack of adult support leads to toddlers who are vulnerable to the impact of trauma from any source. Because of trying so hard to get their basic needs met, they often lag behind secure toddlers in learning, too.

Insecure attachments are most damaging to a person's self-esteem and thus to their mental health. **Figure 13.4** lists several types of insecure attachments, their causes, and outcomes for children during later stages of life. People who have insecure attachments, however, can overcome them and learn new relationship skills.

13.1-5 Expressing Emotions

During the toddler years, children's developing abilities alter how they experience and express emotions. Due to their increasing intellect, toddlers' emotions become more elaborate. They react to more stimuli than infants. They know more people to love and fear, experience more events, and can even imagine unreal things like a monster in the closet. Toddlers can better sense emotions in others, too. Also, emotions become more specific. For example, they may fear a neighbor's dog, but love their dog. In addition, emotions become more intense—sometimes even overwhelming to toddlers.

Due to the intensity of emotions and their increased motor skills, toddlers tend to express emotions physically more often than infants.

Figure 13.4 Insecure Attachments

Anxious-Ambivalent Attachment (also called *resistant*)

Category	Examples
Description	• Toddlers show distress when unfamiliar people are nearby even when caregivers are present. Toddlers stay close to their primary caregiver and react with great distress during separation. Once caregivers return, toddlers resist the adult's offers of comfort. Toddlers' reactions upon reunions are ambivalent and resistant.
Caregivers behaviors*	• Caregivers do not read their infants' and toddlers' signals of needs correctly. They respond in ways that do not fit, such as offering play activities when toddlers are hungry or tired. • Caregivers respond to infants' and toddlers' needs inconsistently. • Caregivers respond in different degrees to the same needs. For example, if the child falls, the adult may ignore the child one time and overly comfort the child the next time.
Long-term child results*	• As toddlers, they are very clingy. • Separation anxiety lasts longer than average. • As school-age children, they want attention and are overemotional. They do not like to work on their own. • As young adults, they fear entering into a close relationship with others. If they do, they are controlling in these relationships. • Throughout life, they are easily frustrated.

Anxious-Avoidant Attachment

Category	Examples
Description	• Toddlers explore toys and show no preference for primary caregiver versus stranger. During separations, toddlers show no distress. Once caregivers return, toddlers ignore and avoid their caregivers.
Caregivers behaviors*	• Caregivers respond to children's physical needs, but not promptly. • Caregivers do not often respond to emotional needs, such as fear, by comforting. Infants and toddlers are left alone to deal with these nonphysical needs. • Caregivers ignore delight or excitement shown by their infants and toddlers.
Long-term child results*	• As infants and toddlers, they see no need to communicate needs. • As toddlers, they appear "mature" during separations because anxiety is not exposed. • As preschool and school-age children, they seem too independent. Even when frustrated, they do not ask for help. They also tend to be aggressive in play. • As school-age children and teens, they show impulsive behaviors, including bullying. • As adults, they prefer to be alone. They value their independence. They rarely admit to having positive feelings for others.

Goodheart-Willcox Publisher
(Continued)

Figure 13.4 Insecure Attachments (Continued)

Disorganized Attachment

Category	Examples
Description	• Toddlers are inconsistent in attachment behaviors. For example, they may act as though they want to be picked up, but they stiffen once held. They make poor eye contact with caregivers and other adults.
Caregivers behaviors*	• Caregivers rarely respond to the needs of their infants or toddlers. • If caregivers respond, the responses do not fit the needs. • Caregivers often neglect or abuse. • Caregivers are often depressed or are on drugs. • Caregivers are absent and children have multiple foster home placements.
Long-term child results*	• As toddlers, they often freeze in their footsteps for no apparent reason. • As preschool and school-age children, they are often hard to understand because of exceptionally fast speech. They have a difficult time understanding other people's feelings. Their pretend play may be violent. • As adults, they do not form lasting intimate relationships and are anxious and depressed. • Throughout life, their behaviors seem different from day to day.

*The way caregivers have responded to the child determines the type of attachment the child has for the adult and the long-term child results. Attachment is very critical to a child's mental health.

On the other hand, toddlers' verbal skills enable them to express emotions verbally, too, if taught. Because of these new and improved abilities, children's expressions of love and affection, fear, anxiety, and anger change during the toddler years.

There are many activities that caregivers can do to help toddlers practice their social and emotional skills. For children with a disability, it may take them longer to reach developmental milestones or understand how to express emotions. For toddlers:

- use pretend play as a chance to talk about feelings. Use a doll or stuffed animal as you play. For example, ask your child, "Doggie is sad because he fell down and got a bump. What can we do to make Doggie feel better?" This will help the child learn empathy.
- make a homemade book about feelings. Toddlers love looking at pictures of themselves, family, and friends. Take pictures of people who are happy, silly, tired, excited, etc. Place in a book and put a feeling word under the photo. Let the child read the book to you and tell what feeling is in each picture.

- use songs to practice feeling words. Change the words to songs like "When You're Happy and You Know It." Add verses to express other emotions, for example, "When you're angry and you know it, stomp your feet", "When you're sad and you know it, get a hug."
- make a cozy place in your home. Children sometimes need time alone to calm down. Give them a space that has soft cushions, blankets, stuffed animals, and favorite stories. Encourage the toddler to use the place when they are feeling overwhelmed.
- suggest ways to manage strong emotions. Telling toddlers what they can do to express big feelings is important. The goal is to teach the toddler that any emotion is okay to feel and that they can learn to express the feelings in healthy, non-hurtful ways.
- develop a feelings vocabulary. Teach toddlers words like safe, peaceful, cranky, silly, bored, proud, confused, cheerful. While toddlers won't understand the words right away, over time and with practice they will grasp the meanings and begin to use the words themselves.

Love and Affection

Toddlers are still attached to their caregivers and express love and affection by wanting to be near them. They seek caregivers when faced with a strange situation. This attachment seems to help other aspects of social-emotional development because the love a toddler feels for caregivers also extends to other adults, children, and pets (**Figure 13.5**).

Fear

Many fears that begin during infancy are evident after the first birthday. Fears increase quickly after two years of age because toddlers know about more things to fear. They know of more objects and situations that can hurt them. Survival fears (such as fears of crossing the street, falling from heights, guns, and poisons), however, are not well-developed. Safety remains in the hands of caregivers.

Toddlers also cannot distinguish real from unreal. They imagine many unreal things, such as monsters. Toddlers may also fear animals, darkness, nightmares, "bad people," injury, gestures, and startling noises.

chachamaliStock via Getty Images Plus

Figure 13.5 Toddlers show affection to personal possessions or objects, including toys. *What are some ways toddlers express love?*

Toddlers tend to act out their fears during play. For example, a 30-month-old who fears dogs may be seen barking and growling in play. Toddlers may imitate bad people seen on television or in books. Adults should handle these fears in a matter-of-fact way, and never tease toddlers about their fears or push them into scary situations.

Anxiety

Toddlers may begin to experience nightmares around two years of age as a way of dealing with anxiety. These nightmares can stem from fears of being left alone, getting hurt, or angering adults. The details of the nightmares are unreal, often including unknown lands and monsters. If toddlers are content during the day, their nightmares do not reveal a problem. For most children, nightmares decrease in time. A trip to the library or bookstore may result in some humorous books to help the child deal with nightmares.

Another form of anxiety is displayed through separation anxiety. Older toddlers between 30 and 35 months of age show less separation anxiety than younger children. Some separation anxiety continues into the toddler stage and sometimes beyond. Many toddlers overcome some of their separation anxiety if they feel a caregiver's love and know the caregiver will return. Increased language skills help toddlers understand why caregivers sometimes leave. Caregivers must make sure their toddler receives good and loving care during separations. Children with insecure attachments may show separation anxiety even well beyond the toddler years.

Anger

Toddlers desire more independence and have a strong will. When defeated in their goal-seeking behaviors, toddlers react with anger. A sudden emotional outburst of anger, called a **temper tantrum**, often appears during the second year of life. A temper tantrum averages about five minutes in length.

The child goes through five stages during the tantrum (**Figure 13.6**).

Tantrums tend to happen when something does not go a toddler's way. Because this is often the case, temper tantrums are common for toddlers. Temper tantrums are meant to attract attention, but often are not directed at anyone. (In the next lesson, you will learn about ideas for handling toddlers' temper tantrums.)

13.1-6 Social-Emotional Developmental Milestones

Children achieve a number of social-emotional developmental milestones during the toddler years. Due to changes in brain development, motor skills, and intellectual/language abilities, toddlers' social-emotional worlds begin to mature, which lays the foundation for development beyond the toddler years. **Figure 13.7** lists some developmental milestones of social-emotional development during the toddler years.

Figure 13.6 **Stages of Temper Tantrums**

1. Experiences anger, shown by throwing self on the floor, kicking, and screaming.
2. Experiences anger and sadness, manifested by crying, whining, and whimpering.
3. Feels anger level drop.
4. Desires cuddling.
5. Forgets about tantrum and engages in other activities.

Goodheart-Willcox Publisher

Juanmonino/iStock via Getty Images Plus

Lesson 13.1 Review and Assessment

1. A toddler's ability to name at least seven of their body parts is called _____. (13.1.1)

   A. sense awareness
   B. gender identity
   C. body awareness
   D. autonomy

2. **True or False.** Autonomy is a form of self-governance in which a toddler seeks to do their own will. (13.1.2)

3. **True or False.** A toddler with a healthy attachment to their caregivers is unlikely to develop a trusting relationship with an adult babysitter. (13.1.3)

4. How might a toddler with an anxious-ambivalent attachment to a parent respond when the parent returns after a separation? (13.1.4)

   A. By ignoring and avoiding the parent
   B. By growing stiff when then parent picks them up
   C. By continuing to cry despite the parent's offers of comfort
   D. By seeking out the parent and showing them affection

5. **True or False.** Toddlers often act out their fears during play. (13.1.5)

6. Which is a social-emotional milestone toddlers often achieve between ages 12 and 18 months? (13.1.6)

   A. Using possessive words like *me* and *mine*
   B. Showing curiosity about their own body parts
   C. Taking turns when playing with other children
   D. Looking at a person who is talking to them

Figure 13.7 **Toddler Social-Emotional Milestones**

12 to 18 months	18 to 24 months	24 to 36 months

eclipse_images/E+ via Getty Images

emholk/iStock via Getty Images Plus

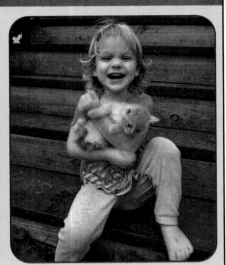
Janell Johnson

12 to 18 months
- Seeks attention.
- Shows affection.
- Protests when frustrated.
- Shows intense separation anxiety.
- Resists napping and bedtime even when tired and sleepy.
- Plays alone on floor with toys for a few minutes.
- Looks at the person who is talking to them.

18 to 24 months
- Directs another's attention to an object.
- Says *hi*, *bye*, and *please* (if reminded).
- Shows some separation anxiety.
- Is shy around strangers.
- Wants things now.
- Becomes more independent and defiant when challenged; may be aggressive when frustrated.
- Often responds with *no*.
- Uses possessive words (*me*, *mine*).
- Shows attachment to a toy or blanket.
- Responds to simple requests.

24 to 36 months
- Verbalizes feelings.
- Shows love to non-caregiving adults, children, and pets.
- Begins to interact more with children, especially by chasing after others.
- Is possessive about toys.
- Fears more real and imaginary things.
- Begins having nightmares.
- Is persistent and demanding.
- Has tantrums.
- Is curious about self (wants to know names of body parts).
- Shows empathy.
- Takes turns, especially on slides.
- Knows much about what is and is not acceptable to parents and regular caregivers, but will test limits.

Goodheart-Willcox Publisher

Meeting Toddlers' Social-Emotional Needs

Key Terms

delay gratification
obedience
premoral
self-assertion
self-restraint
social referencing

Learning Outcomes

After studying this lesson, you will be able to

13.2-1 **plan** activities and toys for stimulating self-awareness in toddlers.

13.2-2 **explain** how caregivers can help toddlers achieve autonomy.

13.2-3 **describe** how caregivers can foster self-assertion and teach obedience in the toddler years.

13.2-4 **give examples** of ways caregivers can help toddlers co-regulate their emotions.

13.2-5 **identify** ways caregivers can help prevent stress in the toddler years.

Reading and Notetaking Activity

Before reading, skim the headings in this chapter. List the headings to create an outline for taking notes during reading and class discussion. Under each heading list any key terms. Finally, write two questions you expect to have answered in class. After completing the chapter, ask your teacher any questions you still have about the concepts or terms you learned.

Introduction

Meeting social-emotional needs in the toddler years differs from meeting needs during infancy. Infants are totally dependent on caregivers to help meet their needs. Toddlers, however, are no longer completely dependent on adults due to their advancing skills. As toddlers learn they can do things on their own, they desire more independence (autonomy).

For toddlers to grow and develop and have self-esteem, caregivers must allow toddlers to do the things they are able to do. Toddlers, however, are far from being ready to be independent. They still need adult help in achieving goals. Adults also need to set limits (exercise authority).

Thus, Galinsky noted that caregivers are still nurturing, but soon will be in the *authority stage* of parenting. The *authority stage* of parenting requires caregivers to find their parenting style often through much trial and error. In sum, the overall adult goal is to find a healthy, overall stress-free balance between toddlers' goals and expressions of emotions and adult control. (You can review Galinsky's parenting stages in Figure 4.4 of the text.)

13.2-1 Supporting the Toddler's Self-Awareness

Self-awareness grows out of the toddler's daily contact with their world. Guardians and caregivers can enhance the toddler's self-awareness and acknowledge the child as a unique person in the following ways:

- Pay attention when a toddler wants to talk. Ask yourself this question, "How would you feel if you wanted to talk and were ignored?" Acknowledge a toddler's feelings with descriptors, such as "You look happy" or "You look so sad." Sit together and talk about how the toddler has grown and how loved they are.
- Provide a place for the toddler's possessions, especially toys, and encourage them to take responsibility for their possessions. Also, let the toddler decide about sharing these possessions.
- Encourage the toddler to self-feed and help with their hygiene. Let the toddler help around the house, too. Comment on the skills and how they helped you.
- Plan a few specific activities to enhance the toddler's self-awareness (**Figure 13.8**).

Self-awareness is well underway by the end of the toddler years but continues to grow throughout life. A happy, secure toddler will develop positive feelings about themselves.

Figure 13.8 **Self-Awareness Activities**

Name the parts of the face. Place the toddler's hands on your face. Name aloud each part of your face as the child feels it. Ask the child to name the parts.

Mirrors. With the toddler on your lap, hold a mirror to reflect the toddler's face. Ask, "Who is that?" If the toddler does not answer, say, "That is you." Say the toddler's name.

Dressing up. Toddlers enjoy dressing up in adults' old hats, clothes, accessories, and shoes. To help the toddler play while dressing up, show the child one object. For example, show the toddler a hat and say, "Look at this pretty hat. I'm going to wear it." Place the hat on your head and talk about how pretty it is. Then say, "Do you want to wear a hat?" Place a hat on the toddler's head, saying how nice it looks. If the toddler enjoys this, try other items.

Pretend. Have a pretend tea party with a toddler. Talk about the pretend foods in much the same way you would talk about real food. If the toddler looks confused, say, "How funny! We can pretend to have a party!"

A book about me. Take pictures of the toddler's daily activities. Place the pictures in a photo album. (Toddlers often take these albums to child care programs to reduce separation anxiety. Be sure to include photos of caregivers, siblings, and other loved ones.)

Photo gallery. Keep a family photo album or place photos of the toddler in various spots around the house (at the toddler's eye level). Toddlers like photos capturing their experiences.

Measuring chart. Measure the toddler's height on a growth chart and keep a running tally of the growth changes.

Goodheart-Willcox Publisher

13.2-2 Helping Toddlers Achieve Autonomy

Autonomy is an important part of the developing toddler's life. Caregivers can help toddlers on this journey toward achieving autonomy by ensuring their safety and encouraging toddlers' efforts.

Ensuring Safety

Guardians and caregivers can help toddlers achieve autonomy by keeping them from harm. Caregivers can make sure toddlers' indoor and outdoor environments are safe. This will decrease the number of times caregivers have to warn a toddler. They can give a toddler safe choices so they can build feelings of independence and use their skills. Caregivers should redirect toddlers before they engage in a forbidden or unsafe action. This is more helpful than waiting to intervene after a toddler is already performing the action. It is also more helpful than simply reacting to the consequences.

When ensuring safety, adults need to recognize that toddlers will sometimes misjudge their skills and need help. Toddlers do not understand possible results of some of their actions. Sometimes, toddlers find limits to their actions through failed attempts. This is frustrating for toddlers. If the goal is unsafe, caregivers need to set limits for a toddler while understanding the child's perspective.

Encouraging Efforts

In addition to ensuring safety, caregivers can encourage toddlers' efforts at achieving autonomy. Caregivers can avoid excessive criticism or correction of toddlers by letting them make mistakes without scolding and by not making demands that are too rigid for toddlers to follow. Adults can encourage a toddler to make choices by offering suggestions on how to complete a task instead of doing the task for the child.

Caregivers can acknowledge toddlers' efforts to become more autonomous and avoid mixing encouragement with criticism. They can celebrate and help toddlers remember personal achievements by taking photos or videos.

13.2-3 Balancing Self-Assertion and Obedience

Because of toddlers' newfound skills, they become willful and curious. Toddlers find it most difficult to **delay gratification** (wait until later to get what is wanted) and inhibit intense emotions (**Figure 13.9**). Problems occur when the personalities and needs of caregivers and other adults conflict with the needs of toddlers.

Toddlers need attachments for protection and comfort as well as for their growing autonomy. They will go back and forth between wanting to be totally independent and wanting to be totally dependent. For adults and other caregivers, getting the balance between allowing autonomy and dependency in toddlers is critical.

These changes in toddlers' wills confuse adults. Most adults find they must give toddlers freedom at times and be firm at other times. Their actions depend on toddlers' needs.

FatCamera/E+ via Getty Images

Figure 13.9 Toddlers find it difficult to control intense, new emotions and may act on these intense emotions around adults and other children. *What can caregivers do to acknowledge toddlers' emotions while still teaching obedience?*

Fostering Self-Assertion

Toddlers need some freedom, and adults need to guide toddlers' **self-assertion** (doing as one chooses rather than what others want). Giving toddlers choices lets them express their preferences. For example, caregivers can let a toddler choose between two sets of clothing to wear that day. A toddler may also choose between self-control and adult-control. The adult may say, "You may color on the paper, or I'll have to put the crayons away." Toddlers seem more willing to accept a firm *no* when given choices at other times. Through choices, toddlers develop *autonomy* and avoid feelings of *shame* for their mistakes and *doubt* about their abilities. (See Erikson's theory in Figure 10.10 of the text.)

Teaching Obedience

Toddlers do not have **self-restraint**, or the ability to control themselves. They also do not know all the rules of acceptable behavior. Adults not only foster self-assertion, but they also teach **obedience** (acting within the limits set by others) to help toddlers understand what is socially acceptable behavior. The best way to teach obedience is to meet toddlers' needs and not punish what they do wrong. There are positive ways to help toddlers learn obedience. Some of these include

- use a soft-spoken tone, stay calm, and provide clear instructions for how you expect the toddler to obey.
- show the child what you want them to do and don't expect the toddler to be able to do things right the first time.
- avoid repeating yourself to avoid the toddler getting the impression that they can put off what the caregiver has requested they do.
- tell the child what you would like them to do; suggest alternate activities or behaviors rather than telling the toddler no repeatedly.
- be consistent with the rules. If you say no be sure to consistently say no. If the child repeats the same misbehavior, couple the disobedience with consequences. For example, if a child throws a toy at another child, take the toy, and put it up.

- encourage the toddler to acknowledge the instructions given.

Setting Limits

Caregivers can help toddlers learn socially acceptable behaviors by setting limits for toddlers. Limits keep toddlers safe and show them how to become more socially acceptable (**Figure 13.10**). Setting limits is part of Galinsky's *authority stage* of parenting. (See Galinsky's parenting stages in Figure 4.4 of the text.) Adults need to decide which limits are necessary ("choose your battles") and whether the limits are appropriate for the toddler. (Am I expecting my toddler to wait too long? Am I always saying *no*?)

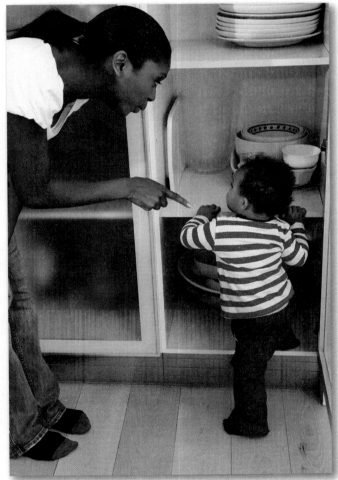

BananaStock/BananaStock/Thinkstock

Figure 13.10 By setting limits, caregivers teach toddlers to behave in socially acceptable ways and to stay safe. *What limits did you have a hard time learning as a young child? Why?*

When setting limits, parents and other adults need to remember toddlers are **premoral** (not self-guided by internal values). Toddlers are guided by outside rules, and they need help learning these rules. Ways in which adults may help toddlers learn rules include

- modeling what is being taught, such as helpfulness, kindness in words, and sharing.
- making simple rules as needs arise. Simple rules may include "Be kind to others," "Always ask for help," "Say *please* and *thank you*," and "Do not hit, bite, or scratch others."
- getting on eye level with the toddler and matching tone of voice to concern. (For example, adults should express by tone of voice more concern about biting than forgetting to say *please*.) Do not yell when talking to the toddler.
- encouraging the toddler to use **social referencing** (evaluating how to respond to a situation by getting a social cue from a more experienced person). When a toddler looks at an adult, he or she is asking, "May I do this?" Adults should send the cue. Toddlers can even notice subtle cues. Social referencing aids the child in learning what is and is not acceptable without direct experience.

- telling the toddler when their behaviors are acceptable.

Providing Guidance

By 18 months of age, many toddlers show definite signs of **contrariness** (tendency to oppose almost everything others do or say). They tend to oppose adults and even other toddlers. They replace *yes* with *no*, even when *yes* is what they really mean. *Me want* is replaced with *No want*.

Adults may find it difficult to help toddlers achieve autonomy while keeping them safe and preventing conflicts. Erikson felt adults should firmly reassure the toddler. Adults do not need to give in to the child's will all the time. When they confront a child, however, parents should stay calm and assure the child they still love them. This protects children from harm without making them feel ashamed or guilty. Oftentimes, adults can prevent the battle of wills. The following ideas may reduce conflicts:

- ***Let the toddler choose.*** Providing the toddler with choices promotes autonomy as well as helps avoid conflicts (**Figure 13.11**). The simplest way to avoid conflict is to let the toddler make some choices. If results are not harmful, allowing toddlers some freedom makes obeying easier.

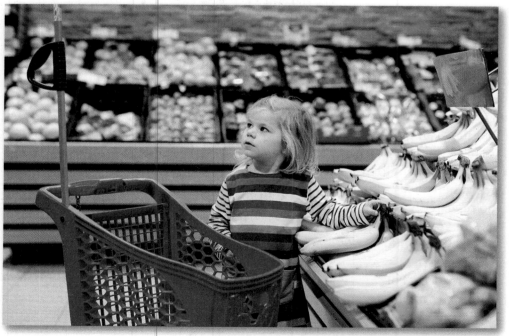

Figure 13.11 Letting a toddler choose between options in some situations, such as which fruit to buy at the grocery store, promotes autonomy and reduces the chance that the toddler will insist on choosing later. *What are safe choices toddlers can be allowed to make?*

romrodinka/iStock via Getty Images Plus

- *Tell the toddler in advance.* Telling the toddler about upcoming events in advance helps reduce contrariness. This lead-time allows the toddler to prepare emotionally for the change of activities. If the toddler resists the change, use calming actions, such as picking up the toddler.
- *Word commands in positive ways.* Wording a command in a playful way can often prevent struggles with the toddler. For example, to let a child know about an upcoming car ride, a parent might say, "Pilot to copilot—it's time to go."
- *Use pretend games.* Playing a pretend game of obedience is another way to reduce contrariness. For example, to get the toddler to wash their hands before meals, the adult might say, "I'm going to wash my hands before you do." (Of course, after much scrubbing, the toddler wins.) Sometimes pretend games of obedience become rituals, such as a chase to the bedroom at naptime.

Toddlers will make frequent mistakes. Even then, adults need to remain positive. When toddlers are always made to feel they are "bad," they may grow to dislike themselves. Adults should label incorrect behavior as a mistake, and not call the child *bad*, *selfish*, *naughty*, or *mean*. Harsh punishment may cause toddlers to feel they are bad, too.

Being Consistent

Consistency helps people feel secure. When there is a conflict between toddler goals and adult expectations, children will test limits. Toddlers are checking adult reactions because they want to know whether these are *real* limits. Consistency in rules and follow-up is the teacher.

From time to time, people need flexible rules. Toddlers may need flexible rules when they are ill or when other problems occur. Once the situation is back to normal, rules can become consistent again. Of course, as children grow, discipline changes and children are often allowed more freedom.

Showing Love and Respect

Toddlers are worthy of the same respect other people receive. Adults should not respond to toddlers' mistakes with hurtful teasing or anger. Respecting toddlers helps them like themselves. It also serves as the model for the growing child's relationships with others.

More than anything else, toddlers need to feel loved by caring adults. They sense love that is shown to them physically and directly (**Figure 13.12**). Toddlers do not seem to sense love shown in indirect ways, such as having cooked meals or clean clothes (although these are important). Toddlers have good days and problem days, just like adults. When limits are set and discipline is firm, yet kind, the toddler will begin to have good days more often. Good days are a sign that toddlers are getting better at balancing self-assertion and the need to obey. Balancing the two is a skill they will need throughout life.

13.2-4 Guiding the Toddler's Emotions

Toddlers show a variety of emotions, ranging from positive to negative. Toddlers have a broader range of negative emotions because of their increased intellectual abilities, lack of inhibition, and immature language skills needed to express needs and resolve conflicts. They need caregivers to help them co-regulate their emotions.

BananaStock/BananaStock/Thinkstock

Figure 13.12 Most toddlers respond to cuddling, loving words, and special times each day when attention is focused on them. *Why do you think toddlers respond best when love is shown in direct ways?*

The goal of co-regulation of emotional expression is to help a child develop a high-level of self-regulating abilities by four or five years of age, which is when the *authority stage* of parenting ends. A child's temperament is involved in co-regulation to some degree, but caregiver behaviors play the central role in the development of children's self-regulation. These behaviors must be guided by a child's developmental level. In infancy and early toddlerhood, co-regulation involves soothing. Between 18 and 30 months, toddlers' emerging intellectual and language abilities increase dramatically and contribute to what works best in co-regulation.

Once a toddler develops language skills, *adult explanation* is considered the best method of co-regulation. An adult explanation might include

- the cause of the problem ("_____ wanted to play with your toy")
- the child's emotional feeling ("You are angry and that is all right because you were playing with _____")
- a response strategy ("Hitting hurts! So just tell _____ that we have another _____. Let's get it. Then you can both play with _____")

Reasoning should be at the child's zone of proximal development (ZPD) to help a toddler learn more sophisticated strategies for coping. Toddlers must grow in their understandings and responses to develop a cache of strategies needed for self-regulation. If you need a refresher on the zone of proximal development (ZPD) look at Figure 12.5.

Another co-regulation method that works with older toddlers who need to delay gratification is *distraction*, which refocuses the toddler's attention. For example, car toys and books or a family game often serve as a distraction for a whining, tired toddler on a long drive.

Love and Empathy

Toddlers who have formed secure attachments know they are loved and protected. In turn, they love their caregivers and other adults. Toddlers show their love by cuddling and snuggling, sharing joy in new experiences and skills, and showing delight when caregivers return after separation.

Toddlers also show love to friends and their "loveys" (attachment items). "Loveys" help toddlers make it through separations. In a way, these attachment items represent family and security and are like the beloved stuffed animals of older children or photographs displayed at the workplace of adults.

Toddlers also begin to learn about empathy. The capacity for **empathy**, the ability to recognize and identify with the emotions of others, is inborn. Developing empathy skills, however, requires learning. Before empathy can develop, toddlers must begin to see the goals and emotions of others (called *taking another's perspective*), which require understanding of self- versus other-awareness. Then, toddlers need to see examples of empathy in their environment.

Toddlers with secure attachments recognize that adults and other caregivers have understood and accepted their needs. These adults have modeled empathy. Toddlers develop empathy by using social referencing as adults model repeated, sincere actions of empathy. Although infants can mimic empathy, two-year-olds can initiate empathy. **Figure 13.13** shows some tips for developing this complex skill.

Figure 13.13 Tips for Developing Empathy

- Verbally reflect on how children are feeling rather than immediately saying, "Everything is (or will be) all right."
- Have children practice "reading" feelings in expressive photographs and drawings.
- Ask older toddlers how specific characters in stories feel in certain situations.
- Read stories about feelings.
- Encourage empathy in pretend play, such as asking, "Does (doll's name) need a nap?"
- Teach words about feelings—happy, mad (or angry), and sad.

Goodheart-Willcox Publisher

Anger and Temper Tantrums

As you read earlier, toddlers express anger through aggressive acts and temper tantrums. Anger is a strong emotion that **bewilders** (confuses) toddlers. The lack of mature language skills is a major challenge in resolving conflicts. Since toddlers cannot articulate their angry feelings, they express anger through aggression.

Many two-year-olds have temper tantrums, but some do not. Toddlers who are lively, under stress (even the stress of being hungry) and cannot yet talk are prone to tantrums.

Caregivers and other adults can learn to handle tantrums by understanding the cause of the child's tantrums. Caregivers can avoid tantrums in some cases by seeing the situation from the toddler's perspective. The following actions may help prevent temper tantrums:

- Meet the toddler's needs before involving the toddler in adult activities. For example, a toddler may need a nutritious snack or a nap before accompanying the adult on errands.
- Avoid making demands when a toddler is tired, hungry, or ill.
- Remove toys or play equipment that frustrates the toddler.
- Have enough toys to prevent boredom or duplicate toys to share with a friend.
- Give in on small demands, such as staying up a few minutes later when cousins are visiting or spending a few more minutes in the park because it was hard to get a turn on the slide.
- Offer help before the toddler becomes too frustrated.
- Find fun ways to gain toddler compliance.
- Acknowledge signs of control.

If a tantrum occurs because the toddler is making demands of their own, tantrums may need to be handled in a different way. Caregivers can tell the toddler beforehand what they can or cannot have or do. They can plan something for the toddler to do in the setting, such as carry a box to the check-out lane in the store (**Figure 13.14**). Most importantly, caregivers and other adults cannot give in, even if the tantrum becomes full blown. (Giving in teaches the child that tantrums work.)

Once a temper tantrum is underway, allow the tantrum to continue. It is a form of release for the child. Stay nearby, but do not try to reason with the child. If a tantrum occurs in public, go to a quiet place, if possible, for the toddler to become calm. Do not act embarrassed if others watch.

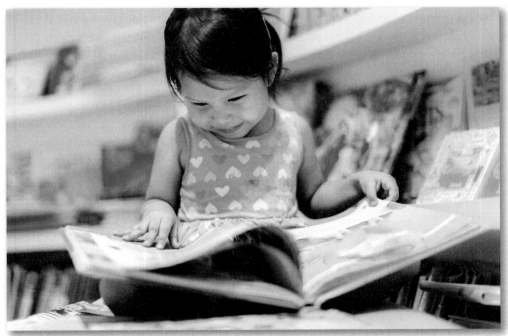

Globalmoments/iStock via Getty Images Plus

Figure 13.14 Making plans for a toddler to follow, such as telling a toddler they can pick out a book from the library, can help reduce temper tantrums. *Why do you think having a plan to follow reduces temper tantrums?*

Avoid using spankings to punish tantrums. If the adult expresses displeasure (or even anger) in a physical way, he or she is modeling that behavior for the toddler. Tantrums, when handled calmly, often decrease during the preschool years. Also, adult calmness serves as a model for children as the best way to deal with anger.

Once the child is calm, adults should acknowledge the feelings of toddlers and show comfort. The adult may say, "I know you really wanted to stay outside. I'm sorry you are so upset about coming in the house." After the tantrum, hugs are often helpful. When adults hold back this comfort, toddlers may feel unlovable.

Fears and Anxieties

For toddlers to overcome fears and anxieties, they need to see and talk about their fears in safe ways. Telling toddlers other children have the same fear may comfort them. Gradual exposure to a feared subject may also help. For example, if the toddler is afraid of dogs, the adult may talk about dogs. Later, the adult may read a story about playful dogs or give a cute toy dog to the child. After some time, the toddler may stand near a friendly puppy or small dog that is safely behind a fence. This method is better for the toddler than suddenly exposing the child to fearful situations.

Focus on Health

Maternal Depression: A Major Child Development Concern

Depression is a sad mood that continues and affects a person's energy level, social functioning, and body functions (eating and sleeping problems, headaches). Even mild forms can affect adults and their families. In fact, depression affects at least 12- to 25-percent of all female caregivers. Common factors causing depression are genetic predisposition, perinatal physical changes, and trauma (violence, abuse).

Toddler risks. Toddler care requires much energy, ingenuity, and calmness. Feeling overwhelmed, depressed adults often withdraw from care tasks (neglect). Others provide controlling, but inconsistent care. They show less affection for, talk and play less with, and seldom encourage their toddlers. The worst problem, however, comes in the parenting style—being too critical of their toddlers' behaviors and reacting with anger, hostility, and even abuse.

Toddler outcomes. When adults withdraw from care, toddler accidents are three times more frequent. This may result in toddlers' intellectual (delays, learning disorders) and behavioral (severe tantrums, biting, conduct disorders) problems, which continue throughout childhood or longer. These toddlers are also prone to depression before adulthood.

Adult support. Almost all depression can be successfully treated. The first task is identifying symptoms. The second task is providing needed treatment, such as antidepressant medications, "talking therapies," and parenting education and support. Depressed adults need to develop routines, have some respite from child care, and take time for themselves. When adults feel a sense of self-control, parenting becomes easier, and the toddler outlook is brighter.

Photo: wavebreakmedia/Shutterstock.com

Giving toddlers security also reduces fear. Night-lights, toys (especially "loveys") in bed, and familiar caregivers add security (**Figure 13.15**). In many cases, adults can avoid situations that cause much fear or anxiety. Some situations, however, such as going to the doctor, cannot be avoided. These situations can be explained to the toddler in a simple, honest way. As they are explained, adults should address only fears the toddler has already shown.

Adults can acknowledge toddlers for their small steps toward overcoming fears. For example, toddlers can receive encouragement for only crying a little or for not running from the puppy behind the fence. Most of the toddler's fears and anxieties will disappear with age. If caregivers handle fear and anxieties in understanding ways, toddlers will be better able to cope with present and future fears and anxieties.

Based on the Harvard Growth Studies, research is leaning toward the belief that some children are genetically vulnerable to stress. These children may be more fearful or anxious throughout life than others. More sensitive and responsive caregiving is needed for these vulnerable children. When a young child has a supportive relationship with adults, the development of healthy stress response systems will occur. However, if the stress response is extreme, long-lasting or there is not a supportive relationship available to the child a damaged, weakened system and brain architecture can have lifelong repercussions.

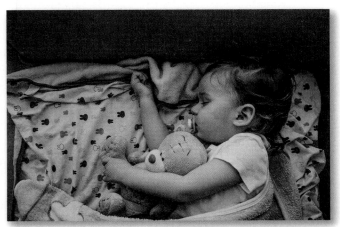

Ijubaphoto/iStock via Getty Images Plus

Figure 13.15 Toys and familiar caregivers give children a sense of security, which reduces fear. *What familiar objects or experiences reduce fear for you?*

13.2-5 Handling Stress in the Toddler Years

One of the best ways to deal with stress is through prevention. Caregivers can help prevent stress in the toddler years by

- meeting toddlers' needs correctly, promptly, and consistently (which encourages secure attachments)
- helping the toddler feel nurtured and loved even when the toddler's actions might be considered unlovable
- aiding the toddler in the control of their emotions through co-regulation
- helping older toddlers communicate needs and feelings by talking

Caregivers might also ask themselves questions, such as: Am I making different child care arrangements too frequently? Is our family life peaceful? Am I allowing my toddler to watch adult-oriented media content, such as scary movies? Am I helping my toddler by being their *security-base* (being the important person in their life)?

Sometimes stress cannot be prevented. Adults and caregivers can, however, respond to the stress and identify stressors. Major stressors that can affect toddlers include adult-toddler conflicts, insecure attachments, concerns and traumatic events in the family, and adult depression in the toddler's second and third years.

Adult depression puts the mental health of the toddler at risk because the toddler's brain systems that generate depression are developing at this time. In the toddler period, the personality and emotional reaction area of the brain is being established. Calm, responsive parenting behaviors are needed to handle the needs of toddlers. Depressed caregivers are often not responsive, or normal toddler behaviors evoke an irritable, even a hostile, response. In turn, cortisol spikes in the toddler's developing brain, including the areas that generate depression. Thus, adult depression begins a chain of events that puts the mental health of the toddler at risk. For many adults, depression is an unavoidable illness, but successful treatments are available.

Caregivers can recognize stress in toddlers by paying attention to signs, such as frequent nightmares, unusually intense fears, and aggressive behaviors. Coping with a toddler's stress involves being patient and supportive. Listening for clues about the source of the stress is important. All toddlers need consistency in their lives. If the symptoms of stress continue or worsen, seek professional help.

FOCUS ON MENTAL HEALTH

The toddler's brain system can generate depression. Stress caused by strong and continuous adult-child conflicts, insecure attachments, and traumatic events can be very damaging to mental health throughout life. Teaching children how to cope with stress by helping them with the physical, emotional/behavioral and regression reactions can be as simple as reassuring the child that they are safe, allowing them to express their emotions through drawing or playing, resuming normal activities as soon as possible or creating a new routine. Physical activities that can help reduce stress include going for a walk, dancing, and playing a game.

Lesson 13.2 Review and Assessment

1. **True or False.** Encouraging a toddler to help brush their teeth is one way to stimulate self-awareness. (13.2.1)
2. Which is the best way for a caregiver to encourage a toddler's efforts at achieving autonomy? (13.2.2)
   A. Correcting them before they make a mistake
   B. Finishing a challenging task for them
   C. Offering them suggestions on how to complete a task
   D. Allowing them to learn from an unsafe action
3. A toddler's ability to control themself is called _____. (13.2.3)
   A. obedience
   B. self-restraint
   C. self-assertion
   D. social referencing
4. **True or False.** Once a toddler develops language skills, adult explanation is considered the best method of co-regulation. (13.2.4)
5. **True or False.** Frequent nightmares, unusually intense fears, and aggressive behaviors are signs of stress in toddlers. (13.2.5)

Chapter 13 Review and Assessment

Summary

Lesson 13.1

13.1-1 During the toddler years, children begin to develop *self-awareness*. Besides seeing themselves as unique people and recognizing themselves, toddlers' self-awareness involves early feelings of self-esteem.

13.1-2 Toddlers are in Erikson's second stage of personality development, known as *autonomy versus shame and doubt*.

13.1-3 During the toddler years, social relations are extended. The caregiver-child relationship, which was solely nurturing during infancy, changes to include socialization and authority.

13.1-3 Toddlers spend more time with adults other than parents. Interactions with other children are brief, though children often imitate each other.

13.1-4 Developing secure attachments is critical for social-emotional outcomes throughout life.

13.1-5 Toddlers experience a wider range of emotions than infants. They are still attached to caregivers, but also begin to show affection for others.

13.1-6 Toddlers are still dependent on adults to meet their social-emotional needs. Changes in brain development, motor skills, and intellectual/language abilities lead to the development of many social-emotional milestones, which lays the foundation for development beyond the toddler years.

Lesson 13.2

13.2-1 Self-awareness is well underway by the end of the toddler years but continues to grow throughout life. A happy, secure toddler will develop positive feelings about themselves.

13.2-2 Caregivers can help toddlers achieve autonomy by ensuring their safety and encouraging toddlers' efforts.

13.2-3 Caregivers must help their toddlers find a balance between self-assertion and obedience.

13.2-4 Caregivers and other adults must guide and co-regulate toddlers' positive and negative emotions.

13.2-5 Stress is common in the toddler years. Most stress is short-lived, but stress associated with insecure attachments or trauma in toddlers, including depressed adults, is serious and requires professional treatment.

College and Career Portfolio

Portfolio Sample Rationale

Portfolio samples are chosen to exhibit your best work in one way or another. Because portfolios can be made up of a variety of pieces, you should be prepared to explain why you chose the portfolio samples you did and how they portray your best work. To determine rationale for your portfolio samples, complete the following activities.

- For each portfolio sample, consider what you like about the sample and what it illustrates about you.
- Write a two- to three-sentence justification for the choice of each sample. Include your explanations in your portfolio or be prepared to repeat them in an interview.

Recall and Application

1. Labels that are often based on physical differences, such as length of hair, contribute to a toddler's _____. (13.1.1)
   A. sense awareness
   B. gender identity
   C. body awareness
   D. cultural assimilation
2. **True or False**. Competence and control are components of a toddler's self-esteem. (13.1.1)
3. According to Erikson, how can caregivers help toddlers develop a sense of autonomy? (13.1.2)
   A. By offering criticism when they do something incorrectly
   B. By helping them complete simple tasks
   C. By allowing them to do things at their own pace
   D. By pointing out things they are too young to do
4. **True or False**. Most toddlers are likely to be possessive of a toy and unwilling to share it with other children. (13.1.3)

5. Toddlers with an anxious-avoidant attachment to their caregivers are more likely to _____. (13.1.4)
   A. appear mature during separations
   B. seem very clingy
   C. freeze in their footsteps for no reason
   D. speak rapidly
6. **True or False**. A toddler's occasional nightmares indicate a deeper, more serious problem, even if they seem content during the day. (13.1.5)
7. Toddlers often achieve which social-emotional milestone between ages 18 to 24 months? (13.1.6)
   A. Showing attachment to a toy or a blanket
   B. Showing curiosity about their own body parts
   C. Resisting bedtime despite being tired
   D. Playing alone on the floor with toys for a few minutes
8. **True or False**. Showing love to a pet is a social-emotional milestone a toddler may achieve between the ages of 24 to 36 months. (13.1.6)

9. Which action is least likely to enhance a toddler's self-awareness? (13.2.1)
   A. Acknowledging a toddler's feelings
   B. Ensuring the toddler shares their possessions
   C. Pointing out the toddler's reflection in a mirror
   D. Paying attention when the toddler wants to talk

10. **True or False.** Caregivers should redirect toddlers before they engage in a forbidden or unsafe action. (13.2.1)

11. A toddler's decision to do as they choose rather than what others want is called _____. (13.2.3)
    A. obedience
    B. delayed gratification
    C. self-assertion
    D. social referencing

12. A caregiver can help reduce a toddler's contrariness by doing what? (13.2.4)
    A. Telling the toddler about upcoming events in advance
    B. Expecting the toddler to complete simple tasks correctly
    C. Allowing the toddler to break some of the rules
    D. Repeating a request multiple times

13. One way a caregiver can help a toddler develop empathy is by _____. (13.2.4)
    A. assuring an unhappy toddler that everything is OK
    B. discussing how a person in a photograph is feeling
    C. distracting the toddler with a toy or book
    D. setting clear and consistent limits on behavior

14. **True or False.** If a toddler's tantrum becomes full-blown, caregivers should give in to the toddler's demands. (13.2.4)

15. **True or False.** Meeting toddlers' needs correctly, promptly, and consistently encourages secure attachments and helps prevent toddler stress. (13.2.5)

Critical Thinking

1. **Identify.** Use the dictionary to find the definitions of the terms *autonomy*, *shame*, and *doubt*. List common situations that toddlers might experience, and identify whether each experience promotes autonomy or shame and doubt. Compare your list to that of a classmate.

2. **Make inferences.** What do you think would be the most challenging part about a toddler's desire for independence? What do you think would be the most gratifying aspect of this for caregivers?

3. **Compare and contrast.** In small groups, compare and contrast behaviors that indicate secure and insecure attachments in toddlers. Create a list of three to five guidelines that caregivers can reference to assess how secure a toddler's attachment is.

4. **Analyze.** Why is it important for caregivers to control their emotions when dealing with toddlers? Analyze what emotional control or loss of control communicates to toddlers and what habits this might teach them.

5. **Draw conclusions.** Draw conclusions about what might happen if a caregiver is permissive and gives in to a toddler's desires all the time.

6. **Cause and effect.** What do you think is the effect on the toddler if an adult fails to respect him or her? List ways that adults frequently fail to respect toddlers and imagine how this lack of respect would affect other relationships in the adult's life, such as a marriage or friendship. How might adults better respect toddlers to prevent a similar outcome?

7. **Evaluate.** Work with a partner to role-play a situation in which a toddler fears the dark and monsters in the closet. Take turns playing the toddler and the caregiver coping with the toddler's fears. Present your role-play to the class and evaluate how well the caregiver copes with the toddler's fears in each role-play you see.

8. **Determine.** How do you think toddlers' temper tantrums and other displays of emotion relate to their central conflict of autonomy versus shame and doubt? Explain your answer.

Core Skills

1. **Math.** Draw a thermometer to illustrate your self-esteem, with 100 being maximum self-esteem and zero being the minimum. Draw a line at the number 50; this will be your baseline self-esteem at the beginning of the day. As you go through your day, make note of any compliments or positive remarks that are made to you. Also note any insults, criticisms, or names you are called. For each positive comment made to you, add one to your self-esteem thermometer. Subtract one for each negative comment made to you. At the end of the day, calculate your self-esteem. What did this exercise teach you about self-esteem? What did it teach you about environment and about how caregivers should conduct themselves around young children?

2. **Listening and speaking.** In small groups, find a children's television show or book that is intended for children as young as toddlers. View or read the show or book and take notes about how young children's struggles for autonomy are referenced or depicted. Do any of the characters in the story yearn for independence? Do any of them end up in dangerous situations as a result? Afterward, discuss the story with your group and compare notes. Together, present an analysis of the story to your class and explain how it speaks to young children's struggles for autonomy.

3. **Research and writing.** When children become toddlers, the adult-child relationship changes as caregivers enter the *authority stage* of parenting. Using reliable online or print resources, research changes in the adult-child relationship during the toddler years. How do other experts and sources explain this transition? Do they have a different perspective than the one covered in this chapter? Read and write summary statements for at least three sources. Finally, write an essay comparing and contrasting these sources and evaluating the information you found. Include a complete bibliography with your essay.

4. **Listening and speaking.** As a class, write all the social-emotional developmental milestones for toddlers on index cards or other pieces of paper. Then, shuffle the cards around the room. Without speaking, try to group yourselves according to the appropriate age range. You can communicate what milestone you are by acting, using hand gestures, or writing words that are not included in your milestone's description. After grouping yourselves, check your accuracy by reading off your milestones.

5. **Technology and speaking.** Imagine you are a child development expert who has been asked to give a presentation to first-time caregivers about fostering self-assertion while teaching obedience to toddlers. In small groups, review this chapter's information about self-assertion and obedience and then research and brainstorm practical ways that caregivers and other adults can encourage self-assertion while communicating to a toddler that he or she must obey. Film a three- to five-minute video demonstrating effective techniques for achieving this balance. Your video should include role-plays of realistic situations involving caregivers and their toddlers. Play your video for the class and answer any questions your classmates have.

6. **Writing.** During the toddler years, children feel emotions they do not understand and do not know how to express and control. For this reason, adults and caregivers should help toddlers co-regulate their emotions. Review this chapter's information about co-regulation and toddlers' emotions and then write three short stories—one about love, empathy, or affection; one about fear or anxiety; and one about anger. Your short stories should be written from a toddler's perspective. These stories should describe how the toddler is feeling and how the caregiver co-regulates the emotion being expressed.

7. **Art.** The toddler years can be difficult for caregivers, and stress in caregivers can easily lead to stress in toddlers. Working with a partner, create a colorful, motivational poster with tips to help caregivers manage the stress of the toddler years and help their toddlers cope with any stress they may experience. Your poster should be informative, encouraging, and visually appealing. Display it somewhere for your classmates to see.

8. **CTE Career Readiness Practice.** As a child care worker at a center for toddlers, it has come to your attention that the local newspaper will soon be interviewing you about what you are doing to teach toddlers self-awareness. You think your lessons for self-awareness are strong and well-researched, but you want to make sure you present the information clearly to the journalist. Describe your plan for teaching toddlers self-awareness—including activities for each day of the week and toys for 10 children—and as preparation for the interview, write and practice a short speech.

As further preparation, consider questions the journalist might ask, and write and practice two to three planned answers. (Writing information organizes a person's thinking, and orally practicing written materials aids fluency, especially if nervous.)

Observations

1. Find a film, online video, or article with pictures that illustrates a caregiver coping with a toddler's temper tantrum. Watch the video or read the article and then assess how well the caregiver handled the tantrum based on what you have learned in this chapter. Write a summary of your assessment, and if the caregiver did not handle the temper tantrum well, explain what he or she could have done differently.

2. Observe several toddlers playing together at a local child care center. Are the toddlers possessive about toys? How do they reclaim a special toy from another child? How do they react when a toy is taken from them? How do adults settle toddlers' disputes?

Unit 5 The Preschool Years

Public Speaking

Public speaking is a competitive event or part of a competitive event you might enter with your CTSO. This allows you to showcase your organizational skills along with nonverbal and verbal communication in making an oral presentation. Public speaking is generally a timed event. You will have time to research, prepare, and practice before attending the competition.

To prepare for a public speaking event, complete the following activities:

1. Read the rules and guidelines your organization provides. Note the topics from which you may choose to make a speech.
2. Locate the rubric or scoring sheet for this event on your organization's website.
3. Confirm whether you can use props or visuals as part of your presentation. Determine how much setup time the guidelines permit.
4. Analyze the rules to confirm whether the judges will ask questions of you or whether you will need to defend a case or situation as part of your speech.
5. Make notes on index cards about important points to remember and use them to study. You may be able to use your notes during the presentation, depending on the guidelines for your event.
6. Practice your presentation. Introduce yourself and the topic of your presentation, defend your position on the topic with supporting evidence, and conclude with a summary.
7. Ask your instructor to give feedback when you practice your speech. You might also have a student audience listen and give feedback.
8. Keep practicing until you are comfortable and can give your speech without flaw.

Chapter 14

Physical Development of Preschoolers

Essential Question

How do children grow and develop during the preschool years, and how can caregivers ensure optimal physical development?

Case Study   Should Preschoolers Be Taught Handwriting?

As a class, read the case study and discuss the questions that follow. After you finish studying the chapter, discuss this case study again. Have your opinions changed based on what you learned?

Brandon, a preschool teacher, took his four-year-old child, Spencer, to the public school for kindergarten entrance testing. Afterward, Brandon told a coworker, "Spencer was tested on writing letters, but we don't teach our preschoolers how to write letters." During the staff meeting that afternoon, Brandon mentioned handwriting for preschoolers.

"I think we need to teach how to write letters," said Brandon. "Not having this skill is not fair to preschoolers when they start kindergarten."

Leigh, a former first-grade teacher, said, "I agree. We could teach straight line capital letters (E, F, H, I, K, L, and T) to our three-year-old preschoolers. The four-year-old class could learn the remaining letters."

Zara, the program director, asked, "What about the three-year-olds who still switch hands while drawing?"

"All the better," said Leigh. "We can teach them how to write right-handed."

"Wait," said Zara. "I was forced to write with my right hand for years before switching to my left hand. I was so uncomfortable."

This jogged Brandon's memory of an article he had seen. "I read an article about how forcing children to go against their hand preferences can lead to stress and other problems."

Zara said, "Before we make any decisions, I'll talk to the curriculum director of the public schools to see what they really expect of children entering kindergarten."

Give It Some Thought

1. Do you think preschoolers should be taught how to write letters? Should they be taught to write only with their right hands? Explain your answers.
2. Do you think preschool programs should teach all the content included on kindergarten entrance tests? Why or why not?
3. If the preschool staff members decide not to teach writing letters, are there other activities that would help prepare the children for learning to write letters? Describe these activities.

Anita_Bonita/iStock via Getty Images Plus

Growth and Development of Preschoolers

Key Terms

ambidextrous
body rotation
dynamic balance
functional specialization
hand preference
internal organs
manipulate
reaction time
static balance
weight shift

Learning Outcomes

After studying this lesson, you will be able to

14.1-1   **describe** the major changes in organ development during the preschool years.

14.1-2   **describe** changes in the skeletal system during the preschool years.

14.1-3   **summarize** major changes in gross- and fine-motor development during the preschool years, including hand preference.

14.1-4   **give examples** of physical developmental milestones children might achieve in the preschool years.

Reading and Notetaking Activity

Before reading, skim the headings in this lesson. List the headings to create an outline for taking notes during reading and class discussion. Under each heading, list any key terms. Finally, write two questions you expect to have answered in class. After completing the lesson, ask your teacher any questions you still have about the concepts or terms you learned.

Introduction

Preschoolers, children between three and five years of age, are looking more grown up. If you were to compare a child at the end of toddlerhood with a child nearing school-age, you would note dramatic physical changes. The maturation of all organs slows but stabilizes during the preschool years. Growth rates during the preschool years are slower than they have been at any other time in the child's life. As the bodies of preschoolers continue to mature, proportionately they begin to look more like adults and less like younger children.

By the beginning of the preschool years, mastery of basic gross-motor movements (walking, bending, stretching) set off an explosion in preschoolers' abilities to control body movements as they develop more gross-motor skills. Preschoolers improve their skills of walking and running and learn jumping, hopping, catching and throwing, and balancing skills. Similarly, they are developing an expansive repertoire of fine-motor skills aided by establishing hand preference. The combined gross- and fine-motor skills allow preschoolers to control body movements to achieve complex goals in both play and self-help tasks.

14.1-1 Maturation of Organs

During the preschool years, the brain is still the fastest growing organ. Because of its rapid growth, the brain uses 30 percent of the body's energy, which makes good nutrition necessary for healthy development. By five years of age, preschoolers' brains are 90 percent of adult brain weight. Children who are biologically male tend to have larger head circumferences than children who are biologically female.

The following three major developments occur in a preschooler's brain:

1. **Functional specialization**, the development of special abilities in different regions (areas) of the brain, occurs. For example, different areas of the brain will store long-term memories and use memory to tell or retell stories or events. Functional specialization of the brain enables people to develop *executive functions* (working memory, cognitive flexibility, and inhibitions), control negative emotions, handle *expressive* (speaking, writing) as well as *receptive* (listening, reading) language, and experience more logical concept development.
2. Greater myelination improves visual-motor coordination and intellectual development.
3. Pruning occurs in unused connections and thus begins to "close" many windows of opportunity if they have not yet been met.

Besides the brain, other organs are also maturing. As the heart matures, heart rate slows and becomes steady. Blood pressure increases. By three years of age, children use adult-like chest breathing. Children's air passages, however, are small. They have large tonsils and *adenoids* (lymphoid tissues).

By four years of age, the stomach capacity of a preschooler is about one-half of the adult stomach. Preschoolers' stomachs are more sensitive than adult stomachs. Digestive upsets can be caused by certain foods or by viruses and bacteria. **Dehydration** (condition in which the body is lacking fluids) is common in the preschool years. The preschooler's bladder is also maturing. Because preschoolers have better control over their bathroom needs, there are fewer trips to the bathroom and fewer "accidents."

14.1-2 Skeletal Growth

Preschoolers grow more slowly than toddlers. The growth rate slows down for most children at an approximately equal rate. This means children who are larger than their peers at three years of age are likely to be larger at five years, too. In addition to changes in height and weight, changes also occur in preschoolers' body proportions, bones and teeth, and fat and muscle.

Height and Weight

Although growth slows during the preschool years as compared to the first three years of life, preschoolers are not finished growing. In the preschool years, height increases about 7 inches, and weight increases by about 12 pounds (approximately 3 to 5 pounds per year). Seventy-five percent of preschoolers' weight gain is due to muscle development. **Figure 14.1** shows the height and weight norms for children from three to five years of age.

Figure 14.1 **Average Height and Weight from Three to Five Years**

Age in Years	Biological Males Height in Inches	Biological Females Height in Inches	Biological Males Weight in Pounds	Biological Females Weight in Pounds
3	37½	37	31¾	30⅝
3½	39	38½	33¾	32⅞
4	40½	40	35¹⁵⁄₁₆	35¹⁄₁₆
4½	41½	41	38⅜	37¼
5	43	42½	40¹³⁄₁₆	39¹¹⁄₁₆
5½	44¼	43¾	43⁵⁄₁₆	42⁵⁄₁₆

Goodheart-Willcox Publisher

Body Proportions

As toddler features begin to disappear, the preschooler's body becomes taller and leaner and body proportions begin to look more like those of an adult. The lower face grows more rapidly than the head, resulting in the preschooler's face looking more like an adult's. Until 30 months of age, a child's waist, hips, and chest measure almost the same. By five years of age, the waist is smaller than the shoulders and hips.

The preschooler's trunk and legs also grow to resemble adult proportions. The trunk grows to allow more space for the **internal organs** (heart, lungs, liver, and others). As the preschooler's trunk grows, the abdomen protrudes less. The legs grow rapidly, too. By five and one-half years, most children's legs are about half the length of the body—the same as an adult's leg-to-body proportions.

Bones and Teeth

Preschoolers' bones continue to ossify and grow larger and longer. Deciduous (baby) teeth typically begin to fall out between four and five years of age (**Figure 14.2**). Although permanent teeth may not erupt until the early school-age years, they are growing under the gums. The jaw **elongates** (lengthens) to accommodate these teeth. Tooth decay is also common during the preschool years. Proper care of teeth is extremely important for lifelong dental health.

Giorgio Rossi/Shutterstock.com

Figure 14.2 Between four and five years of age, children's deciduous teeth begin to fall out. *What does the term* deciduous *mean?*

Science

The Digestion Process

Digestion is the process of breaking down foods into *nutrients* (molecules of proteins, carbohydrates, fats, vitamins, minerals), which the body uses for energy, growth, and cell repair. Every morsel of food must be broken down before nutrients are absorbed by the blood and transported throughout the body.

The digestive system, called the *gastrointestinal (GI) tract*, is comprised of three hollow organs (mouth, stomach, rectum) connected by almost 30 feet of tubes (esophagus and small and large intestines). Two solid organs (pancreas and liver) are part of the digestive system. Besides these organs and tubes, nerve and hormone cells and "good bacteria" (microbiome) help with digestion.

The digestive process begins in the mouth in which chewing and saliva break down some carbohydrates. Swallowing pushes food into the esophagus. From this point on, involuntary muscles, which contract and relax, propel foods through the GI tract (called *peristalsis*). The esophagus empties its contents into the stomach, which mixes foods with stomach enzymes (stomach acids), producing a mixture called *chyme*. Chyme is released into the small intestine where it is mixed with more digestive juices from the pancreas and liver. The molecules are then absorbed into the blood stream. Undigested foods, liquids, and salts move to the large intestine, which creates the stool and stores it in the rectum. During a bowel movement, the stool is pushed through the anus. This completes the digestive process.

Photo: otnaydur/Shutterstock.com

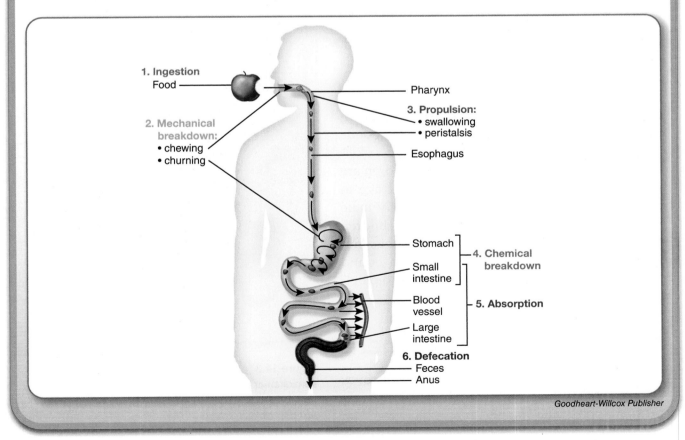

1. Ingestion Food

Pharynx

2. Mechanical breakdown:
• chewing
• churning

3. Propulsion:
• swallowing
• peristalsis

Esophagus

Stomach

4. Chemical breakdown

Small intestine

Blood vessel

5. Absorption

Large intestine

6. Defecation
Feces
Anus

Goodheart-Willcox Publisher

During the preschool years, bone and teeth development can be harmed by malnutrition and other health problems. Bones, muscles, and joints are more prone to injury in preschoolers than in older children. There are two main reasons for injury. First, the *ligaments* (the elastic-like bands that hold bones together) are loose and bones are not fully formed (thinner and less hard than teen bones). This can cause injuries such as bones slipping out of place. Second, certain diseases, such as *osteomyelitis* (infection of a bone), childhood diabetes, Down syndrome, obesity, and sickle-cell anemia can all lead to bone and joint deformities and increase the severity of injuries.

Fat and Muscle

The ratio of fat to muscle tissue continues to decrease slowly during the preschool years. Biologically male children lose baby fat more quickly than biologically female children. With good nutrition and physical activity, most of the baby fat disappears by around kindergarten. At five and one-half years, a child's fat deposits are less than half as thick as they were at one year of age.

As preschoolers' *skeletal muscles* (muscles attached to the bones) and bones are made stronger by ossification, their bodies are strengthened. Muscle fiber, which consists mainly of water, is now being replaced with more protein.

Preschoolers' activity levels also affect muscle development. Besides protein content changes in muscle tissue, the fiber size of muscles responds to physical activity. Thus, a three-year-old's skeletal muscles develop rapidly because children are more active at this age than at any other age in the lifespan. Children who are biologically male have more muscle and bone growth than children who are biologically female. Because of this, biologically male children are, on average, a pound heavier than children their age who are biologically female.

14.1-3 Motor Development

Preschoolers' motor development improves due to physical activity and increasing body growth and development. Preschoolers have an increase in muscle development and develop better balancing skills. Their eye-hand coordination becomes more refined. Their **reaction time** (time required to respond to a sight, sound, or other stimuli) becomes shorter. Preschoolers can perform many physical activities. Through play, their gross- and fine-motor skills develop quickly.

Large-Muscle Development

As preschoolers' large muscles develop, balance develops, too. This complex skill requires coordinating signals from the eyes and the movement of fluids in the semicircular canals of the inner ears (**Figure 14.3**). These signals are sent to the brain and then transmitted to the muscles of the body. Based on these signals, the muscles make constant adjustments to maintain balance, which keeps a person upright and affects many gross-motor activities. A person's ability to maintain balance is also a measure of eye, ear, and brain health.

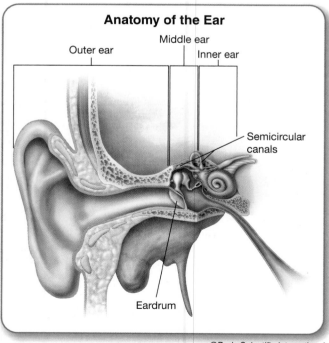

Anatomy of the Ear

Outer ear · Middle ear · Inner ear · Semicircular canals · Eardrum

©Body Scientific International

Figure 14.3 The movements of fluids in the ear's semicircular canals help the body maintain balance. *Which part of the ear are the semicircular canals in—the inner, middle, or outer ear?*

During the preschool years, children differ widely in their balancing skills. Through regular physical activities, children develop two types of balance. **Dynamic balance**, balance maintained while moving, develops when preschoolers walk in a line or on a balance beam. **Static balance**, balance maintained while being still, develops when preschoolers stand on one foot with arms outstretched or folded across their chests. Dynamic balance is easier to develop than static balance. You may realize this if you have ridden a bicycle or watched or participated in dance or gymnastics.

Through muscle development and balancing skills, preschoolers become stronger and more coordinated. Preschoolers walk more smoothly than toddlers and like to try more challenging ways to move. They run faster, and their arms and legs alternate in rhythm. Four-year-olds use a forward arm action to jump higher. With increased courage and better balance, climbing becomes easier. They can catch balls better when they are bounced to them rather than thrown to them. Three-year-olds begin hopping, but older preschoolers can hop and skip faster and for longer distances than younger preschoolers. Older preschoolers' actions become more advanced in all areas.

Two new actions, body rotation and weight shift, help the preschooler's throwing ability. **Body rotation** is the action of turning the hips (pelvis) and then the shoulders backward while the throwing arm comes forward. **Weight shift** is the change of weight from the back leg to the forward leg, which is done by shifting the hips forward. Body rotation and weight shift may begin during the third year, but both become much more pronounced by the end of the preschool years (**Figure 14.4**). Refinement of these skills continues for many years with athletes able to do both actions at the same time. This creates a 20 to 30 percent increase in the force of their throw while allowing the arm and hand to direct the throw.

Small-Muscle Development

Preschoolers' ability to **manipulate**, work with an object by using the hands, is still awkward. As preschoolers play with small objects, however, their small muscles develop and eye-hand coordination improves, which strengthens fine-motor skills. Preschoolers' fine-motor skills change and develop over time.

Figure 14.4 Body rotation and weight shift improve the force behind and thus the speed of the thrown object. *How do body rotation and weight shift improve the accuracy of throwing and protect the throwing arm from injury?*

Huntstock/Disability Images via Getty Images

Hand Preference and the Brain

Hand preference and brain specialization occur at the same time. The brain is divided into two halves called the *right* and *left cerebral hemispheres*. *Brain lateralization* means these halves are not exactly alike. Different skills, called *specializations*, are associated with either the right or left sides. The left side is typically wired for language and logical thinking skills. The right side is typically wired for spatial abilities, visual images, and music. To a great extent, brain dominance is *contralateral* to the body, which means that the right side of the brain controls the left side of the body and vice versa. Thus, the left side of the brain is dominant for right-handed people, who comprise about 95 percent of the population.

Researchers originally thought that brain specialization for hand preference always occurred opposite from brain specialization for language (largely because the brain typically has a left-side language specialization). This, however, is not true for about 60 to 70 percent of left-handed people who have language *and* hand-preference specialization in the left hemisphere. Because left-handed people comprise less than 10 percent of the population, this represents very few people.

The brain link between hand preference and language specialization is high, but not perfect.

In some cases, left-handed people have been pressured to switch their hand preference because left-handedness was seen as negative. In fact, the Latin term for left-handedness is *sinistra* (meaning *evil*) which is also the root word for the English term *sinister*. Other people have switched their hand preference due to accident or illness affecting the preferred hand. Switching can happen because the brain is plastic and can be rewired with effort.

Research Activity

Using reliable resources, research how left-handedness was viewed in a historical period and location of your choosing. Choose a specific date range, such as 1940–1950, and choose one country to research. After conducting your research, write a two- to three-page summary of how left-handed people were viewed and treated in your chosen country during your chosen time. Include a bibliography with citations in APA format.

Photo: Tom Wang/Shutterstock.com

Three Years

At three years of age, children can usually feed themselves using a spoon and fork, but they are still messy. They can build towers from small blocks although the towers may be crooked. Three-year-olds can also draw straight lines and roughly copy circles. They can unbutton buttons and pull large zippers.

Four Years

By four years of age, preschoolers' movements are steadier. In addition to using forks and spoons, four-year-olds may also try to use knives designed for children. They can build straight towers and place blocks with steady hands. Four-year-olds begin to cut along lines with rounded-tip scissors. They can also comb their hair, wash their hands, and begin to lace, but probably will not tie their shoes.

Five Years

At five years of age, eye-hand coordination is greatly improved. Five-year-olds use a spoon, fork, and knife to feed themselves. They can build towers and play with other small toys with skill. They can make simple drawings freehand. Five-year-olds can also fasten large buttons, work large zippers, and may even be able to tie their shoelaces.

Hand Preference

During the preschool years, and sometimes during late toddlerhood, children begin to show hand preference. **Hand preference** is the tendency to use one hand more skillfully than the other hand for most tasks, making this hand the dominant hand (**Figure 14.5**). Hand preference is also called *handedness* and *hand dominance*. Most people think of hand preferences in categories—right, left, and **ambidextrous** (am-bih-DECK-struhs), ability to use the right or left hand, as the preferred hand, almost equally well for many tasks. Today, many researchers see handedness on a continuum with preferences in varying degrees.

Generally, hand preference is not firmly established until the end of the preschool years. During this stage, the brain specializes and myelination allows for better connections between brain areas. This is needed for hand preference. Child development experts believe that other factors, such as genetics, birth trauma, and social pressures, also affect hand preference.

Because researchers believe hand preference is determined by brain wiring, they feel each child should determine their own preference. Adults can help young children develop hand preference by placing or holding objects at a child's *midline* (center of body) rather than to the right or left of the child. This gives the child an easier choice in hand use. Adults can also encourage activities that require the use of both hands for doing different actions, such as bead stringing. Preschoolers need ample time for brain wiring to determine their hand preference. Adults should never force a change in preference.

Figure 14.5 Children who have developed hand preference tend to use one hand more effectively than the other for tasks such as throwing a ball, drawing a picture, or writing. *What is your hand preference? Do you know when you developed this preference?*

miniseries/E+ via Getty Images

14.1-4 Physical Developmental Milestones

Physical capabilities expand during the preschool years. Children are better able to explore and interact with the world around them. **Figure 14.6** describes the physical developmental milestones of preschool children.

Preschoolers need support as they grow and develop physically. Parents and caregivers can support a child's growth and development in many ways, including providing proper nutrition and a healthy diet, which you will learn about in the next lesson.

Figure 14.6 Preschooler Physical Milestones

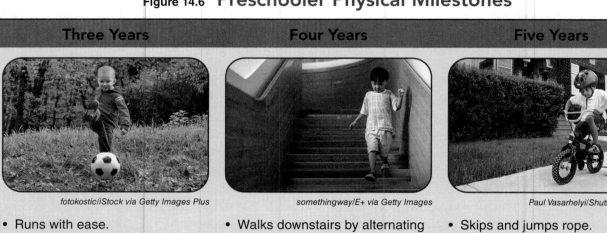

Three Years	Four Years	Five Years
fotokostic/iStock via Getty Images Plus	*somethingway/E+ via Getty Images*	*Paul Vasarhelyi/Shutterstock.com*

Three Years
- Runs with ease.
- Walks upstairs by alternating feet.
- May hop on one foot.
- Turns body slightly when throwing a ball.
- Catches a large ball by trapping ball in arms.
- Kicks a ball.
- Pedals a tricycle.
- Puts on shoes (cannot tie laces).
- Draws a circle.
- Uses a fork.
- Can dress self in some items.
- Washes and dries hands.
- Can string items together (like beads)

Four Years
- Walks downstairs by alternating feet.
- Hops on one foot and may stand on one foot for a few seconds.
- Jumps with ease.
- Pedals and steers tricycle skillfully.
- Throws ball with a slight weight shift from back to front foot when thrown.
- Catches a bounced ball.
- Unbuttons some buttons and may pull zippers up and down.
- Serves themselves food or pours drink with supervision.
- Uses a spoon and fork.
- Grasps marker with thumb and pad of index finger.
- Draws human figure by adding arms and legs extending from face.
- May copy some capital letters.
- Cuts a straight line with rounded-tip scissors.
- Builds a straight block tower.
- Dresses and undresses with assistance needed for tying shoes and working difficult fasteners.

Five Years
- Skips and jumps rope.
- Ascends and descends slide ladders and play structures by alternating feet.
- Can hop several times on one foot and stand on one foot for several seconds.
- Does somersaults.
- Throws ball with definite weight shift.
- Rides bicycle with training wheels.
- Uses a fork, spoon, and sometimes a knife.
- Uses the toilet independently.
- Copies most letters and writes first name from memory.
- Draws human figure with neck, torso, arms and legs extending from torso, and details on face.
- Builds taller towers and other structures (bridges, buildings) with blocks.
- Dresses and undresses without much assistance, including tying shoes.

Goodheart-Willcox Publisher

1. Which major organ change occurs during the ages of 3 to 5 years? (14.1.1)
   A. Stomach capacity is two-thirds that of an adult stomach.
   B. Air passages reach adult size.
   C. Pruning removes unused nerve connections in the brain.
   D. The heart rate becomes faster.

2. **True or False.** Preschoolers develop functional specialization, which allows their brains to store long-term memories. (14.2.5)

3. Which is true about a preschooler's skeletal growth? (14.1.2)
   A. Growth occurs more rapidly for preschoolers than for infants and toddlers.
   B. Seventy-five percent of preschoolers' weight gain is due to bone growth.
   C. Preschoolers' heads grow more rapidly than their lower face and jaw.
   D. The preschooler's trunk and legs grow to resemble adult proportions.

4. What is balance maintained while moving called? (14.1.3)
   A. Static balance
   B. Body rotation
   C. Dynamic balance
   D. Reaction time

5. Three-year-olds commonly achieve which physical developmental milestone? (14.1.4)
   A. Pedaling and steering a tricycle skillfully
   B. Working a 40-piece jigsaw puzzle
   C. Coloring within the lines
   D. Opening and closing twistable lids

Meeting Nutritional Needs of Preschoolers

Key Terms

empty calories
nutrient-dense foods
solid fats

Learning Outcomes

After studying this lesson, you will be able to

14.2-1 **summarize** the importance of meeting preschoolers' nutritional needs and identify healthful eating guidelines.

14.2-2 **identify** ways to foster a positive attitude toward food.

14.2-3 **assess** foods for their appeal to preschoolers.

14.2-4 **explain** ways to make mealtime fun for preschoolers.

Reading and Notetaking Activity

Create a table like the one shown. Include as many rows as you need. Before reading the lesson, list facts you already know about proper nutrition during the preschool years in the Give One column. In the Get One column, list facts you learn as you read the lesson. If you have any questions about what you are reading, raise your hand and ask your teacher. After you finish reading the lesson, team up with a classmate and discuss each other's lists. Are there items you would add to your list?

Proper Nutrition During the Preschool Years	
Give one	**Get one**

Introduction

To meet the preschooler's nutritional needs, adults should provide a variety of healthful foods at regularly scheduled meal and snack times.

Caregivers need to be flexible, however, and listen to their preschooler's indications of fullness or hunger. Children grow at different rates and their energy output can vary from month to month and even day to day. Preschoolers become more interested in foods prepared in different ways. During the preschool years, children may become more interested in eating foods low in nutritional value.

14.2-1 Importance of Nutrition

What people eat affects their growth and development, overall health, general alertness, and emotions. A preschooler's diet must supply nutrients for brain growth and other developing body systems. Children need **nutrient-dense foods** that provide vitamins, minerals, and other beneficial substances, but little or no solid fats, added sugars, refined starches, and sodium (**Figure 14.7**). All vegetables, fruits, whole grains, protein foods, and fat-free or low-fat dairy products are nutrient dense when prepared without added solid fats, sugar, and sodium.

When nutritional needs are not met, children's growth can stall. Children will also be more **susceptible** (prone) to illness, and when they become ill, their recovery time is slower.

Healthful Eating Guidelines

To meet the needs of their growing bodies, preschoolers should be offered nutritious foods at meal and snack times. The MyPlate website is a useful tool for learning about healthy eating. it gives recommended guidelines and amounts needed from different food groups. At this age, children often get hungry between meals. One or two healthful snacks per day may be planned between meals to satisfy hunger pangs. When children are hungry, they should be allowed to eat.

To help children learn to choose healthful amounts of food, parents and caregivers often let them eat only as much as they want. When children are old enough, they can serve themselves appropriate amounts of foods. To teach children how to determine healthful portion sizes, parents and caregivers may suggest children take small portions at first. Children can then come back for more if they are still hungry.

Figure 14.7 Nutrient-dense foods are beneficial to children's growth and development. *What can you do to encourage children to eat nutrient-dense foods?*

Oksana Kuzmina/Shutterstock.com

Rather than forcing children to finish all their food, parents and caregivers should allow them to stop eating once they feel full. A child who learns to pay attention to what their body is signaling is more likely to maintain healthy food habits for a lifetime. When a child needs a special diet for health reasons, adults should consult a doctor or registered dietitian nutritionist.

When planning meals and snacks, foods that contain empty calories should be limited or avoided. **Empty calories** supply the body with energy, but few or no nutrients. Added sugars and solid fats are sources of empty calories in foods. **Solid fats** are fats found mainly in animal foods (not seafood), such as butter and beef. These fats are solid at room temperature. Foods such as cookies, hot dogs, or sugar-sweetened cereals contain both nutrients and empty calories. Other foods such as sodas or candy provide only empty calories and are considered *empty-calorie foods*.

Eating too many empty calories may cause a child to develop negative food habits. When children are eating empty-calorie foods instead of nutrient-dense foods, their bodies are not receiving the nutrients needed for proper growth and development.

Experts say children, as well as adults, should reduce their intake of sugar, salt, and solid fats. Eating excessive amounts of sugar can lead to tooth decay, obesity, and other health concerns that often last for years. Consuming too much fat and salt early in life may increase chances of high blood pressure in later years. Chances are compounded if high blood pressure exists in the family's health history. Snack foods that are high in sugar, salt, and solid fats should be avoided (**Figure 14.8**).

14.2-2 Forming Positive Food Attitudes

The food attitudes preschoolers learn may last a lifetime. Offering a variety of foods in a pleasant atmosphere helps preschoolers form healthful food attitudes.

Figure 14.8 Reducing Added Sugars

Instead of:	Offer:
Flavored milk	Unflavored fat-free or low-fat milk
Sweetened yogurt	Fat-free or low-fat plain yogurt topped with fruit
Ice cream or frozen yogurt	Frozen fruits with no sugar added or frozen 100% fruit bars
Sweetened breakfast cereals	Cereals with little or no added sugars, whole-grain cereals, or oatmeal with fruit
Cookies	Whole-grain crackers, graham crackers, or plain animal crackers
Canned fruit in syrup or sweetened applesauce	Fruit canned in water or 100% fruit juice; unsweetened applesauce
Doughnuts, pies, or cakes for dessert	Fruits (fresh, frozen, or canned in water or 100% juice), fruit salads, or baked fruits (like baked apples or pears)
Jam or jelly	100% fruit spread
Soda, fruit-flavored drinks, fruit cocktails, or fruit punch	Water, fruit-infused water, fat-free or low-fat milk, or 100% fruit juice (no more than one ½-cup serving per day)

Source: teamnutrition.usda.gov/library; Goodheart-Willcox Publisher

For the most part, people like variety in their lives. This includes variety in the foods they eat. Some children may go through phases during which they want the same food(s) day after day. Others eat or drink a few of the same foods daily but vary other foods.

Many healthful options are available within each food group. Children should be able to eat foods they like and still meet their nutritional needs. Forcing children to eat foods they do not like can cause them to have negative feelings toward healthful foods. Using food to reward or punish can also have an adverse effect. Children who are rewarded and punished with food may learn to eat as a way of bribery. For example, some parents reward with food by saying, "If you pick up your toys, you can have an ice cream cone." It would be better to say, "We'll go to the park and play catch as soon as you pick up your toys."

Some parents may punish their picky eaters by threatening to withhold food. A parent might say, "You can't have dessert until you eat your peas." This teaches the child that the dessert is the desirable food and peas are only the means to obtaining the dessert. If access to a food is restricted, it may encourage overeating of that food when it is available.

Preschoolers observe the behavior of those around them. They often copy the actions of the role models in their lives, such as parents, older siblings, and caregivers. If a role model makes negative comments about a food, the preschooler is likely to adopt a negative attitude also. Role models can encourage positive food attitudes in preschoolers by setting a good example and encouraging trying new things (**Figure 14.9**).

Providing a pleasant environment for eating can contribute to a healthful food attitude. Dishes and flatware suited to the child's hands make mealtime easier and lessen the chance of accidents. Children may want to help make the table attractive by choosing the napkins, picking a flower from the garden for the table, or helping set the table.

Food becomes a part of many celebrations. Preschoolers may look forward to helping prepare a special holiday dish or choosing their birthday menu. Trying different eating styles is fun, too. A restaurant, cafeteria, picnic, or cookout provides children with more food experiences.

Figure 14.9 If a child sees an older family member enjoying vegetables or drinking milk, the child is more likely to develop a positive attitude about these foods. *In what ways can family members model healthy eating habits to preschoolers?*

14.2-3 Foods with Preschooler Appeal

Meal and snack time success is more likely when foods are offered that are appropriate for the age group. The tips in this section address some of the unique considerations when serving food to preschool-age children.

Consider the Preschooler's Senses

Children and adults have different senses of taste and smell. For example, many children are "bitter sensitive" to some foods, such as spinach, broccoli, and cabbage. There is an acid in spinach (oxalic acid) that leaves a bitter aftertaste in the mouths of children, but not adults.

Children often prefer mild flavors and aromas over stronger, **acrid** (bitter and unpleasant) flavors and scents. They also tend to dislike foods that are too spicy. Children are influenced by other food tastes and qualities as well. Often by the preschool years, children begin to like their family's favorite cultural dishes. Keeping these differences in mind when offering foods to preschoolers may contribute to a successful meal.

Aim for Visual Appeal

How food looks may influence whether children think they will like it. Children like attractive-looking foods. Foods of different sizes, shapes, colors, textures, and temperatures look better than foods that are **uniform** (look the same). Plates should have some empty space. A plate that appears too full can seem overwhelming before the child has even taken one bite. Instead, serve less food on the plate and offer the child a second helping if they are still hungry. Children also enjoy foods prepared especially for them. Special dishes, napkins, or centerpieces may make eating a meal or snack even more special.

Keep Foods Separate

Children often prefer to eat foods separately rather than eat foods that are combined (**Figure 14.10**). If children see or taste one food they do not like in a casserole, soup, or salad, they may reject the entire dish. They are more likely to accept mixtures of fruits than mixtures of vegetables. Children may eat self-made mixtures more readily than adult-prepared mixtures. For example, children may prefer to mix their own salads from several bowls of precut vegetables.

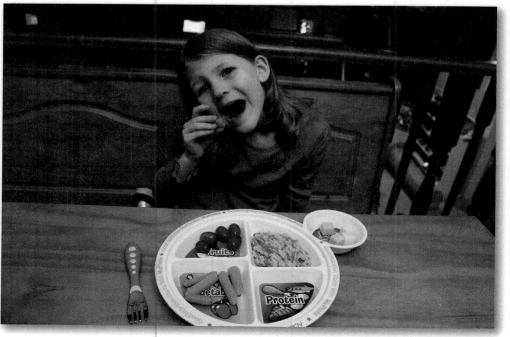

Figure 14.10 Children prefer foods that are separated over foods that are combined. *What are some combined foods adults might separate out for their children?*

Julie Pigors

Serve Foods at Acceptable Temperatures

Preschoolers do not like foods that are served at extreme temperatures. In fact, they can easily burn their mouths on foods that are too hot. Some of these foods (such as hot drinks) can simply be avoided because many children do not like them anyway. Soups are good for children, but young children cannot manage a steamy bowl or cup of soup. One easy solution is to drop a few ice cubes into hot soup just as the child begins to eat. As the ice melts, the temperature of the soup will drop to an acceptable level.

Very cold foods present a problem, too. Children eat these foods very slowly because eating large bites can cause a sharp headache. Thus, there may be more ice cream on the outside of a preschooler than on the inside. Parents can start offering suggestions for managing hot and cold foods during the late preschool years.

Vary Methods of Preparation

Children show likes and dislikes for ways foods are prepared. A child who turns down cooked carrots may eat a crisp, raw carrot. A salad dressing or dip that is mild in flavor may make almost any vegetable or fruit easy to eat. Dressings made from yogurt and cheese can help meet the calcium needs of young children, too.

Offer New Foods in Small Amounts

Children will often taste one bite or a small amount of a food just to see whether they like it. Give children new foods in small amounts (one slice or a tablespoon). Serve new foods with ample portions of foods children like to eat. The new food may be rejected, but do not give up. Foods may need to be offered many times before children will accept them.

Prepare Easy-to-Eat Foods

Foods should be easy for preschoolers to eat (**Figure 14.11**). Bite-sized and finger foods are preferred over foods that are harder to eat. Most children at this age cannot cut food. They may not hold spoons and forks correctly. These problems make eating messier for preschoolers than for older children and adults.

Figure 14.11 Preschooler foods should be fun and easy to eat. *What are some creative ways adults can make foods easier and more fun for their children?*

14.2-4 Making Meals Fun

By helping to prepare food, children have fun while they learn about colors, shapes, tastes, aromas, textures, and appliance names (*blender, oven*). They learn food preparation terms (*cut, boil, poach, bake*) and food names. Cooking teaches math concepts (*measurement, numbers, temperature, time, shapes*) and science as they see changes in foods (*rising, baking, freezing, boiling*). As an added bonus, children are more likely to eat what they help prepare.

Children enjoy eating with others. Meals can be a time to relax, share, and have fun. Enough time should be given for the meal itself because eating with children takes time.

Setting an example by taking turns talking and demonstrating other table manners allows children to learn at mealtimes. Have realistic expectations for behavior at mealtime. The attention span of a preschooler is still relatively short. Preschoolers are often messy eaters because their fine-motor skills are still developing. This behavior is normal. Rather than scolding, include the child in cleanup and praise their efforts.

Lesson 14.2 Review and Assessment

1. Which of the following is an example of an empty-calorie food? (14.2.1)
   A. Hot dogs
   B. Beef
   C. Butter
   D. Soda

2. **True or False.** Restricting a preschooler's access to a certain food may encourage overeating of that food when it is available. (14.2.2)

3. A preschooler would most likely prefer food that is _____. (14.2.3)
   A. very cold
   B. mixed together
   C. cut into bite-sized portions
   D. spicy

4. **True or False.** Foods may need to be offered many times before children will accept them. (14.2.3)

5. **True or False.** Allowing preschoolers to help with food preparation teaches them about colors, shapes, tastes, aromas, textures, and appliance names. (14.2.5)

Meeting Other Physical Needs of Preschoolers

Learning Outcomes

After studying this lesson, you will be able to

14.3-1 **give examples** of features to consider when choosing garments for preschoolers.

14.3-2 **describe** hygiene guidelines for preschoolers, including toileting and dental care.

14.3-3 **summarize** physical activity guidelines for preschoolers.

14.3-4 **explain** preschoolers' need for rest and sleep.

Key Terms

enuresis

plaque

Reading and Notetaking Activity

Before reading this lesson, skim the headings and write each heading in a different color or font on a separate piece of paper or electronically. As you silently read the chapter and then listen to your teacher, take notes in the color or font you chose for each heading. After you finish taking notes for each section, draw or copy and paste a small illustration or visual next to the section that will help you remember what you learned.

Introduction

Preschoolers' physical, intellectual, and social-emotional skills develop at rapid rates. These improved skills help children meet their own needs. Preschoolers want to do tasks for themselves and others. For example, they like to use their motor skills to feed and dress themselves and help parents with everyday tasks. Because their abilities quickly develop, preschoolers need a great deal of support from and time with caring adults.

Although preschoolers can do many tasks on their own, they still need adult help and guidance. Just as in infancy and toddlerhood, parents and caregivers still need to meet preschoolers' physical needs for clothing, good hygiene practices, sleep, and physical activity.

14.3-1 Clothing

Besides protecting a child's body from harsh weather conditions, cuts, and scrapes, clothing also becomes important to a child's growing self-concept during the preschool years. Clothing can also aid the learning of self-help skills as preschoolers learn to dress themselves.

Choosing Garments

Allowing preschoolers to make some choices about their clothes is one way children can express their personality (**Figure 14.12**). Perhaps preschoolers can choose the color they want from similar outfits.

Seiya Kawamoto/Photodisc/Thinkstock

Figure 14.12 During the preschool years, children begin to express their unique personalities through clothing. *What sorts of clothes did you wear as a young child? How did these clothes express your personality?*

Not only will children enjoy clothes they have chosen, but they will also learn to make decisions.

When selecting clothes for preschoolers, fit is an important feature to consider. Hangtags and charts on children's sizes often give measurements for chest, waist, hips, inseam, and other features. Some clothes are also sold in more specialized sizes to fit slender and heavier children. The clothing chosen should give the active child freedom to move and thus should never be too tight in any measurement.

Preschoolers' clothes have most of the same quality fabric and construction features as toddlers' clothes. Preschoolers grow mainly in the length of the arms and legs and the width of the shoulders. For these reasons, their clothes should have features that allow parents to let out the hems as children grow. Adjustable shoulder straps and waistbands also allow room for growth.

Because preschoolers explore indoor and outdoor areas, their clothes need to have certain safety features. Outdoor clothing worn after dark should be light-colored or have a trim of reflective tape that will reflect the light from cars or other vehicles. Hoods attached to coats and rainwear should easily detach if caught on large objects.

Some clothing features may present a safety hazard for children and should be avoided. For example, large, loose headwear can prevent children from seeing traffic or other hazards. Loose or wide pant legs and long shoelaces can cause tripping. Other loose clothing, such as long or wide sleeves, drawstring ties, scarves, and extra-large clothes can also present safety concerns.

Self-Dressing Features

By the end of the preschool years, many children can dress themselves with only a little help from adults. Adults should always be near, however, to help the child and check the child's attempts. The following features aid self-dressing:

- large openings, especially for slipover garments
- easy-to-recognize fronts and backs of garments, such as labels, threads, or tape sewn inside

- front rather than back openings, such as front buttons and attached belts that hook in front (**Figure 14.13**)
- elastic in waistbands and sleeves (at wrist)
- easy-to-work fasteners, such as zippers with large pull tabs
- shoes with self-adhesive straps

In addition to self-dressing features in garments, special toys are available to help children learn to button, snap, zip, and manipulate other closings. These give children extra dressing practice.

Image Source/Image Source via Getty Images

Figure 14.13 Self-dressing features, such as buttons at the front of a shirt, make it easier for preschoolers to dress and undress themselves. *What are some clothing features that would make it difficult for preschoolers to dress or undress?*

Fitting Shoes

Many preschoolers grow one shoe size every four months. Along with size, caregivers should check for the following fitting features in each shoe style:

- *Activity shoes.* Look for flexible soles that are ¼- to 3/8-inch thick to absorb the pounding of walking, running, and jumping.
- *Sneakers and athletic shoes.* Make sure arch support is in correct position. Check fit with the socks to be worn with the shoes. Socks are often bulky, requiring larger shoes.
- *Sandals.* Consider adjustable straps and buckles that do not press into the foot.
- *Dress shoes.* Make sure the sole is as flexible as possible. (Thin soles of dress shoes do not absorb pounding. For this reason, dress shoes should only be worn for short periods.)

14.3-2 Hygiene

By the preschool stage, children have begun to learn and establish hygiene practices (**Figure 14.14**). They still need help and supervision in completing hygiene tasks, however, including using the bathroom and brushing their teeth.

anocha98/iStock/Thinkstock

Figure 14.14 Preschool children often have hygiene practices, such as bathing, already in place. *What are some ways adults can remind preschoolers about their hygiene routines?*

Toileting Accidents

Toileting accidents occur occasionally with preschoolers. Daytime accidents are most often a result of children waiting too long to go to the bathroom. Children may need reminders to go to the bathroom after they wake up in the morning or from naps, before going outside, before and after meals, and before leaving the house.

Time is the major cure for preschoolers' bedtime toileting accidents. Most children are not night-trained in toilet learning until at least three years of age. For a child over three years of age, involuntary urination two or more times a week for at least three months is called **enuresis** (en-yoo-REE-sis). Sometimes, people use the term to apply to bed-wetting when the child no longer has daytime accidents. There may be many causes of bedtime accidents in the late preschool years (and even in the school-age years). Possible causes include:

- inherited problems
- urinary tract problems
- deep sleeping
- constipation causing pressure on the bladder
- too much fluid in the evening hours
- fear of getting up in the dark

Children often outgrow these problems within a few years. For children who are afraid to get up in the middle of the night, a night-light near the child's bed and in the bathroom may help reduce fears. Dim hallway lights or a dimly lit path to the bathroom may also help. If toilet accidents still occur, medical help may be needed.

Dental Care

Preschoolers are prone to **cavities** (areas of decay in teeth). **Plaque**, a sticky, mineral deposit coating the teeth while it colonizes bacteria on food particles left in the mouth, can cause cavities and lead to gum disease. To help prevent tooth decay and gum disease, adults should make sure preschoolers brush their teeth twice a day with a fluoride toothpaste.

To ensure proper brushing, adults should also monitor preschoolers as they brush their teeth. Just as in toilet learning, preschoolers may need reminders or help in the process. For example, preschoolers may need help from an adult to squeeze a pea-sized amount of toothpaste onto their toothbrush. Once children have two or more teeth that are touching, parents or caregivers should also floss a preschooler's teeth once a day. To make sure teeth are clean, healthy, and properly growing, dentists recommend preschoolers have two dental checkups per year.

Focus on Careers

Dental Hygienist

Dental hygienists check teeth and gums and take X-rays to check for non-visible problems with the teeth. They also clean and polish patients' teeth. They assist the dentist as necessary. Dental hygienists also teach people about proper dental care, such as brushing and flossing.

Career cluster: Health science.

Education: Educational requirements include an associate degree in dental hygiene and state licensure.

Job outlook: Future employment opportunities for dental hygienists are expected to grow much faster than the average for all occupations.

To learn more about a career as a dental hygienist, visit the United States Department of Labor's *Occupational Outlook Handbook* website. You will also be able to compare the job responsibilities, educational requirements, job outlook, and average pay of dental hygienists with similar occupations.

Photo: Karin Dreyer/Blend Images/Thinkstock

14.3-3 Physical Activity

As preschoolers' gross-motor skills and eye-hand coordination improve, they become more **agile** (able to move quickly and easily). Because of these improved skills and children's high energy level, preschoolers usually get ample physical activity in their daily routines. These activities might be planned or unplanned. Common physical activities include throwing and catching balls, riding tricycles, or playing tag. Playground activities, such as climbing equipment, swinging on the swings, and running around the playground, are also popular physical activities. **Figure 14.15**

Figure 14.15 Motor Skill Activities

Gross-Motor Activities	Fine-Motor Activities
• Walk backward, sideways, heel-to-toe on a drawn line, or on tiptoes and heels. • March to music. • Run to a given point (tree), run around it, and run back. • Jump off a low, sturdy object. • Jump over two drawn lines or two ropes placed parallel on the floor. *riekephotos/Shutterstock.com* • Hop on one or both feet, in different directions (backward or sideways), or as far as possible. Add music or a rhythmic beat to help the child skip with the beat. • Roll or pass a ball back and forth (while counting). • Throw and catch balls. • Bounce balloons up from the hand or toss balloons to different distances. • Ride tricycles and scooters. • Push strollers and pull wagons. • Climb, slide, and swing on playground equipment. • Crawl through straight and curved tunnels or a tunnel on a hill. • Walk forward and backward on a balance beam. Use specific arm movements, such as a bird flapping its wings while on the balance beam. • Dance freestyle or to songs with movements ("I'm a Little Teapot"). • Use pretend movements to music (plane, animals). • Play "Red Light/Green Light" or circle games. • Sing and use movements to "Head, Shoulders, Knees, and Toes" or the "Hokey Pokey." • Play a modified version of hopscotch.	• Engage in sand play, cooking activities, and art activities, and play with a toy carpenter bench. • Learn finger plays, such as "The Itsy Bitsy Spider." • Use "manipulative toys," such as stringing beads, lacing cards, small blocks and tinker toys, and cube block designs. *emholk/E+ via Getty Image* • Use finger puppets with stories, songs, poems, and finger plays. • Trace with templates or cookie cutters for eye-hand coordination. • Clip clothespins to the rims of containers or to the edges of cardboard. Punch holes with a single-hole punch to strengthen fingers.

Goodheart-Willcox Publisher

shows motor physical activities preschoolers commonly enjoy.

Parents can encourage physical activity and help preschoolers avoid a sedentary lifestyle. The American Academy of Pediatrics recommends limiting screen time to one hour or less per day of high-quality programs. Limiting screen time encourages a physically active lifestyle. Parents can encourage activity by enrolling their children in classes and programs, such as swim or gymnastics classes. Adults can also structure indoor activities for preschoolers when outdoor play is not an option.

14.3-4 Rest and Sleep

Preschoolers need about 10 to 13 hours of sleep daily. Sleep needs are individual, but younger preschoolers often need more sleep than older preschoolers. Most children give up daytime naps during the preschool years.

Preschoolers still want (and need) a bedtime routine. If bedtime rules have been enforced in the toddler years, most children accept them during the preschool years. Fears of the dark and monsters still exist, but many preschoolers develop their own routines to help ease such stress. Locking windows or sleeping with a doll or stuffed animal may comfort the child.

1. Which clothing feature would be most helpful to aid a preschooler with self-dressing? (14.3.1)
   A. An opening in the back of a shirt
   B. A button closure on pants
   C. Tie laces on sneakers
   D. A zipper with a large pull tab
2. **True or False.** For a proper fit, the arch support in a preschooler's sneakers should be in the correct position. (14.3.1)
3. Daytime toileting accidents in preschoolers are most often a result of _____. (14.3-2)
   A. waiting too long to go to the bathroom
   B. experiencing a urinary tract problem
   C. drinking too much fluid
   D. feeling anxious about using the bathroom
4. The American Academy of Pediatrics recommends limiting a preschooler's screen time to _____ per day of high-quality programs. (14.3.3)
   A. 2 hours
   B. 30 minutes or less
   C. 1 hour or less
   D. 3 to 4 hours
5. How many hours of sleep do preschoolers need each day? (14.3.4)
   A. 12–16 hours
   B. 11–14 hours
   C. 10–13 hours
   D. 9–12 hours

Summary

Lesson 14.1

14.1-1 During the preschool years, the three major brain developments are functional specialization, greater myelination, and pruning. The heart, airways, stomach, and bladder also mature.

14.1-2 Preschoolers' height increases by about 7 inches, and their weight increases by about 12 pounds. Their faces begin to look more like those of adults, and their waists become smaller than their shoulders and hips. Bones grow harder, larger, and longer, and deciduous teeth begin to fall out. Fat deposits decrease, and muscle tissue increases in size and strength.

14.1-3 Balance and other gross-motor skills develop through preschoolers' physical activities, and they develop two new actions: body rotation and weight shift.

14.1-3 Fine-motor skills improve as preschoolers manipulate small objects. Eye-hand coordination improves, which strengthens fine-motor skills.

14.1-3 Hand preference develops during the preschool years and is associated with functional specialization, genetics, birth trauma, and social pressures. Each child should determine their own hand preference.

14.1-4 Physical capabilities expand during the preschool years as children are better able to explore and interact with the world around them.

Lesson 14.2

14.2-1 Preschool children need to eat nutrient-dense foods that provide vitamins, minerals, and other beneficial substances, but little or no solid fats, added sugars, refined starches, and sodium.

14.2-1 Caregivers should limit or avoid empty-calorie foods and overall reduce preschoolers' intake of sugar, salt, and solid fats.

14.2-2 Preschoolers learn attitudes about food from others. Caregivers should model positive attitudes toward food, give children choices, and avoid using food as rewards or bribes for behavior.

14.2-3 Preschool children like foods that look good, are separated, are served at acceptable temperatures, are prepared in different ways, are served in small amounts, and are easy to eat.

14.2-4 Involving preschoolers in food preparation teaches them about colors, shapes, tastes, aromas, textures, and appliance names.

14.2-4 Caregivers may set an example by taking turns talking and demonstrating other table manners, but they should have realistic expectations for behavior at mealtime.

Lesson 14.3

14.3-1 Clothing and shoes for preschool children must be appealing and fit properly. When selecting clothing for children, adults should look for safety and self-dressing features.

14.3-2 Preschool children generally have control over their bladders, but some toileting accidents may occur.

14.3-2 Adults should help preschool children maintain basic hygiene, such as using the bathroom and dental care.

14.3-3 Physical activity is vital for preschool children's health and motor skill development.

14.3-4 Preschoolers should get 10 to 13 hours of sleep per night.

College and Career Portfolio

Portfolio Résumé

Whether your portfolio is for a school or for a job, you will need to include a résumé. A *résumé* is an outline of your education and relevant experience. It should be concise, detailed, and attractive, and should advertise why your chosen school or company needs *you*. To create your résumé, complete the following activities.

- Visit your school's career center, writing center, or a local library to learn more about résumés. For more information about résumé writing, you can also read Chapter 25, *Preparing for a Child-Related Career*, in this textbook or view sample résumés online.
- Write a draft of your résumé and have it reviewed by a teacher. Then, edit your résumé accordingly.

Recall and Application

1. What major changes happen in the brain of a preschooler? (14.1.1)
   A. The brain reaches 100 percent of adult volume.
   B. Windows of opportunity for language learning open.
   C. The myelinization of brain neurons concludes.
   D. Functional specialization in different brain areas occurs.

2. Working memory, cognitive flexibility, and inhibitions are examples of _____? (14.1.1)
   A. expressive language
   B. executive functions
   C. receptive language
   D. functional specialization

3. **True or False**. Biologically male children are, on average, a pound heavier than children their age who are biologically female. (14.1.2)

4. Which activity helps a preschooler develop static balance? (14.1.3)
   A. Walking in a straight line
   B. Standing on one foot with arms outstretched
   C. Building a tower using small blocks
   D. Walking on a balance beam

5. A preschooler typically achieves which physical developmental milestone at age 5? (14.1.4)
   A. Pedaling a tricycle
   B. Working a 40-piece jigsaw puzzle
   C. Building a straight block tower
   D. Hopping 8–10 steps on one foot

6. **True or False**. Most five-year-olds can cut and paste simple shapes. (14.1.4)

7. Vegetables, fruits, and whole grains are examples of _____. (14.2.1)
   A. empty-calorie foods
   B. nutrient-dense foods
   C. solid fats
   D. special diets

8. Caregivers can help preschoolers form positive attitudes about food by _____. (14.2.2)
   A. restricting access to desserts and sweets
   B. encouraging them to try new foods
   C. limiting their choices about the foods they can eat
   D. offering them food as rewards for good behavior

9. **True or False.** When first introducing a new food to a preschooler, give them an ample portion to try. (14.2.3)

10. **True or False.** To teach preschoolers proper table manners, caregivers should scold them for being messy eaters. (14.2.4)

11. Because it may present a safety hazard, children should avoid wearing _____. (14.3.1)
    A. jackets with detachable hoods
    B. shoes with self-adhesive straps
    C. pants with wide legs
    D. shirts that open in the front

12. **True or False.** The shoes preschoolers wear for activities should have flexible soles that are 1 inch thick to absorb the pounding of walking, running, and jumping. (14.3.1)

13. Enuresis is involuntary urination that occurs for at least 3 months _____. (14.3.2)
    A. in children of any age
    B. only at night
    C. two or more times a week
    D. during the daytime

14. **True or False.** To help prevent tooth decay and gum disease, adults should make sure preschoolers brush their teeth twice a day with a fluoride toothpaste. (14.3.2)

15. Which physical activity promotes gross-motor skill development in preschoolers? (14.3.3)
    A. Using finger puppets
    B. Playing the "The Itsy-Bitsy Spider"
    C. Pulling a wagon
    D. Tracing with a template

16. **True or False.** Preschoolers still want (and need) a bedtime routine. (14.3.4)

Vocabulary Activities

1. Read the text passages that contain each *Key Term*. Then write the definitions of each term in your own words. Double-check your definitions by re-reading the text and using the text glossary.

Critical Thinking

1. **Compare and contrast.** Obtain two pictures of a child—one as a baby and one at four or five years of age. Compare and contrast the child's physical appearance in these pictures. What physical differences are evident? What physical features have remained the same?

2. **Cause and effect.** The author states that food attitudes learned in the preschool years may last a lifetime. What is meant by a *food attitude*? What food attitudes do you have that you think may have been impacted by your experiences as a young child?

3. **Identify.** Search the internet for creative foods for young children. Choose four food ideas you find especially creative and then identify what makes them so appealing. Also, identify the nutritional content of the food and assess how healthful it would be for a growing preschooler.

4. **Evaluate.** Find a magazine that contains pictures and descriptions of gifts (such as toys and clothes) for preschool children. As you read the magazine, choose three gifts and evaluate their usefulness and appeal based on preschoolers' physical abilities and preferences. Which gifts would preschoolers most like? Which gifts would be too easy or too advanced for preschool children?

5. **Determine.** When Tyler's son, Camden, started preschool, Tyler took advantage of the opportunity to start taking late-afternoon shifts at work. Unfortunately, some of these shifts would run until 8:00 p.m. on weeknights. While Camden's babysitter had already put him to bed by this time, Tyler wanted to hear about Camden's day some nights and woke Camden up to talk. Camden has had trouble sleeping the past few months and always seems tired. How can Tyler help Camden get sufficient sleep? How can Tyler balance the desire to spend time with Camden and help meet Camden's physical needs?

Core Skills

1. **Writing.** Review this chapter's information on the organ maturation and skeletal growth of preschoolers. Then, imagine you have been hired to write a creative and engaging book for parents of preschoolers, with the goal of teaching them what they should expect as their children grow. Write a short, entertaining book chapter covering preschool organ maturation and skeletal growth. Keep your audience in mind and write using a conversational tone.

2. **Reading.** Imagine you are a teacher at a preschool center. Your director has asked you to help preschoolers develop their fine-motor skills through a series of entertaining crafts. In preparation for these activities, search a local library or the internet for fun and simple craft ideas that would help children develop fine-motor skills. Craft a lesson plan based on these activities, including what materials you will need, what additional support you will have to give the children, and how each activity will aid fine-motor development.

3. **Technology and speaking.** In groups of three, review the physical developmental milestones children achieve at three, four, and five years of age. Have each group member select one age, and then, using art supplies or electronic resources, create an easy-to-follow visual representation of the milestones children achieve during these years. Your project should include drawings or pictures of children achieving various milestones during each year and should be an effective study tool and synthesis of the information you learned in this chapter. After completing your project, make a group presentation to the class.

4. **Listening and speaking.** Using MyPlate and the nutritional information covered in this chapter, plan a week's worth of healthful snacks and meals for a preschool child (three meals and two snacks per day). Plan meals that satisfy MyPlate's recommendations in each food group and choose online or print recipes for each food you include.

5. **Technology and art.** Clothing becomes more important to children during the preschool years. Preschool children are developing unique personalities and want to express these personalities in their clothing. Adults, however, still need to ensure that clothing contains appropriate safety and self-dressing features. In small groups, use software or sketch paper to design a preschooler's outfit. First, describe the personality of the preschooler you want to design for and then work together to create a quality outfit that contains some of the safety and self-dressing features covered in this chapter. After completing your design, present it to the class and describe how it meets the preschool child's needs.

6. **Research and speaking.** Lack of dental care in early childhood can lead to serious tooth decay in the teen and even adult years. For children in underserved areas, this can be a complicated problem because dental care is inaccessible or unaffordable. In small groups, research the effects of children's lack of dental care. Document the possible consequences of this problem and identify three organizations that are working to provide dental care to these underserved children. Finally, deliver a five-minute group presentation detailing how lack of dental care affects children and what organizations are doing to remedy the problem.

7. **CTE Career Readiness Practice.** Imagine you are the director of a preschool center, and that recently, one parent complained that their child was not getting enough physical activity. Upon further investigation, you find that children spend more time playing with digital devices than they do playing outside. You gather your three-person team to talk about the problem, but you are afraid of being too harsh with them. In preparation for your team meeting, complete the following steps:

   - **Identify the problem.** Write a two- to three-sentence summary of the problem. Choose words that will challenge your team but will not discourage them.
   - **Create a plan to fix the problem.** Outline a weekly routine that will provide the children with more physical activity.
   - **Delegate the parts of the plan.** Decide who will fulfill each part of the plan (person one, person two, or person three) and document how you will describe each person's job responsibility. After making these preparations, rehearse the meeting in groups of four. Give each other feedback.

Observations

1. As a class, observe preschoolers in a child care program eating lunch or a snack. What foods are they provided? Do the children like some foods and reject others? Why do you think certain foods are rejected? How did adults at the child care center respond to children rejecting the foods? After the observation, have a class discussion concerning how to improve the eating experiences of the preschoolers in this child care program.

2. Interview a teacher at a local preschool center about how the children in the center have physically changed between three and five years of age. Before the interview, identify some questions you want answered. Some possible questions might be: How do children's growing bodies affect their motor development? How do you see hand preference develop? What are some signs that a preschooler's balance is improving? Take notes about your interview and then discuss your findings in small groups.

Chapter 15

Intellectual Development of Preschoolers

Essential Question

How does brain development influence intellectual abilities during the preschool years, and how can parents and other adults provide support for preschoolers' higher-level mental functioning?

Case Study   Can Imaginative Preschoolers Confuse Reality and Fantasy?

As a class, read the case study and answer the questions that follow. After you finish studying the chapter, discuss this case study again. Have your opinions changed based on what you learned?

Four-year-old Marlowe's family went to Disney World before preschool resumed for the fall. Marlowe liked books about princesses, and at Disney World, Marlowe had a day as a "princess," complete with a beautiful dress, makeup, a tiara, and photos. When the day ended, Marlowe's parents had a hard time getting Marlowe to remove the princess accessories.

After that day, Marlowe took on the identity of Cinderella and expected everyone to use that name. Marlowe's preschool teachers chuckled and decided to play along. Almost every day, Marlowe would wear a formal dress from the preschool's dress-up box and play the role of Cinderella. Marlowe expected class friends to be the stepsisters. When Marlowe's friends no longer wanted to play the role of Cinderella's stepsisters, Marlowe could not understand why.

Marlowe no longer played in all the program centers and would not even play outside if the formal dress could not be worn. Marlowe would only

engage in activities for a princess. By this point, some of the teachers and Marlowe's parents were becoming concerned that Marlowe was taking this role too far.

Give It Some Thought

1. Do you think the child truly believes they have become Cinderella? Explain your answer.
2. Do you think Marlowe's dedication to the fantasy role suggests a developmental problem? Explain.
3. Do you think Marlowe's parents and the teachers at the preschool program were right in "playing along" with Marlowe, or should they have insisted that the role could only be played a few minutes each day? Explain your thinking.

FatCamera/E+ via Getty Images

How Preschoolers Learn

Key Terms

centration
egocentrism
episodic memory
intuitive substage
memory capacity
mental images
preconceptual substage
preoperational stage
symbolic thought
transductive reasoning
transformations

Learning Outcomes

After studying this lesson, you will be able to

15.1-1 **summarize** brain development and intellectual (cognitive) changes that occur during the preschool years.

15.1-2 **explain** Jean Piaget's preoperational stage, including the preconceptual and intuitive substages and obstacles to preschoolers' logical thinking.

15.1-3 **explain** the three major origins of abstract thought in preschoolers, as well as scaffolding techniques, as identified by Vygotsky.

Reading and Notetaking Activity

Skim this lesson from top to bottom and from left to right and list all the headings. Then, identify key terms with which you are unfamiliar and scan through the chapter to find their definitions. Write a "topic sentence" and brief summary for each heading, using the key terms to explain what you think you will learn. After you read this lesson, write a new topic sentence and summary for each section, outlining the main points you learned.

Introduction

Preschool children build on what they have learned as infants and toddlers. Because preschoolers have better motor skills, their world broadens. Preschoolers can interact with more objects and people and participate in more events. This enables them to observe more and develop more advanced ideas about the physical attributes of their world.

Preschoolers' intellectual development also broadens their world. Thinking skills are well underway in the preschool years, as brain development allows fast learning. Preschoolers can **conceptualize** (form a concept of) objects and actions. Intellectual (cognitive) changes in pretend play, mental images, drawing, language, and memory help them use their skills more effectively. Preschoolers are in the *preoperational stage*, a developmental stage in which they solve problems first by using only their present perceptions, and later through intuition. Scaffolding is less hands-on during the preschool years, and preschoolers' maturing brains make this stage vital to learning.

15.1-1 Brain Development and Intellectual Changes

Brain development is still rapid during the preschool years. Brain specialization allows for many new abilities, myelination speeds connections between areas, and pruning makes the remaining connections more efficient.

By three years of age, preschoolers use thinking to solve problems even better than before. They do not always have to use trial and error. Their problem-solving skills are affected by past sensory and motor experiences.

Beginning between three and four years of age, one of the most important intellectual advances is *symbolic thought*. **Symbolic thought** is the ability to use symbols (words, sounds, images, toys, household items, etc.) to represent concrete things. Children learn symbolic thought through pretend play, also known as *symbolic play*, where they make associations between their real worlds and the symbols they use (**Figure 15.1**).

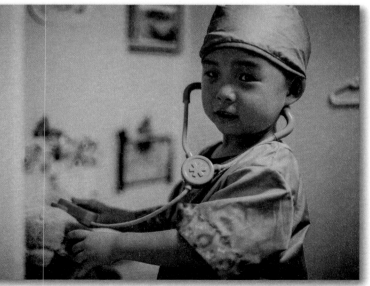

Nikola Stojadinovic/E+ via Getty Images

Figure 15.1 In pretend play, preschoolers associate symbols with real-world objects and events. *What types of pretend play did you engage in as a young child? What symbols did you use while playing?*

For example, a preschooler might use a doll to pretend it is their younger sibling at home. Likewise, they might pretend to cook food by using a stirring motion or cutting motion with their hands. Symbolic thought affects a number of abilities—pretend play, mental images, drawing, language, and memory.

Pretend Play

During late toddlerhood, pretend play begins with the development of deferred imitation. *Deferred imitation* is a child's ability to imitate the actions of a model who is no longer present. Pretend play develops and changes in the following areas during the preschool years:

- *Symbol realism.* Children engaging in early pretend play prefer realistic symbols that closely represent the intended object. Later, children change their pretend play to include objects that may stand for anything they want.
- *Context.* Children's early pretend play takes place within the context of real experience, like things they might do at home or in preschool programs. As pretend play develops, children might choose less realistic contexts like going on a safari or on a trip to outer space.
- *Roles.* Early pretend play involves children role-playing themselves or those like them. Later, children begin to take on a greater variety of roles, such as role-playing adults or even animals.
- *Number of actions.* Early pretend play experiences often involve one action, such as combing hair. Later, children may pretend play a sequence of actions, such as several grooming tasks.
- *Involvement of others.* Early pretend play is usually done alone, but as pretend play develops, children play pretend games with other children and sometimes with adults.

Mental Images

Mental images are symbols of objects and past experiences that are stored in the mind. These images function as a form of mental representation.

The imagery is experienced through all sensory modes, such as the appearance, feel, sound, odor, or flavor of anything. Therefore, mental images resemble a perceptual experience, but occur in the absence of that experience. Mental images are not exact copies of real objects and experiences, but they do relate to the real world (**Figure 15.2**). Mental images are triggered by words, new experiences, memories, and even "What if…" thoughts.

Mental images function in preschoolers' and even adults' thinking in the following ways:

- Memories are often stored as mental images. Through memory a person recalls the past. As you read, *learning* is defined as an adaptation of a past understanding. You modify your current thinking based on recall (memory) and then store the new learning in memory. Thus, learning and memory are interactive processes.
- Imagery is crucial to *language meanings* (semantics). Preschool children store the meanings of concrete words (*cat, apple, building*) as mental images although this does not work for more abstract words, such as *hope* or *joy*. As people of all ages hear or read words, they link the sounds or graphics to meanings through their mental images.

Descriptive writers of both prose and poetry rely on their readers to create mental images from their words.

- Imagery is involved in spatial reasoning as a person "sees" how something would look if rotated, turned over, or *synthesized* (putting together shapes to form new shapes). Playing with jigsaw puzzles or block building aid mental imagery of young children. This early spatial imagery will allow adults to draw images from any perspective. Frank Lloyd Wright, the great American architect, said he used his mental images from childhood block building to create his designs (**Figure 15.3**).
- Mental imagery plays a crucial role in inventive or creative thinking. Creative preschoolers use mental imagery in their pretend play, artistic creations, and language. They imagine new "what if" configurations for a marble chute or a building and refine their physical knowledge concepts. Adult inventors, including Einstein and Tesla, used mental imagery because it allowed them to modify their ideas quickly.

In short, mental imagery plays a crucial role in *all* thought processes.

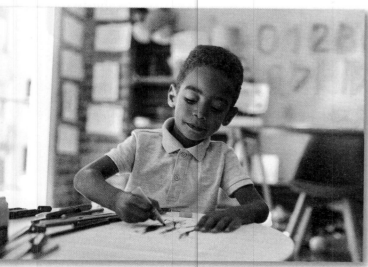

AaronAmat /iStock via Getty Images Plus

Figure 15.2 Mental images exist within a person's mind; they may become observable through drawings. Children's drawings tend to mirror their mental images. *What mental images do you have when you hear the following words: cat, thunderstorm, and flower?*

Photographs in the Carol M. Highsmith Archive, Library of Congress, Prints and Photographs Division

Figure 15.3 Taliesin West, Frank Lloyd Wright's winter home and architectural school, is an example of his great skill at designing attractive and creative buildings and structures. *How much do you think the mental images formed in childhood affect a person's perceptions later in life?*

Drawing

Unlike younger children, preschoolers no longer scribble. Instead, they attempt to draw objects and depict their world through drawings. Preschoolers intend their drawings to be realistic. They draw what they think or know about a person, not what is visually accurate. For example, a side view of a goldfish in a drawing may show both eyes and even a smiling mouth. Drawing mixes the skills involved in pretend play and mental images. Preschool children draw first and then decide what their pictures represent. In contrast, older children decide what to draw, form a mental image of the object, and then draw it.

Language

Spoken and written words are symbols used to represent ideas or actions (referred to as language symbols). Compared with child-created symbols seen in pretend and drawing, language symbols are more abstract and thus more difficult for the child to understand. Unlike symbols used in pretend or in drawing, children do not *decide* on language symbols. Language symbols *already exist* in a culture and must be learned. Therefore, words are more abstract compared with most other symbols.

For example, the word *car* does not look, sound, or move like a car.

Memory

Memory is a complex mental process involved in most, if not all, aspects of thinking and learning. Memory begins at birth when the newborn remembers the rhythm and intonation of a caregiver's voice heard in the prenatal period. Infants have amazing, although short-term, memories. Toddlers remember better and for much longer periods of time, and preschoolers remember even more.

A major change in memory occurs during the preschool years due to brain development and experiences. Preschoolers remember more and retain memories longer than younger children. Preschoolers remember not only images, but also language components. Preschoolers often replay their memories by talking about events or rehearsing what they have learned in a song or a story. **Memory capacity** increases during the preschool years. Memory capacity refers to what a person does with their memory, not how *much* is remembered. Memory capacity increases in both working and long-term memories during the preschool years. (**Figure 15.4**).

Goodheart-Willcox Publisher

Figure 15.4 Memory can be divided into two categories: long-term memory and working memory. Long-term memory can be further divided into implicit and explicit memory, which includes semantic and episodic memory. *What are some examples of memories that fall into each of these categories?*

Working Memory

Working memory (also called *short-term memory*) is critical for executive functioning and is closely related to Galinsky's essential life skills mentioned in Lesson 2.2. Working memory improves a great deal in the preschool years. These improvements allow preschoolers to follow directions, connect events in stories, stay true to the pretend roles they play, play games with several rules, and follow new sequences of rules.

Long-Term Memory

Explicit and implicit memories (also called *long-term memories*) continue to develop in the preschool years. Preschoolers' explicit memory develops as they learn more facts, concepts, and words associated with these facts and concepts. Implicit memories, especially motor skills, also dramatically increase as preschoolers play and learn self-help tasks.

Preschoolers develop what is called *episodic memory*. **Episodic memory**, which is a type of explicit memory, is the memory of personal experiences and events. Episodic memories include the emotion and the context of the event. People usually see themselves as "actors" in these memories. Episodic memories begin between preschoolers' third and fourth birthdays. Even then, children may forget these early memories. Episodic memories are not **crystallized** (KRIS-tuh-lyzd), or clear and fully formed in the mind, until 10 years of age. The inability to remember events before 3 or 4 years of age or the forgetting of recalled events in the preschool and early school years is called *infantile amnesia*. Although more research is needed, the following is known about children's early episodic memories:

- Infants and toddlers do not have the thinking or language skills necessary to store memories of personal events.
- For life experiences to feel real to children, children must have a sense of self and personal identity.
- Cultural differences influence early memories. Individual-oriented cultures stress self-awareness more than group-oriented cultures. Group-oriented cultures talk more about events within the context of the group.

Although there are wide variations among children within any culture, the earliest personal memories of children from group-oriented cultures occur a year or more later than for children from individual-oriented cultures.

- All early memories, including most episodic memories, fade with time or are replaced.

Episodic memories are valuable. They make experiences and understandings more vivid. For example, seeing the Rocky Mountains, as compared with reading some facts about them, would be far more meaningful and lasting in memory. Episodic memories also allow for a special type of cultural communication, binding people with these experiences closer together (**Figure 15.5**). Episodic memories may help in planning or decision making if future events bear similarity to a remembered event. In this case, a child can remember what helped the situation and what did not.

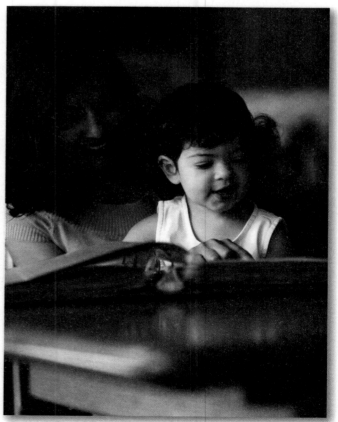

Photodisc/ Photodisc/Thinkstock

Figure 15.5 Episodic memories bind people and cultures together. *What episodic memories bind your family together? What types of memorable experiences have made you feel closer to them?*

15.1-2 Piaget's Cognitive-Developmental Theory

Both Piaget and Vygotsky's theories were discussed in Lesson 9.1. Piaget and Vygotsky both note that children gain new intellectual abilities after infancy and toddlerhood by developing abstract meanings separate from their real world. Piaget focuses on the limitations of these abilities. Both theories shape understanding of the preschooler's intellectual world.

The Preoperational Stage

Piaget describes the second stage of cognitive (intellectual) development as the **preoperational stage**. This is the stage children reach before they acquire logical thinking skills, which Piaget calls *operations*. These logical thinking skills require the mind to think through problems and act accordingly. Examples of logical thinking skills include combining ideas or objects, placing them in order, and engaging in "if-then" (cause and effect) thinking. Preschool children have not entered the logical thinking stage yet. Just as toddlers who are walking are prone to missteps, preschool children are prone to logical thinking errors.

The preoperational stage spans six years of childhood, beginning in the last year of toddlerhood, extending through the preschool years, and ending after the first two school years. The preoperational stage is divided into two substages: the *preconceptual substage* and the *intuitive substage* (**Figure 15.6**).

The Preconceptual Substage

The **preconceptual substage** (also known as the *symbolic substage*) is a substage in which children two to four years of age begin to develop and understand some concepts. These children can form mental images of what they see around them.

Figure 15.6 Piaget's Cognitive-Development Theory

Stages and Substages	Characteristics
Stage 1: Sensorimotor stage (birth to 2 years)	• Children learn through the senses and physical actions in six substages.
Substages 1 and 2	• Involve the baby's own body.
Substages 3 and 4	• Involve people and objects.
Substages 5 and 6 (12 to 24 months)	• Involve creative actions and thinking before acting.
Stage 2: Preoperational stage (2 to 7 years)	• Learning through symbols, such as pretend play, mental images, drawing, language, and memory, but with logical limitations. The word *preoperational* means before (*pre*) logical mental actions (*operations*).
Substage 1: Preconceptual or symbolic (2 to 4 years)	• Begins to develop concepts. • Has rapid development of language. • Does not think logically.
Substage 2: Intuitive (4 to 7 years)	• Figures things out through perception more than through logic; that is, cannot explain "Why." • Shows improvement, especially in classifying, ordering, and numerical skills.
Stage 3: Concrete operational stage (7 to 11 years)	• Children begin to think logically, but base their logic on past experiences.
Stage 4: Formal operational stage (11 years of age and older)	• Older children, teens, and adults reason abstractly.

Goodheart-Willcox Publisher

Many concepts, however, are still incomplete or illogical in the preschooler's mind. Some examples of these incomplete concepts include:

- the identification of an object by one part or attribute rather than by several parts or attributes. For example, a preschooler may identify a dog as any animal that plays with a ball.
- the belief that if an attribute of an object changes or is not present, then that object becomes a different object. For example, a preschooler might believe that an unripe orange is a "ball."
- the inability to distinguish between *similar* and *same*. If two objects share a similar attribute, a preschooler may see them as the same. For example, a preschooler might refer to any dog that is the same breed as their family pet by their pet's name. They might also think that all hot objects are stoves.
- difficulty differentiating between people or objects and their symbols. For example, young preschoolers may see themselves and their photos as the same and may believe that anyone who wears a fire hat is a fire fighter. Because of this incomplete concept, pretend play and reality are not truly separated for preschoolers.

The Intuitive Substage

Growth spurts in the brain always lead to leaps in the thinking processes, which are referred to as substages and stages in intellectual development. A growth spurt in the brain helps preschoolers make a transition from the *preconceptual* to the *intuitive* substage. At this time, brain pruning refines the sensory and motor skills developed earlier. Memory and problem-solving functions increase. Functional specialization and lateralization of the brain begin toward the end of the *intuitive* substage. This refers to the brain having different regions that control specific functions.

In the **intuitive substage**, children are sometimes able to grasp a problem's solution by relying on their mental imagery rather than using logical reasoning. By using their **intuition** (the natural ability to know something without evidence), they "feel their way through" problems instead of thinking logically about them. In the intuitive substage, children can:

- imagine new roles for themselves. For example, they can imagine themselves as parents, police officers, or doctors. They can also imagine relationships between objects—one doll might be a "parent" and the other the parent's "baby."
- understand how one factor affects another. For example, preschoolers can understand that a box being full of blocks makes it harder to push.
- use intuition to solve problems. Older preschoolers may or may not solve problems correctly. For example, a preschooler may try to find an object by envisioning it in their mind instead of by logically thinking through where the object should be.

Obstacles to Logical Thought

While preoperational children in the intuitive substage have many correct ideas due to the accuracy of their intuition, they are not yet logical in their thinking. Logical thinkers, unlike intuitive thinkers, construct "rules" to guide their thinking. For example, in the experiment with the three balls (in the *Focus on Science* feature), the "rule" is that one turn keeps the balls in the same order, but a half turn reverses the order. The intuitive thinker does not use the "rule," but simply forms a mental image of the balls as the tube is turned. The child may track accurately for a few turns, but likely loses track after more turns.

Why are these preschool children intuitive rather than logical? In his work, Piaget notes several obstacles to logical thinking in preoperational children.

Egocentrism

Piaget describes **egocentrism** (ee-goh-SEN-trism) as the preschooler's belief that everyone thinks in the same way and has the same ideas as they do. Egocentrism does not mean children are selfish or too concerned with themselves, but that they view the world in relation to themselves. Egocentrism can cause preschoolers to:

- believe that others like what they like. For example, preschoolers may offer others candy from their mouths because they are enjoying the candy and think others will, too.

- think others see objects the way they do. For example, if a preschooler thinks a slide is tall, they will think adults find it tall, too.
- believe others understand what they are thinking. For example, preschoolers may leave out facts in telling about an event and become exasperated when an adult asks questions to fill in the details.
- experience all events in reference to themselves. For example, a preschooler may believe that rain falls to keep them from playing in the sand.

- believe inanimate objects have attributes like their own. For example, a preschooler may think that if a toy is damaged, that toy is hurting.
- believe that all movements have purposes that relate to them. For example, a preschooler may believe the moon rises to show them a pretty night sky.
- believe they can alter reality by their thinking. For example, in pretend play, preschoolers may believe they have become the person they are role-playing.

Focus on Science

Using Intuition to Solve Problems

During the preschool years, children are more able to solve problems. Problem solving, however, does not rely on logic at this stage. Rather, preschoolers solve problems using their intuition.

One example of a child using intuition to solve a problem is a preschooler keeping track of several balls in an *opaque* (nontransparent) tube. A preschooler can be shown three balls—a blue ball, yellow ball, and a red ball on top—all in a vertical, opaque tube. If the preschooler is asked to find the red ball once the tube is rotated, they will watch as the tube is turned and keep track of the red ball in their "mind's eye." The preschooler will not use logic—such as knowledge about complete and half turns—to find the red ball.

In situations like the one described, preschoolers' reliance on intuition does not make much difference. Many times, however, preschoolers develop incorrect ideas because their intuition misleads them. For example, a preschooler standing on a ladder may say to their parent, "I am taller than you," because the child can see over the parent's head.

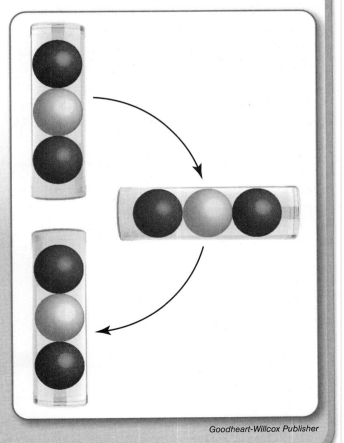

Photo: Anna Marynenko/Shutterstock.com; otnaydur/Shutterstock.com

Goodheart-Willcox Publisher

Centration

Because preschoolers try to solve problems through perception, they may center their attention on only one part of an object or event instead of seeing all parts at the same time. This is known as **centration** (sen-TRAY-shun). Sometimes, centration can cause inaccurate problem solving because the other elements unnoticed by the preschooler may be relevant to the issue. For example, preschool children know that the amount of liquid in two equal-sized glasses is the same. When the liquid of one container is poured into a tall beaker or a wide bowl, however, preschool children incorrectly think the amount of liquid has changed even though it is still the same. They are not paying attention to the fact that nothing else has changed. Another example of centration would be a preschooler becoming upset that a classmate had more cookies than them, even if the cookies were much smaller than the ones the child had. (**Figure 15.7**).

Problems with Transformations and Reversibility

Centration makes it difficult for preschoolers to see **transformations**, which are sequences of changes. Preschool children tend to focus on single steps, stages, or events, and may have difficulty following transformations. Piaget describes preschoolers as focusing on each frame of a film

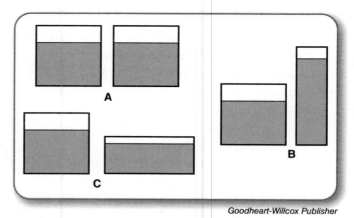

Goodheart-Willcox Publisher

Figure 15.7 Children usually think that *wide* means *more* liquid (B) and that the *lower* height means *less* liquid in the bowl than in the glass (C). *If an adult pours the liquid back and forth from the original-sized glass to the beaker or bowl, do you think a preschooler would say the quantity changes or remains the same with each pour?*

rather than seeing a running story. If shown an object that stands upright and then falls, preoperational children will draw only the first state, in which the object is upright, or the last state, in which the object lies horizontal (**Figure 15.8**).

Because they have difficulty following transformations, preoperational children also struggle to trace actions in reverse, or reverse the transformations. Preschoolers cannot follow a line of reasoning back to where it starts, which is called a *lack of reversibility*. For example, preschoolers cannot reverse or "undo" addition.

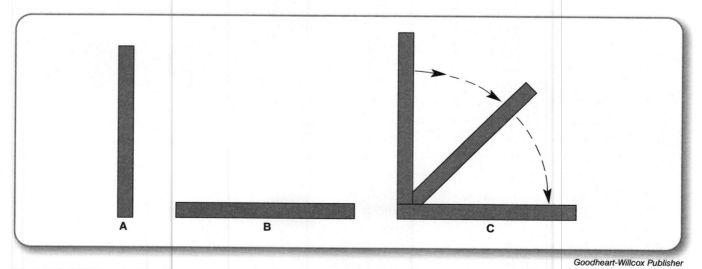

Goodheart-Willcox Publisher

Figure 15.8 When preschool children are asked to watch as a rod is dropped and then draw what they have seen, they draw only the first state (A) or the last state (B). They do not draw any of the in-between states (C). *How do you think preschoolers' difficulty comprehending transformations limits their perceptions of the real world?*

If they know that adding two and three equals five, they will not be able to infer that subtracting two from five equals three. (You will learn more about transformations and reversals later in the text.)

Transductive Reasoning

Preschoolers also use **transductive reasoning**, which is mentally linking events without a logical reason. Preschoolers often link one event or object with another, without any reference to the general big picture. For example, if their parent gets home and it starts raining, they may think it started raining due to their parent getting home rather than it just being a coincidence. Reasoning this way causes flaws in logic, such as overgeneralization. **Overgeneralization** is the assumption that because something is true for one event or object, it is true for all similar events or objects. An example of overgeneralization might be concluding that all dogs are friendly because the child's own dog is friendly.

Problems with Cause-and-Effect Reasoning

Logic is required for understanding cause and effect. Because of this, preschoolers' lack of logic causes many problems with cause-and-effect reasoning. Some of these problems include:

- the belief that any observable attribute of an object can cause an effect (outcome) they have noted. In one recorded interview, Piaget asked the child, "The sun does not fall from the sky. Why?" The child responded, "Because it is hot." In this case, the child is saying the heat of the sun (observable attribute) can affect the outcome (keep the sun from falling). Instead of saying, "Because it is *hot*," the child could have just as easily said, "Because it is *round, yellow,* or *far away*."
- **transposition** (changing of the order) of cause and effect. For example, a preschooler might say, "Because I'm wearing my raincoat, it is raining," instead of recognizing that wearing a raincoat is an effect of the rain.
- mistaken linking of events occurring close in time. If one parent makes coffee just before the other parent comes home from work each day, a preschooler may conclude that the coffee brings their other parent home.
- belief that any event or cause must be recreated in precisely the same way to get the same effect (**Figure 15.9**). For example, if a preschooler experiences many nighttime storms with lightning and thunder, they may conclude that it must be night before lightning causes thunder.

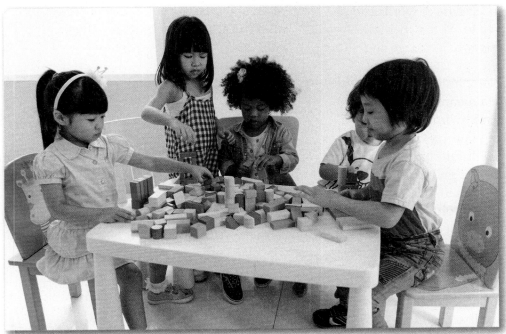

zGel/iStock via Getty Images Plus

Figure 15.9 Preschoolers believe that an event must be reconstructed in precisely the same way each time to achieve the same effect. *How might this belief hinder a preschooler's understanding of an everyday event?*

15.1-3 Vygotsky's Sociocultural Theory

Both Piaget and Vygotsky studied symbolic representation in children but came to different conclusions. Piaget believed imitation, pretend play, and language were indicators of the child's current level of thinking. Conversely, Vygotsky saw these preschool abilities as laying the foundation for more abstract thinking. In fact, Vygotsky identified these abilities as the three important origins of abstract thought in the preschool years:

- *Pretend play props.* Objects used in children's pretend play serve as foundations for imaginative thinking and abstract concepts. During pretend play, children first use realistic props and then they begin to use more abstract ones.

- *Language.* For preschoolers, language becomes more than a means to express knowledge or communicate with others. Currently, language becomes a tool for thinking. Language aids thought and vice versa. Children talk to themselves as they perform tasks, which is a way of thinking about their actions and thus staying on track. Over time, this kind of speech will diminish, but even adults sometimes whisper or talk quietly to themselves while working on challenging tasks. By using language as part of the thinking process, children's language skills increase. Children want to learn more words and varying ways of using them to express their ever-growing knowledge. In this way, language and thinking impact each other.

- *Imitation.* For preschoolers, imitative acts used in pretend play are a means of learning new skills. Lessons learned by imitation vary among cultures. For example, people in different cultures prepare different foods and may use different tools in the process.

Scaffolding techniques also change during the preschool years. Studies of scaffolding for preschoolers note that scaffolding is not as "hands-on" as it is in the toddler years. Generally, scaffolding during the preschool years involves a mentor directing the child's attention to a problem to be solved, suggesting strategies, monitoring the preschooler's attempts with less directive feedback, and then continuing to direct the child through encouragement.

1. Which is true about working memory? (15.1.1)
   A. It is also called long-term memory.
   B. It is critical for executive functioning.
   C. It is the memory of personal experiences and events.
   D. It develops as preschoolers learn more facts and concepts.

2. **True or False.** Rather than scribble, preschoolers attempt to draw objects and depict their world through drawings. (15.1.1)

3. Preschoolers in Piaget's intuitive substage _____. (15.1.2)
   A. identify an object by one part rather than all its parts
   B. understand how one factor affects another
   C. believe two objects sharing similar attributes are the same
   D. think that an object that has changed in some way is a different object

4. Focusing one's attention on only one part of an object or event instead of seeing all parts at the same time is called _____. (15.1.2)
   A. centration
   B. egocentrism
   C. intuition
   D. overgeneralization

5. The least effective scaffolding technique to use with preschoolers is _____. (15.1.3)
   A. directing a child's attention to a problem
   B. encouraging the child's attempts at problem-solving
   C. suggesting possible problem-solving strategies
   D. showing the child how you would solve the problem

What Preschoolers Learn

Learning Outcomes

After studying this lesson, you will be able to

15.2-1 **describe** the major areas of concept learning during the preschool years.

15.2-2 **discuss** preschoolers' progression in communicating more effectively.

15.2-3 **identify** intellectual developmental milestones preschoolers might achieve.

Key Terms

classifying
collective monologue
egocentrism
logical thinking
   concepts
mental maps
monologue
physical attributes
physical knowledge
seriation
tag questions

Reading and Notetaking Activity

Before reading this lesson, scan the lesson headings. Write a paragraph describing what you already know about these topics. Explain where you got the information you have—from conversations, the media, or research, for example. As you are reading, compare and contrast the information in the chapter with your prior knowledge. Organize your notes around the information you already know. After reading, consider how your prior knowledge of the subject matter helped you understand this topic.

Introduction

During the preschool years, brain development and intellectual changes in pretend play, mental images, drawing, language, and memory lead to better comprehension of complex concepts. While preoperational children do not use logic to solve problems, they are capable of symbolic thought and use their perceptions and intuition to reach solutions. Toward the end of the preschool years, children make advances in several areas of concept learning and begin to lay the foundation for understanding and using logical concepts. They also learn new word meanings and develop more complex grammar skills.

15.2-1 Concept Learning

In addition to the development of existing concepts, many new concepts emerge during the preschool years. The major areas of beginning concept learning for preschoolers include the following:

- noting physical attributes
- understanding physical knowledge
- using logical thinking concepts, such as sorting and classifying, ordering by attributes, seeing cause and effect, understanding spatial concepts, understanding number concepts, and noting time concepts

Noting Physical Attributes

From the moment they are born, children use their senses to develop concepts about size, shape, color, texture, and other **physical attributes** (concrete qualities that can be sensed) of objects. During the preschool years, children's sensory organs mature, and their senses become more coordinated. As a result, children's abilities to make sense of their environments improve during the preschool years.

Preschoolers focus on some **physical attributes** more than others. For example, three- and four-year-olds may pay attention to color and size, and five-year-olds may primarily note shapes. Due to centration, preschoolers are limited in the abilities to comprehend a variety of physical attributes at the same time. Therefore, they *center* (focus) on the attribute that stands out to them.

Preschoolers who are learning to note physical attributes may make mistakes. While preschoolers may note many features about an object, they may not note the object's most important features. For example, a preschooler may notice a zebra's ears, but not notice the zebra's stripes, which are most important in distinguishing the zebra from a horse. Because preschoolers tend to focus on individual attributes of an object, they do not always mentally "see" the whole object. When preschoolers are shown drawings such as those in **Figure 15.10**, they tend to recognize the parts, but not the whole.

Figure 15.10 Most preschoolers will see only parts of these drawings, not the whole. *What individual parts of these drawings might distract preschoolers from seeing the faces these parts make up?*

Understanding Physical Knowledge

Starting at four months of age, infants begin learning what happens when objects are used by people or other objects. Piaget calls these types of lessons *physical knowledge*. **Physical knowledge** is knowledge acquired through observations of the physical world, such as attributes of objects (color, shape) and observable phenomenon (how gravity works and the comparative speed of balls rolled on flat surfaces and inclines).

Many physical knowledge concepts, including natural events like evaporation and thunder, are too complex for children to understand. Preschoolers lack the logic needed to understand these concepts, so instead they settle on their own ideas about how the physical world works. Some of these illogical ideas include the following:

- *Animism.* Animism (AN-ih-mism) is the attribution of living qualities to inanimate objects. Preschoolers may assign human qualities to nonhuman objects, such as plants, animals, and possessions. For example, a preschooler who falls off a bike may say, "The bike was mad at me and made me fall." Sometimes, preschoolers use animism to avoid being punished or having to do something they do not want to do (**Figure 15.11**).

- *Artificialism.* Preschoolers may believe that everything is made by a real or imaginary person. For example, a preschooler may say that the sun was rolled into a ball by giants.

- *Finalism.* Preschoolers may see everything as having an identifiable and understandable purpose. For example, a preschooler may say, "The ball rolled away so I would have to chase it." Preschoolers look for reasons for everything because they are trying to learn about how the world around them works.

Teaching physical knowledge concepts by telling preschoolers about the world around them is difficult and usually ineffective. Preschool children best learn physical knowledge concepts through experimentation. Therefore, preschoolers need to be given opportunities to experiment with objects and events they can observe.

Using Logical Thinking Concepts

From an early age, children participate in problem solving. *Problem solving* is a broad term that most often includes noting a problem, observing and questioning what is observed, and solving the problem. By the preschool years, children use both physical (trial and error) and intellectual (intuition) problem-solving skills.

Intellectual problem solving depends on children's understanding of *logical thinking concepts*. **Logical thinking concepts** are those not directly experienced through the senses, but are developed through thought, such as noting similarities and differences in objects and coordinating simple relationships (classifying, ordering by attribute, counting). While these concepts cannot be physically observed, they can be "seen" in the mind. As the name suggests, these concepts will not fully develop until children are able to think logically. As a result, preschoolers' abilities to use logical thinking concepts are immature. Logical thinking concepts that begin to develop during the preschool years include sorting and classifying objects, ordering by attributes, seeing cause and effect, understanding spatial concepts, understanding number concepts, and noting time concepts.

DONOT6_STUDIO/Shutterstock.com

Figure 15.11 In an effort to avoid punishment, preschoolers may blame inanimate objects that they believe have lifelike qualities. For instance, a preschooler may say, "My teddy bear left my toys outside." *Should caregivers be worried if preschoolers blame objects for their actions?*

Sorting and Classifying Objects

During the preschool years, children's abilities to sort objects improve. Preschoolers' sorting techniques differ from adults' techniques. For example, a preschooler might sort a boat, a paper plate, and artificial flowers into one group because these objects were involved in a recent picnic. If sorting by shape, young preschoolers often make a *graphic* (picture-like) collection of shapes (**Figure 15.12**).

Around four years of age, preschoolers develop the executive functions needed to change sorting criteria. *Cognitive flexibility* allows preschoolers to change sorting rules, such as sorting by circles and then by squares. *Working memory* helps preschoolers remember sorting rules. *Inhibitory control* keeps preschoolers focused on the sorting criteria, even if they would like to sort another way. Many older preschoolers sort by attributes, such as color, shape, size, material, patterns, and functions.

Preschoolers also learn how to *classify*. **Classifying** involves choosing an attribute, selecting all objects that contain the given attribute (called the *class*), and then recognizing items that do not contain the attribute (called the *class complement*). Classifying is a more difficult skill than sorting. This is because sorting involves paying attention to a variety of attributes whereas classifying involves focusing on one chosen attribute while considering all others as not belonging to the class. Classifying is not usually mastered until children are school-age.

Ordering by Attributes

During the preschool years, children also begin to learn how to seriate. **Seriation** (seer-ee-AY-shun) is arranging objects in order by the increasing or decreasing magnitude of one of the object's attributes, such as length, shade of a color, texture, or pitch. Preschool children can easily identify extremes in most attributes, such as the largest and smallest square. Because noting extremes is an easy skill, young preschoolers often just alternate between large and small objects rather than truly seriating objects.

Seriating three or more objects is more difficult than finding two extremes in an attribute because it requires a two-way, simultaneous mental comparison of an object's attribute (size, length) to the same attribute in other objects. For example, when a person is seriating on a decreasing (also called *descending*) magnitude, the object placed next must be less in that magnitude than all the preceding objects and more in that magnitude than all the remaining objects.

Figure 15.12 Preschoolers tend to sort shapes into graphic collections. For example, they may be sorting rectangles and see circles as wheels that they can put below the rectangle like a wagon. *How does sorting differ from creating graphic collections of shapes?*

kali9/E+ via Getty Images

As you look at **Figure 15.13**, suppose you are trying to place the fourth rod of the ten rods in descending order of length. The fourth rod must be shorter than the third rod, but longer than the remaining rods. If seriating in increasing (also called *ascending*) magnitude, the reverse would be true, requiring the fourth rod to be longer than the third rod, but shorter than all other rods.

Toward the end of the preschool years, children's seriating skills improve. Many older preschoolers are successful because they use their perceptions and physically manipulate the objects. For example, these preschoolers can arrange dowel rods and sticks in order of their lengths, but to do this, they must physically lay the rods beside one another and align all the bottom ends evenly. To seriate other attributes, they must physically place the objects next to each other often arranging and rearranging them. In contrast, older children can seriate by just pointing to the order without moving the objects.

Seeing Cause and Effect

Because preschool children are not logical thinkers, they have difficulty seeing cause and effect, especially when the cause-effect relationship is not directly observable. As a result, preschoolers tend to create their own explanations of events.

While preschoolers have difficulty with unobservable cause-effect relationships, studies show that preschoolers can understand many visual displays of cause and effect. Preschoolers may still have problems with the complex sentence structure of cause-effect language, however, and may reverse cause and effect when speaking. Unobservable and difficult cause-effect relationships are often misunderstood until the teen years.

Understanding Spatial Concepts

While preschoolers understand the words that indicate spatial relationships, they still have trouble comprehending spatial concepts. Preschoolers think about spatial relationships in reference to themselves. While they understand what is on their right and left, knowing right and left from another person's perspective or in a spatial relationship to an object is much more difficult. Preschoolers tend to draw what they think about a space, rather than what they see.

As early as toddlerhood, children have some spatial memory, usually in the form of *mental maps*. **Mental maps** are remembered mental constructions (seen in the "mind's eye") that organize spatial relationships from an individual's perspective. A mental map enables a person to navigate their own house or other familiar places without thinking and to envision these places without being physically present (**Figure 15.14**). While these mental maps are far from perfect in the preschool years, preschool children exhibit some understanding of mental mapping, especially if mapping in a three-dimensional form.

Figure 15.13 To seriate these number rods, the child must compare each rod in turn with the rod placed on the table just before it (first relationship) and with the remaining rods (second relationship). Thus, seriating is always a two-way comparison. *What other attributes could be used for seriating activities?*

Figure 15.14 Three-dimensional mental mapping enables preschoolers to remember spatial arrangements in their world. *How might this preschooler show his mental mapping of the playground and the complex play structure? What mental maps do you use daily?*

For example, mapping in three-dimensional form means making a mental image of spatial arrangements after seeing a furniture arrangement in a real house or a three-dimensional model of a house (doll house). Conversely, two-dimensional mapping, which preschoolers cannot typically do, means forming mental maps using two-dimensional images, such as maps or floor plans, and being able to envision these spatial arrangements when not looking at the images.

Understanding Number Concepts

From a young age, children have a basic comprehension of quantity. Many young toddlers understand the concept of *more*. Many older toddlers and young preschoolers can imitate adult counting. These children show counting-like behaviors and can say counting words. Such counting, however, does not show they understand numbers. Adults are often misled by a young child's counting skills. For example, these young children may be able to count to five by simply saying the numbers (called *rote counting*) but may have trouble when asked to find five apples in a basket or to count how many of something is present.

Why do young children lack number concepts when they have almost no difficulty rote counting? Number concepts require several complex understandings (**Figure 15.15**). Young preschoolers rote count, but seldom understand the one-to-one relationship that takes place when counting objects (called *rational counting*). Even when watching older children or adults count while touching objects, they often do not understand that one (and only one) number can be assigned to each object and that all objects must be touched once (and only once). Although they go through the counting motions, they will often miss some objects and/or count other objects twice.

During the preschool years, children's comprehension of number concepts increases dramatically due to brain development. The left parietal lobe is being wired for understanding numbers and their functions. Also, synaptic "communication" across many parts of the brain is needed for math success. For example, memory areas are needed for remembering rules and recognizing patterns; language areas are used for understanding vocabulary and rules; and visual-spatial processing is essential for recognizing math symbols and even envisioning math concepts. The approximate benchmarks for preschoolers learning to count are shown in **Figure 15.16**.

Figure 15.15 Number Concept Understandings

- All discrete living or nonliving objects, whether alike or different, can be counted.
- An amount does not change unless another amount is added to or subtracted from it; that is, the size of objects and the way objects are arranged do not affect amount. If the elements of two sets can be paired so that each element is linked with exactly one element from the other set, there is one-to-one correspondence (equivalence) between the two sets.
- Counting involves assigning one and only one number to each item (called the one-on-one principle). Each item must be "counted" only once; no item can be missed; and the order of counting is irrelevant.
- "How many" (called numerosity or cardinal principle) is the last number assigned to the last item counted. Verbal or written number names, called numerals, are symbols for "how many."
- Items can be added to or subtracted from a given amount (called numerical operations). Numerical operations change "how many."

Goodheart-Willcox Publisher

Figure 15.16 Benchmarks for Preschool Counting

Age	Forward Counting	Backward Counting
3 years	Children can count from 1 to 2 or 3.	Children cannot count backward.
4 years	Children can count from 1 to 10.	Children can count back from 5.
5 years	Children can count from 1 to 20.	Children can count back from 10.

Goodheart-Willcox Publisher

Number Concepts at Three Years of Age

Three-year-old preschoolers can handle one-to-one correspondence for groups up to three. When shown two rows of four or more objects in physical one-to-one correspondence, they can identify that they are the "same." However, if one row is slightly spread out or compressed or even if another object is added to a compressed row, these perception-bound children use the end points to determine which row has "more" (**Figure 15.17**). They will focus on the length of the row rather than the number of items in the row.

Number Concepts at Four and Five Years of Age

Around four years of age, children's comprehension of number concepts leaps forward. Math understandings are logical concepts, not physical concepts. Four-year-olds who can count will use counting to determine equivalence or nonequivalence of two rows and can use the one-to-one principle (**Figure 15.18**).

Until about five years of age, **numerosity** (noo-mer-AHS-ih-tee), numerousness, is difficult for preschoolers to comprehend. Numerosity is difficult for preschoolers because, unlike names, which refer to one object, a number does not refer just to the last object named, but also to the entire group of objects being counted. Thus, a child must mentally "see" that the number one is in two and that two is in three. For example, there cannot be three balls if there are not already a ball number one and two present.

One-to-One Correspondence

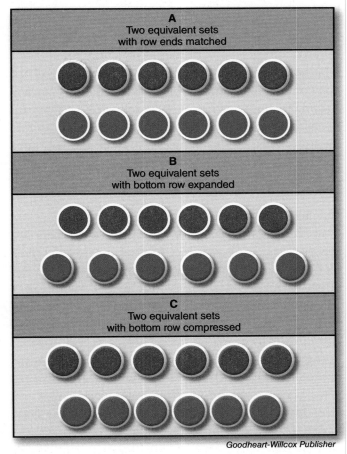

Goodheart-Willcox Publisher

Figure 15.17 Preschoolers may have difficulty understanding that the rows shown in A, B, and C contain the same number of discs. *How would you go about determining whether the rows were equivalent?*

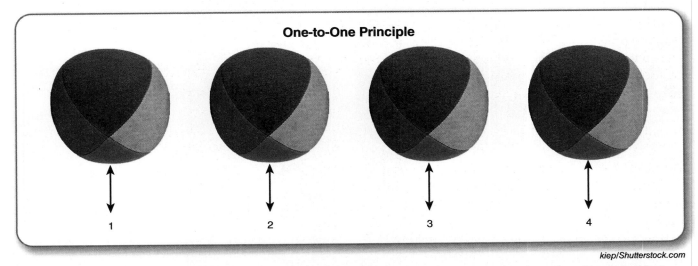

kiep/Shutterstock.com

Figure 15.18 The one-to-one principle in counting holds that one number, and only one number, is assigned to each object. *Why would numerals be difficult to understand without a thorough understanding of the one-to-one principle?*

By five years of age, many preschoolers can add and subtract concrete objects. If they know the number sequence, five-year-olds can make mental comparisons, such as "four is more than three." Older preschoolers can plot numerals on a number line, but the spaces between the consecutive numbers will not be kept equal. In effect, forward counting by ones is *adding* increments of one, and backward counting by ones is *subtracting* increments of one. Counting forward is also *seriating in ascending order* and counting backward is *seriating in descending order*.

Noting Time Concepts

Improvements in working memory during the preschool years help children recall the recent past. Preschoolers may still struggle with long-term memory. They may remember an event that happened yesterday but forget events that occurred a week or a year ago. Children link time with events that occur at specific times, such as home routines or regular activities in a preschool program's schedule. They do not see time passing because daily and seasonal changes are gradual and because no physical changes occur between the days of the week. For these reasons, time concepts are difficult for preschoolers to understand.

Older preschoolers may be introduced to calendars and may learn the names of seasons, the months of the year, and the days of the week. Most of these lessons, however, are **rote memorization** (learning by repetition) without much meaning. Time concepts are among the last concepts to develop in childhood.

15.2-2 Communicating

During the preschool years, language and communication abilities continue to improve. Preschoolers are better able to articulate and are rapidly learning the vocabulary and grammar they will need to communicate their needs and feelings effectively (**Figure 15.19**).

Preschoolers' egocentrism impacts their speaking in that their language often reflects their exact thinking. Preschoolers use **egocentric speech**, which means preschoolers talk as though the listener will understand what they are trying to communicate in the same way as they do. This is because they believe that everyone experiences the world the same as them. Thus, they often do not communicate all the needed information.

Figure 15.19 Having made strides in language development, preschoolers are better able to communicate their needs and feelings. *How do advances in communication impact how adults should meet preschoolers' needs?*

LightFieldStudios/iStock via Getty Images Plus

Examples of preschoolers' egocentric speech include telling a story from the middle instead of the beginning and using pronouns without naming the pronoun's object.

Egocentric speech also includes saying words without speaking to anyone. Sometimes children speak in **monologue** by talking to themselves as though thinking aloud. For example, a preschooler playing with a doll might say, "I'm going to bring you over to the car now." Other times, they engage in **collective monologue** by talking to another person or group of people, but not listening to what the other person is saying. For example, a few preschoolers might all be speaking in monologue but not responding directly to their peers' statements. It is not actual conversation where messages are being received and responded to. All children go through this stage of language development.

Toward the end of the preschool years, egocentric speech gradually disappears, which makes communication easier. Communication also becomes easier as preschoolers are learning articulation, expanding their vocabularies, and learning grammar.

Learning Articulation

In the English language, children can articulate words fluently and **coherently** (clearly and understandably) between three and eight years of age. Although the timing in which preschoolers master the sounds of language varies, the order in which they master these sounds is about the same for most children. Children achieve *total mastery* when they can articulate sounds in different positions within words. **Figure 15.20** shows the typical order and ages for preschoolers' articulation mastery.

Expanding Vocabularies

Children continue to expand their vocabularies as they learn words and their meanings during the preschool years. At three years of age, children know about 900 words in the English language. By four years of age, children know about 1,500 words and at five years of age they know about 2,000 words.

Preschoolers tend to learn the words and names for *concrete items*, such as objects and people, before they learn those that symbolize *abstract ideas*, such as emotions. Preschool children also often assign their own meanings to words. The window of opportunity for vocabulary growth never closes, so vocabulary continues to grow and develop far beyond the preschool years.

Learning Grammar

Brain development research shows that there is a window of opportunity for learning a new language; around age ten, learning a new language becomes increasingly difficult. Because of this, grammar development is critical during the preschool years and becomes more difficult once children are school-age. During the preschool years, children begin to use more complex sentence structures and comprehend correct word order. Children's grammar matures dramatically between three and five years of age.

Figure 15.20 Articulation Mastery of Preschool Children

Age	Sound	Word Examples
3 years	p	pig, happy, cup
	m	monkey, hammer, broom
	h	hand, doghouse
	n	nails, penny, lion
	w	window, bowl
	b	boat, baby, tub
4 years	k	cat, chicken, book
	g	girl, wagon, pig
	d	dog, ladder, bed
	f	fork, telephone, knife
	y	yellow, onion
5-6 years	t	toy, bottle, bat
	ng	fingers, ring
	r	roll, storm, star
	l	loud, flew, ball

Goodheart-Willcox Publisher

Grammar at Three Years of Age

Three-year-olds can begin to understand some grammar rules (**Figure 15.21**). Once they learn these rules, they tend to apply them to sentences and words, including those that are exceptions to the rules. Three-year-old preschoolers may know that *-ed* indicates past tense, but once they know this rule, they may apply it to all verb forms. For example, a preschooler might say, "I eated all of my lunch." Over time, preschoolers will learn the exceptions to these rules.

Young preschoolers do not always comprehend word order. They will use incorrect word order at times and correct word order at other times. Preschoolers may also have a difficult time with questions because of the changed word order. In a statement, the subject comes before the verb, such as "You are tall," but the word order is switched for questions, such as "Are you tall?"

Figure 15.21 Grammar Rules That Three-Year-Olds Begin to Use

Rules of Grammar	Examples
Add –*ing* to the end of a regular verb for present continuous tense.	roll rolling fall falling
Add –*ed* to the end of a regular verb for past tense.	roll rolled walk walked
Change some irregular verbs from simple present tense to simple past tense.	sink sank eat ate
Use a linking verb (*is*, *am*) to link noun to adjective.	The truck *is* red. I *am* good.
Add –*s* to make a plural.	car cars doll dolls
Add an *'s* to form possessive.	*Tyler's* book *Daddy's* car
Use an article (*a*, *the*) to precede or modify a noun.	a toy *the* library
Use a preposition referring to space (*on*, *in*).	*on* the table *in* the room

Goodheart-Willcox Publisher

Negative words are also very difficult for young preschoolers. Once preschoolers know about negatives other than *no*, they may use double or multiple negatives in sentences. For example, sentences such as "I don't never want no more spinach" are common at this age.

Grammar at Four and Five Years of Age

Four- and five-year-old children speak in longer, more complex sentences. They lengthen sentences by using clauses, conjunctions, and prepositions. Instead of saying, "We play games. I had fun," an older preschool child may say, "I had fun because we played games" (**Figure 15.22**).

Four-year-old children may still find word order in questions confusing. They may form questions by moving the question word to the beginning of the statement, such as "What the dog is eating?" Five-year-old children begin using **tag questions**, which are formed by making a statement and then adding *yes* or *no* to ask the question. An example of a tag question is, "The baby is small, yes?" By five years of age, however, children can identify and use correct word order more consistently.

Grammar Problems

Although older preschool children consistently use correct word order and have made large advances in grammar comprehension, they continue to have two problems with grammar.

SDI Productions/E+ via Getty Images

Figure 15.22 As four- and five-year-old preschoolers discover new parts of speech, they become more animated when talking to others. *What characteristics would you use to describe preschoolers' speech?*

One problem is using the correct case for pronouns. Older preschoolers often use objective case pronouns where they should use the subjective case. For example, an older preschooler may say, "Him and me went to town," instead of "He and I went to town."

The second problem older preschoolers have with grammar is that they continue to apply some grammar rules too widely. They may say *eated* instead of *ate*. Once they learn irregular forms, they may even say *ated*. A five-year-old may learn to use the plural form *feet* and ask, "May I go barefeeted?" The many irregular forms in the English language will trouble some children for years, even if they hear and make strides in using correct grammar.

15.2-3 Intellectual Developmental Milestones

Concepts and abilities that develop during the infant and toddler years continue to mature in the preschool years. Although preschoolers are not yet capable of logical thinking, they use both their perceptions and intuition for solving problems that, in turn, lay the foundation for logical thinking. The preschool years are critical times for learning vocabulary and especially grammar. **Figure 15.23** lists some intellectual developmental milestones for preschool children.

Lesson 15.2 Review and Assessment

1. The attribution of living qualities to inanimate objects is called _____. (15.2.1)
   A. artificialism
   B. seriation
   C. classification
   D. animism
2. **True or False.** While preschoolers can typically form two-dimensional mental maps, they are unable to form three-dimensional mental maps. (15.2.1)
3. When a preschooler begins a story about a dog without first making sure the listener knows the story is about a dog, not a person or a cat, this is an example of _____. (15.2.2)
   A. monologue
   B. tag questions
   C. egocentric speech
   D. collective monologue
4. **True or False.** One grammar problem typical of older preschoolers is using objective case pronouns where they should use the subjective case. (15.2.2)
5. Four-year-olds commonly achieve which intellectual milestone? (15.2.3)
   A. Rationally counting two to three objects
   B. Using four-to-five-word sentences
   C. Using the present, past, and future tense when speaking
   D. Knowing 2,000 to 2,200 words

Figure 15.23 Preschool Intellectual Milestones

Three years

Leila Mendez/Image Source via Getty Images

- Expresses thinking through pretend play, drawings, and language.
- Gives illogical "reasons" for events.
- Matches attributes of objects and sorts by shape and color.
- Rationally counts two to three objects.
- Knows about 900 words.
- Knows their own name and the names of family members and friends.
- Knows the names of common objects, some colors, and three basic shapes.
- Articulates sounds with others understanding them about 75 percent of the time.
- Uses four- to five-word sentences.
- Knows some grammar rules (*s* sound for plurals; *ed* sound for past tense), but overgeneralizes rules to include irregular forms (says *singed* instead of *sang*).
- Understands a few prepositions (*on*, *in*, *under*) and a few time words (*now*, *soon*, *later*).
- Tells a simple story but may have some incorrect facts.

Four years

FatCamera/E+ via Getty Images

- Enjoys pretending and has a vivid imagination.
- Solves some problems correctly through intuition (not logic).
- Sorts by shape, color, and size.
- Begins classifying by one attribute (but often changes attributes while classifying).
- Rationally counts 7 to 10 objects and recognizes a few numerals.
- Arranges by size with the help of a baseline.
- Knows about 1,500 words.
- Knows most basic colors by name and knows some opposites, math words, and prepositions.
- Has some sense of time (but says *yesterday* for the past and *tomorrow* for the future).
- Uses five- to six-word sentences.
- Has trouble with the word order of questions and the use of negatives.
- Recognizes a few written words (name, STOP sign, and EXIT sign).
- Follows a three-part command.
- Recalls parts of a story and can play a role in a simple story.

Five years

Jennifer_Sharp/iStock via Getty Images Plus

- Likes to pretend play with themes and uses props.
- Has better problem-solving skills, but still uses intuition.
- Knows own right and left, but finds recognizing right and left from other perspectives is difficult.
- Draws pictures that represent real objects or people (called *representational art*).
- Names basic colors and knows names of some additional colors (*pink*, *grey*, *white*).
- Rationally counts 10 or more objects.
- Extends or makes patterns with beads or blocks.
- Knows 2,000 to 2,200 words.
- Articulates most sounds that are understood about 90 to 95 percent of the time.
- Uses complex sentences.
- Speaks using present, past, and future tense.
- Recognizes several words in books.

Goodheart-Willcox Publisher

Meeting Preschoolers' Intellectual Needs

Learning Outcomes

After studying this lesson, you will be able to

15.3-1 **review** activities to foster the preschooler's motor skills.

15.3-2 **suggest** activities to help build the preschooler's memory skills.

15.3-3 **summarize** activities that aid in preschoolers' comprehension of logical thinking concepts.

15.3-4 **explain** how to stimulate symbolic learning in the preschooler.

15.3-5 **describe** activities that help preschoolers develop language skills.

15.3-6 **evaluate** electronic media activities currently available for preschoolers to determine their educational value.

Key Terms

emergent literacy

interactive media

maturational theory of child development

noninteractive media

reading readiness

Reading and Notetaking Activity

Imagine you are a preschool teacher and your student's parents want to learn more about how to nurture their child's intellectual development. Write a two-paragraph speech recommending steps the parents and other caregivers can take to make sure their child gets appropriate scaffolding and masters key concepts. Incorporate information you already know about helping preschoolers learn, and anything from your personal experiences. As you read this lesson, take detailed notes. After reading the lesson, go back over your speech. With a partner, discuss what you would change about your speech based on any new information you have learned. Present your final speech to the class.

Introduction

During the preschool years, adults continue to help preschool children meet their intellectual needs. As they did during the toddler years, adults direct children's attention to activities and to problems that must be solved. For preschoolers, the home, child care and education programs, and neighborhood play groups are the most important places for learning.

Preschool children are still holistic learners. Their intellectual abilities can and do develop at many times and in many places. Think about how much a child can learn from a simple shopping trip (**Figure 15.24**).

15.3-1 **Motor Activities**

Preschool children are "on the go." Their motor skills usually improve in conjunction with other lessons they are learning. For example, preschoolers use their gross-motor skills when they engage in pretend play and their fine-motor skills when they sort and draw. To help preschoolers hone their motor skills, caregivers can plan activities that, among other skills, involve physical movement.

Preschoolers need lots of opportunities for physical play. Not only are physical activities vital to building motor skills, they are also needed for physical health. (See Figure 14.14 to review motor skill activities parents and caregivers can plan for their preschoolers.)

15.3-2 **Memory Activities**

Memory develops rapidly during the preschool years, as brain development makes way for preschoolers' frequent use of working and episodic memory. Memory is vital to all domains of development, and it is important that caregivers and teachers plan numerous activities to help preschoolers develop and practice their memory skills.

Many memory games are commercially available for preschool learning, but these games do little for children in comparison to everyday activities that caregivers and other adults can plan. Parents and other adults can help preschoolers develop and practice their memory skills in the following ways:

- Help preschoolers understand stories and happenings before asking them to recall. Children have a difficult time recalling what they do not understand.
- Use leading questions and prompting to **pique** (stir up interest in) the child's memory. Instead of asking, "What did you do yesterday?" a caregiver or other adult might ask, "What game did you play with your uncle yesterday?"

Figure 15.24 While shopping, a child can observe attributes of items, such as color, size, shape, and texture; sort and classify items; learn number skills; and learn language skills in naming and describing items. *What other daily activities can help children learn sorting and classifying?*

MBI/Shutterstock.com

- When giving directions, ask the child to repeat the directions before starting on the task. This aids the child's working memory.
- Use photos to remind a child about people, places, or events not regularly seen.
- Use prompting photos to help a child recall specific events from their past.
- Reread stories as often as requested (**Figure 15.25**). When rereading stories or repeating songs and rhymes, change something in the story or song and see whether the child notices.
- Frequently repeat safety rules and other concepts the child is learning. Repeat lessons after a lapse of time to help children remember and easily recall.

15.3-3 Concept Learning Activities

During the preschool years, children are learning a variety of concepts. They learn to note physical attributes, understand physical knowledge, and begin to comprehend logical thinking concepts using their perceptions and intuition.

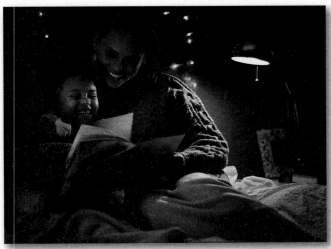

PeopleImages/iStock via Getty Images Plus

Figure 15.25 Rereading books can help children practice their memory skills. In rereading, children can be prompted to identify whether they have heard a story before. *When you reread a book, how easy is it for you to recall what you previously read?*

For each area of concept learning during the preschool years, parents and caregivers can aid intellectual development by planning helpful activities.

Noting Physical Attributes

Preschool children learn to note physical attributes through observation and through their senses of sight, hearing, touch, smell, and taste. During the preschool years, children learn to compare and contrast the attributes of various physical objects.

Adults can help children learn and distinguish between physical attributes by inviting preschoolers to analyze physical attributes with them. When interacting with preschoolers, adults can call attention to physical attributes and then describe or ask the child to describe a sight, sound, texture, odor, or taste. Adults can emphasize the names of attributes and can help preschoolers compare and contrast physical objects. Noting attributes shown in books and other media can also help preschool children process and remember physical attributes. There are many everyday games and activities adults can plan to foster these skills (**Figure 15.26**).

Understanding Physical Knowledge

Preschoolers are fascinated by natural events and ask many *why* questions, even though they do not yet have the logical capabilities to understand the answers. As a result, they produce illogical thoughts of their own. When preschoolers communicate illogical explanations for events they cannot understand, parents and caregivers can correct them, but should not expect the preschooler to comprehend the correct explanation. Caregivers can keep these explanations simple and remember that children have many more years to learn all these facts.

Physical knowledge lessons are closely tied to children's perceptions of cause and effect. Because cause and effect is a logical thinking concept, it is difficult for preschoolers.

Figure 15.26 Attribute Games and Activities

Using the Senses

Attribute	Games and Activities
Seeing	• Give a child a magnifying glass. Help the child look at a leaf, penny, fingernail, piece of food, or other small object. Point out details you want the child to see. Later, ask the child to describe the objects they saw. • Go on an "I Spy" walk or ride. Have the child identify a given attribute, such as a color or shape.
Hearing	• Encourage the child to identify sounds in the environment and use these sounds in pretend play. • As you read stories, ask the child to make the sounds of animals and machines. • Depict emotions through your voice as you read stories.
Touching	• Ask the child to describe textures in the environment and in books in which texture is applied to the photos or drawings. • Ask the child to describe texture before feeling an object. • Ask the child to add texture to Play Doh® creations. • Ask the child to seriate texture from roughest to smoothest or vice versa.
Smelling	• Ask the child to describe odors in their environment or when walking outside. • Ask the child to sniff and describe spices or identify foods by odor. • Read "scratch and sniff" books.
Tasting	• Ask the child to describe how foods taste. • Ask the child to identify texture of foods by tasting.

Comparing and Contrasting Attributes

Attribute	Games and Activities
Alike and different	• Gather pairs of objects or pictures that are exactly alike. Mix up the objects and have the child sort into like pairs. • Have the child explain how some items are similar and different.
Shape sorting	• Have the child fit various shapes through the holes of a shape sorter. As children master simple shape sorters, more advanced ones can be used. • Ask older children to name shapes and explain how they recognized each shape.
Varieties of liquids	• Show the child varieties of liquids, such as water, milk, fruit juice, molasses, cooking oil, tempera paint (in one or more thicknesses), and dish detergent. Have the child describe similarities and differences in the liquids in the following experiments: (A) rub a drop of each liquid between the thumb and forefinger; (B) place a drop of each liquid on wax paper and blow at the drops through a straw. • Have the child watch the pouring of three liquids differing in *viscosities* (thicknesses). Ask the child which liquid pours the fastest and the slowest.

Goodheart-Willcox Publisher

Using Logical Thinking Concepts

Because preschoolers do not think logically, their use of logical thinking concepts does not fully mature during the preschool years. Nevertheless, there are activities that caregivers can plan to help children begin to understand these essential concepts. Preschoolers can benefit from activities that encourage sorting and classifying, ordering by attributes, seeing cause and effect, understanding spatial concepts, understanding number concepts, and noting time concepts.

Sorting and Classifying

To help children practice sorting, parents and caregivers can use commercial sorting materials, such as shape sorters for three-dimensional geometric shapes (**Figure 15.27**). Common household items, such as clothing, toys, flatware, or groceries, can also be used to teach sorting lessons. For example, to turn a grocery shopping trip into a sorting lesson, an adult might say, "Let's put all the foods that are in boxes together and then put all the canned foods together."

Parents and caregivers can also begin to teach preschoolers classifying techniques. For example, after showing a child small blocks that may be classified by color or shape, an adult may ask, "Are any of these alike in some way?" When the child singles out a common attribute, such as some of the blocks are *round*, the adult might say, "Can you find all the round pieces and put them in this box? Then we will put all the other blocks that are not round in the other box."

Ordering by Attributes

While preschool children have trouble putting items in order by a magnitude of an attribute, many activities can help children understand how to practice this concept. Parents and caregivers can plan activities that involve observable differences in height, weight, pitch, or appearance. For example, a caregiver might ask a child to arrange objects from shortest to tallest or from heaviest to lightest. Children can see these differences, which helps them comprehend the arrangement.

When helping preschoolers with seriating activities, caregivers need to keep the difficulty level of the task in mind and make the task appropriate for the child. Following are several factors that can make seriating tasks less difficult:

- having fewer numbers of objects to arrange
- using objects with equal differences in increments, such as shown in Figure 15.13, to be able to seriate by length or height more easily
- using objects that differ in only one attribute, such as different sizes of squares rather than different sizes of mixed shapes
- having greater differences between increments of magnitude, such as 3-, 6-, and 10-inch rods as compared with 3-, 4-, and 5-inch rods

It is difficult to find household items suitable for seriating, especially due to the problem of finding objects that differ in only one attribute. Because of this **stipulation** (specified condition), commercial seriating materials are often better than adult-collected items. Some commercial materials include cylinder blocks, baric tablets, color tablets, nesting objects, unit blocks, and Cuisenaire® rods (**Figure 15.28**).

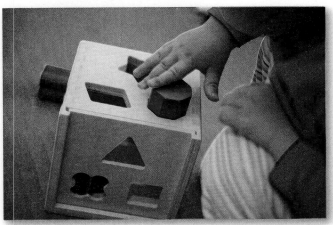

Viki2win/Shutterstock.com

Figure 15.27 Toy shape-sorters help children with their sorting and classifying skills. *How else might caregivers help children develop these skills?*

myboys.me/Shutterstock.com

Figure 15.28 This child is sorting Cuisenaire® rods by attribute. *What other objects can children use to learn to sort by attribute?*

Seeing Cause and Effect

For preschool children, observable cause-effect relationships are easier to understand than non-observable relationships. Parents and caregivers can help preschoolers comprehend cause and effect in the following ways:

- Ask children to predict regular household happenings (**Figure 15.29**). Ask, "What will happen when water is turned on above your glass?" or "What will happen when I open the drain in the bathtub?"
- When reading picture books, read the title, show children the cover, and then ask children to predict what each story is about or who the main characters are. Continue to ask for predictions throughout the story. Choose picture books that involve cause-effect relationships.
- When speaking with children, make cause-effect statements, such as, "The room is sunny because the sun is shining through the windows" or "Your cup is empty because you drank your milk."
- Encourage children to experiment with cause and effect using physical movements. For example, a caregiver could help preschool children build ramps with blocks and then let balls roll down the ramps. Ask questions like, "What makes the ball go *down* the ramp? Which ramp makes the ball go the fastest? The slowest? Which ball rolls the fastest? The slowest? Why do you think so?"

Understanding Spatial Concepts

As preschool children's understanding of spatial concepts deepens, several activities can be used to enhance their learning. The first spatial concepts should pertain to the self. Caregivers can use spatial words in everyday conversation. They can say, "Put your hat *on* your head" or "Put your clothes *in* the closet." They can also use these words in games like "I Spy." Caregivers can encourage children to act out the directional words they hear and can read stories while emphasizing directional actions.

Activities that teach preschool children spatial concepts in relation to themselves are also helpful. Caregivers can play games that require children to position their bodies (**Figure 15.30**). They can tell them to "jump *forward* two jumps" or "put the shoe *under* your chin." "Simon Says" and "Hokey Pokey" are also fun games that require positioning. As preschool children grow older, they can learn more difficult spatial words, such as *away from*, *toward*, *right*, *left*, *center*, and *corner*.

Hands-on projects can help older preschoolers understand spatial concepts that pertain to other objects. Caregivers can help preschoolers grasp spatial concepts by assigning them simple spatial tasks, such as setting the table.

Myboys.me/Shutterstock.com

Figure 15.29 Asking children to predict regular household happenings helps them understand cause and effect. *How is this child learning about cause and effect?*

Daniel Jedzura/Shutterstock.com

Figure 15.30 These children are playing a game that requires them to position their bodies. *What concept can children learn from this game?*

Caregivers can help children build simple bridge-type structures and ask children to place blocks *on*, *under*, *behind*, or *in front of* the bridge. They can ask preschoolers to place objects in different positions on magnetic or flannel boards and can ask children to name the positions of given objects in relation to other objects.

Understanding Number Concepts

Preschoolers learn counting concepts rapidly. Once they can count both forward and backward, they can name numbers that come before or after any given number. Parents and caregivers can help preschoolers learn counting by arranging sets of objects in straight rows or columns and gradually increasing the size of sets children are expected to count. Other ways parents can help preschoolers learn counting may include asking children to touch each item while counting and exposing children to counting picture books, rhymes, and finger plays.

To teach numerals, parents and caregivers can explain that *numerals* are names for "how many." Some activities for learning numerals include matching numerals with sets of objects, identifying numerals in a game, completing a puzzle with numerals, making a "number line," and playing "I Spy" with numerals. Numeral concepts should be taught through activities involved in everyday life. At this stage, numeral concepts presented in workbooks are meaningless and not fun.

Preschoolers may encounter challenges with the language surrounding number concepts. They may equate indefinite terms, such as *less*, *few*, *many*, and *some*, with numbers. When helping preschoolers learn number concepts, caregivers should avoid these indefinite terms and be as clear as possible.

Noting Time Concepts

Time concepts will be difficult for preschoolers, whether caregivers plan activities to encourage these concepts or not. While children will not fully comprehend time concepts until the school-age years, caregivers can use "time words" as they talk with preschoolers. Some time words include: *before*, *after*, *then*, *yesterday*, *tomorrow*, *soon*, *morning*, and *night*. To help preschool children understand the passing of time, caregivers and teachers can use picture schedules of children's daily activities. In these schedules, children can "read" what will happen at each time.

15.3-4 Symbolic Learning Activities

Children's understanding of symbols continues to mature during the preschool years, as preschoolers develop symbolic thought and can imagine scenarios and symbols outside their realms of experience. Parents and caregivers can plan a variety of activities to help preschoolers grasp these concepts.

Using Symbols in Pretend Play

Children use symbols in pretend play by using props and by taking on the representation of another person or object (**Figure 15.31**). To understand these forms of symbolism, preschoolers need many opportunities to play and pretend they are other people and objects. They also need objects that they can pretend represent other things.

Spass/Shutterstock.com

Figure 15.31 By using symbols, preschoolers take on the representation of another person or object. *What symbols help these children pretend to be superheroes?*

For the most part, children need only a little help in pretending. Their imaginations allow them to pretend they are other people with minimal props and encouragement. If an adult suggests a preschooler pretend to be an underwater diver, the preschooler might pretend to be putting on a deep-sea fishing outfit and then "dive" after lost treasures while being careful not to be attacked by sharks. Although "playing pretend" may be difficult for adults, it is important to play along to help preschoolers develop these skills.

Using Symbols in Art

Children also use symbols when they paint, color, or create other forms of art. Younger children tend to create art products first and then decide what they represent. As children mature, however, they are more intentional in planning before they create their end product. As is true of all symbolic representations, children decide what objects and art pieces represent, not adults.

Preschoolers may use a variety of objects, such as crayons, paints, building blocks, or clay, to represent who or what they want. Even if children's art products do not resemble the real-life objects or people they represent, these art products symbolize the real world for the child.

15.3-5 Language Activities

Preschool children learn language by paying attention to what they hear, including how other people articulate sounds, use vocabulary, and use grammar. Through the observation of adults in their lives, preschoolers also learn about the process of reading and writing. For this reason, adults must be the best language and literacy models they can be and should make efforts to talk and read with preschoolers.

Preschool Language Supports

Preschool children need many daily chances to talk with adults and older children and see them engaged in the literacy tasks of reading and writing. When preschool children play only with peers or younger children, they do not learn as quickly as they do by talking with adults. Following are a few suggestions for ways in which adults and older children can support language and literacy development of preschoolers:

- Make language and literacy a part of all activities. Use important words in daily tasks and games.
- Read to children every day. In addition to exposing children to the real world and expanding concepts, reading books to preschoolers helps children understand language and grammar. Preschoolers who are exposed to reading and writing more often are likely to learn these concepts faster and better. What's more, story concepts can be stretched to involve pretend play and other activities.
- After reading a book, talk about story plots with the preschooler by asking more comprehension questions, such as, "Why do you think this happened?" or "Why did the character do what they did?"
- Monitor television viewing, including types of programs and total length of viewing time. While some programs can be helpful, holding actual conversations with adults and other children is a much better learning experience.
- Provide opportunities for preschoolers to observe adults reading and writing, both for work and for pleasure. Use correct grammar and articulation. Children imitate what they see and need to observe how literacy functions in their parents' and caregivers' lives.

Reading Readiness Versus Emergent Literacy

Beyond the need for talking and reading with preschoolers, some parents and teachers in preschool programs are beginning to teach "actual" reading and writing before the school years. This early instruction has become an issue among early childhood educators and has resulted in differing approaches (reading readiness and emergent literacy) to fostering early literacy skills.

Using Symbols in Written Communication

Written word and math symbols are society-determined and the most abstract of all symbols, which makes preschoolers' learning of these symbols difficult. Learning these symbols usually requires direct instruction, which is a practice that is widely debated among early childhood education experts. Why? Experts debate teaching written symbols during the preschool years for the following reasons:

Young children learn best when they create their own symbols. Unlike society-determined symbols, preschoolers' symbols are products of their own symbolic thought. Society-determined symbols generally must be taught to children through rote memorization. Without having rich meanings for these symbols, the child may become what is called a "word caller" (reader without a high level of comprehension).

Preschool children learn best by solving real-world problems. In many cases, the same concepts taught through drill-type lessons and workbooks can be learned in meaningful ways. Preschoolers can see written words while adults read them stories or written signs in their environment. Soon they will be saying, "What does this say?" just as they once questioned the names for objects by asking, "What dat?" They will notice that a letter in their name appears in other words, too. In setting the table, a child will see the need for counting forks. Concrete counting makes numerals meaningful. Thus, instead of using lessons or workbooks to teach preschool children symbols, parents and caregivers can present preschool children with practical applications for their learning as the foundation for using abstract symbols.

Problem-solving skills are best learned through *divergent thinking* (the act of coming up with different possible ideas). Divergent thinking is more often developed through rich, everyday experiences than through formal learning tasks. Formal learning tasks are more likely to encourage *convergent thinking* (the act of producing only one right answer or way to do a task). Workbooks and worksheets call for convergent thinking so that the child's responses match the "answer key." Because convergent thinking is used in teaching written symbols, the child may come to believe that all of life's problems have only one right answer. In short, creativity is stunted when learning this way.

Using "bits and pieces learning," such as learning initial consonant sounds and rhyming words, seldom make sense to preschoolers. Drill techniques are rarely fun either. Thus, many of these young children become frustrated. This frustration may sour a child's attitude toward learning and formal education before they even begin elementary school.

Learning symbols, like so many other skills, is developmental. For these reasons, children need many experiences with real objects first. Next, the child should begin symbolic thinking by using symbols of their own choosing or creation, as seen in pretend play and drawing. Spoken words are vital at both stages. These growing skills will prepare children for reading and writing words and math symbols with comprehension and joy.

Speaking Activity

Imagine you are a child development expert speaking to an audience of caregivers and teachers. You have just delivered a presentation about how preschoolers use symbols in pretend play and art, and one of the teachers asks you whether they should encourage preschoolers to use symbols in written communication. In small groups, practice delivering a concise, but well-supported answer using the information covered in this feature.

Photo: Tom Wang/Shutterstock.com

Reading readiness is a belief that children should be formally taught reading and writing when developmentally ready for instruction. The concept of reading readiness is based on the principles of the *maturational theory of child development*. The **maturational theory of child development** holds to the belief that children mature on a genetic timetable (upon which the environment has little impact) and that skills and concepts should only be taught when children are biologically ready to learn them. These theorists believed that children were biologically mature enough to learn reading and writing at six years of age. Gradually, schools started teaching reading and writing at five years of age and then in some pre-kindergarten programs. The purpose of reading readiness programs is to prepare children for formal reading instruction.

By contrast, many of today's theorists believe in *emergent literacy*. **Emergent literacy** is defined by theorists as all aspects of literacy, including reading and writing, are developmental and learned in interactive ways, beginning in infancy as children learn to understand spoken words. Emergent literacy is based on the theories of Piaget and Vygotsky. Research shows that, beginning in the late toddler or early preschool years, young children pass through several stages in the learning of literacy.

Differences between reading readiness and emergent literacy are shown in **Figure 15.32**. Although preschool and kindergarten programs are divided in the way they approach teaching reading and writing skills prior to first grade, research evidence supports emergent literacy as the more effective method of teaching reading and writing during the preschool years.

Figure 15.32 Reading Readiness Versus Emergent Literacy Concepts

Reading Readiness	Emergent Literacy
Basic concept: At some point between three and five years of age, a child should be introduced to reading readiness. Reading readiness programs teach three basic skills: • *phonemic* awareness (being able to distinguish sounds in words). For example, although *bat* and *light* have a different number of letters, they each have three phonemes or sounds—b/a/t/ and l/igh/t/. Early instruction focuses on hearing initial sounds of words and rhyming sounds at the ends of words. • *letter recognition* (being able to see differences in letter shapes and knowing letter names). Children are taught to recognize letters individually and in words and to write in manuscript (often called *printing*) all the letters in uppercase and lowercase. • *phonics* (the relationship between letters and sounds), such as the letter *b* stands for the sound /b/ heard at the beginning of *bat*. Once children see the relationship between a letter and its sound, they can sound out and read words. Most reading readiness programs use workbooks, worksheets, and audio or digital programs that introduce and review each skill in more or less the same way.	**Basic concept:** At two or three years of age, children spontaneously (without instruction) begin to notice print in their environment and can identify some signs and logos. They also begin scribbling marks characteristic of the writing they see. For example, older preschoolers' scribbling style will be different depending on the language they routinely see in writing. All aspects of literacy are emerging at the same time. Children do not develop these skills in a hard and fast sequence—listen, speak, read, and write. In fact, most children try writing before reading. The knowledge of one aspect of literacy adds to the knowledge of other aspects. In short, the end goal is not to be literate, but to use literacy to achieve other goals. Parents and adults support emergent literacy in these ways: • being a speaking, reading, and writing model. • reading daily to their child. Hearing parents read motivates the child to be a reader. • having books, digital devices, and traditional writing materials available for the child to use as literacy emerges.

Goodheart-Willcox Publisher

Figure 15.32 Reading readiness concepts and emergent literacy concepts are not the same thing. *How do these two concepts differ?*

15.3-6 Electronic Media Activities

Technology devices are **ubiquitous** (yoo-BIH-kwuh-tuhs), found everywhere, and even preschoolers experience technology as a major part of the context of their lives. Technological devices can be classified as either *interactive media* or *noninteractive media*. **Interactive media** refer to media systems, such as games or applications on computers, tablets, or smart phones, which respond to the user's actions. **Noninteractive media** (also called *passive media*) refer to media systems, such as television programs or streaming applications, over which the user has only a limited amount of control. Interactive media systems are used for communication, collaboration, learning, entertainment, and daily life management. Culture demands that people develop digital literacy from an early age.

The *National Association for the Education of Young Children*, in conjunction with the *Fred Rogers Center for Early Learning and Children's Media*, has developed a joint statement concerning media integration in learning environments for young children. This statement holds that media integration needs to be assessed against what is already known about children's development. With this criterion (kry-TIR-ee-uhn) in mind, parents and caregivers can discern what types of media are appropriate for preschoolers. Parents and caregivers can follow some basic principles suggested by experts. Some of these principles include the following:

- *Screen time.* Total screen time for all devices in all settings must be monitored and limited by caregivers. Total daily screen time during the preschool years should be no more than one hour of high-quality programming per day. Total screen time should be broken into short segments of time.
- *Effect.* Parents and caregivers should assess media systems to determine what effect they may have on preschool children.
- *Purpose.* Media should always be used for learning, never just for technology's sake. Media should support and enhance learning, not drive it.
- *Type.* Interactive media should be used rather than noninteractive media. Media should be chosen for its ability to foster active and creative use by the child and for its likelihood to encourage social interactions.
- *Content.* Electronic media should be developmentally appropriate for the child. The content of media systems matters much more than the format.
- *Interactiveness.* Use of media should emphasize co-participation between adults and children and among children.
- *Inclusiveness.* Media use in child care and education programs should be **inclusive** (accessible to a variety of people). Caregivers and teachers should realize that children differ in their home access to digital devices and software just as they do to print media (books).

Parents, caregivers, and teachers should keep in mind that there is conflicting evidence about the value of technology in preschool children's development. Experts have identified some possible negative outcomes, including behavioral issues, problems focusing on tasks, irregular sleep patterns, and negative effects on socialization and language skills. These problems may result from too much screen time, poor-quality software, or incorrect use of technology. Electronic media activities can be beneficial for preschool learning, but parents, caregivers, and teachers should always assess research findings on technology in the lives of young children.

Artist and Animator

Children's multimedia artists and animators create animations and visual effects for children's television, movies, video games, and other forms of media. They also create two- and three-dimensional models for their projects.

Career cluster: Arts, Audio/Video Technology & Communications

Education: Education requirements vary, but artistic and technical skills are required. Many obtain bachelor's degrees in fine art, computer graphics, animation, or a related field.

Job outlook: Future employment opportunities for children's multimedia artists and animators are expected to grow about as fast as average for all occupations.

To learn more about a career as a children's multimedia artist and animator, visit the United States Department of Labor's *Occupational Outlook Handbook* website. You will also be able to compare the job responsibilities, educational requirements, job outlook, and average pay of children's multimedia artists and animators with similar occupations.

Photo: ESB Professional/Shutterstock.com

Lesson 15.3 Review and Assessment

1. **True or False**. Encouraging preschoolers to use specific arm movements, such as pretending to be a bird flapping its wings while walking on the balance beam, helps develop gross-motor ability. (15.3.1)

2. **True or False**. Commercially available memory games designed for preschool learning are the best way to develop a preschooler's memory skills. (15.3.2)

3. Which activity will help a preschooler see cause and effect? (15.3.3)
   A. Using spatial words like in and on as part of conversations
   B. Asking a child to predict what will happen next in a story
   C. Using terms like *less, few, many,* and *some* frequently
   D. Playing "I Spy" with numerals

4. **True or False**. For the most part, children need a lot of help in pretending. (15.3.4)

5. Which is the *least* effective way to help preschoolers develop language skills? (15.3.5)
   A. Use important words in daily tasks and games.
   B. Read to children every day.
   C. Provide children access to educational television.
   D. Use correct grammar and articulation.

6. **True or False**. The purpose of media is to support and enhance learning, not drive it. (15.3.6)

Chapter 15 Review and Assessment

Summary

Lesson 15.1

15.1-1 Preschoolers begin to think rather than depend on trial and error. Through their brain development and new cognitive abilities, they are better able to solve problems and communicate.

15.1-1 Preschoolers' pretend play leads to the development of symbolic play, which allows them to create mental images, think creatively, draw more realistically, and learn language.

15.1-1 Preschoolers remember more and retain memories longer than younger children. Working (short-term) memory is critical for executive functioning. Preschoolers develop episodic memory, and explicit and implicit (long-term) memories continue to develop.

15.1-2 According to Piaget, preschool children are in the preoperational stage and do not yet think logically.

15.1-2 In the preconceptual substage, preschool children learn by developing some concepts using trial and error and their perceptions.

15.1-2 In the intuitive substage, children solve problems using intuition.

15.1-2 Barriers that prevent children from thinking logically include egocentrism, centration, problems with transformations and reversibility, use of transductive reasoning, and problems with cause-and-effect reasoning.

15.1-3 Vygotsky identified three origins of abstract thinking in preschoolers: pretend play props, language, and imitation.

15.1-3 Scaffolding for preschoolers becomes less hands-on.

Lesson 15.2

15.2-1 Preschoolers develop concepts about physical attributes and understand some physical knowledge concepts, such as animism, artificialism, and finalism.

15.2-1 Older preschoolers begin to learn logical thinking concepts, such as sorting and classifying, ordering by attributes, seeing cause and effect, understanding spatial concepts, understanding number concepts, and noting time concepts.

15.2-2 Preschool is an important time in language development, which is now linked to thinking. Communication is easier because preschoolers can articulate better, and their vocabularies have increased.

15.2-2 Sentence structure and grammar rules tend to be difficult. Younger preschoolers may struggle with word order and negative words. Older preschoolers struggle with pronoun case.

15.2-3 Preschoolers are not yet capable of logical thinking, but they use their perceptions and intuition for solving problems that lay the foundation for logical thinking.

15.2-3 The preschool years are critical for learning vocabulary and grammar.

Lesson 15.3

15.3-1 Preschoolers still learn through motor activities, though usually in conjunction with other activities.

15.3-1 Preschoolers need opportunities for physical activities to build gross- and fine-motor skills and for physical health.

15.3-2 Adults should foster preschoolers' growing memory capacities and provide opportunities for concept learning.

15.3-3 During the preschool years, children will learn the most basic physical attributes and enjoy activities involving physical knowledge. Although preschoolers do not master logical thinking skills, they do begin laying a foundation for later logical reasoning.

15.3-4 Learning by creating their own symbols is critical for preschoolers because it prepares them for handling more abstract, society-determined symbols.

15.3-5 Language skills improve through modeling and using language as a part of daily activities.

15.3-5 There are two approaches to reading instruction. Reading readiness believes children between the ages 3 to 5 are developmentally ready for formal reading and writing instruction. Emergent literacy believes that children at ages 2 to 3 years spontaneously notice print in their environment and identify some signs and logos.

15.3-6 Many preschoolers learn using interactive media. Even when using interactive media, screen time should be limited and media content carefully chosen.

College and Career Portfolio

Portfolio Cover Letter

Many school and job applications require a cover letter to accompany a portfolio or résumé. A *cover letter* is an outline and explanation of your experiences. It should explain *why* and *how* your experiences have made you uniquely qualified for your desired school or job.

- Write a cover letter explaining how your experiences have prepared you for your desired role.
- Ask a career counselor or teacher to review your cover letter. Edit your letter according to their feedback.
- Carefully proof your cover letter.

Recall and Application

1. Which is true about the early pretend play of preschoolers? (15.1.1)
   A. It includes less realistic contexts like flying to the moon.
   B. It includes other children or adults.
   C. It involves role-playing about someone like the child.
   D. It includes a sequence of actions like making and baking a cake.

2. **True or False.** Beginning between 3 and 4 years of age, one of the most important intellectual advances is symbolic thought. (15.1.1)

3. Egocentrism may cause a preschooler to _____. (15.1.2)
   A. recognize that other people may not like what they like
   B. focus on only one part of an object instead of seeing all parts at the same time
   C. assume that because something is true for one event, it is true for all similar events
   D. believe inanimate objects have attributes like their own

4. **True or False.** Making a mistake linking events that occur close in time is an example of a preschooler's difficulty seeing transformations. (15.1.2)

5. Vygotsky identified three important origins of abstract thought in the preschool years: pretend play props, language, and _____. (15.1.3)
   A. scaffolding
   B. transformations
   C. imitation
   D. centration

6. **True or False.** Three-year-old preschoolers can handle one-to-one correspondence for groups of up to three. (15.2.1)

7. A 4-year-old can sort blocks by color and then switch to sorting them by size because of _____. (15.2.1)
   A. cognitive flexibility
   B. working memory
   C. finalism
   D. inhibitory control

8. Which is true about a 3-year-old's concept of grammar? (15.2.2)
   A. They speak in longer, more complex sentences.
   B. They begin using tag questions.
   C. They do not understand grammar rules.
   D. They have a difficult time forming questions.

9. Five-year-olds commonly achieve which intellectual milestone? (15.2.3)
   A. Solving some problems correctly through intuition (not logic)
   B. Drawing pictures that represent real objects or people
   C. Telling a simple story with some incorrect facts
   D. Knowing about 900 words

10. **True or False.** Punching holes in paper with a single-hole punch helps to strengthen a preschooler's fingers and develop fine motor skills. (15.3.1)

11. The best way to help preschoolers develop and practice their memory skills is to _____. (15.3.2)
    A. ask the child to recall specific details of a story
    B. sing the same songs to the child without any variation
    C. give the child directions once to test how well they remember them
    D. use photos to remind the child of a person they have not seen in a while

12. Using picture schedules of children's daily activities is one way to help preschoolers learn _____. (15.3.3)
    A. number concepts
    B. sorting and classifying
    C. time concepts
    D. ordering by attributes

13. **True or False.** Children learn problem-solving skills best through divergent thinking. (15.3.4)

14. Which is true about emergent literacy? (15.3.5)
    A. Children between ages 3 and 5 are developmentally ready to learn reading.
    B. It is based on the maturational theory of child development.
    C. It teaches children to recognize and print individual letters.
    D. Children at age 2 or 3 spontaneously notice print.

15. **True or False.** While preschoolers should have limited exposure to any media, they benefit more from exposure to interactive media, like games that respond to a user's actions, than noninteractive media like television. (15.3.6)

Critical Thinking

1. **Draw conclusions.** Preschool children solve problems using intuition and tend to have difficulty following nonobservable cause-and-effect relationships. In small groups, compile a list of nonobservable cause-and-effect relationships that you acknowledge and use each day. Draw conclusions about how your perceptions would change if you did not understand these relationships.

2. **Analyze.** In small groups, pick out children's books that illustrate cause and effect. Read one book aloud in your group and then analyze what the book would teach preschool children about cause-effect relationships. Write a two-page book report containing your analysis.

3. **Identify.** In small groups, assemble a collection of colored shapes or blocks in various shapes, sizes, and colors. Then, identify all the ways the objects can be *sorted* and all the ways they can be *classified*.

Demonstrate to the class one sorting and one classifying activity telling fellow students the criterion used for each.

4. **Cause and effect.** How do your patterns of speech and grammar reflect the language used by your parents or caregivers? How do you think the language models children are exposed to early in life impact their use of grammar?

5. Compare and contrast. Compare and contrast how language development in preschool children relates to language learning in older children and adults. Will learners of a second language have the same obstacles when it comes to language learning? Will they have different obstacles?

6. **Determine.** Anuj, a teacher at a local preschool, has been criticized for the amounts of dramatic play, art, and literature or language activities he incorporates into lessons. Anuj, however, feels these activities are not "just play," but are vital to intellectual development. Determine ways that Anuj can explain this to the parents of his students. Write a short script he can follow.

7. **Evaluate.** Watch a movie or television show for preschool children. While watching, take notes on what preschool children might learn or where an adult could ask a question that prompts learning. Afterward, evaluate the program and rate it on a scale from 1 to 10, with 1 being least educational and 10 being most educational.

Core Skills

1. **Research and writing.** Preschool learning is enabled by brain development leading to changes in cognition. Using reliable online or print resources, research how the brain changes and develops between three and five years of age. Also, research symbolic thought and how it fosters new abilities in preschoolers. Finally, write a three- to five-page report detailing how preschoolers' brains are uniquely prepared to learn and develop skills that are typically understood at this age.

2. **Technology and writing.** With a partner, review this chapter's information about

preschoolers' comprehension of logical thinking concepts and appropriate activities caregivers can use to foster these concepts. Then, create a comprehensive brochure that explains this information to parents and caregivers. Your brochure should both describe reasonable expectations for preschooler logic and advocate for activities that encourage the development of these concepts. Afterward, display your brochure in class.

3. **Art.** In understanding spatial relationships, preschoolers learn mental mapping, which enables them to envision spaces they do not presently see. Using a pencil and paper or a graphics editing software, draw a spatial map of your home from memory. You must be in a location other than your home when you do this activity. After completing your map, compare it to the actual space of your home. How accurately did your mental map resemble the physical space?

4. **Math.** Using reliable print or online resources, research the typical size of an adult's vocabulary. Then, review the sizes of children's vocabularies at three, four, and five years of age. What percentage of their adult vocabularies do children know at each of these ages?

5. **Technology and speaking.** Review the table of intellectual milestones for preschoolers (Figure 15.23), and in small groups, choose one of the three ages covered. Create a checklist for parents and caregivers titled "What My Preschooler Should Understand at Age _____." In your brochure, detail the major milestones a preschooler should achieve and that a parent or caregiver might observe during this time. Make your brochure visually appealing and informative. Finally, distribute the brochure to the class and deliver a presentation about its contents.

6. **Reading.** Research at least three schedules for preschool centers in your area. These schedules should include activities done each day as well as snack and nap times. Read each schedule carefully and note each activity that involves a gross- or fine-motor skill. Are most of these activities primarily structured

as motor activities, or are the motor activities secondary to the intent of the lesson?

7. **Listening and speaking.** As a class, divide into two teams—one team advocating reading readiness and one team advocating emergent literacy. In your teams, interview supporters of your theory and note their arguments. Verify the information given using reliable print or online resources. Finally, compose an opening statement and debate your theory with the opposing team. Be prepared to defend your theory with relevant facts and to create a closing statement based on the discussion that takes place.

8. **CTE Career Readiness Practice.** Presume you are the director of a new preschool center. Recently, parents have been asking you and your staff to explain certain terminology, such as *Piaget's preoperational stage, the preconceptual substage,* and *the intuitive substage.* You have planned a staff meeting to ensure that all your employees know how to respond to the parents' questions. In preparation for this meeting, prepare fact sheets that outline what the staff must know and communicate about the preoperational stage and its substages.

Observations

1. In small groups, make or find an audio recording of preschool children speaking while playing. Listen to the recording in your group and then answer the following questions: What articulation errors did you hear? Did you hear complex sentences—both statements and questions? What incorrect grammar did you hear? Afterward, play your recording and share your findings with the class.

2. In small groups, visit a local child care center and observe preschoolers speaking. Observe any instances of monologue or collective monologue and take notes about the contexts in which these speaking patterns occur. When do preschoolers most often use monologue and collective monologue? For what purpose do they use them? Discuss your findings in class.

Chapter 16

Social-Emotional Development of Preschoolers

Essential Question

How do preschoolers piece together their unique self-portraits while assimilating family and societal expectations, and how do adults serve as mirrors for the children's self-awareness and socializing?

Case Study   How Should Teachers Address Caregivers' Beliefs About Gender Roles?

As a class, read the case study and discuss the questions that follow. After you finish studying the chapter, discuss this case study again. Have your opinions changed based on what you learned?

Three-year-old Sylvan lives with both biologically male and female caregivers in a small town, where he attends preschool with many other children. One day, Sylvan asked his caregivers for a doll to play with in the preschool's housekeeping center.

Sylvan's paternal figure, Mr. Fontenot, was not happy when he heard this request and called Sylvan's preschool teacher, Sheniqua, right away. "If Sylvan plays in the housekeeping center, I have concerns that there will be issues with masculinity," Mr. Fontenot told Sheniqua. "Instead my child will learn to be more feminine and might never grow out of it. I never played with dolls when I was a kid."

Sheniqua replied, "I'm not sure that's what this is, Mr. Fontenot. Sylvan plays in the housekeeping center because a lot of the children that your child interacts with play in the housekeeping center."

Mr. Fontenot asked, "Does my child ever dress up as a different gender?"

Sheniqua pondered how to answer this and said, "Truth be told, Mr. Fontenot, many of the children play in the housekeeping center, and

several dress in male and female clothing and pretend to be caregivers and other adults. Playing multiple gender roles is good for young children."

After this explanation, Mr. Fontenot seemed calm, but Sheniqua worried that Mr. Fontenot might complain to the school.

Give It Some Thought

1. Why do you think Mr. Fontenot was concerned about his child's desire for a doll? Does this contradict Mr. Fontenot's script about masculinity? Why or why not?
2. If Mr. Fontenot complains to the school and scolds his child about playing with dolls, how might the experience affect Sylvan's feelings about gender and gender roles?
3. Sheniqua asserts that there is value in children playing in ways that are traditionally associated with the opposite gender. Do you agree or disagree with Sheniqua? Why?

FatCamera/E+ via Getty Images

The Social-Emotional World of Preschoolers

Key Terms

emotional dependency

fear-conditioning

gender constancy

gender stability

gender-role learning

initiative versus guilt

moral character

moral development

moral emotions

moral judgment and reasoning

repressed jealousy

self-concept

sex typing

sexual stereotyping

Learning Outcomes

After studying this lesson, you will be able to

16.1-1 **explain** how preschoolers learn even more about themselves as they show responsibility, learn gender roles, begin moral development, and expand their self-concept.

16.1-2 **describe** and **analyze** the role of play including problems preschoolers face as they develop initiative and interact with adults, siblings, and peers.

16.1-3 **assess** how feelings and emotions change and review and compare examples of social-emotional milestones preschoolers and children with diverse abilities might achieve.

16.1-4 **identify** social-emotional milestones during the preschool years which can impact growth and development.

16.1-5 **critique** the role and impact of technology on growth and development of preschoolers.

Reading and Notetaking Activity

Before reading, skim the headings in this chapter. List the headings to create an outline for taking notes during reading and class discussions. Under each heading, list any key terms. Finally, write two questions you expect to have answered in class. After completing the chapter, ask your teacher any questions you still have about the concepts or terms you learned.

Introduction

Due to their expanding self-awareness, children's personalities blossom and become more stable during the preschool years. Preschoolers learn more about themselves, including how to answer questions, such as "Who am I?" and "What can I do on my own?" Preschoolers test their skills through a series of successes and mistakes. As they show responsibility, learn gender roles, begin moral development, and expand their self-concept, they make strides toward taking initiative in life.

During the preschool years, children's social worlds expand to include many new adults, friends, peers, and perhaps younger siblings. Preschoolers engage in more friendships, and imaginary friends may become an important part of preschoolers' lives. Preschoolers' emotions also become more complex as they develop a greater understanding of their world. As preschool children grow, they must learn how to control and express emotions. Preschoolers experience stress due to their illogical ideas, lack of language skills, and fearful temperaments, including memories of fearful events that are all typical during this developmental stage. Preschoolers' ever-widening social environments also create more possibilities for stressful situations.

16.1-1 Expanding Self-Awareness

Toddlers begin to develop self-awareness and self-esteem based on how parents and other caregivers react to them. During the preschool years, children learn even more about themselves as they show responsibility, learn gender roles, begin moral development, and expand their self-concept. The feedback children receive during these experiences helps shape the image they have of themselves and determines whether the image is positive or negative.

Showing Responsibility

During the preschool years, children take their first steps toward becoming dependable people. They begin to show *responsibility*, which is a sense of accountability and a sign of trustworthiness. Learning to show responsibility takes time and calls for experience.

Adults can help children learn to show responsibility by setting examples and giving children

tasks they can do based on their abilities. Caregivers may need to show children how to do a task first and then give children time to perform the task (**Figure 16.1**). At home, caregivers may ask children to help with household tasks, such as setting the table, cleaning the kitchen, or folding laundry. In preschool programs, caregivers may ask children to put away toys, distribute snacks, and care for plants and animals. According to Erikson, children can learn responsibility by taking part in the routines of their world in real and important ways.

Mike Watson Images/moodboard/Thinkstock

Figure 16.1 Preschoolers learn to show responsibility when adults teach and then assign them tasks. *What household tasks were you assigned as a child? How did they help you learn responsibility?*

As preschoolers learn to show responsibility, they will have many successes and failures. Adults and caregivers should acknowledge preschoolers' successes and offer support after failures. Children who learn responsibility become more considerate of others and more dependable, which are important qualities as they continue to learn and grow.

Learning Gender Roles

A major part of self-awareness is *gender-role learning*. **Gender-role learning**, which involves knowing what behaviors are expected of males and females within one's society, aids children in their social relations and in their development of self-awareness. Through gender-role learning, children learn what is expected of them because of their genders.

Before preschoolers can understand gender roles, they must grasp the following basic concepts about gender:
- *Gender identity.* *Gender identity* is the ability to label oneself and others as male or female. Children develop gender identity around two years of age.
- *Gender stability.* Between three and four years of age, children begin to grasp **gender stability**, which is the understanding that a person who is either male or female will remain so throughout life. Confusion about gender stability may persist until the early school-age years.
- *Gender constancy.* Older preschoolers begin to comprehend **gender constancy**, which is the understanding that clothing, hairstyles, and actions do not change a person's gender. As with gender stability, confusion about gender constancy may persist into the early school-age years.

Once preschoolers understand these basic concepts about gender, they begin to learn gender roles through *sex typing*. **Sex typing** is the process by which a person adopts the attitudes and behaviors considered culturally appropriate for each gender. Families and even child care programs "teach" sex typing based on how they interpret varying cultural expectations. In the United States, some adults still follow traditional gender roles while other adults stress similarities between male and female roles. The toys and clothing given to a child, how a child's emotional expressions are received, and a child's observations of others filling male and female roles impact sex typing.

Children learn sex typing by observing how others treat them and how others express male or female roles. Preschoolers begin to sense that boys and girls act differently in many situations, and they will often identify with and model themselves after same-gender family members and friends. They may also model themselves after teachers and characters from television, movies, and storybooks. Some of the ways a child typically expresses their gender identity include:
- Clothing or hairstyle
- Preferred name or nickname
- Social behaviors that reflect varying degrees of aggression, dominance, dependency, and gentleness
- Manner and style of behavior and physical gestures and other nonverbal actions identified as masculine or feminine
- Social relationships, including the gender of friends and the people they decide to imitate

In the United States, children who are taught traditional gender roles may learn them at an earlier age compared to children who are taught similarities between male and female roles. Traditional gender-role learning, however, may also lead to sexual stereotyping. **Sexual stereotyping** is stating or even hinting that males and females always behave in certain ways or should always do particular tasks. Examples of sexual stereotyping may be apparent in various books, television programs, movies, and even in some people's conversations. Society has begun to recognize that stereotypes of "masculine" and "feminine" activities and behaviors are inaccurate and limit a child's development. These interests do not determine or influence one's gender identity. Our ability to predict who a child is based on early preferences is not accurate and may be harmful if it leads to shame or attempts to suppress their skills, talents, and genuine self.

When a child's interests and abilities are different from what society expects, they may be subjected to bullying. Caregivers can play an important role in advocating for safe spaces where their child feels comfortable and good about themselves. Regardless of whether children are taught traditional gender roles or similar roles, the gender roles they learn will affect other roles, such as career choices, friendships, dating, and family life.

Learning to Be Moral

During the preschool years, children begin a process known as **moral development**, the process by which children develop proper attitudes toward others (based on sociocultural, familial, school, peer, religious, and societal expectations). Moral development affects children's moral judgment and reasoning, moral character, and moral emotions.

Moral Judgment and Reasoning

Moral judgment and reasoning is the ability to perceive an action as right or wrong. The development of judgment and reasoning coincides with children's development of thinking skills. Jean Piaget and Lawrence Kohlberg researched moral judgment and reasoning.

Piaget exposed children to a number of moral dilemmas and published the findings as part of his *Social Theory of Development*. The theory was called *social*, rather than *intellectual*, because of noted moral judgments that involved not only intellectual reasoning, but also adult limits and peer-group cooperation. Lawrence Kohlberg expanded on Piaget's research by studying children of different ethnic, religious, and social groups. Kohlberg's methods mirrored Piaget's, and the findings were similar.

During the preschool years, both Piaget and Kohlberg noted that children's decisions were regulated by adult limits, not by personal convictions.

Focus on Social Studies

Gender Roles in the United States

For much of the history of the United States, people have adhered to a pattern of gender roles known as *traditional gender roles*. In traditional gender roles, males were typically the economic heads of their families and were seen as having more assertive traits. Females typically stayed home to care for the house and children and were seen as having more nurturing traits. These gender-role norms led to a societal system that encouraged males and females to embrace their respective roles.

Today, people in the United States hold varying beliefs about gender roles. Some people support more traditional gender roles, while others feel that all personality traits are acceptable, regardless of a person's gender at birth. It is more common now for both biological males and females to display traits that were traditionally seen as male (such as being assertive and sharing opinions) and display traits that were traditionally seen as female (such as nurturance and tranquility). Families' gender-role beliefs influence how their children perceive gender during the early years. By the teen and young adult years, however, people's opinions on gender roles may change just as other attitudes and behaviors change.

Photo: wavebreakmedia/Shutterstock.com

In **Figure 16.2**, you can see that preschoolers are in Piaget's *heterogeneous* (HEH-tuh-ruh-JEE-nee-us) stage of morality, which spans from four to seven years of age. In Lawrence Kohlberg's theory, preschoolers occupy the *obedience-punishment orientation* and *individualism and exchange* stages of moral reasoning. Both stages are in Kohlberg's first level called *preconventional morality* (level in which people make moral decisions based on how these decisions will impact them as individuals). During these stages, young children see rules as fixed and see punishments as inhibitors to unacceptable behaviors. Older preschoolers tend to believe that "being good" merits some type of reward. (During the school-age years, children enter the next stages of moral judgment and reasoning, which you will learn about later in this text.)

Moral Character

All studies show that **moral character**, acting in accordance with what is perceived as morally right, never bears a one-to-one correspondence with judgment and reasoning. Character requires having the strength and independence to act in accordance with what is perceived as morally right.

Preschoolers may fail to exhibit moral character because they do not always understand the reasoning behind certain limits. Their natural curiosity leads them beyond adult authority. Because punishment is perceived as a controlling factor, young preschoolers often weigh their chances of being caught and how severe the punishment might be. Older preschoolers often follow adult limits because they understand the reasons for certain behaviors and feel they will be rewarded.

Figure 16.2 **Piaget's and Kohlberg's Stages of Moral Judgement and Reasoning During the Preschool Years**

Jean Piaget

Stage	Characteristics of Stage

Heterogeneous morality* **(also called moral realism)**	• Children are regulated by others (caregivers and teachers), not by personal conviction.
	• Children's beliefs include:
	  • Rules are fixed and inflexible.
	  • Consequences of actions, not intentions, determine the "badness" of actions.
	  • Punishment is automatic.
	  • Not only do adults punish, but objects, such as trees, rocks, and toys, can also punish. This physically implausible connection between objects and punishment is called *immanent justice*.

*Heterogeneous means "from without."

Lawrence Kohlberg's Preconventional Stages of Moral Reasoning

Stage	Characteristics of Stage
Obedience-punishment orientation	• Children obey rules as taught by authority figures. • Children determine how good or bad an action is by its consequences. • Children fear punishment for wrongdoing.
Individualism and exchange	• Children note people have different viewpoints about right and wrong. • Children obey rules if they benefit them, but expect something in return for obedience. • Children exact justice in an eye-for-eye manner because they see this type of justice as fair.

Goodheart-Willcox Publisher

Some older preschoolers may even try to bargain with adults.

Moral Emotions

Moral emotions, which are a person's reactions to acceptable and unacceptable behaviors, emerge first in children who are other-oriented. Other-oriented people behave acceptably out of respect for others and feel remorse when they behave unacceptably. This remorse becomes a person's *inner voice of conscience*. Over time, conscience will take the place of authority figures as a moral guide. Young preschoolers may develop some remorse for wrongdoings, especially when adults emphasize the reasons for acceptable behaviors and how unacceptable behaviors damage others.

Developing a Self-Concept

During the preschool years, children expand their *self-concepts*. **Self-concept** is the picture a person has of themselves. Self-concept is always **cumulative** (KYOO-muh-luh-tihv), meaning it is composed of accumulated parts. A person's experiences can positively and negatively affect their self-concept.

Several factors **constitute** (make up) self-concept (**Figure 16.3**), including the following:
- *Self-recognition.* During the preschool years, children can distinguish the "real me" from symbols of themselves.
- *Self-definition.* Preschoolers begin to develop *self-definition*, which is the describing of oneself. In the preschool years, self-definition is based on one's physical features, gender, physical skills, possessions, and activities. Even though the descriptors change, people continue to practice self-definition throughout their lives.
- *Self-esteem.* In preschoolers, healthy self-esteem is **derived** (sourced) from being unconditionally loved and accepted, having secure attachments, and receiving positive discipline and guidance. Opposite adult behaviors will damage a child's self-esteem.

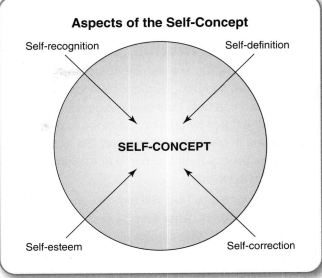

Goodheart-Willcox Publisher

Figure 16.3 Although self-concept evolves and is cumulative for a lifetime, its four aspects begin to emerge during the preschool years. *In your own words, how would you define each of the four aspects of self-concept?*

- *Self-correction.* Preschoolers begin to exhibit *self-correction*, the belief that one can do better and the ability to act on that belief. Preschoolers often self-correct drawings or tasks by starting over and correcting their methods.

As preschoolers develop self-concept, they choose to imitate certain individuals and willingly participate in some experiences. They begin to describe themselves with sayings, such as "I'm good (or bad)" or "I can (or cannot) draw that."

16.1-2 The Role of Play

Play is an essential developmental skill as it contributes to the cognitive, physical, social and emotional well-being of children. Play gives an opportunity for caregivers to engage with children. Today's children are being raised in an atmosphere of pressure and structured learning that limits the time children have for playing. Play allows children to use their creativity while developing their imagination, dexterity, and physical, cognitive, and emotional strengths.

Focus on Mental Health

Preschool children are learning to become independent and have confidence in themselves. Caregivers can help their children develop their self-esteem by offering guidance, but not interfering or giving them solutions. Six activities that caregivers can use at home to reinforce self-esteem include:

1. Pack for a trip. This skill focuses on independence. After they have packed prompt them to think about anything they have missed. An adult might say, "Do you have everything you need for spending the night at Grandma's?"

2. Invent a recipe. This skill focuses on learning from mistakes. Gently encourage mistake-making by asking a child to invent their own pancake recipe. Even if they add something unusual, let them experiment. Afterwards ask them, "What could you have done differently?"

3. Make slime. This skill focuses on teaching others. Children can build self-assuredness and develop confidence by demonstrating newly learned skills when interacting with others.

4. Chore with a purpose. This skill focuses on care of environment. Have the child pick out a special chore like watering the plants, sweeping the floor, etc. Compliment them for good, consistent behavior.

5. Float your boat. This skill focuses on problem-solving. Give children open-ended challenges and let them brainstorm ways to create solutions. Adults can give children items from the recycling bin, tape, glue, and string and let them experiment putting together a boat. Then test their creation to see if it sinks or floats.

6. Serve a snack. This skill focuses on multi-step planning. To develop confidence in cognitive skills, give children a multi-step challenge. Have them plan, prepare and serve a snack to someone coming to their home. This task forces the little ones to think about many different things at once.

Play is also important for healthy brain development and allows children to engage and interact with the world around them. By having a space where they can master skills, conquer fears, practice roles, and interact with others through trial and error, children gain competencies in confidence, decision-making, resiliency, and self-advocacy skills.

Play builds active, healthy bodies and is an easy way to increase the physical activity level in children. When caregivers observe or join their child in play, they can see the world from the child's point of view. This interaction shows children that their caregivers are being attentive to their needs and helps to build enduring relationships. Less verbal children may be able to express their views, experiences and even frustrations through play, allowing caregivers a chance to offer gentle, nurturing guidance. Chapter 20 will explore how to encourage children's play experiences.

Taking Initiative

Between three and six years of age, children grow in independence. Because of their improved abilities and limitless energy, they have a strong desire to learn, explore, and act. These children yearn for many experiences.

Children at this age are in Erikson's third stage of personality development, which is called **initiative versus guilt**. During this stage, children's **initiative** (the ability to think or act without being urged) encourages them to try new activities. At the same time, initiative can lead to failures, and failures may lead to *guilt* (the blaming of oneself for something done wrong) and a fear of trying new things. (You can review Erikson's theory in Figure 10.10 of the text.)

When preschool children make mistakes, they may feel badly about themselves, and if they feel too guilty, their desires to be obedient become so important they are afraid to try new things. Fear and guilt stifle initiative, and to prevent guilty feelings, children must know it is okay to make mistakes.

Extending Social Relations

Preschool children not only improve their motor skills and knowledge through social activities, but they also learn many social lessons, such as

- the social skills needed to form friendships
- the ability to recognize and respond to social cues from others
- the ability to cooperate with and show empathy for others (**Figure 16.4**)
- conflict-resolution skills
- the ability to regulate emotions

Children learn these lessons through their interactions with adults, other children, and even imaginary friends.

Interacting with Adults

Preschoolers continue to depend on caregivers and other adults to meet many of their needs.

ktaylorg/E+ via Getty Images

Figure 16.4 As preschoolers cooperate with others, they begin to develop close relationships with other children. *Who were your first friends? When did you become friends?*

As authority figures, caregivers must impose limits on certain behaviors of their children as well as explain the reasons for the limits. In addition to being caregivers and authority figures, adults also serve as social models for preschoolers. By their examples, adults teach children about responsibility, gender roles, relationships, morals, self-control, manners, and much more. Preschoolers with secure attachments to their caregivers and teachers are more successful at learning tasks and are more self-confident.

Interacting with Other Children

Siblings and peers are more important to preschool children than to toddlers. Among young preschoolers, reactions to siblings and peers differ. Some preschoolers enjoy playing with other children while others do not. It is not until the late preschool years that children form their first real friendships.

A child's ease of making friends depends on the child's friendliness, ability to follow group rules, and lack of dependence on adults. Preschool children tend to prefer making friends with children of the same gender, although within-gender friendships strengthen in the school-age years. While these friendships may last, conflicts can end them just as easily. Older preschoolers do not have the social skills to sustain friendships when conflicts arise.

Preschool children have a self-centered view of friendships. They see friends as people who play with them, help them, and share their toys. Because of this self-centered view, usually two or three preschool children form a close circle of friends. If there are too many friends, one child may not get enough attention from a friend. To protect their interests, preschool children will often call out, "You can't play with us." When a friend does not do as a child desires, feelings quickly change. A child takes a new best friend—at least for the moment.

Preschool children learn many social skills while playing with other children, such as taking turns, giving to others, and receiving from others. They also learn to see from other children's perspectives and to manage their own impulses. Friendships are important for preschoolers, and children with limited peer involvement may experience negative developmental consequences.

Sibling Interactions

In many families, children grow up with at least one sibling. In some families, children have several brothers and sisters. Siblings influence each other's lives in many ways. Siblings can play many roles with each other. They can be teachers and learners, protectors, and even rivals.

Sibling interactions influence both intellectual and social-emotional development as children play roles of teachers and learners. Older children often act like teachers while younger siblings will play the part of eager learners. As teachers, siblings explain, define, describe, show, and offer examples. Older siblings also model social skills, so younger children learn the difference between acceptable and unacceptable social behaviors. From a child's point of view, a sibling shows acceptable social behavior if they play nicely, help with chores, and don't tattle.

If you have ever seen an older child run to a younger sibling's defense, you know that siblings protect each other. Much as they may compete, siblings often have a sense of *family togetherness* and a desire to protect and look after their siblings (especially younger siblings or siblings with special needs). Siblings are more likely to protect each other if they have an age gap of three or more years, come from large families, are in unsupervised places, or if one sibling is attacked physically or verbally by their peers.

Even if siblings teach and protect each other, they may think of each other as *rivals*. Siblings will often compete with one another in both physical and verbal ways for the love and attention of adults and friends. This competition can develop for several reasons. Children may be jealous of siblings who seem more capable than they are. They also may not be able to see a situation from other points of view. Children who have siblings with special needs may become jealous of the amount of time caregivers need to spend meeting these special needs. To young children, *fair* means *equal*, so some children may feel they are being treated unfairly if their siblings are given different treatment, privileges, or responsibilities from those given to them.

Adults cannot prevent rivalry among siblings. As children develop distinct identities and self-concepts, they will unavoidably compare themselves to their siblings and peers. Adults can lessen rivalry, however, by giving each child lots of love and positive feedback. Adults should take care not to compare one child with another. Children are different and comparing them usually makes one child resent the other and feel angry toward the adult. Rather, adults should stress the importance of family togetherness and support and should plan some activities everyone enjoys. Adults should teach children to take pleasure in another's good fortune and should explain that family members love one another although they sometimes get angry at each other. Above all, caregivers should encourage loving behaviors between a child and their siblings.

Writing Activity

Read a story or watch a film or television show in which two young siblings interact. Take notes about the siblings' relationship, including how they teach each other, protect and support each other, and compete with each other. Write a two- to three-page analysis of the relationship identifying these behaviors and discussing how this portrayal of a sibling relationship is or is not realistic.

Photo: Tom Wang/Shutterstock.com

Interacting with Imaginary Friends

During the preschool years, children may also begin to interact with imaginary friends. About two-thirds of children from two to seven years of age have imaginary friends. These "friend-ships" can last long past seven years of age and sometimes even into adulthood. For example, fiction writers talk about their book characters taking on a life of their own. Although these are not "real friendships," imaginary friends can be very important for preschoolers and can occupy much of their time and energy. Often, these friendships involve the entire family. A preschooler may also try to get other adults and children to acknowl-edge the imaginary friend.

In the past, researchers have thought that imaginary friends are created to fill a void in the lives of some children. Recent research, however, does not support this idea and instead has led to many other discoveries (**Figure 16.5**).

16.1-3 Expressing Emotions

During the preschool years, children experi-ence many emotions and express them in intense ways. While preschool children feel many positive emotions, such as love and dependency, they also experience negative emotions when faced with the following types of stressors:

- *Common childlike stressors.* These include short separations from caring adults and fear of monsters.
- *Short-term stressors and "bad days."* These occur when preschoolers' initiative requires more "no" responses from caregivers. These also occur when preschoolers' emotions seem out of control.
- *Long-lasting and serious stressors.* These may include illness, moving, death, adult quarrels, and divorce.

Figure 16.5 Imaginary Friends

Question	Answers
Which children are most likely to have imaginary friends?	• Children who create imaginary friends are outgoing and have many real friends. • Oldest children, only children, and children who do not watch television are most likely to have imaginary friends. These children's unstructured time (not loneliness) enables them to invent friends. • Children who have imaginary friends are not shy or maladjusted.
What are the characteristics of imaginary friends?	• Imaginary friends, estimated to be over 16 million in number, are a diverse group. Researchers cannot categorize these friends. • Imaginary friends can be one friend or a group of friends. For example, one child's imaginary friends were a herd of cattle. Imaginary friends may be as small as a mouse or as large as a dinosaur. • Imaginary friends are rarely younger children. • Imaginary friends often possess the skills that a child desires. • Children can describe imaginary friends in the same detail as they can their real friends.
Which types of relationships do children have with imaginary friends?	• Very few preschoolers insist imaginary friends are real. In fact, over 75 percent voluntarily disclose this information during an interview. • Children with imaginary friends have a very involved form of pretend play. These children expect others to play along. • Unlike play with stuffed animals and dolls, play with imaginary friends treats the imaginary friend as an equal. • Imaginary friends are seldom scapegoats for preschoolers' misbehaviors. In reality, imaginary friends are often role models.

Goodheart-Willcox Publisher

As preschoolers, children are expected to control many of their intense feelings. Controlling outward signs of emotions, such as crying, screaming, or hitting, helps children become socially acceptable. Children need to express their feelings. Statements such as "I am angry," or "I am afraid" are healthy. During the preschool years, children learn how to control and express a variety of emotions, including love and dependency, fear and anxiety, anger, and jealousy.

Love and Dependency

Preschoolers feel love for their caregivers, other family members, teachers, friends, and pets. Preschool children tend to be less defiant than toddlers and express affection with hugs, kisses, and snuggling.

Preschool children often experience conflict between their needs for dependence and independence. Preschoolers show fewer attachment behaviors than do toddlers, but attachment has not disappeared. In times of stress, preschool children may try to recapture the early attachment feelings. These children may cry, cling, show signs of emotional dependence, and have toileting accidents.

Focus on Mental Health

When children repress the feelings underlying their negative emotions, they can become emotionally troubled. Adults should help children admit their negative feelings but should not encourage children to let these feelings override control of their actions. Healthy ways that children can express their feelings include pointing out and giving names to their feelings, discussing how characters in a story are feeling, going to a quiet place when they are upset to calm down, reading books that provide coping strategies, and showing children how to set things right again after an emotional outburst, such as apologizing for their behavior. Praise children when they make progress and teach them that emotions are not right or wrong.

Emotional dependency is the act of seeking attention, approval, comfort, and contact. In emotional dependency, a child is usually dependent on only one or two people. Unlike toddlers, preschoolers are apt to accept comfort from strangers, but still prefer to be comforted by a loved adult or peer.

Around five years of age, children begin to seek help in achieving a goal more often than they seek contact or approval (**Figure 16.6**). In most cases, older preschool children really do need help. From time to time, however, preschoolers may ask for help that is not needed. Usually, preschool children do this to gain reassurance of the adult's love or concern. Thus, older preschoolers still express emotional dependency in asking for help—this emotional dependency is just better disguised.

Fear and Anxiety

Preschoolers' fears often stem from a lack of understanding, the inability to separate reality from fantasy, or a preschooler's own experience of being hurt. Some fears keep preschoolers safe, but preschoolers may also exhibit unhealthy fears.

Many of the fears experienced in the toddler years disappear by the preschool years, and new fears replace the ones that fade. While some preschoolers tend to experience a greater variety of fears, others tend to experience less fears, but will have more intense reactions to these fears. Most

PeopleImages/iStock via Getty Images Plus

Figure 16.6 Older preschool children may ask an adult to tie their shoes or reach toys on a high shelf, even if the preschooler can perform the task. *How should adults respond when preschoolers make these requests?*

preschoolers share common fears, such as fear of the unknown or imagined, fear of physical injury, or fear of pain.

As with fears, preschoolers' anxieties change with their growing minds. Preschoolers understand many new concepts, but their understandings may still be limited. This lack of understanding often creates new fears and anxieties. Children's specific fears may become general anxieties. For example, fear of a tornado may spread to general anxiety during a thunderstorm or even a strong wind.

During the preschool years, separation anxiety often disappears. Preschool children can handle separations better, especially when they see where their caregivers work and what they do. Visiting caregivers' workplaces helps preschoolers develop mental images of the adult at work and understand why the caregiver must go to work. In turn, this causes the preschooler to be less anxious about the separation.

Anger and Aggression

Feelings of anger begin around 10 months of age and peak with displays of temper in the toddler years, sometimes continuing into the preschool years. Anger often stems from stress, fatigue, frustration, and rejection. At times, anger leads to aggression in children. Aggression is associated with the child's temperament, the child's ability to distinguish between accidental and intentional aggression from other children, adult models of aggression, power-assertive discipline techniques, and real and fantasy violence.

Expressions of anger and aggression change in the preschool years. While preschool children tend to hit or bite less than toddlers, they threaten and yell more. This is due to preschoolers' increasing language skills and sometimes due to gender (**Figure 16.7**). Preschoolers' anger and aggression tend to be directed more at siblings and close friends than at casual peers. By the time children reach the preschool years, they appear to have learned that aggression toward adults, especially physical aggression, is not acceptable.

Jealousy

During the preschool years, children commonly experience jealousy. Jealousy begins when children realize they must share love, attention, possessions, and time with others. Preschoolers are trying to figure out who they are as individuals, and to do this, they compare themselves with others. These comparisons often lead to jealousy.

Figure 16.7 Males tend to express anger physically more often than females, whereas females tend to express anger verbally. *In your opinion, are gender differences in expression primarily based in biology or in societal expectations?*

Zabavna/Shutterstock.com

Jealousy may also emerge when there are changes in a family, such as a new sibling. Having to share caregivers' love and attention may make a preschooler feel jealous and less loved. Preschoolers may even experience jealousy over material objects, such as other children's toys.

Some preschool children may experience **repressed jealousy**, which is jealousy that is not directly expressed and may even be denied. Children who repress jealousy may experience the emotion through nightmares or physical problems, such as upset stomachs, headaches, fevers, and changes in appetite.

16.1-4 Social-Emotional Developmental Milestones

As preschool children's worlds expand, they develop self-awareness and learn to take initiative. They also learn new ways to interact with others and express and control their maturing and expanding emotions. Children achieve a number of social-emotional developmental milestones during the preschool years. Some of these milestones are shown in **Figure 16.8**.

Figure 16.8 **Preschool Social-Emotional Milestones**

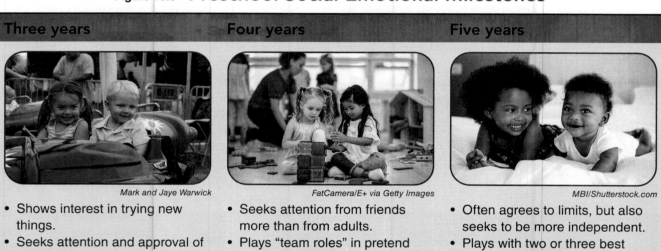

Mark and Jaye Warwick · FatCamera/E+ via Getty Images · MBI/Shutterstock.com

Three years
- Shows interest in trying new things.
- Seeks attention and approval of adults.
- Shows affection for special friends; comforts hurt children.
- Enjoys helping parents with household tasks.
- Takes turns; shares toys at times.
- Expresses a wide range of emotions.
- Fears the unknown, the imagined, pain, and the dark.
- Displays less physical aggression when angry.
- Realizes some actions are wrong and acts "sorry" for some actions.

Four years
- Seeks attention from friends more than from adults.
- Plays "team roles" in pretend play.
- Takes turns, shares, and cooperates (as long as things go their way).
- Resents adult directions and limits and challenges authority.
- Is boastful at times.
- Fears monsters.
- Tattles, uses "shock" words, and lies to protect themself.
- Expresses anger by yelling; sometimes regresses to physical expressions of anger.

Five years
- Often agrees to limits, but also seeks to be more independent.
- Plays with two or three best friends and excludes others.
- Is sensitive to the feelings of other children.
- Protects younger children.
- Begins to follow rules and plays fairly.
- Distinguishes right from wrong (but does not recognize intent).
- Begins to distinguish fantasy from reality.
- Argues, but can negotiate solutions to conflicts.
- Has a gender-role concept.

Goodheart-Willcox Publisher

If a caregiver is concerned about their child not meeting the milestones seen in Figure 16.8 they can talk to the child's doctor about possible developmental delays and ask for developmental screening. When talking to the doctor, caregivers need to be prepared to share specific concerns that they have including examples they have seen. If a developmental delay is found the caregiver may be referred to support services including speech therapy, physical therapy and other types of services based on the child and family's needs (**Figure 16.9**). The connections in a baby's brain are the most adaptable the first three years of life. The neural connections made during this time are the foundation for learning, behavior, and health. Over time, these connections become harder to change so early intervention is important when concerned about developmental delays. Special education is instruction specifically designed to meet the educational and developmental needs of children with disabilities, or those who are experiencing developmental delays. Services for preschool children are provided free of charge through the public school system. These services are available through the Individuals with Disabilities Education Act. In addition to assistance that can come when a child is receiving special education services to address a disability or developmental delay, there are other resources that can be helpful to families, childcare providers, and educators. Figure 16.9 gives a list of some of the resources available.

16.1-5 Recognizing Preschoolers' Stress

Stress and trauma occurring before six years of age have the most powerful negative effects on the developing child. In the United States, there is a growing awareness of children's emotional and behavioral problems and how these problems affect their classroom conduct, abilities to learn, and their friendships with other children. Stress and mental health problems often stem from preschoolers' developmental stage and social environments, including the home, preschool center, and neighborhood.

Figure 16.9 Support Services for Families with Special Needs

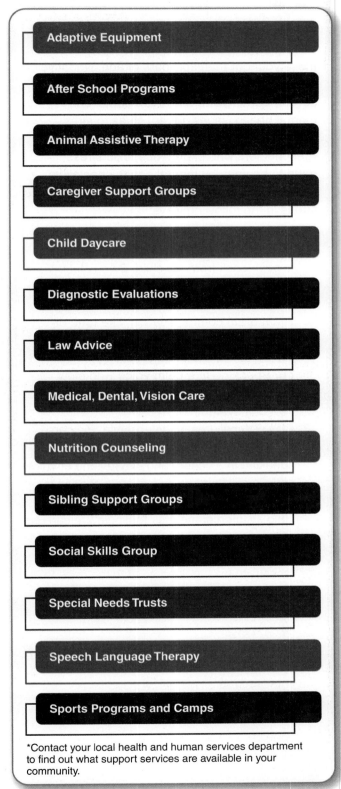

- Adaptive Equipment
- After School Programs
- Animal Assistive Therapy
- Caregiver Support Groups
- Child Daycare
- Diagnostic Evaluations
- Law Advice
- Medical, Dental, Vision Care
- Nutrition Counseling
- Sibling Support Groups
- Social Skills Group
- Special Needs Trusts
- Speech Language Therapy
- Sports Programs and Camps

*Contact your local health and human services department to find out what support services are available in your community.

Goodheart-Willcox Publisher

FOCUS ON MENTAL HEALTH

Toxic stress without adult buffers has powerful, lifelong negative effects on children, especially those younger than six years of age. Negative effects include impaired brain development, severe learning and social problems, and mental health issues. Often, clues to stress can be detected in preschoolers' behaviors. Preschoolers who experience toxic stress need to be seen by mental health specialists. Caregivers can help preschoolers deal with toxic stress in the following ways:

1. Be with them. Simply having someone in the room can be a comfort even when there is push-back from the child. Being alone heightens fear.
2. Be gentle, so as not to startle or jar a child. Right brain communication, like tone of voice, eye contact and body language, are all nonverbal cues children pick up on. Speaking in a calm voice with slow movements helps to avoid startling a fragile nervous system.
3. Play with children when possible. Play helps a child feel better and calm down. Smiling and speaking in a cheery and playful tone of voice gives a child's nervous system a chance to calm down.
4. Help children name their feelings. We can use stories to help children put language on their emotions. Adults can show drawings of little faces with feelings and point to the ones to which they relate.
5. Help children express their feelings. Emotions have impulses of energy and this energy needs to be expressed. For example, if a child is in danger, their brain will trigger fear with an impulse to run.
6. When a child accepts them, give hugs and other physical affection. Holding, rocking, hugging, and swaddling can help soothe a stressed nervous system.

Developmental Stress

Developmental stress during the preschool years involves factors related to preschoolers' developmental stage and personal development. These factors include the following:

- *Way of thinking.* Preschoolers do not always have a firm grasp of reality. Their fears can be worsened by their skewed perspectives of cause and effect and their tendencies to overgeneralize. They also may not understand that the loss of a loved person, pet, or object may be permanent.
- *Lack of language skills.* Preschoolers have few language skills required to explain how they feel or ask for help when they need it. Thus, preschoolers' responses to emotional experiences differ from those of older children and adults. Preschoolers are just beginning to learn how to think about emotions and what triggers them.
- *Fearful temperament.* Some preschoolers have fearful temperaments that lead to anxiety and depression. Preschoolers are vulnerable to **fear-conditioning** (associating a fearful stimulus with a neutral stimulus). For example, if a loud clap of thunder occurs (fearful stimulus) while a preschooler is playing alone in their room (neutral stimulus), the child may then be fearful of playing alone in their room (fear-conditioning). Because of fear-conditioning, preschoolers may experience strong stress responses to the stimuli they associate with fear. As a result, a wide range of conditions can trigger anxiety. Fear-conditioning underlies many anxiety disorders.
- *Episodic memories.* As preschoolers' episodic memories improve, they can relive stressful, fearful experiences. Recall strengthens stress and makes it more difficult to forget. These stressful memories may impair new memory functions, such as learning.
- *Delays or illnesses.* Some preschoolers may experience developmental delays or illnesses. Being delayed or ill is stressful, and stress can make the delay or illness worse.

Clues to Stress in the Preschool Years

Preschoolers respond to stress in several recognizable ways. Some of these behaviors are normal if they last only a short time and are not too intense. Often, the more clues the adult sees, the greater the stress.

- The reliving of a trauma over and over, whether by talking about the event, depicting it through drawings, or acting it out in pretend play. While reliving trauma for a short period of time may relieve stress and help children understand the event, reliving the trauma too many times reinforces it in children's memories and heightens stress.
- Heightened arousal, such as disturbed sleep or being "jumpy."

- Heightened separation anxieties and clinging to adults.
- Regression to toddler-like behaviors.
- Physical complaints, such as tummy aches.
- Changes in appetite.
- Development of new fears not related to the trauma.
- Behavioral changes, such as *defiance* (talking back to adults, temper tantrums, refusing to cooperate), *aggression* (being cruel, destroying toys and other property, fighting peers), and *regression in social competence* (sharing less often, not wanting to play with friends, being more impulsive).

Photo: wavebreakmedia/Shutterstock.com

Environmental Stress

Social environments, such as the preschooler's home, preschool center, and neighborhood, can play a large part in contributing to preschoolers' stress. Preschoolers are much less vulnerable to stress if their caregivers are not experiencing stress or mental health issues. When caregivers face trauma and stress, they have less time to devote to parenting and are less able to provide the predictable and stable home environment needed by a preschooler. Caregivers' problems can spill over into their children's lives. Changes in family life, such as a new baby or an adult's new career, can also be stressful for a preschooler.

Besides adults' stressors that affect preschoolers, other environmental stressors may come from factors associated with low-quality preschool programs (too many children, inappropriate activities, not enough toys), peer aggression, and stressful situations in the neighborhood (violence, poverty).

16.1-6 Technology and Development

Caregivers often struggle with decisions involving technology access for their preschoolers. Technology is in virtually every American home in some form, such as television, tablets, or smart phones. Technology can have both a positive and negative impact on children, so it is important that caregivers are mindful of how their children use technology and the potential effects it can have on their development.

Figure 16.10 shows the positive and negative impacts of technology on children.

The American Academy of Pediatrics recommends children under the age of five receive one hour or less each day of screen time. Screen time includes television, computers, and smart devices like phones and tablets. As a caregiver you need to weigh the pros and cons of technology usage for the child in your care. Adults need to demonstrate the proper use of technology as well as help children make wise choices.

There are several ways that technology can be used to help children develop social and emotional awareness. These include recognizing familiar faces and places, identifying feelings and emotions, and creating awareness and acceptance of change. **Figure 16.11** gives some examples of what you can do to help a preschooler in each of these areas.

Figure 16.10 Positive and Negative Effects of Technology on Children

Negative/Cons	Positives
• Social skills may not develop adequately. Children may not know how to engage with other children or adults, or they have a harder time being empathetic to others' needs. • Relationships are not made. Children become used to being alone and lose the desire to engage with people outside the internet. May lead to difficulties forming friendships. • Can lead to health problems. Technology influences the developing brain and can affect problem-solving skills. Too much sedentary activity can lead to lack of exercise, reduced sleep quality, and overall well-being. • May reduce attention span and ability to focus. Children become easily distracted. • Children are vulnerable to safety risks. It is difficult for caregivers to always monitor what the children are exposed to. • Technology can reduce a child's imagination when they are always shown images instead of being encouraged to imagine on their own. • Creates virtual accomplishments that do not translate into a real ability. • Children with diverse needs struggle to disengage from their digital activities, which can create unwanted behaviors when they can't use technology any longer. • Technology is expensive. Homes with restricted income may find it difficult to pay for technology for their child. • Prolonged exposure to screen-based technology can lead to computer vision syndrome, also known as digital eye strain. Symptoms include eye fatigue, blurred vision, double vision, and headaches.	• Technology can be a rich source of educational entertainment. Children can begin to learn a foreign language, fundamentals of math, and how to count and recognize letters and numbers. • Technology allows access to more information about different cultures, festivals, events, and religions that may not be possible to learn about in the family setting. • Technology prepares children for the future. Exposing children to tech concepts early helps them prepare for school while promoting cognitive development and educational concepts. • Technology improves hand-eye coordination. Eye tracking improves with technology use as the child follows an object on the screen or participates in an activity. • Language skills can improve. Games require a child to follow specific instructions for success. Children can also read e-books to improve vocabulary, and online flashcards promote phonics and mathematical concepts. • Technology can foster connections. Children can stay connected to family members who don't live close by, or with others in their age group while playing games online. • Technology can foster creativity and exploration of interests. Children can explore different areas of interest by a click of a button. • Children learn self-expression. They can share their thoughts, connect with others, and be exposed to different viewpoints as they get older.

Figure 16.11 Technology and Social-Emotional Development

Recognize Familiar Faces and Places	Identify Feelings and Emotions	Create Awareness and Acceptance of Change
• Take photos of family, friends and other important adults, look at the pictures together, and talk about the people in the photos.	• After watching a video, talk about the characters and how they felt and behaved in response to specific events. This helps children label and recognize emotions.	• Help prepare for transitions by visiting new places before the first day the child is to attend. Take pictures of the building, the room, or the people. Take a virtual tour if one is available online.
• Take pictures of the places you go to on a typical day. Reflect on the pictures and talk about what you did and who you saw.	• Relate character experiences and emotions from videos back to your child's everyday life.	• View the photos you took and discuss how the child feels about the change. Encourage acceptance, understanding, and confidence. Review the photos a few months later and reflect on the child's feelings.

Goodheart-Willcox Publisher

Lesson 16.1 Review and Assessment

1. The ability to label oneself and others as male or female is called _____. (16.1.1)
   A. gender stability
   B. sexual stereotyping
   C. sex typing
   D. gender identity
2. **True or False.** Because they are in Kohlberg's level of preconventional morality, older preschoolers tend to believe that "being good" merits some type of reward. (16.1.1)
3. Which of the following is most likely to occur when a preschooler makes a mistake? (16.1.2)
   A. They blame other people.
   B. They are less concerned about being obedient.
   C. They are afraid to try new things.
   D. They learn from their mistake.
4. Which is an example of a serious stressor a preschooler may face? (16.1.3)
   A. Moving to a new town
   B. Being afraid of monsters
   C. Experiencing a temper tantrum
   D. Being away from a caregiver for a few hours

5. Five-year-olds commonly achieve which social-emotional developmental milestone? (16.1.4)
   A. Seeking the approval of adults
   B. Distinguishing between fantasy and reality
   C. Acting "sorry" for some action they realize is wrong
   D. Lying to protect themself
6. **True or False.** A preschooler's fears can be worsened by their skewed perspectives of cause and effect and their tendencies to overgeneralize. (16.1.4)
7. **True or False.** One potential negative associated with a preschooler's use of technology is that it creates virtual accomplishments that do not translate into a real ability. (16.1.5)

Lesson 16.2

Meeting Preschoolers' Social-Emotional Needs

Key Terms

altruistic behaviors
assertive
self-reward
shame
tattling behaviors

Learning Outcomes

After studying this lesson, you will be able to

16.2-1 plan developmentally appropriate activities for supporting self-awareness and teaching responsibility and moral development in preschoolers.

16.2-2 develop social relations by fostering altruistic behavior and teaching preschoolers about avoiding conflicts, having good manners, and guiding emotions to reduce preschoolers' fears, anxieties, and jealousies.

16.2-3 describe how to help preschoolers cope with stress.

Reading and Notetaking Activity

Before reading, skim the headings in this chapter. List the headings to create an outline for taking notes during reading and class discussions. Under each heading, list any key terms. Finally, write two questions you expect to have answered in class. After completing the chapter, ask your teacher any questions you still have about the concepts or terms you learned.

Introduction

Because the preschool years are a time for socialization into the family and other groups, preschoolers have many social-emotional needs. Adults, as the socializing agents, are responsible for teaching children "rules" about how to handle those needs. Due to their growing self-awareness, preschoolers become more and more independent. As they become more independent, one critical source of their self-awareness comes from the reflected appraisals of caregivers and other adults. Children come to see and value themselves in keeping with the positive and negative reactions of others. Preschoolers need gentle guidance to prevent damaging their self-esteem. Preschoolers are eager to master many things to be part of the group—the family, the preschool, and the neighborhood.

Adults need to help preschoolers take the initiative and react calmly when exuberant efforts lead to less than desirable results. Adults must often explain to preschoolers the reasons for limits or requirements and repeat this information frequently in a firm, but fair, way.

Caregivers and other adults should support preschoolers as they attempt to develop positive social relationships with both adults and children. Learning cooperative behaviors takes many lessons. Preschoolers learn best when adults notice and show approval for their positive behaviors and explain specifically the effects of these behaviors on others.

Unlike younger children whose emotions are more general, such as crying when tired, preschoolers' emotions are situation specific. For example, preschoolers may express excitement over plans to go to the park or fear of storms. Adults can help preschoolers learn to seek out situations associated with positive feelings and avoid situations that lead to negative emotions. Adults can also teach preschoolers when and how it is appropriate to display certain emotions. Preschoolers need to learn how to interpret the emotional expressions of others. Because children are especially vulnerable to stress in the preschool years, adults should provide supportive environments and model positive ways of coping with stress.

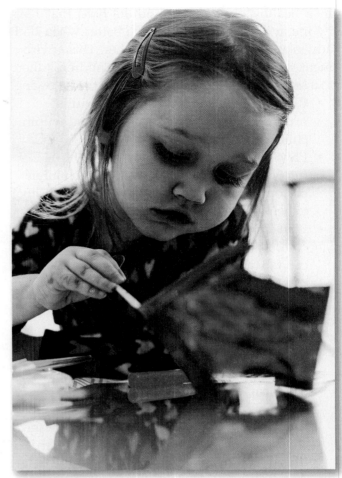

shaunl/E+ via Getty Images

Figure 16.12 As preschoolers discover their own unique traits and abilities, they develop self-awareness. *What unique traits have you observed in preschool children?*

16.2-1 Supporting the Preschooler's Self-Awareness

As early as the toddler years, children begin to develop self-awareness and exert some autonomy. This discovery of self-awareness continues into the preschool years, at which time children begin to understand their own uniqueness, including their physical traits and some skills (**Figure 16.12**). To develop self-awareness, children need to live in environments that promote healthy personal development. Adults, caregivers, and teachers can encourage children to show responsibility, understand gender roles, begin moral development, and develop a healthy self-concept.

Sharing Responsibility

To teach children how to show responsibility, caregivers and teachers can *share* responsibility. Preschool children view tasks as a way of learning new skills, pleasing others and having fun, and taking the initiative. Adults can help children become more dependable and responsible by sharing responsibilities with them.

Caregivers and teachers must strike a careful balance to share the right amount of responsibilities with preschool children. Some adults offer few, if any, opportunities for children to help. These adults may see preschool children as unwilling to help or as unable to do certain tasks. Conversely, some adults may place too many demands on children and expect them to perform at adult standards.

In a healthy environment, adults hold that family life and school life are made better when both adults and children help each other. This environment can be created if adults and children adhere to a set of realistic guidelines, such as the following:

- Children may suggest tasks, but adults must decide which tasks are safe and within children's grasps.
- Physical conditions should be **amenable** (uh-MEH-nuh-buhl), or receptive to, children performing a task, such as having a sturdy stool to help them reach a cabinet (**Figure 16.13**).
- Plans and expectations should be communicated clearly by the adult. Adults can talk about tasks planned for the day and can tell children what they are to do.
- Adults should not expect perfection. If a finished task is not satisfactory, the task should be explained again for the child to do over. When adults redo tasks for children, children feel a sense of failure.
- Tasks can be made fun by incorporating games. For example, if an adult asks a child to pick up their blocks, the adult can ask the child to haul the blocks to the "lumberyard" (the shelf).
- At times, adults should respect children's priorities. There may be no harm in letting a child do a job 10 minutes later. It is healthy for children to decide on some priorities.

- Children should be rewarded for tasks completed. Adults can reward children either with love only or with pay (money or a want fulfilled). Whether adults pay or do not pay, they should thank children and acknowledge their skills.

Helping Children Learn Gender Roles

Preschoolers' learning about gender roles will affect the way they act as children and as adults. Caregivers and teachers should be informed about gender issues and make decisions about what gender roles they want to teach children.

Adults express their feelings about gender roles to children in many ways. The roles they allow or encourage children to try and the day-to-day attitudes they convey affect how children perceive gender. For example, caregivers who model traditional roles in the home may express these roles by the male not doing housework and by females being discouraged from doing heavy outdoor work. On the other hand, caregivers who believe in and practice more **ambiguous** (am-BIH-gyuh-wuhs), less-defined, gender roles might not model these divisions of labor and may allow children to choose activities according to their own interests and skills. Preschool children will rapidly learn gender roles by observing adults (**Figure 16.14**). Toys, media, and books may also affect how children perceive gender roles.

Figure 16.13 If an adult asks a child to help put away laundry, they should make sure the laundry basket and clothes are within the child's reach. *What chores are typically accessible to young children? What chores are typically not accessible?*

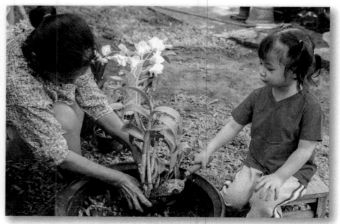

Figure 16.14 Preschoolers may learn gender roles as they help their male and female caregivers with household tasks and errands. *What is this preschooler learning about gender roles while helping her mother garden?*

Encouraging Moral Development

During the preschool years, children look primarily to adults as their guides for moral development. As children begin to learn what is right and wrong and develop conscience, adults can aid them in a number of ways, including the following:

- *Explain the reasoning behind acceptable and unacceptable behaviors.* This will help children understand moral judgment and reasoning and begin to develop personal convictions of their own.
- *Model acceptable behaviors to encourage moral character.* Morality grows out of a child's love for caregivers and teachers. In their parenting styles, adults should model mutual respect and inductive discipline techniques with their children.
- *Explain how unacceptable behaviors damage others.* An explanation given in context of love, respect, and explicit guidance will help children develop moral emotions.
- *Avoid shaming children.* **Shame** is focused on self and involves a loss or threat of a loss to a child's basic security. Examples of shaming include name-calling and negative reactions to a child's wants, feelings, or needs. Corporal punishment also shames because it never feels loving. Shame does not aid character development. Rather, it crushes a young child's curiosity, exuberance, and desire for being independent. Shaming does not model respect so it erodes the young child's self-esteem.

Promoting a Healthy Self-Concept

During the preschool years, a child's self-concept is closely tied to their awareness of physical characteristics and abilities. While forming their self-concepts, children need nurturance, affection, guidance, encouragement, and affirmation. Caregivers and teachers can plan many activities that encourage children to view their physical characteristics in positive ways. Some examples of these activities include setting up a full-length mirror so the child can see themselves at play or having a child draw a self-portrait. Adults can celebrate preschoolers' physical growth by marking a height and weight chart at regular intervals.

Adults can also plan activities that encourage children to view their skills, interests, and abilities in positive ways. Some of these activities include having a child make a collage of favorite things and keeping a scrapbook album of a child's activities. Caregivers and teachers can also have children create a "Me Box," in which a child can collect some of their favorite things, or a "Me Book," in which a child can display their handprint and pictures of favorite foods and activities (**Figure 16.15**). Some picture books and other resources can also help children develop healthy self-concepts.

Figure 16.15 A "Me Book," such as the one shown, can encourage children's skills, interests, and hobbies. *Judging from this "Me Book," what are the skills and interests of this child?*

Helping Preschoolers Take Initiative

As preschool children discover motivation to perform new tasks and struggle against a sense of guilt, the adults in their lives can play an important role. Adults, caregivers, and teachers can help their preschoolers take initiative, thereby reducing the chances of guilt in a number of ways. Some of these ways are as follows:

- Expect preschoolers to exhibit never-ending curiosity, talk often and loudly, and move all the time. Caregivers need to encourage these qualities in children. Children develop initiative when they ask questions, experiment, and explore.
- Understand that preschoolers' initiatives can sometimes lead them to actions that are dangerous, beyond their abilities, or inappropriate.
- Give children some freedom to try, especially in play activities. Children learn more by their own attempts than by having adults perform actions for them or tell them what to do. Adults should model how to do certain tasks and give ample time for children to practice.
- Use positive statements to acknowledge children when they take initiative. For example, adults can say, "It was *nice* of you to be so *loving* toward your baby sister." Caregiver might also say, "You were showing *kindness* when you shared your toys. *Kindness* makes people want to be your friend." In every case, caregivers should use adjectives to refer to a specific case. It is best not to overgeneralize, such as saying, "You are *always* nice, loving, and kind." Case descriptions refine preschool children's self-images and promote feelings of self-esteem.
- Set limits to help preschoolers develop appropriate initiative. During the preschool years, adults and caregivers are in Galinsky's *authority stage* of parenting. Too much or too little guidance will weaken preschoolers' abilities to discover and foster appropriate initiative. (You can review Galinsky's parenting stages in Figure 4.4 of the text.)

Balancing Initiative with Limits

While preschool children want to take initiative and explore, adults and caregivers need to set limits to help children develop initiative and keep them safe (**Figure 16.16**). Preschool children define themselves in terms of what they can do, and to find out what they can do, children try many activities.

Because preschoolers lack inhibitory control, they do many things on impulse without thinking about the results of their actions. Preschool children may often go beyond their abilities and make mistakes. Because preschool children see almost everything as within their control, they often see these mistakes as a defeat. Too many mistakes may bring on guilt.

Although preschoolers can learn from both successes and mistakes, some mistakes are not safe or acceptable behaviors. Preschoolers need limits for safety purposes and to prepare them for the real world. Part of growing up is testing adult limits, and adults must accept that children will try some activities even when adults say "no." Some preschool children may decide the pleasure of doing something is worth the punishment received. Other children may dream up new activities not presently covered by the rules.

Preschool children should be given reasonable, spelled-out limits, and failure to obey should result in loving, yet firm, discipline. Caregivers and other adults need to communicate honestly when guiding and disciplining children. Being honest helps children build trusting relationships. It also helps children realize they should be truthful.

Anna Kuzmenko/Shutterstock.com

Figure 16.16 Limits, such as rules for riding trikes or other activities, keep children safe. *What other limits are important for children's safety?*

Children need to know that adults, too, make mistakes. Children learn this when they hear adults say, "Oops!" or "I'm sorry." In these situations, children begin to understand that all people make mistakes and that making mistakes does not make them bad.

Investigate Special Topics

Helping Children Who Are Shy and Introverted

Some preschoolers may have difficulty making friends due to shyness or introversion. Shyness and introversion are different. Children who are *shy* desire to join groups of children but are not sure how to do so. These children may avoid other people's gazes and appear both physically and verbally hesitant to join conversations and activities. Shyness is caused by temperamental differences among children, lessons a child has learned from their cultural background or family environment, and new and overwhelming social encounters.

Unlike children who are shy, children who are *introverted* are content on their own or with just one or two friends. These children do not have social anxiety. They often have excellent social skills but may feel drained emotionally after prolonged contact with people.

Children who are shy can be helped to overcome their shyness, although they are unlikely to become intensely social. On the other hand, introversion is a personality trait inherent in some children. Trying to change a child's introversion may cause stress and lowered self-esteem. Constant stress and low self-worth can eventually lead to mental health issues. Instead, adults can teach introverts coping strategies for social encounters.

Following are some suggestions for helping preschoolers who are shy and introverted:

Shy

- Have realistic expectations for the child. A shy child rarely becomes the leader of a group.
- Gradually expose the child to new people and novel situations.
- Invite two or three children for play. If only one child is invited, the shy child may feel forced to interact with this child.

- Help the child prepare for new situations by explaining to the child who will be there and what will happen. Role-playing social skills and staying close to the child may also help.
- Allow autonomy.
- Build self-esteem by affirming the child's strengths.

Introverted

- Set aside quiet time before going to a highly social activity and leave early if possible.
- Allow the child to watch from the sidelines and get used to activity and noise.
- Do not overschedule the child.
- Do not allow extroverts to take over conversations and exclude the introvert or supply answers for the introvert.
- Do not allow siblings or peers to make an introverted child a scapegoat for their unacceptable behaviors.
- Find private spaces for the introvert to re-energize.
- Invite just one other child for play.

Research Activity

Strategies for engaging shy and introverted children are widely discussed in childhood education circles. Talking with and including these children can be a challenge for many teachers. In small groups, research strategies for engaging shy and introverted children and "getting them to talk." Choose four or five of these strategies and then deliver a short presentation explaining them and assessing whether they are effective.

Photo: Tom Wang/Shutterstock.com

16.2-2 Helping Preschoolers Develop Social Relations

During the preschool years, children's social worlds extend beyond their caregivers to include other family members and many other adults, such as teachers, friends, and their caregivers' friends. Adults and caregivers can begin to teach preschool children how to interact with others and how to behave in socially acceptable ways. Adults can help preschool children extend their social relations by making time for friendships, fostering altruistic behaviors, reducing conflicts, and teaching manners.

Making Time for Friendships

Friendships become very important to most preschoolers and are a way for children to learn from others. Unlike adults, friends and sometimes siblings treat children as equals. A preschool child's friends will not always give them special favors like a caregiver or other adults would. For example, a child will not always be given the first turn when playing with friends.

Living in a social world involves preschoolers' balancing of *self-assertion* (doing as one chooses rather than what others want) and **cooperation** (the action of helping or working with someone). Friendships with peers help preschool children see the differences in people, and friction, which almost always occurs in play groups, shows children how others see issues differently.

Preschoolers want and need friends. To preschoolers, friends are resources for social play. The preschool period is often called "the play years."

Friendships differ from family relationships in that friendships are formed due to mutual choice. Unlike adult-child relationships, peers interact on an **egalitarian** (belief that all people are equal) basis; that is, children have the same status and authority in the friendship. Because children's friends are often age-mates, too, they are similar developmentally.

Adults can foster preschoolers' friendships in certain ways. Adults can help preschoolers form friendships by giving them both opportunity and time to play with peers. These peers may be neighborhood playmates, children from a preschooler's child care and education program, children in a special interest group (such as swimming or dance classes), or children in a house of worship. Sometimes, peers are introduced through the friendships of caregivers.

Although adults cannot make friends for their preschoolers, they need to teach preschoolers that to have friends, they must be friends. To do this, adults must teach friendship skills—cooperating, sharing, and turn-taking. Adults must explain why trying to gain power by aggression never works. With adult guidance over time, preschoolers move beyond self-focus, become more social, and develop feelings of belonging to a group of friends.

Fostering Altruistic Behaviors

In peer groups, children also witness actions that show concern for others, or **altruistic behaviors**. **Altruism** (ALL-troo-ih-zuhm), a desire to help others, develops as young children sense the needs and wants of others. While helping behaviors may be carried out for some type of reward (concrete or social), altruism is carried out without any expectation of a reward except possibly **self-reward** (a person's good feelings about their actions). Adults can increase the likelihood of a preschooler using altruistic behaviors by

- being a model of kindness
- using supportive rather than punishing discipline to help the child develop moral reasoning skills
- helping children "read" others' emotions
- pointing out the consequences of negative actions
- being supportive of the person who is harmed rather than giving attention to the aggressor
- choosing children's media that is healthy and **prosocial** (encouraging of kind behaviors)
- allowing children to help with projects for those in need or to give some of their money to charity
- acknowledging children for their altruistic behaviors

Reducing Conflicts

Most preschool children's conflicts are disputes about toys or an area of play. Adults should allow children to interact with each other and should not interfere with minor conflicts (except for safety reasons). Adults can reduce conflicts between preschoolers in the following ways:

- Do not make children share any more than an adult would be expected to share. Sometimes adults expect children to share all their toys, even with casual friends. Adults are not expected to share all their belongings, even with close friends.
- Resolve conflicts for younger preschoolers (**Figure 16.17**). To do this, explain the feelings of both children. Often, this will diffuse the conflict.
- Show older preschoolers how to resolve their own conflicts. Adults can teach children conflict-resolution skills, such as asking another child to return a toy, playing with another toy, or asking to take turns with a toy.
- Teach children how to stand up for themselves without being aggressive. Teach children to communicate clearly with statements such as, "Stop hitting me!" or "I do not want to do that."
- Model concern for the hurt child instead of shaming the child who has done wrong.

Children learn more when adults show real concern for the hurt or wronged child while ignoring the child who was in the wrong. Aggressors see that care is given to children who are harmed.

- Teach children to get adult help if needed.

As preschoolers' social worlds extend, they may also start engaging in **tattling behaviors** (behaviors that seek to get another child in trouble by telling adults or other children about something a child has done). To deter tattling behaviors, adults can explain to children when it is appropriate to tell an adult, such as when fighting occurs or someone is hurt. In other cases, when a child tattles, the adult might say to the tattler, "I will worry about that. This is not your job." Then, the adult can deal with the situation when the tattler is not listening; otherwise, tattling will be reinforced.

Teaching Manners

Older preschoolers can begin to learn that everyone likes being treated with good manners. They can also learn appropriate manners for their culture. To teach children manners, adults can make sure to always live by the manners they want to instill. They can explain that manners are a way to be nice to other people and give reasons for using any specific manners they decide to teach. Examples of basic manners adults teach preschoolers include saying "please," "thank you," and "you're welcome"; not interrupting others who are talking; chewing with their mouths closed; and not grabbing food (**Figure 16.18**).

Kenishirotie/ Shutterstock.com

Figure 16.17 In helping children resolve conflicts, adults can explain situations, such as by saying, "Maria needs to play with the shapes for a little while, but when she's finished playing, she will let you know." *What are other ways adults can explain conflicts about sharing?*

MBI/Shutterstock.com

Figure 16.18 Teaching table manners while at the table is often effective. *Why is this a good place for teaching table manners? What other places are good for teaching manners?*

Adults can also explain to preschoolers what good manners are *not*. They can explain that rude remarks and name-calling are always inappropriate. This may be difficult for young children to understand because some rude comments might be true and children are taught that lies are wrong. For example, a child might make a comment about someone who has a disability. In this situation, the adult can apologize for the child and then explain to the preschooler in private why the comment was hurtful.

Guiding Preschoolers' Emotions

Emotions are intense in the preschool years. The growing minds of preschool children not only broaden their emotions, but also help children control how they express their emotions. While preschool children and even adults cannot control their feelings, they can learn to control how they *express* these feelings. When preschoolers express intense emotions, adults should affirm their emotions and address their concerns. For example, a caregiver might say, "I understand why you are angry. I am so sorry your daddy and I could not work out our problems. I can tell you that we will always love you and make sure you are cared for and loved." Adults can also help preschoolers control how they express emotions in the following ways:

- *Expose children to positive examples.* Children imitate how adults do or do not control their emotions. They also imitate the emotional expressions of other children and people seen in television programs or movies.
- *Help children label their emotions.* As preschoolers' language abilities expand, they are more able to name and verbally express their emotions. When emotions are labeled, preschool children can name their emotions to others and often solve or prevent conflicts with peers.
- *Explain that feeling emotions is all right.* Children need to know that it is okay to feel sad, angry, hurt, or happy. They need to know that adults feel and express these emotions, too.
- *Tell children it is okay to express some emotions.* Repressing emotions is unhealthy for children and adults. Children need to

know that it is all right to cry when sad or laugh when happy.
- *Insist that aggression is not an acceptable way to handle anger.* Children need to learn that people must not hurt others, even when they are wronged. Adults can explain this to children by naming the consequences of aggression, such as by saying that hitting hurts people or name-calling makes others feel sad.
- *Talk about how all people must work to control their feelings.* Children need to know they are not alone in trying to control their feelings. Adults can talk about times they have to control their feelings and can help preschoolers read books about feelings. There are many good preschool books on this topic (**Figure 16.19**).

Figure 16.19 Preschool Books on Emotions

- Albee, S. *Sesame Street All About Feelings— My First Manners* 2006
- Bloom, S. *What About Bear?* 2010
- Bowman, C. *Little David and His Best Friend* 2010
- Cain, J. *The Way I Feel* 2008
- Curtis, J. L. *Today I Feel Silly & Other Moods That Make My Day* 2007
- Dewdney, A. *Llama Llama Mad at Mama* 2007
- Finn, C. *Manners on the Playground* 2007
- Graham, B. *"Let's Get a Pup," Said Kate* 2001
- Keats, E. J. *The Snowy Day* 1963
- Mayer, M. *I Was So Mad* 2000
- Mayer, M *All By Myself* 2001
- Offill, J. *17 Things I'm Not Allowed to Do Anymore* 2006
- Shuman, C. *Jenny Is Scared: When Something Happens in the World* 2003
- VanHout, M. *Happy* 2012
- Viorst, J. *Alexander and the Terrible, Horrible, No Good, Very Bad Day* 1987
- Wilhelm, H. *I'll Always Love You* 1988
- Willard, C and O'Leary, W. *Breathing Makes it Better: A Book for Sad Days, Mad Days, Glad Days, and all the Feelings In-Between* 2019

Goodheart-Willcox Publisher

Love and Dependency

When preschoolers express love and dependency, knowing when and how to help them can be difficult. Some children will seek help from adults even when they do not need it. Other children are unable to handle some tasks on their own, but do not want the help adults offer. Adults can help preschoolers by finding a balance between helping and not helping preschoolers with tasks.

Adults can help preschoolers by loving and respecting them. This gives children a secure base from which to try tasks on their own. When children ask for help, adults should be willing to help, but adults should also judge how much help children need. Physically arranging the house in helpful ways can make tasks more manageable for children, and adults should plan tasks for preschoolers that are within their abilities. Children need encouragement when they try tasks on their own. This positive reinforcement will acknowledge children's attempts and help them take pride in their achievements.

Fear and Anxiety

Some fears and anxieties help protect children and urge them to stay safe. Too many fears and anxieties, however, may be harmful. Adults can help preschoolers keep fear and anxiety in check by accepting the expressed fears and anxieties of children and never making fun of them. They can help children feel secure by assuring children they will be kept safe and never threatening them, even in a playful way. Adults can help children face fear by modeling courage and handling a child's fears one at a time. Adults can remind children of the reasons they need not be afraid and can urge children to take small steps in dealing with fears, such as watching from a safe location or drawing one's fear. Lastly, adults should consult a doctor if children's fears seem too prolonged or intense. Sometimes, intense fears can indicate emotional or behavioral problems in children and professional help may be needed.

Focus on Careers

Preschool Teacher

Preschool teachers educate and care for children under five years of age who are not yet in kindergarten. They teach social, language, and motor skills in public and private schools and child care centers. They work in public and private schools, summer camps, parks and recreation centers, youth organizations, and community programs. Preschool teachers organize activities, develop schedules, and watch for signs of emotional or developmental problems in children.

Career cluster: Education and training.

Education: Preschool teachers need a Child Development Associate (CDA) credential or a bachelor's degree.

Job outlook: Future employment opportunities for preschool teachers are expected to grow faster than the average for all occupations.

To learn more about a career as a preschool teacher, visit the United States Department of Labor's *Occupational Outlook Handbook* website. You will also be able to compare the job responsibilities, educational requirements, job outlook, and average pay of preschool teachers with similar occupations.

Photo: MBI/Shutterstock.com

Anger and Aggression

Handling preschoolers' anger and aggression is not only draining, but often stirs up angry feelings in adults. Adults should note the difference between *anger* (a feeling caused by frustration) and *aggression* (an attempt to hurt someone). While it is natural that children feel anger, adults need to help children manage anger in ways other than aggression. One of the first steps in handling preschoolers' anger is to look for reasons the preschooler feels angry. Do they want attention? Are they frustrated in reaching a goal? Are they looking for revenge? Understanding motives makes finding ways to manage anger easier (**Figure 16.20**).

Children are more likely to act aggressively when they see aggression modeled by adults, peers, or people and characters in television programs, films, or other types of media. Even letting a child hit a pillow or kick a tree trunk communicates that aggression is acceptable. Instead, adults should teach children it is all right to feel angry, but that acts of anger must be controlled.

Society tries to teach that, instead of being aggressive, people should be **assertive** (able to speak out, stand up for one's rights, and defend oneself). Finding the line between assertiveness and aggression can be difficult for preschool children, and even for adults, at times. Because of this, preschoolers may act in an aggressive way when they are trying to be assertive.

When children do need to be corrected for aggressive acts, adults should use nonphysical methods of discipline. Studies show that punishment by aggression, such as spanking, increases aggression in preschool children, especially if these punishments are given in response to a child's aggressive acts. Spanking increases children's feelings of anger and **elicits** (calls forth) a negative, aggressive response from the child. Instead of physical punishments, parents and caregivers can discipline children with time-outs or losses of privileges.

Figure 16.20 Ways to Help Preschoolers Manage Anger

Direct preschoolers' energy levels appropriately. When preschoolers spend too much time in quiet activities, they begin to squirm with pent-up energy. Physical play can release some of this energy in more constructive ways than possibly aggravating another child. Conversely, when preschoolers are *overexuberant* (wound-up), they tend to engage in rowdy, physical play that can easily cross-the-line into anger and aggressive acts. Except for resting and sleeping times, make certain preschoolers are not sedentary for more than 60 minutes at a time. When sedentary, preschoolers can engage their brains through reading or fine-motor activities. Excited preschoolers should have a 30-minute wind-down time.

Reduce competitive situations between peers. Competition can be reduced by supplying plenty of toys so that children do not have to wait too long for a turn. If games become aggressive, adults should step in to de-escalate the situation.

Watch peer play groups closely. Often, adults can stop aggression before it occurs by providing a calming touch or encouraging the child to release negative energy in other ways, such as deep breathing or singing.

Reinforce acceptable responses to anger. Acknowledging children for not using aggression will encourage them to express anger in other ways in the future.

Goodheart-Willcox Publisher

japansainlook/Shutterstock.com

Jealousy

Jealousy is common among preschoolers and often leads to anger. In fact, most preschoolers label *jealousy* as being "mad." Learning to tame jealousy is a lifelong process, but the preschool years are the best time to begin helping children control this powerful emotion. Two common sources of jealousy over the preschool years are siblings and friends. Adults can help children control jealousy in both contexts.

Jealousy over Siblings

Preschoolers may be jealous over the attention given to a new baby or other sibling. These feelings occur because preschoolers may think adults love these siblings more than them. Adults can help preschoolers accept their siblings in the following ways:

- Describe what care the sibling requires in a realistic way, including the work involved and other facts. Unlike toddlers, preschool children are better able to understand their caregivers' explanations.
- Spend time alone with the preschooler. This is the best way to say, "I love you."
- Allow the preschooler to help with the new baby or younger sibling (**Figure 16.21**).

twinsterphoto/iStock via Getty Images Plus

Figure 16.21 Allowing preschoolers to help with younger siblings can reduce feelings of jealousy. *What are some ways preschoolers can help with their younger siblings?*

Then thank the preschooler for their help. Preschoolers can feel important by helping with a sibling.

- Expect a preschooler to show some regressive behaviors. It is natural for preschoolers to wish for the attention given to another sibling. Preschoolers enjoy being told or shown with photos how they were once cared for in the same ways.

Jealousy Among Friends

Because preschoolers learn about themselves by comparing themselves with friends, even minor inequalities among friends can seem important. Love, attention, and material goods are all coveted by preschoolers.

To help preschoolers cope with jealousy among friends, adults and caregivers can talk with their children to explain acceptable ways of expressing jealousy. Jealousy may still bubble up and cause the child to be sullen or aggressive. In these situations, adults should validate children's jealous feelings, but should not **placate** (calm; soothe) children by giving in to jealous wishes. Instead, adults can give preschoolers plenty of love and attention and lessen the insecurity that often breeds jealousy.

Repressed Jealousy

Even preschoolers who do not act jealous may be experiencing *repressed jealousy*. Adults, caregivers, and teachers should note any symptoms of repressed jealousy and keep in mind that the continued repression of jealousy can have negative side effects on preschoolers' social-emotional health. When a preschooler has repressed jealousy, adults should find ways to make the child feel special, whether by spending time alone with the preschooler or bringing the preschooler a thoughtful gift.

16.2-3 Helping Preschoolers Cope with Stress

As with all behaviors, preschoolers learn to handle stress by witnessing others' examples.

Caregivers and other adults should take care to model healthy ways of coping with stress (**Figure 16.22**). Adults experiencing overwhelming stress or mental health issues should seek professional help for themselves and their children.

To reduce preschoolers' stress, adults can provide an environment of consistency and predictability and can make sure to give preschoolers personal space and some "alone time." However, overparenting, by overprotecting, is not a good way to reduce stress because the child never learns coping skills.

Adults can alleviate stress in preschoolers by expressing unconditional love and maintaining a supportive relationship. A supportive relationship is the most protective aspect of development. Without it, children are vulnerable to stress for a lifetime.

Figure 16.22 Modeling Healthy Ways to Cope with Stress

Identify the source of the stress. Once stress can be pinpointed, it can be reduced. Encourage children to use language in identifying stressors. When stressed, tell the child, "I am stressed because I have a test tomorrow."

Find positive ways to encourage and distract one's self. Some of these ways might be going for a walk, exercising, talking with a friend, or reading a good book. Adults can invite children to do some of these activities with them.

Express emotions constructively. Adults should express their emotions, but not let their emotions get out-of-control. When children see adults talking or writing in a journal about their emotions, they are more likely to adopt these techniques later in life.

Avoid angry or frustrated outbursts. Children who see these outbursts will learn that outbursts are an acceptable way of dealing with stress.

Seek professional help, if needed. Adults should never feel ashamed in seeking help for stress or other emotional problems. If they feel overwhelmed or out of control, adults should get help and explain to children that it is never bad to ask for help.

Goodheart-Willcox Publisher

Lesson 16.2 Review and Assessment

1. Which is a realistic guideline for teaching preschoolers how to show responsibility? (16.2.1)
   A. Agreeing to let the preschooler help with any task they choose
   B. Redoing a task the preschooler has completed incorrectly
   C. Making it clear to the preschooler that the task is not a game
   D. Giving the preschooler a chance to decide on some priorities

2. **True or False.** An example of modeling ambiguous gender role expectations is assuming boys prefer playing with balls and girls prefer playing with dolls. (16.2.1)

3. Which is the best way to teach preschoolers to handle their anger? (16.2.2)
   A. Allowing them to punch a pillow when they feel angry
   B. Demonstrating ways to be assertive instead of aggressive
   C. Teaching them that feeling angry is normal but needs to be controlled
   D. Using physical punishment to prevent future acts of aggression

4. **True or False.** The best way to handle a preschooler's jealousy among friends is to validate their jealous feelings but not placate them by giving in to jealous wishes. (16.2.2)

5. Which is the least effective way a caregiver can model healthy ways of coping with stress? (16.2.3)
   A. Encouraging children to use language to identify their stress
   B. Choosing a healthy distraction like going for a run
   C. Talking with another adult about the problem
   D. Releasing frustration in a quick outburst of emotion

Summary

Lesson 16.1

16.1-1 Preschool children develop more self-awareness as they learn to show responsibility, learn basic concepts about gender roles, develop morally, and expand their self-concept.

16.1-1 If preschoolers have too many failures or limits from adults, they may feel guilty and fear trying new things on their own.

16.1-2 Play is an essential developmental skill as it contributes to the cognitive, physical, social and emotional well-being of children.

16.1-2 Children between ages 3 and 6 are in Erikson's Initiative versus Guilt stage. Their initiative encourages them to try new activities, while failures may lead to guilt.

16.1-2 While preschool children are still dependent on adults, siblings and friends become more important to them. Creative, outgoing preschoolers often develop imaginary friends.

16.1-3 Preschoolers' emotions are becoming more complex. Most preschoolers show love and are still dependent on adults, especially for emotional support. Some fears and anxieties have disappeared, but others have surfaced.

16.1-4 Preschoolers feel anger but must learn not to express it through aggression. Preschoolers also experience jealousy.

16.1-4 Children achieve a number of social-emotional developmental milestones during the preschool years. Caregivers who are concerned about their child not meeting the milestones can talk to the child's doctor about possible developmental delays and ask for developmental screening.

16.1-5 Preschoolers are vulnerable to both developmental and environmental stress.

16.1-6 Because technology can have positive and negative impacts on children, caregivers must be mindful of how they use technology and its potential effects on their development.

16.1-6 The American Academy of Pediatrics recommends children under the age of 5 receive one hour or less each day of screen time.

Lesson 16.2

16.2-1 Adults can help children expand self-awareness by sharing responsibility, aiding gender roles, encouraging moral development, and promoting a healthy self-concept.

16.2-1 Adults, caregivers, and teachers can help preschoolers take initiative, thereby reducing the chances of guilt.

16.2-2 Adults should also help preschoolers expand their social worlds, especially friendships. This often involves making time for preschoolers' friendships, fostering altruistic behaviors, reducing conflicts, and teaching manners.

16.2-2 While preschool children cannot control their feelings, they can learn to control how they express these feelings, including fear and anxiety, anger and aggression, and jealousy.

16.2-2 When preschoolers feel jealousy, adults can help by giving them plenty of love and attention.

16.2-3 Preschoolers learn to handle stress by witnessing others' examples. Caregivers and other adults should model healthy ways of coping with stress.

College and Career Portfolio

Portfolio Personal Statement

Many portfolios require a *personal statement*, or a short essay describing why one wants to pursue a degree or job and what experiences have honed that vision. Whereas a cover letter focuses primarily on experience, a personal statement includes one's personal drive and interest in a career area.

- Write a personal statement for your intended college or career.
- Seek feedback from a career counselor, teacher, or staff member in the school writing center. Apply the feedback given and proofread your personal statement carefully.

Recall and Application

1. Which self-concept is based on one's physical features, gender, physical skills, possessions, and activities? (16.1.1)
   A. Self-definition
   B. Self-correction
   C. Self-recognition
   D. Self-esteem

2. **True or False.** Moral emotions, which are a person's reactions to acceptable and unacceptable behaviors, emerge first in children who are other-oriented. (16.1.1)

3. **True or False.** Children form their first real friendships around age 3. (16.1.2)

4. A child's ease at making friends depends on their _____. (16.1.2)
   A. dependence on adults
   B. relationship with siblings
   C. ability to follow group rules
   D. belief in an imaginary friend

5. Which is true about the way preschoolers express emotions? (16.1.3)
   A. They show greater attachment behaviors than toddlers.
   B. They know that physical aggression toward adults is unacceptable.
   C. They are unlikely to accept comfort from strangers.
   D. They experience more intense separation anxiety.

6. Four-year-olds commonly achieve which social-emotional developmental milestone? (16.1.4)
   A. Playing with one or two best friends and excluding others
   B. Protecting younger children
   C. Acting sorry for some action they realize is wrong
   D. Playing team roles in pretend play
7. Which is an example of an environmental stressor? (16.1.4)
   A. Developmental delay
   B. Poverty
   C. Fear-conditioning
   D. Episodic memory
8. **True or False.** One potential benefit associated with a preschooler's use of technology is that it helps improve their attention span and ability to focus. (16.1.5)
9. Adults can encourage preschoolers to take initiative while reducing the chance of guilt by _____. (16.2.1)
   A. giving them the freedom to experiment without setting limits
   B. establishing a timeframe during which they may ask questions
   C. using generalized positive statements like "You are always so helpful and nice"
   D. modeling how to do certain tasks and giving them ample time to practice
10. **True or False.** Children need to know that adults, too, make mistakes. (16.2.1)
11. **True or False.** Adults can help preschoolers control how they express emotions by teaching them not to cry in public. (16.2.2)
12. Adults can help preschoolers manage their anger by _____. (16.2.2)
    A. giving excited preschoolers a 10-minute wind-down time
    B. encouraging extended participation in quiet activities to keep them calm
    C. supplying plenty of toys to reduce competition among peers
    D. teaching them to speak out and stand up for their rights

13. **True or False.** To teach children manners, adults can make sure to always live by the manners they want to instill. (16.2.2)
14. **True or False.** Overprotecting children is a good way to reduce their stress. (16.2.3)

Critical Thinking

1. **Identify.** In small groups, identify examples of sexual stereotyping in children's movies or television. What are the most common forms of sexual stereotyping? How should caregivers protect children from this influence? Discuss your group's thoughts and ideas with the rest of the class.
2. **Make inferences.** Based on preschoolers' stage of moral development, how moral can adults expect preschool children to be? How do children's conceptions of morality influence how they should be treated by adults?
3. **Compare and contrast.** Compare and contrast children's interactions with adults in the preschool years and in the infant and toddler years. How do these interactions change when children enter the preschool years? How should adults interpret these changes?
4. **Cause and effect.** Research has shown that imaginary friends do not signal psychological problems in children. Rather, they are beneficial as children learn to interact with their worlds. How do you think interactions with imaginary friends affect children's interactions with adults and other children? How important are imaginary friends for social development?
5. **Analyze.** Analyze the importance of altruistic behaviors in children's lives and futures. How important is it that adults teach children these behaviors? What are the most effective ways adults teach them?
6. **Draw conclusions.** Why is it important to encourage a child to label and discuss their feelings? What could be the effects if a child were never taught to do this?

7. **Determine.** Consider the fears and anxieties you had as a child. What caused these fears and anxieties? How did the adults in your life help you express and cope with fear or anxiety? If you met a child who had the same fear or anxiety, describe two ways you would encourage or help that child.

8. **Evaluate.** In small groups, list five ways that you have seen adults try to teach preschool children manners. The adults' methods should vary in effectiveness. Discuss these methods and evaluate which are healthy and which are not. Finally, present these methods to the class and ask them to evaluate the methods' effectiveness.

Core Skills

1. **Art.** Review the aspects of self-concept discussed in the first lesson of this chapter. Then, using art supplies or a graphics editing software, create visual representations for each of these aspects. Present your illustrations to the class and be prepared to explain your creative decisions.

2. **Research and speaking.** With a partner, research the history of gender roles in the United States and in one other country. While researching, take notes about what roles people filled and how those gender roles were taught to children. Discuss current gender roles in both countries and how those ideas are transmitted to children. Finally, deliver a presentation summarizing your research and discussing how children learn gender roles.

3. **Writing.** Interview a teacher of preschool children and ask this person to give examples of ways in which the preschool's indoor and outdoor spaces, equipment, and materials aid social-emotional development. How do these factors encourage children to take initiative and show responsibility without experiencing guilt? After the interview, write a two- to three-page report reflecting on the teacher's answers. Check your report for correct spelling, grammar, and punctuation.

4. **Math.** In small groups, make a list of 10 behaviors that you would classify as *angry* and 10 behaviors that you would classify as *aggressive*. Discuss these behaviors with your teacher to ensure accuracy and then conduct a survey asking classmates and other people to identify the angry and aggressive behaviors. Calculate what percentage of people classified the behaviors correctly. Discuss your findings with your group, including how society's views of anger and aggression affect what children learn.

5. **Art.** Review Figure 16.8, which lists the social-emotional developmental milestones for preschoolers. Then, create a visual representation of each age range, including as many milestones as you can. Once you are done, place your visual representations on separate desks or on the walls. As a class, walk around the room and identify which age range each visual representation is illustrating. Afterward, share your answers as a class.

6. **Reading and writing.** Find a children's book that discusses a preschool child taking initiative. Read the book, taking notes about ways in which the child expresses initiative and how love and dependency factor into the child's decisions. Finally, rewrite the story from an adult's perspective observing the child. How does the adult interpret the child's initiative? How should the adult balance initiative with limits?

7. **Listening and speaking.** In small groups, interview a caregiver of a preschooler and ask them to describe a time when their preschooler was stressed, as well as how they handled the situation. Then, as a group, discuss the scenario the caregiver described and identify two other ways the situation could have been handled—one more healthy way and one less healthy way. Role-play and film each of these scenarios and then play them for the class. Ask the class to identify which scenario is the least healthy, the healthiest, and the real scenario described.

8. **CTE Career Readiness Practice.** Imagine you are a child care worker and that you are holding an open house for caregivers of your preschoolers. During the open house, one of the preschoolers throws a handful of crayons, and their caregiver responds in loud voices, threatening to spank them. You are concerned because this is a shaming technique (a negative public reaction and a threat of corporal punishment), but you know that there are cultural differences that inform these caregivers behaviors. You have parent-teacher conferences next week, so you begin to plan what you will say about discipline. In preparation, write a script for yourself and include answers to questions the caregivers might ask. Then, role-play the conversation with a classmate until you feel prepared.

Observations

1. Visit a preschool center and observe the children playing. Take note especially of any conflicts that occur between friends. When taking notes, try to identify the source of the conflict and then observe how a child care worker does or does not intervene to reduce the conflict. If the child care worker did intervene, what strategies did they use? If not, why not?

2. Interview a caregiver or teacher about situations in which preschool children act out of jealousy. During the interview, ask for two to three specific examples and take notes about them. Write a narrative describing one of the examples and then exchange narratives with a classmate. Read the narrative you received and make observations about the type of jealousy the child experienced and how the jealousy was handled.

Unit 6 | The School-Age and Adolescent Years

Role-Play or Interview

EVENT PREP

Some competitive events for CTSOs require entrants to complete a role-play or interview. Participants will receive information about situation or topic and time to practice the event. A judge or panel of judges will review the presentations or conduct the interviews. To prepare for the role-play or interview event, complete the following activities:

1. Read and analyze the guidelines your organization provides for this event.
2. Visit the organization's website to look for previous role-play interview events to use in practicing for future competitions. (Many times, organizations also post online videos of top performers in their competitive events.) In addition, locate the evaluation criteria or rubric for this event to help you determine what the judges will look for in your presentation.
3. Practice speaking in front of a mirror. Are you comfortable speaking without directly reading your notes? Do your eye contact, facial expressions, and gestures convey the same message as your words?
4. Ask a friend to practice your role-play or interview with you as your instructor takes the role of competition judge. Give special attention to your posture and how you present yourself. Concentrate on your tone of voice—it should be pleasant and loud enough to hear without shouting. Make eye contact with the listener to engage the person's attention.
5. After making the presentation, ask for constructive feedback from your instructor. Implement any necessary changes and keep practicing.

Chapter 17

Physical Development of School-Age Children and Adolescents

Essential Question

Why do prepubescent school-age children and adolescents appear to be marking time in terms of their physical growth and development, and how can parents ensure optimal development?

Case Study   How Might Parents Approach the Topic of Precocious Puberty with Their Child?

As a class, read the case study and discuss the questions that follow. After you finish studying the chapter, discuss this case study again. Have your opinions changed based on what you learned?

When Valencia went swimsuit shopping along with her second-grade daughter, she was shocked to see that Antonia was developing breasts and growing dark hair under her arms at age seven. Valencia noticed that Antonia was shooting up in height lately but had attributed this to a growth spurt. Now she wasn't so sure.

Valencia made an appointment with Antonia's pediatrician, who ran some tests and said that Antonia has a type of precocious puberty and should see a pediatric endocrinologist. The specialist diagnosed Antonia with central precocious puberty (CPP) and prescribed monthly injections of medication in hopes of delaying further development until Antonia reaches a normal age for puberty to begin. The pediatric endocrinologist also told Valencia that, because of the CPP, her daughter may be shorter than average as an adult, but the drug may help with this and other problems.

This news upset Valencia. Because her daughter is only seven, Valencia hadn't discussed puberty with her, and the school did not cover this topic until fourth or fifth grade. Now, she is concerned about discussing puberty and the CPP diagnosis with Antonia. Valencia doesn't want Antonia to feel like the "odd one out" at school and doesn't want her to grow up too quickly.

Give It Some Thought

1. How do you think Valencia should explain puberty and CPP to Antonia? What might be Antonia's reactions now and in the future?
2. What are some ways in which Antonia's family can help her remain a little girl for several more years?
3. Should Antonia's caregivers and other adults encourage the school to give lessons on puberty at the second-grade level or even before? Why or why not?

Growth and Development of School-Age Children and Adolescents

Key Terms

flexibility
growth pains
growth spurt
permanent teeth
precision
puberty
six-year molars

Learning Outcomes

After studying this lesson, you will be able to

17.1-1 **describe** brain development, organ maturation, skeletal growth, and the process of puberty during the school-age and adolescent years.

17.1-2 **summarize** major changes in motor development during the school-age and adolescent years and give examples of physical developmental milestones school-age children and adolescents might achieve.

Reading and Notetaking Activity

Before reading, skim the headings in the chapter. List the headings to create an outline for taking notes during reading and class discussions. Under each heading, list any key terms. Write two questions you expect to have answered in class. After completing this chapter, ask your teacher any questions you still have about the concepts or terms you learned.

Introduction

School-age children, children between 6 and 12 years of age, are in a period of development known as middle childhood. Children between 13 and 18 years of age are in a period of development known as adolescence, or late childhood. Many physical changes occur during these periods because all of a child's body systems are maturing. The growth rate is rather obscure due to slow and consistent growth and changes in the body proportions. Between 6 and 11 years of age, however, children grow about 2.5 inches a year in height and double their weight. Children born biologically female, who grow a little faster than children born biologically male, reach about 90 percent of their adult height by age 10 or 11 years; males achieve about 80 percent of their adult height by 11 years of age. Overall, until the last two years of middle childhood, this is a period of physical calm.

Averages, however, obscure the wide individual differences in height, weight, and body proportions. If you look at children in the fifth or sixth grades, some children still look like children while others are beginning to look more like teens.

Due to increases in muscle growth and strength and increased myelination in the central nervous system, both children's gross- and fine-motor skills improve to a marked degree. This improvement is often referred to as the "hallmark" of middle childhood. Unless hampered by inadequate nutrition and lack of activity, most school-age children and teens excel in gross-motor skills. Their movements show an ease and grace due to strength and coordination. School-age children and teens become skillful at fine-motor skills, too, such as model building and other crafts, playing musical instruments, and handwriting. Some of these changes may seem awkward to children as they occur, but all changes help them become more coordinated.

17.1-1 Maturation of Organs

With the coming of the school-age years, brain growth slows dramatically. After the preschool years, head circumference only increases one-half inch every five years until maturity. The brain, which reached 90 percent of its adult weight during the preschool years, grows to reach 95 percent of its adult weight by 10 years of age. Instead of growing rapidly, the brain becomes more specialized during the school-age years. Specific areas of the brain coordinate specific tasks. By this time, the brain has established a visual center for processing visual stimuli, a speech center for comprehending speech, and so on. From the school-age years onward, rewiring in the brain is difficult. Brain connections will continue to be made at a rapid pace until about eight years of age. These connections, as well as increased myelination, allow for better memory capacity, language and literacy development, focus and motivation, problem-solving skills, and emotional control.

Besides the brain, other organs continue to mature. The heart grows slowly, and while it does become more efficient at pumping blood,

it is small in relationship to the rest of the body. Too much strain on the heart during this period is dangerous. Blood pressure increases in school-age children and is about the same for both sexes.

Children's lungs continue to grow until eight years of age and breathing becomes less abdominal and more efficient. School-age children's *respiratory rate* (number of breaths per minute) decreases, and children lose less oxygen to exhalation.

As the gastrointestinal system matures, school-age children have fewer stomach upsets, steadier blood sugar levels, and greater stomach capacities than in the preschool years. Bowel and bladder control are usually firmly established.

Children's senses also improve during the school-age years. As the eyes mature, binocular vision is established by 6 years of age and acuity established between 7 and 11 years of age. Auditory (hearing) sensitivity improves until 10 years of age and then declines to adult levels. Maximum hearing sensitivity is established first for mid-range, second for high-range, and last for low-range tones.

During the later school-age years, children begin to enter puberty. **Puberty** is the process by which the body becomes capable of reproduction. Puberty begins in the brain, where the *hypothalamus* (section of the brain responsible for hormone production as well as other functions) releases *GnRH*, gonadotropin (GOH-nad-oh-TROH-puhn) releasing hormone, into the endocrine system. GnRH causes the brain's *pituitary gland* to release two more hormones, *follicle-stimulating hormone* and *luteinizing* (LOO-tee-uh-NY-zing) *hormone*. These hormones cause the ovaries in biological females and the testicles in biological males to produce *sex hormones* (estrogen and testosterone, respectively), which are needed for puberty changes in females and males. Physical changes in **pubescent** (being in puberty) children occur over a period of years (**Figure 17.1**). *Sexual maturity* occurs when females ovulate and when males produce enough sperm for reproduction. The arrival of sexual maturity is signaled by the **menarche** (men-AR-kee), the first menstrual cycle, in females, and by **spermarche** (SPERM-ar-kee), the first ejaculation, in males. After these events, reproductive organs must continue to mature another 12 to 18 months before reproduction can occur.

Figure 17.1 Puberty Changes

Change	Years of Age Girls	Years of Age Boys
Hypothalamus triggers surge of hormones.	8	11
Growth spurt begins.	10½	12½
Growth spurt peaks.	12	14
Growth spurt ends.	16	18
Secondary sex characteristics (visible body changes that distinguish males and females; not directly related to reproduction) develop.	8–14	10–15
Primary sex characteristics (body changes directly related to reproduction) develop.	9–16 average 12½	11–17 average 13½

Goodheart-Willcox Publisher

Focus on
Science

Circulatory System

The heart, a striated muscle, is about the size of a clenched fist. It is located between the lungs in the chest cavity.

Parts of the Heart

The heart has four *chambers*. The two top chambers are called *atria* (RA, right atrium, and LA, left atrium). The two chambers on the bottom are called *ventricles* (RV and LV). The atria pump blood to the ventricles, which then push blood out of the heart. This is felt as pulse.

Each chamber has door-like valves that keep blood flowing forward and prevent backflow. Between the RA and RV is the *tricuspid valve*, and between the LA and the LV is the *mitral valve*. The *pulmonary valve* on the right side and the *aortic valve* on the left side of the heart shut blood out of the heart. As the valves close, a *lub-dub* sound is heard through a stethoscope.

How the Heart Functions

The heart's function is to circulate blood. Blood delivers oxygen to the cells and brings back carbon dioxide and other waste products to the heart. To do this, the blood follows a particular path in and out of the heart. Deoxygenated blood enters the RA and

Heart Anatomy

Right atrium

Left atrium

Left ventricle

Right ventricle

okili77/Shutterstock.com

is pumped to the RV, where it is then pumped to the lungs. The lungs remove waste products when exhaling and intake fresh oxygen when inhaling. Oxygen-rich blood flows into the LA and is pumped into the LV and then out of the heart to the body. The blood flow through the heart is coordinated; when the ventricles contract, the atria refill.

Photo: otnaydur/Shutterstock.com

Skeletal Growth

Children continue to grow slowly and steadily during the early school-age years. In the late school-age years, some children begin a **growth spurt**, a period of rapid growth that **heralds** (signals the beginning of something) pubescence. Other children will experience a growth spurt in adolescence. During these years, body proportions in children change. Children's teeth and jaws grow, and additional changes occur in fat and muscles.

Height and Weight

School-age children's height increases more steadily than their weight. This is because, for the most part, genes determine height. Unlike weight, height is not easily affected by the environment, unless by long-term conditions, such as *malnutrition* or certain illnesses.

Weight increases somewhat parallel to height. Taller children tend to weigh more, and shorter children tend to weigh less. Children's environments also influence their weight because of factors such as nutrition, illness, activity level, and stress.

Biological males are generally taller and heavier than biological females until 10 or 11 years of age (**Figure 17.2**). At this time, most females experience a growth spurt and become taller than males. School-age children are often sensitive to these size differences, especially if they are becoming interested in the opposite gender. The average size difference between school-age males and females is only about one inch at 12 years of age. Most males catch up in size during the early teen years.

Figure 17.2 Average Height and Weight from 6 to 8 Years of Age

Years of Age	Height in Inches Boys	Height in Inches Girls	Weight in Pounds Boys	Weight in Pounds Girls
6	45¾	45	45½	43
7	48	47½	50¼	48½
8	50	49¾	55¾	54¾
9	52	53	62	62¾
10	54¼	54½	69¼	71¾
11	55¾	57	77¾	81¼
12	59	60	90	92¼
13	61½	61⁷⁄₁₀	100	101
14	64½	62½	112	105
15	67	62⁹⁄₁₀	123½	115
16	68³⁄₁₀	64	134	118
17	69	64	142	120
18	69⅕	64⅕	147½	125

Goodheart-Willcox Publisher

Body Proportions

During middle childhood, children's body proportions become more similar to adult proportions. Children's waists and heads begin to look more in proportion to their bodies. The arms and legs grow longer, which gives children a lower center of gravity and better balance. The trunk grows until it is two times as long and two times as wide as it was at birth. Children's abdomens protrude even less than in the preschool years because of their longer trunks (**Figure 17.3**).

Bones and Teeth

The skeletal system continues to mature during the school-age years. Bones ossify and grow larger and longer. The most significant growth occurs in the teeth and jaw, leading to children having a more mature-looking face. School-age children are losing deciduous teeth. They are growing **permanent teeth** (teeth that are intended to last a lifetime; are harder and less sharp than deciduous teeth). Biological females often lose their deciduous teeth and grow permanent teeth before biological males do.

The first two deciduous teeth, often the bottom front teeth, fall out during the late preschool years, and the last of the 20 deciduous teeth (the cuspids) fall out around 12 years of age. The first permanent teeth to come in are **six-year molars** (large

teeth near the back of the jaw that come in around 6 years of age and are used for grinding food). Six-year molars do not replace any lost teeth; rather, they grow behind the second set of deciduous molars (**Figure 17.4**). Subsequent permanent teeth replace lost deciduous teeth. The growth of these permanent teeth changes the look of the lower part of the face in school-age children.

©Body Scientific International

Figure 17.4 Six-year molars grow behind the second set of deciduous molars. *How are permanent teeth different from deciduous teeth?*

A-C: Chase and Hayden Volkmar; D: Jack Hollingsworth/Photosdisc via Getty Images

Figure 17.3 As children grow, their body proportions develop and change to be more adult-like. *In what ways do children's body proportions become more adult-like during middle childhood?*

Precocious Puberty

Typical puberty occurs over a span of years, usually beginning in the late school-age or early teen years. Some children, however, may experience *precocious puberty*. Precocious puberty is the *precocious* (early) onset of puberty and is usually defined by breast development before eight years of age in biological females and by testicle development before nine years of age in biological males.

There are two types of precocious puberty. The first type, *central precocious puberty (CPP)*, begins, as typical puberty does, with the release of hormones in the brain and stimulation of sex hormones. This process is the same as the one described in Figure 17.1 but occurs much earlier than the norm. The second type, *peripheral precocious puberty (PPP)* is less common and is not always triggered in the brain. PPP occurs when sex hormones are released into the body earlier than the typical age, possibly due to problems with the ovaries, testicles, or adrenal glands. Unlike CPP, PPP affects only one or two puberty changes, such as breast or testicle development, but seldom menarche or spermarche.

Causes of Precocious Puberty

The causes of CPP and PPP are numerous. In about 90 percent of females and 50 percent of males, early puberty is considered *idiopathic* (having no known cause). In about 1 percent of females and 5 percent of males, precocious puberty is inherited. Some other risk factors for early puberty include the following:

- infections, head injuries, tumors, and other known medical problems
- high-fat diets
- obesity
- inactivity
- family breakups
- endocrine disruptors, such as fire retardants, plasticizers, pesticides, lead, mercury, nanomaterials, radon, and soy infant formulas
- exposure to estrogen or testosterone creams, ointments, sprays, or oral medications
- radiation treatments for cancers

Effects of Precocious Puberty

Because precocious puberty causes a child to enter the adolescent growth spurt early, they miss several years of regular skeletal growth. Soon after puberty, bone plates fuse. Thus, the child does not reach their genetic potential for height. Precocious puberty increases the risk for estrogen-dependent cancers of the breast and ovaries and can also lead to higher rates of type 2 diabetes, heart problems, and asthma. Social-emotional problems, including poor body image, depression, moodiness, aggression, sexual feelings and behaviors without emotional maturity, and a higher incidence of substance abuse, may also result from early puberty.

Treatments for Precocious Puberty

Pediatricians send suspected cases of early puberty to *pediatric endocrinologists* (doctors who specialize in treating hormone-related conditions in children) for diagnosis and treatment. Generally, only CPP is treated with a drug regimen. These drugs tell the pituitary to ignore GnRH signals, and within a year, stop the puberty process. Physical conditions seen in PPP are usually found and treated in other ways, such as the surgical removal of cysts or tumors.

Research Activity

In small groups, research stories about children who experience precocious puberty. How does precocious puberty affect their social-emotional lives? What are some ways that schools and educational programs are supporting families whose children are experiencing precocious puberty?

Photo: Tom Wang/Shutterstock.com

Fat and Muscle

Fat accounts for about 15 percent of an average school-age child's total body weight. Biological females have more fat than biological males at six years of age, but both accumulate fat at the same rate until puberty. Starting in puberty, females again accumulate fat at a higher rate than males.

Muscles increase in size and strength during middle childhood. Muscle strength doubles during these years, but children's strength is still immature compared to muscle strength in teens. Muscles also become more firmly attached to bones. Because the skeleton grows more quickly than the muscles, school-age children may have a loose-jointed, somewhat awkward look. Children of this age cannot completely keep their muscles from moving. This makes sitting completely still almost impossible.

School-age children and teens may complain of aches and pains. These muscle aches are called **growth pains**, which are caused by muscles trying to catch up with skeletal size. Using strength training or resistance training is a way to build and strengthen muscles. Teens may want to strength train to improve sports performance, treat or prevent injuries, or improve appearance. Strength training improves overall fitness, increases lean body mass (more muscle, less fat), burns more calories, makes bones stronger and can improve mental health. Many schools offer weight training in their gym classes.

17.1-2 Motor Development

The maturation of children's bodies during the school-age and teen years leads to refined motor development. School-age children often have a surplus of energy, which they use in practicing motor activities. Between 6 and 8 years of age, children generally enjoy active games that use their gross-motor skills. This is because children's large muscle coordination is more developed than their small muscle coordination. Children in this age range enjoy running, jumping, climbing, and playing simple games, such as tag and catch. Children between 9 and 12 years of age develop interests in more structured gross-motor activities, such as organized sports, skating, or bicycling. This is due

to children's increased mental abilities as well as improved large-muscle coordination.

Older school-age children and teens have highly developed fine-motor skills. Advances in fine-motor development help children do arts and crafts, build models, play musical instruments, dress themselves, use digital devices, write, and handle other tasks that require fine-motor precision (**Figure 17.5**). These skills seem to increase steadily into adolescence.

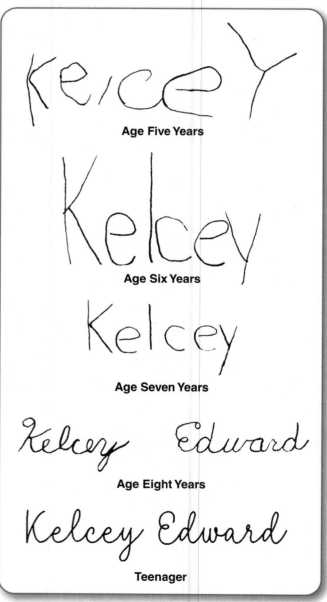

Figure 17.5 Fine-motor skills increase each year, as seen in writing samples. *What other skills improve as fine-motor skills develop?*

In the early part of middle childhood, biological males generally perform better than biological females in tasks requiring power, force, and speed. After females begin their growth spurt, however, they often equal or **surpass** (do better than) males of the same age in these tasks. School-age females tend to perform better than males in tasks requiring flexibility or rhythm. Experts do not know whether these motor differences between genders are due to genes or environment. Children who are highly skilled in one motor activity tend to also excel in others.

Motor skills improve during middle childhood and adolescence due to the following *physiological factors* (changes in physical attributes) (**Figure 17.6**):

- *Reaction time.* School-age children and teens have faster *reaction time* (the time required to respond to a stimulus, such as a thrown ball).
- *Precision.* School-age children and teens have improved **precision** (the ability to perform motor skills accurately). Precision is used in skills such as balancing, steadiness, and aim.
- *Speed and strength.* Children and teens have greater speed and improved strength during the school-age years.
- *Flexibility.* School-age children and teens have a great deal of **flexibility** (ability to move, bend, and stretch easily).

Physical Developmental Milestones

During the school-age and teen years, children grow to look more like adults. Some children begin experiencing puberty changes, as their reproductive organs mature. Children grow in height and weight, grow permanent teeth, and develop stronger muscles. Their gross- and fine-motor skills improve, and they are better able to perform structured and unstructured motor skills.

MBI/Shutterstock.com

Svitlana Bezuhlova/Shutterstock.com

Figure 17.6 Better reaction time and flexibility enable children to participate in more complex and competitive physical activities. *What are some examples of physical activities that require reaction time or flexibility?*

Figure 17.7 lists some physical developmental milestones for school-age children. Other physical changes for school-age children and adolescents include the sweat glands becoming more active and hormonal changes occurring that can cause acne. Caregivers need to work with children and teens on hygiene practices such as using deodorant or antiperspirant and bathing regularly.

Figure 17.7 **School-Age Physical Milestones**

Age	Physical Milestones
Six to Seven Years	• Is constantly active. • May fidget. • Can skate and jump rope with ease. • Has a better sense of balance and timing. • Copies or draws complex shapes. • Ties own shoelaces. • Uses self-care tools, such as combs, brushes, toothbrushes, and flatware. • Has improved eye-hand coordination. • Has established hand preference. • Writes in manuscript style (commonly called *printing*). • Colors within lines and cuts on lines. • Draws pictures.
Eight to Nine Years	• Is in constant motion—jumps, climbs, and chases. • Kicks, throws, catches, and hits balls with growing skill. • Has smooth and quick gross-motor skills. • Enjoys organized games. • Dresses self completely. • Is skillful with hands; uses tools, does handicrafts, plays musical instruments, writes and draws with control. • Is almost as coordinated as an adult.
Ten to Twelve Years	• Shows greater strength and endurance. • Engages in sports and games. • Applies gross-motor skills to sports and games. • May feel awkward during growth spurt. • Has excellent fine-motor coordination.
Thirteen to Fourteen Years	• Female pubic hair, armpit and leg hair reach adult patterns. • Male wet dreams begin. • Male and Female sexual characteristics begin developing. • Applies gross motor skills to sports and games. • Has excellent fine-motor coordination. • May feel awkward during growth spurts. • Sweat glands become more active. • Hormonal changes may cause acne. • Female body fat increases while male muscle mass increases.

Goodheart-Willcox Publisher
(Continued)

Figure 17.7 School-Age Physical Milestones (Continued)

Age	Physical Milestones
Fifteen to Sixteen Years	• Female and Male growth spurt peaks. • Menarche begins for females by age sixteen • Male voice changes. • Applies gross motor skill to sports and games. • Has excellent fine-motor coordination. • Learns how to drive.
Seventeen to Eighteen Years	• Male genitals are adult size and shape. • Male pubic hair, armpit and leg hair reach adult patterns. • Applies gross motor skills to sports and games. • Has excellent fine-motor coordination. • May feel awkward during growth spurts. • Male facial hair begins to appear.

Lesson 17.1 Review and Assessment

1. Which of the following brain developments occur in children during the school-age years? (17.1.1)
   A. Brain growth increases dramatically.
   B. The brain reaches 90 percent of its adult weight.
   C. The brain becomes more specialized.
   D. Brain rewiring is easy.

2. **True or False.** Puberty begins in the reproductive organs. (17.1.1)

3. A school-age child's improved ability to perform motor skills accurately is called _____. (17.1.2)
   A. precision
   B. reaction time
   C. flexibility
   D. puberty

4. **True or False.** School-age females tend to perform better than males in tasks requiring flexibility or rhythm. (17.1.2)

5. Ten- to twelve-year-olds commonly achieve which physical developmental milestone? (17.1.2)
   A. Skates and jumps with ease
   B. Establishes a hand preference
   C. Dresses self completely
   D. Shows excellent fine-motor coordination

Lesson 17.2

Meeting Nutritional Needs of School-Age Children and Adolescents

Key Terms

eating disorder
food-insecure households
heavily processed foods
junk foods
malnutrition
over-nutrition
under-nutrition

Learning Outcomes

After studying this lesson, you will be able to

17.2-1 **summarize** strategies that encourage healthful eating in school-age children and teens by planning healthful lunches and snacks.

17.2-2 **recognize** common causes and risks of being overweight and underweight and recall indications a child or teen may be developing an eating disorder.

Reading and Notetaking Activity

Create a table with two columns and include as many rows as you need. Before reading the chapter, list facts you already know about a healthy diet in the Give One column. In the Get One column, list facts you learn as you read the chapter. If you have any questions about what you are reading, raise your hand and ask your teacher. After you finish reading the chapter, team up with a classmate and discuss each other's list. Are there items you would add to your list?

Healthy Diet	
Give one	**Get one**

Introduction

Although most school-age children and teens can feed themselves, they still rely on adults to meet their nutritional needs. As children and adolescents begin to think for themselves and as peers become more important, meeting these needs becomes more complex. They may express strong preferences in foods, and their food preferences may be heavily influenced by the food choices of their peers. Having a meal similar to a peer's meal may be more important than eating a meal that is nutritious.

Eating nutritious foods is vital to school-age children and adolescents' growth, development, and increased energy demands. They also need to store some nutrients for the rapid growth that occurs in puberty. Eating plans focused on healthful foods also help school-age children and adolescents resist infections and avoid nutrition-related risks.

17.2-1 Healthful Eating in the School-Age Years and Adolescence

During these years, children have more control over the foods they eat. They are more likely to be eating meals away from home with less direct supervision than when they were younger. Meeting the nutritional needs of children this age, however, is no less important than when they were preschoolers. It is important for adults to work with school-age children and adolescents as a team, toward a common goal of healthful eating.

For school-age children and adolescents, lunch is a **pivotal** (crucial or key) meal for a number of reasons. Children who skip lunch have more trouble concentrating in class, have less energy for sports, and are more likely to **binge** (overeat) on unhealthy snacks after school. Furthermore, when children start school, adults are no longer in control of what their children eat at lunchtime (**Figure 17.8**).

Adults and schools can use several strategies to improve the chances of children selecting and eating a nutritious lunch. For instance, some schools publish their weekly menus to help caregivers plan their children's meals and snacks for the day. However, children may not always eat what they are served at school. Even children who carry their lunches to school may give or throw away some of their food. To increase the likelihood of lunches being eaten, caregivers can include children and teens in planning their meals eaten away from home. For example, the adult and child can review the school menu together and discuss healthful choices among the child's preferred foods. If lunches are brought from home, the school-age child or teens can be involved in creating nutritious

recipes, shopping for, and preparing appropriate lunches or snacks. When they are able to participate in planning and preparing their meals, they are more likely to eat them. School staff can also urge children and teens to make nutritious food choices while away from home.

Healthful Eating Plans

During the school-age years and adolescence, children begin to learn about healthful eating plans. A healthful eating plan focuses on colorful fruits and vegetables, lean protein options, low-fat dairy products, and whole grains. **Heavily processed foods** containing hidden sources of solid fats, sodium, and added sugars should be limited or avoided. Examples of heavily processed foods include many ready-to-eat foods, such as cereals, typical snack foods, lunchmeats, and boxed and frozen meals. Too much of a good thing is not always good, however, and even healthful foods must be consumed in appropriate amounts.

Adults can determine the amounts and types of food that are appropriate for their children by creating daily food plans to meet their children's specific needs. Adults can do this on the ChooseMyPlate website. Daily food plans list the recommended amount of foods from each food group based on the average height and weight for children's and adolescents' ages and genders and on how much time the child spends in physical activity on most days.

SolStock/E+ via Getty Images

Figure 17.8 At an age when a nutritious meal has such impact, an adult must rely on their child to consume it. *How can parents increase the likelihood of their child eating their lunch?*

For children nine years of age and older, a daily food plan is calculated using the child's own height and weight, not an average (**Figure 17.9**). For children who are at nutritional risk due to a condition or illness, adults should consult with the child's doctor or a registered dietitian nutritionist.

Healthful Lunches

Whether purchased at school or brought from home, lunches should include some protein, a grain (preferably whole grain), fruit, vegetable, dairy, and a small treat. To make lunch selection easier, consider creating a recipe book of simple, nutritious recipes that the child can make independently.

Figure 17.9 **MyPlate Plan**

Food Group Amounts for 1,800 Calories a Day*

Fruits	Vegetables	Grains	Protein	Dairy	Limit
1½ cups	2½ cups	6 ounces	5 ounces	3 cups	Limit
Focus on whole fruits	Vary your veggies	Make half your grains whole grains	Vary your protein routine	Move to low-fat or fat-free milk or yogurt	Drink and eat less sodium, saturated fat, and added sugars.
Focus on whole fruits that are fresh, frozen, canned, or dried.	Aim for this much **each week:** Dark green veggies—1½ cups Red and orange veggies—5½ cups Beans and peas—1½ cups Starchy veggies—5 cups Other veggies—4 cups	Find whole-grain foods by reading the Nutrition Facts label and ingredients list.	Mix up your protein foods to include seafood, beans and peas, unsalted nuts and seeds, soy products, eggs, and lean meats and poultry.	Choose fat-free milk, yogurt, and soy beverages (soy milk) to cut back on your saturated fat.	Limit: Sodium to **2,200 milligrams** a day. Saturated fat to **20 grams** a day. Added sugars to **45 grams** a day.
Fruits ChooseMyPlate.gov	Vegetables ChooseMyPlate.gov	Grains ChooseMyPlate.gov	Protein ChooseMyPlate.gov	Dairy ChooseMyPlate.gov	Limit ChooseMyPlate.gov

Be active your way: Children 6 to 17 years old should move at least **60 minutes** every day.

*This 1,800-calorie pattern is only an estimate of your needs. Monitor your body weight and adjust your calories if needed.

Courtesy of the United States Department of Agriculture

Figure 17.9 School-age children need a nutritious diet to meet their growth and energy needs. The recommended amounts shown in this sample are for a nine-year-old boy who is active 30–60 minutes daily. *What are some ways to involve children in planning and preparing healthful meals?*

When creating simple recipes for school-age children to prepare, make sure the recipes have few ingredients and easy-to-follow directions. Recipe ingredients should include plenty of colorful fruits and vegetables, lean proteins, low-fat dairy products, and whole grains. The preparation steps in the recipe should take into consideration the child's age, developmental level, and physical skills and abilities. Adults can simplify the child's preparation process by already having vegetables or meats cut up and ready to use. When it is time to prepare the lunch, the caregiver and child can refer to the recipe book and select a recipe that appeals to the child. As the child enters adolescence, allowing them to cook a favorite meal for the family is a good way to incorporate physical, intellectual, and social skills.

It is important that, in addition to meeting the child's nutritional needs, the lunch is also safe. Reusable lunch bags or boxes should be cleaned with warm, soapy water each day. Before assembling the lunch, the kitchen counter should be cleaned, and hands washed. Fruits and vegetables should be washed before packing. Perishable foods must be kept at safe temperatures. Ice packs can be used with insulated lunch bags.

Healthful Snacks

Many school-age children and teens buy snacks, including **junk foods** (foods that are high in calories and low in nutrition), with their spending money. National Cancer Institute research shows that school-age children get up to one-fifth of their calories from sugar. Other studies show that school-age children and teens who participate in sports, such as soccer, burn about 150 calories per game. Often, adults provide these children with postgame, nutrient-poor snacks containing between 300 and 500 calories. Children and teens who eat too much junk food can lose their appetite for nourishing food. These children may receive adequate calories, but they do not receive enough of the nutrients their bodies need for growth. Junk foods also contribute to other health risks, such as obesity and tooth decay.

Adults can promote healthy snacking by keeping nutritious, ready-to-eat snacks readily available **(Figure 17.10)** and placed in the pantry or refrigerator at the child's height. Adults can also urge children to prepare their own nutritious snacks.

Figure 17.10 Healthful Snack Ideas for School-Age Children

- Pita chips with hummus dip
- Whole-grain pretzels with mustard
- Low-fat pudding topped with graham-cracker crumbles
- Yogurt parfait (layers of low-fat plain yogurt, granola, and berries)
- Whole-grain waffles topped with cinnamon applesauce (no sugar added)
- Fruit smoothie (blend low-fat plain yogurt, frozen berries, and 100% fruit juice)
- *Custom trail mix (combine dried fruits, unsalted nuts, and oat cereal)
- Whole-grain English muffin pizza (top-toasted muffin with pizza sauce, chopped vegetables, and low-fat mozzarella cheese; melt in microwave or toaster oven)
- Hard-cooked egg
- Baked tortilla chips with fat-free refried beans
- Baby whole carrots and cherry tomatoes with low-fat ranch dressing
- Toasted whole-grain mini bagel topped with flavored Greek yogurt
- Apple slices dipped in peanut butter
- Whole-grain macaroni floating in a cup of tomato soup
- Whole-wheat English muffin spread with ricotta cheese, sprinkled with lemon pepper, and lightly browned in toaster oven

*For older children

Goodheart-Willcox Publisher

John S. Quinn/Shutterstock.com

Create simple, nutritious snack recipes to put in the child's recipe book. Many good cookbooks are also written for this age group. Simple recipes allow children to prepare foods on their own or with a little help. As children become adolescents, their recipes may become more complex.

17.2-2 Nutrition-Related Risks

Healthful eating every day should be the goal for school-age children and adolescents. For most, the occasional poor food choice causes little or no harm, but when poor food choices are the norm, children and teens are at greater nutrition-related risk.

There are risks associated with both over- and under-nutrition. **Over-nutrition** is the ongoing intake of more calories than is needed for good health. This condition is common in the United States today. It is seen in both children and adults and increases people's risks for a number of chronic diseases. **Under-nutrition** occurs when some food is being eaten but is continuously lacking one or more nutrients required to meet the body's needs. In the United States, under-nutrition is rare and usually due to illness or extreme poverty.

Another nutrition-related risk involves children living in *food-insecure households*. Children in **food-insecure households** (households that are regularly unable to supply healthful meals) do not have enough food available or may have diets that supply adequate calories but are lacking in one or more nutrients. These children may be normal weight or even overweight but are not receiving the nutrients necessary for proper growth and development. These children are experiencing *malnutrition*. **Malnutrition** describes diets that supply an excess, shortage, or imbalance of calories or one or more nutrients. Malnutrition can encompass over- and under-nutrition, both of which pose serious health problems to school-age children and teens, including children being overweight or underweight.

Overweight Children and Adolescents

Today, over-nutrition combined with other factors has contributed to nearly 20 percent of children aged 2-19 being either overweight or obese. Children with obesity may have up to three times the amount of fat tissue as children with normal weight. Children and teens who are overweight or obese are far more likely to become adults who are overweight or obese. Over-nutrition in children is often caused by the consumption of fast foods, snacking on junk foods, and eating takeout or heavily processed foods (**Figure 17.11**).

HandmadePictures/Shutterstock.com

bhofack2/iStock via Getty Images Plus

Figure 17.11 Overnutrition in children can be avoided by making healthful choices, like choosing more nutritious meals when eating out. *What other factors contribute to overweight and obesity in children?*

Overweight or obesity in children and teens can be caused by several factors, such as

- consumption of more calories than are used by the body
- easy access to high-calorie, processed foods
- physical inactivity
- family history of being overweight or obese
- lack of sleep
- depression or other emotional issues
- low metabolic rate

Being overweight or obese increase a person's risk for high blood pressure, type 2 diabetes, and problems with weight-bearing joints (hips, knees, and ankles). These health conditions, which have traditionally been diagnosed in adults, are being observed more frequently in children. Overweight and obese children may also struggle with self-esteem.

Underweight Children

Underweight in school-age children and teens may be the result of inadequate nutrition, heredity, altered bodily responses to foods (such as not absorbing certain nutrients), illness, long-term mental stress, or eating disorders. Sometimes it can be the result of a high metabolism. In the United States, being underweight is more often due to health concerns than to insufficient food.

Incidence of underweight in children has decreased significantly in recent decades. Roughly 3.5 percent of children in the United States are classified as underweight.

Children and teens who are underweight due to illness or abnormal eating patterns should be seen by a doctor. If being underweight is a family trait, however, health risks due to being underweight are unlikely.

Eating Disorders in School-Age Children and Adolescents

More and more, school-age children and adolescents are facing pressure from peers and the media to look "good." Unfortunately, "good" often translates to "thin." Children who are overweight or a healthy weight often want to lose weight. This intense focus on appearance can contribute to the development of *eating disorders*. An **eating disorder** is an illness characterized by distorted behaviors and emotions about food and weight. If untreated, an eating disorder can threaten a child's health and even their life.

Eating disorders, such as *anorexia nervosa*, *bulimia nervosa*, and *binge-eating*, often develop in the school-age years and are observed in biological males, but far more often in biological females (**Figure 17.12**).

Figure 17.12 **Eating Disorders**

Cause	Types
The Academy for Eating Disorders states that the eating disorders of middle childhood stem from a child's, especially a girl's, preoccupation with weight and body shape. Because the child does not have a good understanding of body weight and shape, the eating disorders often lead to growth and health problems and even to death.	*Anorexia nervosa.* To lose weight, these children have an inadequate intake of food and engage in excessive exercise. Regardless of their hunger, they work hard to achieve their weight and body shape goals. *Binge-eating disorder.* Binge eating consists of eating excessive quantities of food at one time. Binge eaters may consume up to four times the amount of food that would constitute a normal meal. *Bulimia nervosa.* These children may try a very restrictive diet, but end up bingeing on foods. Out of guilt, they purge themselves of the foods they have just ingested by vomiting. Alternately, they use laxatives to control their weight. Sometimes they lose weight, but their weight may also be normal or high.

Goodheart-Willcox Publisher

FOCUS ON MENTAL HEALTH

Sometimes school-age children and adolescents develop eating disorders. Caregivers sometimes mistake the symptoms for picky eating patterns or harmless dieting. But eating disorders are serious illnesses that pose a risk to physical and mental health. Thus, an eating disorder requires professional dietetic and mental health diagnosis and treatment. Caregivers can watch for various signs that could be a signal that a child or adolescent is struggling with an eating disorder. When talking to a child about seeking treatment, be sure to clear both the adult and child's schedules and set up a quiet place to talk. Be calm, caring, and non-judgmental. Be prepared for denial and anger as the sufferer feels threatened or exposed when confronted about their behavior. Don't expect insight or buy-in. Often insight does not happen until long into recovery. Insist on a medical check-up and evaluation. Caregivers want to ensure that their children are healthy and will live a long time. Don't be afraid to seek a second opinion. Find a therapist who feels confident they can treat the child, and with whom both the child and adult feel comfortable.

In recent decades, hospitalizations for eating disorders of children under 12 years of age accounted for the largest increase of any age category. An eating disorder is both a physical and mental health issue.

Indications that a child is developing an eating disorder might include

- weight loss
- skipped meals
- baggy clothes
- obsessive exercising
- hoarding food
- crankiness
- difficulty concentrating

Eating disorders can cause malnutrition, imbalance in body chemicals, and death due to heart failure. Puberty, with its growth spurt and other changes, requires adequate nutrition. Children who exhibit warning signs for an eating disorder should be assessed by a physician. Treatment for these disorders often requires a team of health professionals.

Lesson 17.2 Review and Assessment

1. The most effective strategy to improve the chances that a school-age child will eat a nutritious lunch at school is to _____. (17.2.1)
   A. let them eat the lunch served at school
   B. pack them a healthy lunch at home
   C. trust them to make healthy choices
   D. involve them in planning their lunch
2. **True or False.** According to the MyPlate plan, children 6 to 17 years old should move at least 30 minutes every day. (17.2.1)
3. A common cause of being underweight in children is _____. (17.2.2)
   A. physical inactivity
   B. lack of sleep
   C. long-term mental stress
   D. access to processed foods
4. **True or False.** A child who is experiencing malnutrition may be underweight or overweight. (17.2.2)
5. Which is true about eating disorders in school-age children? (17.2.2)
   A. They affect more biological males than biological females.
   B. They rarely require hospitalization.
   C. They increase a child's risk of developing type 2 diabetes.
   D. They are both a physical and mental health issue.

Meeting Other Physical Needs of School-Age Children and Adolescents

Learning Outcomes

After studying this lesson, you will be able to

17.3-1 **name** some features of clothing that school-age children and adolescents need and want and describe how peer pressure affects clothing preferences.

17.3-2 **describe** hygiene needs during the school-age and adolescent years.

17.3-3 **identify** ways parents can encourage their children to get enough physical activity, rest, and sleep.

17.3-4 **analyze** the impact of technology on growth and development and **explain** the impact that digital citizenship, digital footprints, and social media can have on future careers.

Key Terms

digital citizenship
orthopedic problems
peer pressure
pheromones
sleep-deprived

Reading and Notetaking Activity

Skim the headings in this chapter and consider what each concept in this chapter might teach you about body image, disordered eating, eating disorders and the impact of technology. Keep a list, placing a star beside any concept that especially interest you. After reading the chapter, pick three concepts and write a few paragraphs about how these concepts can help you understand the school-age child or adolescent from a caregiver's point of view. Use proper grammar and spelling in your paragraphs.

Introduction

Although school-age children and teens are learning to meet their own needs, they still rely on caregivers to provide them with basic physical necessities, such as clothing and toiletries, and to guide their clothing choices and health practices, such as hygiene, physical activity, and rest and sleep. Although school-age children and teens want more independence and do have less direct adult supervision, caregivers and other significant adults can shape children's choices and behaviors. They can have a positive, moderating effect that overcomes negative external forces, such as unacceptable marketing approaches and peer practices.

Because children's understandings and attitudes develop rapidly during this time, middle and late childhood offers an unprecedented time for children to develop lifelong habits of tasteful dress and health behaviors. During this interpretive stage of parenting, children need to see how even seemingly **innocuous** (not harmful) issues can have a harmful impact. For example, poor hygiene can damage the body and cause a loss of self-esteem due to peer comments. Inadequate rest and sleep affect learning and mood. Lack of regular physical activity endangers health and makes a person feel less physically confident.

17.3-1 Clothing

During the school-age and teen years, children have more say in the types of clothes they wear. They can choose clothing and dress themselves and may express opinions about what clothes they want.

Fit and Construction Features

Like children of all ages, school-age children and teens need clothing that fits and is well constructed. They are still growing, and especially when they hit their growth spurt, they may need garments that have growth features. Because school-age children and teens are active, clothing should be able to withstand stress and strain. Most school-age children can dress themselves, though they may still have trouble with hard-to-reach buttons or a specially tied bow. Younger school-age children may still need to have clothes with some self-dressing features. Shoe and sock sizes change on the average of every six months for children between 6 and 12 years of age.

Clothing Preferences

School-age children and teens begin to develop their own preferences for clothing, such as colors and styles (**Figure 17.13**). Children begin to experience **peer pressure** (the desire to be like their peers) and may choose clothes that will enable them to fit in with a peer group. If clothing and shoes are too different from what others wear, children may feel rejected.

Child development experts advise caregivers to take a close look at how clothing items for school-age children and teens are marketed. Some clothes may have inappropriate logos or be constructed in styles that are more suitable for adults than for young school-age children and teens. Caregivers should assess clothing options and provide guidance to help their children make appropriate choices. Adults should also listen to why a child wants a particular outfit. If a child says, "All my friends are wearing this," a caregiver might ask *why* the child's friends like it. This helps the child become a critic and express their own views. Caregivers can help their children make appropriate choices by offering options within set limits and explaining their reasons for saying "no" to specific outfits.

Due to school-age children and teen's emphasis on clothing, many school systems institute school uniforms. This is usually an effort to improve school performance and reduce negative behaviors. Uniforms seem to improve children's focus on learning and decrease distractions about clothing choices. Uniforms are also often cheaper for caregivers who may not be able to afford an individual school wardrobe. Opponents to school uniforms claim that uniforms do not reduce behavioral problems or create a sense of socioeconomic equality among students. They also claim that uniforms limit the ability of students to express themselves and their cultures. Furthermore, opponents say that one style does not fit all tastes. For example, a typical uniform for biological females may be a skirt or jumper, but some females prefer pants. Finally, some adults point out that buying uniforms for children at the beginning of the school term is hard on the family budget.

Romrodinka/iStock via Getty Images Plus

Figure 17.13 Many school-age children express an interest in picking out their own clothes. *What factors besides peer pressure might influence the clothes a child chooses to wear?*

Caregivers must also buy clothes for nonschool hours in addition to the uniforms.

Allowing children the chance to help pick out clothing that they prefer or is currently popular can be hard for some caregivers. But encouraging school-age children and teens to express their personality through the clothing choices they make is one of the steps adults can take to encourage children to make decisions for themselves. To help school-age children make wise decisions about clothing, remind them of the following:

- Wear well-fitting clothes. Avoid clothes that are too tight or too baggy.
- Wear bright colors. This is a great way to stand out and feel confident. Mix the bright color with neutral or dark colors.
- Choose your fashion style. Try different clothes while finding the perfect combination.
- Showcase your personality. Use creativity and express yourself as you find your style.

17.3-2 Hygiene

Adults should continue stressing the importance of hygiene skills and teaching these skills, if deemed necessary, during the school-age and teen years. Dental hygiene problems often begin in middle childhood. Permanent teeth replace deciduous teeth at a rate of about four per year, yet many children do not receive regular check-ups. Adults often quit brushing their children's teeth in middle childhood, expecting them to do so themselves. Problems may arise because many school-age children regularly snack on sugary foods and drinks, wear dental braces, or use a quick, **cursory** (non-thorough) approach to dental hygiene. By the end of the school years, the majority of children have more than four decayed or filled teeth. Dental hygienists and adults should stress the importance of dental hygiene and the "how to" of keeping teeth clean (**Figure 17.14**).

Body hygiene (also called *personal hygiene*) is a common problem for school-age children. Body odor becomes a problem as children approach puberty. Body chemicals called **pheromones** (FER-uh-mohns) are produced and secreted through sweat. Without regular baths or showers, clean clothing, and **deodorants** (substances that hide body odor) or **antiperspirants** (substances that dry

up sweat), these pheromones will produce body odor due to contact with bacteria. Because young children often play in the water while their parents bathe them, they may not know the importance of or the "how to" of bathing, showering, and shampooing. Once a child has mastered tub baths and is comfortable with water on the head and streaming into the face, they are ready for learning showering techniques. As the child becomes proficient at getting their body clean, shampooing techniques can gradually be introduced. As children head into the teenage years, ensuring they bathe daily will help alleviate body odor. Poor hygiene can lead to skin infections and other preventable illnesses. Hygiene can also impact social interactions. It can be unpleasant to be in close contact with someone who has bad breath or body odor. Children can also be teased or bullied by other children due to poor hygiene. This can lead to low self-esteem and self-concept. Many schools also instruct late school-aged children on the importance of proper hygiene habits like showering regularly and wearing deodorant.

17.3-3 Physical Activity, Rest, and Sleep

School-age children and teens spend many hours attending school and using digital devices. As a result, many children are physically active less than the recommended 60 minutes or more per day.

Figure 17.14 It is important for children to develop good dental hygiene habits to avoid dental problems later in life. Adults should stress the importance of proper dental care. *How can adults encourage children to clean their teeth properly?*

The majority of this time should be spent in moderate or vigorous aerobic activity. Aerobic activity aids physical fitness and brain functioning for both children and adults. Physical activity is known to increase children's levels of concentration. Eye physicians recommend that 10 to 14 hours of outside play per week may reduce nearsightedness in children. Examples of vigorous activities may include brisk walking, running, swimming, cycling, roller skating, jumping rope, dancing, gymnastics, hiking, soccer, and tag games. Exercise may help prevent weight gain and high blood pressure later in life. Benefits of regular physical activity include improved blood circulation, improved stress management, healthy weight maintenance, improved self-image, less risk of anxiety and depression, and increased muscle strength.

Many school-age children are physically active due to participating in competitive sports. Adults should help their children select appropriate sports and coaches and should caution their children about injuries due to sports and "daring feats." Sports injuries often occur because of bone fractures and muscle pulls. Although physical activities help strengthen muscles, **orthopedic problems** (those relating to the bones and muscles) as well as

concussions are the most common physical problems at this age.

In addition to sports taught in schools or youth programs, the family plays an important role in children's physical activity. A good plan is for the family to take up vigorous physical activities adults and children can enjoy together. These activities, unlike some sports, should be potential lifelong activities, such as running, swimming, cycling, hiking, and skiing (**Figure 17.15**).

RyanJLane/E+ via Getty Images

Figure 17.15 Parents can encourage physical exercise by planning fun family activities, such as hiking. These activities encourage children to be physically active and may become lifelong habits. *What are some other activities families can do to stay physically active?*

Focus on

Careers

Coach

Coaches teach children the skills they need to perform a particular sport, such as soccer, swimming, or volleyball. They supervise practice sessions, develop game strategies, instruct and motivate athletes, and keep track of the team's performance. Coaches typically work in schools and recreation industries. They must often work irregular hours, such as evenings and weekends, for practices and games. Travel to sporting events is also required.

Career cluster: Education and training.

Education: Educational requirements include a bachelor's degree and knowledge of a sport.

Job outlook: Future employment opportunities for coaches are expected to grow faster than the average for all occupations.

To learn more about a career as a coach, visit the United States Department of Labor's *Occupational Outlook Handbook* website. You will also be able to compare the job responsibilities, educational requirements, job outlook, and average pay of coaches with similar occupations.

Photo: Creatas Images/Creatas/Thinkstock

FOCUS ON MENTAL HEALTH

School-age children and teens who are depressed or anxious often experience sleep deprivation problems. Conversely, sleep deprivation caused by other factors, such as using digital devices during time for sleep, can result in mental health problems. Sleep deprivation should be professionally diagnosed and treated. Some healthy sleep tips:

- Insist on eight hours of sleep on weekdays and weekends.
- Create a consistent pre-bed routine to help with relaxation and falling asleep faster.
- Avoid caffeine and energy drinks, especially in the afternoon and evening.
- Put away electronic devices at least a half-hour before bed and keep them on silent mode to avoid checking them during the night.
- Keep the bedroom cool, dark, and quiet.

These should not be done for competition, but for purposes of family physical fitness and fun. For many children, these physical activity patterns will last a lifetime.

Research shows that school-age children need 9 to 11 hours of sleep nightly. Younger school-age children tend to need more sleep than those who are older. While school-age children are more likely to want control over their bedtimes, adults should still ensure that their children get enough sleep each night. Teens need 8 to 10 hours of sleep nightly.

Sleep Deprivation

During the school-age and teen years, children may become **sleep-deprived** (having less than the recommended amount of sleep) due to other demands on their lives, such as homework, extracurricular activities, social activities, interest in digital devices, and consumption of caffeine. Sleep deprivation can lead to a number of problems, including

- inability to concentrate, which affects both learning ability and quality of work
- impaired memory
- weakened coping skills, behavioral problems, and low self-esteem

- disruption in hormones affecting appetite and food choices
- inability to use executive functions to achieve goals
- increased chance of mental health problems, such as depression and anxiety

Helping School-Age Children and Teens Get Rest and Sleep

While sleep deprivation is more likely to become a problem in children's lives during the school-age years, adults can use many strategies to help children get **sufficient** (adequate) amounts of rest and sleep. Some of these strategies include

- setting a regular bedtime for each day of the week. Varying bedtimes on weekends is not in the child's best interest.
- getting out in the morning light for a few minutes each day.
- taking all digital devices out of a child's bedroom. If digital devices are in a child's bedroom, the child is likely to use that device instead of sleeping.
- planning a wind-down time of 30 to 60 minutes before bedtime. During this time, digital devices should be put away and the television turned off.
- taking a child to be checked for sleep, respiratory, and emotional disorders if poor sleep habits persist.

FOCUS ON MENTAL HEALTH

Sleep deprivation can have a negative impact on school-age children's academic performance. One study showed that children deprived of one hour of sleep nightly performed more than two years below expectations on academic tasks. Sleep deprivation can affect the development of the frontal lobe, a part of the brain that is critical to control impulsive behavior. Neurodevelopment disorders, such as attention-deficit/hyperactivity disorder (ADHD) and autism spectrum disorder (ASD), can make it harder for children to sleep well and contribute to more pronounced symptoms of these conditions. Caregivers can help by setting a firm bedtime and helping children avoid overstimulation.

17.3.4 School Age Children and Teens and Technology

Digital citizenship refers to the responsible use of technology by anyone who uses computers, the internet, and digital devices to engage with society on any level. As the rate of technological advancement continues to increase, the world is becoming more dependent on the internet for day-to-day activities. School-age children and teens need to learn how to become good digital citizens by learning how to connect with one another, empathize with each other, and create lasting relationships through digital tools. Teaching empathy is a good starting point as it is a crucial skill in understanding how people talk and behave online.

With text-based communication, it's impossible to hear someone's vocal tone, see their facial expressions, or understand other non-verbal cues that you receive when speaking to someone face-to-face. As a result, it's easy for internet users to make quick, harsh judgments about someone's statements online. This in turn allows internet users to trade quick verbal or text-based blows that are intended to hurt someone's feelings instead of carrying on a typical conversation that you might have over a phone call or face to face. In the worst cases, this kind of behavior can devolve into cyberbullying.

Cyberbullying is bullying that takes place over digital devices like cell phones, computers, and tablets. It can occur through messages, texts, apps, or online social media accounts. Cyberbullying includes sending, posting, or sharing negative statements about others on the internet or through social media sites. Because cyberbullying has become an issue with school-age children, most states have enacted laws requiring schools to teach digital citizenship.

Caregivers must face that school-age children and teens don't always use good judgment. Working out how to behave online is a new social skill that will be important for future generations. It used to be when a child was bullied face to face they knew who was saying things about them. With the introduction of the internet and social media, people can hide behind anonymity and bully others. As such many government agencies have provided information on cyberbullying and how to prevent it. Federally funded school have an obligation to resolve harassment when it is discriminatory.

Lesson 17.3 Review and Assessment

1. Caregivers can help their children make appropriate choices about clothing options by ____. (17.3.1)
   A. letting them wear what their friends are wearing
   B. selecting their clothes for them
   C. giving them brightly colored clothing
   D. offering them choices within limits
2. **True or False.** Poor hygiene may lead to teasing or bullying by other children. (17.2.2)
3. All of the following are considered potential benefits of regular physical activity in school-age children except ____. (17.3.3)
   A. improved concentration
   B. muscle strength
   C. concussion
   D. low blood pressure
4. How much sleep do school-age children need each night? (17.3.3)
   A. 10 to 13 hours
   B. 9 to 11 hours
   C. 8 to 10 hours
   D. 7 to 9 hours
5. **True or False.** Teaching empathy is a good starting point, as it is a crucial skill in understanding how people talk and behave online. (17.3.4)

Chapter 17 Review and Assessment

Summary

Lesson 17.1

17.1-1 Brain connections made by about eight years of age and increased myelination permit better memory capacity, language and literacy development, focus and motivation, problem-solving skills, and emotional control.

17.1-1 Heart development lags behind the maturation of the other organs, as the lungs, gastrointestinal system, eyes, and hearing all improve to almost adult levels.

17.1-1 Puberty changes begin in the hypothalamus, and some children complete this process and reach sexual maturity during the school-age years.

17.1-2 School-age children and adolescents achieve several physical developmental milestones. Other physical changes include the sweat glands becoming more active and hormonal changes occurring that can cause acne.

Lesson 17.2

17.2-1 One way adults can teach children and adolescents healthful attitudes about eating is to allow them to participate in planning and preparing meals.

17.2-2 School-age children and teens are prone to some nutrition-related risks related to both over-nutrition and under-nutrition.

17.2-2 Over-nutrition and other factors may cause overweight and obesity in school-age children and teens, increasing the risk for high blood pressure, type 2 diabetes, and problems with weight-bearing joints.

17.2-2 When school-age children and teens are underweight, it may be the result of inadequate nutrition, heredity, altered bodily responses to foods, illness, long-term mental stress, or eating disorders.

17.2-2 Eating disorders are both a physical and mental health issue and include anorexia nervosa, bulimia nervosa, and binge-eating.

Lesson 17.3

17.3-1 School-age children and teens still depend on adults to meet many of their physical needs and to guide their clothing choices and health practices, such as hygiene, physical activity, rest, and sleep.

17.3-1 Adults can encourage children and teens to express their personality through their clothing choices while helping them choose appropriate styles.

17.3-2 Pheromones coming into contact with bacteria produce body odor. Poor hygiene can lead to skin infections, other preventable illnesses, and bullying by peers.

17.3-3 Benefits of regular physical activity include improvements in concentration, blood circulation, stress management, self-image, and muscle strength as well as healthy weight maintenance and less risk of anxiety and depression.

17.3-3 Participation in competitive sports increases the risk of orthopedic problems and concussion.

17.3-3 Sleep deprivation can have harmful effects on children and teen's health and development.

17.3-4 School-age children and teens don't always use good judgment. Caregivers must help them learn how to become good digital citizens by connecting with one another, empathizing with each other, and creating lasting relationships through digital tools.

17.3-4 Cyberbullying is a serious issue with school-age children; most states have enacted laws requiring schools to teach digital citizenship. Many government agencies have information on cyberbullying and how to prevent it.

College and Career Portfolio

Portfolio Design

Using technology effectively in your portfolio gives you an opportunity to demonstrate your skills while making your portfolio look more professional and polished. To create your portfolio design, you can use publishing and design software. To determine the software you would like to use, complete the following activities:

- Research available publishing and design software. View samples of products the software has created. (Keep in mind that your portfolio should look professional and design elements should highlight accomplishments, not take away from them.) After reviewing the samples, choose two types of software you want to use.
- Download a free trial or use a library or school computer to modify one of your portfolio samples in the software. Evaluate if the software makes your sample look more professional.

Recall and Application

1. Which best describes skeletal growth in the late school-age years? (17.1.1)
   A. Growth is slow and steady.
   B. Biological boys tend to be taller than biological girls.
   C. Arms and legs grow more than the trunk.
   D. A growth spurt may occur before puberty.

2. **True or False.** Biological females have more fat than biological males at six years of age, but both accumulate fat at the same rate until puberty. (17.1.1)

3. Eight- to nine-year-olds commonly achieve which physical developmental milestone? (17.1.2)
   A. Enjoys organized games
   B. Colors within the lines
   C. Ties their own shoelaces
   D. Shows greater strength and endurance

4. Improved reaction time enables school-age children to _____. (17.1.2)
   A. balance on one foot
   B. catch a thrown ball
   C. run faster
   D. touch their toes

5. Ideally, a nutritious lunch for a school-age child should include everything except _____. (17.2.1)
   A. colorful vegetables
   B. lean protein
   C. whole milk
   D. fruit

6. **True or False.** Junk foods are high in calories and low in nutrition. (17.2.1)

7. A common cause of being overweight in children is _____. (17.2.2)
   A. inadequate nutrition
   B. high metabolic rate
   C. illness
   D. depression

8. **True or False.** External pressure from peers and the media to look "good" or "thin" can contribute to the development of an eating disorder in a school-age child. (17.2.2)

9. Which is the best response a caregiver might give to a school-age child who wants to wear something just because everyone else is wearing it? (17.3.1)
   A. "No, it's too expensive."
   B. "I don't care if everyone is wearing that."
   C. "Why do your friends like this?"
   D. "Why don't we wait until you're a little older?"

10. **True or False.** Body chemicals called pheromones produce body odor due to contact with bacteria. (17.3.2)

11. All of the following are strategies to help children get sufficient amounts of rest and sleep except _____. (17.3.3)
   A. varying their bedtimes on weekends
   B. removing digital devices from their bedrooms
   C. getting out in the morning light each day
   D. planning a wind-down time 30–60 minutes before bedtime

12. Cyberbullying may occur through all of the following except _____. (17.3.4)
   A. text messages
   B. online social media
   C. apps
   D. phone calls

Critical Thinking

1. **Make inferences.** When did your growth spurt occur? Describe some of the feelings and changes associated with your growth spurt. How can adults help school-age children manage some of these feelings?

2. **Evaluate.** Watch a group of school-age children playing outside and try to determine the children's ages. Then, evaluate the children's motor skills for evidence of reaction time, precision, speed and strength, and flexibility. Cite your evidence. What skills need further improvement?

3. **Cause and effect.** Working with a partner, review this chapter and brainstorm ways that adults can encourage school-age children's healthful eating. How do adults' and schools' attitudes toward eating affect school-age children's food choices? Share some highlights from your conversation with the class.

4. **Analyze.** Research the lunch menu at a local primary or middle school in your community. What lunch options are available for the children? Are children encouraged to bring lunches or eat lunches made at the school? Write a few paragraphs analyzing how healthful the school's lunch menu is and how lunch arrangements might affect children's food choices.

5. **Draw conclusions.** In small groups, discuss why many school-age children worry about their appearance more than the warmth and comfort of their clothing. How can adults and caregivers respect children's clothing preferences while emphasizing appropriate clothing choices?

6. **Identify.** As school-age children approach puberty, they are likely to experience body odor. In small groups, search online or at local stores for deodorants and antiperspirants that are geared toward school-age children. Identify products that you think would appeal to school-age children and discuss how an adult could introduce the concept of body odor to a child.

7. **Determine.** Research local primary and middle schools' start and end times. In small groups, determine what times children would have to wake up to get to school on time. What times, then, should the children go to bed? How could a typical evening be structured for a school-aged child to get sufficient sleep?

Core Skills

1. **Research and writing.** Once children reach the school-age years, their brains begin to specialize rather than rapidly wire new connections. Using reliable online or print resources, research how brain development changes during the school-age years. How do 12-year-olds' brains differ from 6-year-olds' brains? Write a short essay summarizing how the brain changes between 6 and 12 years of age.

2. **Reading and writing.** In small groups, research programs and materials for explaining puberty to school-age children. Choose two programs or materials and read them carefully, paying attention to how the physical changes of puberty are presented. Then, develop your own set of materials for teachers who need to introduce puberty to their students. Be sure to tailor the language to the developmental level of the children and consider how parents, teachers, and school nurses will respond to your materials.

3. **Technology and speaking.** In groups of seven, review the physical developmental milestones children achieve during the school-age years (Figure 17.7). Have each group member select one age, and then create an easy-to-follow visual representation of the milestones children achieve during these years. Your project should include drawings or pictures of children achieving various milestones during each year and should be an effective study tool and synthesis of the information you learned in this chapter.

4. **Technology.** Using a software program of your choice, create a recipe book for school-age children. In the recipe book, create simple, nutritious snacks or meals that are appropriate for children of this age to prepare. Consider the children's age range, developmental levels, and physical skills and abilities as you create the recipes. Be sure to include foods that make up a healthy eating plan, such as colorful fruits and vegetables, lean proteins, low-fat dairy products, and whole grains. Review your cookbooks in class for accuracy and then present them to a nearby middle school.

5. **Research and speaking.** In small groups, research the most current information about factors that contribute to overweight and obesity. What do experts say about the most significant causes of overweight and obesity? What measures can adults take to prevent these conditions in children? What national or local programs are available to educate children about overweight and obesity? Compile your findings into a speech and create a bibliography listing your sources. Present the information to the class.

6. **Technology and speaking.** School-age children develop eating disorders for a number of reasons, including societal pressure to be "thin." In small groups, identify one type of media that school-age children regularly view. Then analyze examples used in this medium and identify pictures, words, or attitudes that might contribute to school-age children's desires to change their bodies. Finally, compile three examples into an electronic presentation and share with the class. Lead a group discussion analyzing the examples and brainstorming ways to combat negative messages about children's bodies.

7. **Listening and speaking.** Interview a dental hygienist or dentist about common problems in dental hygiene during the school-age years. What factors contribute to childhood tooth decay? What methods or activities can be used to teach children proper brushing and flossing techniques? After the interview, compile your notes and share your findings with the class.

8. **Math.** Survey three families with school-age children and ask about the schedules those children follow. If possible, ask the families to account for each hour of time during the day. After the survey, calculate what percentage of the children's time is spent doing physical activities. Also, calculate the average number of hours the children spend being physically active. Identify any hours in the families' schedules that could include more physical activities.

9. **CTE Career Readiness Practice.** Imagine you are a health teacher at a primary school. The principal has asked you to send out a sample weekly lunch plan for adults trying to pack healthful lunches for their nine-year-olds. In preparation, check the MyPlate recommendations for a nine-year-old child of average height and weight. Then, craft a newsletter outlining one week's worth of healthful lunches. Make your newsletter visually appealing with pictures of the foods included.

Observations

1. Visit a local primary or middle school and observe children of a certain age in art and physical education classes. During the observation, take notes about what fine- and gross-motor skills the children exhibit. What motor skills do they possess? What motor skills are they still developing?

2. Observe a primary- or middle-school cafeteria at lunchtime and watch for children who trade lunches or foods with their peers. What foods are children most likely to trade or discard? What foods are they most likely to consume? What role do teachers and other adults play in encouraging children to eat the foods they have been given?

Chapter 18

Intellectual Development of School-Age Children and Adolescents

Essential Question

How do school-age children and adolescents develop more logical and systematic reasoning abilities, and how can adults challenge and nurture their intellectual progress?

Case Study   At What Age Should Children Have Their Own Cell Phones?

As a class, read the case study and discuss the questions that follow. After you finish studying the chapter, discuss this case study again. Have your opinions changed based on what you learned?

Bennett recently turned 11 years old and started asking for a smartphone. When Bennett's parents were less than eager about the idea, Bennett explained that getting a smartphone would help with homework and calling friends. Lastly, Bennett argued, "All of my friends have a smartphone."

*Bennett's parents felt frustrated with their child's persistent asking. After Bennett went to bed that night, they talked about the request. "I don't think it's true that **all** of Bennett's friends have smartphones," one parent said.*

Bennett's other parent went on to say, "I really do not think Bennett is ready for a smartphone. Also, we need to read up on how to protect Bennett while using a smartphone. Maybe we could get a phone that only allows calling and texting until Bennett is 13 or so."

Both parents agreed but were still worried that Bennett might resent them for not buying a smartphone with all the capabilities. They wanted to

talk with some other parents about how they were handling this issue.

Give It Some Thought

1. Do you think it is true that *all* of Bennett's friends have smartphones? What do you think is meant when Bennett says that?
2. What do you think Bennett's parents are talking about with needing to read up on how to protect Bennett while using a smartphone? What types of dangers might school-age children who have personal smartphones or computers face?
3. What do parents need to do before giving smartphones or other digital devices to their children for the first time? What skills and lessons do children need to learn before having their own digital devices?

SDI Productions/E+ via Getty Images

How School-Age Children and Adolescents Learn

Key Terms

concrete operational
  stage
conservation
deductive reasoning
formal operational stage
inductive reasoning
multiple intelligences
nucleus accumbens
prefrontal cortex

Learning Outcomes

After studying this lesson, you will be able to

18.1-1 **explain** brain development and cognitive changes that affect children's learning in the school-age and adolescent years.

18.1-2 **list** major gains in school-age children's and adolescents' thinking skills based on Piaget's theory.

18.1-3 **compare** Vygotsky's theory during the school-age and adolescent years to Piaget's theory.

18.1-4 **summarize** the types of intelligences Gardner proposed in his theory of multiple intelligences.

Reading and Notetaking Activity

Before reading, skim the headings in this lesson. List the headings to create an outline for taking notes during reading and class discussion. Under each heading, list any key terms. Finally, write two questions you expect to have answered in class. After completing the lesson, ask your teacher any questions you still have about the concepts or terms you learned.

Introduction

Children make dramatic gains in intellectual development during the school-age and adolescent years. Advances in brain development and intellectual (cognitive) changes make them more capable of logical thought. As their brains mature, school-age children enter Piaget's last two stages of intellectual development in which they rely less on perception and think more logically. Vygotsky theorized that children's intellectual development is also dependent on the environment for learning. The environment includes the learning opportunities provided and support from peers and adults.

As you have read throughout the text, the intellectual changes from stage to stage have focused on the common features of children's thinking abilities and limitations. Yet, there are wide differences in intellectual abilities of children of the same age and stage, which is commonly called *differences in intelligence*.

Gardner's theory of multiple intelligences represents one of the more recent theories concerning these differences.

18.1-1 Brain Development and Cognitive Changes

During the school-age years, children become capable of logical thought because of several advances in brain development and intellectual changes. Brain development and intellectual advances work together to create the "logical brain." The adolescent brain can perform even more complex tasks and participate in abstract thinking.

The Making of the "Logical" Brain

From the preschool years until 7 or 8 years of age, few structural changes occur in the brain.

Still, this is an important period in brain development because early experiences determine how well or how poorly the brain functions in later stages. Around 8 years of age, when children are completing the third grade, the following two major changes in the brain begin to occur:

- *Wiring in the prefrontal cortex.* During the school-age and adolescent years, wiring in the *prefrontal cortex* allows for higher cognitive functions. The **prefrontal cortex** is a section near the front of the brain that is involved in logical thinking, forming judgments, memory, weighing consequences, decision making, and controlling impulses and emotions **(Figure 18.1)**. As the prefrontal cortex develops, children are better able to engage in these behaviors. The prefrontal cortex is not fully developed until around the age of 25, but important wiring for its functions begins during the school-age years.

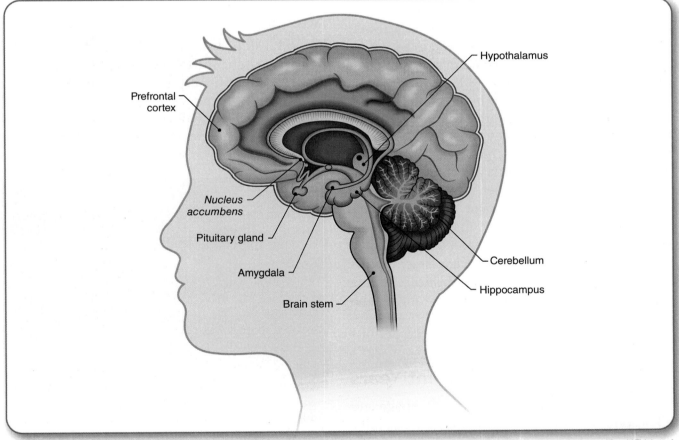

jambojam/iStock/ Thinkstock

Figure 18.1 The prefrontal cortex is located near the front of the brain and allows for higher cognitive functioning in school-age children. *What are some activities in which the prefrontal cortex is involved? How do school-age children engage in these activities with more ease than when they were younger?*

- *Pruning.* Pruning makes for faster and more efficient thinking. Pruning occurs after brain wiring and begins in the back of the brain (where the first connections were made) before moving toward the front of the brain. The prefrontal cortex is last to be pruned and myelinated.

When puberty begins, the brain starts a reorganization process. The exact timing of this process is influenced not only by age, but also by memory, problem-solving skills, and **metacognition** (the awareness of one's own knowledge and thinking). As the brain reorganizes, connections between association areas and language areas allow for richness in communication. Executive functions begin to mature and pruning fosters more efficient thinking and allows for more abstract and hypothetical reasoning. Because decision-making skills do not fully mature until pruning is complete in the prefrontal cortex, the **nucleus accumbens** (NOO-klee-us uh-KUM-buhnz), the pleasure and reward system of the brain, plays a large role in decision-making during these years. As a result, older school-age children, teens, and even young adults may make poor decisions in anticipation of pleasure or reward. (Figure 18.1 shows the location of the *nucleus accumbens* in the brain.)

In the school-age years, children's brains become less plastic than they were in earlier stages (infancy through the preschool years). Traumatic brain injuries (TBIs), which are common among school-age children and teens, may also lead to lessening plasticity. One major change to traditional thinking, however, is that research now shows early childhood is not the only period of increased brain plasticity. The adolescent years mark a second period of neuroplasticity, wiring the teenage brain for learning opportunities and skill acquisition.

Cognitive Advances in the School-Age and Adolescent Years

Brain development during the school-age and adolescent years leads to a number of cognitive changes, all of which make logical thinking more possible. To develop concepts and solve problems, children must acquire and process knowledge.

FOCUS ON MENTAL HEALTH

Traumatic brain injury (TBI) can result in changes to IQ, memory, attention, language, motor skills, and impulse control. It can also affect emotions and mental health. To care for your mental health after a TBI, focus on things like maintaining routines, getting enough sleep and exercise, making lists, and reaching out for help if needed. Being patient with yourself is key to recovery.

To do this, theorists believe that children must absorb relevant information, store it in their memories, and retrieve the information to apply it (**Figure 18.2**). The ability to do these tasks is dependent on cognitive changes in attention and memory.

Attention

To be able to think logically and solve problems, children must be able to pay attention, focus on relevant aspects of the environment, and disregard irrelevant aspects. Preschool and young school-age children often focus on what "stands out" and may miss what is relevant.

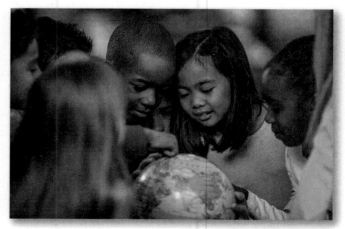

FatCamera/E+ Getty Images

Figure 18.2 Due to cognitive changes during the school-age years, these children can store information about geography and then recall that information to locate countries on the globe. *What are some other activities in which children must recall stored information and apply it?*

For example, in learning the letters *p*, *q*, *b*, and *d*, they may focus on the line and loop and miss what is important, which is the position (*up* or *down*) of the line and the orientation (*left* or *right*) of the loop. Older children and teens learn what is important in solving a task and focus attention on this aspect.

Memory

Memory is vital to logical thinking and problem solving. Children and adults alike draw on what they already know to solve current problems and acquire new information.

Explicit and implicit memories (also known as *long-term memories*) grow significantly during the school-age years. Throughout this time, children develop the following specific skills to help them access their explicit and implicit memories:

- *Rehearsing.* School-age children learn how to *rehearse* (repeat information until it is learned). While a young school-age child might rehearse by repeating one word over and over and then doing the same with the next word, an older school-age child might repeat the first and second words, then the first, second, and third words, and so on (**Figure 18.3**).
- *Organizing information.* School-age children learn to organize information for long-term memory storage. They often do this by categorizing items or events.

FatCamera/E+ Getty Images

Figure 18.3 School-age children can learn stories and facts by rehearsing them, either on their own or in a group. *What songs and stories can you think of that include word sequences that can be rehearsed?*

- *Using visual and verbal aids.* During the school-age years, children learn how to use visual aids, such as charts and outlines, and verbal aids, such as acronyms and sayings, to help them recall information. They continue to use these skills during the teen years.

Working memory (also known as *short-term memory*) improves during the adolescent years, helping solve complex learning tasks and problems. Teenage brains are also more capable of connecting personal experiences to additional information, such as the time, place, or emotions experienced. Besides an increased ability to remember, school-age children and teens have better understandings about how their memories work. These understandings aid school-age children and teens in both selecting the right memory strategies and knowing when information is truly memorized.

18.1-2 Piaget's Cognitive-Developmental Theory

Young school-age children learn in much the same way that older preschoolers do. Around seven or eight years of age, however, changes in thinking begin to occur, and children enter Piaget's third stage of intellectual development. Then, around 12 years of age, young adolescents go through another shift in their intellectual development, placing them in Piaget's fourth and final stage.

The Concrete Operational Stage

Piaget noted that between 7 and 11 years of age, school-age children's thinking skills are no longer dominated by perception. Children gradually learn to use logical thinking concepts to manipulate information, and their thinking becomes more flexible and organized as compared to younger children. Piaget called this third stage of intellectual development the **concrete operational stage**. The concrete operational stage is *concrete* because logic is based on the child's past experiences.

The transition between the preoperational stage and the concrete operational stage is very gradual. Young school-age children do not automatically apply logical thinking to all tasks.

Rather, over time, children become more logical and less dependent on their perceptions. Some children, and even adults, remain in the concrete operational stage for much of their thinking.

The Formal Operational Stage

Piaget's last stage of intellectual development is called the **formal operational stage**. In this last stage, children and adults can reason more abstractly. Some child development experts place the beginning of the formal operational stage at 12 to 14 years of age, but the age at which the stage begins varies from person to person. For most day-to-day activities, even adults reason in the concrete operational stage. People who use formal operations regularly in their occupations are mathematicians, engineers, scientists, and network architects.

The difference between the concrete and formal operational stages can be seen in how a child plays a game of checkers or chess. In the concrete operational stage, the child can play checkers or chess by the rules. They make each move based on which pieces are on the board at that time, but do not think in terms of the next three to five moves. A child in the formal operational stage, however, can think ahead and plan strategies for winning the game. **Figure 18.4** shows the differences in the ways children think in the concrete and formal operational stages.

Figure 18.4 **Piaget's Cognitive-Development Theory**

Stages and Substages	Characteristics
Stage 1: Sensorimotor stage (birth to 2 years)	• Children learn through the senses and physical actions in six substages.
Substages 1 and 2	• Involve the baby's own body.
Substages 3 and 4	• Involve people and objects.
Substages 5 and 6 (12 to 24 months)	• Involve creative actions and thinking before acting.
Stage 2: Preoperational stage (2 to 7 years)	• Children learn through symbols, but with logical limitations.
Substage 1	• Involves the development of concepts.
Substage 2	• Involves the use of perception.
Stage 3: Concrete operational stage (7 to 11 years)	• Children begin to think logically but base their logic on past experiences. • Can see things from various perspectives. • Focus on more than one aspect of something at the same time. • Gradually note transformations (conserve). • Number—5 to 7 years of age • Continuous quantities (liquid)—6 to 8 years of age • Mass (like clay)—6 to 8 years of age • Length—6 to 8 years of age • Area—7 to 9 years of age • Weight—8 to 10 years of age • Volume—10 to 14 years of age • Invert a sequence of steps (reversibility). • Use better reasoning skills.
Stage 4: Formal operational stage (11 years of age and older)	• Older children, teens, and adults reason abstractly. • Can hypothesize. • Do scientific and mathematical abstract reasoning.

Goodheart-Willcox Publisher

Overcoming Obstacles to Logical Thought

As children enter the concrete and formal operational stages, they begin to overcome many of the obstacles to logical thought they experienced during the preschool years. School-age children and teens entering these stages overcome egocentrism by learning to see from the viewpoints of others. They overcome centration by learning to focus on more than one aspect at a time. They also learn to note transformations, understand reversals, and learn to use deductive and inductive reasoning rather than transductive reasoning.

Seeing from the Viewpoints of Others

While preschoolers and younger children are primarily *egocentric* (focused on self), school-age children and teens begin to understand that other people have ideas that differ from their own. They learn to recognize others' points of views and notice how these views compare or contrast with their own ideas. Realizing that others have different ideas leads children to question their previous thoughts and search to find the right answers. School-age children and teens use logic to prove or deny these answers.

During the school-age years, children who try to solve difficult tasks may still exhibit some traces of egocentrism. When a school-age child forms a hypothesis about how or why an object or situation works, the child may force contradictory facts into their hypothesis rather than changing the hypothesis to fit the facts. This is because school-age children want to be right. These traces of egocentrism often disappear during the teen years when abstract thinking becomes more common.

Focusing on More Than One Part

During the school-age years, children begin to overcome their perceptions of *centration* (exclusive focus on one part of an object). School-age children learn to focus on more than one part of an object or situation at a time and can see more than one change at a time. For instance, if you refer again to Figure 15.7, notice that preschoolers were unable to see changes in length and width **simultaneously** (at the same time). In the school-age years, however, children can focus on the different-sized glasses and see that the greater width in the first glass makes up for the greater height in the other glass. Because they can note these changes simultaneously, school-age children are able to understand how the same amount of liquid looks taller in a thinner glass. By the teen years, these changes are even more readily noticed, and the adolescent can focus on several parts of an object at one time.

Focusing on more than one aspect allows school-age children and teens to use *conservation*. **Conservation** is the concept that changing an object's shape, direction, or position does not alter the quantity of the object. Children must be able to understand the principles of conservation before they can form accurate concepts related to number, *continuous quantities* (liquids), mass, length, area, weight, or volume (**Figure 18.5**).

Noting Transformations

Perceptions of centration make noting transformations difficult for children during the preschool years. However, as school-age children learn to note more than one aspect of an object at a time, they are better able to watch and understand certain *transformations* (sequences of changes). School-age children and teens can mentally arrange events to see a series of changes in objects. For example, school-age children can note that a caterpillar transforms into a butterfly or heat transforms ice into water. As shown in Figure 18.5, children understand certain transformations earlier than others.

Understanding Reversibility

School-age children and adolescents are better able to understand reversals. *Reversibility*, the ability to follow a line of reasoning back to where it started, enables children to carry out a task in reverse order. Reversibility depends on the understanding that if an object is changed and then returned to its original shape or form, it will be the same. For example, the school-age child or teen who flattens a ball of clay understands that the flattened clay can be restored to the original ball.

Figure 18.5 Piagetian Conservation Tasks

Type of Conservation	Presentation	
Note	During the initial presentation, the experimenter will ask a basic question (Q) to establish equivalence.	The transformation presentation is always done with the child watching, but without any comment from the experimenter.
Number (5 to 7 years of age)	**Initial Presentation** Two identical rows of objects are aligned.	**Transformation Presentation** One row is lengthened.
Question and Answer	**Q:** Are there the same number of _____ (name of objects) in each row, or does one row have more _____? **A:** A *preconserving* child says the longer row has more _____. A *conserving* child says both have the same number.	
Continuous quantities— liquid (6 to 8 years of age)	**Initial Presentation** Two identical glasses contain the same amount of colored water.	**Transformation Presentation** One glass remains the same; water from the other glass is poured into a third glass with a smaller (or larger) diameter.
Question and Answer	**Q:** Is there the same amount of water in both glasses, and does one glass have more water than the other? **A:** A *preconserving* child will say, "No." Usually, the child points to the glass with the water coming up higher as having more water. A *conserving* child will say, "Both are the same."	
Mass or matter—clay (6 to 8 years of age)	**Initial Presentation** Two identical balls are formed out of clay.	**Transformation Presentation** One ball is kept the same; the other ball is elongated.
Question and Answer	**Q:** Do the two balls have the same amount of clay, or does one ball of clay have more than the other? **A:** A *preconserving* child will say, "No." Usually, the child points to the elongated piece as having more clay. A *conserving* child will say, "Both are the same."	

Note: Piaget indicated the age in which 75 percent of children in his experiments could conserve and justify their answers. More recent researchers now give an age range. Justification of conservation can be done in one of three ways: (1) *Identity*—nothing is added or taken away; therefore, it is identical. (2) *Reversibility*—the alignment or shape of objects can be restored. (3) *Compensation*—one dimension of an object makes up (compensates) for another dimension (longer on one end, but shorter on the other; clay spreads out when flat but is thinner than the ball).

(Continued)

Figure 18.5 **Piagetian Conservation Tasks** (Continued)

Type of Conservation	Presentation	
Length (6 to 8 years of age)	**Initial Presentation** Two rods are aligned.	**Transformation Presentation** One rod is moved to the right.
Question and Answer	**Q:** Are the rods the same length, or is one rod longer than the other? **A:** A *preconserving* child will say, "This one is longer because it sticks out." A *conserving* child will say, "Both are the same."	
Area (7 to 9 years of age)	**Initial Presentation** Two identical sheets of cardboard or wood have one-inch cube blocks.	**Transformation Presentation** One board of blocks remains the same; the other board has the blocks scattered.
Question and Answer	**Q:** Do both boards have the same amount of open space, or does one board have more open space than the other? **A:** A *preconserving* child will say, "This one has more space." Usually, the child points to the board on which the blocks remain clustered. A *conserving* child will say, "Both have the same amount of open space."	
Weight (8 to 10 years of age)	**Initial Presentation** Two sets of three blocks are placed in horizontally aligned rows.	**Transformation Presentation** One set of blocks remains in horizontal position; the other set is stacked vertically.
Question and Answer	**Q:** Do the sets of blocks weigh the same, or does one set of blocks weigh more? **A:** A *preconserving* child will say, "This one weighs more." Usually, the child points to the vertical arrangement. A *conserving* child will say, "Both weigh the same."	
Volume (10 to 14 years of age)	**Initial Presentation** Two identical glasses are filled with the same amount of water. Two identical balls of clay are dropped into the glasses.	**Transformation Presentation** One glass with clay remains untouched; the clay in the other glass is removed, flattened, and laid by the second glass.
Question and Answer	**Q:** Will the two pieces of clay displace the same amount of water, or will one displace more water? **A:** A *preconserving* child will say, "One will displace more water." Usually, the child points to the flattened clay. A *conserving* child will say, "The water displacement will be the same."	

Note: Piaget indicated the age in which 75 percent of children in his experiments could conserve and justify their answers. More recent researchers now give an age range. Justification of conservation can be done in one of three ways: (1) *Identity*—nothing is added or taken away; therefore, it is identical. (2) *Reversibility*—the alignment or shape of objects can be restored. (3) *Compensation*—one dimension of an object makes up (compensates) for another dimension (longer on one end, but shorter on the other; clay spreads out when flat but is thinner than the ball).

Reversibility also means knowing that one change, such as in height, can lead to another change, such as in width. Consider the example of the clay. The school-age child or teen knows that the flattened clay will have a larger diameter than the round ball of clay.

To help school-age children and teens understand intellectual reversals, adults can first expose them to physical reversals, which can be observed and experienced (**Figure 18.6**). After physical reversals are "mastered," adults can ask children and adolescents to form a mental image of what happens during reversibility. Finally, children and teens should understand the principle. (The principle can be stated in one of three ways as shown in the "Note" at the bottom of Figure 18.5.)

Using Deductive and Inductive Reasoning

As preschoolers, children use *transductive reasoning* (linking events without using logic), but during the school-age and adolescent years, children graduate to using *deductive reasoning* and then *inductive reasoning*. **Deductive reasoning** is reasoning from the general to the specific. For example, if a child is presented with the general statement that all fish live in water, and if the child knows that guppies are fish, then the child can use deductive reasoning to conclude that guppies live in water.

Inductive reasoning, reasoning from specific facts to general conclusions, is often used by children 11 years of age and older. Inductive reasoning is also called *scientific reasoning* because it is the form of logic commonly used by scientists. Children who use inductive reasoning can weigh several ideas, test them, and then draw a conclusion. For example, a child who knows that water turns to ice when exposed to cold temperatures might use inductive reasoning to conclude that cold temperatures will also transform other liquids. To test this hypothesis, the child might put water and other fluids, such as juice, milk, and soft drinks, into the freezer. After weighing and testing several ideas, the child concludes that exposure to cold temperatures changes liquids into solids.

18.1-3 **Vygotsky's Sociocultural Theory**

While Piaget concluded that children's intellectual development was primarily due to brain development (*cognitive stage*), Vygotsky saw intellectual development as less dependent on the brain and more dependent on a child's ZPD (*zone of proximal development*). Vygotsky argued that children always learn best when their minds are "stretched" within their ZPDs (**Figure 18.7**). A child has different ZPDs depending on the intellectual (academic) area, such as math, language, and the arts.

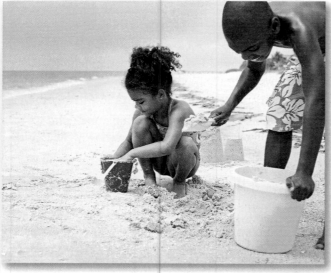

Fuse/Thinkstock

Figure 18.6 An example of a physical reversal might be letting a child pour water or sand from one container into a different container and back again. *What are some other physical reversals that a child can perform?*

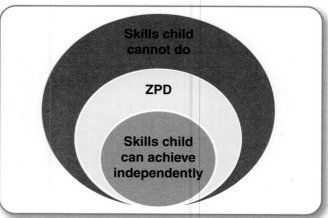

Goodheart-Willcox Publisher

Figure 18.7 The ZPD is the difference between what a child can do independently and what they can do with guidance. *How can adults plan activities that "stretch" children's minds without going beyond their ZPDs?*

Vygotsky also believed that collaboration among peers and between adults and children had a major impact on learning. Like Piaget, Vygotsky believed that children learn by doing, but he also thought that children learn by talking and working with others. He felt it was important for children to persist at tasks until they could perform them.

Piaget felt that language *reflected* learning. On the other hand, Vygotsky saw language *as a way of* learning. For example, children understand the process of learning through verbal interactions, such as explaining what they know and questioning others to clarify. During interactions, children also learn the needed tools and most effective ways to perform tasks. Vygotsky felt that after learning how to do a task, using silent words was important to performing the task independently.

18.1-4 Gardner's Theory of Multiple Intelligences

As children approach middle childhood and adolescence, it becomes very evident that they vary in their abilities to reason and learn new concepts. Howard Gardner's theory of multiple intelligences helps to explain this variance. A person's intellectual competence is usually called *intelligence*. For many years, researchers thought of intelligence as a general capacity or trait and called the measurement of this trait a person's *intelligence quotient* (IQ). These researchers believed that if a person had a high level of intellectual competence (measured as a high IQ), then their cognitive behaviors would be outstanding in all areas. In like manner, people with a low level of competence would not achieve to a high extent in most areas of intellectual performance.

The cognitive theories of Piaget and Vygotsky, as well as other research findings, show that the intellect reflects the diverse and complex skills children develop through their interactions within their natural and social worlds. Thus, more recently, psychologists have come to believe that intelligence consists of separate abilities, not a general overall trait. Howard Gardner goes a step further and defines the intellect as separate, distinct "intelligences."

The many ways that children learn are reflected in Howard Gardner's *theory of multiple intelligences*.

Multiple intelligences are intellectual abilities that contribute to overall intelligence. The types of intelligences Gardner proposed are listed in **Figure 18.8**. All children use all these intelligences to learn but use some to a greater extent than others.

Figure 18.8 Gardner's Multiple Intelligences

Type of Multiple Intelligence	Ability to...
Verbal/ Linguistic	• Understand communication • Communicate
Logical/ Mathematical	• Understand principles of cause and effect • Understand math principles
Bodily/ Kinesthetic	• Control and coordinate one's body to achieve goals • Demonstrate both gross- and fine-motor control and coordination
Visual/Spatial	• "See" space in one's mind • Convey visual and spatial ideas through the visual arts
Musical/ Rhythmic	• Recognize and appreciate tones and rhythmic patterns • Convey tone and rhythm in performing and composing
Naturalist	• Recognize and categorize living and nonliving things in nature • Show sensitivity to features of the natural world
Interpersonal	• Understand motivations and intentions of others and act with empathy • Lead or work with others to achieve goals on behalf of others
Intrapersonal	• Understand oneself, especially one's motivations and emotions • Recognize one's strengths and abilities to accomplish goals
Existential	• Pose questions about beliefs and values • Cause people to think about ethical issues

Goodheart-Willcox Publisher

School learning usually reinforces verbal/linguistic and logical/mathematical intelligences. As a result, school-age children and teens may not have the opportunities to exercise other intelligences. As much as possible, adults should ensure that school-age children and teens learn using the intelligences in which they excel, as well as the intelligences in which they feel challenged (**Figure 18.9**).

SolStock/E+ via Getty Images

Figure 18.9 It is important for school-age children to practice all their intelligences, not just the intelligences that are measured and encouraged in school. *What types of intelligence are involved in children playing outside?*

Lesson 18.1 Review and Assessment

1. Which of the following is true about the brain pruning that occurs in school-age children? (18.1.1)
   A. It permits faster and more efficient thinking.
   B. It occurs before wiring in the prefrontal cortex.
   C. It allows for logical thinking and decision-making.
   D. It begins in the prefrontal cortex.

2. The concept that changing an object's shape, direction, or position does not alter its quantity is _____. (18.1.2)
   A. centration
   B. reversibility
   C. conservation
   D. inductive reasoning

3. An example of reversibility is understanding that _____. (18.1.2)
   A. eggs can be broken and then scrambled
   B. water can freeze and then thaw
   C. glasses with different shapes contain the same amount of liquid
   D. other people have ideas that differ from one's own

4. **True or False.** While Piaget felt that language reflected learning, Vygotsky saw language as a way of learning. (18.1.3)

5. According to Gardner, a school-age child's ability to pose questions about beliefs and values is an example of their _____ intelligence. (18.1.4)
   A. naturalist
   B. musical/rhythmic
   C. existential
   D. intrapersonal

What School-Age Children and Adolescents Learn

Learning Outcomes

After studying this lesson, you will be able to

18.2-1 **explain** developments in concept learning during the school-age and adolescent years and give examples of the different types of concepts.

18.2-2 **chart** school-age children's and adolescents' progress in communicating, including articulation, vocabulary, grammar, and reading abilities.

18.2-3 **identify** intellectual developmental milestones school-age children and teens might achieve.

Key Terms

code-switch
culture-specific knowledge
hierarchical classification

Reading and Notetaking Activity

Before reading this lesson, skim the headings and write each heading in a different color or font on a separate piece of paper or electronically. As you silently read the chapter and then listen to your teacher, take notes in the color or font you chose for each heading. After you finish taking notes for each section, draw or copy and paste a small illustration or visual next to the section that will help you remember what you learned.

Introduction

School-age children's and teens' logical brains enable them to develop and understand many more advanced concepts than those learned in the preschool years. During the school-age and teen years, children understand physical knowledge, use logical thinking concepts, and acquire culture-specific knowledge. School-age children's and adolescents' communication skills improve as they articulate more clearly, expand their vocabularies, and use correct grammar. Their reading skills also improve. During the school-age and teen years, children achieve several significant intellectual developmental milestones.

18.2-1 Concept Learning

As their brains mature and school-age children and adolescents become more capable of logical thought, they develop and understand many new concepts. The major areas of concept learning for school-age children and teens include understanding physical knowledge, using logical thinking concepts, and acquiring culture-specific knowledge.

Understanding Physical Knowledge

Physical knowledge involves learning about attributes of objects and what happens to objects when they are acted upon. Young children acquire physical knowledge by acting upon objects and observing what happens. By the school-age and teen years, children begin to understand general scientific concepts such as gravity, force of wind, and weather. In short, *physical knowledge* is any knowledge of the physical world that is gained through experimentation with objects and includes the academic subjects of chemistry, physics, and astronomy.

During the school-age and teen years, physical knowledge concepts mature as children do more in-depth exploring of their worlds. For example, by nine years of age, children use their eyes or fingertips to trace outlines of objects instead of just glancing at them quickly. By the teen years, they may be asked to describe attributes of objects. This more thorough examination helps children note details in objects.

As they examine objects, children learn what information to act upon and what information to ignore. For example, if a school-age child or teen is tasked with identifying geometric shapes, they will ignore the colors of the shapes. Children also learn to correctly pair visual and auditory stimuli, such as letters with their sounds (**Figure 18.10**). Improved memories help children pay attention to important attributes and recall the names of attributes.

Figure 18.10 Another way children can learn to correctly pair visual and auditory stimuli is by associating written music notes with their pitches. *What other cognitive advances might make school-age children better able to read sheet music?*

Using Logical Thinking Concepts

During the preschool years, children began to grasp *logical thinking concepts*, which are concepts that are not experienced through the senses but are understood intellectually. These concepts were immature in preschool children due to their reliance on physical observation. Due to the development of their logical brains, however, school-age children and teens better understand a number of logical thinking concepts. These concepts include classifying objects; ordering by attributes; understanding cause and effect; applying spatial concepts; using number concepts; and noting distance, time, and speed.

Classifying Objects

Classifying is part of the reasoning process and an efficient way of thinking. Once a new phenomenon is catalogued as part of a particular class about which a person has some knowledge, the new phenomenon can be dealt with quickly. For example, suppose your biology teacher said, "Today, we are going to talk about a mallard duck." Although you may not have seen a mallard, once the word *duck* is said, you already know lots of information about a mallard.

Classification is the grouping of objects into a class and its complement. While preschool children struggled to classify by one stable attribute, such as color or shape, school-age children and teens classify accurately. For example, a school-age child can focus on one attribute and include all objects that contain the attribute for that class. By middle childhood, children fully understand the class and the complement.

School-age children also learn a new classification, called *hierarchical* (HY-uh-RAHR-kuh-kul) *classification*. **Hierarchical classification** is a type of classification in which select classes may contain other classes, or *subclasses*. For example, a large class of *animals* can be divided into subclasses, such as *birds* and *fish*. Groups of *birds* and *fish* can be **subdivided** (divided into smaller parts) as well. School-age children also understand the reverse; that is, subclasses can be combined to form larger classes. This continues into the teen years.

Ordering by Attributes

As preschoolers, children learned to *seriate* (arrange objects in order by the increasing or decreasing magnitude of one of the object's attributes). By the school-age years, children can illustrate relationships among objects by putting them in order according to a variety of attributes.

Ordering attributes might include those that can be seen (color, shape, size), heard (pitch, loudness), or felt (texture and temperature). Other attributes involve time or the order of events. School-age children and teens can order objects by even the smallest differences and use ordering in their daily lives, such as learning to read calendars, write lists, and **alphabetize** (put in alphabetical order).

Understanding Cause and Effect

School-age children begin to comprehend and resolve many of the cause-effect relationships that they could not grasp during the preschool years (**Figure 18.11**). As children become less egocentric, they understand that humans do not always cause natural happenings and begin to adopt a more scientific approach to their thinking.

The preschool belief that nonliving objects have lifelike qualities (called *animism*) is surrendered in favor of scientific answers. Some school-age children may still assign lifelike qualities to especially powerful aspects of nature (the sun and stars, oceans, mountains), but most school-age children understand that inanimate objects are not living. School-age children's and teens' understandings of cause and effect help them learn facts about the natural world.

Figure 18.11 School-age children's knowledge of cause and effect enables them to understand more about their world, including the environment and natural events. *Which, if any, cause-and-effect relationships were children able to understand during the preschool years?*

SDI Productions/E+ Getty Images

Applying Spatial Concepts

School-age children have many correct ideas about spatial relationships. They can identify whether objects are *open* or *closed* and *far* or *near*. They also understand relationships between two or more objects. School-age children can note and apply spatial concepts, such as *close to, connected, behind, in front of, above, below, left,* or *right*. School-age children know that objects, such as flying jets, do not get smaller even though they appear so as they move farther away. Spatial learning concepts can be reinforced into the teen years through Science, Technology, Engineering, and Math (STEM) courses, and through visual arts courses.

Using Number Concepts

During the late preschool and early school-age years, children learn basic concepts about numbers. They start to comprehend number concepts, such as *greater than, less than, equal to,* and others. As they begin to learn math in school, children use the number concepts they learned during the late preschool years and early middle childhood (**Figure 18.12**).

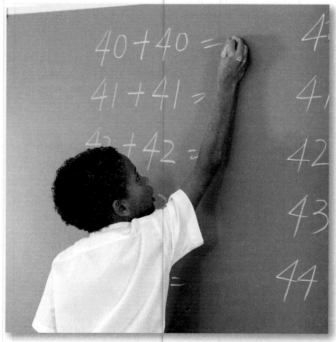

michaeljung/Shutterstock.com

Figure 18.12 School-age children can apply the number concepts they learned during the late preschool years to simple math equations like addition and subtraction. *How do math problems progress in difficulty throughout the school-age years?*

School-age children learn that groups are changed in number if more objects are brought into the group (*added*). They also learn that groups change in number if objects are taken away from the group (*subtracted*). Before the end of middle childhood, children can multiply and divide; understand the concept of measurement; begin to understand the relationships among fractions, decimals, and percentages; develop the ability to work word problems; and can estimate quantities. By the end of the teen years, children should expand on previous knowledge of fractions and decimals and be able to express numbers in bases and variables. Teens should also be able to use numbers in real-life situations, understand the ways math ideas build on each other, and use graphs, maps, and other methods to represent information.

Noting Distance, Time, and Speed

Children younger than eight years of age typically have difficulty grasping distance, time, and speed concepts, especially pertaining to the ways these concepts relate. Time and distance are often confused during the school-age years. For example, a young school-age child might say that walking some place is *far*, but that running makes it *near*. Except for understanding more complex topics regarding time and distance, such as different time zones and very great distances (solar system distances), many older school-age children develop rather accurate concepts of time and distance.

School-age children learn clock time and calendar time in the first or second grade. They do not note calendar time well, however, until 10 or 11 years of age. The timing of historical events can be difficult for children to grasp even into the teen years. Stories written for children often reflect childlike understandings of time. As children grow older, their stories graduate from starting with "once upon a time" to giving hints about seasons or years. By the late school-age and teen years, stories mention exact time periods.

Acquiring Culture-Specific Knowledge

As children interact within their physical world, they develop physical knowledge concepts and logical knowledge concepts. These concepts are universal.

For example, facts about gravity and three plus two equals five are the same in all cultures. **Culture-specific knowledge** is not universal; it is culturally relevant knowledge that one learns by being told or shown. A person does not learn culture-specific knowledge by experimenting within their physical world. Piaget referred to culture-specific knowledge as *social knowledge*. Language and literacy lessons, including vocabulary, articulation, and grammar, are culture-specific knowledge. History concepts, literature, and the arts are also considered culture-specific knowledge.

A culture's educational system often determines what culture-specific knowledge children must learn. Often, this knowledge changes as cultural needs change. For example, lessons in cursive writing have been replaced with other skills in some schools. Additionally, many schools have replaced lessons about telling time using analog clocks with digital clocks.

18.2-2 Communicating

Around six or seven years of age, children's speech becomes more social. School-age children begin to see language as a way of communicating and want to talk with friends and adults. They make great strides in learning articulation, expanding vocabularies, and learning grammar. By the beginning of the school-age years, children learn the basic concepts involved in learning how to read, such as associating letters with sounds.

Focus on Social Studies

The Impact of Culture-Specific Knowledge

Culture is a way of life within a group. With culture comes a collection of culture-specific knowledge that children gain over many years. Through this knowledge, children develop a *cultural lens*, which is a perspective through which they view the world. One example of culture-specific knowledge is history. As children learn their culture's history in school, they learn a distinct outlook on their culture, on other cultures, and on the world. Culture-specific knowledge also affects children's understanding of other subject areas and events. Some of these affected areas include:

Reasoning. Culture-specific knowledge affects which types of reasoning children value. Many European cultures believe that information acquired through scientific reasoning is most valid. Other cultures, such as some African cultures, prefer *affective* (feeling-based) ways of knowing.

Communication. Culture-specific knowledge also affects which types of communication children prefer. Some cultures (especially German- and English-speaking cultures) use explicit and specific communication. Other cultures teach knowledge that will help children "read between the lines."

Relationships. Children's approaches to relationships are also affected by the culture-specific knowledge they learn. Some cultures prefer establishing relationships before performing tasks while other cultures develop relationships as they work. Culture-specific knowledge will typically teach American children to handle conflicts directly. Other cultures will promote quiet and indirect ways of resolving conflict.

In small groups, discuss what subject areas of knowledge affect these habits and behaviors. Are there any school subject areas that are not culture-specific? Explain why or why not.

Photo: wavebreakmedia/Shutterstock.com

By the fourth grade, children have mastered many concepts about learning how to read. They begin to read to learn about social studies concepts, science concepts, and literature. Their learning will continue to build as they move into the teen years.

Learning Articulation

By eight years of age, most children have mastered the articulation of all sounds in their spoken language. Children who begin learning a second language as toddlers are often proficient in both languages by the school-age years. Children with articulation problems at the end of the preschool years, however, often continue to have speech problems in the school-age years. These speech problems are commonly related to reading problems because children need to articulate sounds to decode the sounds of letters, a skill that is needed for reading and spelling.

Expanding Vocabularies

Children's active vocabularies continue to expand in middle childhood. School-age children give more exact definitions than younger children do. If asked to define the word *orange*, a preschool

child may say, "You eat it." A school-age child would give a more precise definition, such as "It is a color or a fruit." Tests in school often ask school-age children to define words. Reading, spelling, and writing all help school-age children's vocabularies grow.

Middle childhood is also an age when children have fun with words. School-age children enjoy using the words they know to perform word rhymes, raps, and chants (**Figure 18.13**).

Viktar Lameika/iStock via Getty Images Plus

Figure 18.13 School-age children often engage in clapping word games with friends. *What word or rhyme games did you like to play at this age?*

Focus on Speech

Bilingualism

Older school-age children and teens trying to learn a second language may have more difficulty articulating the sounds of the new language than younger children learning the same language. Learning language during early childhood allows the child to use a natural approach to language learning. The child will listen to and understand the language, speak it, and then become symbol-literate in interactive ways (such as through reading and writing). After about 10 years of age, most children learn a new language through a more direct-instruction approach instead of a natural approach to language learning.

The window of opportunity for language learning begins in infancy and starts to close in the late school-age years (around 10 years of age). The sensitive periods for language learning close in this order: articulation, grammar, and then vocabulary. Despite this, the window of opportunity for language learning never completely closes. Many teens and adults may also achieve almost total mastery of new languages. Learning a second language is a requirement in most high schools and postsecondary institutions.

Photo: naluwan/Shutterstock.com

They also have fun telling jokes, riddles, and simple puns. As their vocabularies continue to expand, children often engage in more complex word play, such as doing crossword puzzles or word jumbles. They also enjoy board games involving words, such as Scrabble®. Speech, language, and communication continue to expand throughout the teen years. Children who read more tend to have more developed vocabularies than their peers. During the high school years, children will learn new types of language (for example, figurative language and sarcasm). Teens will also continue to add new words to their vocabulary daily during the ages of 14 through 18.

Learning Grammar

School-age children refine their understandings of **syntax** (sentence structure). Until nine years of age, children are often confused by **extraneous** (ek-STRAY-nee-us), nonessential, information in a sentence. For example, in the sentence "The sun, which is almost 93 million miles from Earth, contains gases that are converted into energy for heat and light on Earth," the distance between the sun and the Earth might be considered extraneous information. Sentences in the passive voice are also difficult for children younger than nine or 10 years of age. A sentence in the passive voice might read, "Pete was seen by Bill at the mall." If rewritten into the active voice, the same sentence would read, "Bill saw Pete at the mall."

School-age children often use their own set of grammar rules to make plurals, use pronouns, and show tense. These rules may or may not be those of standard grammar. School-age children speak and write the grammar they hear, and some children may **code-switch** (change their usage of grammar and even vocabulary when communicating with different cultural and age groups). If children have not learned standard grammar by the school-age years, using standard grammar after this age will require breaking incorrect grammar habits and relearning standard grammar. By the teen years, children are expected to have a solid grasp of grammar concepts to complete written and oral work in school. They must understand and use academic language to be successful during the high school years and beyond.

Reading in the School-Age and Adolescent Years

Human brains do not have a specialized location for reading. Many regions of the brain work together to make reading and comprehension occur. Young children begin to read by forming mental pictures of the words they see in their environments. They treat letters as three-dimensional objects, so school-age children often see letters, such as *b*, *d*, *g*, and *p*, as the same.

Because there are too many words for children to mentally map, children will begin to associate letters with sounds; called *grapheme-phoneme* (graf-eem foh-neem) *associations*. This may become difficult when the letter-to-sound relationships are not consistent, such as in the words *rain* and *rein*. Beginning readers must see each letter and then think the sound. Experienced readers begin to process several letters at once. During the school-age years, children become more adept at this and are better able to read quickly and accurately. As children move through the teen years, reading pace and accuracy should continue to improve. New skills for reading comprehension are introduced during these years.

18.2-3 Intellectual Developmental Milestones

School-age children and adolescents are better able to grasp concepts and communication. Their logical brains can now use logical thinking concepts, and they begin to perceive language as a social tool. While school-age children and teens are more capable of reasoning, their prefrontal cortexes are still wiring, which may lead to poor decision-making skills. **Figure 18.14** lists some intellectual developmental milestones for school-age children and adolescents.

Figure 18.14 School-Age and Adolescent Intellectual Milestones

Age	Intellectual Milestones
Six to seven years *MBI/Shutterstock.com*	• Sits and pays attention for about 12 to 21 minutes at a time. • Is eager to learn. • Begins to rely on reason, rather than perception, in problem solving. • Tells and retells stories in logical order. • Begins to note several aspects of a situation at one time. • Begins to note transformations; to understand reversibility; and to conserve numbers, continuous quantities, liquid, mass, and length. • Wants detailed explanations for some complex "why" and "how" questions. • Begins to read, write (with phonetic spellings, such as *kat* for *cat*), and do some arithmetic. • Knows day segments and reads a clock. • Knows left and right. • Uses descriptive phrases in talking. • Is confused by extraneous information, complex sentence construction (including passive voice), and implied word meanings. • Appreciates humor in language. • Locates letters, numbers, and special keys on the computer keyboard; begins learning a word-processing program; uses subject-specific software programs to reinforce school subjects.
Eight to nine years *George Rudy/Shutterstock.com*	• Sits and pays attention for about 16 to 27 minutes at a time. • Considers other peoples' perspectives • Remembers large amounts of information. • Uses oral language to inform, persuade, and entertain. • Knows the days of the week, months of the year, and day's date. • Conserves area. • Draws three-dimensional figures. • Describes objects in detail. • Is a more proficient reader; enjoys recreational reading. • Uses meaning clues in reading (titles, pictures). • Knows key elements of stories (characters, plots, main ideas). • Writes legibly and organizes writing. • Becomes more advanced in keyboarding and using word processing programs; uses computer peripherals (printers and scanners); uses more sophisticated creativity programs to make slide shows and animations; uses search engines on the internet to locate information for school assignments; uses skills to do school assignments.
Ten to twelve years *Ground Picture/Shutterstock.com*	• Sits and pays attention for about 20 to 36 minutes at a time. • Applies math and science concepts to daily activities. • Conserves weight and volume. • Reads for information and recreation. • Can keep informational details straight. • Can put events in the correct time sequence. • Writes notes and letters. • Understands that words can have multiple meanings. • Paraphrases and summarizes content. • Compares and contrasts stories. • Searches for needed information (in books and on the internet). • Develops plans to meet goals. • Writes in different genres (factual essays, creative stories, poems). • Learns computer-use ethics; begins to use spreadsheets and database software; learns basics of multimedia software programs; uses computers for school assignments, hobbies, and socializing; uses other types of digital equipment.

Goodheart-Willcox Publisher
(Continued)

Figure 18.14 **School-Age and Adolescent Intellectual Milestones** (Continued)

Age	Intellectual Milestones
Thirteen to fifteen years *Phovoir/Shutterstock.com*	• Sits and pays attention for about 26 to 45 minutes at a time. • Has more philosophical and futuristic concerns in thinking. • Analyzes and questions frequently and intensely. • Begins to form own code of ethics (what do I think is right and wrong?). • Begins to develop thoughts around their identity. • Continues to consider and plan for future goals. • Begins to think systematically about relationships and how they can be influenced. • Ability to see the big picture and consider consequences to actions, but strong emotions still drive impulsive activity. • Continues to develop reading comprehension skills like inferring, questioning, and summarizing. • Learns new math concepts of using bases, variables, graphs, and other methods of representation. • Continues to expand vocabulary, adding 7-10 new words per day. • Uses numbers in real-life situations. • Uses strategies to find and use information from many sources. • Writes in many different formats about different topics.
Sixteen to eighteen years *Have a nice day Photo/ Shutterstock.com*	• Sits and pays attention for 32 to 48 minutes or more at a time. • Uses more complex thought; is more focused on decision making and less focused on self-centered topics. • Has more interest in global topics: Justice, politics, history. • May form intolerances for opposing views. • Focuses thinking on career decisions and role as an adult in society. • Utilizes better impulse control and can more accurately gauge risks and rewards. • Thinks abstractly and can deal with several concepts at once. • Can solve more complex problems, use analogies, make inferences, and use deductive and inductive reasoning.

Lesson 18.2 Review and Assessment

1. A school-age child's ability to recognize that vegetables can be organized into subcategories like leafy green and root vegetables, and leafy green vegetables can be broken into smaller groups like spinach and lettuce is an example of _____. (18.2.1)
   A. seriation
   B. animism
   C. social knowledge
   D. hierarchical classification

2. **True or False.** A child learns culture-specific knowledge by experimenting within their physical world. (18.2.1)

3. **True or False.** Many regions of the brain work together to make reading and comprehension occur. (18.2.2)

4. Six to seven-year-olds commonly achieve which intellectual developmental milestone? (18.2.3)
   A. Using oral language to inform, persuade, and entertain
   B. Telling and retelling stories in logical order
   C. Writing legibly and organizing writing
   D. Having a vocabulary of 7,200 words

Meeting School-Age Children's Intellectual Needs

Key Terms

after-school programs
enrichment activities
filtering program
flipped classroom
middle school
primary school
special lessons and
  activities

Learning Outcomes

After studying this lesson, you will be able to

18.3-1 **explain** how caregivers can prepare their children for both primary, middle, and high schools.

18.3-2 **describe** ways adults can support their children in school.

18.3-3 **summarize** how parents and caregivers can support their school-age or adolescent child's intellectual abilities outside of school.

18.3-4 **assess** how adults can guide children's electronic media use during the school-age and teen years.

Reading and Notetaking Activity

Before reading this lesson, scan the lesson headings. Write a paragraph describing what you already know about these topics. Explain where you got the information you have—from conversations, the media, or research, for example. As you are reading, compare and contrast the information in the chapter with your prior knowledge. Organize your notes around the information you already know. After reading, consider how your prior knowledge of the subject matter helped you understand this topic.

Introduction

As school-age children and teens mature and their brains become more able to grasp intellectual concepts and activities, it is important that their intellectual needs are met. Most of a child's intellectual needs will be met *in school* once this stage begins. The meeting of intellectual needs in schools, however, does not **mitigate** (lessen) the importance of parents' efforts to meet their children's needs. In fact, children only spend about 20 percent of their total hours each day in school. Thus, the home is also an important learning environment.

During the school-age and teen years, parents and other caregivers can meet children's intellectual needs by preparing their children for school, supporting them in school, planning activities for children to learn outside of school, and guiding children's media use. Having an interest in what a child learns affects the child's achievement.

18.3-1 Preparing Children for School

After completing preschool, school-age children are not automatically prepared to enter school and learn in this new, structured environment. The start of school may be exciting for some children and scary for others. No matter a child's feelings toward school or the grade a child is starting, entering school is a new developmental task for children. School-age children must interact with new people—both children and adults. They must process new concepts and skills and adjust to a different and uncomfortable daily structure (**Figure 18.15**). Adults can help meet school-age children's intellectual needs by:

- helping children make the transition from home to school
- making the new structures of school as enjoyable as possible

How a caregiver helps their child prepare for school may depend on what level of schooling the child is entering. School-age children experience the most **upheaval** (potentially upsetting change) when they enter primary school and when they enter middle school and high school.

miodrag ignjatovic/E+ via Getty Images

Figure 18.15 When children start school, stress may accompany the new hours and routines. *How can parents and caregivers help a child adjust to the start of school?*

Preparing Children for Primary School

After the preschool years, young school-age children enter **primary school** (also called *elementary school*), which usually includes the elementary grades first through fifth or sixth and sometimes kindergarten. (The primary school should not be confused with what early childhood educators call the *primary grades*, kindergarten or first grade through third grades.) Many young school-age children express stress and anxiety about school. Unlike preschool relationships, school relationships are more teacher directed. Children sit, line up, work, eat, and share with other children per their teacher's instructions. School means getting along with other children for many hours.

Figure 18.16 Helping Children Transition to Primary School

- Read and encourage children to read books about starting school. If possible, visit the school and meet the teacher prior to the first day.
- Make transportation plans clear to children. Younger children who walk or take a bus need instructions and practice. Adults or older children should be nearby, and children should be reminded not to talk to or go with strangers. Children should know their full names, as well as parents' names, addresses, and phone numbers.
- Help children view school attendance as a natural course of events. Tell children that "everyone goes to school." Adults can plan a normal routine for the first few days of school. Taking too many photos, sounding anxious, getting children ready too early or too late, or serving a special breakfast may make children even more anxious.
- Say good-byes at the bus stop, on the schoolyard, or at the classroom door. These good-byes should be warm, but not clingy. Teary-eyed children often regain control soon after parents are out of sight.
- Meet the bus or pick up children on time. Being late adds stress to a new beginning.
- Show a strong interest in children's reports about their school days.

Goodheart-Willcox Publisher

Children who are adaptable and have had many interactions with other children usually find it easier to adjust. **Figure 18.16** lists ways that adults can help young school-age children transition to primary school. If the first days go well, children look forward to school. Negative experiences, however, may lead to children wanting to avoid school and stay home.

Preparing Children for Middle and High School

Toward the end of the school-age years, children often enter *middle school*. **Middle school** is school for children approaching the teen years and often includes children in the fifth or sixth through eighth or ninth grades. High school typically includes children from ninth through twelfth grades. Middle school and high school age and grade ranges depend on the school's location and population. Upon entering middle school, children transition from being the most advanced children in their primary school to being the least advanced children in their middle school. Unlike primary schools, middle schools are often large; and children may have six or more teachers and

must walk between classes in crowded halls. Children's friends from primary school may not be in the same classes, and children are more likely to be bullied at this age. A similar transition occurs when children make the shift from middle school to high school. Increased expectations, a more intense focus on grades, and a larger course load can be overwhelming along with new social situations. **Figure 18.17** lists ways adults can help older school-age children and teens make smooth transitions to middle school and high school.

18.3-2 Supporting Children in School

School-age children and teens need daily encouragement and help. Adults can meet children's intellectual needs by working with and helping them with their schoolwork. Help is not effective if given only after the teacher shares negative reports. Parents and caregivers should take active roles in supporting their children at school and work as a team with teachers to give their children the best possible education.

Figure 18.17 Helping Children Transition to Middle and High School

- Visit the school with the child beforehand so the child will know their way around the campus.
- Attend orientation meetings and conferences.
- Check the school website and look at important announcements, bell schedules, and other information that might help the child be successful.
- Purchase the correct supplies and uniforms. If possible, purchase school-spirit items to make the child feel more a part of the school.
- Explain to the child that each teacher will have different expectations and classroom policies. The child will need a planner for writing assignments and testing dates. Offer to help the child study and reinforce strong organizational skills.
- Discuss increased expectations for work, grades, and testing. Make sure there is a dedicated and distraction-free area for the child to complete schoolwork at home.
- Encourage the child to attend clubs for making friends and being involved.
- Have honest talks with the child about teasing and bullying behaviors. Tell the child what they should do if bullied. Become familiar with the school's policies surrounding bullying and other offenses.
- If the child has problems adjusting, ask open-ended questions. Suggest options but try to help the child make decisions about handling these problems. Make time every day to talk about school.
- Adjust home routines, such as bedtime, to work with the new school schedule.
- Encourage and enforce good bedtime habits and routines. No games or screens before bed is a good rule of thumb. Adolescents need 8.5 to 9.5 hours of sleep each night.

Goodheart-Willcox Publisher

Although teens want to be more independent, it is still important for adults to give them opportunities to speak about school and to ask for help. Adults can support their children in school by reinforcing school tasks, strengthening executive functions, and being a school advocate.

Reinforcing School Tasks

Caregivers can help meet children's intellectual needs by reinforcing the tasks their children learn in school. To do this, adults can ensure that children complete any activities or homework assignments the school sends home with them. Parents and caregivers should supervise school-age children's homework. In primary school, homework is most often assigned to reinforce skills learned in the classroom. Some classrooms use a **flipped classroom** mode of teaching in which children learn concepts and facts by reading their textbooks and watching videos at home and then do homework-type assignments while at school.

While adults can help children with their homework, they should not do it for them. Doing children's homework, whether in a traditional or a flipped classroom, causes children to rely on adults to solve their tasks and problems. It also prevents children from getting needed practice and taking responsibility for learning. If the homework assigned seems too difficult, caregivers may want to talk to their children's teachers. Some positive ways adults can help children with their homework are shown in **Figure 18.18**. Children who are younger or who have weak executive functions will need more supervision. By the teen years, adults typically do not have to supervise homework on a day-by-day basis, but it is still important for adults to check in with children to make sure that they are able to handle their workload.

Strengthening Executive Functions

Executive functions (EFs) are skills that people use to manage themselves and their resources to achieve goals. The executive functions are necessary for success in life and school. The most identified executive functions are working memory

Figure 18.18 Supervising School-Age Children's Homework

- Set up a quiet work area without distractions. Supplies should be available at the work area.
- Meet any of the child's needs, such as a nutritious snack, before beginning work.
- Use the child's planner to go through daily assignments. Consult the calendar for progress made on long-term assignments. Help the child prioritize before beginning work on the assignments. The child needs to learn to do more difficult tasks first.
- Monitor the child's work.
- Help the child with any content needing practice, such as learning spelling words, memorizing, and reviewing for tests.
- Explain and provide strategies for problem-solving assignments or projects. Teach the child how to locate resources for papers.
- Help the child check for the completion of the assignment.
- Do not correct assignments but encourage the child to check and self-correct. Have the child pack the assignment in a binder or backpack.

Goodheart-Willcox Publisher

AVAVA/ Shutterstock.com

(also called *short-term memory*), cognitive flexibility (the ability to adjust to changing demands), and inhibition (the ability to filter thoughts and feelings). Weak executive functions, especially in older school-age children, often indicate learning problems or behavioral disorders.

School-age children with weak executive functions are easy to identify. These children tend to be disorganized and take a very long time to do simple tasks. They often fail to record assignments, lose papers and notes, procrastinate, and **belabor** (drag out for too long) the decision-making process in writing a paper or doing a project. Other signs of weak executive functions include a lack of focus and problems managing frustrations.

Caregivers of children with weak executive functions need to do more to help a child through home routines and school assignments. **Figure 18.19** lists ways to help these children. In addition to these suggestions, parents and caregivers should seek professional help for their children through consultation with a pediatrician or school counselor. If children with weak executive functions are not supported during the school-age years, they will face more challenges as they enter middle school and high school, where there are usually more rigid rules about deadlines and requirements for work.

Being a School Advocate

When parents and caregivers become involved in their children's schools and think of themselves as teammates to the school's administrators and teachers, children do better in almost every way.

Figure 18.19 Guiding Children with Weak Executive Functions

Routine	Tips
Home routines	• Develop consistent rituals and routines. • Never try multitasking. Focus on one task at a time. • Reduce distractions. • Make checklists with pictures or words. Include each step for morning and evening routines, household tasks, and homework. • Reduce steps in the morning routine by doing some tasks at night, such as laying out clothes and packing a backpack for the next day.
Homework routines	• Organize workspace with supplies. Some children need separate work areas for different activities. Minimize clutter and clean and organize space regularly. • Make a general checklist for different types of assignments, such as "get pencil and paper," "put name on paper," and so on. • Use a planner to look over all assignments. • Prioritize assignments and make a schedule. Break long assignments into "chunks" with time frames for each "chunk." • Scan directions for each assignment and repeat directions before beginning the task. • Help children learn how to study. • Show children how to use text features, such as headings, words in bold, and figures. • Sequence tasks, such as alphabetizing words before finding meanings in a glossary or dictionary. • Explain that for multiple-choice tests one must study details, but for essay tests one must "tell the story." • Explain that in social studies one looks for main ideas, but in math one works sample problems. • Help children remember by giving other examples of a concept, summarizing, or applying lessons. • Explain the rationale for learning a concept or skill. Children with weak executive functions spend lots of time weighing the worth of a lesson versus the effort to learn it. • Use a pocket folder for storing and transporting school materials.

Goodheart-Willcox Publisher

Adults who are school advocates:

- try to attend orientation meetings and conferences with teachers
- respond to teacher communications
- approach teachers or counselors with any concerns
- participate in follow-up communication if needed
- volunteer in schools
- attend school events when their children are involved

Adult involvements in these activities help children feel more at-home during school and feel more protected. Likewise, this involvement often increases the achievement of students. As teenagers get older, they may feel embarrassed or frustrated if they feel their parents are too involved, so it is important to discuss the level of involvement that the child is comfortable with. It may be appropriate for parents of a high school student to be involved in ways that are more behind the scenes.

18.3-3 Meeting Intellectual Needs Outside of School

Children's intellectual needs are met through schools during the school-age and teen years. Adults can plan many activities to help school-age children and teens learn in their school environments, but the home is also an important place for meeting intellectual needs. Adults can meet children's needs in the home by providing enrichment activities and special lessons and activities.

Providing Enrichment Activities

Intellectual development includes more than the academic subjects taught in schools. It also includes children's reasoning, hobbies, and the multiple intelligences outlined in Gardner's theory of multiple intelligences. Schools tend to emphasize verbal/linguistic and logical/mathematical intelligences.

Focus on Careers

School Counselor

School counselors work with students to help them set academic and career goals and develop a plan to meet these goals. They counsel students individually and in groups depending on their needs. They also provide guidance to help students deal with social and behavioral problems. School counselors work jointly with other teachers and relevant adults to help students succeed.

Career cluster: Education and training.

Education: Educational requirements include a master's degree and state-issued credential.

Job outlook: Future employment opportunities for school counselors are expected to grow faster than average for all occupations.

To learn more about a career as a school counselor, visit the United States Department of Labor's *Occupational Outlook Handbook* website. You will also be able to compare the job responsibilities, educational requirements, job outlook, and average pay of school counselors with similar occupations.

Photo: Creatas/Creatas/Thinkstock

It is important, however, that children practice their strongest intelligences and engage in all intelligences to some degree. Adults can help their children develop these intelligences by planning **enrichment activities** (any activities beyond academic subjects that help children develop intellectually). Through enrichment activities, children often tap **underutilized** (underused) intelligences, increase their self-concepts, and have fun. **Figure 18.20** lists enrichment activities for each type of intelligence. Enrichment activities can occur both in after-school programs and in the actual home.

In After-School Programs

Working caregivers often cannot bring their children home immediately after the school day. As a result, many school-age children attend **after-school programs**, which are programs that supervise, care for, and teach children after school until parents or caregivers finish the workday. When choosing after-school programs for their children, adults can note the enrichment activities that programs provide. Enrichment activities might include helping children with their hobbies and interests and helping children with homework and general academic skills. In high school, many children participate in after school activities such as sports or clubs.

In the Home

Adults can also plan enrichment activities for the hours their children are home. Some examples of these activities include:

- visiting museums, aquariums, zoos, and other places of interest
- enrolling and supporting children in youth groups, such as scouting, 4-H, religious groups, or local sports teams
- involving children in volunteer work
- attending special community programs, such as plays, concerts, dance performances, and sporting events
- engaging in physical activities, such as walking, going to neighborhood parks, playing ball, and using media for physical fitness routines
- engaging in crafts and hobbies
- playing board games and working puzzles

- enjoying books
- going on outings and vacations
- sharing household responsibilities, such as cooking dinner

Figure 18.20 Enrichment Activities for the Multiple Intelligences

Type of Multiple Intelligence	Enrichment Activities
Verbal/Linguistic	• Reading activities • Storytelling • Word puzzles (such as crosswords) • Writing
Logical/Mathematical	• Math • Logical problems • Science experiments • Strategy games
Bodily/Kinesthetic	• Dramatic play • Dancing • Science experiments • Arts and crafts
Visual/Spatial	• Visual art • Puzzles • Mazes
Musical/Rhythmic	• Activities involving hearing • Music • Dancing
Naturalistic	• Outdoor activities • Hands-on activities • Field trips • Journaling
Interpersonal	• Group discussions • Group activities
Intrapersonal	• Reflective activities • Journaling
Existential	• Activities comparing points of view • Develop rubrics for self-evaluation of learning performance-based tasks

Goodheart-Willcox Publisher

Parents and caregivers can also encourage intellectual development in the home by modeling their interests in their own activities. This provides good modeling for children.

Providing Special Lessons and Activities

Very closely related to enrichment activities are **special lessons and activities**, classes, or clubs where children can discover their own interests and talents (**Figure 18.21**). Many of these lessons and activities involve a team aspect, and as children grow older, wider varieties of activities will be available to them. Many school-age children want to sign up for every activity they hear their friends are doing. The best way for children to discover their interests and talents is to have a wide range of experiences. If children stretch themselves too thin, however, they may not excel in the activities they choose. Decisions about participating in these lessons and activities should be made by caregivers and children cooperatively. When deciding among activities, the following criteria should be considered:

- *Fit.* Do the activities fit well with the child's interests and strengths? If the child wants to quit an activity in which they are talented, caregivers may try to negotiate with the child. Some children just need a short break from an activity. If after a waiting period, the child still finds no joy in the activity, they can try another one.
- *Schedule.* How will the activities fit into the child's daily schedule? Children need time to do homework and chores, eat, sleep, play, and relax. The combined schedules of all family members may also affect the child's ability to participate in certain activities.
- *Cost.* Do the lessons and activities involve extra costs, such as prices for instruments and music, sports gear, and dance costumes (**Figure 18.22**)? Some adults borrow or rent expensive items until they know their children are committed to an activity.
- *Competition.* Will the activities be too demanding or competitive for the child's age? Activities for children should be fun and age appropriate. Coaches and other adults who are overly demanding or competitive may put too much pressure on children.
- *Safety.* Are the activities safe for the child's age and health? Is proper safety equipment provided? Leaders of activities should always consider the safety of all participants.

Jose Gil/Shutterstock.com

Figure 18.21 Special lessons and activities, such as karate classes or other clubs, offer a way for children to explore their talents and abilities. *What are some other lessons or activities children can participate in to explore their talents?*

EmirMemedovski/E+ via Getty Images

Figure 18.22 Equipment or clothing for activities, such as costumes for ballet, can become costly. *What are some ways parents can save money on these items?*

18.3-4 Guiding Electronic Media Use

During the school-age and teen years, children become more skilled at using electronic media. They are more independent in their media choices and activities and know how to use electronic media without adult supervision. Adults and caregivers may feel anxious about their children using media, but electronic media activities have many potential benefits for school-age children and teens. For example, quality media can be used to support school lessons and enhance problem solving, decision making, creativity, concepts, language lessons, and even social skills. With good software and access to the internet, children can:

- retrieve information
- communicate (send and receive e-mails, "talk" with experts, and compose stories and poems)
- publish their works
- visit interactive sites

To meet children's intellectual needs and ensure their safety when using electronic media, adults should guide their school-age children's media use. This guidance may mean providing digital devices at appropriate times and protecting children from media-related risks.

FOCUS ON MENTAL HEALTH

Spending too much time on digital devices and social media can contribute to mental health issues. Adults and children of all ages should practice responsible use and limited screen time. Participating in activities like being outdoors, playing, exercising, reading, and being creative can boost mental health. Always follow recommended guidelines on screen time and device use.

Providing Digital Devices at Appropriate Times

Adults often ask, "When is the right time for my child to have their own digital devices, especially mobile devices?" When considering this question, a child's age is typically not as important as a child's developmental maturity. As adults **grapple** (struggle) with this question, they can ask themselves a number of questions, including the following:

- *How have I modeled the use of digital devices to my child?* Adults are models for their children's digital device use. Adults should practice responsible use of their devices if they expect the same from their children.
- *Why does my child need a digital device?* By the middle-school years, children are often more independent and may stay home alone or attend activities on their own. These children may benefit from digital devices that help them stay connected with caregivers.
- *What security controls should I implement?* Adults should consider what security controls they want to put in place for their children and then talk with their children about these controls.
- *What usage rules should I set, and will my child respect these rules?* Adults should set rules for their school-age children's media use and ensure that their children follow these rules. A good indicator of willingness to follow rules may be how well the child followed rules for family-shared devices. As children get older, adults can revisit their guidelines.
- *How will I supervise my child's use of digital devices?* School-age children need guidance in using media devices. Adults should plan how they will supervise their children's media use and discuss this with their children. Adults may change their supervision practices as children get older.

Protecting Children from Media-Related Risks

As positive as media use can be for children, there are also risks involved with children's media use. For example, on the internet, children can be exposed to inappropriate or even illegal content, either on purpose or by accident. They can connect online to strangers who have harmful intentions.

One of the best ways adults can protect their children in a digital age is to establish use guidelines for media and digital devices, set and enforce rules, and supervise use of all internet-enabled devices. Some examples of guidelines might be using safe search engines that forbid inappropriate content, teaching children to use the internet for specific purposes, explaining the difference between private and public information, teaching children about passwords and location systems, and setting safety rules for use of media and digital devices (**Figure 18.23**).

In addition to teaching safety guidelines, parents should establish barriers and modes of supervision for their children's media use. Some adults use *filtering programs*. A **filtering program** is an application designed to prevent children from accessing inappropriate content. Filtering programs:

- provide information concerning children's specific activities on their digital devices and can block access to websites with adult content
- limit access to the internet during set hours
- create a log of visited sites
- track internet discussions in chat rooms
- monitor software downloaded to a personal digital device

Most companies that provide filtering programs also provide parent/caregiver intelligence systems. These systems allow adults to note the calls and texts their children are making, what apps they are using, when they are surfing, and shut-down times. Providers can tailor alerts for child's media devices, such as voice minutes, text messages, data usage, and app downloads (including purchases).

Most basic service providers have parental controls. Even with these barriers in place, however, adult supervision and rule enforcement is still needed. Guiding children's use of digital and media devices involves both safeguards and close supervision. Finally, as with all aspects of life, adults must set a good example for their children when using digital devices.

Figure 18.23 Media and Digital Device Safety Rules for Children

- Use media and digital devices only at times approved by adults. (Some parents collect all mobile devices and laptops during red-light times to lessen temptations.)
- Limit website visits and personal messages to an adult-approved list.
- Do not use chat rooms, bulletin boards, and social networking sites unless approved by adults.
- Demonstrate responsibility in caring for media and digital devices by protecting them from damage, breakage, loss, or theft.
- Do not give out any personal information or send any photos. (Children should use a screen name when on the internet.) Require the child to ask an adult before giving out any personal information.
- Tell adults about any uncomfortable images, information, or message, and never respond to such messages. (Unwanted and inappropriate messages are sent daily to many children, and many children never report this to their caregivers.)
- Do not meet in person with anyone you have met online without a parent with you. Explain the internet is not a place to make friends.
- Never open an e-mail message from someone you do not know.
- Always use ethical behavior.
- Do not try to override technological barriers or erase browser history. Accept the fact adults will supervise media and digital device use.

Goodheart-Willcox Publisher

Assessing Children's Digital Media

With each passing year, school-age children and teens spend more time *using* technology as a means of learning rather than *experimenting* with the tools. School-age children and teens enjoy media programs that make learning fun.

The International Society for Technology in Education (ISTE) has developed seven areas of student standards that should be integrated into media use within the school curriculum. The standards include the following roles for students:

- Empowered Learner
- Digital Citizen
- Knowledge Constructor
- Innovative Designer
- Computational Thinker
- Creative Communicator
- Global Collaborator

Using these standards, caregivers can assess the electronic media software, including websites, apps, and computer programs their children will use both in and outside of school. Teachers may also be able to provide parents and caregivers with a list of suitable software that children use in their classrooms.

Based on this information, adults can choose appropriate media hardware.

Knowing how children use digital media to do homework and projects will enable caregivers to closely supervise their children's media use. If parents and caregivers are uncomfortable with their children's media use, there are many resources they can access. Much literature on children's media use is available through parenting magazines, children's magazines, newspapers, the internet, and in professional books and articles.

Application Activity

In small groups, choose three electronic media devices, software, websites, or apps that school-age children access regularly. Research how these products can be used and test them in your group. Then, evaluate the three products according to the criteria in this lesson. Present your findings to the class.

Photo: Tom Wang/Shutterstock.com

Lesson 18.3 Review and Assessment

1. **True or False.** Preparing a child for primary school includes ensuring children know their full names, their parents' names, addresses, and phone numbers. (18.3.1)

2. A school-age child or teen with weak executive function is likely to demonstrate all the following except _____. (18.3.2)
   A. frequently losing papers
   B. difficulty managing frustration
   C. belaboring decision-making
   D. keeping track of assignments

3. **True or False.** One way a caregiver can be a school advocate is to approach teachers or counselors with any concerns. (18.3.2)

4. Keeping a log of the different songbirds that visit a backyard birdfeeder is an activity that supports _____ intelligence. (18.3.3)
   A. verbal/ linguistic
   B. visual/spatial
   C. logical/ mathematical
   D. intrapersonal

5. **True or False.** Filtering programs and parent/caregiver intelligence systems eliminate the need for adult supervision of children and teens who are using electronic devices. (18.3.4)

Chapter 18 Review and Assessment

Summary

Lesson 18.1

18.1-1 Wiring and pruning in the brain's prefrontal cortex during the school-age years enables children to think logically.

18.1-1 Cognitive advances, including attention and memory, also aid intellectual development. Children develop the specific skills of rehearsing, organizing information, and the ability to use visual and verbal aids to help them access their explicit and implicit memories.

18.1-2 Children enter Piaget's concrete operational stage during the school-age years. They think logically, although logic is based on past experiences. Upon entering the formal operational stage, children reason more abstractly.

18.1-2 School-age children and teens entering these stages overcome egocentrism by learning to see from the viewpoints of others.

18.1-3 According to Vygotsky, school-age children learn because of brain development, of being stretched in their ZPDs, and through collaboration.

18.1-3 Piaget and Vygotsky differed about the role of language in intellectual development. Piaget felt that language reflected learning while Vygotsky saw language as a way of learning.

18.1-4 Howard Gardner's theory of multiple intelligences also outlines the many ways in which children learn.

Lesson 18.2

18.2-1 School-age children's understanding of physical knowledge expands. Logical thinking concepts improve in terms of classification, ordering by attributes, cause and effect, space, number, distance, time, and speed.

18.2-1 Children and teens learn culture-specific knowledge through school and home teachings.

18.2-2 By middle childhood, children have mastered most of the rules of language, including articulation and grammar. Their vocabularies continue to broaden.

18.2-2 School-age children speak and write the grammar they hear, and some children may code-switch.

18.2-2 If children have not learned standard grammar by the school-age years, using standard grammar after this age will require breaking incorrect grammar habits and relearning standard grammar.

18.2-2 Children learn to read by making letter-sound associations. Later in middle childhood, they use reading as a way of learning other subject matter.

18.2-3 School-age children and teens may achieve a number of intellectual developmental milestones.

18.2-3 School-age children and teen's logical brains can now use logical thinking concepts, and they begin to perceive language as a social tool. However, their prefrontal cortexes are still wiring, which may lead to poor decision-making skills.

Lesson 18.3

18.3-1 School-age children's intellectual needs are primarily met through school.

18.3-2 Parents can help children learn in school by preparing them for school experiences and supporting their endeavors by reinforcing school tasks, strengthening executive functions, and being a school advocate.

18.3-3 Outside of school, parents can provide enrichment activities and special lessons and activities.

18.3-4 Parents can guide their children and teen's media use by providing digital devices at appropriate times and protecting them from media-related risks.

College and Career Portfolio

Portfolio Enhancement

A strong portfolio uses technology to enhance its contents. Ways to use technology in your portfolio might include adding a video to your portfolio samples or an audio recording narration to a presentation. Choose one portfolio sample you can improve using technology. Use technology to enhance your portfolio sample and then present that sample to the class.

Recall and Application

1. How do school-age children demonstrate the skill of rehearsing? (18.1.1)
   A. They arrange information into categories.
   B. They commit pictures to memory.
   C. They repeat information until they have learned it.
   D. They focus on what "stands out" in a situation.

2. **True or False.** Reasoning from the general to the specific is inductive reasoning. (18.1.2)

3. **True or False.** Both Piaget and Vygotsky believed that children learn by doing and by talking and working with others. (18.1.3)

4. According to Gardner, a school-age child's ability to lead or work with others to achieve goals on behalf of others is an example of their _____ intelligence. (18.1.4)
   A. visual/spatial
   B. musical/rhythmic
   C. naturalist
   D. interpersonal

5. Which is true about school-age children's ability to master distance, time, and speed concepts? (18.2.1)
   A. Time and distance are often confused during the school-age years.
   B. School-age children do not learn clock time until 10 or 11 years of age.
   C. School-age children understand exact historic time periods by the first or second grade.
   D. Older school-age children understand more complex topics regarding time and distance.

6. Before the end of middle childhood, most children can do all the following except _____. (18.2.1)
   A. multiply and divide
   B. work word problems
   C. use graphs to represent information
   D. estimate quantities

7. An example of code-switching is _____. (18.2.2)
   A. pronouncing air and heir differently
   B. saying "I goed" instead of "I went"
   C. using mamá at home and mom at school
   D. speaking two or more languages fluently

8. Ten- to twelve-year-olds commonly achieve which intellectual developmental milestone? (18.2.3)
   A. Using oral language to inform, persuade, and entertain
   B. Describing objects in detail
   C. Writing legibly and organizing writing
   D. Developing plans to meet goals

9. **True or False.** School-age children experience the most upheaval when they enter high school. (18.3.1)

10. The best way a caregiver can support a child or teen with weak executive function is to _____. (18.3.2)
    A. fix their homework mistakes
    B. reward them with a snack once homework is complete
    C. help them check if an assignment is complete
    D. encourage them to prioritize easier tasks

11. Which extracurricular activity supports a child's visual/spatial intelligence? (18.3.3)
    A. Crossword puzzles
    B. Dancing
    C. Journaling
    D. Mazes

12. **True or False.** Caregivers should teach school-age children that the internet is not a place to make friends. (18.3.4)

Critical Thinking

1. **Analyze.** In small groups, analyze why attention and memory are crucial to a child's ability to process and learn information. Why would learning be difficult without these skills?

2. **Compare and contrast.** Brainstorm examples of transductive, deductive, and inductive reasoning. For each type of reasoning, write a short scenario in which a child reasons accordingly. Then, working with a partner, compare and contrast the three types of reasoning.

3. **Make inferences.** During the school-age years, children gain an understanding of time. Working with a partner, make inferences about why children learn time concepts better once they begin school. Could time concepts that are taught in school be effectively taught in a preschool?

4. **Draw conclusions.** Children's articulation, vocabulary, grammar, and reading skills are interrelated. Draw conclusions about how these aspects of communication relate. Write a brief description for each aspect-pairing.

5. **Determine.** Recall your experience starting primary school, middle school, or high school. What would you have liked to know before starting school? How could the adults in your life have better prepared you? Based on your experience, determine ways adults could prepare children for primary, middle, or high school.

6. **Cause and effect.** Executive functions are critical to a person's motivation and ability to do work. Review the executive functions discussed in this chapter, and in small groups, discuss the long-term effects of weak executive functions in children and teens. Also discuss the long-term effects of strong executive functions.

7. **Identify.** Visit a local library or community center and identify special lessons or activities that are available for children. List at least five activities and explain how they would benefit a school-age child.

8. **Evaluate.** In small groups, research filtering programs and other software that protect children and teens from inappropriate content. Choose two programs and then evaluate them based on customer reviews and the information available. How effective would this program be in protecting children and teens? What other safeguards should adults put into place alongside each program?

Core Skills

1. **Research and writing.** During puberty, the brain reorganizes as the prefrontal cortex continues to mature. Using reliable resources, research brain development in older school-age children and teens. How does the brain begin to reorganize during these years? How do these changes affect children's perceptions and thinking skills? After compiling your research, write a short report based on your findings. Include a bibliography with citations in APA style.

2. **Speaking.** In groups of three, research Piaget's, Vygotsky's, and Gardner's theories about how school-age children learn. During your research, take notes about areas of agreement and disagreement. Then, assign each group member one theorist to portray. In a class presentation, role-play a "conversation" between these three theorists. Each group member should present their theorist's theory and then dialogue with the other theorists. After the conversation, take questions from the class and respond in character.

3. **Reading.** Starting in the school-age years, children understand the logical thinking concepts they had difficulty grasping as preschoolers. In small groups, review this chapter's information about logical thinking concepts and obstacles to logical thought. Also review this text's information about logical thinking during the preschool years. Then, create an informative and visually appealing poster charting children's progress in understanding logical thinking concepts and in overcoming obstacles to logical thought.

Include pictures and use your poster as a studying tool for your group.

4. **Math and writing.** In small groups, research math problems for school-age children and teens. Try to find math problems for various grades. Then, write a brief essay explaining how children learn more complex number concepts with each school grade. Include examples of math problems and relate these problems to how school-age children and teens develop and learn to think logically.

5. **Reading and speaking.** In small groups, find articles on language development geared toward school-age children. Choose two articles and read the information examining vocabulary and articulation. After reading, present a group report assessing each article's effectiveness and relating the content to the information about vocabulary and articulation covered in this chapter.

6. **Speaking.** Review the intellectual developmental milestones for children in the school-age or teen years (Figure 18.14) and then pick one topic you think school-age children or teens should learn. This topic might be a hobby of yours or a piece of information you find interesting. Then, write a short speech as if you were presenting this topic to one age group of school-age children or teens (it could even be a group of children your age). While writing the speech, keep in mind the attention spans and interests of children that age. Consider what milestones those children have achieved. Practice your speech and then deliver it to the class as though speaking to your intended audience.

7. **Listening and technology.** Interview a parent or caregiver of a school-age child about how they help the child with homework. Ask which helping strategies have been most effective. How has help with homework changed as the child grows older? After the interview, work in small groups to film a tutorial about effectively helping school-age children with their homework. Include a list of "dos and don'ts" in your video.

8. **Listening and technology.** Interview three school-age children about the role of electronic media in their lives. What digital devices do the children have? How old were they when they received their first digital device? What do the children like about the role of electronic media in their lives? What do they dislike? Working with a partner, compare findings and create a digital presentation explaining what you discovered about school-age children's electronic media use and comparing it to your own. Deliver your presentation to the class.

9. **CTE Career Readiness Practice.** Presume you are the principal of a middle school. Many of the new middle-school students do not get help with their homework and seem to have weak executive functions. Their parents and guardians do not seem interested in partnering with the school. After a discussion with your staff, you decide to send a letter home to parents and guardians, explaining the importance of supporting children in school. Draft this letter, taking care to be respectful and informative. Have a partner read your letter and give you feedback.

Observations

1. As a class, visit a local primary school and observe children playing at recess or in the classroom. Make observations about the way children play and about how they use logic when interacting with others. Then, discuss how the development of logical thinking concepts alters children's approach to play.

2. Visit a class of school-age children or teens or watch a documentary in which school-age children or teens speak to one another and to teachers. While listening to the children, make observations about how the children use grammar and whether they code-switch during or between conversations. Write a short reflection about your observations.

Chapter 19

Social-Emotional Development of School-Age Children and Adolescents

Lesson 19.1   The Social-Emotional World of School-Age Children and Adolescents
Lesson 19.2   Meeting the Social-Emotional Needs of School-Age Children and Adolescents

Essential Question

How does a child's expanding world present social and emotional challenges during middle childhood and the teen years, and what types of support are needed to help overcome these challenges?

Case Study   Are Friendship Rejections Serious?

As a class, read the case study and discuss the questions that follow. After you finish studying the chapter, discuss this case study again. Have your opinions changed based on what you learned?

Clare and Mia had been friends since preschool. They shared activities, sleepovers, family outings, secrets, and laughter. Clare thought they would be friends forever and was excited as they both prepared to enter middle school.

At the end of the fifth grade, Clare and Mia both tried out for the basketball team. Clare made the team, but Mia did not. Mia was happy for Clare and looked forward to watching Clare play. Little did Mia know that their friendship was about to change.

Clare loved being on the basketball team and quickly became friends with the other players. Now, Clare rarely had time to spend with Mia because Clare was always practicing or hanging out with the team. Even when Mia and Claire did spend time together, all Clare talked about was the basketball team.

Later that school year, Clare asked Mia to hang out and play basketball. Mia jumped at the chance to spend time with Clare. Clare scored

repeatedly, but Mia struggled and often lost track of the ball. Clare became frustrated and left early. After Clare left, Mia went home and cried, feeling sad and alone. That night, Mia's parents asked what was wrong, and Mia shared what happened. Mia's parents wondered how to comfort their child.

Give It Some Thought

1. Was it reasonable for Mia to expect that Mia and Clare would always be best friends? Why or why not?
2. Should Mia's parents view the fading friendship as a serious or a passing problem? Explain your answer.
3. What could Mia's parents say to comfort Mia? What might be some ways they can help their child?

Lesson 19.1

The Social-Emotional World of School-Age Children and Adolescents

Key Terms

domains of
  self-definition
gender schools
goal-corrected
  partnership
guilt
identity versus role
  confusion
industry versus
  inferiority
psychological security
scapegoating
shortcomings
work ethic

Learning Outcomes

After studying this lesson, you will be able to

19.1-1 **explain** how school-age children's and adolescents' self-awareness grows as they show responsibility, learn gender roles, establish a moral conscience, and expand self-concept.

19.1-2 **analyze** how school-age children develop a sense of industry despite the risk of inferiority, and how adolescents develop a sense of identity rather than confusion.

19.1-3 **describe** how school-age children's and adolescents' interactions with adults and other children change.

19.1-4 **summarize** the emotional development of school-age children and adolescents.

19.1-5 **identify** sources of children's stress during the school-age and adolescent years.

19.1-6 **give examples** of social-emotional developmental milestones school-age children and adolescents might achieve.

Reading and Notetaking Activity

Before reading, skim the headings in this lesson. List the headings to create an outline for taking notes during reading and class discussion. Under each heading, list any key terms. Finally, write two questions you expect to have answered in class. After completing the lesson, ask your teacher any questions you still have about the concepts or terms you learned.

Introduction

A whole new social experience begins in middle childhood and adolescence, and children must make many new adjustments. During the school-age and teen years, children work toward becoming competent members of society. Schools prepare children to become independent and productive citizens.

Similarly, parents often give their school-age children chores that help develop responsibility and work ethic, and teenagers usually take on extra responsibilities in the form of leadership roles and jobs outside of school. Children's learning of gender roles is influenced by parents, peers, the school environment, and media. Moral development that began in the preschool years continues in the school-age years. By the end of the school years, children establish a moral conscience, and their self-concepts are well developed.

In many ways, social development becomes the most important aspect of development in middle childhood and the teen years. While parents are still vital in providing security and helping children become more independent, children's peer groups grow in importance. Relationships with peers affect all aspects of development; school-age children and teens often compare themselves with their peers. As children interact more with other adults and peers, they must learn new ways to express their emotions, which are closely connected to their personalities. Because of their increased interactions with others, children often experience more stress during the school-age and teen years. School-age children and teens make great strides in social-emotional development and achieve a number of developmental milestones.

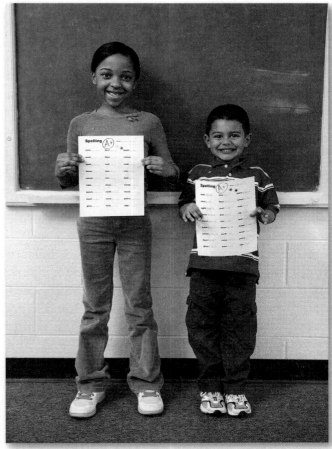

iofoto/Shutterstock.com

Figure 19.1 School-age children take pride in their achievements and acknowledgments. *What achievements and acknowledgments shaped your self-concept as a school-age child?*

19.1-1 Expanding Self-Awareness

During middle childhood and the teen years, children show greater awareness of their responsibilities and roles in society. They try to learn what is expected of them, and their self-concepts often depend on their sense of achievement and the acknowledgment of others (**Figure 19.1**). School-age children's and teens' self-awareness grows as they show responsibility, learn gender roles, establish a moral conscience, and expand their self-concepts.

Showing Responsibility

Doing chores in the home and at school encourages school-age children to show responsibility.

Keeping their rooms clean, doing the dishes, doing homework, and mowing the lawn are just a few ways children demonstrate responsibility during the school-age years. If adults serve as good role models, doing chores will help school-age children develop a healthy *work ethic*. A **work ethic** is a person's sense of responsibility and diligence toward work tasks. By eight years of age, children can do moderately demanding tasks well, though adults are still involved in planning, demonstrating, and supervising. As children grow into teens, they can take on additional responsibilities such as making their own lunch, doing their own laundry, or being expected to advocate for themselves in school and other social settings. Parents and caregivers must give the opportunities for children to show responsibility to nurture this skill.

Learning Gender Roles

School-age children's and teens' gender roles continue to develop and are influenced by a number of sources, including family, peers, the school environment, and media. These influences play a **prodigious** (pruh-DIH-jus), tremendous, role in children's learning of gender roles. Children may get uniform or mixed signals from these influences.

Family

Parents' actions and examples continue to influence children's learning of gender roles during the school-age years. Some children are exposed to traditional gender roles while other children learn similarities between the roles of different genders. As children observe their parents and other caregivers, they often adopt these people's behaviors as their own. Even children's perceptions of career options are influenced by their parents' and caregivers' career attitudes.

Peers

School-age children typically prefer to be friends with peers of the same sex. This preference becomes stronger throughout the school-age years. Thus, groups of same-sex peers become **gender schools** (peer groups that teach members what it means to be masculine or feminine). In gender schools boys teach other boys male behavioral norms, and girls teach other girls female behavioral norms. Some of the behavioral norms that children learn may include preferences in personal appearance, clothing choices, and activities (**Figure 19.2**). Children who do not have a clearly defined gender identity may be part of a gender school that does not match their biological gender. By the teen years, children begin to include other-gendered friends in their social circles, but studies have shown that same-sex friendships still prevail when it comes to close friendships among this age group.

While gender schools teach children masculinity and femininity, children who **deviate** (depart; stray) from acceptable behavioral norms may be faced with sexual stereotyping pressure or gender confusion. These children need positive adult role models to reassure them and promote their self-concepts.

Jupiterimages/Pixland via Getty Images Plus

Figure 19.2 In *gender schools*, boys and girls learn behavioral norms (including clothing choices and appearance) from their same-sex peers. *Do gender schools exist even beyond the school-age years? Explain.*

School Environment

In school, children are exposed to adults and children who have varying gender-role ideas. This affects children's gender-role learning. Historically, schools have treated boys and girls differently, often encouraging children to take different, gender-specific classes. Currently, however, gender-role attitudes in the school environment are **drastically** (greatly) different. Now, care is often taken to ensure that all students are treated equally and not discouraged from taking certain classes. As traditional gender roles and identities change, schools are shifting their practices to include students who do not fit within the typical or traditional parameters of the male or female gender.

Social Studies

Gender-Role Attitudes in Schools

In past decades, school curriculums were constructed to mirror the traditional gender roles of men and women in the home and at work. As a result, boys and girls were often encouraged to take different classes that society deemed more suited to their biological gender. For example, boys were often expected to take math and science classes while girls were not. As a result, boys had somewhat higher achievement in math and science than girls for many years. In many cases, girls simply did not enroll in math and science classes beyond the required courses. Schools justified this difference in achievement by claiming that men and women had different "biological tendencies." Research has shown, however, that these achievement differences were not due to natural differences in *capabilities* (aptitudes).

Since then, schools have worked toward gender equity to boost self-esteem and achievement and prevent gender bias. One positive result of schools' efforts to boost self-esteem and achievements is that the gender gap in math and science classes has almost closed. Gender gaps in other areas, such as physics and technology, still exist, however. This is because males are still encouraged to enter these areas more than females. Today, schools are still making strides to provide more gender equity and prevent achievement gaps. This also ensures equity for students who do not identify with traditional gender roles or their biological gender.

Photo: wavebreakmedia/Shutterstock.com

Even today, though, with changes in educational and career opportunities, some cultures and families still teach their children sexual stereotyping. Because schools must serve all children, regardless of the child's family's beliefs, school-age children and teens may still be exposed to sexual stereotyping in the school environment.

Although schools cannot **infringe** on (restrict) students' personal beliefs about gender roles, they can encourage gender equity and give all children fair opportunities. Some ways that schools can encourage gender equity include:

- making curriculum and teaching practices unbiased
- requiring respect between differently gendered students
- supporting students who make nontraditional choices

Media

School-age children and teens are often more exposed to electronic and print media. Television shows, movies, magazines, books, and social media represent gender roles in many different ways. Children often identify with and model themselves after the characters they see and read about. Therefore, the media messages children view greatly influence their learning of gender roles. As expected, the more stereotyped media children view, the more stereotyped their beliefs become.

Establishing a Moral Conscience

Although moral development begins in the preschool years, **instilling** (gradually establishing) a conscience for acceptable behavior continues in the school-age years. School-age children's moral development is influenced by authority figures and peers. Helping children establish a moral conscience becomes the responsibility of all social institutions and groups entrusted with raising children. Some examples of these groups include families, schools, youth organizations, and religious groups. The family, however, still has the central role in children's moral development during the school-age years. Moral development continues to affect school-age children's moral judgment and reasoning, moral character, and moral emotions. As children move into the teen years, friendships and peer groups become more influential in developing the child's moral conscience.

Moral Judgment and Reasoning

Moral judgment and reasoning refers to the ability to perceive an action as right or wrong. During the school-age years children's moral judgment and reasoning begins to shift from an *egocentric* (self-interested) concern to a consideration for the needs of the social group. School-age children have entered Piaget's *autonomous reality* stage of morality and Kohlberg's level of moral reasoning known as *conventional morality* (**Figure 19.3**). By the teen years and young adulthood, children can move into Kohlberg's *postconventional morality* stage, considering social contracts and ethical principles.

Kohlberg's colleague, Carol Gilligan, questioned Kohlberg's findings because his theory was, for the most part, male-oriented, which limited his ability to generalize to women. Gilligan concluded that women's moral reasoning is centered on caring and empathy in contrast to men's justice-orientation. Unlike Kohlberg, she also concluded that women, like men, can reach the highest stages of moral reasoning (postconventional stages). These findings further explain the importance of gender identity and gender roles during the school-age and teen years.

Figure 19.3 Piaget's and Kohlberg's Stages of Moral Judgment and Reasoning During the School-Age Years

Jean Piaget

Stage	Characteristics of Stage

Autonomous reality	• Children are regulated by rules set with mutual consent and for reasons of fairness and equity.
	• Children's beliefs include the following:
	  • Rules are not "set in stone."
	  • Consequences of actions are determined by intention, not physical damage.
	  • Punishment is based on intent and ability to see rules from the perspectives of others.

Lawrence Kohlberg's Conventional Stages of Moral Reasoning

Stage	Characteristics of Stage
Interpersonal conformity	• Children do what a social group (family, school) says is right or wrong. • Children believe certain behaviors are acceptable because they are good for the social group. • Children want approval by others and want to be considered "good" or "nice" if they live by the code.
Maintaining the social order	• Children believe they must live by the rules of the larger society in which they live. • Children feel compelled to do their duty for society and show respect for authority.

Goodheart-Willcox Publisher

Moral Character

Parents and caregivers are children's first teachers of character. Unlike in the preschool years, school-age children can comprehend the reasoning behind certain limits. Therefore, they are better able to act in accordance with that which is perceived as morally right. As school-age children develop character, they see themselves as socially valued people. (A feeling of worth is an important aspect of a person's self-esteem.)

School-age children and teens are greatly influenced—for good or for bad—by the people around them. Parents and caregivers, however, have the best chance of wielding that influence as compared to others. Showing children love and being a positive role model can make an enormous difference in building children's character. Encouraging teens to make good decisions about their peer group as they get older is another way parents and caregivers can nurture the strong moral character of their children.

Moral Emotions

School-age children and teens who are others-oriented begin to develop a conscience from their feelings of *guilt* after misdeeds. **Guilt** is a feeling of remorse that comes from the inner voice of conscience when a person has behaved unacceptably. Guilt is based in *empathy* (concern for the injured person) and remorse for the misdeed. Generally,

guilt is emotionally healthy because it leads a person to compensate for a misdeed and avoid the mistake in the future.

Instead of feeling guilt for misdeeds, some children feel *shame*. These children have often experienced shaming by those closest to them—parents, other adults, or peers—in the preschool and school-age years. As a result, their remorse for wrongdoings is focused inward and based on how others perceive them rather than on how their actions have affected others.

Shaming does not build character because respect is not the core of these adult-child and peer relationships. The child is not learning how to behave acceptably or respond appropriately to misdeeds. Instead, the child becomes more and more concerned with self and their failure to please adults. Once shame becomes a self-conscious emotion, it erodes self-esteem and can lead to mental health problems that may affect the person throughout their life (**Figure 19.4**).

Expanding Self-Concept

Preschool children begin to develop self-concept and describe themselves (called *self-definition*). They may say comments such as, "I'm good (or bad)." By seven or eight years of age, a child begins to perceive their self-definition in terms of multiple **domains of self-definition** (categories in which children can describe themselves).

Figure 19.4 Results of Shaming

- Creates a perfectionist attitude, an unrealistic goal, which may result in lowered self-esteem when perfection cannot be achieved.
- Promotes overwork or compulsive-type habits (overeating and constant viewing of media) if repressed shame later resurfaces.
- Influences a withdrawal from social relationships due to fear of any form of embarrassment.
- Inhibits emotions except for anger, which may appear in a rage-anger cycle.
- May generate the additional emotions of depression and anxiety.
- Triggers the rise of *defense mechanisms* (blaming others, being supercritical of others, taking revenge, showing exaggerated pride).
- Induces conduct disorders (as discussed later in the text).
- Inhibits moral conscience.
- Leads to a replaying of parents' and others' shame-scripts and using these shame-scripts on the next generation of children.

Goodheart-Willcox Publisher

School-age children are typically able to describe their abilities in each domain shown in **Figure 19.5**. How school-age children evaluate their own abilities (called *self-evaluation*) in each domain can positively or negatively affect self-concept.

Self-evaluation can be complex during the school-age years because children are just coming to understand which domains are **deemed** (considered to be) most important by their cultures. Conflicts between families and peers about the importance of each domain often occur. Children continue to explore the domains throughout adolescence. Until the teen or young adult years, people rarely make decisions about each domain's importance for themselves.

As school-age children evaluate themselves in each domain, they assess how they compare with their peers in terms of abilities. Peers can judge harshly, especially in school environments, and adults usually cannot change how peers judge each other. These peer comparisons cause children to become keenly aware of their **shortcomings** (areas in which they want or need to improve) and failures, which can affect how children define themselves. Unconditional love, acceptance, and acknowledgment of achievements by parents and other adults can help build school-age children's self-esteem during these formative years and are equally important during the teenage years.

19.1-2 Developing a Sense of Industry and Identity

School-age children begin to feel more like members of society. They want to excel alongside their peers and tend to fear rejection or incompetence. School-age children enter Erikson's fourth stage of personality development, which is called **industry versus inferiority**. This stage involves a struggle between children's **industry** (desire to join others in striving to become a competent member of society) and **inferiority** (feeling of incompetence and low value as a member of society).

Goodheart-Willcox Publisher

Figure 19.5 The school-age child's perceived importance for each domain depends on their cultural experiences and family values. *Which three domains of self-definition are most important to you?*

(You can review Erikson's psychosocial theory in Figure 10.10 of the text.)

Industry builds off *initiative*, a sense of motivation children form during the preschool years. Like initiative, industry involves doing and making things. Industry differs from initiative, however. Industry involves the drive to accomplish school tasks and other projects, whereas initiative involves learning tasks that will reduce the need for adult help. Industry also involves joining others and working as a team member, whereas initiative is more personal. Lastly, industry focuses on recognition from peers and important adults, whereas initiative focuses on pleasing self and parents.

Investigate Special Topics

Moral Development in Teens and Adults

According to Kohlberg's theory of moral development, many teens and adults remain at the level of moral reasoning known as *conventional morality*. Conventional morality, which includes interpersonal conformity and maintenance of the social order, guides a person's decisions and views for most of their life. About 10 to 15 percent of people, however, do *not* remain at the conventional level of morality. Rather, they reason in the level of morality known as *postconventional morality*, which includes the stages described in the following chart.

At the postconventional level, morality is viewed more abstractly and concerns what constitutes *universal morality* (morality that goes beyond specific laws). Postconventional morality is similar to Piaget's discussions about "ideal reciprocity," the positive treatment of others because ideally one would also want to be treated well.

In small groups, review the stages of postconventional morality and discuss the required reasoning skills for this level of moral reasoning. Develop a list of questions that would assess the moral level at which a teen or adult is reasoning. Then, survey at least 10 teens and adults using these questions. Evaluate the survey responses and determine the level of morality at which each person is reasoning. Share your group's findings with the rest of the class.

Lawrence Kohlberg's Postconventional Stages of Moral Reasoning

Stage	Characteristics of Stage
Social contract and individual rights	• Teens and adults believe acceptable behaviors are determined by socially agreed-upon standards, which vary among cultures and subgroups within a culture. • Teens and adults believe that the chosen code of conduct is based on the greatest good for the greatest number, even if the code works against the interests of some individuals.
Universal and ethical principles	• Teens and adults believe that all acceptable behaviors are based on justice, human dignity, and equality. • Teens and adults believe they should defend personal principles over laws that are deemed as *aberrant* (diverging) from acceptable principles.

Photo: Tom Wang/Shutterstock.com

If school-age children embrace industry and are successful in this stage, they feel confident and productive. Being industrious increases children's feelings of self-esteem and responsibility. Children will see that what they do makes a difference. If children's efforts and work are demeaned or ignored, the outcome may be a lasting sense of inferiority.

During the school-age years, children learn a lifelong attitude toward work. Though play is still important for school-age children, the play of earlier years is often replaced with more meaningful work (at least by adult standards). School-age children with a sense of industry see work as a route to learning new ideas and skills and to performing in worthwhile ways. They also see work as a way to win approval from parents and caregivers, teachers, and peers. School-age children enjoy doing activities with and for others (**Figure 19.6**). They enjoy learning and practicing cooperation as they interact in their expanding and changing social worlds.

As children shift from the school-age years to the teen years, they move into Erikson's fifth stage of personality development, called **identity versus role confusion**. This stage lasts from around age 13 through age 18 or older. In this stage, teens ask the question, "Who am I?" by examining their values, beliefs, and personal goals.

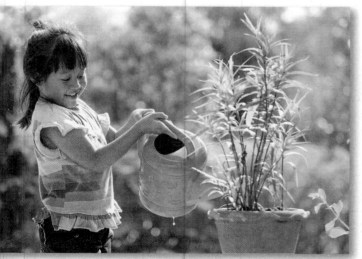

undefined/iStock via Getty Images Plus

Figure 19.6 As they develop a sense of industry, school-age children enjoy doing tasks that bring joy to others, such as watering plants. *What are common tasks that school-age children can do for others?*

Children are becoming more independent and looking to their futures; this brings about the question of where they may belong in society and what type of person they will be. Role confusion occurs when a child is unable to build a sense of self during the teen years, leading to uncertainty and possible experimentation to find a personal identity. Healthy identity development during adolescence leads to a more solid foundation for adulthood and healthier relationships with others.

19.1-3 Changing Social Relations

School-age children's and teens' social relationships grow and become more complicated than the relationships they experienced in the preschool years. During the school-age years children still rely on adults but want to be more independent. This increases during the teen years. School-age children are also trying to develop friendships, which are sometimes difficult. Both school-age children and teens find that mastering the skills needed to fit into society can be stressful. Their relationships change both with adults and with peers.

Interacting with Adults

At the beginning of the school-age years, children enter a **goal-corrected partnership**, a relationship in which children and parents or caregivers are willing to compromise to reach a common goal. The goal between children and their parents or caregivers is for the relationship to be a loving one. Attachments are no longer based on physical proximity, but instead are based on *availability*, which can be both physical and emotional in nature. An adult's physical presence does not mean they are psychologically available. Even the self-reliant child still needs loving adults for guidance and security.

By eight or nine years of age, children and their parents and caregivers move toward a *partner relationship* method of co-regulation if the child acts responsibly. This partner relationship will continue through the teen years. In this relationship, parents and caregivers provide a balance between letting go and holding on.

Parents allow their school-age child or teen some freedom but maintain communication and supervision of the child. This enables children to think of their parents or caregivers as *home base*. They think of home as a safe place where they can go and their needs for food, clothing, shelter, and *psychological security* will be met. **Psychological security** is a feeling that someone cares and will help when needed.

In some cases, children do not make the transition to a partner relationship method of co-regulation because their earlier attachments were not secure. A partnership relationship requires trust on the part of both adult and child.

Interacting with Other Children

As school-age children and teens spend more time with peers, they depend less on adults for company. The peer relationships of school-age children and adolescents require more complex social skills than earlier relationships. To maintain friendships and status within peer groups, children must continually use peer-acceptable social skills. Because these skills are just being learned, most school-age children will have some difficulties interacting with other children. In **Figure 19.7**, you will see that some children are more likely to have negative social experiences with friends and peer groups than others. By the teen years, most children have worked through conflicts and have mastered the social skills needed to maintain positive friendships.

Figure 19.7 **Children at Risk for Negative Peer Relations**

- Children who are aggressive and have disruptive behaviors are often rejected by others.
- Children who are introverted or shy are often unnoticed by their peers.
- Children who are very different from their peers may be ignored.
- Children who are immature in their social skills may be ignored or teased.
- Children with bad reputations may be rejected.

Goodheart-Willcox Publisher

Friendships

The nature of school-age children's friendships changes as children mature. Children tend to choose friends of the same biological gender and generally show dislike for the opposite gender. This can be true until puberty begins, between the ages of 8 and 13 for females and between the ages of 9 and 14 for males, but even during teen years, close friendships tend to be of the same gender.

During the school-age years children often see a friend as someone who helps them. School-age children seldom think in terms of how they can help their friend. The concept of *give and take* is familiar to school-age children, but it often serves the child rather than the mutual interests of their friends. Usually by the end of the school-age years, more close friendships form. Similar interests and tastes often determine these friendships rather than physical nearness. The nature of these friendships becomes one of cooperation and helping each other to achieve group goals.

If a friendship ends, the loss of the friend can be devastating to the school-age child or teen. There are many causes for losing a friendship, such as moving away or attending a different school. Friendship loss hurts the most when a child feels their trust has been broken. Children often see friendship as a place for self-disclosure. When this is violated, the child is hurt and the friendship ends.

Peer Groups

Peer groups are important for school-age children and teens. Belonging to a peer group gives children feelings of sharing and loyalty. Children feel a sense of security when working or playing with others in their group. Peer groups provide emotional support, too. Adults cannot provide the comfort that children feel when they realize others their age share similar feelings. Peer groups also reinforce self-esteem. School-age children and teens are highly concerned about how they appear to others. In peer groups, children tag others with labels, such as *captain of the team* or *the last one chosen*. These labels make children aware of how others feel about them. Once they absorb these peer attitudes, children react to themselves as others have reacted to them.

Through peer groups children learn how to deal with rules and get along with others. Children learn that social relationships involve rules and that rules help groups work as teams. Children must use self-control to follow these rules. Peer groups also help children depend less on adults. Peer groups serve as sifters for thinking through adult-taught values. Peer groups often share information with each other, and peers help children decide which values to keep and which to adjust.

School-age and teen peer groups are smaller as compared with those of the preschool years. Children may feel hurt if one of their friends chooses another child or group for friendship. This often happens when one child enters puberty far ahead of their friend or matures in other ways. It can also be seen in teen friendships when one friend has a new interest, sport, or job and begins spending time with peers from that group instead of the old one.

19.1-4 Expressing Emotions

By the time they enter school, children have fairly well-established patterns of emotional behavior. Personality traits and emotional control continue to emerge and stabilize throughout the school-age and teen years. The emotions felt by school-age children affect their behaviors which, in turn, influence their personalities. As school-age children and teens interact more with adults and other children, they are expected to express their emotions in new, socially acceptable ways. Children learn to express emotions such as love, fear and anxiety, and anger and aggression.

Focus on Health

Helping Children Overcome Rejection

Because peer groups are so important during middle childhood and adolescence, many children experience intense fears of rejection. Every child, at one time or another, feels rejected by peers. A child might say, "Nobody likes me," or "I can never do anything right." If a child struggles with rejection, an adult can help by:

- trying to discover the problem behind the rejection (such as physical appearance or a lack of certain skills)
- giving the child direct help overcoming the problem behind the rejection (encouraging better grooming skills, teaching new activities)
- planning games and activities in which there is not much pressure
- reassuring the child that they are accepted by others and that rejection by a person or group does not alter the child's value as a person or how much the child is loved

If children continue to feel rejected, adults can speak with school counselors or seek professional help for children. If left unaddressed, long-term rejection can lead to mental health problems, such as anxiety and depression.

Photo: wavebreakmedia/Shutterstock.com

FOCUS ON MENTAL HEALTH

Feeling loved is crucial to a child's social and emotional wellbeing. Without feelings of unconditional love, children can develop emotional problems and partake in antisocial behaviors. Parents and caregivers must work to create strong, healthy attachments with their children from birth to avoid potential issues later in life. Love can be shown in a variety of ways and positively contributes to self-concept and other relationships in a child's life.

Love

All children need to feel and express love. They show love to adults and peers who care about them and accept them as they are. Children do not seek relationships in which they must give too much in return. They tend to care for others who share common interests (**Figure 19.8**).

School-age children's and teens' need for love is expressed in their great desire to be accepted by others—both adults and peers. Most children, however, do not express love as openly (with hugs and kisses) as younger children. School-age children and teens may be embarrassed about being openly affectionate with family members. Instead, they may express love for adults by showing kindness and doing activities with them. Children may show affection for peers by wanting to be with them; by sharing secrets; by communicating through phone calls, messages, or notes; and by giving small presents.

School-age children and teens who do not feel loved have a narrowed emotional range, causing them to experience little or no joy, grief, or guilt. These children may turn to antisocial behaviors, such as hostile acts, and may seek acceptance from peers and circles of friends who are poor role models.

Fear and Anxiety

During the school-age and teen years, many fears and worries from a child's early years become less threatening. Children better understand the separation of fantasy and reality. Fear of the dark and fears of the supernatural usually decline during this age. Fears of physical harm (disease, injury, or death) may continue into the school-age years. School-age children's and teens' fears and anxieties tend to center on the future, embarrassment, and people and their actions.

Figure 19.8 School-age children's friendships tend to be grounded in common interests and experiences. *Who were your first friends? What did you have in common?*

pixelfusion3d/Getty Images

The fears and anxieties of middle childhood and adolescence often do not disappear with age. Sometimes, school-age children's fears and anxieties persist into the adult years.

Anger and Aggression

Expressions of anger and aggression change once children enter the school-age years. School-age children do not display anger as physically as younger children do. Older children are better able to control their bodies and express themselves verbally. By this time, they know what is and is not acceptable. Therefore, children in middle childhood and adolescence tend to express their anger indirectly. For example, anger may be expressed in the forms of disrespect, sulkiness, or **scapegoating** (blaming others for one's own mistakes). School-age children and teens also show anger by gossiping, plotting, and even imagining the downfall of their enemies. Withdrawal from a situation, such as quitting or using less ability, may be another sign of anger. Some older school-age children or teens may be physically aggressive, and these acts can have devastating outcomes.

As children grow older, they become angry about different things. Like preschool children, school-age children and teens are angered when their wants are denied, or their possessions are threatened. Unlike preschool children, however, school-age children are also angered by what they see as wrongs to others. In teen years and adulthood, anger at social wrongs may fuel positive social action (**Figure 19.9**).

Jealousy

The feelings of jealousy that children began to experience during the preschool years continue, and sometimes intensify, during the school-age and teen years. School-age children and teens have more social relationships and must interact with other adults and children on a regular basis at school and during activities outside of school. The increase in social interactions makes children more likely to compare themselves with their peers.

Children may also experience intense jealousy due to competitive school environments and school relationships. In the classroom, children are assessed based on a variety of abilities. As they watch their peers being assessed and even acknowledged, children may feel jealous of peers' accomplishments. Jealousy can also develop due to friendships or romantic relationships in the teen years.

Figure 19.9 School-age children are sometimes angered by wrongs done to others. This type of anger can be healthy and, if directed appropriately, can even fuel positive social action. *What are some examples of ways school-age children can take positive social action?*

izusek/E+ via Getty Images

19.1-5 Recognizing Stress in School-Age Children and Adolescents

As the school-age child's and teen's world expands to include new relationships and responsibilities, stress can originate from many new and different sources. For this reason, stress often increases in the school-age and adolescent years. Some new sources of stress for children include the following:

- *Home life.* Stress may come from a lack of family routines and from overscheduling activities. Adults who have unclear or unreasonable expectations (such as being intolerant of anything less than excellence) may cause stress in their children. Stress can also come from changes in the family situation, such as divorce, deaths, financial problems, and domestic and community violence.
- *School life.* School life brings major changes for school-age children and teens. Play evolves into competitive sports, and curiosity and fun learning activities can turn into a struggle to excel. The most stress occurs when the classroom environment is unstructured, when teachers have unclear or unreasonable expectations, and when children realistically or unrealistically fear failure, especially on major tests.
- *Peer relations.* Children may experience stress due to peer rejection, dealing with bullies, and dealing with "unknown peers" due to changing schools.

- *Internal stress.* Stress can occur due to poor nutrition, sleep deprivation, or illnesses. Stress hormones increase during puberty. Mental health disorders are also closely related to stress.

Due to added stressors during the school-age and teen years, it can sometimes be difficult for adults to distinguish between typical adjustment behaviors and true stress-related problems. School-age children and teens often communicate less with adults because they want to be independent, and adults have less supervision of their children during these years. Nevertheless, some changes may indicate stress-related problems in children. **Figure 19.10** lists some of these warning signs.

19.1-6 Social-Emotional Developmental Milestones

Children's social-emotional worlds transform when they enter school and continue to develop through the teenage years. Self-awareness expands as they learn to take responsibility, understand gender roles, and develop their self-concept. School-age children and adolescents strive to be industrious and form a personal identity. They are exposed to numerous new social relations and situations in which they must express their emotions carefully. **Figure 19.11** lists social-emotional developmental milestones that children achieve during the school-age and adolescent years.

Figure 19.10 Warning Signs of Stress in School-Age Children

- Disordered eating
- Sleep difficulty or nightmares
- Overreactions to minor problems
- Trouble concentrating or completing schoolwork
- Drop in grades
- Withdrawal from family and friends
- Hyperactive behavior
- Increased aggression
- Unexplained headaches or stomachaches
- Negativism and lying
- Regressive behaviors
- Experimentation with alcohol and other drugs

Goodheart-Willcox Publisher

Figure 19.11 School-Age Social-Emotional Milestones

Age	Social-Emotional Milestones
Six to seven years *MBI/Shutterstock.com*	• Friendship is becoming important; friendships are based on play interest. • Has friends of the same gender. • Can cooperate and share. • Wants to be more independent from parents and family. • May be afraid of monsters and the dark and may have nightmares. • Tattles to check sense of right and wrong. • Wants approval from adults and peers; wants to be liked.
Eight to nine years *FatCamera/E+ via Getty Images*	• Is able to be sensitive to what others think. • Wants to look and act like peers. • Likes friendship groups and enjoys group activities. Starts to have friends of different gender. • Is more self-critical and competitive. • Wants more independence from parents. • Has preference for certain friends. • Can be sensitive, dramatic, and express anger or frustration. • Starts to be modest about their body.
Ten to twelve years *PeopleImages/E+ via Getty Images*	• Shows growing independence. • Is friend-focused, shares secrets with friends, and constantly talks about friends. May have a best friend. • May show romantic interests. • Conforms to peer groups. • Is self-conscious. • Has reality-based fears. • Gets feelings easily hurt. • More aware of their body as puberty occurs. Body image problems may be an issue.
Thirteen to fifteen years *New Africa/Shutterstock.com*	• Shows more concern about appearance and body image. • Experiences more impulsiveness and moodiness. • Shows more interest and is more influenced by peer groups. • May begin dating. • Expresses less affection toward parents or caregivers; may appear to be rude or embarrassed by family. • Fluctuates between high expectations of self and low confidence. • Experiences stress in relation to schoolwork. • May experience feelings of sadness or depression. • Starts to analyze their own feelings.
Sixteen to eighteen years *Prostock-studio/Shutterstock.com*	• Relates better to parents/caregivers and family. • Has a stronger sense of self and is able to identify strengths and contributions. • Can voice emotions and try to find solutions when conflicts arise. • Develops more interest in romantic relationships and sexuality. • Explores sexual identity. • Has more mature emotions, causing more intimate relationships. • May continue to experience feelings of sadness or depression. • Spends most of their time with friends rather than family.

Goodheart-Willcox Publisher

1. Teens and young adults move into _____ stage, considering social contracts and ethical principles. (19.1.1)
   A. Piaget's autonomous reality
   B. Kohlberg's postconventional morality
   C. Kohlberg's conventional morality
   D. Piaget's concrete operational

2. **True or False.** By the teen years, most children have an equal number of other-gendered and same-sex friends in their social circles. (19.1.1)

3. Initiative is different from industry because it _____. (19.1.2)
   A. involves the drive to accomplish school tasks and other projects
   B. focuses on recognition from peers and important adults
   C. involves learning tasks that will reduce the need for adult help
   D. focuses on others and working as a team member

4. **True or False.** Attachments between children and caregivers at the beginning of the school-age years are based on availability, which can be both physical and emotional in nature. (19.1.3)

5. Which statement about school-age children's expression of emotions is correct? (19.1.4)
   A. They tend to display anger physically.
   B. They have an increased fear of the dark and of the supernatural.
   C. They are attracted to peers with interests different than their own.
   D. They express their love for adults by showing kindness.

6. **True or False.** Trouble concentrating or completing schoolwork is a possible warning sign of stress in a school-age child or adolescent. (19.1.5)

7. Eight- to nine-year-olds typically achieve which social-emotional developmental milestone? (19.1.6)
   A. Showing embarrassment if parents are around when with friends
   B. Defining *self* in terms of appearance, possessions, and activities
   C. Conforming to peer groups
   D. Tattling to check their sense of right and wrong

Lesson 19.2

Meeting the Social-Emotional Needs of School-Age Children and Adolescents

Key Terms

interdependent stage
interpretive stage
society of children

Learning Outcomes

After studying this lesson, you will be able to

19.2-1 **summarize** ways to boost self-awareness and foster a healthy self-concept in school-age children and adolescents.

19.2-2 **explain** how adults and caregivers can help children be industrious and develop a positive identity.

19.2-3 **describe** ways adults can support social interactions for school-age children and adolescents.

19.2-4 **identify** ways adults can help school-age children and adolescents control their emotions.

19.2-5 **discuss** how adults can help reduce children's stress during the school-age and adolescent years.

Reading and Notetaking Activity

Before reading this lesson, scan the lesson headings. Write a paragraph describing what you already know about these topics. Explain where you got the information you have—from conversations, the media, or research, for example. As you are reading, compare and contrast the information in the chapter with your prior knowledge. Organize your notes around the information you already know. After reading, consider how your prior knowledge of the subject matter helped you understand this topic.

Introduction

Although the peer group becomes an important part of school-age children's and teens' social lives, adults still play a significant role in meeting their children's social-emotional needs. As children's self-awareness expands, adults can encourage children's successes, support them through their failures, and appreciate them as unique children. Parents can serve as the physical and psychological home base while providing time for friendships. Parents should also realize that school-age children and teens have mood swings and emotional difficulties from time to time, which are normal. Lack of emotional control, however, may signal the need for professional help.

19.2-1 Promoting Self-Awareness

By the school-age years, children are very self-aware. Their self-awareness is influenced by how they believe others (parents and caregivers, teachers, and peers) think of them. Because their self-concepts are fragile, they need support and encouragement throughout the school-age and teen years. Adults can promote their children's self-awareness by giving children responsibility, supporting their gender roles, instilling morality, and building a healthy self-concept.

Giving Responsibility

As school-age children and teens learn to take responsibility for their schoolwork and other tasks, adults can support them by *giving* them responsibilities. Adults should supervise school and household tasks at first but may give children more responsibility and freedom as children prove themselves to be **diligent** (hardworking).

While adults should not assign children too many tasks, they can give responsibility by asking children to do chores. Chores help teach children skills and aid them in developing a work ethic. Some chores are best seen as "labors of love," even if parents want to pay the child for some extra work. Teaching responsibility and the value of work requires effort on the part of parents and other adults. **Figure 19.12** lists some other ways parents and caregivers can give responsibility to school-age children and teens.

Supporting Gender Roles

School-age children's and adolescents' perceptions of gender roles are under constant influence from families, peers, the school environment, and media. As societal views change and children develop narrower areas of interest, it is important for parents and caregivers to support their children's learning of gender roles and help children understand the information they are influenced by.

Figure 19.12 Giving Responsibility to School-Age Children

- As a parent or caregiver, be a model of good work ethic in the home.
- Explain to the child that chores come before recreational activities and that some chores have to be done at specific times to prevent harm.
- Compile a list of chores that the child is able to do or learn to do.
- Allow the child some choices among chores and rotate tasks from time to time.
- Teach the child the needed skills to complete a task.
- If the child completes a task poorly, find out why. Reteach needed skills, or have the child repeat the chore if the results were a matter of not trying.
- Allow flexibility in completing chores if another responsibility takes priority but encourage the child to plan ahead next time.
- Show appreciation for what the child does. For example, say "thank you" for a job well done or provide a special treat for doing all chores for a week.
- If a child earns money for going beyond the chore list, then parents and caregivers need to help the child learn about saving, giving, and spending earnings.

Goodheart-Willcox Publisher

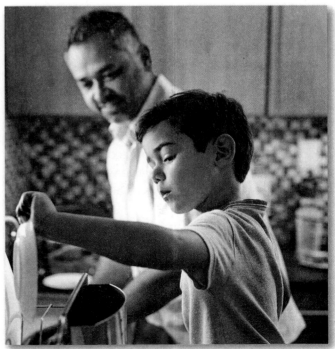

PeopleImages/iStock via Getty Images Plus

For the most part, children learn gender roles through adult models. All children are influenced by the male and female adults and caregivers in their lives, which affects the child's perspective of feminine and masculine gender roles. Learning and absorbing information about gender roles affects a child's goals in the world of work and at home. Adults who model warmth and sureness in their own masculine or feminine roles affect masculinity and femininity in the children they care for. Traditional gender roles have changed a great deal over time; many children associate a mix of feminine and masculine roles to each gender, especially if they see their parents or caregivers taking on tasks that are seen as both masculine and feminine. For example, a child may see their biologically male parent doing most of the cooking or cleaning at home, while another child's biologically female parent may handle much of the yard work or home repairs. Many adults in today's families share gender roles more equally than couples have in the past.

Instilling Morality

Children learn morality through the examples of the adults in their lives. As children begin to develop their own moral consciences, adults are responsible for instilling morality and encouraging the growth of that conscience. Parents and other adults can aid children's moral development by teaching them to:

- *respect others.* Respect is always a two-way street between an adult and a child or among peers.
- *show responsibility.* Giving children responsibilities in the family and other social groups helps them become *altruistic* (selflessly concerned for the welfare of others) and act on these feelings as a universal moral principle (**Figure 19.13**).
- *follow established limits.* School-age children, teens, and even adults accept limits if they believe the imposed limits are for their welfare.
- *behave acceptably.* Children need to understand why certain behaviors are unacceptable. For example, children need to know that bullying hurts, lying destroys

trust, and stealing violates the owner of the property. (This is part of Galinsky's *interpretive stage* of parenting. You can review Galinsky's parenting stages in Figure 4.4 of the text.)

- *express remorse for misdeeds.* Children need to take appropriate actions to restore their **solidarity** (sense of belonging) within their social groups when they make a mistake, such as returning stolen property with an apology for the misdeed.
- *think for themselves before acting on moral issues.* Children need to put themselves in another person's shoes, such as by asking, "How would I feel if ____?" They also need to ask themselves, "What will the consequences be?"

Building a Healthy Self-Concept

Children's feelings about themselves are influenced by how those who are important in their lives treat them. School-age children and teens need to know they are important to their families. As children seek parental affection and approval, parents need to communicate their love and acceptance to their children. Parents, caregivers, and other adults who provide love, appreciation, and encouragement form the foundation for a child's positive self-concept.

Carlos Horta/Shutterstock.com

Figure 19.13 Showing compassion for others is one way school-age children may act altruistically. *What is an example of an altruistic act that you or someone you know has performed?*

Every child has special talents and abilities. Parents can help build healthy self-concepts in their children by acknowledging and encouraging these traits. They can also offer positive feedback for tasks children did well. "You did a good job," is an important message for children to hear. Helping children believe in their own abilities can help school-age children and teens build their confidence. With love and support, adults can help children in their struggle for a healthy self-concept (**Figure 19.14**).

When children need to be disciplined, parents should discipline their children in ways that express caring and love. Research shows that the authoritative parenting style produces better self-concepts in children than the authoritarian, permissive, or overparenting styles. (You can review possible results of parenting styles on children in Figure 4.13 of the text.) Adults should discipline children privately, not in front of their peers or others. If criticism must be given, the act should be criticized and not the child. If done this way, criticism can teach school-age children that their actions were wrong, but they can still be trusted and loved as a person.

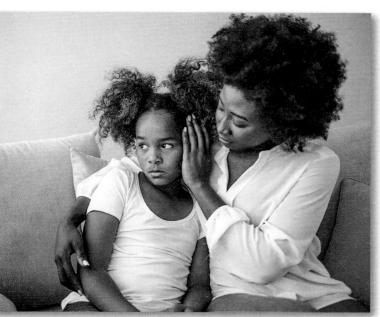

Figure 19.14 School-age children need love and support to help them establish healthy self-concepts. *How do love and support from a caregiver differ from the acknowledgment of a teacher?*

19.2-2 Helping Children Be Industrious and Form a Positive Identity

In middle childhood, children develop a sense of industry, which begins to prepare them for adult work. To help children develop positive feelings about work, adults can lead children to focus on their abilities rather than on their faults. Adults should set reasonable standards. When standards are too high, children feel they cannot reach them and will not try. If standards are set too low, children may not work at their potential. Even small successes help children feel positive about their work, which increases their self-esteem. (You can review Erikson's psychosocial theory in Figure 10.10 of the text.)

Adults can also help children be industrious by encouraging them to succeed in school. Children do better in school when they have loving, caring adults who want them to do well than when they have adults who show little or no concern.

In order to help children form a positive personal identity during the teen years, parents and caregivers should be active listeners and sources of unconditional love. It is also important for parents and caregivers to maintain the boundaries and limits they have set for their teens and be good role models as their children navigate their own values and beliefs. Being patient and open-minded as teens try out different versions of themselves is crucial to allowing teens to explore and make decisions about who they want to be. Finally, parents and caregivers can help nurture a positive identity by helping their children identify their strengths and providing opportunities for those strengths to be explored and developed.

19.2-3 Supporting Social Relations

Despite children's growing reliance on peer groups, the parent-child relationship is still the most important influence in a child's life. Children whose parents or caregivers have high expectations, but who are also responsive to the child's growing independence, have children who thrive.

In most families, the parent-child relationship is well established by the school-age years. Unlike the parent-child relationship, friendships are just being developed and are thus not well established until the later school-age or teen years. Parents and caregivers can support children's relationships by making time for friendships, expanding children's horizons, guiding and modeling behaviors, and managing conflicts.

Making Time for Friendships

School-age children and teens spend more and more time with peers. Parents and other caregivers should encourage children to form friendships and relationships with other children. Children need time to be with friends. If parents and caregivers have too many other plans for children, then children do not always have a chance to form friendships.

The peer groups children form, called a **society of children** by sociologists, prepare children for independence from parents when children grow up. Parents should understand that children will like their best friends almost as much as their families and will want to include their friends in family outings. Making friends welcome in the home and encouraging peer activities will help children establish these relationships.

Expanding Horizons

During the school-age and teen years, children's social worlds expand, and parents and caregivers can help children form relationships by expanding their children's horizons. One way parents can help is to encourage their children to participate in activities with their peers at school and in the community. Parents can support children in their endeavors by helping them organize their activity schedules, ensuring that needed equipment is ready, and then driving children to and from activities until they can drive themselves.

Another way to help children form relationships is to plan family activities that can extend the skills children learn in peer groups. Family activities can **bolster** (lend support to) children's physical, intellectual, and social skills. Suggesting hobbies in which their children can succeed is another good way for parents to help children expand their horizons. Children enjoy the tasks involved in their hobbies and like to display their new abilities and knowledge in their peer groups.

Focus on

Careers

Sociologist

Sociologists study their own societies and other societies around the world. They examine social behaviors and traditions by studying individuals, cultures, groups, institutions, and human development. They typically work at colleges or universities, in research organizations, or as consultants.

Career cluster: Human services.

Education: Educational requirements include a master's degree or Ph.D.

Job outlook: Future employment opportunities for sociologists are expected to show little to no change. There are relatively few jobs available in this field, so there will be much competition for positions.

To learn more about a career as a sociologist, visit the United States Department of Labor's *Occupational Outlook Handbook* website. You will also be able to compare the job responsibilities, educational requirements, job outlook, and average pay of sociologists with similar occupations.

Guiding and Modeling Behaviors

During the school-age years, parents and caregivers enter Galinsky's **interpretive stage** of parenting, and by the teen years, they have entered Galinsky's **interdependent stage**. Parents in these stages are tasked with modeling their values and attitudes about almost all aspects of life while finding a balance between giving freedom and boundaries to their child. (You can review Galinsky's parenting stages in Figure 4.4 of the text.) Children watch and listen to important adults in their lives. They pattern many of their thoughts and actions after these adults. Parents and caregivers should provide guidance and continue to support the parent-child relationship. Some ways that parents and caregivers can support this relationship include the following:

- *Keep family communication open.* It is important for parents and children to talk about and express their feelings openly.

By 9 or 10 years of age, children begin to see parents' mistakes, which may strain family communication. As a result, parents and their children need to keep the lines of communication open (**Figure 19.15**). If good communication patterns are established during middle childhood, the parent-child relationship during the teen years will be much better.

- *Teach morals and values.* School-age children face moral decisions daily. At school they may be exposed to cheating, lying, stealing, and other negative activities. Parents and caregivers can help children build an internal moral system by providing love, respect, and mutual trust; by modeling what they expect; and by setting rules, giving reasons for rules, and applying logical consequences when the child makes mistakes.

Figure 19.15 How to Keep Parent-Child Communication Open

Type of Problem	Parent-Child Communication Skills
Parent has a concern, such as a child coming home late.	• Parent can take a few moments to calm down. • Parent and child can communicate clearly and effectively using I-statements, such as "I became worried when I didn't know where you were after school." I-statements allow children to have points of view whether or not they are right. Avoid you-statements, such as "You should have at least called me." • Child can present their point of view. Parent can ask the child, "How can we solve this problem?"
Child makes a general accusation, such as "You always pick on me."	• Parent can listen until the child finishes talking. If the child is angry, the parent can say, "We will talk about this later," and then follow up. • Child can explain feelings and parent can paraphrase the child's feelings to ensure understanding. • Parent can ask, "Can you give me an example?" Avoid interrupting the child. • Parent and child can ask, "How can we both work on this problem so we do not have negative feelings?"
Child comes to parent with a problem.	• Child can come to parent and clearly explain feelings and problem. • Parent can focus on the child and their message, show interest, and clarify anything not understood. • Parent can say, "I can see that this is important to you," and ask, "What would you like to do about it? Do you have any ideas?" Parent can offer some suggestions if the child seems willing. • If the problem is severe and beyond what the child can handle, the parent can explain how they will handle it. • Parent can confirm interest and concern for the child by saying, "Let me know how this works out. Thanks for telling me."

Goodheart-Willcox Publisher

- *Balance dependence with independence.* School-age children and teens often question caregivers' guidance. They need parents and caregivers to listen to them and, at times, to advise and set limits. Parents must learn the balance between letting go and being there for children, which is not easy. Parents do not always know whether they should protect children from problems with friends or let them cope on their own. Parents may be torn between trying to enforce their teachings and allowing children to make some of their own decisions. Parents and caregivers should communicate with children about how to strike this balance and be responsive to their children's needs and concerns.

Managing Conflicts

For the most part, children are reluctant to tell adults about what goes on in their world of peers. This becomes especially true during the late school-age and teen years. When children experience conflicts and friendship difficulties, adults should be ready to encourage and support them. Ways that adults can help children manage conflicts and difficulties include the following:

- Give direct assistance to children who experience rejection. Some children may need counseling for aggression or shyness.
- Realize that children often need help when they lose their best friends, whether because of conflicts, new interests, moves, or death (**Figure 19.16**). Children can suffer great pain, even depression, from ended friendships. Depression can cause eating and sleeping problems, as well as indifference toward working or playing. Adults can help children who are depressed by talking about emotions, staying neutral if the ended friendship was caused by a conflict, and by preparing children for future friendship losses.
- Set firm limits on risky or inappropriate behaviors. Adults should not allow children to attend parties or events in which the activities make them uncomfortable as a parent or caregiver. Parents can also tell children that they can always say, "My parent will not let me," if they feel an activity or

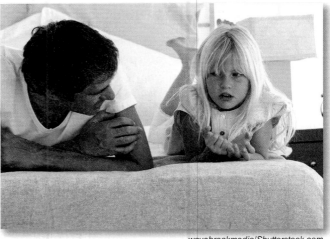

wavebreakmedia/Shutterstock.com

Figure 19.16 School-age children may struggle with the sadness of losing a friend. Talking with a parent may help these children process the loss. *Think of a time when you lost a friend as a child. How did you feel at the time? How did you express your feelings?*

situation is inappropriate. Many children are relieved by this option because it removes the blame from themselves, hopefully preventing rejection from peers.

- Watch for inappropriate friendships and talk about inappropriate behaviors of peer groups (such as bullying, using alcohol or drugs, participating in sexual activities, and shoplifting). Adults can explain to children why these behaviors are wrong and outline the consequences. Adults can also offer guidance on what children might do if such a situation arises.

19.2-4 Helping Children Control Their Emotions

During the school-age and teen years, children continue working toward self-regulation. Older school-age children and teens can often self-regulate emotions consistently and analyze the causes of their feelings and the consequences of certain behaviors. They are capable of thinking before they act, even though they remain impulsive through the teen years. At times, however, children may still experience some mood swings and outbursts and need adults to help them control their emotions.

Some ways adults continue to guide children's emotions during the school-age and teen years include the following:

- *Modeling emotional control.* Children need to observe parents modeling control of their own emotions. Children learn by watching adults handle frustration and anger.
- *Normalizing emotions.* Children need to know that all people have strong feelings. School-age children may be helped by reading about the struggles of other children and adults to control feelings. Adults may want to talk about their own struggles, too, such as controlling their tempers or managing jealousy. Talking through emotions can be beneficial for both school-age children and teens.
- *Respecting others.* Children need to learn that control of emotions is done out of respect for others.
- *Using loving discipline.* Parents and caregivers can model acceptable ways of guiding and disciplining their children. Physical punishment can show a loss of control by the adult.
- *Suggesting indirect outlets.* Children need indirect ways to control emotions, such as physical activity and creative tasks (**Figure 19.17**).
- *Teaching skills.* Caregivers and other adults can teach skills that help children overcome fears and anxieties, as well as other strong emotions.

FOCUS ON MENTAL HEALTH

Children who cannot control their emotions may experience depression and be unable to participate in the joys of life. To help prevent feelings of depression in their children, adults can make sure that communication is strong in the parent-child relationship. Maintaining a sense of love and acceptance through difficult times is vital in helping children manage conflicts and develop a strong sense of self.

In some cases, children need professional help if their behavior goes beyond the boundaries (in intensity and length of time) of what most children do. Two common problems that require professional help are sad and withdrawn behaviors and aggressive and defiant behaviors.

Sad and withdrawn behaviors often suggest depression. Children cannot just "get over" depression. Aggressive and defiant behaviors may signal poor anger management. These children may interpret many actions as hostile and immediately react with anger. The risk factors for this problem are having an irritable temperament and being exposed to models of poor anger management. Often these problems occur together. Professionals have to train children how to evaluate situations and how to be assertive rather than aggressive.

Figure 19.17 Engaging in physical activity can help school-age children control their emotions. *What indirect outlets help you control emotions?*

Jupiterimages/The Image Bank via Getty Images

19.2-5 Helping School-Age Children and Adolescents Cope with Stress

Parents and caregivers, along with other influential adults, can work together to try and prevent chronic and toxic stress in school-age children and teens. One way to do this is by watching for signs of stress, which can appear as both physical and psychological symptoms. Some of these symptoms may be prolonged or severe. Listening for signs of stress is also important. Most children will not say, "I'm stressed," but they may say, "I'm angry" or "I'm worried." Stressed children are more likely to say negative things about themselves, about others, or about the world around them.

At home, parents and caregivers can reduce stress by giving children constant love and support. They can provide a stable home environment and monitor children's eating and sleeping habits. Parents can also seek to understand the causes of mistakes in behavior rather than just punishing children. Avoiding unrealistic expectations is important, too. Parents can let children know they can help them with their problems through open communication and possible suggestions. Lastly, working with a licensed mental health professional may be necessary if stress seems to overwhelm the child.

FOCUS ON MENTAL HEALTH

Children who experience chronic or toxic stress are at higher risk of developing mental health issues. Parents and caregivers can reduce stress by giving constant love and support, knowing the risk factors, looking for warning signs, having open communication, and teaching healthy coping skills. Children who learn how to deal with stress in a healthy way are more likely to be well-adjusted adults.

Lesson 19.2 Review and Assessment

1. When disciplining a child, a caregiver should _____. (19.2.1)
   A. reprimand them in front of a sibling or peer
   B. temporarily withdraw their affection
   C. explain that their behavior will be hard to forgive
   D. criticize the act, not the child
2. **True or False.** Children do better in school when adults show little or no concern about their success. (19.2.2)
3. To foster open communication with their school-age child, a parent should _____. (19.2.3)
   A. use you-statements instead of I-statements
   B. interrupt the child as needed to clarify information
   C. thank the child for sharing a problem with them
   D. make sure the child knows they are upset with them
4. **True or False.** Children may pattern many of their thoughts and actions after the important adults in their lives. (19.2.3)
5. Which is the least effective way caregivers can guide school-age children's emotions? (19.2.4)
   A. Suggesting physical activity to redirect strong emotion
   B. Using physical punishment to control behavior
   C. Sharing their own struggles with anger
   D. Modeling emotional control themselves
6. **True or False.** Children under stress are more likely to say negative things about themselves, about others, or about the world around them. (19.2.5)

Chapter 19

Review and Assessment

Summary

Lesson 19.1

19.1-1 School-age children's self-awareness expands as they take on and show new responsibilities. Their self-concepts often depend on their sense of achievement and the acknowledgment of others.

19.1-1 Adults who serve as good role models will help school-age children and teens develop a healthy work ethic.

19.1-1 Children's awareness of gender roles is influenced by family, peers, school environment, and the media. Children without a clearly defined gender identity may be part of a gender school that does not match their biological gender.

19.1-1 School-age children's moral development is influenced by authority figures and peers.

19.1-1 Children who are others-oriented begin to develop a conscience from their feelings of guilt after misdeeds. Conversely, shame erodes self-esteem and can lead to mental health problems.

19.1-1 Comparisons with other peers affect the self-concepts of school-age children.

19.1-2 School-age children are in Erikson's fourth stage of personality development, industry versus inferiority.

19.1-2 Teenagers enter Erikson's fifth stage of personality development, identity versus role confusion, as they ask, "Who am I?" by examining their values, beliefs, and personal goals.

19.1-3 During the early school-age years, children enter into a goal-corrected partnership with caregivers. Attachments are no longer based on physical proximity; they are instead based on physical and emotional availability.

19.1-3 By age 8 or 9, children and their caregivers move toward a partner relationship method of co-regulation. Caregivers provide a balance between letting go and holding on, giving children a sense of psychological security as they consider caregivers their "home base."

19.1-3 Peers and friends become much more important in children's lives as compared with their importance during the preschool years.

19.1-3 Peer groups help children learn how to deal with rules, get along with others, depend less on adults, and process adult-taught values.

19.1-4 School-age children are learning to control their emotions. They express love, fear and anxiety, anger and aggression, and jealousy in socially acceptable ways.

19.1-5 As school-age children adjust to their new responsibilities and relationships, adults should watch for signs of stress, which include eating disorders, sleeping difficulties, hyperactive behavior, and negativism and lying, to name a few.

19.1-6 School-age children and adolescents may achieve many social-emotional developmental milestones as their worlds transform when they enter school. Their self-awareness expands; they strive to be industrious; and they begin to form a personal identity.

Lesson 19.2

19.2-1 Adults can promote their children's self-awareness by giving children responsibility, supporting their gender roles, instilling morality, and building a healthy self-concept.

19.2-1 Instilling morality involves teaching children to respect others, show responsibility, follow established limits, behave acceptably, express remorse for misdeeds, and think for themselves before acting on moral issues.

19.2-2 To help teens form a positive personal identity, parents should be active listeners and sources of unconditional love. They should maintain set boundaries and limits, be good role models, be patient and open-minded, and help teens identify and explore their strengths.

19.2-3 In guiding school-age children's social relationships, caregivers can make time for children's friendships, expand children's horizons, guide and model important behaviors, and help manage conflicts with friends.

19.2-3 To support the parent-child relationship, caregivers should keep family communication open, teach morals and values, and balance dependence with independence.

19.2-4 Children who exhibit sad and withdrawn behaviors and aggressive and defiant behaviors require professional help.

19.2-5 Adults should watch for signs of stress, which can appear as both physical and psychological symptoms, and take steps to help children cope.

College and Career Portfolio

Portfolio Website

Making your portfolio available electronically can make it easier for colleges and employers to review the portfolio's contents. Some professionals make their portfolios available through a website.

Research platforms for making your portfolio available online.

Use one platform to create a sample portfolio. Then, evaluate whether the platform is right for your portfolio.

Recall and Application

1. During which stage are school-age children regulated by rules set with mutual consent and for reasons of fairness and equity? (19.1.1)
   A. Piaget's autonomous reality
   B. Kohlberg's postconventional morality
   C. Kohlberg's conventional morality
   D. Piaget's concrete operational

2. **True or False.** Current gender-role attitudes in the school environment are drastically different than they were in decades past. (19.1.1)

3. Which is least accurate about how school-age children with a sense of industry see work? (19.1.2)
   A. It is a route to learning new ideas and skills.
   B. It is a chance to perform in worthwhile ways.
   C. It is a way to win approval from others.
   D. It is an opportunity to have fun.

4. In the partner relationship method of co-regulation, all of the following are true except _____. (19.1.3)
   A. caregivers provide a balance between letting go and holding on
   B. children and caregivers share the goal of creating a loving relationship
   C. children think of their caregivers as home base
   D. caregivers maintain communication and supervision of the child

5. **True or False.** The fears and anxieties of middle childhood and adolescence usually disappear with age and rarely persist into the adult years. (19.1.4)

6. An example of an internal source of stress that may affect a school-age child is _____. (19.1.5)
   A. community violence
   B. divorce
   C. sleep deprivation
   D. peer rejection

7. Ten- to twelve-year-olds typically achieve which social-emotional developmental milestone? (19.1.6)
   A. Feeling anxious about school failure
   B. Defining self in terms of appearance, possessions, and activities
   C. Feeling sensitive to what others think
   D. Constantly talking about friends

8. **True or False.** All children are influenced by the male and female adults and caregivers in their lives, which affects the child's perspective of feminine and masculine gender roles. (19.2.1)

9. Adults can help children develop a positive sense of industry by _____. (19.2.2)
   A. focusing on their traits that need improvement
   B. setting low standards they can easily achieve
   C. encouraging their success in school
   D. leaving them alone to figure out complex tasks

10. To help children build an internal moral system, caregivers should do all of the following *except* _____. (19.2.3)
    A. setting rules for them to follow
    B. teaching them not to question rules
    C. applying logical consequences to their mistakes
    D. modeling expected behavior

11. **True or False.** Most children can get over depression without professional help. (19.2.4)

12. **True or False.** To reduce a child's stress, parents can seek to understand the causes of mistakes in behavior rather than just punishing children. (19.2.5)

Critical Thinking

1. **Evaluate.** Choose one media depiction of a school-age child or teen. Then, evaluate how this child shows responsibility. What tasks do they perform to demonstrate responsibility? How might the child show *more* responsibility? Share your thoughts with the rest of the class.

2. **Draw conclusions.** As children develop a sense of industry, play can take a different role in their lives. In small groups, discuss how the importance of play changes during the school-age years. Should play take a "backseat" to industrious activities? Why or why not?

3. **Analyze.** During the school-age and adolescent years, peers become increasingly important to children. Children may rely more on friendships than they do on their parents and caregivers. Analyze why peer relationships become so important during this stage of development. What factors contribute to this importance? How does this importance affect the way children behave?

4. **Make inferences.** Children in the school-age and teen years compare themselves with one another and tend to judge harshly. Why do you think this is? What developmental changes contribute to these behaviors? What societal factors influence peers' judgments?

5. **Determine.** Choose one emotion discussed in this chapter and determine concrete ways parents and caregivers can help children control this emotion. How well were you able to control this emotion as a school-age child, or how well are you able to control it now as a teen?

6. **Cause and effect.** Forming a self-concept becomes more complex for children during the school-age years. In small groups, identify and summarize reasons for this complexity. Then, analyze how these reasons affect school-age children's self-esteem. Finally, discuss ways adults can help children build healthy self-concepts.

7. **Compare and contrast.** Review the ways adults and caregivers can help children manage conflicts. Choose two of these ways to compare and contrast. How do the two ways help manage a conflict? How effective are the two ways? Is one way more effective than the other?

8. **Identify.** Many children experience difficulties adjusting to relationships with peers. Some of these children may benefit from outside help, whether in the form of a social group or counselor. In small groups identify helpful community resources for children who have difficulties with peer relationships. Create an easy-to-follow list of these resources and their objectives.

Core Skills

1. **Research, listening, and speaking.** Using reliable resources, research how gender roles develop during the school-age and teen years. Where do children learn about gender roles? How do they express them? Take notes about your findings and compile a short bibliography. Then interview a school counselor (at a primary, middle, or high school) and discuss your research. Does the school counselor agree with your research findings? What, if anything, would the school counselor add or change? After the interview, deliver an oral presentation summarizing your research and interview.

2. **Listening, speaking, and writing.** Interview a primary, middle school, or high school teacher about school-age children's or teens' morality. According to the teacher, what kind of morality do school-age children or teens possess? How do they act on that morality? During the second half of your interview, discuss Kohlberg's theory of moral reasoning with the teacher. Draw connections between Kohlberg's theory and the teacher's real-life experience. After the interview, write a short reflection about what you learned from the discussion.

3. **Writing.** Review this chapter's information about the school-age child's struggle between *industry* and *inferiority* or the adolescent's struggle between *identity* and *role confusion*. Then, write a short story for school-age children or teens exploring this struggle and encouraging children to keep striving for industry or identity while avoiding inferiority or role confusion. Include a summary for your short story explaining how it will help children in their struggle.

4. **Technology and speaking.** In small groups, arrange to visit a primary or middle school. Interview 5 to 10 school-age children of various ages about their friendships and experiences with peers. Ask questions about how important the children's friendships are, what makes a good friend, and what concerns the child has when it comes to friendships. If possible, obtain permission to film the children's responses to these questions and compile the responses into a video. Play your video for the class and then discuss what your video reveals about school-age children's social worlds.

5. **Listening and speaking.** As a class, write a different social-emotional developmental milestone for school-age children and teens (Figure 19.11) on index cards or other pieces of paper. Then, shuffle the cards around the room. Try to group yourselves according to the appropriate age range. After grouping yourselves, check for accuracy by reading off your milestones.

6. **Listening and math.** Interview a parent and their school-age child or teen. During the interview, ask the parent and child to identify behaviors they have in common and behaviors they do not have in common. Which behaviors does the parent think the child learned from them? Which behaviors of the parent does the child reject? After the interview, tally the number of behaviors in common and the number of behaviors not in common. What percentage of the child's behaviors were guided or modeled by the parent?

7. **Reading.** Research and locate two scholarly articles about stress in school-age children or teens. Read these articles and take notes about what causes stress, how stress impacts children, and how adults can help alleviate stress. Afterward, write a comprehensive summary for each article. Print your summaries and place them on the walls of the classroom. As a class, walk around the room and read about articles your classmates found.

8. **CTE Career Readiness Practice.** Presume you are a social counselor at a middle school and your principal has asked you to deliver a presentation at sixth-grade orientation about children's emotional control. Your presentation will be for parents and caregivers and should highlight how children are learning to control emotions and ways in which adults can help them. Write a script for your presentation and memorize it. Practice until you feel confident. Finally, deliver your presentation to the class.

Observations

1. As a class, visit a local primary or middle school, or observe in your own high school. Sit near the outside of the school's lunchroom and observe how children interact in their peer groups. How much are the children trying to impress one another? Do you see signs of peers judging one another? Of peers comparing abilities and skills? Discuss your observations as a class.

2. Find a documentary about school-age children's or teens' stress and the social-emotional risks these children face. Watch the documentary in a small group and take notes about what you learn. Then, discuss how your group members have witnessed these social-emotional risks, either personally or at their former schools.

Unit 7 Guiding and Caring for Children

Job Interview

Job interviewing is an event you might enter with your CTSO organization. By participating in the job interview, you will showcase your presentation skills, communication techniques, and ability to actively listen to the interviewer's questions. Written expectations for this event often include the creation of a cover letter, résumé, portfolio, and completion of a job application.

To prepare for a job interview event, complete the following activities:

1. Use internet and print resources to research the job-application process and interview techniques.
2. Write your cover message, résumé, and complete the job application (if provided for the event).
3. Prepare your portfolio. Include a table of contents, cover message, resume, job application, and relevant samples of your work. Check the rules and regulations for your CTSO event for any other items to include in your portfolio and for presentation format (print or digital). (Note: Your organization may require that you submit these materials prior to the event or at the event.)
4. Make certain each piece of communication is complete and free of errors.
5. Solicit feedback regarding your written materials from peers, instructors, and family members.
6. Ask a peer to take the role of interviewer as you practice answering interview questions. Your instructor or classmates may serve as competition judges during your practice sessions. Incorporate suggestions for improvement in your responses.

Chapter 20

Encouraging Children's Play Experiences

Essential Question

How does play serve as children's context for development?

Case Study · How Do Children Learn Through Art?

As a class, read the case study and discuss the questions that follow. After you finish studying the chapter, discuss this case study again. Have your opinions changed based on what you learned?

After completing his degree in early childhood education, Hiroto was excited to land a job teaching preschoolers. From the moment he received the job offer, Hiroto started planning creative art activities that would promote holistic learning. Hiroto excelled at his job and received only praise from his director for the first few months.

One Friday, Hiroto's preschoolers engaged in a messy activity using tempera paint. Later that day, the director called Hiroto into her office and said, "Please change these messy activities. The children will only produce scribbles, and parents expect art projects to look real." The director pulled a butterfly art pattern from a file in her office. She explained, "We usually copy art patterns like this one for the children to color and decorate."

Hiroto felt crushed that the director wanted him to use this "cookie cutter" art instead of the "real art" he had been organizing. He thought, I've been taught so many ideas for helping children do creative art. Why can't the center embrace my ideas even if some of the art projects are messy?

During the next week or so, Hiroto followed the director's instructions, although sending home "cookie cutter" art projects made him unhappy. Hiroto wondered, Are my ideas about art for preschoolers wrong? How can I please the director while still giving my students the best education?

Give It Some Thought

1. Whose ideas about art are most appropriate for preschoolers? How much of a difference does the type of art project make? Explain your answer.
2. Do you think Hiroto would be better off following the director's ideas or the ones he recently learned? Explain your answer.
3. Do you think parents really want "cookie cutter" art as the director indicated? Why or why not?

Renata Angerami/E+ via Getty Images

Lesson 20.1 The Importance of Play

Key Terms

active-physical play

imitative-imaginative play

language-logic play

manipulative-constructive play

play therapy

Learning Outcomes

After studying this lesson, you will be able to

20.1-1 **eplore** and **identify** the stages of play, the different types of play, and why they are important in children's lives.

20.1-2 **identify** ways that adults can encourage play in children and the benefits children derive from play.

Reading and Notetaking Activity

Skim this chapter from top to bottom and from left to right and list all the headings. Then, identify key terms with which you are unfamiliar and scan through the chapter to find their definitions. Write a "topic sentence" and brief summary for each heading, using the key terms to explain what you think you will learn. After you read this chapter, write a new topic sentence and summary for each section, outlining the main points you learned.

wundervisuals/E+ via Getty Images

Figure 20.1 While playing with bubbles, a child can *express* what they know while *learning* more about the nature of air and bubbles. *What was your favorite type of play as a child? How did that type of play allow you to express yourself while learning more?*

Introduction

Play affects all domains of child development. In fact, play can be seen as the context of child development. Research on play supports the benefits of play. Theorists, however, do not agree on how play affects children's development.

According to Piaget, play is a way for children to practice concepts they already know, which leads to mastery. In contrast to Piaget, Vygotsky believed that play enables children to learn new concepts if the play is within their zone of proximal development (ZPD). Perhaps both theorists were correct in their ideas about the intellectual benefits of play (**Figure 20.1**).

Piaget, Vygotsky, and Erikson all studied the relationship between play and social-emotional development. Piaget believed that play aids children's ability to see from other perspectives—a step in moral development. Vygotsky found that pretend play aids self-regulation because children learn to be true to the roles they are playing and to cooperate with other children. Erikson saw play as a way for children to try new social skills, to learn about cultural and gender roles, and to dramatize child-adult conflicts in a safe way.

To help children learn and express themselves through play, adults must recognize the importance of play. Adults should also be familiar with the stages of play and types of play so they can encourage children to express and refine their learning in each stage of their development.

20.1-1 Stages of Play

Play, often referred to as the *highest level of child development*, reflects changes that take place in children's physical, intellectual, and social-emotional development. As such, play proceeds through a series of stages as children grow and develop new skills.

Children's stages of play build on one another. Very young children will not begin to play in advanced stages until they have mastered early stages. Older children learn to play in advanced stages, but they can still play in earlier stages, too (**Figure 20.2**). New objects and people may cause a child to play at a less advanced stage until the child is accustomed to the change.

Child development experts describe the stages of play in several ways, depending on the aspects of play on which they focus. Piaget identified three stages of play, which correspond with Piaget's first three stages of cognitive development. Other theorists have approached play from different perspectives. Stages of play involve children's play with objects and with people. **Figure 20.3** shows some of these stages of play with objects and with people although other child development experts may describe stages of play in different ways.

©iStock.com/acfrank

Figure 20.2 When older children play with younger children, the stage of play most often fits the ZPD for the younger child. However, older children may provide ideas that slightly "stretch" younger children's thinking. *Why do you think play most often fits the ZPD for the younger child?*

Types of Play

Children play in many different ways depending on their interests, stages of development, and materials available. Different types of play encourage different skills and strengthen different areas of development. While play classifications may vary, some common types of play include *active-physical play, manipulative-constructive play, imitative-imaginative play*, and *language-logic play*. Knowing the types of play can help caregivers and other adults foster healthful and appropriate play in children.

Figure 20.3 Stages of Play

Age Range	Play with Objects*	Play with People**
Infancy and the Toddler Years	*Practice play.* Children explore objects by picking them up or tracking them with their eyes. Play involves putting objects in mouth, moving body, listening to noises, exploring surroundings, and imitating others' actions. Play activities are repeated. (Also known as *sensory motor play*.)	*Solitary play.* Infants ignore other children who are nearby. Sometimes infants treat others as objects to be pushed or walked on, to be poked in the eyes or nose, or to have hair pulled. *Onlooker play.* Toddlers watch others play, but do not join in their play. *Parallel play.* Children play near other children and often play with the same or similar toys. They note that others have interests and skills much like their own. There is no real interaction among children, however.
Preschool and the Early School-Age Years	*Symbolic play.* Children engage in pretend play. They pretend they are someone else. Also, they project mental images on objects. For example, a stick can become a horse. Symbolic play becomes more complex as children age.	*Associative play.* Two or more children play at a common activity. The children share ideas. The play is not well organized in terms of goals or roles, however. For example, one child may decide to run a food store and another may be a mother, but the mother never shops at the food store.
Late School-Age Years	*Rule play.* Children make rules to govern their games or carefully follow established rules. Play becomes more logical and interactive.	*Cooperative play.* Two or more children share common goals and play complementary roles, such as the chaser and the chased.

* The stages of play with objects were outlined by Piaget and follow Piaget's first three stages of cognitive development. *Practice play* corresponds to Piaget's sensorimotor stage; *symbolic play* to Piaget's preoperational stage; and *rule play* to Piaget's concrete operational stage.
** The stages of play with people are based on Parten's research.

Active-Physical Play

Active-physical play is a type of play in which children use their gross-motor skills. Gross-motor skills are used in activities such as walking, running, hopping, jumping, twisting, bending, skipping, galloping, catching, throwing, balancing, pushing, pulling, and rocking. Through active-physical play, children test and improve various physical skills. They learn how strong they are by pushing, pulling, lifting, and carrying objects. Children learn how to spring up to lift their bodies, which is a skill they often need. They also learn how to catch themselves on impact, which protects the body from injury. Active-physical play also improves a child's reaction time and balance. Children need balance for almost every gross-motor movement. Active-physical play helps children become more **graceful** (able to move smoothly and elegantly). Grace improves as gross-motor skills develop and helps a person engage in many more fun activities.

Through active-physical play, children learn about spatial concepts. For example, they learn about the positions of objects and about the movements of their bodies in space. Names for movements and positions in space take on meaning.

Until about 60 years ago, play was not an area of much research in child development. Before this time, play was seen as both difficult to define and as a frivolous pastime of children. Today, play is known to be a vital aspect of a child's development and thus worthy of research. Following are six researchers whose mini theories have contributed to people's understanding of children's play.

Mildred Parten, a sociologist, began the study of play before most researchers began to study child's play. Parten's main interest was how play stimulated social development in children. Parten noted six stages of play: unoccupied—the random movements of infants, solitary, onlooker, parallel, associative, and cooperative. Parten found that children progress through these stages in a somewhat linear way but can play at different stages when playing with older or younger children.

Sara Smilansky, a psychologist, helped Piaget develop his theory of play. Smilansky accepted Piaget's three stages of play—practice, symbolic, and rule play—and added another stage, called *constructive play* (using materials to create objects), which was placed as the second stage in the sequence. Smilansky made major contributions to the understanding of dramatic play (same as Piaget's *symbolic play*), such as understanding the child's use of objects and words in play roles, persistence in playing a role, and social interactions during play. Smilansky felt that dramatic play prepared a child for school, and children who did not have rich dramatic play experiences suffered academically.

Kenneth H. Rubin, professor of human development, researched the correlation between social and cognitive aspects of play by using a matrix format to combine some of Parten's and Smilansky's stages of play. These studies led to the development of a play observation scale, which is valuable as an authentic assessment of a child's stage of social-cognitive development in play.

Jerome L. Singer and **Dorothy G. Singer**, clinical psychologists, specialized in children's imaginations and daydreaming. They concluded that the use of imagination in childhood led children to become adults who could engage successfully in new situations. They also researched the use of play therapy as a means of helping children with mental health problems.

Brian Sutton-Smith, a developmental psychologist, lectured throughout the world and helped in the preparation of televised films on toys and play. Sutton-Smith categorized the many forms of play from a child's early play to sports, jokes, drama, and celebrations. A few of the diverse topic areas researched were the history of games, toys, and children's play; the folk games of children; the importance of play in learning; and how adults should play with children. Sutton-Smith felt that playful caregiver-child relationships are associated with children who are flexible, friendly, and happy, and found that direct intervention by adults in a child's play added stress to the child's life.

Speaking Activity

Choose one of the theorists discussed and research that theorist's ideas about play. Take notes of your findings and then write a persuasive speech about the importance of play from that theorist's point of view. Present your speech to the class.

Photo: Tom Wang/Shutterstock.com

These names include *forward, backward, big, little, fast, slow, under, over, up, down, behind, in front of, through, beside,* and *between.* Children will also develop physical knowledge concepts through active-physical play. For example, they will become aware of the force of gravity on objects and on their bodies. They will experience going faster on a steep slide as compared to a slide with a gentle slope.

Older school-age children participate in active-physical play through joining community and school sports, and interscholastic league teams like drill team, band, cheerleading and other athletic programs found in both public and private schools. Throughout the high school years, these students continue working on gross-motor skills, spatial concepts, and exercise. Older school-age children not involved in sports or athletics also benefit with physical activity as well. When a child is active the brain releases endorphins and serotonin which help create feelings of happiness, well-being, and a heightening of appetite. Both help children feel good about themselves and benefit their heart, lungs, muscles, and bones. Being active is also a great way to reduce stress and keep a clear head. For both adults and children physical activity helps reduce body fat and helps with maintaining a healthy weight.

Manipulative-Constructive Play

Manipulative-constructive play is a type of play that involves the use of children's fine-motor skills. Children's fine-motor skills develop after basic gross-motor skills. For example, most children will not learn the fine-motor skill of writing until after they learn the gross-motor skill of walking. Even early in life, though, some fine-motor skills start to develop. Crawling infants can pick up small objects (such as gravel and paper) on a carpet. They can put objects in their mouths, ears, and noses. Manipulative-constructive play also benefits eye-hand coordination, which is crucial for children's writing and artwork (**Figure 20.4**).

Many toys and materials promote children's development of fine-motor skills. These include jigsaw puzzles, small blocks and other construction materials, beads for stringing, pegs and pegboards, art materials, woodworking tools, and cooking gadgets.

portishead1/E+ via Getty Images

Figure 20.4 Manipulative-constructive play involves handling objects and may include art activities and fine-motor games. *What are some other examples of manipulative-constructive play?*

Toys that promote fine-motor skills are made for little, unskilled hands as well as for more skilled hands.

In addition to promoting fine-motor skills, manipulative-constructive play helps children mentally picture objects. Furthermore, many visual and intellectual concepts, such as recognition of shapes and understandings of distance, math, sorting and classifying, and reversibility, are developed as children play with manipulative toys. Finally, manipulative-constructive play helps children create abstract models of what they see (such as by drawing their houses and yards).

By the time children enter the late school-age and adolescent time frames, their fine-motor skills are used often in their day to day lives. These children can continue working on fine motor skills and eye-hand coordination by participating in activities like checkers or chess, drawing, basketball, tennis, and bowling.

Imitative-Imaginative Play

During **imitative-imaginative play**, children use words and actions to pretend to be objects or people other than themselves. Imitative-imaginative play has great value and involves creativity as children invent their own worlds. As children put themselves in different situations, they learn to plan, solve problems, and make decisions.

Children choose props and actions in their play and can use imitative-imaginative play to test many roles. They can imagine or picture themselves as if they are other people and objects and can begin to understand others' real-life roles. Children can use pretend actions to depict holiday, work, family, and other rituals that begin to prepare them for adult life. In group play, leadership roles often emerge, too.

Imitative-imaginative play also helps improve children's memories because children must recall events to play. Children's language improves as they listen and speak during play. There is much freedom in expression as children try to bridge the gap between what they know and what they do not know. Children use their bodies to extend their language. For example, a child may say, "I'm a barber," while moving their fingers in a cutting motion.

Through imitative-imaginative play, children can also express fears, resentments, and even hostile feelings in ways that are socially acceptable. Role-playing has many healing qualities, which are utilized in activities like **play therapy** (the use of play between a child and a trained counselor to help the child resolve certain problems).

There are three stages of imitative-imaginative play. These stages are called *imitative play*, *dramatic play*, and *socio-dramatic play* (**Figure 20.5**). As children grow and progress through these stages, their roles and imaginations become more and more complex. Caregivers can encourage pretend play to help children use imagination and creativity, this helps with thinking for themselves and understanding another point of view. Other benefits include supporting social and emotional development and helping with self-esteem and self-awareness development, improving language and communication skills, developing and building thinking, learning and problem-solving abilities, and enhancing physical development.

As children enter the adolescent years the skills translate over into learning and exhibiting sportsmanship behaviors like taking turns, being a good winner or loser, and abstract thinking.

Figure 20.5 Stages of Imitative-Imagination Play

Stage	Characteristics	Example
Imitative play	• Begins at about two years of age, or just as children start to use symbolic thought. • Involves the child doing one imitative action to an object. • Occurs in short periods of time, but repeatedly over days, weeks, and even months.	For ten minutes every day, a child throws a stuffed animal into the air to pretend it is a spaceship.
Dramatic play	• Begins when the child is three or four years of age. • Involves role-playing with more than one child, but each child's role is independent of others' roles. • Often includes children engaging in collective monologue. • Involves several behaviors associated with a role.	Three children pretend to be space creatures by running around a room, but they are all playing different and sometimes contradictory roles.
Socio-dramatic play	• Is common in children between five and seven years of age. • Involves play associated with a theme. • Involves assigning special roles to each child.	Three children assign each other roles as explorers (a navigator, an astronaut, and a scientist) and pretend to look for new planets together.

Goodheart-Willcox Publisher

Adolescents learn to think outside of the box when it comes to solving problems or scenarios they are presented with. At the same time, they can practice leadership roles which they will use throughout their lives. Many teens also participate in plays, musicals, and dramas where they are able to act out characters while expressing emotions and enjoying interacting with others.

Language-Logic Play

Language-logic play is a form of intellectual play most often seen in school-age children. Language-logic play can include many different types of language and word games. In some language games, children compete by using vocabulary skills. Other language games include humor that is based on language, such as puns. Logic games, such as chess, object puzzles, word problems, and checkers, require much thought about one's actions. In these games, children must think ahead and **strategize** (plan strategies).

20.1-2 Encouraging Play in Children

Play is important for children's development and health, and it is important that adults (both caregivers and other adults who work with children) encourage children to play. Children need support and need to know that adults recognize the importance of and approve of their play. Although how an adult specifically encourages a child's play will depend on the child and the type of play they enjoy, there are several principles adults can keep in mind when supporting play.

First, adults can allow freedom for children to explore and play. Children need time to explore on their own. While adults can observe play and, at times, model ideas or add materials, children need freedom to decide whether they will use these ideas. Rather than directing play, adults can add to play by playing along with children's pretend play in supportive roles and by explaining new concepts. As much as possible, children should take the lead in their own play. While some limits (such as rules for safety) are necessary, too many limits set by

adults and sometimes children's peers may discourage a child.

In addition to letting children lead, adults can encourage play by displaying positive attitudes toward play. Adults' attitudes toward play influence how children view play. What adults do and say can promote or hamper children's creativity. To encourage children, adults can recognize the importance of play and then express that to children by providing plenty of playtime and by acknowledging children's learning, creativity, and fun.

Finally, adults can encourage play in children by providing toys that children will like. Children's preferences in toys change as children grow and develop. **Figure 20.6** lists toys that are attractive to children in different stages of development.

Figure 20.6 Attractive Toys for Children

Age Range	Toys
Infancy and the Toddler Years	• Texture toys • Squeeze toys • Stuffed toys and dolls • Large balls • Toys that make sounds • Push-and-pull toys
Preschool Years	• Toys for gross-motor play (balls, pedal toys, and climbing toys) • Toys for fine-motor play (puzzles, beads, and pegs) • Floor blocks • Dress-up clothes and props • Toy cars, trucks, and planes • Toy animals • Puppets and toy people
School-Age Years	• Sports equipment • Bicycles • Board games • Digital games • Crafts and puzzles • Advanced construction sets • Collectibles

Goodheart-Willcox Publisher

1. When a child plays with the same toy near another child, noting the other child but without interacting with them, this is called _____ play. (20.1.1)
   A. associative
   B. cooperative
   C. parallel
   D. onlooker

2. Which is the best example of symbolic play? (20.1.1)
   A. Imitating another person's gestures
   B. Creating new rules for checkers
   C. Deciding who will be "it" in freeze tag
   D. Pretending a wagon is a race car

3. An example of an activity that promotes manipulative-constructive play is _____. (20.1.1)
   A. balancing on a balance beam
   B. completing a jigsaw puzzle
   C. pretending to be a deep-sea diver
   D. doing a word-search puzzle

4. The best way an adult can support a child's ability to play is by _____. (20.1.2)
   A. directing the child's actions during play
   B. setting limits on when they can play
   C. giving the child freedom to explore on their own
   D. observing the child as they play with others

5. **True or False.** Push-and-pull toys are most appropriate for preschoolers. (20.1.2)

Lesson 20.2

Play Activities for Children

Key Terms

sand tables
unit blocks
visual arts
visual literacy
water tables

Learning Outcomes

After studying this lesson, you will be able to

20.2-1 **compare** and **contrast** the pros and cons of various types of learning experiences, including blocks, water, cooking, art, music, science, and literature.

20.2-2 **discuss** the benefits of literature experiences and identify age-appropriate reading techniques for children of all ages.

Reading and Notetaking Activity

Skim this chapter from top to bottom and from left to right and list all the headings. Then, identify key terms with which you are unfamiliar and scan through the chapter to find their definitions. Write a "topic sentence" and brief summary for each heading, using the key terms to explain what you think you will learn. After you read this chapter, write a new topic sentence and summary for each section, outlining the main points you learned.

20.2-1 Learning Experiences

Adults have a major role in children's play. Their abilities to recognize and implement various play activities impact children's play experiences. Quality play experiences should both entertain children and teach them. Because children learn through play, the potential benefits of planning quality play activities are enormous. Through play, children can become physically stronger and more coordinated, can practice new intellectual concepts, and can learn social skills that will strengthen their relationships.

Many play activities and games are available for children, but the best play activities tend to be open-ended and benefit all areas of development. Quality play activities that adults can plan for children include block building, sand play, water play, cooking experiences, art experiences, music experiences, science experiences, and literature experiences. By planning these activities and allowing children freedom to explore, adults foster children's development.

Block Building

Blocks are one of the most important play experiences and learning tools for children. Block building is a flexible, open-ended activity that extends to all areas of development, allowing for holistic learning. As children develop, they experience several stages of block building that correspond to their development of spatial concepts (**Figure 20.7**). Progress in block building also complements children's other understandings.

Figure 20.7 **Stages in Unit Block Building**

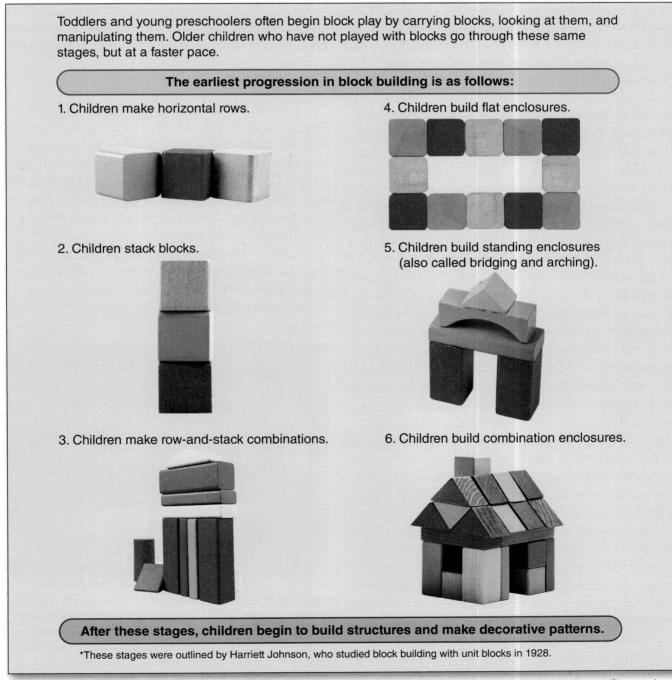

Toddlers and young preschoolers often begin block play by carrying blocks, looking at them, and manipulating them. Older children who have not played with blocks go through these same stages, but at a faster pace.

The earliest progression in block building is as follows:

1. Children make horizontal rows.

2. Children stack blocks.

3. Children make row-and-stack combinations.

4. Children build flat enclosures.

5. Children build standing enclosures (also called bridging and arching).

6. Children build combination enclosures.

After these stages, children begin to build structures and make decorative patterns.

*These stages were outlined by Harriett Johnson, who studied block building with unit blocks in 1928.

1–4: Nenov Brothers Images/Shutterstock.com; 5: Tomas Hilger/Shutterstock.com; 6: Vladimir Prusakov/Shutterstock.com

For example, at three years of age, children can express symbolic understandings, such as saying a pile of blocks is a house. By four years of age, children express understandings about how environmental features are related, such as depicting houses by the side of a road. By seven years of age, children build more to scale, such as building a chair smaller than a house.

Unlike sand, water, and art materials, blocks are solid, constant shapes that create a stable environment, permit self-correction, and allow for endless repetitions. Block building has benefits in all areas of development. Through running, jumping, lifting, carrying, bending, reaching, grasping, and balancing, children develop gross- and fine-motor skills and eye-hand coordination. Block building enhances thinking skills and aids the beginning of logical thought by promoting **visual literacy** (the ability to draw meaning from observable and **tangible**—perceived by touch—objects). Concepts that children learn through visual literacy include spatial concepts, classification, seriation, and number and shape concepts. Block building may also promote physics concepts (such as gravity), social studies concepts (such as space planning), art concepts (through making designs), and language and literacy concepts (through using blocks in dramatic play). Finally, block building encourages social skills (such as taking turns and sharing), requires patience and persistence, and strengthens children's self-concepts. School-age children use block play to explore cause and effect and experimentation using problem-solving skills, testing hypotheses and practicing scientific learning. Older school-age children experience a sense of achievement as they create and develop something new or unique. Many teenagers enjoy building models of different items that they build from a kit or from their own imaginations.

To support children's block building, adults can provide blocks, space for block building, and time for children to build. Different types of blocks offer different learning opportunities for children. *Unit blocks* (commonly called *floor blocks*) are often considered the best set of blocks for preschool and school-age children. **Unit blocks** are naturally finished wooden blocks that are multiples or divisions of the basic unit size (1⅜″ × 2¾″ × 5½″).

As children grow, the size of the blocks that they use may get smaller, and by the time they are teenagers they are using very small blocks to build models which helps with their eye-hand coordination and fine motor skills. It is important that adults allow children freedom to play with blocks. Rather than taking the lead or attempting to teach concepts, adults can help children by giving occasional suggestions, such as "Do you think another block might fit?" Adults can also support block building through expressions of pride in their children's creations, such as by taking photos and encouraging children to talk about their structures.

Sand Play

Because sand is a natural substance, children have probably played in it throughout history (**Figure 20.8**). Children are attracted to natural substances, whether on beaches or in sandboxes or sand tables. Sand is a highly **tactile** (perceived by touch) and open-ended substance with properties that change depending on moisture, making it ideal for children's play.

Sand play, like block building, promotes holistic learning that extends to all areas of development. Children use gross-motor skills when digging, moving, or cleaning up sand.

Irina Fischer/Shutterstock.com

Figure 20.8 In the late 1800s, the sand gardens of Germany inspired the first children's playgrounds in the United States. Although playground equipment has replaced sandboxes in some areas, there is a movement toward natural play spaces for children, including sand, water, and gardens. *What natural play spaces exist in your community?*

They use fine-motor skills for filling, pouring, smoothing, and sifting sand and for using sand tools, such as spades or tubing. Sand play enhances physical knowledge as children move sand buckets with pulleys. Children learn logical thinking concepts by discerning the weight of dry and wet sand and learn environmental concepts by observing sandy beaches and deserts. By writing letters and making patterns in the sand, children learn language and literacy concepts and creativity. As with block building, sand play refines children's social skills and emotional regulation when children work together.

The adult's role in sand play is one of support. Adults set the stage for sand play by providing equipment and accessories. Most sand play occurs in outdoor sandboxes or in **sand tables**, which are designed to hold sand and encourage experimental play (**Figure 20.9**). During play, adults can scaffold children's learning by asking questions, such as "What do you think would happen if you sprinkled more sand on top?" or "What shape are you making with that sand?" Finally, adults can show appreciation for children's sand play through photos, videos, drawings, and children's stories.

Sand tables are essential to the classroom for higher-level learning. These centers allow children to learn with hands-on material and take in information through their senses. These sensory experiences can assist some children when calming down their bodies. Sand tables also introduce higher-level thinking concepts like volume and develop language skills through question-and-answer sessions as the child talks to adults about what they have created.

LightField Studios/Shutterstock.com

Figure 20.9 Sandboxes, like the one shown, are ideal places for sand play and experimentation. Froebel, a German educator, created the first sandboxes for his kindergarten. *In what other places can children play with sand?*

Teachers and other caregivers can encourage sand play by making it available to children each day, modeling the behavior expected in the sand area and setting up the environment to optimize learning. Teachers can include access to materials like measuring cups, ladles, funnels, sifters, colanders or small manipulatives like plastic animals.

Water Play

Children can spend countless hours playing with water—pouring it back and forth between containers, making it spill over a container, or directing the flow by pushing water with their hands or a paddle (**Figure 20.10**). Besides having fun, children can also learn new concepts through water play.

Figure 20.10 Children can play with water in many places, including lakes, water tables, and pools. *What experiences did you have with water play as a child?*

wundervisuals/E+ via Getty Images

Water play is an open-ended activity that allows for children's explorations over many years. Because water, unlike other natural substances, can exist in three states (solid, liquid, and gas), water promotes even more lessons than many other activities. Children use gross-motor skills to run from sprinklers, wash toys, or water a garden. They use fine-motor skills and eye-hand coordination for filling, pouring, and emptying containers with water and for handling tubing and funnels. Although understanding the scientific concepts of water will take many years, water play can lay the foundations for these concepts. Children can learn physical knowledge concepts by watching water conform to the shape of its container. They can learn logical thinking concepts by practicing the conservation of continuous quantities and the conservation of volume (see Figure 18.5). They can also work on scientific concepts where they can make predictions and then experiment to see if those predictions were correct. Through learning about the states of water, precipitation, weight, and volume, children can learn science and math concepts. During water play, children can learn to work independently or cooperatively and can develop social skills through collaborating with peers.

As with block building and sand play, adults have the responsibility for supervising and supporting water play activities. Adults can provide equipment and materials for water play, such as **water tables**, which are designed to hold water and accessories for water play. As with other open-ended activities, adults can scaffold children's learning by planning activities in response to children's discoveries and questions. Adults should refrain from taking the lead during water play, over teaching, or expecting young children to understand concepts they cannot yet grasp (such as floating and sinking).

Cooking Experiences

Young children explore cooking in much the same way they do sand and water play. Children experiment with cooking tools and ingredients—making pretend foods—and then graduate to trying recipes.

Focus on Careers

Playground Designer

Playground designers are *landscape architects* who plan and design land and space for children. They design and create playgrounds, including playground equipment and areas for play activities (such as sand play and block building).

Playground designers analyze who will be using the space and for what purpose, the nature around the space, and how the environment will be impacted. They use sketches, models, and photographs to explain their ideas. Playground designers also work with building architects and engineers to complete a task.

Career cluster: Architecture and construction.

Education: Most playground designers have a bachelor's or master's degree in landscape architecture or a related subject. Most states require playground designers to be licensed.

Job outlook: Future employment opportunities for playground designers are expected to grow as fast as the average for all occupations.

To learn more about a career as a playground designer, visit the United States Department of Labor's *Occupational Outlook Handbook* website. You will also be able to compare the job responsibilities, educational requirements, job outlook, and average pay of playground designers with similar occupations.

Photo: Solis Images/Shutterstock.com

Health

Water Play Safety

Because of the risk for drowning, safety during water play is important. The most important factor in safe water play is adult supervision. Adults should never leave a child alone with standing water, even if the water is in a water table. For outdoor water play in pools, water parks, or natural bodies of water, adults should provide children with life jackets and watch to make sure children do not get into deep water if they cannot swim.

Sanitation is also a safety concern during water play. Outdoor bodies of water can contain harmful bacteria and poisonous plants. Children may consume or play with dangerous objects. Even the water in a water table may grow bacteria and become hazardous if the water is not changed daily. Adults can guard against these hazards by changing water regularly for indoor water play and by closely supervising children and removing dangerous objects during outdoor water play.

Photo: wavebreakmedia/Shutterstock.com

Cooking experiences promote learning in all areas of development. Children use fine-motor skills as they stir, shake, pour, knead, and use many other cooking techniques and basic cooking tools. As children learn concepts about quality food (as opposed to "junk food") and the need for safety and health practices, they also begin to understand and practice good nutritional habits for physical growth. Almost every cooking and eating experience leads to intellectual learning. Children learn physical knowledge concepts as they observe changes in foods during freezing, thawing, or baking. They learn logical thinking concepts by using numerical measurements. Seeing math symbols and words in recipes helps teach children language concepts. Children learn to cooperate while cooking, and cooking aids self-concept as children learn to meet their basic needs for nourishment. Cooking also requires self-regulation, especially in the areas of inhibition (where children must carefully follow a recipe and use tools correctly) and the delay of gratification (when food preparation requires time before eating).

In *real* (as opposed to *pretend*) cooking activities, adults help children more directly than they do in block building, water play, and sand play. Cooking experiences generally require more adult guidance and supervision. Adults can support children's cooking experiences by

- purchasing or collecting appropriate equipment
- assigning a child developmentally appropriate cooking tasks
- supervising carefully
- demonstrating the use of equipment
- scaffolding learning with the child's safety in mind
- reinforcing cooking lessons by applying them to other areas, such as science, art, math, and language

School-age children can create a recipe book of healthy snacks or easy-to-make meals that they can use when they are hungry. As they get older, school-age children can take turns preparing their families' meals. As school-age children become teenagers and involved in more activities, they may not be able to eat meals at the same time as the rest of the family. Having a list of quick and easy-to-prepare meals will ensure they are eating healthy foods rather than junk foods. As teenagers go off to college or live on their own, having recipes that they made with their family helps bring a taste of home to their lives.

Art Experiences

Art is important in children's lives. **Visual arts**, such as painting, molding, and photography, create products that appeal to children's sense of sight. Because a child's total development (including physical, intellectual, and social-emotional development) determines they use crayons, paints, clay, and other art materials, the child will progress through several stages of development in artistic expression (**Figure 20.11**).

Art experiences promote learning for children in all areas of development. As children learn to handle art tools, they develop the motor skills needed to draw, paint, or mold carefully and accurately.

Figure 20.11 **Stages of Development in Visual Arts**

Stage	Characteristics
Manipulative stage (birth–3½ years of age) *AnRo brook/ Shutterstock.com*	• Children play with the art materials themselves instead of using them to create artwork. • Children under 2 years of age enjoy art for motor reasons. Around 2 to 2½ years of age, children begin *scribbling* (using hands and eyes together to draw dots, lines, and loops). • Around 2½ to 3½ years of age, children begin to draw basic shapes.
Transition between manipulative and representation stage (3½–5 years of age) *AnRo brook/Shutterstock.com*	• Children create their first symbols. • Around 2½ years of age, children begin to draw human figures. • Children draw no spatial relationships among objects.
Representation stage (5–6 years of age and older) *s_oleg/Shutterstock.com*	• Children create symbols that represent objects, experiences, and feelings. • Children decide what a symbol is before creating it. • Children show spatial relationships among objects. • In the early part of the representation stage, children may draw *mixed perspectives*, *exaggerated images*, and *transparencies*. • Children draw more details and more accurate perspectives. • Around 9 to 10 years of age, children can draw objects from their perspectives *and* from the perspectives of others.

Goodheart-Willcox Publisher

Reading

Learning Math Through Cooking

Because of the measurements involved in following a recipe, cooking experiences can be excellent opportunities for children to learn about math. Using the Internet, research articles about teachers who successfully used lessons in cooking to reinforce math concepts. What strategies did they use to help children understand measurement? What follow-up activities did they plan?

After reading the article, choose your favorite recipe and read it carefully. Take notes about ingredients and steps in the recipe that a teacher could use to reinforce math concepts. Working with a partner, follow the recipe and cook your favorite foods. Afterward, discuss how you would adapt the recipe to strengthen math concepts in an early childhood education classroom.

Photo: Andy-pix/Shutterstock.com

Art experiences improve general intellectual functioning, such as focused attention and motivation to improve. Sensory experiences help children expand their concepts of color, line, shape, form, texture, and size. Children also use spatial concepts when creating art. Young children illustrate what they know about their world. For example, a young child's drawing of a wagon will show all four wheels. Later in the school-age years, children will create perceptually correct representations, such as a wagon showing only two wheels if drawn from the front, one side, or back. Art also helps children develop socially and emotionally. Children make choices about what they want to do and how they want to do an art activity. As children play, they can use art to express feelings. (Some children who have experienced trauma or social-emotional disturbances receive *art therapy*, which encourages them to express fears or repressed emotions through creativity.) Finally, taking pride in art and knowing that others accept their products builds children's self-esteem.

Adults can support art experiences by introducing children to art tools and art activities suited to their stages of development. Once children understand how to use art tools, adults need to let children do their own work. Children's works should reflect their physical skills in handling art tools and their intellectual ways of seeing the world, not adults' physical skills and artistic stage of representation. If an adult corrects or redoes a child's artwork, the child may experience self-doubt and lower self-esteem. Adults can also encourage children by showing interest in their artwork and joining children in art activities (**Figure 20.12**). They can display children's artwork to support self-esteem.

monzenmachi/E+ via Getty Images

Figure 20.12 When children show adults their artwork, adults should always be supportive. Instead of asking, "What is that?" adults can ask children to tell them about the artwork. *Why is asking a child to talk about their artwork better than asking a direct question?*

Music Experiences

Music surrounds people from birth. Children who have been exposed to a rich world of sound and movement will have good backgrounds for later learning and pleasure.

Music experiences promote growth in all areas of development. For young children, movement and music are viewed as one. Even toddlers move to music without being prompted by adults. During these movements, motor skills are enhanced. Preschool and school-age children who play instruments practice fine-motor skills and increase their dexterity, often in both hands. Some instruments, such as string instruments, require two different fine-motor movements at the same time.

Intellectual skills are also enhanced through music. Young children who learn to play musical instruments tend to be high achievers in spatial concepts and math in later years. In addition, music provides chances for sensory and expressive experiences. Listening to the sounds of music can improve children's listening skills in general. As children become more attuned to the sounds around them, they learn to translate these sounds in musical ways. They may say that sounds have a high or low pitch or an even or uneven rhythm. Like pitch and rhythm, language is also involved in music. Singing involves adding words to pitch and rhythm (**Figure 20.13**). Singing and playing instruments seem to make children feel good and can be collaborative (such as in choirs, combos, bands, and orchestras), which fosters social learning. Finally, making music is fun for children.

To guide music experiences, adults can introduce children to music activities suited to their interests. These areas may include moving to music, listening, playing instruments, and singing. In addition to providing activities, including music lessons, adults can provide an environment that is rich in sound. They can model enthusiasm and enjoyment for various types of music (called *genres*, such as classical, modern, pop, folk, country, rock, and blues).

SpeedKingz/Shutterstock.com

Figure 20.13 Although young children do enjoy singing, they often cannot carry a tune. To sing with others, children must hear their own voices, the voices of other singers or instruments, and the unison sound. *Why do you think it is difficult for young children to match their pitches and thus produce a unison sound?*

Perhaps the adult's most difficult role is listening to a child's early attempts to play an instrument. However, caregivers need to encourage children's musical attempts if they are to practice enough to gain musical skills. Adults can encourage older children by attending their musical events, keeping programs of these events in a scrapbook or on display, and even recording their children's musical performances to show other family members who were unable to attend the performance. Other activities caregivers can do is taking their children to musicals, plays, and theater productions. Adults can encourage their teenage student to participate in school plays and productions. Children who participate in theater arts in high school and college gain skills in oral communication, creative problem solving, commitment and motivation, cooperation and team work as well as the ability to work independently. Theater students also need to be able to memorize lines or learn technical aspects of a production quickly and accurately. These are all skills that 21st-century employers are looking for.

Science Experiences

Children are born scientists. They wonder and seek answers and test their answers repeatedly. To children, *science* is wondering about the world and everything in it, appreciating beauty, and caring for the world. Children experience science when they catch a cricket, put it in a jar, and watch it. They experience science when they watch water freeze and see snow melt. Children can learn about science when they ask, "Why do I need to eat my green beans?" or "How do clouds move?" Science can also be incorporated into many other activities, such as block building, sand play, water play, and cooking experiences.

Science activities foster growth in all areas of development. In exploring their worlds, children use their gross-motor skills for running, walking, jumping, and bending. They also practice fine-motor skills when they handle objects and creatures with care. During science experiences, intellectual development is also stimulated. Sensory experiences abound. For example, children explore *substances* (the physical matter of objects) and handle liquid, granular, and solid objects.

Through many science experiences in which children observe and experiment, children learn cause-and-effect relationships and math skills. By using science resources, such as science magazines and websites, children practice and use their language and reading skills, too. Science aids social-emotional development. Through watching, listening to, and touching living things, when appropriate, children learn about and develop respect for the world around them. Children can also overcome some fears with science facts. For example, children may learn not to fear thunderstorms after learning how and why thunderstorms happen.

Adults can promote science experiences by encouraging children to appreciate the beauty of their world. For example, adults can call attention to the beauty of the environment, such as light coming through a prism, colors on butterflies' wings, the fragrance of roses, and the songs of birds. Along with appreciation, lessons on caring for nature can also begin early for children. Starting in the toddler years, adults can give children developmentally appropriate tasks in caring for living creatures and the environment. Adults can also read books about nature and science to children. They can visit zoos, gardens, and forests together (**Figure 20.14**). Adults should never present science as a magic show. Instead, adults can explain science so children can learn about their world.

Figure 20.14 Children experience science through their everyday lives, including their encounters with nature and new locations. *What science experiences do you best remember from your childhood?*

20.2-2 Literature Experiences

Literature opens a world of magic and new ideas for children, and literature experiences aid children in all areas of development. During literature experiences, children use fine-motor skills for turning pages and learn to move their eyes for reading. Literature activities arouse curiosity and spark imagination in children as children learn many new concepts and then expand these concepts by reading books that answer their endless questions. Literature experiences also help children enjoy learning and want to learn.

As would be expected, literature activities expand language skills. Literature activities aid children in developing vocabulary as well as sentence structure and grammar. Through quality stories and poems, children hear the rhythm of language, the rise and fall of the voice, and tongue-tickling phrases. Children build reading skills, such as reading direction (reading top to bottom and left to right) and print knowledge about letters, words, sentences, paragraphs, punctuation marks, and spacing. Children who are heavily exposed to literature often become good writers of stories, poems, and essays.

Literature expands children's understandings of themselves and others. Young children like to hear stories about others their age and about familiar people and objects. These young children better understand themselves by hearing stories that draw on their backgrounds. As older children read about people and places beyond their own immediate environment, they come to understand and respect diversity in their world. Finally, literature activities strengthen the adult-child relationship. Reading time is quality time. As adults, people often recall family reading experiences.

Adults have a primary responsibility in nurturing children's love of literature. Although most caregivers are not professional readers, children are an appreciative, uncritical audience. In fostering literature experiences, adults can begin to read aloud to children during the first few months of life and continue until the child learns to read well (**Figure 20.15**). Adults and children can read interesting stories to each other throughout the school-age and teen years, too. Adults can also extend children's understandings of what they read through story stretchers (additional activities in other areas that relate to the story, such as art, music, cooking, and dramatic play).

Figure 20.15 Age-Appropriate Reading

Stage of Development	Reading Methods
Infancy	• Point to, name, and talk about pictures. • Allow the infant to touch, grasp, and turn pages.
Toddler years	• Ask the toddler to point to or name pictures, make story-related sounds, and repeat repetitive phrases. • Substitute the toddler's name for the character's name to engage interest. • Compare story experiences to the toddler's experiences. • Use props.
Preschool years	• Look at the cover, read the title, and then read the author's and illustrator's names together. • Ask the preschooler to guess what the book is about. • Engage the preschooler by asking questions, such as "What might happen next?" or "Why did the character do this?" • Look closely at illustrations together. • Repeat interesting words and phrases. • Run fingers under the text while reading. • Talk about the story while reading it.
School-age years	• Set the stage before reading. • Relate the book to similar books (author, genre, content). • Ask questions such as "What would you do in a similar situation?"

Goodheart-Willcox Publisher

Reading Techniques

Developing reading comprehension skills is incredibly important for early readers, starting as early as picture books. As school-age children get older, it will help them understand textbooks, newspapers, and other complex texts. Contrary to what some people believe, learning to read is not a "natural" process that happens on its own. It's a complex one that requires the proper teaching of various skills and strategies, such as phonics (knowing the relationship between letters and sounds) and phonemic awareness. Caregivers and other adults can work with school-age children by using many methods. Some of these methods include using songs and nursery rhymes to build phonemic awareness, making sight word cards at home to use to help them recognize the words, playing word games at home or in the car. Other activities include letting children play with letter magnets by spelling out words that use a consonant-vowel-consonant, for example cat. Adults can also harness the power of technology to help keep children engaged. There are many programs available on the internet as well as apps that can be downloaded to devices that can help motivate and keep children on track. **Figure 20.16** has some general strategies that adults can use to help school-age children of all ages with reading comprehension.

Figure 20.16 **General Strategies for Reading Comprehension**

Strategy	Instructions
Use Prior Knowledge/Previewing— when students preview text, they tap into what they already know that will help them to understand the text they are about to read. This helps provide a framework for any new information they read.	**Ages 5–8**—have students look at the book front and tell the caregiver what the story will be about from the illustration or name. **Ages 9–18**—questions to ask before, during and after reading—What are you interested in about this book? What doesn't interest you? What's going on in the book? Is it turning out the way you thought it would? What do you think will happen next? What did you like or dislike about the book?
Predicting—when students make predictions about what they are about to read, it sets up expectations based on their prior knowledge about similar topics. As they read, they may mentally revise their prediction as they gain more information.	**Ages 5–18**—questions to ask—What do you think is going to happen and why? What do you think will happen next? Is it turning out the way you thought it would? Why or why not?
Identifying the Main Idea and Summarization—requires students to determine what is important and put it into their own words.	**Ages 5–8**—have them read aloud, provide books as the right level, reread to build fluency. **Ages 9–18**—question the topic—What does the author want me to know about this topic? Identify the topic sentence, use headings and subheadings, look for repeated words or phrases,
Questioning—helps students focus on the meaning of text by answering questions. Teachers can help by modeling both the process of asking good questions and strategies for finding the answers in the text.	**Ages 5–8**—questions might include—What characters are in the book? What items do you see in the illustrations? **Ages 9–13**—questions might include—What are the similarities or differences between the character and you? What would you have done if you were the character? **Ages 14–19**—questions might include—What information about the characters culture were mentioned in the story? After learning about the traditions of the characters culture, compare and contrast your own cultural background to that of the character.

Goodheart-Willcox Publisher
(Continued)

Figure 20.16 **General Strategies for Reading Comprehension** (Continued)

Strategy	Instructions
Making Inferences—students must learn to draw on prior knowledge and recognize clues in the text itself.	**Ages 5–10**—might have students looking for clues about what will happen next. **Ages 11–19**—might have students using information they already know about a subject and inferring what will happen next based on that information.
Visualizing—readers can take advantage of illustrations that are embedded in the text or create their own mental images or drawings when reading text without illustrations.	**Ages 5–8**—have children explain what is going on in the story only using the pictures. **Ages 9–19**—have the students create their own drawing of a story they read from their mental image.
Retelling—ask students to retell the story in their own words. This encourages them to analyze the content to determine what is important. Teachers and caregivers can encourage the child to go beyond the recounting to draw their own conclusions.	**Ages 5–10**—have students tell in their own words what the story was about. **Ages 11–9**—have students explain what they think would happen if something changed in the story.

Lesson 20.2 Review and Assessment

1. Which is not a benefit of playing with blocks? (20.2.1)
   A. They create a stable environment.
   B. They allow for endless repetition.
   C. They have changeable properties.
   D. They permit self-correction.

2. **True or False.** Children learn spatial concepts, classification, seriation, and number and shape concepts through visual literacy. (20.2.1)

3. During the manipulative stage of visual art development, children _____. (20.2.1)
   A. begin to draw human figures
   B. begin to draw basic shapes
   C. show spatial relationships among objects
   D. draw mixed perspectives

4. Which reading method is *most* appropriate for using with a toddler? (20.2.2)
   A. Allowing them to touch, grasp, and turn the pages
   B. Asking them to guess what the book is about
   C. Relating the story to other stories
   D. Substituting their name for the character's name

5. **True or False.** To foster literature experiences, adults can begin to read aloud to children during the first few months of life and continue until the child learns to read well. (20.2.2)

Chapter 20

Review and Assessment

Summary

Lesson 20.1

20.1-1 Play is a *holistic* way of learning that is fun and tends to reflect changes in children's developmental levels. It is often referred to as the highest level of child development.

20.1-1 The stages of play with objects correspond to Piaget's first three levels of cognitive development. They include practice play (infants and toddlers), symbolic play (preschoolers and early school-age children), and rule play (late school-age children).

20.1-1 The stages of play with people involve children's social skills and development and are based on Mildred Parten's research. They include solitary, onlooker, and parallel play (infants and toddlers); associative play (preschoolers and early school-age children); and cooperative play (late school-age children).

20.1-1 Many types of play exist. *Active-physical play* involves gross-motor skills, and *manipulative-constructive play* uses fine-motor skills. *Imitative-imaginative play* includes pretend play and involves imitative, dramatic, and socio-dramatic stages as children learn to use symbols. *Language-logic play* usually occurs in school-age children and involves logical thinking and strategy.

20.1-2 Adults can encourage play experiences by allowing children freedom, displaying positive attitudes about play, and providing age-appropriate, attractive toys.

Lesson 20.2

20.2-1 Block building, sand play, and water play help children develop motor skills, intellectual understandings, and social skills. Block play is especially ideal as it benefits all areas of development and aids the beginning of logical thought by promoting visual literacy.

20.2-1 Cooking experiences, which enhance all areas of development, require more adult guidance than other enrichment activities. Cooking experiences help children learn about math.

20.2-1 Art activities promote fine-motor skills, perceptual learning, and social-emotional health. Music experiences also aid children's motor skills, intellectual development (including language concepts), and social-emotional development.

20.2-1 Science activities foster growth in all areas of development. Such experiences can be incorporated into many play activities and thus enhance all types of learning as well as respect for one's physical world.

20.2-2 Literature experiences can stimulate creativity, take children to any real or imagined place, expose children to quality language, and reinforce the adult-child relationship.

20.2-2 Learning to read is not a natural process that happens on its own. Children need to work on and practice reading often.

20.2-3 Caregivers and teachers have a variety of techniques they can use when helping school-age children learn to read.

College and Career Portfolio

Portfolio Presentation Research

Depending on the purpose of your portfolio, the way in which you present the portfolio may vary. For example, schools may expect you to submit your portfolio electronically. Employers may expect you to bring a physical copy of your portfolio to the interview and walk an interviewer through the portfolio's highlights.

- Talk to a college or career counselor or search online to find out how portfolios in your field are generally presented.
- Confirm the information you find with one or more sources and write a short summary about the presentation guidelines.

Recall and Application

1. When two or more children play at a common, yet unorganized activity, this is called _____ play. (20.1.1)
   A. associative
   B. cooperative
   C. practice
   D. onlooker

2. The game of chess is an example of _____ play. (20.1.1)
   A. imitative-imaginative
   B. manipulative-constructive
   C. language-logic
   D. active-physical

3. A type of play that is common between ages 5 and 7 that involves assigning special roles to each child is _____ play. (20.1.1)
   A. imitative
   B. socio-dramatic
   C. symbolic
   D. dramatic

4. Which type of toy is most appropriate for a school-age child? (20.1.2)
   A. floor blocks
   B. large balls
   C. puppets
   D. board games

5. **True or False.** Adults' attitudes toward play influence how children view play. (20.1.2)

6. During the transition between the manipulative and the representation stage of visual art development, children _____. (20.2.1)
   A. enjoy art for motor reasons
   B. begin to draw basic shapes
   C. show spatial relationships among objects
   D. create their first symbols

7. **True or False.** The sensory experiences associated with sand play can assist some children with calming down their bodies. (20.2.1)

8. **True or False.** Learning science facts may help a child overcome some fears. (20.2.1)

9. Which reading method is most appropriate for use with a preschooler? (20.2.2)
   A. Using props to act out the story while reading it
   B. Asking them what they'd do in a similar situation
   C. Comparing the story experiences to their own experiences
   D. Asking what they think might happen next in the story
10. **True or False.** Young children like to hear stories about children who are older than them and who live in unfamiliar places. (20.2.2)

Critical Thinking

1. **Cause and effect.** The stages of play with objects were developed by Piaget to correspond to the first three stages of cognitive development. Working with a partner, review your notes about the sensorimotor, preoperational, and concrete operational stages of cognitive development. Then, analyze how the qualities of these stages connect to the stages of play with objects. Explain these cause-and-effect relationships to the class.

2. **Evaluate.** In small groups, create two active-physical play activities that you enjoy. Try these with children and then observe the children playing. What skills is the play activity helping children develop? Are children enjoying the activity? Evaluate your activity based on its value and fun.

3. **Compare and contrast.** Review the stages of imitative-imaginative play outlined in Figure 20.5. Read the examples for each stage carefully and then compare and contrast the key similarities and differences among the examples. Finally, write your own examples illustrating changes that occur among the stages of imitative-imaginative play.

4. **Identify.** Providing children with toys that they like encourages children to play. Use this text's list of attractive toys for children at each stage of development to identify current toys that would encourage play in children. Find toys in catalogs or visit a toy store and find three examples of attractive toys for infants, toddlers, preschoolers, and school-age children. Write a brief explanation about why each toy is attractive and appropriate in your opinion.

5. **Analyze.** Experiences in block building promote *visual literacy*, which is a key element influencing children's learning of intellectual concepts. Analyze how visual literacy influences concepts and give examples of other concepts children learn by developing this skill.

6. **Determine.** Obtain drawings by four- and six-year-olds and compare the drawings, keeping in mind the stages of visual arts development. What differences do you note among the drawings? Determine what developmental abilities or changes might account for these differences.

7. **Draw conclusions.** Art activities can be fun and useful ways for children to learn more about their worlds. Review the text's information about the benefits of art activities and then draw conclusions about other related benefits. Why are art activities important for children? Why is it important to allow a child freedom of expression?

8. **Make inferences.** In small groups, review the guidelines for age-appropriate reading during literature experiences (Figure 20.15). Then, organize a time for your group to visit a local library or bookstore. During your visit, explore books in the children's section. As a group, identify books that you think would provide the best literature experiences for infants, toddlers, preschoolers, and school-age children. Bring pictures of the books (or if possible, the books themselves) to class and deliver an oral presentation about how the books you chose would support quality literature experiences.

Core Skills

1. **Technology.** Children pass through five stages of "play with people." Review these stages of play (Figure 20.3) and then work in small groups to brainstorm real-life examples for each of the five stages. After your discussion, create a visual representation of the stages of "play with people." Use digital or drawn artwork or videos to illustrate each stage. Also summarize how each stage of play reflects children's social worlds and development. Present your project to the class.

2. **Speaking.** In small groups, visit a beach, lake, water park, playground with a sandbox, or other location where sand play or water play could take place. Once at the location, plan water-play or sand-play activities that you think would be beneficial for all areas of children's development. Test these activities in your group and keep brainstorming activities until your group is confident you have devised the best and most helpful activity you can. Finally, present and explain your activity to the class.

3. **Reading and speaking.** Working with a partner, review this text's information about logical thinking concepts for preschoolers and school-age children. Take notes about what concepts children understand, when, and what types of activities support these lessons. Then, create one or two play activities to support or teach all the logical thinking concepts children learn. Explain in detail how children will learn each concept and how adults can scaffold learning. Present your activities to the class and ask for feedback.

4. **Reading and science.** Visit a local library or search online to find magazines, articles, or books that outline science experiences for young children. Choose two resources and read them carefully, noting any activities you find especially interesting or fun.

What concepts do your favorite activities teach? Are they stand-alone science activities or are they science experiences incorporated into other play activities? Choose one favorite activity and conduct it with your class. After the activity, explain the concepts taught and how easily the activity or experience could be incorporated into an early childhood education setting.

5. **Math and listening.** Math experiences can be incorporated into a wide range of play activities. Interview a preschool teacher about how they teach math through other types of activities. What activities best lend themselves to math experiences? How does the teacher first introduce math concepts to children? What benefits do math experiences have on children's physical, intellectual, and social-emotional development?

6. **Research and writing.** Using reliable online or print resources, research the effects of music on social and emotional well-being. Read scientific studies about these effects and take notes, documenting your sources in a bibliography. Write a three- to four-page essay detailing your findings and explaining the importance of music for social-emotional development.

7. **Technology.** Electronic media can be a powerful tool for enhancing children's learning and play activities. Using reliable online or print resources, research ways in which technology and electronic media can be used in play activities. Share your findings with a partner. Then, work together with your partner to create a digital presentation illustrating how technology can be incorporated into two types of play activities. Be sure to include visuals in your presentation and explain how the use of technology reinforces and benefits the play experience.

8. **CTE Career Readiness Practice.** Imagine you are a recent graduate from a well-known early childhood education program. After being hired by a long-established child care center, you learn that the director of the center prioritizes academic learning and strict adherence to education standards more than he does children's play experiences. Concerned about the children in your care, you ask your director if you can meet with him. You know that you are relatively inexperienced, but you want to express why you think play is important. Write a short speech that respectfully and accurately describes the importance of play. Practice your speech with a partner and ask for feedback about whether you are approaching the issue tactfully.

Observations

1. Visit a local school or art fair and view children's artwork. As you view the artwork, take notes about each child's art skills, and determine the child's stage of development in the visual arts. If the ages of the children are displayed, check your answers. If not, write short summaries explaining each identification.

2. As a class, visit a local child care center, preferably one with infants, toddlers, and preschoolers enrolled. Observe the children at the center playing and try to identify the children's stages of play. Back up your identifications with concrete examples and facts. Afterward, discuss as a class.

Protecting Children's Physical Health and Safety

Lesson 21.1 Maintaining Children's Health

Lesson 21.2 Ensuring Children's Safety

Lesson 21.3 Treating Children's Illnesses and Injuries

Essential Question

What can caregivers and other adults do to keep children healthy and safe, and how can caregivers treat children's illnesses, injuries, and traumas when they do occur?

Case Study What Does It Take to Keep a Child Safe?

As a class, read the case study and discuss the questions that follow. After you finish studying the chapter, discuss this case study again. Have your opinions changed based on what you learned?

One cold, wintry morning, four-year-old Joaquin and Joaquin's caregiver, Lupita, went to the grocery store. As they pulled into their driveway, Joaquin's other caregiver, Martin, called out, "Leave the car running. I just need to take this phone call and then I have to get to my meeting." Lupita nodded, quickly got Joaquin into the house, then hurried back to the car to get the groceries.

Martin rushed through the call, impatient and already late for the meeting. Suddenly Martin was shocked to see the car, with Joaquin in it, rolling into the street. Martin rushed outside but was too late to stop the car from being struck by a speeding minivan. Joaquin's caregivers frantically called 911. The paramedics took Joaquin to the hospital for treatment of a severe and potentially life-threatening blow to the head.

Phone records showed that Martin's call lasted less than one minute. Joaquin's caregivers did not know whether Joaquin returned to the car when Lupita went to get the groceries or if Joaquin

slipped past Martin during the phone call. They had thoroughly childproofed their home and yard. As caregivers they modeled safety practices and taught Joaquin safety lessons, which were usually obeyed.

After weeks in the hospital, Joaquin's caregivers decided they wanted to do something to prevent other families from experiencing the terror they experienced. They wanted to tell their story and reach out to caregivers and adults of preschoolers and school-age children about safety practices.

Give It Some Thought

1. How do children play their own role in injury protection? What role does the environment play? the caregivers' forethought and supervision? cultural norms?
2. What are some ways Joaquin's caregivers might reach out to other adults about safety?

Maintaining Children's Health

Key Terms

allergen

allergy

asthma

communicable diseases

epilepsy

foodborne diseases

health screenings

immunization

non-communicable
  diseases

preventive health care

vaccination

vaccines

well-child checkups

Learning Outcomes

After studying this lesson, you will be able to

21.1-1 describe aspects involved in basic health care for children, including recommended immunizations, physical exams, and oral hygiene.

21.1-2 compare and **contrast** communicable diseases and non-communicable diseases including how to prevent foodborne illness, causes of diabetes, epilepsy, allergies, and asthma; and identify community resources to help families with these issues.

21.1-3 explore current legislation and public policies affecting children.

Reading and Notetaking Activity

Skim this chapter from top to bottom and left to right and list all the headings. Then, identify key terms with which you are unfamiliar and scan through the chapter to find their definitions. Write a "topic sentence" and brief summary for each heading, using the key terms to explain what you think you will learn. After you read this chapter, write a new topic sentence and summary for each section, outlining the main points you learned.

Introduction

Today's advances in health and safety are greater than ever before. Growing up is still risky business, however. Each day infants and children face the risks of illness, injury, and even death. Sometimes adults can control these risks; at other times they cannot. Adults who care for children bear an enormous responsibility when it comes to keeping children healthy and safe.

Adults can promote their children's health and wellness by making sure they receive basic health care. Basic health care involves meeting children's physical needs for good nutrition, rest, physical activity, and cleanliness. Regular medical and dental appointments, health screenings, and immunizations are also necessary to support children's health and wellness. When children are in good health, they are better able to fight common childhood diseases.

21.1-1 Basic Health Care for Children

Children, like adults, need basic health care to ensure their bodies are developing properly and to treat infections and diseases. When health concerns are prevented, detected early, or treated properly, children have a better chance of leading a healthy and happy life. When disease or injury occurs, children who are otherwise healthy tend to recover quickly and completely. Neglecting health needs for long periods can cause health conditions with lasting effects. To promote children's health and safety, adults must meet children's physical needs and provide children with preventive health care.

Meeting Children's Physical Needs

Every person has basic physical needs. As you may recall, children's needs vary depending on a child's stage. Young children rely on adults to meet all their physical needs. As children grow older, they become capable of meeting some of their own needs. Adults, however, still pay careful attention to and meet many of children's needs.

Adults help meet children's physical needs by ensuring children eat healthfully, get plenty of rest, and are physically active. Maintaining cleanliness can protect children from certain illnesses, such as the flu or common cold. Adults can reduce children's risk of infection by

- encouraging proper hand washing (**Figure 21.1**)
- teaching children to cover their sneezes and coughs
- teaching children to not touch their eyes or mouth when around sick children
- modeling good health practices

Providing Children with Preventive Health Care

Part of meeting children's basic health needs involves adults providing children with preventive health care. **Preventive health care** consists of measures taken to keep children well. Preventive health care includes regular doctor and dental appointments, health screenings, and immunizations.

Figure 21.1 Proper Hand-Washing Steps

1. Wet hands with water and apply soap. (Children like colorful, foamy soap. Antibacterial products are not any more effective than other types of soap and may give rise to antibiotic-resistant bacteria.)
2. Rub soap between hands, on backs of hands, between fingers, and under fingernails.
3. Scrub lathered hands for at least 20 seconds. (Some sources say 30 seconds of scrubbing is needed. Sing the "Happy Birthday" song twice to time scrubbing.)
4. Rinse hands thoroughly.
5. Dry hands with a clean towel or air dry.

Goodheart-Willcox Publisher

PeopleImages/iStock via Getty Images Plus

Regular Doctor and Dental Appointments

Proper preventive health care for children involves regular **well-child checkups** (doctor's appointments while the child is not sick). During these visits, doctors monitor children's health and wellness and check their growth and development. They note children's eating, sleeping, and playing habits. Doctors also answer caregivers' questions about their child's development. Well-child checkups may **unearth** (reveal) possible health concerns before they become serious or cannot be repaired. These visits may even prevent certain health conditions altogether.

Because well-child checkups are so important, doctors suggest a schedule for regular visits. The schedule varies slightly among doctors, but the American Academy of Pediatrics (AAP) suggests children have 11 well-child checkups during the first three years of life (**Figure 21.2**).

FatCamera/E+ via Getty Images

Figure 21.2 The AAP schedule recommends that children receive well-child checkups at 1, 2, 4, 6, 9, 12, 15, 18, 24, 30, and 36 months of age. Doctors may schedule additional or fewer visits depending on the child's health needs and parents' experience. *How do you think parents' experience impacts how often a child should receive well-child checkups?*

Focus on Health

Supporting Children During an Exam

Some children may be nervous about the prospect of going to a doctor or receiving routine care. Children under two years of age often cry while being examined. Two- and three-year-olds may cry and hide from, kick, or push the doctor to get rid of the person. Children often feel *situation stress* that is relieved within minutes after the examination.

The caregivers' role during a medical examination is to help the child feel more comfortable. To help the child during an examination, adults can try the following tips:

- Stay with the child and remain within the child's line of vision (unless the doctor or dentist prefers that caregivers stay in the waiting room).

- Use a soft, soothing voice. A child may stop crying to hear whispered words.
- Hold the child if the doctor asks.
- Do not tell the child a procedure will *not* hurt if, in fact, it will. Instead, tell the child, "It will be all right" or "Soon it will be over." If the child cries, reassure them that crying is all right. Say, "I know this hurts, but it will stop hurting soon."
- Do not distract a baby or child by making noises, such as jingling keys. Such sounds interfere with a doctor's ability to hear internal sounds. Some babies and children cry louder when an adult tries to distract them.

Photo: wavebreakmedia/Shutterstock.com

This does not include checkups made between birth and discharge from the hospital. Yearly examinations are recommended after three years of age. Infants of nursing parents and premature infants may have extra checkups during their early weeks to ensure they are thriving. Children also need regular, preventive dental care from a pediatric or family dentist. Dental care usually begins by the first birthday with follow-up appointments every six months afterward.

Adults often have difficulty choosing health care for their children because there are so many health care providers available. In most regions, pediatricians and dentists abound, and caregivers are not always sure how to decide which health care services will best meet their children's needs.

Caregivers need to assess prospective medical personnel. To choose the best health care services for their children, adults need to consider several factors. Is the medical provider within the caregivers' insurance coverage network, and will the provider accept their insurance? Are office hours and location accessible? Is the medical professional open to caregivers' questions? Will they answer caregivers' questions clearly and calmly? Are they accepting of emergency calls?

While all licensed pediatric doctors and dentists are qualified to work with a child, caregivers often consider the child's preference when choosing a medical professional. Choosing a doctor or dentist the child likes will make the child less anxious during examinations. Children generally like friendly medical personnel who greet them by name and smile. They also prefer colorful treatment rooms and pleasant waiting areas.

Focus on Science

Types of Immunity

Children's health is partially dependent on their *immunity* (the body's defense against infection and disease). There are two types of immunity—*active immunity* and *passive immunity*. *Active immunity* results when a person's body produces *antibodies* (AN-ti-bah-deez), which are proteins in the blood that destroy toxins and disease-carrying organisms. Active immunity occurs through direct exposure to an illness or through vaccination and takes several days or even weeks to become effective. Once developed, however, active immunity lasts several years or a lifetime.

Passive immunity results when antibodies are produced by one person's exposure to a disease and then passed to another person. This is what happens when pregnant people pass antibodies to their unborn babies across the placenta. People also receive transfusions of antibodies that are made by someone else's body (called *antiserums*). Unlike active immunity, passive immunity takes effect immediately, but lasts only a few weeks.

Immunity can be naturally or artificially acquired. *Naturally acquired immunity* (sometimes called *natural immunity*) is developed after direct contact with infection or by receiving antibodies from the pregnant person during pregnancy or breast-feeding. *Artificially acquired immunity* (sometimes called *acquired immunity*) forms as a person's reaction to antibodies or an antigen received through medical care. *Antigens* (AN-ti-juhns) are substances made from bacteria, viruses, or toxins that prompt the body to produce antibodies that fight a disease. These substances are made in a laboratory and transferred to people in the form of vaccines.

Photo: otnaydur/Shutterstock.com

Health Screenings

Health screenings are standard tests that look for potential conditions or diseases that may affect children's health and development. These screenings are given before symptoms appear, which helps prevent developmental lags and some medical conditions. Besides the screenings of infancy, children should continue to get hearing and vision tests every six months before the age of 3 and every two years between 3 and 12 years of age. The American Academy of Pediatrics recommends more thorough hearing test at ages 4, 5, 6, 8, and 10. If a child needs their vision corrected then they should have eye exams yearly. Lead tests should be given to children with high-risks and repeated if the screening was performed before 2014 due to prior test inaccuracy. All children between 9 and 11 years of age should be screened for high blood cholesterol levels and beginning earlier for children with high-risk due to the growing epidemic of obesity in children according to the American Academy of Pediatrics.

Health screenings also exist for certain special needs (such as autism and mental health problems) and some infections (such as sexually transmitted infections—STIs). The AAP website contains more information about health screenings recommended at each age.

Immunization

Providing children with preventive health care includes **immunization** (process to protect children, as well as adults, from certain serious diseases). Substances used to produce **immunity** (the body's ability to resist infection) from diseases are called **vaccines**. Vaccines can be administered through *injections* (shots), oral medications, or aerosol sprays. Some illnesses require a series of vaccines to produce immunity. The process of administering vaccines is known as **vaccination**.

From birth children are given vaccines to cause immunity. In the United States, all states require children to receive certain vaccinations for school admission. Although vaccination laws vary from state to state, some of the diseases children must be vaccinated against include diphtheria, *pertussis* (whooping cough), measles, *rubella* (German measles), mumps, tetanus, polio, and *varicella* (chicken pox). **Figure 21.3** outlines the *immunization schedule* often recommended for children from birth through 18 years of age. (Recommendations are reviewed and updated regularly.)

Doctors record children's vaccines on immunization records and then check these records before giving more vaccines. Caregivers should keep records, too, for their own information. Children's immunization records often need to be provided for entry into child care and education programs, schools, and camps. In rare cases, caregivers may submit a request for their children to be exempt from immunization due to religious or personal beliefs. If children who are not vaccinated become infected, however, these diseases can cause serious illness and even death. Unvaccinated children may also pose a greater disease-transmission risk to other children and adults who cannot be vaccinated due to age or medical conditions.

21.1-2 Childhood Diseases

Adults who care for children should be aware of diseases that are often contracted or developed during childhood (called *childhood diseases*). If left untreated, children can suffer negative effects and even die from some childhood diseases. Serious effects usually occur when adults are unaware of the diseases and their symptoms and do not seek early treatment. Childhood diseases can be either *communicable diseases* or *non-communicable diseases*.

Communicable Diseases

Communicable diseases are diseases that can be transmitted from an object to an individual or between individuals. Thus, these diseases are contracted. *Influenza* (the flu) is just one example of a communicable disease. **Figure 21.4** shows other examples of communicable childhood diseases. Some of these diseases can be prevented with a vaccine.

Immunization Schedules

Recommended Immunizations for Children from Birth Through 6 Years Old

Shaded boxes indicate the vaccine can be given during shown age range.

NOTE: If your child misses a shot, you don't need to start over, just go back to your child's doctor for the next shot. Talk with your child's doctor if you have questions about vaccines.

For more information, visit the Centers for Disease Control and Prevention website at http://www.cdc.gov/vaccines

Recommended Immunizations for Children from 7 Through 18 Years Old

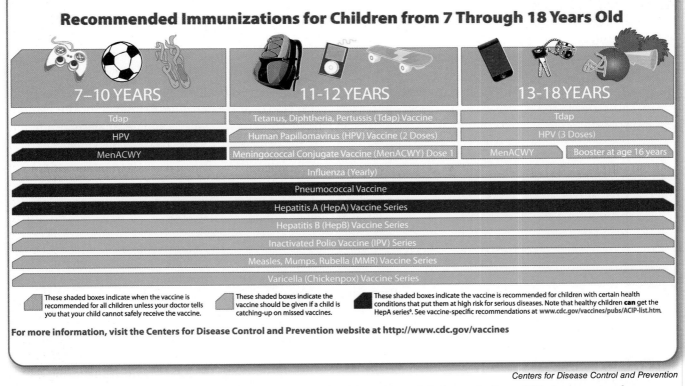

These shaded boxes indicate when the vaccine is recommended for all children unless your doctor tells you that your child cannot safely receive the vaccine.

These shaded boxes indicate the vaccine should be given if a child is catching-up on missed vaccines.

These shaded boxes indicate the vaccine is recommended for children with certain health conditions that put them at high risk for serious diseases. Note that healthy children **can** get the HepA series⁶. See vaccine-specific recommendations at www.cdc.gov/vaccines/pubs/ACIP-list.htm.

For more information, visit the Centers for Disease Control and Prevention website at http://www.cdc.gov/vaccines

Centers for Disease Control and Prevention

Figure 21.3 Immunization schedules outline when children should receive certain immunizations. *What memories do you have about receiving vaccines? How did your caregivers explain immunization to you?*

Figure 21.4 Communicable Childhood Diseases

Condition	Cause	Symptoms	Comments
*Chicken pox, or varicella	Virus	Fever; runny nose; cough; rash (pimples, blisters, and scabs)	Seek medical treatment. Keep child away from others for six days after rash begins.
Cold	Virus	Runny nose; scratchy throat; coughing; sneezing; watery eyes	Seek medical treatment if child looks and acts very ill.
Conjunctivitis (kun-JUNK-ti-VY-tus), or pink eye	Virus and bacteria	Watery eyes; mucus in eyes; red or pink color in whites of eyes; eyelid redness	Seek medical treatment. Keep child away from others for 24 hours after starting treatment.
Covid-19	Virus	Fever; chills; cough; shortness of breath, fatigue; muscle/body aches; headache; loss of taste/smell; sore throat; nausea or vomiting; diarrhea	Seek medical treatment for trouble breathing or other symptoms surface. Quarantine/stay home and keep child away from others; rest and stay hydrated; stay in touch with your doctor; wash bedding frequently.
Coxsackie (kahk-SA-kee) virus	Digestive-tract virus	High fever; headaches; muscle aches; painful red blisters in the throat and mouth	Seek medical treatment if other symptoms surface. Keep child away from others; virus is spread through unwashed hands and surfaces.
*Diphtheria (dif-THIR-ee-uh)	Bacteria	Headache; fever; severe sore throat with white fluid over tonsils and throat; cough	Seek medical treatment. Keep child away from others for two weeks after fever starts or when throat cultures are clear.
*Haemophilus (hee-MAHF-uh-lus) influenzae type b (Hib)	Bacteria	Fever; lethargy; vomiting; poor appetite; earache; breathing and swallowing difficulties; cough; purple area on skin near eyes	Seek medical treatment. Keep child away from others until fever is gone or physician approves contact.
Head lice	Parasite	Visible lice and lice eggs; small red, itchy bumps on head and shoulders	Obtain medications for treatment. Do not share hats, combs, or other contaminated objects with others.
*Hepatitis B	Virus	Fever; jaundice; loss of appetite; nausea; joint pain; rash	Seek medical treatment. Keep child away from others until fever is gone and skin rash is dry.

* Vaccine may prevent disease.

Goodheart-Willcox Publisher
(Continued)

Figure 21.4 **Communicable Childhood Diseases** (Continued)

Condition	Cause	Symptoms	Comments
Impetigo (im-PUH-tee-go)	Bacteria	Red, cracking, oozing blister-like pimples often seen on the face	Seek medical treatment. Keep child away from others until 24 hours after starting treatment.
*Influenza	Virus	Fever; headache; fatigue; cough; sore throat; body aches; vomiting	Seek medical treatment. Keep child away from others until 24 hours after fever is gone.
*Measles	Virus	Fever; cough; runny nose; watery eyes; brownish red and blotchy rash	Seek medical treatment. Keep child away from others for six days after rash begins.
Meningitis (men-un-JYT-us)	Virus and bacteria	Fever; lethargy; poor appetite; vomiting; irritability; headache; stiff neck	Seek emergency medical help. Physician will determine if child can have contact with others.
*Mumps	Virus	Fever; swelling of one or more salivary glands; earache; headache	Seek medical treatment. Keep child away from others for nine days after onset of swelling.
*Pertussis (pur-TUS-us), or whooping cough	Bacteria	Runny nose; coughing spells; vomiting	Seek medical treatment. Keep child away from others for three weeks after onset of cough.
*Poliomyelitis (PO-lee-oh-my-uh-LYT-us), or polio	Virus	Fever; vomiting; irritability; headache; stiff neck and back; paralysis in some cases	Seek medical treatment. Physician will determine when child may have contact with others.
Ringworm	Parasite	Scaly patches on the scalp	Treat for six weeks with medication. Can be spread through contact or contaminated objects.
Roseola (roh-zee-OH-luh) infantum	Virus	Fever followed by rash	Seek medical treatment. Keep child away from others until fever is gone.
*Rubella, or German measles	Virus	Red rash; enlarged lymph nodes; joint pain	Seek medical treatment. Keep child away from others for six days after rash begins.
Scarlet fever, or scarlatina	Bacteria	Fever; rash that causes skin to peel	Seek medical treatment. Keep child away from others until 24 hours after starting treatment.
Strep throat	Bacteria	Sore throat; skin infections	Seek medical treatment. Keep child away from others until 24 hours after starting treatment.

* Vaccine may prevent disease.

Another type of communicable disease is spread through food. **Foodborne diseases** (also called *foodborne illnesses*) are caused by eating foods contaminated with harmful bacteria and other pathogens during food production or preparation. Examples of foodborne illnesses include *botulism, E. coli, listeria*, and *salmonella*. Young children are at high risk for foodborne illnesses and can suffer serious side effects.

To prevent foodborne illness, adults should pay careful attention to food safety, which involves

- keeping the food preparation area clean to avoid the spread of harmful bacteria
- washing utensils, dishes, and preparation supplies thoroughly with soap and water to prevent *cross-contamination* (the spread of bacteria from one food to another via an object)
- ensuring that all meats and egg dishes are cooked to the proper temperatures (**Figure 21.5**)
- storing foods safely before preparation and storing leftovers safely after preparation
- keeping foods at recommended temperatures (keep hot foods hot and cold foods cold)
- returning foods on recall and notifying your physician if these foods were eaten prior to knowledge of the recall

Non-communicable Diseases

Non-communicable diseases are diseases that cannot be transmitted between an object and an individual or between individuals. Thus, these diseases are developed in a person's body. Examples of non-communicable childhood diseases include diabetes, epilepsy, allergies, and asthma.

Diabetes

Diabetes is a disease that occurs as a result of the body's inability to produce enough insulin, which causes too much sugar in the blood. Children may develop two types of diabetes: *type 1 diabetes* and *type 2 diabetes*. *Type 1 diabetes* is a condition in which the pancreas produces little or no insulin. This type of diabetes typically begins before the adult years. The cause is mainly genetic, but other unknown factors may contribute as well. *Type 2 diabetes* occurs when the body becomes resistant

to the effects of insulin or when the pancreas does not produce enough insulin to maintain a normal blood sugar. The onset often occurs in the adult years, but school-age children are becoming more and more vulnerable. Causes of type 2 diabetes are genetic and lifestyle related. Genetic factors include a person's ethnicity and age. Lifestyle-related factors include poor diet and lack of physical activity.

The symptoms are similar for both type 1 and type 2 diabetes. Symptoms include increased thirst and urination, intense hunger, weight loss, fatigue, blurred vision, and slow-healing sores.

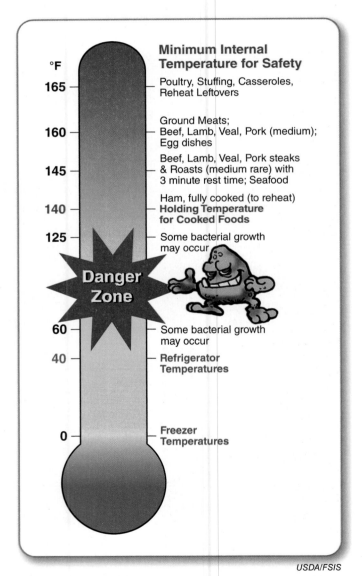

Figure 21.5 Adequate cooking kills the harmful bacteria that can reside in foods. *Is a casserole cooked to an internal temperature of 140°F safe to eat?*

If blood sugar drops too low, a person can go into a diabetic coma and die. Type 1 diabetes requires consistent care, blood sugar monitoring, and insulin delivery. Type 2 diabetes is treated by diet and physical activity to manage weight. If the condition worsens, oral medications or insulin treatments are needed.

Epilepsy

Epilepsy is a neurological disorder in which abnormal activity in brain cells causes seizures. *Seizures* are sudden attacks that vary in intensity from a blank stare for a few seconds (*petit mal*) to convulsions with loss of consciousness (*grand mal*). Although seizures vary in frequency and intensity, most people have repeated seizures. (Seizures may be infrequent or occur repeatedly throughout the day.) Epilepsy often begins in childhood and may be caused by defective genes or traced to accidents, diseases with high fevers, or medical trauma. Medications can help control epilepsy.

Patients with severe seizures may wear helmets to prevent head trauma during a seizure. Knee pads and elbow pads may also be worn to help prevent injuries. Some children have service dogs that sense and warn them of upcoming seizures, allowing these children to get to a safe place quickly.

Allergies

Allergies are the greatest cause of chronic health conditions in young children, affecting over one-fourth of all children. An **allergy** is a negative reaction by the body's immune system to an allergen. An **allergen** (AL-lur-jun) is a substance that causes an allergic reaction. **Figure 21.6** shows types of allergens from which children may suffer. Symptoms of allergies may vary from cold-like symptoms or wheezing to **anaphylaxis** (AN-uh-fuh-LAK-sus)—life-threatening shock. Immediate treatment for severe allergic reactions requires epinephrine (EH-puh-NEH-frun) injections.

Figure 21.6 Types of Allergens

Agent	Symptoms
Foods (often cow's milk, tree nuts, chocolate, wheat, peanuts, eggs, soy, fish, and shellfish) and medicines taken by mouth*	Tingling mouth Swelling of tongue, face, or throat Hives *Anaphylaxis* (a potentially life-threatening allergic reaction)
Insect bites and stings, thorns, and medicines that are injected	*Edema* (swelling) at the site of the injection Cough, wheezing, or shortness of breath Hives Anaphylaxis
Latex and other touched substances	Itchy skin Flaking or peeling skin Redness of skin
Airborne allergens	Congestion Itchy, runny nose Itchy, watery eyes Dark circles under eyes (called *allergic shiners*)

*Children with milk allergies are likely to be allergic to dustless chalk, which contains casein (a substance found in both chalk and milk).

Goodheart-Willcox Publisher

Allergies may also be treated by

- removing or limiting contact with the substance (cleaning regularly to remove dust mites or staying inside as much as possible when the pollen count is high)
- using drugs that control allergic reactions (antihistamines, decongestants, and bronchodilators)
- receiving injections or other forms of administration of some allergens to desensitize the body (called *desensitization therapy*)

Asthma

Asthma, inflammation of the airways, is the most common chronic disease of childhood. Onset of asthma in children usually begins before five years of age. Eighty-five percent of asthma cases are triggered by allergens. Symptoms of asthma vary from coughing and wheezing to shortness of breath. Asthma can be aggravated by a virus, secondhand smoke, cold or dry air, and exercise. Asthma may lead to a number of other respiratory problems. Adults can take some measures to reduce children's risk of asthma (**Figure 21.7**). Oral, inhaled, and injected medications can be used to help prevent attacks and to treat ongoing ones.

21.1-3 Legislation Affecting Children

There is both state and federal legislation that affects families and children. Some of these laws and regulations range from the age of mandatory education to how and who is responsible for reporting child abuse. **Figure 21.8** lists some legislation impacting families and children. Other laws include who is listed on the birth certificate—for example, in Texas, if a woman who gives birth is not married, the male's name is not listed on the birth certificate unless the male fills out an acknowledgement of paternity form. The Texas Office of the Attorney General has put together a parenting and paternity awareness program that focuses on the importance of paternal involvement, the value of paternity establishment, legal realities of child support as well as relationship violence prevention and healthy relationship skills. This program complies with Texas state law requiring high-school health to include a parenting and paternity awareness curriculum. Many child development courses teach the information as well. Other states also have laws regarding what curriculum must be taught.

Figure 21.7 Reducing the Risk of Asthma and Allergies

- Breast-feed children for at least the first six months of life.
- Introduce solids around six months of age. Give only one tablespoon or less of a new food and wait five or more days between the introductions of new foods.
- Reduce children's exposure to some allergens, including dust mites, mold, air pollution, secondhand smoke, and cockroaches.
- Expose children to pets (cats or dogs) early in life. Children raised on farms are less likely than other children to develop allergies and asthma.

Goodheart-Willcox Publisher

FatCamera /E+ via Getty Images

Figure 21.8 Common Laws and Legislation Regarding Children

Topic	Description
Child Custody and Support	• Includes who gets custody of children and how must child support will be paid to the custodial caregiver if non-custodial caregiver refuses to pay.
Rights and Responsibilities of Caregiver to children	• Caregiver guidance, survival, development, nationality, identify, freedom of expression and thought, privacy, education, healthcare, etc.
Child Abuse Protection Laws	• Definitions of abuse, neglect, and abandonment; who is a mandatory reporter; and the process to report suspected child abuse.
Child Labor Laws	• Cover any employee under the age of 18 and what they are and are not allowed to do, work hours, etc.
Education Code	• Allows caregivers to see all written records a school district keeps on their children, including attendance records, test scores, grades, disciplinary action, counseling, psychological testing and teacher and counselor evaluations.
Child Safety Seat Laws and Seat Belt Laws	• 1969: seat belts required in cars but not required to wear. • 1984: front seat riders required to wear seat belts but not required of back seat. • Today age and weight of required use of car seats, booster seats, when a child can sit in the front seat, etc.
Head Start Program	• Launched as an eight-week summer program in 1965 to help break the cycle of poverty by providing preschool children of low-income families with a comprehensive program. • Today it is an all-year program.
National Mental Health Act	• 1983 law that covers the assessment, treatment, and rights of people with a mental health disorder.
Bike Helmet Laws	• Began in 1987, each state has different regulations in place, and some do not have laws about helmets.

Goodheart-Willcox Publisher

Lesson 21.1 Review and Assessment

1. All of these are examples of preventive health care except _____. (21.1.1)
   A. scheduling a child for a six-month teeth cleaning
   B. following the approved child immunization schedule
   C. taking a sick child to the emergency room
   D. performing a vision screening on a child

2. An infant who is breast-fed receives which type of immunity? (21.1.1)
   A. Natural immunity
   B. Acquired immunity
   C. Artificially acquired immunity
   D. Active immunity

3. Which is an example of a communicable disease? (21.1.2)
   A. Diabetes   C. Asthma
   B. Covid-19   D. Epilepsy

4. Which is considered the "danger zone" for internal food temperatures because bacterial growth may occur in this range? (21.1.2)
   A. 160°–165° F
   B. 145°–160° F
   C. 60°–125° F
   D. 0°–40° F

5. **True or False.** All U.S. states have passed bike helmet laws to protect children. (21.1.3)

Lesson 21.2

Ensuring Children's Safety

Key Terms

certified child safety seat
childproofing
cluttering
idle
rigorous
safety recall
ventilated

Learning Outcomes

After studying this lesson, you will be able to

21.2-1 **explain** why adequate supervision is essential throughout childhood and how safety measures should change with the growth and development of the child.

21.2-2 **identify** strategies for selecting, maintaining, and storing toys.

21.2-3 **summarize** guidelines for teaching safety lessons to children.

Reading and Notetaking Activity

Skim this chapter from top to bottom and left to right and list all the headings. Then, identify key terms with which you are unfamiliar and scan through the chapter to find their definitions. Write a "topic sentence" and brief summary for each heading, using the key terms to explain what you think you will learn. After you read this chapter, write a new topic sentence and summary for each section, outlining the main points you learned.

Introduction

Accidents claim the lives of more children than any of the major childhood diseases. High accident rates among children are due to many factors, such as lack of supervision and unsafe equipment and toys. By the toddler years, children have the gross- and fine-motor skills to reach almost anything and get into potentially dangerous places. Children depend on adults to protect them by supervising them and creating a safe environment. Teaching safety lessons can make children aware of the need for safety.

21.2-1 Supervising Children

Caregivers and other adults worry about how to protect children from violence and strangers who may hurt them. Many adults do not think about the two major threats to children's safety—lack of constant and adequate supervision and home hazards. Children are much more likely to be injured in an accident at home than by a stranger's crime.

No safety device or lesson in the home can take the place of an adult's eyes and ears. Accidents happen more often when adults do not carefully supervise children. When adults are talking or texting on the phone, watching television, working on the computer, visiting a friend, feeling ill, or in any way **preoccupied** (focused on another task), accidents are more likely to occur. Accidents may also take place when supervision is unsuitable or lacking, such as when older children supervise younger children or when children (especially school-age children) are home alone for a brief time.

Part of supervising children is watching closely to anticipate the possible hazards a child may face as they grow and develop. Adults often refer to developmental milestones, which outline the *sequence of skills* their children will learn, to identify upcoming potential hazards. **Figure 21.9** shows common accidents children are likely to experience during each stage of development.

Figure 21.9 Common Accidents of Children

Developmental Stage	Types of Accidents
Infancy	• Bath scalding and burns from hot water faucets, open heaters, and floor furnaces • Falls from changing tables, carriers, stairs, or other high places • Injuries from swallowing small objects or putting them into eyes, ears, or nose • Drowning • Strangling on cords or smothering from items, such as dry-cleaning bags or balloons • Suffocation under blankets, pillows, or soft objects • Injuries from sharp or broken objects, such as glass, plastics, knives, or sharp-edged furniture • Injuries caused by pulling on cords of kitchen appliances, pulling, or grasping containers filled with hot foods or beverages • Injuries from electrical outlets • Mishaps while using walkers, strollers, and riding toys
Toddler years	• Drowning in bathtubs, water features, or pools • Burns from cigarette lighters, matches, open flames, and stoves • Poisoning from medications and cleaning agents • Injuries from dangerous objects, such as knives, electrical outlets, breakable objects, toys with small parts, and sharp-edged objects • Injuries caused by getting into almost anything that is not locked or equipped with special devices • Injuries caused by falls from high places, jumps onto dangerous surfaces (such as concrete), falls off ride-on toys, swings, and slides • Injuries caused by playing in driveways and roads and darting across streets • Injuries caused by swallowing small objects or putting them into eyes, ears, and nose • Eye injuries due to dust and sand

Goodheart-Willcox Publisher
Continued

Figure 21.9 **Common Accidents of Children** (Continued)

Developmental Stage	Types of Accidents
Preschool years	• Poisoning from medications and household products • Injuries from being around or using home, shop, and garden tools • Injuries related to action games, bicycles, and rough play • Various injuries from hazards, such as old refrigerators, deep holes, trash heaps, and construction sites • Drowning • Burns from electrical outlets, appliances, and open flames • Traffic injuries • Injuries from vehicle doors, getting locked in car trunks, and putting the car in gear
School-age years	• Sports-related injuries • Drowning • Firearm and fireworks accidents • Traffic injuries • Head injuries/concussion

Creating a Safe Environment

After potential hazards are identified within a child's environment, adults can implement safety measures to **neutralize** (reduce the effect of) those hazards. For example, a child who can crawl up one step or onto any low object can soon climb an entire flight of steep stairs. To prevent the child from falling, an adult might install a child safety gate with locks for the stairs as soon as the child begins to crawl. As adults carefully supervise children's development and see growth occur, they can adjust and implement different safety measures accordingly. Adults can create a safe environment, both indoors and outdoors, through childproofing and selecting and using safe child items and toys.

Childproofing

Childproofing is the process in which adults note dangers in a child's environment and then make the area safe for the child. Childproofing an environment often takes place before the baby is even born. Caregivers can choose to childproof either through a professional childproofing service or on their own. A professional *childproofer* inspects the home so they can assess the need for safety devices. The service is expensive, but includes the costs of the advice, safety devices, and installation.

Indoor and outdoor environments in or around the home pose the greatest hazards to children. A home's structure, general furnishings, rooms, and household items kept in or near the residence all hold threats for young children. Each home is alike in some ways (containing doors, windows, electrical outlets) and different in others (stairs or no stairs, furnishings). The dangers adults look for will vary based on the layout of the home. There are, however, common indoor and outdoor hazards. These hazards may include unstable furniture, blinds and curtains, loose rugs, windows, firearms, hinged doors, poisonous plants, rocks, broken glass, ruts, holes, and old or homemade playground equipment (**Figure 21.10**).

Childproofing measures in or around the home will also vary based on the temperament of the child. Sometimes a child's personality (such as being especially curious or loving to climb) may call for additional childproofing measures. By taking measures to create a safe environment in and around the home, adults can help prevent, or at least minimize, various injuries that might befall children.

Figure 21.10 Indoor and Outdoor Safety

Indoor Hazards

Artazum/Shutterstock.com

- Glass doors may cause collision or pinched fingers.
- Electrical outlets may cause electrocution.
- Windows can be broken and cause cuts or falls.
- Rugs may cause children to trip and fall.
- Blind cords may cause strangulation.
- Curtains may cause suffocation or strangulation.

Childproofing Measures
- Put colorful decals on doors at children's eye level; use doorstops and door holders to prevent pinched fingers.
- Use electrical outlet covers or other safety devices; if safe, place heavy furniture in front of outlets.
- Never put climbable furniture near windows; install window guards.
- Use nonskid pads under rugs; tape loose edges of rugs to floor.
- Cut or loop blind cords or place them on cleats; use cordless blinds if possible.
- Keep young children away from curtains; use short curtains if possible.

Outdoor Hazards

Artazum/Shutterstock.com

- Landscaping around playground may cause falls.
- If old, playground equipment may not adhere to most current safety standards.
- Wood chips can get in children's eyes or cause scrapes.
- If eaten, outdoor plants may be poisonous.

Childproofing Measures
- As much as possible, remove places where children can fall, such as landscaping and uneven surfaces.
- Research most current safety standards and ensure equipment adheres to these standards.
- Use rubber or another gentle material instead of wood chips.
- Make sure all outdoor plants are non-harmful if eaten. Keep children away from poisonous plants.

Goodheart-Willcox Publisher

Using Safe Child Items and Toys

Children require many *child items*, such as highchairs and cribs, and play with a variety of toys. Unfortunately, children's items and toys cause many injuries each year. These are injuries that could be avoided if adults knew which safety features to look for when selecting child items and toys. Properly storing and maintaining items and toys can also help in avoiding injuries. All items and toys need to be used under adult supervision, even if the items and toys are deemed safe.

Selecting Safe Child Items

Children's items do not just include items used in the home, such as a crib, changing table, high-chair, or play yard. Items also include those used by children outside the home, such as a stroller or a *certified child safety seat*. A **certified child safety seat** (also called a *car seat*) is a restraint system for children under the age of 13, which is required when riding in a motor vehicle. Certified child safety seats, which are fitted to the child's size, have been tested and approved by federal agencies.

Over the years child items have evolved to meet more **rigorous** (demanding) safety standards. Some safety standards, such as no lead paint and 23/8 inch-spaced slats on cribs and play yards, are now required by law. Items that are homemade or made prior to the enactments of these laws may not meet safety standards. **Figure 21.11** lists features that make a child item safe or unsafe.

All child items are sometimes subject to *safety recalls* issued by the manufacturers. In a **safety recall**, the manufacturer of a product issues a notice stating the product has been found to be unsafe. Consumers are asked to stop using the recalled, unsafe product unless the manufacturer can provide additional parts that will make the product safe.

Figure 21.11 Safety Standards for Child Items

Item	Safety Standards
Baby vehicle (carriage or stroller)	• Pretested for balance and weight distribution • Safety brake that can be set quickly • Protective padded bumpers should be securely attached
Bassinet	• Sturdy bottom and wide, stable base • Smooth surfaces and secure leg locks • Firm mattress with snug fit
Bed (toddler)	• Detachable rails with openings no more than 3½ inches apart • Padding on floor next to bed in case child rolls out
Changing table	• Sturdy with safety strap • Guardrails are at least 2 inches high
Child safety seat	• *Rear-facing* if the child is younger than 2 years of age and weighs 22–40 pounds • *Convertible* if the child is younger than 8 years of age and weighs 40–80 pounds • *Three-in-one* if the child is younger than 12 years of age and weighs 80–120 pounds • *Booster* if the child is 8 through 12 years of age and is at least 4 feet 9 inches tall
Crib	• Slats must not be more than 2⅜ inches apart • Height of crib side from bottom of mattress to top of railing should be no less than 26 inches • Child has outgrown crib when side rail is less than three-fourths of child's height • Children 35 inches and taller must be removed from portable cribs • Side rails must be fixed (not drop) and not adjustable • Paint should be lead free • Teething rails are preferred and should have a plastic covering • No horizontal bars inside crib because a baby can climb on them • Bumper pads should not be used • Corner posts should be flush with the headboard or should be 16 inches or higher for canopy beds • Placed away from windows, heaters, lamps, wall decorations, curtains, blinds, cords, and climbable furniture • Remove crib mobiles and hanging toys at five months; do not use stuffed animals or pillows until the toddler years • No cutout designs on head- or footboards • Crib hardware must have anti-loosening devices • All new cribs should have permanently fixed sides and come with a certificate of conformity—certificate indicates the crib has been rigorously tested and meets the Consumer Product Safety Commission (CPSC) standards

Goodheart-Willcox Publisher
Continued

Figure 21.11 **Safety Standards for Child Items** (Continued)

Item	Safety Standards
Crib mattress	• The top of the mattress support and the top of the rail should be no less than 9 inches for standard crib and 5 inches for portable crib • Mattress should be covered with durable plastic with air vents and then covered with a fitted sheet; torn mattress covers should be discarded • Mattress should be firm rather than soft and fit snugly in crib • Move mattress to the lowest point once child can pull self up to stand • Required marking, labeling and instructional literature reduces the risks of SIDS and suffocation related to infant positioning, soft bedding, and gap entrapment
Diaper pails and wastebaskets	• Keep out of reach of children • Choose models with child-resistant lids
Highchair	• Wide-spread legs improve stability • Tray should lock in place • Crotch-snap and wrap-around seat straps are needed • Nonskid rubber mats placed on seat help prevent baby from sliding
Play yard	• Slats should be no more than 2⅜ inches apart • Any mesh netting weave should be smaller than tiny baby buttons • Floor should not collapse • Hinges on folding models should lock tightly • If a *rivet* (screw like fastener) sticks out ¼ inch or more, stop using the play yard (May cause strangulation if clothing catches on rivet.) • Stop using play yard when child can crawl out of it

When selecting safe child items, the use and installation of these items is as important as the initial selection. For example, unless certified child safety seats are installed and used properly, they offer little or no protection for a child in a crash. For this reason, it is important to read directions for all child items carefully.

21.2-2 Toy Safety

Most new toys that are unsafe for infants and toddlers carry warnings, such as "Not Intended for Children Under Three Years of Age." Other items, such as lawn darts, cannot be sold in toy departments or toy stores because they are dangerous for children to use. When selecting children's toys, adults need to carefully examine the toy for safety features, read all warning labels, and heed recommendations. Toys should be checked for durability and any unsafe small parts. Adults can also ensure children's safety by testing noisemakers for volume, avoiding toys that fly or shoot, and purchasing proper safety gear (such as helmets and pads) for ride-on toys.

Adults can select age-stage appropriate toys for their children by remembering that age is only a clue to stage. Toys need to be appropriate for the child's physical skills (ability to use the toy), intellectual abilities (understanding of how to use the toy), and interests. Age-stage safety features can make appropriate toys even safer (**Figure 21.12**). After purchasing a toy, it is important to discard toy packaging. Styrofoam®; plastic; small, plastic ties; and other packaging materials are safety hazards for young children. Keeping safety information about child items in a file folder can help adults check recall information or make a complaint, if necessary.

Figure 21.12 Safety Features for Toys

Age Stage	Safety Features
Infants and Toddlers	• *Size should be larger than the child's two fists.* Even large toys can break, exposing small parts. Laws ban small parts in new toys intended for children under three years of age. Older and handmade toys may still have small parts. • *Nonbreakable.* Toys that break may expose small parts or break into small pieces. Toys made of glass or brittle plastic are the most unsafe. • *No sharp edges or points.* Laws ban new toys with sharp edges or points intended for children under eight years of age. Broken toys often have sharp edges. Wires with sharp points are often inside stuffed toys. • *Nontoxic.* Painted toys should be labeled nontoxic. Avoid all painted toys for children who put playthings in their mouth. • *No long cords or strings.* Toys with long cords or strings should not be used with infants and young children because they may present a strangulation hazard. • *Nonflammable, flame retardant, or flame resistant.* Dolls and stuffed toys should be made of materials not likely to ignite. • *Washable and hygienic materials.* Dolls and stuffed toys must be clean when bought and must be easy to keep clean. • *No broken or uninflated balloons.* These balloons are the most dangerous objects for suffocation. (Inflated balloons are not safe for children under five years of age.) • *No toys or games with marbles or balls smaller than 1¾ inches in diameter.* These items are a choking hazard. • *No small parts.* Laws ban small parts intended for children under three years of age. Older and handmade toys may still have small parts. • *No detachable clothing on dolls or stuffed animals.* Fasteners used on clothing items for dolls or stuffed animals are very small and thus present a choking hazard. • *No toys with springs or hinges.* Springs and hinges can pinch fingers. • *Sounds at acceptable decibel levels.* The law requires a label on toys that produce sounds above a certain decibel level. The label warns, "Do not use within one foot of the ear. Do not use indoors." Toys making sounds that can result in hearing damage are banned.
Older Children	• *Safe electric toys.* Electric toys must meet requirements for maximum surface temperatures, electrical wiring, and display of warning labels. Electrical toys that heat are intended for children over eight years of age. • *Items used for age intended.* Chemistry sets, hobby sets, balloons, and games and toys with small parts are extremely dangerous if misused or left within the reach of younger children. • *Sturdy, safe, large outdoor equipment.* Space between moving parts is wide enough to not pinch or crush fingers. Bolt ends should be covered with plastic end caps. Swing seats should be lightweight and have smooth, rolled edges. All swing sets, gyms, and other large equipment should be anchored firmly to the ground. • *Paints and crayons marked with designation ASTM D4236.* The designation means the material has been examined and is either nontoxic or carries a warning. • *No toys that are projectiles.* Projectiles cause many eye injuries. • *Safe tricycles and bicycles.* Tricycles and bicycles need to be assembled properly and seats adjusted to the rider's height. (Size of tricycle or bicycle should be suitable for child's current size.) Pedals should have skid-resistant surfaces. Reflectors (at least two inches in diameter) should be used on bicycles. A proper fitting helmet should be worn at all times.

Goodheart-Willcox Publisher

Storing and Maintaining Child Items and Toys

Child items and toys require appropriate space for storage. In some cases, the size of a toy during use and nonuse is about the same, such as a toy truck. In other cases, toys in use require much more space than they do when stored, such as building blocks. When storing toys, adults should consider the following: find indoor storage places near where each toy can be safely used; store outdoor toys where they can be secured when not in use; store all toys in spaces without **cluttering** (filling with many objects); and use special storage cabinets or shelves as needed.

Toys and child items tend to be used often and sometimes roughly. Adults can take care to maintain these objects and should always check for the following:

- recalls issued by the manufacturer or the Consumer Product Safety Commission
- sharp points, jagged edges, and loose parts
- removable parts that are small enough to fit inside a child's mouth

- rust on outdoor equipment
- stuffed toys and dolls that must be repaired and cleaned (**Figure 21.13**)
- batteries not secured by a cover with a screw to prevent removal

yaoinlove/iStock via Getty Images Plus

Figure 21.13 Stuffed toys need to be cleaned and checked regularly. Otherwise, they may grow bacteria or have unsafe parts. *What types of hazards do unwashed stuffed toys pose for young children?*

Focus on Careers

Toy Designer

Toy designers combine art, business, and engineering to develop toys that are safe and appeal to children. They create designs on paper or computers, select construction materials, and fabricate prototypes. Toy designers work with other specialists to evaluate design feasibility and cost before presenting to clients.

Career cluster: Arts, Audio/Video Technology & Communications.

Education: Educational requirements include a bachelor's degree, preferably in industrial design or engineering. Most programs include courses in drawing, computer-aided design and drafting, and three-dimensional modeling.

Job outlook: Future employment opportunities for toy designers are expected to grow slower than average for all occupations.

To learn more about a career as a toy designer, visit the United States Department of Labor's *Occupational Outlook Handbook* website. You will also be able to compare the job responsibilities, educational requirements, job outlook, and average pay of toy designers with similar occupations.

Photo: Stock Rocket/Shutterstock.com

Children can seriously injure themselves with broken toys. Adults should remove any broken toys from use, properly dispose of those that cannot be fixed, and repair any other broken items before they are put back into use.

Adults can also add safety devices to child items and toys. If a toy chest is not properly **ventilated** (accessible to air), an adult can drill a few air holes. If skates move too fast, adults can place a piece of adhesive tape around the wheel edge. To remind children not to hold the chains of a swing too low, adults can mark chains with tape at the proper holding height.

21.2-3 Teaching Safety Lessons

In addition to supervising children and using safe items and toys, adults can ensure children's safety by teaching their children *how* to be safe. Children often engage in unsafe behaviors because they are trying to achieve goals. While adults cannot always change children's goals, they can help children meet these goals safely. For example, when an infant wants to climb, a caregiver might let the infant climb up and down a single carpeted step. This environment is safe to explore, even if the infant takes small tumbles. Small risks teach children to cope with possible dangers. A steep staircase, however, poses too great a safety risk for such a young child.

Teaching safety is an ongoing process that begins almost at birth and continues for life. The first lessons occur in the home and yard. They expand to include the total environment, such as school, water, traffic, and job safety.

Adults can teach safety to young children in the following ways:

- *Be a model for children.* A child will absorb adults' approaches to everyday actions and safety measures, such as buckling seat belts and looking before crossing streets. Adults may even exaggerate behaviors to make safety measures clearer for the young child. They may stop, look, and say, "I don't see a car coming, so we can cross now," before walking across a street.
- *Explain the boundaries of play.* Show, as well as tell children, what they can and cannot do. Warnings are more helpful if they are stated in positive ways. An adult may say, "Grass is for playing, and streets are for cars and trucks." Warnings stated in negative ways may tempt children to act unsafely. Also, warnings that are repeated too often lose their meanings.

Focus on

Speech

Safety Around Strangers

As they grow older and meet more people, children will most likely encounter *strangers*, or adults whom they do not know. While adult supervision can reduce children's risks of being harmed by strangers or dangerous situations, children still need to be taught lessons about stranger safety. In learning about strangers, children first need to distinguish between *safe strangers*, such as police officers and firefighters, and *unsafe*

strangers, such as unfamiliar adults who offer them rides home.

Using reliable online or print resources, research strategies for teaching children the difference between safe and unsafe strangers. Also, research tips for teaching children stranger safety. After you research, deliver a short oral presentation summarizing what you learn.

Photo: naluwan/Shutterstock.com

- *Couple warnings with reasons.* When communicating safety rules, adults can explain the reasons for these rules. For example, an adult may say, "I want you to put on your seat belt because it will protect you if we make a fast stop or get into a crash."
- *Insist on obedience.* To insist on obedience means acting against wrongdoings, not simply making **idle** (inactive) threats of punishment. Acting does not call for physical punishment, but discipline appropriate for the action. For example, an adult may say, "If you do not put on your life jacket, you will not be allowed to play in the water." The adult could then enforce that limit (**Figure 21.14**).
- *Practice safety measures with children.* Adults can practice many safety measures with children, including safe walks to school or to other places, fire drills, and evacuation plans. To support safety lessons, adults can encourage children to talk about, act out, or illustrate safety actions.

Trauma and Injury

No matter how careful an adult is, children easily slip past adults and get into things they should not. Sometimes this leads to the child being hurt, other times things outside of adult's control cause the child to be hurt. Trauma is an experience, body wound or shock that causes a physical or psychological injury. Traumatic experiences can initiate strong emotions and physical reactions that persist long after the event. Children may feel terror, helplessness, or fear as well as physiological reactions such as heart pounding, vomiting, or loss of bowel or bladder control. Even though adults work hard to keep children safe, dangerous events can still occur. Sometimes the danger comes from outside of the family (a natural disaster, car accident, school shooting, or community violence) or from within the family such as domestic violence, physical or sexual abuse, or the unexpected death of a loved one. We go more into this in Chapter 22.

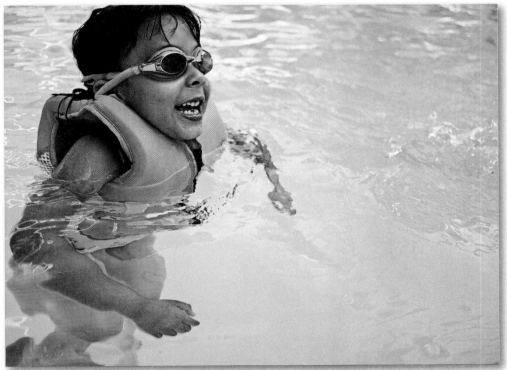

Figure 21.14 Insisting on obedience involves setting and then enforcing limits. For example, a child may not be allowed to go into the water unless they are wearing a life jacket. *How did your caregivers insist on obedience?*

Marilyn Nieves/iStock via Getty Images Plus

1. Accidents from firearm and fireworks most commonly occur in ____. (21.2.1)
   A. infants
   B. preschoolers
   C. toddlers
   D. school-age children

2. Which of the following is not considered a safety standard for a child's crib? (21.2.1)
   A. Adjustable side rails
   B. Slats no more than 2 3/8 inches apart
   C. Plastic-covered teething rails
   D. Crib hardware with anti-loosening devices

3. **True or False.** Adults should select age-stage appropriate toys for their children by remembering that age is only a clue to stage. (21.2.2)

4. A safety feature for a toy that is intended for use by children aged 12 and older would be ____. (21.2.2)
   A. ensuring the toy is larger than the child's two fists
   B. making balls larger than 1 ¾ inches in diameter
   C. ensuring the toy is unbreakable
   D. marking paints with designation ASTM D4236

5. When an adult encounters a broken toy among their child's things, they should do all of the following except ____. (21.2.2)
   A. try to fix it
   B. donate it
   C. dispose of it
   D. remove it from use

6. Which is the most effective guideline for teaching a safety lesson to a child? (21.2.3)
   A. Repeat warnings about unsafe behavior frequently.
   B. Begin all warnings with "never do" or "do not."
   C. Use the threat of a spanking as a consequence of noncompliance.
   D. Include a reason as part of a warning.

Treating Children's Illnesses and Injuries

Learning Outcomes

After studying this lesson, you will be able to

21.3-1 **explore** how to treat a child's illness by identifying symptoms that reveal a need for prompt medical attention, essentials in giving medication, and how to make a child comfortable.

21.3-2 **identify** and **describe** first aid for treating wounds including burns, fractures, bruises, sprains, splinters, bites, poisonings, and stings.

21.3-3 **list** steps to take for medical emergencies and demonstrate infant, child and adult cardiopulmonary resuscitation skills (CPR).

Key Terms

emergency situations
first aid
first-degree burns
fractures
second-degree burns
shock
splinters
sprains
third-degree burns
wounds

Reading and Notetaking Activity

As you read this lesson, put sticky notes next to sections that interest you or next to sections in which you have questions. Write your questions or comments on the sticky notes. After reading, find a partner and share your questions and comments. Ask your teacher any questions you and your partner cannot answer together.

Introduction

Even with preventive and basic health care, children still experience illness at times. Adults may be able to treat some minor illnesses children experience without medical help, but more serious illnesses may require immediate medical attention. To effectively care for children who are ill, adults must be able to recognize symptoms of illness and then make sure children receive the necessary treatment to get well. Sometimes treatment for an illness can be handled at home, and other times an illness may require immediate medical treatment from a doctor. If the illness is serious, children may need to stay in the hospital. Whether children are recovering from an illness at home or in the hospital, adults can help children by making them feel as comfortable as possible.

Similarly, even with proper safety measures in place, not all accidents can be prevented. Children will still experience many scrapes, bumps, and bruises as they learn what their bodies can and cannot do (**Figure 21.15**). Many injuries that occur during childhood are often minor, but some injuries can be serious, requiring immediate medical attention. Adults who work with children need to know basic first aid to treat children's injuries. They also need to know how to handle emergency situations.

21.3-1 Treating a Child's Illness

Most adults who work with children will eventually care for an ill child. To treat a child's illness, adults must recognize the need for medical intervention. In some cases, children need to be taken to a medical professional for treatment. In other cases, caregivers can care for children at home and treat them without assistance from medical professionals, often by giving medications and keeping children comfortable.

Imgorthand/E+ via Getty Images

Figure 21.15 As children grow and develop, their curiosity and energy motivate them to explore their worlds and test what they can do. *How can adults encourage exploration while ensuring children's health and safety?*

Recognizing the Need for Medical Intervention

Young children, especially those under seven or eight years of age, have many common illnesses, such as colds and digestive upsets. Minor illnesses such as these are typically taken care of at home without seeking professional medical attention. Other minor illnesses, which caregivers can often handle at home, include mild fevers (under 101°F), diarrhea, a runny nose, and short-term vomiting.

To safely treat children's illnesses, adults must first be able to recognize symptoms that require medical (sometimes immediate) intervention (**Figure 21.16**). For these illnesses, adults should take children to a doctor or seek urgent care if appropriate. For minor illnesses being handled at home, treatment usually involves taking children's temperatures, preparing specific foods, and sometimes giving children medications. Keeping children comfortable, hydrated, and ensuring they get plenty of rest are also important.

Giving Medications

For many illnesses, children need medication to get well. Medications for children include both *prescription medications* (medications prescribed by a doctor) and *over-the-counter medications* (medications that can be bought without a prescription). Parents and other adults should always read instructions for medications before giving them to children. Some over-the-counter medications, such as aspirin, should *never* be given to children. Any questions caregivers have about children's medications should be directed to the pharmacist or the child's doctor.

Medications are best given in accurate, medically defined measuring devices. Incorrect dosages may deliver too little medication and hinder infections from clearing up. Too much medication may poison the child. Medications work best when they are given in ways that are easy for children to consume.

Figure 21.16 **Symptoms Requiring Medical Intervention**

Areas of Concern	Symptoms	
Blood	• Large amount lost in bleeding • Bleeding that will not stop	
Body movement	• *Convulsions* (seizures) • Immobility in any part of the body	• Shaking • Stiffness of the body
Bones and muscles	• Swelling • Pain	• Difficulty in movement • *Bone fracture* (crack or break)
Brain	• Dizziness • Visual problems • Strange actions or appearance	• Unconsciousness • Headache
Breathing	• Difficulty breathing • Slow or rapid breathing • Continued coughing, sneezing, or wheezing	
Digestive system	• Sudden decrease in appetite • Nausea or forceful vomiting • Vomiting for several hours with inability to retain fluids • Abdominal pain or tenderness • Sudden increase or decrease in number of bowel movements • Stools or urine unusual in amount, color, odor, or consistency	
Eyes	• Irritation or redness • Sensitivity to light	• Blurred vision • Uneven pupils
Fever	• Rectal temperature of 101°F or higher • Mild fever that lasts several days	
General behavior	• Extremely ill appearance or demeanor that worsens quickly • Unusual quietness, irritability, confusion, or drowsiness • Strange behavior after a fall or other accident • If already ill, a rise in fever or new symptoms • Sharp screaming • Ear rubbing, head rolling, or drawing of legs toward abdomen	
Nose	• Nasal discharge (note color, amount, and consistency), congestion, or bleeding • Continuous clear drainage from the nose after a head injury	
Skin	• Dryness or hotness • Excessive perspiration • Rash or hives	• Severe cuts or *abrasions* (scrapes) • Deep bruising • Flushed or pale skin
Throat	• Soreness • Redness	• Choking or coughing

Goodheart-Willcox Publisher

For example, infants may suck medication through a nursing nipple with a ring attached, and some children may take medication from a dropper or syringe (without a needle) inserted far back at the side of the mouth (**Figure 21.17**). A pharmacist can advise caregivers on how to give medications so children receive accurate dosages.

Medications are to be kept in *child-resistant containers* and disposed of properly (such a through a pharmacy, hospital, or trash service). Child-resistant caps need to be replaced carefully after use and medications kept in an out-of-reach place, such as a locked cabinet. Medication should never be given in the dark, referred to as "candy," or given in baby bottles or juice glasses. Lastly, adults can avoid taking medication (even vitamins) in front of young children and keep medication away from children's reach.

Making a Child Comfortable

When children are ill, they need extra attention. Infants and young children will need lots of holding and rocking. Older children may need their illness and the treatment explained to them. Most children who are ill also enjoy little surprises, such as a small gift of a new book or a stuffed animal. Above all, adults can appear cheerful and confident so they will not cause ill children to worry. If the child's attitude is positive, this can speed recovery.

As children begin to feel well, they often do not want to stay in bed. Keeping an active child in bed at this time can be quite challenging for adults. Quiet games, books, movies, music, and paper and crayons can help children pass time. Visits from adults and other children (if the illness is not contagious) also help.

Making a child comfortable can be especially important if the child is in a hospital. Adults can prepare children for hospital care by explaining hospital life, touring the hospital, and using play and other means to introduce hospital concepts. During the hospital stay, caregivers should stay with their children and, as much as possible, make the hospital feel like home.

21.3-2 Knowing Basic First Aid

In the case of a severe illness or injury, adults may be required to administer first aid. **First aid** is emergency treatment for an illness or injury that is given before professional medical help arrives. Training in first aid can be very helpful to caregivers and is required as part of teacher training.

Figure 21.17 Many infants receive medication from a syringe inserted into the mouth. *Why is this method of delivering medication developmentally appropriate for infants?*

hilllander/iStock via Getty Images Plus

First-aid supplies, including a first-aid chart or book, should be kept current and nearby (**Figure 21.18**).

First aid includes guidelines for the treatment of wounds; burns; fractures, bruises, and sprains; splinters, bites, and stings; and poisonings. First aid also includes methods for dealing with emergency situations.

Wounds

Wounds are damage to the body's skin or tissue. Wounds may be caused by falls, punctures, collisions, and a variety of other accidents involving objects and other people. To properly treat wounds, adults should first identify the child's type of wound. Types of wounds include shallow cuts, abrasions, and deep cuts with heavy bleeding.

Shallow Cuts and Abrasions

Children can get shallow cuts from falling, handling an object incorrectly, or running into objects.

Figure 21.18 First-Aid Items

- Adhesive bandages (various sizes)
- Adhesive tape
- Antiseptic for cuts and scratches
- Calamine lotion (for insect bites)
- Gauze bandages and squares
- Scissors
- Activated charcoal (prevents poisons from entering the bloodstream)
- First-aid chart or book (for quick reference)
- Warm blanket (for shock)

*Note: First-aid items need to be kept both in the home and in all vehicles in which a child is transported.

Goodheart-Willcox Publisher

omphoto/Shutterstock.com

These cuts may bleed a little, but usually only damage the first layer of skin. If a child has a shallow cut that bleeds, first stop the bleeding by applying pressure using sterile gauze. After the bleeding has stopped, wash the wound using soap and warm water and apply an **antiseptic** (substance that kills bacteria) to prevent infection. Cover the cut with an adhesive bandage or other dressing (**Figure 21.19**).

If a child has an **abrasion** (uh-BRAY-zhun)—a scrape—follow these same guidelines. Make sure to wash the affected area carefully so particles do not remain in the wound and infect it.

Deep Cuts and Bleeding

If a child experiences a deep cut with much bleeding or bleeding that will not stop, seek medical attention immediately. While waiting for medical help, continue trying to stop the bleeding by applying pressure to the wound using a sterile dressing. Some children who experience much blood loss may go into **shock**, a condition in which the heartbeat and breathing slow. If a child goes into shock while awaiting medical help, lay the child on their back and elevate the child's legs. Keep the child warm until medical help arrives.

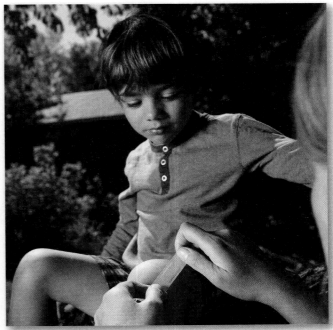

Fertnig/E+ via Getty Images

Figure 21.19 To prevent infection, shallow cuts should be covered with an adhesive bandage or other dressing. *How might an adult explain to a child the importance of wearing a bandage?*

Burns

Children who experience burns are at risk for shock and infection. When treating a burn, first identify the degree of burn (**Figure 21.20**). **First-degree burns** occur when heat or radiation burns the top layer of skin. First-degree burns include mild sunburns, in which the skin turns pink but does not peel or blister. **Second-degree burns** affect layers of skin beneath the first layer. Symptoms include blistering, peeling, discoloration, swelling, or severe pain in the skin. Finally, **third-degree burns** affect the innermost layer of skin and sometimes the muscle and bone beneath. Symptoms include blackened or whitened skin. Following are methods for treating burns:

- *First-degree burns.* Run cool water over affected area 15 to 20 minutes. Dry area and keep it clean. Cover the burn with a clean dressing.
- *Second-degree burns.* Run cool water over affected area 15 to 20 minutes. Dry area and keep it clean. Cover the burn with a clean dressing.

If the second-degree burn is deep or large, seek emergency medical attention immediately.
- *Third-degree burns.* Seek emergency medical attention immediately. Do *not* try to clean a severe burn. Observe the child for signs of shock and respond accordingly.

Fractures, Bruises, and Sprains

Falls or collisions can cause fractures or sprains in children. **Fractures** are cracks and breaks in bones, and **sprains** are injuries to joint ligaments. Symptoms for both fractures and sprains include swelling and pain around the site of the injury. If a child experiences a fracture or sprain, seek medical help immediately. There is no way of knowing the severity of the injury without examination by a medical professional. If the injury occurs in the neck or spinal region, do *not* try to move the child. Rather, call for emergency medical help.

Epidermis

Dermis

Hypodermis-Subcutaneous fat

First-degree burn   **Second-degree burn**   **Third-degree burn**

Medical Media/Shutterstock.com

Figure 21.20 Burns that affect the innermost layer of skin (third-degree burns) are more serious than burns that affect the outermost layer of skin (first-degree burns). When treating a burn, it is not recommended that you use ointments or apply ice directly to the burn. *What is the most serious type of burn you have experienced?*

Splinters, Bites, and Stings

Children who like to explore are prone to a number of injuries from their environment, including splinters, bites, and stings. **Splinters** are pieces of wood or plastic that become lodged in a child's skin. Shallow splinters can be removed with care using tweezers, but deep or large splinters should be removed by a medical professional. If a child is bitten or stung, check carefully for an allergic reaction. If the child is not allergic, wash the wound thoroughly to avoid infection. If a child is bitten by an animal, note the type of animal. Some animals can carry dangerous diseases; if a child is bitten by one of these animals, seek medical help immediately. Also, certain insect and animal bites are poisonous, thus requiring emergency medical treatment.

Poisonings

Most childhood poisonings happen when children **ingest** (consume) dangerous substances found around the house. Implementing safety measures around the home can help lessen the chance of children being poisoned. Reading all product labels and warnings can help caregivers identify which products are dangerous (**Figure 21.21**). Storing household products high above floor level (rather than under sinks) and locking up household products may help keep them away from children. Potentially dangerous products should not be left unattended or within reach, even for a minute.

Poisonings can be deadly to children. If a child has ingested a poison, adults should take immediate action and call a hospital or poison control center. The person at the hospital or center will determine whether the child needs emergency medical attention. Symptoms of a poisoning might include fever, rash, choking or coughing, nausea, labored breathing, or irritation around the mouth or eyes.

Figure 21.21 **Poisonous Household Products**

Cleaning Products	Garage and Garden Products	Medications	Personal Products
• Air fresheners • Ammonia (used in many cleaning products) • Bleach • Cleaners • Dishwasher and dishwashing products • Disinfectant • Drain opener • Floor wax • Furniture polish • Laundry products • Lye (sometimes found in soaps) • Metal polish • Oven cleaner • Rust remover • Spot remover • Toilet bowl cleaner • Water softener	• Antifreeze • Caustic lime • Fertilizer • Gasoline, kerosene, lighter fluid, oil, and other petroleum products • Oils • Paint • Pesticides • Putty • Strychnine • Turpentine • Varnish • Weed killer • Windshield solution	• Acetaminophen • Amphetamines • Analgesic creams • Antibiotics • Anticonvulsants • Antidepressants • Antidiarrheals • Blood pressure drugs • Camphor • Cold preparations • Cough medications • Diabetes drugs • Ear medications • Heart drugs • Iron, vitamins with iron • Nasal sprays • Oil of wintergreen • Pain relievers • Sleeping pills • Topical anesthetics • Tranquilizers • Vitamins	• Aftershave • Baby and bath oils • Cosmetics • Deodorant • Hair coloring products • Hair removal products • Hand sanitizers • Lotion • Mouthwash • Nail polish and polish remover • Perfume • Permanent wave solution • Powder, talcum (baby and body powder) • Water softener • Rubbing alcohol • Shampoo • Soap

Goodheart-Willcox Publisher

Emergency Preparedness

Emergency situations tend to be unexpected and stressful, especially when young children are involved. These situations, however, can be managed well if preparations are made ahead of time. *Emergency preparedness* usually refers to a collection of plans made in case of emergency situations. These plans might include evacuation plans, disaster plans, and preparations. For adults who work with young children, emergency preparedness can mean the difference between a serious accident and safety.

Establishing Emergency Plans

For most families and child care programs, emergency plans include preparations for fires, natural disasters (such as tornadoes), violence, and other dangerous situations. Adults should plan evacuation routes, establish safe locations, and compile emergency preparedness kits. For violence, lockdowns are used. If the violence is near the building, schools practice *soft lockdowns* (keeping children in a locked classroom and continuing with the regular activities). If violence is occurring inside the building, schools practice *hard lockdowns* (keeping children in a locked room, turning off the lights, and hiding the children from view). Typically, these plans must be taught to and practiced by children, which helps them remember the procedure and lessens panic.

Guiding Children Through Emergency Plans

Children, especially children who are too young to understand an emergency, may feel upset and react strongly to emergency situations. Part of emergency preparedness is planning to help young children cope and guiding them through emergency plans. Young children cannot help their intense reactions to stressful events. Caregivers and other adults can keep in mind their children's developmental stages during emergency situations and can remain calm, reminding children of the plans that have been established and soothing fears as much as possible.

Research Activity

Working with a partner, search the internet for reliable sources of information about emergency preparedness. These sources should be governmental websites or websites of authoritative organizations, such as the American Red Cross (ARC). During your research, take notes about tips for emergency preparedness. Afterward, create a short slideshow presentation of these tips. Present the slideshow to your class.

Photo: Tom Wang/Shutterstock.com

21.3-3 Handling Emergency Situations

Sometimes, adults will face emergency situations with children. **Emergency situations** are dangerous, often unexpected, or life-threatening events that require immediate action. Medical emergencies can arise from both illnesses and accidents. In a medical emergency, adults should always call for immediate medical help (**Figure 21.22**).

iStock.com/katifcam

Figure 21.22 The first step in handling any emergency situation is to call for emergency help. *Why should calling for emergency help be the first step?*

When responding to emergency situations, adults need to know how to use choking maneuvers; *cardiopulmonary resuscitation* (CAR-dee-oh-PUL-muh-nar-ee ree-SUH-suh-TAY-shun), or *CPR*; and *automatic external defibrillators* (dee-FIH-bruh-lay-turs), or *AEDs*. Procedures for using these methods and devices are listed in **Figure 21.23**. Adults should continue first aid until professional help arrives and then not interfere with the assistance. The ARC and the American Heart Association (AHA) both offer first-aid and CPR training so adults can become certified to effectively and safely treat children's injuries.

Sometimes emergency situations occur due to fire, explosions, or weather situations. In these cases, adults or teachers should comfort children and follow the evacuation or safety plans that have been practiced. A caregiver or teacher could have a flashlight and first-aid kit next to the evacuation doors or in a safe area for easy access while helping children remain safe. The ARC's first-aid guides, available in both print and digital media formats, contain further pointers for preparing for emergencies.

Figure 21.23 **Handling Emergency Situations**
Conscious Choking

Adults trained to handle choking emergencies use the following steps if an infant, child, or adult is conscious and is choking. If the person is an infant or child, obtain parental consent, if possible.

Steps	Infants	Children and Adults
Step 1 Give five back blows.	Give back blows with heel of hand between infant's shoulder blades.	Bend child or adult forward at waist and give back blows with heel of hand between shoulder blades.
Step 2 Give five thrusts.	Give five *chest thrusts* with two to three fingers at center of infant's chest just below nipple line. Compress breastbone about 1½ inches.	Give five *abdominal thrusts* with fist in middle of child's or adult's abdomen (thumb side against body; fist covered with other hand).
Step 3	Continue sets of five back blows and five thrusts until object is forced out, person can cough or breathe, or person becomes unconscious. If person becomes unconscious, call 911, send someone for an AED and begin CPR.	Continue sets of five back blows and five thrusts until object is forced out, person can cough or breathe, or person becomes unconscious. If person becomes unconscious, call 911, send someone for an AED and begin CPR.

Cardiopulmonary Resuscitation (CPR)

Adults trained in handling CPR use the following steps if an infant, child, or adult is unconscious and not breathing. If the person is an infant or child, obtain parental consent, if possible.

Steps	Infants	Children and Adults
Step 1 Give 30 chest compressions in about 18 seconds.	Place two or three fingers in center of chest (on lower half of sternum, just below nipple line) can also use both thumbs in center of chest with hands wrapped around chest. Compress chest about 1½ inches.	Place two hands in center of chest (on lower half of sternum). Compress chest about 2 inches.
Step 2	Give two rescue breaths until the chest clearly rises (about one second per breath).	Give two rescue breaths until the chest clearly rises (about one second per breath).
Step 3	Continue cycle. Do not stop unless situation becomes unsafe, person shows sign of life, another person takes over, you are too exhausted to continue, or AED becomes available.	Continue cycle. Do not stop unless situation becomes unsafe, person shows sign of life, another person takes over, you are too exhausted to continue, or AED becomes available.

Goodheart-Willcox Publisher
Continued

Figure 21.23 Handling Emergency Situations (Continued)
Using an Automated External Defibrillator (AED)

Adults trained in using an AED use the following steps if an infant, child, or adult is unconscious and not breathing. If the person is an infant or child, obtain parental consent, if possible.

Steps	Infants	Children and Adults
Step 1	Turn on AED.	Turn on AED.
Step 2	Wipe bare chest dry.	Wipe bare chest dry.
Step 3	1. Attach pads. 2. Use *pediatric pads* if possible. 3. Place one pad on the upper right side of the chest and the other pad on the left side of the chest. 4. For infants, place one pad in the middle of the chest and one pad in the middle of the back. 5. For adults, place one pad on the upper right side of the chest and the other pad on the left side of the chest.	1. Attach pads. 2. Use *pediatric pads* if possible. 3. Place one pad on the upper right side of the chest and the other pad on the left side of the chest. 4. For infants, place one pad in the middle of the chest and one pad in the middle of the back. 5. For adults, place one pad on the upper right side of the chest and the other pad on the left side of the chest.
Step 4	If necessary, plug in connector.	If necessary, plug in connector.
Step 5	Tell everyone to stand clear and follow the instructions from the AED.	Tell everyone to stand clear and follow the instructions from the AED.
Step 6	Deliver shock.	Deliver shock.
Step 7	Perform about five cycles of CPR.	Perform about five cycles of CPR.

Lesson 21.3 Review and Assessment

1. A child with which symptom requires immediate medical attention? (21.3.1)
   A. Infrequent runny nose
   B. Fever under 101°F
   C. Difficulty breathing
   D. One episode of diarrhea

2. **True or False.** Adults should avoid taking medication, even vitamins, in front of young children; and they should keep medication away from children's reach. (21.3.1)

3. The first step in treating a child's shallow cut is to _____. (21.3.2)
   A. apply an antiseptic to the wound
   B. wash the wound with soap and warm water
   C. cover the cut with an adhesive
   D. stop the bleeding with pressure

4. **True or False.** If a child has a suspected fracture or injury in their neck or spinal region, do not try to move the child but instead call for immediate emergency assistance. (21.3.2)

5. The first step in providing emergency treatment to an infant who is choking is to _____. (21.3.3)
   A. give 5 chest thrusts with 2 to 3 three fingers at the center of their chest
   B. give back blows with the heel of the hand between their shoulder blades
   C. give 5 abdominal thrusts with a fist in middle of their abdomen
   D. bend them forward at the waist and give back blows with the heel of a hand between the shoulder blades

Chapter 21 — Review and Assessment

Summary

Lesson 21.1

21.1-1 Adults help meet children's physical needs by ensuring they eat healthfully, get plenty of rest, and are physically active. Adults can take specific measures to protect children from certain illnesses and reduce their risk of infection.

21.1-1 Health screenings are also an important part of children's health care. Screenings exist for potential conditions or diseases, hearing and vision, and certain special needs such as autism and mental health problems.

21.1-1 Immunizations protect children from many serious diseases, and regular immunization schedules are recommended by doctors.

21.1-1 Although vaccination laws vary by state, to attend public school all children must be vaccinated against diphtheria, pertussis (whooping cough), measles, rubella (German measles), mumps, tetanus, polio, and varicella (chicken pox).

21.1-2 Numerous communicable diseases can be transmitted from an object to an individual or between individuals; these include chicken pox, the cold, conjunctivitis, Covid-19, and poliomyelitis, to name a few.

21.1-2 Young children are at a high risk for foodborne diseases or illnesses that are caused by eating foods contaminated with harmful bacteria and other pathogens during food production or preparation. Examples include botulism, E. coli, listeria, and salmonella.

21.1-2 Non-communicable diseases cannot be transmitted between an object and an individual or between individuals, but they develop in a person's body. Examples of these diseases include diabetes, epilepsy, allergies, and asthma.

21.1-3 Both state and federal legislation affects families and children.

Lesson 21.2

21.2-1 Adults are responsible for ensuring children's safety, and the most important element of safety is supervision. Supervision involves anticipating and removing possible hazards for children.

21.2-1 Adults can implement safety measures to neutralize hazards, including childproofing and using child-safe items and toys.

21.2-2 Adults should take care to select safe child items and toys for children. They should carefully examine toys for safety features, read all warning labels, heed recommendations, and check toys for durability and any unsafe small parts.

21.2-2 Adults should remember that toys need to be appropriate for the child's physical skills (ability to use the toy), intellectual abilities (understanding of how to use the toy), and interests.

21.2-2 Adults should pay attention to safety recalls, and they should store and maintain items well.

21.2-3 Teaching safety is an ongoing process that begins almost at birth and continues for life.

21.2-3 As children grow older, adults can teach them safety lessons to help them take precautions to keep themselves safe. Guidelines include being a model for children, explaining the boundaries of play, coupling warnings with reasons, insisting on obedience, and practicing safety precautions with children.

21.2-3 Dangerous or traumatic events can still occur from outside of the family or from within the family.

Lesson 21.3

21.3-1 Even with health care and adequate supervision, children may experience illnesses or injuries. In treating illness, adults need to recognize symptoms requiring medical intervention, know how to give medications, and make children comfortable.

21.3-1 Medications are best given in accurate, medically defined measuring devices. Incorrect dosages may deliver too little medication and affect treatment, while too much may poison the child.

21.3-1 Medications should be kept in child-resistant containers, disposed of properly, and kept in an out-of-reach place. They should never be given in the dark, referred to as "candy," or given in baby bottles or juice glasses.

21.3-2 First aid includes guidelines for the treatment of wounds; burns; fractures, bruises, and sprains; splinters, bites, and stings; poisonings; and knowing methods for dealing with emergencies.

21.3-3 Emergency situations are dangerous, often unexpected, or life-threatening events that require immediate action. They can arise from both illnesses and accidents.

21.3-3 In emergency situations, adults can help by calling for help and knowing choking maneuvers, cardiopulmonary resuscitation (CPR), and how to use an automatic external defibrillator (AED).

College and Career Portfolio

Portfolio Review

Once you have selected, created, and compiled the elements of your portfolio, you can begin finalizing your work and preparing to present it. Now is a good time to have someone review your portfolio. The feedback you gain from a review can be extremely helpful.

- Select one adult (such as a teacher or counselor) to review your portfolio. Ask the adult for honest feedback.
- Listen to the adult's feedback and brainstorm how you can implement their advice at this stage.

Recall and Application

1. At what age should most children first begin screening for high blood cholesterol levels? (21.1.1)
   A. Between ages 1 and 3 years
   B. Between ages 5 and 7 years
   C. Between 9 and 11 years
   D. Between ages 13 and 15 years

2. **True or False.** Although vaccination laws vary from state to state, to attend public school, children must be vaccinated against diphtheria, pertussis, measles, rubella, mumps, tetanus, polio, and varicella. (21.1.1)

3. Which is an example of a non-communicable disease? (21.1.2)
   A. Allergies
   B. Head lice
   C. Diphtheria
   D. Impetigo

4. **True or False.** One recommendation to prevent foodborne illness is to keep all foods hot. (21.1.2)

5. Child labor laws _____. (21.1.3)
   A. determine mandatory reporters for child abuse
   B. protect children who are under age 18
   C. allow parents to view their children's school records
   D. set child support requirements for custodial caregivers

6. Accidental suffocation under blankets, pillows, or soft objects most commonly occurs in _____. (21.2.1)
   A. infants
   B. preschoolers
   C. toddlers
   D. school-age children

7. Which child safety seat is most appropriate for child younger than 2 years who weighs 22–40 pounds? (21.2.1)
   A. Rear-facing
   B. Convertible
   C. Three-in-one
   D. Booster

8. **True or False.** To select age-stage appropriate toys for their children, adults should buy toys their children have the physical ability to use. (21.2.2)

9. Which is the most effective example of teaching a child about safety? (21.2.3)
   A. "Never, ever follow a ball into the road."
   B. "If you don't wear your bike helmet you can't have dessert tonight."
   C. "I don't need to wear a life jacket because I'm an adult and can swim."
   D. "Matches are tools, not toys, because they are used to start fires, which can burn you badly and be dangerous."

10. **True or False.** To make it easier to give a reluctant child their medication, a caregiver might refer to it as "candy." (21.3.1)

11. Which is true of a first-degree burn? (21.3.2)
    A. It affects only the top layer of skin.
    B. It may cause skin blistering and peeling.
    C. It requires immediate emergency medical attention.
    D. It causes blackened or whitened skin.

12. When performing CPR on a person of any age, the rescuer should provide two rescue breaths of about one second per breath until the person's chest clearly rises. (21.3.3)

Critical Thinking

1. **Cause and effect.** Part of basic health care is meeting the physical needs of children. In small groups, review this text's chapters about meeting the physical needs of infants, toddlers, preschoolers, and school-age children. Then discuss how meeting these needs impacts the success of health care.

2. **Draw conclusions.** Write a short essay answering the question, *Why is supervision still important even in a thoroughly childproofed environment?* Draw conclusions about supervisory effects on physical, intellectual, and social-emotional development.

3. **Compare and contrast.** Safety precautions differ depending on the environment that must be childproofed. Working with a partner, compare and contrast the safety measures that might be taken in a house and in a child care center. How is childproofing similar in these two locations? How is it different?

4. **Evaluate.** Obtain a catalog or search online to review popular toys for children. As you view the toys, identify five toys as safe or unsafe. What safety features do the toys have? How, if at all, are the toys still hazardous? For what ages are the toys appropriate?

5. **Analyze.** It is not recommended that adults use old or antique child items or toys with their children. Why do experts make this recommendation? How would you explain to a caregiver the need for new or current child items and toys?

6. **Make inferences.** Choose one of the guidelines for teaching safety lessons discussed in this chapter. Then, working with a partner, discuss how the guideline is developmentally appropriate for young children.

7. **Identify.** Review the list of common household poisons in this chapter and then take an inventory of the items in your home's bathrooms and kitchen. What poisonous items does your family have? What childproofing measures would you take if a toddler or a preschooler were to stay in your home?

8. **Determine.** In small groups, write a short case study about a child who becomes injured. Then trade case studies with another group. Read the new case study in your group and determine the first-aid measures that should be taken to treat the child.

Core Skills

1. **Listening and speaking.** In small groups, conduct research and visit local health care services for children. What features (such as colorful waiting rooms or books for reading) do they offer that appeal to children? Talk with someone who works at the health care service and ask what advice they might give families who are choosing health care services for their children. Finally, deliver your findings to the class in an oral presentation.

2. **Science.** Knowing the causes of common communicable and non-communicable diseases can help adults prevent and treat these conditions. In small groups, choose one communicable and one non-communicable disease. Research the causes and treatments of these diseases and create a public service announcement detailing your findings.

3. **Research and technology.** Food safety is a key component of ensuring children's health. To learn more about food safety, visit Foodsafety.gov and research the recommended temperatures, cooking times, and storage methods for various types of food. Then choose three meals that you prepare or eat on a regular basis. Create a slideshow presentation explaining how these meals are prepared and stored to ensure food safety.

4. **Listening and math.** Interview at least 10 families with school-age children about the childproofing measures they took when their children were younger. What childproofing devices did they install and when? How far ahead of their children's development did they try to childproof? After the interviews, compile your data and calculate, on average, how far ahead of their children's development adults childproofed.

5. **Research and reading.** Research current safety standards for children's cribs and other child items. The most current safety standards should be outlined by the U.S. Consumer Product Safety Commission (U.S. CPSC). Then obtain three catalogs (one current, one from a few years ago, and one from more than a decade ago) with pictures of children's cribs and other child items. Review and assess the cribs and other items according to current safety standards to determine which items are safe or unsafe. What changes could be made to unsafe items to *make* them safe?

6. **Reading and writing.** Search the internet to find examples of three recent safety recalls for child items or toys. For each recall, identify why the recall has been made and the manufacturer's recommended remediation. After reading these examples, choose one unsafe historical child item or toy. Write a recall for the product based on the examples you read. Share your recall with the class.

7. **Listening and writing.** Interview someone who works with children (such as a teacher, child care worker, or babysitter) and ask questions about how to recognize the need for medical intervention. Has the person ever called for emergency help while working with children? Has the person ever taken a child to the doctor? If so, how did the person decide that the child's condition required medical intervention? What advice does the person have about recognizing this need? After the interview, write a short summary about what you learned.

8. **CTE Career Readiness Practice.** Presume you are the director of a child care center and have planned a short training session to refresh your employees on the basics of performing choking maneuvers, administering CPR, and using AEDs. In preparation for the session, research the most current recommendations for these emergency procedures. Then create handouts to summarize each of the emergency procedures. Make your handouts professional and easy to follow. Use your handouts to remind or teach a partner about these techniques.

Observations

1. Search the internet for videos of young children crawling or walking for the first time. During the video, pay attention to the environment around the children. What childproofing measures are evident in the environment? Does the environment seem safe or unsafe? What additional childproofing measures would you recommend?

2. As a class, visit a local child care center and observe a group of toddlers or preschoolers at play. As you observe, take notes about what developmental traits make the children prone to accidents. Give specific examples. (Refer to children's developmental milestones if need be.) How do adult actions or the environment of the center prevent or lessen potential accidents? After the observation, discuss your findings.

Chapter 22

Handling Family-Life Challenges

Essential Question

What types of challenges affect children and adolescents, and how can caregivers and other adults protect and help children and adolescents develop resilience?

Case Study · What Does It Mean to Be a Mandated Reporter?

As a class, read the case study and discuss the questions that follow. After you finish studying the chapter, discuss this case study again. Have your opinions changed based on what you learned?

Alexandra has been a child care worker at a local preschool for six months and has enjoyed working with a diverse group of young children and their caregivers. About one month ago, a preschooler named Josh started attending the center. Since Josh joined the center, Alexandra has had several meetings with Josh's family. From these meetings, Alexandra surmises that one of Josh's caregivers may have severe depression after losing their job. Alexandra also thinks that Josh's other caregiver is overwhelmed by the stress of caring for a new baby while working to support the family.

Lately, Josh has been coming to the center dressed in tattered clothes. Josh is always hungry and eats large amounts of food very quickly. One week ago, Josh contracted a rash while playing outside, and the rash has still not cleared up. When Alexandra asked Josh's caregivers about the rash, they said they had not taken Josh to the doctor yet. For the past few days, Josh has been unusually tired and hesitant about engaging in physical activities.

When helping Josh wash their hands, Alexandra noticed several bruises on Josh's arms.

Alexandra knows that Josh's caregivers are in difficult emotional and financial straits but is worried about Josh and knows that by law daycare workers are mandated reporters for neglect and abuse.

Give It Some Thought

1. What signs of neglect or abuse are present in Josh's behavior? Does Alexandra have a reason to be worried?
2. Alexandra knows about the difficulties Josh's primary caregivers are facing. As such, should someone at the daycare center try to talk with the caregivers? Why or why not?
3. What are Alexandra's responsibilities as a mandated reporter of child neglect and abuse? What do those responsibilities mean concerning the action(s) they should take?

wavebreakmedia/iStock via Getty Images Plus

Lesson 22.1

Helping Children and Adolescents Cope with Challenges

Key Terms

buffers
custody plans
impoverished
resilient children
stages of grief
terminally ill

Learning Outcomes

After studying this lesson, you will be able to

22.1-1 **identify** how parents and other adults can help children and teens cope with family challenges such as moving, financial strain, addiction, divorce, violence, and disaster.

22.1-2 **summarize** how adults can help children and teens understand and cope with illness and death and how resilience can be fostered in children.

22.1-3 **identify** resources for children and teens in crises and the types of counseling and therapeutic services available to help.

Reading and Notetaking Activity

Before reading this lesson, interview someone who works in a child-related career (such as a child care worker, pediatrician, or school counselor). Ask the person why it is important to know about the lesson topic and how this topic affects the person's job. Then, as you read the lesson, take notes about items you talked about that are discussed in the lesson.

22.1-1 Challenges in the Family

As children grow up, they will encounter challenges. Many of these challenges stem from within the family—the child's foundation for living and learning. Family life can be complex. Stressful events may occur that cause tensions and problems for many families. Family challenges, whether due to life circumstances or decisions, affect children and teens. Family-life challenges include moving, financial strain, addiction, violence and disaster, divorce, and illness and death.

In Chapter 2, you learned about adverse childhood experiences (ACEs) and the best practices for helping a child or teen who has experienced an ACE: trauma informed care (TIC). In this chapter, you will take a closer look at some of the ACEs that children and teens experience.

How ACEs affect a child depends on how the child learns to cope. It also depends on how caregivers and other adults (such as teachers) help the child in handling the ACE. Through learning to cope with ACEs, many children and teens will develop resilience. Resources for children and teens in crisis situations are available.

Moving

Today, many societies are *mobile societies*, meaning that people move from place to place. Moving can be stressful for children and teens, especially as they make friends and extend their social relations in a region. Family moves can lead to **severed** (ended) friendships, unfamiliar schools, and new dangers. During moves, children and teens may experience loneliness, long for stability, and need some time to adjust.

To help children and teens cope with moving, caregivers and other adults need to work together to create stability. Adults can help their children and teens by trying to plan moves so they fit well in children's lives. For example, a move that coincides with the death of a family member, divorce, or poor grades will be especially stressful. On the other hand, moving at the beginning or end of a school term may be less stressful. Caregivers can also help children and teens by expressing why they are pleased about the move (better paying job, nearer relatives, safer neighborhood). Before the move, adults can involve children and teens in the moving process and explain what will happen during the move. After the move, they can encourage children and teens to invest in new relationships and local activities (**Figure 22.1**).

Other adults who interact with children and teens, such as teachers or other caregivers, can help children cope by providing as much stability as possible. This may mean allowing the preschool child to carry a favorite toy or photo or helping the teenager settle into new routines at high school. Teachers and other adults can help young children cope by giving them opportunities to learn about moving. They may provide books or stories that talk about moving or may encourage a child to act out the move in play. For school-age children and teens, teachers can help children catch up in new classes and encourage them to connect with new friends.

FOCUS ON MENTAL HEALTH

As they grow older, children tend to place more importance on social relationships, especially peer relationships. For this reason, older children and teens may have a more difficult time adjusting to a move than younger children. To help elevate some of the stress, caregivers can break the news in advance to allow children time to adjust to the idea. Next, acknowledge their feelings. It is completely normal for children to feel confusion, anger, and unhappiness when facing a major change. Check on children regularly and be available to talk or answer questions. Involve children and teens in the moving process by having them go through old toys and books to donate or sell. If possible, let them choose their new room and decorate it themself. Finally, be sure to allow them to say goodbye to their old home, friends, and loved ones. Remind them there will be opportunities to keep in touch.

FatCamera/E+ via Getty Images

Figure 22.1 Becoming involved in activities and social groups can help children adjust after a family move. *Are peer relations more important for older children than for younger children? Why or why not?*

This might involve providing workbooks or hand-outs that outline material already covered in class or referring children to tutoring resources or clubs.

Children and teens adjust best to a move when caregivers and other adults work as a team to provide stability and help the child. During or after a move, caregivers and teachers can collaborate by having caregiver-teacher conferences and by actively communicating about the child's needs.

Financial Strain

Lack of financial resources can cause significant stress for children and teens. Families may lack financial resources for a number of reasons, including unemployment, underemployment, illness, unforeseen expenses (such as medical expenses), addiction, or lack of money-management skills. Some families experiencing financial strain may be **impoverished**, meaning they have inadequate funds to reasonably provide for family members' needs. No matter the reasons, financial strain can negatively impact children from before birth even into adulthood (**Figure 22.2**).

Figure 22.2 Effects of Financial Strain on Children

Developmental Stage	Effects
Before Birth	• Low-quality prenatal care puts children at risk for complications and conditions. • Maternal stress and malnutrition may hinder children's development.
Infancy	• Family stress and lack of quality care may hinder infant attachments and social-emotional development. • Lack of nutritious foods may slow infants' physical development. • Lack of quality care and developmental experiences may affect infants' brain development and have adverse effects on intellectual development.
Toddler Years	• Lack of quality care and developmental experiences may cause missed windows of opportunity and stunt learning. • Family stress and lack of quality care may damage toddlers' relationships and cause social-emotional disturbances. • Lack of nutritious foods and physical activity may adversely affect toddlers' health and development.
Preschool Years	• Lack of nutritious foods and physical activity may adversely affect children's health and development. • Family stress may harm familial relationships. Children learn to express emotions and stress by watching adults. • As children build peer relationships, rejection may cause sadness and a poor self-concept. • Lack of quality care and developmental experiences may cause missed windows of opportunity and slow learning.
School-Age and Teen Years	• Lack of quality care and experiences may cause poor habits. • Family stress may cause depression or aggression in children. • Children may receive poor grades due to lack of help at home, feelings of inadequacy, or depression. • Children may experience rejection from peers due to family circumstances. • Teenagers may act out the behaviors they see at home in their own financial dealings and relationships.

Goodheart-Willcox Publisher

Children and teens best cope with financial strain when their caregivers and the other adults in their lives work together to support their development. Caregivers and other adults can help by accessing appropriate resources to support their children's development. Examples of these types of resources may include organizations that provide healthful lunches for children and not-for-profit child care programs. Caregivers can also seek to address issues that cause financial strain and do everything in their power to provide for their children's needs. For older children and teens, caregivers may want to explain the financial strain, but not make children and teens feel as though it is their problem to solve.

Teachers and other adults also play a key role in helping children cope with financial strain. Judgments passed by other adults and children's peers may hurt children's self-concepts. Teachers and other adults can help children cope in the following ways:

- *Always model respect.* Regardless of their opinions, teachers and other adults should always show respect for children and their families. This includes not making judgmental or insulting remarks. It also includes involving children in decisions and challenging them to excel.

- *Encourage social interactions.* Children whose families are experiencing financial strain may feel isolated or out of place among their peers. Teachers and other adults can help children cope by teaching younger children basic social skills and encouraging older children to form positive relationships with their peers. They can make children feel important by giving them responsibility and appreciating their contributions in class.

- *Ensure that programs are inclusive.* Programs or schools that require large donations, tuitions, or fees tend to exclude or place pressure on families experiencing financial strain. Teachers and other adults can help children cope by reducing the barriers to children participating in programs through scholarships and donations of school supplies and uniforms. They can be sure to thank children and families for their contributions (monetary or otherwise) to the program.

- *Refer families to available resources.* Teachers and other adults can help children cope with financial strain by referring children's families to appropriate resources. These resources may include programs that provide food, low-cost housing, and community- or government-subsidized child care programs (**Figure 22.3**).

SDI Productions/iStock via Getty Images Plus

Figure 22.3 Government programs, such as the National School Lunch Program (NSLP), provide healthful lunches for children at little or no cost. *What are your state's regulations regarding which children are eligible for free or reduced-price lunches?*

FOCUS ON MENTAL HEALTH

Mental health problems of feeling anxious, depressed, or inferior are associated with being unemployed, homeless, or on public assistance. Many times, children do not want their peers to know that their families are in these types of situations. Schools and communities have programs to help these children discretely by sending food, clothing, and other necessary items home with children. Examples include Backpack Friends, which provides school supplies; the free and reduced lunch program; and local food banks, some of which will prepare a backpack of food for children to take home over the weekend.

Addiction

Family members' behaviors always affect children. *Addiction* (the dependency on a substance, such as alcohol or drugs, or action, such as gambling) causes a pattern of destructive behaviors that negatively affect children. People who are addicted to a substance or action feel they cannot continue to live without the substance or action in their life. As a result, people with addictions may hurt their families in order to **feed** (continue) their addiction. They may speak hurtful words, lie to their family members, and use family resources to feed the addiction. They may also physically harm their family or be emotionally distant. People with addictions may also struggle to keep a job and contribute to their family.

Children and teens are influenced by the behaviors and addictions of their family members. Children and teens with caregivers or other family members who abuse substances are likely to abuse substances later in life. Children and teens also suffer under the stress caused by addicted behaviors.

Caregivers and other adults can help children and teens cope by limiting children's contact with those who have addictions. They can assure children and teens that the addiction is not their fault and can protect them from the hurtful words or actions of people who have addictions. Most importantly, caregivers and other adults can ensure that the person with the addiction is receiving help, either through a support group or other intervening organization.

Teachers and other adults can help children and teens cope by being available to talk and lend support. Children and teens may confide in teachers, counselors, or therapists and may express their feelings about the addiction. Teachers and adults can work with caregivers to provide a stable environment. If a child or teen is in danger, teachers and adults may need to contact outside help. A *state department of child protective services* is a state agency that protects children's safety by intervening in potentially hazardous family situations.

Violence and Disasters

Even children and teens who are loved and protected in the home may be exposed to violence and disaster in the world around them. Violence and disasters can occur unexpectedly and can happen to children, families, communities, and even countries. Children and teens are affected by violence and disaster, whether it happens to them, to a person they know, or to a person or place the child or teen has never encountered.

FOCUS ON MENTAL HEALTH

Children's and teen's mental health problems stem from the following:

- trying to act as a surrogate "spouse" for the adult who is addicted
- developing elaborate systems of denial to protect themselves against the reality of the caregivers' addiction
- trying to compensate for a caregiver-deficiency if in a single-parent family
- dealing with a caregiver who is mentally ill in addition to having an addiction

Focus on Speech

Media Depictions of Violence

Children and teens do not have to be direct witnesses to be exposed to violence and disaster. Media depictions of violence—whether on the news, in films, or in video games—can be upsetting. These media depictions of violence are especially upsetting if children and teens are experiencing other challenges or have witnessed other forms of trauma. Over the years, experts have conducted several studies about the effects of violence in the media on children and teens.

Work with a partner to find and read one of the more recent studies. After reading, prepare a two-minute oral presentation for the class in which you and your partner summarize the study and discuss its relevance to child development.

Reactions to violence and disaster will vary depending on the child's age and development (**Figure 22.4**). News of violence and disaster can travel quickly by word of mouth and through the media.

Caregivers can help children and teens cope with violence and disaster by attempting to limit their exposure to these events. For example, if a robbery occurs in the child's town, caregivers might explain as needed, but then limit how much news coverage the child accesses. News and media coverage of violence and disaster can upset children and cause stress.

Figure 22.4 Children's Reactions to Violence and Disaster

Age of Child	Typical Reactions
Infants and toddlers	• Being extremely afraid • Clinging to a caregiver • Screaming • Crying • Whimpering • Trembling • Moving violently • Not moving • Regressing in behaviors (such as returning to thumb sucking or clinging behaviors)
Preschoolers, school-age children, and teenagers	• Isolating self and not talking with others • Showing social-emotional disturbances, such as angry outbursts, depression, or feelings of numbness • Having trouble sleeping • Experiencing physical problems, such as digestive upsets • Losing interest in favored activities • Doing poorly in school or being unable to concentrate

Goodheart-Willcox Publisher

traumatic event and note any especially severe or dangerous reactions. In these situations, adults may need to recommend help, such as therapy, for a child.

Divorce

In the United States, many couples divorce for a variety of reasons. Divorce affects both adults and children. Caregivers are challenged to overcome their negative feelings and adjust to a new lifestyle. Children and teens are affected during the separation process and often for years following the divorce. Even children who were infants when their caregivers divorced still deal with these issues in their school-age and adolescent years. Couples seeking to divorce may find professional counseling helpful. Counselors or members of support groups can discuss the effects of divorce on adults and their children. Both caregivers and children may need a support system for many years.

It is difficult to predict how divorce will affect a particular child. Age and gender tend to affect how children cope (**Figure 22.5**). Divorce usually confuses young children. They do not understand the divorce process, but they know that one caregiver is not living with the family. A child's personality will also affect how they will cope. Some children are more positive than others and have fewer coping problems.

Unfortunately, limiting children's exposure to violence and disaster is not always possible. Caregivers should be prepared to help their children process the event and related feelings. If a child has encountered violence or disaster, caregivers can allow the child to express how they feel about the event. They should not dismiss or encourage children to stifle their emotions, but rather should give children opportunities to talk about their feelings. Adults and caregivers can be understanding of children's *regressive reactions* (such as bedwetting or thumb sucking), can engage children in standard routines, and can give children choices to reduce feelings of helplessness. If a child is **traumatized** (seriously disrupted socially or emotionally) by an event, caregivers can help the child get appropriate treatment.

Teachers and other adults can help children cope by being understanding and not reacting harshly if children act out or express their emotions inappropriately. Instead of expecting children to overcome their emotions, adults can encourage emotional expression and listen carefully. As children heal, adults can reduce other stressors (such as school pressure and social tension) in the child's life and remind children that adults love them. Adults should pay attention to children as they recover from a

Adults and caregivers can help preschoolers and older children cope by giving honest, but appropriate, answers to their questions. Adults should not discuss problems of the marriage or divorce with young children. Children cannot understand these complex issues, and because they cannot help solve the problems of marriage, they should not be burdened with them. Instead, both adults should explain and repeat the message that the divorce is not the child's fault and that both caregivers still love the child.

Figure 22.5 Reactions to Loss of a Parent Through Divorce or Death

Age	Common Behaviors and Feelings
Toddlers	• Whining, crying, and clinging • Acting fretful • Having sleep and appetite problems • Experiencing possible regression (occurring most often at a time of day when the absent parent was usually with the child)
Preschoolers	• Whining and crying • Hitting or biting others • Feeling anxious • Seeming moody and restless • Acting aggressively • Wanting physical contact with others • Denying the loss and even pretending parents will be together again • Having problems in creative play • Feeling they caused the divorce or death
School-age children and teenagers	• Daydreaming more and worrying more about the future • Denying the loss • Feeling angry and bitter (blaming the adult whom they think is responsible) • Feeling lonely, abandoned, and rejected by the absent adult • Showing antisocial behaviors, such as lying or stealing • Having more headaches and stomachaches than usual • Having school problems, such as not being able to pay attention • Showing premature detachment, rejecting the adult who is gone, and the qualities shared with this absent caregiver • Becoming the confidant (close friend to whom secrets are entrusted) of the remaining caregiver and thus having too much adult-like pressure

Gender	Common Behaviors and Feelings
Boys	• Acting oblivious and inattentive • Having a drop in school achievement • Acting more aggressively • Having more problems during the divorce process and for the first two years after the divorce • Doing better if they have a positive relationship with the absent adult
Girls	• Feeling grief and frustration • Crying • Withdrawing • Blaming themselves • Being more troubled a year after the divorce than at the time of the divorce

Goodheart-Willcox Publisher

As much as possible, caregivers should support the child during the divorce. They can do this by keeping routines normal, helping the child stay in touch with other family members, listening to the child, and developing a positive new lifestyle for the child (**Figure 22.6**). Once **custody plans** (legal plans outlining who will care for the child and to what extent) are firm, adults should tell children about them if they are old enough to understand. Finally, caregivers can help children cope by alerting teachers and other adults in the child's life when the family structure changes.

Teachers and other adults can help children cope by offering support once they are aware of the situation. Children often need neutral adults who can help them express their sadness or anger in acceptable ways and cope with loneliness and a new lifestyle. Teachers and other adults can also serve as role models for expressing emotions and adjusting. Other ways that teachers and neutral adults can help children cope with divorce include

- keeping routines and discipline consistent
- supporting children's feelings of worth and confidence even when children struggle to concentrate or act out due to stress at home
- listening to children without judgment
- advocating for children, especially if parents are engaging in behaviors that harm them
- involving both parents in the children's care and education
- recommending therapy for children, if appropriate

22.1-2 Illness and Death

Illness and death are basic parts of life, and even young children need to come to terms with them. Some children may lose a caregiver before they finish elementary school. Many more witness the illness or death of a close friend, relative, or even a pet during childhood and adolescence. Caregivers and other adults can help children and teens understand and cope with illness and death.

MBI/Shutterstock.com

Figure 22.6 After a divorce, creating a new, appealing space for children can help them positively embrace their new lifestyles. *Why do you think children respond positively to having their own space?*

Helping Children and Adolescents Understand Illness and Death

Children's understanding of illness and death develops gradually. Understandings of illness may focus on the effects of the illness (such as weakness or fatigue) rather than on the causes of or treatments for the illness. Death may be an even harder concept for children to grasp. Around six or seven months of age, an infant will notice separations from caring adults. These separations, most of which are brief, are the earliest experiences of loss in a child's life. Early separation may set the stage for later responses to separation, loss, and even death. Until three or four years of age, children have little, if any, understanding of death. Preschool children may try to learn the physical facts of death but will find many facts difficult to believe and thus question them. Even older preschoolers may find it difficult to understand their family's beliefs about death.

Usually, adults do not talk about illness or death with children unless a person or pet is sick or dies. These concepts, however, are important for children to grasp. In helping children understand illness, adults and caregivers need to answer children's questions about the illness honestly. These answers might include age-appropriate explanations of the illness, details about the effects of the illness, and treatments for the illness. If a family member or close friend is **terminally ill** (having an incurable disease that will result in death), adults can prepare the child for the upcoming death with simple, truthful statements. For example, a caregiver may say, "You know Grandma is very sick. The nurses and doctors are trying to help, but Grandma is getting sicker. She may soon die." Adults should not lie about a terminally ill person's **prognosis** (the predicted outcome of a disease or condition). In some cases, a child may be terminally ill. How a child perceives their condition greatly depends on the child's age. What and how much information a family tells a terminally ill child should depend on how much the sick child wants or needs to understand about their illness.

When death occurs, adults can explain at the child's level what has happened. They can answer questions honestly and say what they believe to be true about death. Children become worried if they feel adults are keeping facts from them or avoiding their questions. When explaining, adults can ensure that children do not expect the deceased person (or pet) to return. Instead of telling a child that the deceased person is sleeping, an adult may say, "Uncle Bill is dead. This means he does not move or breathe anymore." Adults can assure children that they did not cause the death. For a long time after the death, caregivers and other adults who work with children can be prepared to answer questions and repeat facts. At first, for example, a child may seem to understand the death. A week later, however, the child may again ask about the death.

Special challenges occur when explaining suicide to children. Suicides are difficult for all survivors to understand. Older children and teens will need some special guidance. In these situations, adults should give children clear facts about the suicide, but not overexplain. They can recall the good traits of the person, assure children the suicide was not their fault, and emphasize that everyone has choices.

Suicide is the second leading cause of death for children, adolescents, and young adults ages 15 to 24 years old. A teenager's suicide attempt may be associated with feelings of stress, self-doubt, pressure to succeed, financial uncertainty, disappointment, and loss. For some teens, suicide appears to be a solution to their problems.

FOCUS ON MENTAL HEALTH

As children begin to understand death, they may become afraid that an adult or caregiver will die. Caregivers can reassure their children they will probably live a long time. They should never promise children they will not die. If a caregiver does die after such a promise, the child might feel betrayed and develop a lack of trust in others. Reassuring young children will help them refocus on life around them rather than focusing on possible death. Keeping promises also helps develop trust in others.

Teenagers can talk to someone about their feelings and stresses in their life or get professional help with a qualified mental health professional.

Helping Children and Adolescents Cope with Grief

Once children understand and react to death, caregivers and other adults can help children cope. When it comes to death, children, like adults, experience *stages of grief*. The **stages of grief**, outlined in **Figure 22.7**, are feelings or mind-sets that most people experience when **mourning** (feeling sad about a loss). Although these grieving stages are universal, they do not always occur in order. Sometimes stages may be revisited or skipped.

Caregivers can help children and teens cope with grief by supporting children at home. Some ways they can help include

- watching for signs of grief and offering support (**Figure 22.8**)
- providing opportunities for close contact with other loved ones
- seeing teaching opportunities when the child or teen expresses inappropriate reactions to grief
- setting an example by not trying to mask sadness
- allowing children and teens to talk about death and grieve in their own developmental ways, such as through pretend play or by carrying photos of a loved one

Figure 22.8 **Signs of Grief in Children**

Response	Sign
Verbal	• Talking or not talking about the loss • Asking or not asking questions about the loss • Wanting or not wanting to hear about what happened • Having dreams about the person or pet who died • Trying to get attention from others • Wishing to see the person or pet again • Voicing worries about other people or pets becoming sick or injured
Emotional	• Crying • Overreacting to insignificant situations with tears or anger • Not focusing on tasks • Being irritable • Wanting to be near adults and close friends • Being noncompliant about "rules" and requests
Physical	• Experiencing changes in appetite • Experiencing changes in sleeping habits • Having urine and bowel accidents • Having stomachaches or headaches • Regressing in behaviors • Feeling tired

Goodheart-Willcox Publisher

Figure 22.7 **Stages of Grief**

Stage	Description
Shock and denial	This stage protects the child from immediately experiencing the entire intensity of the loss. It should never be confused with "not caring."
Anger	The child feels angry about the loss. This anger may extend to others who were involved with the person, such as doctors.
Bargaining	The child thinks about what "could have been done" to prevent the loss. Unless the child gets past the "if only" and lives in the present, they may always carry intense feelings of guilt.
Depression	The child now feels the entire intensity of the loss. Physical symptoms often appear.
Acceptance	The child comes to terms with the loss and integrates the loss into their other life experiences. The child recognizes the loss as the new reality.

Goodheart-Willcox Publisher

Children and teens best cope with grief when caregivers and other adults (such as teachers) collaborate to help them. Caregivers should inform teachers and others who work with the child about the tragedy. Teachers and other adults can be understanding with the child. Teachers should maintain normal routines but can also give the child room to grieve and express their feelings. They can also use inappropriate reactions to grief as opportunities to teach children about expressing emotions. Beliefs about death should be left for caregivers to explain. While teachers cannot share in the child's grief, they can demonstrate and encourage empathy and reduce other stressors in the child's life.

Resilience in Children and Adolescents

All children and teens will cope with some challenges in their lives. How they react often depends on their *resilience* (their abilities to recover from stressful situations). **Resilient children** are children who adapt well, even when faced with **adversity** (risks and stress) in their lives. These children can adapt and survive even in difficult circumstances. Resilient children are autonomous, flexible, resourceful, and caring and can communicate their needs to others. Studies have shown that resilience at 10 years of age predicts how well people will adapt to life's circumstances by 40 years of age.

Resilience is a result of a person's inner qualities, as well as what **buffers** (protections or support systems) they have, such as family or community supports (**Figure 22.9**). For example, if family stress is toxic, a child or teen might rely on a community buffer or on other relatives. If a child's community is violent, the child or teen may be buffered by a protective family member.

Resilience is important for every child. Adults cannot correct or undo every mistake (such as replace a lost toy or ask a teacher for a retake of a test). They cannot shield children from all problems (such as financial problems or divorce). Adults also cannot remove all the obstacles children face (such as homework and social challenges). Adults can, however, help children develop resilience and protect children while encouraging them to cope with the stressors in their lives.

Figure 22.9 ## Qualities of Resilient Children

Inner Qualities of Resilient Children
- Easy temperaments
- Affectionate and engaging personalities
- Vigorous
- Assertive
- Autonomous
- Healthy self-concept
- Able to distance themselves from their problems
- Believe they can beat the odds
- Communicate easily

Family or Community Buffers
- A trusting, secure, and ongoing relationship based on unconditional love from at least one person. (This person might be a caregiver, other relative, child care provider or teacher, or youth leader.)
- Resilience modeled by someone else.
- External supports given by teachers, youth leaders, or friends who validate and reinforce the inner qualities, competencies, and values of the child.
- Outside interests (extracurricular activities or youth groups) that relieve stress or remove the child from a stressful setting.

Goodheart-Willcox Publisher

SeventyFour/iStock via Getty Images Plus

Overprotecting or over-parenting children does not aid resilience. To help children develop resilience, adults can ensure children

- develop secure attachments
- develop social skills needed to make friends
- see situations from different perspectives and deal with problems they can change
- be autonomous
- be confident in their abilities
- trust that adults will handle the "big problems" (finances, addiction, divorce) and will protect them

If children are not resilient, they may benefit from professional help. Professional help might be a counselor or therapist, a school counselor, or one of many other resources for children who struggle to cope with challenges.

22.1-3 Resources for Children and Adolescents in Crises

Many resources are available to help children and teens in crises (**Figure 22.10**). Some of these resources directly assist children and their families. Others provide information, registries, and referrals to local support groups or counselors.

Available resources include departments and agencies of federal, state, or local governments. Other resources are national private agencies funded by membership dues and contributions. Still other resources are the work of religious groups, hospitals and medical associations, mental health centers, and crises intervention centers.

Figure 22.10 **Resources for Children in Crises**

Resource	Description
Supplemental Nutritional Assistant Program (SNAP)	Provides financial support to help families purchase foods
Special Supplemental Program for Women, Infants, and Children (WIC)	Provides food assistance for infants, children four years of age or younger, and pregnant women
National School Lunch Program (NSLP)	Provides nutritious lunches to children in schools (at a reduced price or free for qualifying students)
Public Housing Program	Provides affordable housing for families experiencing financial strain
Child Protective Services	Handles reports of child neglect or abuse and investigates reports of unsafe environments
Early Intervention	Provides services for families with children under three years of age who have special needs
Medicaid and Children's Health Insurance Program (CHIP)	Provides health insurance coverage for children from families experiencing financial strain
Save the Children	In the event of a disaster, provides food, medical attention, and education to children
United Nations Children Fund (UNICEF)	Provides education, health care, safe environments, food, and emergency relief for children in crises
Child Crisis Centers and Crisis Nurseries	Provide shelter, food, and care for children in crisis situations
Crisis Mental Health Services	Provide help for children experiencing mental-health emergencies

Goodheart-Willcox Publisher

Law enforcement agencies, legal associations, counseling services, schools, and civic or volunteer organizations are all resources as well (**Figure 22.11**).

Many resources for children and teens in crises have online bookstores for purchasing books and other materials designed to aid children and families facing different challenges. When searching for items on a specific topic of interest, an online bookstore might also offer resources for parents, children, or families. Other books and materials can be located through online publishers and libraries. Conducting an internet search and visiting the local library are other ways to find good resources for helping children in crises.

Overcoming Trauma

A trauma is a tragic, violent, and/or dangerous event that overwhelms a child's or teen's ability to cope. No matter how hard adults work to keep children safe, ACEs can still occur. ACEs initiate strong emotions and physical reactions that can persist long after the event. Children and teens may feel terror, helplessness, or fear as well as physiological reactions, such as heart pounding,

vomiting, or loss of bowel or bladder control. Sometimes the danger comes from outside of the family (a natural disaster, car accident, school shooting, or community violence) or from within the family (domestic violence, physical or sexual abuse, or the unexpected death of a loved one). Below you will learn more about the methods that help promote resilience in children and teens who have experienced ACEs.

Counseling and Therapeutic Services

Sometimes adults and children need to seek help from mental health professionals after traumatic events. There are many types of therapy available to families and children and it does not necessarily need to be a traumatic event like a hurricane, death, or assault. Other events impacting a family can include drug or alcohol abuse, eating disorders, and temporary foster care situations due to arrests, prison sentences, or even hospitalizations. Some of the counseling and therapeutic services available include pharmacotherapy, cognitive-behavioral therapy, family therapy, trauma-focused therapy and play therapy.

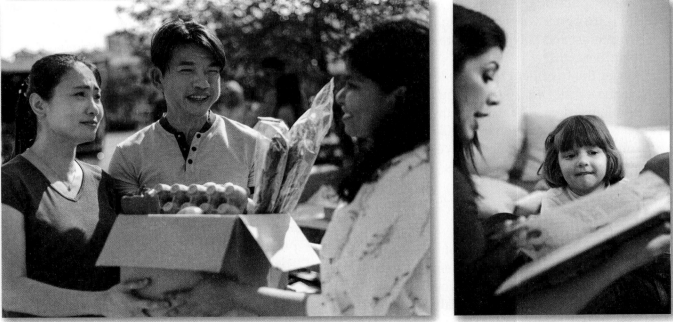

gahsoon/E+ via Getty Images

iStock.com/diego_cervo

Figure 22.11 There are many types of volunteer organizations that serve families in crises, such as organizations that provide food for families in need or child care centers that provide safe places for children in danger. *What volunteer organizations serve families in crises in your community?*

Pharmacotherapy

Pharmacotherapy is the treatment of a disorder or disease with medication. Many times, in the treatment for addiction, medications are used to reduce the intensity of withdrawal symptoms and reduce the likelihood of relapse. Pharmacotherapy also includes mood-stabilizing medications that treat conditions such as depression and anxiety. The length of time a person takes the medication depends upon the severity of the illness and the number of previous illnesses, but also the life situation of the person taking the medication.

Cognitive Behavioral Therapy

Cognitive behavioral therapy (CBT) is a form of talk therapy that can be used with kids, teens, and adults. CBT is based on the idea that how we think, feel, and act are all closely related. These treatments are used for depression, anxiety disorders, alcohol and drug abuse, marital problems, eating disorders, and severe illness. CBT is based on several principles:

- Psychological problems are based in part on faulty or unhelpful ways of thinking.
- Psychological problems are based on learned patterns of unhelpful behavior.
- People suffering from psychological problems can learn better ways of coping, relieving symptoms, and becoming more effective in their lives.

Part of the treatment involves learning to recognize one's distortions in thinking that are creating problems, then reevaluating them in light of reality. Using problem-solving skills to cope with difficult situations will help develop a greater sense of confidence in the child's or teen's own abilities.

Family Therapy

Family therapy is a type of psychological counseling that can help family members improve communication and resolve conflicts. It is usually provided by a psychologist, clinical social worker, or licensed therapist. Family therapy is often short term and includes all family members or just those able or willing to participate. These therapy sessions can teach skills to deepen family connections and get through stressful times, even after the family is finished with the therapy sessions. Family therapy can be used for marital or financial problems, conflict between parents and children, or the impact of substance abuse or mental illness on the entire family. Family therapy can be useful in any family situation that causes stress, grief, anger, or conflict. During family therapy participants will examine their family's ability to solve problems and express thoughts and emotions in a productive manner. They will explore family roles, rules, and behavior patterns to identify issues that contribute to conflict and discover ways to work through the issues. They will also identify family strengths and weaknesses.

Trauma-Focused Therapy

Trauma-focused therapy is a type of TIC that recognizes and emphasizes understanding how the traumatic experience impacts a child's or teen's mental, behavioral, emotional, and physical well-being. The purpose of this type of therapy is to offer skills and strategies to assist children in better understanding, coping with and processing ACEs, with the end goal of enabling the child to create a healthier and more adaptive meaning of the experience that took place in their life. Trauma-focused therapy can be beneficial to youth who have experienced a traumatic event. The child learns more about what they are experiencing, how to address the concern, and develops healthier ways of coping. Trauma-focused therapy focuses on:

- learning about the trauma
- re-establishing safety
- identifying triggers
- developing healthy coping skills
- decreasing the traumatic stress symptoms, and
- practicing trauma processing or integration

There are a large variety of different activities and strategies that are used within the treatment process. These activities may look different based on age, the nature of the trauma, setting, or location.

Play Therapy

Play therapy is a psychotherapeutic approach used to help children ages three to twelve explore their lives and freely express repressed thoughts and emotions through play. Therapeutic play will take place in a safe, comfortable playroom, where very few rules or limits are imposed on the child, encouraging free expression and allowing the therapist to observe the child's choices, decisions, and play style. The goal is to help children learn to express themselves in healthier ways, become more respectful and empathetic, and discover new and more positive ways to solve problems. Many times, play therapy is used to help children with social or emotional deficits learn to communicate better, change their behavior, develop problem-solving skills, and relate to others in positive ways. It is appropriate for children undergoing or witnessing stressful event in their lives, such as a serious illness or hospitalization, domestic violence, abuse, trauma, family crisis, or an upsetting change in their environment.

Lesson 22.1 Review and Assessment

1. Which is the least helpful way caregivers can help a child cope with a move? (22.1.1)
   A. Explaining why they are pleased about the move
   B. Involving the child in the moving process
   C. Reading the child books about other children who have moved
   D. Planning the move at the beginning of the school year

2. **True or False.** Family stress and lack of quality care may hinder infant attachments and social-emotional development. (22.1.1)

3. A typical reaction of a preschooler who has been exposed to violence or disaster is _____. (22.1.1)
   A. regressing in behaviors
   B. clinging to a caregiver
   C. having trouble sleeping
   D. whimpering

4. A child feels the entire intensity of the loss of a loved one during which stage of grief? (22.1.2)
   A. Bargaining
   B. Depression
   C. Anger
   D. Shock and denial

5. Which resource provides services for families with children under three years of age who have special needs? (22.1.3)
   A. Early Intervention
   B. Save the Children
   C. Child Protective Services
   D. Medicaid

6. The idea that psychological problems are based on learned patterns of unhelpful behavior is a principle of _____ therapy. (22.1.3)
   A. play
   B. family
   C. cognitive behavioral
   D. trauma-focused

Lesson 22.2

Protecting Children and Adolescents from Neglect and Abuse

Key Terms

bullying

child abuse

child neglect

child protection agencies

cyberbullying

educational neglect

emotional abuse

emotional neglect

home visitation

mandated reporters

medical neglect

moral neglect

peer abuse

physical abuse

physical neglect

sexual abuse

Shaken Baby Syndrome (SBS)

sibling abuse

six core strengths

social abuse

verbal abuse

Learning Outcomes

After studying this lesson, you will be able to

22.2-1 **identify** and **explain** the types and causes of child neglect and abuse.

22.2-2 **describe** the effects of child neglect and abuse on children's physical, intellectual, and social-emotional development.

22.2-3 **list** and **describe** the types of sibling and peer abuse.

22.2-4 **summarize** how neglect and abuse are recognized and reported.

22.2-5 **explain** how cases of neglect and abuse are treated as well as strategies for prevention.

Reading and Notetaking Activity

Write all of this lesson's key terms on a piece of paper, and before reading, record what you think each term means. As you read, update or correct definitions according to the lesson. Finally, highlight any definitions that changed significantly while reading. Make flashcards for these terms.

Introduction

Tragically, some children face the challenges of neglect and abuse. Neglect and abuse, whether inflicted by a caregiver, other adult, or children's siblings or peers, have devastating physical, intellectual, and social-emotional effects on children. Neglect and abuse are not challenges children should expect or for which they should need to learn protective coping skills. Rather, neglect and abuse should be reported so children can be protected from all of these criminal behaviors. In facing these challenges, adults should know how to identify and report all cases of neglect and abuse. They should also take part in measures designed to prevent these happenings in society.

22.2-1 Child Neglect and Abuse

Neglect and abuse are very serious problems that threaten children's health and welfare. **Child neglect** is the failure of an adult to provide for a child's basic needs. While states' legal definitions of neglect vary, neglect usually involves adults' failures to meet needs for food, clothing, shelter, hygiene, medical attention, or supervision. In contrast to neglect, **child abuse** refers to an intentional act committed by an adult that harms or threatens to harm a child's well-being.

Most cases of neglect and abuse occur in the home and are **perpetrated** (done) by a person the child knows and trusts. The vast majority of cases involve at least one caregiver although some cases involve other relatives or adults close to the family. Very few cases involve adults working in child care education programs or in foster care settings and even fewer cases involve strangers.

About one-fourth of all abuse cases involve more than one type of neglect or abuse. Many times, the reason abuse occurs is unknown although various factors (called *risk factors*) may contribute to incidences of neglect and abuse. The effects of neglect and abuse are harmful to children's physical, intellectual, and social-emotional development. People who work in **child protection agencies** (organizations that work to prevent and rescue children from neglect and abuse) try to protect children from further neglect or abuse (**Figure 22.12**).

Types of Child Neglect and Abuse

Child neglect and abuse can take many forms. Not all neglect and abuse are physical in nature. Children have many needs, including physical needs, intellectual needs, and social-emotional needs. The neglect of any of these needs can cause harm to a child.

Child neglect refers to harm or endangerment of a child caused by an adult's failure to do something legally expected of them. There are several types of neglect, which include the following:

- **Physical neglect** refers to endangering a child's health or safety by failing to provide basic needs (such as food, clothing, and shelter) and supervision. Physical neglect also refers to situations in which caregivers troubled mental states (whether due to substance abuse or illness) make them unaware of their children's lack of basic necessities.

Figure 22.12 Children who have experienced neglect or abuse need comfort and protection from further neglect or abuse. *Why is it important that children's traumatic experiences not be repeated?*

Imagesbybarbara/E+ via Getty Images

- **Educational neglect** is the failure to conform to state legal requirements regarding school attendance. In educational neglect, children do not experience sufficient learning. The standards for meeting children's educational needs are determined by the state and new standards are frequently implemented.
- **Medical neglect** is the harm or endangerment of a child caused by failure to seek treatment for health problems or accidents. Medical neglect can lead to serious health problems and even death.

- **Moral neglect** is the failure to teach a child right from wrong in terms of general social expectations. For example, a child who has been morally neglected might believe or have been taught that stealing is not wrong.
- **Emotional neglect** is the failure to meet a child's social-emotional needs at each stage of development. It may involve inadequate care and attention or violence and drug use in the home.

Investigate Special Topics

Domestic Violence

Abuse within the family, even if not directed at a child, can have serious negative effects on children's development. One type of abuse that may occur in families is *domestic violence* (also known as *intimate partner violence*). Domestic violence is *any* type of physical, sexual, emotional, or verbal abuse directed at a partner (such as a current or former spouse or nonmarried partner).

Domestic violence can take many forms. Some signs of domestic violence include
- physical injuries (such as bone fractures, cuts, or bruises) or the wearing of excessive clothing to hide injuries
- social-emotional disturbances, such as anxiety attacks and sleeping problems
- fear of a partner or over eagerness to please a partner
- lack of trust in others, resulting in poor relationships
- low self-esteem, as indicated by self-hate, self-blame, and sensitivity to rejection
- workplace problems, such as frequent absences, heated phone calls or e-mails, isolation, and crying
- limited access to social interactions, finances, and transportation

Domestic violence has serious consequences on children and on the family. Over ten million children witness domestic violence each year, and 30 to 60 percent of children from violent homes experience child neglect and abuse. Children who witness domestic violence are more likely to abuse others, have academic problems, display anxiety and depression, and resort to substance abuse and other risky behaviors.

Speaking Activity

Domestic violence, like most abuse, is a complex cycle that is difficult to escape. In small groups, visit the website of The National Domestic Violence Hotline. Record the website's definition of *abuse* and research tips for recognizing signs of domestic violence and for escaping from an abusive situation. Afterward, arrange your findings into a short oral presentation for the class.

Photo: Tom Wang/Shutterstock.com

While neglect may be unintentional in nature, child abuse involves an intentional act that harms or threatens to harm a child. As with neglect, there are many types of child abuse. The types of child abuse include the following:

- **Physical abuse** is any intentional physical act that results in pain, injuries, or both, to a child. Physical abuse may involve violence or even physical punishment in the name of *discipline*.
- **Sexual abuse** is *any* act of a sexual nature that involves an adult and a child. Whether a child understands or does not resist a sexual act is irrelevant. Some states define *sexual abuse* as any act of a sexual nature between a child and someone who is at least five years older than the child. **Figure 22.13** explains some of the myths and realities related to child sexual abuse.
- **Emotional abuse** is the abuse of power through devaluing, undermining, and coercing a child. This type of abuse tends to be indirect, but not unconscious. Emotional abuse harms a child's self-esteem.
- **Verbal abuse** is the use of words to control and debase (degrade) a child. It also harms a child's self-esteem.

FOCUS ON MENTAL HEALTH

Even partner abuse can result in mental health problems in children, such as anxiety, depression, addictions, and violence. These problems may last a lifetime. Stopping the cycle of abuse can be difficult for adults. Seeking help and getting out of an abusive relationship requires the person leaving to have a support network they can fall back on. This support network can be family, friends, or organizations that help abused people.

Causes of Child Neglect and Abuse

There is no simple cause-and-effect explanation for why adults neglect or abuse a child. Very different reasons and causes can lead to the same results. For example, neglect may occur when caregivers cannot afford to meet a child's needs or when adults think only about their own needs.

Figure 22.13 Myths and Realities about Child Sexual Abuse

Myth	Reality
Child sexual abuse is rare.	Child sexual abuse occurs often and can take many forms, such as pornography or incest.
The person who abuses is usually an unknown, dangerous person.	In the vast majority of cases, the person who abuses is a known person, such as a relative or friend of the family.
The abuse occurs suddenly, such as when an adult who does not abuse is momentarily out of the room.	The abuse is usually repeated over and over again and may continue for several years.
Child sexual abuse is usually a violent attack.	More often, child sexual abuse happens through subtle "force." The person who abuses may tell the child it is a "new game."
Children often make up stories of sexual abuse.	Children rarely make up stories about sexual abuse. In fact, they are often reluctant to talk about sexual abuse because they fear the person who abused them or feel guilty for being involved.
Children who recant stories of sexual abuse were lying about the first report.	People who abuse may have pressured children to change their stories.

Goodheart-Willcox Publisher

Sometimes neglect occurs when caregivers do not know how to provide proper care for children. In investigating instances of child neglect and abuse, experts have come across several principles that describe some of the causes.

- *Parents who are neglectful and abusive come from all income, intelligence, and education levels.* Generally, adults who are abusive do not exhibit obvious and observable signs of their problems. Caregivers who are abusive may seem nice, quiet, and kind when they are at work or with friends.

- *Risk factors do exist for neglect and abuse.* Experts who study neglect and abuse believe it is important to look at the entire family system for answers (**Figure 22.14**). Although experts cannot weigh the degree of risk for each factor, studies show that alcohol and drug abuse, financial problems, and inadequate housing are the most common risk factors.

Figure 22.14 **Risk Factors for Child Neglect and Abuse**

Type of Risk Factor	Contributing Factors
Societal	• Poverty • Overcrowding • Illegal drug culture • High crime rates • High unemployment rates • Few social services • Unaffordable health care
Family	• Unwanted pregnancy • Single or teen parent • Physical, sexual, or emotional abuse as a child • Emotional neglect as a child • Use of violence to express anger • Lack of self-esteem • Emotional immaturity • Poor coping skills • Alcohol or illegal drug abuse • Marriage problems • Financial stress • Recent stressful events (divorce, recent move, death in family) • Illness (physical or mental health, especially depression) • Lack of parenting skills, including no preparation for the extreme stress of a new baby • Lack of knowledge of child development, leading to unrealistic expectations for the child • Heavy parenting responsibility (multiple births or single children less than 18 months apart in age) • Weak bonding or attachment to a child (often due to child's care in ICU after birth) • Use of physical punishment (also called *corporal punishment*) • Isolation (lack of family or friend support)
Child	• Under five years of age, especially under one year of age • Low birth weight or premature birth • Possession of the traits of a disliked relative • Irritability or frequent crying (sometimes due to colic or postnatal drug withdrawal) • Frequent disobedience or arguing

Goodheart-Willcox Publisher

- *Experts cannot always predict from the risk factors which form the abuse will take.* Experts identify two exceptions to this principle. First, a caregiver who physically abuses a spouse is likely to physically abuse a child. Second, a person who has a history of sexual abuse is more likely to sexually abuse others.
- *Abuse is a complex, interactive process.* Some adults may abuse only one child in the family or may abuse a child only during times of high parental stress. An unplanned pregnancy might lead to more financial stress, causing a woman not to get prenatal care. The baby may be born at a low birth weight and have feeding problems that cause the child to cry for hours at a time. The caregiver, who already has problems in coping, abuses the infant "to stop the crying." The fact that abuse is complex and interactive does *not* mean the child is to blame for the abuse. People who abuse are *always* responsible for their own actions.

22.2-2 Effects of Child Neglect and Abuse

Most children who experience neglect and abuse are left with deep and long-lasting scars. Neglect and abuse affect every aspect of a child's development. In many cases, the idea that "time heals all wounds" does not apply to those who have been neglected or abused as children. Child neglect and abuse can have serious physical, intellectual, and social-emotional effects.

Effects on Physical Development

Many children who are neglected lack adequate food, clothing, or housing. Poor hygiene and other unsafe living conditions can hinder infants and young children from growing and thriving. Children who are abused may be beaten, bruised, burned, or cut. Their bones and teeth may be broken (**Figure 22.15**). Even without physical marks, they may experience pain from slapping and other physical attacks. Children who are sexually abused may have internal and external injuries, contract STIs, and may become pregnant.

FatCamera/E+ via Getty Images

Figure 22.15 Children who have experienced neglect or abuse may need physical therapy to recover from their injuries. *What health care services in your community offer physical therapy for children?*

Statistics show that the youngest children are the most prone to die from physical neglect and abuse. For example, infants who are shaken in frustration may die as a result of *Shaken Baby Syndrome*. **Shaken Baby Syndrome (SBS)** is a condition in which the "whiplash" shaking motion causes an infant's brain to hit the skull repeatedly. These hits cause the eye retina to bleed and veins in the brain to break, filling the area around the brain with blood resulting in swelling. Swelling damages brain cells and puts pressure on the brain stem, which controls breathing and heartbeat. As a result, these babies may develop cerebral palsy, paralysis, brain seizures, blindness, deafness, and learning and behavioral problems. Approximately 25 percent of children with SBS will die from their injuries.

Effects on Intellectual Development

Child neglect and abuse can stunt and hinder children's intellectual development. Abuse may cause brain injuries, which make it harder for children to learn. Educational neglect and an inability to concentrate during learning tasks due to abuse may cause children to lag behind in learning and in school. Lack of brain stimulation during children's windows of opportunity can cause them not to learn vital skills. Studies indicate that children who are abused are more likely to have some type of language or learning problem and have difficulty in school.

Effects on Social-Emotional Development

The social-emotional effects of child neglect and abuse are often referred to as *invisible,* but these effects can be clearly seen in children's behaviors. Child neglect and abuse can cause children to lack self-esteem; have feelings of anger, anxiety, shame, and guilt; and experience depression. Children who are neglected or abused are more likely to have social-emotional problems.

In one study, Dr. Bruce Perry, a pediatric psychiatrist at the Child Trauma Academy in Houston, Texas, found that children develop **six core strengths**, building blocks that make up children's foundation for future health, productivity, and happiness. These core strengths are attachment, self-regulation, affiliation, awareness (of how people are alike and different), tolerance, and respect. Children need nurturing and supportive caregivers to develop these core strengths. Children who are neglected and abused often need extensive treatment to overcome their past or ongoing traumas and develop these core strengths.

22.2-3 Sibling and Peer Abuse

In addition to abuse at the hands of adults, children can also experience abuse from siblings and peers. **Sibling abuse** is physical, verbal, emotional, or sexual abuse of one sibling by another. Sibling abuse happens to over one-third of all children, and the incidence is rising. It is more common than child abuse by adults. This form of abuse is much more than squabbles between siblings. The abuse takes several forms. Sibling abuse can range from pushing, shoving, and hitting to violent behavior, such as using weapons. Abuse often takes the form of stealing or breaking the sibling's possessions. *Incest* (sexual acts between closely related individuals) is a common form of sibling abuse. Adults often do not see sibling abuse for what it is.

Peer abuse is some form of abuse (physical, verbal, social, or emotional) directed at a child or teen by someone in the same peer group. Based on self-reports, the majority of school-age children have both abused peers and been abused by peers. Peer abuse can have negative physical and social-emotional effects on children and can be deadly.

Bullying, the most common form of peer abuse, involves inflicting physical, verbal, and emotional abuse on another person. Some examples of actions that are considered physical bullying or emotional bullying are listed in **Figure 22.16**. It also involves **social abuse**, which is restricting or intentionally harming a person's relationships with others. Bullying may include **cyberbullying**, which involves bullying through a digital medium. Peer abuse may also include sexual abuse in the form of sexual acts or *sexting* (sending photographs of a sexual nature and explicit sexual messages through digital devices).

Figure 22.16 Types of Bullying

Bullying	Examples
Physical	• Hitting or punching • Pushing or shoving • Kicking • Biting • Choking • Physical intimidation
Emotional	• Teasing or mocking • Gossiping or spreading rumors • Name-calling or embarrassing • Threatening • Excluding • Stealing

Goodheart-Willcox Publisher

Rawpixel.com/Shutterstock.com

Some children may be exposed to peer abuse in the form of *gang violence,* which involves groups of people who use their power over others. Gang violence is more often seen in teen groups but may be seen in the later school-age years. Gangs may target rival gang members and may also hurt and kill innocent bystanders.

Peer abuse often occurs in schools, where it may be known as *school violence* (violence that occurs on school property or at a school event). Often, school violence is done out of revenge, and many are hurt or killed who were not in any way connected with the perpetrator. Although school violence is a very high-profile form of peer abuse, most deaths among school-age children and teens are *not* due to school violence. The number of incidences of school violence is increasing, however.

22.2-4 Recognizing and Reporting Neglect and Abuse

Untold numbers of children experience neglect and abuse by caregivers, friends, relatives, child care and education teachers and other staff members, siblings, and peers. Statistics never tell the whole story. Many cases of neglect or abuse are never reported. Some reported cases are not investigated due to heavy caseloads of social workers. Still other cases are never confirmed or proven due to lack of evidence or legal definitions of neglect and abuse as given in a state's laws. Some experts believe these legal definitions should be expanded to include more cases.

To end neglect and abuse, people must recognize and report it. Knowing what behaviors are neglectful or abusive is the first step. Adults should be alert to signs that neglect and abuse may be occurring. Some common signs of child neglect and abuse are listed in **Figure 22.17**. Adults can look for signs of sibling or peer abuse by keeping the lines of communication open with their children and taking note of any physical injuries or disturbed behaviors.

Figure 22.17 Signs of Child Neglect and Abuse

Child Neglect

Type of Neglect	Signs
Physical and medical	• Is malnourished • Fails to receive needed health care (unless caregiver has objection, such as for religious reasons) • Fails to receive proper hygiene (is not washed or bathed; has poor oral hygiene; has skin, nails, and hair that are not groomed) • Has insufficient clothing or clothing that is dirty, tattered, or inappropriate for the weather • Lives in filthy conditions or inadequate shelter
Moral and educational	• Lacks moral training • Lacks constructive discipline • Does not receive positive examples from adults • Does not have adequate supervision • Is left alone for hours • Fails to attend school regularly because caregivers do not make certain their children attend school • Fails to receive adult stimulation toward learning or education suited to their ability • Is not allowed to take part in wholesome recreational activities
Emotional	• Experiences constant friction in the home • Is denied normal experiences that produce feelings of being wanted, loved, and protected • Is rejected through indifference • Is overly rejected, such as through abandonment

Goodheart-Willcox Publisher
(Continued)

Figure 21.17 Signs of Child Neglect and Abuse (Continued)

Child Abuse

Type of Abuse	Signs
Physical	• Seems fearful or quiet around caregivers, but has no close feeling for them • Is wary of physical contact initiated by an adult • Has little or no reaction to pain and seems much less afraid than most children the same age • Has unexplained injuries or shows evidence of repeated injuries, such as having bruises in various stages of healing or repeated fractures • Is dressed inappropriately (such being dressed in pajamas after being injured on a "bicycle" or being dressed in a turtleneck in the summer to cover bruises) • Shows a history of past injuries to long bones • Has injuries not reported on previous health records • Has been taken by caregivers to many hospitals and doctors without appropriate explanation • Has caregivers who refuse further diagnostic studies of their child's injuries • Has caregivers who show detachment or see the child as bad or "different" during medical treatment • Has caregivers who give too many minute details about the cause of injury • Tries to protect caregivers when they are questioned about the child's injuries
Verbal and emotional	• Lacks self-esteem • Is either too quiet and polite or uses harsh and improper language when dealing with others, especially those who are smaller or younger • Expresses long-term feelings of damage and isolation
Sexual	• Has extreme and sudden changes in behavior, such as loss of appetite or sudden drop in grades • Has nightmares and other sleep problems • Regresses to previous behaviors, such as renewed thumb sucking • Has torn or stained underwear • Has infections (with symptoms like bleeding or other discharges and itching) or swollen genitals • Fears a person or shows an intense dislike of being left alone with that person • Has an STI or is pregnant • Has unusual interest in or knowledge of sexual matters for their age

When adults suspect and recognize signs of neglect or abuse, they should immediately report this to an agency or authority that can help. Some of these agencies include the local or state departments of human services. For child abuse, adults can also call hotlines to report suspected abuse. Some professionals who work with children are **mandated reporters**, meaning they are legally bound to report any known or suspected cases of neglect or abuse. Mandated reporters include health care workers, teachers, counselors, social service workers, and child care providers. In many states, mandated reporters can be charged with a criminal offense if they fail to report known or suspected cases of neglect or abuse. For cases of peer abuse, adults can report to a principal or school social worker, and in extreme cases, to the state justice system.

Cases of neglect and abuse are handled through the appropriate state agency within the state government. A social service caseworker is assigned a reported case. They investigate by making a visit to the home and talking to all family members and by interviewing others with whom the child has contact. A decision is made within the state agency on whether there is or is not enough evidence to pursue the case. If the case is confirmed, steps will be taken to handle the perpetrator and treat the child. In most cases, the name and information of the person initially reporting the case remains confidential. Even if the investigation does not conclude that neglect or abuse is occurring, the reporter is protected unless they willfully reported just to get another adult in trouble.

22.2-5 Treating Cases of Neglect and Abuse

Documented cases of neglect and abuse will be dealt with by the proper authorities. In child neglect or abuse, the case will be brought before the courts if there is enough evidence. In working with adults, courts and caseworkers will consider the severity of the neglect or abuse, the adult's relationship to the child, and any past history of neglectful or abusive behaviors. Several actions may be taken, including the following:

- Children may be returned to their caregivers with the requirement that the adults have therapy. This therapy could include treatment for mental illness or substance abuse, individual or group counseling, or education for adults who are neglectful and abusive. The reason behind these treatments is to deter the adult from choosing further neglectful or abusive actions.
- Children may be put into the foster care system until the caregivers fulfill therapy and other requirements of the courts (**Figure 22.18**).
- Adults may be restricted from seeing the child or they may have their parental rights **rescinded** (ree-SIND-ed), or taken away.
- Adults may be convicted of a crime or they may be ordered to receive therapy.

When a case of neglect or abuse is confirmed, children can begin to receive the help and treatment they need.

Figure 22.18 Foster care provides a temporary home and family life for children who need shelter after a case of neglect or abuse. *What qualities do you think foster adults need to have?*

SDI Productions/E+ via Getty Images

Physical treatment for the child experiencing neglect or abuse is the first priority. As a doctor examines and treats the child, they will take a history (from the child, an older sibling, or adult) and document the examination. Records will include the doctor's observations, lab reports, and photographs or drawings (**Figure 22.19**).

Caseworkers or advocates from a child abuse prevention agency may also be involved in helping the child. These professionals make decisions about the child's welfare and advocate on their behalf. As caseworkers make decisions about the child, they keep the following questions in mind:

- What is the relationship of the child to the person who abused them?
- What risks are present for further abuse?
- What role, if any, should the courts have in this case?
- Should the child remain with the family?
- What support services could help both the child and family?

The services recommended will depend on the particulars of the case and the age of the child. Foster care, residential treatment facilities, child advocacy centers, counseling, Head Start programs, group therapy, play therapy, family intervention therapy, and individual therapy are examples of support services that are often used.

In cases of peer abuse, the situation may be handled by a school counselor or principal, or in severe cases, by a court. The school may take measures to discipline people who abuse others and protect people who have been abused. Both will likely receive therapy.

Preventing Neglect and Abuse

Neglect and abuse have many causes. As such, these complex problems do not have a single, quick solution. Work must be done on many fronts to put an end to them. Preventing neglect and abuse will take the efforts of individuals, families, communities, and society at large. Each person's involvement counts in the fight against these crimes.

Promoting Public Awareness

The future of any society depends on the health and well-being of the next generation. Awareness of a problem is the first step in prevention. Neglect and abuse can be prevented by encouraging *public*

Figure 22.19 Treating children's physical injuries is a top priority after a case of neglect or abuse. *Why is physical health a top priority for children?*

awareness, which is people's knowledge about a problem and what constitutes it. Public awareness can help prevent neglect and abuse when people

- are made to understand what behaviors are neglectful or abusive
- learn more about how certain problems threaten children and affect families' lives
- are informed about how the public can help fight against these crimes
- are made aware of the legal consequences of neglect and abuse
- understand that reporting suspected cases of neglect and abuse, although very important, is intervention, not prevention
- understand that prevention keeps children safe and healthy and helps avoid spending billions of dollars each year on intervention services

Many organizations are leading the way to increase public awareness about neglect and abuse. These organizations provide a variety of information on prevention and support services. Some of these agencies host websites at which people can learn more about neglect and abuse.

Improving the Social Climate

Neglect and abuse are more likely to occur in a society where people feel undervalued, financial problems abound, and violence is condoned. To effectively prevent abuse, problems that contribute to a negative social climate must be addressed. Adults and organizations can help change the social climate that causes abuse by

- rejecting violence and aggression
- promoting better economic security for families
- reducing the numbers of women who do not receive adequate prenatal care
- educating adults and other caregivers about child development
- providing high-quality child care facilities, including crisis child care programs that provide **respite** (rest) for caregivers through child care
- collaborating with service providers who support families
- increasing the emphasis on respecting children, their needs, and their rights

Focus on Careers

Recreational Therapist

Recreational therapists are mental health or physical therapists who use recreational activities (such as arts and crafts, play, drama, sports, games, or music) to improve people's physical or social-emotional well-being. They work with a variety of people, including people with mental health disorders, people with physical disabilities, and people recovering from traumatic events.

Career cluster: Human services.

Education: Educational requirements include a bachelor's degree in recreational therapy or a related field such as mental health. Many employers expect recreational therapists to be state certified.

Job outlook: Future employment opportunities for recreational therapists are expected to grow as fast as the average for all occupations.

To learn more about a career as a recreational therapist, visit the United States Department of Labor's *Occupational Outlook Handbook* website. You will also be able to compare the job responsibilities, educational requirements, job outlook, and average pay of recreational therapists with similar occupations.

Photo: wavebreakmedia/ Shutterstock.com

Being active in groups that promote these changes can help prevent abuse. Making elected officials aware of needed changes is important, too. Schools and communities are establishing codes of behavior that prohibit peer abuse. Setting clear behavioral expectations about violence and using a framework focused on prevention and academic success can create a positive social climate in schools.

Providing Professional Support

Doctors and other professionals who come into contact with families need to be aware of risk factors that lead to neglect or abuse. They should note any risk factors they observe and connect high-risk families to the appropriate social programs.

Doctors can provide professional support by talking with caregivers and assessing a situation during a prenatal visit, well-child checkup, or medical visit. During a prenatal visit, a doctor might ask about how the pregnancy affects others in the family. If the family is facing problems, the doctor could make referrals for the family to seek other needed support services and social programs. During well-child checkups, doctors can talk with caregivers about child development. They can answer questions and offer advice about expected behaviors and issues, such as toilet learning, teething, crying, and sleep or eating problems. Understanding child development can help people form more realistic expectations of their children. Appropriate expectations for children can reduce frustration and prevent some abusive outbursts. During each medical visit, doctors can assess a child's home life by asking simple questions, such as the following:

- What is it like for you taking care of your child?
- Do you get time for yourself?
- Do you get any help with your children from family or friends?
- How do you deal with your child's behavior problems?

It is not enough for professional support individuals and organizations just to assess, however. Support services must be available in the community. One type of support program is *home visitation*. In **home visitation**, a professional comes to the home to monitor the health of the caregiver and infant, to provide one-on-one parenting education, and to suggest other helpful community programs caregivers can access. Additionally, some hospitals and other agencies provide support services for new caregivers and respite child care for caregivers. Schools may also provide professional support by employing social workers who can talk with children and their families about any source of abuse.

Educating Adults

Adults can benefit from learning more about children and their care. This education may include life-skills training for children, teens, and young adults and education in child development and parenting. Learning more about healthy relationships, communication, stress and anger management, and coping skills will also help people prepare themselves to work with or care for children.

In addition, caregivers can also benefit from learning parenting techniques from parent-education programs, such as

- Parent Effectiveness Training (PET)
- Nurturing Parent Programs® (NPPs)
- Systematic Training for Effective Parenting (STEP)

In peer-abuse situations, adults should be educated about how to notice and follow up about instances in which children are being abused. **Figure 22.20** lists some principles adults should follow when dealing with these situations. Many schools are also developing programs to educate adults about lessening peer violence and its effects.

Figure 22.20 Preventing Children from Becoming Victims of Sibling or Peer Abuse

- Listen to the child and support their problem.
- Document ongoing abuse and seek adult help in the setting in which it occurs.
- Help the child learn the best strategies for dealing with abuse of other children. This does not include ignoring the people who abuse, walking away, or fighting. Teach the child self-assertive techniques and where to go for help.
- Help the child know how to make friends and be self-confident. People who abuse often target other children with low self-confidence or those who irritate others. Although abuse by another is never right, every child needs to learn social skills that lessen the chance of abuse.
- Teach the child to not send or post anything on the Internet that they would not want shared with others.
- Teach the child to never hurt or embarrass anyone.
- Teach the child to share with an adult anything that makes them uncomfortable.
- Contact the appropriate authority to report incidences of bullying.
- Address the emotional bruises of violence inflicted by another child. Without treatment, children who are abused may experience depression, anxiety, and other mental health issues even many years after the abuse.
- Teach the child how to avoid people who bully them.

Goodheart-Willcox Publisher

Stopping the Cycle of Neglect and Abuse

Stopping abusive cycles is a critical component of ending neglect and abuse. Children and teenagers must not be allowed to go through life being neglected, abused, or both. They need to receive help as soon as possible to end the harm and heal the wounds they have already experienced. Healing lessens children's chances of repeating these behaviors.

Another important piece of the puzzle lies within the adults who abuse. These adults perhaps play the biggest role in stopping abuse. Adults who are abusive need to recognize that what they are doing is wrong and find help to stop. When people who abuse sincerely want to change their behaviors, the chances for success are much higher. If caregivers feel out of control and think they may abuse a child, they should call a national organization like *Parents Anonymous*®, which forms local chapters that provide support services any time. Adults can also call a crisis hotline to ask for help.

In situations in which sibling or peer abuse is a risk, adults can help prevent their children from becoming perpetrators of sibling and peer abuse by

- modeling respectful relationships with colleagues, family, and friends. "Putting people down" teaches bullying.
- developing a close relationship with the child by keeping the lines of communication open.
- teaching the child respectful self-assertion. A child needs to use words, not aggression, to stick up for themselves.
- involving the child in community activities and home chores.
- including good role models in the child's life.
- monitoring violence in media content.
- involving the child in physical activities.
- taking even early, minor abuse seriously. Abuse that is not stopped is likely to escalate.
- checking the child's use of social media. Explain the dangers of media use.

1. Failing to bring a child who has fallen and broken their arm to the hospital is an example of _____ neglect. (22.2.1)
   A. moral
   B. medical
   C. emotional
   D. educational

2. **True or False.** Parents who are neglectful and abusive come from all income, intelligence, and education levels. (22.2.1)

3. A possible social-emotional effect of neglect and abuse on a child is a/n _____. (22.2.2)
   A. inability to concentrate
   B. internal injury
   C. lack of self-esteem
   D. language problem

4. Which statement about sibling abuse is correct? (22.2.3)
   A. It is less uncommon than child abuse by adults.
   B. It involves bullying through a digital medium.
   C. It is most often seen in teen groups.
   D. Its seriousness often goes unnoticed by adults.

5. Which is an example of a possible sign of physical child abuse? (22.2.4)
   A. A child uses improper language when dealing with younger children.
   B. A child has a history of past injuries to long bones.
   C. An older child regresses to sucking their thumb.
   D. A child has an unusual interest in sexual matters for their age.

6. The most effective strategy a child can use to deal with abuse by other children is to _____. (22.2.5)
   A. walk away from the abuser
   B. use respectful self-assertion to stick up for themself
   C. ignore the abuser until they stop
   D. fight the abuser

Chapter 22 Review and Assessment

Summary

Lesson 22.1

22.1-1 When families encounter challenges, it is important that parents and teachers work together to help children cope. When families move, parents and other adults working with children can strive to give children a sense of stability and can try to reduce other stressors.

22.1-1 Families facing financial strain can help children cope by providing as best they can and by seeking appropriate help to meet children's needs.

22.1-1 Caregivers can help children and teens cope with family members who have addictions by limiting their contact with them. Families also need to ensure family members with addictions receive help.

22.1-1 Children who have experienced violence and disaster need support and comfort. Caregivers should be prepared to help their children process the event and their related feelings.

22.1-2 Illness and death are especially hard challenges for children because children need help understanding these concepts and must experience grief. Adults and caregivers need to answer children's questions about illness honestly.

22.1-2 Adults should give children clear facts about the suicide, but not overexplain. They can recall the good traits of the person, assure children the suicide was not their fault, and emphasize that everyone has choices.

22.1-2 Many children who face challenges develop resilience, the ability to recover from stressful situations. By fostering resilience and seeking appropriate resources for children in crises, adults can help children cope well.

22.1-3 Resources for children and teens in crises include departments and agencies of federal, state, or local governments; national private agencies; religious groups; hospitals and medical associations; mental health centers; crises intervention centers; law enforcement agencies; legal associations; counseling services; schools; and civic or volunteer organizations.

22.1-3 Counseling and therapeutic services available to help children in crises include pharmacotherapy, cognitive behavioral therapy, family therapy, trauma-focused therapy, and play therapy.

Lesson 22.2

22.2-1 Types of child neglect are physical, educational, medical, moral, and emotional. Types of child abuse are physical, sexual, emotional, and verbal.

22.2-1 Each type of neglect or abuse has many complex causes and risk factors. Abuse is a complex, interactive process.

22.2-2 Child neglect and abuse can have serious physical, intellectual, and social-emotional effects.

22.2-3 Besides abuse by adults, abuse of children by siblings and peers occurs. Sibling abuse happens to over one-third of all children, and the incidence is rising. It takes the same forms as adult abuse.

22.2-3 Peer abuse takes the forms of physical or emotional bullying, cyberbullying, gang violence, and school violence. Sibling and peer abuse leaves much the same scars as abuse by adults.

22.2-4 Recognition and reporting is an important step in stopping neglect and abuse, and some people are mandated reporters.

22.2-5 When people report suspected cases of neglect and abuse, the children and adults involved can get the treatment they need. Children may be returned to their caregivers or placed in foster care, while caregivers may undergo therapy, be restricted from or denied access to their children, or convicted of a crime.

22.2-5 Many people are working to prevent and stop the cycle of neglect and abuse.

College and Career Portfolio

Portfolio Presentation Preparation

Presenting your portfolio well requires a great deal of preparation. At a job or school interview, you likely will not have time to present your entire portfolio. It is important, therefore, to highlight special achievements you want your audience to see.

Complete the following activities as part of your portfolio presentation preparation:
- Identify two or three components of your portfolio of which you are especially proud.
- Brainstorm ways to make these components the first and most important thing a potential employer or school would see.

Recall and Application

1. **True or False.** Regardless of their opinions, teachers and other adults should always show respect for children and their families. (22.1.1)

2. A common response of teenagers who experienced the loss of a parent through death or divorce is to _____. (22.1.1)
   A. believe they somehow caused the death or divorce
   B. become the confidant of the remaining caregiver
   C. exhibit problems with sleep or appetite
   D. begin hitting or biting others

3. **True or False.** Suicide is the second leading cause of death for children, adolescents, and young adults ages 15 to 24 years old. (22.1.2)

4. The *best* way for a child's teacher to help them cope with grief is to _____. (22.1.2)
   A. alter the child's normal routine
   B. share their beliefs about death with the child
   C. tell the child about their own experiences with death
   D. give the child room to express their feelings

5. One way for caregivers to build resilience in children is to give them a role in handling "big problems" like financial struggles or addiction. (22.1.2)

6. A therapeutic service that focuses on re-establishing safety and identifying triggers following a traumatic event is _____ therapy. (22.1.3)
   A. play
   B. family
   C. cognitive behavioral
   D. trauma-focused

7. A caregiver who frequently tells their child they are "stupid" or "unteachable" is committing _____ abuse. (22.2.1)
   A. physical
   B. sexual
   C. verbal
   D. emotional

8. **True or False.** Children often make up stories of sexual abuse. (22.2.1)

9. **True or False.** The idea that "time heals all wounds" does not apply to those who have been neglected or abused as children. (22.2.2)

10. An example of emotional bullying is _____. (22.2.3)
    A. gossiping or spreading rumors
    B. physical intimidation
    C. pushing or shoving
    D. choking

11. Health care workers, teachers, counselors, social service workers, and child care providers are mandated reporters and are legally required to report any known or suspected cases of neglect or abuse. (22.2.4)

12. Adults who are guilty of child abuse may be restricted from seeing the child or they may have their parental rights rescinded. (22.2.4)

Critical Thinking

1. **Determine.** Interview three young children about their experiences moving. If you cannot find children to interview, read three different stories about children who have moved. How did the children feel about the move? How did their caregivers help them cope with the move? After the interviews, determine which factors most helped the children cope with their family moving and why.

2. **Draw conclusions.** Often, teachers and other adults who work with children are not aware of sensitive family issues, such as addiction in a child's family. Some signs, however, can alert adults to possible challenges in the child's family. In small groups, interview a social worker at a primary or middle school and ask about signs that indicate a child's family is struggling with addiction. Draw conclusions about why these signs might signify a problem.

3. **Analyze.** Research guidelines and instructions for caregivers helping their children cope with violence and disaster. Choose three suggestions given and analyze how the suggestions are or are not developmentally appropriate for young children.

4. **Make inferences.** When explaining illness and death to children, many adults are tempted to use *euphemisms* (such as *to pass away* instead of *to die*). Are euphemisms a good way to explain illness and death to children? Why or why not?

5. **Compare and contrast.** Working with a partner, research your state's definitions of *child neglect* and *child abuse*. According to your state, what is the primary difference between *neglect* and *abuse*? How do your state's definitions compare to the definitions in this text?

6. **Cause and effect.** In groups of three, assign each group member one area of development (physical, intellectual, social-emotional). Study the effects of *each type* of child neglect or abuse in your assigned area of development and create a spreadsheet documenting your thoughts. Finally, compare notes in your group and create a comprehensive spreadsheet detailing how each type of neglect or abuse affects all three areas of development.

7. **Identify.** Using reliable resources, find and read a scholarly study about the causes of child neglect and abuse. Identify which cause or causes are being researched and explain how the findings affect the likelihood of neglect or abuse.

8. **Evaluate.** Research school initiatives that seek to combat peer abuse. Choose one initiative and research its history, mission, and implementation. What services does the initiative offer? In your opinion, how effective is the initiative? Evaluate the initiative using examples from experience.

Core Skills

1. **Reading and speaking.** Search for articles written about families coping with financial strain. These articles should outline resources for families in these situations and should propose ways that caregivers and teachers can help children cope. Read two of the articles and summarize them in a short oral presentation. During the presentation, lead a class discussion analyzing whether you think the methods suggested in the articles would be helpful to children.

2. **Math.** Over the course of one day, tally every time that you are exposed to violence and disaster or reports of violence and disaster. This tally includes violence and disaster experienced, seen on the news, discussed at school, or read online. At the end of the day, calculate your total tally. As a class, average the individual tallies and discuss whether children are exposed to more or less violence and disaster.

3. **Writing and speaking.** Imagine you are a preschool teacher and one of your preschoolers, Raphael, is coping with caregiver divorce. Raphael has been acting out, crying, and refusing to participate. Working with a partner, write a short skit in which you help Raphael cope with the emotional outbursts. Role-play your skit for the class and ask for feedback.

4. **Technology.** In small groups, review the information about illness and death in this chapter. Then, adapt the information into an interactive digital presentation and film about helping children cope. Include a sequential exploration of how children come to understand illness and death and select some practical videos that demonstrate effective techniques for helping children cope. Make your presentation visually appealing and easy to follow. Finally, present to the class.

5. **Research and technology.** Working with a partner, research resources for children in crises in your state. Resources might include federal or state agencies, crisis centers or nurseries, and hotlines for families in need. Create a five-panel pamphlet of these resources, including their names, contact information, and brief summaries of their services. Share your pamphlets with the class.

6. **Listening and technology.** Interview a school counselor about the most common types of peer abuse in school-age children. How has peer abuse changed over the past decade? Why do children abuse their peers? What can children do to protect themselves from abuse? Also ask about current measures that are being taken to reduce peer abuse. After the interview, create a digital poster highlighting your findings. Present your poster to the class.

7. **Research and speaking.** In groups of five, review the information on preventing neglect and abuse in this chapter. Assign each group member one method of prevention. Research examples of your method of prevention.

Take notes about what made these examples successful or unsuccessful. Then, create your own movement, initiative, or club that uses your prevention method. Write a persuasive speech selling your movement, initiative, or club. Finally, practice in your group and deliver your persuasive speeches to the class.

8. **CTE Career Readiness Practice.** Imagine you are a child protective services caseworker who has been asked by a local child care center to deliver a presentation about recognizing abuse and mandated reporting requirements. In preparation for your presentation, research definitions of *neglect* and *abuse* in your state and tips for recognizing these problems. Also research the guidelines for mandated reporters and the legal penalties for failing to report neglect and abuse as a mandated reporter. Compile this information into a professional slideshow and oral presentation. Practice your presentation with the class. Ask for feedback about your professionalism and speaking skills (clarity and volume).

Observations

1. As a class, view a documentary about helping children recover from neglect or abuse. What behaviors or symptoms are typical of children who have been neglected or abused? What treatments do pediatricians and therapists administer to these children? How are caseworkers involved in children's treatment? After the documentary, discuss these questions in class.

2. In small groups, visit a local crisis child care center or disaster relief organization and interview someone about the effects of violence and disaster on children. How do children typically react to violence and disaster? How does the organization help these children obtain treatment? Write a brief report about your findings.

Meeting Children's Special Needs

Types of Special Needs

Supporting Children with Special Needs

Essential Question

How do special needs impact children's development, and what support is available for children with special needs?

Case Study   How Do Special Needs Affect Children and Families?

As a class, read the case study and discuss the questions that follow. After you finish studying the chapter, discuss this case study again. Have your opinions changed based on what you learned?

For the first three years of his life, Theo excelled at motor and physical activities. Theo was an active child who liked to run outside and kick the ball. Theo's parents noticed a change in their child's physical development when Theo entered the preschool years. Before, Theo had been growing stronger and testing new skills eagerly. Now, Theo seemed tired and had trouble running across the backyard. At first, Theo's parents thought their child just needed more sleep.

Theo's parents hoped the new schedule of preschool would benefit Theo. Unfortunately, Theo only grew weaker. One day, Theo's preschool teacher met with the parents and expressed concerns that Theo had seemed stiff lately, was having trouble sitting down and standing up, and had started showing signs of toe walking. The teacher recommended a visit to the pediatrician.

Worried for their child, Theo's parents acted promptly and told the pediatrician about the situation. The pediatrician examined Theo and referred the family to a specialist for further

testing. The tests revealed Theo has a condition known as muscular dystrophy. Theo's parents felt overwhelmed, wondering: How will we tell Theo? What will this mean for our child? What will it mean for our family? How will this change the way we live our lives?

Give It Some Thought

1. What behaviors and signs caused Theo's parents and the preschool teacher to worry? Why were these behaviors and signs alarming?
2. What does this new condition mean for Theo's family? How might this change the way they live?
3. What advice would you give to Theo's parents about how they should explain this condition to Theo and how they should treat their child as they adjust?

olesiabilkei/iStock via Getty Images Plus

Types of Special Needs

Key Terms

anxiety disorder

attention-deficit hyperactivity disorder (ADHD)

autism spectrum disorder (ASD)

behavioral disorder

developmental dyscalculia

developmental dyslexia

intellectual disability

intelligence quotient (IQ) test

language disorder

learning disorder

oppositional defiant disorder (ODD)

physical disability

speech disorder

typical development

Learning Outcomes

After studying this lesson, you will be able to

23.1-1 **explain** the principles and guidelines to consider for children with special needs.

23.1-2 **describe** physical special needs children may experience.

23.1-3 **summarize** intellectual special needs that affect children.

23.1-4 **explain** the social-emotional special needs of children.

23.1-5 **identify** special needs that affect multiple areas of children's development.

Reading and Notetaking Activity

Imagine you are in college to become a special education teacher and for a class project, you have to give a speech about the types of special needs in children. Write a two-paragraph speech explaining the different types of needs and what each entails. Incorporate information you already know about children's special needs, and anything from your personal experiences. As you read this lesson, take detailed notes. After reading the lesson, go back over your speech. With a partner, discuss what you would change about your speech based on any new information you have learned. Present your final speech to the class.

Introduction

Many children develop in similar ways, achieving typical milestones in each stage of development. These children have basic needs that must be met. Sometimes, though, children's development differs from that which is expected. Children who experience developmental accelerations or delays have special needs, which need to be met in different ways.

There are many types of special needs, and not all these types are fully understood. Children with physical special needs differ in their physical development. Intellectual special needs, such as intellectual disabilities and giftedness, both impact children's intellectual development. Learning disorders affect how children learn. Several social-emotional special needs, including anxiety disorders, depression, childhood schizophrenia, and oppositional defiant disorder (ODD) can also affect children's development. Sometimes children have special needs due to the complex interactions among multiple areas of development, as seen in attention disorders and autism spectrum disorder (ASD). Understanding these special needs is the first step in helping children who possess them.

23.1-1 Who Are Children with Special Needs?

Although each child is unique, children typically grow and develop in similar ways. Through research, child development experts have determined which developmental milestones (physical, intellectual, and social-emotional) children generally attain within each stage of development. A child whose development follows these patterns exhibits **typical development**. Some children, however, do not follow typical patterns of development. These children are known as *children with special needs*. *Special needs* are needs that go *beyond* the basic needs of all children (**Figure 23.1**).

Children with special needs may have abilities that differ from most other children. They may exhibit differences in motor skills, seeing, hearing, speech, intellectual abilities, learning, language, and social behaviors. In discussing children with special needs, it is important to consider several guidelines. These guidelines include the following:

- *Special needs may occur in one or more areas of development.* Children with special needs may differ from typical development in any area of development—physical, intellectual, or social-emotional. Just because a child has a special need in one developmental area does not mean they have special needs in another area. For example, one child may differ from typical development in language development alone. Another child may differ from typical development in both language development and social interactions.
- *Special needs may develop due to acceleration or delay.* Children who develop faster or achieve higher degrees of development than most other children are referred to as having *gifts* or *talents*. Children who experience *developmental delays* (the late achievement of a developmental milestone) are referred to as having *conditions*, *disabilities*, or *disorders*.

Figure 23.1 Even though children with special needs have additional needs that must be met, they have much in common with children who do not have special needs. *What are examples of basic needs all children have in common?*

FatCamera/E+ via Getty Images

- *Special needs are identified through observations and tests.* To determine a child's type of special need, professionals (such as doctors or psychologists) make observations and perform tests. Some special needs are apparent at birth, but many special needs are not evident for several years or more.
- *Special needs vary in intensity.* Special needs exist on a spectrum of intensity, ranging from *borderline* to *profound* (**Figure 23.2**). The term *borderline* indicates that a talent or delay differs *very little* from typical development. The term *profound* indicates that a talent or delay differs *very much* from typical development.
- *Special needs vary in duration and permanence.* Types of special needs may be described as *correctable* or *chronic*. The term *correctable* indicates that a special need may be overcome or may subside with appropriate support and time. For example, many speech disorders are correctable through speech therapy. The term *chronic* indicates that a special need may exist for a long time, perhaps a lifetime. For example, Down syndrome presents a chronic, lifelong special need.

Children may possess different types of special needs, including needs that affect physical development (such as physical disabilities), needs that affect intellectual development (such as intellectual disabilities and gifts and talents), and needs that affect social-emotional development (such as anxiety disorders and other mental health disorders). Some types of special needs affect more than one area of development (such as attention disorders).

23.1-2 Children with Physical Special Needs

Physical special needs are needs that affect a child's physical development. Types of physical special needs include physical disabilities (such as gross-motor, vision, and hearing conditions) and speech disorders. Physicians and therapists often identify physical special needs by noting *physical developmental delays*. Developmental delays may occur during any stage of development, as shown in **Figure 23.3**.

Figure 23.3 Signs of Physical Developmental Delays

- Child does not meet physical or language milestones for their age.
- Child's pediatrician expresses concern from results of developmental screenings.
- Muscle stiffness or weakness.
- Child gets tired easily.
- Child cannot keep up with other children their age.
- Clumsiness.
- Losing skills the child once had.
- Unable to perform self-care tasks such as brushing teeth, dressing, washing hands, and toileting (for older children).

Goodheart-Willcox Publisher

Special Needs Spectrum

	Borderline	Mild	Moderate	Severe	Profound	
Least intense	differs *very little* from typical development	differs *little* from typical development	differs *somewhat* from typical development	differs *much* from typical development	differs *very much* from typical development	**Most intense**

Degree of Intensity

Goodheart-Willcox Publisher

Figure 23.2 The spectrum of special needs reflects the varying intensities of children's needs. *Give an example of a special need at each point on the spectrum.*

Children with Physical Disabilities

A **physical disability** is a condition that affects a person's body or its function. Physical disabilities indicate that a child is developing behind the typical physical development of most other children the same age. Children with physical disabilities differ from typical physical development for many reasons. Some of these reasons include:

- genetic disorders
- congenital conditions
- serious illnesses, such as **meningitis** (MEH-nun-JY-tis), an inflammation of the thin membranes that cover the spinal cord and brain
- spinal cord, brain, or other bodily injuries

Children with Gross-Motor Conditions

One type of physical disability is a *gross-motor condition*. Gross-motor conditions may result from any of the following issues: Bodily trauma; bone, joint, nerve, or muscle diseases; or damage to the brain or nervous system. Some gross-motor conditions include

- *muscular dystrophy*, a genetic disease that weakens the muscles
- *spina bifida*, a congenital disorder in which the spine does not completely cover the spinal cord, leading to physical complications and sometimes **paralysis** (the inability to move or feel parts of the body)
- *cerebral palsy*, a disorder resulting from damage to the brain that affects muscle coordination
- paralysis, which may be caused by a brain or spinal injury or disease
- amputated or missing limbs, which may lead to limited mobility

Any gross-motor condition may cause delays in gross-motor development. Children with gross-motor conditions may need special aids, such as artificial limbs, walkers, crutches, braces, or wheelchairs, to participate fully in daily life.

Focus on Reading

Developmental Delays

Developmental milestones measure children's progress at each stage of their physical, intellectual, and social-emotional development. Children who achieve a developmental milestone late or do not achieve a milestone at all are experiencing a *developmental delay*. Developmental delays can be difficult for caregivers and teachers to identify, and adults often have questions about how to identify a delay, when a delay is serious, and what to do about a delay. Questions that adults often have include the following:

- Do developmental milestones and their ages still apply to premature infants?

- If children regress in their skills, is this cause for concern?
- How absolute are the ages given for developmental milestones? When does the nonachievement of a milestone become a *developmental delay*?
- If children achieve milestones early, does that mean they have *gifts and talents*?

In small groups, conduct research to answer these questions. Be sure to cite your sources in a short bibliography. Write your answers as a group and then compare answers with another group.

Photo: Andy-pix/Shutterstock.com

Children with Vision Conditions

Another type of physical disability is a *vision condition*, which causes children to experience challenges seeing. Signs of vision conditions include squinting, holding objects close to the face, and rubbing the eyes frequently. Poor depth perception may also signal that a child has a vision condition. Certain vision conditions may cause children only to see light, colors, shadow forms, or large pictures. Other conditions may cause children to be unable to see anything at all.

While some vision conditions are correctable because of wearing eyeglasses or having surgery, other vision conditions are chronic and cannot be corrected (**Figure 23.4**). One chronic vision condition is *legal blindness*, which occurs when a person's better eye has a corrected visual acuity of 20/200 and/or in which the visual field is 20 degrees or less.

Children with Hearing Conditions

A third type of physical disability is a *hearing condition*, which causes children to have difficulty hearing. This difficulty may include hearing loss ranging from borderline to profound. Profound hearing loss may result in *deafness*. Signs of a hearing condition include unresponsiveness to sounds, incorrect formation of speech sounds, or major delays in talking.

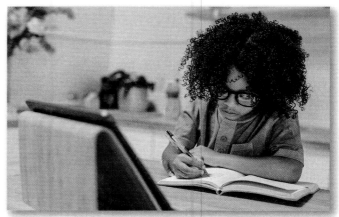

kate_sept2004/E+ via Getty Images

Figure 23.4 Some vision conditions, such as nearsightedness or farsightedness, are often correctable, usually through eyeglasses or contacts. *What other methods are used to help children with correctable vision conditions?*

Newborns are often tested for hearing conditions before they leave the hospital. Hearing conditions, however, can develop months or years after birth due to illnesses or exposure to loud sounds.

Children with hearing conditions may excel in some areas not affected by hearing loss. Many children with hearing conditions use their sense of touch far more than other children. They also watch other people's faces and mouths closely to understand messages that are being communicated.

Focus on Health

Continued Stuttering

Most cases of stuttering resolve over time and sometimes with therapy. Sometimes, however, stuttering does not resolve on its own. Some children may be at risk for *continued stuttering* (stuttering that continues over life). Children who are at risk for continued stuttering tend to:

- have a family history of stuttering
- have delayed development or other speech problems
- experience extreme family stress
- show physical tension while speaking (such as jaw clenching or blinking eyes)
- be male

Children with continued stuttering should receive professional help from speech and language therapists. Continued stuttering can hinder children's abilities to be understood and can lead to poor self-concept if children are criticized for their speech habits.

Photo: wavebreakmedia/Shutterstock.com

Children with Speech Disorders

Some children with physical special needs have *speech disorders*. A **speech disorder** is a condition that causes a child to have difficulty speaking or being understood. For the most part, speech disorders involve children's physical development. Children with speech disorders typically face challenges in one or more of the following areas:

- *Articulation.* Articulation is the ability to pronounce words understandably. Children who face articulation challenges may substitute one sound for another, distort sounds, leave out sounds in words, or add sounds to words.
- *Voice.* Children who face voice challenges may speak with voices that are exceptionally high in pitch, low in pitch, loud, quiet, nasal, or husky. These qualities can hinder children's abilities to be understood by others.
- *Rhythm.* Everyone speaks at a certain rhythm. Children who face rhythm challenges may repeat sounds and words, have pauses between sounds, or use prolonged sounds (called *stuttering* or *stammering*). Other children may also speak especially fast, stumble on words or phrases, or double back to try to communicate meaning (called *cluttering*).

Speech disorders are often identified by doctors and teachers rather than by parents. Parents or caregivers may not hear differences in their children's speech because they are accustomed to these differences. Sometimes children even learn speech differences *from* their parents or caregivers.

Children with suspected speech disorders need to be evaluated by a speech therapist (also called a *speech pathologist*). Speech therapists are also trained to treat speech disorders.

23.1-3 Children with Intellectual Special Needs

Children with intellectual special needs have needs that affect their intellectual development or their abilities to learn. Intellectual special needs may be indicated by *intellectual developmental delays*, such as those shown in **Figure 23.5**. They may also be indicated by accelerated intellectual development. Struggling to learn academic subjects or having difficulties understanding language may also be indicators that children have intellectual special needs. Types of intellectual special needs include intellectual disabilities, gifts and talents, learning disorders, and language disorders.

Children with Intellectual Disabilities

An **intellectual disability** is a condition in which a child has significant delays or deficits in learning and daily functioning. Causes of intellectual disabilities include genetic disorders, congenital conditions, birth complications, and injuries to or infections of the brain after birth. A lack of basic experiences within the child's environment may also lead to intellectual delays.

Figure 23.5 Signs of Intellectual Developmental Delays

- Child has a known cause of intellectual disability (for example, Down syndrome, fragile X syndrome, fetal alcohol syndrome, or other conditions).
- Child has experienced head injury, stroke, or certain infections.
- Child does not meet intellectual milestones for their age.
- Delays in sitting up or walking without support.
- Delays in speech.
- Has trouble remembering things.
- Does not readily see the consequences of their actions.
- Difficulty with solving problems.
- Immature social skills, self-care skills, school and learning skills, financial skills, or personal safety skills (referred to as adaptive behavior skills).

Goodheart-Willcox Publisher

Indications of intellectual disabilities vary widely, but most intellectual disabilities do share some characteristics. Children with intellectual disabilities tend to:

- experience delays in motor skills
- have delays or difficulty with speech
- have a hard time understanding social rules
- have trouble remembering things
- have difficulty with problem solving and logical thinking

Intellectual disabilities can vary from borderline to profound. These disabilities are usually identified by doctors or other professionals through a combination of testing and assessment. Testing for intellectual disabilities may involve the administering of a specialized test called an *intelligence quotient (IQ) test*. An **intelligence quotient (IQ) test** measures how quickly a person can learn and how well a person can reason using words, numbers, and spatial concepts. Children with intellectual disabilities tend to score below 70 on IQ tests. IQ tests, however, do not totally define whether a child has an intellectual disability. True identification depends on assessment of children's functioning and overall ability, including multiple intelligences.

Children with Gifts and Talents

Although all children have strengths, *children with gifts and talents* are children who experience *accelerated intellectual development*, meaning they develop far ahead of most other children's intellectual development. Children with gifts and talents show high performance in one or more of the following areas:

- general intellectual ability (showing above-average intelligence)
- specific academic aptitude (excelling in one or more subject areas)
- creative or productive thinking (writing or inventing)
- leadership ability (planning or organizing)
- high skill in visual or performing arts (excelling in art, music, or dance)
- high **psychomotor ability**—the ability to coordinate muscle movements with mental processes (excelling in sports)

Just as all children are unique, so are children with gifts and talents. Some children with gifts and talents

seem to be gifted or talented in almost all areas. Other children are talented in only one or two areas.

Children who are gifted and talented are not necessarily children who excel in school. Children who are gifted and talented may not excel in areas other than their area of giftedness. Just because a child is gifted or talented does not mean that child will not experience typical development or a developmental delay in another area. Giftedness and talent are not the same. **Figure 23.6** shows some traits that are characteristic of children with gifts and talents.

Figure 23.6 Traits of Children with Gifts and Talents

- Advanced development in any or several areas.
- Very observant.
- Intense curiosity, motivation, and enthusiasm for learning.
- Extremely good memory and absorb information quickly.
- Advanced ability to focus and concentrate.
- Learn well independently.
- High personal standard of achievement.
- Advanced vocabulary and speech.
- Preference for speaking to older children or adults.
- Imaginative and creative.
- Strong reasoning and problem-solving skills.
- Emotional maturity and/or sensitivity.
- Ask big picture questions about global issues.
- Have intense interests.
- Focus on issues of justice and right vs. wrong.
- Intense frustration when standards are not met or with threats of shortcomings and failure.

Goodheart-Willcox Publisher

Robertprzybysz/iStock via Getty Images Plus   *Jose Girarte/iStock via Getty Images Plus*

Children with Gifts and Talents

Children with gifts were traditionally thought to excel largely in language and mathematical intelligence, scoring significantly higher (115 or higher) on individual IQ tests than children who follow typical development. An IQ score between 145 and 159 indicates that a child is *highly gifted*, a score between 160 and 179 indicates that a child is *exceptionally gifted*, and a score of 180 or higher indicates that a child is *profoundly gifted*. Today's definition of gifted includes other areas where children may excel. For example, a preschooler who plays the violin more like a school-age child or teen is gifted in music.

If a child is borderline gifted, parents may not recognize the child's giftedness. Often teachers see potential giftedness by noting high scores on *standardized* (not teacher-constructed) school achievement tests, although many children achieve high scores without being truly gifted. Based on children's scores on these tests, children may be recommended by their teachers for further testing, such as being given an IQ test. To determine giftedness, children may also be given a college-admission aptitude test, such as the *Scholastic Aptitude Test (SAT)*, at a younger age than is typical. Researchers widely agree that the potential for giftedness in children is mostly *genetic* (inherited). These gifts must be nurtured, however, for children to reach their full potential.

Children's gifts are both genetic and environmental. While these traits do run in families, a supportive environment to meet these children's special needs is also required. The words gifted and talented are used in conjunction in today's educational world, but the difference between them is the child's potential. A child can be born with predisposed gifts, but if those gifts are not nurtured, they will not have the opportunity to flourish and turn into talents. Likewise, some children are born without a higher ability to perform but hone their skills to become talented in their area of interest. Pediatricians, teachers, and other professionals may help parents identify areas of giftedness and talents that their children might possess.

Many children with gifts are *also* children with talents. Because children with gifts have such high intelligence, they often perform well in many other areas (such as academics, music, art, leadership, or sports). Thus, these children are considered to have both gifts *and* talents.

Children with Learning Disorders

A **learning disorder** is a challenge that impacts a child's spoken or written language, math, or *spatial orientation* (the ability to see relationships among objects in space). Children with learning disorders have average or above-average intelligence. Nevertheless, the academic achievement of children with learning disorders is below what would be expected for their intelligence and grade level.

Studies show that learning disorders usually result from neural misfires in the brain. **Misfires** are electrical signals that either fail to cross neuron synapses or cross these synapses incorrectly. What causes these misfires is unknown. Some contributing factors, however, may include prenatal complications (such as lack of oxygen for the fetus), trauma during birth, accidents, and breathing or nutritional problems after birth. The type of learning disorder depends on the part of the brain in which the misfiring repeatedly occurs. Children with learning disorders have a number of defining traits that vary from children's typical development (**Figure 23.7**).

Figure 23.7 Traits of Children with Learning Disabilities*

- Issues with attentiveness or memory.
- Problems with speech, reading, written expression, or math.
- Difficulty following directions.
- Eye-hand coordination or motor problems; clumsiness.
- Disorganization.
- Inconsistent performance.
- Difficulty with telling time or understanding time concepts.
- Difficulty adjusting to change.
- Problems understanding words or concepts.
- Impulsive behavior or "acting out."
- Difficulties with listening or correctly expressing thoughts.

*Some children who follow typical development may also experience these traits. While children who follow typical development are able to correct some of these traits, children with learning disorders still struggle with them regularly.

Goodheart-Willcox Publisher

Two common types of learning disorders identified in childhood are *developmental dyslexia* and *developmental dyscalculia*. **Developmental dyslexia** (dis-LEK-see-uh) affects a child's ability to read. Children with developmental dyslexia may also have problems writing and spelling. They may find it difficult to connect words with their written forms and may reverse words and letters when reading or writing. They may also confuse the order of letters in words or read words backward. Currently, dyslexia is more common in biological males than in biological females. **Developmental dyscalculia** (DIS-kal-KYOO-lee-uh) affects a child's mathematical abilities. Children with dyscalculia may reverse numerals and may not develop a mental number line necessary for calculating. Unlike dyslexia, dyscalculia is equally common among all children.

Children with Language Disorders

A **language disorder** involves a child's lack of ability to understand and use language. Language disorders tend to involve the brain and intellectual development, which makes them more serious and less correctable than speech disorders.

The most serious language disorder of childhood is *acquired childhood aphasia*, which is the partial or total loss of the ability to understand words and use language. The term *acquired* is used because this disorder occurs after children have developed some language skills. Acquired childhood aphasia develops due to a brain injury, which may be caused by head trauma, brain infection, a brain tumor, stroke, seizures, or other brain disorders. The possibility of recovery depends on the severity of the brain damage.

23.1-4 Children with Social-Emotional Special Needs

Children with special needs do not just experience these needs in their physical and intellectual lives. Children may also have social-emotional special needs. Social-emotional special needs are usually identified by serious changes in the ways children behave socially or regulate their emotions (**Figure 23.8**). These needs can also be signaled by lags or delays in children's achievement

of social-emotional developmental milestones. The *social-emotional developmental delays* for infants, preschoolers, toddlers, and school-age children are outlined in **Figure 23.9**.

Figure 23.8 Behaviors That May Indicate Social-Emotional Special Needs

- Appears excessively fearful and cannot be easily soothed.
- Appears sad or withdrawn.
- Shows inappropriate or aggressive behaviors, especially toward family members and familiar children.
- Displays hyperactivity and impulsive behaviors.
- Has violent temper tantrums or frequent tantrums.
- Exhibits distorted thinking or extreme anxiety.
- Is extremely defiant.
- Displays changes in eating or sleeping behaviors.
- Talks excessively or interrupts others.
- Has trouble waiting their turn.
- Difficulty playing alone quietly.

Goodheart-Willcox Publisher

Figure 23.9 Signs of Social-Emotional Developmental Delays

- Child does not meet social-emotional milestones for their age.
- Does not pick up on social cues.
- Difficulty beginning or sustaining simple conversation.
- Prolonged tantrums.
- Difficulty with changes to routine, even if they are minor.
- Does not seem interested in interacting with others.
- Has trouble regulating their behavior.
- Loses previously acquired skills.
- Does not understand simple directions.
- Does not participate in make-believe.
- Has a small range of emotions.
- Shows extreme behavior.

Goodheart-Willcox Publisher

There are many types of social-emotional special needs. Many times, these needs take the form of *mental health disorders*. Some social-emotional special needs include anxiety disorders, depression, childhood schizophrenia, and oppositional defiant disorder (ODD).

Children with Anxiety Disorders

One type of social-emotional special need common in children is an *anxiety disorder*. *Anxiety* is a form of stress that all people feel from time to time, and some anxiety is healthy. An **anxiety disorder**, however, is a specific anxiety that interferes with a child's ability to achieve goals or enjoy life. Children with anxiety disorders are at increased risk for other conditions, such as eating disorders and sleep problems. All these risks also have the potential to interfere with children's lives and health.

Several types of anxiety disorders occur in children, and each type of disorder has different symptoms (**Figure 23.10**). General symptoms of anxiety disorders include the following:

- excessive and prolonged worry
- trouble sleeping and fatigue during the day
- stomach aches or other physical problems
- inability to focus on schoolwork and other goals
- irritability
- withdrawn behaviors and avoiding certain situations
- poor self-concept

Experts do not yet know exactly what causes anxiety disorders. Two people may have similar life experiences, and one person may develop an anxiety disorder while the other person may not. Several factors seem to contribute to anxiety disorders, such as genetics, brain chemistry, stressful life circumstances (such as neglect and abuse), and learned behaviors.

Children with Depression

Depression is a common social-emotional special need in the United States. *Depression* is a serious mental health disorder characterized by a persistent sadness and loss of interest. Children with depression can be as young as newborns. Children with depression may also experience *bipolar disorder*, a condition in which a child's mood alternates between depression and *high-energy mania* (happy, irritable, or energetic behavior). Depression can be caused by low levels of certain neurotransmitters in the brain, genetics, significant life events, and stress. Many children show improvement in their symptoms of depression through therapy, medication, or both.

Children with Childhood Schizophrenia

Childhood schizophrenia (also known as *pediatric schizophrenia, childhood-onset schizophrenia,* or *early-onset schizophrenia*) is one of the most serious social-emotional special needs children can experience. Although it is rare in children under 13 years of age, it is usually more severe than adult-onset schizophrenia. Children with schizophrenia often develop lags in motor and language skills and have poor school performance. Later, they may have **hallucinations** (seeing, hearing, or smelling objects that seem real, but are not), **delusions** (beliefs that are not true), and deterioration of even basic self-care behaviors. They may also lack impulse control and thus become aggressive. Genetics and the environment both play a role in schizophrenia. Early identification and treatment by a psychiatrist improve the child's long-term outcome.

Children with Oppositional Defiant Disorder (ODD)

Some children with special needs have behavioral disorders. A **behavioral disorder** is a pattern of challenges that surfaces in a person's behavior. (Behavioral disorders are also called *conduct* or *disruptive disorders*.) Such disorders are often marked by extremes of behaviors. One such behavioral disorder is **oppositional defiant disorder (ODD)**, which involves *aggressive behaviors*, such as name-calling, fighting, arguing, and bullying without being provoked into such actions. These behaviors are common at times to most children, but for children with ODD, these behaviors gradually worsen rather than improve. ODD usually begins before eight years of age.

Figure 23.10 Types and Symptoms of Anxiety Disorders

Type	Symptoms
Generalized anxiety disorder (GAD)	• Worrying excessively about many situations. • Thinking of the worst that can happen. • Indecisiveness due to fear of making the wrong choice. • Inability to overcome worries or relax. • Exhibiting physical symptoms, such as headaches, stomachaches, sweating, trouble sleeping, etc.
Obsessive compulsive disorder (OCD)	• Having repeated and unwanted thoughts; also called *obsessions*. • Performing repetitive behaviors or mental acts (handwashing, counting, repeating words silently) to reduce anxiety; also called *compulsions*
Separation anxiety disorder	• Having separation anxiety continuing during the school-age years. • Believing something terrible will occur when a loved one is away. • Worrying that an event will occur that will take a loved one away (such as a kidnapping or death). • Refusing to go to school, sleepovers with friends, and even to other relatives' homes if caregiver is not present. • Crying or hiding when caregivers are preparing to leave. • Having nightmares about separation. • Taking a long time to calm after being left by a caregiver. • Wanting to frequently check on caregiver's well-being, such as calling them, when separated. • Physical symptoms such as headaches or stomachaches when separation is approaching.
Panic disorder	• Having *panic attacks* (increased heart rate, difficulty breathing, hot or cold flashes, dizziness, chest pain, nausea, and tingling in legs or arms). • Displaying fears of panic attacks, dying, or losing control. • Avoiding settings in which one may experience panic attacks.
Specific phobia	• Becoming very fearful of something specific (storms, flying, dogs, enclosed spaces, blood, insects). • Attempting to avoid the feared object or situation. • Awareness that fears are unreasonable but powerless in overcoming them. • Cannot function normally due to the fear. • Crying, clinging, trying to run away, or having sudden physical symptoms around feared object or situation.
Social anxiety disorder	• Having an intense fear of social or performance situations. • Fear of being embarrassed in a social situation. • Fear of embarrassment from physical symptoms such as sweating, blushing, or having a shaky voice. • Avoiding social situations with peers, talking with authority figures (teachers or group leaders), and speaking in public. • Avoiding being the center of attention.
Post-traumatic stress disorder (PTSD)	• Having directly witnessed a traumatic event or suffered because of it. (These events may be sudden, unexpected, or chronic, such as abuse.) • Withdrawing from people and activities related to the event. • Having flashbacks, nightmares, and distress or physical reactions when reminded of the event. • Seeming tense (including sleep problems and being easy to startle). • Feeling detached from family and friends. • Losing interest in previously enjoyed activities.

Goodheart-Willcox Publisher

A professional identification is needed to recognize the difference between a child with sometimes difficult and challenging behavior and a child with ODD. Certain symptoms, such as those listed in **Figure 23.11**, are common identifiers. There is no known clear cause of ODD. ODD may have genetic components, such as gene mutations. Some environmental factors are also associated with ODD. These factors include:

- abuse and neglect
- harsh or inconsistent discipline
- lack of positive parental involvement
- family instability
- depression and ADHD

FOCUS ON MENTAL HEALTH

Children with mental health disorders may have difficulty leading fulfilling lives. If left untreated, mental health issues can continue into the adult years. Early diagnosis and professional treatment are key to ensuring that children will grow into well-adjusted adults. Mental health affects all areas of life, and children can be taught from an early age how to boost their mental wellbeing. It's never too early to help your child develop their mental health toolkit.

23.1-5 Children with Other Types of Special Needs

While some special needs primarily affect one area of development, other special needs involve complex interactions between multiple areas of development. Special needs such as attention disorders and autism spectrum disorder (ASD) are some of the most difficult special needs to identify and treat.

Children with Attention Disorders

Children with attention disorders experience difficulty paying attention. People must use attention and memory to learn, retain information, and solve problems. To pay attention, a person has to focus one or more of the senses on a certain aspect of the environment and ignore irrelevant information. For example, to pay attention to music, a person must focus their senses on the music recording and ignore irrelevant sounds, such as humming fans.

Although all children can be distracted, some children are highly distractible. Traditionally, attention disorders included *attention-deficit hyperactivity disorder (ADHD)* and *attention-deficit disorder (ADD)*.

Figure 23.11 **Common Traits of Children with ODD**

- Lose their temper, even over small situations.
- Argue with authority figures.
- Actively defy or refuse to comply with adults' requests or rules.
- Deliberately annoy others.
- Blame others for personal mistakes or misbehaviors.
- Are angry and resentful.
- Are aggressively spiteful.

Goodheart-Willcox Publisher

Antonio_Diaz/iStock via Getty Images Plus

ADHD involved lack of attention, impulsivity, and *hyperactivity* (behavior that is extremely active beyond a child's normal energy level). ADD involved lack of attention but did not include hyperactive behaviors.

Currently, experts identify only one attention disorder, **attention-deficit hyperactivity disorder (ADHD)**, which is classified into three types. These types are:

- *inattentive type* (which was formerly known as ADD).
- *hyperactive/impulsive type* (formerly known as ADHD).
- *combined hyperactive/impulsive and inattentive type* (including characteristics of what was formerly known as ADD *and* what was formerly known as ADHD). This is the most common type of ADHD.

ADHD is difficult to identify. In children, identification is based on observation rather than on tests. ADHD has characteristics in common with childhood anxiety and depression, as well as some learning disorders. Common traits of children with ADHD are listed in **Figure 23.12**.

The causes of attention disorders are not yet clear. Brain studies show that children with attention disorders have brains with reduced regions for motor and some cognitive skills. Some experts think that attention disorders result from challenges in executive functions, and recent research suggests that genetics play a large role. Some environmental factors are associated with ADHD, including oxygen deprivation before birth, alcohol or tobacco use during pregnancy, low birth weight or premature birth, and exposure to secondhand smoke and pesticides used on produce. Additional research is needed before more causes can be identified. Attention disorders are often identified in the school-age years by doctors and professionals.

Figure 23.12 Traits of Children with ADHD

Inattentive Type
- Seem to be inattentive; easily distracted; forgetful.
- Act disinterested ("tune-out") or daydream.
- Do not finish a task or play activity.
- Appear not to listen.
- Cannot organize work.
- Loses important items.
- Avoids tasks that require focus.

Hyperactive/Impulsive Type
- Exhibit hyperactive and impulsive behaviors.*
- Are fidgety; may constantly run, climb, or move in other ways; get out of their chairs or their places in group settings, tap feet, squirm.
- Have trouble doing anything quietly and talk excessively.
- Have difficulty waiting for their turns.
- Interrupt others.

Combined Hyperactive/Impulsive and Inattentive Type
- Have characteristics of both the inattentive and hyperactive/impulsive types.

*Hyperactivity is present in most of the cases involving attention disorders. Hyperactivity, however, is difficult to diagnose, especially in biological females. For this reason, attention disorders seem to be diagnosed in males more often than females.

Goodheart-Willcox Publisher

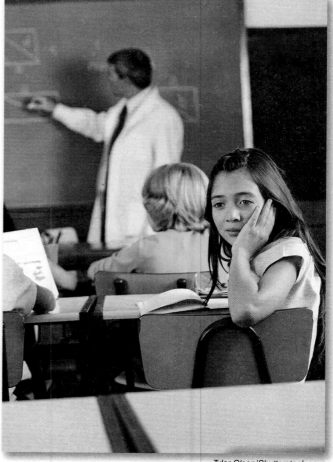

Tyler Olson/Shutterstock.com

Children with Autism Spectrum Disorder (ASD)

A number of children with special needs are children with *autism spectrum disorder (ASD)*. **Autism spectrum disorder (ASD)** is a general term used to describe complex communication, social, learning, and behavioral developmental disabilities. The term *spectrum* indicates that these disabilities vary in severity and supports needed. ASD is categorized into three levels based on severity of needs: Level 1, Level 2, and Level 3.

Major indications of ASD include language, social, and behavioral challenges. The three main commonalities among all people with ASD include difficulty with social interaction, restricted interests, and repetitive behaviors. Children with ASD often have other challenges associated with ASD, such as *sensory conditions* (inabilities to process and integrate sensory information), digestive conditions, sleep disturbances, seizures, and mental health disorders. At the same time, children with ASD often have exceptional strengths in some areas, such as in drawing, math, computers, music, or memory. There are no definitive medical tests that can be used to identify ASD. For the most part, a developmental pediatrician or a team of specialists identify ASD by the observation of signs and symptoms such as those listed in **Figure 23.13**.

The exact cause of ASD is not known. Research suggests that ASD may be caused by genetic factors as well as several environmental factors. ASD is associated with genetic mutations. However, many genes are involved in the development of ASD, making ASD very complex and difficult to analyze.

Many environmental factors are associated with ASD, but these factors may or may not be **causal** (related to the cause). Some of these factors include close spacing between children, diabetes in the pregnant person (including gestational diabetes), parental age, lack of folic acid supplements prior to pregnancy and during the first two stages of pregnancy, induced labor, and inflammation before birth.

Figure 23.13 Characteristics of Children with ASD

Area	Characteristics
Interactions	• Does not share interests or enjoyment with caregivers. • Does not show interest in other children. • Does not imitate others or pretend. • Does not show a range of emotions. • Does not partake in interactive play. • Does not notice the emotions of others. • Preference for being alone. • Shows atypical object exploration or attachment to objects. • Repetitive behaviors with objects.
Communication	• Lack of eye contact or smiling. • Does not consistently respond to their name. • Difficulty understanding simple one-step instructions. • Does not use gestures to communicate. • Does not make conversational babble when learning to speak.
Other	• Difficulty adjusting to any type of change; insists on rigid rituals. • Delayed skills in other areas. • Other health conditions or learning issues. • Hyperactivity, impulsivity, inattentiveness. • Extremely sensitive to some sounds, sights, textures, or other sensory experiences, while seeking others. • Repetitive or unusual body movements such as flapping their hands or rocking their body.

Goodheart-Willcox Publisher

Recently, vaccines were ruled out as an environmental factor for ASD (**Figure 23.14**). Studies of potential environmental causes are just beginning.

FOCUS ON MENTAL HEALTH

Many mental health disorders are diagnosed as symptoms of ASD rather than as additional conditions. About 70 percent of children with ASD, however, have an additional diagnosis, including social anxiety disorder, ADHD, or ODD.

Prostock-Studio/iStock via Getty Images Plus

Figure 23.14 It was once thought that vaccines administered during early childhood were an environmental factor for children developing ASD. Recent research, however, has shown this not to be true. *Where could you go for reliable information about recent research concerning vaccines?*

Lesson 23.1 Review and Assessment

1. A child with a borderline special need differs _____ from a child with typical development. (23.1.1)
   A. somewhat
   B. little
   C. very little
   D. much

2. A gross-motor condition that affects a child's muscle coordination is _____. (23.1.2)
   A. cerebral palsy
   B. spina bifida
   C. muscular dystrophy
   D. paralysis

3. A child with an articulation disorder would most likely _____. (23.1.2)
   A. speak in a nasal pitch
   B. pause between sounds
   C. use prolonged sounds
   D. substitute one sound for another

4. **True or False.** Children who are gifted and talented usually excel in school. (23.1.3)

5. A child with developmental dyscalculia has problems with _____. (23.1.3)
   A. math
   B. reading
   C. articulation
   D. social rules

6. Having repeated and unwanted thoughts and performing repetitive behaviors are symptoms of _____ disorder. (23.1.4)
   A. social anxiety
   B. oppositional defiant
   C. obsessive-compulsive
   D. panic

7. Individuals with autism spectrum disorder share all of the following commonalities except _____. (23.1.5)
   A. difficulty with social interaction
   B. sleep disturbances
   C. restricted interests
   D. repetitive behaviors

Supporting Children with Special Needs

Learning Outcomes

After studying this lesson, you will be able to

23.2-1 **summarize** how to support children with physical special needs.

23.2-2 **describe** types of support available for children with intellectual special needs.

23.2-3 **explain** the types of support available for children with social-emotional special needs.

23.2-4 **identify** support that is available for children with other types of special needs.

23.2-5 **describe** education and services guidelines in place for children with special needs.

23.2-6 **describe** the role of support groups in helping families who have children with special needs.

Key Terms

antidepressants

antipsychotics

Braille system

cognitive-behavioral therapy

Early Intervention Program for Infants and Toddlers with Disabilities

inclusion

Individualized Education Plan (IEP)

Individualized Family Service Plan (IFSP)

Individuals with Disabilities Education Act (IDEA)

mainstreaming

special education teachers

Reading and Notetaking Activity

Before reading this lesson, scan the lesson headings. Write a paragraph describing what you already know about these topics. Explain where you got the information you have—from conversations, the media, or research, for example. As you are reading, compare and contrast the information in the chapter with your prior knowledge. Organize your notes around the information you already know. After reading, consider how your prior knowledge of the subject matter helped you understand this topic.

Introduction

An estimated 1 out of every 10 children has special needs. These needs can affect physical, intellectual, and social-emotional development (**Figure 23.15**). Special needs may vary from borderline to profound and may be chronic or correctable. Also, many children have more than one special need.

Figure 23.15 Special Needs in Children

Special Needs	Examples
Physical	• Gross-motor conditions • Muscular dystrophy • Spina bifida • Cerebral palsy • Paralysis • Amputated or missing limbs • Vision conditions • Legal blindness • Nearsightedness • Farsightedness • Hearing conditions • Hearing loss • Deafness • Speech disorders
Intellectual	• Intellectual disabilities • Gifts and talents • Learning disorders • Language disorders
Social-emotional	• Anxiety disorders • Generalized anxiety disorder • Obsessive compulsive disorder (OCD) • Separation anxiety disorder • Panic disorder • Specific phobia • Social anxiety disorder • Post-traumatic stress disorder (PTSD) • Depression • Bipolar disorder • Childhood schizophrenia • Oppositional defiant disorder
Other types of special needs	• Attention-deficit hyperactivity disorder (ADHD) • Autism spectrum disorder (ASD)

Goodheart-Willcox Publisher

When considering the types of support needed for children with special needs, it is important to remember that *children are more alike than they are different*. All children have the same basic needs. They need physical care, intellectual stimulation, positive relationships with caregivers, and love. Support for children with special needs is based on the idea that, in addition to basic needs, children with special needs have additional needs that require different care. In addition to helping care for children's specific special needs, the government provides some services for the education and care of children with special needs. Lastly, supporting children with special needs also involves providing support for these children's families.

23.2-1 Supporting Children with Physical Special Needs

Helping children with physical special needs involves providing resources for the child to function well among other children and teaching the child to use these resources. The types of resources provided depend on the type of physical special need. Different types of physical disabilities and speech disorders require different types of help.

Support for Children with Physical Disabilities

Support for children with physical disabilities varies depending on the child's type of disability. For example, *orthopedic surgeons* can perform surgery to correct conditions involving bone structure or muscles. *Physiotherapists* (therapists who treat injuries with exercises and other physical treatments) often coordinate therapy plans with orthopedic surgeons. They can also aid caregivers in learning how to safely assist a child (by lifting, positioning, and using special equipment).

Children with vision conditions can see *pediatric ophthalmologists*, doctors who specialize in eye treatment. Children with vision conditions can also use services and aids, such as special readers that magnify and or change the display of print to help them function daily. Children with legal blindness may be eligible to receive certain services.

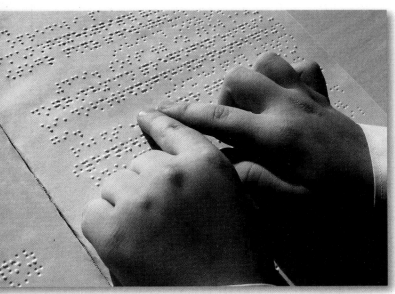

Focus on Speech

Early Identification

The first step in providing support for children with special needs is to *identify* the special need. Once a special need is identified, children with special needs should be given extra support or support that differs from that of most other children. According to brain development research, early identification and intervention make assistance more effective. Caregivers generally begin by seeking help from a pediatrician. Pediatricians can refer children for needed tests and can explain a

child's condition to caregivers and discuss ways to help the child.

In small groups, research the importance of early identification for children with special needs. Also research the common challenges that pediatricians and parents face in identifying special needs. Then, as a group, write a speech to persuade classmates of this importance. Give a group presentation of your speech in class.

Photo: naluwan/Shutterstock.com

They might learn to use the **Braille system**, a system of raised dots enabling people with vision conditions to read by touch (**Figure 23.16**).

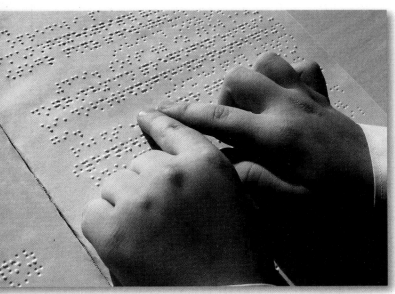

Alsu/Shutterstock.com

Figure 23.16 The Braille system is a written system of raised dots that helps people with vision conditions read signs, papers, and books by touch. *Why do you think Braille is important for communities?*

Audiologists, doctors who specialize in hearing, can provide support for children with hearing conditions. Children with hearing conditions might need a *cochlear implant* (electronic device that has an external part placed behind the ear and an implanted part under the skin) or hearing aids to help them hear and communicate. In cases in which the cochlear implant or hearing aids do not significantly help, children with hearing loss can use sign language or lip reading to communicate with others.

Support for Children with Speech Disorders

Children with speech disorders need encouragement and sometimes therapy to communicate clearly. Some children need encouragement to speak more slowly. Children may also need to see speech therapists who will help them devise solutions to their communication challenges. In many cases, speech disorders resolve without assistance. For example, stuttering typically begins between the ages of 18 months and 5 years old but resolves within one to two years in most cases.

23.2-2 Supporting Children with Intellectual Special Needs

Helping children with intellectual special needs involves tailoring activities and tasks to the children's intellectual developmental level. This may include providing additional instruction, therapy, and modified activities.

Support for Children with Intellectual Disabilities

The overall goal for helping children with intellectual disabilities is to develop their intellectual abilities to the fullest. As such, helping children with intellectual disabilities usually involves providing the children with additional, specialized instruction. Such help usually comes in the form of *special education teachers*. **Special education teachers** are teachers trained to work with children with special needs. In helping children with intellectual disabilities, they seek to teach and help these children grasp necessary information and life skills at the appropriate level.

They may also help assess children with intellectual disabilities. Special education teachers tend to work directly with parents and caregivers.

Support for Children with Gifts and Talents

Supporting children with gifts and talents usually involves the placement of these children in groups of other children with gifts and talents. Children with gifts and talents who learn in typical classrooms may feel bored or distracted, act out, and not reach their full potential. As such, children with gifts and talents are helped by learning environments that include other children with gifts and talents and more rigorous standards in the child's area of accelerated intellectual development (**Figure 23.17**).

Some schools provide special curriculum programs for children with gifts and talents, and other schools only admit children with gifts and talents. When schools do not have these programs, parents may often find extracurricular programs or private schools geared toward meeting their children's special needs.

Figure 23.17 Children with gifts and talents perform well in rigorous educational programs suited to their areas of giftedness or talent. *What schools for children with gifts and talents are in your community?*

Jose Girarte/iStock via Getty Images Plus

Support for Children with Learning Disorders

Because learning disorders emerge as academic challenges, they are often identified in school settings. Identification of learning disorders is usually done by a psychologist or school psychologist, and early identification is most helpful. Once a learning disorder is identified, schools and teachers can take measures to meet children's special needs. Usually, these measures focus on helping the child build on strengths and on developing ways to compensate for the child's areas of weakness. For example, if a child has dyslexia, they may have materials read orally by someone else or be given spoken directions. Many experts on learning disorders believe these children can succeed if given a customized educational strategy.

Support for Children with Language Disorders

Children with language disorders may benefit from therapy to recover their use of language. Aphasia therapy works to restore language as much as possible. Therapy also aids children in using remaining language skills and learning other methods of communicating (drawings, gestures, writing, or technology) as a way "to talk." Treatment for aphasia usually begins with a *neurologist* (a doctor who treats brain conditions). Once the neurologist's work is completed, the child will work with a speech-language pathologist.

23.2-3 Supporting Children with Social-Emotional Special Needs

Supporting children with social-emotional needs usually involves some form of therapy. Therapy helps children sort through their social anxieties and emotions and develop ways to respond to social-emotional challenges. The type of help provided depends on the type of need.

Support for Children with Anxiety Disorders

Helping children with anxiety disorders who live in stressful life circumstances involves removing or shielding these children from these circumstances.

Stressful life circumstances may include neglect, abuse, and a violent home or community.

For children with anxiety disorders who do not live in highly stressful environments, help involves regular appointments with a mental health specialist (**Figure 23.18**). Mental health specialists treat anxiety disorders using **cognitive-behavioral therapy**. This therapy teaches children to recognize their anxieties and develop coping strategies. Caregivers are included in the treatment and are taught how to reduce their children's anxieties and encourage them for their successes. Children with anxiety disorders benefit from having people who provide unconditional love and serve as "safety nets" (buffers). Cognitive-behavioral therapy for many anxiety disorders is highly successful. Medication is also needed along with coping strategies in some instances to help minimize feelings of anxiety and the physical symptoms that are associated with anxiety.

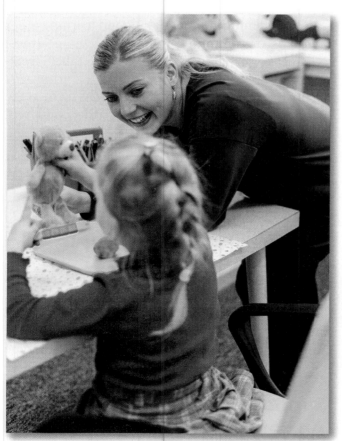

Figure 23.18 Children with anxiety disorders benefit from regular therapy with a mental health specialist. *Why is it important that therapy sessions be regular?*

Support for Children with Depression

Children with depression can be helped by identification, therapy, and medications. Identification is perhaps the most important part of helping these children. Children with depression can go for years without their needs being identified due to fears of admitting their feelings of sadness and due to misconceptions about what depression is.

Once depression is identified, children can receive help in the form of therapy. Therapy helps children process their emotions and talk about possible roots of their feelings. Children with depression may be helped by **antidepressants**, which are medications used to correct the chemical imbalance in neurotransmitters, especially serotonin, in the brain and boost mood. Supports vary depending on the child and the severity of their depression.

Support for Children with Childhood Schizophrenia

Providing support for children with childhood schizophrenia will usually involve the intervention of a *psychiatrist* who will prescribe appropriate medications and organize a plan for therapy. Helping children with childhood schizophrenia usually involves administering **antipsychotics**, medications that reduce symptoms of **psychosis** (a serious mental state characterized by delusions). Helping these children also involves individual and family therapy, training for children in academic and social skills, and in severe cases, hospitalization (**Figure 23.19**).

Figure 23.19 Hospitalization may be necessary to help a child with childhood schizophrenia. *How might hospitalization be helpful?*

Support for Children with ODD

Supporting children with ODD usually involves both child and family therapy and training. During these therapy sessions, professionals teach children effective social skills. In addition, parents and caregivers are given strategies for more effective guidance. Therapy for children with ODD is usually long term.

23.2-4 Supporting Children with Other Types of Special Needs

Special needs that affect multiple areas of development are some of the most difficult to identify. Supporting children with these types of special needs can also be difficult. Helping children with special needs that affect multiple areas of development usually involves therapy and, at times, medications.

Support for Children with Attention Disorders

Children with attention disorders may need specific types of environmental and instructional changes to help them concentrate on tasks and stay motivated. Some ways schools and teachers help these students include:

- restricting stimuli (providing fewer items for children to see, hear, or touch) during times when children need to concentrate
- establishing and enforcing adherence to a routine
- giving short, clear instructions (**Figure 23.20**)
- using acknowledgement and rewards
- providing experiences that are challenging, but manageable
- offering physical activities while **curtailing** (reducing) overexcitement
- ensuring the child has a healthful diet

When carefully monitored by doctors, some children with attention disorders are helped by medications. Giving medication without careful observations has been criticized for several reasons, including potential side effects on children and the concern that some parents may use medication as a quick fix without considering other alternatives. Parents and caregivers must make the best choice for their family when it comes to any type of medication for social and emotional disorders.

Figure 23.20 Clear and concise instructions help children with attention disorders better grasp information. *What is an example of a clear and concise instruction?*

monkeybusinessimages/ iStock via Getty Images Plus

Focus on Science

Antidepressants and the Brain

Some studies show that depression in children and adults is linked to an imbalance in the levels of certain neurotransmitters in the brain. The brain is made up of many neurons, and as you may recall, neurotransmitters are chemicals that travel across neuron synapses. These neurotransmitters help transmit electrical signals. The neurotransmitters possibly linked with depression include *serotonin* (sir-uh-TOH-nun), *norepinephrine* (NOR-eh-puh-NEH-frun), and *dopamine* (DOH-puh-meen).

Antidepressants treat depression in several ways depending on the type of medication. The most common antidepressants prevent neurons from *reuptaking* (reabsorbing) neurotransmitters, especially serotonin. Preventing the uptake of serotonin leaves more serotonin available to help communication between neurons, which seems to boost mood.

Antidepressants ease symptoms of moderate to severe depression in about 40 to 60 percent of people. Treatment-resistant depression, however, requires psychological therapy. Because brain chemistry is not fully understood, antidepressants are not considered the final answer to treating depression. For example, research is being conducted on the growth of new synapses and the generation and migration of new neurons as potentially causative of depression. Thus, before effective treatment of depression for all victims can occur, much more research will be needed. Even with the use of medication, doctors generally recommend therapy to help understand stressors and teach coping strategies.

Photo: otnaydur/Shutterstock.com

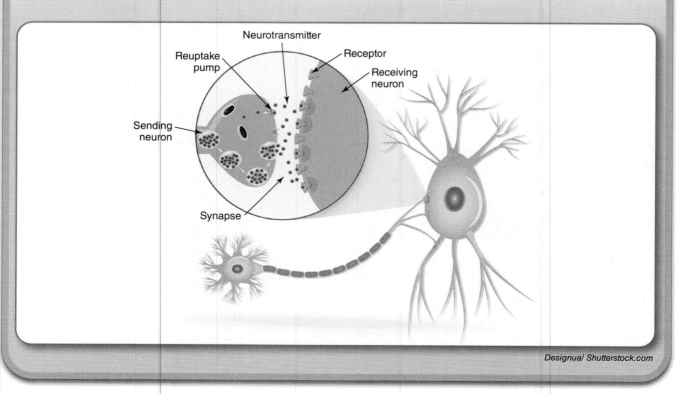

Designua/ Shutterstock.com

Support for Children with ASD

Support for children with ASD is most successful when ASD is identified early. Children with ASD can be taught how to socially interact, recognize facial expressions for emotions, and use gestures. They can also learn how to regulate their emotions although learning these skills may require intensive behavioral therapy. With help, many children with ASD can be fulfilled and manage their ASD throughout life. Children with more severe ASD will need more intense or frequent therapies and interventions.

23.2-5 Education and Services for Children with Special Needs

The United States government ensures that both education and appropriate services are available for children with special needs. To help meet children's special needs, the government has passed several acts and established a number of plans.

In 1990, the United States government passed the **Individuals with Disabilities Education Act (IDEA)**, a federal law governing the education of children with special needs. IDEA guarantees qualifying children with special needs the right to receive free and appropriate public education (**Figure 23.21**). Unless children with gifts and talents also have disabilities, disorders, or conditions, they do *not* qualify for help under IDEA. State and local funds are sometimes used to help these children develop their gifts and talents. On the whole, however, parents of children with gifts or talents are responsible for finding and financing services to meet their children's needs.

IDEA outlines ways for helping children with special needs and their families. IDEA includes three written documents that *outline* (specify; state clearly) required services for qualifying children with special needs.

wavebreakmedia/ iStock via Getty Images Plus

Figure 23.21 Under the provisions of IDEA, children with many types of special needs are guaranteed access to appropriate education. *What does it mean that IDEA guarantees appropriate education?*

Individualized Family Service Plan (IFSP)

The first document outlined by IDEA is the **Individualized Family Service Plan (IFSP)**. This plan guarantees that families can get the help they need for qualifying children with special needs from birth to three years of age. The IFSP focuses on the entire family's needs. The plan includes the formation of a team composed of parents or caregivers and experts from various agencies (such as from schools or social service agencies). One member of the team serves as a coordinator and ensures that the child and their parents receive all the services for which they are eligible under the IFSP. Usually, these services are administered near the family's home. An IFSP outlines the special caregiving skills parents and other caregivers need to perform to meet a child's special needs.

Individualized Education Plan (IEP)

The second document outlined by IDEA states that all qualifying children with special needs between 3 and 21 years of age are eligible to receive appropriate educational services. To receive these services, the child must be referred for testing, which requires parental consent (**Figure 23.22**).

aldomurillo/E+ via Getty Images

Figure 23.22 To be eligible for government services, children with special needs must undergo testing. This can sometimes be an obstacle for families because parents do not always want to give consent for this testing. *Why do you think some parents struggle with giving consent for their child to be tested?*

Based on testing results, an **Individualized Education Plan (IEP)**, which is tailored to the child's specific educational needs, is written. An IEP includes very specific goals for the child and a placement (typical class or special education class) agreement. The most common educational placement for children with special needs is **inclusion** (full-time placement in a regular classroom) rather than **mainstreaming** (a former term used for placing a child with special needs in a regular classroom for only part of the day). Together, parents, teachers, and school administrators design and implement the IEP. Parents also meet with their child's teachers on a regular basis. The child is retested routinely, and the plan is adjusted, as needed, to fit the child's changing educational needs and goals.

Early Intervention Program for Infants and Toddlers with Disabilities

The third part outlined in IDEA, the **Early Intervention Program for Infants and Toddlers with Disabilities**, serves infants and toddlers (through two years of age) who have developmental delays or who have identified physical and intellectual conditions that will likely cause developmental delays. High-quality early intervention services prepare children to successfully transition to preschool and kindergarten.

23.2-6 Support Groups for Families of Children with Special Needs

Family members are often shocked when they first learn their child has special needs. Gifts or talents children possess may shock parents because the active minds or special talents of these children often **baffle** (confuse) adults. Children with disabilities may also baffle adults and cause them to feel stress. Caregivers may need some time to adjust and learn how to meet their child's special needs. Sometimes families face this adjustment when a child is born.

Early Childhood Education Programs for Children with Special Needs

As with schools and educational institutions, early childhood education programs are also evolving to practice inclusion for children with special needs. In early childhood education programs, *inclusion* involves placing children with special needs and other children in the same group while providing special help for the children who need it. In these programs, teachers and caregivers work in teams and collaborate with other adults who provide help for children with special needs.

Programs that enroll children with special needs do have some unique features. In inclusionary programs, rooms are arranged with children's special needs in mind. For example, some programs provide space for the easy movement of children with wheelchairs and walkers. Other programs may provide *adaptive equipment* (objects such as eating utensils or chairs that can be adjusted to accommodate children with special needs) or *assistive technology* (programs that help children with special needs use technology).

The staff in programs that enroll children with special needs use *teamwork* to plan activities. While all children work on many of the same concepts and skills, some activities must be adapted for children with special needs. For these activities, teachers enlist the help of adults who work with children with special needs. For example, while a child with a physical disability may not be able to do the same puzzle as some other children, the child could enjoy puzzle time with the other children by using a puzzle with fewer pieces or knobs attached to each piece. An adult who works with children with special needs might make this accommodation and suggest other appropriate accommodations.

Programs enrolling children with special needs also utilize many group activities. In group activities, many children can do all parts of an activity, and children with special needs can enjoy at least some parts. The nature of each child's needs determines specific tasks they can perform. For example, a child with a physical disability may not be able to squat or toss a beanbag, but they could learn a song. A child with a hearing condition could enjoy squatting and tossing the beanbag, even if they could not learn the song. By planning group activities, teachers can meet the needs of all children in the program.

Research Activity

Working with a partner, identify two early childhood education programs that enroll children with special needs. If possible, these programs should be local. Using reliable online resources, research the programs and take notes about types of accommodations the programs use to include children with special needs. If information is not available online, obtain needed information by visiting the program or interviewing the director or a teacher at the program site. Summarize your findings in a short essay.

Photo: Tom Wang/Shutterstock.com

Other times, a special need may not be identified until the school-age years. For still other parents, an accident or illness may cause a child to have a special need.

Members of families who have children with special needs often join support groups (**Figure 23.23**). At the national level, these groups provide family members with the latest information on children with special needs. National groups also seek money for research and assistance for families of children who need costly training or equipment. At the local level, groups support the goals of national groups. They also provide helpful contacts and services among those with similar needs.

MBI/Shutterstock.com

Figure 23.23 Support groups provide relationships and education for families who have children with special needs. These groups might discuss common feelings or struggles and often refer families to helpful resources. *What support groups for families of children with special needs are available in your community?*

Lesson 23.2 Review and Assessment

1. A cochlear implant is used in the treatment of a _____ condition. (23.2.1)
   A. vision
   B. speech
   C. hearing
   D. muscle

2. **True or False.** Special education teachers tend to work directly with parents and caregivers. (23.2.2)

3. Treatment for childhood schizophrenia usually involves _____. (23.2.3)
   A. cognitive-behavioral therapy
   B. antidepressants
   C. speech therapy
   D. antipsychotics

4. Providing experiences that are challenging, but manageable is a suggestion for helping students with _____. (23.2.4)
   A. attention disorders
   B. childhood depression
   C. childhood schizophrenia
   D. anxiety disorders

5. **True or False.** Children with gifts and talents qualify for help under the Individuals with Disabilities Education Act, even if they do not also have disabilities, disorders, or conditions. (23.2.5)

6. An Individualized Education Plan (IEP) _____. (23.2.5)
   A. allows a school to test a child without parental consent
   B. includes specific educational goals for a child
   C. focuses on an entire family's needs
   D. serves the needs of infants and children under age 3

7. **True or False.** One objective of national support groups for families of children with special needs is to support research efforts related to that condition or disorder. (23.2.6)

Summary

Lesson 23.1

23.1-1 Children with special needs are children who differ from children with typical development in one or more ways. They may exhibit differences in motor skills, seeing, hearing, speech, intellectual abilities, learning, language, and social behaviors.

23.1-1 Special needs may occur in one or more areas of development, may develop due to acceleration or delay, are identified through observations and tests, and vary in intensity, duration, and permanence.

23.1-1 Special needs exist on a spectrum, and a child will be typical in all areas other than the area(s) of need.

23.1-2 Physical special needs are often identified by physical developmental delays. Possible causes include genetic disorders, congenital conditions, serious illnesses, and spinal cord, brain, or other bodily injuries.

23.1-2 Types of physical special needs include physical disabilities (such as gross-motor conditions, hearing conditions, and vision conditions) and speech disorders.

23.1-3 Children whose intellectual development differs from children with typical development have intellectual special needs, often identified by intellectual developmental delays or accelerations.

23.1-3 Children with intellectual developmental delays may experience delays in motor skills, speech, problem-solving, and logical thinking. They may also have a hard time understanding social rules and remembering things.

23.1-3 Children with gifts and talents show high performance in one or more of the following areas: general intellectual ability, specific academic aptitude, creative or productive thinking, leadership ability, high skill in the visual or performing arts, and high psychomotor ability.

23.1-3 Children with learning disorders have average or above-average intelligence, but their academic achievement is below what would be expected for their intelligence and grade level. Developmental dyslexia and developmental dyscalculia are two common examples.

23.1-3 Children with language disorders lack the ability to understand and use language. Acquired childhood aphasia, the most serious language disorder of childhood, is the partial or total loss of the ability to understand words and use language.

23.1-4 Children who differ socially and emotionally from those with typical development have social-emotional special needs, which are identified by behavioral changes and by social-emotional developmental delays.

23.1-4 Social-emotional special needs include anxiety disorders (generalized anxiety disorder, obsessive-compulsive disorder, separation anxiety disorder, panic disorder, specific phobia, social anxiety disorder, and post-traumatic stress disorder), depression, childhood schizophrenia, and oppositional defiant disorder (ODD).

23.1-5 Some special needs affect many areas of development. These special needs include attention disorders, such as Attention Deficit Hyperactivity Disorder (ADHD) and Autism Spectrum Disorder (ASD).

Lesson 23.2

23.2-1 Help for children with special needs hinges on the idea that children are more alike than they are different. The first step in providing support is to identify the special need.

23.2-1 Children with physical special needs may receive physical therapy and accommodations, such as adaptive equipment or correction devices. Specialists who assist children with physical special needs include physiotherapists, pediatric ophthalmologists, orthopedic surgeons, speech therapists, and audiologists.

23.2-2 Intellectual special needs are met through additional services, such as special education teachers in classrooms, programs or schools for children with gifts and talents, and aid for children with learning disorders.

23.2-2 Children with language disorders may benefit from aphasia therapy to recover their use of language.

23.2-3 Social-emotional special needs are met through therapy and some medications.

23.2-3 Mental health specialists treat anxiety disorders using cognitive-behavioral therapy.

23.2-3 Children with depression can be helped by identification, therapy, and medications (antidepressants).

23.2-3 Children with childhood schizophrenia usually requires a psychiatrist who will prescribe appropriate medications, such as antipsychotics, and organize a plan for therapy.

23.2-3 Supporting children with ODD is usually long-term and involves child and family therapy and training.

23.2-4 Special needs involving multiple areas of development are some of the most difficult to meet, but help is available. Help usually involves therapy and sometimes medications.

23.2-5 Through a federal law, the Individuals with Disabilities Education Act (IDEA), the U.S. government funds and outlines three programs that provide for the identification of and services for children with special needs.

23.2-5 The Individualized Family Service Plan (IFSP) guarantees that families can get help for qualifying children with special needs from birth to three years of age.

23.2-5 An Individualized Education Plan (IEP) is tailored to the child's specific educational needs and includes very specific goals for the child and a placement agreement.

23.2-5 The Early Intervention Program for Infants and Toddlers with Disabilities serves infants and toddlers who have developmental delays or who have identified physical and intellectual conditions that will likely cause developmental delays.

23.2-6 Support groups can help families struggling to meet children's special needs.

College and Career Portfolio

Portfolio Presentation Notes

As you prepare to present your portfolio, it is wise to prepare notes that you can quickly reference before or during the presentation. These notes will ensure that you do not forget anything important.

- Identify the highlights of your portfolio presentation. Verify these highlights with a teacher or career counselor.
- Create note cards or some other type of notes you can study or quickly reference in case you forget.

Recall and Application

1. An anxiety disorder is most likely to affect which area of a child's development? (23.1.1)
   A. Physical
   B. Intellectual
   C. Social-emotional
   D. Physical, intellectual, and social-emotional

2. A gross-motor condition that is the result of a genetic disease that weakens a child's muscles is _____. (23.1.2)
   A. cerebral palsy
   B. spina bifida
   C. muscular dystrophy
   D. paralysis

3. All of the following are signs of a possible vision condition in a child except _____. (23.1.2)
   A. squinting
   B. holding objects far away from the face
   C. showing difficulty with depth perception
   D. rubbing the eyes frequently

4. Which of the following behaviors are considered possible signs of an intellectual developmental delay? (23.1.3)
   A. Difficulty managing frustration when standards are not met or with threats of shortcomings and failure
   B. Difficulty with telling time or understanding time concepts
   C. Difficulty remembering things and not readily seeing the consequences of actions
   D. Difficulty with listening or correctly expressing thoughts

5. Which statement about oppositional defiant disorder is correct? (23.1.4)
   A. It is an anxiety disorder.
   B. It is caused by a genetic mutation.
   C. It usually begins during puberty.
   D. Its symptoms generally worsen rather than improve.

6. **True or False.** Vaccines are not an environmental factor associated with autism spectrum disorder. (23.1.5)

7. **True or False.** The identification of attention-deficit hyperactivity disorder in a child is based on observation rather than on tests. (23.1.5)

8. **True or False.** When considering the types of support needed for children with special needs, it is important to remember that children are more alike than they are different. (23.2.1)

9. A child with a vision condition would most likely receive treatment from a/n _____. (23.2.1)
   A. physiotherapist
   B. pediatric ophthalmologist
   C. orthopedic surgeon
   D. audiologist

10. **True or False.** The identification of a learning disorder in a child is usually done by a parent or caregiver. (23.2.2)

11. Which of the following is true about childhood depression? (23.2.3)
    A. It is typically treated with antipsychotic medications.
    B. It is uncommon in the United States.
    C. It may be caused by a chemical imbalance in brain neurotransmitters.
    D. It is easily identified and treated.

12. **True or False.** Children with autism spectrum disorder can be taught how to socially interact, recognize facial expressions for emotions, and use gestures. (23.2.4)

13. **True or False.** Mainstreaming is the most common educational placement for children with special needs. (23.2.5)

14. **True or False.** Local support groups are a valuable asset for families seeking information about services related to their children's conditions. (23.2.6)

Critical Thinking

1. **Identify.** Draw the spectrum of special needs on a board or whiteboard and, as a class, brainstorm examples of specific types of special needs that fall in various places on the spectrum. Try to discuss an example of each special need covered in this chapter.

2. **Cause and effect.** While speech disorders and language disorders both affect children's communication abilities, the causes of these needs are different. Review this text's information about speech and language

disorders and then read at least one reliable article about the causes of these disorders. Write a short essay comparing the causes of these needs.

3. **Draw conclusions.** Imagine a parent confides in you that their child is failing in school, and they suspect the child may have an intellectual disability. You know the child is of average intelligence, so you doubt the parent's assumption. To organize your thoughts, create a T-chart and list the characteristics of children with intellectual disabilities and children with learning disorders. Draw conclusions about how you would explain the difference to this parent.

4. **Compare and contrast.** In small groups, compare and contrast the traits of children with gifts and children with talents. Create two films in which you explain and demonstrate the characteristics of each special need. Also discuss traits of children with gifts *and* talents.

5. **Determine.** Working with a partner, discuss why depression and childhood schizophrenia are considered special needs. What qualities of special needs do they possess? If someone challenged the idea that these disorders were special needs, determine how you would explain your position.

6. **Analyze.** The way attention disorders are classified has changed since ADHD was first identified. In small groups, analyze why classifications for attention disorders changed as they did. What does the new classification achieve? How does the new classification affect the ways adults help children with attention disorders?

7. **Evaluate.** Imagine a local family with these three children: an infant who is legally blind, a preschooler who is gifted, and a school-age child who has ASD. Working with a partner, evaluate the educational and other services that these three children and their parents are eligible to receive according to the programs under the federal law, IDEA. Research the next steps the family would need to take to obtain these services.

8. **Make inferences.** Learning that a child has special needs can be stressful for parents

and caregivers, especially if parents did not foresee the need. Working with a partner, interview a parent whose child has a special need. How did the parent feel when their child's need was identified? What resources or support groups helped the parent?

Core Skills

1. **Technology.** In groups of four, review the physical, intellectual, and social-emotional developmental delays for infants, toddlers, preschoolers, and school-age children. Assign each group member one stage of development and study the developmental delays in detail. For each delay, write a real-life example and one way the delay could be identified. Then, as a group, combine your projects into a comprehensive digital presentation outlining examples and methods for identifying developmental delays. Deliver your presentation to the class and then lead a discussion about ways to optimize the development of children with these delays.

2. **Reading and speaking.** Visit a local library or search online to find articles or books describing types of physical disabilities. Choose one article or book and skim the material. Identify two types of physical disabilities not covered in this text and write a short summary of each, including the characteristics, causes, and treatments for each disability. Present the information orally to the class.

3. **Research and technology.** Techniques for identifying intellectual disabilities have changed over the years to rely less on IQ tests. Using reliable online or print resources, research the role of IQ tests in identifying intellectual disabilities and the most current methods for identification. Read at least three scholarly sources and compile them into a bibliography. Finally, present your findings in a slideshow presentation to the class.

4. **Reading and listening.** Visit the National Institute of Mental Health's website and read more about the causes, identification, and treatment for ASD. As you are reading, write questions you have about the material on the website. Then, arrange an interview with a special education teacher or other adult who works with children who have ASD. Ask questions and discuss your notes to increase your understanding of ASD.

5. **Research and writing.** Legislation and public policies for children with special needs have changed as new special needs and practices have developed. Using reliable online or print resources, research historical legislation, policies, or practices for educating and caring for children with special needs. Conduct research covering at least two historical periods and then write a three-page essay comparing historical practices to current policy.

6. **CTE Career Readiness Practice.** Imagine you are a crisis child care worker in a low-income area of the U.S. Many families in your area have children with special needs but are not always aware of or able to access needed services. To help these families, research federal and state resources for low-income families who have children with special needs. How can families access government services? What other services are available for them? Create a professional-looking pamphlet including these services and their contact information. Working with a partner, practice walking a parent through the pamphlet.

Observations

1. In small groups, find and watch a documentary about the life of a person with a special need. During the documentary, take notes about the person's feelings toward the special need and how the person's needs were met. Afterward, discuss the documentary in your group.

2. As a class, visit an early childhood education program or classroom that has children with special needs. Observe how, if at all, the classroom or program accommodates children with special needs (such as: makes environmental changes; has special education teachers available; makes curriculum changes for those with differing needs). How are the children's needs being met?

Chapter
24

Providing Early Childhood Education in Group Settings

Essential Question

What are the program options for early childhood care, and what factors should be considered when choosing a program?

Case Study   How Do Early Learning Standards Impact Preschool Programs?

As a class, read the case study and discuss the questions that follow. After you finish studying the chapter, discuss this case study again. Have your opinions changed based on what you learned?

When Bri's state announced the adoption of new early learning standards, Bri was worried along with all the other preschool teachers about the effect on their careers. No one wanted to lose their current preschool program and the developmentally appropriate practices (DAP) they had worked so hard to implement.

*The preschool director called a meeting and distributed the new learning standards, listened to the teachers' comments, and expressed understanding for their concerns. "The new learning standards should be viewed as an **outline** of possible learning content," the director said. "It is up to us, as teachers, to **embed** the learning standards into quality learning experiences based on DAP. Unlike standards that focus primarily on language arts, literacy, and mathematics, early learning standards focus on **all** domains of child development. Over the next few days, we will take*

one standard daily and talk about how our current learning activities are already meeting this standard."

Bri said, "Many parents do not seem to understand our use of DAP. How can we help parents see the value of our approach?"

"That is a good question," the director said. "As we review these standards, let us consider how we might share our thinking with parents."

Give It Some Thought

1. Why are DAP important when helping children meet standards in preschool programs?
2. What would happen if teachers taught content without adapting it to children's needs?

Lesson 24.1

Early Childhood Education Programs

Key Terms

center-based child care

child care programs

child care resources and referral (CCR&R) agencies

child development laboratories

early childhood education programs

family child care

fingerplays

for-profit programs

Head Start

in-home child care

kindergartens

Montessori schools

not-for-profit program

on-site child care programs

pre-K programs

preschools

private programs

public programs

school-age child care (SACC) programs

universal preschool programs

Learning Outcomes

After studying this lesson, you will be able to

24.1-1 **differentiate** between the various types of child care and early childhood education options.

24.1-2 **identify** current trends in early childhood education programs.

Reading and Notetaking Activity

Before reading this lesson, scan the lesson headings. Write a paragraph describing what you already know about these topics. Explain where you got the information you have—from conversations, the media, or research, for example. As you are reading, compare and contrast the information in the chapter with your prior knowledge. Organize your notes around the information you already know. After reading, consider how your prior knowledge of the subject matter helped you understand this topic.

Introduction

As children grow and develop, they will likely participate in an early childhood education program. **Early childhood education programs** are child care and education arrangements. These programs may be informal arrangements (such as in-home care and family care programs) or formal arrangements (such as center-based child care and preschools). Formal arrangements are more likely to have a planned educational program in addition to care.

Many types of early childhood education programs exist, and types vary depending on the ages of the children participating, the children's developmental levels, and parents' preferences. Over the past few decades, the numbers of early childhood education programs have increased. The landscape of early childhood education programs continues to shift as new trends shape child care and education practices and programs.

24.1-1 Types of Early Childhood Education Programs

There are many types of early childhood education programs, but all are either public or private in sponsorship. **Public programs** are early childhood education programs funded by local, state, or federal governments. **Private programs** are early childhood education programs owned by individuals and religious or other nongovernment groups. Whether public or private, types of early childhood education programs cater to families with varying needs. Some types of early childhood education programs include child care programs, child development laboratories, Head Start programs, prekindergarten programs, Montessori schools, kindergartens, and primary school programs (**Figure 24.1**). These programs differ in several ways.

Child Care Programs

Child care programs refer to programs that provide care for children for extended hours, usually between 9 and 12 hours a day. The main purpose of child care programs is to provide *custodial care* (basic care) for children when parents or guardians are not available. Most child care programs also provide education for children from infancy through the preschool years. They may even serve school-age children at times when school is not in session. Typically, by the high school years, children are involved in sports, clubs, or other activities that are provided through the school, but many participate in programs that are not school-related. Other teens get their first jobs during the high school years or stay home unsupervised in self-care.

There are four main types of child care programs—*in-home child care*, *family child care*, *center-based child care*, and *school-age child care*. Some caregivers use combinations of these arrangements, such as a center-based child care program for work hours and family child care for other hours. The type of care parents choose depends on many factors, including the number and ages of children, costs of care, family goals for children, locations of employment, work hours, and types of child care locally available. No one type of child care program is best for every family; each type has its advantages and disadvantages.

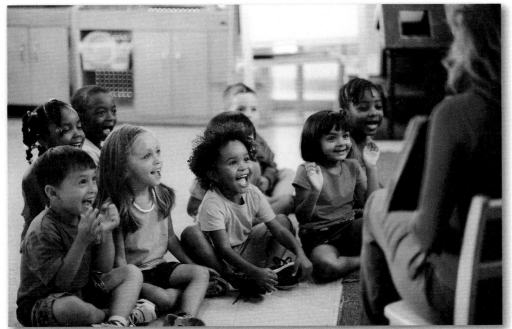

FatCamera/iStock via Getty Images Plus

Figure 24.1 Early childhood education programs vary from those that only care for basic needs to those that provide many special activities to enhance all areas of development. *Which local early childhood education programs are you familiar with?*

In-Home Child Care

In-home child care takes place in the child's own home. In these arrangements, parents can likely be assured that children receive all of a caregiver's attention. These children stay in a home atmosphere during care and can be cared for even if they are ill. While these child care programs provide limited education for children, they can be convenient and assuring for parents of young children.

In-home care can be provided by parents, relatives, or nonrelatives. Care by a parent may involve one parent staying home to care for the children. In families in which both parents work, parents may provide this type of care by working alternate schedules so one parent is always home or working from home. In-home care by a parent is more common for infants and toddlers than for preschoolers. *Homeschooling*, in which parents educate their children in the home, is also a type of in-home child care. Some homeschooling arrangements include several families.

Besides in-home care by a parent, in-home care by a relative is very common. For this type of care, parents may ask grandparents, aunts or uncles, cousins, or older siblings to care for their children. This type of in-home child care is convenient for parents whose families live nearby or are available to care for children.

Only a small percentage of children have care provided by nonrelatives in the home. For the most part, nonrelative caregivers in the home are *housekeepers*, *au pairs* (oh PERS), or *nannies* (**Figure 24.2**).

Family Child Care

Family child care is care provided by a person for a small number of children in their own home. Some family child care homes are operated by people wanting a small business in their home. Other family child care homes are run by a parent of young children. The parent stays home with their own children and provides care for other children, too. Child care laws vary among the states, but most family child care homes serve a maximum of six or seven children, including the caregiver's own children. If any child is under two years of age, the maximum number of children served is often four or five.

The type of children's activities in family child care varies greatly. Some child care homes are run much like child care centers. For example, these homes might offer a structured schedule, meals and snacks, and activities. Many family child care homes follow less rigid schedules than child care centers. Children in family child care may do homelike activities, such as helping the caregiver do housekeeping tasks, visiting with friends who come to the home, and even going on shopping trips as well as playing with toys.

Figure 24.2 In-Home Child Care by Nonrelatives

Nonrelative Caregivers	Characteristics
Au pairs	• Provide child care for a host family as part of a cultural exchange program • Receive room, board, cultural experiences, and transportation from the host family for services • Can share their culture and customs with the host family
Nannies	• Are professionals who work for a family to provide in-home child care • May be temporary or long-term • May live in a family's home or come to the home daily, but do not do housework beyond preparing meals for the children unless those duties are outlined in their job offer • May have training beyond high school in early childhood education, health and safety, and nutrition • May be certified as *Certified Household Managers*, *Certified Professional Nannies*, or *Certified Professional Governesses*

Goodheart-Willcox Publisher

Many parents rely on family child care arrangements because they need more flexible hours than those often provided by other child care programs. Other families need family child care because other child care programs may not be available in their communities. Furthermore, many parents want family child care because they see this arrangement as similar to the type of care they would provide if not employed, and others see the program more like that of a small child care center. Other advantages of family child care programs are listed in **Figure 24.3**.

Family child care homes may be regulated or unregulated. *Regulated family child care homes* are homes that have reported their business to the state and have a state license or a certificate of registration to operate. In this type of home, parents can be assured of at least a minimum standard of quality.

Unregulated family child care homes are homes that do *not* report their business to the state. Therefore, they do not have a state license or certificate of registration to operate. If the state is unaware of a family child care home, it cannot regulate the care provided there. Some of these unregulated homes have too many children or do not provide

safe care. The operator of the child care home may or may not be following the state laws regarding number of children or other safety issues. Caregivers in these homes may not have had a criminal background check. Because parents cannot be certain of the quality of care provided in these homes, it is recommended that parents only enroll their children in regulated family child care homes.

Center-Based Child Care

Center-based child care is group child care provided in a center (not a home). For the most part, center-based child care serves parents who are full-time employees, but other at-home parents may also enroll their children for the benefits of the program. Sometimes, child care centers are called **preschools** because they serve preschool-age children.

Child care centers differ in the number of children they serve. Many centers serve 20 or fewer children who are cared for in a building with one or two large rooms. Others enroll several hundred children who are grouped by age and placed in classrooms with each group under the care of one teacher and an assistant teacher. Large centers are multiroom buildings resembling a school.

Figure 24.3 Advantages of Family Child Care

Type of Children	Advantages
Infants and toddlers	Using family child care for infants and toddlers is often less expensive than using center-based child care. Also, infants and toddlers need much individual attention, which may be more available in a family child care home.
Children who are prone to mild illnesses, such as colds, sore throats, and ear infections	Pediatricians often advise parents of these children to limit the children's contact with large groups of children. Because family child care homes have fewer children, these may be a better choice than center-based child care.
Children who need part-time or flexible-schedule care	Part-time or flexible-schedule care is more often available in family child care homes than in center-based child care. Centers try to maximize their profits by filling as many placements as they can with children who need full-time care. Some centers charge the same rate for part- and full-time care, while many family child care providers charge a reduced rate for part-time care.
School-age children	Most center-based child care programs are designed for young children. These programs may not meet the needs of children who are school-age. Furthermore, many older children only need part-time care.
Children who live in rural areas	Many rural areas do not have much selection in center-based child care. In these areas, many more children attend family child care homes than centers.

Goodheart-Willcox Publisher

State licensing laws set the standards for all aspects of center-based child care programs (such as staff qualifications, numbers of children per teacher, building and outside requirements, food services, and basic program activities). Program activities can vary a great deal, but most programs have basic play areas, such as reading, block building, dramatic play, art, science, and computer centers for play. Most groups have activities, too, such as story time, group games, music, outdoor time, and field trips. Due to the number of children and the emphasis on socialization of children, caregivers emphasize cooperative play and social living (**Figure 24.4**).

There are many advantages to center-based child care. Large centers are often open long hours, meeting the needs of many working parents. They all have programs for preschool children, and some have programs for infants and toddlers, too. Thus, children can stay in the same center for several years, and siblings can typically be at the same center, too. Center-based child care programs must be licensed, ensuring the basic minimum quality of care. Many parents like the

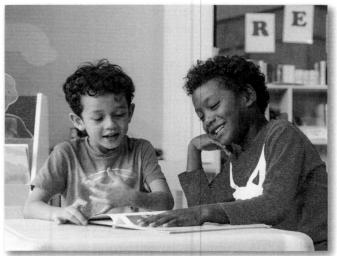

Weedezign/iStock via Getty Images Plus

Figure 24.4 Center-based child care can have positive effects on children's social and collaboration skills. *What types of collaborative activities might take place in a child care center?*

activities and equipment provided for children in these programs. Some programs also provide helpful special services, such as transportation for children and special classes, such as dance.

Focus on
Health

Center-Based Child Care Can Reduce Risk of Child Neglect and Abuse

Center-based child care programs can have a large role in reducing risks of child neglect and abuse. These programs can be a service to at-risk families and can be a source of information for parents and caregivers who do not understand the development and needs of their children. Center-based child care programs reduce the risks of child neglect and abuse by:

- providing parents and caregivers with social connections to other adults (thus reducing feelings of isolation)

- providing knowledge about parenting, child development, and developmentally appropriate behaviors
- sharing guidance and discipline strategies with knowledge about the behaviors of children
- caring for children several hours a day and allowing parents or caregivers respite from full-time child care

Photo: wavebreakmedia/Shutterstock.com

Center-based programs are divided between two types of ownership/sponsorship. These include the following:

- *for-profit programs.* Most center-based child care programs are **for-profit programs**, meaning they are set up to make money and run as businesses. These centers are owned either by individuals or corporations. Other for-profit center-based programs are *national chains* and *franchises*. **National chains** are a group of businesses owned by one company. **Franchises** are a group of businesses originally owned by a corporation and sold to different owners. These owners use the same name, building design and equipment, and often provide the same services. Franchise owners also receive business advice from the franchiser. Because child care is labor intensive and for-profit centers are businesses, these centers are often more expensive and thus not affordable for all families.
- *not-for-profit programs.* Other center-based programs are **not-for-profit programs** (also called *nonprofit programs*). A not-for-profit center's income only covers current costs and the surplus needed to keep the center operating on an ongoing basis or to expand services. Most not-for-profit programs are sponsored and partially funded by religious or service groups, businesses, hospitals, branches of the

armed services, or colleges. Not-for-profit programs sponsored by businesses for their employees' children are called **on-site child care programs** and are an employee benefit. Child care cooperatives (co-ops) are another type of not-for-profit program funded by families of enrolled children. In co-ops, parents offer their time and services to help keep costs low. Because income is not generated for making a profit and sponsors partially pay for the programs, not-for-profit programs are less expensive for parents than for-profit ones.

School-Age Child Care

School-age child care (SACC) programs, also known as *before- and after-school programs* or *out-of-school programs*, provide child care for children between 5 and 14 years of age. These programs provide care when school is not in session, including before and after school, on school holidays or vacations, and during the summer or track out periods for year-round schools. The majority of households with school-age children have working parents, and a typical school day is shorter than the standard workday. Many families prefer to find part-time care for these times rather than leave their children unsupervised in self-care. Because part-time care can be difficult to find, however, quality SACC programs are needed and important to communities (**Figure 24.5**).

Figure 24.5 SACC programs benefit children, families, and communities. If a SACC program or youth program is not available, parents can advocate for programs in their area. *What SACC programs are available in your community?*

monkeybusinessimages/iStock via Getty Images Plus

Many children in the United States do not attend early childhood education programs. Instead, they care for themselves while parents or other caregivers are not available. These children are known as *children in self-care*.

There are few states with laws about the age at which children can legally be left in self-care. In addition to the child's age, the success of self-care is dependent on several other factors. These include the child's maturity, the safety of the home and the neighborhood, and the child's and caregivers' feelings about self-care.

Successful self-care also depends on how well parents and caregivers prepare their children. Children who are left in self-care need to learn effective self-care skills from their parents or other adults in their lives. To prepare children for self-care, parents and other caregivers can do the following:

- Make sure the child learns safety rules, such as those shown in the *Rules for Safe Self-Care* chart.
- Ensure that children communicate where they are, what they are doing, and whom they are with.
- Set rules for children about using appliances, digital media devices, power tools, and other equipment. Other rules may involve having friends over and leaving the house.
- Establish a routine for children to follow.
- Begin self-care gradually, if possible. Start with a short period when the child stays alone as the parent or caregiver does a quick, nearby errand or visits briefly with a neighbor. As the child shows confidence, adults can gradually increase the time to cover the amount of time between school and the adults' arrival home.

Research Activity

In small groups, use reliable resources to research the positive and negative effects of self-care on children, families, and communities. After researching, discuss your findings in your group. Share the highlights from your discussion with the class.

Rules for Safe Self-Care

- Keep house keys with you at all times.
- If walking home from school, walk with friends; come straight home unless other plans are first approved by parent or caregiver.
- Call parent or caregiver upon arrival.
- Do not enter the house if a door is open or a window is broken.
- Tell a trusted adult if anything or anyone frightens you.
- Call 911 in case of emergency and know how to give the address to your house.
- Practice what to do while waiting for emergency responders. (For example, in the case of fire, evacuate house, call 911, and wait at a designated place for emergency responders.)
- Upon entering the house, use locks and set alarm system if you have one.
- Never open the door at home; talk through the door if needed.
- If there is a landline phone, only answer phone calls if the caller is your parent/caregiver or an approved person.
- Never tell people at the door or over the phone that you are home alone.
- Arrange an emergency evacuation plan.

Goodheart-Willcox Publisher

Photo: Tom Wang/Shutterstock.com

SACC programs have many advantages. These programs ensure the safety and health of children who might otherwise be in self-care. Programs often have a wide variety of activities from which children may choose. In some SACC programs called *clubs*, parents choose from a menu of activities for their children. Most SACC programs provide

- care (protection, shelter, food, and guidance)
- recreation (supervised play or specific skill development activities, such as dance, ball games, or swimming)
- diversion (crafts, drama, or field trips)
- education (such as help with homework or lessons in music or dance)

The majority of SACC programs are affiliated with schools or agencies that serve youth. In schools, SACC programs are often operated by non-school sponsors, such as the YMCA. Other groups that operate SACC programs include religious groups, park and recreation facilities, housing authorities, military bases, family child care homes, child care centers, and companies.

As is true of all types of child care, parents may have trouble finding quality SACC programs and affording the costs for quality. For providers, the challenges of running a SACC program include finding suitable housing for a part-time program and planning details if space must be shared with other programs.

Child Development Laboratories

Child development laboratories provide education and physical care for children who are under five years of age while serving as child development research sites. They also offer training opportunities for adults in child-related careers or for students training to get degrees in child-related fields. To enroll children in child development laboratories, parents must sign a release that allows the child to be part of all research studies being conducted and to be under the care and guidance of adults in child care and education training. Parents are guaranteed that observations and reports used for research or training purposes will follow ethical guidelines. Parents also get detailed oral and written reports about their child's development.

When child development laboratories first opened in the United States, child development was becoming a science. These child care programs opened as laboratory schools directed by staff members associated with research and teaching hospitals and colleges.

Focus on Careers

Child Development Professor

Child development professors are *postsecondary teachers*, meaning they teach at colleges, universities, and other professional schools. Many child development laboratories are run by these professors, who conduct research and teach classes to students. Child development professors are considered to be experts in their field.

Career cluster: Education and training.

Education: Educational requirements include a related master's degree or Ph.D. depending on the college or university.

Job outlook: Future employment opportunities for postsecondary teachers are expected to grow much faster than the average for all occupations.

To learn more about a career as a child development professor, visit the United States Department of Labor's *Occupational Outlook Handbook* website. You will also be able to compare the job responsibilities, educational requirements, job outlook, and average pay of child development professors with similar occupations.

Photo: sirtravelalot/Shutterstock.com

Soon, the programs began to study children and train parents and teachers to care for and teach children.

Today, many child development laboratories are still part of research and teaching universities. These programs operate in some high schools, too. These high-quality programs employ university-associated child development professionals who oversee adults' research and teaching. The director and staff members of the children's program plan children's activities and establish a play setting that is rich with materials, equipment, other children, and teachers who are caring and well trained. The costs of these programs can make it difficult for child development laboratories to stay open, but there are still many throughout the United States that have become well known.

Head Start Programs

In the 1960s, Americans became concerned with the effects of poverty on young children. Studies had shown how important the early years were to a child's development. Americans wanted to help children living in poverty have quality experiences that were vital to their development. Therefore, in 1965, the federal government launched **Head Start**, a program for three- and four-year-old children from low-income families (**Figure 24.6**). As Head Start researchers realized that quality experiences

for infants and toddlers were also critical for all later development, they launched the *Early Head Start program* in 1995 to serve children from birth through 35 months of age.

Today, the Office of Head Start provides grants to local public and private not-for-profit agencies to provide educational, health, nutritional, social, and other services to children and their low-income families. Parents and families play a key part in planning and operating local Head Start programs. Head Start often helps these parents progress toward their educational, literacy, and employment goals.

Head Start programs can have long-term benefits for children when the programs are of good quality and when families and schools follow through on children's basic goals. Overall, children from quality Head Start programs achieve greater school success and higher high school graduation rates than their peers from similar backgrounds who are not enrolled in Head Start. Head Start graduates also show better social behaviors as adults, including acting more responsibly in family, work, and community settings. Experience with Head Start has helped researchers learn more about how to meet the needs of children from low-income families. This research is being applied toward new Head Start goals and toward other early childhood education programs.

Figure 24.6 Children in Head Start programs may be in need of food and medical care and may need additional help in learning important concepts and language skills. *Why is meeting children's basic needs so important to learning?*

alvarez/iStock via Getty Images Plus

Pre-K Programs

Pre-K programs, also called *prekindergartens,* refer to state-financed programs for three- and four-year-olds from low-income families. The majority of these programs operate in public school settings, but some programs are affiliated with local Head Start programs. A few operate as research laboratories at universities. A few states offer **universal preschool programs** (state-financed preschool programs for children from families of all income levels), and other states may soon follow as funding becomes available.

Because Head Start and state-funded preschool programs basically serve the same population of children and have many of the same program goals, many professionals believe that these two programs should be combined to form a national prekindergarten initiative. Unlike Head Start programs, however, preschool programs tend to offer fewer supportive services, such as medical and social services.

Montessori Schools

Another type of early childhood education program is a Montessori school. These schools are based on the educational theory and practice of Maria Montessori, an Italian medical doctor and educator. Montessori's methods came to the United States in the early 1900s but gained popularity in the 1950s. Montessori education can begin at birth and go through age 12, although many environments can support up to age 15. In Montessori classrooms, children are free to move about the classroom, work with other children, and use any materials they understand (**Figure 24.7**). Montessori programs are also available for school-age and secondary children.

The primary principle of **Montessori schools** is that young children should learn independently through the use of highly specialized materials rather than through direct input from teachers. These materials, which are called *self-correcting materials* (such as puzzles that work only one way), aid children's independent work. Teachers trained in Montessori methods, called *directors* or *directresses,* guide (direct) children's use of materials, but they do *not* use direct teaching. In this way,

Daria Kolpakova/iStock via Getty Images Plus

Figure 24.7 In Montessori classrooms, children learn through their own explorations of materials and ideas. *How might the Montessori approach be beneficial to young children?*

Montessori schools strive to put each child more in charge of their own learning. Other Montessori education principles include an emphasis on work for work's sake. Therefore, traditional play is not part of the Montessori program. For example, children prepare foods to eat rather than pretend-play food preparation and eating. Montessori programs operate on the belief that children absorb and learn from their world as they work at common tasks.

Montessori school curriculum begins with sensory learning involving specialized materials called sensorial materials. Learning from these materials is the major focus of the early childhood Montessori curriculum. These materials work to refine the sensory perceptions for all senses beyond what is typical in other early childhood curricula. For example, children learn to recognize small differences in shades of colors rather than just the typical eight colors seen in crayon boxes.

Materials are also designed to teach math and literacy concepts, as well as cultural studies. Thus, the curriculum moves the child from sensorimotor learning to some logical concept learning during the early childhood program.

Another curricular goal is for children to develop self-help skills. Children work to learn grooming techniques (handwashing, handling clothes fasteners), household chores (pouring liquids, cutting foods, washing dishes, scrubbing tables, and cleaning the floor), and gardening. All of these activities are real-world skills, not play.

Kindergartens

Kindergartens are early childhood education programs for four- and five-year-old children. In the United States, kindergartens are part of each state's public education system although many private schools offer kindergarten, too.

Friedrich Froebel chose the name *kindergarten* (German for *children's garden*) because he thought children needed nurturing like plants. Froebel felt a school for young children should be different from the "harsh" academic schools typical for older children of his day.

Unlike Montessori, Froebel felt that play was the "highest level of child development." Children learned through an activity-oriented curriculum that was teacher-directed. The major emphasis of the curriculum was art and math activities. He developed many of the play activities that occur in today's kindergartens and other programs for young children. Examples include block building, stringing beads, drawing and paper folding, sand play, nature walks, gardening, animal care, stories, and music (**Figure 24.8**). Froebel also wrote **fingerplays** (poems and rhymes acted out with the hands) that taught moral lessons to children.

Due to today's academic focus, kindergartens are seen as an entrance to primary school education. While play is still used as the means for some kindergarten learning activities, current kindergarten programs tend to be more like first-grade classrooms with emphases on academic subjects. There is an ongoing debate among professionals in regard to the effectiveness of this academic focus in kindergarten classrooms.

nmedia/Shutterstock.com

Figure 24.8 Froebel's emphasis on play set his activities apart from the drill methods used in other schools of Froebel's time. In fact, Froebel's statement that "play is the highest level of child development" was scorned by many of his contemporaries. *Why do you think some parents still question the importance of play for young children?*

Primary School Programs

Primary school programs are an important part of the education setting for young children. The United States has long mandated school attendance for primary school children. These children may attend private schools—including religious schools called **parochial** (puh-ROH-kee-ul) schools—or public schools.

Educational standards used in primary school programs are relatively consistent throughout the nation. Children in all primary school programs learn the core subjects of language arts, mathematics, science, and social studies. Many primary schools offer music, art, computer literacy, and physical education as parts of their programs, too.

24.1-2 Trends in Early Childhood Education Programs

Early childhood education programs have not always been common. For several decades, however, the numbers of these programs have been rapidly growing. This growth is partly due to the increasing numbers of parents and caregivers in the workforce. It is also due to society's greater understanding about the benefits of early childhood education programs and the need for children's quality education.

As early childhood education programs grow and expand, new trends shape and will continue to shape the types of programs available. Current trends of early childhood education programs include the following:

- **Growth in infant and toddler programs.** The majority of families with children have two working parents or caregivers. Despite the growth in programs for infants and toddlers, these programs are still difficult to find and are often very expensive, making them unaffordable for many families.
- **Growth in school-age child care (SACC) programs.** Most SACC programs are in urban and suburban areas and serve children mainly in grades three and below. More programs are needed, especially programs with activities that interest older children.
- **Growth in employer support for child care programs.** Some businesses provide on-site child care programs for their employees. Many other businesses promote the growth of child care programs within their communities and pay some child care costs. As a result of the COVID-19 pandemic, many businesses are considering and implementing new policies and supports for working parents/caregivers.
- **Growth in child care resource and referral (CCR&R) agencies. Child care resources and referral (CCR&R) agencies** promote local early childhood education programs and help parents identify child care options (**Figure 24.9**). These agencies are funded by the state or by community business and civic groups. In CCR&R agencies, experts research the needs for and availability of local early childhood education programs. They then communicate information to providers about what types of care are most needed and about how to provide quality care. Although CCR&R staff members do not recommend specific programs to parents, they share listings of local providers, information about programs, and current openings. They also help parents learn how to select quality programs.

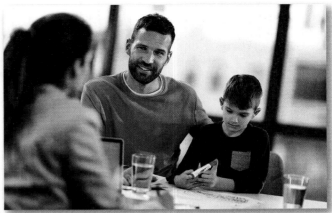
skynesher/iStock via Getty Images Plus

Figure 24.9 CCR&R agencies help parents choose quality early childhood education programs. *Why do you think some parents need help finding appropriate programs for their children?*

Lesson 24.1 Review and Assessment

1. The main purpose of a child care program is to provide _____. (24.1.1)
   A. education
   B. religious instruction
   C. custodial care
   D. sensory education
2. An au pair is associated with _____ child care. (24.1.1)
   A. family
   B. in-home
   C. center-based
   D. school-age
3. **True or False.** Caregivers in unregulated family child care homes may not have had a criminal background check. (24.1.1)
4. While visiting a Montessori school, you would be least likely to see children _____. (24.1.1)
   A. using self-correcting materials
   B. washing dishes
   C. distinguishing between shades of blue
   D. playing kickball
5. **True or False.** Most school-age child care programs are in urban and suburban areas and serve children mainly in grades three and below. (24.1.2)

Lesson 24.2

Choosing an Early Childhood Education Program

Key Terms

accredited programs

adult-child ratio

culture shock

developmentally appropriate practices (DAP)

early learning standards

field trips

hidden added costs

hidden cost credits

lesson plan

regulations

staff turnover

Learning Outcomes

After studying this lesson, you will be able to

24.2-1 **summarize** factors to consider when choosing an early childhood education program.

24.2-2 **describe** ways to help children adjust to early childhood education programs.

Reading and Notetaking Activity

Imagine you are an early childhood specialist, and your client wants to learn more about program options for their child. Write a two-paragraph speech recommending steps your client can take to make sure they choose the best care for their child. Incorporate information you already know about program options, and anything from your personal experiences. As you read this lesson, take detailed notes. After reading the lesson, go back over your speech. With a partner, discuss what you would change about your speech based on any new information you have learned. Present your final speech to the class.

Introduction

For many families, deciding on an early childhood education program is difficult, and it is even more difficult for families to find *quality* programs. When choosing programs, parents and caregivers need to look for programs that meet the needs of their family and promote their beliefs and priorities. These needs differ depending on the family, and not all programs will meet each family's needs. To ensure a good fit in a quality early childhood education program, all families should consider a few basic factors.

Even in a quality program, children may have difficulty adjusting to new care. To support the transition to an early childhood education program, parents and caregivers can be prepared to help their children adjust and find new care if needed.

24.2-1 Factors to Consider When Choosing a Program

Choosing high-quality early childhood programs is vital to the successful care and education of children. Children are defenseless clients of the programs they attend. They cannot measure the quality of a program for themselves or take action if the quality is poor. Children depend on their parents or caregivers to find quality programs for them.

Often, parents and caregivers cannot judge a program by only meeting staff members, checking the indoor and outdoor areas, or seeing a posted certificate that states the program meets state standards. Rather, when assessing the quality of a program, parents and caregivers should consider a number of factors and observe the program's day-to-day activities. Important factors to consider when choosing an early childhood education program include:

- adherence to regulations
- housing and equipment
- quality and number of staff
- parent/caregiver communication and participation
- use of early learning standards
- quality activities
- cultural diversity
- costs of child care
- special services

FOCUS ON MENTAL HEALTH

Early childhood education programs can have long-lasting effects on children. High-quality early childhood education programs can have many positive effects on children, such as strong social-emotional skills and a positive self-esteem. Parents and caregivers can help boost their child's mental health by enrolling them in high-quality programs that focus on needs of the whole child rather than just one aspect.

Adherence to Regulations

All quality early childhood education programs are governed by regulations. **Regulations** are standards that govern how a program operates. Regulations for different types of early childhood programs vary. Some regulations, such as fire safety, apply to all programs. Other regulations apply to either private programs or public programs or to either center-based or family child care programs. The most common set of regulations for group programs is called a *license*. Licensing regulations address program housing, equipment, staff, children's services, and business operations. Certificates awarded to programs meeting regulations must be periodically renewed.

When choosing an early childhood education program, parents should ensure that these programs meet all appropriate regulations. Adherence to regulations, however, does not *guarantee* high quality. This is due to the following reasons:

- *Most regulations are minimum standards.* Programs may almost completely meet regulations, barely meet regulations, or fall somewhere in between these extremes. Licensing regulations vary because these regulations are not federal standards. Rather, licensing regulations are state-determined standards and thus vary from state to state; so, quality varies with whatever regulations are in place.
- *Some regulations are easier to observe than others.* Concrete regulations, such as having a fence around the outside play area, are easy to observe. More abstract regulations, such as the warmth and nurturance of staff, are much more difficult to observe and can be shown for an evaluation but not used routinely.
- *Regulations are not always enforced.* Some regulations have little to no enforcement. For example, there are many regulations for family child care homes, but due to the number of homes and limited state funding for inspections, these programs are seldom checked. Regulations difficult to observe are not as likely to be enforced as those that are easy to observe.

To ensure quality beyond adherence to mandated regulations, adults may look for the *accreditation* of a program. **Accredited programs** are not only licensed but have met even higher standards of quality set forth by a professional organization. Thus, accredited programs are like high achievers on tests. Accreditation attests to the fact that the program has voluntarily met standards of high quality.

Housing and Equipment

The types of housing and equipment in an early childhood education program will vary with the program's goals. For example, a family child care home will have different housing than a kindergarten, and a kindergarten will provide different materials than a Montessori program. Furniture, equipment, and materials should always meet the needs of the children in the program.

Regardless of the type of housing and equipment that are provided, all housing and equipment must be safe, sanitary, and meet health standards **(Figure 24.10)**. Equipment should be plentiful enough to prevent long waits and possible aggressive acts among children. Housing and equipment should also include adequate space for activities and comfort of both children and adults.

FatCamera/iStock via Getty Images Plus

Figure 24.10 Early childhood education programs must stay up to date on current safety standards. *Where can early childhood education workers go to research the most current safety standards?*

Quality and Number of Staff

Another major factor in the quality of an early childhood education program is the quality and number of adult caregivers. Young children are dependent on program caregivers and need plenty of adult help and supervision. Positive caregiver interactions can aid children's development, but negative caregiver interactions can have damaging effects. When choosing an early childhood education program, parents should consider the quality of the caregivers, the adult-child ratio, and staff turnover.

Quality of Caregivers

Caregivers for children should be in good physical and mental health. For a positive experience, children must feel secure, loved, and wanted, knowing they matter to others. Children need adults who hug, comfort, listen to them, talk with them, and say *no* and correct them when needed.

Quality caregivers provide guidance for children. They apply their knowledge of child development at each stage in a child's development. For example, quality caregivers of infants will cuddle them and accept their dependency. Quality caregivers of toddlers will encourage them to explore and learn, and quality caregivers of preschool children will welcome children's curiosity, questions, and energy.

Quality staff members must also be able to work well with coworkers as a team. They must communicate effectively with parents and caregivers for the child, be sensitive to parents' and caregivers' concerns, and convey needed information.

Adult-Child Ratio and Group Size

State regulations identify the minimum required adult-child ratio and group sizes for various types of early childhood education programs. As is true of other licensing regulations, adult-child ratio and group-size requirements vary from state to state. All states, however, base their numbers on professional recommendations.

An **adult-child ratio** (read as *adult to child ratio*) is the number of adults per the number of children in a program. An adult-child ratio of 1:10 (read as *adult to child ratio of 1 to 10*) means 1 adult per 10 children. The way of presenting the ratio can be reversed by saying that the child-adult ratio is 10:1 (read as *child to adult ratio is 10 to 1*).

This means exactly the same thing—there are 10 children for each adult. Support staff and regular volunteers, though vital to quality programs, are *not* counted when the adult-child ratio is calculated. Adult-child ratios tend to be highest for accredited programs and for programs enrolling very young children and children with special needs.

Group sizes refer to the number of children in one room who will interact with each other throughout the day. Accredited programs, programs for young children, and programs serving children with special needs tend to have the smallest group sizes. Because older children and those without disabilities tend to require less physical care compared with other children, they can be safely cared for and educated in rooms with a lower adult-child ratio and in groups that are somewhat larger.

When choosing early childhood education programs, parents can inquire about adult-child ratios and group size (**Figure 24.11**). After enrolling a child, they can also spot-check these numbers at different times throughout the day. (Some directors enroll the maximum number of children and then allow drop-in children to attend, which increases the number beyond licensing limits.)

Figure 24.11 Recommended Adult-Child Ratios

Age of Children	Adult-Child Ratio*	Group Size*
Birth to one year	1:4	8
One to two years	1:6	12
Two to three years	1:6	12
Three to six years (excluding first grade)	1:10	20
School age**	1:15	30

*Numbers for children per adult and group size should be reduced if children with special needs are included.

**Recommendations go up to third grade. An ideal adult-child ratio or class size has not been determined for older students, but research continues to prove that smaller class sizes have bigger learning payoffs.

Goodheart-Willcox Publisher

Focus on Careers

Child Care Center Director

Child care center directors supervise and lead the staff in a child care center. They oversee children's activities, plan schedules and budgets, keep staff updated on educational and safety standards, and advise staff in handling situations.

Career cluster: Human services.

Education: Educational requirements include a high school diploma and sometimes a college degree. Child care center directors must have experience in early childhood education, and in some states, must have a Child Development Associate (CDA) certification.

Job outlook: Future employment opportunities for child care center directors are expected to grow faster than the average for all occupations.

To learn more about a career as a child care center director, visit the United States Department of Labor's *Occupational Outlook Handbook* website. You will also be able to compare the job responsibilities, educational requirements, job outlook, and average pay of child care center directors with similar occupations.

Photo: mangostock/Shutterstock.com

Staff Turnover

Beyond parents, caregivers, and other family members, staff members are the most important people in children's lives. Infants and toddlers in child care can become deeply attached to these caregivers. They often spend more *waking hours* with their program caregivers than with their own parents. Despite this, most early childhood education programs experience some *staff turnover*. **Staff turnover** is a term used to describe caregivers who leave a program and are replaced (often statistically presented as a rate). Early childhood education programs with high staff turnover can be damaging to infants, toddlers, and children with special needs. Children need consistency, and it is recommended that they have the same caregivers for over a year. High rates of staff turnover may also indicate that there is something unfavorable at the child care program that is causing staff to leave.

In the United States, the annual staff turnover rate for early childhood education programs is about 30 percent. This is largely due to low pay, as caregivers leave programs to seek better-paying jobs. The median annual income for caregivers is about $25,790 annually. If wages were higher, staff turnover would decrease; however, higher wages would increase the cost of child care even more for parents, making programs even less affordable.

Focus on Speech

Safety for Early Childhood Education Staff

Early childhood education staff members face unique challenges as they work with young children. Child care can expose caregivers to some illnesses and to risks associated with guiding children and regulating their behaviors. The *Occupational Safety and Health Administration (OSHA)* sets and enforces standards to protect employees in the workplace, including staff in early childhood education programs.

In small groups, research OSHA standards for health and safety. Take notes about standards that apply to early childhood education programs. After conducting your research, choose two standards and lead a class discussion about how these standards apply to programs. Also discuss ways in which directors and staff can ensure employee health and safety in a child care center.

Photo: naluwan/Shutterstock.com

Parent/Caregiver Communication and Participation

In high-quality programs, staff members encourage parent and caregiver involvement. Children benefit when all of their caregivers work together as a team. When choosing early childhood education programs, adults should look for programs that practice the following:

- *Work with parents/caregivers as a team.* Quality programs employ teachers who know a great deal about child development and understand parents' and caregivers' specific goals for their children. These teachers respect parents' and caregivers' goals and work together to achieve them (**Figure 24.12**). An exception to this is when parents' or caregivers' wishes violate program policy or professional ethics.
- *Convey the importance of parent/caregiver participation in the program.* A quality program will communicate to parents and caregivers that they play the most important role in their children's lives. These programs emphasize that staff members respect parents and caregivers as children's first teachers and encourage participation from home. They acknowledge that the parent-child or caregiver-child relationship influences a child's development more than any other aspect of a child's life.
- *Know about each family they serve.* Staff members at quality programs work to understand the cultures represented in the program and how these cultures affect families. They acknowledge that a family's culture might influence parenting practices and child development. They respect each culture and make efforts to get to know each child's family.
- *Provide opportunities for communication and participation.* Quality programs communicate frequently with parents and caregivers and provide ample opportunities for those who want to participate (**Figure 24.13**). Programs should respect parents' and caregivers' rights to refuse involvement, however.

Figure 24.12 An Example of Combining Caregiver and Teacher Goals

Goal area: Discipline

Teacher's goal and reason: Children should begin to learn self-control. Through learning self-control, children use problem-solving skills to resolve conflicts and gain self-esteem.

Caregiver's goal and reason: Children should respect authority. Children have to respect caregivers, just as adults have to respect the authority of their employers.

Using both goals: After discussing the teacher's and caregivers' goals, the teacher may suggest how both can be met. For example, children will be asked to resolve some of their conflicts with the teacher's help. They will also be expected to follow rules and show respect for other people and property. In some situations (such as safety issues), children will be expected to comply immediately with what the teacher says.

Goodheart-Willcox Publisher

FatCamera/iStock via Getty Images Plus

Use of Early Learning Standards

All quality early childhood education programs are based on goals for children's development. Early childhood education program goals sometimes differ, however, making all programs unique. This is because various programs were founded at different periods in history and were based on the child development knowledge of that time.

Figure 24.13 Opportunities for Parent/Caregiver Communication and Involvement

Area	Opportunities
Entrance or reception area	• Photos of and stories about program activities are displayed. • Materials, including videos and handouts on child development, are available for caregivers to read and view. • Informal networks often form among caregivers.
Group meetings and workshops	• Orientation meetings are helpful for caregivers and children. • Discussion groups or workshops on child development, program activities or policies, or community concerns can be planned as needed.
Open house	• Caregivers see facilities and view displayed materials, such as children's drawings and stories. • Caregivers may participate in some of the children's activities. • Caregivers and other family members meet staff members and other families.
Individual conferences	• Teachers and caregivers set goals for children in the program. • Teachers and caregivers review children's goals and accomplishments.
Home visits	• Teachers see the child and family in a home setting. • Caregivers share some of the child's home life.
Newsletters	• Caregivers receive descriptions of current program activities, suggestions for home learning and fun activities, and information about new child-related books, websites, TV shows, or community events. • Caregivers receive newsletters weekly or monthly in a print or electronic format.
Informal notes to family members	• Caregivers learn about a child's activity or achievement. • Staff members recognize each family's special events (new baby, new job) and show concern for family challenges (illness, death).
Advisory board	• Caregivers help plan activities for program. • Caregivers can advise director or administration on desired program goals. • Caregivers can discuss general concerns.
Volunteering	• Caregivers can be regular volunteers by assisting in program activities or making learning materials for the children's use. • Caregivers can serve as occasional volunteers by helping teachers during children's outings or special activities in which extra adult help is needed.

Goodheart-Willcox Publisher

Today, many preschool programs follow their states' **early learning standards** (also called *foundations* and *guidelines*), which are expectations for young children's development. Some learning standards include *benchmarks* under broader outcomes. All states have identified learning standards for preschool children. Besides preschool learning standards developed by each state, Head Start has defined outcomes for children enrolled in this federal program.

Early learning standards are used for deciding on program goals. They benefit program planners because they outline the rich potential for children's growth and development. How these standards are actually used by program planners and teachers depends on the early childhood education program.

Teachers in quality programs follow early learning standards, but plan how to meet them by using **developmentally appropriate practice (DAP)**. DAP is based on knowledge about:

- child development
- the strengths, needs, and interests of each child within a group
- the social and cultural contexts in which children enrolled in a given program live

A program that incorporates early learning standards using without using DAP is not desirable for young children.

To determine whether a practice is developmentally appropriate or not, a person would consider not only the practice, but also the child and how the practice is conducted. For example, asking two-year-olds to sit still for a 15-minute story is not a DAP. This same activity, however, would likely be a DAP for five-year-olds, depending on their attention spans. Also, a well-presented story for a young audience makes the sit-still time seem less lengthy to children. In choosing a quality early childhood education program, caregivers can look for how these programs use DAP to incorporate early learning standards.

Quality Activities

Quality early childhood education programs provide appropriate and high-quality activities for children. Young children are holistic learners who learn best through play. Quality programs should acknowledge this importance and then *guide* play so it is goal-oriented, not random or chaotic.

Quality Activities for Infants and Toddlers

For infants and toddlers, quality activities mostly involve *primary care*. In primary care, one primary caregiver feeds, diapers, soothes, plays with, and reads to a given child. (Most primary caregivers are assigned three or four children.) Other caregivers who help the child are called *secondary*. Secondary caregivers provide care consistent with the primary caregiver. Because infants and young toddlers have their own learning agendas, caregivers plan quality activities by providing an interesting environment and following each child's lead.

Quality Activities for Preschoolers

During the preschool years, quality activities involving primary care are replaced by activities that promote learning in all domains, satisfy curiosity, and build confidence. Quality activities enable preschool children to develop feelings that they can handle tasks with just a little adult help.

Quality preschool programs use DAP in their day-to-day routines and planned activities. For example, in these programs, eating serves a purpose beyond curbing hunger. Snacks and meals also offer time to learn about foods and styles of eating, practice table manners, and talk with others. During day-to-day routines, children also learn self-care, independence, and self-help skills.

In quality preschool programs, all activities are planned to help children develop. These program activities often include the following:

- *language activities*, which improve language skills and involve talking, listening, reading (or looking at) books, and writing or pretending to write (for example, a grocery list in the housekeeping center or "signing" a drawing).
- *math activities*, which improve math skills and involve counting, matching shapes in puzzles, measuring, and noting the use of math symbols in everyday life.

- *social activities*, which improve social interactions and involve children trying new roles, helping each other, recognizing emotions in others and showing empathy, and helping plan events (**Figure 24.14**).
- *science activities*, which teach children about their living and nonliving world. These activities involve pets, plants, foods, water, sand, weather and seasonal changes, and more.
- *creative activities*, which allow children to enjoy expressing themselves through art, dramatic play, music, and storytelling.
- *motor activities*, which help develop motor skills. Gross-motor skills develop through active play, especially outdoor play. Fine-motor skills become refined as children manipulate materials, such as art materials, writing tools, puzzles, and building materials.
- *multidevelopmental activities*, which aid multiple areas of development. For example, activities such as block building, sand and water play, cooking, visual arts, music, science, and literature impact many areas of development.

Quality activities might also include **field trips** (outings) to take children to new places. Field trips teach children about their communities and develop multicultural understandings. For example, a field trip to the fire station might help children learn about firefighters, fire safety skills, and fire prevention.

Presenting worthwhile activities for children requires careful planning. In a quality program, teachers plan specific activities and materials to meet selected goals. Written plans for learning are usually formatted as *lesson plans*.

gpointstudio/iStock via Getty Images Plus

Figure 24.14 Many high-quality programs encourage social activities by inviting adults who are not on staff to share special skills or stories with children. *What are the benefits of volunteer participation for adults? for children?*

A **lesson plan** for kindergarten or school-age children contains a specific goal objective (related to an early learning standard), activities to help the child meet the objective, and assessment of the learning (**Figure 24.15**). Lesson plans for preschool children usually incorporate several standards at the same time (for more holistic learning), potential activities to aid learning, and an informal assessment. In these plans, most activities are guided by a unifying *theme* (such as farms, weather, or families) that is carried through both large-group and individual learning activities (**Figure 24.16**). Lesson plans for preschool children tend to be more open-ended so children can take the lead in their activities and teachers can scaffold children's learning. Lesson plans for preschool children usually last several days.

Cultural Diversity

High-quality early childhood education programs take steps to become culturally diverse. Cultural diversity provides opportunities for children's *multicultural education*, an important part of children's education in a global society.

Understanding of cultural diversity develops as a result of a positive approach by the parents or caregivers and employees in an early childhood education program. In multicultural education, young children work to develop self-awareness and notice differences among themselves and others. In a carefully planned program, children will have the chance to establish their cultural identities, respect diversity, and develop unbiased attitudes.

Example of a Lesson Plan for Kindergarten Children

Content area	Measurement and Data
Early learning standard	Classify objects and count the number of objects in each category.
Learning objective	Given 15 parquetry blocks in three colors and five shapes, the children will form a class and its complement and count the number of blocks in each. They will then do a second classification using different criteria and counting again.
Materials per child	15 parquetry blocks in various shapes and colors; two small, plastic trays
Procedure	1. Distribute materials. 2. Ask children how the materials are alike in some way (color or shape). 3. Ask children to choose *one* color or shape and put all other objects of the same color or shape on one tray. Have them name their color or shape and correct objects in the chosen class if necessary. Then count them. 4. Ask children to put all of the other objects on the other tray. Have them call these objects their *not group*, such as "not red" or "not square." Then count these objects. 5. Repeat steps 3 and 4 using a different group for the class and the complement.
Assessment	Using a check-and-comment assessment form, check each child's ability to *classify objects* (form the class and complement), *name the class and complement*, and *count the number of objects* in the class and complement.

Goodheart-Willcox Publisher

Figure 24.15 Lesson plans are usually written to address one early learning standard. These plans are for kindergarten and early school-age children. *What are the components of the lesson plan shown?*

Example of a Lesson Plan for Preschool Children

Theme Farms

Early learning standards
- Develop and use models to represent their ideas, observations, and explanations through approaches, such as drawing, building, or modeling with clay.
- Use vocabulary that describes length, height, weight, capacity, and size.
- With teacher assistance, discuss illustrations in books and make personal connections to the pictures and stories.

Originating idea and goal The children had been playing with model barns and farm animals in the dramatic play center. One child said, "My horses are running away; there is no fence." Another child put his arms around a barn and said, "I can be a fence!" It would be a good experience for the children to build fences for their barn animals in the block center.

Materials
- Model barns, farm animals, and unit blocks
- Pictures and illustrated books
- Paper for measuring
- Field trip (to see fences and fencing materials)

Developmentally appropriate practices
1. Build enclosures and gates for their animals with blocks. Children could do the following:
   a. discuss the size of enclosures needed and use different block lengths to make the enclosures
   b. discuss why gates are needed and build these
   c. determine whether the enclosure is a *rectangle*, a *square*, or *another shape*
2. Find pictures of and talk about different types of animal enclosures—*backyard fence*; *cage*; *bird cage*; *stall*; *aquarium*; or *butterfly house*.
3. Discuss why some fences are taller than others; made of different materials; and have or do not have tops.
4. Read picture books about farms and fences:
   - H. Moser's *Snoopy the Sheep*, (Christian Light Publications, 2013).
   - A. Hunter. *On Grandpa's Farm*, (HMH Books, 1997).
5. Discuss purposes of fences—keep animals from getting away and protect them by keeping other animals out.
6. Take a community field trip to see various animal enclosures.
7. Discuss other uses of fences beyond animal protection, such as a fence around a swimming pool or around dangerous equipment.
8. Draw or make fences with art materials.

Assessment Write notes or use check sheets that indicate children's knowledge, such as:
William B. showed spatial orientation in block building by using both horizontal enclosures for pens and vertical enclosures for gates.

Possible follow-up ideas*
1. Children may need more experiences with other categories of animals, such as zoo animals, pets, insects, or fish.
2. Children could be introduced to other types of farms—*crop farms* or *fish farms*.

*These may lead to new originating ideas.

Goodheart-Willcox Publisher

Figure 24.16 The format of a written plan sets the tone of the teacher's approach to children's learning (holistic or "bits and pieces") and determines the teacher's preparation (to allow children to take the lead or make the experience teacher-directed). *How are lesson plans different for preschool children?*

In a culturally diverse program, staff and other adults do the following:

- *Affirm children's identities.* Staff learn how to pronounce children's names and say some words in each child's language. They help children learn to describe themselves and their activities. Affirming children's identities can help children who are experiencing **culture shock** (an uncomfortable response to an unfamiliar culture).
- *Help children learn about people who are different from them.* Staff aid children in noting differences, especially physical differences among people. Children are able to note these differences around 30 months of age and need experiences with people who are different from them. Programs with little diversity can find ways for children to explore differences outside of the classroom, such as through community resources.
- *Encourage children to see people as individuals, not groups.* Staff can affirm individual identities and **dismantle** (tear apart) cultural generalizations. They can provide multicultural and anti-bias books that point out the inaccuracies of sweeping generalizations. For example, children could read to learn that not all older people are inactive.
- *Listen to and answer children's questions.* Staff can use questions, even questions that reflect bias, as learning experiences. For example, if children mention skin color or eye shape, adults may say, "We are born with differences. These differences make all of us special." Instead of criticizing children for biased statements, staff can acknowledge statements with an explanation and show positive acceptance of differences. With older children, staff can explain that biased statements and behaviors hurt.
- *Help children learn that almost all human activities can be done in different ways.* Staff can affirm differences in the ways people speak, act out family roles and activities, appreciate art and music, and learn at home or school.

- *Respect diversity by making the program culturally rich.* Staff can work to include children representing many different cultures. They can include diverse materials, activities, and people in their programs (**Figure 24.17**).

Ensuring cultural diversity in early childhood education programs can be challenging for two reasons. First, many programs are fairly **homogeneous** (hoh-MUH-jee-nyus), more alike than different. This is because parents tend to choose programs similar to their family and religious backgrounds; cultures; and views on early education, guidance, and discipline. Second, multicultural education is not taught as directly as other types of learning. These understandings are not developed through specific curriculum activities, but rather through incorporation into many activities.

Costs of Child Care

Child care is considered affordable if it is no more than 7 percent of a family's annual income, but many families pay more than this amount each year. This can mean paying more per year for child care than a family would on a home mortgage or a year of college tuition. Low-income families are especially burdened by the costs of high-quality child care.

While the quality of a program does not necessarily correlate to its cost, high-quality programs for young children do tend to be expensive. Costs of programs include costs of staff salaries, buildings, equipment, food, and supplies. These costs vary with the type of program, days and hours of care, age groups served, and location. For example, staffing costs for programs with infants, toddlers, and children with special needs may be higher than staffing costs for pre-K programs. Before- and after-school programs serving only school-age children cost more per hour than most full-time child care programs. These costs increase with any added special services, such as transportation or special program activities (dance, gymnastics, and foreign languages).

Figure 24.17 Characteristics of a Culturally Rich Program

Characteristics	Examples
Materials	• Books about all types of children and families, books that show positive roles, and books that celebrate various cultural activities and customs • Housekeeping centers filled with inclusive dolls; tools, play foods, and cooking utensils from various cultures • Puzzles, pictures, and posters depicting families from various cultures • Crayons, paints, and paper to represent all skin tones • Musical instruments and recordings from various cultures • Toys and games from around the world • Photos and posters of multicultural activities shared in the program
Activities	• Reading stories, singing songs, learning poems, cooking foods, or playing games that have their origins in various cultures • Learning words, phrases, songs, or rhymes in various languages • Using art materials to depict oneself and others, various celebrations, and multicultural program activities • Sharing an object from home or showing photos of a family activity • Attending parades and festivals in the community • Making a book of multicultural activities using photos, children's artwork, and child-dictated stories about these activities
People	• Welcoming diverse volunteers • Having parents and caregivers from various cultures share activities involving favorite foods, songs, stories, and games • Seeing people of various cultures and different genders engaged in their work roles

Goodheart-Willcox Publisher

Besides direct costs, parents who enroll their children in early childhood education programs have both additional costs and cost credits, such as:

- **hidden added costs** (costs that add to direct costs). Examples are costs of transportation, supplies, and disposable diapers (if cloth diapers would have otherwise been used). Services or items donated to an early childhood education program are hidden added costs, too.
- **hidden cost credits** (credits that lower direct costs of child care). These include money earned from a second income, money saved in the cost of utilities or food, and child-care tax credits.

When choosing an early childhood education program, parents must assess program costs. While cost may sometimes indicate the high quality of a program, many families cannot afford these programs.

Special Services

When choosing early childhood education programs, some families look for programs that offer *special services*. These services might include transportation to and from the program, child care for children with special needs, or extended-hour care. Programs with these services are not always conveniently located or affordable.

If several families need the same services, they may be able to persuade programs to add these services. On-site child care programs are good examples of businesses that meet the special child care needs of their employees. For example, some hospital child care programs are open 24 hours a day to serve employees' children.

24.2-2 Helping Children Adjust to Care

Some children may experience difficulty or uneasiness transitioning from home care to an early childhood education program. These children may experience separation anxiety or may feel nervous for the first few days or weeks away from home.

Once caregivers have chosen a quality program, they can help make the adjustment seem casual. Rather than talking often about the change and seeming anxious, caregivers can stay calm and confident about their children's ability to adjust (**Figure 24.18**). They may say, "I know there are many new faces, but you will make new friends. Everyone is new for a while."

About a month before enrolling a child in an early childhood education program, a parent or caregiver can explain to the child what the program is like. They may explain there will be other children, toys, and activities. The adult and child can also visit the program and get to know children who are enrolled if possible.

If children do not adjust well to a program, even after a few weeks, parents and caregivers should investigate the cause. Unannounced visits to the program might reveal serious problems, but parents and caregivers should also ask teachers what problems they have noted and what efforts are being made to help the child adjust. Children can be encouraged to share why the program makes them uncomfortable if they are old enough to communicate. Parents and caregivers should take children's answers seriously.

If no care problems are found, parents and caregivers can find other ways to help the child adjust. They might offer the child more chances to play with other children or ask their child's doctor for advice.

If caregivers do find problems with the care, they should immediately start to look for a new placement. With their children's safety and well-being as a primary concern, caregivers can monitor the situation closely until a new program can be found. They can also give the child extra love and support as they search for a more acceptable program. Once a new program is selected, parents and caregivers may want to begin care gradually if possible.

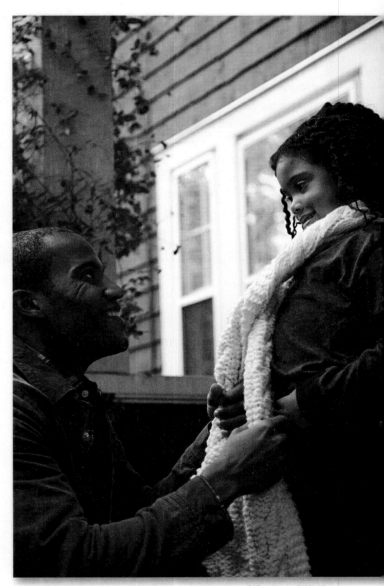

©iStock.com/XiXinXing

Figure 24.18 Being calm and confident about children's abilities can help these children believe they are capable of adjusting. *What was your most difficult adjustment as a young child?*

FINANCIAL LITERACY

Comparing Costs of Early Childhood Education Programs

When deciding on an early childhood education program, families often compare the costs of several programs. Costs of early childhood education programs vary depending on location, hours, quality of care, activities and special services provided, and the ages of the children.

In small groups, gather information on at least 10 early childhood education programs in your community. If possible, gather information about each of the types of programs discussed in this chapter. Try to include both for-profit and not-for-profit programs. During your research, determine the cost of care for one child for the operational hours of the program.

Make a spreadsheet tracking the quality of the programs you researched, their costs, and the hours of operation. Present your spreadsheet to the class. Compare the costs and discuss possible factors affecting the cost. Indicate which program you would choose for a child in each stage of development.

Photo: Noam Armonn/Shutterstock.com

Lesson 24.2 Review and Assessment

1. When choosing an early childhood program, caregivers should know that _____. (24.2.1)
   A. programs that adhere to licensing regulations are guaranteed to be of high quality
   B. states routinely perform regular unannounced inspections to enforce licensing regulations
   C. programs are not required to renew licenses once they have been awarded
   D. accredited programs have voluntarily met standards of high quality

2. What is the recommended adult to child ratio for children who are age birth to one year? (24.2.1)
   A. 1:4   C. 1:8
   B. 1:6   D. 1:10

3. An example of a multi-developmental activity in a preschool program is _____. (24.2.1)
   A. drawing with crayons
   B. playing in a sandbox
   C. counting balls
   D. listening to a story

4. In contrast to lesson plans for kindergarten or school-age children, a lesson plan for preschool children typically contains a/n _____. (24.2.1)
   A. single specific goal objective
   B. early learning standard
   C. series of activities to aid learning
   D. formal assessment

5. **True or False.** If a child shares why an early childhood education program makes them uncomfortable, caregivers should take children's answers seriously. (24.2.2)

Chapter 24

Review and Assessment

Summary

Lesson 24.1

24.1-1 Parents may choose public or private early childhood education options.

24.1-1 Child care programs provide custodial care for children for extended hours, usually between 9 and 12 hours a day; and most also provide education for children from infancy through the preschool years. Options include in-home child care, family child care, for-profit or non-profit center-based child care, or school-age child care (SACC) programs.

24.1-1 Parents can also look for programs that provide more direct educational activities for their children, such as child development laboratories, Head Start programs, pre-K programs, Montessori schools, and kindergartens.

24.1-1 Young school-age children attend primary schools, which is mandated in the United States.

24.1-2 Current trends in early childhood education programs include growth in these areas: infant and toddler programs, school-age child care (SACC) programs, employer support for child care programs, and child care resource and referral (CCR&R) agencies.

24.1-2 Despite more infant and toddler programs, they are difficult to find and unaffordable for many families.

24.1-2 Despite more SACC programs, they are mostly located in urban and suburban, rather than rural, areas and focus mainly on children in grades three and below.

Lesson 24.2

24.2-1 When choosing early childhood education programs, parents can consider a combination of factors, including adherence to regulations, voluntary accreditation, housing and equipment, quality and number of staff, parent communication and participation, use of early learning standards, quality activities, cultural diversity, costs, and special services.

24.2-1 The caregiver should remember that a program's adherence to regulations does not guarantee high quality.

24.2-1 Teachers in quality programs follow early learning standards, but they plan how to meet them by using developmentally appropriate practice (DAP). Quality programs acknowledge that children are holistic learners who learn best through play; and then they guide play so it is goal-oriented, not random or chaotic.

24.2-2 Parents may need to help children adjust to group care. If children are not adjusting easily to group care, adults should investigate the source of their child's discomfort by speaking with the child and their teachers. They can also visit the program, give the child outside opportunities to socialize with the other children, or speak with the child's doctor.

24.2-2 If caregivers find problems with the care, they should immediately start to look for a new placement while monitoring their children's safety and well-being until a new program can be found.

College and Career Portfolio

Portfolio Presentation Practice

Before presenting your portfolio, you will want to practice. Practice can help you remain calm during a presentation and can help you choose the right words to communicate your skills and experiences.

- Practice presenting your portfolio by yourself. Time your presentation and pay attention to your body language and enunciation.
- Practice presenting your portfolio to a trusted adult or friend. Ask for feedback about your public speaking skills. Practice until you feel comfortable with your presentation.

Recall and Application

1. School-age child care programs ____. (24.1.1)
   A. have programs for infants and toddlers
   B. are typically provided in the home
   C. provide care when school is not in session
   D. do not require state licensure to operate

2. Which is considered an advantage of using center-based child care for infants and toddlers? (24.1.1)
   A. They limit the exposure of illness-prone children to other children.
   B. They are open long hours to meet the needs of working parents.
   C. They are usually less expensive than family child care.
   D. They provide children with a home-like atmosphere.

3. An example of a for-profit center-based child care program is a/n ____. (24.1.1)
   A. child care cooperative
   B. on-site child care program
   C. child development laboratory
   D. national chain

4. **True or False.** As a result of the COVID-19 pandemic, many businesses are considering and implementing new policies and support for working parents or caregivers. (24.1.2)

5. Which is not a goal of a child care resource and referral (CCR&R) agency? (24.1.2)
   A. To recommend a specific local program to caregivers
   B. To share listings of local child care providers
   C. To promote local early childhood education programs
   D. To help caregivers learn how to select quality programs

6. **True or False.** Affordable, high-quality infant and toddler programs are now easier for families to find than in years' past. (24.1.2)

7. What is the recommended group size for 2- to 3-year-olds? (24.2.1)
   A. 8
   B. 12
   C. 15
   D. 20

8. **True or False.** When calculating an adult-child ratio in an early education program, support staff and regular volunteers are not counted. (24.2.1)

9. A quality activity for an infant and toddler is designed to _____. (24.2.1)
   A. promote learning in all domains
   B. build confidence
   C. provide primary care
   D. satisfy curiosity

10. **True or False.** In a high-quality early childhood education program, staff respect children by learning how to pronounce their names and saying some words in each child's language. (24.2.1)

11. Which is an example of a hidden added cost related to sending a child to an early childhood education program? (24.2.1)
    A. Staffing
    B. Child care tax credits
    C. Food
    D. Supplies

12. If a child fails to adjust well to an early childhood education program after a few weeks, as a first step caregivers should do all of the following *except* _____. (24.2.2)
    A. ask teachers what problems they are seeing
    B. immediately withdraw their child from the program
    C. encourage the child to share why they dislike the program
    D. show up to the program for an unannounced visit

Critical Thinking

1. **Determine.** In small groups, review the information about child care programs in this chapter. Create a poster identifying the types of child care programs, their advantages, and their disadvantages. Present your poster to the class and "sell" each type of program by explaining its benefits.

2. **Cause and effect.** Trends in early childhood education programs are often influenced by historical events and societal changes. Working with a partner, research one historical decade and discuss how events and changes in that decade affected the development and types of early childhood education programs.

3. **Identify.** Research current licensing regulations for preschools in your state. Make a list of these standards and research and explain any standards you do not understand. Rewrite the standards in your own words for understandability.

4. **Compare and contrast.** Research the NAEYC accreditation standards available from the Academy for Early Childhood Program Accreditation. Note similarities and differences between accreditation standards and your state's licensing regulations, which you researched in question #5. (Be sure that both sets of standards being considered are for the same ages of children.) Are accreditation standards more rigorous? Why or why not?

5. **Analyze.** Working with a partner, discuss important personal and professional characteristics of a quality program caregiver. How should caregiving practices change as children grow older? Analyze what makes a quality caregiver for children at each stage of development. Do some characteristics of a quality caregiver remain the same for children at each stage of development?

6. **Draw conclusions.** In small groups, brainstorm ways that early childhood education programs can provide opportunities for parent/caregiver communication and involvement. Choose one idea discussed in your group and then draw conclusions about how it could be implemented in an early childhood education program of your choice.

7. **Evaluate.** Research a local early childhood education program for a list of play activities that the program provides. What types of activities are offered? Evaluate any "holes" in the program's activity offerings. What types of activities would you suggest they add to their list?

8. **Make inferences.** Interview a parent of a young child about how their child adjusted to an early childhood education program. Was the transition difficult at first? Why or why not? What did the parent do to ease the child's transition? After the interview, discuss your findings with a partner. Discuss the differences and similarities between the parents you interviewed.

Core Skills

1. **Research and technology.** Choose one type of early childhood education program covered in this chapter. Then, use reliable resources to research the program's history, principles and practices, prevalence, any standards that apply, and current considerations (such as current changes in the program or legislation that has affected the program's practices). After conducting your research, create a digital presentation outlining your findings.
2. **Research and speaking.** Using reliable resources, research Head Start and other early childhood education programs for low-income families. What are the goals of these programs? What new initiatives or programs are they starting? How do staff members in these programs interact with children and families? Organize your findings and deliver an oral presentation to the class.
3. **Reading and writing.** Find scholarly articles about the effects of early childhood education programs on children. Read at least three articles and take notes about how group care affects children's physical, intellectual, and social-emotional development. After reading, write a three- to four-page essay discussing your research. Include a bibliography in APA format with your essay.
4. **Math.** Research the required adult-child ratio for one type of early childhood education program in your state. Then, calculate how many adults would be required if the program enrolled 5, 15, 25, and 50 children.
5. **Research and speaking.** Research current early learning standards in your state.

Read the standards and take notes about the key areas they cover. What do you think are the goals of the standards? Are there any places in the standards where it would be difficult to incorporate DAP? In small groups, discuss your answers. Share the highlights from your discussion with the class.

6. **Technology.** In small groups, identify three activities or tasks (such as math activities, science experiences, or diapering) that might occur in an early childhood education program. Then, make a list of DAP in each activity or task area. (Be sure to identify the ages of the children you are discussing. DAP will vary based on children's stages of development.) After your discussion, create a short video illustrating and explaining DAP for all three areas. In your video, explain why each practice is developmentally appropriate or inappropriate. Show your video to the class.
7. **Writing.** Review the information in this chapter about lesson plans for different age groups. Then, choose an activity that you think would be enjoyable and educational for young children. Using your state's early learning standards and your knowledge about child development, write a lesson plan for preschool children and a lesson plan for kindergarten children incorporating your activity. Be sure to tailor the activity to the children's developmental stages. Finally, trade plans with a partner and peer review each other's work.
8. **CTE Career Readiness Practice.** Imagine you are a health and safety inspector and have been asked to visit a local child care center to ensure they meet state regulations. In preparation for your visit, you decide to refresh your memory about health and safety standards and create a checklist you can use during the inspection. Using reliable online or print resources, research current health and safety standards for child care centers in your state. Include standards about cleanliness, group size, adult-child ratio, and equipment safety. Then, create a checklist of the qualities you will assess during your visit. Compare checklists with a partner and ask for constructive criticism.

Observations

1. As a class, visit a local early childhood education program. Take notes about the multicultural materials available in the program. Which cultures are represented by materials? Do the cultures represented by the materials correspond with the cultures of the children enrolled in the program? How might the materials be used to present culturally diverse activities to the children enrolled in the program? After your visit, discuss what the staff members might do to make their program more culturally rich.

2. In small groups, search online for early childhood education programs in your community. List as many programs as you can find and then review the programs' websites or visit the programs. Categorize each program by type using the classifications given in Lesson 24.1. Explain your reasoning for each identification.

Preparing for a Child-Related Career

Essential Question

What types of child-related careers are available, and what qualities and actions prepare someone for a successful career?

Case Study   Which Method of Instruction Is Best?

As a class, read the case study and discuss the questions that follow. After you finish studying the chapter, discuss this case study again. Have your opinions changed based on what you learned?

Addison, who graduated from high school two years ago, was speaking to a high school child development class about beginning a career in child development. Addison had just received the Child Development Associate (CDA) certification and was an associate teacher in a large early childhood education program. Addison told the students about planning to get a bachelor's degree in early childhood education as the next step in the process.

After Addison's presentation, one of the students raised a hand and asked, "What is the most difficult aspect of your job?"

Addison replied: "I think it is being uncomfortable when you are not sure whether your decision is the correct one or even if there is a correct decision. I am not even sure experience teaches you everything. For example, some preschool teachers require children to sit in a certain way and not move during story time. Other teachers allow children to get comfortable and move during the reading of a story. All teachers can explain their reasons for these practices."

Addison continued, "I talked about these differences with my director once and was told that educators must develop what early childhood education advocate and icon Gwen Morgan called a greater tolerance for ambivalence, which means you have to learn to cope with different feelings or attitudes about the same topic. This is what I find most difficult in my career. Some things you know for sure, but other things are unclear."

Give It Some Thought

1. Why do you think teachers make different decisions about the same situation? How can people learn the same material, but arrive at different conclusions and ideas?
2. Do you agree with Addison's director that early childhood educators need to develop what Gwen Morgan called a *greater tolerance for ambivalence* in their profession? Why or why not?

monkeybusinessimages/iStock via Getty Images Plus

Lesson 25.1

Making Career Decisions

Key Terms

abilities
aptitudes
career plan
employability skills
job shadowing
occupational categories
personal plan of study
professional
 organization
self-assessment
values

Learning Outcomes

After studying this lesson, you will be able to

25.1-1 **differentiate** between interests, *aptitudes,* and *abilities.*

25.1-2 **explain** how to research careers using occupational categories, market analysis, education and training requirements, and inside views.

25.1-3 **summarize** the steps to creating a career plan.

Reading and Notetaking Activity

Before reading, skim the headings in this lesson. List the headings to create an outline for taking notes during reading and class discussion. Under each heading, list any key terms. Finally, write two questions you expect to have answered in class. After completing the lesson, ask your teacher any questions you still have about the concepts or terms you learned.

Introduction

A career is more than just an occupation (a job). A career is a progression of related jobs that results in employment with opportunities for professional and personal growth.

Choosing a career will affect many factors in your lifestyle. Your career choices will likely influence where you live, what skills you develop, who your associates might be, what free time you have, and what your financial picture might look like.

Making career decisions involves learning about yourself and about different types of career paths, employment trends, and qualifications needed to reach a career outcome. Understanding your personal preferences, skill sets, and career options are important in making career choices and developing a career plan. To make informed career decisions, begin by assessing your interests, aptitudes, and abilities. Then continue by exploring careers and developing a career plan.

25.1-1 Assessing Your Interests, Aptitudes, and Abilities

One of the most difficult and important steps in career planning is **self-assessment** (identifying your interests, aptitudes, and abilities). Completing a self-assessment helps you learn more about who you are as a person and which types of jobs are likely a good fit. Self-assessment is worth the effort because it often leads to finding a career that is personally fulfilling. Without this step, some people might pursue a career that is unsatisfying.

Interests

Your *interests* include the objects or causes you care about, the achievements or qualities you are proud of, and the situations or activities that challenge you. Some of your deeper interests might be **values**, which are ideas, beliefs, and objects that are important and meaningful to you (**Figure 25.1**).

Interests are a key part of your career decision, affecting what you feel motivated to do, what you feel satisfied doing, and what fulfills you. Many people seek and stay in careers that align with their interests and values. Showing interest in your work, however, is only one factor. Your abilities and aptitudes also play a role in your career decisions.

Aptitudes

Aptitudes are talents with which people are born; they are natural and a part of heredity. Some of your aptitudes may be quite obvious. These may be subjects or activities that come naturally to you. Other aptitudes may not be obvious to you. For example, if you have a natural talent for nurturing children, you may not realize this until you have an opportunity to interact with children.

Most people enjoy doing activities that come naturally, so aptitudes often align with interests. Sometimes, however, aptitudes and interests can differ. You might not have an *interest* in an area even if you have a *talent* in that area. For example, you might dislike math, but excel at setting up and solving problems. On the contrary, you might have interests in areas, such as music or performing arts, for which you have no natural talents.

Aptitudes influence career choices. To do well in a career, you must develop certain skills that enable you to perform the tasks of your chosen career. These career skills will come more quickly and easily if they align with your natural talents.

A guidance or career counselor can help you identify your aptitudes with an aptitude test.

Figure 25.1 Your family, culture, experiences, and personality traits all help shape your values. *What are two of your values?*

monkeybusinessimages/iStock via Getty Images Plus

An *aptitude test* identifies areas in which you have aptitudes based on your responses to given questions and scenarios. The test may also reveal some employability skills you already possess (**Figure 25.2**).

Abilities

Unlike aptitudes, people are not born with abilities. Instead, **abilities** are skills you learn or develop and acquire through effort and practice. For example, while you might have an *aptitude* for leading others, you will have to *develop* leadership abilities. Also, while you might not have an *aptitude* for teaching children, you can still develop *abilities* to interact well with them.

In careers, people need two types of abilities. First, they need **employability skills**—general abilities that employers desire of all employees. Second, they need *career-specific skills*, which are abilities that employees must have for certain careers. For example, illustrating children's books requires general communication skills, but also certain career-specific skills in drawing and graphic design. Developing abilities is a lifelong learning process.

Figure 25.2 **Employability Skills**

Skills	Examples
Applied knowledge	• Reading, writing, mathematical strategies, scientific principles • Critical thinking skills, problem-solving skills, decision-making skills
Effective relationships	• Interpersonal skills (collaboration skills, communication, positive attitude, work ethic) • Responsibility, self-discipline, flexibility, integrity, initiative, professionalism
Workplace skills	• Resource management, time management, role management, collaborative skills, systems thinking, technology use

Goodheart-Willcox Publisher

Many workplaces continue to teach new abilities to their employees or require ongoing trainings or credentials to maintain employability.

Focus on Careers

Career Counselor

Career counselors focus on helping people with career decisions. They may assist college students entering the workforce, professionals advancing their careers, or people seeking to change fields. Career counselors explore and evaluate their clients' education, training, work history, interests, skills, and personality traits. They also work with clients to develop job-search skills and assist them in locating and applying for jobs. Career counselors provide support to people experiencing job loss, job stress, or other career transition issues.

Career cluster: Human services.

Education: Educational requirements include a master's degree. State requirements vary, but licensure and certification are typically required.

Job outlook: Future employment opportunities for career counselors are expected to grow faster than average for all occupations.

To learn more about a career as a career counselor, visit the United States Department of Labor's *Occupational Outlook Handbook* website. You will also be able to compare the job responsibilities, educational requirements, job outlook, and average pay of career counselors with similar occupations.

Photo: MBI/ Shutterstock.com

25.1-2 Exploring Careers

As you learn about your interests, aptitudes, and abilities, you may begin to discover various types of careers and industries. You can use several sources of information to research career areas, opportunities, and realistic pictures of what it is like to work in a career field. As you examine career options, you can learn more by researching occupational categories, analyzing the market, researching the required education and training, and taking an inside view at the career field.

Research Occupational Categories

As you explore careers, you can begin by researching *occupational categories* (also known as *career clusters*). **Occupational categories** are industry areas that encompass a variety of different careers. There are 16 common occupational categories and industries, and each category contains groupings of similar or related careers (**Figure 25.3**). Most child-related careers fall into the education and training and human services categories. Learning about careers by category can help you discover a career path and multiple careers of interest.

Figure 25.3 Common Occupational or Industry Categories

Category	Type of Job Emphasis
Agriculture, food, and natural resources	Agricultural products such as food, natural fibers, wood, plants, and animal products; the production, distribution, marketing, and financing of these products
Architecture and construction	Design, plan, or construct building structures; building management and maintenance
Arts, A/V technology, and communications	Visual and performing arts, journalism, and entertainment; designing, directing, exhibiting, writing, performing, and producing multimedia products
Business management and administration	Plan, organize, and evaluate business operations; sales, support services, and administration
Education and training	Teach in various learning environments; educational support services and administration
Finance	Investments, banking, insurance, financial planning, and financial management
Government and public administration	Local, state, and national government jobs
Health science	Health and medical services
Hospitality and tourism	Foodservice, lodging, travel, and tourism
Human services	Child and adult care services, counselors, therapists, home care assistants, and consumer services
Information technology	Relate information through communication systems, computers (including hardware, software, internet), and other media
Law, public safety, corrections, and security	Public safety and security
Manufacturing	Production of goods; sourcing and distribution
Marketing	Sale of goods; advertising, marketing, forecasting, and planning
Science, technology, engineering, and mathematics	Scientific research, scientific services, and product development
Transportation, distribution, and logistics	Movement of people or goods through flight, rail, car, biking, trucking, walking, or by other means

Goodheart-Willcox Publisher

Analyze the Market

An important step in learning about careers is analyzing the labor market for career opportunities. Learning about careers can help you identify career fields that are growing. Learning about an entire career field can also help you identify any specific careers that may be becoming **obsolete** (no longer useful; out of practice). When researching the outlook for a career, look for the following information:

- current and future employment opportunities for specific occupations
- required education and training
- work conditions and environment
- typical work hours or time commitment
- salaries for entry-level and advanced positions

Many career information sources are readily available online. You can also analyze the labor market by reading national and local newspapers, business magazines, and trade or professional journals published within a certain career field.

Determine Needed Education and Training

All careers, including some training programs, have education and training requirements that a person must meet. If you know which career you would like to pursue, you can find out exactly what the requirements are and begin to work toward them while you are still in high school.

Once you know what education or training you need, you can search for the best place to acquire it. Some education and training options are listed in **Figure 25.4**. Most colleges and other training programs have information available online. As you search, you might wish to talk with a career counselor or meet with faculty at colleges or other training programs. After reviewing the requirements for your chosen career, you can move toward finalizing your educational and training plans.

Figure 25.4 Education and Training Options

Type of Education or Training	Characteristics
Colleges and universities	• Students select *majors* (programs of study). • Upon completion of program of study, students receive an *associate's degree* (two-year), a *bachelor's degree* (four-year), or an advanced degree, such as a *master's degree* or a *Ph.D.*
Career and technical education	• Students receive occupational training in areas that require hands-on skills (such as working with children and culinary arts). • Programs usually involve a combination of education through a classroom setting and hands-on training and experience. • Classes may begin in high school and continue after graduation. • Students may earn a *credential* (proof of having certain skills, such as a college degree, license, or certificate) after successfully completing all required training.
Military training	• Soldiers receive hands-on training in various occupational categories that are useful both while in the military as well as in a nonmilitary job. • Aptitude tests are used to determine placement. • Programs may offer scholarships and degrees for agreed-upon service.
Employer training (also called in-service education)	• Workers attend specialized courses or sessions that teach them about their job functions. • Programs may be short-term, involving only a few classes, or long-term, lasting one year or more.

Get an Inside View

Getting an inside view is the best way to learn about a particular career. An inside view allows you to witness the day-to-day functions of a certain career and compare your career expectations with your interests, aptitudes, and abilities. You can get an inside view of various careers by talking to people in the career field and by gaining related work experience.

When talking with people in a career field, get as many perspectives as possible. Ask each employer what qualities they desire in new employees. You can ask employees what they find to be most rewarding and challenging about the job. You can also learn more about job duties and typical job demands through *job shadowing*. **Job shadowing** is following a competent worker through their workday. By job shadowing, you can experience the work environment, note the career skills in practice, and get a realistic feel for what a typical day on the job is like.

Another way to get an inside view is to join a **professional organization** (group of professionals who meet to discuss and advance their career field). Professional organizations offer opportunities to meet people working in a particular career area and to become knowledgeable about industry-specific jargon, current events related to the field, and career opportunities.

Another way to get an inside look at careers is to work at a job related to your career of interest. For example, you might consider taking a babysitting class or volunteering at a children's program to learn more about working with and providing care for young children. Even jobs not related to the career you are considering can help you develop general skills, and job experience during high school is considered positive for college applications.

Many high schools offer *work-based learning programs*, school programs that aid students in getting quality experiences in the world of work. In these programs, students take classes and are placed at a work site. A school program coordinator works with both the student and the work-site **mentor** (a person who counsels and advises) to make the student's learning meaningful. There are three different forms of work-based learning programs (**Figure 25.5**). In some cases, students may find entry-level positions with the employer who supervised their work-based learning.

25.1-3 Developing a Career Plan

After you have completed a self-assessment, investigated careers and occupational categories, and chosen a possible career path, you are ready to develop a career plan. A **career plan** is a detailed list of steps a person works to complete to enter a chosen career path. A career plan will help you identify your *goals* (what you want to achieve or obtain), including short-term goals and long-term goals.

Figure 25.5 Types of Work-Based Learning Programs

Type	Description
Co-op programs	Students enroll in a cooperative education class to learn more about a career area and develop the general skills they need. Students receive paid, on-the-job training through part-time work.
Apprenticeships	Students take a specific career class, such as child care, and then apply what they learn in class by working under the supervision of a highly-skilled tradesperson.
Internships	Students work at a company for a specified amount of time and learn about professional organizations, career options, and the related industry. Interns are supervised and may be paid or unpaid. Some students may be able to earn academic credits for internships.

Goodheart-Willcox Publisher

Reading

Career Narratives

Most workers are willing and even eager to share about their personal experiences on the job. There are many first-person accounts available describing how people in various occupational categories first chose and started their career paths. These career narratives often outline both the challenges and the rewards of a particular career and workplace. They may describe professionals' career paths and how they launched their careers as young adults. Some career narratives are books.

Other narratives are articles published online or in trade or professional journals. You can also learn a lot about workers' experiences in various careers through videos online.

Search online or visit the local library to find career narratives that might interest you. Select books, articles, or videos to explore. After you finish the career narrative(s), summarize what you have learned and then share this information with the class.

Photo: Andy-pix/Shutterstock.com

Short-term goals are achievable in the near future while *long-term goals* may take months or even years to achieve. The short-term goals you set to meet your long-term goal help break the goal down into manageable steps. For example, a long-term goal might be to obtain a bachelor's degree. Short-term goals for obtaining this degree may include applying for a scholarship or passing a difficult class.

When planning for a career, short-term goals include the steps you need to take as you work toward your long-term goal of entry in your career field. To achieve your long-term career goal, you will probably create and achieve many short-term goals along the way.

When developing your goals, make sure they are effective. Effective goals are *SMART goals*, which are specific, measurable, achievable, relevant, and timely (**Figure 25.6**). By setting SMART goals, you are more likely to stay motivated and be successful.

Figure 25.6 Creating SMART Goals

SMART Stands for...	Questions to Answer with SMART Goals
Specific	Does this goal outline what you want to accomplish, who will be involved, and how it will be accomplished?
Measurable	How will you measure whether or not the goal has been reached?
Achievable	Will this goal be challenging, but still possible? Do you have the knowledge, skills, and abilities to achieve this goal?
Relevant	Does this goal relate to your long-term goal and overall career plan?
Timely	Can you achieve this goal within a set time frame? Have you established a completion date for this goal?

Goodheart-Willcox Publisher

Part of your career plan also involves developing a **personal plan of study**. This plan identifies the courses and other learning experiences you need to complete to meet your educational and career goals. Teachers and counselors can help you identify these courses. You may wish to design a plan that leads to several related occupations within an occupational group. You often have greater flexibility job hunting when your skills are broader. Because child development knowledge is used in all careers dealing with children, a course in child development is considered broader than a course in teaching music at the elementary school level.

When developing a career plan, identify your *resources*, which are tools you can use in achieving your goals. Your goals and resources should be realistic and should challenge, but not overwhelm you. As you follow your career plan, keep a log of your achievements. This log will help you track your progress and motivate you to accomplish other goals. Reviewing your log and revising your goals when necessary can help you as you continue to make decisions about careers.

Lesson 25.1 Review and Assessment

1. **True or False.** Abilities are talents with which people are born; they are natural and a part of heredity. (25.1.1)
2. Which employability skill is most critical to forming effective relationships with others? (25.1.1)
   A. Time management
   B. Reading ability
   C. Technology use
   D. Positive attitude
3. To receive occupational training in a career area that requires hands-on skills, a student would most likely attend a/n _____. (25.1.2)
   A. college
   B. technical school
   C. university
   D. in-service training

4. An example of a short-term career goal is _____. (25.1.3)
   A. passing a final exam
   B. obtaining a teaching certification
   C. graduating from college
   D. working with children
5. All of the following are characteristics that define SMART goals except _____. (25.1.3)
   A. timely
   B. ambitious
   C. specific
   D. measurable

Learning About Careers That Involve Children

Key Terms

Childhood Education
  International (CEI)

career burnout

Child Development
  Associate (CDA)

direct intervention

entrepreneurship

health services

indirect intervention

leader

National Association
  for the Education
  of Young Children
  (NAEYC)

personal qualifications

professional
  qualifications

protective services

Learning Outcomes

After studying this lesson, you will be able to

25.2-1 **describe** child-related careers in different fields.

25.2-2 **identify** the personal qualifications important for child-related careers.

25.2-3 **identify** the professional qualifications important for child-related careers.

Reading and Notetaking Activity

Before reading this lesson, scan the lesson headings. Write a paragraph describing what you already know about these topics. Explain where you got the information you have—from conversations, the media, or research, for example. As you are reading, compare and contrast the information in the chapter with your prior knowledge. Organize your notes around the information you already know. After reading, consider how your prior knowledge of the subject matter helped you understand this topic.

Introduction

If you are interested in children and their development, then a career in a child-related field may be for you. Many opportunities exist for working in a career that involves children. Child-related careers are constantly growing, and the widespread effort to improve children's quality of life is one trend that makes child-related work a fulfilling career choice for many.

Learning more about the many types of careers that relate to children can help you decide whether this field is right for you. To be successful in child-related careers, workers will need certain personal and professional qualifications.

25.2-1 Types of Child-Related Careers

Child-related careers involve varying amounts of contact with children. In some careers, adults work and interact with children directly; this is called **direct intervention**. People in such careers include teachers and pediatricians. In other child-related careers, adults work on behalf of children, but not directly with children. Working indirectly with children is called **indirect intervention** (**Figure 25.7**). All adults in child-related careers, whether working directly or indirectly with children, must understand children and their needs to be successful on the job.

Careers in child-related fields can be grouped into several areas. The most common areas include health and protective services; care and education; entertainment; design; advertising, marketing, and management; research, consulting, and advocacy; and entrepreneurship.

Health and Protective Services

Professionals in health and protective services attend to the health needs and protection of children. This career field encompasses two types of services: *health services* and *protective services*.

Workers in **health services** ensure that children receive adequate physical and mental health care. Adults in these services understand children's health needs and have the knowledge and skills needed to provide quality care. **Figure 25.8** lists examples of careers in children's health services.

Other workers in health services may not work *exclusively* with children, but still should know children's needs and how to meet them. Some of these health professionals include eye doctors, speech therapists, hearing specialists, sports medicine doctors, physical therapists, occupational therapists, play therapists, emergency room and hospital staff, and pharmacists.

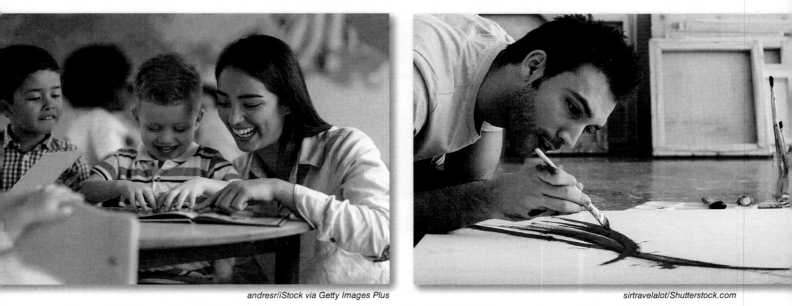

andresr/iStock via Getty Images Plus

sirtravelalot/Shutterstock.com

Figure 25.7 Examples of child-related careers in direct intervention include child care workers and therapists. Examples of child-related careers in indirect intervention include child development professors, artists who design children's spaces, and manufacturers of children's products and toys. *Would you prefer to work in direct or indirect intervention with children? Why?*

Figure 25.8 Child-Related Careers in Health Services

Career	Description
Child psychiatrists	Physicians who specialize in the treatment of children's mental health conditions.
Clinical child psychologists	Professionals who specialize in delivering psychological services to address the social-emotional and mental health of children from infancy to adolescence.
Clinical social workers	Social workers who offer diagnostic services, therapy, and counseling in a variety of settings.
Counseling psychologists	Professionals who help families and children cope with life challenges and improve well-being with a special focus on lifespan development.
Developmental psychologists	Professionals who research and assess development across the lifespan; some may make recommendations or treat conditions directly.
Infant mental health specialists	Specialists trained to provide comprehensive and intensive mental health services to families with infants and toddlers. This includes focusing on social-emotional health of the infant and caregiver and identifying any relationship issues between the infant and caregiver. They may also help to identify any delays or disabilities.
Neonatal nurses	Registered nurses who provide critical care to premature or sick newborns and offer support to caregivers of those infants.
Pediatric and school nurses	Nurses who specialize in the care of children.
Pediatric dentists	Dentists who specialize in the care of children.
Pediatricians	Doctors who specialize in the care of children.
Registered dietitians	Nutrition specialists who may plan healthy diets or help work through food issues for children and families, including children with special food and medical needs.
School foodservice personnel	People who plan school menus and prepare and serve food to meet children's needs.
School psychologists	Professionals who help school-age children and teens with educational diagnoses and decisions. They work with families, students, teachers, and administrators to create supportive learning environments for children with academic, social, emotional, or behavioral issues at school.

Goodheart-Willcox Publisher

Some of these professionals, however, may specialize in pediatric work (pediatric eye doctors or pediatric dentists) or be employed in a setting that deals only with children (children's hospital).

Adults with careers in **protective services** work to identify injustices to children and to correct or remove children from dangerous situations. Careers in protective services are growing as society becomes more concerned about the rights and needs of children. Some positions in protective services are listed in **Figure 25.9**.

Care and Education

Another area of child-related careers involves care and education. The career area of care and education includes parents, caregivers, teachers, and other caregiving or education professionals. Due to increased enrollments in early childhood education programs and to governmental commitments to children's education, these types of careers are always in demand. **Figure 25.10** lists some common careers in care and education.

Figure 25.9 Child-Related Careers in Protective Services

Career	Description
Child, family, and school social workers	Professionals who assist children and families in crisis, place foster children, arrange adoptions, and serve as a link between students' families and the schools.
Child protective services social workers	Professionals who investigate reports of neglect and abuse and intervene, if necessary. They can initiate legal action to remove children to a safe place until the case comes into the courts.
Juvenile officers and family court judges	Professionals who make legal decisions about children and their families' rights and responsibilities.
Licensing personnel	Professionals who check the quality of services for children, such as the quality of child care centers.
Medical and public health social workers	Professionals who help children and their families cope with chronic and terminal illnesses, help advocate for patients, and help plan for the child's needs after hospital discharge.
Mental health and substance abuse social workers	Professionals who provide individual and group therapy, crisis intervention, and other supportive interventions.

Goodheart-Willcox Publisher

Figure 25.10 Child-Related Careers in Care and Education

Career	Description
Child and youth leaders	People who plan, organize, and work with children and their instructors in religious programs or youth organizations, such as scouting groups, recreational programs, and camps.
Child care providers	People who care for infants, toddlers, preschoolers, and school-age children (when school is not in session).
Children's librarians	Librarians trained to work in school libraries or in children's sections of other libraries.
Family life coordinators	People who connect and coordinate support, services, and resources for children and their families.
Family life educators	People who provide direct services to children and families or train professionals in providing services for children and families.
Elective high school teachers and college professors	Teachers who instruct high school or college students in child-related courses, such as health, education, child or lifespan development, and parenting.
Leaders, managers, and administrators	Directors of child care and education programs as well as principals and supervisors of school programs.
Parent educators	People who teach parents and caregivers about child development and parenting.
Recreational instructors	People who guide or teach children in areas such as music, art, sports, and hobbies.
Special education teachers	Teachers who work with children who have special needs.
Teachers and teachers' assistants	People trained to teach or assist teachers in public and private school programs for children in pre-K or Kindergarten through high school.

Goodheart-Willcox Publisher

Entertainment

In recent years, the business of children's entertainment has expanded greatly. Many new children's television programs, movies, and live programs have been produced. A wider variety of children's books and games (including video games, other interactive games, and apps) are available.

People in entertainment careers include producers, directors, actors, technicians, video game developers, writers, and performers.

Design

Due to their changing development, children need items especially designed to meet their physical, intellectual, and social-emotional needs. Items designed for children include clothing, personal care items, dishes and flatware, furniture, books, and toys.

People who work in design may include interior or playground designers, product developers, and illustrators or other artists involved in children's books or films. *Designers* plan indoor and outdoor spaces for children, such as playgrounds and child care centers. Other designers may also work in the entertainment industry, such as in set design or costuming for children's productions. *Product developers* may design toys or other items made especially for children. *Illustrators and other artists* bring print and electronic media to life with their developmentally appropriate and child-appealing artwork.

Advertising, Marketing, and Management

As children's products are produced, businesses need employees who are trained to advertise and market these products. Another growing career choice is managing the businesses that produce and sell children's products. Positions for advertising, marketing, and managing can be found in corporations, agencies, firms, and small businesses.

Research, Consulting, and Advocacy

Many career areas, such as health, education, entertainment, design, and business, conduct research on children and their needs. Research studies provide knowledge that allows people to serve children well. Because thousands of research studies on children and their caregivers are published each year, a massive amount of child-related research and information is available. Workers in research, consulting, and advocacy are involved in both the research and application of this information. Examples of careers in this area include consultants and child advocates.

As the body of child development research grows, *consultants* will continue to be important in child-related career fields. Consultants work on behalf of children. They serve as a link between researchers and those in direct intervention, product development, and sales. Some consultants are child development experts who provide state and federal lawmakers with information. Others write informational papers or deliver oral presentations (**Figure 25.11**).

Figure 25.11 Consultants often share child development information through oral presentations that can be delivered to a variety of audiences. *In your opinion, what would be the benefits of a career as a consultant? What drawbacks would there be?*

Child advocates are professionals who focus on research addressing mental health, education, and legal or medical issues that affect children. Most advocates specialize in one issue, such as child support, substance abuse, **delinquency** (misbehavior; illegal behavior), or housing. Advocates work in the judicial and legislative branches of government and through professional associations. They conduct and compile research on an issue, observe the issue, seek support for needed changes, and keep others informed on the issue's status.

Entrepreneurship

Many child-related careers offer chances for **entrepreneurship**, the creation of one's own business. Family child care homes are one of the most common child-related businesses started by entrepreneurs. Some entrepreneurs own and operate child care centers. Entrepreneurs can start many other types of businesses as well, such as: child photography; recreational instruction; private medical practice; children's retail, such as clothing, furniture, and toys; and writing for and about children. Entrepreneurship in a child-related field can be satisfying and rewarding. Creativity, knowledge, self-motivation, and hard work are keys to making a business profitable.

25.2-2 Personal Qualifications for a Child-Related Career

Success in a child-related career involves a number of **personal qualifications**, traits you possess that cannot be learned in career training. Personal qualifications are sometimes hard to define and measure, so they are less specific than professional qualifications. Personal qualifications for success in a child-related career include concern for children, flexibility, and leadership.

Focus on Speech

Qualities of Entrepreneurs

Entrepreneurs need many skills other than those directly related to their specialties. For example, a person who owns and operates a child care center must know much more than how to teach and care for children. This entrepreneur must also be able to manage money, coordinate advertising, hire and supervise staff, oversee enrollment, know and follow laws and regulations, maintain the facilities, and communicate with caregivers. Many entrepreneurs want to have the freedom to run business in their own ways and like the variety of roles to be filled.

Research stories about entrepreneurs with successful businesses. What were the advantages of starting a business? What were the drawbacks? In the person's opinion, what key qualities make a good entrepreneur? Deliver an oral presentation to the class summarizing what you learn.

Photo: naluwan/Shutterstock.com

Concern for Children

For a person in a child-related career, the most important personal qualification is a **genuine** (JEN-yuh-wun), real, concern for children. Sometimes, in the effort to perform well, people lose sight of the most important concern of all—the children. If you work directly or indirectly with children, you must always make decisions based on what is best for them.

When working directly with children, concern is expressed as an authentic liking for children. Adults show they like children through their **benevolence** (well-meaning attitudes) toward children. **Figure 25.12** describes behaviors of adults who display a genuine concern for children.

Flexibility

In working with children, it is important to be *flexible* (to remain open to new ideas). Children can be unpredictable, and research has shown that the constant changes required when working with children can cause people to have *career burnout*. **Career burnout** is emotional exhaustion with a career. A person who is flexible will adapt more easily to change and will be less likely to have career burnout.

Leadership

Being able to lead others is very important when working in a child-related career. Children see adults and teens as leaders, and those working in child-related careers should model positive forms of leadership. A **leader** is a person who inspires or motivates the thoughts, feelings, or actions of others. Effective leaders are self-confident, which helps children feel secure (**Figure 25.13**).

Figure 25.12 Behaviors of Adults Who Are Concerned for Children

- Respect the uniqueness of each child
- Show kindness and patience with children and families
- Tolerate noise and physical activity
- Enjoy the child's world—games, songs, stories, concepts, play, and humor
- Feel comfortable helping young children with physical needs—dressing, toileting, and caring for scrapes, bruises, and common childhood illnesses
- Accept physical closeness—the child's touching of hair, clothing, and jewelry; hugging and kissing; and clinging when hurt or distraught

Goodheart-Willcox Publisher

kali9/iStock via Getty Images Plus

Figure 25.13 Qualities of Effective Leaders

- Have a positive outlook and motivate others; excite people about possibilities
- Handle responsibility by following through to complete tasks, accepting blame for mistakes, and keeping promises
- Are honest; are trusted because they do not take advantage of others
- Show acceptance of others; are flexible and open to others' ideas
- Are aware of differing points of view and work to resolve conflicts
- Share reasons and explain their positions
- Seek positive group interaction through open and ongoing communication
- Listen to get other people's perspectives and seek common ground
- Know how to set and articulate goals to help the team achieve its purpose
- Assign responsibilities to others
- Develop team support by getting all members to participate
- Make sound decisions and are confident in their choices

Goodheart-Willcox Publisher

They provide clear instructions for the group or individual and set firm limits with children when needed.

Leaders in child-related careers teach self-discipline and listen patiently to understand what a child is saying. Leadership skills are also needed in working with adults, such as other staff members or the children's caregivers.

Like other personal qualifications, leadership qualities are a part of your whole life, not just your working hours. For some people, leadership is an aptitude. These people seem to have more natural leadership talent than others. If leadership is not one of your aptitudes, you can improve your ability to lead through practice. Babysitting or providing child care could give you practice at making decisions and being responsible.

25.2-3 Professional Qualifications for a Child-Related Career

In addition to personal qualifications, workers need certain professional qualifications to succeed in child-related careers. **Professional qualifications** are the physical, intellectual, and social-emotional skills you need to perform well in a career. People most often learn these skills from education, training, or entry-level work experience.

Training might include classes in high school or college as well as on-the-job training. Professional qualifications for child-related careers often include specialized knowledge and training, education and certification, and lifelong learning.

Knowledge of Child Development

Child development is the science of understanding children. If you want to have a career in a child-related field, you must have a thorough knowledge of child development and know how to use and apply child development concepts. Because physical, intellectual, and social-emotional development are interrelated, workers in child-related careers must study *all* aspects of child development, even if professional training for a career only stresses one aspect. For example, although pediatricians primarily deal with children's physical aspects of development, they must also be aware of children's levels of comprehension (intellectual development) and social-emotional development.

Career Specialization

In addition to learning about child development, workers in child-related careers must obtain specialized knowledge in their career areas. Specialized knowledge might include understanding the following:

- how children learn
- what to teach and in what order to teach certain concepts and skills
- the best methods and materials for teaching
- how to assess children's knowledge

For some careers, people must learn specialties within a specialty. Specialties require in-depth learning. For example, a *pediatric ophthalmologist* (AWF-thuhl-mawl-oh-jist) is a children's eye doctor. These professionals first learn general medicine, then how to treat diseases of the eye, and finally how to care for children's eye conditions. As more professionals have specialties within specialties, these professionals are becoming more available to all children, but particularly those residing in areas that have more access to health care.

Setting Short- and Long-Term SMART Goals in Child-Related Careers

Obtaining professional qualifications for and making progress toward a career choice can seem *daunting* (difficult), especially while you are still learning about career possibilities. Creating a career plan with short- and long-term SMART goals, however, can help make your educational and professional steps clearer and more manageable.

As you read in Lesson 25.1, short- and long-term SMART goals can help break down major career goals. For example, if your goal is to earn a CDA certification, you would need to:

- hold a high school diploma or a GED or be a junior or senior enrolled in a high school career and technical program in early childhood education
- complete 120 hours of training
- complete 480 hours of experience working with children in the age group matching your type of CDA application
- complete *Family Questionnaires* and *Professional Portfolio*
- successfully complete a *Verification Visit* and pass a CDA exam online

Because one professional qualification is to complete 120 hours of training, you might focus on dividing that long-term goal into smaller, short-term goals. First, you could focus on finding an organization that provides training. Thus, one short-term goal may be to spend time each week researching early education programs. Another short-term goal may be to decide whether to take the training for college credit or no credit, which also affects where you might receive the training. Along with this decision, another short-term goal is to get a good estimate of the total cost of getting the CDA and develop a savings plan for this expenditure. These short-term goals will help you reach your long-term goal of achieving 120 clock-hours of formal training.

Dividing your career plan into short- and long-term goals will make your career plans clearer and will keep you focused on the short-term goals you can achieve now. Achieving these goals can strengthen your motivation to achieve your long-term goals. Using SMART goals increases the likelihood that you will accomplish your overall career plan.

Writing Activity

List one or more child-related careers that interest you. What are the professional requirements you would need to reach this career goal? Outline a career plan that identifies the major long-term goals (five to ten years) for reaching a career. How could you meet those long-term goals with short-term goals (within a year or a few months)? After creating your outline, write down your short- and long-term goals and identify how these are SMART goals.

Photo: Tom Wang/Shutterstock.com

Education and Certification

There are many levels of positions within child-related fields. Most child-related careers require a college degree. Teachers, especially those in public school programs, must have a bachelor's degree in education. Public school supervisors and directors generally have at least bachelor's degrees, and many have master's degrees in child development, early childhood education, or related areas. Most have had previous experience as teachers. Consultants for public school programs are usually employed by higher education institutions and are hired just for specific training purposes. They usually have a master's degree or a doctoral degree.

In addition to a college degree, most child-related careers also require a *specific certification* (state-required documentation that proves someone is qualified to perform a job). Examples of a specific certification include a teaching certificate for specific grade levels or subject matter areas, a school administrator certificate, or a counseling certificate. *Certification* is also called a *license* in some professions. Earning a certification often includes:

- passing a background check
- meeting certain education and experience requirements
- successfully completing a specific test
- obtaining the endorsement of the training institution

Certification requirements vary from state to state. Therefore, professionals who move to a different state must reapply for certification and meet any additional requirements. Certifications often expire within a couple years and must be renewed.

A common certification in child-related careers is the **Child Development Associate (CDA)** certification. The CDA is an entry-level position qualification for teaching in an early childhood education program or working as a teacher's assistant in a preschool program. Earning a CDA requires students to:

- select a specialization
- complete a certain number of hours of study and experience
- pass an exam

Generally, the amount of training a job requires depends on the level of responsibility it demands. Teachers have greater professional responsibilities than teachers' assistants. Some careers, such as a neonatal nurse or an infant mental health specialist, require study in schools and colleges and supervised work in the career field. People may earn professional qualifications for other careers (such as entertainment) through on-the-job training rather than through schools and colleges. Many in these fields, however, also have degrees from colleges and other institutions. Some professionals continue their education to get degrees and certifications while they are working in their jobs.

Lifelong Learning

In addition to basic career training, adults in child-related careers are expected to keep up with the latest knowledge and practices in their field. Continuing to learn about a field of study even after earning a degree is called *lifelong learning*.

Keeping up in a child-related career may require more classroom study, seminar or webinar attendance, or on-the-job training. Independent study helps keep professionals informed. An example of independent study may include reading about current research and the application of research findings in journals and books. Lifelong learning may also involve exchanging knowledge and practices among those working in the many child-related careers. This type of exchange often occurs at professional meetings.

One way to foster lifelong learning in a career path is to join a professional organization. Two of the many professional organizations for those in child-related careers in care and education include the *National Association for the Education of Young Children (NAEYC)* and the *Association for Childhood Education International (ACEI)*.

- The **National Association for the Education of Young Children (NAEYC)** is an organization that works on behalf of young children. Members receive educational materials, have access to child development research, and can attend conferences with opportunities for workshops, seminars, and networking with professionals in the field.
- **Childhood Education International (CE International)** is an organization that focuses on the education and healthy development of children. Members receive educational resources, attend programs and conferences, and may qualify for scholarships, awards, or grants.

Lesson 25.2 — Review and Assessment

1. An example of a career path that involves direct intervention with children is _____. (25.2.1)
   A. pediatric medicine
   B. toy design
   C. illustration
   D. acting
2. A juvenile officer works in which child-related career area? (25.2.1)
   A. Entertainment
   B. Care and education
   C. Health
   D. Protective services
3. A personal trait that would most likely help someone be successful in a child-related career is _____. (25.2.2)
   A. being open to new ideas
   B. preferring silence over noise
   C. taking direction from others
   D. feeling most comfortable with order
4. **True or False.** A person who is flexible will adapt more easily to change and will be less likely to have career burnout. (25.2.2)
5. An entry-level qualification for teaching in an early childhood education program or working as a teacher's assistant in a preschool program is a/n _____. (25.2.3)
   A. bachelor's degree in education
   B. secondary education certification
   C. master's degree in education
   D. child development associate certification

Developing Skills for Career Success

Learning Outcomes

After studying this lesson, you will be able to

25.3-1 **identify** interpersonal skills needed for career success.

25.3-2 **describe** good collaboration skills.

25.3-3 **explain** the importance of critical thinking, problem-solving, and conflict-resolution skills.

25.3-4 **describe** professionalism, executive function, and role-management skills.

Key Terms

codes of professional ethics
collaboration skills
critical thinking skills
interpersonal skills
mediation
negotiation
problem-solving skills
professionalism
role guilt
role strain
time management

Reading and Notetaking Activity

Create a table like the one shown. Include as many rows as you need. Before reading the lesson, list facts and skills you already know in the Give One column. In the Get One column, list facts you learn as you read the lesson. If you have any questions about what you are reading, raise your hand and ask your teacher. After you finish reading the lesson, team up with a classmate and discuss each other's lists. Are there items you would add to your list?

Give One	Get One
Facts and skills known	*Facts you learned*

Introduction

You live in a changing world where careers are increasingly part of a global, diverse economy. In this information age (also known as the *digital age*), jobs increasingly require knowledge-based and versatile skills.

Jobs are constantly changing, and schools are educating children for jobs that have not even been created yet, making the focus on skills more important than ever before. A modern-day economy needs an employee who:

- adapts and copes with the stress of change
- learns quickly and is willing to learn new skills continuously
- possesses skills that are portable, meaning they can be useful in more than one career area
- is eager and able to learn about using new types of technology (**Figure 25.14**)

Career success today is defined more by the career skills gained and used than by keeping one job until retirement. Success also means finding work that is rewarding and fulfilling.

At this point in your life, you may not know exactly what type of career you want. You still have time to make this decision. You can start today, however, to develop employability skills, which are skills all employers seek in job candidates regardless of career area.

jeffbergen/iStock via Getty Images Plus

Figure 25.14 Most employees today are expected to be well-versed in technology and eager to learn and adapt to new types of work. *Why is knowledge about technology important for today's workplace?*

Employability skills include interpersonal skills, collaboration skills, critical thinking and problem-solving skills, conflict resolution skills, professionalism skills, strong executive function skills, and role-management skills. Chances are that you have already begun to develop some of these skills, but you can refine and enhance these skills throughout life. If you begin now, you will be much more prepared when it is time to enter the job market.

25.3-1 Interpersonal Skills

Interpersonal skills are skills you use to relate to and work with other people. These skills are perhaps the most important you will develop both professionally and personally. Interpersonal skills will often determine whether you will get a desired job, keep your job, or be promoted. Outside of the workplace, your interpersonal skills, or lack thereof, can strengthen or damage your relationships with family and friends. Interpersonal skills include a positive attitude, strong work ethic, good manners, and excellent communication skills.

Positive Attitude

Although a person's basic temperament is largely determined by genes, basic attitudes are influenced by the environment and begin to develop early in life. Attitude development is influenced by role models, such as family members, friends, and others, as well as by the media. Parents and caregivers, teachers, and youth leaders often encourage children to develop positive attitudes. For example, they teach children to show respect and solve conflicts in a **diplomatic** (agreeable; polite) manner.

As adults, people are responsible for their own attitudes. To a great extent, work performance is linked to attitude. Employers need employees who have positive attitudes and who are friendly, cheerful, and considerate of others in the workplace. Employees with positive attitudes are generally liked and respected. Maintaining a positive attitude also involves respecting differences among people and getting along with coworkers, supervisors, and clients or customers (**Figure 25.15**).

Strong Work Ethic

In the workplace, *work ethic* refers to a standard of actions, behaviors, and values for job performance. A good employee is said to have a *strong work ethic*. This person understands what behaviors are appropriate for the workplace and is honest, hardworking, and dependable. A *dependable* employee shows up for work on time and works steadily through the workday except for normal breaks. They work independently and do more than that which is asked by the employer. An employee with a strong work ethic strives to get along with others, does the best work possible, and cares about their quality of work.

Good Manners

Manners are behaviors that make you comfortable around others and make others comfortable around you. Employers must trust you will not embarrass them in any situation. Furthermore, good manners help others take you seriously. The following are basic guidelines you can follow to practice good manners:

- avoid gossip
- have empathy
- be professional in meetings and in verbal and written communications
- apologize if you must interrupt a meeting, conversation, or someone's concentration on a task
- keep any conflicts situation-related rather than personal
- keep your voice moderated in loudness and pitch
- be polite and respectful with everyone
- be thoughtful of coworkers and clients

Excellent Communication Skills

Interpersonal communication skills involve the ability to read, write, speak, and listen well. In general, communication skills, especially writing skills, are listed as the **scarcest** (rarest) skills in the workforce.

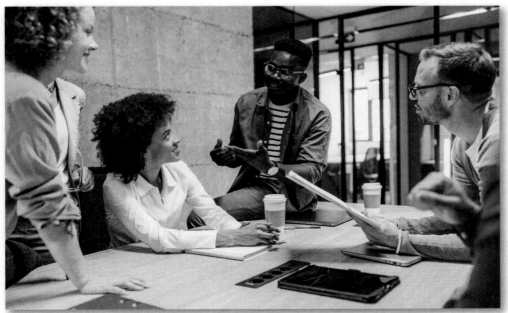

Figure 25.15 Having a positive attitude makes it easier to get along and work together with coworkers and clients. *Why is a positive attitude helpful for business relationships?*

filadendron/iStock via Getty Images Plus

Employees with good communication skills are expected to:

- have good listening skills. *Active listening* involves devoting your full attention to the person communicating with you and then repeating or rephrasing what you have heard to ensure correct understanding.
- have excellent reading comprehension.
- use good *verbal communication skills* (communication involving words, such as speaking clearly and choosing words carefully).
- use good *nonverbal communication skills* (communication not involving words, such as appropriate body language and eye contact).
- communicate using standard English (grammar, mechanics, and spelling). For some careers, fluency in more than one language may be required.
- have needed computer and other technology skills.

In addition to these expectations, specific skill requirements vary with each career. Some of the communication skills that contribute to these expectations include those listed in **Figure 25.16**. Boosting these communication skills can greatly increase your chances of job success.

Figure 25.16 Interpersonal Communication Skills

Skills	Examples
Listening skills	• Following directions • Grasping information • Clarifying information • Asking questions
Speaking skills	• Giving instructions • Responding to phone calls and voice mail • Actively participating in personal conversations • Participating in meetings and conferences • Giving presentations
Reading skills	• Understanding office signs and maps, such as evacuation plans • Comprehending office correspondence and manuals • Understanding career-specific vocabulary • Interpreting statistical data and understanding graphs and diagrams
Writing skills	• Writing messages and memos • Making records • Composing business letters • Drafting business reports
Nonverbal communication skills	• Appearing to be alert and interested • Focusing on the speaker • Smiling and greeting others with a friendly voice and firm handshake
Technology-based skills	• Organizing work tasks • Writing and responding to e-mail for business purposes • Using reputable sources for gathering work-related information • Using word processing software and any company-specific software • Making spreadsheets and creating databases • Creating drawings and images (computer graphics) • Preparing multimedia presentations

Goodheart-Willcox Publisher

25.3-2 Collaboration Skills

The information-age economy has resulted in a more team-oriented workplace. Most workplaces require employees to have **collaboration skills** (the skills needed to work well with others to combine knowledge, solve problems, reach common goals, and make decisions). Most careers, and especially child-related careers, involve team efforts.

Good teamwork involves getting along well with others. Team members work to develop problem-solving and decision-making skills. They learn to brainstorm, compromise, build **consensus** (group agreement) for ideas, and evaluate results of decisions. Good team players participate by listening and speaking. They also:

- respect others' differences and ideas
- take responsibility for assigned tasks
- accept accountability for the team as well as for themselves
- are adaptable and open to new ideas
- share roles with team members (**Figure 25.17**)
- deal with personality clashes and manage conflicts
- present an agenda and help the team follow it
- keep the team focused on goals

- encourage every member to participate
- analyze ideas presented
- keep records of ideas and decisions

Developing collaboration skills takes time and usually begins in the early years of schooling. Working on group projects is the best way to learn teamwork. You can also build teamwork skills through participation in clubs, organizations, youth groups, and volunteer activities.

Collaboration skills also involve being an effective leader. Most effective leaders are also good team players. They have the skills to get along with others and work together. Leadership skills have their roots in the early years of life. As children, future leaders develop autonomy, responsibility, and self-confidence even in the face of risks or challenges. Young leaders-to-be often have leadership role models in their lives.

You can gain leadership skills through formal and informal leadership positions. A formal leadership position might be a position in a school organization. Career and technical student organizations (CTSOs), such as Family, Career and Community Leaders of America (FCCLA), also offer leadership opportunities. An informal leadership position might include taking charge during a group project.

gpointstudio/iStock via Getty Images Plus

Figure 25.17 A person's willingness and ability to share roles with team members is a sign of excellent collaboration skills. *Why is collaboration important for the workplace?*

25.3-3 Critical Thinking, Problem-Solving, and Conflict-Resolution Skills

Critical thinking skills are the skills needed to analyze and evaluate situations to make reasonable judgments and decisions. Critical thinking skills are essential in every career and in everyday situations.

People use critical thinking to develop **problem-solving skills**, which are skills used to analyze problems and formulate solutions. This process includes defining and analyzing the problem, setting and implementing goals, and monitoring and evaluating the plan. People need good problem-solving skills to handle issues at home, at school, and at work.

Conflict-resolution skills are the skills required to resolve a situation in which a disagreement could lead to hostile behavior. **Figure 25.18** lists steps for resolving conflicts in a workplace setting. **Negotiation** occurs when individuals involved in a conflict come together to discuss a compromise. In a compromise, each party is willing to give up something to meet the other party in the middle. Sometimes, formal methods are required to settle conflicts. **Mediation** is the inclusion of a neutral person, called a *mediator*, to help the conflicting parties resolve their dispute and reach an agreement.

Figure 25.18 Conflict-Resolution Model

Step 1

Identify the issue. Have all parties state their perspectives. Listen carefully and calmly.

Step 2

Identify possible solutions. Keep an open mind and do not rule out any suggestions.

Step 3

Begin the negotiation process. Evaluate each possible solution. Calmly discuss the issue until an agreement is reached that is acceptable to all parties.

Step 4

Carry out the decision. Be sure everyone follows through on the agreement. If the solution is not working, renegotiation may be necessary.

Goodheart-Willcox Publisher

Focus on Reading

Confidentiality in Child-Related Careers

Part of professionalism is following the ethical guidelines set by your employer. Child-related careers are especially concerned with ethical behaviors and with protecting children. Because of this, most child-related careers have established guidelines about confidentiality and information sharing. Guidelines about confidentiality affect how much information child care workers share with other parents and caregivers about children's circumstances. They also affect how and to whom a pediatrician shares a child's health information.

Choose one child-related career and research typical guidelines about confidentiality in that career. Read two articles about these guidelines (or the guidelines themselves, if possible) and then write a short summary about typical guidelines in that career.

Photo: Andy-pix/Shutterstock.com

Professionalism Skills

Many experts believe professionalism has declined in the workplace. **Professionalism** involves the skills, good judgment, and the attitudes and behaviors expected from any person trained to do a job well. When professionalism is present, people who work together feel positive about each other and their work. There is also mutual respect present.

Professionalism requires the following:

- being skilled in your area of expertise and constantly searching for opportunities to grow in expertise
- being willing to go slightly above and beyond the minimum requirements or expectations
- being courteous and pleasant and maintaining a humble attitude in daily interactions
- having a strong sense of individual and group purpose
- taking personal responsibility, being accountable, and following through on your word
- being motivated to do your work and willing to share knowledge and information that help achieve group goals
- striving for excellence in each task
- bringing out strengths of others

Professionalism also involves following a code of ethics. Some people develop a *personal code of ethics* to guide them in everyday life. Many professions have written standards of conduct for workers in a certain career field. These written standards are called **codes of professional ethics**. An employee is expected to follow any codes of professional ethics that apply to their profession (**Figure 25.19**). For example, the first principle within NAEYC's code of ethical conduct is never to harm a child in any manner.

In some careers, violating the code of professional ethics can result in **suspension** (temporary removal from a job) or **termination** (permanent removal from a job). People can develop professionalism skills by learning about career-specific ethics and professionalism requirements and by practicing good conduct before, as well as during, employment.

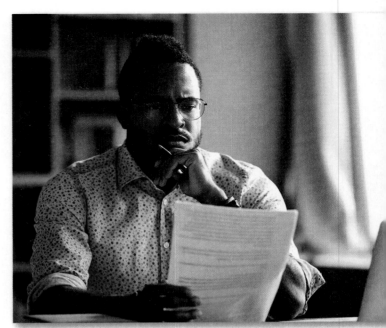

fizkes/iStock via Getty Images Plus

Figure 25.19 It is important to read and carefully follow a workplace's code of professional ethics. Following these codes demonstrates professionalism and one's seriousness about a job. *What types of ethical standards are typical in child-related careers?*

Strong Executive Function Skills

The executive functions (EFs) of working memory, cognitive flexibility, and inhibition allow people to self-regulate behavior. People with strong EF skills exhibit a number of characteristics, including those shown in **Figure 25.20**.

Figure 25.20 Characteristics of People with Strong Executive Function Skills

- Able to problem-solve and overcome obstacles
- Create plans and prioritize to accomplish tasks
- Self-evaluate to check progress and fix errors
- Control impulses and emotions
- Retain and use learned information easily
- Use time management and organizational skills to complete tasks
- Focus and sustain attention on tasks and projects
- Handle multiple tasks simultaneously by employing skills to manage each task

Goodheart-Willcox Publisher

One important EF skill is **time management**, the practice of organizing time and work assignments to increase personal efficiency. Time management involves prioritizing tasks by determining which ones should be completed before others. Time-management skills aid effectiveness when working independently or in a team and can be practiced in the daily management of a person's schedule and tasks. These skills are essential to success in the workplace, where an employee must regularly schedule time for and prioritize tasks.

Role-Management Skills

Most adults have more than one role, and each role comes with expectations. Many adults are simultaneously workers, spouses, family members, parents, consumers, and community members. Conflicts can occur among these many roles and their demands, and even the most satisfying roles can cause stress.

Focus on
Social Studies
Children and Role Management

Decisions about how to handle multiple roles affect the entire family, including any children. In families in which parents or caregivers experience role strain and role guilt, children may be affected by familial stress and lack of time with caregivers. To minimize the effects of role-management stress, adults can give themselves outlets for relieving stress and can help children cope.

Adults can cope with role-management stress by making time to relax. During the early evening hours, when adults and children are tired and hungry, children are most likely to express their feelings. Parents, however, may need to relax for a few minutes after long hours at work. To do this, parents or caregivers can take a brisk, short walk with their children or could set out a light snack and a board game for their children while they change into home clothes and take a few deep breaths before starting the evening routines.

To help children cope with role-management stress, adults can ensure that some of the time at home is *quality time* (time when caregivers are totally attentive to their children). Adults can also ensure that children's needs are met and can make time to attend school events or meet with children's teachers.

Photo: wavebreakmedia/Shutterstock.com

For social-emotional and physical health, a person must achieve a sense of balance between their roles. When a person's roles do not balance well, *role strain* can occur. **Role strain** is a feeling of having too many tasks to do at one time. Role strain can lead to **role guilt**, the feeling that one is not doing the best job at any role because of role strain. Role strain and role guilt can make people feel stressed, guilty, and unhappy.

People who want to be successful workers must have role-management skills. They need to learn to lead well-balanced lives using time management, prioritization, and healthful stress management skills. People can begin to practice these skills at any stage of life. You can practice role-management skills by managing the roles you have now, such as the roles of student, child, and friend.

Lesson 25.3 Review and Assessment

1. An example of an interpersonal nonverbal communication skill is _____. (25.3.1)
   A. comprehending office correspondence
   B. organizing work tasks
   C. smiling and greeting others with a friendly voice
   D. giving presentations
2. The term for a standard of actions, behaviors, and values for job performance is _____. (25.3.1)
   A. dependability
   B. active listening
   C. manners
   D. work ethic
3. **True or False.** Working on independent projects is the best way to learn teamwork. (25.3.2)
4. The second step in resolving a conflict with the conflict-resolution model is to _____. (25.3.3)
   A. carry out a decision
   B. identify possible solutions
   C. begin negotiating
   D. identify the issue
5. **True or False.** Professionalism requires being skilled in one's area of expertise and constantly searching for opportunities to grow in expertise. (25.3.4)

Lesson 25.4

Finding, Succeeding in, and Leaving a Job

Key Terms

cover letter
job fair
networking
portfolio
references
résumé

Learning Outcomes

After studying this lesson, you will be able to

25.4-1 **identify** resources for searching for jobs.

25.4-2 **discuss** the steps in applying for a job.

25.4-3 **summarize** the process of interviewing for a job.

25.4-4 **describe** guidelines for succeeding on the job.

25.4-5 **explain** considerations for leaving a job.

Reading and Notetaking Activity

Before reading this lesson, skim the headings and write each heading in a different color or font on a separate piece of paper or electronically. As you silently read the chapter and then listen to your teacher, take notes in the color or font you chose for each heading. After you finish taking notes for each section, draw or copy and paste a small illustration or visual next to the section that will help you remember what you learned.

Introduction

Once you have chosen a career, finding the job you want takes effort. Being qualified is only one part of gaining employment in a child-related career. Another part is looking for and securing a job in that career. There are many steps involved in the job-searching process. Knowing what to expect and how to handle yourself at each stage will increase your chances of job-search success. As you apply for jobs, you will need to write a strong résumé and cover letter and prepare a portfolio. Applying for jobs most often involves one or more interviews, which is a critical part of your search for a job. After a successful interview process, it is important to know how to hone your skills, succeed on the job, and correctly leave a job if need be.

25.4-1 Searching for Jobs

Many resources are available to help you find employment opportunities. The most common method of job searching is using the internet. Online, you can visit credible websites dedicated to posting job opportunities in multiple industries. You can also visit specific company websites to view career opportunities available within a company.

You may also find job leads in your community. Jobs may be posted on bulletin boards located in shopping areas and recreational centers or at employment agencies or advertised in newspapers. Attending a **job fair**—a gathering of employers and job seekers to exchange information—can be helpful in finding job opportunities (**Figure 25.21**). Many people find job opportunities through **networking** (making professional contacts with family, friends, and others, especially professionals in your career area, for job information or referrals). Through networking, you can learn more about industry information, including potential job openings. Often, a combination of search methods is best used to find employment opportunities.

25.4-2 Applying for Jobs

Applying for jobs requires presenting your credentials and completing a job application. While seeking employment, it is wise to have your credentials ready before applying. Before applying for jobs, you should prepare a résumé and cover letter, prepare a portfolio, and complete a job application. Different jobs will require different elements to be submitted for consideration.

Preparing a Résumé and Cover Letter

To apply for jobs, you will need a résumé and a cover letter. A **résumé** is a brief account of your career goals, education, work experience, and other employment qualifications. The purpose of the résumé is to acquire an opportunity for an interview. A **cover letter** is a letter or e-mail message that accompanies a résumé. Its purpose is to invite potential employers to review your

Rawpixel/ Shutterstock.com

Figure 25.21 Going to a job fair can be an excellent way to meet potential employers and other professionals. *What job fairs are usually held near your community?*

résumé by highlighting your biggest strengths and why you would be a good candidate for the position.

Writing a Résumé

Prospective employers look at your résumé to understand more about your experiences. Your résumé helps them decide whether you are qualified for a job.

There are two types of résumés—functional résumés and chronological résumés. A *functional résumé* is best suited to applicants with much experience and emphasizes qualifications, skills, and achievements. A *chronological résumé* focuses on your experiences and how they make you an excellent candidate. An example of a chronological résumé is shown in **Figure 25.22**.

When preparing your résumé, keep it easy to review—use a bullet format, short phrases instead of full sentences, and clear, bold headings. Many employers and online job postings require the use of an *electronic résumé*, a text-only file without any special formatting. A text-only résumé allows potential employers to view your résumé regardless of the compatibility of computer programs.

It is important to carefully select educational and work history highlights when creating a personal résumé. High school students who have not had the opportunity to have much job or education experience should focus on skills, accomplishments, and extracurricular experience.

Mia Holtz

1603 Green Street
Southland Township, Wisconsin 66732
(262) 555-7472
miaholtz@provider.com

name and personal information

| OBJECTIVE | To become employed as a summer camp counselor. | career objective |

EDUCATION

Southland High School   20XX to present
Southland Township, Wisconsin

- Focus on human services with an emphasis in child development courses
- Southland High Honor Roll, 20XX
- Graduating in June 20XX

education and degree type

EXPERIENCE

Southland High School-Age Child Care Program   20XX to present
Volunteer

- Provide care for toddlers and preschoolers
- Develop lesson plans and activities
- Prepare nutritious snacks

Babysitter   20XX to present

- Provide quality child care for five families with children ages 10 months to 12 years

work experience

HONORS AND ACTIVITIES

- Southland High Ray Scholarship, 20XX
- Member, FCCLA, Southland High Chapter, 20XX to present
- Member, Southland High Writing Club, 20XX to present
- Team Captain, Southland High Volleyball Team, 20XX

honors, awards, achievements, memberships, and professional organizations

SKILLS AND INTERESTS

- Computer skills include Microsoft Office, Word, Excel, and PowerPoint; word processing; Adobe Photoshop
- Fluent in both English and Spanish

skills and interests

Figure 25.22 A résumé usually includes the components labeled in this figure. The order in which these components are presented depends on the résumé's intended purpose and audience. *How does order impact the effectiveness of a résumé?*

For example, volunteering at a local summer camp every year shows that you are dedicated and have years of experience working with young children. The words you use in your résumé have never been more important. Many employers use applicant-tracking systems that perform *key word searches* based on the job description. These employers will view or not view your résumé depending on how many words it has in common with that description. Working with a career counselor or recruiter can help you determine which key words might best fit the job you are applying for.

When writing a résumé, be sure to obtain permission to list people as references. **References** are people other than your family members who know you well enough to discuss your qualifications for a job, such as teachers, youth leaders, and former employers. Do not include references on your résumé, but always have a list available upon request.

Be sure that you carefully proofread your résumé and are as specific as possible. Customizing your résumé to the job description and using a professional sounding e-mail address can also increase your chances of getting an interview. For more information about résumé writing, you can attend a résumé writing workshop at your school or public library.

Writing a Cover Letter

When applying for jobs, you may also need to submit a cover letter with your résumé (**Figure 25.23**). In your cover letter, you will introduce yourself and summarize the reason you are applying for the position without repeating your attached résumé.

1603 Green Street
Southland Township, Wisconsin
66732
April 15, 20XX

Ms. Anna Martinez
Program Director
Big Lake Day Camp
Rural Route 3
Southland Township, Wisconsin 66732

Dear Ms. Martinez:

I am interested in working as a counselor-in-training at Big Lake this summer. My guidance counselor at Southland High School, Mr. O'Brien, suggested I write you.

This job would be a good learning experience for me. I also have much to offer you as an employee. I have taken three child development classes in high school. Two of the classes included working eight hours per week in the school child care center. My duties involved planning a variety of activities for children, such as puppet shows, crafts, games, and snacks. I enjoy being with children and helping them learn. My long-term career goal is to open my own child care center.

My résumé is attached. I would appreciate the opportunity to meet for an interview. I will call your office next week to see whether we can schedule an appointment. If you would like to speak with me sooner or have any questions, please contact me at (262) 555-7472 or at miaholtz@provider.com. Thank you for your time and consideration.

Sincerely,

Mia Holtz

Mia Holtz

Figure 25.23 A cover letter should introduce you as a candidate and highlight the important parts of your education and experience. *What parts of your résumé would you highlight in a cover letter?*

Remember, the purpose of a cover letter is to highlight some of your job-related skills and qualifications and to capture the interest of the employer enough to arrange an interview with you. For online applications, a cover letter is often transmitted in the body of an e-mail you send to a potential employer. Cover letters can make a lasting impression. A good letter is brief, positive, customized to the job description, and follows specific instructions. Make sure your letter is neat and follows standard business format. Be sure to check the spelling, grammar, and punctuation. Many people seeking jobs have the qualifications that match the job description, but are not interviewed because of grammatical errors and misspellings in cover letters. Consider having several people proofread your letter and offer advice on improvements.

Preparing a Portfolio

Many job seekers prepare a portfolio to show when interviewing with prospective employers. A **portfolio** is an organized collection of materials that supports your job qualifications and reflects your work, academic, and personal experiences.

Your portfolio may be a physical copy that you take with you to interviews or a digital copy (called an *electronic portfolio*). Electronic portfolios can be shared digitally or uploaded as websites. Whichever format you choose, make sure to update your portfolio on a regular basis to reflect new skills and qualifications.

Preparing a portfolio involves accumulating items for your portfolio over time and assembling them in an organized format. These portfolio items should be organized around an *objective*, or a purpose for your portfolio. For example, the objective of a portfolio might be to showcase your experience in child care to a hiring child care center. Some of the items you might want to include in a portfolio are:

- your résumé and cover letter
- transcripts from your education and standardized test scores
- samples of your best job- or school-related work, such as videos or writing samples

- pictures of you working with young children in various settings
- letters of recommendation documenting work-related skills
- honors and awards
- proof of membership in student or professional organizations
- a personal statement describing your goals and how they came to be important to you
- summaries of volunteer work
- certifications or licenses
- a list of references that can **vouch** (guarantee; verify) for your character and qualifications

If you are unsure what items to showcase in a portfolio, consider your career plan. If you are seeking an entry-level job upon graduation, showcase both the general and career-specific skills you need. For example, in child-related careers, experience working with children and families is most important. Your portfolio should reflect experience working with children and your understanding of child development. Your portfolio might include essays written for a child development course, lists of activities planned while working with children, or a summary of your experiences.

When using your portfolio to apply for college and scholarships, match your portfolio to admission and scholarship requirements. Student portfolios should contain samples of academic and extracurricular experiences.

Completing a Job Application

Prospective employers may ask you to complete a *job application*. The application asks for information such as your name, address, Social Security number, educational background, and work history. Information on your application and résumé should match. Job applications often ask for references, too. Employers may contact your references to find out more about you before making a hiring decision. Your references may include past employers, teachers, coaches, and other adults whom you know well.

25.4-3 Interviewing for a Job

After an employer has reviewed your job application or résumé and cover letter, they may contact you for an interview (**Figure 25.24**). At the interview, you need to put your best foot forward by preparing before the interview, presenting yourself well during the interview, and following up well after the interview.

Figure 25.24 Types of Interviews

- Screening and phone interviews
- Teleconferencing/video call interviews
- One-on-one interviews
- Candidate group interviews (multiple applicants)
- Panel or committee interviews (multiple interviewers)
- Mealtime interviews (outside of the office setting)
- Behavioral interviews (part of other interviews, to determine how you have handled different situations)
- Stress interviews (to determine how you react to unexpected pressure)

Goodheart-Willcox Publisher

Before an Interview

The first step in preparing for a job interview is to learn as much as you can about the job and the employer. If the company has a website, thoroughly study the site. Use your network to find people who are familiar with the employer and learn as much information as you can from them.

As you prepare for the interview, consider some of the questions you might be asked and how you would answer them. It is also a good idea to prepare some questions for the interviewer. These questions should focus on information about the business, agency, or program and on the work duties required for the job position. Asking these questions shows you are interested in the job and the employer. Avoid asking any questions about pay, vacation time, or other benefits until you receive a job offer.

Before the interview, ensure that your personal appearance is professional and neat and that your clothes are clean and appropriate for the type of job you want. Be on time and be sure all of your digital devices are turned off before the interview begins. Do not turn them on again until the interview is over.

Focus on Speech

Practice Interviewing

You may want to rehearse for a job interview with a friend or family member before you go. This will help you prepare answers to some of the questions interviewers often ask. Consider the questions listed in Figure 25.25. Reflect how you might answer each question. What other questions might interviewers expect you to answer during an interview?

Conduct online research to view common interview questions. Select three questions to add to the list in Figure 25.25. Then work with a partner to conduct a mock interview. Take turns being the interviewer and the prospective employee. Offer each other constructive criticism, helpful advice and feedback that states how well your partner did and how they could strengthen their interviewing skills.

Photo: naluwan/Shutterstock.com

During an Interview

When you arrive for the interview, introduce yourself and thank the interviewer for meeting with you. Be sure to indicate your pleasure and enthusiasm for the interview opportunity. Offer a strong professional first impression by making direct eye contact and offering a firm handshake.

Let the interviewer lead the interview and ask you a variety of questions. Questions may be related to your educational background, work experience, goals, interests, and activities. Interviewers cannot, however, ask you certain questions. **Figure 25.25** lists common types of interview questions and questions interviewers cannot ask. If you are asked an illegal interview question, you can politely refuse to answer the question. Be sure to speak clearly and confidently and be yourself. Have a print copy of your résumé in your hands to consult if need be. It is also good practice to bring an extra copy for the interviewer; it shows that you are prepared and organized.

If you are given the opportunity, present your portfolio to the interviewer. If the interviewer asks you to explain one of your portfolio projects, be brief and to the point. Avoid talking while the interviewer examines your work. If the interviewer wants additional information, they will ask for it.

After the interview, you might be offered the job. Employers often have other applicants to interview, however, before making hiring decisions. If there are many applicants, you might be asked to interview a second or third time before the employer makes a decision. Potential employees may be called back to demonstrate their competencies, such as interacting with children in a center or using a specified computer application.

After an Interview

Immediately after the interview, send a *thank-you message* to the person who interviewed you. Thank the interviewer for taking the time to talk with you about the job and your career interests. Restate any important points that were made and reinforce your strong interest in the job.

A thank-you may be in the form of a printed letter sent through the mail or an e-mail. Keep the letter brief and to the point. Remind the interviewer of your name and **reiterate** (restate; emphasize) your enthusiasm, but do not be pushy.

Figure 25.25 Interview Questions

Questions	Examples
Common interview questions	• Tell me about yourself. Discuss your résumé. • Why are you interested in this job, and why do you think you would be a good fit for the position? • What are your strengths? • What are your weaknesses? • Tell me about your experience as a volunteer/babysitter/employee/member of an organization. What were your responsibilities? • Have you had to assume a leadership role? What are some of your qualities as a leader? • List one mistake you have made in the past. How did you correct this mistake, and how do you plan to prevent it from happening again? • How do you keep yourself organized when working on more than one project at the same time? • Where do you see yourself professionally in five years? • Do you prefer to work alone or as part of a team? • Why is there a gap in your employment? • Do you have any questions for me?
Questions interviewers cannot ask	• Are you in a relationship? • Are you married? • Do you have children? • When do you plan on having children? • What is your ethnicity? • What is your religion? • Do you have a disability? • How old are you? • What is your gender or sexual orientation?

Goodheart-Willcox Publisher

Remember that employment decisions can take a long time. Some companies notify all applicants when a decision has been made, but some do not. If you have not heard anything for a week or two after the interview, it is appropriate to send a brief follow-up message. A *follow-up message* is a message you send to the employer to ask about the status of the job position. Be sure your tone is positive. Avoid sounding impatient or demanding. Simply restate your interest in the job and politely inquire whether a decision has been made.

A message or phone call accepting a job offer is fulfilling. When accepting an offer, remain professional and ensure your message is error free. Think of this as your first official act as a new employee. Let your natural enthusiasm show, be positive and thank the employer, and mention that you look forward to starting the job (**Figure 25.26**). You may also use this opportunity to confirm your understanding of the employment process going forward. If you decline the job or are not offered the position, it is still important to be polite and friendly. The employer may consider you for a future position and likely has colleagues who are employers in the same career areas.

fizkes/iStock via Getty Images Plus

Figure 25.26 When accepting a job offer, express your enthusiasm and reiterate your interest in the job you have been offered. *Why is it important to let your excitement show when accepting a job offer?*

25.4-4 Succeeding on the Job

Once you have been offered a job and accepted a position, put in your best effort to keep your position and succeed on the job. Continue to maintain your employability skills, such as interpersonal, communication, collaboration, and strong EF skills. Recall your work-ethic standards. Maintain a level of professionalism in interactions with coworkers, supervisors, and clients or customers. Show respect for your position by being reliable, dependable, and timely when you carry out job responsibilities.

Also make sure to follow safety practices in your workplace. The *Occupational Safety and Health Act* established a set of health and safety guidelines to follow in the workplace. These guidelines are regulated by the Occupational Safety and Health Administration (OSHA) of the U.S. Department of Labor. Under this act, the employer is responsible for providing a safe workplace. This includes ensuring employees use proper safety gear and the workplace is free of potential hazards. The employee is responsible for following established safety guidelines.

25.4-5 Leaving a Job

Few people stay in the same workplace for a career lifetime. People change jobs for many reasons. Sometimes people discover after working in a certain career that it is not a good match for them. Others outgrow their jobs for various reasons. Sometimes families move due to one spouse being transferred to another location, requiring the other spouse to seek new employment. If you plan to voluntarily leave a job, it is best to secure employment elsewhere before leaving your current job. You should not use your work time at the current job to search for another job. You can look for another job, however, in your nonworking hours.

Even when leaving your current job, you have an obligation to treat your employer fairly. See **Figure 25.27** for guidelines to follow when you wish to leave a job. Regardless of why you are leaving, strive to end the job on a positive note.

Leaving in this way helps others to remember you in a good light. In the future, you might need a reference or recommendation from your employer or coworkers.

Figure 25.27 Guidelines
When Leaving a Job

- Leave when the business is less busy, if possible. For example, a retailer might not want to lose employees during a busy holiday season.
- Avoid bragging about your new job.
- Show appreciation to your supervisor and coworkers for helping you to learn needed skills or for being positive role models.
- Consult the employee handbook or company policies to learn the correct procedure for terminating (ending) employment. Adhere to this procedure as you notify the employer you wish to leave the job.
- Provide ample notice so the employer can find a suitable replacement. The company policy may state the required time of termination notice. If it does not, you will need to decide how much notice to give the employer. An acceptable amount of notice depends on the level of skills required in the job. Employers often need more time to fill a high-skill job than an entry-level job. Two weeks' notice is generally the minimum for an entry-level job.
- Complete a letter of resignation and any other termination forms, if required by the employer. Address your notice to your direct supervisor. You may also have an exit interview. In this interview, employers may ask questions, such as "Why are you leaving?" or "What do you expect to find in another job?" Be honest but remain professional and respectful.
- Try to complete all current tasks. Employers expect and are paying for your work through the final day. You may be expected to help train the employee who will take your place.

Goodheart-Willcox Publisher

1. Which is the most common method of searching for a job? (25.4.1)
   A. Attending a job fair
   B. Viewing a job bulletin board
   C. Using the internet
   D. Networking with friends
2. The least appropriate individual to include on a reference list when applying for a job is a/n _____. (25.4.2)
   A. previous supervisor
   B. high school teacher
   C. parent
   D. coach
3. An organized collection of materials that supports a person's job qualifications and reflects their work, academic, and personal experiences is a/n _____. (25.4.2)
   A. cover letter   C. reference list
   B. résumé   D. portfolio
4. During a job interview, the applicant should avoid asking the interviewer about _____. (25.4.3)
   A. job duties
   B. vacation time
   C. company history
   D. start date
5. **True or False.** It is the responsibility of the employee to follow established safety guidelines while on the job. (25.4.4)
6. An example of what not to do when voluntarily leaving a job is _____. (25.4.5)
   A. provide at least two weeks' notice
   B. show appreciation to your supervisor
   C. discuss how your new job is a step up
   D. complete a letter of resignation

Summary

Lesson 25.1

25.1-1 To begin the process of choosing a career, begin with a self-assessment by assessing your interests, aptitudes, and abilities. Interests include objects or causes you care about, the achievements or qualities you are proud of, situations or activities that challenge you, and your values.

25.1-1 Aptitudes are the natural talents with which people are born, while abilities are skills you learn or develop and acquire through effort and practice.

25.1-2 Researching careers begins by examining the 16 occupational categories and sub-categories and analyzing the labor market to discover trends, work conditions, and salary information.

25.1-2 It is important to find out the education and training requirements of different careers, along with the best places to acquire it. Also get inside views by talking to people in the career field.

25.1-3 A career plan includes short-term and long-term SMART goals, a personal plan of study, and resources necessary to achieve your goals.

Lesson 25.2

25.2-1 Careers in child-related fields are diverse and growing. They exist in the areas of health and protective services; care and education; entertainment; design; advertising, marketing, and management; research, consulting, and advocacy; and entrepreneurship.

25.2-2 Personal qualifications for success in a child-related career include concern for children, flexibility, and leadership.

25.2-3 Professional qualifications for child-related careers often include specialized knowledge and training, education and certification, and lifelong learning.

25.2-3 Because physical, intellectual, and social-emotional development are interrelated, workers in child-related careers must study all aspects of child development, even if the professional training for a career only stresses one aspect.

25.2-3 Workers in child-related careers must obtain specialized knowledge in their career areas. Most child-related careers require a college degree and a specific certification (license); certification requirements vary from state to state.

25.2-3 The Child Development Associate (CDA) certification is an entry-level qualification for teaching in an early childhood education program or working as a teacher's assistant in a preschool program.

Lesson 25.3

25.3-1 Interpersonal skills needed for career success include a positive attitude, a strong work ethic, good manners, and excellent communication skills.

25.3-2 Most workplaces require employees to have collaboration skills, or the skills needed to work well with others to combine knowledge, solve problems, reach common goals, and make decisions.

25.3-3 Critical thinking skills are essential in every career and in everyday situations. They are the skills needed to analyze and evaluate situations to make reasonable judgments and decisions.

25.3-3 The problem-solving process includes defining and analyzing the problem, setting and implementing goals, and monitoring and evaluating the plan.

25.3-3 Conflict-resolution skills are the skills required to resolve a situation in which a disagreement could lead to hostile behavior. They may include negotiation, compromise, and mediation.

25.3-4 Professionalism involves the skills, good judgment, and the attitudes and behaviors expected from any person trained to do a job well, as well as following a personal—and sometimes also a professional—code of ethics.

25.3-4 Executive function skills are the ability to problem-solve and overcome obstacles, create plans and prioritize to accomplish tasks, self-evaluate, control impulses and emotions, retain and use learned information easily, use time management and organizational skills to complete tasks, focus and sustain attention, and handle multiple tasks simultaneously.

25.3-4 For social-emotional and physical health and to avoid role strain and role guilt, a person must achieve a sense of balance between their roles.

Lesson 25.4

25.4-1 Means of searching for jobs include using the internet, checking job bulletin boards and postings, attending job fairs, and networking.

25.4-2 To apply for a job, you will need to write a résumé and cover letter, create a reference list, and possibly compile a portfolio.

25.4-2 Prospective employers may also require you to complete a job application.

25.4-3 To prepare for a job interview, learn as much as possible about the job and the employer. Consider some of the questions you might be asked and how you would answer them, and prepare your own questions for the interviewer.

25.4-3 Your performance during an interview will greatly affect your chances of getting a job. Following an interview, send a thank-you message to the interviewer.

25.4-4 To succeed on the job, maintain your employability skills, recall your work-ethic standards, maintain a level of professionalism in interactions with others, and show respect for your position when you carry out job responsibilities.

25.4-4 Make sure to follow safety practices in your workplace; be aware of the guidelines stated in the Occupational Safety and Health Act.

25.4-5 Considerations for leaving a job include securing employment elsewhere first, giving adequate notice, following company procedures for leaving a job, treating your employer fairly, and leaving on a positive note.

College and Career Portfolio

Portfolio Presentation

The portfolio you have been creating over the course of this text is now ready to present. Review your notes for your presentation, and in small groups of three, practice presenting your portfolios.

- Present your portfolio as if to a college admissions officer or employer.
- Ask your peers for feedback on your presentation. Also give feedback on your peers' presentations.

Recall and Application

1. Which is an example of a career-specific skill? (25.1.1)
   - A. Problem-solving
   - B. Website design
   - C. Self-discipline
   - D. Professionalism

2. Students working under the supervision of a highly skilled tradesperson to apply what they have learned in a specific career class in a/n _____. (25.1.2)
   - A. internship
   - B. co-op program
   - C. apprenticeship
   - D. job-shadowing program

3. The best time to develop a career plan is _____. (25.1.3)
   - A. before completing a self-assessment
   - B. after developing your SMART goals
   - C. before investigating occupational categories
   - D. after choosing a possible career path

4. Determining if a career goal outlines what you want to accomplish and how you will accomplish it addresses which component of a SMART goal? (25.1.3)
   - A. Is it achievable?
   - B. Is it specific?
   - C. Is it relevant?
   - D. Is it timely?

5. The career path of a person who created their own business selling cloth diapers for infants is _____. (25.2.1)
   - A. advocacy
   - B. care
   - C. entrepreneurship
   - D. entertainment

6. Professionals who focus on research addressing mental health, education, and legal or medical issues that affect children are _____. (25.2.1)
   - A. product developers
   - B. child advocates
   - C. social workers
   - D. consultants

7. **True or False.** The most important personal qualification in a child-related career is a genuine, real, concern for children. (25.2.2)

8. **True or False.** One way to foster lifelong learning in a career path is to join a professional organization. (25.2.3)

9. Understanding career-specific vocabulary is an example of an interpersonal communication _____ skill. (25.3.1)
   - A. speaking
   - B. reading
   - C. nonverbal communication
   - D. technology-based

10. An example of nonverbal communication is _____. (25.3.1)
    - A. rephrasing another person's words
    - B. choosing words carefully
    - C. using standard English
    - D. making eye contact

11. An effective team player _____. (25.3.2)
    - A. avoids dealing with personality clashes
    - B. only accepts accountability for themself
    - C. rejects new ideas that require further investigation
    - D. shares roles with other team members

12. **True or False.** Mediation occurs when the individuals involved in a conflict come together to discuss a compromise. (25.3.3)

13. A feeling of having too many tasks to do at one time is _____. (25.3.3)
    - A. mediation
    - B. role strain
    - C. collaboration
    - D. time management

14. **True or False.** Letting family members and friends know you are looking for a job is an example of networking. (25.4.1)

15. A chronological résumé focuses on a job applicant's _____. (25.4.2)
    - A. experiences
    - B. skills
    - C. qualifications
    - D. achievements

16. **True or False.** During a job interview, it is best to let the interviewer lead the interview and ask you a variety of questions. (25.4.3)

17. **True or False.** A prospective employer may not call you for a job interview if your cover letter contains grammatical errors and misspellings, regardless of your experience and qualifications. (25.4.3)

18. Which is an example of a question an interviewer cannot ask during a job interview? (25.4.3)
    A. Why is there a gap in your employment?
    B. What are your weaknesses?
    C. When do you plan on having children?
    D. Where do you see yourself professionally in five years?

19. **True or False.** The Occupational Safety and Health Act requires an employer to provide a safe workplace. (24.4.4)

20. If you decide to voluntarily leave a job, you should _____. (25.4.5)
    A. use your work time to conduct a job search
    B. give your supervisor at least two days' notice
    C. use the exit interview to air your grievances
    D. find another job elsewhere before resigning

Critical Thinking

1. **Compare and contrast.** Working with a partner, brainstorm examples of short- and long-term SMART goals in child-related careers. Then, compare and contrast these goals. How are short- and long-term goals different? How do these SMART goals contribute toward your future career?

2. **Identify.** Choose one workplace with child-related careers and research the workplace's code of professional ethics. Identify ethical standards the workplace enforces. For each standard, list situations in which an employee would have to adhere to the standards.

3. **Analyze.** Collaboration skills are vital to success in the workplace. Analyze your current teamwork skills. In what ways can you improve? How can poor collaboration skills affect a work environment?

4. **Determine.** In small groups, discuss examples of critical thinking and problem-solving skills in practice. In what everyday situations do people use these skills? Then, determine practical ways you can practice these skills.

5. **Draw conclusions.** How do you use leadership skills in your life today? Are there ways you want to improve your leadership skills? Write a short essay drawing conclusions about how leadership skills affect you now and will affect your future career.

6. **Evaluate.** The online job market is always changing as new websites emerge. Using the internet, research current websites with job postings. You might also talk to a career counselor about which websites are most common. Identify five websites and evaluate how effectively they would aid your job search.

Core Skills

1. **Math and technology.** In small groups, research current statistics for how long the typical worker holds a job. What percentage of workers holds one job over an entire career? How long do workers typically stay at careers? Also discuss what cultural, economic, and field-related influences impact how long the typical worker holds a job. Use a digital device to create a graph illustrating your statistics.

2. **Research and technology.** In small groups, research child-related careers not discussed in this chapter. Each group member should choose one career to research in detail. For your chosen career, note typical job responsibilities, required education, average pay, and how much demand there is for the career. Use your findings to create a digital presentation for your class.

3. **Speaking.** Entrepreneurs need to know about many aspects of running a business to be successful. In small groups, research essential business knowledge and skills for entrepreneurs. Some of these essential skills might be setting tuition amounts, coordinating payroll deductions and insurance, or completing tax forms. Choose three essential skills and write a group speech explaining each skill and how entrepreneurs would apply it in an early childhood education business setting. Deliver your speech to the class and take notes about skills described by your classmates. Afterward, as a class, discuss the importance of business knowledge to child-related entrepreneurship.

4. **Research.** Speak to your school's career counselor to find an aptitude test. This test should analyze your interests, aptitudes, and abilities to determine what career areas are the best fit for you. Take this test and evaluate the results. Do the results match with career areas you were already considering? Did the results suggest a career area you had not previously considered?

5. **Listening and speaking.** Working with a partner, interview someone in a career of your interest about how they balance multiple roles. Has the person ever experienced role strain or role guilt? How did the person cope with these feelings? In the person's opinion, how are role-management skills important for career success? After the interview, present your findings in an oral presentation to the class.

6. **Writing and listening.** Find a job posting for a child-related career of interest to you. Then, review your education and experiences to create a résumé. Tailor your résumé to the job description and make sure your résumé is as professional as possible. Then take your résumé to a writing center or college and career center and ask someone to review it. Take notes about their suggestions and implement them, if appropriate.

7. **Writing.** Reread the job description for which you wrote your résumé and then write a cover letter as if you were applying for the job. In your cover letter, explain why you are the ideal candidate. Be sure to check for grammar and spelling. Exchange cover letters with a partner for peer review.

8. **Reading.** Visit a local library or search online to find books or articles about interviewing techniques. Read two articles or chapters from a book and summarize the authors' main points. According to the authors, what questions are usually asked during interviews? What tips do they give for responding to interview questions?

9. **CTE Career Readiness Practice.** Imagine your life 10 years from now. Where do you see yourself living? What is your dream job? Research the cost of living in one or two possible locations and compare this to the average salary for various child-related careers. Would you be able to afford the cost of living? How do your personal life plans compare to your career plan and your financial plan? Write down a few short- and long-term SMART goals to help you accomplish your career, financial, and personal life plans.

Observations

1. As a class, arrange to visit a local workplace with child-related careers. Before the visit, research the workplace and write questions you have about the career and work environment. During the visit, ask your questions. Afterward, think about your visit and what you learned. Do you think the child-related career is one that might interest you? How well does the career align with your interests, aptitudes, and abilities?

2. In small groups, interview a worker in a child-related career who is a member of NAEYC. How did the person become a member of NAEYC? What privacy laws, professional practices and standards, and codes of professional ethics does NAEYC advocate? What are the benefits of participating in NAEYC? After the interview, discuss the benefits of professional organizations in your small group.

Glossary

A

abilities. Skills people learn or develop and acquire through effort and practice. (25.1)

abnormalities. Flaws or irregularities. (5.2)

abrasion (uh-BRAY-zhun). Scrape. (21.3)

abstinence. Refusal to engage in a sexual relationship. (6.2)

abundance. Large amount. (2.1)

accredited programs. Early childhood education programs that are not only licensed but have met even higher standards of quality set forth by a professional organization. (24.2)

active listening. Communication technique in which the receiver of a message provides feedback to the speaker, indicating that the message is understood. (3.1)

active-physical play. Type of play in which children use their gross-motor skills. (20.1)

active vocabulary. Words a person uses in talking or writing. (9.2)

adoption. Process by which a child of one pair of parents legally becomes the child of other parents (or parent). (3.2)

adoption agency. State-funded or private agency licensed by the state to handle adoptions. (3.2)

adult-child ratio. Number of adults per the number of children in an early childhood education program. (24.2)

adversely. Unfavorably. (6.2)

adversity. Risks and stress. (22.1)

advocates. People who actively support a cause. (1.3)

after-school programs. Programs that supervise, care for, and teach children after school until parents or caregivers finish the work day. (18.3)

age-appropriate behaviors. Proper or expected ways to express emotions at certain ages. (10.1)

age norm. Typical time when a developmental milestone, such as walking or talking, occurs. An age norm can be expressed as an average age or an age range. (1.2)

age of viability. Time from when a baby can survive if born early; possibly as early as 23 weeks, but 24–28 weeks improves chances. (5.1)

AIDS. Acquired immunodeficiency syndrome; disease caused by the human immunodeficiency virus (HIV), which attacks the body's immune system. (5.2)

allergen. (AL-lur-jun). Substance that causes an allergic reaction. (21.1)

allergy. Negative reaction by the body's immune system to an allergen. (21.1)

altruistic behaviors. Actions that show concern for others, but without an expectation for a reward. (16.2)

ambidextrous (am-bih-DECK-struhs). Ability to use the right or left hand, as the preferred hand, almost equally well for many tasks. (14.1)

amniocentesis (AM-nee-oh-sen-TEE-sis). Prenatal test in which a needle is inserted through the woman's abdomen into the amniotic sac and a sample of the fluid is removed for cell study. (5.3)

amnion. Fluid-filled sac that surrounds the baby in the uterus. (5.1)

ample. A generous amount. (4.1)

anaphylaxis (AN-uh-fuh-LAK-sus). Life-threatening shock. (21.1)

anemia. Condition that occurs when the level of healthy red blood cells, which carry oxygen to all parts of the body, becomes too low. (7.3)

antidepressants. Medications that treat depression by working to correct the chemical imbalance in neurotransmitters, especially serotonin, in the brain and boost mood. (23.2)

antipsychotics. Medications that reduce symptoms of psychosis and help children with schizophrenia. (23.2)

antiseptic. Substance that kills bacteria. (21.3)

anxiety disorder. Specific anxiety that interferes with a child's ability to achieve goals or enjoy life. (23.1)

Note: The number in parentheses following each definition indicates the lesson in which the term can be found.

Apgar test. Test that measures the newborn's chance of survival by checking the baby's pulse, breathing, muscle tone, responsiveness, and skin color. (7.3)

apt. Likely. (3.2)

aptitudes. Talents with which people are born; they are natural and a part of heredity. (25.1)

articulation. Person's ability to pronounce words that can be understood by others. (12.2)

artificial insemination. Assisted reproductive technology (ART) procedure that involves introducing sperm into the vagina or uterus by a medical procedure rather than by intercourse; also called *intrauterine insemination*. (6.1)

aspects. Parts of something. (4.2)

assertive. Able to speak out, stand up for one's rights, and defend one's self. (16.2)

assisted reproductive technologies (ARTs). Methods infertile couples can use to help them conceive. (6.1)

Association for Childhood Education International (ACEI). Professional organization that focuses on the education and healthy development of children by providing educational resources, programs and conferences, scholarships, awards, and grants. (25.2)

asthma. Chronic inflammation of the airways. (21.1)

attachment. Closeness between people that remains over time. (10.1)

attention-deficit hyperactivity disorder (ADHD). Disorder that involves lack of attention and extremely active behavior that exceeds a typical high energy level. (23.1)

auditory. Relating to hearing. (9.2)

authoritarian. Parenting style in which the main objective is to make children completely obedient. (4.2)

authoritative. Parenting style in which parents set some rules but allow children some freedom. Also called *assertive-democratic*. (4.2)

autism spectrum disorder (ASD). General term used to describe complex communication, social, and behavioral developmental disabilities. (23.1)

autonomy versus shame and doubt. Conflict toddlers must resolve according to the second stage of Erikson's psychosocial theory. (13.1)

axons. Long, thick cables that transmit all the signals from a neuron to other neurons. (2.1)

B

babbling. Infant speech using the tongue and the front of the mouth to make a consonant-vowel sound, such as *ba*. (9.2)

baby agenda. Term that describes how all infants, regardless of culture, are born with the internal drive to learn certain concepts and skills in holistic ways and at approximately the same age. (9.3)

baby blues. Mild postpartum mood disorder that goes away on its own. (7.4)

bassinet. Basketlike bed newborns may use during the first few weeks after birth. (8.3)

behavioral disorder. Pattern of challenges that surfaces in a person's behavior. (23.1)

beneficial. Helpful. (3.1)

benevolence. Well-meaning attitudes. (25.2)

bias. Favoring; unequal treatment. (3.1)

bilingual. Person who is fluent in two languages. (12.2)

binocular vision. Vision achieved when using both eyes in unison, equally, and accurately to fuse in the brain the two images into one image. (9.1)

biochemistry. The chemistry of living organisms. (2.1)

birth control methods. Measures couples use to help prevent pregnancy. (4.1)

body language. Type of nonverbal communication that involves sending and receiving messages through body movements, such as facial expressions, eye contact, gestures, and posture. (3.1)

body proportions. Relative size of body parts. (8.1)

body rotation. Using the axis of the spine for rotation, the hips (pelvis) and then the shoulders turn toward the back while the throwing arm comes forward. (14.1)

botanist. Person who studies plant life. (5.2)

Braille system. System of raised dots enabling people with vision conditions to read by touch. (23.2)

Brazelton scale. Test doctors use to determine whether a baby has problems interacting with the environment, handling motor processes, controlling his or her physical state, or responding to stress. (7.3)

breech birth position. Common abnormal birth position in which a baby enters the birth canal feet-, legs-, or buttocks-first. (7.2)

buffers. Protections or support systems. (22.1)

bullying. Most common form of peer abuse; involves inflicting physical, verbal, and emotional abuse on another person. (22.2)

C

career. Progression of related jobs that results in employment with opportunities for professional and personal growth. (25.1)

career burnout. State in which a person becomes emotionally exhausted with a career. (25.2)

career plan. Detailed list of steps a person works to complete to enter a chosen career path. (25.1)

categorization. Grouping similar objects or events into a group. (9.2)

cell. Smallest unit of life that is able to reproduce itself. (5.1)

center-based child care. Group child care that is provided in a center rather than in a home. (24.1)

centration (sen-TRAY-shun). Focusing on only one part of an object or event instead of seeing all parts at the same time. (15.1)

cephalocaudal (sef-uh-lo-KAW-dahl) development. Progression of development beginning with the head and moving down to the feet; also called *head-to-foot development*. (8.1)

certified child safety seat. Restraint system for children under the age of 13, which is required when riding in a motor vehicle; also called a *car seat*. (21.2)

certified nurse-midwife (CNM). Nurse who has special training in delivering babies during low-risk pregnancies. (7.1)

cervix (SER-viks). Lower, narrow portion of the uterus that connects the uterus to the vagina, or *birth canal*. (5.1)

cesarean (sih-ZARE-ee-uhn) section. Delivery method in which the person's abdomen and uterus are surgically opened and the baby is removed; also called *C-section*. (7.2)

character. Principles and beliefs that guide a person's conduct and define his or her personality and behavior. (4.2)

child abuse. Intentional act committed by an adult that harms or threatens to harm a child's well-being. (22.2)

child care programs. Early childhood education programs that provide care for children for extended hours, usually between 9 and 12 hours a day. (24.1)

child care resources and referral (CCR&R) agencies. Agencies that promote local early childhood education programs and help parents identify child care options. (24.1)

child-centered society. Society that sees children as important, cares about their well-being, and works to meet their needs. (1.3)

child development. Scientific study of children from conception to adolescence. (1.1)

Child Development Associate (CDA). Entry-level position qualification for teaching in a child care and education program or working as a teacher's assistant in a preschool program. (25.2)

child development laboratories. Early childhood education programs for children under five years of age that also serve as child development research sites and offer training programs for adults in child-related careers; formerly called *nursery schools*. (24.1)

child neglect. Failure of an adult to provide for a child's basic needs. (22.2)

child protection agencies. Organizations that work to prevent and rescue children from neglect and abuse. (22.2)

child support order. Judgment of the court that states how much the noncustodial parent must pay toward the children's expenses. (3.2)

childproofing. Process in which adults note dangers in a child's environment and then make the area safe for the child. (21.2)

chorion (CORE-ee-ahn). Outermost membrane that surrounds the baby in the uterus. (5.1)

chorionic villus sampling (CVS). Prenatal procedure for finding abnormalities in the fetus by testing a small sample of the chorion. (5.3)

chromosomal disorders. Defects in the chromosomes that usually occur due to an error in cell division. (5.2)

chromosomes (KRO-muh-zomes). Threadlike structures that carry genes in living cells. (5.2)

circumstances. Situations or conditions. (3.2)

classifying. Ability to choose an attribute and group all the objects from a set (either physically or mentally) that possess that attribute. (15.2)

closed adoption. Adoption in which the identity of the birthparents and adopting family are not revealed; also called *confidential adoption*. (3.2)

closed-ended questions. Questions that only require a one- or two-word response. (12.3)

cluttering. Filling a space with many objects. (21.2)

codes of professional ethics. Sets of standards created by various professions to govern the conduct of employees in these careers. (25.3)

code-switch. Change grammar and vocabulary usage when communicating with different cultural and age groups. (18.2)

codified. Arranged in an orderly way. (1.2)

cognition. Act or process of knowing or understanding. (9.1)

cognitive-behavioral therapy. Therapy that teaches children to recognize their anxieties and develop coping strategies. (23.2)

cognitive development. Development that concerns how people learn, what people learn, and how people express what they know through language. (1.1)

cognitive flexibility. Being able to adjust to changing demands. (2.2)

colic. Condition in which a baby has intense abdominal pain and cries inconsolably. (8.2)

collaboration skills. Skills needed to work well with others to combine knowledge, solve problems, reach common goals, and make decisions. (25.3)

collective monologue. Talking to another person, but not listening to what the other person has said. (15.2)

collective symbolism. Second level of pretense in which the toddler uses one set of objects to represent another set of objects and pretends to do something that involves other people (parents) or objects (stuffed animals). (12.1)

communicable diseases. Diseases that can be transmitted from an object to an individual or between individuals. (21.1)

communication. Exchange of messages and information between at least two people. (3.1)

complementary foods. Solid foods that provide the nutrients infants and toddlers need in addition to their breast milk, formula, or whole cow's milk. (11.2)

comprise. Make up. (3.1)

concept. Idea formed by combining what is known about a person, object, place, quality, or event. (9.2)

conception. Joining of the ovum and sperm cells. (5.1)

concrete operational stage. Piaget's third stage of intellectual development in which children begin to think logically, but base their logic on past experiences. (18.1)

conduct. Person's actions and manners. (4.2)

congenital condition. Physical or biochemical problem that is present at birth and may be caused by genetic or environmental factors. (5.3)

consenting. Giving permission. (3.2)

conservation. Concept that changing an object's shape, direction, or position does not alter the quantity of the object. (18.1)

constancy. Unchanging. (1.2)

contraction. Tightening or shortening of a muscle. (7.2)

coo. Light, happy, vowel-like sound babies use to communicate between six and eight weeks after birth. (9.2)

coordination. Working together of muscles to form movements. (9.3)

cope. Handle challenges in a healthy manner. (3.2)

co-regulation. Soothing the baby to aid him or her to calm down. (10.2)

cover letter. Letter or e-mail message that accompanies a résumé to invite potential employers to review the résumé. (25.4)

crawl. Moving by pulling with the arms, but not lifting the abdomen from the floor. (8.1)

creep. Moving by using the hands and knees or the hands and feet with the abdomen off the floor. (8.1)

critical periods. Times when some part of the body is very vulnerable to lack of stimulation or to negative experiences. (2.1)

critical thinking skills. Skills needed to analyze and evaluate situations in order to make reasonable judgments and decisions. (25.3)

cruising. Walking by holding onto something for support. (8.1)

cultural diversity. Having more than one culture represented. (3.1)

culture. Way of life within a group of people that includes language, beliefs, attitudes, values, rituals, and skills. (3.1)

culture shock. Uncomfortable response to an unfamiliar culture. (24.2)

culture-specific knowledge. Culturally relevant knowledge that one learns by being told or shown. (18.2)

custodial parent. Parent who heads the household and has legal responsibility for caregiving. (3.2)

custody plans. Legal plans outlining who will care for the child and to what extent. (22.1)

cyberbullying. Bullying through a digital medium. (22.2)

D

debase. Degrade. (22.2)

deciduous (deh-SID-joo-uhs) teeth. First set of teeth, which will later be replaced by permanent teeth; also called *nonpermanent teeth* or *baby teeth*. (8.1)

deductive reasoning. Reasoning from the general to the specific. (18.1)

defective. Flawed; imperfect. (6.1)

deferred imitation. Ability to recall and later imitate someone's behavior. (12.1)

deflected. Changing direction. (5.3)

delay gratification. Wait until later to get what is wanted. (13.2)

delinquency. Misbehavior; illegal behavior. (25.2)

dendrites (DEHN-drights). Short, bushy cables that allow each neuron to receive signals sent by other neurons. (2.1)

depleted. Used up the supply of something. (4.1)

depth perception. Ability to tell how far away something is. (9.2)

detrimental. Unhelpful or harmful. (3.1)

development. Gradual process of change through many stages, such as before birth, infancy, childhood, adolescence, and adulthood. (1.1)

developmental acceleration. When a child performs like an older child. (1.2)

developmental delay. When a child performs like a younger child. (1.2)

developmental dyscalculia (DIS-kal-KYOO-lee-uh). Learning disorder that affects a child's mathematical abilities. (23.1)

developmental dyslexia (dis-LEK-see-uh). Learning disorder that affects a child's ability to read, write, and spell. (23.1)

developmentally appropriate practices (DAPs). Child care and education practices that use knowledge about child development and consider each child's strengths, needs, interests, and culture. (24.2)

developmental milestones. Physical, intellectual, and social-emotional tasks most children learn to accomplish by a certain age. (8.1)

developmental tasks. Skills that should be mastered at a certain stage in life. (2.2)

dexterity. Fine-motor movements that are smooth and rather effortless. (11.1)

diabetes. Disorder caused by the body's inability to use sugar properly. (5.2)

digital citizenship. The responsible use of technology by anyone who uses computers, the internet, and digital devices to engage with society on any level. (17.3)

dilation. First stage of labor during which the cervix opens. (7.2)

diplomatic. Agreeable; polite. (25.3)

direct costs. Expenses related to raising a child, such as clothing, food, housing, child care and education, transportation, and toys and activities. (4.1)

direct intervention. Term used to describe a child-related career in which a person works in close contact with children. (25.2)

direct observation. Watching children in their natural environments. (1.3)

discipline. Use of methods and techniques to teach children self-control. (4.2)

discontentment. Unhappiness. (3.1)

disposition. General mood of a person. (10.1)

domains. Areas. (1.1)

domains of self-definition. Categories (physical, intelligence, social skills, and self-regulation of emotions) in which children can describe themselves. (19.1)

dominant traits. Traits that are always expressed in a person even if only one gene of the pair is inherited for that trait. (5.2)

Down syndrome. Chromosomal condition that occurs when each body cell has three copies of chromosome 21 instead of two copies. (5.2)

dynamic balance. Balance maintained while moving. (14.1)

E

early childhood education programs. Child care and education arrangements; may be informal or formal. (24.1)

Early Intervention Program for Infants and Toddlers with Disabilities. Program that provides intervention services for infants and toddlers (through two years of age) with developmental delays or who have been diagnosed with physical and intellectual conditions that will likely cause developmental delays. (23.2)

early learning standards. Expectations for young children's development; also called *foundations* and *guidelines*. (24.2)

eating disorder. Illness characterized by distorted behaviors and emotions about food and weight. (17.2)

educational neglect. Failure to conform to state legal requirements regarding school attendance. (22.2)

egocentrism (ee-goh-SEN-trism). Child's belief that everyone thinks in the same way and has the same ideas as he or she does. (15.1)

embed. Attach. (5.1)

embryo. Medical term used to describe the unborn baby in the embryonic stage of development—weeks three through eight of the pregnancy. (5.1)

embryonic stage. Second stage of prenatal development, lasting six weeks. (5.1)

emergency situations. Dangerous, often unexpected or life-threatening events that require immediate action. (21.3)

emergent literacy. Conceived as all aspects of literacy, including reading and writing, are developmental and acquired in interactive ways, beginning in infancy as children learn to understand spoken words. (15.3)

emotional abuse. Abuse of power through devaluing, undermining, and coercing a child. (22.2)

emotional dependency. Act of seeking attention, approval, comfort, and contact. (16.1)

emotional neglect. Failure to meet a child's social-emotional needs at each stage of development. (22.2)

emotions. Thoughts that lead to feelings and cause changes in the body. (10.1)

empathize. Understand and relate to others. (1.3)

employability skills. Skills all employers seek in job candidates; includes interpersonal skills, collaboration skills, critical thinking and problem-solving skills, professionalism skills, strong executive function skills, and role-management skills. (25.1)

empty calories. Contained in foods supplying the body with energy, but having few or no nutrients, such as fats and sugars. (14.2)

endeavors. Attempts to achieve plans and goals. (6.1)

endorse. To support. (4.2)

enriched environment. Setting that offers a person many chances to learn. (9.3)

enrichment activities. Any activities beyond academic subjects that help children develop intellectually. (18.3)

entitlement. Having a right to particular privileges or benefits. (4.2)

entrepreneurship. Creation of one's own business. (25.2)

enuresis (en-yoo-REE-sis). *Involuntary* (by accident) urination two or more times a week for at least three months by a child over three years of age. (14.3)

environment. Sum of all the conditions and situations that surround and affect a child's growth and development. (1.1)

environmental factors. Factors caused by a person's surroundings. (5.2)

epigenome (eh-pih-JEE-nohm). Chemicals that can turn genes on and off. (1.1)

epilepsy. Neurological disorder in which abnormal activity in brain cells causes seizures. (21.1)

episiotomy (ih-pea-zee-AW-tuh-mee). Incision made to widen the birth canal and prevent tearing. (7.2)

episodic memory. Memory of personal experiences and events, including the emotion and context of the event. (15.1)

essential life skills. Intellectual, social, and emotional skills that prepare children for the pressures of modern life, according to Galinsky. (2.2)

executive functions (EFs). Intellectual functions people use to manage themselves and their resources (knowledge, time) to achieve goals. (2.2)

exert. Forcibly place. (5.2)

expenditures. Expenses. (4.1)

explicit. Clearly described. (2.2)

explicit memory. Involves a person's conscious, intentional recalling of experiences and facts. (9.1)

exponentially. Rapidly. (5.2)

expulsion. Forcing out. (6.1)

extended family. Family that extends past the parent or parents and their children to include other adult relatives who interact within the same household. (3.2)

eye-hand coordination. Ability to coordinate sight with movement of the hands. (11.1)

F

failure to thrive. Condition in which a child fails to grow at a healthy rate. (8.1)

fallopian tubes. Two hollow tubes that extend from the right and left sides of the uterus and have fingerlike projections that reach toward each ovary. (5.1)

Family and Medical Leave Act (FMLA). Law that protects the rights of qualified employees to take unpaid leave for various family-related reasons, such as maternity or paternity leave. (7.1)

family child care. Child care provided by a person for a small number of children in his or her own home. (24.1)

family life cycle. Series of six stages that many families go through over the years. (3.1)

family planning. Decisions couples make about whether or not they want to have children and when to have them. (4.1)

fear-conditioning. Associating a fearful stimulus with a neutral stimulus. (16.1)

feed. Continue. (22.1)

fertility counseling. Medical evaluation that seeks to determine the reasons for fertility problems and explore available treatment options. (6.1)

fetal alcohol spectrum disorders (FASDs). Group of symptoms that occurs in infants whose parent drank during pregnancy. (5.2)

fetal stage. Third stage of prenatal development, lasting from nine weeks after conception until birth. (5.1)

fetus. Medical term used to describe the unborn baby in the fetal stage of development—week nine until the end of pregnancy. (5.1)

filtering program. Application designed to prevent children from accessing inappropriate content when using electronic media. (18.3)

fine-motor skills. Being able to use and control the small muscles, especially those in the fingers and hands. (8.1; 11.1)

fingerplays. Poems and rhymes acted out with the hands. (24.1)

firing. Process by which a neurotransmitter leaves the axon of one neuron and jumps the synapse to travel to the dendrite of another neuron. (2.1)

first aid. Emergency treatment for an illness or injury that is given before professional medical help arrives. (21.3)

first-degree burns. Damage to body tissue when heat or radiation burns the top layer of skin. (21.3)

flexibility. Ability to move, bend, and stretch easily. (17.1)

flipped classroom. Mode of teaching in which children learn concepts and facts by reading their textbooks and watching videos at home, and then do homework-type assignments while at school. (18.3)

folic acid. B-vitamin that reduces the baby's risk for neural tube defects. (5.3)

food allergy. Abnormal response to a food triggered by the body's immune system. (11.2)

foodborne diseases. Diseases caused by eating foods contaminated with harmful bacteria and other pathogens during food production or preparation; also called *foodborne illnesses*. (21.1)

food-insecure households. Households that are regularly unable to supply healthful meals. (17.2)

forceps. Curved instrument that fits around the sides of a baby's head and is used to help the doctor ease the baby down the birth canal during a contraction. (7.2)

foregone income. Potential income given up by a parent who leaves the workforce and stays home to raise a child. (4.1)

formal operational stage. Piaget's final stage of intellectual development in which a person can reason abstractly. (18.1)

formative. Shaping. (5.1)

for-profit programs. Early childhood education programs set up to make money and run as businesses by individuals or corporations. (24.1)

foster family. Family in which an adult provides a temporary home for a child who cannot live with his or her birthparents. (3.2)

fractures. Cracks and breaks in bones. (21.3)

fraternal births. Term used to describe children from multiple pregnancies who develop from two or more fertilized ova and differ in genetic makeup; also called *dizygotic* (DYE-zye-GAW-tik) *births*. (6.1)

friction. Conflict; tension. (6.2)

functional specialization. Development of special abilities in different regions (areas) of the brain. (14.1)

G

gamete intrafallopian transfer (GIFT). Assisted reproductive technology (ART) procedure in which a mixture of sperm and eggs is placed in the woman's fallopian tubes, where fertilization can occur. (6.1)

gender constancy. Understanding that clothing, hairstyles, and actions do not change a person's gender. (16.1)

gender identity. Ability to label self and others as male or female (also called *gender labeling*). (13.1)

gender-role learning. Knowing what behaviors are expected of males and females within one's society. (16.1)

gender schools. Same-sex peer groups that teach members what it means to be masculine or feminine. (19.1)

gender stability. Understanding that a person who is born either male or female will remain so throughout life. (16.1)

General Educational Development (GED) test. Opportunity for people who do not graduate from high school to earn a state-issued certificate of high school equivalency. (6.2)

genes. Sections of the DNA molecule found in a person's cells that determine his or her individual traits. (1.1)

genetic disorder. Defect caused by one or more abnormalities in the genome. (5.2)

genetic factors. Person's inherited traits passed to him or her through the parents' genes at conception. (5.2)

genetics (juh-NET-iks). Study of the factors involved in the passing of traits in living beings from one generation to the next. (1.1)

germinal stage. First stage of prenatal development, lasting two weeks after conception. (5.1)

glial cells. Brain cells that support neurons. (2.1)

goal-corrected partnership. Relationship in which both parties are willing to compromise to reach a common goal. (19.1)

grammar. Study of word usage and order in a given language. (12.2)

gross-motor skills. Being able to use the large muscles to roll over, sit, crawl, stand, and walk. (8.1; 11.1)

growth. Change in size, such as height, or in quantity, such as vocabulary. (1.1)

growth pains. Muscle aches caused by muscles growing rapidly to catch up with increasing skeletal size during the school-age years. (17.1)

growth spurt. Period of rapid growth that heralds pubescence. (17.1)

guardian. Person who is legally appointed by the court to take responsibility for a child in the event of the birthparents' death or extended absence. (3.2)

guidance. Words and actions parents use to influence their children's behavior. (4.2)

guilt. Feeling of remorse that comes from the inner voice of conscience when a person has behaved unacceptably; is based in empathy and remorse for the misdeed. (19.1)

H

hamper. Interfere with. (6.1)

hand preference. Tendency to use one hand more skillfully than the other hand for most tasks; also called *handiness* and *hand dominance*. (14.1)

Head Start. Federal program for three- and four-year-old children from low-income families. (24.1)

health screenings. Standard tests that look for potential conditions or diseases that may affect children's health or development. (21.1)

health services. Career area in which workers ensure children receive adequate physical and mental health care. (25.2)

heavily processed foods. Foods containing hidden sources of solid fats, sodium, and added sugars. (17.2)

heredity. Sum of all the traits that are passed to a child from blood relatives. (1.1)

hidden added costs. Costs of child care that add to the direct costs. (24.2)

hidden cost credits. Credits that lower the direct costs of child care. (24.2)

hierarchical (HY-uh-RAHR-kuh-kul) classification. Type of classification in which select classes may contain subclasses. (18.2)

hierarchy. Rank order. (1.3)

high-reactive infants. Infants who react to anything new with caution and can easily become physically agitated and distressed; formerly called *difficult infants*. (10.1)

HIV. Human immunodeficiency virus; STI that causes the disease AIDS. (5.2)

holistic. Whole; complete. (9.3)

home visitation. Type of support in which a professional comes to the home to monitor the health of the birth giver and infant, to provide one-on-one parenting education, and to suggest other helpful community programs parents can access. (22.2)

hysterectomy (HIS-ter-ECK-toh-mee). Surgical removal of a woman's uterus. (7.2)

I

identical births. Term used to describe children from multiple pregnancies who develop from one fertilized ovum and have the same genetic makeup; also called *monozygotic* (MAWN-oh-zye-GAWT-ik) *births*. (6.1)

idle. Inactive. (21.2)

illegal market adoption. Adoption in which a child is bought or sold, which is against the law in all states. (3.2)

imitative-imaginative play. Type of play in which children use words and actions to pretend to be objects or people other than themselves. (20.1)

immerse. Cover in liquid. (8.3)

immunity. Body's ability to resist infection. (21.1)

immunization. Process to protect children, as well as adults, from certain serious diseases. (21.1)

impart. Give or share. (4.2)

implicit. Implied or understood without describing in detail. (2.2)

implicit memory. Involves a person's unconscious awareness of past experiences to perform tasks. (9.1)

impoverished. Having inadequate funds to reasonably care for one's family. (22.1)

incessantly. Constantly; without break. (4.2)

inclusion. Full-time placement of a child with special needs in a regular classroom. (23.2)

inclusive. Accessible to a variety of people. (15.3)

income. Money received for working. (3.1)

inconsolable. Unable to be soothed. (6.2)

independent adoption. Adoption in which a person, such as a lawyer or physician, works out the details between the birthparents and adoptive parents. (3.2)

indirect costs. Resources used to meet child-related expenses that could have been used to meet other goals. (4.1)

indirect intervention. Term used to describe a child-related career in which a person works on behalf of, but not directly with, children. (25.2)

indirect observation. Observation done by methods other than watching children, including asking other people questions about the children and observing the products children make. (1.3)

Individualized Education Plan (IEP). Educational plan tailored to the specific educational needs of a child who has special needs and who is between 3 and 21 years of age. (23.2)

Individualized Family Service Plan (IFSP). Plan that guarantees families can get the help they need for qualifying children with special needs from birth to three years of age. (23.2)

individual life cycle. Description of the stages of change people experience throughout life. (1.1)

Individuals with Disabilities Education Act (IDEA). Federal law governing the education of children with special needs. (23.2)

induction. Technique in which parents discipline their children by reasoning and explaining to them why they should or should not use certain behaviors. (4.2)

inductive reasoning. Reasoning from specific facts to general conclusions; also called *scientific reasoning*. (18.1)

Industrial Revolution. Time in history in which society began to focus on industry and manufacturing. (3.1)

industry versus inferiority. Erikson's fourth stage of personality development in which children strive to be industrious, but may feel inferior if criticized. (19.1)

infancy. Stage of development during the first year of life. (8.1)

infertile. Term used to refer to a person who is unable to conceive after a year of trying. (6.1)

inflections. Changes of pitch. (9.2)

ingest. Consume. (21.3)

inherent. Basic. (3.1)

inhibition. Filtering thoughts and feelings so as not to act impulsively. (2.2)

in-home child care. Child care that takes place in the child's own home. (24.1)

initiate. Start. (6.2)

initiative versus guilt. Erikson's third stage of personality development in which children want to take initiative, but may be hindered by guilt. (16.1)

intellectual disability. Condition in which a child's intellectual abilities are a year or more delayed when compared with other children the same age. (23.1)

intelligence quotient (IQ) test. Test that measures how quickly a person can learn and how well a person can reason using words, numbers, and spatial concepts. (23.1)

interactive media. Media systems, such as computers, that respond to the user's actions. (15.3)

internal organs. Collections of tissues that independently carry out special functions and are located inside the body, such as heart, lungs, and liver. (14.1)

interpersonal skills. Skills a person uses to relate to and work with other people. (25.3)

interpretive stage. Galinsky's parenting stage during which parents are tasked with modeling their values and attitudes about almost all aspects of life. (19.2)

intolerance. Negative physical reaction that eating a certain food can cause. (8.2)

intonation. Rise and fall of a person's voice while speaking. (12.3)

intuitive substage. Substage of the preoperational stage during which children rely on their mental imagery rather than logical reasoning to grasp a problem's solution. (15.1)

in vitro fertilization (IVF). Assisted reproductive technology (ART) procedure in which some of the person's eggs are surgically removed, fertilized with sperm in a laboratory dish, and then implanted in the their uterus. (6.1)

irreducible. Impossible to make smaller or simpler. (1.3)

J

jaundice. Liver condition that can make the skin, tissues, and body fluids look yellow. (7.3)

job fair. Gathering of employers and job seekers to exchange information. (25.4)

job shadowing. Following a competent worker through his or her workday. (25.1)

joint custody. Shared legal right of parents who are not married to provide care for and make decisions about their children's lives. (3.2)

junk foods. Foods that are high in calories and low in nutrition. (17.2)

K

kindergartens. Early childhood education programs for four- and five-year-old children; serve as an entrance to primary school education. (24.1)

kin care. The care of children by relatives other than the parents. (3.2)

L

labor. Process that moves the baby out of the birth giver's body. (7.1)

lactation consultant. Breast-feeding expert. (8.2)

Lamaze method. Delivery method in which the pregnant woman is trained to use breathing patterns to keep her mind off the pain. (7.1)

language disorder. Condition involving a child's lack of ability to understand and use language. (23.1)

language-logic play. Form of intellectual play common in school-age children that involves words and logical concepts. (20.1)

large-muscle development. Development of the trunk and arm and leg muscles. (11.1)

learning disorder. Challenge in spoken or written language, math, or spatial orientation. (23.1)

lesson plan. Teacher plan that contains a specific goal objective (related to a standard), activities to help the child meet the objective, and assessment of the learning; usually written for kindergarten and school-age children. (24.2)

lifelong learning. The ongoing pursuit of learning throughout life. (2.2)

lightening. Change in the baby's position in which the uterus settles downward and forward, and the baby descends lower into the pelvis. (7.2)

logical thinking concepts. Concepts that are not directly experienced through the senses, but are developed through thought, such as noting similarities and differences in objects and coordinating simple relationships (classifying, ordering by attribute, counting). (15.2)

love withdrawal. Discipline technique in which parents threaten children with being unloved or suggest some form of parent/child separation. (4.2)

low birthweight. Weight under 5.5 pounds at birth for a single birth and under 3.3 pounds per baby in a multiple birth. (6.1)

low-reactive infants. Infants who tend to be sociable and bold (trying new challenges); formerly called *easy infants.* (10.1)

M

mainstreaming. Former term used for placing a child with special needs in a regular classroom for only part of the day. (23.2)

malnutrition. Condition in which one's diet supplies an excess, shortage, or imbalance of calories or one or more nutrients. (17.2)

mandated reporters. Professionals who are legally bound to report any known or suspected cases of neglect or abuse. (22.2)

manipulate. Using the hands to work with objects. (14.1)

manipulating. Moving or changing. (2.2)

manipulative-constructive play. Type of play that involves the use of children's fine-motor skills. (20.1)

marriage. Legal contract and, ideally, an emotional and social union between two partners. (3.1)

maternity leave. Time a woman takes off from work for the birth or adoption of a child. (7.1)

maturational theory of child development. Based on the premise that children mature on a genetic timetable (upon which the environment has little impact) and that skills and concepts should only be taught when children are biologically ready to learn them. (15.3)

maturity. Having the intellectual and emotional capacity of a healthy, responsible adult. (4.1)

mediation. Inclusion of a neutral person, called a mediator, to help the conflicting parties resolve their dispute and reach an agreement. (25.3)

medical neglect. Harm or endangerment of a child caused by failure to seek treatment for health problems or accidents. (22.2)

memory capacity. What a person does with his or her memory (not how *much* is remembered). (15.1)

mental imagery. Seeing in the "mind's eye" or hearing in the "mind's ear" in the absence of a stimulus. (12.1)

mental maps. Remembered mental constructions (seen in the "mind's eye") that organize spatial relationships from an individual's perspective. (15.2)

mentor. Person who counsels and advises. (25.1)

metabolize. Break down in the digestive system. (7.3)

middle school. School including children in the fifth or sixth through eighth or ninth grades. (18.3)

miscarriage. Expulsion of a baby from the body before week 20 of pregnancy. (6.1)

mixed-type births. Term used to describe children from higher multiple pregnancies (three or more children) some of whom are identical and one or more fraternal. (6.1)

monolingual. Person who speaks only one language. (12.2)

monologue. Talking to oneself as though thinking aloud. (15.2)

Montessori schools. Early childhood education programs that encourage children to learn independently through the use of highly specialized materials rather than through direct input from teachers. (24.1)

moral character. Acting in accordance with what is perceived as morally right. (16.1)

moral development. Process by which children develop proper attitudes towards others (based on sociocultural, familial, school, peer, religious, and societal expectations). (16.1)

moral emotions. Person's reactions to acceptable and unacceptable behaviors. (16.1)

moral judgment and reasoning. Ability to perceive an action as right or wrong. (16.1)

moral neglect. Failure to teach a child right from wrong in terms of general social expectations. (22.2)

mortality rate. Rate of death. (6.2)

motivation. Desire to achieve. (1.2)

motor development. Use and control of muscles that direct body movements. (8.1)

mourning. Feeling sad about a loss. (22.1)

multicultural family. Family with members from two or more cultural groups. (3.1)

multiple intelligences. Intellectual abilities that contribute to overall intelligence. (18.1)

multiple pregnancy. Pregnancy in which two or more babies develop. (6.1)

myelin. Fatty substance formed by glial cells that wraps around longer axons and cushions the cell bodies of neurons. (2.1)

MyPlate. Food guidance system developed by the U.S. Department of Agriculture to help people two years of age and older make nutritious food choices. (5.3)

N

National Association for the Education of Young Children (NAEYC). Professional organization that works on behalf of young children by providing educational materials, child development research, and conferences. (25.2)

natural childbirth. Delivery method in which the pregnant woman learns about the birth process and uses breathing and relaxation techniques to reduce fear and pain during labor. (7.1)

negotiation. Process of individuals involved in a conflict coming together to discuss a compromise. (25.3)

neonatal intensive care unit (NICU). Part of a hospital where premature, low-birthweight, or other high-risk babies can receive immediate, specialized, round-the-clock care and treatment; also called *intensive care nursery*. (7.3)

neonate. Medical term used to describe the baby from birth to one month of age. (7.3)

neonatology (NEE-oh-nay-TAW-lo-gee). Branch of medicine concerned with the care, development, and diseases of newborns. (7.3)

networking. Term used for making professional contacts with family, friends, and others, especially professionals in your career area, for job information or referrals. (25.4)

neurons. Brain cells that send and receive chemical and electrical impulses amongst each other to direct the various tasks of the brain. (2.1)

neuroscience. Study of the brain. (2.2)

neutralize. Reduce the effect of. (21.2)

noncommunicable diseases. Diseases that cannot be transmitted between an object and an individual or between individuals. (21.1)

noncustodial parent. Parent who lives separately from his or her children. (3.2)

nonessential. Not vital. (6.2)

noninteractive media. Media systems, such as television programs, over which the user has only a limited amount of control; also called *passive media*. (15.3)

noninvasive. Not requiring insertion or cutting. (5.3)

norm. Normal, socially acceptable pattern. (3.1)

not-for-profit programs. Early childhood education programs for which income only covers current costs and the surplus needed to keep the center operating on an ongoing basis or to expand services; also called *nonprofit programs*. (24.1)

nuclear family. Family consisting of a father, a mother, and their biological child or children who live together. (3.2)

nucleus accumbens **(NOO-klee-us uh-KUM-buhnz).** Pleasure and reward system of the brain. (18.1)

nurturance. Providing all aspects of care for a child, which includes meeting physical, intellectual, and social-emotional needs. (4.2)

nutrient-dense foods. Foods that are high in lean protein, complex carbohydrates, healthy fats, vitamins, and minerals and contain relatively few calories. (14.2)

nutrients. Substances that give the body what it needs to grow and function. (5.3)

O

obedience. Acting within the limits set by others. (13.2)

object concept. Ability to understand that objects, people, and events are separate from a person's interactions with them. (9.2)

object constancy. Ability to understand that objects remain the same even if they appear different. (9.2)

object identity. Ability to understand that an object stays the same from one time to the next. (9.2)

object permanence. Ability to understand that people, objects, and places still exist even when they are no longer seen, felt, or heard. (9.2)

obstetricians. Doctors who specialize in pregnancy and birth. (5.3)

occupation. Job. (25.1)

occupational categories. Sixteen industry areas that encompass a variety of different careers. (25.1)

oils. Fats that are liquid at room temperature. (11.2)

open adoption. Adoption that involves some degree of communication between the birthparent(s) and adoptive family. (3.2)

open-ended questions. Questions that require a descriptive response for an answer. (12.3)

oppositional defiant disorder (ODD). Behavioral disorder involving aggressive behaviors that are not provoked and worsen over time. (23.1)

optimum. Best. (5.3)

orthopedic problems. Problems relating to the bones and muscles. (17.3)

ossification (AWS-sih-fih-CAY-shun). Hardening of bones caused by the depositing of the minerals *calcium* and *phosphorus*. (8.1)

ovaries. Female reproductive glands. (5.1)

overindulgent. Providing everything a child wants. (4.2)

overnutrition. Condition in which the body's ongoing intake of calories is more than is needed for good health. (17.2)

overparenting. Parenting style in which parents desire to provide for and protect their children beyond what is in the best interest of children. Also called *helicopter parenting*. (4.2)

ovum. Female sex cell; also called *the egg*. (5.1)

P

parental responsibilities. Parents must meet their child's basic needs including food, clothing, housing, education, medical care, emotional and physical needs, and financial needs. (4.2)

parental rights. The right to have a child. (4.2)

parentese. Infant-directed, sing-song, high-pitched style in which parents and other adults speak to babies (9.2)

parochial (puh-ROH-kee-ul). Religious. (24.1)

passive vocabulary. Words a person understands, but does not say or write. (9.2)

paternal postpartum depression (PPPD). Mood disorders in men that may occur after the birth of a child. (7.4)

paternity leave. Time a man takes off from work (usually without pay) for a set period after a child's birth or adoption. (7.1)

pediatrician. Doctor who cares for infants, children, and teens until adulthood when physical growth is complete. (7.3)

peer abuse. Some form of abuse (physical, verbal, social, or emotional) directed at a child or teen by someone in the same peer group. (22.2)

peer pressure. Desire to be like one's peers. (17.3)

perception. Organizing information that comes through the senses. (9.1)

perceptual learning. Process of making sense out of sensory stimuli. (9.1)

perinatal (per-ih-NAY-tuhl) depression. Mood disorder that can occur during pregnancy or during the postpartum period or even afterward. (7.4)

period of gestation. Time between conception and birth; also called *pregnancy*. (5.1)

permanent teeth. Teeth that are intended to last a lifetime; are harder and less sharp than deciduous teeth. (17.1)

permissive. Parenting style in which parents give children almost no guidelines or rules. (4.2)

perpetrated. Done. (22.2)

personal plan of study. Plan that identifies the core courses and other learning experiences a person needs to complete to meet his or her educational and career goals. (25.1)

personal qualifications. Traits a person has that cannot be learned in career training. (25.2)

pheromones (FER-uh-mohns). Substances that are produced and secreted through sweat; cause body odor through contact with bacteria on skin and clothing. (17.3)

physical abuse. Any intentional physical act that results in pain, injuries, or both to a child. (22.2)

physical attributes. Concrete qualities of objects that can be sensed. (15.2)

physical development. Growth of the body and development of the large and small motor skills. (1.1)

physical disability. Limitation of a person's body or its function. (23.1)

physical knowledge. Knowledge acquired through observations of the physical world, such as attributes of objects (color, shape) and observable phenomenon (how gravity works and the comparative speed of balls rolled on flat surfaces and inclines). (15.2)

physical neglect. Endangering a child's health or safety by failing to provide basic needs (food, clothing, and shelter) and supervision. (22.2)

pique. Stir up interest in. (15.3)

placenta (pluh-SENT-uh). Organ filled with blood vessels that nourish the baby in the uterus. (5.1)

plaque. Sticky, mineral deposit coating the teeth while it colonizes bacteria on food particles left in the mouth causing cavities and leading to gum disease. (14.3)

plasticity. Ability of the brain to be shaped and reshaped, which is greatest early in life. (2.1)

play therapy. Use of play between a child and a trained counselor to help the child resolve certain problems. (20.1)

play yard. Enclosed play space for babies; formerly called a *playpen*. (8.3)

portfolio. Organized collection of materials that supports a person's job qualifications and reflects work, academic, and personal experiences. (25.4)

postpartum care. Care the birthing person receives during the six to eight weeks following the birth of her baby; also called *postnatal care*. (7.4)

postpartum depression (PPD). Less frequent than "baby blues," but a serious form of depression that may occur after giving birth. (7.4)

postpartum mood disorder (PPMD). Mental health condition, characterized by feelings of sadness, guilt, or depression, that men and women may experience after the birth of their baby. (7.4)

postpartum psychosis (PPP). Rare and extremely severe mental illness that may result after giving birth. (7.4)

potential. Greatest amount or level possible. (1.1)

power assertion. Discipline technique in which parents use or threaten to use some form of physical punishment or deny privileges. (4.2)

practical. Usable; applicable. (6.2)

precision. Ability to perform motor skills accurately. (17.1)

preconceptual substage. Substage of the preoperational stage in which children two to four years of age begin to develop and understand some concepts; also known as the *symbolic substage*. (15.1)

prefrontal cortex. Section near the front of the brain that is involved in logical thinking, forming judgments, memory, weighing consequences, decision making, and controlling impulses and emotions. (18.1)

Pregnancy Discrimination Act (PDA). Law that protects the rights of pregnant women who work. (7.1)

pregnancy-induced hypertension (PIH). High blood pressure caused by pregnancy. (5.2)

pregnancy leave. Leave from work taken by parents-to-be who cannot work for part or all of the pregnancy due to health reasons. (7.1)

premature birth. Born too soon. (5.3)

premoral. Not self-guided by internal values. (13.2)

prenatal development. Development that takes place between conception and birth. (5.1)

prenatal supplement. Supplement containing extra folic acid, iron, calcium, and other important vitamins and minerals that pregnant women take during pregnancy. (5.3)

preoccupied. Focused on another task. (21.2)

preoperational stage. Second of Piaget's stages of cognitive development in which children begin to think through problems rather than solve all their problems through physical actions. (15.1)

pre-K programs. State-financed early childhood education programs for three- and four-year-olds from low-income families; also called *prekindergartens*. (24.1)

preschools. Child care centers that serve preschool-age children. (24.1)

pretense. Symbolic actions seen in play that mimic real situations. (12.1)

preterm birth. Delivery that occurs before 39 weeks of pregnancy. (6.1)

preventive health care. Measures taken to keep children well, including regular doctor and dental appointments, health screenings, and immunization. (21.1)

primary school. School including the elementary grades first through fifth or sixth and sometimes the kindergarten; also called *elementary school*. (18.3)

principles of growth and development. Statements of the general patterns in which growth and development take place in people. (1.2)

private programs. Early childhood education programs owned by individuals and religious or other nongovernment groups. (24.1)

problem-solving skills. Skills used to analyze problems and formulate solutions. (25.3)

procreation. The producing of children. (4.1)

professionalism. Involves the skills, good judgment, and the attitudes and behaviors expected from any person trained to do a job well. (25.3)

professional organization. Group of professionals who meet to discuss their career field. (25.1)

professional qualifications. Physical, intellectual, and social-emotional skills a person needs to perform well in a career. (25.2)

prognosis. Predicted outcome of a disease or condition. (22.1)

prompt. Immediate. (5.3)

prone. Likely. (4.2)

protective services. Career area in which workers identify injustices to children and correct or remove children from dangerous situations. (25.2)

proximodistal (prahk-sum-oh-DIS-tahl) development. Direction of development from the center of the body to the extremities; also called *center-to-extremities development*. (8.1)

pruning. Process of weeding out underused or weak pathways between neurons. (2.1)

psychological security. Feeling that someone cares and will help when needed. (19.1)

psychosocial theory. Erik Erikson's theory that indicates that people go through eight stages of personality development in their lifespan. (10.2)

puberty. Process by which the body becomes capable of reproduction. (17.1)

public programs. Early childhood education programs funded by local, state, or federal government. (24.1)

Q

quickening. Movements of the fetus that can be felt by the birthing person. (5.1)

R

reaction time. Time required to respond to a sight, sound, or other stimuli. (14.1)

reading readiness. Belief that children should be formally taught reading and writing when developmentally ready for instruction; also refers to pre-reading programs taught through direct instruction. (15.3)

recession. Economic period with minimal or no growth. (3.2)

recessive traits. Traits that are not typically expressed in a person unless both genes for the trait are inherited. (5.2)

references. People other than family members who know a person well enough to discuss his or her qualifications for a job. (25.4)

reflexes. Automatic, unlearned movements in response to stimuli. (8.1)

regression. Going back to an earlier stage of development. (11.3)

regulations. Standards that govern how an early childhood education program operates. (24.2)

reinforcement. Rewards. (2.2)

repressed jealousy. Jealousy that is not directly expressed and may even be denied. (16.1)

rescinded (ree-SIND-ed). Taken away. (22.2)

resilient children. When faced with adversity in their lives, children who adapt well. (22.1)

respite. Rest. (22.2)

résumé. Brief account of a person's career goals, education, work experience, and other employment qualifications. (25.4)

resuscitate. Bring to an active state; revitalize. (7.3)

Rh factor. Protein substance found in the red blood cells of about 85 percent of the population. (5.2)

rigid. Stiff; restricted. (11.1)

rigorous. Demanding. (21.2)

role guilt. Feeling that one is not doing the best job at any role because of role strain. (25.3)

role strain. Feeling of having too many tasks to do at one time. (25.3)

rubella. Virus that can cross the placenta and affect the baby during the first three months of pregnancy. (5.2)

S

safety recall. Notice issued by a product manufacturer stating a product has been found to be unsafe. (21.2)

sand tables. Large, wooden or plastic containers on legs that are designed to hold sand and sand accessories for play. (20.2)

satiety. Being full. (8.2)

scaffolding. Varying levels of instructional support given to help children learn a new concept or skill. (9.1)

scapegoating. Blaming others for one's own mistakes. (19.1)

school-age child care (SACC) programs. Child care programs that provide child care for children between 5 and 14 years of age when school is not in session; also called *before- and after-school programs* or *out-of-school programs*. (24.1)

second-degree burns. Damage to body tissue when heat or radiation burns the middle layer of skin. (21.3)

seldom. Rarely. (2.1)

self-actualization. To grow and feel fulfilled as a person. (1.3)

self-assertion. Doing as one chooses rather than what others want. (13.2)

self-assessment. Step in career planning that involves a person identifying his or her interests, aptitudes, and abilities. (25.1)

self-awareness. Understanding someone has of him- or herself as a person. (10.2)

self-concept. Picture a person has of him- or herself. (16.1)

self-esteem. Confidence a person has in his or her own worth (feelings of being valued by others), competence (confidence in one's abilities to achieve goals), and control (sense one can affect outcomes and events in his or her life). (13.1)

self-restraint. Ability to control oneself. (13.2)

self-reward. Person's good feelings about his or her actions. (16.2)

sensitive periods. Times when the brain is best able to wire specific skills for all children. (2.1)

sensorimotor stage. First of Piaget's stages of cognitive (intellectual) development in which children use their senses and motor skills to learn and communicate. (9.1)

sensory stimulation. Using the senses to learn about the environment. (9.3)

separation anxiety. Anxiety common in infants caused by the fear that loved ones who leave them in the care of others will not return. (10.1)

sequenced steps. Steps in growth and development that follow one another in a set order. (1.2)

seriation (seer-ee-AY-shun). Arranging objects in order by the increasing or decreasing magnitude of one of the object's attributes, such as length, shade of a color, texture, or pitch. (15.2)

sever. End or cut off. (3.2)

severed. Ended. (22.1)

severity. Seriousness. (5.3)

sex typing. Process by which a person adopts the attitudes and behaviors considered culturally appropriate for his or her gender. (16.1)

sexual abuse. Any act of a sexual nature that involves an adult and a child. (22.2)

sexually transmitted infections (STIs). Infectious illnesses contracted primarily through sexual intercourse. (5.2)

sexual stereotyping. Stating or even hinting that men and women always behave in certain ways or should always do particular tasks, but not other tasks. (16.1)

shaken baby syndrome (SBS). Condition in which the "whiplash" shaking motion causes an infant's brain to hit the skull repeatedly. These hits cause the eye retina to bleed and veins in the brain to break, filling the area around the brain with blood resulting in swelling; also called *traumatic brain injury abuse.* (22.2)

shame. Self-focused feeling that involves a loss or threat of a loss to a child's basic security. (16.2)

shock. Condition in which the heartbeat and breathing slow. (21.3)

sibling abuse. Physical, verbal, emotional, or sexual abuse of one sibling by another. (22.2)

single-parent family. Family headed by one adult. (3.2)

six core strengths. Building blocks developed by Perry that make up children's foundation for future health, productivity, and happiness; includes attachment, self-regulation, affiliation, awareness (of how people are alike and different), tolerance, and respect. (22.2)

six-year molars. Large teeth near the back of the jaw that come in around six years of age and are used for grinding food (17.1)

skeletal system. Framework of the body that consists of cartilage, bones, and teeth. (8.1)

sleep-deprived. Having less than the recommended amount of sleep. (17.3)

small-muscle development. Development of muscles, especially those in the hands and fingers. (11.1)

social abuse. Restricting or intentionally harming a person's relationships with others. (22.2)

social-emotional development. Development that involves interactions with people and social groups, disposition, and emotions. (1.1)

socialize. To train a child to live as part of a group, such as the family, culture, or society. (4.2)

social referencing. Evaluating how to respond to a situation by getting a social cue from a more experienced person. (13.2)

society of children. Peer groups that prepare children for independence. (19.2)

sociocultural. Relating to social and cultural factors. (9.1)

socioeconomic. Social and economic factors. (4.1)

solid fats. Found mainly in animal-based foods, such as butter and beef fat. (14.2)

solids. Semiliquid and mushy foods fed to an infant by spoon. (8.2)

solitary symbolic play. First level of pretense in which the toddler uses real objects or realistic toys and pretends to do something that has to do with him- or herself. (12.1)

spatial. Pertaining to space. (9.2)

special education teachers. Teachers trained to work with children with special needs. (23.2)

special lessons and activities. Classes or clubs where children can discover their own interests and talents. (18.3)

speech disorder. Condition that causes a child to have difficulty speaking or being understood. (23.1)

sperm. Male sex cell. (5.1)

splinters. Pieces of wood or plastic that become lodged in the skin. (21.3)

sponge bath. Using a washcloth to wash the baby's body instead of immersing the baby in water. (8.3)

sprains. Injuries to joint ligaments. (21.3)

staff turnover. Term used to describe caregivers who leave a program and are replaced; often statistically presented as a rate. (24.2)

stages of grief. Feelings or mind-sets that most people experience when mourning; includes shock and denial, anger, bargaining, depression, and acceptance. (22.1)

static balance. Balance maintained while being still. (14.1)

stature. A person's height. (11.1)

stepfamily. Family that forms when a single parent marries another person. (3.2)

sterile. Condition of being permanently unable to conceive or carry fully biological children. (6.1)

stifle. To suppress. (4.1)

stillbirth. Loss of a fetus after 20 weeks of pregnancy. (6.1)

stimuli. Changes in the environment, such as light, sound, heat, or texture, that affect the sensory organs causing the person to react. (9.1)

stipulation. Specified condition. (15.3)

stressors. Situations that cause worry and anxiety. (1.1)

subsequent. Following. (5.1)

sudden infant death syndrome (SIDS). Condition in which a sleeping baby dies without warning and for medically unexplained reasons. (8.3)

surrogate. Person who bears (sometimes both conceives and bears) a child for a couple. (6.1)

suspension. Temporary removal from a job. (25.3)

symbolic thought. Ability to use symbols to represent objects, actions, or events from a person's world of experiences. (15.1)

synapse. Tiny gap between a dendrite of one neuron and the axon of another across which electrical impulses can be transmitted. (2.1)

synthetic. Not natural. (5.3)

T

table foods. Foods prepared for the entire family. (11.2)

tag questions. Making a statement and then adding *yes* or *no* to ask a question. (15.2)

tattling behaviors. Behaviors that seek to get another child in trouble by telling adults or other children about something a child has done. (16.2)

teachable moment. Optimal time when a person can learn a new task. (1.2)

temperament. Inherited tendency to react in a certain way to events. (10.1)

temper tantrum. Sudden emotional outburst of anger commonly displayed by a toddler. (13.1)

tentative. Not permanent; may change. (2.1)

terminally ill. Having an incurable disease that will result in death. (22.1)

termination. Nontemporary removal from a job. (25.3)

testes. Male reproductive glands. (5.1)

theory. Set of statements offered as a possible explanation for a phenomenon, such as child growth and development. (1.2)

third-degree burns. Damage to body tissue when heat or radiation burns the innermost layer of skin or the muscle and bone beneath. (21.3)

time management. Practice of organizing time and work assignments to increase personal efficiency. (25.3)

timid. Shy. (11.1)

toilet learning. Process by which adults help children control their excretory systems, namely bowel movements and urination. (11.3)

training pants. Special underpants or pants made of disposable diaper material that help lessen the mess of accidents during toilet learning. (11.3)

transductive (trans-DUCT-ihv) reasoning. Mentally linking events without using logic. (15.1)

transformations. Sequences of changes. (15.1)

trauma. Experiences characterizes by high levels of negative stress. (1.1)

traumatized. Seriously disrupted socially or emotionally. (22.1)

trimester. Period of three months. (5.1)

trust versus mistrust. Conflict infants must resolve according to the first stage of Erikson's psychosocial theory. (10.2)

typical development. Development that follows typical patterns of achieving developmental milestones. (23.1)

U

ubiquitous (yoo-BIH-kwuh-tuhs). Found everywhere. (15.3)

ultrasound. Prenatal test in which sound waves bounce off the fetus to produce an image of the fetus inside the womb. (5.3)

umbilical cord. Contains three blood vessels that connect the baby to the placenta. (5.1)

unconditional love. Deep affection without limitations. (10.2)

undernutrition. Condition in which food is being eaten, but is continuously lacking one or more nutrients required to meet the body's needs. (17.2)

unearth. Reveal. (21.1)

uninvolved. A parenting style in which the caregiver has little or no knowledge of what their children are doing. (4.2)

unit blocks. Naturally finished wooden blocks that are multiples or divisions of the basic unit size (1 3/8" X 2 3/4" X 5 1/2"); also called *floor blocks*. (20.2)

universal preschool programs. State-financed early childhood education programs for preschool children from families of all income levels. (24.1)

uterus. Organ in which the baby develops and is protected until birth. (5.1)

V

vaccination. Process of administering vaccines. (21.1)

vaccines. Substances used to produce immunity from diseases. (21.1)

vacuum extraction. Technique that uses suction to help the doctor move the baby down the birth canal as the birthing person pushes. (7.2)

values. Ideas, beliefs, or objects that are important and meaningful to a person. (25.1)

ventilated. Accessible to air. (21.2)

verbal abuse. Use of words to control and debase a child. (22.2)

vigor. Strength and energy. (3.2)

visual arts. Two- and three-dimensional art forms appealing to the sense of sight. (20.2)

visual literacy. Ability to draw meaning from observable and tangible objects and images. (20.2)

voluntary grasping. The intentional grasping of objects. (8.1)

vulnerable. Easily affected; sensitive. (5.2)

W

water tables. Large, plastic containers (tub-like and on legs) that are designed to hold water and accessories for play. (20.2)

weaning. Gradual process of taking infants off the breast or bottle. (8.2)

weight shift. Shifting the hips (pelvis) forward to transfer body weight onto the forward leg in order to offset equal weight on both legs. (14.1)

well-baby checkup. Routine medical visit in which the doctor examines a baby for signs of good health and proper growth. (7.3)

well-child checkups. Doctor's appointments while the child is not sick. (21.1)

window of opportunity. Prime period in a child's life for developing a particular skill if given the opportunity. (2.1)

wiring. Network of fibers that carry brain signals between neurons. (2.1)

working memory. Storing, organizing, and manipulating information while working on a task. (2.1)

wounds. Damage to the body's skin or tissue. (21.3)

X, Y, Z

zone of proximal development (ZPD). Level in which a child can learn with help. (9.1)

zygote (ZIGH-goht). Single cell formed at conception; also called a *fertilized egg*. (5.1)

Index

A

AAP. *See* American Academy of Pediatrics (AAP)
abilities assessment for careers involving children, 808
abrasions, 687
abstinence, 176
Academy for Eating Disorders, 545
accelerated intellectual development, 744–745
accidents of children, 673–674
accredited programs, 786
acquired childhood aphasia, 746
Acredolo, Linda, 279
active immunity, 663
active listening, 66
active-physical play, 634, 636
active vocabulary, 278–279
activity quality in early childhood education programs, 791–794
acuity of vision, 263–264
adaptive equipment, 763
addiction, 704
ADHD (attention-deficit/ hyperactivity disorder), 551, 749–750
adolescence stage of life cycle, 8
adoption, 80–81, 83–85
adoption agencies, 82, 83–84
adoption coordinators, 83
ADPKD (autosomal dominant polycystic kidney disease), 135
adult-child ratio, in early childhood education programs, 786–787
adults
    enrichment activities planned by, 585–587
    helping with homework, 583
    infant interactions with, 310–314
    preschooler interaction with, 497
    as school advocates, 584–585
    school-age and adolescent years interactions with, 606–607
    as strangers, safety around, 680
    supervising digital devices for children, 588–590
    toddler interaction with, 390–391

adverse childhood experiences (ACEs), 46, 700–701, 713. *See also* families, challenges to
advertising careers, 818
advocates
    careers as, 25, 818–819
    local citizens groups as, 23
    school, 584–585
AEDs (automatic external defibrillators), 691–692
after-school programs, 586
age
    age-appropriate behaviors, 304
    of biological parents, 136–137
    norms related to, 16
    of viability, 126
aggression
    oppositional defiant disorder (ODD), 747, 749, 759
    preschoolers, 501, 518
    school-age and adolescent years, 610
AHA (American Heart Association), 690
AIDS (acquired immunodeficiency syndrome)., 138–139
Ainsworth, Mary, 301
alarmist behavior of caregivers, 298
alcohol-related birth defects (ARBD), 140
alcohol-related neurodevelopmental disorder (ARND), 140
alcohol use, 140–142
allergens, 669–670
allergies, 341, 669–670
alphabetizing, 573
altruistic behaviors, 514
ambidextrous, 425
American Academy of Pediatrics (AAP)
    on corporal punishment, 108
    on health screenings, 664
    no blankets on infants, 248
    on nutrition for infants, 240, 243–244
    on screen time for children, 44, 379, 506
    on well-child checkups, 662

American Heart Association (AHA), 690
American Red Cross (ARC), 690–691
American Sign Language (ASL), 279
amniocentesis, 149–150
amnion, 125–126
anemia, 208
anger
    infants, 304
    preschoolers, 501, 518
    school-age and adolescent years, 610
    toddlers, 395–396, 405–406
animators and artists, 482
animism, 461
antibodies, 663
antidepressants, 758, 760
antigens, 663
antiperspirants and deodorants, 549
antipsychotic medications, 758
anti-Rh-immune globulin, 138
anxiety. *See also* stress
    infants, 303
    preschoolers, 500–501, 517
    school-age and adolescent years, 609–610
    toddlers, 395, 406–407
anxiety disorders, 747–748, 757–758
anxious-ambivalent attachments, 393
anxious-avoidant attachments, 393
Apgar test, 207
applying for careers involving children, 835–838
aptitude assessment for careers involving children, 807–808
ARBD (alcohol-related birth defects), 140
ARC (American Red Cross), 690–691
ARND (alcohol-related neurodevelopmental disorder), 140
art, 478, 646–648
articulation, 366, 467, 576
artificial insemination, 163–164
artificialism, 461
artificially acquired immunity, 663
artists and animators, 482
ARTs (assisted reproductive technologies), 163–166

ASD (autism spectrum disorder),
370, 551, 750–751, 761
ASL (American Sign Language), 279
assertiveness in preschoolers, 518
assessment of abilities, aptitudes,
and interests, 807–808
assimilation of culture, 387
assisted reproductive technologies
(ARTs), 163–166
asthma, 670
astrocytes (glial cells), 41
attachments
early childhood education
programs and, 788
infancy, 299–301, 314
toddler years, 392–394
attention-deficit/hyperactivity
disorder (ADHD), 551, 749–750
attention disorders, 749–750, 759–760
attention span, 562–563
attributes
ordering by, 573
preschoolers distinguishing, 460,
462–463, 473–475
school-age and adolescent years,
573
toddlers distinguishing, 364
auditory maps, 275
authoritarian parenting style,
110–111
authoritative parenting style, 110,
112
authority stage of parenting, 391,
399, 401, 512
autism spectrum disorder (ASD),
370, 551, 750–751, 761
automatic external defibrillators
(AEDs), 691–692
autonomous reality stage of
development (Piaget), 602
autonomy of toddlers, 390, 400
autosomal dominant polycystic
kidney disease (ADPKD), 135
autosomes, 133–134
axons in neurons, 40–41

B

babbling by infants, 278
Babinski reflex, 233
baby-adult interactions, 310–314
baby agenda, 283
baby blues, 214–215
baby-led weaning, 245–246
Baby Signs (Acredolo and Goodwin),
279
Backpack Friends, 703
balance, physical, 422–423

Bandura, Albert, 18
bassinets, 253
bathing toddlers, 346
behavioral disorders, 747
behaviors, guiding and modeling,
619–620
beneficial family dynamics, 66
bias, 73
Big Brothers Big Sisters of America, 78
bilingualism, 366, 370, 576
binocular vision, 265, 273
biochemistry, 39
birth control methods, 102–103
bites, 689
bleeding, 687
blended families, 80
block building play, 641–642
blood tests, prenatal, 148
body awareness of toddlers, 387
body language, 66
body part recognition, 315
body proportions
infants, 230–231
preschoolers, 420
school-age and adolescent years,
534
toddlers, 328–329
body rotation, 423
bonding, 205, 299
bones
infants, 231
preschoolers, 420–422
school-age and adolescent years,
534
toddlers, 329
Bowlby, John, 301
Braille system, 755
brain, 36–47. *See also* knowledge
acquisition
antidepressants and, 760
biology, 39–41
connections, 42
experiences, 45–47
functional specialization of, 419
hand preference and, 424–425
language wiring in, 275
learning process, 39
mental imagery in toddlers, 357
overview, 38–39
plasticity, 42–43
protection, 47
timing in development, 43–45
brain, growth of
infancy, 229, 263–267
preschool years, 449–452
school-age and adolescent years,
561–563
toddlers, 327

Brazelton scale, 209
Brazelton, T. Berry, 26, 209, 301
breast feeding, 240–241
breech birth position, 200
Bronfenbrenner, Urie, 18
bruises, 688
buffers (support systems), 711
bullying, 582, 722
burnout, career, 820–821
burns, 688
burping babies, 242

C

caffeine, 151
carbohydrates, 145
cardiac muscle, 331
cardiopulmonary resuscitation
(CPR), 691–692
care and education careers, 816–817
career and technical student
organizations (CTSOs), 3, 829
career counselors, 808
careers involving children,
804–847
abilities assessment, 808
aptitude assessment, 807–808
career plan for, 811–813
collaboration skills for, 829
conflict-resolution skills for,
830
critical thinking skills for, 830
education and training needed,
810
executive function skills for,
831–832
inside view of, 811
interest assessment, 807
interpersonal skills for,
826–828
job application in, 835–838
job changing, 841–842
job interview in, 839–841
job search in, 835
job success in, 841
market analysis, 810
occupational categories, 809
overview, 806
personal qualifications for,
819–821
problem-solving skills for, 830
professionalism skills for, 831
professional qualifications for,
821–824
in research, consulting, and
advocacy, 818–819
role-management skills for,
832–833

careers involving children, specific
adoption coordinator, 83
advertising, marketing, and
management, 818
artist and animator, 482
care and education, 816–817
career counselor, 808
certified nurse-midwife, 193
child advocate, 23
child care center director, 787
child care worker, 23
child development professor, 779
coaching, 550
dental hygienists, 438
design careers, 818
diagnostic medical sonographer,
149
elementary school teacher, 49
in entertainment, 818
entrepreneurship, 819
genetic counselors, 137
health and protective services,
815–817
marriage and family therapists,
69
mental health counselor, 317
parenting, 100
pediatric ophthalmologist, 265
physical therapists, 249
physician-neonatologist, 210
playground designer, 644
preschool teacher, 517
recreational therapist, 727
recreation worker, 102
registered dietitian, 342
school counselor, 585
social and human service
assistant, 181
social worker, 83
sociologists, 618
special education teacher, 757
speech-language pathologist,
368
survey researcher, 388
toy designer, 679
career narratives, 812
career portfolios, 32, 58, 86, 114, 156,
184, 219, 256, 290, 319, 351, 381,
410, 442, 484, 522, 554, 592, 624,
654, 694, 732, 767, 800, 838, 844
caregivers, needs after childbirth,
216–217
catching balls, in toddler years,
332–333
cause and effect
infant learning, 315
preschooler problems with, 457,
463, 476

school-age and adolescent years,
573
toddlers distinguishing,
364–365
CBT (cognitive-behavioral therapy),
714, 758
CCHD (critical congenital heart
disease), 209
CCRR (Child Care Resource and
Referral Agency), 182
CCR&R (child care resources and
referral) agencies, 783
CDA (Child Development Associate)
credential, 517
CE International (Childhood
Education International), 824
center-based child care, 775–777
Centers for Disease Control and
Prevention (CDC), 46, 138, 235
center-to extremities development,
in infants, 236
central precocious puberty (CPP),
529
centration, 456, 565
cephalocaudal development, 234
cephalocaudal principle, 327
certified child safety seat (car seat),
675–676
certified nurse-midwife, 193–194
cervix, 123–124
cesarean section deliveries, 204
character building, 107–108
chiari malformation, 171
childbirth, 188–223. *See also*
pregnancy
caregiver needs, 216–217
complications of, 203–204
delivery considerations,
194–197
employment considerations,
192–193
family considerations, 191–192
first medical care of baby,
207–210
high-risk newborns, 210–211
hospital stay, 204–205
labor signs, 200
labor stages, 201–202
overview, 190
postpartum mood disorders,
213–216
postpartum physical care, 213
child care center directors, 787
Child Care Resource and Referral
Agency (CCRR), 182
child care resources and referral
(CCR&R) agencies, 783
child care worker, 23

child-centered society, 21
child development, 6–35
description of, 6–7
domains of, 7
factors influencing, 9–12
growth and development
principles, 13–17
growth and development
theories, 17–19
hierarchy of needs, 25–26
individual life cycle, 7–8
irreducible needs, 26–27
knowledge about, 821
observing children, 27–29
studying children, 21–24
Child Development Associate (CDA)
credential, 517
child development laboratories,
779–782
child development professors, 779
childhood, infant intellectual
development *versus*, 283
Childhood Education International
(CE International), 824
childhood schizophrenia, 747, 758
child items, safety of, 675–677
childproofing measures, 674–675
child protection agencies, 717
Child Protective Services (CPS), 23
child-related careers. *See* careers
involving children
Children's Bureau, U.S. Department
of Health and Human Services., 23
children's rights, 22
children with gifts and talents,
744–745, 756
children with special needs, 737–769
attention disorders, 749–750,
759–760
autism spectrum disorder
(ASD), 750–751, 761
description of, 739–740
education and services for,
761–762
intellectual special needs,
743–746, 756–757
overview, 738–739
physical special needs, 740–743,
754–755
social-emotional special needs,
746–749, 757–759
support for families of, 762–764
child-resistant containers for
medications, 686
child support orders, 77
chlamydia, 139
choking maneuvers, 690
chorionic villus sampling (CVS), 149

chorion membrane, 125–126
chromosomes, 132–133, 136
circadian rhythms, 252
circulatory system, 532
circumcision, 209
circumference of head, in infants, 231
classifying objects, 462, 475, 572–573
cleft lip/palate, 171
climbing in toddler years, 332
closed adoption, 84–85
closed-ended questions, 376
clothing needs
    infants, 248–249
    preschool years, 436–437
    school-age and adolescent years, 548–549
    toddlers, 344–346
CMV (cytomegalovirus), 138
coaches, 550
cochlear implants, 755
codes of professional ethics, 831
code-switching in school-age and adolescent years, 577
codified steps in growth and development, principle of, 14–16
cognitive-behavioral therapy (CBT), 714, 758
cognitive change in school-age and adolescent years, 561–563
cognitive development theories, 18, 268–270
cognitive flexibility, 54–56
colic, 244
collaboration skills, 829
collective monologues, 467
collective symbolism, 360, 376
college portfolios, 114
color sensitivity, in vision, 265
communicable diseases, 664–668
communication
    in child-related careers, 827–828
    in families, 66
    by infants, 277–278
    parent-child, 619
    in parenting, 99
    in preschool years, 466–469
    in school-age and adolescent years, 575–577
    symbols in, 479
    by toddlers, 366–370
competence, 389
complementary foods, 338
comprising culture, 70
concept activities for toddlers, 375
conception, 122–124
concept learning
    infants, 272–275
    play and, 632–633

preschool years, 448, 460–466, 473–477
    school-age and adolescent years, 572–575
    toddlers, 363–366
concrete operational stage (Piaget), 563–564
confidentiality in child-related careers, 830
conflict-resolution skills, 830
conflicts, 515, 620
congenital conditions, 149–150, 170–172
conscience, 495
consensus building, 829
consenting to adoption, 85
conservation, 565–567
consistency in rules and follow-up, 403
constancy principle of growth and development, 14–15
constructivist approach to education, 53
consulting careers, 818–819
continued stuttering, 742
contractions, 200
contrast sensitivity, 265
control, toddlers assuming, 389
conventional morality (Kohlberg), 602, 605
Convention on the Rights of the Child (United Nations International Children's Education Fund), 22
convergent thinking, 479
cooing, 277
cooking as play, 644–645, 647
coordination, motor, 286
coping, 78
cord-blood banking, 197
co-regulation
    newborns, 312
    school-age and adolescent years, 606–607
    toddlers, 404
cost
    child rearing, 78, 100–101
    early childhood education programs, 795–796, 798
counseling on fertility, 163
counseling services, 713
counselors, school, 585
counting numbers in preschooler years, 464–466
cover letters, 835, 837–838
CPP (central precocious puberty), 529
CPR (cardiopulmonary resuscitation), 691–692
CPS (Child Protective Services), 23

crawling, 235
creeping, 235
crises resources, 712–715
critical congenital heart disease (CCHD), 209
critical periods in brain development, 44
critical thinking skills in careers involving children, 830
cruising, in infants, 235
CTSOs (career and technical student organizations), 3, 829
cultural diversity, 793, 795–796
cultural influences
    episodic memory and, 452
    on families, 63, 70–73
    on language learning, 368
    on socialization of children, 106
    toddler assimilation of, 387
culturally sensitive trauma-informed care, 74
culture shock, 795
culture-specific knowledge in school-age and adolescent years, 574–575
cumulative self-concept, 495
Curry, Julie, 10
Curry, Sara, 10
custodial parents, 77
custody of children, in divorce, 708
CVS (chorionic villus sampling), 149
cyberbullying, 552, 722
cystic fibrosis, 135, 171
cytomegalovirus (CMV), 138

D

DAP (developmentally appropriate practice), 791
death, 708–712
deciduous teeth, 232
deductive reasoning, 568
deep cuts, 687
deferred imitation, 360, 449
dehydration in preschoolers, 419
delayed gratification, 400, 404
delivery considerations, in childbirth, 194–197
dendrites in neurons, 40–41
dental care, 438, 663
dental hygiene, 438, 549
deodorants and antiperspirants, 549
dependency, emotional, 500
depression
    children with, 747, 758
    maternal, 406
    school-age and adolescent years, 621

deprivation, sleep, 551
depth perception, 273
design careers, 818
detrimental family dynamics, 66
developmental acceleration, 16–17
developmental delays
    intellectual, 743–744
    overview, 16–17, 739
    physical, 740
    in reading, 741
    social-emotional, 746–747
developmental dyscalculia, 746
developmental dyslexia, 746
developmentally appropriate
    practice (DAP), 791
developmental stress, 504
developmental tasks, 52–53
DeVries, Rheta, 18, 53
dexterity, 333
diabetes
    in children, 668–669
    as congenital condition, 171
    pregnancy and, 137–138
diagnostic medical sonographers,
    149
diapering babies, 250–251
dietitians, registered, 342
different rates of growth and
    development, principle of, 14,
    16–17
digestion, 421
digital citizenship, 552
dilation of cervix, in labor, 201
direct costs of child rearing, 100–101
direct intervention, in child-related
    careers, 815
direct observations, 28
disabilities
    intellectual, 743, 756
    physical, 741, 754–755
discontentment, 66
diseases
    communicable, 664–668
    non-communicable, 668–670
disorganized attachments, 394
disposition of infants, 297
dissociation, 706
distance concepts, 574
distraction, as co-regulation, 404
divergent thinking, 479
diversity, cultural, 70–72
divorce, 706–708
domains of child development, 7
domains of self-definition, 603–604
domestic violence, 718
dominant traits, 133, 135
doulas, 195
Down syndrome, 136, 171

drawing by preschoolers, 451
dressing babies, 248–249
drugs
    illegal, 140–142
    for labor and delivery, 196,
        203–204
Duchenne muscular dystrophy, 136
dynamic balance, 423

E

early childhood education programs,
    770–803
    activity quality, 791–794
    center-based child care, 775–777
    child development laboratories,
        779–782
    children adjusting to, 797
    for children with special needs,
        763
    cost of, 795–796, 798
    cultural diversity, 793, 795–796
    family child care, 774–775
    housing and equipment in, 786
    in-home child care, 774
    learning standards for, 771
    overview, 771–773
    parent-caregiver communication
        and participation, 789–791
    regulatory adherence in,
        785–786
    school-age child care, 777–779
    special services in, 796
    staff quality and number,
        786–788
    trends in, 782–783
Early Head Start programs, 780
Early Intervention Program for
    Infants and Toddlers with
    Disabilities, 762
early learning standards, 789, 791
ears, 422
eating disorders, 545–546
eating in toddler years, 336–337
ecological systems theory of growth
    and development, 18
economic recession, 79
ectopic pregnancies, 170
education, knowledge acquisition
    links to, 52–53
educational neglect, 718
education and care careers, 816–817
education and training for careers
    involving children, 810, 823
Educators Rising, 3
EFs (executive functions), 54–55,
    583–584
egocentricity, 454–455, 466, 565

electronic media
    in preschool years, 481–482
    in school-age and adolescent
        years, 588–590
    for toddlers, 379
elementary school teachers, 49
embryonic stage, 125
emergencies, 690–692. *See also*
    violence and disasters
emergent literacy, 478–480
emotional abuse, 719
emotional dependency, 500
emotional neglect, 718
emotions
    infants, 297, 300–304
    moral emotions, 495, 603
    preschoolers, 499–502, 516
    school-age and adolescent years,
        608–610, 620–621
    toddlers, 392, 403–407
empathy, 26, 404, 603
employability skills, 808
employment considerations,
    192–193, 783
empty calories, 430
energy, as parenting resource, 99
enriched environment for infants,
    282, 285
enrichment outside of school, 585–587
entertainment careers, 818
entrepreneurship, 819
enuresis (involuntary urination), 438
environmental influence
    on development, 9
    hereditary factors affected by,
        10–12
    in preschool years, 505
    on unborn babies, 136–143
ependymal glial cells, 41
epigenome, 11
epilepsy, 669
episiotomy, 202
episodic memory, 452, 504
Erikson, Erik, 18, 309, 390, 604
Erikson's psychosocial theory,
    309–310, 633
essence of family, 65
executive functions (EFs), 54–55,
    583–584
executive function skills, 831–832
experiences, need for, 45–47
experts, knowledge about, 51–52
explicit knowledge, 50
explicit memory, 267, 286
extended families, 79–80
extrusion reflex in infants, 244
eye-hand coordination, 334
eyes, 263–266

F

"face time," 277
failure to thrive, 227, 230
fallopian tubes, 123–125
families
    adopted children in, 80–81,
        83–85
    childbirth and, 191–192
    children with special needs and,
        737, 762–764
    cultural influences on, 70–73
    description of, 65–67
    extended, 79–80
    foster, 81
    gender roles influenced by, 600
    guardians with, 82
    healthy, 73–75
    kin care, 82
    life cycle of, 67–70
    nuclear, 76–77
    overview, 64–65
    single-parent, 77–79
    societal influences on, 73
    stepfamilies and blended, 80
families, challenges to, 698–735
    addiction, 704
    child neglect and abuse, 717–730
    crises resources, 712–715
    divorce, 706–708
    financial strain, 702–704
    illness and death, 708–712
    moving, 701–702
    overview, 700–701
    sibling and peer abuse, 722–723
    violence and disasters, 704–706
Family, Career and Community
    Leaders of America (FCCLA), 3, 829
Family and Medical Leave Act
    (FMLA), 193
family child care, 774–775
family names, toddler knowledge
    of, 387
family planning, 102–103
family therapists, 69
family therapy, 714
FASDs (fetal alcohol spectrum
    disorders), 140, 142
fat
    overview, 145
    preschooler bodies, 422
    school-age and adolescent years,
        536
    solid, 430
    toddler bodies, 329–330
FCCLA (Family, Career and
    Community Leaders of America),
    3, 829

FEA (Future Educators of America),
    3
fear. *See also* anxiety; stress
    infants, 302
    preschoolers, 500–501, 504, 517
    school-age and adolescent years,
        609–610
    toddlers, 395, 406–407
fear-conditioning, 504
feeding problems of toddlers, 341
feeding schedules for infants, 242
fetal alcohol spectrum disorders
    (FASDs), 140, 142
fetal stage, 125
fiberoptic phototherapy, 208
field trips, in early childhood
    education programs, 792
filtering programs, 589
finalism, 461
financial literacy, 78
financial strain on families, 702–704
fine-motor skills
    infants, 233
    manipulative-constructive play
        for, 636
    toddlers, 333–334, 374
fingerplays (Froebel), 782
firing process in brain, 43
first aid, 686–689
first-degree burns, 688
first words, in infants, 278
flexibility, 537, 820
flipped classroom mode of teaching,
    583
FMLA (Family and Medical Leave
    Act), 193
folic acid, 145, 150–151
fontanels (soft spots) in infant skulls,
    231
food
    appeal in preschool years,
        432–433
    attitudes in preschool years,
        430–431
    junk foods, 543
    making meals fun in preschool
        years, 434
    nutritional needs in preschool
        years, 429–430
    nutritional risks in school-age
        and adolescent years, 544–546
    school-age and adolescent years,
        541–544
food allergies, 341
food assistance programs, 177
foodborne diseases, 668
food-insecure households, 544
forceps, 204

foregone income, with child rearing,
    101
formal operational stage (Piaget),
    564
formula feeding, 240–242
for-profit center-based child care,
    777
foster families, 81
fractures, 688
franchised for-profit center-based
    child care, 777
fraternal births, 166–168
Fred Rogers Center for Early
    Learning and Children's Media,
    481
Freud, Anna, 18
Freud, Sigmund, 18
friends
    imaginary, 499
    preschooler jealousy and, 519
    preschool years, 514
    rejection by, 597
    school-age and adolescent years,
        607, 618
Froebel, Friedrich, 782
functional specialization of brain,
    419
Future Educators of America (FEA),
    3

G

galactosemia, 209
Galinsky, Ellen, 55–56
    parenting stages, 97, 299, 391,
        399, 401, 512, 619
    seven essential life skills, 55–56
Galton, Francis, 10–11
games (inquiry-based learning
    activities), 53
gamete intrafallopian transfer
    (GIFT), 163–164
gang violence, 723
Gardner, Howard, 569
Gardner's theory of multiple
    intelligences, 569–570
GED (General Educational
    Development) test., 180
gender constancy, 492
gender identity, 387, 492
gender roles
    adult feelings about, 510
    caregivers' beliefs impact, 489
    learning, 492–493
    in school-age and adolescent
        years, 600–601, 615–616
gender schools, 600
gender stability, 492

General Educational Development
(GED) test., 180
genetic counselors, 137
genetics
    affecting unborn baby, 132–134
    disorders affecting unborn baby,
      134–136
    gene function, 9
    overview, 10
Gerber, Magda, 311
germinal stage, 124
Gesell, Arnold, 18
gestation, 124
gestational diabetes, 138
GIFT (gamete intrafallopian
    transfer), 163–164
gifts and talents, children with,
    744–745, 756
Gilligan, Carol, 602
glial cells, 40–41
goals
    goal-corrected partnerships, 606
    SMART, 812, 822
    working toward, 359–360
gonorrhea, 139
Goodwin, Susan, 279
gradual and continuous growth and
    development, principle of, 14–15
grammar
    preschooler years, 467–469
    school-age and adolescent years,
      577
    toddler years, 368–369
grasping skills, 236
gratification, delayed, 400, 404
gravity, 274
Greenspan, Stanley I., 26
grief, 710
gross-motor skills
    active-physical play for, 634, 636
    disabilities reducing, 741
    infancy, 233
    toddler years, 330, 374
group presentations, 52
growth and development
    definition of, 7
    growth spurts, 532–533
    principles of, 13–17
    theories of, 17–19
growth pains, 536
guardians with families, 82
guidance and discipline, 91, 107–109
guilt, 603

H

hand preference, 424
hand regard, by infants, 315

hand-washing steps, 661
hard lockdowns at schools, 690
Harvard Growth Studies, 407
Havighurst, Robert, 52
head and neck control, in infants, 234
Head Start programs, 780–781
head-to-foot development, 234
head-to-foot principle, 327
health
    communicable diseases, 664–668
    emotional, during pregnancy,
      141–143
    first aid, 686–689
    illness treatment for children,
      684–686
    non-communicable diseases,
      668–670
    physical, during pregnancy,
      137–141
    physical needs of children for,
      661
    during pregnancy, 147–153
    preventative health care,
      661–664
    prior to pregnancy, 145
health and protective services
    careers, 815–817
health screenings, 664
healthy eating
    school-age and adolescent years,
      541–544
    toddlers, 337–341
healthy families, 73–75
hearing, 209, 742
heart, 209, 532
heavily processed foods, 541
height
    preschoolers, 419–420
    school-age and adolescent years,
      533
    toddlers, 328
helicopter parenting, 110, 112
hemophilia, 136
hereditary influence, 9–12
herpes simplex, 139
heterogeneous morality stage
    (Piaget), 494
hidden objects, searching for, 361
hierarchical classification of objects,
    573
higher-multiple births, 167–169
high-reactive infants, 297–298
high-risk newborns, 210–211
high school, preparing for, 582
HIV (human immunodeficiency
    virus), 138–139
home care, as parenting resource,
    99–100

home visitation, 728
homework, helping children with,
    583
Honig, Alice S., 311
hormone therapy for fertility, 164
hospital stay in childbirth, 204–205
HPV (human papillomavirus), 139
Huntington's disease, 135, 172
hydrocephalus, 172
hygiene, 437–438, 549
hyper-arousal, 706
hypothyroidism, 209

I

IDEA (Individuals with Disabilities
    Education Act), 761–762
identical births, 167
identity *versus* role confusion stage
    of development (Erikson), 606
IEP (Individualized Education Plan),
    762
IFSP (Individualized Family Service
    Plan), 762
illegal market adoption, 84
illness, 708–712
imaginary friends, 499
imitation
    deferred, 449
    learning language via, 277
    by preschoolers, 458
    by toddlers, 359–360
imitative-imaginative play, 636–638
immunity, 663
immunizations, 664–665
implicit knowledge, 50
implicit memory, 267, 286
impoverishment, 702
inadequate soothing of high-reactive
    infants, 298
inclusion, of children with special
    needs, 762–763
independent adoption, 83–84
indirect costs of child rearing, 101
indirect intervention, in child-related
    careers, 815
indirect observations, 28
Individualized Education Plan (IEP),
    762
Individualized Family Service Plan
    (IFSP), 762
individual life cycle, 7–8
Individuals with Disabilities
    Education Act (IDEA), 761–762
induction discipline technique,
    108–109
inductive reasoning, 568
Industrial Revolution, 73

industry and identity in school-age and adolescent years, 604–606, 617

industry *versus* inferiority stage of development (Erikson), 604–606

infancy, intellectual development in, 260–293
 brain development, 263–267
 childhood learning *versus*, 283
 cognitive development theories, 268–270
 communicating, 277–278
 concept learning, 272–275
 helping infants learn, 283–288
 language learning, 275–277
 milestones in, 278–281
 overview, 261–262
 perceptual learning, 267–268

infancy, physical development in, 226–259
 bathing, 249–250
 clothing and dressing, 248–249
 diapering, 250–251
 milestones in, 236–238
 motor development, 233–236
 nutrition from six to twelve months, 243–245
 nutrition in first six months, 240–243
 organ maturation, 229
 physical activity, 253–254
 reflexes, 232–233
 resting and sleeping, 251–253
 self-feeding, 245–246
 skeletal growth, 230–232

infancy, social-emotional development in, 294–321
 baby-adult interactions, 310–314
 emotional expression of, 300–304
 Erikson's psychosocial theory, 309–310
 milestones in, 304–307
 self-awareness in, 315
 social relations of, 298–300
 stress and special problems, 316–317
 temperamental differences in, 297–298

infancy stage of life cycle, 8

infant rage, 304

infants, early education programs for, 783, 791

infertility and sterility, 163–166

inflections, in infant sounds, 278

influenza, 664

informed knowledge, 20

inherent essence of family, 65

inhibition, 54–56

in-home child care, 774

initiative
 industry builds from (Erikson), 605
 initiative *versus* guilt stage (Erikson), 495
 in preschool years, 512–513

injury, in children, 681

inquiry-based learning activities (games), 53

insecure attachments, 392–394

intellectual development, 7, 721. *See also* infancy, intellectual development in; preschool years, intellectual development in; school-age and adolescent years, intellectual development in; toddler years, intellectual development in

intellectual special needs, 743–746, 756–757

intelligence quotient (IQ) test, 744–745

interactive media, 481

interdependent stage of parenting (Galinsky), 619

interest assessment in careers involving children, 807

internal organs of preschoolers, 420

International Society for Technology in Education (ISTE), 590

interneurons, 40–41

interpersonal communication skills, 827–828

interpersonal skills, 826–828

interpretive stage of parenting (Galinsky), 619

interrelatedness of growth and development, principle of, 17

interviews, for careers involving children, 839–841

intolerance to foods, in infants, 245

intonation, 376

introverted children, 513

intrusive behavior of caregivers, 298

intuition, 455

intuitive substage of development (Piaget), 454

in vitro fertilization (IVF), 163–164

involuntary urination (enuresis), 438

IQ (intelligence quotient) test, 744–745

irreducible needs of children, 26–27

ISTE (International Society for Technology in Education), 590

IVF (in vitro fertilization), 163–164

J

jaundice, 208

jealousy, 501–502, 519, 610

job fairs, 835

jobs. *See* careers involving children

job shadowing, 811

joint custody of children, 77

jumping by toddlers, 332

junk foods, 543

K

Kagan, Jerome, 297–298

Kamii, Constance, 18, 53

karyotype, 134

Kennell, John, 301

kin care, 82

kindergarten programs, 782, 793

Klaus, Marshall, 301

knowledge acquisition, 48–56. *See also* brain
 education links to, 52–53
 effective use of, 53–55
 Galinsky's seven essential life skills, 55–56
 overview, 48–49
 types of, 49–52

knowledge-based economy, 53

Kohlberg, Lawrence, 493–494, 602

L

labor, in childbirth, 194, 200–202

lactation consultants, 241

laissez-faire parenting style, 110–111

Lally, Ronald, 283

Lamaze method of natural childbirth, 195

language
 infant activities for, 287–288
 infant learning of, 275–277
 of instruction, 355
 language-rich environment for infants, 277
 meanings of, 450
 Piaget *versus* Vygotsky views of, 569
 preschool activities for, 478–480
 of preschoolers, 451, 504
 toddler activities for, 366, 376–378

language disorders, 746, 757

language-logic play, 638

large-muscle development
 preschoolers, 422–423
 toddler years, 330–333

leadership skills, 820–821
learning. *See also* brain; knowledge
    acquisition
      concepts by infants, 272–275
      concepts by toddlers, 363–366
      enrichment outside of school,
        585–587
      gender roles, 492–493
      language activities, 287–288
      language in infancy, 275–277
      lifelong, 50, 823–824
      math by cooking, 647
      motor activities, 286
      perceptual, by infants, 267–268
      problem-solving activities, 287
      scaffold for children's, 362
      sensory activities, 286
      from stimuli, 263
      word meanings, 367–370
learning disorders, 745–746, 757
learning theory of growth and
    development, 18
leg control, in infants, 235
legislation, children affected by,
    670–671
length and weight in infancy, 230
lesson plans, in early childhood
    education programs, 793–794
Lewis, Jim, 10
life cycle of families, 67–70
lifelong learning, 50, 823–824
lightening, in labor, 200
literature experiences as play, 650–652
locomotor skills, in infants, 236
"logical" brain, 561–562
logical thinking
    activities for, 474–477
    concepts for problem-solving in,
      461–467
    obstacles in preschool years,
      454–457
    obstacles in school-age and
      adolescent years, 565–568
    use in school-age and adolescent
      years, 572–573
long-term memory, 452
love and affection
    preschoolers, 500, 517
    school-age and adolescent years,
      609
    toddlers, 395, 403–404
love withdrawal discipline
    technique, 108
low birthweights, in multiple births,
    166
low-reactive infants, 297–298
lunches in school-age and adolescent
    years, 542–543

M

magnetic resonance imaging (MRI),
    39
mainstreaming, of children with
    special needs, 762
malnutrition, 544
management careers, 818
mandated reporters, 699, 724
manipulating information, 54
manipulating objects, 423
manipulative-constructive play, 636
manners, 515–516, 827
mapping words to objects, 276
Marfan syndrome, 135
mark and mirror experiments, 388
market analysis of careers involving
    children, 810
marketing careers, 818
marriage, 65
marriage and family therapists, 69
Maslow, Abraham, 25–26, 247
Maslow's hierarchy of needs, 25–26
maternal depression, 406
maternity leave, 192, 195
math knowledge, 647
maturational theory of child
    development, 480
maturational theory of growth and
    development, 18
measles-mumps-rubella (MMR)
    vaccination, 140
media, 601, 705. *See also* technology
media-related risks, 589
mediation, 830
medical neglect, 718
medications for children, 141,
    684–686
memory
    capacity of, 451
    centers of brain for, 267
    episodic, 504
    preschoolers, 451–452, 472–473
    school-age and adolescent years,
      563
menarche (menstruation), 531
Mendel, Gregor, 133
Mendelian inheritance, 133
mental health, 12, 79. *See also*
    mental health features in each
    chapter
mental health counselors, 317
mental imagery, 357, 449–450
mental maps, 463–464
metacognition, 562
microglia (glial cells), 41
microsurgery, 164
middle school, preparing for, 582

milestones, infant
    intellectual development,
      278–281
    infant physical development,
      236–238
    infant social-emotional
      development, 304–307
milestones, preschool
    intellectual development,
      469–470
    physical development, 426
    social-emotional development,
      502–503
milestones, school-age and
    adolescent
    intellectual development,
      577–579
    physical development,
      537–539
    social-emotional development,
      611–612
milestones, toddler
    intellectual development,
      370–371
    physical development,
      334–335
    social-emotional development,
      396–397
minerals, 145
mirror play, 315
miscarriage, 173
mixed-type births, 167–168
MMR (measles-mumps-rubella)
    vaccination, 140
monolingualism, 367
monologues in preschooler years,
    467
Montessori, Maria, 781
Montessori schools, 781–782
month-by-month development
    during pregnancy, 126–129
mood disorders, postpartum,
    213–216
moral development
    moral character, 494–495
    preschool years, 493–495, 511
    school-age and adolescent years,
      605, 616
moral emotions, 495, 603
moral judgment and reasoning,
    493–494
moral neglect, 718
moral reasoning (Kohlberg), 605
moro (startle) reflex, 233
mortality rate, in teen pregnancies,
    179
motivation, 17
motor center of brain, 266

motor development. *See also* physical
   activity
      infancy, 233–236, 286
      preschool years, 422–425, 472
      school-age and adolescent years,
         536–537
      toddler years, 330–334, 374
motor neurons, 40–41
movement and coordination in eyes,
   265
moving, as family challenge, 701–702
MRI (magnetic resonance imaging),
   39
multicultural families, 72–73
multigenerational families, 7
multiple intelligences, Gardner's
   theory of, 569–570, 586
multiple pregnancies, 163, 166–169
muscle development
      preschoolers, 422–424
      school-age and adolescent years,
         536
      toddler years, 329–334
muscular dystrophy, 172
music, as play, 648–649
mutations, 134
myelination, 327
myocardium muscles, 331
MyPlate food guidance system
   (USDA)
      overview, 145, 150
      school-age and adolescent years,
         541–542
      toddlers, 338–340

N

name recognition, 315
National Association for the
   Education of Young Children
   (NAEYC), 373, 481, 824
National Campaign to Prevent Teen
   Pregnancy, 183
national chains of for-profit
   center-based child care, 777
National Child Abuse Hotline, 81
National Child Traumatic Stress
   Network, 46
National Domestic Violence Hotline,
   718
National Resource Center for Child
   Protective Services (NRCCPS), 23
National School Lunch Program
   (NSLP), 703
natural childbirth, 195
natural immunity, 663
nature *versus* nurture, 10–11

neglect and abuse of children
      causes of, 719–721
      center-based child care to reduce
         risk of, 776
      effects on child, 721–722
      recognizing and reporting,
         723–725
      siblings and peers, 722–723
      treating, 725–730
      types of, 717–719
negotiation, 830
Neonatal Behavioral Assessment
   Scale, 209
neonatal discontinuation, 142
neonatal intensive care unit (NICU),
   210–211
neonatal stage of life cycle, 8
neonatal withdrawal symptoms,
   141–142
neonates, 207
neonatology, 210
networking for jobs, 835
neurons, 40–41, 43
neuroscience, 55
newborns
      first medical care of, 207–210
      high-risk, 210–211
      interacting with, 311–313
      learning activities for, 283–285
      visual preferences of, 284
nicotine, 140
NICU (neonatal intensive care unit),
   210–211
non-communicable diseases, 668–670
noncustodial parents, 77
noninteractive media, 481
nonrelative caregivers, 774
norms of living, 73
not-for-profit center-based child
   care, 777
NRCCPS (National Resource Center
   for Child Protective Services), 23
NSLP (National School Lunch
   Program), 703
nuclear families, 76–77
nucleus accumbens, 562
number concepts, 464–466, 477, 574
number sense, 273
numerosity, 465
nurse-midwifes, 193
nurturance, 105
nutrition. *See also* infancy, physical
   development in
      pregnancy, 145, 150–152
      preschool years, 429–430
      school-age and adolescent years,
         544–546

O

obedience, 400–403, 681
object concept, 272–273
object constancy, 272
object identity, 272–273
object permanence, 273, 360
object possession, 315, 387
object solidity, 274
observations, 27–29, 373
obstetricians, 147
occupational categories, in careers
   involving children, 809
Occupational Outlook Handbook
   (United States Department of
   Labor), 23, 25
Occupational Safety and Health
   Administration (OSHA), 788,
   841
ODD (oppositional defiant disorder),
   747, 749, 759
oils, in food, 339
oligodendrocytes (glial cells), 41
onomatopoeic words, 374
on-site child care programs, 777,
   783
open adoption, 84–85
open-ended questions, 376
oppositional defiant disorder (ODD),
   747, 749, 759
organizing information, 563
organ maturation
      infancy, 229
      preschool years, 419
      school-age and adolescent years,
         531–532
      toddler years, 327–328
orthopedic problems, 550
ossification, 232
ovaries, 123–125
overgeneralization in preschool
   years, 457
over-nutrition, 544
overparenting, 110, 112
overweight children and
   adolescents, 544–545
ovum (female germ cell), 123

P

palmar (grasping) reflex, 232
parent-caregiver communication
   and participation in early
   childhood education programs,
   789–791
"parentese" language, 276

parenting, 90–117
    choosing, 92–94
    family planning, 102–103
    guidance and discipline in,
        107–109
    knowledge about, 94–95
    maturity for, 95
    relationships affected by, 95–99
    resources needed for, 99–102
    roles and responsibilities in,
        105–106
    styles of, 110–112, 391
Parents Anonymous, 729
Parents Without Partners, 78
Parten, Mildred, 635
passive immunity, 663
passive vocabulary, 278–279
paternal postpartum depression
    (PPPD), 215
paternity leave, 193, 195
PDA (Pregnancy Discrimination
    Act), 192
pediatric endocrinologists, 535
pediatricians, 207
pediatric ophthalmologists, 265
peers
    neglect and abuse of, 722–723,
        729
    pressure from, 548
    school-age and adolescent years,
        607–608
pelvic inflammatory disease (PID),
    139
perceptual learning, 267–268, 272–274
perinatal depression, 213–214
period of gestation, 124
peripheral precocious puberty (PPP),
    535
permanent teeth, 534
permissive parenting style, 110–111
Perry, Bruce, 722
personal plan of study, 813
personal qualifications for careers
    involving children, 819–821
pharmacotherapy, 714
phenylketonuria (PKU), 135, 172, 208
pheromones, 549
phonics, 366
phototherapy, 208
physical abuse, 719
physical activity. *See also* motor
    development
    infancy, 253–254
    preschool years, 439–440
    school-age and adolescent years,
        549–551
    toddlers, 348

physical attributes, 460, 473–474
physical concepts, 274
physical development, 7, 721. *See
    also* infancy, physical development
    in; preschool years, physical
    development in; school-age
    and adolescent years, physical
    development in; toddler years,
    physical development in
physical health, postpartum, 213
physical knowledge, 460–461, 473,
    572
physical neglect, 717
physical special needs, 740–743,
    754–755
physician-neonatologist, 210
Piaget, Jean, 18, 53, 268, 286, 493–494,
    602
Piaget's cognitive-development
    theory
    infancy, 268–269
    play stages, 632–633, 635
    preschool years, 453–457
    school-age and adolescent years,
        563–568
    toddler years, 358–361
PID (pelvic inflammatory disease),
    139
PIH (pregnancy-induced
    hypertension), 138, 170
pincer grasp, 333
PKU (phenylketonuria), 135, 172, 208
placenta, 125–126
placenta abruptio, 170
placenta previa, 170
plantar (grasping) reflex, 233
plasticity of brain, 42–43
play, 630–657
    art as, 646–648
    block building, 641–642
    boundaries of, for safety, 680
    cooking as, 644–645, 647
    encouraging, 638
    Froebel on, 782
    literature experiences as,
        650–652
    music as, 648–649
    overview, 632–633
    in preschool years, 495–499
    sand, 642–643
    science experiences as, 649
    stages of, 633–638
    theories of, 635
    water, 643–645
playground designers, 644
play therapy, 637, 715
play yards, 253

poisonings, 689
portfolios, 32, 58, 86, 114, 156, 184,
    219, 256, 290, 319, 351, 381, 410,
    442, 484, 522, 554, 592, 624, 654,
    694, 732, 767, 800, 838, 844
positive attitude, for child-related
    careers, 826–827
positive stress, 12
postconventional morality
    (Kohlberg), 605
postpartum depression (PPD), 214,
    312
postpartum mood disorders
    (PPMD), 213–216
postpartum physical care, 213
postpartum psychosis (PPP), 214
postural skills, in infants, 236
potential traits, 9
power assertion discipline
    technique, 108
PPD (postpartum depression), 214,
    312
PPMD (postpartum mood
    disorders), 213–216
PPP (peripheral precocious puberty),
    535
PPP (postpartum psychosis), 214
PPPD (paternal postpartum
    depression) (PPPD), 215
precision, 537
precocious puberty, 529, 535
preconceptual substage of
    development (Piaget), 453–454
preconventional morality stage
    (Kohlberg), 494
preferences of infants, 267
prefrontal cortex of brain, 561
pregnancy, 120–159. *See also*
    childbirth
    biological parents' ages,
        136–137
    conception, 122–124
    emotional health of mother,
        141–143
    genetic and chromosomal
        disorders affecting unborn
        baby, 134–136
    genetic factors affecting unborn
        baby, 132–134
    health habits during, 147–153
    health habits prior to, 145
    month-by-month development,
        126–129
    physical health of mother,
        137–141
    prenatal development, 124–127
    signs of, 146

pregnancy, special circumstances, 160–187
    congenital conditions, 170–172
    infertility and sterility, 163–166
    miscarriage, 173
    multiple pregnancies, 166–169
    preterm birth, 173
    stillbirth, 173–174
    teen pregnancy, 176–183
Pregnancy Discrimination Act (PDA), 192
pregnancy-induced hypertension (PIH), 138, 170
pregnancy leave, 192
pre-K (prekindergarten) programs, 781
premature birth, 150, 189
premoral, toddlers as, 402
prenatal development, 124–127
prenatal stage of life cycle, 8
prenatal supplements, 150–151
prenatal testing, 148
preoperational stage of development (Piaget), 453
pre-schools, child care in, 775
preschool stage of life cycle, 8
preschool teachers, 517
pre-school years. *See also* early childhood education programs
    center-based child care for, 775–776
    early learning standards for, 771, 791
    quality activities for, 791–793
    universal preschool programs for, 781
preschool years, intellectual development in, 446–487
    brain development, 449–452
    communicating, 466–469
    concept learning, 460–466
    concept learning activities, 473–477
    electronic media activities, 481–482
    language activities, 478–480
    memory activities, 472–473
    milestones in, 469–470
    motor activities, 472
    overview, 447–449
    Piaget's cognitive-developmental theory, 453–457
    symbolic learning activities, 477–478
    Vygotsky's sociocultural theory, 458

preschool years, physical development in, 416–445
    clothing needs in, 436–437
    food appeal in, 432–433
    food attitudes in, 430–431
    hygiene in, 437–438
    making meals fun, 434
    milestones in, 426
    motor development in, 422–425
    nutritional needs in, 429–430
    organ maturation in, 419
    overview, 418–419
    physical activity in, 439–440
    rest and sleep in, 440
    skeletal growth in, 419–422
preschool years, social-emotional development in, 488–525
    emotions, expressing, 499–502
    milestones in, 502–503
    overview, 490–491
    play in, 495–499
    self-awareness expansion, 491–495, 509–513
    social relations, developing, 514–519
    stress, 503–505
    stress, coping with, 519–520
    technology access in, 505–507
presentations, group, 52
President's Teen Pregnancy Prevention Initiative (TPPI), 183
pretend play, 449, 458, 477–478
pretense by toddlers, 360
preterm birth, 173
preventative health care, 661–664
primary school, preparing for, 581–582
primary school programs, 782
problem-solving
    activities for, 287
    in careers involving children, 830
    by divergent thinking, 479
    in families, 67
    intuition for, 455
    by toddlers, 365
processed foods, 541
procreation, 96
professionalism skills, 831
professional organizations, 811
professional qualifications for careers involving children, 821–824
protection of brain, 47
protective services careers, 815–817
proteins, 145
protowords, 278

proximodistal development, 236
pruning, in brain development, 43, 562
psychoanalytic theory of growth and development, 18
psychological security, 607
psychomotor ability, 744
puberty
    brain reorganization in, 562
    central precocious puberty (CPP), 529, 535
    overview, 531–532
    peripheral precocious puberty (PPP), 535
pulse oximetry, 209

Q

quantity, toddler understanding of, 365
questioning by toddlers, 376
quickening, in pregnancy, 126

R

radiation exposure, 140
RDs (registered dietitians), 342
reaction time, 537
reading
    age-appropriate, 650
    career narratives, 812
    comprehension strategies, 651–652
    developmental delays in, 741
    readiness for, 478–480
    school-age and adolescent years, 577
recession, economic, 79
recessive traits, 133, 135–136
recreational therapists, 727
recreation workers, 102
references, 836
referential meaning, in language, 276
reflexes of infants, 232–233
registered dietitians (RDs), 342
regression in development, 347, 706
regulated family child care homes, 775
regulatory adherence in early childhood education programs, 785–786
rehearsing in school-age and adolescent years, 563
reinforcement, 52
rejection, fear of, 597, 608
relationship concepts, 274–275

repressed jealousy, 502, 519
research careers, 818–819
resilience, 46, 711–712
resources, parenting, 99–102
responsibility
  preschool years, 491–492,
    509–510
  school-age and adolescent years,
    599, 615–616
rest and sleep
  infancy, 251–253
  preschool years, 440
  school-age and adolescent years,
    551
  toddlers, 348–349
résumés, 835–837
reversibility, 456–457, 565, 568
Rh factor, 138
risks
  media-related, 589
  negative peer relations, 607
  nutritional, 544–546
  teen sexual relationships, 176
role guilt, 833
role-management skills, 832–833
role strain, 833
rote memorization, 52
rubella (German measles), 139–140
Rubin, Kenneth, 635
running, in toddler years, 330–331

S

SACC (school-age child care)
  programs, 777–779, 783
safety
  of child items, 675–677
  of children in self-care, 778
  for early childhood education
    staff, 788
  in emergencies, 690–692
  lessons for children on, 680–681
  for preschoolers, 473
  supervising children for, 673–
    677
  teachable moment on, 16
  for toddlers, 400
  of toys, 677–680
  in water play, 645
safety recalls, 675
SAMHSA (Substance Abuse
  and Mental Health Services
  Administration), 12
sand play, 642–643
sand tables, 643
SAT (Scholastic Aptitude Test), 745

SBS (Shaken Baby Syndrome), 721
scaffolding
  children's learning, 362
  in instructional support, 270
  with preschoolers, 458
scapegoating behavior, 610
schizophrenia, childhood, 747, 758
Scholastic Aptitude Test (SAT), 745
school
  enrichment outside of, 585–587
  gender role learning and,
    600–601
  hard lockdowns at, 690
  preparing children for, 581–582
  supporting children in,
    582–585
school-age and adolescent years,
  intellectual development in,
  558–595
  brain development and
    cognitive changes, 561–563
  cognitive-development theory,
    563–568
  communicating, 575–577
  concept learning, 572–575
  electronic media use, 588–590
  enrichment outside of school,
    585–587
  milestones in, 577–579
  multiple intelligences theory,
    569–570
  overview, 560–561
  preparing children for school,
    581–582
  sociocultural theory, 568–569
  supporting children in school,
    582–585
school-age and adolescent years,
  physical development in, 528–557
  body proportions in, 534
  bones and teeth in, 534
  clothing needs in, 548–549
  fat and muscle in, 536
  healthful eating in, 541–544
  height in, 533
  hygiene in, 549
  milestones in, 537–539
  motor development in, 536–537
  nutritional risks in, 544–546
  organ maturation in, 531–532
  overview, 530–531
  physical activity in, 549–551
  rest and sleep in, 551
  skeletal growth in, 533
  technology access in, 552
  weight in, 533

school-age and adolescent years,
  social-emotional development in,
  596–627
  controlling emotions, 620–621
  expressing emotions, 608–610
  industry and identity, sense of,
    604–606, 617
  milestones in, 611–612
  overview, 598–599
  self-awareness, 599–604, 615–617
  social relations, 606–608, 617–620
  stress, 611, 622
school-age child care (SACC)
  programs, 777–779, 783
school-age stage of life cycle, 8
school counselors, 585
school uniforms, 548
school violence, 723
science experiences as play, 649
scientific knowledge, 51
scientific reasoning, 568
searching for careers involving
  children, 835
second-degree burns, 688
secure attachments, 392, 404
sedentary toddlers, 348
self-actualization, 27
self-assertion and obedience balance,
  400–403
self-assessment in career choice, 807
self-awareness
  infants, 315
  preschool years, 491–495, 509–513
  school-age and adolescent years,
    599–604, 615–617
  toddler years, 387–389, 399
self-care, children in, 778
self-concept
  preschool years, 495, 511
  school-age and adolescent years,
    603–604, 616–617
self-correction, 495
self-definition, 495, 603–604
self-dressing features, 345, 436–437
self-esteem, 389, 495
self-evaluation, 604
self-feeding, by babies, 245–246
self-recognition, 388, 495
self-restraint, 401
self-reward, 514
semantics, 450
sense awareness of toddlers, 387
sensitive periods in brain
  development, 44
sensorimotor stage, in cognitive
  development (Piaget), 268

sensory activities, 266, 286
sensory neurons, 40–41
sensory stimulation activities for toddlers, 373–375
separation anxiety, 303, 385
sequenced steps in growth and development, principle of, 14–16
seriation, 462–463
severing rights of birthparents, 81
sex chromosomes, 133–134
sex typing, 492
sexual abuse, 719
sexually transmitted infections (STIs), 138–139, 176
sexual maturity, 531
sexual stereotyping, 492
Shaken Baby Syndrome (SBS), 721
shallow cuts, 687
shame and doubt, autonomy *versus*, 390
shaming, 511, 603–604
shock, 687
shoes
    preschoolers, 437
    toddlers, 345–346
shortcomings, awareness of, 604
short-term memory, 583–584
shy children, 513
siblings
    neglect and abuse of, 722–723, 729
    preschooler interaction with, 498, 519
sickle-cell anemia, 135, 172, 209
SIDS (sudden infant death syndrome), 251–253
Singer, Dorothy G., 635
Singer, Jerome L., 635
single-parent families, 77–79
situation stress, 662
six core strengths, in children, 722
six-year molars, in permanent teeth, 534
skeletal growth
    infancy, 230–232
    preschool years, 419–422
    toddler years, 328–330
skeletal muscles, 331
SkillsUSA, 3
Skinner, B. F., 18
skin-to-skin contact, 316
sleep and rest
    infancy, 251–253
    preschool years, 440
    school-age and adolescent years, 551
    toddlers, 348–349
sleep deprivation, 551
sleep-wake cycles, 252

small-muscle development, 333–334, 423–424
SMART goals, 812
Smilansky, Sara, 635
smooth muscles, 331
snacks, in school-age and adolescent years, 543–544
SNAP (Supplemental Nutrition Assistance Program), 177, 182
social abuse, 722
social and human service assistants, 181
social climate, 727
social-emotional development, 7, 722. *See also* infancy, social-emotional development in; preschool years, social-emotional development in; school-age and adolescent years, social-emotional development in; toddler years, social-emotional development in
social-emotional special needs, 746–749, 757–759
social interaction, language involved in, 275–276
socialization, 106
social referencing, 402
social relations
    infants, 298–300
    preschool years, 514–519
    school-age and adolescent years, 606–608, 617–620
    toddler years, 390–391
Social Theory of Development (Piaget), 493
social workers, 83
societal influences on families, 73
society of children, 618
sociocultural theory of growth and development, 18
socioeconomic issues for families, 100
sociologists, 618
solidarity, 616
solid fats, 430
solid foods for infants, 243–244
solitary symbolic play, 360
SONAR (Sound Navigation and Ranging), 150
sorting and classifying objects, 462, 475
sorting process in brain, 43
spatial relationships
    infant learning of, 273
    preschooler problems with, 463, 476–477
    school-age and adolescent years, 574
    toddlers distinguishing, 365
special education teachers, 757

special lessons and activities, 587
special needs. *See* children with special needs
Special Supplemental Nutrition Program for Women, Infants and Children (WIC), 177, 182
speech, 52
speech disorders, 743, 755
speech-language pathologists, 368
speed and strength, 537
speed concepts, 574
sperm (male germ cell), 123
spermarche (ejaculation), 531
spina bifida, 172
splinters, 689
sponge baths for infants, 249
spoon-feeding infants, 244
sprains, 688
Springer, Jim, 10
staff, early childhood education programs
    quality and number, 786–788
    turnover, 788
stages of development, 41
stages of grief, 710
standing, in infants, 235
static balance, 423
stepfamilies, 80
sterility, infertility and, 163–166
stillbirth, 173–174
stimuli, learning from, 263, 285–286
stings, 689
STIs (sexually transmitted infections), 138–139, 176
storage of child items and toys, 679–680
strangers, safety around, 302, 680
Strange Situation (Ainsworth), 301
stress. *See also* anxiety; fear
    infants, 316–317
    preschool years, 503–505, 519–520
    school-age and adolescent years, 611, 622
    situation, 662
    toddler years, 407–408
stress hormones, 141
stressors, 11–12, 499–500
striated muscles, 331
studying children, 21–24
stuttering, 742–743
Substance Abuse and Mental Health Services Administration (SAMHSA), 12, 79
sucking reflex, 232
sudden infant death syndrome (SIDS), 251–253
sudden unexpected infant death (SUID), 251–253

suicide, 709–710

SUID (sudden unexpected infant death), 251–253

Supplemental Nutrition Assistance Program (SNAP), 177, 182

surrogates, 164

survey researchers, 388

suspension from job, 831

Sutton-Smith, Brian, 635

symbolic thought, 449

symbols

    collective symbolism, 360, 376

    preschool learning activities on, 477–478

    solitary symbolic play by toddlers, 360

    toddler learning activities on, 375–376

    toddler use of, 366

    in written communication, 479

syntax, in school-age and adolescent years, 577

syphilis, 139

T

table foods, 337

tag questions in preschooler years, 468

talking, rates of learning, 369–370

TANF (Temporary Assistance for Needy Families), 182

tattling behaviors, 515

Tay-Sachs disease, 135, 172

TBI (traumatic brain injury), 562

teachable moments, 16

teachers, elementary school, 49

teamwork, 323

technology

    developing brain and, 44

    preschool years, 505–507

    school-age and adolescent years, 552, 559, 588–590

teen pregnancy

    negative impacts of, 176–182

    prevention of, 183

    sexual relationship risks, 176

    support systems for, 182–183

teeth

    dental care, 438

    infants, 232

    preschool years, 420–422

    school-age and adolescent years, 534

    toddler years, 329

temperament of infants, 297–298, 310–311

temper tantrums in toddlers, 395–396, 405–406

Temporary Assistance for Needy Families (TANF), 182

terminal illness, 709

termination from job, 831

testes, 123

therapeutic services, 713

thinking center of brain, 266

third-degree burns, 688

3-D vision, 266

throwing, in toddler years, 332–333

TIC (trauma-informed care), 46, 74, 700

time

    management of, 832

    as parenting resource, 99, 101

    preschooler years, 466, 477

    school-age and adolescent years, 574

timing in brain development, 43–45

toddlers, early education programs for, 783, 791

toddler years, intellectual development in, 354–383

    cognitive-development theory, 358–361

    communicating, 366–370

    concept activities for, 375

    concept learning, 363–366

    electronic media activities for, 379

    language activities for, 376–378

    learning time in, 357–358

    milestones in, 370–371

    motor activities for, 374

    overview, 356

    sensory simulation activities for, 374–375

    sociocultural theory, 361–362

    symbolic learning activities for, 375–376

toddler years, physical development in, 323–353

    bathing, 346

    clothing needs, 344–346

    eating, 336–337

    feeding problems, 341

    healthy food choices, 337–341

    large-muscle development, 330–333

    as life cycle stage, 8

    milestones in, 334–335

    organ maturation, 327–328

    overview, 325–327

    physical activity, 348

    rest and sleep, 348–349

    skeletal growth, 328–330

    small-muscle development, 333–334

    special nutritional needs, 341

    toilet learning, 346–348

toddler years, social-emotional development in, 384–413

    attachments, 392–394

    autonomy, 390, 400

    emotions, 392, 394–396, 403–407

    milestones in, 396–397

    overview, 386–387

    self-assertion and obedience balance, 400–403

    self-awareness, 387–389, 399

    social relations, 390–391

    stress, 407–408

toilet learning, 346–348, 438

tolerable stress, 12

Touch Points (Brazelton), 301

toxic stress, 12, 504

toy designers, 679

TPPI (President's Teen Pregnancy Prevention Initiative)., 183

training pants for toddlers, 348

traits, 9, 133–136

transductive reasoning, 457, 568

transformations, 456–457, 565

trauma, 11–12, 46, 681

trauma-focused therapy, 714

trauma-informed care (TIC), 46, 74, 700

traumatic brain injury (TBI), 562

trunk control, in infants, 234–235

tummy time, 234, 254

turn-taking in conversations, 275, 287

twin studies, 10

U

ultrasound, 148–150

umbilical cord, 125–126

unconditional love, 314

under-nutrition, 544

underutilized intelligences, 586

underweight children and adolescents, 545

uninvolved parenting style, 111–112

unit blocks, as toys, 642

United Nations International Children's Education Fund, 22

universal morality (Kohlberg), 605

universal preschool programs, 781

unregulated family child care homes, 775

urination, involuntary (enuresis), 438

US Census Bureau, 64

US Department of Agriculture (USDA), 145

    MyPlate food guidance system of, 145, 150, 339–340, 541–542

US Department of Health and
Human Services., 23
US Department of Labor (DOL), 23,
25, 841
uterus, 123–125

V

vaccinations, 664
vacuum extraction, 204
vaginal-assisted deliveries, 204
values, 807
verbal abuse, 719
verbal aids, 563
violence and disasters, 704–706, 718.
See also emergencies
virtual twins, 10
visceral muscles, 331
vision center of brain, 263–266
vision conditions, 742
visual aids, 563
visual arts, 645
visual literacy, 642
visual preferences of newborns, 284
vitamins, 145
vocabulary
passive and active, 278–279
preschooler years, 467
school-age and adolescent years,
576–577
toddler years, 367–368
Vygotsky, Lev, 18, 53, 268, 270

Vygotsky's sociocultural theory of
development
infancy, 268, 270
play in, 632–633
preschool years, 458
school-age and adolescent years,
568–569
toddler years, 361–362

W

walking, 233, 235, 330–331
water, 145
water play, 643–645
water tables, 644
weaning babies, 242–243, 245–246
weight
infancy, 230
pregnancy and, 152
of preschoolers, 419–420
school-age and adolescent years,
533
toddlers, 328
weight shift, 423
well-baby checkups, 210
well-child checkups, 662
WIC (Special Supplemental
Nutrition Program for Women,
Infants and Children), 177, 182
windows of opportunity in brain
development, 45
wiring process in brain, 43–44

words, 367–370, 376
work-based learning programs,
811
work ethic, 599, 827
working memory
essential life skills related to,
56
as executive function (EF), 54,
583–584
preschool years, 452
school-age and adolescent years,
563
worth, feelings of, 389
wounds, 687
writing, toddlers' grasping tools for,
333
written communication, symbols in,
479

Z

zone of proximal development
(ZPD)
in infancy, 283
intellectual development
reliance on, 568–569
overview, 270
play in, 632–633
reasoning with child at, 404
in toddler years, 361–362, 377
zygote (fertilized egg), 123–125